Oxford
COLOR FRENCH
Dictionary Plus

Third edition

FRENCH–ENGLISH
ENGLISH–FRENCH

FRANÇAIS–ANGLAIS
ANGLAIS–FRANÇAIS

OXFORD
UNIVERSITY PRESS

OXFORD

UNIVERSITY PRESS

Great Clarendon Street, Oxford OX2 6DP

Oxford University Press is a department of the University of Oxford.
It furthers the University's objective of excellence in research, scholarship,
and education by publishing worldwide in

Oxford New York

Auckland Cape Town Dar es Salaam Hong Kong Karachi
Kuala Lumpur Madrid Melbourne Mexico City Nairobi
New Delhi Shanghai Taipei Toronto

With offices in

Argentina Austria Brazil Chile Czech Republic France Greece
Guatemala Hungary Italy Japan Poland Portugal Singapore
South Korea Switzerland Thailand Turkey Ukraine Vietnam

Oxford is a registered trade mark of Oxford University Press
in the UK and in certain other countries

Published in the United States
by Oxford University Press Inc., New York

© Oxford University Press 2007

The moral rights of the authors have been asserted
Database right Oxford University Press (maker)

First published as the Oxford French Minidictionary, 2005
Supplementary material published by OUP in 2001, 2005, and 2006
This edition published 2007

brary Cataloguing in Publication Data

ble
Da
Typ   gress Cataloging in Publication Data
Print

ISBN 9 e Sciences Ltd, Gloucester
ISBN 97 orint S.p.A.

10 9 8 5
US edition)

Contents

Preface

This dictionary is designed primarily for students of French. Its clear presentation and use of color make it easily accessible. This new edition contains new material, not found in the previous edition, on texting. In addition, the notes on French life and culture have been expanded. It also contains a list of the French words you must know, making it even more useful for students who wish to improve their vocabulary.

Contributors

Third Edition

Editors:

Nicholas Rollin
Jean Benoit Ormal-Grenon

Supplementary Material:

Marianne Chalmers
Martine Pierquin
Glynnis Chantrell
Valerie Grundy
Natalie Pomier
Joanna Rubery
Lexus Ltd

Second Edition Revised

Marianne Chalmers

Second Edition

Marianne Chalmers
Rosalind Combley
Catherine Roux
Laura Wedgeworth

First Edition

Michael Janes
Dora Latiri-Carpenter
Edwin Carpenter

Introduction

This dictionary has been designed to be a practical reference tool for the student, adult learner, traveller and business professional. It provides user-friendly treatment of core vocabulary across a broad spectrum of written and spoken language.

Enhanced coverage

The wordlist has been revised to reflect recent additions to both languages.

The more complex grammatical words, or *function words*, are given special treatment in highlighted entries to make them easily accessible. All verbs in the French-English section are cross-referenced to the verb tables at the end of the book. Here information is given on regular, irregular and reflexive verbs as well as the translation of French verb tenses.

Easy reference

The dictionary layout has been designed to be clear, streamlined and easy to use. Bullet points separate each new part of speech within an entry. Nuances of meaning or usage are pinpointed by semantic indicators or by typical collocates with which the headword frequently occurs. Extra help is given with symbols to mark the register of language. A boxed exclamation mark ▯ indicates colloquial language and a cross ✖ indicates slang.

The pronunciation of French is given in the International Phonetic Alphabet. Irregular parts of French verbs appear as headwords with a cross-reference to the main entry of the verb.

A new feature for this edition is the list of French words you must know, which can be found in the centre section of the dictionary. A ▣ symbol next to the headword means that there is more information on this subject in the A–Z of French life and culture found in the centre section. France has recently undergone a spelling review. All words that can have a new spelling are marked with an asterisk * in the main text. For a full list of all the spelling changes see pp.xiv–xvii.

Pronunciation of French

Vowels

a	*as in*	patte	/pat/	ɑ	*as in*	pâte	/pɑt/
ã		clan	/klã/	e		dé	/de/
ɛ		belle	/bɛl/	ɛ̃		lin	/lɛ̃/
ə		demain	/dəmɛ̃/	i		gris	/gʀi/
o		gros	/gʀo/	ɔ		corps	/kɔʀ/
ɔ̃		long	/lɔ̃/	œ		leur	/lœʀ/
œ̃		brun	/bʀœ̃/	ø		deux	/dø/
u		fou	/fu/	y		pur	/pyʀ/

Semi-Vowels

j	*as in*	fille	/fij/
ɥ		huit	/ɥit/
w		oui	/wi/

Consonants

Aspiration of 'h'
Where it is impossible to make a liaison this is indicated by /'/ immediately after the slash e.g. *haine* /'ɛn/.

b	*as in*	bal	/bal/	ŋ	*as in*	camping	/kɑ̃piŋ/
d		dent	/dã/	p		porte	/pɔʀt/
f		foire	/fwaʀ/	ʀ		rire	/ʀiʀ/
g		gomme	/gɔm/	s		sang	/sã/
k		clé	/kle/	ʃ		chien	/ʃjɛ̃/
l		lien	/ljɛ̃/	t		train	/tʀɛ̃/
m		mer	/mɛʀ/	v		voile	/vwal/
n		nage	/naʒ/	z		zèbre	/zɛbʀ/
ɲ		oignon	/ɲɔ̃/	ʒ		jeune	/ʒœn/

Glossary of grammatical terms

Abbreviation
A shortened form of a word or phrase made by leaving out some letters or by using only the initial letter of each word: **etc., DNA**

Active
In the active form the subject of the verb performs the action: **she whistled = elle a sifflé**

Adjective
A word describing a noun: **a** *red* **pencil = un crayon** *rouge*

Adverb
A word that describes or changes the meaning of a verb, an adjective, or another adverb: **he drives** *fast* **= il conduit** *vite*; *fairly* **often = assez souvent**

Article
The definite article, **the = le, la, l', les**, and indefinite article, **a/an = un, une**, are used in front of a noun

Attributive
An adjective or noun is attributive when it is used directly before a noun: **the** *big* **dog = le** *grand* **chien;** *birthday* **card = carte** *d'anniversaire*

Auxiliary verb
One of the verbs used to form the perfect, pluperfect, and future perfect tenses. In French the auxiliary verbs are **avoir** and **être: I have read the letter = j'** *ai* **lu la lettre; he had already gone = il** *était* **déjà parti**

Cardinal number
A whole number representing a quantity: **one, two, three = un/une, deux, trois**

Clause
A self-contained section of a sentence that contains a subject and a verb

Collective noun
A noun that is singular in form but refers to a group of persons or things, e.g. **royalty, grain**

Collocate
A word that regularly occurs with another; in French **livre** is a typical collocate of the verb **lire**

Comparative
The form of an adjective or adverb for comparing two or more nouns or pronouns, often using **more, less** or **as (plus, moins, aussi): smaller = plus petit; more frequently = plus fréquemment; as intelligent = aussi intelligent**

Compound adjective
An adjective formed from two separate words : **tout-puissant = all-powerful; nord-américain = North American**

Compound noun
A noun formed from two or more separate words: **porte-clés = keyring**

Conditional tense
A tense of a verb that expresses what would happen if something else

Glossary of grammatical terms

occurred: **I would invite them = je les inviterais**

Conjugation
Variation of the form of a verb to show tense, person, mood, etc.

Conjunction
A word used to link clauses: **and = et, because = parce que**

Definite article:
the = le, la, l', les

Demonstrative pronoun
A pronoun indicating the person or thing referred to: *this one* is cheaper = *celui-ci* est moins cher

Determiner
A word that comes before a noun to show how it is being used: **the = le, la, l', les; some = du/de l'/de la/des; my = mon/ma/mes**

Direct object
The noun or pronoun directly affected by the verb: **she ate *the apple* = elle a mangé *la pomme***

Direct speech
A speaker's actual words or the use of these in writing

Ending
Letters added to the stem of verbs, as well as to nouns and adjectives, according to tense, number, gender

Exclamation
A sound, word, or remark expressing a strong feeling such as anger, fear, or joy: **ouch! = aïe!**

Feminine
One of the two noun genders in French: **la femme = the woman; la carte = the card**

Future tense
The tense of a verb that refers to

something that will happen in the future: **I will go = j'irai**

Gender One of the two groups of nouns in French: masculine and feminine

Imperative
A form of a verb that expresses a command: **hurry up! = dépêche-toi!**

Imperfect tense
The tense of a verb that refers to an uncompleted or a habitual action in the past: **I went there every day = j'y allais tous les jours**

Impersonal verb
A verb used in English only with **'it'** and in French only with **'il': it is raining = il pleut**

Indefinite article:
a/an = un, une

Indefinite pronoun
A pronoun that does not identify a specific person or object: **one = on; something = quelque chose**

Indicative form
The form of a verb used when making a statement of fact or asking questions of fact: **we like animals = nous aimons les animaux**

Indirect object
The noun or pronoun indirectly affected by the verb, at which the direct object is aimed: **she gave *him* the key = elle *lui* a donné la clé**

Indirect speech
A report of what someone has said which does not reproduce the exact words

Infinitive
The basic part of a verb: **to play = jouer**

Glossary of grammatical terms

Inflect
To change the ending or form of a word to show its tense or its grammatical relation to other words: **donne** and **donnez** are inflected forms of the verb **donner**

Interrogative pronoun
A pronoun that asks a question: **who? = qui?**

Intransitive verb
A verb that does not have a direct object: **he died yesterday = il est mort hier**

Invariable adjective
An adjective that has the same form in the feminine as the masculine, as French **ivoire, transmanche**

Invariable noun
A noun that has the same form in the plural as the singular as. English **sheep, species,** French **précis, rabais**

Irregular verb
A verb that does not follow one of the set patterns and has its own individual forms, e.g. English **to be**, French **être**

Masculine
One of the two noun genders in French: **le garçon = the boy; le livre = the book**

Modal verb
A verb that is used with another verb to express permission, obligation, possibility, such as **might, should.** The French modal verbs are **devoir, pouvoir, savoir, vouloir, falloir**

Negative
Expressing refusal or denial: **there aren't any = il n'y en a pas; he won't go = il ne veut pas partir**

Noun
A word that names a person or thing

Number
The state of being either singular or plural

Object
The word or group of words which is immediately affected by the action indicated by the verb, as **livre** in **il a lu le livre**, or **voiture** in **elle lave la voiture**

Ordinal number
A number that shows the position of a person or thing in a series: **the** *third* **time = la** *troisième* **fois, the** *fourth* **door on the left = la** *quatrième* **porte à gauche**

Part of speech
A grammatical term for the function of a word; noun, verb, adjective, etc., are parts of speech

Passive
In the passive form the subject of the verb experiences the action rather than performs it: **he was punished = il a été puni**

Past participle
The part of a verb used to form past tenses: **she had** *gone* **= elle était** *partie*

Perfect tense
The tense of a verb that refers to an action that has taken place in a period of time that includes the present: **I have already eaten = j'ai déjà mangé; my bike has been stolen = on m'a volé mon vélo**

Person
Any of the three groups of personal pronouns and forms taken by verbs. In the singular the **first person** (e.g.

I/je refers to the person speaking; **the second person** (e.g. **you/tu**) refers to the person spoken to; the **third person** (e.g. **he, she, it/il, elle**) refers to the person spoken about. The corresponding plural forms are **we/nous, you/vous, they/ils, elles**

Personal pronoun
A pronoun that refers to a person or thing

Phrasal verb
A verb in English combined with a preposition or an adverb to have a particular meaning: **run away = se sauver**

Phrase
A self-contained section of a sentence that does not contain a full verb

Pluperfect tense
The tense of a verb that refers to something that happened before a particular point in the past: **when I arrived, he *had* already *left* = quand je suis arrivé, il *était* déjà *parti***

Plural
Of nouns, etc., referring to more than one: **the children = les enfants**

Possessive adjective
An adjective that shows possession, belonging to someone or something: **my = mon/ma/mes**

Possessive pronoun
A pronoun that shows possession, belonging to someone or something: **mine = le mien/la mienne/les miens/les miennes**

Predicative
An adjective is predicative when it comes after a verb such as **be** or **become** in English, or after **être** or

devenir in French: **she is beautiful = elle est belle**

Prefix
A group of letters added to the beginning of a word to change its meaning, e.g. **anti-, ultra-, non-**

Preposition
A word that stands in front of a noun or pronoun, usually indicating movement, position or time: *on* **the chair = *sur* la chaise;** *towards* **the car = *vers* la voiture**

Present participle
The part of a verb in English that ends in **-ing**; the corresponding ending in French is **-ant**

Present tense
The tense of a verb that refers to something happening now: **I make = je fais**

Pronoun
A word that stands instead of a noun: **he = il, she = elle, mine = le mien/la mienne/ les miens/les miennes**

Proper noun
A name of a person, place, institution etc. written with a capital letter at the start; **France, the Alps, Madeleine, l'Europe** are all proper nouns

Reflexive pronoun
A pronoun that goes with a reflexive verb: in French **me, te, se, nous, vous, se**

Reflexive verb
A verb whose object is the same as its subject. In French it is used with a reflexive pronoun and conjugated with **être: you should wash yourself = tu devrais te laver**

Regular verb
A verb that follows a set pattern in its

different forms

Relative pronoun
A pronoun that introduces a subordinate clause, relating to a person or thing mentioned in the main clause: **the book *which* I chose = le livre *que* j'ai choisi**

Reported speech
Another name for **Indirect speech**

Sentence
A sequence of words, with a subject and a verb, that can stand on their own to make a statement, ask a question, or give a command

Singular
Of nouns, etc., referring to just one: **the tree = l'arbre**

Stem
The part of a verb to which endings are added; **donn-** is the stem of **donner**

Subject
In a clause or sentence, the noun or pronoun that causes the action of the verb: ***he* caught the ball = *il* a attrapé le ballon**

Subjunctive
A verb form that is used to express doubt or uncertainty in English. It is more widely used in French, particularly after certain conjunctions and with verbs of wishing, fearing,

ordering, forbidding followed by **que: I want you to be good = je veux que tu sois sage; you may be right = il est possible que tu aies raison**

Subordinate clause
A clause which adds information to the main clause of a sentence, but cannot function as a sentence by itself, e.g. **when it rang** in **she answered the phone when it rang**

Suffix
A group of letters joined to the end of a word to form another word, as **-eur** in **grandeur** or **-able** in **véritable**

Superlative
The form of an adjective or adverb that makes it the 'most' or 'least': **the *biggest* house = *la plus grande* maison; the *cheapest* CD = le CD *le moins cher***

Tense
The form of a verb that tells when the action takes place: present, future, imperfect, perfect, pluperfect are all tenses

Transitive verb
A verb that is used with a direct object: **I wrote the letter = j'ai écrit la lettre**

Verb
A word or group of words that describes an action: **the children are playing = les enfants jouent**

Abbreviations

adjective	*adj*	adjectif
abbreviation	*abbr, abrév*	abréviation
adverb	*adv*	adverbe
anatomy	*Anat*	anatomie
archaeology	*Archaeol, Archéol*	archéologie
architecture	*Archit*	architecture
motoring	*Auto*	automobile
auxiliary	*aux*	auxiliaire
aviation	*Aviat*	aviation
botany	*Bot*	botanique
commerce	*Comm*	commerce
computing	*Comput*	informatique
conjunction	*conj*	conjonction
cookery	*Culin*	culinaire
determiner	*det, dét*	déterminant
electricity	*Electr, Électr*	électricité
figurative	*fig*	sens figuré
geography	*Geog, Géog*	géographie
geology	*Geol, Géol*	géologie
grammar	*Gram*	grammaire
humorous	*hum*	humoristique
interjection	*interj*	interjection
invariable	*inv*	invariable
law	*Jur*	droit
linguistics	*Ling*	linguistique
literal	*lit*	littéral
phrase	*loc*	locution
medicine	*Med, Méd*	médecine
military	*Mil*	armée
music	*Mus*	musique
noun	*n*	nom
nautical	*Naut*	nautisme
feminine noun	*nf*	nom féminin
masculine noun	*nm*	nom masculin
masculine and feminine noun	*nm,f* or *nmf* or *nm/f*	nom masculin et féminin
computing	*Ordinat*	informatique

pejorative	*pej, péj*	péjoratif
philosophy	*Phil*	philosophie
photography	*Photo*	photographie
plural	*pl*	pluriel
politics	*Pol*	politique
possessive	*poss*	possessif
past participle	*pp*	participe passé
prefix	*pref, préf*	préfixe
preposition	*prep, prép*	préposition
present participle	*pres p*	participe présent
pronoun	*pron*	pronom
psychology	*Psych*	psychologie
past	*pt*	prétérit
something	*qch*	quelque chose
somebody	*qn*	quelqu'un
railway	*Rail*	chemin de fer
relative pronoun	*rel pron, pron rel*	pronom relatif
religion	*Relig*	religion
somebody	*sb*	quelqu'un
school	*School, Scol*	scolaire
sport	*Sport*	sport
something	*sth*	quelque chose
technology	*Tech*	technologie
theatre	*Theat, Théât*	théâtre
television	*TV*	télévision
university	*Univ*	université
American English	*US*	anglais américain
auxiliary verb	*v aux*	verbe auxiliaire
intransitive verb	*vi*	verbe intransitif
reflexive verb	*vpr*	verbe pronominal
transitive verb	*vt*	verbe transitif
transitive and intransitive verb	*vt/i*	verbe transitif et intransitif
approximate translation	≈	équivalent approximatif
trademark	®	marque déposée
colloquial	!	familier
slang	✖	argot
alternative spelling	*	
see A–Z of French life and culture	▣	
verb table number	**1**	
phrasal verb	■	

Words affected by the French spelling review

France has recently undergone a spelling review. All words that appear in this dictionary that can have a new spelling are listed here and are marked with an asterisk (*) in the main text. The *Académie française* has stated that "neither of the two written forms can be considered incorrect."

Previously, words that were invariable in the plural, i.e. did not change in the plural, marked in this list as *inv*, now have plural forms.

Existing spelling	New spelling	Existing spelling	New spelling
abat-jour *nm inv*	abat-jour *des abat-jours*	asseoir	assoir
abîme	abime	auto-école	autoécole
abîmer	abimer	auto-stop	autostop
accroître	accroitre		
acupuncture	acuponcture	avant-goût	avant-gout
affûter	affuter	baby-foot *nm inv*	babyfoot *des babyfoots*
aide-mémoire *nm inv*	aide-mémoire *des aide-mémoires*		
aigu, aiguë	aigu, aigüe	basse-cour	bassecour
aîné	ainé	bien-aimé	bienaimé
allô	allo	boîte	boite
ambigu, ambiguë	ambigu, ambigüe	boîtier	boitier
amuse-gueule *nm inv*	amuse-gueule *des amuse-gueules*	bonneterie	bonnèterie
		boursoufler	boursouffler
août	aout		
apparaître	apparaitre	brûlant	brulant
appui-tête *des appuis-têtes*	appuie-tête *des appuie-têtes*	brûlé	brulé
après-midi *nm inv*	après-midi *des après-midis*	brûler	bruler
		brûlure	brulure
après-ski *nm inv*	après-ski *des après-skis*	bûche	buche
		bûcher (*nom*)	bucher
après-vente *adj inv*	après-vente *après-ventes*	bûcher (*verbe*)	bucher
		bûcheron	bucheron
a priori *loc adj inv, loc adv*	à priori	bulldozer	bulldozeur
		cacahuète	cacahouète
arrache-pied (d')	arrachepied (d')	cache-cache *nm inv*	cachecache *des cachecaches*
arrière-goût	arrière-gout		

Existing spelling	New spelling	Existing spelling	New spelling
cachottier	cachotier	dîner	diner
casse-cou *adj inv,*	casse-cou	*(verbe et nom)*	
nm inv, nmf inv	*(des) casse-cous*	disparaître	disparaitre
casse-pied *nm inv*	casse-pied	eczéma	exéma
	(des) casse-pieds	emboîter	emboiter
casse-tête *nm inv*	casse-tête	en-cas	encas
	des casse-têtes	enchaînement	enchainement
céleri	cèleri	enchaîner	enchainer
chaîne	chaine	entraînement	entrainement
		entraîner	entrainer
chaînette	chainette	entraîneur	entraineur
chaînon	chainon	entre-temps	entretemps
chariot	charriot	essuie-mains	essuie-main
		nm inv	*des essuie-mains*
chausse-pied	chaussepied	événement	évènement
chauve-souris	chauvesouris	exigu, exiguë	exigu, exigüe
cloche-pied (à)	clochepied (à)	extra *adj inv,*	extra *(des) extras*
cloître	cloitre	*nm inv*	
cloîtrer	cloitrer	fac-similé	facsimilé
combatif	combattif	faire-part *nm inv*	fairepart
comparaître	comparaitre		*des faireparts*
compte-gouttes	compte-goutte	faîte	faite
nm inv	*des compte-*	fast-food	fastfood
	gouttes	féerie	féérie
connaître	connaitre	féerique	féérique
contigu, contiguë	contigu, contigüe	ferry *des ferries*	ferry *des ferrys*
contre-attaque	contrattaque	flash *des flashes*	flash *des flashs*
contre-attaquer	contrattaquer	flipper *(nom)*	flippeur
contre-indiqué	contrindiqué	flûte	flute
contre-jour	contrejour	fourre-tout *nm inv*	fourretout
coût	cout		*des fourretouts*
coûter	couter	fraîchement	fraichement
croche-pied (à)	crochepied (à)	fraîcheur	fraicheur
croque-monsieur	croquemonsieur	fraîchir	fraichir
nm inv	*des*	frais, fraîche	frais, fraiche
	croquemonsieurs	free-lance	freelance
croque-mort	croquemort	freezer	freezeur
croûte	croute	fût *(nom)*	fut
croûton	crouton	gageure	gageüre
cure-dents *nm inv*	cure-dent	gagne-pain *nm inv*	gagne-pain
	des cure-dents		*des gagne-pains*
déboîter	déboiter	gaiement	gaiment
déchaîner	déchainer	gaieté	gaité
décroître	décroitre	gîte	gite
dégoût	dégout	goût	gout
dégoûtant	dégoutant	goûter	gouter
dégoûter	dégouter	graffiti *nmpl*	graffiti *des graffitis*
diesel	diésel		

Existing spelling	New spelling	Existing spelling	New spelling
gratte-ciel *nm inv*	gratte-ciel *des gratte-ciels*	oignon	ognon
		ouvre-boîtes *nm inv*	ouvre-boite *des ouvre-boites*
grelotter	greloter		
grille-pain *nm inv*	grille-pain *des grille-pains*	ouvre-bouteilles *nm inv*	ouvre-bouteille *des ouvre-bouteilles*
haut-parleur	hautparleur		
hors-bord *adj,* *nm inv*	hors-bord *(des) hors-bords*	paître	paitre
		papeterie	papèterie
hors-jeu *nm inv*	hors-jeu *des hors-jeux*	paraître	paraitre
		pare-brise *nm inv*	pare-brise *des pare-brises*
hors-piste *nm inv*	hors-piste *des hors-pistes*		
huître	huitre	pare-chocs *nm inv*	pare-choc *des pare-chocs*
île	ile		
îlot	ilot	passe-partout *adj inv, nm inv*	passepartout *(des) passepartouts*
in extremis	in extrémis		
interpeller	interpeler	passe-temps	passetemps
knock-out	knockout	pêle-mêle *nm inv*	pêlemêle *des pêlemêles*
lance-missiles *nm inv*	lance-missile *des lance-missiles*		
		pique-nique	piquenique
lance-pierres *nm inv*	lance-pierre *des lance-pierres*	piqûre	piqure
		plate-bande	platebande
lasagnes *nfpl*	lasagne *des lasagnes*	porte-avions *nm inv*	porte-avion *des porte-avions*
lave-linge *nm inv*	lave-linge *des lave-linges*		
		porte-bagages *nm inv*	porte-bagage *des porte-bagages*
lave-vaisselle *nm inv*	lave-vaisselle *des lave-vaisselles*		
		porte-bonheur *nm inv*	porte-bonheur *des porte-bonheurs*
main-forte	mainforte		
maître	maitre		
maîtresse	maitresse	porte-documents *nm inv*	porte-document *des porte-documents*
maître-assistant	maitre-assistant		
maître-chanteur	maitre-chanteur		
maître-nageur	maitre-nageur	porte-jarretelles *nm inv*	porte-jarretelle *des porte-jarretelles*
maîtrise	maitrise		
maîtriser	maitriser		
maraîcher	maraicher	porte-monnaie *nm inv*	portemonnaie *des portemonnaies*
méconnaître	méconnaitre		
médico-légal	médicolégal	porte-parole *nm inv*	porte-parole *des porte-paroles*
méli-mélo	mélimélo		
mille-pattes *nm inv*	millepatte *des millepattes*	post-scriptum *nm inv*	post-scriptum *des post-scriptums*
monte-charge *nm inv*	monte-charge *des monte-charges*	presqu'île	presqu'ile
		pull-over	pullover
mûre *(nom)*	mure	punch *(boisson)*	ponch
mûrir	murir	quincaillier	quincailler
naître	naitre	quote-part	quotepart
nénuphar	nénufar	rabat-joie *adj inv, nm inv*	rabat-joie *des rabat-joies*
nu *nm inv*	nu *des nus*		
		rafraîchir	rafraichir
		rafraîchissant	rafraichissant

Existing spelling	New spelling	Existing spelling	New spelling
rafraîchissement	rafraichissement	sécheresse	sècheresse
ragoût	ragout	senior	sénior
receler	recéler	serpillière	serpillère
reconnaître	reconnaitre	shampooing	shampoing
refréner	réfréner	sketch	sketch
réglementaire	règlementaire	*des sketches*	*des sketchs*
réglementation	règlementation	soûl	soul
réglementer	règlementer	soûler	souler
relais	relai	supporter (*nom*)	supporteur
remue-ménage	remue-ménage	surcroît	surcroit
nm inv	*des remue-*	sûreté	sureté
	ménages	taille-crayons	taille-crayon
renouvellement	renouvèlement	*nm inv*	*des taille-crayons*
repartie	répartie	terre-plein	terreplein
réveille-matin	réveille-matin	tire-bouchon	tirebouchon
nm inv	*des réveille-matins*	traîne	traine
revolver	révolver	traîneau	traineau
rond-point	rondpoint	traînée	trainée
saccharine	saccarine	traîner	trainer
sage-femme	sagefemme	traître, traîtresse	traitre, traitresse
des sages-femmes	*des sagefemmes*	veto	véto
sans-abri *nmf inv*	sans-abri	vide-greniers	vide-grenier
	des sans-abris	*nm inv*	*des vide-greniers*
sans-faute *nm inv*	sans-faute	vide-ordures	vide-ordure
	des sans-fautes	*nm inv*	*des vide-ordures*
sans-gêne *adj inv*,	sans-gêne	volley(-ball)	volleyball
nmf inv	(*des*) *sans-gênes*	volte-face *nf inv*	volte-face
sans-papiers	sans-papier		*des volte-faces*
nm inv	*des sans-papiers*	voûte	voute
saute-mouton	saute-mouton	waters *nmpl*	water *des waters*
nm inv	*des saute-moutons*	week-end	weekend
scotch	scotch	whisky	whisky
des scotches	*des scotchs*	*des whiskies*	*des whiskys*
sèche-cheveux	sèche-cheveu	yo-yo	yoyo
nm inv	*des sèche-cheveux*		

Aa

a /a/ ▸AVOIR **5**.

à /a/
● préposition

! à+le = au
■ à+les = aux

⋯▸ (avec verbe de mouvement) to.

⋯▸ (pour indiquer où l'on se trouve) ~ **la maison** at home; ~ **Nice** in Nice.

⋯▸ (âge, date, heure) ~ **l'âge de...** at the age of...; **au XIXe siècle** in the 19th century; ~ **deux heures** at two o'clock.

⋯▸ (description) with; **aux yeux verts** with green eyes.

⋯▸ (appartenance) ~ **qui est ce stylo?** whose pen is this?; **c'est** ~ **vous?** is this yours?

⋯▸ (avec nombre) ~ **90 km/h** at 90 km per hour; ~ **10 minutes d'ici** 10 minutes from here; **des tomates** ~ **2 euros le kilo** tomatoes at 2 euros a kilo; **un timbre** ~ **2 euros** a 2-euro stamp; **nous avons fait le travail** ~ **deux** two of us did the work; **mener 5** ~ **4** to lead 5 (to) 4.

⋯▸ (avec être) **c'est** ~ **moi** it's my turn; **je suis** ~ **vous tout de suite** I'll be with you in a minute; **c'est** ~ **toi de décider** it's up to you to decide.

⋯▸ (hypothèse) ~ **ce qu'il paraît** apparently; ~ **t'entendre** to hear you talk.

⋯▸ (exclamatif) ~ **ta santé!** cheers!; ~ **demain/bientôt!** see you tomorrow/soon!

⋯▸ (moyen) ~ **la main** by hand; ~ **vélo** by bike; ~ **pied** on foot; **chauffage au gaz** gas heating.

abaissement /abɛsmɑ̃/ nm (de taux, de prix) cut; (de seuil) lowering.

abaisser /abese/ **1** vt lower; (levier) pull *ou* push down; (fig) humiliate. ■ **s'~** vpr go down, drop; (fig) demean oneself; **s'~ à** stoop to.

abandon /abɑ̃dɔ̃/ nm abandonment; (de personne) desertion; (de course) withdrawal; (naturel) abandon; **à l'~** in a state of neglect.

abandonner /abɑ̃dɔne/ **1** vt abandon; (épouse, cause) desert; (renoncer à) give up, abandon; (céder) give (**à** to); (course) withdraw from; (Ordinat) abort. ■ **s'~ à** vpr give oneself up to.

abasourdir /abazurdir/ **2** vt stun.

abat-jour* /abaʒur/ nm inv lampshade.

abats /aba/ nmpl offal.

abattement /abatmɑ̃/ nm dejection; (faiblesse) exhaustion; (Comm) reduction; ~ **fiscal** tax allowance.

abattre /abatr/ **11** vt knock down; (arbre) cut down; (animal) slaughter; (avion) shoot down; (affaiblir) weaken; (démoraliser) demoralize; **ne pas se laisser ~** not let things get one down. ■ **s'~** vpr come down, fall (down).

abbaye /abei/ nf abbey.

abbé /abe/ nm priest; (supérieur d'une abbaye) abbot.

abcès /apsɛ/ nm abscess.

abdiquer /abdike/ **1** vt/i abdicate.

abdomen /abdɔmɛn/ nm abdomen.

abdominal (mpl -aux) /abdɔminal/ adj abdominal.

a

abdominaux nmpl (Sport) stomach exercises.

abeille /abɛj/ nf bee.

aberrant, ~e /abɛʀɑ̃, -t/ adj absurd.

abêtir /abetiʀ/ **2** vt turn into a moron.

abîme* /abim/ nm abyss.

abîmer* /abime/ **1** vt damage, spoil. ∎ s'~ vpr get damaged *ou* spoilt.

ablation /ablasjɔ̃/ nf removal.

aboiement /abwamɑ̃/ nm bark, barking; ~s barking.

abolir /abɔliʀ/ **2** vt abolish.

abondance /abɔ̃dɑ̃s/ nf abundance; (prospérité) affluence. **abondant**, ~e adj abundant, plentiful.

abonder /abɔ̃de/ **1** vi abound (**en** in); ~ **dans le sens de qn** agree wholeheartedly with sb.

abonné, ~e /abɔne/ nm, f (lecteur) subscriber; (voyageur, spectateur) season-ticket holder.

abonnement /abɔnmɑ̃/ nm (à un journal) subscription; (de bus, Théât) season-ticket; (au gaz) standing charge.

abonner (s') /(s)abɔne/ **1** vpr subscribe (**à** to).

abord /abɔʀ/ nm access; ~s surroundings; **d'**~ first.

abordable /abɔʀdabl/ adj (prix) affordable; (personne) approachable; (texte) accessible.

aborder /abɔʀde/ **1** vt approach; (lieu) reach; (problème) tackle. • vi reach land.

aborigène /abɔʀiʒɛn/ nm aborigine.

aboutir /abutiʀ/ **2** vi succeed, achieve a result; ~ **à** end (up) in, lead to; **n'**~ **à rien** come to nothing.

aboutissement /abutismɑ̃/ nm outcome; (de carrière, d'évolution) culmination.

aboyer /abwaje/ **31** vi bark.

abrégé /abreʒe/ nm summary.

abréger /abreʒe/ **14 40** vt (texte) shorten, abridge; (mot) abbreviate, shorten; (visite) cut short.

abreuver /abrœve/ **1** vt water; (fig) overwhelm (**de** with). ∎ s'~ vpr drink.

abréviation /abrevjasjɔ̃/ nf abbreviation.

abri /abri/ nm shelter; **à l'**~ under cover; (en lieu sûr) safe; **à l'**~ **de** sheltered from; **se mettre à l'**~ take shelter.

abricot /abriko/ nm apricot.

abriter /abrite/ **1** vt shelter; (recevoir) house. ∎ s'~ vpr (take) shelter.

abrupt, ~e /abrypt/ adj steep, sheer; (fig) abrupt.

abruti, ~e /abryti/ nm, f **1** idiot.

absence /apsɑ̃s/ nf absence; **il a des** ~s sometimes his mind goes blank.

absent, ~e /apsɑ̃, -t/ adj (personne) absent, away; (chose) missing; **il est toujours** ~ he's still away; **d'un air** ~ absently. • nm, f absentee.

absenter (s') /(s)apsɑ̃te/ **1** vpr go *ou* be away; (sortir) go out, leave.

absolu, ~e /apsɔly/ adj absolute.

absorbant, ~e /apsɔʀbɑ̃, -t/ adj (travail) absorbing; (matière) absorbent.

absorber /apsɔʀbe/ **1** vt absorb; **être absorbé par qch** be engrossed in sth.

abstenir (s') /(s)apstəniʀ/ **58** vpr abstain; **s'**~ **de** refrain from.

abstrait, ~e /apstrɛ, -t/ adj & nm abstract.

absurde /apsyʀd/ adj absurd.

abus /aby/ nm abuse, misuse; (injustice) abuse; ~ **de confiance** breach of trust.

abuser /abyze/ **1** vt deceive. •vi go too far; ~ **de** abuse, misuse; (profiter de) take advantage of; (alcool) overindulge in. ∎ s'~ vpr be mistaken.

abusif, -ive /abyzif, -v/ adj excessive; (impropre) wrong; (injuste) unfair.

académie /akademi/ nf academy; (circonscription) local education authority.

acajou /akaʒu/ nm mahogany.

accablant, ~e /akablɑ̃, -t/ adj (chaleur) oppressive; (fait, témoignage) damning.

accabler /akable/ **1** vt overwhelm; ~ **d'impôts** burden with taxes; ~ **d'injures** heap insults upon.

accéder /aksede/ **14** vi ~ **à** (lieu) reach; (pouvoir, trône) accede to; (requête) grant; (Ordinat) access; ~ **à la propriété** become a homeowner.

accélérateur /akseleratœr/ nm accelerator.

accélérer /akselere/ **14** vt/i accelerate. ∎ s'~ vpr speed up.

accent /aksɑ̃/ nm accent; (sur une syllabe) stress; **mettre l'~ sur** stress; ~ **aigu/grave/ circonflexe** acute/grave/ circumflex accent.

accentuer /aksɑ̃tɥe/ **1** vt (lettre, syllabe) accent; (fig) emphasize, accentuate. ∎ s'~ vpr become more pronounced, increase.

accepter /aksɛpte/ **1** vt accept; ~ **de faire** agree to do.

accès /aksɛ/ nm access; (porte) entrance; (de fièvre) bout; (de colère) fit; (d'enthousiasme) burst; (Ordinat) access; **les ~ de** (voies) the approaches to; **facile d'~** easy to get to.

accessoire /akseswar/ adj secondary, incidental. •nm accessory; (Théât) prop.

accident /aksidɑ̃/ nm accident; ~ **de train/d'avion** train/plane crash; **par ~** by accident.

accidenté, ~e adj (personne) injured (in an accident); (voiture) damaged; (terrain) uneven, hilly.

accidentel, ~le adj accidental.

acclamer /aklame/ **1** vt cheer, acclaim.

accommoder /akɔmode/ **1** vt adapt (**à** to); (cuisiner) prepare; (assaisonner) flavour. ∎ s'~ **de** vpr make the best of.

accompagnateur, -trice /akɔ̃paɲatœr, -tris/ nm, f (Mus). accompanist; (guide) guide; ~ **d'enfants** accompanying adult.

accompagner /akɔ̃paɲe/ **1** vt accompany. ∎ s'~ **de** vpr be accompanied by.

accomplir /akɔ̃plir/ **2** vt carry out, fulfil. ∎ s'~ vpr take place, happen; (vœu) be fulfilled.

accord /akɔr/ nm agreement; (harmonie) harmony; (Mus) chord; **être d'~** agree (**pour** to); **se mettre d'~** come to an agreement, agree; **d'~!** all right **1**, OK!

accorder /akɔrde/ **1** vt grant; (couleurs) match; (Mus) tune; (attribuer) (valeur, importance) assign. ∎ s'~ vpr (se mettre d'accord) agree; (s'octroyer) allow oneself; **s'~ avec** (s'entendre avec) get on with.

accotement /akɔtmɑ̃/ nm verge; ~ **non stabilisé** soft verge.

accouchement /akuʃmɑ̃/ nm childbirth; (travail) labour.

accoucher /akuʃe/ **1** vi give birth (**de** to); (être en travail) be in labour. •vt deliver. **accoucheur** nm **médecin** ~ obstetrician.

accoudoir /akudwar/ nm arm-rest.

accoupler /akuple/ **1** vt (Tech) couple. ∎ s'~ vpr mate.

accourir /akurir/ **20** vi run up.

accoutumance /akutymɑ̃s/ nf familiarization; (Méd) addiction.

accoutumer /akutyme/ **1** vt accustom. ∎ s'~ vpr get accustomed.

accro /akʀo/ nmf 🚹 (drogué) addict;
(amateur) fan.

accroc /akʀo/ nm tear, rip; (fig)
hitch.

accrochage /akʀoʃaʒ/ nm
hanging; hooking; (Auto)
collision; (dispute) clash; (Mil)
encounter.

accrocher /akʀoʃe/ 🚹 vt
(suspendre) hang up; (attacher)
hook, hitch; (déchirer) catch;
(heurter) hit; (attirer) attract. ■ s'~
vpr cling, hang on (**à** to); (se
disputer) clash.

accroissement /akʀwasmɑ̃/ nm
increase (**de** in).

accroître* /akʀwatʀ/ 24 vt
increase. ■ s'~ vpr increase.

accroupir (s') /(s)akʀupiʀ/ 2 vpr
squat.

accru, ~e /akʀy/ adj increased,
greater.

accueil /akœj/ nm reception,
welcome.

accueillant, ~e /akœjɑ̃, -t/ adj
friendly, welcoming.

accueillir /akœjiʀ/ 25 vt receive,
welcome; (film, livre) receive;
(prendre en charge) (réfugiés, patients)
take care of, cater for.

accumuler /akymyle/ 🚹 vt
(énergie) store up; (capital)
accumulate. ■ s'~ vpr (neige,
ordures) pile up; (dettes) accrue.

accusation /akyzasjɔ̃/ nf
accusation; (Jur) charge; **l'~**
(magistrat) the prosecution.

accusé, ~e /akyze/ adj marked.
• nm, f defendant, accused.

accuser /akyze/ 🚹 vt accuse (**de**
of); (blâmer) blame (**de** for); (Jur)
charge (**de** with); (fig)
emphasize; ~ **réception de**
acknowledge receipt of.

acharné, ~e /aʃaʀne/ adj
relentless, ferocious.
acharnement nm (énergie)
furious energy; (ténacité)
determination.

acharner (s') /(s)aʃaʀne/ 🚹 vpr
persevere; **s'~ sur** set upon;
(poursuivre) hound; **s'~ à faire**
(s'évertuer) try desperately;
(s'obstiner) keep on doing.

achat /aʃa/ nm purchase; ~**s**
shopping; **faire l'~ de** buy;
faire des ~s do some shopping.

acheminer /aʃ(ə)mine/ 🚹 vt
dispatch, convey; (courrier)
handle. ■ s'~ **vers** vpr head for.

acheter /aʃ(ə)te/ 6 vt buy; ~ **qch
à qn** (pour lui) buy sth for sb;
(chez lui) buy sth from sb.
acheteur, -euse nm, f buyer;
(client de magasin) shopper.

achèvement /aʃɛvmɑ̃/ nm
completion.

achever /aʃ(ə)ve/ 6 vt finish
(off). ■ s'~ vpr end.

acide /asid/ adj acid, sharp.
• nm acid.

acier /asje/ nm steel.

acné /akne/ nf acne.

acompte /akɔ̃t/ nm deposit, part-
payment.

à-côté (pl ~s) /akote/ nm side
issue; ~**s** (argent) extras.

acoustique /akustik/ nf acoustics
(+ sg). • adj acoustic.

acquéreur /akeʀœʀ/ nm
purchaser, buyer.

acquérir /akeʀiʀ/ 7 vt acquire,
gain; (biens) purchase, acquire.

acquis, ~e /aki, -z/ adj acquired;
(fait) established; **tenir qch pour
~** take sth for granted. • nm
experience. **acquisition** nf
acquisition; purchase.

acquitter /akite/ 🚹 vt acquit;
(dette) settle. ■ s'~ **de** vpr
(promesse) fulfil; (devoir) discharge.

âcre /ɑkʀ/ adj acrid.

acrobatie /akʀobasi/ nf
acrobatics (+ pl); ~ **aérienne**
aerobatics (+ pl).

acte /akt/ nm act, action, deed;
(Théât) act; (Jur) deed; ~ **de**

naissance/mariage birth/ marriage certificate; **~s** (compte rendu) proceedings; **prendre ~ de** note.

acteur /aktœʀ/ nm actor.

actif, -ive /aktif, -v/ adj active; (population) working. • nm (Comm) assets; **avoir à son ~** have to one's credit *ou* name.

action /aksjɔ̃/ nf action; (Comm) share; (Jur) action; (effet) effect; (initiative) initiative. **actionnaire** nmf shareholder.

activer /aktive/ **1** vt speed up; (feu) boost. ∎ **s'~** vpr hurry up; (s'affairer) be very busy.

activité /aktivite/ nf activity; **en ~** (volcan) active; (fonctionnaire) working; (usine) in operation.

actrice /aktʀis/ nf actress.

actualité /aktyalite/ nf topicality; **l'~** current affairs; **les ~s** news; **d'~** topical.

actuel, -le /aktyɛl/ adj current, present; (d'actualité) topical. **actuellement** adv currently, at the present time.

acupuncture* /akypɔ̃ktyʀ/ nf acupuncture.

adaptateur /adaptatœʀ/ nm (Électr) adapter.

adapter /adapte/ **1** vt adapt; (fixer) fit. ∎ **s'~** vpr adapt (oneself); (Tech) fit.

additif /aditif/ nm (note) rider; (substance) additive.

addition /adisjɔ̃/ nf addition; (au café) bill; (US) check. **additionner** **1** vt add; (totaliser) add (up).

adepte /adɛpt/ nmf follower; (d'activité) enthusiast.

adéquat, ~e /adekwa, -t/ adj suitable; (suffisant) adequate.

adhérent, ~e /adeʀɑ̃, -t/ nm, f member.

adhérer /adeʀe/ **14** vi adhere, stick (à to); **~ à** (club) be a

member of; (s'inscrire à) join.

adhésif, -ive /adezif, -v/ adj adhesive; **ruban ~** sticky tape.

adhésion /adezjɔ̃/ nf membership; (soutien) support.

adieu (pl **~x**) /adjø/ interj & nm goodbye, farewell.

adjectif /adʒɛktif/ nm adjective.

adjoint, ~e /adʒwɛ̃, -t/ nm, f assistant; **~ au maire** deputy mayor. • adj assistant.

adjuger /adʒyʒe/ **40** vt award; (aux enchères) auction. ∎ **s'~** vpr take (for oneself).

ADM abrév fpl (armes de destruction massive) WMD.

admettre /admɛtʀ/ **42** vt let in, admit; (tolérer) allow; (reconnaître) admit, acknowledge; (candidat) pass.

administrateur, -trice /administʀatœʀ, -tʀis/ nm, f administrator, director; (Jur) trustee; **~ de site Internet** Webmaster.

administratif, -ive /administʀatif, -v/ adj administrative; (document) official.

administration nf administration; (gestion) management; **l'A~** Civil Service.

administrer /administʀe/ **1** vt run, manage; (justice, biens, antidote) administer.

admirateur, -trice /admiʀatœʀ, -tʀis/ nm, f admirer.

admiration /admiʀasjɔ̃/ nf admiration.

admirer /admiʀe/ **1** vt admire.

admission /admisjɔ̃/ nf admission.

ADN abrév m (**acide désoxyribonucléique**) DNA.

adolescence /adɔlesɑ̃s/ nf adolescence. **adolescent, ~e** nm, f adolescent, teenager.

adopter /adɔpte/ **1** vt adopt. **adoptif, -ive** adj (enfant) adopted;

(parents) adoptive.

adorer /adɔʀe/ **1** vt love; (plus fort) adore; (Relig) worship, adore.

adosser /adose/ **1** vt lean (**à, contre** against). ■ s'~ vpr lean back (**à, contre** against).

adoucir /adusiʀ/ **2** vt soften; (boisson) sweeten; (chagrin) ease. ■ s'~ vpr soften; (chagrin) ease; (temps) become milder.
adoucissant nm (fabric) softener.

adresse /adʀɛs/ nf address; (habileté) skill; ~ **électronique** email address.

adresser /adʀese/ **1** vt send; (écrire l'adresse sur) address; (remarque) address; ~ **la parole à** speak to. ■ s'~ à vpr address; (aller voir) (personne) go and ask ou see; (bureau) enquire at; (viser, intéresser) be directed at.

adroit, ~e /adʀwa, -t/ adj skilful, clever.

ADSL abrév m (asymmetrical digital subscriber line) ADSL.

adulte /adylt/ nmf adult. •adj adult; (plante, animal) fully grown.

adultère /adyltɛʀ/ adj adulterous. •nm adultery.

adverbe /advɛʀb/ nm adverb.

adversaire /advɛʀsɛʀ/ nmf opponent, adversary.

aérer /aeʀe/ **1** vt air; (texte) space out. ■ s'~ vpr get some air.

aérien, ~ne /aeʀjɛ̃, -jɛn/ adj air; (photo) aerial; (câble) overhead.

aérobic /aeʀɔbik/ nm aerobics (+ sg).

aérogare /aeʀɔgaʀ/ nf air terminal.

aéroglisseur /aeʀɔglisœʀ/ nm hovercraft.

aérogramme /aeʀɔgʀam/ nm airmail letter; (US) aerogram.

aéronautique /aeʀɔnotik/ adj aeronautical. •nf aeronautics (+ sg).

aéroport /aeʀɔpɔʀ/ nm airport.

aérospatial, ~e (mpl **-iaux**) /aeʀɔspasjal, -jo/ adj aerospace.

affaiblir /afebliʀ/ **2** vt weaken. ■ s'~ vpr get weaker.

affaire /afɛʀ/ nf affair, matter; (Jur) case; (histoire, aventure) affair; (occasion) bargain; (entreprise) business; (transaction) deal; (question, problème) matter; ~**s** (Comm) business; (Pol) affairs; (problèmes personnels) business; (effets personnels) things; **c'est mon** ~ that's my business; **avoir** ~ **à** deal with; **ça fera l'**~ that will do the job; **ça fera leur** ~ that's just what they need; **tirer qn d'**~ help sb out of a tight spot; **se tirer d'**~ get out of trouble.

affairé, ~e /afeʀe/ adj busy.

affaisser (s') /(s)afese/ **1** vpr (terrain, route) sink, subside; (poutre) sag; (personne) collapse.

affamé, ~e /afame/ adj starving.

affectation /afɛktasjɔ̃/ nf (nomination) (à une fonction) appointment; (dans un lieu) posting; (de matériel, d'argent) allocation; (comportement) affectation.

affecter /afɛkte/ **1** vt (feindre) affect; (toucher, affliger) affect; (destiner) assign; (nommer) appoint, post.

affectif, -ive /afɛktif, -v/ adj emotional.

affection /afɛksjɔ̃/ nf affection; (maladie) complaint.

affectueux, -euse /afɛktɥø, -z/ adj affectionate.

affichage /afiʃaʒ/ nm billposting; (électronique) display.

affiche /afiʃ/ nf (public) notice; (publicité) poster; (Théât) bill; **être à l'**~ (film) be showing; (pièce) be on.

afficher /afiʃe/ **1** vt (annonce) put up; (événement) announce;

(sentiment) display; (Ordinat) display.

affirmatif, -ive /afiʀmatif, -v/ adj affirmative. **affirmation** nf assertion.

affirmer /afiʀme/ **1** vt assert; (soutenir) maintain.

affligé, ~e /afliʒe/ adj distressed; **~ de** afflicted with.

affluer /aflye/ **1** vi flood in; (sang) rush.

affolant, ~e /afɔlɑ̃, -t/ adj alarming.

affoler /afɔle/ **1** vt throw into a panic. ■ **s'~** vpr panic.

affranchir /afʀɑ̃ʃiʀ/ **2** vt stamp; (à la machine) frank; (esclave) emancipate; (fig) free. **affranchissement** nm (tarif) postage.

affreux, -euse /afʀø, -z/ adj (laid) hideous; (mauvais) awful.

affrontement /afʀɔ̃tmɑ̃/ nm confrontation.

affronter /afʀɔ̃te/ **1** vt confront. ■ **s'~** vpr confront each other.

affûter* /afyte/ **1** vt sharpen.

afin /afɛ̃/ prép & conj **~ de faire** in order to do; **~ que** so that.

africain, ~e /afʀikɛ̃, -ɛn/ adj African. **A~, ~e** nm, f African.

Afrique /afʀik/ nf Africa; **~ du Sud** South Africa.

agacer /agase/ **10** vt irritate, annoy.

âge /aʒ/ nm age; (vieillesse) (old) age; **quel ~ avez-vous?** how old are you?; **~ adulte** adulthood; **~ mûr** maturity; **d'un certain ~** middle-aged.

âgé, ~e /aʒe/ adj elderly; **~ de cinq ans** five years old.

agence /aʒɑ̃s/ nf agency, bureau, office; (succursale) branch; **~ d'intérim** employment agency; **~ de voyages** travel agency; **~ publicitaire** advertising agency.

agenda /aʒɛ̃da/ nm diary; **~**

électronique electronic organizer.

agent /aʒɑ̃/ nm agent; (fonctionnaire) official; **~ (de police)** policeman; **~ de change** stockbroker; **~ commercial** sales representative.

agglomération /aglɔmeʀasjɔ̃/ nf town, built-up area.

aggraver /agʀave/ **1** vt aggravate, make worse. ■ **s'~** vpr get worse.

agile /aʒil/ adj agile, nimble.

agir /aʒiʀ/ **2** vi act; (se comporter) behave; (avoir un effet) work, take effect. ■ **s'~ de** vpr (être nécessaire) **il s'agit de faire** we/you *etc.* must do; (être question de) **il s'agit de faire** it is a matter of doing; **dans ce livre il s'agit de** this book is about; **dont il s'agit** in question; **il s'agit de ton fils** it's about your son; **de quoi s'agit-il?** what is it about?

agitation /aʒitasjɔ̃/ nf bustle; (trouble) agitation; (malaise social) unrest.

agité, ~e /aʒite/ adj restless, fidgety; (troublé) agitated; (mer) rough.

agiter /aʒite/ **1** vt (bras, mouchoir) wave; (liquide, boîte) shake; (troubler) agitate; (discuter) debate. ■ **s'~** vpr bustle about; (enfant) fidget; (foule, pensées) stir.

agneau (pl **~x**) /aɲo/ nm lamb.

agrafe /agʀaf/ nf hook; (pour papiers) staple. **agrafeuse** nf stapler.

agrandir /agʀɑ̃diʀ/ **2** vt enlarge; (maison) extend. ■ **s'~** vpr expand, grow. **agrandissement** nm extension; (de photo) enlargement.

agréable /agʀeabl/ adj pleasant.

agréé, ~e /agʀee/ adj (agence) authorized; (nourrice, médecin) registered; (matériel) approved.

agréer /agʀee/ **15** vt accept; **~ à** please; **veuillez ~, Monsieur,**

a

mes salutations distinguées (personne non nommée) yours faithfully; (personne nommée) yours sincerely.

agrégation /agʀegasjɔ̃/ nf *highest examination for recruitment of teachers.* **agrégé, ~e** nm, f teacher (who has passed the agrégation).

agrément /agʀemɑ̃/ nm charm; (plaisir) pleasure; (accord) assent.

agresser /agʀese/ **1** vt attack; (pour voler) mug.

agressif, -ive /agʀesif, -v/ adj aggressive. **agression** nf attack; (pour voler) mugging; (Mil) aggression.

agricole /agʀikɔl/ adj agricultural; (ouvrier, produit) farm. **agriculteur, -trice** nm, f farmer. **agriculture** nf agriculture, farming.

agripper /agʀipe/ **1** vt grab. ■ **s'~** vpr cling (**à** to).

agroalimentaire /agʀɔalimɑ̃tɛʀ/ nm food industry.

agrumes /agʀym/ nmpl citrus fruit(s).

ai /e/ ▷ AVOIR **5**.

aide /ɛd/ nf help, assistance; (en argent) aid; **à l'~ de** with the help of; **venir en ~ à** help; **~ à domicile** carer, home help; **~ familiale** mother's help; **~ sociale** social security; (US) welfare. ● nmf assistant. **aide-éducateur, -trice** nm, f classroom assistant. **aide-mémoire*** nm inv handbook of key facts.

aider /ede/ **1** vt/i help, assist; (subventionner) aid, give aid to; **~ à faire** help to do. ■ **s'~ de** vpr use.

aïeul, ~e /ajœl/ nm, f grandparent.

aigle /ɛgl/ nm eagle.

aigre /ɛgʀ/ adj sour, sharp; (fig) sharp.

aigrir /egʀiʀ/ **2** vt embitter. ■ **s'~**

vpr turn sour; (personne) become embittered.

aigu, ~ë* /egy/ adj (douleur, problème) acute; (objet) sharp; (voix) shrill; (Mus) high(-pitched); (accent) acute.

aiguille /egɥij/ nf needle; (de montre) hand; (de balance) pointer; **~ à tricoter** knitting needle.

aiguilleur /egɥijœʀ/ nm pointsman; **~ du ciel** air traffic controller.

aiguiser /eg(ɥ)ize/ **1** vt sharpen; (fig) stimulate.

ail (pl **~s** ou **aulx**) /aj, o/ nm garlic.

aile /ɛl/ nf wing.

ailier /elje/ nm winger; (US) end.

aille /aj/ ▷ ALLER **8**.

ailleurs /ajœʀ/ adv elsewhere, somewhere else; **d'~** besides, moreover; **nulle part ~** nowhere else; **par ~** moreover, furthermore; **partout ~** everywhere else.

aimable /ɛmabl/ adj kind.

aimant /ɛmɑ̃/ nm magnet.

aimer /eme/ **1** vt like; (d'amour) love; **j'aimerais faire** I'd like to do; **~ bien** quite like; **~ mieux** ou **autant** prefer.

aîné*, ~e /ene/ adj eldest; (de deux) elder. ● nm, f eldest (child); (premier de deux) elder (child); **~s** elders; **il est mon ~** he is older than me ou my senior.

ainsi /ɛ̃si/ adv like this, thus; (donc) so; **et ~ de suite** and so on; **pour ~ dire** so to speak, as it were; **~ que** as well as; (comme) as.

air /ɛʀ/ nm air; (mine) look, air; (mélodie) tune; **~ conditionné** air-conditioning; **avoir l'~** look, appear; **avoir l'~ de** look like; **avoir l'~ de faire** appear to be doing; **en l'~** (up) in the air; (promesses) empty; **prendre l'~** get some fresh air.

aire /ɛʀ/ nf area; ~ **d'atterrissage** landing-strip; ~ **de pique-nique** picnic area; ~ **de repas** rest area; ~ **de services** (motorway) services.

aisance /ɛzɑ̃s/ nf ease; (richesse) affluence.

aise /ɛz/ nf joy; **à l'**~ (sur un siège) comfortable; (pas gêné) at ease; (fortuné) comfortably off; **mal à l'**~ uncomfortable; ill at ease; **aimer ses** ~**s** like one's creature comforts; **mettre qn à l'**~ put sb at ease; **se mettre à l'**~ make oneself comfortable.

aisé, ~e /eze/ adj easy; (fortuné) well-off.

aisselle /ɛsɛl/ nf armpit.

ait /ɛ/ ▷AVOIR **5**.

ajourner /aʒuʀne/ **1** vt postpone; (débat, procès) adjourn.

ajout /aʒu/ nm addition.

ajouter /aʒute/ **1** vt add (**à** to); ~ **foi à** lend credence to. ▪ s'~ vpr be added.

ajuster /aʒyste/ **1** vt adjust; (cible) aim at; (adapter) fit; ~ **son coup** adjust one's aim.

alarme /alaʀm/ nf alarm; **donner l'**~ raise the alarm.

alarmer /alaʀme/ **1** vt alarm. ▪ s'~ vpr become alarmed (**de** at).

Albanie /albani/ nf Albania.

alcool /alkɔl/ nm alcohol; (eau de vie) brandy; ~ **à brûler** methylated spirit. **alcoolique** adj & nmf alcoholic. **alcoolisé, ~e** adj (boisson) alcoholic. **alcoolisme** nm alcoholism.

alcootest /alkɔtɛst/ nm breath test; (appareil) Breathalyser®.

aléa /alea/ nm hazard. **aléatoire** adj unpredictable, uncertain; (Ordinat) random.

alentours /alɑ̃tuʀ/ nmpl surroundings; **aux ~ de** (de lieu) around; (de chiffre, date) about, around.

alerte /alɛʀt/ adj (personne) alert; (vif) lively. ▪nf alert; ~ **à la bombe** bomb scare. **alerter 1** vt alert.

algèbre /alʒɛbʀ/ nf algebra.

Algérie /alʒeʀi/ nf Algeria.

algue /alg/ nf seaweed; **les** ~**s** (Bot) algae.

aliéné, ~e /aljene/ nm, f insane person.

aliéner /aljene/ **14** vt alienate; (céder) give up. ▪ s'~ vpr alienate.

aligner /aliɲe/ **1** vt (objets) line up, make lines of; (chiffres) string together; ~ **sur** bring into line with. ▪ s'~ vpr line up; **s'**~ **sur** align oneself on.

aliment /alimɑ̃/ nm food.

alimentaire /alimɑ̃tɛʀ/ adj (industrie) food; (habitudes) dietary; **produits** ~**s** foodstuffs.

alimentation /alimɑ̃tasjɔ̃/ nf feeding, supply(ing); (régime) diet; (aliments) food; **magasin d'**~ grocery shop *ou* store.

alimenter /alimɑ̃te/ **1** vt feed; (fournir) supply; (fig) sustain. ▪ s'~ vpr eat.

allaiter /alete/ **1** vt (bébé) breast-feed; (US) nurse; (animal) suckle.

allée /ale/ nf path, lane; (menant à une maison) drive(way); (dans un cinéma, magasin) aisle; (rue) road; ~**s et venues** comings and goings.

allégé, ~e /aleʒe/ adj diet; (beurre, yaourt) low-fat.

alléger /aleʒe/ **14 40** vt make lighter; (fardeau, chargement) lighten; (fig) (souffrance) alleviate.

allégresse /alegʀɛs/ nf gaiety, joy.

alléguer /alege/ **14** vt (exemple) invoke; (prétexter) allege.

Allemagne /alman/ nf Germany.

allemand, ~e /almɑ̃, -d/ adj German. ●nm (Ling) German. **A**~, ~**e** nm, f German.

a

aller /ale/ 🔟
● verbe auxiliaire
••••➤ **je vais l'appeler** I'm going to call him; **j'allais partir** I was about to leave; **va savoir!** who knows?; **~ en s'améliorant** be improving.
● verbe intransitif
••••➤ (se déplacer) go; **allons-y!** let's go!; **allez!** come on!
••••➤ (se porter) **comment allez-vous?, comment ça va?** how are you?; **ça va (bien)** I'm fine; **qu'est-ce qui ne va pas?** what's the matter?; **ça ne va pas la tête?** 🔟 are you mad? 🔟.
••••➤ (mettre en valeur) **~ à qn** suit sb; **ça te va bien** it really suits you.
••••➤ (convenir) **ça va ma coiffure?** is my hair OK?; **ça ne va pas du tout** that's no good at all.
■ **s'en aller** verbe pronominal
••••➤ **va-t'en!** go away!; **ça ne s'en va pas** (tache) it won't come out.
● nom masculin
••••➤ outward journey; **~ (simple)** single (ticket); (US) one-way (ticket); **~ retour** return (ticket); (US) round trip (ticket); **à l'~** on the way out.

allergie /alɛrʒi/ nf allergy. **allergique** adj allergic (**à** to).

alliance /aljɑ̃s/ nf alliance; (bague) wedding-ring; (mariage) marriage.

allier /alje/ 🔠 vt combine; (Pol) ally. ■ **s'~** vpr combine; (Pol) form an alliance; (famille) become related (**à** to).

allô* /alo/ interj hallo, hello.

allocation /alɔkasjɔ̃/ nf allowance; **~ chômage** unemployment benefit; **~s familiales** family allowance.

allonger /alɔ̃ʒe/ 🔟 vt lengthen; (bras, jambe) stretch (out); (coucher) lay down. ■ **s'~** vpr get longer; (s'étendre) lie down; (s'étirer) stretch (oneself) out.

allouer /alwe/ 🔟 vt allocate; (prêt) grant.

allumer /alyme/ 🔟 vt (bougie, gaz) light; (lampe, appareil) turn on; (pièce) switch the light(s) on in; (fig) arouse. ■ **s'~** vpr (lumière, appareil) come on.

allumette /alymɛt/ nf match.

allure /alyr/ nf speed, pace; (démarche) walk; (apparence) appearance; **à toute ~** at full speed; **avoir de l'~** have style; **avoir des ~s de** look like; **avoir une drôle d'~** be funny-looking.

allusion /alyzjɔ̃/ nf allusion (**à** to); (implicite) hint (**à** at); **faire ~ à** allude to; hint at.

alors /alɔr/ adv (à ce moment-là) then; (de ce fait) so; (dans ce cas-là) then; **ça ~!** well!; **et ~?** so what? ● conj **~ que** (pendant que) while; (tandis que) when, whereas.

alouette /alwɛt/ nf lark.

alourdir /alurdir/ 🔟 vt weigh down; (rendre plus important) increase.

aloyau (pl **~x**) /alwajo/ nm sirloin.

Alpes /alp/ nfpl **les ~** the Alps.

alphabet /alfabɛ/ nm alphabet. **alphabétique** adj alphabetical.

alphabétiser /alfabetize/ 🔟 vt teach to read and write.

alpinist /alpinist/ nmf mountaineer.

altérer /altere/ 🔟 vt (fait, texte) distort; (abîmer) spoil; (donner soif à) make thirsty. ■ **s'~** vpr deteriorate.

alternance /altɛrnɑ̃s/ nf alternation; **en ~** alternately.

altitude /altityd/ nf altitude, height.

amabilité /amabilite/ nf kindness.

amaigrir /amegrir/ 🔟 vt make thin(ner).

amande /amãd/ nf almond; (d'un fruit à noyau) kernel.

amant /amã/ nm lover.

amarre /amaʀ/ nf (mooring) rope; ~s moorings.

amas /amɑ/ nm heap, pile.

amasser /amɑse/ **1** vt amass, gather; (empiler) pile up. ∎ s'~ vpr pile up; (gens) gather.

amateur /amatœʀ/ nm amateur; ~ **de** lover of; **d'**~ amateur; (péj) amateurish.

ambassade /ãbasad/ nf embassy. **ambassadeur, -drice** nm, f ambassador.

ambiance /ãbjãs/ nf atmosphere. **ambiant, ~e** adj surrounding.

ambigu, ~ë* /ãbigy/ adj ambiguous.

ambitieux, -ieuse /ãbisjø, -z/ adj ambitious. **ambition** nf ambition.

ambulance /ãbylãs/ nf ambulance.

ambulant, ~e /ãbylã, -t/ adj itinerant, travelling.

âme /ɑm/ nf soul; ~ **sœur** soul mate.

amélioration /ameljɔʀasjõ/ nf improvement.

améliorer /ameljɔʀe/ **1** vt improve. ∎ s'~ vpr improve.

aménagement /amenaʒmã/ nm (de magasin) fitting out; (de grenier) conversion; (de territoire) development; (de cuisine) equipping.

aménager /amenaʒe/ **40** vt (magasin) fit out; (transformer) convert; (territoire) develop; (cuisine) equip.

amende /amãd/ nf fine; **faire ~ honorable** make amends.

amener /am(ə)ne/ **6** vt bring; (causer) bring about; ~ **qn à faire** cause sb to do. ∎ s'~ vpr **1** turn up.

amer, -ère /ameʀ/ adj bitter.

américain, ~e /ameʀikɛ̃, -ɛn/ adj American. A~, ~e nm, f American.

Amérique /ameʀik/ nf America; ~ **centrale/latine** Central/Latin America; ~ **du Nord/Sud** North/South America.

amertume /ameʀtym/ nf bitterness.

ami, ~e /ami/ nm, f friend; (amateur) lover; **un ~ des bêtes** an animal lover. ∎ adj friendly.

amiable /amjabl/ adj amicable; **à l'**~ (divorcer) by mutual consent; (se séparer) on friendly terms; (séparation) amicable.

amical, ~e (mpl **-aux**) /amikal, -o/ adj friendly.

amiral (pl **-aux**) /amiʀal, -o/ nm admiral.

amitié /amitje/ nf friendship; ~s (en fin de lettre) kind regards; **prendre qn en ~** take a liking to sb.

amnistie /amnisti/ nf amnesty.

amoindrir /amwɛ̃dʀiʀ/ **2** vt reduce.

amont: en ~ /ãnamõ/ loc upstream.

amorcer /amɔʀse/ **10** vt start; (hameçon) bait; (pompe) prime; (arme à feu) arm.

amortir /amɔʀtiʀ/ **2** vt (choc) cushion; (bruit) deaden; (dette) pay off; ~ **un achat** make a purchase pay for itself.

amortisseur /amɔʀtisœʀ/ nm shock absorber.

amour /amuʀ/ nm love; **pour l'**~ **de** for the sake of.

amoureux, -euse /amuʀø, -z/ adj (personne) in love; (relation, regard) loving; (vie) love; ~ **de qn** in love with sb. ∎ nm, f lover.

amour-propre /amuʀpʀɔpʀ/ nm self-esteem.

amphithéâtre /ãfiteatʀ/ nm amphitheatre; (d'université) lecture hall.

ampleur /ɑ̃plœʀ/ nf extent, size; (de vêtement) fullness; **prendre de l'~** spread, grow.

amplifier /ɑ̃plifje/ 45 vt amplify; (fig) expand, develop. ∎ s'~ vpr (son) grow; (scandale) intensify.

ampoule /ɑ̃pul/ nf (électrique) bulb; (sur la peau) blister; (Méd) phial, ampoule.

amusant, ~e /amyzɑ̃, -t/ adj (blague) funny; (soirée) enjoyable, entertaining.

amuse-gueule* /amyzgœl/ nm inv cocktail snack.

amusement /amyzmɑ̃/ nm amusement; (passe-temps) entertainment.

amuser /amyze/ 1 vt amuse; (détourner l'attention de) distract. ∎ s'~ vpr enjoy oneself; (jouer) play.

amygdale /amidal/ nf tonsil.

an /ɑ̃/ nm year; **avoir dix ~s** be ten years old; **un garçon de deux ~s** a two-year-old boy; **à soixante ~s** at the age of sixty; **les moins de dix-huit ~s** under eighteens.

analogie /analɔʒi/ nf analogy.

analogue /analɔg/ adj similar, analogous (**à** to).

analphabète /analfabɛt/ adj & nmf illiterate.

analyse /analiz/ nf analysis; (Méd) test. **analyser** 1 vt analyse; (Méd) test.

ananas /anana(s)/ nm pineapple.

anarchie /anaʀʃi/ nf anarchy.

anatomie /anatɔmi/ nf anatomy.

ancêtre /ɑ̃sɛtʀ/ nm ancestor.

anchois /ɑ̃ʃwa/ nm anchovy.

ancien, ~ne /ɑ̃sjɛ̃, -jɛn/ adj old; (de jadis) ancient; (meuble) antique; (précédent) former, ex-, old; (dans une fonction) senior; **~ combattant** veteran. ∎nm, f senior; (par l'âge) elder. **anciennement** adv formerly.

ancienneté nf age, seniority.

ancre /ɑ̃kʀ/ nf anchor; **jeter/lever l'~** cast/weigh anchor.

andouille /ɑ̃duj/ nf sausage (filled with chitterlings); (idiot 🔢) fool; **faire l'~** fool around.

âne /ɑn/ nm donkey, ass; (imbécile 🔢) dimwit 🔢.

anéantir /aneɑ̃tiʀ/ 2 vt destroy; (exterminer) annihilate; (accabler) overwhelm.

anémie /anemi/ nf anaemia.

ânerie /ɑnʀi/ nf stupid remark.

anesthésie /anɛstezi/ nf (opération) anaesthetic.

ange /ɑ̃ʒ/ nm angel; **aux ~s** in seventh heaven.

angine /ɑ̃ʒin/ nf throat infection.

anglais, ~e /ɑ̃glɛ, -z/ adj English. ∎nm (Ling) English. **A~, ~e** nm, f Englishman, Englishwoman.

angle /ɑ̃gl/ nm angle; (coin) corner.

Angleterre /ɑ̃glətɛʀ/ nf England.

anglophone /ɑ̃glɔfɔn/ adj English-speaking. ∎nmf English speaker.

angoissant, ~e /ɑ̃gwasɑ̃, -t/ adj alarming; (effrayant) harrowing.

angoisse /ɑ̃gwas/ nf anxiety. **angoissé, ~e** adj anxious. **angoisser** 1 vi worry.

animal (pl **-aux**) /animal, -o/ nm animal; **~ familier**, **~ de compagnie** pet. ∎adj (mpl **-aux**) animal.

animateur, -trice /animatœʀ, -tʀis/ nm, f organizer, leader; (TV) host, hostess.

animation /animasjɔ̃/ nf liveliness; (affairement) activity; (au cinéma) animation; (activité dirigée) organized activity.

animé, ~e /anime/ adj lively; (affaire) busy; (être) animate.

animer /anime/ 1 vt liven up; (débat, atelier) lead; (spectacle) host; (pousser) drive; (encourager) spur on. ∎ s'∼ vpr liven up.

anis /ani(s)/ nm (Culin) aniseed; (Bot) anise.

anneau (pl ∼x) /ano/ nm ring; (de chaîne) link.

année /ane/ nf year; ∼ **bissextile** leap year; ∼ **civile** calendar year.

annexe /anɛks/ adj (document) attached; (question) related; (bâtiment) adjoining. ●nf (bâtiment) annexe; (US) annex; (document) appendix; (électronique) attachment. **annexer** ❶ vt annex; (document) attach.

anniversaire /anivɛʀsɛʀ/ nm birthday; (d'un événement) anniversary. ●adj anniversary.

annonce /anɔ̃s/ nf announcement; (publicitaire) advertisement; (indice) sign.

annoncer /anɔ̃se/ ❿ vt announce; (prédire) forecast; (être l'indice de) herald. ∎ s'∼ vpr (crise, tempête) be brewing; **s'∼ bien/mal** look good/bad. **annonceur** nm advertiser.

annuaire /anɥɛʀ/ nm year-book; ∼ **(téléphonique)** (telephone) directory.

annuel, ∼**le** /anɥɛl/ adj annual, yearly.

annulation /anylasjɔ̃/ nf cancellation; (de sanction, loi) repeal; (de mesure) abolition.

annuler /anyle/ ❶ vt cancel; (contrat) nullify; (jugement) quash; (loi) repeal. ∎ s'∼ vpr cancel each other out.

anodin, ∼**e** /anɔdɛ̃, -in/ adj insignificant; (sans risques) harmless, safe.

anonymat /anɔnima/ nm anonymity; **garder l'**∼ remain anonymous. **anonyme** adj anonymous.

anorexie /anɔʀɛksi/ nf anorexia.

anormal, ∼**e** (mpl **-aux**) /anɔʀmal, -o/ adj abnormal.

anse /ãs/ nf handle; (baie) cove.

Antarctique /ãtaʀktik/ nm Antarctic.

antenne /ãtɛn/ nf aerial; (US) antenna; (d'insecte) antenna; (succursale) agency; (Mil) outpost; **à l'**∼ on the air; ∼ **chirurgicale** mobile emergency unit; ∼ **parabolique** satellite dish.

antérieur, ∼**e** /ãteʀjœʀ/ adj previous, earlier; (placé devant) front; ∼ **à** prior to.

antiaérien, ∼**ne** /ãtiaeʀjɛ̃, -ɛn/ adj anti-aircraft; **abri** ∼ air-raid shelter.

antiatomique /ãtiatɔmik/ adj **abri** ∼ nuclear fall-out shelter.

antibiotique /ãtibjɔtik/ nm antibiotic.

anticipation /ãtisipasjɔ̃/ nf d'∼ (livre, film) science fiction; **par** ∼ in advance.

anticiper /ãtisipe/ ❶ vt ∼ **(sur)** anticipate; (effectuer à l'avance) bring forward.

anticorps /ãtikɔʀ/ nm antibody.

antidater /ãtidate/ ❶ vt backdate, antedate.

antigel /ãtiʒɛl/ nm antifreeze.

Antilles /ãtij/ nfpl **les** ∼ the West Indies.

antipathique /ãtipatik/ adj unpleasant.

antiquaire /ãtikɛʀ/ nmf antique dealer.

antiquité /ãtikite/ nf (objet) antique; **l'A**∼ antiquity.

antisémite /ãtisemit/ adj anti-Semitic.

antiseptique /ãtisɛptik/ adj & nm antiseptic.

antivirus /ãtiviʀys/ nm inv (Ordinat) antivirus software.

antivol /ãtivɔl/ nm anti-theft device; (Auto) steering lock.

anxiété /ãksjete/ nf anxiety.

anxieux, -ieuse /ãksjø, -z/ adj

a

anxious. •nm, f worrier.

août* /u(t)/ nm August.

apaiser /apeze/ **1** vt calm down; (colère, militant) appease; (douleur) soothe; (faim) satisfy. ■ s'~ vpr (tempête) die down.

apathie /apati/ nf apathy. **apathique** adj apathetic.

apercevoir /apεʀsəvwaʀ/ **52** vt see. ■ s'~ de vpr notice; s'~ que notice ou realize that.

aperçu /apεʀsy/ nm (échantillon) glimpse, taste; (intuition) insight.

apéritif /apeʀitif/ nm aperitif, drink.

aphte /aft/ nm mouth ulcer.

apitoyer /apitwaje/ **31** vt move (to pity). ■ s'~ vpr s'~ sur (le sort de) qn feel sorry for sb.

aplanir /aplaniʀ/ **2** vt level; (fig) iron out.

aplatir /aplatiʀ/ **2** vt flatten (out). ■ s'~ vpr (s'immobiliser) flatten oneself.

aplomb /aplɔ̃/ nm balance; (fig) self-confidence; **d'~** (en équilibre) steady; **je ne suis pas bien d'~** **1** I don't feel very well.

apogée /apɔʒe/ nm peak.

apologie /apɔlɔʒi/ nf panegyric.

apostrophe /apɔstʀɔf/ nf apostrophe; (remarque) remark.

apothéose /apoteoz/ nf high point; (d'événement) grand finale.

apparaître* /apaʀɛtʀ/ **18** vi appear; **il apparaît que** it appears that.

appareil /apaʀɛj/ nm device; (électrique) appliance; (Anat) system; (téléphone) phone; (avion) plane; (Culin) mixture; (système administratif) apparatus; ~ **(dentaire)** brace; (dentier) dentures; ~ **(photo)** camera; **c'est Gabriel à l'**~ it's Gabriel on the phone; ~ **auditif** hearing aid; ~ **électroménager** household electrical appliance.

appareiller /apaʀeje/ **1** vi (navire) cast off, put to sea.

apparemment /apaʀamɑ̃/ adv apparently.

apparence /apaʀɑ̃s/ nf appearance; **en** ~ outwardly; (apparemment) apparently.

apparent, ~e /apaʀɑ̃, -t/ adj apparent; (visible) conspicuous.

apparenté, ~e /apaʀɑ̃te/ adj related; (semblable) similar.

apparition /apaʀisjɔ̃/ nf appearance; (spectre) apparition.

appartement /apaʀtəmɑ̃/ nm flat; (US) apartment.

appartenir /apaʀtəniʀ/ **58** vi belong (à to); **il lui appartient** **de** it is up to him to.

appât /apɑ/ nm bait; (fig) lure.

appauvrir /apovʀiʀ/ **2** vt impoverish. ■ s'~ vpr become impoverished.

appel /apεl/ nm call; (Jur) appeal; (supplique) appeal, plea; (Mil) call-up; (US) draft; **faire** ~ appeal; **faire** ~ **à** (recourir à) call on; (invoquer) appeal to; (évoquer) call up; (exiger) call for; **faire l'**~ (Scol) call the register; (Mil) take a roll-call; ~ **d'offres** (Comm) invitation to tender; **faire un** ~ **de phares** flash one's headlights.

appeler /aple/ **38** vt call; (téléphoner) phone, call; (nécessiter) call for; **en** ~ **à** appeal to; **appelé à** (destiné) destined for. ■ s'~ vpr be called; **il s'appelle** **Tim** his name is Tim ou he is called Tim.

appellation /apεlasjɔ̃/ nf name, designation.

appendice /apɛ̃dis/ nm appendix. **appendicite** nf appendicitis.

appesantir /apəzɑ̃tiʀ/ **2** vt weigh down. ■ s'~ vpr grow heavier; s'~ **sur** dwell upon.

appétissant, ~e /apetisɑ̃, -t/ adj appetizing.

appétit /apeti/ nm appetite; **bon ~!** enjoy your meal!

applaudir /aplodiʀ/ ② vt/i applaud. **applaudissements** nmpl applause.

application /aplikasjɔ̃/ nf (soin) care; (de loi) (respect) application; (mise en œuvre) implementation; (Ordinat) application program.

appliqué, ~e /aplike/ adj (travail) painstaking; (sciences) applied; (élève) hard-working.

appliquer /aplike/ ① vt apply; (loi) enforce. ■ **s'~** vpr apply oneself (**à** to), take great care (**à faire** to do); **s'~ à** (concerner) apply to.

appoint /apwɛ̃/ nm support; **d'~** extra; **faire l'~** give the correct money.

apport /apɔʀ/ nm contribution.

apporter /apɔʀte/ ① vt bring; (aide, précision) give; (causer) bring about.

appréciation /apʀesjasjɔ̃/ nf estimate, evaluation; (de monnaie) appreciation; (jugement) assessment.

apprécier /apʀesje/ ⑮ vt appreciate; (évaluer) assess; (objet) value, appraise.

appréhender /apʀeɑ̃de/ ① vt dread, fear; (arrêter) apprehend.

apprendre /apʀɑ̃dʀ/ ⑤ vt learn; (être informé de) hear, learn; (de façon indirecte) hear of; **~ qch à qn** teach sb sth; (informer) tell sb sth; **~ à faire** learn to do; **~ à qn à faire** teach sb to do; **~ que** learn that; (être informé) hear that.

apprenti, ~e /apʀɑ̃ti/ nm, f apprentice. **apprentissage** nm apprenticeship; (d'un sujet) learning.

apprêter /apʀete/ ① vt prepare; (bois) prime; (mur) size. ■ **s'~ à** vpr prepare to.

apprivoiser /apʀivwaze/ ① vt tame.

approbation /apʀɔbasjɔ̃/ nf approval.

approchant, ~e /apʀɔʃɑ̃, -t/ adj close, similar.

approcher /apʀɔʃe/ ① vt (objet) move near(er) (**de** to); (personne) approach; **~ de** get nearer ou closer to. ● vi approach. ■ **s'~ de** vpr approach, move near(er) to.

approfondir /apʀɔfɔ̃diʀ/ ② vt deepen; (fig) (sujet) go into sth in depth; (connaissances) improve.

approprié, ~e /apʀɔpʀije/ adj appropriate.

approprier (s') /(s)apʀɔpʀije/ ⑮ vpr appropriate.

approuver /apʀuve/ ① vt approve; (trouver louable) approve of; (soutenir) agree with.

approvisionner /apʀɔvizjɔne/ ① vt supply (**en** with); (compte en banque) pay money into. ■ **s'~** vpr stock up.

approximatif, -ive /apʀɔksimatif, -v/ adj approximate.

appui /apɥi/ nm support; (de fenêtre) sill; (pour objet) rest; **à l'~ de** in support of; **prendre ~ sur** lean on.

appui-tête* (pl **appuis-tête**) /apɥitɛt/ nm headrest.

appuyer /apɥije/ ㉛ vt lean, rest; (presser) press; (soutenir) support, back. ● vi **~ sur** press (on); (fig) stress. ■ **s'~ sur** vpr lean on; (compter sur) rely on.

après /apʀɛ/ prép after; (au-delà de) after, beyond; **~ avoir fait** after doing; **~ tout** after all; **~ coup** after the event; **d'~** (selon) according to; (en imitant) from; (adapté de) based on. ● adv after (wards); (plus tard) later; **le bus d'~** the next bus. ● conj **~ qu'il est parti** after he left. **après-demain** adv the day after tomorrow. **après-guerre** (pl **~s**) nm ou f postwar period. **après-midi*** nm ou f inv afternoon.

a

après-rasage (pl ~s) nm aftershave. **après-shampooing** nm conditioner. **après-ski*** nm inv moon boot. **après-vente*** adj inv after-sales.

a priori* /apRijɔRi/ adv (à première vue) offhand, on the face of it; (sans réfléchir) out of hand. ●nm preconception.

à-propos /apRɔpo/ nm timing, timeliness; (fig) presence of mind.

apte /apt/ adj capable (**à** of); (ayant les qualités requises) suitable (**à** for); (en état) fit (**à** for).

aptitude /aptityd/ nf aptitude, ability.

aquarelle /akwaRɛl/ nf water-colour.

aquatique /akwatik/ adj aquatic; (Sport) water.

arabe /aRab/ adj Arab; (Ling) Arabic; (désert) Arabian. ●nm (Ling) Arabic. A~ nmf Arab.

Arabie /aRabi/ nf ~ **Saoudite** Saudi Arabia.

arachide /aRaʃid/ nf groundnut; **huile d'**~ groundnut oil.

araignée /aRɛɲe/ nf spider.

arbitraire /aRbitRɛR/ adj arbitrary.

arbitre /aRbitR/ nm referee; (au cricket, tennis) umpire; (expert) arbiter; (Jur) arbitrator. **arbitrer** ◼ vt (match) referee, umpire; (Jur) arbitrate in.

arbre /aRbR/ nm tree; (Tech) shaft.

arbuste /aRbyst/ nm shrub.

arc /aRk/ nm (arme) bow; (courbe) curve; (voûte) arch; ~ **de cercle** arc of a circle.

arc-en-ciel (pl **arcs-en-ciel**) /aRkãsjɛl/ nm rainbow.

arche /aRʃ/ nf arch; ~ **de Noé** Noah's ark.

archéologie /aRkeɔlɔʒi/ nf archaeology.

archevêque /aRʃəvɛk/ nm archbishop.

architecte /aRʃitɛkt/ nmf architect. **architecture** nf architecture.

Arctique /aRktik/ nm Arctic.

ardent, ~e /aRdã, -t/ adj burning; (passionné) ardent; (foi) fervent. **ardeur** nf ardour; (chaleur) heat.

ardoise /aRdwaz/ nf slate; ~ **électronique** notepad computer.

arène /aRɛn/ nf arena; ~s amphitheatre; (pour corridas) bullring.

arête /aRɛt/ nf (de poisson) bone; (bord) ridge.

argent /aRʒã/ nm money; (métal) silver; ~ **comptant** cash; **prendre pour** ~ **comptant** take at face value; ~ **de poche** pocket money.

argenté, ~e /aRʒãte/ adj silver(y); (métal) (silver-)plated.

argenterie /aRʒãtRi/ nf silverware.

Argentine /aRʒãtin/ nf Argentina.

argile /aRʒil/ nf clay.

argot /aRgo/ nm slang.

argument /aRgymã/ nm argument; ~ **de vente** selling point. **argumenter** ◼ vi argue.

aristocratie /aRistɔkRasi/ nf aristocracy.

arithmétique /aRitmetik/ nf arithmetic. ●adj arithmetical.

armature /aRmatyR/ nf framework; (de tente) frame.

arme /aRm/ nf arm, weapon; ~ **à feu** firearm; ~s (blason) coat of arms; ~s **de destruction massive** weapons of mass destruction.

armée /aRme/ nf army; ~ **de l'air** Air Force; ~ **de terre** Army.

armer /aRme/ ◼ vt arm; (fusil) cock; (navire) equip; (renforcer) reinforce; (Photo) wind on. ◼ s'~ **de** vpr arm oneself with.

armoire /aʀmwaʀ/ nf cupboard; (penderie) wardrobe; (US) closet; ~ **à pharmacie** medicine cabinet.

armure /aʀmyʀ/ nf armour.

arnaque /aʀnak/ nf 🄵 swindling; **c'est de l'~** it's a swindle🄵.

arobas(e) /aʀɔbas, aʀɔbaz/ nm at sign.

aromate /aʀɔmat/ nm herb, spice.

aromatisé, ~e /aʀɔmatize/ adj flavoured.

arôme /aʀom/ nm aroma; (additif) flavouring.

arpenter /aʀpɑ̃te/ 🛈 vt pace up and down; (terrain) survey.

arqué, ~e /aʀke/ adj arched; (jambes) bandy.

arrache-pied: d'~* /daʀaʃpje/ loc relentlessly.

arracher /aʀaʃe/ 🛈 vt pull out *ou* off; (plante) pull *ou* dig up; (cheveux, page) tear *ou* pull out; (par une explosion) blow off; ~ **à** (enlever à) snatch from; (fig) force *ou* wrest from. ▪ s'~ **qch** vpr fight over sth.

arranger /aʀɑ̃ʒe/ 🛈 vt arrange, fix up; (réparer) put right; (régler) sort out; (convenir à) suit. ▪ s'~ vpr (se mettre d'accord) come to an arrangement; (se débrouiller) manage (**pour** to).

arrestation /aʀɛstasjɔ̃/ nf arrest.

arrêt /aʀɛ/ nm stopping; (de combats) cessation; (de production) halt; (lieu) stop; (pause) pause; (Jur) ruling; **aux ~s** (Mil) under arrest; **à l'~** (véhicule) stationary; (machine) idle; **faire un ~** (make a) stop; **sans ~** (sans escale) nonstop; (sans interruption) constantly; ~ **maladie** sick leave; ~ **de travail** (grève) stoppage; (Méd) sick leave.

arrêté /aʀete/ nm order; ~ **municipal** bylaw.

arrêter /aʀete/ 🛈 vt stop; (date) fix; (appareil) turn off; (renoncer à) give up; (appréhender) arrest. ▪ vi

stop. ▪ s'~ vpr stop; **s'~ de faire** stop doing.

arrhes /aʀ/ nfpl deposit; **verser des ~** pay a deposit.

arrière /aʀjɛʀ/ adj inv back, rear. ● nm back, rear; (football) back; **à l'~** in *ou* at the back; **en ~** behind; (marcher, tomber) backwards; (marcher, tomber) backwards; **en ~ de** behind. **arrière-boutique** (pl ~s) nf back room (of the shop). **arrière-garde** (pl ~s) nf rearguard. **arrière-goût*** (pl ~s) nm aftertaste. **arrière-grand-mère** (pl **arrière-grands-mères**) nf great-grandmother. **arrière-grand-père** (pl **arrière-grands-pères**) nm great-grandfather. **arrière-pays** nm inv backcountry. **arrière-pensée** (pl ~s) nf ulterior motive. **arrière-plan** nm (pl ~s) background.

arrimer /aʀime/ 🛈 vt secure; (cargaison) stow.

arrivage /aʀivaʒ/ nm consignment.

arrivée /aʀive/ nf arrival; (Sport) finish.

arriver /aʀive/ 🛈 vi (aux être) arrive, come; (réussir) succeed; (se produire) happen; ~ **à** (atteindre) reach; ~ **à faire** manage to do; **je n'arrive pas à faire** I can't do; **en ~ à faire** get to the stage of doing; **il arrive que** it happens that; **il lui arrive de faire** he (sometimes) does.

arriviste /aʀivist/ nmf go-getter, self-seeker.

arrondir /aʀɔ̃diʀ/ 🛈 vt (make) round; (somme) round off. ▪ s'~ vpr become round(ed).

🄲**arrondissement** /aʀɔ̃dismɑ̃/ nm district.

arroser /aʀoze/ 🛈 vt water; (repas) wash down (with a drink); (rôti) baste; (victoire) drink to. **arrosoir** nm watering can.

art /aʀ/ nm art; (don) knack (**de**

🄲 *see* A-Z of French life and culture

a

faire of doing); ∼**s et métiers** arts and crafts; ∼**s ménagers** home economics (+ sg).

artère /aʀtɛʀ/ nf artery; **(grande)** ∼ main road.

arthrite /aʀtʀit/ nf arthritis.

arthrose /aʀtʀoz/ nf osteoarthritis.

artichaut /aʀtiʃo/ nm artichoke.

article /aʀtikl/ nm article; (Comm) item, article; **à l'**∼ **de la mort** at death's door; ∼ **de fond** feature (article); ∼**s de voyage** travel goods.

articulation /aʀtikylasjɔ̃/ nf articulation; (Anat) joint.

articuler /aʀtikyle/ 1 vt articulate; (structurer) structure; (assembler) connect (**sur** to).

artificiel, ∼**le** /aʀtifisjɛl/ adj artificial.

artisan /aʀtizɑ̃/ nm artisan, craftsman; **l'**∼ **de** (fig) the architect of.

artisanal, ∼**e** (mpl ∼**aux**) /aʀtizanal/ adj craft; (méthode) traditional; (amateur) home-made; **de fabrication** ∼**e** hand-made, hand-crafted.

artiste /aʀtist/ nmf artist. **artistique** adj artistic.

as¹ /a/ ▷AVOIR 5.

as² /ɑs/ nm ace.

ascenseur /asɑ̃sœʀ/ nm lift; (US) elevator.

ascension /asɑ̃sjɔ̃/ nf ascent; **l'A**∼ Ascension.

aseptiser /asɛptize/ 1 vt disinfect; (stériliser) sterilize; **aseptisé** (péj) sanitized.

asiatique /azjatik/ adj Asian. **A**∼ nmf Asian.

Asie /azi/ nf Asia.

asile /azil/ nm refuge; (Pol) asylum; (pour malades, vieillards) home; ∼ **de nuit** night shelter.

··
▣ see A–Z of French life and culture

aspect /aspɛ/ nm appearance; (facettes) aspect; (perspective) side; **à l'**∼ **de** at the sight of.

asperge /aspɛʀʒ/ nf asparagus.

asperger /aspɛʀʒe/ 40 vt spray.

asphyxier /asfiksje/ 45 vt (personne) asphyxiate; (entreprise, réseau) paralyse. ■ **s'**∼ vpr suffocate; gas oneself; (entreprise, réseau) become paralysed.

aspirateur /aspiʀatœʀ/ nm vacuum cleaner.

aspirer /aspiʀe/ 1 vt inhale; (liquide) suck up. ● vi ∼ **à** aspire to.

aspirine® /aspiʀin/ nf aspirin.

assainir /aseniʀ/ 2 vt clean up.

assaisonnement /asɛzɔnmɑ̃/ nm seasoning.

assassin /asasɛ̃/ nm murderer; (Pol) assassin. **assassiner** 1 vt murder; (Pol) assassinate.

assaut /aso/ nm assault, onslaught; **donner l'**∼ **à, prendre d'**∼ storm.

assemblage /asɑ̃blaʒ/ nm assembly; (combinaison) collection; (Tech) joint.

▣**assemblée** /asɑ̃ble/ nf meeting; (gens réunis) gathering; (Pol) assembly.

assembler /asɑ̃ble/ 1 vt assemble, put together; (réunir) gather. ■ **s'**∼ vpr gather, assemble.

asseoir* /aswaʀ/ 9 vt sit (down), seat; (bébé, malade) sit up; (affermir) establish; (baser) base. ■ **s'**∼ vpr sit (down).

assez /ase/ adv (suffisamment) enough; (plutôt) quite, fairly; ∼ **grand/rapide** big/fast enough (**pour** to); ∼ **de** enough; **j'en ai** (∼ **de**) I've had enough (of).

assidu, ∼**e** /asidy/ adj (zélé) assiduous; (régulier) regular; ∼ **auprès de** attentive to. **assiduité** nf assiduousness, regularity.

assiéger /asjeʒe/ 14 40 vt besiege.

assiette /asjɛt/ nf plate; (équilibre) seat; ~ **anglaise** assorted cold meats; ~ **creuse/plate** soup-/dinner-plate; **ne pas être dans son** ~ feel out of sorts.

assigner /asiɲe/ 1 vt assign; (limite) fix.

assimilation /asimilasjɔ̃/ nf assimilation; (comparaison) likening, comparison.

assimiler /asimile/ 1 vt ~ **à** liken to; (classer) class as. ■ s'~ vpr assimilate; (être comparable) be comparable (**à** to).

assis, ~e /asi, -z/ adj sitting (down), seated. ●▷ASSEOIR 9.

assise /asiz/ nf (base) foundation; ~**s** (tribunal) assizes; (congrès) conference, congress.

assistance /asistɑ̃s/ nf audience; (aide) assistance; **l'A~ (publique)** welfare services.

assistant, ~e /asistɑ̃, -t/ nm, f assistant; (Scol) foreign language assistant; ~**s** (spectateurs) members of the audience; ~**e sociale** social worker; ~ **personnel numérique** personal digital assistant, PDA.

assister /asiste/ 1 vt assist; ~ **à** attend, be (present) at; (accident) witness; **assisté par ordinateur** computer-assisted.

association /asɔsjasjɔ̃/ nf association.

associé, ~e /asɔsje/ nm, f partner, associate. ●adj associate.

associer /asɔsje/ 45 vt associate; (mêler) combine (**à** with); ~ **qn à** (projet) involve sb in; (bénéfices) give sb a share of. ■ s'~ vpr (sociétés, personnes) become associated, join forces (**à** with); (s'harmoniser) combine (**à** with); s'~ **à** (joie, opinion de qn) share; (projet) take part in.

assommer /asɔme/ 1 vt knock out; (animal) stun; (fig) overwhelm; (ennuyer 1) bore.

Assomption /asɔ̃psjɔ̃/ nf Assumption.

assortiment /asɔrtimɑ̃/ nm assortment.

assortir /asɔrtir/ 2 vt match (**à** with, to); ~ **de** accompany with. ■ s'~ vpr match; s'~ **à qch** match sth.

assoupir (s') /(s)asupir/ 2 vpr doze off; (s'apaiser) subside.

assouplir /asuplir/ 2 vt make supple; (fig) make flexible.

assourdir /asurdir/ 2 vt (personne) deafen; (bruit) muffle.

assouvir /asuvir/ 2 vt satisfy.

assujettir /asyʒetir/ 2 vt subjugate, subdue; ~ **à** subject to.

assumer /asyme/ 1 vt assume; (coût) meet; (accepter) come to terms with, accept.

assurance /asyrɑ̃s/ nf (self-)assurance; (garantie) assurance; (contrat) insurance; ~**s sociales** social insurance; ~ **automobile/maladie** car/health insurance.

assuré, ~e /asyre/ adj certain, assured; (sûr de soi) confident, assured. ●nm, f insured party.

assurer /asyre/ 1 vt ensure; (fournir) provide; (exécuter) carry out; (Comm) insure; (stabiliser) steady; (frontières) make secure; ~ **à qn que** assure sb that; ~ **qn de** assure sb of; ~ **la gestion/ défense de** manage/defend. ■ s'~ vpr take out insurance; s'~ **de/que** make sure of/that; s'~ **qch** (se procurer) secure sth. assureur nm insurer.

astérisque /asterisk/ nm asterisk.

asthmatique /asmatik/ adj & nmf asthmatic.

asthme /asm/ nm asthma.

asticot /astiko/ nm maggot.

astreindre /astrɛ̃dr/ 22 vt ~ **qn à qch** force sth on sb; ~ **qn à faire** force sb to do.

astrologie /astʀɔlɔʒi/ nf astrology. **astrologue** nmf astrologer.

astronaute /astʀonot/ nmf astronaut.

astronomie /astʀɔnɔmi/ nf astronomy.

astuce /astys/ nf smartness; (truc) trick; (plaisanterie) wisecrack.

astucieux, -ieuse /astysjø, -z/ adj smart, clever.

atelier /atəlje/ nm (local) workshop; (de peintre) studio; (séance de travail) workshop.

athée /ate/ nmf atheist. ●adj atheistic.

athlète /atlɛt/ nmf athlete. **athlétisme** nm athletics.

Atlantique /atlɑ̃tik/ nm Atlantic (Ocean).

atmosphère /atmosfɛʀ/ nf atmosphere.

atomique /atɔmik/ adj atomic; (énergie, centrale) nuclear.

atomiseur /atɔmizœʀ/ nm spray.

atout /atu/ nm trump (card); (avantage) asset.

atroce /atʀɔs/ adj atrocious.

attabler (s') /(s)atable/ ∎ vpr sit down at table.

attachant, ~e /ataʃɑ̃, -t/ adj charming.

attache /ataʃ/ nf (agrafe) fastener; (lien) tie.

attaché, ~e /ataʃe/ adj **être ~ à** (aimer) be attached to. ●nm, f (Pol) attaché.

attacher /ataʃe/ ∎ vt tie (up); (ceinture, robe) fasten; (bicyclette) lock; **~ à** (attribuer à) attach to. ●vi (Culin) stick. ∎ **s'~ à** vpr fasten, do up; **s'~ à** (se lier à) become attached to; (se consacrer à) apply oneself to.

attaquant, ~e /atakɑ̃, -t/ nm, f attacker; (au football) striker; (au football américain) forward.

attaque /atak/ nf attack; **~**

(cérébrale) stroke; **il va en faire une ~** he'll have a fit; **~ à main armée** armed attack.

attaquer /atake/ ∎ vt attack; (banque) raid. ●vi attack. ∎ **s'~ à** vpr attack; (problème, sujet) tackle.

attardé, ~e /atarde/ adj backward; (idées) outdated; (en retard) late.

attarder (s') /(s)atarde/ ∎ vpr linger.

atteindre /atɛ̃dʀ/ 22 vt reach; (blesser) hit; (affecter) affect.

atteint, ~e /atɛ̃, -t/ adj **~ de** suffering from.

atteinte /atɛ̃t/ nf attack (à on); **porter ~ à** attack; (droit) infringe.

atteler /atle/ 38 vt (cheval) harness; (remorque) couple. ∎ **s'~ à** vpr get down to.

attelle /atɛl/ nf splint.

attenant, ~e /atnɑ̃, -t/ adj **~ (à)** adjoining.

attendant: en ~ /ɑ̃natɑ̃dɑ̃/ loc meanwhile.

attendre /atɑ̃dʀ/ 3 vt wait for; (bébé) expect; (être le sort de) await; (escompter) expect; **~ que qn fasse** wait for sb to do. ●vi wait; (au téléphone) hold. ∎ **s'~ à** vpr expect.

attendrir /atɑ̃dʀiʀ/ 2 vt move (to pity). ∎ **s'~** vpr be moved to pity.

attendu¹ /atɑ̃dy/ prép given, considering; **~ que** considering that.

attendu², ~e /atɑ̃dy/ adj (escompté) expected; (espéré) long-awaited.

attentat /atɑ̃ta/ nm assassination attempt; **~ (à la bombe)** (bomb) attack.

attente /atɑ̃t/ nf wait(ing); (espoir) expectations (+ pl).

attenter /atɑ̃te/ ∎ vi **~ à** make an attempt on; (fig) violate.

attentif, -ive /atɑ̃tif, -v/ adj

attentive; (scrupuleux) careful; ∼ **à** mindful of; (soucieux) careful of.

attention /atɑ̃sjɔ̃/ nf attention; (soin) care; ∼ **(à)!** watch out (for)!; **faire** ∼ **à** (écouter) pay attention to; (prendre garde à) watch out for; (prendre soin de) take care of; **faire** ∼ **à faire** be careful to do. **attentionné,** ∼**e** adj considerate.

attentisme /atɑ̃tism/ nm wait-and-see policy.

atténuer /atenɥe/ **1** vt (violence) reduce; (critique) tone down; (douleur) ease; (faute) mitigate. ■ s'∼ vpr subside.

atterrir /ateʀiʀ/ **2** vi land. **atterrissage** nm landing.

attestation /atɛstasjɔ̃/ nf certificate.

attester /atɛste/ **1** vt testify to; ∼ **que** testify that.

attirant, ∼**e** /atiʀɑ̃, -t/ adj attractive.

attirer /atiʀe/ **1** vt draw, attract; (causer) bring. ■ s'∼ vpr bring upon oneself; (amis) win.

attiser /atize/ **1** vt (feu) poke; (sentiment) stir up.

attitré, ∼**e** /atitʀe/ adj accredited; (habituel) usual, regular.

attitude /atityd/ nf attitude; (maintien) bearing.

attraction /atʀaksjɔ̃/ nf attraction.

attrait /atʀɛ/ nm attraction.

attraper /atʀape/ **1** vt catch; (corde, main) catch hold of; (habitude, accent) pick up; (maladie) catch; **se faire** ∼ **1** get told off.

attrayant, ∼**e** /atʀɛjɑ̃, -t/ adj attractive.

attribuer /atʀibɥe/ **1** vt allocate; (prix) award; (imputer) attribute. ■ s'∼ vpr claim (for oneself). **attribution** nf awarding, allocation.

attrouper (s') /(s)atʀupe/ **1** vpr gather.

au /o/ ▷**À**.

aubaine /obɛn/ nf godsend, opportunity.

aube /ob/ nf dawn, daybreak.

auberge /obɛʀʒ/ nf inn; ∼ **de jeunesse** youth hostel.

aubergine /obɛʀʒin/ nf aubergine; (US) eggplant.

aucun, ∼**e** /okœ̃, okyn/ adj (dans une phrase négative) no, not any; (positif) any. ●pron (dans une phrase négative) none, not any; (positif) any; ∼ **des deux** neither of the two; **d'**∼**s** some. **aucunement** adv not at all, in no way.

audace /odas/ nf daring; (impudence) audacity.

audacieux, -ieuse /odasjø, -z/ adj daring.

au-delà /od(ə)la/ adv beyond. ●prép ∼ **de** beyond.

au-dessous /od(ə)su/ adv below. ●prép ∼ **de** below; (couvert par) under.

au-dessus /od(ə)sy/ adv above. ●prép ∼ **de** above.

au-devant /od(ə)vɑ̃/ prép **aller** ∼ **de qn** go to meet sb; **aller** ∼ **des désirs de qn** anticipate sb's wishes.

audience /odjɑ̃s/ nf audience; (d'un tribunal) hearing; (succès, attention) success.

audimat® /odimat/ nm **l'**∼ the TV ratings.

audiovisuel, ∼**le** /odjovizɥɛl/ adj audio-visual.

auditeur, -trice /oditœʀ, -tʀis/ nm, f listener.

audition /odisjɔ̃/ nf hearing; (Théât, Mus) audition.

auditoire /oditwaʀ/ nm audience.

augmentation /ogmɑ̃tasjɔ̃/ nf increase; ∼ **(de salaire)** (pay) rise; (US) raise.

augmenter /ogmɑ̃te/ **1** vt/i increase; (employé) give a pay rise *ou* raise to.

augure /ogyʀ/ nm (devin) oracle; **être de bon/mauvais ~** be a good/ bad sign.

aujourd'hui /oʒuʀdɥi/ adv today.

auparavant /opaʀavɑ̃/ adv (avant) before; (précédemment) previously; (en premier lieu) beforehand.

auprès /opʀɛ/ prép **~ de** (à côté de) beside, next to; (comparé à) compared with; **s'excuser/se plaindre ~ de** apologize/ complain to.

auquel /okɛl/ ▸LEQUEL.

aura, aurait /oʀa, oʀɛ/ ▸AVOIR **5**.

aurore /oʀoʀ/ nf dawn.

aussi /osi/ adv (également) too, also, as well; (dans une comparaison) as; (si, tellement) so; **~ bien que** as well as. ●conj (donc) so, consequently.

aussitôt /osito/ adv immediately; **~ que** as soon as, the moment; **~ arrivé** as soon as he arrived.

austère /ostɛʀ/ adj austere.

Australie /ostʀali/ nf Australia.

australien, ~ne /ostʀaljɛ̃, -ɛn/ adj Australian. **A~, ~ne** nm, f Australian.

autant /otɑ̃/ adv (travailler, manger) as much (**que** as); **~ (de)** (quantité) as much (**que** as); (nombre) as many (**que** as); (tant) so much, so many; **~ faire** one had better do; **d'~ plus que** all the more than; **en faire ~** do the same; **pour ~** for all that.

autel /otɛl/ nm altar.

auteur /otœʀ/ nm author; **l'~ du crime** the perpetrator of the crime.

authentifier /otɑ̃tifje/ **45** vt authenticate.

authentique /otɑ̃tik/ adj authentic.

auto /oto/ nf car; **~**

tamponneuse dodgem, bumper car.

autobus /otobys/ nm bus.

autocar /otokaʀ/ nm coach.

autochtone /otoktɔn/ nmf native.

autocollant, ~e /otokɔlɑ̃, -t/ adj self-adhesive. ●nm sticker.

autodidacte /otodidakt/ nmf self-taught person.

auto-école* (pl **~s**) /otoekɔl/ nf driving school.

automate /otomat/ nm automaton, robot.

automatique /otomatik/ adj automatic.

automatisation /otomatizasjɔ̃/ nf automation.

automne /otɔn/ nm autumn; (US) fall.

automobile /otomɔbil/ adj motor, car; (US) automobile. ●nf (motor) car; **l'~** the motor industry; (Sport) motoring. **automobiliste** nmf motorist.

autonome /otonɔm/ adj autonomous; (Ordinat) stand-alone.

autoradio /otoʀadjo/ nm car radio.

autorisation /otoʀizasjɔ̃/ nf permission, authorization; (permis) permit.

autorisé, ~e /otoʀize/ adj (opinions) authoritative; (approuvé) authorized.

autoriser /otoʀize/ **1** vt authorize, permit; (rendre possible) allow (of); (donner un droit) **~ qn à faire** entitle sb to do.

autoritaire /otoʀitɛʀ/ adj authoritarian.

autorité /otoʀite/ nf authority; **faire ~** be authoritative.

⧉autoroute /otoʀut/ nf motorway; (US) highway; **~ de l'information** (Ordinat) information superhighway.

auto-stop* /otostɔp/ nm hitchhiking; **faire de l'~** hitch-hike; **prendre qn en ~** give a lift to sb.

autour /otur/ adv around; **tout ~** all around. • prép **~ de** around.

autre /otr/ adj other; **un ~ jour/ livre** another day/book; **~ chose/part** something/ somewhere else; **quelqu'un/ rien d'~** somebody/ nothing else; **quoi d'~?** what else?; **d'~ part** on the other hand; (de plus) moreover, besides; **vous ~s Anglais** you English. • pron **un ~, une ~** another (one); **l'~** the other (one); **les ~s** the others; (autrui) others; **d'~s** (some) others; **l'un l'~** each other; **l'un et l'~** both of them; **d'un jour à l'~** (bientôt) any day now; **entre ~s** among other things.

autrefois /otrəfwa/ adv in the past; (précédemment) formerly.

autrement /otrəmã/ adv differently; (sinon) otherwise; (plus ❶) far more; **~ dit** in other words.

Autriche /otriʃ/ nf Austria.

autrichien, ~ne /otriʃjɛ̃, -jɛn/ adj Austrian. A~, ~ne nm, f Austrian.

autruche /otryʃ/ nf ostrich.

autrui /otrɥi/ pron others, other people.

aux /o/ ▷À.

auxiliaire /oksiljɛr/ adj auxiliary. • nmf (assistant) auxiliary. • nm (Gram) auxiliary.

auxquels, -quelles /okɛl/ ▷LEQUEL.

aval: en ~ /ãnaval/ loc downstream.

avaler /avale/ ❶ vt swallow.

avance /avãs/ nf advance; (sur un concurrent) lead; **~ (de fonds)** advance; **à l'~** in advance; **d'~** already; **en ~** early; (montre) fast; **en (~ sur)** (menant) ahead (of).

avancement /avãsmã/ nm promotion.

avancé, ~e /avãse/ adj advanced.

avancer /avãse/ ❿ vi move forward, advance; (travail) make progress; (montre) be fast; (faire saillie) jut out. • vt move forward; (dans le temps) bring forward; (argent) advance; (montre) put forward. ■ **s'~** vpr move forward, advance; (se hasarder) commit oneself.

avant /avã/ nm front; (Sport) forward. • adj inv front. • prép before; **~ de faire** before doing; **en ~ de** in front of; **~ peu** shortly; **~ tout** above all. • adv (dans le temps) before, beforehand; (d'abord) first; **en ~** (dans l'espace) forward(s); (dans le temps) ahead; **le bus d'~** the previous bus. • conj **~ que** before; **~ qu'il (ne) fasse** before he does.

avantage /avãtaʒ/ nm advantage; (Comm) benefit.

avantager /avãtaʒe/ ❹ vt favour; (embellir) show off to advantage.

avantageux, -euse /avãtaʒø, -z/ adj advantageous, favourable; (prix) attractive.

avant-bras /avãbra/ nm inv forearm.

avant-centre (pl **avants-centres**) /avãsãtr/ nm centre forward.

avant-coureur (pl **~s**) /avãkuroer/ adj precursory, foreshadowing.

avant-dernier, -ière (pl **~s**) /avãdernje, -jɛr/ adj & nm, f last but one.

avant-goût* (pl **~s**) /avãgu/ nm foretaste.

avant-hier /avãtjɛr/ adv the day before yesterday.

avant-poste (pl **~s**) /avãpɔst/ nm outpost.

avant-première (pl **~s**) /avãprəmjɛr/ nf preview.

avant-propos /avɑ̃pRɔpo/ nm inv foreword.

avare /avaR/ adj miserly; ~ **de** sparing with. •nmf miser.

avarié, ~e /avaRje/ adj (aliment) spoiled.

avatar /avataR/ nm misfortune.

avec /avɛk/ prép with. •adv 🔢 with it *ou* them.

avènement /avɛnmɑ̃/ nm advent; (d'un roi) accession.

avenir /avniR/ nm future; **à l'~** in future; **d'~** with (future) prospects.

aventure /avɑ̃tyR/ nf adventure; (sentimentale) affair. **aventureux, -euse** adj adventurous; (hasardeux) risky.

avérer (s') /(s)aveRe/ 🔢 vpr prove (to be).

averse /avɛRs/ nf shower.

avertir /avɛRtiR/ 🔢 vt inform; (mettre en garde, menacer) warn. **avertissement** nm warning.

avertisseur /avɛRtisœR/ nm alarm; (Auto) horn; ~ **d'incendie** fire-alarm; ~ **lumineux** warning light.

aveu (pl ~x) /avø/ nm confession; **de l'~ de** by the admission of.

aveugle /avœgl/ adj blind. •nmf blind man, blind woman.

aviateur, -trice /avjatœR, -tRis/ nm, f aviator.

aviation /avjasjɔ̃/ nf flying; (industrie) aviation; (Mil) air force.

avide /avid/ adj greedy (**de** for); (anxieux) eager (**de** for); ~ **de faire** eager to do.

avion /avjɔ̃/ nm plane, aeroplane, aircraft; (US) airplane; ~ **à réaction** jet.

aviron /aviRɔ̃/ nm oar; **l'~** (Sport) rowing.

avis /avi/ nm opinion; (conseil) advice; (renseignement) notification; (Comm) advice; **à mon ~** in my opinion; **changer d'~** change

one's mind; **être d'~ que** be of the opinion that; ~ **au lecteur** foreword.

avisé, ~e /avize/ adj sensible; **être bien/mal ~ de** be well-/ill-advised to.

aviser /avize/ 🔢 vt advise, notify. •vi decide what to do. ■ s'~ **de** vpr suddenly realize; **s'~ de faire** take it into one's head to do.

avocat, ~e /avɔka, -t/ nm, f barrister; (US) attorney; (fig) advocate; ~ **de la défense** counsel for the defence. •nm (fruit) avocado (pear).

avoine /avwan/ nf oats (+ pl).

---

avoir /avwaR/ 🔢

• verbe auxiliaire

····▶ have; **il nous a appelés hier** he called us yesterday.

• verbe transitif

····▶ (possession) have (got).

····▶ (obtenir) get; (au téléphone) get through to.

····▶ (duper) 🔢 have; **on m'a eu!** I've been had!

····▶ ~ **chaud/faim** be hot/hungry.

····▶ ~ **dix ans** be ten years old.

• **avoir à** verbe + préposition

····▶ to have to; **j'ai beaucoup à faire** I have a lot to do; **tu n'as qu'à leur écrire** all you have to do is write to them.

• **en avoir pour** verbe + préposition

····▶ **j'en ai pour une minute** I will only be a minute; **j'en ai eu pour 100 euros** it cost me 100 euros.

• **il y a** verbe impersonnel

····▶ there is; (pluriel) there are; **qu'est-ce qu'il y a?** what's the matter?; **il est venu il y a cinq ans** he came here five years ago; **il y a au moins 5 km jusqu'à la gare** it's at least 5 km to the station.

● nom masculin
····➤ (dans un magasin) credit note.
····➤ (biens) asset (+ pl).

avortement /avɔʀtəmã/ nm (Méd) abortion.

avorter /avɔʀte/ **1** vi (projet) abort; **(se faire)** ~ have an abortion.

avoué, ~e /avwe/ adj avowed.
● nm solicitor; (US) attorney.

avouer /avwe/ **1** vt (amour, ignorance) confess; (crime) confess to, admit. ● vi confess.

avril /avʀil/ nm April.

axe /aks/ nm axis; (essieu) axle; (d'une politique) main line(s), basis; ~ **(routier)** main road.

ayant /ɛjã/ ▷AVOIR **5**.

azote /azɔt/ nm nitrogen.

azur /azyʀ/ nm sky-blue.

Bb

baba /baba/ nm ~ **(au rhum)** (rum) baba; **en rester** ~ **1** be flabbergasted.

babillard /babijaʀ/ nm ~ **électronique** (Internet) bulletin board system, BBS.

babines /babin/ nfpl **se lécher les** ~ lick one's chops.

babiole /babjɔl/ nf trinket.

bâbord /babɔʀ/ nm port (side).

baby-foot* /babifut/ nm inv table football.

bac /bak/ nm (Scol) ▷BACCALAURÉAT; (bateau) ferry; (récipient) tub; (plus petit) tray.

🄲baccalauréat /bakalɔʀea/ nm school leaving certificate.

bâche /baʃ/ nf tarpaulin.

🄲bachelier, -ière /baʃəlje, -jɛʀ/ nm, f holder of the baccalauréat.

bachoter /baʃɔte/ **1** vi cram (for an exam).

bâcler /bakle/ **1** vt botch (up).

bactérie /bakteʀi/ nf bacterium; ~**s** bacteria.

badaud, ~e /bado, -d/ nm, f onlooker.

badigeonner /badiʒɔne/ **1** vt whitewash; (barbouiller) daub.

badiner /badine/ **1** vi banter.

baffe /baf/ nf **1** slap.

baffle /bafl/ nm speaker.

bafouiller /bafuje/ **1** vt/i stammer.

bagage /bagaʒ/ nm bag; (connaissances) knowledge; ~**s** luggage; ~ **à main** hand luggage.

bagarre /bagaʀ/ nf fight.

bagatelle /bagatɛl/ nf trifle; (somme) trifling amount.

bagnard /baɲaʀ/ nm convict.

bagnole /baɲɔl/ nf **1** car.

bague /bag/ nf (bijou) ring.

baguette /bagɛt/ nf stick; (de chef d'orchestre) baton; (chinoise) chopstick; (pain) baguette; ~ **magique** magic wand; ~ **de tambour** drumstick.

baie /bɛ/ nf (Géog) bay; (fruit) berry; (Ordinat) bay; ~ **(vitrée)** picture window.

baignade /bɛɲad/ nf swimming.

baigner /beɲe/ **1** vt bathe; (enfant) bath. ● vi ~ **dans l'huile** swim in grease. ■ **se** ~ vpr have a

🄲 see A-Z of French life and culture

swim. **baigneur, -euse** nm, f swimmer.

baignoire /bɛɲwaʀ/ nf bath(tub).

bail (pl **baux**) /baj, bo/ nm lease.

bâiller /baje/ **1** vi yawn; (être ouvert) gape.

bailleur /bajœʀ/ nm ~ **de fonds** (Comm) sleeping partner.

bain /bɛ̃/ nm bath; (baignade) swim; **prendre un ~ de soleil** sunbathe; ~ **de bouche** mouthwash; **être dans le ~** (fig) be in the swing of things; **se remettre dans le ~** get back into the swing of things; **prendre un ~ de foule** mingle with the crowd.

bain-marie (pl **bains-marie**) /bɛ̃maʀi/ nm double boiler.

baiser /beze/ **1** vt (main) kiss; ✖ screw ✖. ●nm kiss.

baisse /bɛs/ nf fall, drop; **être en ~** be going down.

baisser /bese/ **1** vt lower; (radio, lampe) turn down. ●vi (niveau) go down, fall; (santé, forces) fail. ■ **se ~** vpr bend down.

bal (pl ~**s**) /bal/ nm dance; (habillé) ball; (lieu) dance-hall; ~ **costumé** fancy-dress ball.

balade /balad/ nf stroll; (en auto) drive.

balader /balade/ **1** vt take for a stroll. ■ **se ~** vpr (à pied) (go for a) stroll; (en voiture) go for a drive; (voyager) travel.

baladeur /baladœʀ/ nm personal stereo.

balafre /balafʀ/ nf gash; (cicatrice) scar.

balai /balɛ/ nm broom.

balance /balɑ̃s/ nf scales (+ pl); **la B~** Libra.

balancer /balɑ̃se/ **10** vt swing; (doucement) sway; (lancer **1**) chuck! (se débarrasser de **1**) chuck out **1**. ●vi sway. ■ **se ~** vpr swing; sway; **s'en ~ 1** not to give a damn **1**.

balancier /balɑ̃sje/ nm (d'horloge) pendulum; (d'équilibriste) pole.

balançoire /balɑ̃swaʀ/ nf swing.

balayage /balejaʒ/ nm sweeping; (cheveux) highlights.

balayer /baleje/ **31** vt sweep (up); (vent) sweep away; (se débarrasser de) sweep aside.

balbutiement /balbysimɑ̃/ nm stammering; **les ~s** (fig) the first steps.

balcon /balkɔ̃/ nm balcony; (Théât) dress circle.

baleine /balɛn/ nf whale.

balise /baliz/ nf beacon; (bouée) buoy; (Auto) (road) sign. **baliser** **1** vt mark out (with beacons); (route) signpost; (sentier) mark out.

balivernes /balivɛʀn/ nfpl nonsense.

ballant, -e /balɑ̃, -t/ adj dangling.

balle /bal/ nf (projectile) bullet; (Sport) ball; (paquet) bale.

ballerine /balʀin/ nf (danseuse) ballerina; (chaussure) ballet pump.

ballet /balɛ/ nm ballet.

ballon /balɔ̃/ nm (Sport) ball; ~ **(de baudruche)** balloon; ~ **de football** football.

ballonné, -e /balɔne/ adj bloated.

balnéaire /balneɛʀ/ adj seaside.

balourd, -e /baluʀ, -d/ nm, f oaf. ●adj uncouth.

balustrade /balystʀad/ nf railing.

ban /bɑ̃/ nm round of applause; ~**s** (de mariage) banns; **mettre au ~ de** cast out from.

banal, -e (mpl ~**s**) /banal/ adj commonplace, banal.

banane /banan/ nf banana.

banc /bɑ̃/ nm bench; (de poissons) shoal; ~ **des accusés** dock; ~ **d'essai** (test) testing ground.

bancaire /bɑ̃kɛʀ/ adj (secteur)

b

banking; (chèque) bank.

bancal, ~**e** (mpl ~**s**) /bɑ̃kal/ adj
wobbly; (solution) shaky.

bande /bɑ̃d/ nf (groupe) gang; (de
papier) strip; (rayure) stripe; (de
film) reel; (pansement) bandage;
🌅**dessinée** comic strip; ~
(**magnétique**) tape; ~ **sonore**
sound-track.

bande-annonce (pl **bandes-
annonces**) /bɑ̃danɔ̃s/ nf trailer.

bandeau (pl ~**x**) /bɑ̃do/ nm
headband; (sur les yeux) blindfold;
~ **publicitaire** (Ordinat) banner.

bander /bɑ̃de/ **1** vt bandage; (arc)
bend; (muscle) tense; ~ **les yeux
à** blindfold.

banderole /bɑ̃dʀɔl/ nf banner.

bandit /bɑ̃di/ nm bandit.
banditisme nm crime.

bandoulière: en ~ /bɑ̃duljɛʀ/
loc across one's shoulder.

banlieue /bɑ̃ljø/ nf suburbs; **de**
~ suburban. **banlieusard**, ~**e**
nm, f (suburban) commuter.

bannir /baniʀ/ **2** vt banish.

banque /bɑ̃k/ nf bank; (activité)
banking; ~ **de données**
databank.

banqueroute /bɑ̃kʀut/ nf
bankruptcy.

banquet /bɑ̃kɛ/ nm banquet.

banquette /bɑ̃kɛt/ nf seat.

banquier, -ière /bɑ̃kje, -jɛʀ/ nm, f
banker.

baptême /batɛm/ nm baptism,
christening. **baptiser 1** vt
baptize, christen; (nommer) call.

bar /baʀ/ nm (lieu) bar.

baragouiner /baʀagwine/ **1** vt/i
gabble; (langue) speak a few
words of.

baraque /baʀak/ nf hut, shed;
(maison 🌅) house.

baratin /baʀatɛ̃/ nm 🌅 sweet ou
smooth talk.

barbare /baʀbaʀ/ adj barbaric.
• nmf barbarian.

barbe /baʀb/ nf beard; ~ **à papa**
candy-floss; (US) cotton candy;
quelle ~**!** 🌅 what a drag! 🌅.

barbelé /baʀbəle/ adj **fil** ~
barbed wire.

barber /baʀbe/ **1** vt 🌅 bore.

barboter /baʀbɔte/ **1** vi (dans
l'eau) paddle, splash. • vt (voler 🌅)
pinch.

barbouiller /baʀbuje/ **1** vt
(souiller) smear (**de** with); **tu es
tout barbouillé** your face is all
dirty; **être barbouillé** feel
queazy.

barbu, ~**e** /baʀby/ adj bearded.

barème /baʀɛm/ nm list, table;
(échelle) scale.

baril /baʀil/ nm barrel.

bariolé, ~**e** /baʀjɔle/ adj
multicoloured.

baromètre /baʀɔmɛtʀ/ nm
barometer.

baron, ~ne /baʀɔ̃, -ɔn/ nm, f
baron, baroness.

barque /baʀk/ nf (small) boat.

barrage /baʀaʒ/ nm dam; (sur
route) roadblock.

barre /baʀ/ nf bar; (trait) line,
stroke; (Naut) helm; ~ **de
boutons** (Ordinat) toolbar.

barreau (pl ~**x**) /baʀo/ nm bar;
(d'échelle) rung; la ~ (Jur) the bar.

barrer /baʀe/ **1** vt block; (porte)
bar; (rayer) cross out; (Naut) steer.
■ **se** ~ vpr 🌅 leave.

barrette /baʀɛt/ nf (hair) slide.

barrière /baʀjɛʀ/ nf (porte) gate;
(clôture) fence; (obstacle) barrier.

bar-tabac (pl **bars-tabac**)
/baʀtaba/ nm café (selling stamps and
cigarettes).

bas, basse /bɑ, bɑs/ adj (niveau,
table) low; (action) base; **au** ~
mot at the lowest estimate; **en**
~ **âge** young; ~ **morceaux**
(viande) cheap cuts. • nm bottom;

🌅 *see* A-Z of French life and culture

b

(chaussette) stocking; **~ de laine**
(fig) nest-egg. ●adv low; **en ~**
down below; (dans une maison)
downstairs; **en ~ de la page** at
the bottom of the page; **plus ~**
further *ou* lower down; **mettre
~** give birth (to). **bas de casse**
nm inv lower case. **bas-côté** (pl
~s) nm (de route) verge; (US)
shoulder.

bascule /baskyl/ nf (balance) scales
(+ pl); **cheval/fauteuil à ~**
rocking-horse/-chair.

basculer /baskyle/ **1** vi topple
over; (benne) tip up.

base /baz/ nf base; (fondement)
basis; (Pol) rank and file; **de ~**
basic. **base de données** nf
database.

baser /baze/ **1** vt base. ■**se ~
sur** vpr go by.

bas-fonds /bafɔ̃/ nmpl (eau)
shallows; (fig) dregs.

basilic /bazilik/ nm basil.

basilique /bazilik/ nf basilica.

basque /bask/ adj Basque. **⛊B~**
nmf Basque.

basse /bas/ ▷**BAS.**

basse-cour* (pl **basses-cours**)
/baskur/ nf farmyard.

bassesse /bases/ nf baseness;
(action) base act.

bassin /basɛ̃/ nm (pièce d'eau) pond;
(de piscine) pool; (Géog) basin;
(Anat) pelvis; (plat) bowl; **~
houiller** coalfield.

bassine /basin/ nf bowl.

basson /basɔ̃/ nm bassoon.

bas-ventre (pl **~s**) /bavɑ̃tr/ nm
lower abdomen.

bat /ba/ ▷**BATTRE 11.**

bataille /bataj/ nf battle; (fig)
fight.

bâtard, **~e** /batar, -d/ adj (solution)
hybrid. ●nm, f bastard.

bateau (pl **~x**) /bato/ nm boat; **~**

pneumatique rubber dinghy.
bateau-mouche (pl **bateaux-
mouches**) nm sightseeing boat.

bâti, **~e** /bati/ adj **bien ~** well-
built.

bâtiment /batimɑ̃/ nm building;
(industrie) building trade; (navire)
vessel.

bâtir /batir/ **2** vt build.

bâton /batɔ̃/ nm stick;
conversation à ~s rompus
rambling conversation; **~ de
rouge** lipstick.

battant /batɑ̃/ nm (vantail) flap;
porte à deux ~s double door.

battement /batmɑ̃/ nm (de cœur)
beat(ing); (temps) interval;
(Mus) beat.

batterie /batri/ nf (Mil, Électr)
battery; (Mus) drums; **~ de
cuisine** pots and pans.

batteur /batœr/ nm (Mus)
drummer; (Culin) whisk.

battre /batr/ **11** vt/i beat; (cartes)
shuffle; (Culin) whisk; (l'emporter
sur) beat; **~ des ailes** flap its
wings; **~ des mains** clap; **~ des
paupières** blink; **~ en retraite**
beat a retreat; **~ la semelle**
stamp one's feet; **~ son plein**
be in full swing. ■**se ~** vpr fight.

baume /bom/ nm balm.

bavard, **~e** /bavar, -d/ adj
talkative. ●nm, f chatterbox.

bavardage /bavardaʒ/ nm
chatter, gossip. **bavarder 1** vi
chat; (jacasser) chatter, gossip.

bave /bav/ nf dribble, slobber; (de
limace) slime. **baver 1** vi dribble,
slobber; (stylo) leak. **baveux, -euse** adj
dribbling; (omelette) runny.

bavoir /bavwar/ nm bib.

bavure /bavyr/ nf smudge; (erreur)
blunder; **~ policière** police
blunder.

bazar /bazar/ nm bazaar; (objets **1**)
clutter.

BCBG abrév mf (**bon chic bon
genre**) posh.

⛊ *see A-Z of French life and culture*

BD abrév f (**bande dessinée**) comic strip.

béant, ~e /beɑ̃, -t/ adj gaping.

béat, ~e /bea, -t/ adj (hum) blissful; **~ d'admiration** wide-eyed with admiration.

beau (**bel** before vowel or mute h), **belle** (mpl **~x**) /bo, bɛl/ adj beautiful; (femme) beautiful; (homme) handsome; (temps) fine, nice. ● nm beauty. ● adv **il fait ~** the weather is nice; **au ~ milieu** right in the middle; **bel et bien** well and truly; **de plus belle** more than ever; **faire le ~** sit up and beg; **on a ~ essayer/ insister** however much one tries/insists.

beaucoup /boku/ adv a lot, very much; **~ de** (nombre) (quantité) a lot of; **pas ~ (de)** not many; (quantité) not much; **~ plus/mieux** much more/better; **~ trop** far too much; **de ~** by far.

beau-fils (pl **beaux-fils**) /bofis/ nm (remariage) stepson.

beau-frère (pl **beaux-frères**) /bofʀɛʀ/ nm brother-in-law.

beau-père (pl **beaux-pères**) /bopɛʀ/ nm father-in-law; (remariage) stepfather.

beauté /bote/ nf beauty; **finir en ~** end magnificently.

beaux-arts /bozaʀ/ nmpl fine arts.

beaux-parents /boparɑ̃/ nmpl parents-in-law.

bébé /bebe/ nm baby. **bébé-éprouvette** (pl **bébés-éprouvette**) nm test-tube baby.

bec /bɛk/ nm beak; (de théière) spout; (de casserole) lip; (bouche 🎏) mouth; **~ de gaz** gas street-lamp.

bécane /bekan/ nf 🎏 bike.

bêche /bɛʃ/ nf spade.

bégayer /begeje/ 31 vt/i stammer.

bègue /bɛg/ nmf stammerer. ● adj

être ~ stammer.

bégueule /begœl/ adj prudish.

beige /bɛʒ/ adj & nm beige.

beignet /bɛɲɛ/ nm fritter.

bel /bɛl/ ▷BEAU.

bêler /bele/ 🚹 vi bleat.

belette /bəlɛt/ nf weasel.

belge /bɛlʒ/ adj Belgian. **B~** nmf Belgian.

Belgique /bɛlʒik/ nf Belgium.

bélier /belje/ nm ram; **le B~** Aries.

belle /bɛl/ ▷BEAU.

belle-fille (pl **belles-filles**) /bɛlfij/ nf daughter-in-law; (remariage) stepdaughter.

belle-mère (pl **belles-mères**) /bɛlmɛʀ/ nf mother-in-law; (remariage) stepmother.

belle-sœur (pl **belles-sœurs**) /bɛlsœʀ/ nf sister-in-law.

belliqueux, -euse /belikø, -z/ adj warlike.

bémol /bemɔl/ nm (Mus) flat.

bénédiction /benediksjɔ̃/ nf blessing.

bénéfice /benefis/ nm (gain) profit; (avantage) benefit.

bénéficiaire /benefisjɛʀ/ nmf beneficiary.

bénéficier /benefisje/ 45 vi **~ de** benefit from; (jouir de) enjoy, have.

bénéfique /benefik/ adj beneficial.

Bénélux /benelyks/ nm Benelux.

bénévole /benevɔl/ adj voluntary.

bénin, -igne /benɛ̃, -iɲ/ adj minor; (tumeur) benign.

bénir /beniʀ/ 2 vt bless. **bénit, ~e** adj (eau) holy; (pain) consecrated.

benjamin, ~e /bɛ̃ʒamɛ̃, -in/ nm, f youngest child.

benne /bɛn/ nf (de grue) scoop; **~**

b

à ordures (camion) waste disposal truck; (conteneur) skip; ~ **(basculante)** dump truck.

béquille /bekij/ nf crutch; (de moto) stand.

berceau (pl ~x) /bɛʀso/ nm (de bébé, civilisation) cradle.

bercer /bɛʀse/ [10] vt (balancer) rock; (apaiser) lull; (leurrer) delude.

béret /beʀɛ/ nm beret.

berge /bɛʀʒ/ nf (bord) bank.

berger, -ère /bɛʀʒe, -ɛʀ/ nm, f shepherd, shepherdess.

berne: en ~ /ɑ̃bɛʀn/ loc at halfmast.

berner /bɛʀne/ [1] vt fool.

besogne /bəzɔɲ/ nf task, job.

besoin /bəzwɛ̃/ nm need; **avoir ~ de** need; **au ~** if need be; **dans le ~** in need.

bestiole /bɛstjɔl/ nf [1] bug.

bétail /betaj/ nm livestock.

bête /bɛt/ adj stupid. ●nf animal; **~ noire** pet hate; **~ sauvage** wild beast; **chercher la petite ~** be overfussy.

bêtise /betiz/ nf stupidity; (action) stupid thing.

béton /betɔ̃/ nm concrete; **~ armé** reinforced concrete; **en ~** (mur) concrete; (argument [1]) watertight. **bétonnière** nf concrete mixer.

betterave /bɛtʀav/ nf beet; **~ rouge** beetroot.

beugler /bøgle/ [1] vi bellow; (radio) blare out.

beur /bœʀ/ nmf & adj [1] second-generation North African living in France.

beurre /bœʀ/ nm butter. **beurré, ~e** adj buttered; [1] drunk. **beurrier** nm butter-dish.

bévue /bevy/ nf blunder.

biais /bjɛ/ nm (moyen) way; **par le ~ de** by means of; **de ~, en ~** at an angle.

bibelot /biblo/ nm ornament.

biberon /bibʀɔ̃/ nm (feeding) bottle; **nourrir au ~** bottle-feed.

bible /bibl/ nf bible; **la B~** the Bible.

bibliographie /biblijɔgʀafi/ nf bibliography.

bibliothécaire /biblijɔtekɛʀ/ nmf librarian.

bibliothèque /biblijɔtɛk/ nf library; (meuble) bookcase.

bic® /bik/ nm Biro®.

bicarbonate /bikaʀbɔnat/ nm ~ **(de soude)** bicarbonate (of soda).

biceps /bisɛps/ nm biceps.

biche /biʃ/ nf doe; **ma ~** darling.

bichonner /biʃɔne/ [1] vt pamper.

bicyclette /bisiklɛt/ nf bicycle.

bide /bid/ nm (ventre [1]) paunch; (échec [1]) flop.

bidet /bidɛ/ nm bidet.

bidon /bidɔ̃/ nm can; (plus grand) drum; (ventre [1]) belly; **c'est du ~!** it's a load of hogwash [1]. ●adj inv [1] phoney.

bidonville /bidɔ̃vil/ nm shanty town.

bidule /bidyl/ nm [1] thing.

Biélorussie /bjelɔʀysi/ nf Byelorussia.

bien /bjɛ̃/ adv well; (très) quite, very; **~ des** (nombre) many; **tu as ~ de la chance** you are very lucky; **j'aimerais ~** I would like to; **ce n'est pas ~ de** it is not nice to; **~ sûr** of course. ●nm good; (patrimoine) possession; **~s de consommation** consumer goods. ●adj inv good; (passable) all right; (en forme) well; (à l'aise) comfortable; (beau) attractive; (respectable) nice, respectable. ●conj **~ que** (al-)though; **~ que ce soit** although it is. **bien-aimé*, ~e** adj & nm, f beloved. **bien-être** nm wellbeing.

bienfaisance /bjɛ̃fəzɑ̃s/ nf charity; **fête de ~** charity event. **bienfaisant, ~e** adj beneficial.

bienfait /bjɛ̃fɛ/ nm (kind) favour; (avantage) beneficial effect. **bienfaiteur, -trice** nm, f benefactor.

bien-pensant, ~e /bjɛ̃pɑ̃sɑ̃, -t/ adj right-thinking.

bienséance /bjɛ̃seɑ̃s/ nf propriety.

bientôt /bjɛ̃to/ adv soon; **à ~** see you soon.

bienveillance /bjɛ̃vɛjɑ̃s/ nf kind-(li)ness.

bienvenu, ~e /bjɛ̃vny/ adj welcome. ●nm, f **être le ~, être la ~e** be welcome.

bienvenue /bjɛ̃vny/ nf welcome; **souhaiter la ~ à** welcome.

bière /bjɛʀ/ nf beer; (cercueil) coffin; **~ blonde** lager; **~ brune** ≈ stout; **~ pression** draught beer.

bifteck /biftɛk/ nm steak.

bifurquer /bifyʀke/ [1] vi branch off, fork.

bigarré, ~e /bigaʀe/ adj motley.

bigoudi /bigudi/ nm curler.

bijou (pl ~x) /biʒu/ nm jewel; **~x en or** gold jewellery. **bijouterie** nf (boutique) jewellery shop; (Comm) jewellery. **bijoutier, -ière** nm, f jeweller.

bilan /bilɑ̃/ nm outcome; (d'une catastrophe) (casualty) toll; (Comm) balance sheet; **faire le ~ de** assess; **~ de santé** check-up.

bile /bil/ nf bile; **se faire de la ~** 🄸 worry.

bilingue /bilɛ̃g/ adj bilingual.

billard /bijaʀ/ nm billiards (+ pl); (table) billiard-table.

bille /bij/ nf (d'enfant) marble; (de billard) billiard-ball.

billet /bijɛ/ nm ticket; (lettre) note; (article) column; **~ (de banque)** (bank) note; **~ de 50 euros** 50-euro note.

billetterie /bijɛtʀi/ nf cash dispenser.

billion /biljɔ̃/ nm billion; (US) trillion.

bimensuel, ~le /bimɑ̃sɥɛl/ adj fortnightly, bimonthly.

binette /binɛt/ nf hoe; (visage) face; (Internet) smiley.

biochimie /bjoʃimi/ nf biochemistry.

biodégradable /bjodegʀadabl/ adj biodegradable.

biographie /bjɔgʀafi/ nf biography.

biologie /bjɔlɔʒi/ nf biology. **biologique** adj biological; (produit) organic.

bioterrorisme /bjɔtɛʀɔʀism/ nm bioterrorism.

bis /bis/ nm & interj encore.

biscornu, ~e /biskɔʀny/ adj crooked; (bizarre) cranky 🄸.

biscotte /biskɔt/ nf continental toast.

biscuit /biskɥi/ nm biscuit; (US) cookie; **~ salé** cracker; **~ de Savoie** sponge-cake.

bise /biz/ nf 🄸 kiss; (vent) north wind.

bison /bizɔ̃/ nm buffalo.

bisou /bizu/ nm 🄸 kiss.

bistro(t) /bistʀo/ nm 🄸 café, bar.

bit /bit/ nm (Ordinat) bit.

bitume /bitym/ nm asphalt.

bizarre /bizaʀ/ adj odd, strange. **bizarrerie** nf peculiarity.

blafard, ~e /blafaʀ, -d/ adj pale.

blague /blag/ nf 🄸 joke; **sans ~!** no kidding! 🄸.

blaguer /blage/ 🄸 vi 🄸 joke.

blaireau (pl ~x) /blɛʀo/ nm shaving-brush; (animal) badger.

blâmer /blame/ 🄸 vt criticize.

blanc, blanche /blɑ̃, blɑ̃ʃ/ adj white; (papier, page) blank. •nm white; (espace) blank; ~ **d'œuf** egg white; ~ **de poireau** white part of the leek; ~ **(de poulet)** chicken breast; **le** ~ (linge) whites; **laisser en** ~ leave blank. **B~, Blanche** nm, f white man, white woman. **blanche** nf (Mus) minim.

blanchiment /blɑ̃ʃimɑ̃/ nm (d'argent) laundering.

blanchir /blɑ̃ʃiʀ/ **2** vt whiten; (personne: fig) clear; (argent) launder; (Culin) blanch; ~ **(à la chaux)** whitewash. •vi turn white.

blanchisserie /blɑ̃ʃisʀi/ nf laundry.

blason /blazɔ̃/ nm coat of arms.

blasphème /blasfɛm/ nm blasphemy.

blé /ble/ nm wheat.

blême /blɛm/ adj pallid.

blessant, ~e /blesɑ̃, -t/ adj hurtful.

blessé, ~e /blese/ nm, f casualty, injured person.

blesser /blese/ **1** vt injure, hurt; (par balle) wound; (offenser) hurt. ∎se ~ vpr injure *ou* hurt oneself. **blessure** nf wound.

bleu, ~e /blø/ adj blue; (Culin) very rare; ~ **marine/turquoise** navy blue/turquoise; **avoir une peur ~e** be scared stiff. •nm blue; (contusion) bruise; ~ **(de travail)** overalls (+ pl).

bleuet /bløɛ/ nm cornflower.

blindé, ~e /blɛ̃de/ adj armoured; (fig) immune (**contre** to); **porte ~e** security door. •nm armoured car, tank.

blinder /blɛ̃de/ **1** vt armour; (fig) harden.

bloc /blɔk/ nm block; (de papier) pad; **serrer à ~** tighten hard; **en ~** (matériau) in a block; (nier) outright.

blocage /blɔkaʒ/ nm (des prix) freeze, freezing; (des roues) locking; (Psych) block.

bloc-notes (pl **blocs-notes**) /blɔknɔt/ nm note-pad.

blocus /blɔkys/ nm blockade.

blond, ~e /blɔ̃, -d/ adj fair, blond. •nm, f fair-haired man, fairhaired woman.

bloquer /blɔke/ **1** vt block; (porte, machine) jam; (roues) lock; (prix, crédits) freeze. ∎se ~ vpr (prix, roues) lock; (freins) jam; (ordinateur) crash; **bloqué par la neige** snowbound.

blottir (se) /(sə)blɔtiʀ/ **2** vpr snuggle, huddle (**contre** against).

blouse /bluz/ nf overall. **blouse blanche** nf white coat.

blouson /bluzɔ̃/ nm jacket, blouson.

bluffer /blœfe/ **1** vt/i bluff.

bobine /bɔbin/ nf (de fil, film) reel; (Électr) coil.

bobo /bɔbo/ **1** sore, cut; **avoir ~** have a pain.

bocal (pl **-aux**) /bɔkal, -o/ nm jar.

bœuf (pl **~s**) /bœf, bø/ nm bullock; (US) steer; (viande) beef; **~s** oxen.

bogue /bɔg/ nm (Ordinat) bug.

bohème /bɔɛm/ adj & nmf bohemian.

boire /bwaʀ/ **12** vt/i (personne, plante) drink; (argile) soak up; ~ **un coup** **1** have a drink.

bois /bwa/ ▷**BOIRE** **12**. •nm (matériau, forêt) wood; **de ~, en ~** wooden. •nmpl (de cerf) antlers.

boiseries /bwazʀi/ nfpl panelling.

boisson /bwasɔ̃/ nf drink.

boit /bwa/ ▷**BOIRE** **12**.

boîte* /bwat/ nf box; (de conserves) tin, can; (entreprise **1**) firm; **en ~** tinned, canned; **~ à gants** glove compartment; **~ aux lettres**

letterbox; ~ **aux lettres électronique** mailbox; ~ **de nuit** night-club; ~ **postale** post-office box; ~ **de vitesses** gear box.

boiter /bwate/ **1** vi limp. **boiteux, -euse** adj lame; (raisonnement) shaky.

boîtier* /bwatje/ nm case.

bol /bɔl/ nm bowl; ~ **d'air** abreath of fresh air; **avoir du ~!** be lucky.

bolide /bɔlid/ nm racing car.

Bolivie /bɔlivi/ nf Bolivia.

bombardement /bɔ̃bardəmɑ̃/ nm bombing; shelling.

bombarder /bɔ̃barde/ **1** vt bomb; (par obus) shell; ~ **qn de** (fig) bombard sb with. **bombardier** nm (Aviat) bomber.

bombe /bɔ̃b/ nf bomb; (atomiseur) spray, aerosol.

bombé, ~e /bɔ̃be/ adj rounded; (route) cambered.

bon, bonne /bɔ̃, bɔn/ adj good; (qui convient) right; ~ **à/pour** (approprié) it to/for; **bonne année** happy New Year; ~ **anniversaire** happy birthday; ~ **appétit/voyage** enjoy your meal/trip; **bonne chance/nuit** good luck/night; ~ **sens** common sense; **bonne femme** (péj) woman; **de bonne heure** early; **à quoi ~?** what's the point? ●adv **sentir ~** smell nice; **tenir ~** stand firm; **il fait ~** the weather is mild. ●interj right, well. ●nm (billet) voucher, coupon; ~ **de commande** order form; **pour de ~** for good. **bonne** nf (domestique) maid.

bonbon /bɔ̃bɔ̃/ nm sweet; (US) candy.

bonbonne /bɔ̃bɔn/ nf demijohn; (de gaz) cylinder.

bond /bɔ̃/ nm leap; **faire un ~** (de surprise) jump.

bonde /bɔ̃d/ nf plug; (trou) plughole.

bondé, ~e /bɔ̃de/ adj packed.

bondir /bɔ̃dir/ **2** vi leap; (de surprise) jump.

bonheur /bɔnœr/ nm happiness; (chance) (good) luck; **au petit ~** haphazardly; **par ~** luckily.

bonhomme (pl **bonshommes**) /bɔnɔm, bɔzɔm/ nm fellow; ~ **de neige** snowman. ●adj inv good hearted.

bonifier (se) /(sə)bɔnifje/ **45** vpr improve.

bonjour /bɔ̃ʒur/ nm & interj hallo, hello, good morning *ou* afternoon.

bon marché /bɔ̃marʃe/ adj inv cheap. ●adv cheap(ly)

bonne /bɔn/ ▷**BON**.

bonne-maman (pl **bonnes-mamans**) /bɔnmamɑ̃/ nf **1** granny.

bonnement /bɔnmɑ̃/ adv **tout ~** quite simply.

bonnet /bɔnɛ/ nm hat; (de soutien-gorge) cup; ~ **de bain** swimming cap. **bonneterie*** nf hosiery.

bonsoir /bɔ̃swar/ nm good evening; (en se couchant) good night.

bonté /bɔ̃te/ nf kindness.

bonus /bɔnys/ nm (Auto) no-claims bonus.

boots /buts/ nmpl ankle boots.

bord /bɔr/ nm edge; (rive) bank; **à** (~ **de**) on board; **au ~ de la mer** at the seaside; **au ~ des larmes** on the verge of tears; ~ **de la route** road-side.

bordeaux /bɔrdo/ adj inv maroon. ●nm inv Bordeaux.

bordel /bɔrdɛl/ nm brothel; (désordre **1**) shambles.

border /bɔrde/ **1** vt line, border; (tissu) edge; (personne, lit) tuck in.

bordereau (pl ~**x**) /bɔrdəro/ nm (document) slip.

bordure /bɔrdyr/ nf border; **en ~**

de on the edge of.

borgne /bɔʀɲ/ adj one-eyed.

borne /bɔʀn/ nf boundary marker; (pour barrer le passage) bollard; **~ (kilométrique)** ≈ milestone; **~s** limits.

borné, ~e /bɔʀne/ adj (esprit) narrow; (personne) narrow minded.

borner (se) /(sə)bɔʀne/ **1** vpr confine oneself (**à** to).

bosniaque /bɔsnjak/ adj Bosnian. **B~** nmf Bosnian.

Bosnie /bɔsni/ nf Bosnia.

bosse /bɔs/ nf bump; (de chameau) hump; **avoir la ~ de 1** have a gift for; **avoir roulé sa ~** have been around. **bosselé, ~e** adj dented; (terrain) bumpy.

bosser /bɔse/ **1** vi **1** work (hard).

bossu, ~e /bɔsy/ adj hunchbacked. ● nm, f hunchback.

botanique /bɔtanik/ nf botany.● adj botanical.

botte /bɔt/ nf boot; (de fleurs, légumes) bunch; (de paille) bundle, bale; **~s de caoutchouc** wellingtons.

botter /bɔte/ **1** vt **1** **ça me botte** I like the idea.

bottin® /bɔtɛ̃/ nm phone book.

bouc /buk/ nm (billy-)goat; (barbe) goatee; **~ émissaire** scapegoat.

boucan /bukã/ nm **1** din.

bouche /buʃ/ nf mouth; (lèvres) lips; **~ bée** open-mouthed; **~ d'égout** manhole; **~ d'incendie** (fire)hydrant; **~ de métro** entrance to the underground *ou* subway (US). **bouche-à-bouche** nm inv mouth-to-mouth resuscitation. **bouche-à-oreille** nm inv word of mouth.

bouché, ~e /buʃe/ adj (profession, avenir) oversubscribed; (stupide: péj) stupid.

bouchée /buʃe/ nf mouthful.

boucher[1] /buʃe/ **1** vt block; (bouteille) cork. ■ **se ~** vpr get blocked; **se ~ le nez** hold one's nose.

boucher[2]**, -ère** /buʃe, -ɛʀ/ nm, f butcher. **boucherie** nf butcher's (shop); (carnage) butchery.

bouchon /buʃɔ̃/ nm stopper; (en liège) cork; (de stylo, tube) cap; (de pêcheur) float; (embouteillage) traffic jam; **~ de cérumen** plug of earwax.

boucle /bukl/ nf (de ceinture) buckle; (de cheveux) curl; (forme) loop; **~ d'oreille** earring. **bouclé, ~e** adj (cheveux) curly.

boucler /bukle/ **1** vt fasten; (enfermer **1**) shut up; (encercler) seal off; (budget) balance; (terminer) finish off. ● vi curl.

bouclier /buklije/ nm shield.

bouddhiste /budist/ adj & nmf Buddhist.

bouder /bude/ **1** vi sulk. ●vt stay away from.

boudin /budɛ̃/ nm black pudding.

boue /bu/ nf mud.

bouée /bwe/ nf buoy; **~ de sauvetage** lifebuoy.

boueux, -euse /buø, -z/ adj muddy.

bouffe /buf/ nf **1** food, grub.

bouffée /bufe/ nf puff, whiff; (d'orgueil) fit; **~ de chaleur** (Méd) hot flush.

bouffi, ~e /bufi/ adj bloated.

bouffon, ~ne /bufɔ̃, -ɔn/ adj farcical. ●nm buffoon.

bougeoir /buʒwaʀ/ nm candlestick.

bougeotte /buʒɔt/ nf **avoir la ~ 1** have the fidgets.

bouger /buʒe/ **40** vt/i move. ■ **se ~** vpr **1** move.

bougie /buʒi/ nf candle; (Auto) spark(ing)-plug.

bouillant, ~e /bujɑ̃, -t/ adj

boiling; (très chaud) boiling hot.

bouillie /buji/ nf (pour bébé) baby cereal; (péj) mush; **en ~** crushed, mushy.

bouillir /bujiʀ/ [13] vi boil; (fig) seethe; **faire ~** boil.

bouilloire /bujwaʀ/ nf kettle.

bouillon /bujɔ̃/ nm (de cuisson) stock; (potage) broth.

bouillonner /bujɔne/ [1] vi bubble.

bouillotte /bujɔt/ nf hot-water bottle.

boulanger, -ère /bulɑ̃ʒe, -ɛʀ/ nm, f baker. **boulangerie** nf bakery. **boulangerie-pâtisserie** nf bakery (selling cakes and pastries).

boule /bul/ nf ball; ▣**~s** (jeu) boules; **jouer aux ~s** play boules; **une ~ dans la gorge** a lump in one's throat; **~ de neige** snowball.

bouleau (pl **~x**) /bulo/ nm (silver) birch.

boulet /bulɛ/ nm (de forçat) ball and chain; **~ (de canon)** cannonball; **~ de charbon** coal nut.

boulette /bulɛt/ nf (de pain, papier) pellet; (bévue) blunder; **~ de viande** meat ball.

boulevard /bulvaʀ/ nm boulevard.

bouleversant, ~e /bulvɛʀsɑ̃, -t/ adj deeply moving. **bouleversement** nm upheaval. **bouleverser** [1] vt turn upside down; (pays, plans) disrupt; (émouvoir) upset.

boulimie /bulimi/ nf bulimia.

boulon /bulɔ̃/ nm bolt.

boulot, ~te /bulo, -ɔt/ adj (rond ▣) dumpy. ●nm (travail ▣) work.

boum /bum/ nm & interj bang. ●nf (fête ▣) party.

bouquet /bukɛ/ nm (de fleurs) bunch, bouquet; (d'arbres) clump; **c'est le ~!** ▣ that's the last straw!

bouquin /bukɛ̃/ nm ▣book. **bouquiner** [1] vt/i ▣read. **bouquiniste** nmf second-hand bookseller.

bourbier /buʀbje/ nm mire; (fig) tangle.

bourde /buʀd/ nf blunder.

bourdon /buʀdɔ̃/ nm bumble bee. **bourdonnement** nm buzzing.

bourg /buʀ/ nm (market) town (centre), village town.

bourgeois, ~e /buʀʒwa, -z/ adj & nm,f middle-class (person); (péj) bourgeois. **bourgeoisie** nf middle class(es).

bourgeon /buʀʒɔ̃/ nm bud.

bourgogne /buʀgɔɲ/ nm Burgundy.

bourlinguer /buʀlɛ̃ge/ [1] vi ▣ travel about.

bourrage /buʀaʒ/ nm **~ de crâne** brainwashing.

bourratif, -ive /buʀatif, -v/ adj stodgy.

bourreau (pl **~x**)/buʀo/ nm executioner; **~ de travail** (fig) workaholic.

bourrelet /buʀlɛ/ nm weather strip, draught excluder; (de chair) roll of fat.

bourrer /buʀe/ [1] vt cram (**de** with); (pipe) fill; **~ de** (nourriture) stuff with; **~ de coups** thrash; **~ le crâne à qn** brainwash sb.

bourrique /buʀik/ nf donkey; ▣ pig-headed person.

bourru, ~e /buʀy/ adj gruff.

bourse /buʀs/ nf purse; (subvention) grant; **la B~** the Stock Exchange.

boursier, -ière /buʀsje, -jɛʀ/ adj (valeurs) Stock Exchange. ●nm, f grant holder.

boursoufler* /buʀsufle/ [1] vt (visage) cause to swell; (peinture) blister.

▣ *see* A-Z of French life and culture

b

bousculade /buskylad/ nf crush; (précipitation) rush. **bousculer** 1 vt (pousser) jostle; (presser) rush; (renverser) knock over.

bousiller /buzije/ 1 vt 𝕀 wreck.

boussole /busɔl/ nf compass.

bout /bu/ nm end; (de langue, bâton) piece; (morceau) bit; **à ∼** exhausted; **à ∼ de souffle** out of breath; **à ∼ portant** point-blank; **au ∼ de** (après) after; **venir à ∼ de** (finir) manage to finish; **d'un ∼ à l'autre** throughout; **au ∼ du compte** in the end; **∼ filtre** filtertip.

bouteille /butɛj/ nf bottle; **∼ d'oxygène** oxygen cylinder.

boutique /butik/ nf shop; (de mode) boutique.

bouton /butɔ̃/ nm button; (sur la peau) spot, pimple; (pousse) bud; (de porte, radio) knob; **∼ de manchette** cuff-link. **boutonner** 1 vt button (up). **boutonnière** nf buttonhole. **bouton-pression** (pl **boutons-pression**) nm press-stud; (US) snap.

bouture /butyʀ/ nf cutting.

bovin, **∼e** /bɔvɛ̃, -in/ adj bovine. **bovins** nmpl cattle (pl).

box (pl **∼ ou boxes**) /bɔks/ nm lock-up garage; (de dortoir) cubicle; (d'écurie) (loose) box; (Jur) dock.

boxe /bɔks/ nf boxing.

boyau (pl **∼x**) /bwajo/ nm gut; (corde) catgut; (galerie) gallery; (de bicyclette) tyre; (US) tire.

boycotter /bɔjkɔte/ 1 vt boycott.

BP abrév f (**boîte postale**) PO Box.

bracelet /braslɛ/ nm bracelet; (de montre) watchstrap.

braconnier /brakɔnje/ nm poacher.

brader /brade/ 1 vt sell off. **braderie** nf clearance sale.

braguette /bragɛt/ nf fly.

braille /braj/ nm & adj Braille.

brailler /braje/ 1 vt/i bawl.

braise /brez/ nf embers (+ pl).

braiser /breze/ 1 vt (Culin) braise.

brancard /brākar/ nm stretcher; (de charrette) shaft.

branche /brāʃ/ nf branch.

branché, **∼e** /brāʃe/ adj 𝕀 trendy.

branchement /brāʃmā/ nm connection. **brancher** 1 vt (prise) plug in; (à un réseau) connect.

brandir /brādir/ 2 vt brandish.

branler /brāle/ 1 vi be shaky.

braquer /brake/ 1 vt (arme) aim; (regard) fix; (roue) turn; (banque: 𝕀) hold up; **∼ qn contre** turn sb against. ●vi (Auto) turn (the wheel). ■**se ∼** vpr dig one's heels in.

bras /bra/ nm arm; (de rivière) branch; (Tech) arm; **∼ dessus ∼ dessous** arm in arm; **∼ droit** (fig) right hand man; **∼ de mer** sound; **en ∼ de chemise** in one's shirtsleeves. ●nmpl (fig) labour, hands.

brasier /brazje/ nm blaze.

brassard /brasar/ nm armband.

brasse /bras/ nf breast-stroke; **∼ papillon** butterfly (stroke).

brasser /brase/ 1 vt mix; (bière) brew; (affaires) handle a lot of. 𝕔**brasserie** nf brewery; (café) brasserie.

brave /brav/ adj (bon) good; (valeureux) brave. **braver** 1 vt defy.

bravo /bravo/ interj bravo. ●nm cheer.

bravoure /bravur/ nf bravery.

break /brɛk/ nm estate car; (US) station-wagon.

brebis /brabi/ nf ewe.

brèche /brɛʃ/ nf gap, breach; **être sur la ∼** be on the go.

bredouille /bʀəduj/ adj emptyhanded.

bredouiller /bʀəduje/ **1** vt/i mumble.

bref, brève /bʀɛf, -v/ adj short, brief. ●adv in short; **en ~** in short.

Brésil /bʀezil/ nm Brazil.

Bretagne /bʀətaɲ/ nf Brittany.

bretelle /bʀətɛl/ nf (de sac, maillot) strap; (d'autoroute) access road; **~s** (pour pantalon) braces; (US) suspenders.

breton, ~ne /bʀətɔ̃, -ɔn/ adj & nm (Ling) Breton. **B~, ~ne** nm, f Breton.

breuvage /bʀœvaʒ/ nm beverage.

brève /bʀɛv/ ▷**BREF.**

brevet /bʀəvɛ/ nm (diplôme) diploma; **~ (d'invention)** patent.

breveté, ~e /bʀəvte/ adj patented.

bribes /bʀib/ nfpl scraps.

bricolage /bʀikɔlaʒ/ nm do-it yourself (jobs).

bricole /bʀikɔl/ nf trifle.

bricoler /bʀikɔle/ **1** vi do DIY; (US) fix things, tinker with.

bricoleur, -euse /bʀikɔlœʀ, -øz/ nm, f handyman, handywoman.

bride /bʀid/ nf bridle.

bridé, ~e /bʀide/ adj **yeux ~s** slanting eyes.

brider /bʀide/ **1** vt (cheval) bridle; (fig) keep in check.

brièvement /bʀijɛvmɑ̃/ adv briefly.

brigade /bʀigad/ nf (de police) squad; (Mil) brigade; (fig) team. **brigadier** nm (de gendarmerie) sergeant.

brigand /bʀigɑ̃/ nm robber.

brillant, ~e /bʀijɑ̃, -t/ adj (couleur) bright; (luisant) shiny; (remarquable) brilliant. ●nm (éclat) shine;

(diamant) diamond.

briller /bʀije/ **1** vi shine.

brimade /bʀimad/ nf vexation. **brimer** **1** vt bully, harass; **se sentir brimé** feel put down.

brin /bʀɛ̃/ nm (de muguet) sprig; (d'herbe) blade; (de paille) wisp; **un ~ de** (un peu) a bit of.

brindille /bʀɛ̃dij/ nf twig.

brioche /bʀijɔʃ/ nf brioche, sweet bun; (ventre **1**) paunch.

brique /bʀik/ nf brick.

briquet /bʀikɛ/ nm (cigarette-)lighter.

brise /bʀiz/ nf breeze.

briser /bʀize/ **1** vt break. ■**se ~** vpr break.

britannique /bʀitanik/ adj British. **B~** nmf Briton; **les B~s** the British.

brocante /bʀɔkɑ̃t/ nf bric-à-brac trade; (marché) flea market.

broche /bʀɔʃ/ nf brooch; (Culin) spit; **à la ~** spit-roasted.

broché, ~e /bʀɔʃe/ adj paperback.

brochet /bʀɔʃɛ/ nm pike.

brochette /bʀɔʃɛt/ nf skewer.

brochure /bʀɔʃyʀ/ nf brochure, booklet.

broder /bʀɔde/ **1** vt/i embroider. **broderie** nf embroidery.

broncher /bʀɔ̃ʃe/ **1** vi **sans ~** without turning a hair.

bronchite /bʀɔ̃ʃit/ nf bronchitis.

bronze /bʀɔ̃z/ nm bronze.

bronzé, ~e /bʀɔ̃ze/ adj (sun-) tanned.

bronzer /bʀɔ̃ze/ **1** vi (personne) get a (sun-)tan.

brosse /bʀɔs/ nf brush; **~ à dents** toothbrush; **~ à habits** clothes brush; **en ~** (coiffure) in a crew cut.

⚏ *see A-Z of French life and culture*

b

brosser /bʀɔse/ **1** vt brush; (fig) paint. ■ se ~ vpr se ~ les dents/ les cheveux brush one's teeth/hair.

brouette /bʀuɛt/ nf wheelbarrow.

brouhaha /bʀuaa/ nm hubbub.

brouillard /bʀujaʀ/ nm fog.

brouille /bʀuj/ nf quarrel.

brouiller /bʀuje/ **1** vt (vue) blur; (œufs) scramble; (amis) set at odds; ~ les pistes cloud the issue. ■ se ~ vpr (ciel) cloud over; (amis) fall out.

brouillon, ~ne /bʀujɔ̃, -ɔn/ adj untidy. ●nm (rough) draft.

brousse /bʀus/ nf la ~ the bush.

brouter /bʀute/ **1** vt/i graze.

broyer /bʀwaje/ **31** vt crush; (moudre) grind.

bru /bʀy/ nf daughter-in-law.

bruine /bʀɥin/ nf drizzle.

bruissement /bʀɥismã/ nm rustling.

bruit /bʀɥi/ nm noise; ~ de couloir (fig) rumour.

bruitage /bʀɥitaʒ/ nm sound effects.

brûlant*, ~e /bʀylã, -t/ adj burning (hot); (sujet) red-hot; (passion) fiery.

brûlé* /bʀyle/ nm burning; ça sent le ~ I can smell something burning. ●▷BRÛLER **1**.

brûler* /bʀyle/ **1** vt/i burn; (essence) use (up); (cierge) light (à to); ~ un feu (rouge) jump the lights; ~ d'envie de faire be longing to do. ■ se ~ vpr burn oneself.

brûlure* /bʀylyʀ/ nf burn; ~s d'estomac heartburn.

brume /bʀym/ nf mist. **brumeux, -euse** adj misty; (esprit) hazy.

brun, ~e /bʀœ̃, -yn/ adj brown, dark. ●nm brown. ●nm, f dark haired person. **brunir** **2** vi turn brown; (bronzer) get a tan.

brushing /bʀœʃiŋ/ nm blow-dry.

brusque /bʀysk/ adj (personne) abrupt; (geste) violent; (soudain) sudden.

brusquer /bʀyske/ **1** vt be abrupt with; (précipiter) rush.

brut, ~e /bʀyt/ adj (diamant) rough; (champagne) dry; (pétrole) crude; (Comm) gross.

brutal, ~e (mpl -aux) /bʀytal, -o/ adj brutal. **brutalité** nf brutality.

brute /bʀyt/ nf brute.

Bruxelles /bʀysɛl/ npr Brussels.

bruyant, ~e /bʀɥijã, -t/ adj noisy.

bruyère /bʀyjɛʀ/ nf heather.

bu /by/ ▷BOIRE **12**.

bûche* /byʃ/ nf log; ~ de Noël Christmas log; ramasser une ~ **1** fall.

bûcher* /byʃe/ **1** vt/i **1** slog away (at) **1**. ●nm (supplice) stake.

bûcheron* /byʃʀɔ̃/ nm lumberjack.

budget /bydʒɛ/ nm budget. **budgétaire** adj budgetary.

buée /bɥe/ nf condensation.

buffet /byfɛ/ nm sideboard; (table garnie) buffet.

buffle /byfl/ nm buffalo.

buisson /bɥisɔ̃/ nm bush.

buissonnière /bɥisɔnjɛʀ/ adj faire l'école ~ play truant.

bulbe /bylb/ nm bulb.

bulgare /bylgaʀ/ adj & nm Bulgarian. B~ nmf Bulgarian.

Bulgarie /bylgaʀi/ nf Bulgaria.

bulldozer* /byldozɛʀ/ nm bulldozer.

bulle /byl/ nf bubble.

bulletin /byltɛ̃/ nm bulletin, report; (Scol) report; ~ d'information news bulletin; ~ météorologique weather report; ~ (de vote) ballot-paper; ~ de salaire pay-slip.

buraliste /byʀalist/ nmf
tobacconist.

bureau (pl ∼**x**) /byʀo/ nm office;
(meuble) desk; (comité) board; ∼
d'études design office; ∼ **de
poste** post office; ∼ **de tabac**
tobacconist's (shop); ∼ **de vote**
polling station.

bureaucrate /byʀokʀat/ nmf
bureaucrat. **bureaucratie** nf
bureaucracy. **bureaucratique** adj
bureaucratic.

bureautique /byʀotik/ nf office
automation.

burlesque /byʀlɛsk/ adj (histoire)
ludicrous; (film) farcical.

bus /bys/ nm bus.

business /biznɛs/ nm inv (affaires
commerciales) business; (affaires
privées) affairs.

buste /byst/ nm bust.

but /by(t)/ nm target; (dessein) aim,
goal; (football) goal; **avoir pour** ∼

de aim to; **de** ∼ **en blanc** point-
blank; **dans le** ∼ **de** with the
intention of; **aller droit au** ∼
go straight to the point.

butane /bytan/ nm butane,
Calor gas®.

buté, ∼**e** /byte/ adj obstinate.

buter /byte/ **1** vi ∼ **contre** knock
against; (problème) come up
against. ●vt antagonize. ■ **se** ∼
vpr (s'entêter) become obstinate.

buteur /bytœr/ nm (au football)
striker.

butin /bytɛ̃/ nm booty, loot.

butte /byt/ nf mound; **en** ∼ **à**
exposed to.

buvard /byvar/ nm blotting-
paper.

buvette /byvɛt/ nf
(refreshment) bar.

buveur, -euse /byvœr, -øz/ nm, f
drinker.

Cc

c' /s/ ▷CE.

ça /sa/
● pronom démonstratif
····▷ (sujet) it; that; ∼ **flotte** it
floats; ∼ **suffit!** that's enough!;
∼ **y est!** that's it!; ∼ **sent le
brûlé** there's a smell of burning;
∼ **va?** how are things?
····▷ (objet) (proche) this; (plus
éloigné) that; **c'est** ∼ that's right.
····▷ (dans expressions) **où** ∼**?**
where?; **quand** ∼**?** when?; **et
avec** ∼**?** anything else?

çà /sa/ adv ∼ **et là** here and there.

cabane /kaban/ nf hut; (à
outils) shed.

cabaret /kabaʀɛ/ nm cabaret.

cabillaud /kabijo/ nm cod.

cabine /kabin/ nf (à la piscine)
cubicle; (de bateau) cabin; (de
camion) cab; (d'ascenseur) cage; ∼
d'essayage fitting room; ∼ **de
pilotage** cockpit; ∼ **de plage**
beach hut; ∼ (**téléphonique**)
phone booth, phone box.

cabinet /kabinɛ/ nm (de médecin)
surgery; (US) office; (d'avocat)
office; (clientèle) practice; (cabinet
collectif) firm; (Pol) Cabinet; (pièce)
room; ∼**s** (toilettes) toilet; (US)
bathroom; ∼ **de toilette**
bathroom.

câble /kɑbl/ nm cable; (corde)
rope; (TV) cable TV. **câbler** vt **1**

 see A-Z of French life and culture

C

cable; (TV) install cable television in.

cabosser /kabɔse/ **1** vt dent.

cabotage /kabɔtaʒ/ nm coastal navigation.

cabrer (se) /(sə)kabʀe/ **1** vpr (cheval) rear; **se ~ contre** rebel against.

cabriole /kabʀijɔl/ nf **faire des ~s** caper about.

cacahuète* /kakawɛt/ nf peanut.

cacao /kakao/ nm cocoa.

cachalot /kaʃalo/ nm sperm whale.

cache /kaʃ/ nm mask. ●nf hiding place; **~ d'armes** arms cache.

cache-cache* /kaʃkaʃ/ nm inv hide-and-seek.

cache-nez /kaʃne/ nm inv scarf.

cacher /kaʃe/ **1** vt hide, conceal (**à** from). ■ **se ~** vpr hide; (se trouver caché) be hidden.

cachet /kaʃɛ/ nm (de cire) seal; (à l'encre) stamp; (de la poste) postmark; (comprimé) tablet; (d'artiste) fee; (chic) style, cachet.

cachette /kaʃɛt/ nf hiding-place; **en ~** in secret.

cachot /kaʃo/ nm dungeon.

cachottier,* -ière /kaʃɔtje, -jɛʀ/ adj secretive.

cacophonie /kakɔfɔni/ nf cacophony.

cactus /kaktys/ nm cactus.

cadavérique /kadaveʀik/ adj (teint) deathly pale.

cadavre /kadavʀ/ nm corpse; (de victime) body.

caddie /kadi/ nm (de supermarché®) trolley; (au golf) caddie.

cadeau (pl **~x**) /kado/ nm present, gift; **faire un ~ à qn** give sb a present.

cadenas /kadna/ nm padlock.

cadence /kadɑ̃s/ nf rhythm, cadence; (de travail) rate; **en ~** in

time; (marcher) in step.

cadet, ~te /kadɛ, -t/ adj youngest; (entre deux) younger. ●nm, f youngest (child); younger (child).

cadran /kadʀɑ̃/ nm dial; **~ solaire** sundial.

cadre /kadʀ/ nm frame; (lieu) setting; (milieu) surroundings; (limites) scope; (contexte) framework; **dans le ~ de** (à l'occasion de) on the occasion of; (dans le contexte de) in the framework of. ●nm (personne) executive; **les ~s** the managerial staff.

cadrer /kadʀe/ **1** vi **~ avec** tally with. ●vt (photo) centre.

cafard /kafaʀ/ nm (insecte) cockroach; **avoir le ~** be down in the dumps.

café /kafe/ nm coffee; (bar) café; **~ crème** espresso with milk; **~ en grains** coffee beans; **~ au lait** white coffee.

cafetière /kaftjɛʀ/ nf coffee-pot; **~ électrique** coffee machine.

cage /kaʒ/ nf cage; **~ d'ascenseur** lift shaft; **~ d'escalier** stairwell; **~ thoracique** rib cage.

cageot /kaʒo/ nm crate.

cagibi /kaʒibi/ nm storage room.

cagneux, -euse /kaɲø, -z/ adj **avoir les genoux ~** be knock-kneed.

cagnotte /kaɲɔt/ nf kitty.

cagoule /kagul/ nf hood; (passe-montagne) balaclava.

cahier /kaje/ nm notebook; (Scol) exercise book; **~ de textes** homework notebook; **~ des charges** (Tech) specifications (+ pl).

cahot /kao/ nm bump, jolt. **cahoteux, -euse** adj bumpy.

caïd /kaid/ nm big shot.

caille /kɑj/ nf quail.

cailler /kɑje/ **1** vi curdle; **ça caille** **1** it's freezing. ■ se ~ vpr (sang) clot; (lait) curdle. **caillot** nm (blood) clot.

caillou (pl ~**x**) /kaju/ nm stone; (galet) pebble.

caisse /kɛs/ nf crate, case; (tiroir, machine) till; (guichet) cash desk; (au supermarché) check-out; (bureau) office; (Mus) drum; ~ **enregistreuse** cash register; ~ **d'épargne** savings bank; ~ **de retraite** pension fund. **caissier, -ière** nm, f cashier.

cajoler /kaʒɔle/ **1** vt coax.

calcaire /kalkɛʀ/ adj (sol) chalky; (eau) hard.

calciné, ~e /kalsine/ adj charred.

calcul /kalkyl/ nm calculation; (Scol) arithmetic; (différentiel) calculus; ~ **biliaire** gallstone.

calculatrice /kalkylatʀis/ nf calculator. **calculer** **1** vt calculate. **calculette** nf (pocket) calculator.

cale /kal/ nf wedge; (pour roue) chock; (de navire) hold; ~ **sèche** dry dock.

calé, ~e /kale/ adj **1** clever.

caleçon /kalsɔ̃/ nm boxer shorts (+ pl); underpants (+ pl); (de femme) leggings.

calembour /kalɑ̃buʀ/ nm pun.

calendrier /kalɑ̃dʀije/ nm calendar; (fig) schedule, timetable.

calepin /kalpɛ̃/ nm notebook.

caler /kale/ **1** vt wedge. ●vi stall; (abandonner **1**) give up.

calfeutrer /kalføtʀe/ **1** vt (fissure) stop up; (porte) draught proof.

calibre /kalibʀ/ nm calibre; (d'un œuf, fruit) grade.

calice /kalis/ nm (Relig) chalice; (Bot) calyx.

califourchon: à ~ /akalifuʀʃɔ̃/ loc astride.

câlin, ~e /kɑlɛ̃, -in/ adj (regard, ton) affectionate; (personne) cuddly.

calmant /kalmɑ̃/ nm sedative.

calme /kalm/ adj calm. ●nm peace; calm; (maîtrise de soi) composure; **du ~!** calm down!

calmer /kalme/ **1** vt (personne) calm down; (situation) defuse; (douleur) ease; (soif) quench. ■ se ~ vpr (personne, situation) calm down; (agitation, tempête) die down; (douleur) ease.

calomnie /kalɔmni/ nf (orale) slander; (écrite) libel. **calomnier** **45** vt slander; libel. **calomnieux, -ieuse** adj slanderous; libellous.

calorie /kalɔʀi/ nf calorie.

calque /kalk/ nm tracing; **(papier)** ~ tracing paper; (fig) exact copy.

calquer /kalke/ **1** vt trace; (fig) copy; ~ **qch sur** model sth on.

calvaire /kalvɛʀ/ nm (croix) Calvary; (fig) suffering.

calvitie /kalvisi/ nf baldness.

camarade /kamaʀad/ nmf friend; (Pol) comrade; ~ **de jeu** playmate. **camaraderie** nf friendship.

cambouis /kɑ̃bwi/ nm dirty oil.

cambrer /kɑ̃bʀe/ **1** vt arch. ■ se ~ vpr arch one's back.

cambriolage /kɑ̃bʀijɔlaʒ/ nm burglary. **cambrioler** **1** vt burgle. **cambrioleur, -euse** nm, f burglar.

camelot /kamlo/ nm **1** street vendor.

camelote /kamlɔt/ nf **1** junk.

caméra /kameʀa/ nf (cinéma, télévision) camera.

caméscope® /kameskɔp/ nm camcorder.

camion /kamjɔ̃/ nm lorry, truck. **camion-citerne** (pl **camions-citernes**) nm tanker. **camionnage** nm haulage. **camionnette** nf van. **camionneur** nm lorry ou truck

C

driver; (entrepreneur) haulage contractor.

camisole /kamizɔl/ nf ~ **(de force)** straitjacket.

camoufler /kamufle/ **1** vt camouflage.

camp /kã/ nm camp; (Sport, Pol) side.

campagnard, ~**e** /kãpaɲaʀ, -d/ adj country. ●nm, f countryman, countrywoman.

campagne /kãpaɲ/ nf country; countryside; (Mil, Pol) campaign.

campement /kãpmã/ nm camp, encampment.

camper /kãpe/ **1** vi camp. ●vt (esquisser) sketch. ■ **se** ~ vpr plant oneself. **campeur**, -**euse** nm, f camper.

camping /kãpiŋ/ nm camping; **faire du** ~ go camping; **(terrain de)** ~ campsite. **camping-car** (pl ~**s**) nm camper-van; (US) motorhome. **camping-gaz**® nm inv (réchaud) camping stove.

Canada /kanada/ nm Canada.

canadien, ~**ne** /kanadjẽ, -ɛn/ adj Canadian. **C**~, ~**ne** nm, f Canadian. **canadienne** nf (veste) fur-lined jacket; (tente) ridge tent.

canaille /kanɑj/ nf rogue.

canal (pl -**aux**) /kanal, -o/ nm (artificiel) canal; (bras de mer) channel; (Tech, TV) channel; (moyen) channel; **par le** ~ **de** through. **canalisation** nf (tuyaux) mains (+ pl). **canaliser** **1** vt (eau) canalize; (fig) channel.

canapé /kanape/ nm sofa.

canard /kanaʀ/ nm duck; (journal 1) rag.

canari /kanaʀi/ nm canary.

cancans /kãkã/ nmpl 1 gossip.

cancer /kãsɛʀ/ nm cancer; **le C**~ Cancer. **cancéreux**, -**euse** adj cancerous. **cancérigène** adj carcinogenic.

cancre /kãkʀ/ nm dunce.

candeur /kãdœʀ/ nf ingenuousness.

candidat, ~**e** /kãdida, -t/ nm, f (à un examen, Pol) candidate; (à un poste) applicant, candidate (**à** for).

candidature /kãdidatyʀ/ nf application; (Pol) candidacy; **poser sa** ~ **à un poste** apply for a job.

candide /kãdid/ adj ingenuous.

cane /kan/ nf (female) duck. **caneton** nm duckling.

canette /kanɛt/ nf (bouteille) bottle; (boîte) can.

canevas /kanva/ nm canvas; (ouvrage) tapestry; (plan) framework, outline.

caniche /kaniʃ/ nm poodle.

canicule /kanikyl/ nf scorching heat; (vague de chaleur) heatwave.

canif /kanif/ nm penknife.

canine /kanin/ nf canine (tooth).

caniveau (pl -**x**) /kanivo/ nm gutter.

cannabis /kanabis/ nm cannabis.

canne /kan/ nf (walking) stick; ~ **à pêche** fishing rod; ~ **à sucre** sugar cane.

cannelle /kanɛl/ nf cinnamon.

cannibale /kanibal/ adj & nmf cannibal.

canoë /kanɔe/ nm canoe; (Sport) canoeing.

canon /kanõ/ nm (big) gun; (ancien) cannon; (d'une arme) barrel; (principe, règle) canon.

canot /kano/ nm dinghy, (small) boat; ~ **de sauvetage** lifeboat; ~ **pneumatique** rubber dinghy. **canotier** nm boater.

cantatrice /kãtatʀis/ nf opera singer.

cantine /kãtin/ nf canteen.

cantique /kãtik/ nm hymn.

cantonner /kɑ̃tɔne/ ■ vt (Mil) billet. ■ se ~ dans vpr confine oneself to.

canular /kanylaʀ/ nm hoax.

caoutchouc /kautʃu/ nm rubber; (élastique) rubber band; ~ **mousse** foam rubber.

cap /kap/ nm cape, headland; (direction) course; (obstacle) hurdle; **franchir le ~ de la cinquantaine** pass the fifty mark; **mettre le ~ sur** steer a course for.

capable /kapabl/ adj capable (**de** of); ~ **de faire** able to do, capable of doing.

capacité /kapasite/ nf ability; (contenance, potentiel) capacity.

cape /kap/ nf cape; **rire sous ~** laugh up one's sleeve.

capillaire /kapileʀ/ adj (lotion, soins) hair; **(vaisseau)** ~ capillary.

capitaine /kapitɛn/ nm captain.

capital, ~**e** (mpl **-aux**) /kapital,-o/ adj key, crucial, fundamental; (peine, lettre) capital. ● nm (pl **-aux**) (Comm) capital; (fig) stock; **capitaux** (Comm) capital; ~**-risque** venture capital; ~**-risqueur** venture capitalist. **capitale** nf (ville, lettre) capital.

capitalisme /kapitalism/ nm capitalism.

capitonné, ~**e** /kapitɔne/ adj padded.

capituler /kapityle/ ■ vi capitulate.

caporal (pl **-aux**) /kapɔʀal, -o/ nm corporal.

capot /kapo/ nm (Auto) bonnet; (US) hood.

capote /kapɔt/ nf (Auto) hood; (US) top; (préservatif ▯) condom.

capoter /kapɔte/ ■ vi overturn; (fig) collapse.

câpre /kɑpʀ/ nf (Culin) caper.

caprice /kapʀis/ nm whim; (colère) tantrum; **faire un ~** throw a

tantrum. **capricieux, -ieuse** adj capricious; (appareil) temperamental.

Capricorne /kapʀikɔʀn/ nm **le ~** Capricorn.

capsule /kapsyl/ nf capsule; (de bouteille) cap.

capter /kapte/ ■ vt (eau) collect; (émission) get; (signal) pick up; (fig) win, capture.

captif, -ive /kaptif, -v/ adj & nm, f captive.

captiver /kaptive/ ■ vt captivate.

capturer /kaptyʀe/ ■ vt capture.

capuche /kapyʃ/ nf hood. **capuchon** nm hood; (de stylo) cap.

car /kaʀ/ conj because, for. ● nm coach; (US) bus.

carabine /kaʀabin/ nf rifle.

caractère /kaʀaktɛʀ/ nm (lettre) character; (nature) nature; ~**s d'imprimerie** block letters; **avoir bon/mauvais ~** be good-natured/bad-tempered; **avoir du ~** have character.

caractériel, ~**le** /kaʀakteʀjɛl/ adj (trait) character; (enfant) disturbed.

caractériser /kaʀakteʀize/ ■ vt characterize. ■ se ~ par vpr be characterized by. **caractéristique** adj & nf characteristic.

carafe /kaʀaf/ nf carafe.

Caraïbes /kaʀaib/ nfpl **les ~** the Caribbean.

carambolage /kaʀɑ̃bɔlaʒ/ nm pile-up.

caramel /kaʀamɛl/ nm caramel; (bonbon) toffee.

carapace /kaʀapas/ nf shell.

caravane /kaʀavan/ nf (Auto) caravan; (US) trailer; (convoi) caravan.

carbone /kaʀbɔn/ nm carbon; **(papier)** ~ carbon (paper). **carboniser** ■ vt burn (to ashes).

carburant /kaʀbyʀɑ̃/ nm (motor) fuel.

carburateur /kaʀbyʀatœʀ/ nm carburettor; (US) carburetor.

carcan /kaʀkɑ̃/ nm constraints (+ pl).

carcasse /kaʀkas/ nf (squelette) carcass; (armature) frame; (de voiture) shell.

cardiaque /kaʀdjak/ adj heart. • nmf heart patient.

cardinal, ~e (mpl **-aux**) /kaʀdinal, -o/ adj & nm cardinal.

Carême /kaʀɛm/ nm **le ~** Lent.

carence /kaʀɑ̃s/ nf shortcomings (+ pl); inadequacy; (Méd) deficiency; (absence) lack.

caresse /kaʀɛs/ nf caress; (à un animal) stroke. **caresser 1** vt caress, stroke; (espoir) cherish.

cargaison /kaʀgɛzɔ̃/ nf cargo.

cargo /kaʀgo/ nm cargo boat.

caricature /kaʀikatyʀ/ nf caricature.

carie /kaʀi/ nf (trou) cavity; **la ~ (dentaire)** tooth decay.

carillon /kaʀijɔ̃/ nm chimes (+ pl); (horloge) chiming clock.

caritatif, -ive /kaʀitatif, -v/ adj **association caritative** charity.

carnage /kaʀnaʒ/ nm carnage.

carnassier, -ière /kaʀnasje, -jɛʀ/ adj carnivorous.

carnaval (pl **~s**) /kaʀnaval/ nm carnival.

carnet /kaʀnɛ/ nm notebook; (detickets, timbres) book; **~ d'adresses** address book; **~ de chèques** chequebook.

carotte /kaʀɔt/ nf carrot.

carpe /kaʀp/ nf carp.

carré, ~e /kaʀe/ adj (forme, mesure) square; (fig) straightforward; **un mètre ~** one square metre. • nm square; (de terrain) patch.

⬛ see A-Z of French life and culture

carreau (pl **~x**) /kaʀo/ nm (window) pane; (par terre, au mur) tile; (dessin) check; (aux cartes) diamonds (+ pl); **à ~x** (tissu) check(ed); (papier) squared.

carrefour /kaʀfuʀ/ nm crossroads (+ sg).

carrelage /kaʀlaʒ/ nm tiling; (sol) tiles.

carrément /kaʀemɑ̃/ adv (complètement) completely; (stupide, dangereux) downright; (dire) straight out; **elle a ~ démissionné** she went straight ahead and resigned.

carrière /kaʀjɛʀ/ nf career; (terrain) quarry.

carrossable /kaʀɔsabl/ adj suitable for vehicles.

carrosse /kaʀɔs/ nm (horse-drawn) coach.

carrosserie /kaʀɔsʀi/ nf (Auto) body(work).

carrure /kaʀyʀ/ nf shoulders; (fig) necessary qualities, calibre.

cartable /kaʀtabl/ nm satchel.

carte /kaʀt/ nf card; (Géog) map; (Naut) chart; (au restaurant) menu; **~s** (jeu) cards; **à la ~** (manger) à la carte; (horaire) personalized; **donner ~ blanche à** give a free hand to; ⬛**~ bleue**® credit card; **~ de crédit** credit card; **~ de fidélité** loyalty card; ⬛**~ grise** (car) registration document; ⬛**~ d'identité** identity card; **~ magnétique** swipe card; **~ de paiement** debit card; **~ postale** postcard; **à puce** smart card; **~ de séjour** resident's permit; **~ des vins** wine list; **~ de visite** (business) card; **~ vitale** social insurance smart card.

cartilage /kaʀtilaʒ/ nm cartilage.

carton /kaʀtɔ̃/ nm cardboard; (boîte) (cardboard) box; **~ à dessin** portfolio; **faire un ~** ⬛ do well.

cartonné, ~e /kaʀtɔne/ adj **livre ~** hardback.

cartouche /kaʀtuʃ/ nf cartridge;

(de cigarettes) carton.
cartouchière nf cartridge-belt.

cas /kɑ/ nm case; **au ~ où** in case; **~ urgent** emergency; **en aucun ~** on no account; **en ~ de** in the event of, in case of; **en tout ~** in any case; (du moins) at least; **faire ~ de** set great store by; **~ de conscience** moral dilemma.

casanier, -ière /kazanje, -jɛʀ/ adj home-loving.

cascade /kaskad/ nf waterfall; (au cinéma) stunt; (fig) spate, series (+ sg).

cascadeur, -euse /kaskadœʀ, -øz/ nm, f stuntman, stuntwoman.

case /kɑz/ nf hut; (de damier) square; (compartiment) pigeon-hole; (sur un formulaire) box.

caser /kaze/ 1 vt 🔲 (mettre) put; (loger) put up; (dans un travail) find a job for; (marier: péj) marry off.

caserne /kazɛʀn/ nf barracks; **~ de sapeurs-pompiers** fire station.

casier /kazje/ nm pigeon-hole, compartiment; (à bouteilles, chaussures) rack; **~ judiciaire** criminal record.

casque /kask/ nm (de motard) crash helmet; (de cycliste) cycle helmet; (chez le coiffeur) (hair-)drier; **~ (à écouteurs)** headphones; **~ anti-bruit** ear defenders; **~ de protection** safety helmet.

casquette /kaskɛt/ nf cap.

cassant, ~e /kasɑ̃, -t/ adj brittle; (brusque) curt.

cassation /kasasjɔ̃/ nf **cour de ~** appeal court.

casse /kɑs/ nf (objets) breakages; (lieu) breaker's yard; **mettre à la ~** scrap.

casse-cou* /kasku/ nmf inv daredevil.

casse-croûte* /kaskʀut/ nm inv snack.

casse-noix /kasnwa/ nm inv nutcrackers (+ pl).

casse-pieds* /kaspje/ nmf inv 🔲 pain (in the neck) 🔲.

casser /kase/ 1 vt break; (annuler) annul; **~ les pieds à qn** 🔲 annoy sb. •vi break. ■**se ~** vpr break; (partir 🔲) be off 🔲.

casserole /kasʀɔl/ nf saucepan.

casse-tête* /kastɛt/ nm inv (problème) headache; (jeu) brain teaser.

cassette /kasɛt/ nf casket; (de magnétophone) cassette, tape; (de vidéo) video tape; **~ audio numérique** digital audio tape.

cassis /kasi(s)/ nm inv blackcurrant.

cassure /kasyʀ/ nf break.

castor /kastɔr/ nm beaver.

castration /kastrasjɔ̃/ nf castration.

catalogue /katalɔg/ nm catalogue.

catalyseur /katalizœr/ nm catalyst; (Auto) catalytic convertor.

catastrophe /katastʀɔf/ nf disaster, catastrophe.
catastrophique adj catastrophic.

catch /katʃ/ nm (all-in) wrestling.

catéchisme /kateʃism/ nm catechism.

catégorie /kategɔʀi/ nf category.
catégorique adj categorical.

cathédrale /katedʀal/ nf cathedral.

catholique /katɔlik/ adj Catholic; **pas très ~** a bit fishy.

catimini: en ~ /ɑ̃katimini/ loc on the sly.

cauchemar /koʃmaʀ/ nm nightmare.

cause /koz/ nf cause; (raison) reason; (Jur) case; **à ~ de** because of; **en ~** (en jeu, concerné) involved; **pour ~ de** on account of; **mettre en ~** implicate;

remettre en ~ call into question.

causer /koze/ **1** vt cause; (discuter de **1**) **~ travail** talk shop; **~ de** talk about. ●vi chat. **causerie** nf talk.

causette /kozɛt/ nf (Internet) chat; **faire la ~** have a chat.

caution /kosjɔ̃/ nf surety; (Jur) bail; (appui) backing; (garantie) deposit; **libéré sous ~** released on bail. **cautionner** **1** vt guarantee; (soutenir) back.

cavalcade /kavalkad/ nf stampede, rush.

cavalier, -ière /kavalje, -jɛʀ/ adj offhand; **allée cavalière** bridle path. ●nm, f rider; (pour danser) partner. ●nm (aux échecs) knight.

cave /kav/ nf cellar. ●adj sunken.

caveau (pl ~**x**) /kavo/ nm vault.

caverne /kavɛʀn/ nf cave.

CCP abrév m (**compte chèque postal**) post office account.

CD abrév m (**compact disc**) CD.

CD-ROM abrév m inv (**compact disc read only memory**) CD-ROM.

---

ce, c', cet, cette (pl **ces**) /sə, s, sɛt, se/

! **c'** before e. **cet** before vowel or mute h.

●**ce, cet, cette** (pl **ces**) adjectif démonstratif

····▸ this; (plus éloigné) that; **ces** these; (plus éloigné) those; **cette nuit** (passée) last night; (à venir) tonight.

●**ce, c'** pronom démonstratif

····▸ **c'est** it's ou it is; **c'est un policier** he's a policeman; **~ sont eux qui l'ont fait** they did it; **qui est-~?** who is it?

····▸ **ce que/qui** what; **~ que je ne comprends pas** what I don't understand; **elle est**

---

venue, **~ qui est étonnant** she came, which is surprising; **~ que tu as de la chance!** how lucky you are! **tout ~ qu'elle trouve/peut** everything she finds/can

CE abrév f (**Communauté européenne**) EC.

ceci /səsi/ pron this.

cécité /sesite/ nf blindness.

céder /sede/ **14** vt give up; **~ le passage** give way; (vendre) sell. ●vi (se rompre) give way; (se soumettre) give in.

cédérom /sedeʀɔm/ nm CD-ROM.

cédille /sedij/ nf cedilla.

cèdre /sɛdʀ/ nm cedar.

CEI abrév f (**Communauté des États indépendants**) CIS.

ceinture /sɛ̃tyʀ/ nf belt; (taille) waist; **~ de sauvetage** lifebelt; **~ de sécurité** seatbelt.

cela /səla/ pron it, that; (pour désigner) that; **~ va de soi** it is obvious; **~ dit/fait** having said/done that.

célèbre /selɛbʀ/ adj famous. **célébrer** **14** vt celebrate. **célébrité** nf fame; (personne) celebrity.

céleri* /selʀi/ nm (en branches) celery. **céleri-rave** (pl **céleris-raves**) nm celeriac.

célibat /seliba/ nm celibacy; (état) single status.

célibataire /selibatɛʀ/ adj single. ●nm bachelor. ●nf single woman.

celle, celles /sɛl/ ▷CELUI.

cellulaire /selylɛʀ/ adj cell; **emprisonnement ~** solitary confinement; **fourgon** ou **voiture ~** prison van; **téléphone ~** cellular phone.

cellule /selyl/ nf cell; **~ souche** stem cell.

celui, celle (pl **ceux, celles**) /səlɥi, sɛl, sø/ pron the one; **~ de**

mon ami my friend's; **~-ci** this (one); **~-là** that (one); **ceux-ci** these (ones); **ceux-là** those (ones).

cendre /sɑ̃dʀ/ nf ash.

cendrier /sɑ̃dʀije/ nm ashtray.

censé, **~e** /sɑ̃se/ adj **être ~ faire** be supposed to do.

censeur /sɑ̃sœʀ/ nm censor; (Scol) administrator in charge of discipline.

censure /sɑ̃syʀ/ nf censorship. **censurer** ▯ vt censor; (critiquer) censure.

cent /sɑ̃/ adj (a) hundred; **20 pour ~** 20 per cent.•n (quantité) hundred; **~ un** a hundred and one; (centième d'euro) cent.

centaine /sɑ̃tɛn/ nf hundred; **une ~ (de)** (about) a hundred.

centenaire /sɑ̃tnɛʀ/ nm (anniversaire) centenary.

centième /sɑ̃tjɛm/ adj & nmf hundredth.

centimètre /sɑ̃timɛtʀ/ nm centimetre; (ruban) tape-measure.

central, **~e** (mpl **-aux**) /sɑ̃tʀal,-o/ adj central. •nm (pl **-aux**) **~ (téléphonique)** (telephone) exchange. **centrale** nf power-station.

centre /sɑ̃tʀ/ nm centre; **~ commercial** shopping centre; (US) mall; **~ d'appels** call centre; **~ de formation** training centre; **~ hospitalier** hospital. **centrer** ▯ vt centre. **centre-ville** (pl **centres-villes**) nm town centre.

centuple /sɑ̃typl/ nm **le ~ de** a hundred times; **au ~** a hundredfold.

cep /sɛp/ nm vine stock.

cépage /sepaʒ/ nm grape variety.

cèpe /sɛp/ nm cep.

cependant /səpɑ̃dɑ̃/ adv however.

céramique /seʀamik/ nf ceramic; (art) ceramics (+ sg).

cercle /sɛʀkl/ nm circle; (cerceau) hoop; (association) society, club; **~ vicieux** vicious circle.

cercueil /sɛʀkœj/ nm coffin.

céréale /seʀeal/ nf cereal; **~s** (Culin) (breakfast) cereal.

cérébral, **~e** (mpl **-aux**) /seʀebʀal, -o/ adj cerebral.

cérémonie /seʀemɔni/ nf ceremony; **sans ~s** (repas) informal; (recevoir) informally.

cerf /sɛʀ/ nm stag.

cerfeuil /sɛʀfœj/ nm chervil.

cerf-volant (pl **cerfs-volants**) /sɛʀvɔlɑ̃/ nm kite.

cerise /s(ə)ʀiz/ nf cherry. **cerisier** nm cherry tree.

cerner /sɛʀne/ ▯ vt surround; (question) define; **avoir les yeux cernés** have rings under one's eyes.

certain, **~e** /sɛʀtɛ̃, -ɛn/ adj certain; (sûr) certain, sure (**de** of; **que** that); **d'un ~ âge** no longer young; **un ~ temps** some time. **certainement** adv (probablement) most probably; (avec certitude) certainly. **certains, -es** pron some people.

certes /sɛʀt/ adv (sans doute) admittedly; (bien sûr) of course.

certificat /sɛʀtifika/ nm certificate.

certifier /sɛʀtifje/ ▮ vt certify; **~ qch à qn** assure sb of sth; **copie certifiée conforme** certified true copy.

certitude /sɛʀtityd/ nf certainty.

cerveau (pl **~x**) /sɛʀvo/ nm brain.

cervelle /sɛʀvɛl/ nf (Anat) brain; (Culin) brains.

ces /se/ ▷CE.

césarienne /sezaʀjɛn/ nf Caesarean (section).

cesse /sɛs/ nf **n'avoir de ~ que** have no rest until; **sans ~** constantly, incessantly.

cesser /sese/ ▯ vt stop; **~ de**

faire stop doing. ●vi cease; **faire ~** put an end to.

cessez-le-feu /seselfø/ nm inv ceasefire.

cession /sesjɔ̃/ nf transfer.

c'est-à-dire /setadiʀ/ conj that is (to say).

cet, cette /set/ ▷CE.

ceux /sø/ ▷CELUI.

chacun, ~e /ʃakœ̃, -yn/ pron each (one), every one; (tout le monde) everyone; **~ d'entre nous** each (one) of us.

chagrin /ʃagʀɛ̃/ nm sorrow; **avoir du ~** be sad.

chahut /ʃay/ nm row, din.

chahuter /ʃayte/ **1** vi make a row. ●vt (enseignant) be rowdy with; (orateur) heckle.

chaîne* /ʃɛn/ nf chain; (de télévision) channel; **~ (d'assemblage)** assembly line; **~s** (Auto) snow chains; **~ de montagnes** mountain range; **~ de montage/fabrication** assembly/production line; **~ hi-fi** hi-fi system; **~ laser** CD player; **en ~** (accidents) multiple; (réaction) chain. **chaînette*** nf (small) chain. **chaînon*** nm link.

chair /ʃɛʀ/ nf flesh; **bien en ~** plump; **en ~ et en os** in the flesh; **~ à saucisses** sausage meat; **la ~ de poule** goose-pimples. ●adj inv **(couleur) ~** flesh-coloured.

chaire /ʃɛʀ/ nf (d'église) pulpit; (Univ) chair.

chaise /ʃɛz/ nf chair; **~ longue** deckchair.

châle /ʃɑl/ nm shawl.

chaleur /ʃalœʀ/ nf heat; (moins intense) warmth; (d'un accueil, d'une couleur) warmth. **chaleureux, -euse** adj warm.

chalumeau (pl ~**x**) /ʃalymo/ nm blowtorch.

chalutier /ʃalytje/ nm trawler.

chamailler (se) /(sə)ʃamaje/ **1** vpr squabble.

chambre /ʃɑ̃bʀ/ nf (bed) room; (Pol, Jur) chamber; **faire ~ à part** sleep in separate rooms; **~ à air** inner tube; **~ d'amis** spare *ou* guest room; **~ de commerce (et d'industrie)** Chamber of Commerce; **~ à coucher** bedroom; **~ à un lit/deux lits** single/twinroom; **~ pour deux personnes** double room; **~ forte** strong-room; **~ d'hôte** bed and breakfast, B and B. **chambrer** **1** vt (vin) bring to room temperature.

chameau (pl ~**x**) /ʃamo/ nm camel.

chamois /ʃamwa/ nm chamois.

champ /ʃɑ̃/ nm field; **~ de bataille** battlefield; **~ de courses** racecourse; **~ de tir** firing range.

champêtre /ʃɑ̃pɛtʀ/ adj rural.

champignon /ʃɑ̃piɲɔ̃/ nm mushroom; (moisissure) fungus; **~ de Paris** button mushroom.

champion, ~ne /ʃɑ̃pjɔ̃, -ɔn/ nm, f champion. **championnat** nm championship.

chance /ʃɑ̃s/ nf (good) luck; (possibilité) chance; **avoir de la ~** be lucky; **quelle ~!** what luck!

chanceler /ʃɑ̃sle/ 38 vi stagger; (fig) falter, waver.

chancelier /ʃɑ̃səlje/ nm chancellor.

chanceux, -euse /ʃɑ̃sø, -z/ adj lucky.

chandail /ʃɑ̃daj/ nm sweater.

chandelier /ʃɑ̃dəlje/ nm candlestick.

chandelle /ʃɑ̃dɛl/ nf candle; **dîner aux ~s** candlelight dinner.

change /ʃɑ̃ʒ/ nm (foreign) exchange; (taux) exchange rate.

changement /ʃɑ̃ʒmɑ̃/ nm change; **~ de vitesse** (dispositif) ears.

changer /ʃɑ̃ʒe/ **40** vt change; ~ **qch de place** move sth; (échanger) change (**pour, contre** for); ~ **de nom/voiture** change one's name/car; ~ **de place/train** change places/trains; ~ **de direction** change direction; ~ **d'avis** *ou* **d'idée** change one's mind; ~ **de vitesse** change gear. ◾ **se** ~ vpr change, get changed.

chanson /ʃɑ̃sɔ̃/ nf song.

chant /ʃɑ̃/ nm singing; (chanson) song; (Relig) hymn.

chantage /ʃɑ̃taʒ/ nm blackmail.

chanter /ʃɑ̃te/ **1** vt sing; **si cela vous chante** 🖪 if you feel like it. ●vi sing; **faire** ~ (délit) blackmail. **chanteur, -euse** nm, f singer.

chantier /ʃɑ̃tje/ nm building site; ~ **naval** shipyard; **mettre en** ~ get under way, start.

chaos /kao/ nm chaos.

chaparder /ʃaparde/ **1** vt 🖪 pinch 🖪, filch.

chapeau (pl ~**x**) /ʃapo/ nm hat; ~**!** well done!

chapelet /ʃaplɛ/ nm rosary; (fig) string.

chapelle /ʃapɛl/ nf chapel.

chapelure /ʃaplyr/ nf (Culin) breadcrumbs.

chaperonner /ʃaprɔne/ **1** vt chaperone.

chapiteau (pl ~**x**) /ʃapito/ nm marquee; (de cirque) big top; (de colonne) capital.

chapitre /ʃapitr/ nm chapter; (fig) subject.

chaque /ʃak/ adj every, each.

char /ʃar/ nm (Mil) tank; (de carnaval) float; (charrette) cart; (dans l'antiquité) chariot.

charabia /ʃarabja/ nm 🖪 gibberish.

charade /ʃarad/ nf riddle.

charbon /ʃarbɔ̃/ nm coal; (Méd) anthrax; ~ **de bois** charcoal.

🖪**charcuterie** /ʃarkytri/ nf pork butcher's shop; (aliments) (cooked) pork meats. **charcutier, -ière** nm, f pork butcher.

chardon /ʃardɔ̃/ nm thistle.

charge /ʃarʒ/ nf load, burden; (Mil, Electr, Jur) charge; (responsabilité) responsibility; **avoir qn à** ~ be responsible for; ~**s** expenses; (de locataire) service charges; **être à la** ~ **de** (personne) be the responsibility of; (frais) be payable by; ~**s sociales** social security contributions; **prendre en** ~ take charge of.

chargé, ~e /ʃarʒe/ adj (véhicule) loaded; (journée, emploi du temps) busy; (langue) coated. ●nm, f ~ **de mission** head of mission; ~ **d'affaires** chargé d'affaires; ~ **de cours** lecturer.

chargement /ʃarʒəmɑ̃/ nm loading; (objets) load.

charger /ʃarʒe/ **40** vt load; (Ordinat, Photo) load; (attaquer) charge; (batterie) charge; ~ **qn de** (fardeau) weigh sb down with; (tâche) entrust sb with; ~ **qn de faire** make sb responsible for doing. ●vi (attaquer) charge. ◾ **se** ~ **de** vpr take charge *ou* care of.

chariot* /ʃarjo/ nm (à roulettes) rolley; (US) cart; (charrette) cart.

charitable /ʃaritabl/ adj charitable.

charité /ʃarite/ nf charity; **faire la** ~ **à** give (money) to.

charlatan /ʃarlatɑ̃/ nm charlatan.

charmant, ~e /ʃarmɑ̃, -t/ adj charming.

charme /ʃarm/ nm charm; (qui envoûte) spell. **charmer** **1** vt charm. **charmeur, -euse** nm, f charmer.

charnel, ~le /ʃarnɛl/ adj carnal.

charnière /ʃarnjɛr/ nf hinge; **à la**

....

🖪 *see* A-Z of French life and culture

~ **de** at the meeting point between.

charnu, ~e /ʃaʀny/ adj plump, fleshy.

charpente /ʃaʀpɑ̃t/ nf framework; (carrure) build.

charpentier /ʃaʀpɑ̃tje/ nm carpenter.

charrette /ʃaʀɛt/ nf cart.

charrue /ʃaʀy/ nf plough.

🄳**chasse** /ʃas/ nf hunting; (au fusil) shooting; (poursuite) chase; (recherche) hunt(ing); ~ **(d'eau)** (toilet) flush; ~ **sous-marine** harpoon fishing.

chasse-neige /ʃasnɛʒ/ nm inv snowplough.

chasser /ʃase/ 🄸 vt hunt; (au fusil) shoot; (faire partir) chase away; (odeur, employé) get rid of. ●vi go hunting; (au fusil) go shooting.

chasseur, -euse /ʃasœʀ, -øz/ nm, f hunter. ●nm bellboy; (US) bellhop; (avion) fighter plane.

châssis /ʃasi/ nm frame; (Auto) chassis.

chasteté /ʃastəte/ nf chastity.

chat[1] /ʃa/ nm cat; (mâle) tomcat.

chat[2] /tʃat/ nm (Internet) chat.

châtaigne /ʃatɛɲ/ nf chestnut. **châtaignier** nm chestnut tree. **châtain** adj inv chestnut (brown).

château (pl ~x) /ʃato/ nm castle; (manoir) manor; ~ **d'eau** water tower; ~ **fort** fortified castle.

châtiment /ʃatimɑ̃/ nm punishment.

chaton /ʃatɔ̃/ nm (chat) kitten.

chatouillement /ʃatujmɑ̃/ nm tickling. **chatouiller** 🄸 vt tickle. **chatouilleux, -euse** adj ticklish; (susceptible) touchy.

châtrer /ʃatʀe/ 🄸 vt castrate; (chat) neuter.

chatte /ʃat/ nf female cat.

....

🄳 *see A-Z of French life and culture*

chaud, ~e /ʃo, -d/ adj warm; (brûlant) hot; (vif: fig) warm. ●nm heat; **au** ~ in the warm(th); **avoir** ~ be warm; be hot; **il fait** ~ it is warm; it is hot; **pour te tenir** ~ to keep you warm. **chaudement** adv warmly; (disputé) hotly.

chaudière /ʃodjɛʀ/ nf boiler.

chaudron /ʃodʀɔ̃/ nm cauldron.

chauffage /ʃofaʒ/ nm heating; ~ **central** central heating.

chauffard /ʃofaʀ/ nm (péj) reckless driver.

chauffer /ʃofe/ 🄸 vt/i heat (up); (moteur, appareil) overheat. ■ se ~ vpr warm oneself up.

chauffeur /ʃofœʀ/ nm driver; (aux gages de qn) chauffeur.

chaume /ʃom/ nm (de toit) thatch.

chaussée /ʃose/ nf road (way).

chausse-pied* /ʃospje/ (pl ~s) /ʃospje/ nm shoehorn.

chausser /ʃose/ 🄸 vt (chaussures) put on; (enfant) put shoes on (to). ●vi ~ **bien** (aller) fit well; ~ **du 35** take a size 35 shoe. ■ se ~ vpr put one's shoes on.

chaussette /ʃosɛt/ nf sock.

chausson /ʃosɔ̃/ nm slipper; (de bébé) bootee; ~ **de danse** ballet shoe; ~ **aux pommes** apple turnover.

chaussure /ʃosyʀ/ nf shoe; ~ **de ski** ski boot; ~ **de marche** hiking boot.

chauve /ʃov/ adj bald.

chauve-souris* (pl **chauves-souris**) /ʃovsuʀi/ nf bat.

chauvin, ~e /ʃovɛ̃, -in/ adj chauvinistic. ●nm, f chauvinist.

chavirer /ʃaviʀe/ 🄸 vt (bateau) capsize; (objets) tip over.

chef /ʃɛf/ nm leader, head; (supérieur) boss, superior; (Culin) chef; (de tribu) chief; **architecte en** ~ chief *ou* head architect; ~ **d'accusation** (Jur) charge; ~

d'équipe foreman; (Sport) captain; ~ **d'État** head of State; ~ **de famille** head of the family; ~ **de file** (Pol) leader; ~ **de gare** stationmaster; ~ **d'orchestre** conductor; ~ **de service** department head; ~ **de train** guard; (US) conductor.

chef-d'œuvre (pl **chefs-d'œuvre**) /ʃɛdœvʀ/ nm masterpiece.

chef-lieu (pl **chefs-lieux**) /ʃɛfljø/ nm county town, administrative centre.

chemin /ʃəmɛ̃/ nm road; (étroit) lane; (de terre) track; (pour piétons) path; (passage) way; (direction, trajet) way; **avoir du ~ à faire** have a long way to go; ~ **de fer** railway; **par ~ de fer** by rail; ~ **de halage** towpath; ~ **vicinal** country lane.

cheminée /ʃəmine/ nf chimney; (intérieure) fireplace; (encadrement) mantelpiece; (de bateau) funnel.

cheminot /ʃəmino/ nm railwayman; (US) railroad man.

chemise /ʃəmiz/ nf shirt; (dossier) folder; (de livre) jacket; ~ **de nuit** nightdress. **chemisette** nf short-sleeved shirt. **chemisier** nm blouse.

chêne /ʃɛn/ nm oak.

chenil /ʃəni(l)/ nm (pension) kennels (+ sg).

chenille /ʃənij/ nf caterpillar; **véhicule à ~s** tracked vehicle.

cheptel /ʃɛptɛl/ nm livestock.

chèque /ʃɛk/ nm cheque; ~ **sans provision** bad cheque; ~ **de voyage** traveller's cheque. **chéquier** nm chequebook.

cher, chère /ʃɛʀ/ adj (coûteux) dear, expensive; (aimé) dear; (dans la correspondance) dear. ●adv (coûter, payer) a lot (of money); (en importance) dearly. ●nm, f **mon ~, ma chère** my dear.

chercher /ʃɛʀʃe/ **1** vt look for; (aide, paix, gloire) seek; **aller ~** go

and get ou fetch, go for; ~ **à faire** attempt to do; ~ **la petite bête** be finicky.

chercheur, -euse /ʃɛʀʃœʀ, -øz/ nm, f research worker.

chèrement /ʃɛʀmɑ̃/ adv dearly.

chéri, ~e /ʃeʀi/ adj beloved. ●nm, f darling.

chérir /ʃeʀiʀ/ **2** vt cherish.

chétif, -ive /ʃetif, -v/ adj puny.

cheval (pl **-aux**) /ʃəval, -o/ nm horse; **à ~** on horseback; **à ~ sur** astride, straddling; **faire du ~** ride, go horse-riding.

chevalerie /ʃəvalʀi/ nf chivalry.

chevalet /ʃəvalɛ/ nm easel; (de menuisier) trestle.

chevalier /ʃəvalje/ nm knight.

chevalière /ʃəvaljɛʀ/ nf signet ring.

cheval-vapeur (pl **chevaux-vapeur**) /ʃəvalvapœʀ/ nm horsepower.

chevaucher /ʃəvoʃe/ **1** vt sit astride. ■ **se ~** vpr overlap.

chevelu, ~e /ʃəvly/ adj (péj) long-haired; (Bot) hairy.

chevelure /ʃəvlyʀ/ nf hair.

chevet /ʃəvɛ/ nm **au ~ de** at the bedside of; **livre de ~** bedside book.

cheveu (pl ~**x**) /ʃəvø/ nm (poil) hair; ~**x** (chevelure) hair; **avoir les ~x longs** have long hair.

cheville /ʃəvij/ nf ankle; (fiche) peg, pin; (pour mur) (wall) plug.

chèvre /ʃɛvʀ/ nf goat.

chevreuil /ʃəvʀœj/ nm roe (deer); (Culin) venison.

chevron /ʃəvʀɔ̃/ nm (poutre) rafter; **à ~s** herringbone.

chez /ʃe/ prép (au domicile de) at the house of; (parmi) among; (dans le caractère ou l'œuvre de) in; **aller ~ qn** go to sb's house; ~ **le boucher** at ou to the butcher's; ~ **soi** at home; **rentrer ~ soi** go home. **chez-soi** nm inv home.

chic /ʃik/ adj inv smart; (gentil) kind. ●nm style; **avoir le ~ pour** have a knack for; **~ (alors)!** great!

chicane /ʃikan/ nf double bend; **chercher ~ à qn** pick a quarrel with sb.

chiche /ʃiʃ/ adj mean (**de** with); **~ que je le fais!** 🆃 I bet you I can do it.

chichis /ʃiʃi/ nmpl 🆃 fuss.

chicorée /ʃikɔʀe/ nf (frisée) endive; (à café) chicory.

chien /ʃjɛ̃/ nm dog; **~ d'aveugle** guide dog; **~ de garde** watchdog. **chienne** nf dog, bitch.

chiffon /ʃifɔ̃/ nm rag; (pour nettoyer) duster; **~ humide** damp cloth. **chiffonner** 🆃 vt crumple; (préoccuper 🆃) bother.

chiffre /ʃifʀ/ nm figure; (numéro) number; (code) code; **~s arabes/ romains** Arabic/Roman numerals; **~s (statistiques)** statistics; **~ d'affaires** turnover.

chiffrer /ʃifʀe/ 🆃 vt put a figure on, assess; (texte) encode. ■se **~ à** vpr come to.

chignon /ʃiɲɔ̃/ nm bun, chignon.

Chili /ʃili/ nm Chile.

chimère /ʃimɛʀ/ nf fantasy.

chimie /ʃimi/ nf chemistry. **chimique** adj chemical. **chimiste** nmf chemist.

chimpanzé /ʃɛ̃pɑ̃ze/ nm chimpanzee.

Chine /ʃin/ nf China.

chinois, ~e /ʃinwa, -z/ adj Chinese. ●nm (Ling) Chinese. **C~, ~e** nm, f Chinese.

chiot /ʃjo/ nm pup(py).

chipoter /ʃipɔte/ 🆃 vi (manger) pick at one's food; (discuter) quibble.

chips /ʃips/ nf inv crisp; (US) chip.

chirurgie /ʃiʀyʀʒi/ nf surgery; **~**

esthétique plastic surgery. **chirurgien** nm surgeon.

chlore /klɔʀ/ nm chlorine.

choc /ʃɔk/ nm (heurt) impact, shock; (émotion) shock; (collision) crash; (affrontement) clash; (Méd) shock; **sous le ~** in shock.

chocolat /ʃɔkɔla/ nm chocolate; (à boire) drinking chocolate; **~ au lait** milk chocolate; **~ chaud** hot chocolate; **~ noir** plain ou dark chocolate.

chœur /kœʀ/ nm (antique) chorus; (chanteurs, nef) choir; **en ~** in chorus.

choisir /ʃwaziʀ/ ② vt choose, select.

choix /ʃwa/ nm choice, selection; **fromage ou dessert au ~** a choice of cheese or dessert; **de ~** choice; **de premier ~** top quality.

chômage /ʃomaʒ/ nm unemployment; **au ~, en ~** unemployed; **mettre en ~ technique** lay off.

chômeur, -euse /ʃomœʀ, -øz/ nm, f unemployed person; **les ~s** the unemployed.

choquer /ʃɔke/ 🆃 vt shock; (commotionner) shake.

choral, ~e (mpl ~s) /kɔʀal/ adj choral. **chorale** nf choir, choral society.

chorégraphie /kɔʀegʀafi/ nf choreography.

choriste /kɔʀist/ nmf (à l'église) chorister; (à l'opéra) member of the chorus ou choir.

chose /ʃoz/ nf thing; **(très) peu de ~** nothing much; **pas grand ~** not much.

chou (pl **~x**) /ʃu/ nm cabbage; **~ (à la crème)** cream puff; **~ de Bruxelles** Brussels sprout; **mon petit ~** 🆃 my dear.

chouchou, ~te /ʃuʃu, -t/ nm, f (de professeur) pet; (du public) darling.

choucroute /ʃukʀut/ nf sauerkraut.

chouette /ʃwɛt/ nf owl. ● adj 𝟙 super.

chou-fleur (pl **choux-fleurs**) /ʃuflœʀ/ nm cauliflower.

choyer /ʃwaje/ 𝟛𝟙 vt pamper.

chrétien, ~ne /kʀetjɛ̃, -jɛn/ adj & nm, f Christian.

Christ /kʀist/ nm **le ~** Christ.

chrome /kʀom/ nm chromium, chrome.

chromosome /kʀomozom/ nm chromosome.

chronique /kʀonik/ adj chronic. ● nf (rubrique) column; (nouvelles) news; (annales) chronicle.

chronologique /kʀonoloʒik/ adj chronological.

chronomètre /kʀonomɛtʀ/ nm stopwatch. **chronométrer** 𝟙𝟜 vt time.

chrysanthème /kʀizɑ̃tɛm/ nm chrysanthemum.

chuchoter /ʃyʃote/ 𝟙 vt/i whisper.

chut /ʃyt/ interj shh, hush.

chute /ʃyt/ nf fall; (déchet) offcut; **~ (d'eau)** waterfall; **~ de pluie** rainfall; **~ des cheveux** hair loss; **~ des ventes ~** drop in sales; **~ de 5%** 5% drop. **chuter** 𝟙 vi fall.

Chypre /ʃipʀ/ nf Cyprus.

ci /si/ adv here; **~-gît** here lies; **cet homme-~** this man; **ces maisons-~** these houses.

ci-après /siapʀɛ/ adv below.

cible /sibl/ nf target.

ciboulette /sibulɛt/ nf (Culin) chives (+ pl).

cicatrice /sikatʀis/ nf scar.

cicatriser /sikatʀize/ 𝟙 vt heal. ■ **se ~** vpr heal.

ci-dessous /sidəsu/ adv below.

ci-dessus /sidəsy/ adv above.

cidre /sidʀ/ nm cider.

ciel (pl **cieux, ciels**) /sjɛl, sjø/ nm sky; (Relig) heaven; **cieux** (Relig) heaven.

cierge /sjɛʀʒ/ nm (church) candle.

cigale /sigal/ nf cicada.

cigare /sigaʀ/ nm cigar.

cigarette /sigaʀɛt/ nf cigarette.

cigogne /sigoɲ/ nf stork.

ci-joint /siʒwɛ̃/ adv enclosed.

cil /sil/ nm eyelash.

cime /sim/ nf peak, tip.

ciment /simɑ̃/ nm cement.

cimetière /simtjɛʀ/ nm cemetery, graveyard; **~ de voitures** breaker's yard.

cinéaste /sineast/ nmf film-maker.

cinéma /sinema/ nm cinema; (US) movie theater. **cinémathèque** nf film archive; (salle) film theatre. **cinématographique** adj cinema.

cinéphile /sinefil/ nmf film lover.

cinglant, ~e /sɛ̃glɑ̃, -t/ adj (vent) biting; (remarque) scathing.

cinglé, ~e /sɛ̃gle/ adj 𝟙 crazy.

cinq /sɛ̃k/ adj & nm five.

cinquante /sɛ̃kɑ̃t/ adj & nm fifty.

cinquième /sɛ̃kjɛm/ adj & nmf fifth.

cintre /sɛ̃tʀ/ nm coat-hanger; (Archit) curve.

cirage /siʀaʒ/ nm polish.

circoncision /siʀkɔ̃sizjɔ̃/ nf circumcision.

circonflexe /siʀkɔ̃flɛks/ adj circumflex.

circonscription /siʀkɔ̃skʀipsjɔ̃/ nf district; **~ électorale** constituency; (US) district; (de conseiller, maire) ward.

circonscrire /siʀkɔ̃skʀiʀ/ 𝟛𝟘 vt (incendie, épidémie) contain; (sujet) define.

circonspect, ~e /siʀkɔ̃spɛkt/ adj circumspect.

circonstance /siʀkõstɑ̃s/ nf circumstance; (situation) situation; (occasion) occasion; ~s **atténuantes** mitigating circumstances.

circuit /siʀkɥi/ nm circuit; (trajet) tour, trip.

circulaire /siʀkylɛʀ/ adj & nf circular.

circulation /siʀkylasjõ/ nf circulation; (de véhicules) traffic.

circuler /siʀkyle/ ◩ vi (se répandre, être distribué) circulate; (aller d'un lieu à un autre) get around; (en voiture) travel; (piéton) walk; (être en service) (bus, train) run; **faire** ~ (badauds) move on; (rumeur) spread.

cire /siʀ/ nf wax.

ciré /siʀe/ nm oilskin.

cirer /siʀe/ ◩ vt polish.

cirque /siʀk/ nm circus; (arène) amphitheatre; (désordre: fig) chaos; **faire le** ~◩ make a racket ◩.

ciseau (pl ~x) /sizo/ nm chisel; ~x scissors.

ciseler /sizle/ ◪ vt chisel.

citadelle /sitadɛl/ nf citadel.

citadin, ~e /sitadɛ̃, -in/ nm, f city-dweller. ●adj city.

citation /sitasjõ/ nf quotation; (Jur) summons.

cité /site/ nf city; (logements) housing estate; ~ **universitaire** (university) halls of residence.

citer /site/ ◩ vt quote, cite; (Jur) summon.

citerne /sitɛʀn/ nf tank.

citoyen, ~ne /sitwajɛ̃, -ɛn/ nm, f citizen.

citron /sitʀõ/ nm lemon; ~ **vert** lime. **citronnade** nf lemon squash, (still) lemonade.

citrouille /sitʀuj/ nf pumpkin.

civet /sivɛ/ nm stew; ~ **de lièvre** jugged hare.

civière /sivjɛʀ/ nf stretcher.

civil, ~e /sivil/ adj civil; (non militaire) civilian; (poli) civil. ●nm civilian; **dans le** ~ in civilian life; **en** ~ in plain clothes.

civilisation /sivilizasjõ/ nf civilization.

civiliser /sivilize/ ◩ vt civilize. ■ **se** ~ vpr become civilized.

civique /sivik/ adj civic.

clair, ~e /klɛʀ/ adj clear; (éclairé) light, bright; (couleur) light; **le plus** ~ **de** most of. ●adv clearly; **il faisait** ~ it was already light. ●nm ~ **de lune** moonlight; **tirer une histoire au** ~ get to the bottom of things. **clairement** adv clearly.

clairière /klɛʀjɛʀ/ nf clearing.

clairsemé, ~e /klɛʀsəme/ adj sparse.

clamer /klame/ ◩ vt proclaim.

clameur /klamœʀ/ nf clamour.

clan /klɑ̃/ nm clan.

clandestin, ~e /klɑ̃dɛstɛ̃, -in/ adj secret; (journal) underground; (immigration, travail) illegal; **passager** ~ stowaway.

clapier /klapje/ nm (rabbit) utch.

clapoter /klapote/ ◩ vi lap.

claquage /klakaʒ/ nm strained muscle; **se faire un** ~ pull a muscle.

claque /klak/ nf slap.

claquer /klake/ ◩ vi bang; (porte) slam, bang; (fouet) crack; (se casser ◩) conk out; (mourir ◩) snuff it!; ~ **des doigts** snap one's fingers; ~ **des mains** clap one's hands; **il claque des dents** his teeth are chattering. ●vt (porte) slam, bang; (dépenser ◩) blow; (fatiguer ◩) tire out.

claquettes /klakɛt/ nfpl tap-dancing.

clarifier /klaʀifje/ ◪ vt clarify.

clarinette /klaʀinɛt/ nf clarinet.

clarté /klaʀte/ nf light, brightness; (netteté) clarity.

classe /klas/ nf class; (salle: Scol)

classroom; (cours) class, lesson; **aller en** ~ go to school; **faire la** ~ **teach;** ~ **ouvrière/moyenne** working/middle class.

classement /klasmɑ̃/ nm classification; (d'élèves) grading; (de documents) filing; (rang) place, grade; (de coureur) placing.

classer /klase/ **1** vt classify; (par mérite) grade; (papiers) file; (Jur) (affaire) close. ■ **se** ~ vpr rank.

classeur /klasœʀ/ nm (meuble) filing cabinet; (chemise) file; (à anneaux) ring binder.

classification /klasifikasjɔ̃/ nf classification.

classique /klasik/ adj classical; (de qualité) classic; (habituel) classic, standard. • nm classic; (auteur) classical author.

clavecin /klavsɛ̃/ nm harpsichord.

clavicule /klavikyl/ nf collarbone.

clavier /klavje/ nm keyboard; ~ **numérique** keypad.

clé, clef /kle/ nf key; (outil) spanner; (Mus) clef; ~ **anglaise** (monkey-)wrench; ~ **de contact** ignition key; ~ **à molette** adjustable spanner; ~ **de voûte** keystone.• adj inv key.

clémence /klemɑ̃s/ nf (de climat) mildness; (indulgence) leniency.

clergé /klɛʀʒe/ nm clergy.

clérical, ~e (mpl **-aux**) /kleʀikal, -o/ adj clerical.

clic /klik/ nm (Ordinat) click.

cliché /kliʃe/ nm cliché; (Photo) negative.

client, ~e /klijɑ̃, -t/ nm, f customer; (d'un avocat) client; (d'un médecin) patient; (d'hôtel) guest; (de taxi) passenger.

clientèle /klijɑ̃tɛl/ nf customers, clientele; (d'un avocat) clients, practice; (d'un médecin) patients, practice; (soutien) custom.

cligner /kliɲe/ **1** vi ~ **des yeux** blink; ~ **de l'œil** wink.

clignotant /kliɲɔtɑ̃/ nm (Auto) indicator, turn.

clignoter /kliɲɔte/ **1** vi blink; (lumière) flicker; (comme signal) flash.

climat /klima/ nm climate.

climatisation /klimatizasjɔ̃/ nf air-conditioning.

clin d'œil /klɛ̃dœj/ nm wink; **en un** ~ in a flash.

clinique /klinik/ adj clinical. • nf (private) clinic.

clinquant, ~e /klɛ̃kɑ̃, -t/ adj showy.

clip /klip/ nm video.

cliquer /klike/ **1** vi (Ordinat) click (**sur** on).

cliqueter /klikte/ **38** vi (couverts) clink; (clés, monnaie) jingle; (ferraille) rattle. **cliquetis** nm clink(ing), jingle, rattle.

clivage /klivaʒ/ nm divide.

clochard, ~e /klɔʃaʀ, -d/ nm, f tramp.

cloche /klɔʃ/ nf bell; (imbécile **1**) idiot; ~ **à fromage** cheese-cover.

cloche-pied*: à ~ /aklɔʃpje/ loc **sauter à** ~ hop on one leg.

clocher /klɔʃe/ nm bell-tower; (pointu) steeple; **de** ~ parochial.

cloison /klwazɔ̃/ nf partition; (fig) barrier.

cloître* /klwatʀ/ nm cloister. **cloîtrer (se)* 1** vpr shut oneself away.

clonage /klonaʒ/ nm clonage.

cloner /klone/ **1** vt clone.

cloque /klɔk/ nf blister.

clos, ~e /klo, -z/ adj closed.

clôture /klotyʀ/ nf fence; (fermeture) closure; (de magasin, bureau) closing; (de débat, liste) close; (en Bourse) close of trading. **clôturer 1** vt enclose, fence in; (festival, séance) close.

clou /klu/ nm nail; (furoncle) boil;

(de spectacle) star attraction; **les
~s** (passage) pedestrian crossing;
(US) crosswalk.

clouer /klue/ **1** vt nail down; (fig)
pin down; **être cloué au lit** be
confined to one's bed; **~ le bec
à qn** shut sb up.

clouté, ~e /klute/ adj studded;
passage ~ pedestrian crossing;
(US) crosswalk.

CMU abrév f *free health care for
people on low incomes.*

coaliser (se) /(sə)kɔalize/ **1** vpr
join forces.

coalition /kɔalisjɔ̃/ nf coalition.

cobaye /kɔbaj/ nm guinea-pig.

cocaïne /kɔkain/ nf cocaine.

cocasse /kɔkas/ adj comical.

coccinelle /kɔksinɛl/ nf ladybird;
(US) ladybug.

cocher /kɔʃe/ **1** vt tick (off),
check. ●nm coachman.

cochon, ~ne /kɔʃɔ̃, -ɔn/ nm, f
(personne **1**) pig. ●adj **1** filthy.
●nm pig. **cochonnerie** nf (saleté
1) filth; (marchandise **1**)
rubbish, junk.

cocon /kɔkɔ̃/ nm cocoon.

cocorico /kɔkɔʀikɔ/ nm cock-
a-doodle-doo.

cocotier /kɔkɔtje/ nm
coconut palm.

cocotte /kɔkɔt/ nf (marmite)
casserole; **~ minute®** pressure-
cooker; **ma ~** **1** my dear.

cocu, ~e /kɔky/ nm, f **1** deceived
husband, deceived wife.

code /kɔd/ nm code; **~s** dipped
headlights; **se mettre en ~s**
dip one's headlights; **~ (à)
barres** bar code; **~
confidentiel (d'identification)**
PIN number; **~ postal** post
code; (US) zip code; **~ de la
route** Highway Code. **coder** **1**
vt code, encode.

coéquipier, -ière /kɔekipje, -jɛʀ/
nm, f team mate.

cœur /kœʀ/ nm heart; (aux cartes)
hearts (+ pl); **~ d'artichaut**
artichoke heart; **~ de palmier**
palm heart; **à ~ ouvert**
(opération) open-heart; (parler)
freely; **avoir bon ~** be kind-
hearted; **de bon ~** willingly;
(rire) heartily; **par ~** by heart;
avoir mal au ~ feel sick *ou*
nauseous; **je veux en avoir le
~ net** I want to be clear in my
own mind (about it).

coffre /kɔfʀ/ nm chest; (pour argent)
safe; (Auto) boot; (US) trunk.
coffre-fort (pl **coffres-forts**)
nm safe.

coffret /kɔfʀɛ/ nm casket, box; (de
livres, cassettes) boxed set.

cogner /kɔɲe/ **1** vt/i knock. ■se
~ vpr knock oneself; **se ~ la
tête** bump one's head.

cohabiter /kɔabite/ **1** vi live
together.

cohérent, ~e /kɔeʀɑ̃, -t/ adj
coherent; (homogène) consistent.

cohue /kɔy/ nf crowd.

coi, ~te /kwa, -t/ adj silent.

coiffe /kwaf/ nf headgear.

coiffer /kwafe/ **1** vt do the hair
of; (chapeau) put on; (surmonter)
cap; **~ qn d'un chapeau** put a
hat on sb; **coiffé de** wearing;
être bien/mal coiffé have tidy/
untidy hair. ■se ~ vpr do
one's hair.

coiffeur, -euse /kwafœʀ, -øz/ nm,
f hairdresser. **coiffeuse** nf
dressing-table.

coiffure /kwafyʀ/ nf hairstyle;
(métier) hairdressing;
(chapeau) hat.

coin /kwɛ̃/ nm corner; (endroit)
spot; (cale) wedge; **au ~ du feu**
by the fireside; **dans le ~**
locally; **du ~** local.

coincer /kwɛ̃se/ **10** vt jam; (caler)
wedge; (attraper **1**) catch. ■se ~
vpr get jammed.

coïncidence /kɔɛ̃sidɑ̃s/ nf
coincidence.

coing /kwɛ̃/ nm quince.

coït /kɔit/ nm intercourse.

col /kɔl/ nm collar; (de bouteille) neck; (de montagne) pass; ~ **blanc** white-collar worker; ~ **roulé** polo-neck; (US) turtle-neck; ~ **de l'utérus** cervix; **se casser le ~ du fémur** break one's hip.

colère /kɔlɛʀ/ nf anger; (accès) fit of anger; **en ~** angry; **se mettre en ~** lose one's temper; **faire une ~** throw a tantrum.

coléreux, -euse /kɔleʀø, -z/ adj quick-tempered.

colin /kɔlɛ̃/ nm (merlu) hake; (lieu noir) coley.

colique /kɔlik/ nf diarrhoea; (Méd) colic.

colis /kɔli/ nm parcel.

collaborateur, -trice /kɔlabɔʀatœʀ, -tʀis/ nm, f collaborator; (journaliste) contributor; (collègue) colleague.

collaboration /kɔlabɔʀasjɔ̃/ nf collaboration (**à** on); (à ouvrage, projet) contribution (**à** to).

collaborer /kɔlabɔʀe/ 🚺 vi collaborate (**à** on); ~ **à** (journal) contribute to.

collant, ~e /kɔlɑ̃, -t/ adj (moulant) kin-tight; (poisseux) sticky. ●nm (bas) tights; (US) panty hose.

colle /kɔl/ nf glue; (en pâte) paste; (problème 🚹) poser; (Scol 🚹) detention.

collecter /kɔlɛkte/ 🚺 vt collect.

collectif, -ive /kɔlɛktif, -v/ adj collective; (billet, voyage) group.

collection /kɔlɛksjɔ̃/ nf collection; (ouvrages) series (+ sg); (du même auteur) set.
collectionner 🚺 vt collect.
collectionneur, -euse nm, f collector.

collectivité /kɔlɛktivite/ nf community; ~ **locale** local authority.

college /kɔlɛʒ/ nm secondary school (up to age 15); (US) junior high school; (assemblée) college.
collégien, ~ne nm, f schoolboy, schoolgirl.

collègue /kɔlɛg/ nmf colleague.

coller /kɔle/ 🚹 vt stick; (avec colle liquide) glue; (affiche) stick up; (mettre 🚹) stick; (par une question 🚹) stump; (Scol 🚹) **se faire ~** get a detention; **je me suis fait ~ en maths** I failed ou flunked maths. ●vi stick (**à** to); (être collant) be sticky; ~ **à** (convenir à) fit, correspond to.

collet /kɔlɛ/ nm (piège) snare; ~ **monté** prim and proper; **mettre la main au ~ de qn** collar sb.

collier /kɔlje/ nm necklace; (de chien) collar.

colline /kɔlin/ nf hill.

collision /kɔlizjɔ̃/ nf (choc) collision; (lutte) clash; **entrer en ~ (avec)** collide (with).

collyre /kɔliʀ/ nm eye drops (+ pl).

colmater /kɔlmate/ 🚹 vt plug, seal.

colombe /kɔlɔ̃b/ nf dove.

Colombie /kɔlɔ̃bi/ nf Colombia.

colon /kɔlɔ̃/ nm settler.

colonel /kɔlɔnɛl/ nm colonel.

colonie /kɔlɔni/ nf colony; 🅲~ **de vacances** children's holiday camp.

colonne /kɔlɔn/ nf column; ~ **vertébrale** spine; **en ~ par deux** in double file.

colorant /kɔlɔʀɑ̃/ nm colouring.

colorier /kɔlɔʀje/ 45 vt colour (in).

colosse /kɔlɔs/ nm giant.

colza /kɔlza/ nm rape(-seed).

coma /kɔma/ nm coma; **dans le ~** in a coma.

combat /kɔ̃ba/ nm fight; (Sport)

🅲 see A-Z of French life and culture

match; ~s fighting. **combatif*, -ive** adj eager to fight; (esprit) fighting.

combattre /kɔ̃batʀ/ ◈ vt/i fight.

combien /kɔ̃bjɛ̃/ adv ~ **(de)** (quantité) how much; (nombre) how many; (temps) how long; ~ **il a changé!** (comme) how he has changed!; ~ **y a-t-il d'ici à...?** how far is it to...?; **on est le ~ aujourd'hui?** what's the date today?

combinaison /kɔ̃binɛzɔ̃/ nf combination; (de femme) slip; (bleu de travail) boiler suit; (US) overalls; ~ **d'aviateur** flying-suit; ~ **de plongée** wetsuit.

combine /kɔ̃bin/ nf trick; (fraude) fiddle; (intrigue) scheme.

combiné /kɔ̃bine/ nm (de téléphone) receiver, handset.

combiner /kɔ̃bine/ ◈ vt (réunir) combine; (calculer) devise; ~ **de faire** plan to do.

comble /kɔ̃bl/ adj packed. ● nm height; (mansarde) attic, loft; **c'est le ~!** that's the (absolute) limit!

combler /kɔ̃ble/ ◈ vt fill; (perte, déficit) make good; (désir) fulfil; ~ **qn de cadeaux** lavish gifts on sb.

combustible /kɔ̃bystibl/ nm fuel.

comédie /kɔmedi/ nf comedy; (histoire⧗) fuss; ~ **musicale** musical; **jouer la** ~ put on an act. **comédien, ~ne** nm, f actor, actress.

comestible /kɔmɛstibl/ adj edible.

comète /kɔmɛt/ nf comet.

comique /kɔmik/ adj comical, funny; (genre) comic. ● nm (acteur) comic; (comédie) comedy; (côté drôle) comical aspect.

commandant /kɔmɑ̃dɑ̃/ nm commander; (dans l'armée de terre) major; ~ **(de bord)** captain; ~ **en chef** Commander-in-Chief.

commande /kɔmɑ̃d/ nf (Comm)

order; (Tech) control; ~s (d'avion) controls.

commandement /kɔmɑ̃dmɑ̃/ nm command; (Relig) commandment.

commander /kɔmɑ̃de/ ◈ vt command; (acheter) order; (étude, œuvre d'art) commission; ~ **à** (maîtriser) control; ~ **à qn de** command sb to. ● vi be in command.

comme /kɔm/ adv ~ **c'est bon!** it's so good!; ~ **il est mignon!** isn't he sweet!; ● conj (dans une comparaison) as; (dans une équivalence, illustration) like; (en tant que) as; (puisque) as, since; (au moment où) as; **vif** ~ **l'éclair** as quick as a flash; **travailler** ~ **sage-femme** work as a midwife; ~ **ci** ~ **ça** so-so; ~ **il faut** properly; ~ **pour faire** as if to do; **jolie** ~ **tout** as pretty as anything; **qu'est-ce qu'il y a** ~ **légumes?** what is there in the way of vegetables?

commencer /kɔmɑ̃se/ ◈ vt/i begin, start; ~ **à faire** begin ou start to do.

comment /kɔmɑ̃/ adv how; ~**?** (répétition) pardon?; (surprise) what?; ~ **est-il?** what is he like?; **le** ~ **et le pourquoi** the whys and wherefores.

commentaire /kɔmɑ̃tɛʀ/ nm comment; (d'un texte, événement) commentary. **commentateur, -trice** nm, f commentator.

commenter /kɔmɑ̃te/ ◈ vt comment on; (film, visite) provide a commentary for; (radio, TV) commentate.

commérages /kɔmeʀaʒ/ nmpl gossip.

commerçant, ~e /kɔmɛʀsɑ̃, -t/ adj (rue) shopping; (personne) business-minded. ● nm, f shopkeeper.

commerce /kɔmɛʀs/ nm trade, commerce; (magasin) business; **faire du** ~ be in business; ~ **électrique** e-commerce.

commercial, ~e (mpl **-iaux**)
kɔmɛʀsjal, -jo/ adj commercial.
commercialiser 1 vt market.

commettre /kɔmɛtʀ/ 42 vt
commit.

commis /kɔmi/ nm (de magasin)
assistant; (de bureau) clerk.

commissaire /kɔmisɛʀ/ nm
commissioner; (Sport) steward; ~
(de police) (police)
superintendent. **commissaire-
priseur** (pl **commissaires-
priseurs**) nm auctioneer.

commissariat /kɔmisaʀja/ nm ~
(de police) police station.

commission /kɔmisjɔ̃/ nf
commission; (course) errand;
(message) message; **~s** shopping.

commode /kɔmɔd/ adj handy,
convenient; (facile) easy; **il n'est
pas** ~ he's a difficult customer.
• nf chest (of drawers).
commodité nf convenience.

commotion /kɔmosjɔ̃/ nf ~
(cérébrale) concussion.

commun, ~e /kɔmœ̃, -yn/ adj
common; (effort, action) joint; (frais,
pièce) shared; **en** ~ jointly; **avoir
ou mettre en** ~ share; **le** ~ **des
mortels** ordinary mortals.
communal, ~e (mpl **-aux**) adj of
the commune, local.

communauté /kɔmynote/ nf
community.

commune /kɔmyn/ nf
(circonscription, collectivité) commune.

communicatif, -ive
/kɔmynikatif, -v/ adj (personne)
talkative; (gaieté) infectious.

communication /kɔmynikasjɔ̃/
nf communication; (téléphonique)
call; **~s** (relations)
communications (+ pl); **voies ou
moyens de** ~ communications
(+ pl).

communier /kɔmynje/ 45 vi
(Relig) receive communion; (fig)
commune.

communiqué /kɔmynike/ nm

statement; (de presse)
communiqué.

communiquer /kɔmynike/ 1 vt
pass on, communicate; (date,
décision) announce. • vi
communicate. ■ **se** ~ **à** vpr
spread to.

communiste /kɔmynist/ adj & nmf
communist.

commutateur /kɔmytatœʀ/ nm
(Électr) switch.

compagne /kɔ̃paɲ/ nf
companion.

compagnie /kɔ̃paɲi/ nf company;
tenir ~ **à** keep company; **en** ~
de together with; ~ **aérienne**
airline.

compagnon /kɔ̃paɲɔ̃/ nm
companion.

comparable /kɔ̃paʀabl/ adj
comparable (**à** to).
comparaison nf comparison;
(littéraire) simile.

comparaître* /kɔ̃paʀɛtʀ/ 18 vi
(Jur) appear (**devant** before).

comparatif, -ive /kɔ̃paʀatif, -v/
adj & nm comparative.

comparer /kɔ̃paʀe/ 1 vt compare
(**à** with). ■ **se** ~ vpr compare
oneself; (être comparable) be
comparable.

compartiment /kɔ̃paʀtimɑ̃/ nm
compartment.

comparution /kɔ̃paʀysjɔ̃/ nf (Jur)
appearance.

compas /kɔ̃pa/ nm (pair of)
compasses; (boussole) compass.

compassion /kɔ̃pasjɔ̃/ nf
compassion.

compatible /kɔ̃patibl/ adj
compatible.

compatir /kɔ̃patiʀ/ 2 vi
sympathize; ~ **à** share in.

compatriote /kɔ̃patʀijɔt/ nmf
compatriot.

compensation /kɔ̃pɑ̃sasjɔ̃/ nf

....

G see A-Z of French life and culture

compensation. compenser 1 vt compensate for, make up for.

compère /kɔ̃pɛʀ/ nm accomplice.

compétence /kɔ̃petɑ̃s/ nf competence; (fonction) domain, sphere; **entrer dans les ~s de qn** be in sb's domain. **compétent, ~e** adj competent.

compétition /kɔ̃petisjɔ̃/ nf competition; (sportive) event; **de ~** competitive.

complaire (se)* /(sə)kɔ̃plɛʀ/ 47 vpr **se ~ dans** delight in.

complaisance /kɔ̃plɛzɑ̃s/ nf kindness; (indulgence) indulgence.

complément /kɔ̃plemɑ̃/ nm supplement; (Gram) complement; **~ (d'objet)** (Gram) object; **~ d'information** further information. **complémentaire** adj complementary; (renseignements) supplementary.

complet, -ète /kɔ̃plɛ, -t/ adj complete; (train, hôtel) full. •nm suit.

compléter /kɔ̃plete/ 14 vt complete; (agrémenter) complement. ■ **se ~** vpr complement each other.

complexe /kɔ̃plɛks/ adj complex.• nm (sentiment, bâtiments) complex.

complexé, ~e /kɔ̃plekse/ adj **être ~** have a lot of hang-ups.

complice /kɔ̃plis/ nm accomplice.

compliment /kɔ̃plimɑ̃/ nm compliment; **~s** (félicitations) compliments, congratulations.

compliquer /kɔ̃plike/ 1 vt complicate. ■ **se ~** vpr become complicated.

complot /kɔ̃plo/ nm plot.

comportement /kɔ̃pɔʀtəmɑ̃/ nm behaviour; (de joueur, voiture) performance.

comporter /kɔ̃pɔʀte/ 1 vt (être composé de) comprise; (inclure) include; (risque) entail. ■ **se ~** vpr behave; (joueur, voiture) perform.

composant /kɔ̃pozɑ̃/ nm component.

composé, ~e /kɔ̃poze/ adj composite; (salade) mixed; (guindé) affected. •nm compound.

composer /kɔ̃poze/ 1 vt make up, compose; (chanson, visage) compose; (numéro) dial; (page) typeset. •vi (transiger) compromise. ■ **se ~ de** vpr be made up ou composed of. **compositeur, -trice** nm, f (Mus) composer.

composter /kɔ̃pɔste/ 1 vt (billet) punch.

compote /kɔ̃pɔt/ nf stewed fruit; **~ de pommes** stewed apples.

compréhensible /kɔ̃pʀeɑ̃sibl/ adj understandable; (intelligible) comprehensible.

compréhensif, -ive /kɔ̃pʀeɑ̃sif, -v/ adj understanding.

compréhension /kɔ̃pʀeɑ̃sjɔ̃/ nf understanding, comprehension.

comprendre /kɔ̃pʀɑ̃dʀ/ 50 vt understand; (comporter) comprise, be made up of. ■ **se ~** vpr (personnes) understand each other; **ça se comprend** that is understandable.

compresse /kɔ̃pʀɛs/ nf compress.

comprimé /kɔ̃pʀime/ nm tablet.

comprimer /kɔ̃pʀime/ 1 vt compress; (réduire) reduce.

compris, ~e /kɔ̃pʀi, -z/ adj included; (d'accord) agreed; **~ entre** (contained) between; **service (non) ~** service (not) included; **tout ~** (all) inclusive; **y ~** including.

compromettre /kɔ̃pʀɔmɛtʀ/ 42 vt compromise. **compromis** nm compromise.

comptabilité /kɔ̃tabilite/ nf accountancy; (comptes) accounts; (service) accounts department.

comptable /kɔ̃tabl/ adj accounting. •nmf accountant.

comptant /kɔ̃tɑ̃/ adv (payer) (in)

cash; (acheter) for cash.

compte /kɔ̃t/ nm count; (facture, comptabilité) account; (nombre exact) right number; **~ bancaire, ~ en banque** bank account; **prendre qch en ~, tenir ~ de qch** take sth into account; **se rendre ~ de** realize; **demander/rendre des ~s** ask for/give an explanation; **à bon ~** cheaply; **s'en tirer à bon ~** get off lightly; **travailler à son ~** be self-employed; **faire le ~ de** count; **pour le ~ de** on behalf of; **sur le ~ de** about; **au bout du ~** all things considered; **~ à rebours** countdown.

compte-gouttes* /kɔ̃tgut/ nm inv (Méd) dropper; **au ~** (fig) in dribs and drabs.

compter /kɔ̃te/ 🔟 vt count; (prévoir) allow, reckon on; (facturer) charge for; (avoir) have; (classer) consider; **~ faire** intend to do. • vi (calculer, importer) count; **~ avec** reckon with; **~ parmi** (figurer) be considered among; **~ sur** rely on, count on.

compte(-)rendu /kɔ̃trɑ̃dy/ nm report; (de film, livre) review.

compteur /kɔ̃tœr/ nm meter; **~ de vitesse** speedometer.

comptine /kɔ̃tin/ nf nursery rhyme.

comptoir /kɔ̃twar/ nm counter; (de café) bar.

comte /kɔ̃t/ nm count.

comté /kɔ̃te/ nm county.

comtesse /kɔ̃tɛs/ nf countess.

con, ~ne /kɔ̃, kɔn/ adj 🗙 stupid 🗙. • nm, f 🗙 bloody fool 🗙.

concentrer /kɔ̃sɑ̃tre/ 🔟 vt concentrate. ■ **se ~** vpr be concentrated.

concept /kɔ̃sɛpt/ nm concept.

concerner /kɔ̃sɛrne/ 🔟 vt concern; **en ce qui me**

concerne as far as I am concerned.

concert /kɔ̃sɛr/ nm concert; **de ~** in unison.

concerter /kɔ̃sɛrte/ 🔟 vt organize, prepare. ■ **se ~** vpr confer.

concession /kɔ̃sesjɔ̃/ nf concession; (terrain) plot.

concevoir /kɔ̃svwar/ 🗗🗗 vt (imaginer, engendrer) conceive; (comprendre) understand; (élaborer) design.

concierge /kɔ̃sjɛrʒ/ nmf caretaker.

concilier /kɔ̃silje/ 🗗🗗 vt reconcile. ■ **se ~** vpr (s'attirer) win (over).

concis, ~e /kɔ̃si, -z/ adj concise.

conclure /kɔ̃klyr/ 🗗🗗 vt conclude; **~ à** conclude in favour of. • vi **~ en faveur de/contre** find in favour of/against. **conclusion** nf conclusion.

concombre /kɔ̃kɔ̃br/ nm cucumber.

concordance /kɔ̃kɔrdɑ̃s/ nf agreement.

concourir /kɔ̃kurir/ 🗗🗗 vi compete. • vt **~ à** contribute towards.

🄲**concours** /kɔ̃kur/ nm competition; (examen) competitive examination; (aide) help; (de circonstances) combination.

concret, -ète /kɔ̃krɛ, -t/ adj concrete.

concrétiser /kɔ̃kretize/ 🔟 vt give concrete form to. ■ **se ~** vpr materialize.

conçu, ~e /kɔ̃sy/ adj **bien/mal ~** well/badly designed.

concubinage /kɔ̃kybinaʒ/ nm cohabitation; **vivre en ~** live together, cohabit.

concurrence /kɔ̃kyrɑ̃s/ nf competition; **faire ~ à** compete

....

🄲 see A-Z of French life and culture

C

with; **jusqu'à** ∼ **de** up to a limit of.

concurrencer /kɔ̃kyRɑ̃se/ 🔟 vt compete with.

concurrent, ∼e /kɔ̃kyRɑ̃, -t/ nm, f competitor; (Scol) candidate. ●adj rival.

condamnation /kɔ̃danasjɔ̃/ nf condemnation; (peine) sentence; ∼ **centralisée des portières** central locking. **condamné, ∼e** nm, f condemned man, condemned woman. **condamner** 🔟 vt (censurer, obliger) condemn; (Jur) sentence; (porte) block up.

condition /kɔ̃disjɔ̃/ nf condition; ∼**s** (prix) terms; **à** ∼ **de** *ou* **que** provided (that); **sans** ∼ unconditional(ly); **sous** ∼ conditionally.

conditionnel, ∼le /kɔ̃disjɔnɛl/ adj conditional. ●nm conditional (tense).

conditionnement /kɔ̃disjɔnmɑ̃/ nm conditioning; (emballage) packaging.

condoléances /kɔ̃dɔleɑ̃s/ nfpl condolences.

conducteur, -trice /kɔ̃dyktœr, -tRis/ nm, f driver.

conduire /kɔ̃dɥiR/ 🔟 vt take (**à** to); (guider) lead; (Auto) drive; (affaire) conduct; ∼ **à** (faire aboutir) lead to. ●vi drive. ■ **se** ∼ vpr behave.

conduit /kɔ̃dɥi/ nm duct.

conduite /kɔ̃dɥit/ nf conduct, behaviour; (Auto) driving; (tuyau) pipe; **voiture avec** ∼ **à droite** right-hand drive car.

confection /kɔ̃fɛksjɔ̃/ nf making; **de** ∼ ready-made; **la** ∼ the clothing industry.

conférence /kɔ̃feRɑ̃s/ nf conference; (exposé) lecture; ∼ **au sommet** summit meeting. **conférencier, -ière** nm, f lecturer.

confesser /kɔ̃fese/ 🔟 vt confess. ■ **se** ∼ vpr go to confession.

confiance /kɔ̃fjɑ̃s/ nf trust; **avoir** ∼ **en** trust.

confiant, ∼e /kɔ̃fjɑ̃, -t/ adj (assuré) confident; (sans défiance) trusting.

confidence /kɔ̃fidɑ̃s/ nf confidence.

confidentiel, ∼le /kɔ̃fidɑ̃sjɛl/ adj confidential.

confier /kɔ̃fje/ 🔟 vt ∼ **à qn** entrust sb with; ∼ **un secret à qn** tell sb a secret. ■ **se** ∼ **à** vpr confide in.

configuration /kɔ̃figyRasjɔ̃/ nf configuration.

configurer /kɔ̃figyRe/vt configure.

confiner /kɔ̃fine/ 🔟 vt confine; ∼ **à** border on. ■ **se** ∼ vpr confine oneself (**à, dans** to).

confirmation /kɔ̃fiRmasjɔ̃/ nf confirmation. **confirmer** 🔟 vt confirm.

confiserie /kɔ̃fizRi/ nf sweet shop; ∼**s** confectionery.

confisquer /kɔ̃fiske/ 🔟 vt confiscate.

confit, ∼e /kɔ̃fi, -t/ adj candied; (fruits) crystallized. ●nm ∼ **de canard** confit of duck.

confiture /kɔ̃fityR/ nf jam.

conflit /kɔ̃fli/ nm conflict.

confondre /kɔ̃fɔ̃dR/ 🔟 vt confuse, mix up; (étonner) confound. ■ **se** ∼ vpr merge; **se** ∼ **en excuses** apologize profusely.

conforme /kɔ̃fɔRm/ adj **être** ∼ **à** comply with; (être en accord) be in keeping with.

conformer /kɔ̃fɔRme/ 🔟 vt adapt. ■ **se** ∼ **à** vpr conform to.

conformité /kɔ̃fɔRmite/ nf compliance, conformity; **agir en** ∼ **avec** act in accordance with.

confort /kɔ̃fɔR/ nm comfort; **tout** ∼ with all mod cons. **confortable** adj comfortable.

confrère /kɔ̃fRɛR/ nm colleague.

confronter /kɔ̃fRɔ̃te/ 🔟 vt

confront; (textes) compare. ■ se
~ à vpr be confronted with.

confus, ~e /kɔ̃fy, -z/ adj
confused; (gêné) embarrassed.

congé /kɔ̃ʒe/ nm holiday; (arrêt
momentané) time off, leave; (avis de
départ) notice; **en ~** on holiday
ou leave; **~ de maladie/
maternité** sick/maternity leave;
jour de ~ day off; **prendre ~
de** take one's leave of.

congédier /kɔ̃ʒedje/ 45 vt
dismiss.

congélateur /kɔ̃ʒelatœʀ/ nm
freezer.

congeler /kɔ̃ʒle/ 6 vt freeze.

congère /kɔ̃ʒɛʀ/ nf snowdrift.

congrès /kɔ̃gʀɛ/ nm conference;
(Pol) congress.

conjoint, ~e /kɔ̃ʒwɛ̃, -t/ nm, f
spouse. ●adj joint.

conjonctivite /kɔ̃ʒɔ̃ktivit/ nf
conjunctivitis.

conjoncture /kɔ̃ʒɔ̃ktyʀ/ nf
situation; (économique) economic
climate.

conjugaison /kɔ̃ʒygɛzɔ̃/ nf
conjugation.

conjugal, ~e (mpl **-aux**)
/kɔ̃ʒygal, -o/ adj conjugal,
married.

conjuguer /kɔ̃ʒyge/ 1 vt (Gram)
conjugate; (efforts) combine. ■ se
~ vpr (Gram) be conjugated;
(facteurs) be combined.

conjurer /kɔ̃ʒyʀe/ 1 vt (éviter)
avert; (implorer) beg.

connaissance /kɔnɛsɑ̃s/ nf
knowledge; (personne)
acquaintance; **~s** (science)
knowledge; **faire la ~ de** meet;
(apprécier une personne) get to know;
perdre/reprendre ~ lose/
regain consciousness; **sans ~**
unconscious.

connaisseur /kɔnɛsœʀ/ nm
expert, connoisseur.

connaître* /kɔnɛtʀ/ 18 vt know;

(difficultés, faim, succès) experience;
faire ~ make known. ■ se ~ vpr
(se rencontrer) meet; **s'y ~ en**
know (all) about.

connecter /kɔnɛkte/ 1 vt
connect; **être/ne pas être
connecté** be on-/off-line. ■ se ~
à vpr (Ordinat) log on to.

connerie /kɔnʀi/ nf 🗵 **faire une
~** do something stupid; **dire
des ~s** talk rubbish.

connexion /kɔnɛksjɔ̃/ nf (Ordinat)
connection.

connu, ~e /kɔny/ adj well-
known.

conquérant, ~e /kɔ̃keʀɑ̃, -t/ nm,
f conqueror.

conquête /kɔ̃kɛt/ nf conquest.

consacrer /kɔ̃sakʀe/ 1 vt devote;
(Relig) consecrate; (sanctionner)
sanction. ■ se ~ à vpr devote
oneself to.

conscience /kɔ̃sjɑ̃s/ nf
conscience; (perception) awareness;
(de collectivité) consciousness;
avoir/prendre ~ de be/become
aware of; **perdre/reprendre ~**
lose/regain consciousness; **avoir
bonne/mauvaise ~** have a
clear/guilty conscience.

conscient, ~e /kɔ̃sjɑ̃, -t/ adj
conscious; **~ de** aware *ou*
conscious of.

conseil /kɔ̃sɛj/ nm (piece of)
advice; (assemblée) council,
committee; (séance) meeting;
(personne) consultant; **~
d'administration** board of
directors; **~ en gestion**
management consultant; **~ des
ministres** Cabinet; **~
municipal** town council.

conseiller¹ /kɔ̃seje/ 1 vt advise;
~ à qn de advise sb to; **~ qch à
qn** recommend sth to sb.

conseiller², -ère /kɔ̃seje, -jɛʀ/
nm, f adviser, counsellor; **~
municipal** town councillor; **~
d'orientation** careers adviser.

C

consentement /kɔ̃sɑ̃tmɑ̃/ nm
consent.

conséquence /kɔ̃sekɑ̃s/ nf
consequence; **en ~** (comme il
convient) accordingly; **en ~ (de
quoi)** as a result of which.

conséquent, ~e /kɔ̃sekɑ̃, -t/ adj
consistent, logical; (important)
substantial; **par ~** consequently,
therefore.

conservateur, -trice
/kɔ̃sɛʀvatœʀ, -tʀis/ adj
conservative. ● nm, f (Pol)
conservative; (de musée) curator.
● nm preservative.

conservation /kɔ̃sɛʀvasjɔ̃/ nf
preservation; (d'espèce, patrimoine)
conservation.

conservatoire /kɔ̃sɛʀvatwaʀ/ nm
academy.

conserve /kɔ̃sɛʀv/ nf tinned *ou*
canned food; **en ~** tinned,
canned; **boîte de ~** tin, can.

conserver /kɔ̃sɛʀve/ 1 vt keep;
(en bon état) preserve; (Culin)
preserve. ■ se ~ vpr (Culin) keep.

considérer /kɔ̃sidere/ 14 vt
consider; (respecter) esteem; ~
comme consider to be.

consigne /kɔ̃siɲ/ nf (de gare) left-
luggage office; (US) baggage
checkroom; (somme) deposit;
(ordres) orders; ~ **automatique**
left-luggage lockers; (US)
baggage lockers.

consistance /kɔ̃sistɑ̃s/ nf
consistency; (fig) substance,
weight. **consistant, ~e** adj solid;
(épais) thick.

consister /kɔ̃siste/ 1 vi ~
en/dans consist of/in; ~ **à faire**
consist in doing.

consoler /kɔ̃sɔle/ 1 vt console.
■ se ~ vpr find consolation; **se ~
de qch** get over sth.

consolider /kɔ̃sɔlide/ 1 vt
strengthen; (fig) consolidate.

consommateur, -trice
/kɔ̃sɔmatœʀ, -tʀis/ nm, f (Comm)
consumer; (dans un café) customer.

consommation /kɔ̃sɔmasjɔ̃/ nf
consumption; (accomplissement)
consummation; (boisson) drink;
de ~ (Comm) consumer.

consommer /kɔ̃sɔme/ 1 vt
consume, use; (manger) eat; (boire)
drink; (mariage) consummate. ■ se
~ vpr (être mangé) be eaten; (être
utilisé) be used.

consonne /kɔ̃sɔn/ nf consonant.

constat /kɔ̃sta/ nm (official)
report; ~ **(à l')amiable** accident
report drawn up by those
involved.

constatation /kɔ̃statasjɔ̃/ nf
observation, statement of fact.
constater 1 vt note, notice;
(certifier) certify.

consternation /kɔ̃stɛʀnasjɔ̃/ nf
dismay.

constipé, ~e /kɔ̃stipe/ adj
constipated; (fig) uptight.

constituer /kɔ̃stitɥe/ 1 vt
(composer) make up, constitute;
(organiser) form; (être) constitute;
constitué de made up of. ■ se
~ vpr **se ~ prisonnier** give
oneself up.

constitution /kɔ̃stitysjɔ̃/ nf
formation, setting up; (Pol, Méd)
constitution.

constructeur /kɔ̃stʀyktœʀ/ nm
manufacturer, builder.

construction /kɔ̃stʀyksjɔ̃/ nf
building; (structure, secteur)
construction; (fabrication)
manufacture.

construire /kɔ̃stʀɥiʀ/ 17 vt build;
(système, phrase) construct.

consulat /kɔ̃syla/ nm consulate.

consultation /kɔ̃syltasjɔ̃/ nf
consultation; (réception: Méd)
surgery; (US) office; **heures de
~** surgery *ou* office (US) hours.

consulter /kɔ̃sylte/ 1 vt consult.
● vi (médecin) hold surgery, see
patients. ■ se ~ vpr consult
together.

contact /kɔ̃takt/ nm contact;

(toucher) touch; **au ~ de** on contact with; (personne) by contact with; by seeing; **mettre/couper le ~** (Auto) switch on/off the ignition; **prendre ~ avec** get in touch with. **contacter** 1 vt contact.

contagieux, -ieuse /kɔ̃taʒjø, -z/ adj contagious.

conte /kɔ̃t/ nm tale; **~ de fées** fairy tale.

contempler /kɔ̃tãple/ 1 vt contemplate.

contemporain, ~e /kɔ̃tɑ̃pɔrɛ̃, -ɛn/ adj & nm,f contemporary.

contenance /kɔ̃t(ə)nãs/ nf (volume) capacity; (allure) bearing; **perdre ~** lose one's composure.

contenir /kɔ̃t(ə)nir/ 58 vt contain; (avoir une capacité de) hold. ■ se ~ vpr contain oneself.

content, ~e /kɔ̃tã, -t/ adj pleased, happy (**de** with); **~ de faire** pleased ou happy to do.

contenter /kɔ̃tãte/ 1 vt satisfy. ■ se ~ de vpr content oneself with.

contenu /kɔ̃t(ə)ny/ nm (de récipient) contents (+ pl); (de texte) content.

conter /kɔ̃te/ 1 vt tell, relate.

contestation /kɔ̃tɛstasjɔ̃/ nf dispute; (opposition) protest.

contester /kɔ̃tɛste/ 1 vt question, dispute; (s'opposer) protest against. ●vi protest.

conteur, -euse /kɔ̃tœr, -øz/ nm, f storyteller.

contigu, ~ë* /kɔ̃tigy/ adj adjacent (**à** to).

continent /kɔ̃tinã/ nm continent.

continu, ~e /kɔ̃tiny/ adj continuous.

continuer /kɔ̃tinɥe/ 1 vt continue. ●vi continue, go on; **~ à** ou **de faire** carry on ou go on ou continue doing.

contorsionner (se) /(se) kɔ̃tɔrsjɔne/ 1 vpr wriggle.

contour /kɔ̃tur/ nm outline, contour; **~s** (d'une route) twists and turns, bends.

contourner /kɔ̃turne/ 1 vt go round, by-pass; (difficulté) get round.

contraceptif, -ive /kɔ̃trasɛptif, -v/ adj contraceptive. ●nm contraceptive. **contraception** nf contraception.

contracter /kɔ̃trakte/ 1 vt (maladie) contract; (dette) incur; (muscle) tense; (assurance) take out. ■ se ~ vpr contract.

contractuel, ~le /kɔ̃traktɥɛl/ nm, f (agent) traffic warden.

contradictoire /kɔ̃tradiktwar/ adj contradictory; (débat) open.

contraignant, ~e /kɔ̃trɛɲã, -t/ adj restricting.

contraindre /kɔ̃trɛ̃dr/ 22 vt force, compel (**à faire** to do).

contrainte /kɔ̃trɛ̃t/ nf constraint.

contraire /kɔ̃trɛr/ adj opposite; **~ à** contrary to. ●nm opposite; **au ~** on the contrary; **au ~ de** unlike.

contrarier /kɔ̃trarje/ 45 vt annoy; (projet, volonté) frustrate; (chagriner) upset.

contraste /kɔ̃trast/ nm contrast.

contrat /kɔ̃tra/ nm contract.

contravention /kɔ̃travãsjɔ̃/ nf (parking) ticket; **en ~** in breach (**à** of).

contre /kɔ̃tr(ə)/ prép against; (en échange de) for; **par ~** on the other hand; **tout ~** close by. **contre-attaque*** (pl ~s) nf counterattack. **contre-attaquer*** 1 vt counter-attack. **contre-balancer** 10 vt counterbalance.

contrebande /kɔ̃trəbãd/ nf contraband; **faire la ~ de** smuggle.

contrebas: en ~ /ɑ̃kɔ̃trəba/ loc below.

contrebasse /kɔ̃tʀəbɑs/ nf double bass.

contrecœur: à /akɔ̃tʀəkœʀ/ loc reluctantly.

contrecoup /kɔ̃tʀəku/ nm effects, repercussions.

contredire /kɔ̃tʀədiʀ/ **37** vt contradict. ▪ **se** ~ vpr contradict oneself.

contrée /kɔ̃tʀe/ nf region; (pays) land.

contrefaçon /kɔ̃tʀəfasɔ̃/ nf (objet imité, action) forgery.

contre-indiqué*, ~**e** /kɔ̃tʀɛ̃dike/ adj (Méd) contra-indicated; (déconseillé) not recommended.

contre-jour*: à ~ /akɔ̃tʀəʒuʀ/ loc against the light.

contrepartie /kɔ̃tʀəpaʀti/ nf compensation; **en** ~ in exchange, in return.

contreplaqué /kɔ̃tʀəplake/ nm plywood.

contresens /kɔ̃tʀəsɑ̃s/ nm misinterpretation; (absurdité) nonsense; **à** ~ the wrong way.

contretemps /kɔ̃tʀətɑ̃/ nm hitch; **à** ~ (fig) at the wrong time.

contribuable /kɔ̃tʀibɥabl/ nmf taxpayer.

contribuer /kɔ̃tʀibɥe/ **1** vt contribute (**à** to, towards).

contrôle /kɔ̃tʀol/ nm (maîtrise) control; (vérification) check; (des prix) control; (poinçon) hallmark; (Scol) test; ~ **continu** continuous assessment; ~ **des changes** exchange control; ~ **des naissances** birth control; ~ **de soi-même** self-control; ~ **technique (des véhicules)** MOT (test).

contrôler /kɔ̃tʀole/ **1** vt (vérifier) check; (surveiller, maîtriser) control. ▪ **se** ~ vpr control oneself.

contrôleur, -euse /kɔ̃tʀolœʀ, -øz/ nm, f inspector.

convaincre /kɔ̃vɛ̃kʀ/ **59** vt convince; ~ **qn de faire** persuade sb to do.

convalescence /kɔ̃valesɑ̃s/ nf convalescence; **être en** ~ be convalescing.

convenable /kɔ̃vnabl/ adj (correct) decent, proper; (approprié) suitable; (acceptable) reasonable, acceptable.

convenance /kɔ̃vnɑ̃s/ nf **à ma** ~ to my satisfaction; **les** ~**s** convention.

convenir /kɔ̃vniʀ/ **58** vt/i be suitable; ~ **à** suit; ~ **que** admit that; ~ **de qch** (avouer) admit sth; (s'accorder sur) agree on sth; ~ **de faire** agree to do; **il convient de** it is advisable to; (selon les bienséances) it would be right to.

convention /kɔ̃vɑ̃sjɔ̃/ nf agreement, convention; (clause) article, clause; ~**s** (convenances) convention; **de** ~ conventional; ~ **collective** industrial agreement.

convenu, ~e /kɔ̃vny/ adj agreed.

conversation /kɔ̃vɛʀsasjɔ̃/ nf conversation.

convertir /kɔ̃vɛʀtiʀ/ **2** vt convert (**à** to; **en** into). ▪ **se** ~ vpr be converted, convert.

conviction /kɔ̃viksjɔ̃/ nf conviction; **avoir la** ~ **que** be convinced that.

convivial, ~e (mpl **-iaux**) /kɔ̃vivjal, -jo/ adj convivial; (Ordinat) user-friendly.

convocation /kɔ̃vɔkasjɔ̃/ nf (Jur) summons; (d'une assemblée) convening; (document) notification to attend.

convoi /kɔ̃vwa/ nm convoy; (train) train; ~ **(funèbre)** funeral procession.

convoquer /kɔ̃vɔke/ **1** vt (assemblée) convene; (personne) summon; **être convoqué pour un entretien** be called for interview.

coopération /koopeRasjɔ̃/ nf cooperation; (Mil) civilian national service abroad.

coordination /kooRdinasjɔ̃/ nf coordination. **coordonnées** nfpl coordinates; (adresse) address and telephone number.

copain /kopɛ̃/ nm friend; (petit ami) boyfriend.

copie /kopi/ nf copy; (Scol) paper; ~ **d'examen** exam paper *ou* script; ~ **de sauvegarde** back-up copy.

copier /kopje/ 45 vt/i copy; ~ **sur** (Scol) copy *ou* crib from.

copieux, -ieuse /kopjø, -z/ adj copious.

copine /kopin/ nf friend; (petite amie) girlfriend.

coq /kok/ nm cockerel.

coque /kok/ nf shell; (de bateau) hull.

coquelicot /kokliko/ nm poppy.

coqueluche /koklyʃ/ nf whooping cough.

coquet, ~te /kokɛ, -t/ adj flirtatious; (élégant) pretty; (somme ①) tidy.

coquetier /koktje/ nm eggcup.

coquillage /kokijaʒ/ nm shellfish; (coquille) shell.

coquille /kokij/ nf shell; (faute) misprint; ~ **Saint-Jacques** scallop.

coquin, ~e /kokɛ̃, -in/ adj mischievous. ●nm, f rascal.

cor /kor/ nm (Mus) horn; (au pied) corn.

corail (pl **-aux**) /koRaj, -o/ nm coral.

corbeau (pl ~**x**) /koRbo/ nm (oiseau) crow.

corbeille /koRbɛj/ nf basket; ~ **à papier** waste-paper basket.

corbillard /koRbijaR/ nm hearse.

cordage /koRdaʒ/ nm rope; ~**s** (Naut) rigging.

corde /koRd/ nf rope; (d'arc, de violon) string; ~ **à linge** washing line; ~ **à sauter** skipping-rope; ~ **raide** tightrope; ~**s vocales** vocal cords.

cordon /koRdɔ̃/ nm string, cord; ~ **de police** police cordon.

cordonnier /koRdonje/ nm cobbler.

Corée /koRe/ nf Korea.

coriace /koRjas/ adj tough.

corne /koRn/ nf horn.

corneille /koRnɛj/ nf crow.

cornemuse /koRnəmyz/ nf bagpipes (+ pl).

corner /koRne/ 1 vt (page) turn down the corner of; **page cornée** dog-eared page. ●vi (Auto) hoot, honk.

cornet /koRnɛ/ nm (paper) cone; (crème glacée) cornet, cone.

corniche /koRniʃ/ nf cornice; (route) cliff road.

cornichon /koRniʃɔ̃/ nm gherkin.

corporel, ~le /koRpoRɛl/ adj bodily; (châtiment) corporal.

corps /koR/ nm body; (Mil) corps; **combat** ~ **à** ~ hand-to-hand combat; ~ **électoral** electorate; ~ **enseignant** teaching profession.

correct, ~e /koRɛkt/ adj proper, correct; (exact) correct.

correcteur, -trice /koRɛktœR, -tRis/ nm, f (d'épreuves) proofreader; (Scol) examiner; ~ **liquide** correction fluid; ~ **d'orthographe** spell-checker.

correction /koRɛksjɔ̃/ nf correction; (d'examen) marking, grading; (punition) beating.

correspondance /koRɛspɔ̃dɑ̃s/ nf correspondence; (de train, d'autobus) connection; **vente par** ~ mail order; **faire des études par** ~ do a correspondence course.

correspondant, ~e /koRɛspɔ̃dɑ̃, -t/ adj corresponding. ●nm, f correspondent; penfriend; (au téléphone) **votre** ~ the person you are calling.

correspondre /kɔʀɛspɔ̃dʀ/ 🔢 vi (s'accorder, écrire) correspond; (chambres) communicate. • v + prép ~ **à** (être approprié à) match, suit; (équivaloir à) correspond to. ■ se ~ vpr correspond.

corrida /kɔʀida/ nf bullfight.

corriger /kɔʀiʒe/ 🔢 vt correct; (devoir) mark, grade, correct; (punir) beat; (guérir) cure.

corsage /kɔʀsaʒ/ nm bodice; (chemisier) blouse.

corsaire /kɔʀsɛʀ/ nm pirate.

Corse /kɔʀs/ nf Corsica. •nmf Corsican. **corse** adj Corsican.

corsé, ~e /kɔʀse/ adj (vin) full-bodied; (café) strong; (scabreux) racy; (problème) tough.

cortège /kɔʀtɛʒ/ nm procession; ~ **funèbre** funeral procession.

corvée /kɔʀve/ nf chore.

cosmonaute /kɔsmonot/ nmf cosmonaut.

cosmopolite /kɔsmɔpɔlit/ adj cosmopolitan.

cosse /kɔs/ nf (de pois) pod.

cossu, ~e /kɔsy/ adj (gens) well-to-do; (demeure) opulent.

costaud, ~e /kɔsto, -d/ 🔢 adj strong. •nm strong man.

costume /kɔstym/ nm suit; (Théât) costume.

cote /kɔt/ nf (classification) mark; (en Bourse) quotation; (de cheval) odds (**de** on); (de candidat, acteur) rating; ~ **d'alerte** danger level; **avoir la** ~ be popular.

côte /kot/ nf (littoral) coast; (pente) hill; (Anat) rib; (Culin) chop; ~ **à** ~ side by side; **la C**~ **d'Azur** the (French) Riviera.

côté /kote/ nm side; (direction) way; **à** ~ nearby; **voisin d'à** ~ next-door neighbour; **à** ~ **de** next to; (comparé à) compared to; **à** ~ **de**

la cible wide of the target; **aux** ~**s** by the side of; **de** ~ (regarder) sideways; (sauter) to one side; **mettre de** ~ put aside; **de ce** ~ this way; **de chaque** ~ on each side; **de tous les** ~**s** on every side; (partout) everywhere; **du** ~ **de** (vers) towards; (proche de) near.

côtelette /kotlɛt/ nf chop.

coter /kɔte/ 🔢 vt (Comm) quote; **coté en Bourse** listed on the Stock Exchange; **très coté** highly rated.

cotiser /kɔtize/ 🔢 vi pay one's contributions (**à** to); (à un club) pay one's subscription. ■ se ~ vpr club together.

coton /kɔtɔ̃/ nm cotton; ~ **hydrophile** cotton wool.

cou /ku/ nm neck.

couchant /kuʃɑ̃/ nm sunset.

couche /kuʃ/ nf layer; (de peinture) coat; (de bébé) nappy; (US) diaper; ~**s** (Méd) childbirth; ~**s sociales** social strata.

coucher /kuʃe/ 🔢 vt put to bed; (loger) put up; (étendre) lay down; ~ **(par écrit)** set down. •vi sleep. ■ se ~ vpr go to bed; (s'étendre) lie down; (soleil) set. •nm ~ **de soleil** sunset.

couchette /kuʃɛt/ nf (de train) couchette; (Naut) berth.

coude /kud/ nm elbow; (de rivière, chemin) bend; ~ **à** ~ side by side.

cou-de-pied (pl **cous-de-pied**) /kudpje/ nm instep.

coudre /kudʀ/ 🔢 vt/i sew.

couette /kwɛt/ nf duvet, quilt.

couler /kule/ 🔢 vi flow, run; (fromage, nez) run; (fuir) leak; (bateau) sink; (entreprise) go under; **faire** ~ **un bain** run a bath. •vt (bateau) sink; (sculpture, métal) cast. ■ se ~ vpr slip (**dans** into).

couleur /kulœʀ/ nf colour; (peinture) paint; (aux cartes) suit; ~**s** (teint) colour; **de** ~ (homme, femme) coloured; **en ~s** (télévision, film) colour.

couleuvre /kulœvʀ/ nf grass snake.

coulisse /kulis/ nf (de tiroir) runner; **à ~** (porte, fenêtre) sliding; **~s** (Théât) wings; **dans les ~s** (fig) behind the scenes.

couloir /kulwaʀ/ nm corridor; (Sport) lane; **~ de bus** bus lane.

coup /ku/ nm blow; (choc) knock; (Sport) stroke; (de crayon, chance, cloche) stroke; (de fusil, pistolet) shot; (fois) time; (aux échecs) move; **donner un ~ de pied/poing à** kick/punch; **à ~ sûr** definitely; **après ~** after the event; **boire un ~** 🔲 have a drink; **~ sur ~** in rapid succession; **du ~** as a result; **d'un seul ~** in one go; **du premier ~** first go; **sale ~** dirty trick; **sous le ~ de la fatigue/colère** out of tiredness/anger; **sur le ~** instantly; **tenir le ~** hold out; **manquer son ~** 🔲 blow it 🔲; **~ de chiffon** wipe (with a rag); **~ de coude** nudge; **~ de couteau** stab; **~ d'envoi** kick-off; **~ d'État** (Pol) coup; **~ franc** free kick; **~ de main** helping hand; **~ d'œil** glance; **~ de soleil** sunburn; **~ de téléphone** telephone call; **~ de vent** gust of wind.

coupable /kupabl/ adj guilty.

coupe /kup/ nf cup; (de champagne) goblet; (à fruits) dish; (de vêtement) cut; (dessin) section; **~ de cheveux** haircut.

couper /kupe/ 🟦 vt cut; (arbre) cut down; (arrêter) cut off; (voyage) break up; (appétit) take away; (vin) water down; **~ par** take a short cut via; **~ la parole à qn** cut sb short. ●vi cut. ■**se ~** vpr cut oneself; **se ~ le doigt** cut one's finger; (routes) intersect; **se ~ de** cut oneself off from.

couple /kupl/ nm couple; (d'animaux) pair.

coupure /kupyʀ/ nf cut; (billet de banque) note; (de presse) cutting; (pause, rupture) break; (**~ de courant**) power cut.

cour /kuʀ/ nf (court) yard; (du roi) court; (tribunal) court; (**~ de récréation**) playground; **~ martiale** court-martial; **faire la ~ à** court.

courageux, -euse /kuʀaʒø, -z/ adj courageous.

couramment /kuʀamɑ̃/ adv frequently; (parler) fluently.

courant, ~e /kuʀɑ̃, -t/ adj standard, ordinary; (en cours) current. ●nm current; (de mode, d'idées) trend; **~ d'air** draught; **dans le ~ de** in the course of; **être/mettre au ~ de** know/tell about; (à jour) be/bring up to date on.

courbature /kuʀbatyʀ/ nf ache; **avoir des ~s** be stiff, ache.

courber /kuʀbe/ 🟦 vt bend.

coureur, -euse /kuʀœʀ, -øz/ nm, f (Sport) runner; **~ automobile** racing driver; **~ cycliste** racing cyclist. ●nm womanizer.

courgette /kuʀʒɛt/ nf courgette; (US) zucchini.

courir /kuʀiʀ/ 🟩 vi run; (se hâter) rush; (nouvelles) go round; **~ après qn/qch** chase after sb/sth. ●vt (risque) run; (épreuve sportive) run ou compete in; (fréquenter) do the rounds of; (filles) chase (after).

couronne /kuʀɔn/ nf crown; (de fleurs) wreath.

couronnement /kuʀɔnmɑ̃/ nm coronation, crowning; (fig) crowning achievement.

courriel /kuʀjɛl/ nm email.

courrier /kuʀje/ nm post, mail; (à écrire) letters; **~ du cœur** problem page; **~ électronique** email.

cours /kuʀ/ nm (leçon) class; (série de leçons) course; (prix) price; (cote) (de valeur, denrée) price; (de devises) exchange rate; (déroulement, d'une

rivière) course; (allée) avenue; **au
~ de** in the course of; **avoir ~**
(monnaie) be legal tender; (fig) be
current; (Scol) have a lesson; **~
d'eau** river, stream; **~ du soir**
evening class; **~ particulier**
private lesson; **~ magistral**
(Univ) lecture; **en ~** current;
(travail) in progress; **en ~ de
route** along the way.

course /kuʀs/ nf running; (épreuve
de vitesse) race; (activité) racing;
(entre rivaux: fig) race; (de projectile)
flight; (voyage) journey;
(commission) errand; **~s** (achats)
shopping; (de chevaux) races; **faire
la ~ avec qn** race sb.

coursier, -ière /kuʀsje, -jɛʀ/ nm, f
messenger.

court, ~e /kuʀ, -t/ adj short. ● adv
short; **à ~ de** short of; **pris de
~** caught unawares. ● nm **~ (de
tennis)** (tennis) court.

courtier, -ière /kuʀtje, -jɛʀ/ nm, f
broker.

courtiser /kuʀtize/ **1** vt woo,
court.

courtois, ~e /kuʀtwa, -z/ adj
courteous. **courtoisie** nf
courtesy.

cousin, ~e /kuzɛ̃, -in/ nm, f
cousin; **~ germain** first cousin.

coussin /kusɛ̃/ nm cushion.

coût* /ku/ nm cost; **le ~ de la
vie** the cost of living.

couteau (pl **~x**) /kuto/ nm knife;
~ à cran d'arrêt flick knife.

coûter* /kute/ **1** vt/i cost; **coûte
que coûte** at all costs; **au prix
coûtant** at cost (price).

coutume /kutym/ nf custom.

couture /kutyʀ/ nf sewing; (métier)
dressmaking; (points) seam.
couturier nm fashion designer.
couturière nf dressmaker.

couvée /kuve/ nf brood.

couvent /kuvɑ̃/ nm convent.

couver /kuve/ **1** vt (œufs) hatch;
(personne) overprotect, pamper;

(maladie) be coming down with,
be sickening for. ● vi (feu)
smoulder; (mal) be brewing.

couvercle /kuvɛʀkl/ nm (de
marmite, boîte) lid; (qui se visse)
screwtop.

couvert, ~e /kuvɛʀ, -t/ adj
covered (**de** with); (habillé)
covered up; (ciel) overcast. ● nm (à
table) place setting; (prix) cover
charge; **~s** (couteaux etc.) cutlery;
mettre le ~ lay the table; (abri)
cover; **à ~** (Mil) under cover; **à
~ de** (fig) safe from.

couverture /kuvɛʀtyʀ/ nf cover;
(de lit) blanket; (toit) roofing; (dans
la presse) coverage; **~ chauffante**
electric blanket.

couvre-feu (pl **~x**) /kuvʀəfø/ nm
curfew.

couvre-lit (pl **~s**) /kuvʀəli/ nm
bedspread.

couvrir /kuvʀiʀ/ **21** vt cover. ■ se
~ vpr (s'habiller) wrap up; (se coiffer)
put one's hat on; (ciel) become
overcast.

covoiturage /kɔvwatyʀaʒ/ nm car
sharing.

cracher /kʀaʃe/ **1** vi spit; (radio)
crackle. ● vt spit (out); (fumée)
belch out.

crachin /kʀaʃɛ̃/ nm drizzle.

craie /kʀɛ/ nf chalk.

craindre /kʀɛ̃dʀ/ **22** vt be afraid
of, fear; (être sensible à) be easily
damaged by.

crainte /kʀɛ̃t/ nf fear (**pour** for);
de ~ de/**que** for fear of/that.
craintif, -ive adj timid.

crampon /kʀɑ̃pɔ̃/ nm (de
chaussure) stud.

cramponner (se) /(sə)kʀɑ̃pɔne/
1 vpr **se ~ à** cling to.

cran /kʀɑ̃/ nm (entaille) notch; (trou)
hole; (courage **1**) guts **1**,
courage; **~ de sûreté** safety
catch.

crâne /kʀɑn/ nm skull.

crapaud /kʀapo/ nm toad.

craquer /kʀake/ **1** vi crack, snap; (plancher) creak; (couture) split; (fig) (personne) break down; (céder) give in. •vt (allumette) strike; (vêtement) split.

crasse /kʀas/ nf grime.

cravache /kʀavaʃ/ nf (horse) whip.

cravate /kʀavat/ nf tie.

crayon /kʀɛjɔ̃/ nm pencil; **~ de couleur** coloured pencil; **~ à bille** ballpoint pen; **~ optique** light pen.

créateur, -trice /kʀeatœʀ, -tʀis/ adj creative. •nm, f creator, designer.

crèche /kʀɛʃ/ nf day nursery, crèche; (Relig) crib.

crédit /kʀedi/ nm credit; (somme allouée) funds; **à ~** on credit; **faire ~** give credit (**à** to).

créer /kʀee/ **15** vt create; (produit) design; (société) set up.

crémaillère /kʀemajɛʀ/ nf **pendre la ~** have a housewarming party.

crème /kʀɛm/ adj inv cream. •nm (café) **~** espresso with milk. •nf cream; (dessert) cream dessert; **~ anglaise** egg custard; **~ fouettée** whipped cream; **~ pâtissière** confectioner's custard. **crémerie** nf dairy. **crémeux, -euse** adj creamy. **crémier, -ière** nm, f dairyman, dairywoman.

créneau (pl **~x**) /kʀeno/ nm (trou, moment) slot, window; (dans le marché) gap; **faire un ~** to parallel-park.

crêpe /kʀɛp/ nf (galette) pancake. •nm (tissu) crêpe; (matière) crêpe (rubber).

crépitement /kʀepitmɑ̃/ nm crackling; (d'huile) sizzling.

crépuscule /kʀepyskyl/ nm twilight, dusk.

cresson /kʀəsɔ̃/ nm (water) cress.

crête /kʀɛt/ nf crest; (de coq) comb.

crétin, ~e /kʀetɛ̃, -in/ nm, f 🔟 moron 🔟.

creuser /kʀøze/ **1** vt dig; (évider) hollow out; (fig) go into in depth. ■ **se ~** vpr (écart) widen; **se ~ (la cervelle)** 🔟 rack one's brains.

creux, -euse /kʀø, -z/ adj hollow; (heures) off-peak. •nm hollow; (de l'estomac) pit; **dans le ~ de la main** in the palm of the hand.

crevaison /kʀəvɛzɔ̃/ nf puncture.

crevasse /kʀəvas/ nf crack; (de glacier) crevasse; (de la peau) chap.

crevé, ~e /kʀəve/ adj 🔟 worn out.

crever /kʀəve/ **1** vt burst; (pneu) puncture, burst; (exténuer 🔟) exhaust; (œil) put out. •vi (pneu, sac) burst; (mourir 🔟) die.

crevette /kʀəvɛt/ nf **~ grise** shrimp; **~ rose** prawn.

cri /kʀi/ nm cry; (de douleur) scream, cry; **pousser un ~** cry out, scream.

criard, ~e /kʀijaʀ, -d/ adj (couleur) garish; (voix) shrill.

crier /kʀije/ **45** vi (fort) shout, cry (out); (de douleur) scream; (grincer) creak. •vt (ordre) shout (out).

crime /kʀim/ nm crime; (meurtre) murder.

criminel, ~le /kʀiminɛl/ adj criminal. •nm, f criminal; (assassin) murderer.

crinière /kʀinjɛʀ/ nf mane.

crise /kʀiz/ nf crisis; (Méd) attack; (de colère) fit; **~ cardiaque** heart attack; **~ de foie** bilious attack; **~ de nerfs** hysterics (+ pl).

crisper /kʀispe/ **1** vt tense; (énerver 🔟) irritate. ■ **se ~** vpr tense; (mains) clench.

critère /kʀitɛʀ/ nm criterion.

critique /kʀitik/ adj critical. •nf criticism; (article) review;

(commentateur) critic; **la ~** (personnes) the critics. **critiquer** ◾ vt criticize.

Croate /kʀɔat/ adj Croatian. **C~** nmf Croatian.

Croatie /kʀɔasi/ nf Croatia.

croche /kʀɔʃ/ nf quaver.

croche-pied* (pl ~s) /kʀɔʃpje/ nm ◾ **faire un ~ à** trip up.

crochet /kʀɔʃɛ/ nm hook; (détour) detour; (signe) (square) bracket; (tricot) crochet; **faire au ~** crochet.

crochu, ~e /kʀɔʃy/ adj hooked.

crocodile /kʀɔkɔdil/ nm crocodile.

croire /kʀwaʀ/ ◾ vt believe (**à, en** in); (estimer) think, believe (**que** that). •vi believe.

croisade /kʀwazad/ nf crusade.

croisement /kʀwazmɑ̃/ nm crossing; (fait de passer à côté de) passing; (carrefour) crossroads.

croiser /kʀwaze/ ◾ vi (bateau) cruise. •vt cross; (passant, véhicule) pass; **~ les bras** fold one's arms; **~ les jambes** cross one's legs; (animaux) crossbreed. ◾ **se ~** vpr (véhicules, piétons) pass each other; (lignes) cross. **croisière** nf cruise.

croissance /kʀwasɑ̃s/ nf growth.

croissant, ~e /kʀwasɑ̃, -t/ adj growing. •nm crescent; (pâtisserie) croissant.

croix /kʀwa/ nf cross; **~ gammée** swastika; **C~-Rouge** Red Cross.

croquant, ~e /kʀɔkɑ̃, -t/ adj crunchy.

croque-monsieur* /kʀɔkmǝsjø/ nm inv toasted ham and cheese sandwich.

croque-mort* (pl ~s) /kʀɔkmɔʀ/ nm ◾ undertaker.

croquer /kʀɔke/ ◾ vt crunch; (dessiner) sketch; **chocolat à ~** plain chocolate. •vi be crunchy.

croquis /kʀɔki/ nm sketch.

crotte /kʀɔt/ nf dropping.

crotté, ~e /kʀɔte/ adj muddy.

crottin /kʀɔtɛ̃/ nm (horse) dropping.

croupir /kʀupiʀ/ ◾ vi stagnate.

croustillant, ~e /kʀustijɑ̃, -t/ adj crispy; (pain) crusty; (fig) spicy.

croûte* /kʀut/ nf crust; (de fromage) rind; (de plaie) scab; **en ~** (Culin) in pastry.

croûton* /kʀutɔ̃/ nm (bout de pain) crust; (avec potage) croûton.

CRS abrév m (**Compagnie républicaine de sécurité**) French riot police; **un ~** a member of the French riot police.

cru¹ /kʀy/ ▷ CROIRE ◾.

cru², ~e /kʀy/ adj raw; (lumière) harsh; (propos) crude. •nm vineyard; (vin) vintage wine.

crû /kʀy/ ▷ CROÎTRE ◾.

cruauté /kʀyote/ nf cruelty.

cruche /kʀyʃ/ nf jug, pitcher.

crucial, ~e (mpl **-iaux**) /kʀysjal, -jo/ adj crucial.

crudité /kʀydite/ nf (de langage) crudeness; **~s** (Culin) raw vegetables.

crue /kʀy/ nf rise in water level; **en ~** in spate.

crustacé /kʀystase/ nm shellfish.

cube /kyb/ nm cube. •adj (mètre) cubic.

cueillir /kœjiʀ/ ◾ vt pick, gather; (personne) ◾ pick up.

cuiller, cuillère /kɥijɛʀ/ nf spoon; **~ à soupe** soup spoon; (mesure) tablespoonful.

cuir /kɥiʀ/ nm leather; **~ chevelu** scalp.

cuire /kɥiʀ/ ◾ vt cook; **~ (au**

four) bake. •vi cook; **faire ~** cook.

cuisine /kɥizin/ nf kitchen; (art) cookery, cooking; (aliments) food; **faire la ~** cook.

cuisiner /kɥizine/ **1** vt cook; (interroger **1**) grill. •vi cook.

cuisinier, -ière /kɥizinje, -jɛʁ/ nm, f cook. **cuisinière** nf (appareil) cooker, stove.

cuisse /kɥis/ nf thigh; (de poulet) thigh; (de grenouille) leg.

cuisson /kɥisɔ̃/ nf cooking.

cuit, ~e /kɥi, -t/ adj cooked; **bien ~** well done ou cooked; **trop ~** overdone.

cuivre /kɥivʁ/ nm copper; **~ (jaune)** brass; **~s** (Mus) brass.

cul /ky/ nm (derrière **X**) backside, bottom, arse **X**.

culbuter /kylbyte/ **1** vi (personne) tumble; (objet) topple (over). •vt knock over.

culminer /kylmine/ **1** vi reach its highest point ou peak.

culot /kylo/ nm (audace **1**) nerve, cheek; (Tech) base.

culotte /kylɔt/ nf (de femme) pants (+ pl), knickers (+ pl); (US) panties (+ pl); **~ de cheval** riding breeches; **en ~ courte** in short trousers.

culpabilité /kylpabilite/ nf guilt.

culte /kylt/ nm cult, worship; (religion) religion; (office protestant) service.

cultivateur, -trice /kyltivatœr, -tʁis/ nm, f farmer.

cultiver /kyltive/ **1** vt cultivate; (plantes) grow.

culture /kyltyʁ/ nf cultivation; (de plantes) growing; (agriculture) farming; (éducation) culture; (connaissances) knowledge; **~s** (terrains) lands under cultivation; **~ physique** physical training.

culturel, ~le /kyltyʁɛl/ adj cultural.

cumuler /kymyle/ **1** vt accumulate; (fonctions) hold concurrently.

cure /kyʁ/ nf (course of) treatment.

curé /kyʁe/ nm (parish) priest.

cure-dent* (pl **~s**) /kyʁdɑ̃/ nm toothpick.

curer /kyʁe/ **1** vt clean. ■ **se ~** vpr **se ~ les dents/ongles** clean one's teeth/nails.

curieux, -ieuse /kyʁjø, -z/ adj curious. •nm, f (badaud) onlooker.

curiosité /kyʁjozite/ nf curiosity; (objet) curio; (spectacle) unusual sight.

curriculum vitae /kyʁikylɔm vite/ nm inv curriculum vitae; (US) résumé.

curseur /kyʁsœʁ/ nm cursor.

cutané, ~e /kytane/ adj skin.

cuve /kyv/ nf vat; (à mazout, eau) tank.

cuvée /kyve/ nf (de vin) vintage.

cuvette /kyvɛt/ nf bowl; (de lavabo) (wash) basin; (des cabinets) pan, bowl.

CV abrév m (**curriculum vitae**) CV.

cyberbranché, ~e /sibɛʁbʁɑ̃ʃe/ adj cyberwired.

cybercafé /sibɛʁkafe/ nm cybercafe.

cyberespace /sibɛʁsɛpas/ nm cyberspace.

cybernaute /sibɛʁnot/ nmf Netsurfer.

cybernétique /sibɛʁnetik/ nf cybernetics (+ pl).

cyclisme /siklism/ nm cycling.

cycliste /siklist/ nmf cyclist. •nm cycling shorts. •adj cycle.

cyclone /siklon/ nm cyclone.

cygne /siɲ/ nm swan.

cynique /sinik/ adj cynical. •nm cynic.

Dd

d' /d/ ▸DE.

d'abord /dabɔʀ/ adv first; (au début) at first.

dactylo /daktilo/ nf typist. **dactylographier** 45 vt type.

dada /dada/ nm hobby-horse.

daim /dɛ̃/ nm (fallow) deer; (cuir) suede.

dallage /dalaʒ/ nm paving. **dalle** nf slab.

daltonien, ∼ne /daltɔnjɛ̃, -ɛn/ adj colour-blind.

dame /dam/ nf lady; (cartes, échecs) queen; **∼s** (jeu) draughts; (US) checkers.

damier /damje/ nm draught board; (US) checker-board; **à ∼** chequered.

damner /dane/ 1 vt damn.

dandiner (se) /(sə)dɑ̃dine/ 1 vpr waddle.

Danemark /danmaʀk/ nm Denmark.

danger /dɑ̃ʒe/ nm danger; **en ∼** in danger; **mettre en ∼** endanger.

dangereux, -euse /dɑ̃ʒ(ə)ʀø, -z/ adj dangerous.

danois, ∼e /danwa, -z/ adj Danish. ●nm (Ling) Danish. **D∼, ∼e** nm, f Dane.

dans /dɑ̃/ prép in; (mouvement) into; (à l'intérieur de) inside, in; **être ∼ un avion** be on a plane; **∼ dix jours** in ten days' time; **boire ∼ un verre** drink out of a glass; **∼ les 10 euros** about 10 euros.

danse /dɑ̃s/ nf dance; (art) dancing.

danser /dɑ̃se/ 1 vt/i dance. **danseur, -euse** nm, f dancer.

darne /daʀn/ nf steak (of fish).

date /dat/ nf date; **∼ limite** deadline; **∼ limite de vente** sell-by date; **∼ de péremption** use-by date.

dater /date/ 1 vt/i date; **à ∼ de** as from.

datte /dat/ nf (fruit) date.

daube /dob/ nf casserole.

dauphin /dofɛ̃/ nm (animal) dolphin.

davantage /davɑ̃taʒ/ adv more; (plus longtemps) longer; **∼ de** more; **je n'en sais pas ∼** that's as much as I know.

de, d' /də, d/

! d' before vowel or mute h.

● préposition

••••▸ of; **le livre ∼ mon ami** my friend's book; **un pont ∼ fer** an iron bridge.

••••▸ (provenance) from.

••••▸ (temporel) from; **∼ 8 heures à 10 heures** from 8 till 10.

••••▸ (mesure, manière) **dix mètres ∼ haut** ten metres high; **pleurer ∼ rage** cry with rage.

••••▸ (agent) by; **un livre ∼ Marcel Aymé** a book by Marcel Aymé.

● **de, de l', de la, du,** (pl **des**) déterminant

••••▸ some; **du pain** (some) bread; **des fleurs** (some) flowers; **je ne bois jamais ∼ vin** I never drink wine.

! de + le = du
 ▪ de + les = des

dé /de/ nm (à jouer) dice; (à coudre) thimble; ~**s** (jeu) dice.

débâcle /debɑkl/ nf (Géog) breaking up; (Mil) rout.

déballer /debale/ **1** vt unpack; (révéler) spill out.

débarbouiller /debaʀbuje/ vt wash the face of. ■ se ~ vpr wash one's face.

débarcadère /debaʀkadɛʀ/ nm landing-stage.

débardeur /debaʀdœʀ/ nm (vêtement) tank top.

débarquement /debaʀkəmɑ̃/ nm disembarkation. **débarquer** **1** vt/i disembark, land; (arriver **⊺**) turn up.

débarras /debaʀɑ/ nm junk room; **bon** ~**!** good riddance!

débarrasser /debaʀase/ **1** vt clear (**de** of); ~ **qn de** relieve sb of; (défaut, ennemi) rid sb of. ■ se ~ **de** vpr get rid of.

débat /deba/ nm debate.

débattre /debatʀ/ **11** vt debate. ● vi ~ **de** discuss. ■ se ~ vpr struggle (to get free).

débauche /deboʃ/ nf debauchery; (fig) profusion.

débaucher /deboʃe/ **1** vt (licencier) lay off; (distraire) tempt away.

débile /debil/ adj weak; **⊺** stupid. ● nmf moron **⊺**.

débit /debi/ nm (rate of) flow; (élocution) delivery; (de compte) debit; ~ **de tabac** tobacconist's shop; ~ **de boissons** bar; **haut** ~ broadband.

débiter /debite/ **1** vt (compte) debit; (fournir) produce; (vendre) sell; (dire: péj) spout; (couper) cut up.

débiteur, -trice /debitœʀ, -tʀis/ nm, f debtor. ● adj (compte) in debit.

déblayer /debleje/ **31** vt clear.

déblocage /deblɔkaʒ/ nm (de prix) deregulating. **débloquer** **1** vt (prix, salaires) unfreeze.

déboiser /debwaze/ **1** vt clear (of trees).

déboîter* /debwate/ **1** vi (véhicule) pull out. ● vt (membre) dislocate.

débordement /debɔʀdəmɑ̃/ nm (de joie) excess.

déborder /debɔʀde/ **1** vi overflow. ● vt (dépasser) extend beyond; ~ **de** (joie etc.) be brimming over with.

débouché /debuʃe/ nm opening; (carrière) prospect; (Comm) outlet; (sortie) end, exit.

déboucher /debuʃe/ **1** vt (bouteille) uncork; (évier) unblock. ● vi come out (**de** from); ~ **sur** (rue) lead into.

débourser /debuʀse/ **1** vt pay out.

debout /dəbu/ adv standing; (levé, éveillé) up; **être** ~, **se tenir** ~ be standing, stand; **se mettre** ~ stand up.

déboutonner /debutɔne/ **1** vt unbutton. ■ se ~ vpr unbutton oneself; (vêtement) come undone.

débrancher /debʀɑ̃ʃe/ **1** vt (prise) unplug; (système) disconnect.

débrayer /debʀeje/ **31** vi (Auto) declutch; (faire grève) stop work.

débris /debʀi/ nmpl fragments; (détritus) rubbish (+ sg); debris.

débrouillard, ~e /debʀujaʀ, -d/ adj **⊺** resourceful.

débrouiller /debʀuje/ **1** vt disentangle; (problème) solve. ■ se ~ vpr manage.

début /deby/ nm beginning; **faire ses** ~**s** (en public) make one's début; **à mes** ~**s** when I started out. **débutant, ~e** nm, f beginner. **débuter 1** vi begin; (dans un métier etc.) start out.

déca /deka/ nm **⊺** decaf.

deçà: en ~ /ɑ̃dəsa/ loc this side. ● prép **en** ~ **de** this side of.

décacheter /dekaʃte/ **6** vt open.

décade /dekad/ nf ten days; (décennie) decade.

décadent, ~e /dekadɑ̃, -t/ adj decadent.

décalage /dekalaʒ/ nm (écart) gap; **~ horaire** time difference. **décaler** 🔟 vt shift.

décalquer /dekalke/ 🔟 vt trace.

décamper /dekɑ̃pe/ 🔟 vi clear off.

décanter /dekɑ̃te/ vt allow to settle. ■ se ~ vpr settle.

décapant /dekapɑ̃/ nm chemical agent; (pour peinture) paint stripper. ● adj (humour) caustic.

décapotable /dekapɔtabl/ adj convertible.

décapsuleur /dekapsylœr/ nm bottle-opener.

décédé, ~e /desede/ adj deceased. **décéder** 🔢 vi die.

déceler /desle/ 🔢 vt detect; (démontrer) reveal.

décembre /desɑ̃br/ nm December.

décemment /desamɑ̃/ adv decently. **décence** nf decency. **décent, ~e** adj decent.

décennie /deseni/ nf decade.

décentralisation /desɑ̃tralizasjɔ̃/ nf decentralization. **décentraliser** 🔟 vt decentralize.

déception /desɛpsjɔ̃/ nf disappointment.

décerner /desɛrne/ 🔟 vt award.

décès /desɛ/ nm death.

décevant, ~e /des(ə)vɑ̃, -t/ adj disappointing. **décevoir** 🔢 vt disappoint.

déchaîner* /deʃene/ 🔟 vt (enthousiasme) rouse. ■ se ~ vpr go wild.

décharge /deʃarʒ/ nf (de fusil) discharge; **~ électrique** electric shock; **~ publique** municipal dump.

décharger /deʃarʒe/ 🔠 vt unload; **~ qn** relieve sb from. ■ se ~ vpr (batterie, pile) go flat.

déchausser (se) /(sə)deʃose/ 🔟 vpr take off one's shoes; (dent) work loose.

dèche /dɛʃ/ nf 🔟 **dans la ~** broke.

déchéance /deʃeɑ̃s/ nf decay.

déchet /deʃɛ/ nm (reste) scrap; (perte) waste; **~s** (ordures) refuse.

déchiffrer /deʃifre/ 🔟 vt decipher.

déchiqueter /deʃikte/ 🔢 vt tear to shreds.

déchirement /deʃirmɑ̃/ nm heartbreak; (conflit) split.

déchirer /deʃire/ 🔟 vt (par accident) tear; (lacérer) tear up; (arracher) tear off ou out; (diviser) tear apart. ■ se ~ vpr tear. **déchirure** nf tear.

décibel /desibɛl/ nm decibel.

décidément /desidemɑ̃/ adv really.

décider /deside/ 🔟 vt decide on; (persuader) persuade; **~ que/de** decide that/to; **~ de qch** decide on sth. ■ se ~ vpr make up one's mind (**à** to).

décimal, ~e (mpl ~aux) /desimal, -o/ adj & nf decimal.

décisif, -ive /desizif, -v/ adj decisive.

décision /desizjɔ̃/ nf decision.

déclaration /deklarasjɔ̃/ nf declaration; (commentaire politique) statement; **~ d'impôts** tax return.

déclarer /deklare/ 🔟 vt declare; (naissance) register; **déclaré coupable** found guilty; **~ forfait** (Sport) withdraw. ■ se ~ vpr (feu) break out.

déclencher /deklɑ̃ʃe/ 🔟 vt (Tech) set off; (conflit) spark off; (avalanche) start; (rire) provoke. ■ se ~ vpr (Tech) go off.

déclencheur nm (Photo) shutter release.

déclic /deklik/ nm click.

déclin /deklɛ̃/ nm decline.

déclinaison /deklinɛzɔ̃/ nf (Ling) declension.

décliner /dekline/ **1** vt (refuser) decline; (dire) state; (Ling) decline.

décocher /dekɔʃe/ **1** vt (coup) fling; (regard) shoot.

décollage /dekɔlaʒ/ nm take-off.

décoller /dekɔle/ **1** vt unstick. •vi (avion) take off. ■ se ∼ vpr come off.

décolleté, ∼e /dekɔlte/ adj lowcut. •nm low neckline.

décolorer /dekɔlɔʀe/ **1** vt fade; (cheveux) bleach. ■ se ∼ vpr fade.

décombres /dekɔ̃bʀ/ nmpl rubble.

décommander /dekɔmɑ̃de/ **1** vt cancel.

décomposer /dekɔ̃poze/ **1** vt break up; (substance) decompose. ■ se ∼ vpr (pourrir) decompose.

décompte /dekɔ̃t/ nm deduction; (détail) breakdown.

décongeler /dekɔ̃ʒle/ **6** vt thaw.

déconseillé, ∼e /dekɔ̃seje/ adj not recommended, inadvisable.

déconseiller /dekɔ̃seje/ **1** vt ∼ **qch à qn** advise sb against sth.

décontracté, ∼e /dekɔ̃tʀakte/ adj relaxed.

déconvenue /dekɔ̃vny/ nf disappointment.

décor /dekɔʀ/ nm (paysage) scenery; (de cinéma, théâtre) set; (cadre) setting; (de maison) decor.

décoratif, -ive /dekɔʀatif, -v/ adj decorative.

décorateur, -trice /dekɔʀatœʀ, -tʀis/ nm, f (de cinéma) set designer. **décoration** nf decoration. **décorer** **1** vt decorate.

décortiquer /dekɔʀtike/ **1** vt shell; (fig) dissect.

découdre (se) /(sə)dekudʀ/ **19** vpr come unstitched.

découler /dekule/ **1** vi ∼ **de** follow from.

découper /dekupe/ **1** vt cut up; (viande) carve; (détacher) cut out.

découragement /dekuʀaʒmɑ̃/ nm discouragement.

décourager /dekuʀaʒe/ **40** vt discourage. ■ se ∼ vpr become discouraged.

décousu, ∼e /dekuzy/ adj (vêtement) which has come unstitched; (idées) disjointed.

découvert, ∼e /dekuvɛʀ, -t/ adj (tête) bare; (terrain) open. •nm (de compte) overdraft; **à ∼** exposed; (fig) openly.

découverte /dekuvɛʀt/ nf discovery; **à la ∼ de** in search of.

découvrir /dekuvʀiʀ/ **21** vt discover; (voir) see; (montrer) reveal. ■ se ∼ vpr (se décoiffer) take one's hat off; (ciel) clear.

décrasser /dekʀase/ **1** vt clean.

décrépit, ∼e /dekʀepi, -t/ adj decrepit. **décrépitude** nf decay.

décret /dekʀɛ/ nm decree. **décréter** **14** vt order; (dire) declare.

décrié, ∼e /dekʀije/ adj criticized.

décrire /dekʀiʀ/ **30** vt describe.

décroché, ∼e /dekʀɔʃe/ adj (téléphone) off the hook.

décrocher /dekʀɔʃe/ **1** vt unhook; (obtenir **1**) get. •vi (abandonner **1**) give up; ∼ (**le téléphone**) pick up the phone.

décroître* /dekʀwatʀ/ **24** vi decrease.

déçu, ∼e /desy/ adj disappointed.

décupler /dekyple/ **1** vt/i increase tenfold.

dédaigner /dedɛɲe/ **1** vt scorn.

dédain /dedɛ̃/ nm scorn.

dédale /dedal/ nm maze.

dedans /dədɑ̃/ adv & nm inside; **en ~** on the inside.

dédicacer /dedikase/ 🔟 vt dedicate; (signer) sign.

dédier /dedje/ 45 vt dedicate.

dédommagement /dedɔmaʒmɑ̃/ nm compensation. **dédommager** 40 vt compensate (**de** for).

déduction /dedyksjɔ̃/ nf deduction; **~ d'impôts** tax deduction.

déduire /deduir/ 17 vt deduct; (conclure) deduce.

déesse /deɛs/ nf goddess.

défaillance /defajɑ̃s/ nf (panne) failure; (évanouissement) blackout. **défaillant, ~e** adj (système) faulty; (personne) faint.

défaire /defɛʀ/ 33 vt undo; (valise) unpack; (démonter) take down. ■ **se ~** vpr come undone; **se ~ de** rid oneself of.

défait, ~e /defɛ, -t/ adj (cheveux) ruffled; (visage) haggard; (nœud) undone. **défaite** nf defeat.

défaitiste /defetist/ adj & nmf defeatist.

défalquer /defalke/ 🔟 vt (somme) deduct.

défaut /defo/ nm fault, defect; (d'un verre, diamant, etc.) flaw; (pénurie) shortage; **à ~ de** for lack of; **pris en ~** caught out; **faire ~** (argent etc.) be lacking; **par ~** (Jur) in one's absence; **~ de paiement** non-payment.

défavorable /defavɔʀabl/ adj unfavourable.

défavoriser /defavɔʀize/ 🔟 vt discriminate against.

défectueux, -euse /defɛktɥø, -z/ adj faulty, defective.

défendre /defɑ̃dʀ/ 🔢 vt defend; (interdire) forbid; **~ à qn de** forbid sb to. ■ **se ~** vpr defend

oneself; (se protéger) protect oneself; (se débrouiller) manage; **se ~ de** (refuser) refrain from.

défense /defɑ̃s/ nf defence; **~ de fumer** no smoking; (d'éléphant) tusk. **défenseur** nm defender. **défensif, -ive** adj defensive.

déferler /defɛʀle/ 🔢 vi (vagues) break; (violence) erupt.

défi /defi/ nm challenge; (provocation) defiance; **mettre au ~** challenge.

déficience /defisjɑ̃s/ nf deficiency. **déficient, ~e** adj deficient.

déficit /defisit/ nm deficit. **déficitaire** adj in deficit.

défier /defje/ 45 vt challenge; (braver) defy.

défilé /defile/ nm procession; (Mil) parade; (fig) (continual) stream; (Géog) gorge; **~ de mode** fashion parade.

défiler /defile/ 🔢 vi march; (visiteurs) stream; (images) flash by; (chiffres, minutes) add up. ■ **se ~** vpr 🔢 sneak off.

défini, ~e /defini/ adj (Ling) definite.

définir /definiʀ/ 🔢 vt define.

définitif, -ive /definitif, -v/ adj final, definitive; **en définitive** in the end.

définition /definisjɔ̃/ nf definition; (de mots croisés) clue.

définitivement /definitivmɑ̃/ adv definitively, permanently.

déflagration /deflagʀasjɔ̃/ nf explosion.

déflation /deflasjɔ̃/ nf deflation. **déflationniste** adj deflationary.

défoncé, ~e /defɔ̃se/ adj (terrain) full of potholes; (siège) broken; (drogué: 🔢) high.

défoncer /defɔ̃se/ 🔟 vt (porte) break down; (mâchoire) break. ■ **se ~** vpr 🔢 to give one's all.

déformation /defɔʀmasjɔ̃/ nf

distortion. déformer 1 vt put out of shape; (faits, pensée) distort.

défouler (se) /(sə)defule/ 1 vpr let off steam.

défrayer /defʀeje/ 31 vt (payer) pay the expenses of; ~ **la chronique** be the talk of the town.

défricher /defʀiʃe/ 1 vt clear.

défroisser /defʀwase/ 1 vt smooth out.

défunt, ~e /defœ̃, -t/ adj (mort) late. • nm, f deceased.

dégagé, ~e /degaʒe/ adj (ciel) clear; (front) bare; **d'un ton ~** casually.

dégagement /degaʒmɑ̃/ nm clearing; (football) clearance.

dégager /degaʒe/ 40 vt (exhaler) give off; (désencombrer) clear; (faire ressortir) bring out; (ballon) clear. ■ se ~ vpr free oneself; (ciel, rue) clear; (odeur) emanate.

dégarnir (se) /(sə)degaʀniʀ/ 2 vpr clear, empty; (personne) be going bald.

dégâts /dega/ nmpl damage (+ sg).

dégel /deʒɛl/ nm thaw. **dégeler** 6 vi thaw (out).

dégénéré, ~e /deʒeneʀe/ adj & nm,f degenerate.

dégivrer /deʒivʀe/ 1 vt (Auto) de-ice; (réfrigérateur) defrost.

déglinguer /deglɛ̃ge/ 1 1 vt bust. ■ se ~ vpr break down.

dégonflé, ~e /degɔ̃fle/ adj (pneu) flat; (lâche 1) yellow.

dégonfler /degɔ̃fle/ 1 vt deflate. • vi (blessure) go down. ■ se ~ vpr 1 chicken out.

dégouliner /deguline/ 1 vi trickle.

dégourdi, ~e /deguʀdi/ adj smart.

dégourdir /deguʀdiʀ/ 2 vt (membre, liquide) warm up. ■ se ~ vpr **se ~ les jambes** stretch one's legs.

dégoût* /degu/ nm disgust.

dégoûtant*, ~e /degutɑ̃, -t/ adj disgusting.

dégoûter* /degute/ 1 vt disgust; ~ **qn de qch** put sb off sth.

dégradant, ~e /degʀadɑ̃, -t/ adj degrading.

dégradation /degʀadasjɔ̃/ nf damage; **commettre des ~s** cause damage.

dégrader /degʀade/ 1 vt (abîmer) damage. ■ se ~ vpr (se détériorer) deteriorate.

dégrafer /degʀafe/ 1 vt unhook.

degré /dəgʀe/ nm degree; (d'escalier) step.

dégressif, -ive /degʀesif, -v/ adj graded; **tarif ~** tapering charge.

dégrèvement /degʀɛvmɑ̃/ nm ~ **fiscal** ou **d'impôts** tax reduction.

dégringolade /degʀɛ̃gɔlad/ nf tumble.

dégrossir /degʀosiʀ/ 2 vt (bois) trim; (projet) rough out.

déguerpir /degɛʀpiʀ/ 2 vi clear off.

dégueulasse /degœlas/ adj ✖ disgusting, lousy.

dégueuler /degœle/ 1 vt ✖ throw up.

déguisement /degizmɑ̃/ nm (de carnaval) fancy dress; (pour duper) disguise.

déguiser /degize/ 1 vt dress up; (pour duper) disguise. ■ se ~ vpr (au carnaval etc.) dress up; (pour duper) disguise oneself.

déguster /degyste/ 1 vt taste, sample; (savourer) enjoy.

dehors /dəɔʀ/ adv **en ~ de** outside; (hormis) apart from; **jeter/ mettre ~** throw/put out. • nm outside. • nmpl (aspect de qn) exterior.

déjà /deʒa/ adv already; (avant) before, already.

déjeuner /deʒœne/ 1 vi have

lunch; (le matin) have breakfast. ●nm lunch; **petit ∼** breakfast.

delà /dəla/ adv & prép **au ∼ (de) par ∼** beyond.

délai /delɛ/ nm time-limit; (attente) wait; (sursis) extension (of time); **sans ∼** immediately; **dans un ∼ de 2 jours** within 2 days; **finir dans les ∼s** finish within the deadline; **dans les plus brefs ∼s** as soon as possible.

délaisser /delese/ **1** vt (négliger) neglect.

délassement /delasmã/ nm relaxation.

délation /delasjõ/ nf informing.

délavé, ∼e /delave/ adj faded.

délayer /deleje/ **31** vt mix (with liquid); (idée) drag out.

délecter (se) /(sə)delɛkte/ **1** vpr **se ∼ de** delight in.

délégué, ∼e /delege/ nm, f delegate.

délibéré, ∼e /delibeRe/ adj deliberate; (résolu) determined.

délicat, ∼e /delika, -t/ adj delicate; (plein de tact) tactful. **délicatesse** nf delicacy; (tact) tact. **délicatesses** nfpl (kind) attentions.

délice /delis/ nm delight. **délicieux, -ieuse** adj (au goût) delicious; (charmant) delightful.

délier /delje/ **45** vt untie; (délivrer) free. ■ **se ∼** vpr come untied.

délimiter /delimite/ **1** vt determine, demarcate.

délinquance /delɛ̃kãs/ nf delinquency. **délinquant, ∼e** adj & nm, f delinquent.

délirant, ∼e /deliRã, -t/ adj delirious; (frénétique) frenzied; Ⅰ wild.

délire /deliR/ nm delirium; (fig) frenzy. **délirer** **1** vi be delirious (**de** with); Ⅰ be off one's rocker Ⅰ.

délit /deli/ nm offence.

délivrance /delivRãs/ nf release; (soulagement) relief; (remise) issue. **délivrer** **1** vt free, release; (pays) liberate; (remettre) issue.

déloyal, ∼e (mpl **-aux**) /delwajal, -jo/ adj disloyal; (procédé) unfair.

deltaplane /dɛltaplan/ nm hangglider.

déluge /delyʒ/ nm downpour; **le D∼** the Flood.

démagogie /demagoʒi/ nf demagogy. **démagogue** nmf demagogue.

demain /dəmɛ̃/ adv tomorrow.

demande /dəmãd/ nf request; **∼ d'emploi** job application; **∼ en mariage** marriage proposal.

demander /dəmãde/ **1** vt ask for; (chemin, heure) ask; (nécessiter) require; **∼ que/si** ask that/if; **∼ qch à qn** ask sb sth; **∼ à qn de** ask sb to; **∼ en mariage** propose to. ■ **se ∼** vpr **se ∼ si/où** wonder if/where.

demandeur, -euse /dəmãdœR, -øz/ nm, f **∼ d'emploi** job seeker; **∼ d'asile** asylum-seeker.

démangeaison /demãʒezõ/ nf itch(ing).

démanteler /demãtle/ **6** vt break up.

démaquillant /demakijã/ nm make-up remover. **démaquiller (se)** **1** vpr remove one's make-up.

démarchage /demarʃaʒ/ nm door-to-door selling.

démarche /demarʃ/ nf walk, gait; (procédé) step.

démarcheur, -euse /demarʃœR, -øz/ nm, f (door-to-door) canvasser.

démarrage /demaraʒ/ nm start.

démarrer /demare/ **1** vi (moteur) start (up); (partir) move off; (fig) get moving. ●vt Ⅰ get moving.

démarreur /demarœR/ nm starter.

démêlant /demelɑ̃/ nm conditioner. **démêler** ▯ vt disentangle.

déménagement /demenaʒmɑ̃/ nm move; (transport) removal.

déménager /demenaʒe/ ▯ vi move (house). ● vt (meubles) remove.

déménageur /demenaʒœʀ/ nm removal man.

démence /demɑ̃s/ nf insanity.

démener (se) /(sə)demne/ ▯ vpr move about wildly; (fig) put oneself out.

dément, ~e /demɑ̃, -t/ adj insane. ● nm, f lunatic.

démenti /demɑ̃ti/ nm denial.

démentir /demɑ̃tiʀ/ ▯ vt deny; (contredire) refute; **~ que** deny that.

démerder (se) /(sə)demɛʀde/ ▯ vpr ▨ manage.

démettre /demɛtʀ/ ▯ vt (poignet etc.) dislocate; **~ qn de** relieve sb of. ■ **se ~** vpr resign (**de** from).

demeure /dəmœʀ/ nf residence; **mettre en ~ de** order to.

demeurer /dəmœʀe/ ▯ vi live; (rester) remain.

demi, ~e /dəmi/ adj half(-). ● nm, f half. ● nm (bière) (half-pint) glass of beer; (football) half-back. ● adv **à ~** half; (ouvrir, fermer) halfway; **à la ~e** at half past; **une heure et ~e** an hour and a half; (à l'horloge) half past one; **une ~-journée/-livre** half a day/ pound. **demi-cercle** (pl **~s**) nm semicircle. **demi-finale** (pl **~s**) nf semifinal. **demi-frère** (pl **~s**) nm half-brother, stepbrother. **demi-heure** (pl **~s**) nf half-hour, half an hour. **demi-litre** (pl **~s**) nm half a litre. **demi-mesure** (pl **~s**) nf half-measure. **à demi mot** adv without having to express every word. **demi-pension** nf half-board. **demi-queue** nm boudoir grand piano.

demi-sel adj inv slightly salted.

demi-sœur (pl **~s**) nf half-sister, stepsister.

démission /demisjɔ̃/ nf resignation.

demi-tarif (pl **~s**) /dəmitaʀif/ nm half-fare.

demi-tour (pl **~s**) /dəmituʀ/ nm about turn; (Auto) U-turn; **faire ~** turn back.

démocrate /demɔkʀat/ nmf democrat. ● adj democratic. **démocratie** nf democracy.

démodé, ~e /demɔde/ adj oldfashioned.

demoiselle /dəmwazɛl/ nf young lady; (célibataire) single lady; **~ d'honneur** bridesmaid.

démolir /demɔliʀ/ ▯ vt demolish.

démon /demɔ̃/ nm demon; **le D~** the Devil. **démoniaque** adj fiendish.

démonstration /demɔ̃stʀasjɔ̃/ nf demonstration; (de force) show.

démonter /demɔ̃te/ ▯ vt take apart, dismantle; (installation) take down; (fig) disconcert. ■ **se ~** vpr come apart.

démontrer /demɔ̃tʀe/ ▯ vt demonstrate; (indiquer) show.

démoraliser /demɔʀalize/ ▯ vt demoralize.

démuni, ~e /demyni/ adj impoverished; **~ de** without.

démunir /demyniʀ/ ▯ vt **~ de** deprive of. ■ **se ~ de** vpr part with.

dénaturer /denatyʀe/ ▯ vt (faits) distort.

dénigrement /denigʀəmɑ̃/ nm denigration.

dénivellation /denivɛlasjɔ̃/ nf (pente) slope.

dénombrer /denɔ̃bʀe/ ▯ vt count.

dénomination /denɔminasjɔ̃/ nf designation.

d

dénommé, ~e /denɔme/ nm, f **le ~ X** the said X.

dénoncer /denɔ̃se/ 🔟 vt denounce. ■ se ~ vpr give oneself up. **dénonciateur, -trice** nm, f informer.

dénouement /denumɑ̃/ nm outcome; (Théât) dénouement.

dénouer /denwe/ 🔟 vt undo. ■ se ~ vpr (nœud) come undone.

dénoyauter /denwajote/ 🔟 vt stone.

denrée /dɑ̃ʀe/ nf ~ **alimentaire** foodstuff.

dense /dɑ̃s/ adj dense. **densité** nf density.

dent /dɑ̃/ nf tooth; **faire ses ~s** teethe; ~ **de lait** milk tooth; ~ **de sagesse** wisdom tooth; (de roue) cog. **dentaire** adj dental.

denté, ~e /dɑ̃te/ adj (roue) toothed

dentelé, ~e /dɑ̃tle/ adj jagged.

dentelle /dɑ̃tɛl/ nf lace.

dentier /dɑ̃tje/ nm dentures (+ pl), false teeth (+ pl).

dentifrice /dɑ̃tifʀis/ nm toothpaste.

dentiste /dɑ̃tist/ nmf dentist.

dentition /dɑ̃tisjɔ̃/ nf teeth, dentition.

dénudé, ~e /denyde/ adj bare.

dénué, ~e /denɥe/ adj ~ **de** devoid of.

dénuement /denymɑ̃/ nm destitution.

déodorant /deɔdɔʀɑ̃/ nm deodorant.

dépannage /depanaʒ/ nm repair; (Ordinat) troubleshooting. **dépanner** 🔟 vt repair; (fig) help out. **dépanneuse** nf breakdown lorry.

dépareillé, ~e /depaʀeje/ adj odd, not matching.

································
🄰 *see A-Z of French life and culture*

départ /depaʀ/ nm departure; (Sport) start; **au ~ de Nice** from Nice; **au ~** (d'abord) at first.

🄲**département** /depaʀtəmɑ̃/ nm department.

dépassé, ~e /depɑse/ adj outdated.

dépasser /depɑse/ 🔟 vt go past, pass; (véhicule) overtake; (excéder) exceed; (rival) surpass; **ça me dépasse** 🄸 it's beyond me. ●vi stick out.

dépaysement /depeizmɑ̃/ nm change of scenery; (désagréable) disorientation.

dépêche /depɛʃ/ nf dispatch.

dépêcher /depeʃe/ 🔟 vt dispatch. ■ se ~ vpr hurry (up).

dépendance /depɑ̃dɑ̃s/ nf dependence; (à une drogue) dependency; (bâtiment) outbuilding.

dépendre /depɑ̃dʀ/ 🄳 vt take down. ●vi depend (~ **de** on); ~ **de** (appartenir à) belong to.

dépens /depɑ̃/ nmpl **aux ~ de** at the expense of.

dépense /depɑ̃s/ nf expense; expenditure.

dépenser /depɑ̃se/ 🔟 vt/i spend; (énergie etc.) use up. ■ se ~ vpr get some exercise.

dépérir /depeʀiʀ/ 🄿 vi wither.

dépêtrer (se) /(sə)depetʀe/ 🔟 vpr get oneself out (**de** of).

dépeupler /depœple/ 🔟 vt depopulate. ■ se ~ vpr become depopulated.

déphasé, ~e /defɑze/ adj 🄸 out of step.

dépilatoire /depilatwaʀ/ adj & nm depilatory.

dépistage /depistaʒ/ nm screening. **dépister** 🔟 vt detect; (criminel) track down.

dépit /depi/ nm resentment; **par ~** out of pique; **en ~ de** despite; **en ~ du bon sens** in a very illogical way. **dépité, ~e** adj vexed.

déplacé, ~e /deplase/ adj (remarque) uncalled for.

déplacement /deplasmɑ̃/ nm (voyage) trip.

déplacer /deplase/ **10** vt move. ■ **se ~** vpr move; (voyager) travel.

déplaire /deplɛR/ **47** vi ~ **à** (irriter) displease; **ça me déplaît*** I don't like it.

déplaisant, ~e /deplɛzɑ̃, -t/ adj unpleasant, disagreeable.

dépliant /deplijɑ̃/ nm leaflet.

déplier /deplije/ **45** vt unfold.

déploiement /deplwamɑ̃/ nm (démonstration) display; (militaire) deployment.

déplorable /deplɔRabl/ adj deplorable. **déplorer** **1** vt (trouver regrettable) deplore; (mort) lament.

déployer /deplwaje/ **31** vt (ailes, carte) spread; (courage) display; (armée) deploy.

déportation /depɔRtasjɔ̃/ nf (en 1940) internment in a concentration camp.

déposer /depoze/ **1** vt put down; (laisser) leave; (passager) drop; (argent) deposit; (plainte) lodge; (armes) lay down. ●vi (Jur) testify. ■ **se ~** vpr settle.

dépositaire /depozitɛR/ nmf (Comm) agent.

déposition /depozisjɔ̃/ nf (Jur) statement.

dépôt /depo/ nm (entrepôt) warehouse; (d'autobus) depot; (particules) deposit; (garantie) deposit; **laisser en ~** give for safe keeping; **~ légal** formal deposit of a publication with an institution.

dépouille /depuj/ nf skin, hide; (**~ mortelle**) mortal remains.

dépouiller /depuje/ **1** vt (courrier) open; (scrutin) count; (écorcher) skin; **~ qn de** strip sb of.

dépourvu, ~e /depuRvy/ adj ~ **de** devoid of; **prendre au ~** catch unawares.

déprécier /depResje/ **45** vt depreciate. ■ **se ~** vpr depreciate.

déprédations /depRedasjɔ̃/ nfpl damage (+ sg).

dépression /depResjɔ̃/ nf depression; **~ nerveuse** nervous breakdown.

déprimer /depRime/ **1** vt depress.

---

depuis /dəpɥi/

● préposition

····▸ (point de départ) since; **~ quand attendez-vous?** how long have you been waiting?

····▸ (durée) for; **~ toujours** always; **~ peu** recently.

● adverbe

····▸ since; **il a eu une attaque le mois dernier, ~ nous sommes inquiets** he had a stroke last month and we've been worried ever since.

● **depuis que** conjunction

····▸ since, ever since; **Sophie a beaucoup changé depuis que Camille est née** Sophie has changed a lot since Camille was born.

---

député /depyte/ nm ≈ Member of Parliament.

déraciné, -e /deRasine/ nm, f rootless person.

déraillement /deRajmɑ̃/ nm derailment.

dérailler /deRaje/ **1** vi be derailed; (fig **1**) be talking nonsense; **faire ~** derail. **dérailleur** nm (de vélo) derailleur.

déraisonnable /deRɛzɔnabl/ adj unreasonable.

dérangement /deRɑ̃ʒmɑ̃/ nm bother; (désordre) disorder, upset; **en ~** out of order; **les ~s** the fault reporting service.

....

◨ see A-Z of French life and culture

déranger /deʀɑ̃ʒe/ 40 vt (gêner)
bother, disturb; (dérégler) upset,
disrupt. ■ se ~ vpr (aller) go; (fig)
put oneself out; **ça te
dérangerait de...?** would you
mind...?

dérapage /deʀapaʒ/ nm skid.
déraper 1 vi skid; (fig) (prix) get
out of control.

déréglé, **~e** /deʀegle/ adj (vie)
dissolute; (estomac) upset;
(mécanisme) (that is) not running
properly.

dérégler /deʀegle/ 14 vt make go
wrong. ■ se ~ vpr go wrong.

dérision /deʀizjɔ̃/ nf mockery;
tourner en ~ ridicule.

dérive /deʀiv/ nf **aller à la ~**
drift.

dérivé /deʀive/ nm by-product.

dériver /deʀive/ 1 vi (bateau)
drift; **~ de** stem from.

dermatologie /dɛʀmatɔlɔʒi/ nf
dermatology.

dernier, **-ière** /dɛʀnje, -jɛʀ/ adj
last; (nouvelles, mode) latest; (étage)
top. ●nm, f last (one); **ce ~** the
latter; **le ~ de mes soucis** the
least of my worries.

dernièrement /dɛʀnjɛʀmɑ̃/ adv
recently.

dérober /deʀɔbe/ 1 vt steal. ■ se
~ vpr slip away; **se ~ à** (obligation)
shy away from.

dérogation /deʀɔgasjɔ̃/ nf special
authorization.

déroger /deʀɔʒe/ 40 vi **~ à**
depart from.

déroulement /deʀulmɑ̃/ nm
(d'une action) development.

dérouler /deʀule/ 1 vt (fil etc.)
unwind. ■ se ~ vpr unwind; (avoir
lieu) take place; (récit, paysage)
unfold.

déroute /deʀut/ nf (Mil) rout.

dérouter /deʀute/ 1 vt
disconcert.

derrière /dɛʀjɛʀ/ prép & adv

behind. ●nm back, rear; (postérieur
🔲) behind 🔲; **de ~** (fenêtre)
back, rear; (pattes) hind.

des /de/ ▷DE.

dès /dɛ/ prép (right) from; **~ lors**
from then on; **~ que** as soon as.

désabusé, **~e** /dezabyze/ adj
disillusioned.

désaccord /dezakɔʀ/ nm
disagreement.

désaffecté, **~e** /dezafɛkte/ adj
disused.

désagréable /dezagʀeabl/ adj
unpleasant.

désagrément /dezagʀemɑ̃/ nm
annoyance, inconvenience.

désaltérer (se) /(sa)dezalteʀe/
14 vpr quench one's thirst.

désamorcer /dezamɔʀse/ 10 vt
(situation, obus) defuse.

désapprobation /dezapʀɔbasjɔ̃/
nf disapproval. **désapprouver** 1
vt disapprove of.

désarçonner /dezaʀsɔne/ 1 vt
throw.

désarmement /dezaʀməmɑ̃/ nm
(Pol) disarmament.

désarroi /dezaʀwa/ nm distress.

désastre /dezastʀ/ nm disaster.
désastreux, **-euse** adj
disastrous.

désavantage /dezavɑ̃taʒ/ nm
disadvantage. **désavantager** 40
vt put at a disadvantage.

désaveu (pl **~x**) /dezavø/ nm
denial. **désavouer** 1 vt deny.

descendance /desɑ̃dɑ̃s/ nf
descent; (enfants) descendants (+
pl). **descendant**, **~e** nm, f
descendant.

descendre /desɑ̃dʀ/ 3 vi (aux être)
go down, come down; (venir)
(passager) get off ou out; (nuit)
fall; **~ à pied** walk down; **~ par
l'ascenseur** take the lift down;
~ de (être issu de) be descended
from; **~ à l'hôtel** go to a hotel;
~ dans la rue (Pol) take to the

streets. ●vt (aux avoir) (escalier etc.) go *ou* come down; (objet) take down; (abattre 🔢) shoot down.

descente /desɑ̃t/ nf descent; (à ski) downhill; (raid) raid; **dans la ~ downhill; ~ de lit** bedside rug.

descriptif, -ive /dɛskʀiptif, -v/ adj descriptive. **description** nf description.

désemparé, ~e /dezɑ̃paʀe/ adj distraught.

désendettement /dezɑ̃dɛtmɑ̃/ nm reduction of the debt.

déséquilibré, ~e /dezekilibʀe/ adj unbalanced; 🔢 crazy. ●nm, f lunatic. **déséquilibrer** 🔢 vt throw off balance.

désert, ~e /dezɛʀ, -t/ adj deserted. ●nm desert.

déserter /dezɛʀte/ 🔢 vt/i desert. **déserteur** nm deserter.

désertique /dezɛʀtik/ adj desert.

désespérant, ~e /dezɛspeʀɑ̃, -t/ adj utterly disheartening.

désespéré, ~e /dezɛspeʀe/ adj in despair; (état, cas) hopeless; (effort) desperate.

désespérer /dezɛspeʀe/ 🔢 vt drive to despair. ●vi despair, lose hope; **~ de** despair of. ■se ~ vpr despair.

désespoir /dezɛspwaʀ/ nm despair; **en ~ de cause** as a last resort.

déshabillé, ~e /dezabije/ adj undressed. ●nm négligee.

déshabiller /dezabije/ 🔢 vt undress. ■se ~ vpr get undressed.

désherbant /dezɛʀbɑ̃/ nm weedkiller.

déshérité, ~e /dezeʀite/ adj (région) deprived; (personne) the underprivileged.

déshériter /dezeʀite/ 🔢 vt disinherit.

déshonneur /dezɔnœʀ/ nm disgrace.

déshonorer /dezɔnɔʀe/ 🔢 vt dishonour.

déshydrater /dezidʀate/ 🔢 vt dehydrate. ■se ~ vpr get dehydrated.

désigner /deziɲe/ 🔢 vt (montrer) point to *ou* out; (élire) appoint; (signifier) designate.

désillusion /dezilyzjɔ̃/ nf disillusionment.

désinence /dezinɑ̃s/ nf (Gram) ending.

désinfectant /dezɛ̃fɛktɑ̃/ nm disinfectant. **désinfecter** 🔢 vt disinfect.

désintéressé, ~e /dezɛ̃teʀese/ adj (personne, acte) selfless.

désintéresser (se) /(sə)dezɛ̃teʀese/ 🔢 vpr **se ~ de** lose interest in.

désintoxiquer /dezɛ̃tɔksike/ 🔢 vt detoxify; **se faire ~** to undergo detoxification.

désinvolte /dezɛ̃vɔlt/ adj casual. **désinvolture** nf casualness.

désir /deziʀ/ nm wish, desire; (convoitise) desire.

désirer /deziʀe/ 🔢 vt want; (sexuellement) desire; **vous désirez?** what would you like?

désireux, -euse /deziʀø, -z/ adj **~ de faire** anxious to do.

désistement /dezistəmɑ̃/ nm withdrawal.

désobéir /dezɔbeiʀ/ 🔢 vi (**~ à**) disobey. **désobéissant, ~e** adj disobedient.

désobligeant, ~e /dezɔbliʒɑ̃, -t/ adj disagreeable, unkind.

désodorisant /dezɔdɔʀizɑ̃/ nm air freshener.

désodoriser /dezɔdɔʀize/ 🔢 vt freshen up.

désœuvré, ~e /dezœvʀe/ adj at a loose end. **désœuvrement** nm lack of anything to do.

désolation /dezɔlasjɔ̃/ nf distress.

désolé, ~e /dezɔle/ adj (au regret)

sorry; (région) desolate.

désoler /dezɔle/ **1** vt distress.
■ se ~ vpr be upset (**de qch**
about sth).

désopilant, ~e /dezɔpilɑ̃, -t/ adj
hilarious.

désordonné, ~e /dezɔrdɔne/ adj
untidy; (mouvements)
uncoordinated.

désordre /dezɔrdʀ/ nm
untidiness; (Pol) disorder; **en ~**
untidy.

désorganiser /dezɔrganize/ **1** vt
disorganize.

désorienter /dezɔrjɑ̃te/ **1** vt
disorient.

désormais /dezɔrmɛ/ adv from
now on.

desquels, desquelles /dekɛl/
▷ LEQUEL.

dessécher /deseʃe/ **1** vt dry out.
■ se ~ vpr dry out, become dry;
(plante) wither.

dessein /desɛ̃/ nm intention; **à ~**
intentionally.

desserrer /desere/ **1** vt loosen; **il
n'a pas desserré les dents** he
never once opened his mouth.
■ se ~ vpr come loose.

dessert /desɛʀ/ nm dessert; **en ~**
for dessert.

desservir /desɛʀviʀ/ **46** vt/i
(débarrasser) clear away; (autobus)
serve.

dessin /desɛ̃/ nm drawing; (motif)
design; (discipline) art; (contour)
outline; **professeur de ~** art
teacher; **~ animé** (cinéma)
cartoon; **~ humoristique**
cartoon.

dessinateur, -trice /desinatœʀ,
-tʀis/ nm, f artist; (industriel)
draughtsman.

dessiner /desine/ **1** vt/i draw;
(fig) outline. ■ se ~ vpr appear,
take shape.

dessoûler /desule/ **1** vt/i
sober up.

dessous /dəsu/ adv underneath.
●nm underside, underneath.
●nmpl underwear; **les ~ d'une
histoire** what is behind a story;
du ~ bottom; (voisins)
downstairs; **en ~, par-~**
underneath. **dessous-de-plat** nm
inv (heat resistant) table-mat.
dessous-de-table nm inv
backhander. **dessous-de-verre**
nm inv coaster.

dessus /dəsy/ adv on top (of it),
on it. ●nm top; **du ~** top; (voisins)
upstairs; **avoir le ~** get the
upper hand. **dessus-de-lit** nm inv
bedspread.

déstabiliser /destabilize/ **1** vt
destabilize, unsettle.

destin /dɛstɛ̃/ nm (sort) fate;
(avenir) destiny.

destinataire /dɛstinatɛʀ/ nmf
addressee.

destination /dɛstinasjɔ̃/ nf
destination; (fonction) purpose;
vol à ~ de flight to.

destinée /dɛstine/ nf destiny.

destiner /dɛstine/ **1** vt ~ **à**
intend for; (vouer) destine for; **le
commentaire m'est destiné**
this comment is aimed at me;
être destiné à faire be
intended to do; (obligé) be
destined to do. ■ se ~ **à** vpr
(carrière) intend to take up.

destituer /dɛstitɥe/ **1** vt
discharge.

destructeur, -trice /dɛstʀyktœʀ,
-tʀis/ adj destructive.
destruction nf destruction.

désuet, -ète /dezɥɛ, -t/ adj
outdated.

détachant /detaʃɑ̃/ nm stain
remover.

détacher /detaʃe/ **1** vt untie;
(ôter) remove, detach; (déléguer)
second. ■ se ~ vpr come off,
break away; (nœud etc.) come
undone; (ressortir) stand out.

détail /detaj/ nm detail; (de compte)
breakdown; (Comm) retail; **au ~**

détaillant, ~e /detajɑ̃, -t/ nm, f retailer.

détaillé, ~e /detaje/ adj detailed.

détailler /detaje/ **1** vt (rapport) detail; ~ **ce que qn fait** scrutinize what sb does.

détaler /detale/ **1** vi **1** bolt.

détartrant /detartrɑ̃/ nm descaler.

détecter /detɛkte/ **1** vt detect. **détecteur** nm detector.

détective /detɛktiv/ nm detective.

déteindre /detɛ̃dʀ/ **22** vi (dans l'eau) run (**sur** on to); (au soleil) fade; ~ **sur** (fig) rub off on.

détendre /detɑ̃dʀ/ **3** vt slacken; (ressort) release; (personne) relax. ■ **se** ~ vpr (ressort) slacken; (personne) relax. **détendu**, ~e adj (calme) relaxed.

détenir /det(ə)niʀ/ **58** vt hold; (secret, fortune) possess.

détente /detɑ̃t/ nf relaxation; (Pol) détente; (saut) spring; (gâchette) trigger; **être lent à la** ~ **1** be slow on the uptake.

détenteur, **-trice** /detɑ̃tœʀ, -tʀis/ nm, f holder.

détention /detɑ̃sjɔ̃/ nf detention; ~ **provisoire** custody.

détenu, ~e /detny/ nm, f prisoner.

détergent /detɛʀʒɑ̃/ nm detergent.

détérioration /deteʀjɔʀasjɔ̃/ nf deterioration; (dégât) damage.

détériorer /deteʀjɔʀe/ **1** vt damage. ■ **se** ~ vpr deteriorate.

détermination /detɛʀminasjɔ̃/ nf determination. **déterminé**, ~e adj (résolu) determined; (précis) definite. **déterminer** **1** vt determine.

déterrer /deteʀe/ **1** vt dig up.

détestable /detɛstabl/ adj (caractère, temps) foul.

détester /detɛste/ **1** vt hate. ■ **se** ~ vpr hate each other.

détonation /detɔnasjɔ̃/ nf explosion, detonation.

détour /detuʀ/ nm (crochet) detour; (fig) roundabout means; (virage) bend.

détournement /detuʀnəmɑ̃/ nm hijack(ing); (de fonds) embezzlement.

détourner /detuʀne/ **1** vt (attention) divert; (tête, yeux) turn away; (avion) hijack; (argent) embezzle. ■ **se** ~ **de** vpr stray from.

détraquer /detʀake/ **1** vt make go wrong; (estomac) upset. ■ **se** ~ vpr (machine) go wrong.

détresse /detʀɛs/ nf distress; **dans la** ~, **en** ~ in distress.

détritus /detʀity(s)/ nmpl rubbish (+ sg).

détroit /detʀwa/ nm strait.

détromper /detʀɔ̃pe/ **1** vt set straight. ■ **se** ~ vpr **détrompe-toi!** you'd better think again!

détruire /detʀɥiʀ/ **17** vt destroy.

dette /dɛt/ nf debt.

deuil /dœj/ nm (période) mourning; (décès) bereavement; **porter le** ~ be in mourning; **faire son** ~ **de qch** give sth up as lost.

deux /dø/ adj & nm two; ~ **fois** twice; **tous** (**les** ~) both. **deuxième** adj & nmf second. **deux-pièces** nm inv (maillot de bain) two-piece; (logement) two-room flat. **deux-points** nm inv (Gram) colon. **deux-roues** nm inv two-wheeled vehicle.

dévaliser /devalize/ **1** vt rob, clean out.

dévalorisant, ~e /devalɔʀizɑ̃, -t/ adj demeaning.

dévaloriser /devalɔʀize/ **1** vt (monnaie) devalue. ■ **se** ~ vpr (personne) put oneself down.

dévaluation /devalyasjɔ̃/ nf devaluation.

dévaluer /devalɥe/ **1** vt devalue. ■ se ∼ vpr devalue.

devancer /dəvɑ̃se/ **10** vt be ou go ahead of; (arriver) arrive ahead of; (prévenir) anticipate.

devant /d(ə)vɑ̃/ prép in front of; (distance) ahead of; (avec mouvement) past; (en présence de) in front of; (face à) in the face of; **avoir du temps ∼ soi** have plenty of time. ●adv in front; (à distance) ahead; **de ∼** front. ●nm front; **prendre les ∼s** take the initiative.

devanture /dəvɑ̃tyʀ/ nf shop front; (vitrine) shop window.

développement /devlɔpmɑ̃/ nm development; (de photos) developing.

développer /devlɔpe/ **1** vt develop. ■ se ∼ vpr (corps, talent) develop; (entreprise) grow, expand.

devenir /dəvniʀ/ **58** vi (aux être) become; **qu'est-il devenu?** what has become of him?

dévergondé, ∼e /devɛʀgɔ̃de/ adj & nm,f shameless (person).

déverser /devɛʀse/ **1** vt (liquide) pour; (ordures, pétrole) dump. ■ se ∼ vpr (rivière) flow; (égout, foule) pour.

dévêtir /devetiʀ/ **61** vt undress. ■ se ∼ vpr get undressed.

déviation /devjɑsjɔ̃/ nf diversion.

dévier /devje/ **45** vt divert; (coup) deflect. ●vi (ballon, balle) veer; (personne) deviate.

devin /dəvɛ̃/ nm soothsayer.

deviner /dəvine/ **1** vt guess; (apercevoir) distinguish.

devinette /dəvinɛt/ nf riddle.

devis /dəvi/ nm estimate, quote.

dévisager /devizaʒe/ **40** vt stare at.

devise /dəviz/ nf motto; ∼s (monnaie) (foreign) currency.

dévisser /devise/ **1** vt unscrew.

dévitaliser /devitalize/ **1** vt (dent) carry out root canal treatment on.

dévoiler /devwale/ **1** vt reveal.

---

devoir /dəvwaʀ/ **28**
●verbe auxiliaire
····▸ ∼ **faire** (obligation, hypothèse) must do; (nécessité) have got to do; **je dois dire que...** I have to say that...; **il a dû partir** (nécessité) he had to leave; (hypothèse) he must have left.
····▸ (prévision) **je devais lui dire** I was to tell her; **elle doit rentrer bientôt** she's due back soon.
····▸ (conseil) **tu devrais** you should.
●verbe transitif
····▸ (argent, excuses) owe; **combien je vous dois?** (en achetant) how much is it?
■ se devoir verbe pronominal
····▸ **je me dois de le faire** it's my duty to do it.
●nom masculin
····▸ duty; **faire son ∼** do one's duty.
····▸ (Scol) ∼ (**surveillé**) test; **les ∼s** homework (+ sg); **faire ses ∼s** do one's homework.

---

dévorer /devɔre/ **1** vt devour.

dévot, ∼e /devo, -ɔt/ adj devout.

dévoué, ∼e /devwe/ adj devoted. **dévouement** nm devotion.

dévouer (se) /(sə)devwe/ **1** vpr devote oneself (**à** to); (se sacrifier) sacrifice oneself.

dextérité /dɛksteʀite/ nf skill.

diabète /djabɛt/ nm diabetes. **diabétique** adj & nmf diabetic.

diable /djɑbl/ nm devil.

diagnostic /djagnɔstik/ nm diagnosis. **diagnostiquer** **1** vt diagnose.

diagonal, ∼e (mpl **-aux**)

/djagɔnal, -o/ adj diagonal.
diagonale nf diagonal; **en ~e** diagonally.

diagramme /djagʀam/ nm diagram; (graphique) graph.

dialecte /djalɛkt/ nm dialect.

dialogue /djalɔg/ nm dialogue. **dialoguer** ⬛ vi have talks, enter into a dialogue.

diamant /djamɑ̃/ nm diamond.

diamètre /djamɛtʀ/ nm diameter.

diapositive /djapozitiv/ nf slide.

diarrhée /djaʀe/ nf diarrhoea.

dictateur /diktatœʀ/ nm dictator.

dicter /dikte/ ⬛ vt dictate. **dictée** nf dictation.

dictionnaire /diksjɔnɛʀ/ nm dictionary.

dicton /diktɔ̃/ nm saying.

dièse /djɛz/ nm (Mus) sharp.

diesel* /djezɛl/ nm & adj inv diesel.

diète /djɛt/ nf restricted diet.

diététicien, ~ne /djetetisjɛ̃, -ɛn/ nm, f dietician.

diététique /djetetik/ nf dietetics. • adj **produit** ou **aliment ~** dietary product; **magasin ~** health food shop ou store.

dieu (pl ~**x**) /djø/ nm god; **D~** God.

diffamation /difamasjɔ̃/ nf slander; (par écrit) libel. **diffamer** ⬛ vt slander; (par écrit) libel.

différé: en ~ /ɑ̃difeʀe/ loc (émission) pre-recorded.

différemment /difeʀamɑ̃/ adv differently.

différence /difeʀɑ̃s/ nf difference; **à la ~ de** unlike.

différencier /difeʀɑ̃sje/ 🔢 vt differentiate. ■ se ~ vpr differentiate oneself; **se ~ de** (différer de) differ from.

différend /difeʀɑ̃/ nm difference (of opinion).

différent, ~e /difeʀɑ̃, -t/ adj different (**de** from).

différer /difeʀe/ 🔢 vt postpone. • vi differ (**de** from).

difficile /difisil/ adj difficult; (exigeant) fussy. **difficilement** adv with difficulty.

difficulté /difikylte/ nf difficulty; **faire des ~s** raise objections.

diffus, ~e /dify, -z/ adj diffuse.

diffuser /difyze/ ⬛ vt (émission) broadcast; (nouvelle) spread; (lumière, chaleur) diffuse; (Comm) distribute. **diffusion** nf broadcasting; diffusion; distribution.

digérer /diʒeʀe/ 🔢 vt digest; (endurer ⬛) stomach. **digeste** adj digestible.

digestif, -ive /diʒɛstif, -v/ adj digestive. • nm after-dinner liqueur.

digital, ~e (mpl -**aux**) /diʒital, -o/ adj digital.

digne /diɲ/ adj (noble) dignified; (approprié) worthy; **~ de** worthy of; **~ de foi** trustworthy.

digue /dig/ nf dyke; (US) dike.

dilater /dilate/ ⬛ vt dilate. ■ se ~ vpr dilate; (estomac) distend.

dilemme /dilɛm/ nm dilemma.

dilettante /diletɑ̃t/ nmf amateur.

diluant /dilɥɑ̃/ nm thinner.

diluer /dilɥe/ ⬛ vt dilute.

dimanche /dimɑ̃ʃ/ nm Sunday.

dimension /dimɑ̃sjɔ̃/ nf (taille) size; (mesure) dimension; (aspect) dimension.

diminuer /diminɥe/ ⬛ vt reduce, decrease; (plaisir, courage) dampen; (dénigrer) diminish. • vi (se réduire) decrease; (faiblir) (bruit, flamme) die down; (ardeur) cool. **diminutif** nm diminutive; (surnom) pet name. **diminution** nf decrease (**de** in); (réduction) reduction; (affaiblissement) diminishing.

dinde /dɛ̃d/ nf turkey.

dîner* /dine/ **1** vi have dinner.
• nm dinner.

dingue /dɛ̃g/ adj **1** crazy.

dinosaure /dinozɔʀ/ nm dinosaur.

diphtongue /diftɔ̃g/ nf
diphthong.

diplomate /diplɔmat/ nmf
diplomat. • adj diplomatic.
diplomatique adj diplomatic.

diplôme /diplom/ nm certificate,
diploma; (Univ) degree. **diplômé,
∼e** adj qualified.

dire /diʀ/ **27** vt say; (secret, vérité,
heure) tell; (penser) think; **∼ que**
say that; **∼ à qn que** tell sb
that; **∼ à qn de** tell sb to; **ça
me dit de faire** I feel like
doing; **on dirait que** it would
seem that, it seems that; **dis/
dites donc!** hey! ■ **se ∼** vpr (mot)
be said; (penser) tell oneself; (se
prétendre) claim to be. • nm **au ∼
de, selon les ∼s de**
according to.

direct, ∼e /diʀɛkt/ adj direct. • nm
(train) express train; **en ∼**
(émission) live.

directeur, -trice /diʀɛktœʀ,
-tʀis/ nm, f director; (chef de service)
manager, manageress; (de journal)
editor; (d'école) headteacher; (US)
principal; **∼ de banque** bank
manager; **∼ commercial** sales
manager; **∼ des ressources
humaines** human resources
manager.

direction /diʀɛksjɔ̃/ nf (sens)
direction; (de société)
management; (Auto) steering; **en
∼ de** (going) to.

dirigeant, ∼e /diʀiʒɑ̃, -t/ nm, f
(Pol) leader; (Comm) manager. • adj
(classe) ruling.

diriger /diʀiʒe/ **40** vt (service, école,
parti, pays) run; (entreprise, usine)
manage; (travaux) supervise;
(véhicule) steer; (orchestre) conduct;
(braquer) aim; (tourner) turn. ■ **se
∼** vpr (s'orienter) find one's way; **se
∼ vers** head for, make for.

dis /di/ ▷ DIRE **27**.

discernement /disɛʀnəmɑ̃/ nm
discernment.

disciplinaire /disiplinɛʀ/ adj
disciplinary. **discipline** nf
discipline.

discontinu, ∼e /diskɔ̃tiny/ adj
intermittent.

discordant, ∼e /diskɔʀdɑ̃, -t/ adj
discordant.

discothèque /diskɔtɛk/ nf record
library; (boîte de nuit) disco-
(thèque).

discours /diskuʀ/ nm speech;
(propos) views.

discret, -ète /diskʀɛ, -t/ adj
discreet.

discrétion /diskʀesjɔ̃/ nf
discretion; **à ∼** (vin) unlimited;
(manger, boire) as much as one
desires.

discrimination /diskʀiminasjɔ̃/
nf discrimination.
discriminatoire adj
discriminatory.

disculper /diskylpe/ **1** vt
exonerate. ■ **se ∼** vpr vindicate
oneself.

discussion /diskysjɔ̃/ nf
discussion; (querelle) argument.

discutable /diskytabl/ adj
debatable; (critiquable)
questionable.

discuter /diskyte/ **1** vt discuss;
(contester) question. • vi (parler)
talk; (répliquer) argue; **∼ de**
discuss.

disette /dizɛt/ nf food shortage.

disgrâce /disgʀɑs/ nf disgrace.

disgracieux, -ieuse /disgʀasjø,
-z/ adj ugly, unsightly.

disjoindre /disʒwɛ̃dʀ/ **22** vt take
apart. ■ **se ∼** vpr come apart.

disloquer /dislɔke/ **1** vt (membre)
dislocate; (machine) break (apart).
■ **se ∼** vpr (parti, cortège) break up;
(meuble) come apart.

disparaître* /dispaʀɛtʀ/ **18** vi

disappear; (mourir) die; **faire ~** get rid of. **disparition** nf disappearance; (mort) death.

disparate /dispaʀat/ adj illassorted.

disparu, ~e /dispaʀy/ adj missing. ●nm, f missing person; (mort) dead person.

dispensaire /dispɑ̃sɛʀ/ nm clinic.

dispense /dispɑ̃s/ nf exemption.

dispenser /dispɑ̃se/ **1** vt exempt (**de** from). ■ se ~ **de** vpr avoid.

disperser /dispɛʀse/ **1** vt (éparpiller) scatter; (répartir) disperse. ■ se ~ vpr disperse.

disponibilité /disponibilite/ nf availability. **disponible** adj available.

dispos, ~e /dispo, -z/ adj **frais et ~** fresh and alert.

disposé, ~e /dispoze/ adj **bien/mal ~** in a good/bad mood; **~ à** prepared to; **~ envers** disposed towards.

disposer /dispoze/ **1** vt arrange; **~ à** (engager à) incline to. ●vi **~ de** have at one's disposal. ■ se ~ **à** vpr prepare to.

dispositif /dispozitif/ nm device; (ensemble de mesures) operation.

disposition /dispozisjɔ̃/ nf arrangement, layout; (tendance) tendency; **~s** (humeur) mood; (préparatifs) arrangements; (mesures) measures; (aptitude) aptitude; **mettre à la ~ de** place ou put at the disposal of.

disproportionné, ~e /dispʀopɔʀsjone/ adj disproportionate; **~ à** out of proportion with.

dispute /dispyt/ nf quarrel.

disputer /dispyte/ **1** vt (match) play; (course) run in; (prix) fight for; (gronder **1**) tell off. ■ se ~ vpr quarrel; (se battre pour) fight over; (match) be played.

disquaire /diskɛʀ/ nmf record dealer.

disque /disk/ nm (Mus) record; (Sport) discus; (cercle) disc, disk; (Ordinat) disk; **~ compact** compact disc; **~ dur** hard disk; **~ optique compact** CD-ROM; **~ souple** floppy disk.

disquette /diskɛt/ nf floppy disk, diskette; **~ de sauvegarde** back-up disk.

disséminer /disemine/ **1** vt spread, scatter.

dissertation /disɛʀtasjɔ̃/ nf essay, paper.

disserter /disɛʀte/ **1** vi **~ sur** speak about; (par écrit) write about.

dissident, ~e /disidɑ̃, -t/ adj & nm, f dissident.

dissimulation /disimylasjɔ̃/ nf concealment; (fig) deceit.

dissimuler /disimyle/ **1** vt conceal (**à** from). ■ se ~ vpr conceal oneself.

dissipé, ~e /disipe/ adj (élève) unruly.

dissiper /disipe/ **1** vt (fumée, crainte) dispel; (fortune) squander; (personne) distract. ■ se ~ vpr disappear; (élève) grow restless.

dissolvant /disɔlvɑ̃/ nm solvent; (pour ongles) nail polish remover.

dissoudre /disudʀ/ 53 vt dissolve. ■ se ~ vpr dissolve.

dissuader /disɥade/ **1** vt dissuade (**de** from).

dissuasion /disɥazjɔ̃/ nf dissuasion; **force de ~** deterrent force.

distance /distɑ̃s/ nf distance; (écart) gap; **à ~** at ou from a distance.

distancer /distɑ̃se/ 10 vt outdistance.

distendre /distɑ̃dʀ/ **3** vt (estomac) distend; (corde) stretch.

distinct, ~e /distɛ̃(kt), -ɛkt/ adj distinct.

distinctif, -ive /distɛ̃ktif, -v/ adj

d

(trait) **distinctive**; (signe, caractère) **distinguishing**.

distinction /distɛ̃ksjɔ̃/ nf distinction; (récompense) honour.

distinguer /distɛ̃ge/ **1** vt distinguish.

distraction /distʀaksjɔ̃/ nf absent-mindedness; (passe-temps) entertainment, leisure; (détente) recreation.

distraire /distʀɛʀ/ **29** vt amuse; (rendre inattentif) distract; ~ **qn de qch** take sb's mind off sth. ∎ **se** ~ vpr amuse oneself.

distrait, ~**e** /distʀɛ, -t/ adj absentminded; (élève) inattentive.

distrayant, ~**e** /distʀɛjɑ̃, -t/ adj entertaining.

distribuer /distʀibɥe/ **1** vt hand out, distribute; (répartir) distribute; (tâches, rôles) allocate; (cartes) deal; (courrier) deliver.

distributeur /distʀibytœʀ/ nm (Auto, Comm) distributor; ~ **(automatique)** vending-machine; ~ **de billets (de banque)** cash dispenser. **distribution** nf distribution; (du courrier) delivery; (acteurs) cast; (secteur) retailing.

district /distʀikt/ nm district.

dit¹, dites /di, dit/ ▷ DIRE **27**.

dit², ~**e** /di, dit/ adj (décidé) agreed; (surnommé) known as.

diurne /djyʀn/ adj diurnal; (activité) daytime.

divagations /divagasjɔ̃/ nfpl ravings.

divergence /divɛʀʒɑ̃s/ nf divergence. **divergent,** ~**e** adj divergent. **diverger** **40** vi diverge.

divers, ~**e** /divɛʀ, -s/ adj (varié) diverse; (différent) various; (frais) miscellaneous; **dépenses** ~**es** sundries. **diversifier** **45** vt diversify.

diversité /divɛʀsite/ nf diversity, variety.

divertir /divɛʀtiʀ/ **2** vt amuse, entertain. ∎ **se** ~ vpr amuse oneself; (passer du bon temps) enjoy oneself. **divertissement** nm amusement, entertainment.

dividende /dividɑ̃d/ nm dividend.

divin, ~**e** /divɛ̃, -in/ adj divine. **divinité** nf divinity.

diviser /divize/ **1** vt divide. ∎ **se** ~ vpr become divided; **se** ~ **par sept** be divisible by seven. **division** nf division.

divorce /divɔʀs/ nm divorce.

divorcé, ~**e** /divɔʀse/ adj divorced. ●nm, f divorcee.

divorcer /divɔʀse/ **10** vi ~ **(d'avec)** divorce.

dix /dis/ (/di/ before consonant, /diz/ before vowel) adj & nm ten.

dix-huit /dizɥit/ adj & nm eighteen.

dixième /dizjɛm/ adj & nmf tenth.

dix-neuf /diznœf/ adj & nm nineteen.

dix-sept /disɛt/ adj & nm seventeen.

docile /dɔsil/ adj docile.

docteur /dɔktœʀ/ nm doctor.

doctorat /dɔktɔʀa/ nm doctorate, PhD.

document /dɔkymɑ̃/ nm document. **documentaire** adj & nm documentary.

documentaliste /dɔkymɑ̃talist/ nmf information officer; (Scol) librarian.

documentation /dɔkymɑ̃tasjɔ̃/ nf information, literature; **centre de** ~ resource centre.

documenté, ~**e** /dɔkymɑ̃te/ adj well-documented.

documenter /dɔkymɑ̃te/ **1** vt provide with information. ∎ **se** ~ vpr collect information.

dodo /dodo/ nm **faire** ~ (langage enfantin) sleep.

dodu, ~e /dɔdy/ adj plump.

dogmatique /dɔgmatik/ adj dogmatic. **dogme** nm dogma.

doigt /dwa/ nm finger; **un ~ de** a drop of; **montrer qch du ~** point at sth; **à deux ~s de** a hair's breadth away from; **~ de pied** toe. **doigté** nm (Mus) fingering, touch; (diplomatie) tact.

dois, doit /dwa/ ▶DEVOIR 26.

doléances /dɔleɑ̃s/ nfpl grievances.

dollar /dɔlaʀ/ nm dollar.

domaine /dɔmɛn/ nm estate, domain; (fig) domain, field.

domestique /dɔmɛstik/ adj domestic. ● nmf servant. **domestiquer** 1 vt domesticate.

domicile /dɔmisil/ nm home; **à ~** at home; (livrer) to the home.

domicilié, ~e /dɔmisilje/ adj resident; **être ~ à Paris** live ou be resident in Paris.

dominant, ~e /dɔminɑ̃, -t/ adj dominant. **dominante** nf dominant feature.

dominer /dɔmine/ 1 vt dominate; (surplomber) tower over, dominate; (sujet) master; (peur) overcome. ● vi dominate; (équipe) be in the lead; (prévaloir) stand out.

domino /dɔmino/ nm domino.

dommage /dɔmaʒ/ nm (tort) harm; **~s** (dégâts) damage; **c'est ~ de** (fruits, résultats) produce; (film) show; (pièce) put on; **ça donne soif/faim** it makes one thirsty/ hungry; **~ qch à réparer** take sth to be repaired; **~ lieu à** give rise to. ● vi **~ sur** look out on to; **~ dans** tend towards. ■ **se ~ à** vpr devote oneself to; **se ~ du mal** go to a lot of trouble (**pour faire** to do).

dompter /dɔ̃te/ 1 vt tame. **dompteur, -euse** nm, f tamer.

DOM-TOM /dɔmtɔm/ abrév mpl (**départements et territoires d'outre-mer**) French overseas departments and territories.

don /dɔ̃/ nm (cadeau, aptitude) gift. **donateur, -trice** nm, f donor. **donation** nf donation.

donc /dɔ̃k/ conj so, then; (par conséquent) so, therefore; **quoi ~?** what did you say?; **tiens ~!** fancy that!

donjon /dɔ̃ʒɔ̃/ nm (tour) keep.

donné, ~e /dɔne/ adj (fixé) given; (pas cher 1) dirt cheap; **étant ~ que** given that.

donnée /dɔne/ nf (élément d'information) fact; **~s** data.

donner /dɔne/ 1 vt give; (vieilles affaires) give away; (distribuer) give out; (fruits, résultats) produce; (film) show; (pièce) put on; **ça donne soif/faim** it makes one thirsty/hungry; **~ qch à réparer** take sth to be repaired; **~ lieu à** give rise to. ● vi **~ sur** look out on to; **~ dans** tend towards. ■ **se ~ à** vpr devote oneself to; **se ~ du mal** go to a lot of trouble (**pour faire** to do).

dont /dɔ̃/
● pronom
····▸ (personne) **la fille ~ je te parlais** the girl I was telling you about; **l'homme ~ la fille a dit...** the man whose daughter said...
····▸ (chose) which. **l'affaire ~ il parle** the matter which he is referring to; **la manière ~ elle parle** the way she speaks; **ce ~ il parle** what he's talking about
····▸ (provenance) from which.
····▸ (parmi lesquels) **deux personnes ~ toi** two people, one of whom is you; **plusieurs thèmes ~ l'identité et le racisme** several topics including identity and racism.

dopage /dɔpaʒ/ nm (de cheval) doping; (d'athlète) illegal drug-use.

doper /dɔpe/ 1 vt dope. ■ **se ~** vpr take drugs.

doré, ~e /dɔʀe/ adj (couleur d'or) golden; (qui rappelle l'or) gold; (avec de l'or) gilt; **la jeunesse ~e** gilded youth.

dorénavant /dɔrenavɑ̃/ adv henceforth.

dorer /dɔre/ **1** vt gild; (Culin) brown.

dormir /dɔrmir/ **46** vi sleep; (être endormi) be asleep; ~ **debout** be asleep on one's feet; **une histoire à ~ debout** a cock-and-bull story.

dortoir /dɔrtwar/ nm dormitory.

dorure /dɔryr/ nf gilding.

dos /do/ nm back; (de livre) spine; **à ~ de** riding on; **au ~ de** (chèque) on the back of; **de ~** from behind; ~ **crawlé** backstroke.

dosage /dozaʒ/ nm (mélange) mixture; (quantité) amount, proportions. **dose** nf dose. **doser 1** vt measure out; (contrôler) use in a controlled way.

dossier /dɔsje/ nm (documents) file; (Jur) case; (de chaise) back; (TV, presse) special feature.

dot /dɔt/ nf dowry.

douane /dwan/ nf customs.

douanier, -ière /dwanje, -jɛr/ adj customs. •nm customs officer.

double /dubl/ adj & adv double. •nm (copie) duplicate; (sosie) double; **le ~ (de)** twice as much *ou* as many (as); **le ~ messieurs** the men's doubles.

double-cliquer /dublklike/ **1** vt double-click.

doubler /duble/ **1** vt double; (dépasser) overtake; (vêtement) line; (film) dub; (classe) repeat; (cap) round. •vi double.

doublure /dublyr/ nf (étoffe) lining; (acteur) understudy.

douce /dus/ ▷DOUX.

doucement /dusmɑ̃/ adv gently; (sans bruit) quietly; (lentement) slowly.

douceur /dusœr/ nf (mollesse) softness; (de climat) mildness; (de personne) gentleness; (friandise) sweet; (US) candy; **en ~** smoothly.

douche /duʃ/ nf shower.

doucher (se) /duʃe/ **1** vpr have *ou* take a shower.

doudoune /dudun/ nf **1** down jacket.

doué, ~e /dwe/ adj gifted; ~ **de** endowed with.

douille /duj/ nf (Électr) socket.

douillet, ~te /dujɛ, -t/ adj cosy, comfortable; (personne: péj) soft.

douleur /dulœr/ nf pain; (chagrin) sorrow, grief. **douloureux, -euse** adj painful.

doute /dut/ nm doubt; **sans ~** no doubt; **sans aucun ~** without doubt.

douter /dute/ **1** vt ~ **de** doubt; ~ **que** doubt that. •vi doubt. ■ **se ~ de** vpr suspect; **je m'en doutais** I thought so.

douteux, -euse /dutø, -z/ adj dubious, doubtful.

Douvres /duvr/ npr Dover.

doux, douce /du, dus/ adj (moelleux) soft; (sucré) sweet; (clément, pas fort) mild; (pas brusque, bienveillant) gentle.

douzaine /duzɛn/ nf about twelve; (douze) dozen; **une ~ d'œufs** a dozen eggs.

douze /duz/ adj & nm twelve. **douzième** adj & nmf twelfth.

doyen, ~ne /dwajɛ̃, -ɛn/ nm, f dean; (en âge) most senior person.

dragée /draʒe/ nf sugared almond.

draguer /drage/ **1** vt (rivière) dredge; (filles **1**) chat up.

drainer /drene/ **1** vt drain.

dramatique /dramatik/ adj dramatic; (tragique) tragic. •nf (television) drama.

dramatiser /dramatize/ **1** vt dramatize.

dramaturge /dramatyrʒ/ nmf dramatist.

drame /dʀam/ nm (genre) drama; (pièce) play; (événement tragique) tragedy.

drap /dʀa/ nm sheet; (tissu) (woollen) cloth.

drapeau (pl ∼x) /dʀapo/ nm flag.

drap-housse (pl **draps-housses**) /dʀaus/ nm fitted sheet.

dressage /dʀesaʒ/ nm training; (compétition équestre) dressage.

dresser /dʀese/ **1** vt put up, erect; (tête) raise; (animal) train; (liste, plan) draw up; **∼ l'oreille** prick up one's ears. ■ **se ∼** vpr (bâtiment) stand; (personne) draw oneself up. **dresseur, -euse** nm, f trainer.

dribbler /dʀible/ **1** vi (Sport) dribble.

drive /dʀajv/ nm (Ordinat) drive.

drogue /dʀɔg/ nf drug; **la ∼** drugs.

drogué, ∼e /dʀɔge/ nm, f drug addict.

droguer /dʀɔge/ **1** vt (malade) drug heavily; (victime) drug. ■ **se ∼** vpr take drugs.

🔲**droguerie** /dʀɔgʀi/ nf hardware shop. **droguiste** nmf owner of a hardware shop.

droit, ∼e /dʀwa, -t/ adj (contraire de gauche) right; (non courbe) straight; (loyal) upright; **angle ∼** right angle. ●adv straight. ●nm right; **∼(s)** (taxe) duty; **le ∼** (Jur) law; **avoir ∼ à** be entitled to; **avoir le ∼ de** be allowed to; **être dans son ∼** be in the right; **∼ d'auteur** copyright; **∼ d'inscription** registration fee; **∼s d'auteur** royalties.

droite /dʀwat/ nf (contraire de gauche) right; **à ∼** on the right; (direction) (to the) right; **la ∼** the right (side); (Pol) the right (wing); (ligne) straight line.
droitier, -ière adj right-handed.

drôle /dʀol/ adj (amusant) funny; (bizarre) funny, odd. **drôlement** adv funnily; (très **1**) really.

dru, ∼e /dʀy/ adj thick; **tomber ∼** fall thick and fast.

drugstore /dʀœgstɔʀ/ nm drugstore.

DTD abrév m (**document type definition**) DTD.

du /dy/ ▷DE.

dû, due /dy/ adj due. ●nm due; (argent) dues; **∼ à** due to.
●▷DEVOIR **26**.

duc, duchesse /dyk, dyʃɛs/ nm, f duke, duchess.

duo /dɥo/ nm (Mus) duet; (fig) duo.

dupe /dyp/ nf dupe.

duplex /dyplɛks/ nm split-level apartment; (US) duplex; (émission) link-up.

duplicata /dyplikata/ nm inv duplicate.

duquel /dykɛl/ ▷LEQUEL.

dur, ∼e /dyʀ/ adj hard; (sévère) harsh, hard; (viande) tough; (col, brosse) stiff; **∼ d'oreille** hard of hearing. ●adv hard. ●nm, f tough nut **1**; (Pol) hardliner.

durable /dyʀabl/ adj lasting.

durant /dyʀɑ̃/ prép (au cours de) during; (avec mesure de temps) for; **∼ des heures** for hours; **des heures ∼** for hours and hours.

durcir /dyʀsiʀ/ **2** vt harden. ●vi (terre) harden; (ciment) set; (pain) go hard. ■ **se ∼** vpr harden.

durée /dyʀe/ nf length; (période) duration; **de courte ∼** short-lived; **pile longue ∼** long-life battery.

durer /dyʀe/ **1** vi last.

dureté /dyʀte/ nf hardness; (sévérité) harshness.

duvet /dyvɛ/ nm down; (sac) sleeping-bag.

DVD abrév m (**digital versatile disc**) DVD.

dynamique /dinamik/ adj dynamic.

dynamite /dinamit/ nf dynamite.

dynamo /dinamo/ nf dynamo.

🔲 *see A-Z of French life and culture*

Ee

eau (pl ~**x**) /o/ nf water; ~ **courante** running water; ~ **de mer** seawater; ~ **de source** spring water; ~ **douce/salée** fresh/salt water; ~ **de pluie** rainwater; ~ **potable** drinking water; ~ **de Javel** bleach; ~ **minérale** mineral water; ~ **gazeuse** sparkling water; ~ **plate** still water; ~ **de toilette** eau de toilette; ~**x usées** dirty water; ~**x et forêts** forestry commission (+ sg); **tomber à l'~** (fig) fall through; **prendre l'~** take in water. **eau-de-vie** (pl **eaux-de-vie**) nf brandy.

ébahi, ~**e** /ebai/ adj dumbfounded.

ébauche /eboʃ/ nf (dessin) sketch; (fig) attempt.

ébéniste /ebenist/ nm cabinet-maker.

éblouir /ebluiʀ/ 2 vt dazzle.

éboueur /ebwœʀ/ nm dustman.

ébouillanter /ebujɑ̃te/ 1 vt scald.

éboulement /ebulmɑ̃/ nm landslide.

ébouriffé, ~**e** /ebuʀife/ adj dishevelled.

ébrécher /ebʀeʃe/ 14 vt chip.

ébruiter /ebʀɥite/ 1 vt spread about. ■ s'~ vpr get out.

ébullition /ebylisjɔ̃/ nf boiling; **en** ~ boiling.

écaille /ekaj/ nf (de poisson) scale; (de peinture, roc) flake; (matière) tortoiseshell.

écarlate /ekaʀlat/ adj scarlet.

écarquiller /ekaʀkije/ 1 vt ~ **les yeux** open one's eyes wide.

écart /ekaʀ/ nm gap; (de prix) difference; (embardée) swerve; ~ **de conduite** lapse in behaviour; **être à l'~** be isolated; **se tenir à l'~ de** stand apart from; (fig) keep out of the way of.

écarté, ~**e** /ekaʀte/ adj (lieu) remote; **les jambes** ~**es** (with) legs apart; **les bras** ~**s** with one's arms out.

écarter /ekaʀte/ 1 vt (séparer) move apart; (membres) spread; (branches) part; (éliminer) dismiss; ~ **qch de** move sth away from; ~ **qn de** keep sb away from. ■ s'~ vpr (s'éloigner) move away; (quitter son chemin) move aside; **s'~ de** stray from.

ecchymose /ekimoz/ nf bruise.

écervelé, ~**e** /eseʀvəle/ adj scatterbrained. ● nm, f scatterbrain.

échafaudage /eʃafodaʒ/ nm scaffolding; (amas) heap.

échalote /eʃalɔt/ nf shallot.

échancré, ~**e** /eʃɑ̃kʀe/ adj lowcut.

échange /eʃɑ̃ʒ/ nm exchange; **en** ~ **(de)** in exchange (for). **échanger** 40 vt exchange (**contre** for).

échangeur /eʃɑ̃ʒœʀ/ nm (Auto) interchange.

échantillon /eʃɑ̃tijɔ̃/ nm sample.

échappatoire /eʃapatwaʀ/ nf way out.

échappement /eʃapmɑ̃/ nm exhaust.

échapper /eʃape/ 1 vi ~ **à** escape; (en fuyant) escape (from); ~ **des mains de** slip out of the hands of; **ça m'a échappé** (fig) it just slipped out; **l'~ belle**

have a narrow *ou* lucky escape. ■ s'~ vpr escape.

écharde /eʃaʀd/ nf splinter.

écharpe /eʃaʀp/ nf scarf; (de maire) sash; **en ~** (bras) in a sling.

échasse /eʃas/ nf stilt.

échauffement /eʃofmɑ̃/ nm (Sport) warm-up.

échauffer /eʃofe/ **1** vt heat; (fig) excite. ■ s'~ vpr warm up.

échéance /eʃeɑ̃s/ nf due date (for payment); (délai) deadline; (obligation) (financial) commitment.

échéant: le cas ~ /ləkazeʃeɑ̃/ loc if need be.

échec /eʃɛk/ nm failure; **~s** (jeu) chess; **~ et mat** checkmate.

échelle /eʃɛl/ nf ladder; (dimension) scale.

échelon /eʃlɔ̃/ nm rung; (hiérarchique) grade; (niveau) level.

échevelé, ~e /eʃəvle/ adj dishevelled.

écho /eko/ nm echo; **~s** (dans la presse) gossip.

échographie /ekɔgʀafi/ nf (ultrasound) scan.

échouer /eʃwe/ **1** vi (bateau) run aground; (ne pas réussir) fail; **~ à un examen** fail an exam. ● vt (bateau) ground. ■ s'~ vpr run aground.

échu, ~e /eʃy/ adj (délai) expired.

éclabousser /eklabuse/ **1** vt splash.

éclair /eklɛʀ/ nm (flash of) lightning; (fig) flash; (gâteau) éclair. ● adj inv (visite) brief.

éclairage /eklɛʀaʒ/ nm lighting.

éclaircie /eklɛʀsi/ nf sunny interval.

éclaircir /eklɛʀsiʀ/ **2** vt lighten; (mystère) clear up. ■ s'~ vpr (ciel) clear; (mystère) become clearer. **éclaircissement** nm clarification.

éclairer /eklɛʀe/ **1** vt light (up);

(personne) (fig) enlighten; (situation) throw light on. ● vi give light. ■ s'~ vpr become clearer.

éclaireur, -euse /eklɛʀœʀ, -øz/ nm, f (boy) scout, (girl) guide.

éclat /ekla/ nm fragment; (de lumière) brightness; (splendeur) brilliance; **~ de rire** burst of laughter.

éclatant, ~e /eklatɑ̃, -t/ adj brilliant; (soleil) dazzling.

éclater /eklate/ **1** vi burst; (exploser) go off; (verre) shatter; (guerre) break out; (groupe) split up; **~ de rire** burst out laughing.

éclipse /eklips/ nf eclipse.

éclosion /eklozjɔ̃/ nf hatching, opening.

écluse /eklyz/ nf (de canal) lock.

écœurant, ~e /ekœʀɑ̃, -t/ adj (gâteau) sickly; (fig) disgusting. **écœurer** **1** vt sicken.

éco-guerrier, -ière /ekogɛʀje, jɛʀ/ nmf eco-warrior.

🔲**école** /ekɔl/ nf school; 🔲**~ maternelle**/🔲**primaire**/ 🔲**secondaire** nursery/primary/ secondary school; **~ normale** teachers' training college. **écolier, -ière** nm, f schoolboy, schoolgirl.

écologie /ekɔlɔʒi/ nf ecology. **écologique** adj ecological, green. **écologiste** nmf (chercheur) ecologist; (dans l'âme) environmentalist; (Pol) Green.

économie /ekɔnɔmi/ nf economy; (discipline) economics; **~s** (argent) savings; **une ~ de** (gain) a saving of. **économique** adj (Pol) economic; (bon marché) economical.

économiser /ekɔnɔmize/ **1** vt/i save.

écorce /ekɔʀs/ nf bark; (de fruit) peel.

écorcher /ekɔʀʃe/ **1** vt (genou)

🔲 *see* A-Z of French life and culture

graze; (animal) skin. ∎ s'∼ vpr graze oneself. **écorchure** nf graze.

écossais, ∼e /ekɔsɛ, -z/ adj Scottish. É∼, ∼e nm, f Scot.

Écosse /ekɔs/ nf Scotland.

écoulement /ekulmɑ̃/ nm flow.

écouler /ekule/ **1** vt dispose of, sell. ∎ s'∼ vpr (liquide) flow; (temps) pass.

écourter /ekuʀte/ **1** vt shorten.

écoute /ekut/ nf listening; **à l'∼ (de)** listening in (to); **heures de grande ∼** prime time; **∼s téléphoniques** phone tapping.

écouter /ekute/ **1** vt listen to. ∙vi listen; **∼ aux portes** eavesdrop. **écouteur** nm earphones (+ pl); (de téléphone) receiver.

écran /ekʀɑ̃/ nm screen; **∼ total** sun-block.

écraser /ekʀaze/ **1** vt crush; (piéton) run over; (cigarette) stub out. ∎ s'∼ vpr crash (**contre** into).

écrémé, ∼e /ekʀeme/ adj skimmed; **demi-∼** semi-skimmed.

écrevisse /ekʀəvis/ nf crayfish.

écrier (s') /(s)ekʀije/ **45** vpr exclaim.

écrin /ekʀɛ̃/ nm case.

écrire /ekʀiʀ/ **30** vt/i write; (orthographier) spell. ∎ s'∼ vpr (mot) be spelt.

écrit /ekʀi/ nm document; (examen) written paper; **par ∼** in writing.

écriteau (pl ∼x) /ekʀito/ nm notice.

écriture /ekʀityʀ/ nf writing; **∼s** (Comm) accounts.

écrivain /ekʀivɛ̃/ nm writer.

écrou /ekʀu/ nm (Tech) nut.

écrouler (s') /(s)ekʀule/ **1** vpr collapse.

écru, ∼e /ekʀy/ adj (couleur) natural; (tissu) raw.

écueil /ekœj/ nm reef; (fig) danger.

éculé, ∼e /ekyle/ adj (soulier) worn at the heel; (fig) well-worn.

écume /ekym/ nf foam; (Culin) scum.

écumer /ekyme/ **1** vt skim. ∙vi foam.

écureuil /ekyʀœj/ nm squirrel.

écurie /ekyʀi/ nf stable.

écuyer, -ère /ekɥije, -jɛʀ/ nm, f (horse) rider.

eczéma* /ɛgzema/ nm eczema.

EDF abrév f (**Électricité de France**) French electricity board.

édifice /edifis/ nm building.

édifier /edifje/ **45** vt construct; (porter à la vertu) edify.

Édimbourg /edɛ̃buʀ/ npr Edinburgh.

édit /edi/ nm edict.

éditer /edite/ **1** vt publish; (annoter) edit. **éditeur, -trice** nm, f publisher; (réviseur) editor.

édition /edisjɔ̃/ nf (activité) publishing; (livre, disque) edition.

éditique /editik/ nf electronic publishing.

éditorial, ∼e (pl **-iaux**) /editɔʀjal, -jo/ adj & nm editorial.

édredon /edʀədɔ̃/ nm eiderdown.

éducateur, -trice /edykatœʀ, -tʀis/ nm, f youth worker.

éducatif, -ive /edykatif, -v/ adj educational.

éducation /edykasjɔ̃/ nf (façon d'élever) upbringing; (enseignement) education; (manières) manners; **∼ physique** physical education.

éduquer /edyke/ **1** vt (élever) bring up; (former) educate.

effacé, ∼e /efase/ adj (modeste) unassuming.

effacer /efase/ **10** vt (gommer) rub out; (à l'écran) delete; (souvenir) erase. ∎ s'∼ vpr fade; (s'écarter) step aside.

effarer /efaʀe/ 1 vt alarm; **être effaré** be astounded.

effaroucher /efaʀuʃe/ 1 vt scare away.

effectif, -ive /efɛktif, -v/ adj effective. ●nm (d'école) number of pupils; **~s** numbers.
effectivement adv effectively; (en effet) indeed.

effectuer /efɛktɥe/ 1 vt carry out, make.

efféminé, ~e /efemine/ adj effeminate.

effervescent, ~e /efɛʀvesã, -t/ adj **comprimé ~** effervescent tablet.

effet /efɛ/ nm effect; (impression) impression; **~s** (habits) clothes, things; **sous l'~ d'une drogue** under the influence of drugs; **en ~** indeed; **faire de l'~** have an effect, be effective; **faire bon/mauvais ~** make a good/bad impression; **ça fait un drôle d'~** it feels strange.

efficace /efikas/ adj effective; (personne) efficient. **efficacité** nf effectiveness; (de personne) efficiency.

effleurer /eflœʀe/ 1 vt touch lightly; (sujet) touch on; **ça ne m'a pas effleuré** it did not cross my mind.

effondrement /efɔ̃dʀəmã/ nm collapse. **effondrer (s')** 1 vpr collapse.

efforcer (s') /(s)efɔʀse/ 10 vpr try (hard) (**de** to).

effort /efɔʀ/ nm effort.

effraction /efʀaksjɔ̃/ nf **entrer par ~** break in.

effrayant, ~e /efʀejã, -t/ adj frightening; (fig) frightful.

effrayer /efʀeje/ 31 vt frighten; (décourager) put off. ■ **s'~** vpr be frightened.

effréné, ~e /efʀene/ adj wild.

effriter (s') /(s)efʀite/ 1 vpr crumble.

effroi /efʀwa/ nm dread.

effronté, ~e /efʀɔ̃te/ adj cheeky. ●nm, f cheeky boy, cheeky girl.

effroyable /efʀwajabl/ adj dreadful.

égal, ~e (mpl **-aux**) /egal, -o/ adj equal; (surface, vitesse) even. ●nm, f equal; **ça m'est/lui est ~** it is all the same to me/him; **sans ~** matchless; **d'~ à ~** between equals. **également** adv equally; (aussi) as well. **égaler** 1 vt equal.

égaliser /egalize/ 1 vt/i (Sport) equalize; (niveler) level out; (cheveux) trim.

égalitaire /egalitɛʀ/ adj egalitarian.

égalité /egalite/ nf equality; (de surface) evenness; **être à ~** be level.

égard /egaʀ/ nm consideration; **~s** respect (+ sg); **par ~ pour** out of consideration for; **à cet ~** in this respect; **à l'~ de** with regard to; (envers) towards.

égarer /egaʀe/ 1 vt mislay; (tromper) lead astray. ■ **s'~** vpr get lost; (se tromper) go astray.

égayer /egeje/ 31 vt (personne) cheer up; (pièce) brighten up.

église /egliz/ nf church.

égoïsme /egoism/ nm selfishness, egoism.

égoïste /egoist/ adj selfish. ●nmf egoist.

égorger /egoʀʒe/ 40 vt slit the throat of.

égout /egu/ nm sewer.

égoutter /egute/ 1 vt drain. ■ **s'~** vpr (vaisselle) drain; (lessive) drip dry. **égouttoir** nm draining-board.

égratigner /egʀatiɲe/ 1 vt scratch. **égratignure** nf scratch.

Égypte /eʒipt/ nf Egypt.

éjecter /eʒɛkte/ 1 vt eject.

élaboration /elabɔʀasjɔ̃/ nf

elaboration. **élaborer** [1] vt elaborate.

élan /elɑ̃/ nm (animal) moose; (Sport) run-up; (vitesse) momentum; (fig) surge.

élancé, ~e /elɑ̃se/ adj slender.

élancement /elɑ̃smɑ̃/ nm twinge.

élancer (s') /(s)elɑ̃se/ [10] vpr leap forward, dash; (arbre, édifice) soar.

élargir /elaʀʒiʀ/ [2] vt (route) widen; (connaissances) broaden. ▪ **s'~** vpr (famille) expand; (route) widen; (écart) increase; (vêtement) stretch.

élastique /elastik/ adj elastic. ●nm elastic band; (tissu) elastic.

électeur, -trice /elɛktœʀ, -tʀis/ nm, f voter. **élection** nf election. **électoral, ~e** (mpl -aux) adj (réunion) election. **électorat** nm electorate, voters (+ pl).

électricien, ~ne /elɛktʀisjɛ̃, ɛn/ nm, f electrician. **électricité** nf electricity.

électrifier /elɛktʀifje/ [45] vt electrify.

électrique /elɛktʀik/ adj electric; (installation) electrical.

électrocuter /elɛktʀɔkyte/ [1] vt electrocute.

électroménager /elɛktʀɔmenaʒe/ nm l'~ household appliances (+ pl).

électron /elɛktʀɔ̃/ nm electron. **électronicien, ~ne** nm, f electronics engineer.

électronique /elɛktʀɔnik/ adj electronic. ●nf electronics.

élégance /elegɑ̃s/ nf elegance. **élégant, ~e** adj elegant.

élément /elemɑ̃/ nm element; (meuble) unit. **élémentaire** adj elementary.

éléphant /elefɑ̃/ nm elephant.

élevage /ɛlvaʒ/ nm (stock-) breeding.

élévation /elevasjɔ̃/ nf rise; (hausse) rise; (plan) elevation; ~

de terrain rise in the ground.

élève /elɛv/ nmf pupil.

élevé, ~e /ɛlve/ adj high; (noble) elevated; **bien ~** well-mannered.

élever /ɛlve/ [6] vt (lever) raise; (enfants) bring up, raise; (animal) breed. ▪ **s'~** vpr rise; (dans le ciel) soar up; **s'~ à** amount to. **éleveur, -euse** nm, f (stock-)breeder.

éligible /eliʒibl/ adj eligible.

élimination /eliminasjɔ̃/ nf elimination.

éliminatoire /eliminatwaʀ/ adj qualifying. ●nf (Sport) heat.

éliminer /elimine/ [1] vt eliminate.

élire /eliʀ/ [39] vt elect.

elle /ɛl/ pron she; (complément) her; (chose) it. **elle-même** pron herself; itself. **elles** pron they; (complément) them. **elles-mêmes** pron themselves.

élocution /elɔkysjɔ̃/ nf diction.

éloge /elɔʒ/ nm praise; **faire l'~ de** praise; **~s** praise (+ sg).

éloigné, ~e /elwaɲe/ adj distant; **~ de** far away from; **parent ~** distant relative.

éloigner /elwaɲe/ [1] vt take away ou remove (**de** from); (danger) ward off; (visite) put off. ▪ **s'~** vpr go ou move away (**de** from); (affectivement) become estranged (**de** from).

élongation /elɔ̃gasjɔ̃/ nf strained muscle.

éloquent, ~e /elɔkɑ̃, -t/ adj eloquent.

élu, ~e /ely/ adj elected. ●nm, f (Pol) elected representative.

élucider /elyside/ [1] vt elucidate.

éluder /elyde/ [1] vt evade.

émacié, ~e /emasje/ adj emaciated.

e-mail /imɛl/ nm email; **envoyer**

un ~ a qn email sb.

émail (pl -aux) /emaj, -o/ nm enamel.

émanciper /emɑ̃sipe/ **1** vt emancipate. ■ s'~ vpr become emancipated.

émaner /emane/ **1** vi emanate.

emballage /ɑ̃balaʒ/ nm (dur) packaging; (souple) wrapping.

emballer /ɑ̃bale/ **1** vt pack; (en papier) wrap; **ça ne m'emballe pas** 🔢 I'm not really taken by it. ■ s'~ vpr (moteur) race; (cheval) bolt; (personne) get carried away; (prices) shoot up.

embarcadère /ɑ̃baʀkadɛʀ/ nm landing-stage.

embarcation /ɑ̃baʀkasjɔ̃/ nf boat.

embardée /ɑ̃baʀde/ nf swerve.

embarquement /ɑ̃baʀkəmɑ̃/ nm (de passagers) boarding; (de fret) loading.

embarquer /ɑ̃baʀke/ **1** vt take on board; (frêt) load; (emporter 🔢) cart off. ●vi board. ■ s'~ vpr board; **s'~ dans** embark upon.

embarras /ɑ̃baʀa/ nm (gêne) embarrassment; (difficulté) difficulty.

embarrasser /ɑ̃baʀase/ **1** vt (encombrer) clutter (up); (fig) embarrass. ■ s'~ **de** vpr burden oneself with.

embauche /ɑ̃boʃ/ nf hiring. **embaucher** **1** vt hire, take on.

embaumer /ɑ̃bome/ **1** vt (pièce) fill; (cadavre) embalm. ●vi be fragrant.

embellir /ɑ̃beliʀ/ **2** vt make more attractive; (récit) embellish.

embêtant, ~e /ɑ̃bɛtɑ̃, -t/ adj 🔢 annoying.

embêter /ɑ̃bete/ **1** vt bother. ■ s'~ vpr be bored.

emblée: d'~ /dɑ̃ble/ loc right away.

emblème /ɑ̃blɛm/ nm emblem.

emboîter* /ɑ̃bwate/ **1** vt fit together; ~ **le pas à qn** (imiter) follow suit. ■ s'~ vpr fit together; **(s')~ dans** fit into.

embonpoint /ɑ̃bɔ̃pwɛ̃/ nm stoutness.

embourber (s') /(s)ɑ̃buʀbe/ **1** vpr get stuck in the mud; (fig) get bogged down.

embouteillage /ɑ̃butɛjaʒ/ nm traffic jam.

emboutir /ɑ̃butiʀ/ **2** vt (Auto) crash into.

embraser (s') /(s)ɑ̃bʀaze/ **1** vpr catch fire.

embrasser /ɑ̃bʀase/ **1** vt kiss; (adopter, contenir) embrace. ■ s'~ vpr kiss.

embrayage /ɑ̃bʀɛjaʒ/ nm clutch. **embrayer** 🔢 vi engage the clutch.

embrouiller /ɑ̃bʀuje/ **1** vt confuse; (fils) tangle. ■ s'~ vpr become confused.

embryon /ɑ̃bʀijɔ̃/ nm embryo.

embûches /ɑ̃byʃ/ nfpl traps.

embuer (s') /(s)ɑ̃bɥe/ **1** vpr mist up.

embuscade /ɑ̃byskad/ nf ambush.

émeraude /ɛmʀod/ nf emerald.

émerger /emɛʀʒe/ 🔢 vi emerge; (fig) stand out.

émeri /ɛmʀi/ nm emery.

émerveillement /emɛʀvɛjmɑ̃/ nm amazement, wonder.

émerveiller /emɛʀveje/ **1** vt fill with wonder. ■ s'~ vpr marvel at.

émetteur /emɛtœʀ/ nm transmitter.

émettre /emɛtʀ/ 🔢 vt (son) produce; (message) send out; (timbre, billet) issue; (opinion) express.

émeute /emøt/ nf riot.

émietter /emjete/ **1** vt crumble. ■ s'~ vpr crumble.

émigrant, ~e /emigʁɑ̃, -t/ nm, f emigrant. **émigration** nf emigration. **émigrer** 1 vi emigrate.

émincer /emɛ̃se/ 10 vt cut into thin slices.

éminent, ~e /eminɑ̃, -t/ adj eminent.

émissaire /emisɛʀ/ nm emissary.

émission /emisjɔ̃/ nf (programme) programme; (de chaleur, gaz) emission; (de timbre) issue.

emmagasiner /ɑ̃magazine/ 1 vt store.

emmanchure /ɑ̃mɑ̃ʃyʀ/ nf armhole.

emmêler /ɑ̃mele/ 1 vt tangle. ■ s'~ vpr get mixed up.

emménager /ɑ̃menaʒe/ 40 vi move in; ~ **dans** move into.

emmener /ɑ̃mne/ 6 vt take; (comme prisonnier) take away.

emmerder /ɑ̃mɛʀde/ 1 ⊠ vt ~ **qn** get on sb's nerves. ■ s'~ vpr be bored.

emmitoufler /ɑ̃mitufle/ 1 vt wrap up warmly. ■ s'~ vpr wrap oneself up warmly.

émoi /emwa/ nm turmoil; (plaisir) excitement.

émotif, -ive /emotif, -v/ adj emotional. **émotion** nf emotion; (peur) fright. **émotionnel, ~le** adj emotional.

émousser /emuse/ 1 vt blunt.

émouvant, ~e /emuvɑ̃, -t/ adj moving.

empailler /ɑ̃paje/ 1 vt stuff.

empaqueter /ɑ̃pakte/ 38 vt package.

emparer (s') /(s)ɑ̃paʀe/ 1 vpr s'~ **de** get hold of.

empêchement /ɑ̃pɛʃmɑ̃/ nm **avoir un ~** to be held up.

empêcher /ɑ̃peʃe/ 1 vt prevent; ~ **de faire** prevent ou stop (from) doing; **(il) n'empêche**

que still. ■ s'~ vpr **il ne peut pas s'en ~** he cannot help it.

empereur /ɑ̃pʀœʀ/ nm emperor.

empester /ɑ̃pɛste/ 1 vt stink out; (essence) stink of. ●vi stink.

empêtrer (s') /(s)ɑ̃petʀe/ 1 vpr become entangled.

empiéter /ɑ̃pjete/ 14 vi ~ **sur** encroach upon.

empiffrer (s') /(s)ɑ̃pifʀe/ 1 vpr 1 stuff oneself.

empiler /ɑ̃pile/ 1 vt pile up. ■ s'~ vpr pile up.

empire /ɑ̃piʀ/ nm empire.

emplacement /ɑ̃plasmɑ̃/ nm site.

emplâtre /ɑ̃plɑtʀ/ nm (Méd) plaster.

emploi /ɑ̃plwa/ nm (travail) job; (embauche) employment; (utilisation) use; **un ~ de chauffeur** a job as a driver; ~ **du temps** timetable. **employé, ~e** nm, f employee.

employer /ɑ̃plwaje/ 31 vt (personne) employ; (utiliser) use. ■ s'~ vpr be used; **s'~ à** devote oneself to. **employeur, -euse** nm, f employer.

empoigner /ɑ̃pwaɲe/ 1 vt grab. ■ s'~ vpr come to blows.

empoisonnement /ɑ̃pwazɔnmɑ̃/ nm poisoning.

empoisonner /ɑ̃pwazɔne/ 1 vt poison; (embêter 1) annoy. ■ s'~ vpr to poison oneself.

emporter /ɑ̃pɔʀte/ 1 vt take (away); (entraîner) sweep away; (arracher) tear off. ■ s'~ vpr lose one's temper; **l'~** get the upper hand (**sur** of); **plat à ~** take-away.

empoté, ~e /ɑ̃pɔte/ adj clumsy.

empreinte /ɑ̃pʀɛ̃t/ nf mark; ~ **(digitale)** fingerprint; ~ **de pas** footprint.

empressé, ~e /ɑ̃pʀese/ adj eager, attentive.

empresser (s') /(s)ɑ̃pʀese/ 1 vpr s'~ **de** hasten to; **s'~ auprès**

de be attentive to.

emprise /ɑ̃pʀiz/ nf influence.

emprisonnement /ɑ̃pʀizɔnmɑ̃/ nm imprisonment. **emprisonner** ◼ vt imprison.

emprunt /ɑ̃pʀœ̃/ nm loan; **faire un ~** take out a loan.

emprunté, ~e /ɑ̃pʀœ̃te/ adj awkward.

emprunter /ɑ̃pʀœ̃te/ ◼ vt borrow (**à** from); (route) take; (fig) assume. **emprunteur, -euse** nm, f borrower.

ému, ~e /emy/ adj moved; (intimidé) nervous.

émule /emyl/ nmf imitator.

---

en /ɑ̃/

▷ Pour les expressions comme **en principe, en train de, s'en aller**, etc. ▷**principe, train, aller**, etc.

● préposition

····▸ (lieu) in.

····▸ (avec mouvement) to.

····▸ (temps) in.

····▸ (manière, état) in; **~ faisant** by ou while doing; **je t'appelle ~ rentrant** I will call you when I get back.

····▸ (en qualité de) as.

····▸ (transport) by.

····▸ (composition) made of; **table ~ bois** wooden table.

● pronom

····▸ **en avoir/vouloir** have/want some; **ne pas ~ avoir/vouloir** not have/want any; **j'~ ai deux** I've got two; **prends-~ plusieurs** take several; **il m'~ reste un** I have one left; **j'~ suis content** I am pleased with him/her/it/them; **je m'~ souviens** I remember it.

····▸ **~ êtes-vous sûr?** are you sure?

encadrement /ɑ̃kadʀəmɑ̃/ nm framing; (de porte) frame.
encadrer ◼ vt frame; (entourer

d'un trait) circle; (superviser) supervise.

encaisser /ɑ̃kese/ ◼ vt (argent) collect; (chèque) cash; (coups ◼) take.

encart /ɑ̃kaʀ/ nm **~ publicitaire** (advertising) insert.

en-cas* /ɑ̃kɑ/ nm (stand-by) snack.

encastré, ~e /ɑ̃kastʀe/ adj built-in.

encaustique /ɑ̃kɔstik/ nf wax polish.

enceinte /ɑ̃sɛ̃t/ adj f pregnant; **~ de 3 mois** 3 months pregnant. ●nf enclosure; **~ (acoustique)** speaker.

encens /ɑ̃sɑ̃/ nm incense.

encercler /ɑ̃sɛʀkle/ ◼ vt surround.

enchaînement* /ɑ̃ʃɛnmɑ̃/ nm (suite) chain; (d'idées) sequence.

enchaîner* /ɑ̃ʃene/ ◼ vt chain (up); (phrases) link (up). ●vi continue. ◼ **s'~** vpr follow on.

enchanté, ~e /ɑ̃ʃɑ̃te/ adj (ravi) delighted. **enchanter** ◼ vt delight; (ensorceler) enchant.

enchère /ɑ̃ʃɛʀ/ nf bid; **mettre** ou **vendre aux ~s** sell by auction.

enchevêtrer /ɑ̃ʃəvetʀe/ ◼ vt tangle. ◼ **s'~** vpr become tangled.

enclave /ɑ̃klav/ nf enclave.

enclencher /ɑ̃klɑ̃ʃe/ ◼ vt engage.

enclin, ~e /ɑ̃klɛ̃, -in/ adj **~ à** inclined to.

enclos /ɑ̃klo/ nm enclosure.

enclume /ɑ̃klym/ nf anvil.

encoche /ɑ̃kɔʃ/ nf notch.

encolure /ɑ̃kɔlyʀ/ nf neck.

encombrant, ~e /ɑ̃kɔ̃bʀɑ̃, -t/ adj cumbersome.

encombre /ɑ̃kɔ̃bʀ/ nm **sans ~** without any problems.

encombrement /ɑ̃kɔ̃bʀəmɑ̃/ nm (Auto) traffic congestion; (volume) bulk.

encombrer /ɑ̃kɔ̃bʀe/ 🛈 vt clutter (up); (obstruer) obstruct. ∎ s'∼ **de** vpr burden oneself with.

encontre: à l'∼ de /alɑ̃kɔ̃tʀədə/ loc against.

encore /ɑ̃kɔʀ/ adv (toujours) still; (de nouveau) again; (de plus) more; (aussi) also; ∼ **plus grand** even larger; ∼ **un café** another coffee; **pas** ∼ not yet; **si** ∼ if only; **et puis quoi** ∼? 🛈 what next?

encouragement /ɑ̃kuʀaʒmɑ̃/ nm encouragement. **encourager** 🛈 vt encourage.

encourir /ɑ̃kuʀiʀ/ 🛈 vt incur.

encrasser /ɑ̃kʀase/ 🛈 vt clog up (with dirt).

encre /ɑ̃kʀ/ nf ink. **encrier** nm ink-well.

encyclopédie /ɑ̃siklɔpedi/ nf encyclopaedia.

endettement /ɑ̃dɛtmɑ̃/ nm debt.

endetter /ɑ̃dete/ 🛈 vt put into debt. ∎ s'∼ vpr get into debt.

endiguer /ɑ̃dige/ 🛈 vt dam; (fig) curb.

endimanché, ∼e /ɑ̃dimɑ̃ʃe/ adj in one's Sunday best.

endive /ɑ̃div/ nf chicory.

endoctriner /ɑ̃dɔktʀine/ 🛈 vt indoctrinate.

endommager /ɑ̃dɔmaʒe/ 🛈 vt damage.

endormi, ∼e /ɑ̃dɔʀmi/ adj asleep; (apathique) sleepy.

endormir /ɑ̃dɔʀmiʀ/ 🛈 vt send to sleep; (médicalement) put to sleep; (duper) dupe (**avec** with). ∎ s'∼ vpr fall asleep.

endosser /ɑ̃dose/ 🛈 vt (vêtement) put on; (assumer) take on; (Comm) endorse.

endroit /ɑ̃dʀwa/ nm place; (de tissu) right side; **à l'∼** the right way round; **par ∼s** in places.

enduire /ɑ̃dɥiʀ/ 🛈 vt coat. **enduit** nm coating.

endurance /ɑ̃dyʀɑ̃s/ nf endurance. **endurant, ∼e** adj tough.

endurcir /ɑ̃dyʀsiʀ/ 🛈 vt strengthen. ∎ s'∼ vpr become hard (hardened).

endurer /ɑ̃dyʀe/ 🛈 vt endure.

énergétique /enɛʀʒetik/ adj energy; (food) high-calorie. **énergie** nf energy; (Tech) power. **énergique** adj energetic.

énervant, ∼e /enɛʀvɑ̃, -t/ adj irritating, annoying.

énerver /enɛʀve/ 🛈 vt irritate. ∎ s'∼ vpr get worked up.

enfance /ɑ̃fɑ̃s/ nf childhood; **la petite** ∼ infancy.

enfant /ɑ̃fɑ̃/ nmf child. **enfantillage** nm childishness. **enfantin, ∼e** adj simple, easy; (puéril) childish; (jeu, langage) children's.

enfer /ɑ̃fɛʀ/ nm (Relig) Hell; (fig) hell.

enfermer /ɑ̃fɛʀme/ 🛈 vt shut up. ∎ s'∼ vpr shut oneself up.

enfiler /ɑ̃file/ 🛈 vt (aiguille) thread; (vêtement) slip on; (rue) take.

enfin /ɑ̃fɛ̃/ adv (de soulagement) at last; (en dernier lieu) finally; (résignation, conclusion) well; ∼ **presque** well nearly.

enflammé, ∼e /ɑ̃flame/ adj (Méd) inflamed; (discours) fiery; (lettre) passionate.

enflammer /ɑ̃flame/ 🛈 vt set fire to. ∎ s'∼ vpr catch fire.

enfler /ɑ̃fle/ 🛈 vt (histoire) exaggerate. •vi (partie du corps) swell (up); (mer) swell; (rumeur, colère) spread. ∎ s'∼ vpr (colère) mount; (rumeur) grow.

enfoncer /ɑ̃fɔ̃se/ 🛈 vt (épingle) push ou drive in; (chapeau) push down; (porte) break down. •vi sink. ∎ s'∼ vpr sink (**dans** into).

enfouir /ɑ̃fwiʀ/ 🛈 vt bury.

enfourcher /ɑ̃fuʀʃe/ 🛈 vt mount.

enfreindre /ãfʀɛdʀ/ 22 vt
infringe, break.

enfuir (s') /(s)ãfɥiʀ/ 35 vpr
run away.

enfumé, ~e /ãfyme/ adj filled
with smoke.

engagé, ~e /ãɡaʒe/ adj
committed.

engagement /ãɡaʒmã/ nm
(promesse) promise; (Pol, Comm)
commitment.

engager /ãɡaʒe/ 40 vt (lier) bind,
commit; (embaucher) take on;
(commencer) start; (introduire) insert;
(investir) invest. ■ s'~ vpr
(promettre) commit oneself;
(commencer) start; (soldat) enlist;
(concurrent) enter; s'~ à faire
undertake to do; s'~ dans (voie)
enter.

engelure /ãʒlyʀ/ nf chilblain.

engendrer /ãʒãdʀe/ 1 vt (causer)
generate.

engin /ãʒɛ̃/ nm device; (véhicule)
vehicle; (missile) missile.

engloutir /ãɡlutiʀ/ 2 vt
swallow (up).

engouement /ãɡumã/ nm
passion.

engouffrer /ãɡufʀe/ 1 vt 1
gobble up. ■ s'~ dans vpr
rush in.

engourdir /ãɡuʀdiʀ/ 2 vt numb.
■ s'~ vpr go numb.

engrais /ãɡʀɛ/ nm manure;
(chimique) fertilizer.

engrenage /ãɡʀənaʒ/ nm gears (+
pl); (fig) spiral.

engueuler /ãɡœle/ 1 ⬛ vt shout
at. ■ s'~ vpr have a row.

enhardir (s') /(s)ãaʀdiʀ/ 2 vpr
become bolder.

énième /ɛnjɛm/ adj umpteenth.

énigmatique /enigmatik/ adj
enigmatic. **énigme** nf enigma;
(devinette) riddle.

enivrer /ãnivʀe/ 1 vt intoxicate.
■ s'~ vpr get intoxicated.

enjambée /ãʒãbe/ nf stride.
enjamber 1 vt step over;
(pont) span.

enjeu (pl ~x) /ãʒø/ nm stake.

enjoué, ~e /ãʒwe/ adj cheerful.

enlacer /ãlase/ 10 vt entwine.

enlèvement /ãlɛvmã/ nm (de
colis) removal; (d'ordures)
collection; (rapt) kidnapping.

enlever /ãlve/ 6 vt remove (à
from); (vêtement) take off; (tache,
organe) take out, remove;
(kidnapper) kidnap; (gagner) win.

enliser (s') /(s)ãlize/ 1 vpr get
bogged down.

enneigé, ~e /ãneʒe/ adj snow-
covered.

ennemi, ~e /ɛnmi/ adj & nm
enemy; ~ (fig) hostile to.

ennui /ãnɥi/ nm problem; (tracas)
boredom; **s'attirer des ~s** run
into trouble.

ennuyer /ãnɥije/ 31 vt bore;
(irriter) annoy; (préoccuper) worry;
si cela ne t'ennuie pas if you
don't mind. ■ s'~ vpr get bored.

ennuyeux, -euse /ãnɥijø, -z/ adj
boring; (fâcheux) annoying.

énoncé /enõse/ nm wording, text;
(Gram) utterance.

énoncer /enõse/ 10 vt express,
state.

enorgueillir (s') /(s)ãnɔʀɡœjiʀ/
2 vpr s'~ de pride oneself on.

énorme /enɔʀm/ adj enormous.

enquête /ãkɛt/ nf (Jur)
investigation, inquiry; (sondage)
survey; **mener l'~** lead the
inquiry. **enquêter** 1 vi ~ (sur)
investigate. **enquêteur**, -euse
nm, f investigator.

enquiquinant, ~e /ãkikinã, -t/
adj 1 irritating.

enraciné, ~e /ãʀasine/ adj deep
rooted.

enragé, ~e /ãʀaʒe/ adj furious;
(chien) rabid; (fig) fanatical.

enrager /ãʀaʒe/ 40 vi be furious;

faire ~ qn annoy sb.

enregistrement /ɑ̃ʀ(ə)ʒistʀəmɑ̃/ nm recording; (des bagages) check-in. **enregistrer** ◼ vt (Mus, TV) record; (mémoriser) take in; (bagages) check in.

enrhumer (s') /(s)ɑ̃ʀyme/ ◼ vpr catch a cold.

enrichir /ɑ̃ʀiʃiʀ/ ◪ vt enrich. ◼ s'~ vpr grow rich(er). **enrichissant, ~e** adj (expérience) rewarding.

enrober /ɑ̃ʀɔbe/ ◼ vt coat (**de** with).

enrôler /ɑ̃ʀole/ ◼ vt recruit. ◼ s'~ vpr enlist, enrol.

enroué, ~e /ɑ̃ʀwe/ adj hoarse.

enrouler /ɑ̃ʀule/ ◼ vt wind, wrap. ◼ s'~ vpr wind; **s'~ dans une couverture** roll oneself up in a blanket.

ensanglanté, ~e /ɑ̃sɑ̃glɑ̃te/ adj bloodstained.

enseignant, ~e /ɑ̃sɛɲɑ̃, -t/ nm, f teacher. ●adj teaching.

enseigne /ɑ̃sɛɲ/ nf sign.

enseignement /ɑ̃sɛɲəmɑ̃/ nm (profession) teaching; (instruction) education.

enseigner /ɑ̃seɲe/ ◼ vt/i teach; **~ qch à qn** teach sb sth.

ensemble /ɑ̃sɑ̃bl/ adv together. ●nm group; (Mus) ensemble; (vêtements) outfit; (cohésion) unity; (maths) set; **dans l'~** on the whole; **d'~** (idée) general; **l'~ de** (totalité) all of, the whole of.

ensevelir /ɑ̃səvliʀ/ ◪ vt bury.

ensoleillé, ~e /ɑ̃sɔleje/ adj sunny.

ensorceler /ɑ̃sɔʀsəle/ ◈◈ vt bewitch.

ensuite /ɑ̃sɥit/ adv next, then; (plus tard) later.

ensuivre (s') /(s)ɑ̃sɥivʀ/ ◈◈ vpr follow; **et tout ce qui s'ensuit** and all the rest of it.

entaille /ɑ̃taj/ nf cut; (profonde)

gash; (encoche) notch.

entamer /ɑ̃tame/ ◼ vt start; (inciser) cut into; (ébranler) shake.

entasser /ɑ̃tase/ ◼ vt (livres) pile; (argent) hoard; (personnes) cram (**dans** into). ◼ s'~ vpr (objets) pile up (**dans** into); (personnes) squeeze (**dans** into).

entendement /ɑ̃tɑ̃dmɑ̃/ nm understanding; **ça dépasse l'~** it's beyond belief.

entendre /ɑ̃tɑ̃dʀ/ ◈ vt hear; (comprendre) understand; (vouloir dire) mean; **~ dire que** hear that. ◼ s'~ vpr (être d'accord) agree; **s'~ (bien)** get on (**avec** with); **cela s'entend** of course.

entendu, ~e /ɑ̃tɑ̃dy/ adj (convenu) agreed; (sourire, air) knowing; **bien ~** of course; **(c'est) ~!** all right!

entente /ɑ̃tɑ̃t/ nf understanding; **bonne ~** good relationship.

enterrement /ɑ̃tɛʀmɑ̃/ nm funeral.

enterrer /ɑ̃teʀe/ ◼ vt bury.

en-tête /ɑ̃tɛt/ nm heading; **à ~** headed.

entêté, ~e /ɑ̃tete/ adj stubborn. **entêtement** nm stubbornness. **entêter (s')** ◼ vpr persist (**à, dans** in).

enthousiasme /ɑ̃tuzjasm/ nm enthusiasm. **enthousiasmer** ◼ vt fill with enthusiasm. **enthousiaste** adj enthusiastic.

enticher (s') /(s)ɑ̃tiʃe/ ◼ vpr **s'~ de** become infatuated with.

entier, -ière /ɑ̃tje, -jɛʀ/ adj whole; (absolu) absolute; (entêté) unyielding. ●nm whole; **en ~** entirely.

entonnoir /ɑ̃tɔnwaʀ/ nm funnel; (trou) crater.

entorse /ɑ̃tɔʀs/ nf sprain; (fig) **~ à** (loi) infringement of.

entortiller /ɑ̃tɔʀtije/ ◼ vt wind, wrap (**autour** around); (duper ◼) get round.

entourage /ɑ̃tuʀaʒ/ nm circle of family and friends; (bordure) surround.

entouré, ~e /ɑ̃tuʀe/ adj (personne) supported.

entourer /ɑ̃tuʀe/ **1** vt surround (**de** with); (réconforter) rally round; **~ qch de mystère** shroud sth in mystery.

entracte /ɑ̃tʀakt/ nm interval.

entraide /ɑ̃tʀɛd/ nf mutual aid. **entraider (s')** **1** vpr help each other.

entrain /ɑ̃tʀɛ̃/ nm zest, spirit.

entraînement* /ɑ̃tʀɛnmɑ̃/ nm (Sport) training.

entraîner* /ɑ̃tʀene/ **1** vt (emporter) carry away; (provoquer) lead to; (Sport) train; (actionner) drive. ∎ **s'~** vpr train. **entraîneur*** nm trainer.

entrave /ɑ̃tʀav/ nf hindrance. **entraver** **1** vt hinder.

entre /ɑ̃tʀ(ə)/ prép between; (parmi) among(st); **~ autres** among other things; **l'un d'~ nous/ eux** one of us/them.

entrebâillé, ~e /ɑ̃tʀəbaje/ adj ajar, half-open.

entrechoquer (s') /(s)ɑ̃tʀəʃɔke/ **1** vpr knock against each other.

entrecôte /ɑ̃tʀəkot/ nf rib steak.

entrecouper /ɑ̃tʀəkupe/ **1** vt **~ de** intersperse with.

entrecroiser (s') /(s)ɑ̃tʀəkʀwaze/ **1** vpr (routes) intertwine.

entrée /ɑ̃tʀe/ nf entrance; (vestibule) hall; (accès) admission, entry; (billet) ticket; (Culin) starter; (Ordinat) **tapez sur E~** press Enter; '**~ interdite**' 'no entry'.

entrejambes /ɑ̃tʀəʒɑ̃b/ nm crotch.

entremets /ɑ̃tʀəmɛ/ nm dessert.

entremise /ɑ̃tʀəmiz/ nf intervention; **par l'~ de** through.

entreposer /ɑ̃tʀəpoze/ **1** vt store.

entrepôt /ɑ̃tʀəpo/ nm warehouse.

entreprenant, ~e /ɑ̃tʀəpʀənɑ̃, -t/ adj (actif) enterprising; (séducteur) forward.

entreprendre /ɑ̃tʀəpʀɑ̃dʀ/ **50** vt start on, undertake; (personne) buttonhole; **~ de faire** undertake to do.

entrepreneur /ɑ̃tʀəpʀənœʀ/ nm (de bâtiment) contractor; (chef d'entreprise) firm manager.

entreprise /ɑ̃tʀəpʀiz/ nf (projet) undertaking; (société) firm, business, company.

entrer /ɑ̃tʀe/ **1** vi (aux être) go in, enter; (venir) come in, enter; **~ dans** go ou come into, enter; (club) join; **~ en collision** collide (**avec** with); **faire ~** (personne) show in; **laisser ~** let in; **~ en guerre** go to war. ∎vt (données) enter.

entre-temps* /ɑ̃tʀətɑ̃/ adv meanwhile.

entretenir /ɑ̃tʀət(ə)niʀ/ **58** vt (appareil) maintain; (vêtement) look after; (alimenter) (feu) keep going; (amitié) keep alive; **~ qn de** converse with sb about. ∎ **s'~** vpr speak (**de** about; **avec** to). **entretien** nm maintenance; (discussion) talk; (pour un emploi) interview.

entrevoir /ɑ̃tʀəvwaʀ/ **63** vt make out; (brièvement) glimpse.

entrevue /ɑ̃tʀəvy/ nf meeting.

entrouvert, ~e /ɑ̃tʀuvɛʀ, -t/ adj ajar, half-open.

énumération /enymeʀasjɔ̃/ nf enumeration. **énumérer** **14** vt enumerate.

envahir /ɑ̃vaiʀ/ **2** vt invade, overrun; (douleur, peur) overcome.

enveloppe /ɑ̃vlɔp/ nf envelope; (emballage) wrapping; **~ budgétaire** budget. **envelopper** **1** vt wrap (up); (fig) envelop.

envergure /ɑ̃vɛʀgyʀ/ nf

wingspan; (importance) scope; (qualité) calibre.

envers /ɑ̃vɛʀ/ prép toward(s), to. • nm (de tissu) wrong side; **à l'~** (tableau) upside down; (devant derrière) back to front; (chaussette) inside out.

envie /ɑ̃vi/ nf urge; (jalousie) envy; **avoir ~ de qch** feel like sth; **avoir ~ de faire** want to do; (moins urgent) feel like doing; **faire ~ à qn** make sb envious.

envier /ɑ̃vje/ 45 vt envy. **envieux, -ieuse** adj envious.

environ /ɑ̃viʀɔ̃/ adv about.

environnant, ~e /ɑ̃viʀɔnɑ̃, -t/ adj surrounding.

environnement /ɑ̃viʀɔnmɑ̃/ nm environment.

environs /ɑ̃viʀɔ̃/ nmpl vicinity; **aux ~ de** (lieu) in the vicinity of; (heure) round about.

envisager /ɑ̃vizaʒe/ 40 vt consider; (imaginer) envisage; **~ de faire** consider doing.

envoi /ɑ̃vwa/ nm dispatch; (paquet) consignment; **faire un ~** send; **coup d'~** (Sport) kick-off.

envoler (s') /(s)ɑ̃vɔle/ 1 vpr fly away; (avion) take off; (papiers) blow away.

envoyé, ~e /ɑ̃vwaje/ nm, f envoy; **~ spécial** special correspondent.

envoyer /ɑ̃vwaje/ 32 vt send; (lancer) throw.

éolienne /eɔljɛn/ nf windmill; **ferme d'~s** wind farm.

épais, ~se /epɛ, -s/ adj thick. **épaisseur** nf thickness.

épaissir /epesiʀ/ 2 vt/i thicken. ■ **s'~** vpr thicken; (mystère) deepen.

épanoui, ~e /epanwi/ adj (personne) beaming, radiant.

épanouir (s') /(s)epanwiʀ/ 2 vpr (fleur) open out; (visage) beam; (personne) blossom.

épanouissement nm (éclat) blossoming, full bloom.

épargne /epaʀɲ/ nf savings.

épargner /epaʀɲe/ 1 vt/i save; (ne pas tuer) spare; **~ qch à qn** spare sb sth.

éparpiller /epaʀpije/ 1 vt scatter. ■ **s'~** vpr scatter; (fig) dissipate one's efforts.

épars, ~e /epaʀ, -s/ adj scattered.

épatant, ~e /epatɑ̃, -t/ adj 1 amazing.

épaule /epol/ nf shoulder.

épave /epav/ nf wreck.

épée /epe/ nf sword.

épeler /ɛple/ 6 vt spell.

éperdu, ~e /epɛʀdy/ adj wild, frantic.

éperon /epʀɔ̃/ nm spur.

éphémère /efemɛʀ/ adj ephemeral.

épi /epi/ nm (de blé) ear; (mèche) tuft of hair; **~ de maïs** corn cob.

épice /epis/ nf spice. **épicé, ~e** adj spicy.

épicerie /episʀi/ nf grocery shop; (produits) groceries. **épicier, -ière** nm, f grocer.

épidémie /epidemi/ nf epidemic.

épiderme /epidɛʀm/ nm skin.

épier /epje/ 45 vt spy on.

épilepsie /epilɛpsi/ nf epilepsy. **épileptique** adj & nmf epileptic.

épiler /epile/ 1 vt remove unwanted hair from; (sourcils) pluck.

épilogue /epilɔg/ nm epilogue; (fig) outcome.

épinard /epinaʀ/ nm **~s** spinach (+ sg).

épine /epin/ nf thorn, prickle; (d'animal) prickle, spine; **~ dorsale** backbone. **épineux, -euse** adj thorny.

épingle /epɛ̃gl/ nf pin; **~ de**

nourrice, ∼ **de sûreté** safety-pin.

épisode /epizɔd/ nm episode; **à** ∼**s** serialized.

épitaphe /epitaf/ nf epitaph.

épluche-légumes /eplyʃlegym/ nm inv (potato) peeler.

éplucher /eplyʃe/ **1** vt peel; (examiner, fig) scrutinize.

épluchure /eplyʃyʀ/ nf ∼**s** peelings.

éponge /epɔ̃ʒ/ nf sponge. **éponger** **40** vt (liquide) mop up; (surface, front) mop; (fig) (dettes) wipe out.

épopée /epɔpe/ nf epic.

époque /epɔk/ nf time, period; **à l'**∼ at the time; **d'**∼ period.

épouse /epuz/ nf wife.

épouser /epuze/ **1** vt marry; (forme, idée) adopt.

épousseter /epuste/ **38** vt dust.

épouvantable /epuvɑ̃tabl/ adj appalling.

épouvantail /epuvɑ̃taj/ nm scarecrow.

épouvante /epuvɑ̃t/ nf terror. **épouvanter** **1** vt terrify.

époux /epu/ nm husband; **les** ∼ the married couple.

éprendre (s') /(s)epʀɑ̃dʀ/ **50** vpr **s'**∼ **de** fall in love with.

épreuve /epʀœv/ nf test; (Sport) event; (malheur) ordeal; (Photo, d'imprimerie) proof; **mettre à l'**∼ put to the test.

éprouver /epʀuve/ **1** vt (ressentir) experience; (affliger) distress; (tester) test.

éprouvette /epʀuvɛt/ nf test tube.

EPS abrév f (**éducation physique et sportive**) PE.

épuisé, ∼**e** /epɥize/ adj exhausted; (livre) out of print. **épuisement** nm exhaustion.

épuiser /epɥize/ **1** vt (fatiguer, user)

exhaust. ∎ **s'**∼ vpr become exhausted.

épuration /epyʀasjɔ̃/ nf purification; (Pol) purge. **épurer** **1** vt purify; (Pol) purge.

équateur /ekwatœʀ/ nm equator.

équilibre /ekilibʀ/ nm balance; **être** ou **se tenir en** ∼ (personne) balance; (objet) be balanced. **équilibré**, ∼**e** adj well-balanced.

équilibrer /ekilibʀe/ **1** vt balance. ∎ **s'**∼ vpr balance each other.

équilibriste /ekilibʀist/ nmf acrobat.

équipage /ekipaʒ/ nm crew.

équipe /ekip/ nf team; ∼ **de nuit/jour** night/day shift.

équipé, ∼**e** /ekipe/ adj equipped; **cuisine** ∼**e** fitted kitchen.

équipement /ekipmɑ̃/ nm equipment; ∼**s** (installations) amenities, facilities.

équiper /ekipe/ **1** vt equip (**de** with). ∎ **s'**∼ vpr equip oneself.

équipier, -ière /ekipje, -jɛʀ/ nm, f team member.

équitable /ekitabl/ adj fair.

équitation /ekitasjɔ̃/ nf (horse-) riding.

équivalence /ekivalɑ̃s/ nf equivalence. **équivalent**, ∼**e** adj equivalent.

équivaloir /ekivalwaʀ/ **60** vi ∼ **à** be equivalent to.

équivoque /ekivɔk/ adj equivocal; (louche) questionable. ∎ nf ambiguity.

érable /eʀabl/ nm maple.

érafler /eʀafle/ **1** vt scratch. **éraflure** nf scratch.

éraillé, ∼**e** /eʀaje/ adj (voix) raucous.

ère /ɛʀ/ nf era.

éreintant, ∼**e** /eʀɛ̃tɑ̃, -t/ adj exhausting. **éreinter (s')** **1** vpr wear oneself out.

e

ériger /eʁiʒe/ 40 vt erect. ■ s'~ **en** vpr set (oneself) up as.

éroder /eʁɔde/ 1 vt erode. **érosion** nf erosion.

errer /eʁe/ 1 vi wander.

erreur /eʁœʁ/ nf mistake, error; **dans l'~** mistaken; **par ~** by mistake; **~ judiciaire** miscarriage of justice.

erroné, ~e /eʁɔne/ adj erroneous.

érudit, ~e /eʁydi, -t/ adj scholarly. ●nm, f scholar.

éruption /eʁypsjɔ̃/ nf eruption; (Méd) rash.

es /ɛ/ ▸ÊTRE 4.

escabeau (pl ~x) /ɛskabo/ nm step-ladder.

escadron /ɛskadʁɔ̃/ nm (Mil) company.

escalade /ɛskalad/ nf climbing; (Pol, Comm) escalation. **escalader** 1 vt climb.

escale /ɛskal/ nf (d'avion) stopover; (port) port of call; **faire ~ à** (avion, passager) stop over at; (navire, passager) put in at.

escalier /ɛskalje/ nm stairs (+ pl); **~ mécanique** ou **roulant** escalator.

escalope /ɛskalɔp/ nf escalope.

escargot /ɛskaʁgo/ nm snail.

escarpé, ~e /ɛskaʁpe/ adj steep.

escarpin /ɛskaʁpɛ̃/ nm court shoe; (US) pump.

escient: à bon ~ /abɔnesjɑ̃/ loc wisely.

esclandre /ɛsklɑ̃dʁ/ nm scene.

esclavage /ɛsklavaʒ/ nm slavery. **esclave** nmf slave.

escompte /ɛskɔ̃t/ nm discount. **escompter** 1 vt expect; (Comm) discount.

escorte /ɛskɔʁt/ nf escort.

escrime /ɛskʁim/ nf fencing.

escroc /ɛskʁo/ nm swindler.

escroquer /ɛskʁɔke/ 1 vt

swindle; **~ qch à qn** swindle sb out of sth. **escroquerie** nf swindle.

espace /ɛspas/ nm space; **~s verts** gardens and parks.

espacer /ɛspase/ 10 vt space out. ■ s'~ vpr become less frequent.

espadrille /ɛspadʁij/ nf rope sandal.

Espagne /ɛspaɲ/ nf Spain.

espagnol, ~e /ɛspaɲɔl/ adj Spanish. ●nm (Ling) Spanish. E~, ~e nm, f Spaniard.

espèce /ɛspɛs/ nf kind, sort; (race) species; **en ~s** (argent) in cash; **~ d'idiot!** 🔲 you idiot! 🔲.

espérance /ɛspeʁɑ̃s/ nf hope.

espérer /ɛspeʁe/ 14 vt hope for; **~ faire/que** hope to do/that. ●vi hope.

espiègle /ɛspjɛgl/ adj mischievous.

espion, ~ne /ɛspjɔ̃, -ɔn/ nm, f spy. **espionnage** nm espionage, spying. **espionner** 1 vt spy (on).

espoir /ɛspwaʁ/ nm hope; **reprendre ~** feel hopeful again.

esprit /ɛspʁi/ nm (intellect) mind; (humour) wit; (fantôme) spirit; (ambiance) atmosphere; **perdre l'~** lose one's mind; **reprendre ses ~s** come to; **faire de l'~** try to be witty.

esquimau, ~de (mpl ~x) /ɛskimo, -d/ nm, f Eskimo.

esquinter /ɛskɛ̃te/ 1 vt 🔲 ruin.

esquisse /ɛskis/ nf sketch; (fig) outline.

esquiver /ɛskive/ 1 vt dodge. ■ s'~ vpr slip away.

essai /ese/ nm (épreuve) test, trial; (tentative) try; (article) essay; (au rugby) try; **~s** (Auto) qualifying round (+ sg); **à l'~** on trial.

essaim /esɛ̃/ nm swarm.

essayage /esejaʒ/ nm fitting; **salon d'~** fitting room.

essayer /eseje/ 31 vt/i try;

(vêtement) try (on); (voiture) try (out); ~ **de faire** try to do.

essence /esɑ̃s/ nf (carburant) petrol; (nature, extrait) essence; ~ **sans plomb** unleaded petrol.

essentiel, ~**le** /esɑ̃sjɛl/ adj essential. •nm l'~ the main thing; (quantité) the main part.

essieu (pl ~**x**) /esjø/ nm axle.

essor /esɔʀ/ nm expansion; **prendre son** ~ expand.

essorage /esɔʀaʒ/ nm spin drying. **essorer** 1 vt (linge) spin-dry; (en tordant) wring.

essoreuse /esɔʀøz/ nf spin-drier; ~ **à salade** salad spinner.

essoufflé, ~**e** /esufle/ adj out of breath.

essuie-glace /esɥiglas/ nm inv windscreen wiper.

essuie-mains* /esɥimɛ̃/ nm inv hand-towel.

essuie-tout /esɥitu/ nm inv kitchen paper.

essuyer /esɥije/ 31 vt wipe; (subir) suffer. ■ s'~ vpr dry ou wipe oneself.

est[1] /ɛ/ ▷ÊTRE 4.

est[2] /ɛst/ nm east. •adj inv east; (partie) eastern; (direction) easterly.

estampe /ɛstɑ̃p/ nf print.

esthète /ɛstɛt/ nmf aesthete.

esthéticienne /ɛstetisjɛn/ nf beautician.

esthétique /ɛstetik/ adj aesthetic.

estimation /ɛstimasjɔ̃/ nf (de coûts) estimate; (valeur) valuation.

estime /ɛstim/ nf esteem.

estimer /ɛstime/ 1 vt (tableau) value; (calculer) estimate; (respecter) esteem; (considérer) consider (**que** that).

estival, ~**e** (mpl -**aux**) /ɛstival, -o/ adj summer. **estivant,** ~**e** nm, f summer visitor.

estomac /ɛstɔma/ nm stomach.

estomaqué, ~**e** /ɛstɔmake/ adj 🗓 stunned.

Estonie /ɛstɔni/ nf Estonia.

estrade /ɛstʀad/ nf platform.

estragon /ɛstʀagɔ̃/ nm tarragon.

estropié, ~**e** /ɛstʀɔpje/ nm, f cripple. •adj crippled.

estuaire /ɛstɥɛʀ/ nm estuary.

et /e/ conj and; ~ **moi?** what about me?; ~ **alors?** so what?

étable /etabl/ nf cow-shed.

établi, ~**e** /etabli/ adj established; **un fait bien** ~ a well-established fact. •nm work-bench.

établir /etablir/ 2 vt establish; (liste, facture) draw up; (personne, camp, record) set up. ■ s'~ vpr (personne) settle; **s'~ à son compte** set up on one's own.

établissement /etablismɑ̃/ nm (entreprise) organization; (institution) establishment; ~ **scolaire** school.

étage /etaʒ/ nm floor, storey; (de fusée) stage; **à l'~** upstairs; **au premier** ~ on the first floor.

étagère /etaʒɛʀ/ nf shelf; (meuble) shelving unit.

étain /etɛ̃/ nm pewter.

étais, était /etɛ/ ▷ÊTRE 4.

étalage /etalaʒ/ nm display; (vitrine) shop-window; **faire** ~ **de** flaunt. **étalagiste** nmf window-dresser.

étaler /etale/ 1 vt spread; (journal) spread (out); (pâte) roll out; (exposer) display; (richesse) flaunt. ■ s'~ vpr (prendre de la place) spread out; (tomber 🗓) fall flat; **s'~ sur** (paiement) be spread over.

étalon /etalɔ̃/ nm (cheval) stallion; (modèle) standard.

étanche /etɑ̃ʃ/ adj watertight; (montre) waterproof.

étancher /etɑ̃ʃe/ 1 vt (soif) quench.

étang /etɑ̃/ nm pond.

étant /etɑ̃/ ▷ÊTRE 🖪.

étape /etap/ nf stage; (lieu d'arrêt) stopover; (fig) stage.

état /eta/ nm state; (liste) statement; (métier) profession; **en bon/mauvais ∼** in good/bad condition; **en ∼ de** in a position to; **en ∼ de marche** in working order; **faire ∼ de** (citer) mention; **être dans tous ses ∼s** be in a state; **∼ civil** civil status; **∼ des lieux** inventory of fixtures. **État** nm State.

état-major (pl **états-majors**) /etamaʒɔʀ/ nm (officiers) staff (+ pl).

États-Unis /etazyni/ nmpl **∼ (d'Amérique)** United States (of America).

étau (pl **∼x**) /eto/ nm vice.

étayer /eteje/ 🟤 vt prop up.

été¹ /ete/ ▷ÊTRE 🖪.

été² /ete/ nm summer.

éteindre /etɛ̃dʀ/ 🟤 vt (feu) put out; (lumière, radio) turn off. ∎**s'∼** vpr (feu, lumière) go out; (appareil) go off; (mourir) die. **éteint, ∼e** adj (feu) out; (volcan) extinct.

étendard /etɑ̃daʀ/ nm standard.

étendre /etɑ̃dʀ/ 🟤 vt (nappe) spread (out); (bras, jambes) stretch (out); (linge) hang out; (agrandir) extend. ∎**s'∼** vpr (s'allonger) lie down; (se propager) spread; (plaine) stretch; **s'∼ sur** (sujet) dwell on.

étendu, ∼e /etɑ̃dy/ adj extensive. **étendue** nf area; (d'eau) stretch; (importance) extent.

éternel, ∼le /etɛʀnɛl/ adj (vie) eternal; (fig) endless.

éterniser (s') /(s)etɛʀnize/ 🟤 vpr (durer) drag on.

éternité /etɛʀnite/ nf eternity.

éternuement /etɛʀnymɑ̃/ nm sneeze. **éternuer** 🟤 vi sneeze.

êtes /ɛt/ ▷ÊTRE 🖪.

éthique /etik/ adj ethical. ∎nf ethics (+ sg).

ethnie /ɛtni/ nf ethnic group. **ethnique** adj ethnic.

étincelant, ∼e /etɛ̃slɑ̃, -t/ adj sparkling. **étinceler** 🟤 vi sparkle. **étincelle** nf spark.

étiqueter /etikte/ 🟤 vt label. **étiquette** nf label; (protocole) etiquette.

étirer /etiʀe/ 🟤 vt stretch. ∎**s'∼** vpr stretch.

étoffe /etɔf/ nf fabric.

étoffer /etɔfe/ 🟤 vt expand. ∎**s'∼** vpr fill out.

étoile /etwal/ nf star; **à la belle ∼** in the open; **∼ filante** shooting star; **∼ de mer** starfish.

étonnant, ∼e /etɔnɑ̃, -t/ adj (curieux) surprising; (formidable) amazing. **étonnement** nm surprise; (plus fort) amazement.

étonner /etɔne/ 🟤 vt amaze. ∎**s'∼** vpr be amazed (**de** at).

étouffant, ∼e /etufɑ̃, -t/ adj stifling.

étouffer /etufe/ 🟤 vt/i suffocate; (sentiment, révolte) stifle; (feu) smother; (bruit) muffle; **on étouffe** it is stifling. ∎**s'∼** vpr suffocate; (en mangeant) choke.

étourderie /etuʀdəʀi/ nf thoughtlessness; (acte) careless mistake.

étourdi, ∼e /etuʀdi/ adj absent-minded. ∎nm, f scatterbrain.

étourdir /etuʀdiʀ/ 🟤 vt stun; (fatiguer) make sb's head spin. **étourdissant, ∼e** adj stunning.

étourneau (pl **∼x**) /etuʀno/ nm starling.

étrange /etʀɑ̃ʒ/ adj strange.

étranger, -ère /etʀɑ̃ʒe, -ɛʀ/ adj (inconnu) strange, unfamiliar; (d'un autre pays) foreign. ∎nm, f foreigner; (inconnu) stranger; **à l'∼** abroad; **de l'∼** from abroad.

étrangler /etʀɑ̃gle/ 🟤 vt strangle; (col) throttle. ∎**s'∼** vpr choke.

être /ɛtʀ/ 4
● verbe auxiliaire
••••▸ (du passé) have; **elle est partie/venue hier** she left/came yesterday.
••••▸ (de la voix passive) be.
● verbe intransitif (aux avoir)
••••▸ be; **~ médecin** be a doctor; **je suis à vous** I'm all yours; **j'en suis à me demander si...** I'm beginning to wonder whether...; **qu'en est-il de...?** what's the news about...?
••••▸ (appartenance) be, belong to.
••••▸ (heure, date) be; **nous sommes le 3 mars** it's March 3.
••••▸ (aller) be; **je n'y ai jamais été** I've never been; **il a été le voir** he went to see him.
••••▸ **c'est** it is or it's; **c'est moi qui l'ai fait** I did it; **est-ce que tu veux du thé?** do you want some tea?
● nom masculin
••••▸ being; **~ humain** human being.
••••▸ (personne) person; **un ~ cher** a loved one.

étreindre /etʀɛ̃dʀ/ 22 vt embrace. **étreinte** nf embrace.

étrennes /etʀɛn/ nfpl (New Year's) gift (+ sg); (argent) money.

étrier /etʀije/ nm stirrup.

étriqué, ~e /etʀike/ adj tight.

étroit, ~e /etʀwa, -t/ adj narrow; (vêtement) tight; (liens, surveillance) close; **à l'~** cramped. **étroitement** adv closely. **étroitesse** nf narrowness.

étude /etyd/ nf study; (enquête) survey; (bureau) office; **(salle d')~** (Scol) prep room; **à l'~** under consideration; **faire des ~s (de)** study; **il n'a pas fait d'~s** he didn't go to university; **~ de marché** market research.

étudiant, ~e /etydjɑ̃, -t/ nm, f student.

étudier /etydje/ 45 vt/i study.

étui /etɥi/ nm case.

étuve /etyv/ nf steam room.

eu, ~e /y/ ▷AVOIR 5.

euro /øʀo/ nm euro.

Europe /øʀɔp/ nf Europe.

européen, ~ne /øʀɔpeɛ̃, -ɛn/ adj European. **E~, ~ne** nm, f European.

euthanasie /øtanazi/ nf euthanasia.

eux /ø/ pron they; (complément) them. **eux-mêmes** pron themselves.

évacuation /evakɥasjɔ̃/ nf evacuation; (d'eaux usées) discharge. **évacuer** 1 vt evacuate.

évadé, ~e /evade/ adj escaped. ● nm, f escaped prisoner. **évader (s')** 1 vpr escape.

évaluation /evalɥasjɔ̃/ nf assessment. **évaluer** 1 vt assess.

évangile /evɑ̃ʒil/ nm gospel; **l'É~** the Gospel.

évanouir (s') /(s)evanwiʀ/ 2 vpr faint; (disparaître) vanish.

évaporation /evapɔʀasjɔ̃/ nf evaporation. **évaporer (s')** 1 vpr evaporate.

évasif, -ive /evazif, -v/ adj evasive.

évasion /evazjɔ̃/ nf escape.

éveil /evɛj/ nm awakening; **en ~** alert.

éveillé, ~e /eveje/ adj awake; (intelligent) alert.

éveiller /eveje/ 1 vt awake(n); (susciter) arouse. ■ **s'~** vpr awake.

événement* /evɛnmɑ̃/ nm event.

éventail /evɑ̃taj/ nm fan; (gamme) range.

éventrer /evɑ̃tʀe/ 1 vt (sac) rip open.

éventualité /evɑ̃tɥalite/ nf possibility; **dans cette ~** in that event.

e

éventuel, ∼le /evãtɥɛl/ adj
possible. **éventuellement** adv
possibly.

évêque /evɛk/ nm bishop.

évertuer (s') /(s)evɛʀtɥe/ 1 vpr
s'∼ à struggle hard to.

éviction /eviksjɔ̃/ nf eviction.

évidemment /evidamã/ adv
obviously; (bien sûr) of course.

évidence /evidãs/ nf obviousness;
(fait) obvious fact; **être en ∼** be
conspicuous; **mettre en ∼** (fait)
highlight. **évident, ∼e** adj
obvious, evident.

évier /evje/ nm sink.

évincer /evɛ̃se/ 10 vt oust.

éviter /evite/ 1 vt avoid (**de
faire** doing); **∼ qch à qn**
(dérangement) save sb sth.

évocateur, -trice /evɔkatœʀ,
-tʀis/ adj evocative. **évocation** nf
evocation.

évolué, ∼e /evɔlɥe/ adj highly
developed.

évoluer /evɔlɥe/ 1 vi evolve;
(situation) develop; (se déplacer)
glide. **évolution** nf evolution;
(d'une situation) development.

évoquer /evɔke/ 1 vt call to
mind, evoke.

exacerber /ɛgzasɛʀbe/ 1 vt
exacerbate.

exact, ∼e /ɛgza(kt), -akt/ adj
(précis) exact, accurate; (juste)
correct; (personne) punctual.
exactement adv exactly.
exactitude nf exactness;
punctuality.

ex æquo /ɛgzeko/ adv **être ∼** tie
(**avec qn** with sb).

exagération /ɛgzaʒeʀasjɔ̃/ nf
exaggeration. **exagéré, ∼e** adj
excessive.

exagérer /ɛgzaʒeʀe/ 14 vt/i
exaggerate; (abuser) go too far.

exalté, ∼e /ɛgzalte/ nm, f fanatic.
exalter 1 vt excite; (glorifier)
exalt.

examen /ɛgzamɛ̃/ nm
examination; (Scol) exam.
examinateur, -trice nm, f
examiner. **examiner** 1 vt
examine.

exaspération /ɛgzaspeʀasjɔ̃/ nf
exasperation. **exaspérer** 14 vt
exasperate.

exaucer /ɛgzose/ 10 vt grant;
(personne) grant the wish(es) of.

excédent /ɛksedã/ nm surplus; **∼
de bagages** excess luggage; **∼
de la balance commerciale**
trade surplus. **excédentaire** adj
excess, surplus.

excéder /ɛksede/ 14 vt (dépasser)
exceed; (agacer) irritate.

excellence /ɛksɛlãs/ nf
excellence. **excellent, ∼e** adj
excellent. **exceller** 1 vi excel
(**dans** in).

excentricité /ɛksãtʀisite/ nf
eccentricity. **excentrique** adj &
nmf eccentric.

excepté, ∼e /ɛksɛpte/ adj & prép
except.

excepter /ɛksɛpte/ 1 vt except.

exception /ɛksɛpsjɔ̃/ nf
exception; **à l'∼ de** except for;
d'∼ exceptional; **faire ∼** be an
exception. **exceptionnel, ∼le**
adj exceptional.
exceptionnellement adv
exceptionally.

excès /ɛksɛ/ nm excess; **∼ de
vitesse** speeding.

excessif, -ive /ɛksesif, -v/ adj
excessive.

excitant, ∼e /ɛksitã, -t/ adj
stimulating; (palpitant) exciting.
● nm stimulant.

exciter /ɛksite/ 1 vt excite; (irriter)
get excited. ■ s'∼ vpr get excited.

exclamer (s') /(s)ɛksklame/ 1
vpr exclaim.

exclure /ɛksklyʀ/ 16 vt exclude;
(expulser) expel; (empêcher)
preclude.

exclusif, -ive /ɛksklyzif, -v/ adj exclusive.

exclusion /ɛksklyzjɔ̃/ nf exclusion.

exclusivité /ɛksklyzivite/ nf (Comm) exclusive rights (+ pl); **projeter en ~** show exclusively.

excursion /ɛkskyRsjɔ̃/ nf excursion; (à pied) hike.

excuse /ɛkskyz/ nf excuse; ~s apology (+ sg); **faire des ~s** apologize.

excuser /ɛkskyze/ ◻ vt excuse; **excusez-moi** excuse me. ■ s'~ vpr apologize (**de** for).

exécrable /ɛgzekRabl/ adj dreadful. **exécrer** ◻ vt loathe.

exécuter /ɛgzekyte/ ◻ vt carry out, execute; (Mus) perform; (tuer) execute.

exécutif, -ive /ɛgzekytif, -v/ adj & nm (Pol) executive.

exécution /ɛgzekysjɔ̃/ nf execution; (Mus) performance.

exemplaire /ɛgzãplɛR/ adj exemplary. ● nm copy.

exemple /ɛgzãpl/ nm example; **par ~** for example; **donner l'~** set an example.

exempt, ~e /ɛgzã, -t/ adj ~ **de** exempt (**de** from).

exempter /ɛgzãte/ ◻ vt exempt (**de** from). **exemption** nf exemption.

exercer /ɛgzɛRse/ ◻ vt exercise; (influence, contrôle) exert; (former) train, exercise; ~ **un métier** have a job; ~ **le métier de...** work as a... ■ s'~ vpr practise.

exercice /ɛgzɛRsis/ nm exercise; (de métier) practice; **en ~** in office; (médecin) in practice.

exhaler /ɛgzale/ ◻ vt emit.

exhaustif, -ive /ɛgzostif, -v/ adj exhaustive.

exhiber /ɛgzibe/ ◻ vt exhibit.

exhorter /ɛgzɔRte/ ◻ vt exhort (**à** to).

exigeant, ~e /ɛgziʒã, -t/ adj demanding; **être ~ avec qn** demand a lot of sb. **exigence** nf demand. **exiger** ◻ vt demand.

exigu, ~ë* /ɛgzigy/ adj tiny.

exil /ɛgzil/ nm exile. **exilé, ~e** nm, f exile.

exiler /ɛgzile/ ◻ vt exile. ■ s'~ vpr go into exile.

existence /ɛgzistãs/ nf existence. **exister** ◻ vi exist.

exode /ɛgzɔd/ nm exodus.

exonérer /ɛgzɔneRe/ ◻ vt exempt (**de** from).

exorbitant, ~e /ɛgzɔRbitã, -t/ adj exorbitant.

exorciser /ɛgzɔRsize/ ◻ vt exorcize.

exotique /ɛgzɔtik/ adj exotic.

expansé, ~e /ɛkspãse/ adj (Tech) expanded.

expansif, -ive /ɛkspãsif, -v/ adj expansive. **expansion** nf expansion.

expatrié, ~e /ɛkspatRije/ nm, f expatriate.

expectative /ɛkspɛktativ/ nf **être dans l'~** wait and see.

expédient /ɛkspedjã/ nm expedient; **vivre d'~s** live by one's wits; **user d'~s** resort to expedients.

expédier /ɛkspedje/ ◻ vt send, dispatch; (tâche) polish off. **expéditeur, -trice** nm, f sender.

expéditif, -ive /ɛkspeditif, -v/ adj quick.

expédition /ɛkspedisjɔ̃/ nf (envoi) dispatching; (voyage) expedition.

expérience /ɛkspeRjãs/ nf experience; (scientifique) experiment.

expérimental, ~e (mpl -aux) /ɛkspeRimãtal, o/ adj experimental. **expérimentation** nf experimentation. **expérimenté, ~e** adj experienced. **expérimenter** ◻ vt

e

test, experiment with.

expert, ∼**e** /ɛkspɛʀ, -t/ adj expert. ●nm expert; (d'assurances) adjuster. **expert-comptable** (pl **experts-comptables**) nm accountant.

expertise /ɛkspɛʀtiz/ nf valuation; (de dégâts) assessment. **expertiser** ◻ vt value; (dégâts) assess.

expier /ɛkspje/ 45 vt atone for.

expiration /ɛkspiʀasjɔ̃/ nf expiry.

expirer /ɛkspiʀe/ ◻ vi breathe out; (finir, mourir) expire.

explicatif, -ive /ɛksplikatif, -v/ adj explanatory.

explication /ɛksplikasjɔ̃/ nf explanation; (fig) discussion; ∼ **de texte** (Scol) literary commentary.

explicite /ɛksplisit/ adj explicit.

expliquer /ɛksplike/ ◻ vt explain. ■ s'∼ vpr explain oneself; (discuter) discuss things; (être explicable) be understandable.

exploit /ɛksplwa/ nm exploit.

exploitant, ∼**e** /ɛksplwatã, -t/ nm, f ∼ **(agricole)** farmer.

exploitation /ɛksplwatasjɔ̃/ nf exploitation; (d'entreprise) running; (ferme) farm.

exploiter /ɛksplwate/ ◻ vt exploit; (ferme) run; (mine) work.

explorateur, -trice /ɛksplɔʀatœʀ, -tʀis/ nm, f explorer. **exploration** nf exploration. **explorer** ◻ vt explore.

exploser /ɛksploze/ ◻ vi explode; **faire** ∼ explode; (bâtiment) blow up.

explosif, -ive /ɛksplozif, -v/ adj & nm explosive. **explosion** nf explosion.

exportateur, -trice /ɛkspɔʀtatœʀ, -tʀis/ nm, f exporter. ●adj exporting. **exportation** nf export. **exporter** ◻ vt export.

exposant, ∼**e** /ɛkspozã, -t/ nm, f exhibitor.

exposé, ∼**e** /ɛkspoze/ nm talk (**sur** on); (d'une action) account; **faire l'**∼ **de la situation** give an account of the situation. ●adj ∼ **au nord** facing north.

exposer /ɛkspoze/ ◻ vt display, show; (expliquer) explain; (soumettre, mettre en danger) expose (**à** to); (vie) endanger. ■ s'∼ à vpr expose oneself to.

exposition /ɛkspozisjɔ̃/ nf (d'art) exhibition; (de faits) exposition; (géographique) aspect.

exprès¹ /ɛkspʀɛ/ adv specially; (délibérément) on purpose.

exprès², -esse /ɛkspʀɛs/ adj express.

express /ɛkspʀɛs/ adj & nm inv **(café)** ∼ espresso; **(train)** ∼ fast train.

expressif, -ive /ɛkspʀesif, -v/ adj expressive. **expression** nf expression.

exprimer /ɛkspʀime/ ◻ vt express. ■ s'∼ vpr express oneself.

expulser /ɛkspylse/ ◻ vt expel; (locataire) evict; (joueur) send off. **expulsion** nf (d'élève) expulsion; (de locataire) eviction; (d'immigré) deportation.

exquis, ∼**e** /ɛkski, -z/ adj exquisite.

extase /ɛkstɑz/ nf ecstasy.

extasier (s') /(s)ɛkstazje/ 45 vpr s'∼ **sur** be ecstatic about.

extensible /ɛkstɑ̃sibl/ adj (tissu) stretch.

extension /ɛkstɑ̃sjɔ̃/ nf extension; (expansion) expansion.

exténuer /ɛkstenye/ ◻ vt exhaust.

extérieur, ∼**e** /ɛksteʀjœʀ/ adj outside; (signe, gaieté) outward; (politique) foreign. ●nm outside, exterior; (de personne) exterior; **à l'**∼ **(de)** outside. **extérioriser** ◻ vt show, externalize.

extermination /ɛkstɛʀminasjɔ̃/

nf extermination. **exterminer** ◗
vt exterminate.

externe /ɛkstɛʀn/ adj external.
● nmf (Scol) day pupil.

extincteur /ɛkstɛ̃ktœʀ/ nm fire
extinguisher.

extinction /ɛkstɛ̃ksjɔ̃/ nf
extinction; **avoir une ~ de
voix** have lost one's voice.

extorquer /ɛkstɔʀke/ ◗ vt extort.

extra* /ɛkstʀa/ adj inv first-rate.
● nm inv (repas) (special) treat.

extraction /ɛkstʀaksjɔ̃/ nf
extraction.

extrader /ɛkstʀade/ ◗ vt
extradite.

extraire /ɛkstʀɛʀ/ 29 vt extract.
extrait nm extract.

extraordinaire /ɛkstʀaɔʀdinɛʀ/
adj extraordinary.

extravagance /ɛkstʀavagɑ̃s/ nf
extravagance. **extravagant, ~e**
adj extravagant.

extraverti, ~e /ɛkstʀavɛʀti/ nm, f
extrovert.

extrême /ɛkstʀɛm/ adj & nm
extreme. **extrêmement** adv
extremely.

Extrême-Orient /ɛkstʀɛmɔʀjɑ̃/
nm Far East.

extrémiste /ɛkstʀemist/ nmf
extremist.

extrémité /ɛkstʀemite/ nf end;
(mains, pieds) extremity.

exubérance /ɛgzybeʀɑ̃s/ nf
exuberance. **exubérant, ~e** adj
exuberant.

e
f

Ff

F abrév f (**franc, francs**) franc,
francs.

fabricant, ~e /fabʀikɑ̃, -t/ nm, f
manufacturer. **fabrication** nf
making; manufacture.

fabrique /fabʀik/ nf factory.
fabriquer ◗ vt make;
(industriellement) manufacture; (fig)
make up.

fabuler /fabyle/ ◗ vi fantasize.

fabuleux, -euse /fabylø, -z/ adj
fabulous.

fac /fak/ nf 🖪 university.

façade /fasad/ nf front; (fig)
façade.

face /fas/ nf face; (d'un objet) side;
en (~ de), d'en ~ opposite; **en
~ de** (fig) faced with; **~ à**
facing; (fig) faced with; **faire ~
à** face. **face-à-face** nm inv (débat)
one-to-one debate.

fâcher /fɑʃe/ ◗ vt anger; **fâché**

angry; (désolé) sorry. ■ **se ~** vpr
get angry; (se brouiller) fall out.

facile /fasil/ adj easy; (caractère)
easygoing.

facilité /fasilite/ nf easiness;
(aisance) ease; (aptitude) ability; **~s**
(possibilités) facilities,
opportunities; **~s
d'importation** import
opportunities; **~s de paiement**
easy terms.

faciliter /fasilite/ ◗ vt facilitate,
make easier.

façon /fasɔ̃/ nf way; (de vêtement)
cut; **de cette ~** in this way; **de
~ à** so as to; **de toute ~**
anyway; **~s** (chichis) fuss; **faire
des ~s** stand on ceremony; **sans
~s** (repas) informal;
(personne) unpretentious.
façonner ◗ vt shape;
(faire) make.

fac-similé* (pl ~s) /faksimile/
nm facsimile.

facteur, -trice /faktœʀ, -tʀis/ nm,
f postman, postwoman. ●nm
(élément) factor.

facture /faktyʀ/ nf bill; (Comm)
invoice; ~ **détaillée** itemized
bill. **facturer** 🛘 vt invoice.
facturette nf credit card slip.

facultatif, -ive /fakyltatif, -v/ adj
optional.

🖪**faculté** /fakylte/ nf faculty;
(possibilité) power; (Univ) faculty.

fade /fad/ adj insipid.

faible /fɛbl/ adj weak; (espoir,
quantité, écart) slight; (revenu,
intensité) low; ~ **d'esprit** feeble-
minded. ●nm (personne) weakling;
(penchant) weakness. **faiblesse** nf
weakness. **faiblir** 🛘 vi weaken.

faïence /fajɑ̃s/ nf earthenware.

faillir /fajiʀ/ 🛘 vi **j'ai failli
acheter** I almost bought.

faillite /fajit/ nf bankruptcy; (fig)
collapse.

faim /fɛ̃/ nf hunger; **avoir** ~ be
hungry; **rester sur sa** ~ (fig) be
left wanting more.

fainéant, -e /feneɑ̃, -t/ adj idle.

---

faire /fɛʀ/ 🔢

▷ Pour les expressions comme
faire attention, faire la
cuisine, etc. ▷ attention,
cuisine etc.

●verbe transitif
••••➤ (préparer, créer) make; ~ **une
tarte/une erreur** make a tart/a
mistake.
••••➤ (se livrer à une activité) do; ~
du droit do law; ~ **du foot/
du violon** play football/the
violin; **qu'est-ce qu'elle fait?**
(dans la vie) what does she do?;
(en ce moment précis) what is she

doing?
••••➤ (dans les calculs, mesures,
etc.) **10 et 10 font 20** 10 and
10 make 20; **ça fait 25 euros**
that's 25 euros; ~ **60 kilos**
weigh 60 kilos; **il fait 1,75 m**
he's 1.75 m tall.
••••➤ (dans les expressions de
temps) **ça fait une heure que
j'attends** I have been waiting
for an hour.
••••➤ (imiter) ~ **le clown** act the
clown; **faire le malade** pretend
to be ill.
••••➤ (parcourir) ~ **10 km** do ou
cover 10 km; ~ **les musées** go
round the museums.
••••➤ (entraîner, causer) **ça ne fait
rien** it doesn't matter;
l'accident a fait 8 morts 8
people died in the accident.
••••➤ (dire) say; **'excusez-moi',
fit-elle** 'excuse me', she said.
●verbe auxiliaire
••••➤ (**faire** + infinitif + qn) make;
~ **pleurer qn** make sb cry.
••••➤ (**faire** + infinitif + qch) have,
get; ~ **réparer sa voiture** have
ou get one's car mended.
••••➤ (**ne faire que** + infinitif)
(continuellement) **ne** ~ **que
pleurer** do nothing but cry;
(seulement) **je ne fais qu'obéir**
I'm only following orders.
●verbe intransitif
••••➤ (agir) do, act; ~ **vite** act
quickly; **fais comme tu veux**
do as you please; **fais comme
chez toi** make yourself at home.
••••➤ (paraître) look; ~ **joli** look
pretty; **ça fait cher** it's
expensive.
••••➤ (en parlant du temps) **il fait
chaud/gris** it's hot/overcast.
■ **se faire** verbe pronominal
••••➤ (obtenir, confectionner) make;
se ~ **des amis** make friends; **se**
~ **un thé** make (oneself) a cup
of tea.
••••➤ (**se faire** + infinitif) **se** ~
gronder be scolded; **se** ~
couper les cheveux have one's

🖪 see A-Z of French life and culture

hair cut.

····▸ (devenir) **il se fait tard** it's getting late.

····▸ (être d'usage) **ça ne se fait pas** it's not the done thing.

····▸ (emploi impersonnel) **comment se fait-il que tu sois ici?** how come you're here?

····▸ ■ **se faire à** get used to; **je ne m'y fais pas** I can't get used to it.

····▸ ■ **s'en faire** worry; **ne t'en fais pas** don't worry.

1 Lorsque **faire** remplace un verbe plus précis, on traduira quelquefois par ce dernier: **faire une visite** pay a visit, **faire un nid** build a nest.

faire-part* /fɛʀpaʀ/ nm inv announcement.

fais /fɛ/ ▷FAIRE 33.

faisan /fəzɑ̃/ nm pheasant.

faisceau (pl ~x) /fɛso/ nm (rayon) beam; (fagot) bundle.

fait, ~e /fɛ, fɛt/ adj done; (fromage) ripe; ~ **pour** made for; **tout** ~ ready made; **c'est bien ~ pour toi** it serves you right. ● nm fact; (événement) event; **au** ~ **(de)** informed (of); **de ce** ~ therefore; **du** ~ **de** on account of; ~ **divers** (trivial) news item; ~ **nouveau** new development; **prendre qn sur le** ~ catch sb in the act. ● ▷FAIRE 33.

faîte* /fɛt/ nm top; (fig) peak.

faites /fɛt/ ▷FAIRE 33.

falaise /falɛz/ nf cliff.

falloir /falwaʀ/ 34 vi **il faut qch/qn** we/you etc. need sth/sb; **il lui faut du pain** he needs bread; **il faut rester** we/you etc. have to ou must stay; **il faut que j'y aille** I have to ou must go; **il faudrait que tu partes** you should leave; **il aurait fallu le faire** we/you etc. should have done it; **comme il faut** (manger, se tenir) properly; (personne) respectable, proper. ■ **s'en** ~ vpr

il s'en est fallu de peu qu'il gagne he nearly won; **il s'en faut de beaucoup que je sois** I am far from being.

falsifier /falsifje/ 45 vt falsify; (signature, monnaie) forge.

famé, ~e /fame/ adj **mal** ~ disreputable, seedy.

fameux, **-euse** /famø, -z/ adj famous; (excellent **1**) first-rate.

familial, ~e (mpl **-iaux**) /familjal, -jo/ adj family.

familiale /familjal/ nf estate car; (US) station wagon.

familiariser /familjaʀize/ **1** vt familiarize (**avec** with). ■ **se** ~ vpr familiarize oneself.

familier, **-ière** /familje, -jɛʀ/ adj familiar; (amical) informal.

famille /famij/ nf family; **en** ~ with one's family.

famine /famin/ nf famine.

fanatique /fanatik/ adj fanatical. ● nmf fanatic.

fanfare /fɑ̃faʀ/ nf brass band; (musique) fanfare.

fantaisie /fɑ̃tezi/ nf imagination, fantasy; (caprice) whim; **(de)** ~ (boutons etc.) fancy. **fantaisiste** adj unorthodox; (personne) eccentric.

fantasme /fɑ̃tasm/ nm fantasy.

fantastique /fɑ̃tastik/ adj fantastic.

fantôme /fɑ̃tom/ nm ghost; **cabinet(-)**~ (Pol) shadow cabinet.

faon /fɑ̃/ nm fawn.

FAQ abrév f (**Foire aux questions**) (Internet) FAQ, Frequently Asked Questions.

farce /faʀs/ nf (practical) joke; (Théât) farce; (hachis) stuffing.

farcir /faʀsiʀ/ **2** vt stuff.

fard /faʀ/ nm make-up; ~ **à paupières** eye-shadow; **piquer un** ~ blush.

fardeau (pl ~x) /faʀdo/ nm burden.

farfelu, ~e /faʀfəly/ adj & nm,f eccentric.

farine /faʀin/ nf flour. **farineux, -euse** adj floury. **farineux** nmpl starchy food.

farouche /faʀuʃ/ adj shy; (peu sociable) unsociable; (violent) fierce.

fascicule /fasikyl/ nm (brochure) booklet; (partie d'un ouvrage) fascicule.

fasciner /fasine/ **1** vt fascinate.

fascisme /faʃism/ nm fascism.

fasse /fas/ ▷FAIRE 33.

fast-food* /fastfud/ nm fast-food place.

fastidieux, -ieuse /fastidjø, -z/ adj tedious.

fatal, ~e (mpl ~s) /fatal/ adj inevitable; (mortel) fatal. **fatalité** nf (destin) fate.

fatigant, ~e /fatigã, -t/ adj tiring; (ennuyeux) tiresome.

fatigue /fatig/ nf fatigue, tiredness.

fatigué, ~e /fatige/ adj tired.

fatiguer /fatige/ **1** vt tire; (yeux, moteur) strain. ●vi (moteur) labour. ■**se ~** vpr get tired, tire (**de** of).

faubourg /fobuʀ/ nm suburb.

faucher /foʃe/ **1** vt (herbe) mow; (voler **1**) pinch; **~ qn** (véhicule, tir) mow sb down.

faucon /fokɔ̃/ nm falcon, hawk.

faudra, faudrait /fodʀa, fodʀɛ/ ▷FALLOIR 34.

faufiler (se) /(sə)fofile/ **1** vpr edge one's way, squeeze.

faune /fon/ nf wildlife, fauna.

faussaire /fosɛʀ/ nmf forger.

fausse /fos/ ▷FAUX².

fausser /fose/ **1** vt buckle; (fig) distort; **~ compagnie à qn** give sb the slip.

faut /fo/ ▷FALLOIR 34.

faute /fot/ nf mistake; (responsabilité) fault; (délit) offence;

(péché) sin; **en ~** at fault; **~ de** for want of; **~ de quoi** failing which; **sans ~** without fail; **~ de frappe** typing error; **~ de goût** bad taste; **~ professionnelle** professional misconduct.

fauteuil /fotœj/ nm armchair; (de président) chair; (Théât) seat; **~ roulant** wheelchair.

fautif, -ive /fotif, -v/ adj guilty; (faux) faulty. ●nm, f guilty party.

fauve /fov/ adj (couleur) fawn, tawny. ●nm wild cat.

faux¹ /fo/ nf scythe.

faux², fausse /fo, fos/ adj false; (falsifié) fake, forged; (numéro, calcul) wrong; (voix) out of tune; **c'est ~!** that is wrong!; **~ témoignage** perjury; **faire ~ bond à qn** stand sb up; **fausse couche** miscarriage; **~ frais** incidental expenses. ●adv (chanter) out of tune. ●nm forgery. **faux-filet** (pl ~s) nm sirloin.

faveur /favœʀ/ nf favour; **de ~** (régime) preferential; **en ~ de** in favour of.

favorable /favɔʀabl/ adj favourable.

favori, ~te /favɔʀi, -t/ adj & nm,f favourite. **favoriser** **1** vt favour.

fax /faks/ nm fax. **faxer** **1** vt fax.

fébrile /febʀil/ adj feverish.

fécond, ~e /fekɔ̃, -d/ adj fertile. **féconder** **1** vt fertilize. **fécondité** nf fertility.

fédéral, ~e (mpl -aux) /federal, -o/ adj federal. **fédération** nf federation.

fée /fe/ nf fairy. **féerie*** nf magical spectacle. **féerique*** adj magical.

feindre /fɛ̃dʀ/ 22 vt feign; **~ de** pretend to.

fêler /fele/ **1** vt crack. ■**se ~** vpr crack.

félicitations /felisitasjɔ̃/ nfpl congratulations (**pour** on).

féliciter ◼ vt congratulate (**de** on).

félin, ~e /felɛ̃, -in/ adj & nm feline.

femelle /fəmɛl/ adj & nf female.

féminin, ~e /feminɛ̃, -in/ adj feminine; (sexe) female; (mode, équipe) women's. ● nm feminine. **féministe** nmf feminist.

femme /fam/ nf woman; (épouse) wife; ~ **au foyer** housewife; ~ **de chambre** chambermaid; ~ **de ménage** cleaning lady.

fémur /femyr/ nm thigh-bone.

fendre /fɑ̃dR/ ◼ vt (couper) split; (fissurer) crack. ◼ **se** ~ vpr crack.

fenêtre /fənɛtR/ nf window.

fenouil /fənuj/ nm fennel.

fente /fɑ̃t/ nf (ouverture) slit, slot; (fissure) crack.

féodal, ~e (mpl **-aux**) /feodal, -o/ adj feudal.

fer /fɛR/ nm iron; ~ **(à repasser)** iron; ~ **à cheval** horseshoe; ~ **de lance** spearhead; ~ **forgé** wrought iron.

fera, ferait /fəra, fərɛ/ ▷FAIRE 33.

férié, ~e /ferje/ adj **jour** ~ public holiday.

ferme /fɛRm/ nf farm; (maison) farm(house); ~ **éolienne** wind farm. ● adj firm. ● adv (travailler) hard.

fermé, ~e /fɛRme/ adj closed; (gaz, radio) off.

fermenter /fɛRmɑ̃te/ ◼ vi ferment.

fermer /fɛRme/ ◼ vt/i close, shut; (cesser d'exploiter) close *ou* shut down; (gaz, robinet) turn off. ◼ **se** ~ vpr close, shut.

fermeté /fɛRməte/ nf firmness.

fermeture /fɛRmətyR/ nf closing; (dispositif) catch; ~ **annuelle** annual closure; ~ **éclair**® zip(-fastener); (US) zipper.

fermier, -ière /fɛRmje, -jɛR/ adj farm. ● nm farmer. **fermière** nf farmer's wife.

féroce /feros/ adj ferocious.

ferraille /fɛRɑj/ nf scrap-iron.

ferrer /fɛRe/ ◼ vt (cheval) shoe.

ferroviaire /fɛRɔvjɛR/ adj rail(way).

ferry* /fɛRi/ nm ferry.

fertile /fɛRtil/ adj fertile; ~ **en** (fig) rich in. **fertiliser** ◼ vt fertilize. **fertilité** nf fertility.

fervent, ~e /fɛRvɑ̃, -t/ adj fervent. ● nm, f enthusiast (**de** of).

fesse /fɛs/ nf buttock. **fessée** nf spanking, smack.

festin /fɛstɛ̃/ nm feast.

festival (pl ~s) /fɛstival/ nm festival.

fêtard, ~e /fɛtaR, -d/ nm, f ◼ party animal.

fête /fɛt/ nf holiday; (religieuse) feast; (du nom) name-day; (réception) party; (en famille) celebration; (foire) fair; (folklorique) festival; ~ **des Mères** Mother's Day; ~ **foraine** fun-fair; **faire la** ~ live it up; **les** ~**s (de fin d'année)** the Christmas season. **fêter** ◼ vt celebrate; (personne) give a celebration for.

fétiche /fetiʃ/ nm fetish; (fig) mascot.

feu¹ (pl ~**x**) /fø/ nm fire; (lumière) light; (de réchaud) burner; **à** ~ **doux/vif** on a low/high heat; ~ **rouge/vert/orange** red/green/amber light; **aux** ~**x, tournez à droite** turn right at the traffic lights; **avez-vous du** ~? (pour cigarette) have you got a light?; **au** ~! fire!; **mettre le** ~ **à** set fire to; **prendre** ~ catch fire; **jouer avec le** ~ play with fire; **ne pas faire long** ~ not last; ~ **d'artifice** firework display; ~ **de joie** bonfire; ~ **de position** sidelight.

feu² /fø/ adj inv (mort) late.

feuillage /fœjaʒ/ nm foliage.

feuille /fœj/ nf leaf; (de papier)

sheet; (formulaire) form; ~
d'impôts tax return; ~ **de paie**
payslip.

feuilleté, ~e /fœjte/ adj **pâte ~e**
puff pastry. ●nm savoury pasty.

feuilleter /fœjte/ **1** vt leaf
through.

feuilleton /fœjtõ/ nm (à suivre)
serial; (histoire complète) series.

feutre /føtʀ/ nm felt; (chapeau) felt
hat; (crayon) felt-tip (pen).

fève /fɛv/ nf broad bean.

février /fevʀije/ nm February.

fiable /fjabl/ adj reliable.

fiançailles /fjãsaj/ nfpl
engagement.

fiancé, ~e /fjãse/ adj engaged.
●nm fiancé. **fiancée** nf fiancée.
fiancer (se) **10** vpr become
engaged (**avec** to).

fibre /fibʀ/ nf fibre; ~ **de verre**
fibreglass.

ficeler /fisle/ **38** vt tie up.

ficelle /fisɛl/ nf string.

fiche /fiʃ/ nf (index) card;
(formulaire) form, slip; (Électr) plug.

ficher¹ /fiʃe/ **1** vt (enfoncer) drive
(**dans** into).

ficher² /fiʃe/ **1** **1** vt (faire) do;
(donner) give; (mettre) put; ~ **le
camp** clear off. ■ se ~ **de** vpr
make fun of; **il s'en fiche** he
couldn't care less.

fichier /fiʃje/ nm file.

fichu, ~e /fiʃy/ adj **1** (mauvais)
rotten; (raté) done for; **mal ~**
terrible.

fictif, -ive /fiktif, -v/ adj fictitious.
fiction nf fiction.

fidèle /fidɛl/ adj faithful. ●nmf
(client) regular; (Relig) believer;
~**s** (à l'église) congregation.
fidélité nf fidelity.

fier¹, fière /fjɛʀ/ adj proud
(**de** of).

fier² (se) /(sə)fje/ **45** vpr **se ~ à**
trust.

fierté /fjɛʀte/ nf pride.

fièvre /fjɛvʀ/ nf fever; **avoir de
la ~** have a temperature; ~
aphteuse foot-and-mouth
disease. **fiévreux, -euse** adj
feverish.

figer /fiʒe/ **40** vi (graisse) congeal;
(sang) clot; **figé sur place** frozen
to the spot. ■ se ~ vpr (personne,
sourire) freeze; (graisse) congeal;
(sang) clot.

figue /fig/ nf fig.

figurant, ~e /figyʀã, -t/ nm, f (au
cinéma) extra.

figure /figyʀ/ nf face; (forme,
personnage) figure; (illustration)
picture.

figuré, ~e /figyʀe/ adj (sens)
figurative.

figurer /figyʀe/ **1** vi appear. ●vt
represent. ■ se ~ vpr imagine.

fil /fil/ nm thread; (métallique,
électrique) wire; (de couteau) edge; (à
coudre) cotton; **au ~ de** with the
passing of; **au ~ de l'eau** with
the current; ~ **de fer** wire; **au
bout du ~** **1** on the phone.

file /fil/ nf line; (voie: Auto) lane; ~
(d'attente) queue; (US) line; **en
~ indienne** in single file.

filer /file/ **1** vt spin; (suivre)
shadow; ~ **qch à qn** **1** slip sb
sth. ●vi (bas) ladder, run; (liquide)
run; (aller vite **1**) speed along, fly
by; (partir **1**) dash off; (disparaître
1) ~ **entre les mains** slip
through one's fingers; ~ **doux**
do as one's told.

filet /filɛ/ nm net; (d'eau) trickle;
(de viande) fillet; ~ **(à bagages)**
(luggage) rack; ~ **à provisions**
string bag (for shopping).

filiale /filjal/ nf subsidiary
(company).

filière /filjɛʀ/ nf (official)
channels; (de trafiquants) network;
passer par ou **suivre la ~**
(employé) work one's way up.

fille /fij/ nf girl; (opposé à fils)
daughter. **fillette** nf little girl.

filleul /fijœl/ nm godson.

filleule /fijœl/ nf goddaughter.

film /film/ nm film; ~ **d'épouvante/muet/parlant** horror/silent/talking film; ~ **dramatique** drama. **filmer 1** vt film.

filon /filɔ̃/ nm (Géol) seam; (travail lucratif 1) money spinner; **avoir trouvé le bon** ~ be onto a good thing.

fils /fis/ nm son.

filtre /filtʀ/ nm filter. **filtrer 1** vt/i filter; (personne) screen.

fin¹ /fɛ̃/ nf end; **à la** ~ finally; **en** ~ **de compte** all things considered; ~ **de semaine** weekend; **mettre** ~ **à** put an end to; **prendre** ~ come to an end.

fin², ~**e** /fɛ̃, fin/ adj fine; (tranche, couche) thin; (taille) slim; (plat) exquisite; (esprit, vue) sharp; ~**es herbes** mixed herbs. ● adv (couper) finely.

final, ~**e** (mpl **-aux**) /final, -o/ adj final.

finale /final/ nm (Mus) finale. ● nf (Sport) final; (Gram) final syllable. **finalement** adv finally; (somme toute) after all. **finaliste** nmf finalist.

finance /finɑ̃s/ nf finance. **financer 10** vt finance.

financier, -ière /finɑ̃sje, -jɛʀ/ adj financial. ● nm financier.

finesse /fines/ nf fineness; (de taille) slimness; (acuité) sharpness; ~**s** (de langue) niceties.

finir /finiʀ/ 2 vt/i finish, end; (arrêter) stop; (manger) finish (up); **en** ~ **avec** have done with; ~ **par faire** end up doing; **ça va mal** ~ it will turn out badly.

finlandais, ~**e** /fɛ̃lɑ̃dɛ, -z/ adj Finnish. F~, ~**e** nm, f Finn.

Finlande /fɛ̃lɑ̃d/ nf Finland.

finnois, ~**e** /finwa/ adj Finnish. ● nm (Ling) Finnish.

firme /fiʀm/ nf firm.

fisc /fisk/ nm tax authorities. **fiscal,** ~**e** (mpl **-aux**) adj tax, fiscal. **fiscalité** nf tax system.

fissure /fisyʀ/ nf crack.

FIV abrév f (**fécondation in vitro**) IVF.

fixe /fiks/ adj fixed; (stable) steady; **à heure** ~ at a set time; **menu à prix** ~ set menu. ● nm basic pay.

fixer /fikse/ 1 vt fix; ~ **(du regard)** stare at; **être fixé** (personne) have made up one's mind. ■ se ~ vpr (s'attacher) be attached; (s'installer) settle down.

flacon /flakɔ̃/ nm bottle.

flagrant, ~**e** /flagʀɑ̃, -t/ adj flagrant, blatant; **en** ~ **délit** in the act.

flair /flɛʀ/ nm (sense of) smell; (fig) intuition.

flamand, ~**e** /flamɑ̃, -d/ adj Flemish. ● nm (Ling) Flemish. F~, ~**e** nm, f Fleming.

flamant /flamɑ̃/ nm flamingo.

flambeau (pl ~**x**) /flɑ̃bo/ nm torch.

flambée /flɑ̃be/ nf blaze; (fig) explosion.

flamber /flɑ̃be/ 1 vi blaze; (prix) shoot up. ● vt (aiguille) sterilize; (volaille) singe.

flamme /flam/ nf flame; (fig) ardour; **en** ~**s** ablaze.

flan /flɑ̃/ nm custard tart.

flanc /flɑ̃/ nm side; (d'animal, d'armée) flank.

flâner /flɑne/ 1 vi stroll. **flânerie** nf stroll.

flanquer /flɑ̃ke/ 1 vt flank; (jeter 1) chuck; (donner 1) give; ~ **à la porte** kick out.

flaque /flak/ nf (d'eau) puddle; (de sang) pool.

flash* (pl ~**es**) /flaʃ/ nm (Photo) flash; (information) news flash; ~

publicitaire commercial.

flatter /flate/ **1** vt flatter. ■ se ~ de vpr pride oneself on.

flatteur, -euse /flatœr, -øz/ adj flattering. ●nm, f flatterer.

fléau (pl ~x) /fleo/ nm (désastre) scourge; (personne) pest.

flèche /flɛʃ/ nf arrow; (de clocher) spire; **monter en** ~ spiral; **partir en** ~ shoot off.

flécher /fleʃe/ **14** vt mark ou signpost (with arrows). **fléchette** nf dart.

fléchir /fleʃir/ **2** vt bend; (personne) move, sway. ●vi (faiblir) weaken; (prix) fall; (poutre) sag, bend.

flemme /flɛm/ nf **1** laziness; **j'ai la** ~ **de faire** I can't be bothered doing.

flétrir (se) /(sə)fletrir/ **2** vpr (plante) wither; (fruit) shrivel; (beauté) fade.

fleur /flœr/ nf flower; **à** ~ **de terre/d'eau** just above the ground/water; **à** ~**s** flowery; ~ **de l'âge** prime of life; **en** ~**s** in flower.

fleurir /flœrir/ **2** vi flower; (arbre) blossom; (fig) flourish. ●vt decorate with flowers. **fleuriste** nmf florist.

fleuve /flœv/ nm river.

flic /flik/ nm **1** cop.

flipper* /flipœr/ nm pinball (machine).

flirter /flœrte/ **1** vi flirt.

flocon /flɔkɔ̃/ nm flake.

flore /flɔr/ nf flora.

florissant, ~**e** /flɔrisɑ̃, -t/ adj flourishing.

flot /flo/ nm flood, stream; **être à** ~ be afloat; **les** ~**s** the waves.

flottant, ~**e** /flɔtɑ̃, -t/ adj (vêtement) loose; (indécis) indecisive.

flotte /flɔt/ nf fleet; (pluie **1**) rain; (eau **1**) water.

flottement /flɔtmɑ̃/ nm (incertitude) indecision.

flotter /flɔte/ **1** vi float; (drapeau) flutter; (nuage, parfum, pensées) drift; (pleuvoir **1**) rain. **flotteur** nm float.

flou, ~**e** /flu/ adj out of focus; (fig) vague.

fluctuer /flyktɥe/ **1** vi fluctuate.

fluet, ~**te** /flyɛ, -t/ adj thin.

fluide /flɥid/ adj & nm fluid.

fluor /flyɔr/ nm (pour les dents) fluoride.

fluorescent, ~**e** /flyɔrɛsɑ̃, -t/ adj fluorescent.

flûte* /flyt/ nf flute; (verre) champagne glass.

fluvial, ~**e** (mpl **-iaux**) /flyvjal, -jo/ adj river.

flux /fly/ nm flow; ~ **et reflux** ebb and flow.

FM abrév f (**frequency modulation**) FM.

fœtus /fetys/ nm foetus.

foi /fwa/ nf faith; **être de bonne/ mauvaise** ~ be acting in good/ bad faith; **ma** ~**!** well (indeed)!

foie /fwa/ nm liver.

foin /fwɛ̃/ nm hay.

foire /fwar/ nf fair; **faire la** ~ **1** live it up.

fois /fwa/ nf time; **une** ~ once; **deux** ~ twice; **à la** ~ at the same time; **des** ~ (parfois) sometimes; **une** ~ **pour toutes** once and for all.

fol /fɔl/ ▷ FOU.

folie /fɔli/ nf madness; (bêtise) foolish thing, folly; **faire une** ~**, faire des** ~**s** be extravagant.

folklore /fɔlklɔr/ nm folklore. **folklorique** adj folk; **1** eccentric.

folle /fɔl/ ▷ FOU.

foncé, ~**e** /fɔ̃se/ adj dark.

foncer /fɔ̃se/ **10** vt darken. ●vi

(s'assombrir) darken; (aller vite 🔟) dash along; ~ **sur** 🔟 charge at.

foncier, -ière /fɔ̃sje, -jɛʀ/ adj fundamental; (Comm) real estate.

fonction /fɔ̃ksjɔ̃/ nf function; (emploi) position; ~**s** (obligations) duties; **en** ~ **de** according to; ~ **publique** civil service; **voiture de** ~ company car. **fonctionnaire** nmf civil servant. **fonctionnement** nm working.

fonctionner /fɔ̃ksjɔne/ 🔟 vi work; **faire** ~ work.

fond /fɔ̃/ nm bottom; (de salle, magasin, etc.) back; (essentiel) basis; (contenu) content; (plan) background; (Sport) long-distance running; **à** ~ thoroughly; **au** ~ basically; **de** ~ (bruit) background; **de** ~ **en comble** from top to bottom; **au** ou **dans le** ~ really; ~ **de teint** foundation, make-up base.

fondamental, ~e (mpl **-aux**) /fɔ̃damɑ̃tal, -o/ adj fundamental.

fondateur, -trice /fɔ̃datœʀ, -tʀis/ nm, f founder. **fondation** nf foundation.

fonder /fɔ̃de/ 🔟 vt found; (baser) base (**sur** on); **(bien) fondé** wellfounded. ■ **se** ~ **sur** vpr be guided by, be based on.

fonderie /fɔ̃dʀi/ nf foundry.

fondre /fɔ̃dʀ/ 🔟 vt/i melt; (dans l'eau) dissolve; (mélanger) merge; **faire** ~ melt; dissolve; ~ **en larmes** burst into tears; ~ **sur** swoop on. ■ **se** ~ vpr merge.

fonds /fɔ̃/ nm fund; ~ **de commerce** business. ● nmpl (capitaux) funds.

fondu, ~e /fɔ̃dy/ adj melted; (métal) molten.

font /fɔ̃/ ▸**FAIRE** 🔟.

fontaine /fɔ̃tɛn/ nf fountain; (source) spring.

fonte /fɔ̃t/ nf melting; (fer) cast iron; ~ **des neiges** thaw.

foot /fut/ nm 🔟 football.

football /futbol/ nm football.

footing /futiŋ/ nm jogging.

forain /fɔʀɛ̃/ nm fairground entertainer; **marchand** ~ stallholder.

forçat /fɔʀsa/ nm convict.

force /fɔʀs/ nf force; (physique) strength; (hydraulique etc.) power; ~**s** (physiques) strength; **à** ~ **de** by sheer force of; **de** ~, **par la** ~ by force; ~ **de dissuasion** deterrent; ~ **de frappe** strike force, deterrent; ~ **de l'âge** prime of life; ~**s de l'ordre** police (force) ; ~**s de marché** market forces.

forcé, ~e /fɔʀse/ adj forced; (inévitable) inevitable; **c'est** ~ **qu'il fasse** 🔟 he's bound to do. **forcément** adv necessarily; (évidemment) obviously.

forcené, ~e /fɔʀsəne/ adj frenzied. ● nm, f maniac.

forcer /fɔʀse/ 🔟 vt force (**à faire** to do); (voix) strain; ~ **la dose** 🔟 overdo it. ● vi force; (exagérer) overdo it. ■ **se** ~ vpr force oneself.

forer /fɔʀe/ 🔟 vt drill.

forestier, -ière /fɔʀɛstje, -jɛʀ/ adj forest. ● nm, f forestry worker.

forêt /fɔʀɛ/ nf forest.

forfait /fɔʀfɛ/ nm (Comm) (prix fixe) fixed price; (offre promotionnelle) package. **forfaitaire** adj (prix) fixed.

forger /fɔʀʒe/ 🔟 vt forge; (inventer) make up.

forgeron /fɔʀʒəʀɔ̃/ nm blacksmith.

formaliser (se) /(sə)fɔʀmalize/ 🔟 vpr take offence (**de** at).

formalité /fɔʀmalite/ nf formality.

format /fɔʀma/ nm format. **formater** 🔟 vt (Ordinat) format.

formation /fɔʀmasjɔ̃/ nf formation; (professionnelle)

training; (culture) education; ~ **permanente** *ou* **continue** continuing education.

forme /fɔʀm/ nf form; (contour) shape, form; ~**s** (de femme) figure; **être en** ~ be in good shape, be on form; **en** ~ **de** in the shape of; **en bonne et due** ~ in due form.

formel, ~le /fɔʀmɛl/ adj formal; (catégorique) positive.

former /fɔʀme/ ◻ vt form; (instruire) train. ◼ **se** ~ vpr form.

formidable /fɔʀmidabl/ adj fantastic.

formulaire /fɔʀmylɛʀ/ nm form.

formule /fɔʀmyl/ nf formula; (expression) expression; (feuille) form; ~ **de politesse** polite phrase, letter ending. **formuler** ◻ vt formulate.

fort, ~e /fɔʀ, -t/ adj strong; (grand) big; (pluie) heavy; (bruit) loud; (pente) steep; (élève) clever; **au plus** ~ **de** at the height of; **c'est une** ~**e tête** she/he's headstrong. ●adv (frapper) hard; (parler) loud; (très) very; (beaucoup) very much. ●nm (atout) strong point; (Mil) fort.

fortifiant /fɔʀtifjɑ̃/ nm tonic. **fortifier** ◻ vt fortify.

fortune /fɔʀtyn/ nf fortune; **de** ~ (improvisé) makeshift; **faire** ~ make one's fortune.

forum /fɔʀɔm/ nm forum; ~ **de discussion** (Internet) newsgroup.

fosse /fos/ nf pit; (tombe) grave; ~ **d'orchestre** orchestra pit; ~ **septique** septic tank.

fossé /fose/ nm ditch; (fig) gulf; ~ **numérique** digital divide.

fossette /fosɛt/ nf dimple.

fossile /fosil/ nm fossil.

fou (**fol** before vowel or mute h) , **folle** /fu, fɔl/ adj mad; (course, regard) wild; (énorme ◻) tremendous; ~ **de** crazy about; **le** ~ **rire** the giggles. ●nm

madman; (bouffon) jester. **folle** nf madwoman.

foudre /fudʀ/ nf lightning.

foudroyant, ~e /fudʀwajɑ̃, -t/ adj (mort, maladie) violent.

foudroyer /fudʀwaje/ ◻ vt (orage) strike; (maladie etc.) strike down; ~ **qn du regard** look daggers at sb.

fouet /fwɛ/ nm whip; (Culin) whisk.

fougère /fuʒɛʀ/ nf fern.

fougue /fug/ nf ardour. **fougueux, -euse** adj ardent.

fouille /fuj/ nf search; (Archéol) excavation.

fouiller /fuje/ ◻ vt/i search; (creuser) dig; ~ **dans** (tiroir) rummage through.

fouillis /fuji/ nm jumble.

foulard /fulaʀ/ nm scarf.

foule /ful/ nf crowd; **une** ~ **de** (fig) a mass of.

foulée /fule/ nf stride; **il l'a fait dans la** ~ he did it while he was at *ou* about it.

fouler /fule/ ◻ vt (raisin) press; (sol) set foot on; ~ **qch aux pieds** trample sth underfoot; (fig) ride roughshod over sth. ◼ **se** ~ vpr **se** ~ **le poignet/le pied** sprain one's wrist/foot; **ne pas se** ~ ◻ not strain oneself.

four /fuʀ/ nm oven; (de potier) kiln; (Théât) flop; ~ **à micro-ondes** microwave oven; ~ **crématoire** crematorium.

fourbe /fuʀb/ adj deceitful.

fourche /fuʀʃ/ nf fork; (à foin) pitchfork. **fourchette** nf fork; (Comm) bracket, range.

fourgon /fuʀgɔ̃/ nm van.

fourmi /fuʀmi/ nf ant; **avoir des** ~**s** have pins and needles.

fourmiller /fuʀmije/ ◻ vi swarm (**de** with).

fourneau (pl ~**x**) /fuʀno/ nm stove.

fourni, ~e /furni/ adj (épais)
thick.

fournir /furnir/ ☑ vt supply,
provide; (client) supply; (effort) put
in; **~ à qn** supply sb with. ▪ se
~ chez vpr shop at.

fournisseur /furnisœr/ nm
supplier; **~ d'accès à l'Internet**
Internet service provider.

fourniture /furnityr/ nf supply.

fourrage /furaʒ/ nm fodder.

fourré, ~e /fure/ adj (vêtement)
fur-lined; (gâteau etc.) filled (with
jam, cream, etc.). ●nm thicket.

fourre-tout* /furtu/ nm inv (sac)
holdall.

fourreur /furœr/ nm furrier.

fourrière /furjɛr/ nf (lieu) pound.

fourrure /furyr/ nf fur.

foutre /futr/ ☒ vt ▣= **ficher²** ▣.

foutu, ~e /futy/ adj ▣ = **fichu**.

foyer /fwaje/ nm home; (âtre)
hearth; (club) club; (d'étudiants)
hostel; (Théât) foyer; (Photo)
focus; (centre) centre.

fracas /fraka/ nm din; (de train)
roar; (d'objet qui tombe) crash.
fracassant, ~e adj (bruyant)
deafening; (violent) shattering.

fraction /fraksjɔ̃/ nf fraction.

fracture /fraktyr/ nf fracture; **~
du poignet** fractured wrist.

fragile /fraʒil/ adj fragile; (peau)
sensitive; (cœur) weak. **fragilité**
nf fragility.

fragment /fragmã/ nm bit,
fragment. **fragmenter** ☐ vt
split, fragment.

fraîchement* /frɛʃmã/ adv
(récemment) freshly; (avec froideur)
coolly. **fraîcheur*** nf coolness;
(nouveauté) freshness. **fraîchir*** ☑
vi freshen, become colder.

frais¹, fraîche* /frɛ, -ʃ/ adj fresh;
(temps, accueil) cool; (peinture) wet;
~ et dispos fresh; **il fait ~** it is
cool. ●adv (récemment) newly,
freshly. ●nm **mettre au ~** put in

a cool place; **prendre le ~** get
some fresh air.

frais² /frɛ/ nmpl expenses; (droits)
fees; **aux ~ de** at the expense
of; **faire des ~** spend a lot of
money; **~ généraux** (Comm)
overheads, running expenses; **~
de scolarité** school fees.

fraise /frɛz/ nf strawberry.
fraisier nm strawberry plant;
(gâteau) strawberry gateau.

framboise /frãbwaz/ nf
raspberry. **framboisier** nm
raspberry bush.

franc, franche /frã, -ʃ/ adj frank;
(regard) frank, candid; (cassure)
clean; (net) clear; (libre) free;
(véritable) downright. ●nm franc.

français, ~e /frãsɛ, -z/ adj
French. ●nm (Ling) French. F**~,
~e** nm, f Frenchman,
Frenchwoman.

France /frãs/ nf France.

franchement /frãʃmã/ adv
frankly; (nettement) clearly; (tout à
fait) really.

franchir /frãʃir/ ☑ vt (obstacle) get
over; (distance) cover; (limite)
exceed; (traverser) cross.

franchise /frãʃiz/ nf (qualité)
frankness; (Comm) franchise;
(exemption) exemption; **~
douanière** exemption from
duties.

franc-maçon (pl **francs-
maçons**) /frãmasɔ̃/ nm
Freemason. **franc-maçonnerie**
nf Freemasonry.

franco /frãko/ adv postage paid.

francophone /frãkɔfɔn/ adj
French-speaking. ●nmf French
speaker.

franc-parler /frãparle/ nm inv
outspokenness.

frange /frãʒ/ nf fringe.

frappe /frap/ nf (de texte) typing.

frappé, ~e /frape/ adj chilled.

frapper /frape/ ☐ vt/i strike;

(battre) hit, strike; (monnaie) mint; (à la porte) knock, bang; **frappé de panique** panic-stricken.

fraternel, ~le /fʀatɛʀnɛl/ adj brotherly. **fraternité** nf brotherhood.

fraude /fʀod/ nf fraud; (à un examen) cheating; **passer qch en ~** smuggle sth in. **frauder** ⓵ vt/i cheat. **fraudeux, -euse** adj fraudulent.

frayer /fʀeje/ ㉛ vt open up. ■ se **~** vpr **se ~ un passage** force one's way (**à travers, dans** through).

frayeur /fʀejœʀ/ nf fright.

fredonner /fʀədɔne/ ⓵ vt hum.

free-lance* /fʀilɑ̃s/ adj & nmf freelance.

freezer* /fʀizœʀ/ nm freezer.

frein /fʀɛ̃/ nm brake; **mettre un ~ à** curb; **~ à main** hand brake.

freiner /fʀene/ ⓵ vt slow down; (modérer, enrayer) curb. ●vi (Auto) brake.

frêle /fʀɛl/ adj frail.

frelon /fʀəlɔ̃/ nm hornet.

frémir /fʀemiʀ/ ② vi shudder, shake; (feuille, eau) quiver.

frêne /fʀɛn/ nm ash.

frénésie /fʀenezi/ nf frenzy. **frénétique** adj frenzied.

fréquemment /fʀekamɑ̃/ adv frequently. **fréquence** nf frequency. **fréquent, ~e** adj frequent. **fréquentation** nf frequenting.

fréquentations /fʀekɑ̃tasjɔ̃/ nfpl acquaintances; **avoir de mauvaises ~** keep bad company.

fréquenter /fʀekɑ̃te/ ⓵ vt frequent; (école) attend; (personne) see.

frère /fʀɛʀ/ nm brother.

fret /fʀɛt/ nm freight.

friand, ~e /fʀijɑ̃, -d/ adj **~ de** very fond of.

friandise /fʀijɑ̃diz/ nf sweet; (US) candy; (gâteau) cake.

fric /fʀik/ nm 🔲 money.

friction /fʀiksjɔ̃/ nf friction; (massage) rub-down.

frigidaire ® /fʀiʒidɛʀ/ nm refrigerator.

frigo /fʀigo/ nm 🔲 fridge. **frigorifique** adj (vitrine etc.) refrigerated.

frileux, -euse /fʀilø, -z/ adj sensitive to cold.

frime /fʀim/ nf 🔲 **c'est de la ~** it's all pretence; **pour la ~** for show.

frimousse /fʀimus/ nf 🔲 face.

fringale /fʀɛ̃gal/ nf 🔲 ravenous appetite.

fringant, ~e /fʀɛ̃gɑ̃, -t/ adj dashing.

fringues /fʀɛ̃g/ nfpl 🔲 gear.

friper /fʀipe/ ⓵ vt crumple, crease. ■ se **~** vpr crumple, crease.

fripon, ~ne /fʀipɔ̃, -ɔn/ nm, f rascal. ●adj mischievous.

fripouille /fʀipuj/ nf rogue.

frire /fʀiʀ/ ㊱ vt/i fry; **faire ~** fry.

frise /fʀiz/ nf frieze.

friser /fʀize/ ⓵ vt/i (cheveux) curl; (personne) curl the hair of; **frisé** curly.

frisson /fʀisɔ̃/ nm (de froid) shiver; (de peur) shudder. **frissonner** ⓵ vi shiver; shudder.

frit, ~e /fʀi, -t/ adj fried.

frite /fʀit/ nf chip; **avoir la ~** 🔲 feel good.

friteuse /fʀitøz/ nf chip pan; (électrique) (deep) fryer.

friture /fʀityʀ/ nf fried fish; (huile) (frying) oil ou fat.

frivole /fʀivɔl/ adj frivolous.

froid, ~e /fʀwa, -d/ adj & nm cold; **avoir/prendre ~** be/catch cold; **il fait ~** it is cold. **froidement** adv coldly; (calculer) coolly.

froideur nf coldness.

froisser /fʀwase/ ◻1 vt crumple; (fig) offend. ▪ **se ~** vpr crumple; (fig) take offence; **se ~ un muscle** strain a muscle.

frôler /fʀole/ ◻1 vt brush against, skim; (fig) come close to.

fromage /fʀɔmaʒ/ nm cheese.

fromager, -ère /fʀɔmaʒe, -ɛʀ/ adj cheese. ●nm, f (fabricant) cheesemaker; (marchand) cheesemonger.

froment /fʀɔmã/ nm wheat.

froncer /fʀõse/ ◻10 vt gather; **~ les sourcils** frown.

front /fʀõ/ nm forehead; (Mil, Pol) front; **de ~** at the same time; (de face) head-on; (côte à côte) abreast; **faire ~ à** face up to. **frontal, ~e** (mpl **-aux**) adj frontal; (Ordinat) front-end.

frontalier, -ière /fʀõtalje, -jɛʀ/ adj border; **travailleur ~** commuter from across the border.

frontière /fʀõtjɛʀ/ nf border, frontier.

frottement /fʀɔtmã/ nm rubbing; (Tech) friction. **frotter** ◻1 vt/i rub; (allumette) strike.

frottis /fʀɔti/ nm **~ vaginal** cervical smear.

frousse /fʀus/ nf ◻1 fear; **avoir la ~** ◻1 be scared.

fructifier /fʀyktifje/ ◻45 vi **faire ~** put to work.

fructueux, -euse /fʀyktɥø, -z/ adj fruitful.

frugal, ~e (mpl **-aux**) /fʀygal, -o/ adj frugal.

fruit /fʀɥi/ nm fruit; **des ~s** (some) fruit; **~s de mer** seafood. **fruité, ~e** adj fruity.

frustrant, ~e /fʀystʀã, -t / adj frustrating. **frustrer** ◻1 vt frustrate.

fuel /fjul/ nm fuel oil.

fugitif, -ive /fyʒitif, -v/ adj (passager) fleeting. ●nm, f fugitive.

fugue /fyg/ nf (Mus) fugue; **faire une ~** run away.

fuir /fɥiʀ/ ◻35 vi flee, run away; (eau, robinet, etc.) leak. ●vt (quitter) flee; (éviter) shun.

fuite /fɥit/ nf flight; (de liquide, d'une nouvelle) leak; **en ~** on the run; **mettre en ~** put to flight; **prendre la ~** take flight.

fulgurant, ~e /fylgyʀã, -t/ adj (vitesse) lightning.

fumé, ~e /fyme/ adj (poisson, verre) smoked.

fumée /fyme/ nf smoke; (vapeur) steam.

fumer /fyme/ ◻1 vt/i smoke.

fumeur, -euse /fymœʀ, -øz/ nm, f smoker; **zone non-~s** no smoking area.

fumier /fymje/ nm manure.

funambule /fynãbyl/ nmf tightrope walker.

funèbre /fynɛbʀ/ adj funeral; (fig) gloomy.

funérailles /fyneʀaj/ nfpl funeral.

funéraire /fyneʀɛʀ/ adj funeral.

funeste /fynɛst/ adj fatal.

fur: au ~ et à mesure /ofyʀea- məzyʀ/ loc as one goes along, progressively; **au ~ et à mesure que** as.

furet /fyʀɛ/ nm ferret.

fureur /fyʀœʀ/ nf fury; (passion) passion; **avec ~** furiously; passionately; **mettre en ~** infuriate; **faire ~** be all the rage.

furieux, -ieuse /fyʀjø, -z/ adj furious.

furoncle /fyʀõkl/ nm boil.

furtif, -ive /fyʀtif, -v/ adj furtive.

fuseau (pl **~x**) /fyzo/ nm ski trousers; (pour filer) spindle; **~ horaire** time zone.

fusée /fyze/ nf rocket.

fusible /fyzibl/ nm fuse.

fusil /fyzi/ nm rifle, gun; (de chasse) shotgun; ~ **mitrailleur** machine-gun.

fusion /fyzjõ/ nf fusion; (Comm) merger. **fusionner** 1 vt/i merge.

fut /fy/ ▶ÊTRE 5.

fût* /fy/ nm (tonneau) barrel; (d'arbre) trunk.

futé, ~**e** /fyte/ adj cunning.

futile /fytil/ adj futile.

futur, ~**e** /fytyR/ adj future; ~**e femme/maman** wife-/mother-to-be. ●nm future.

fuyant, ~**e** /fɥijã, -t/ adj (front, ligne) receding; (personne) evasive.

fuyard, ~**e** /fɥijaR, -d/ nm, f runaway.

Gg

gabardine /gabaRdin/ nf raincoat.

gabarit /gabaRi/ nm size; (patron) template; (fig) calibre.

gâcher /gɑʃe/ 1 vt (gâter) spoil; (gaspiller) waste.

gâchette /gɑʃɛt/ nf trigger.

gâchis /gɑʃi/ nm waste.

gaffe /gaf/ nf 1 blunder; **faire** ~ be careful (**à** of).

gage /gaʒ/ nm security; (de bonne foi) pledge; (de jeu) forfeit; ~**s** (salaire) wages; **en** ~ **de** as a token of; **mettre en** ~ pawn; **tueur à** ~**s** hired killer.

gageure* /gaʒyR/ nf challenge.

gagnant, ~**e** /gaɲã, -t/ adj winning. ●nm, f winner.

gagne-pain* /gaɲpɛ̃/ nm inv job.

gagner /gaɲe/ 1 vt (match, prix) win; (argent, pain) earn; (temps) save; (atteindre) reach; (convaincre) win over; ~ **sa vie** earn one's living. ●vi win; (fig) gain.

gai, ~**e** /ge/ adj cheerful; (ivre) merry. **gaiement*** adv cheerfully. **gaieté*** nf cheerfulness.

gain /gɛ̃/ nm (salaire) earnings; (avantage) gain; (économie) saving; ~**s** (Comm) profits; (au jeu) winnings.

gaine /gɛn/ nf (corset) girdle; (étui) sheath.

galant, ~**e** /galã, -t/ adj courteous; (amoureux) romantic.

galaxie /galaksi/ nf galaxy.

gale /gal/ nf (de chat etc.) mange.

galère /galɛR/ nf (navire) galley; **c'est la** ~! 1 what an ordeal!

galérer /galere/ 14 vi 1 (peiner) have a hard time.

galerie /galRi/ nf gallery; (Théât) circle; (de voiture) roof-rack; ~ **marchande** shopping arcade.

galet /galɛ/ nm pebble.

galette /galɛt/ nf flat cake; ~ **des Rois** Twelfth Night cake.

Galles /gal/ nfpl **le pays de** ~ Wales.

gallois, ~**e** /galwa, -z/ adj Welsh. ●nm (Ling) Welsh. **G**~, ~**e** nm, f Welshman, Welshwoman.

galon /galõ/ nm braid; (Mil) stripe; **prendre du** ~ be promoted.

galop /galo/ nm canter; **aller au** ~ canter; **grand** ~ gallop; ~ **d'essai** trial run. **galoper** 1 vi (cheval) canter; (au grand galop) gallop; (personne) run.

galopin /galɔpɛ̃/ nm 1 rascal.

gambader /gɑ̃bade/ **1** vi leap about.

gamelle /gamɛl/ nf (de soldat) mess kit; (d'ouvrier) lunch-box.

gamin, ~e /gamɛ̃, -in/ adj childish; (air) youthful. ●nm, f **1** kid.

gamme /gam/ nf (Mus) scale; (série) range; **haut de ~** up-market, top of the range; **bas de ~** down-market, bottom of the range.

gang /gɑ̃g/ nm **1** gang.

ganglion /gɑ̃glijɔ̃/ nm ganglion.

gangster /gɑ̃gstɛʀ/ nm gangster; (escroc) crook.

gant /gɑ̃/ nm glove; **~ de ménage** rubber glove; **~ de toilette** face-flannel, face-cloth.

garage /gaʀaʒ/ nm garage. **garagiste** nmf garage owner; (employé) car mechanic.

garant, ~e /gaʀɑ̃, -t/ nm, f guarantor. ●adj **se porter ~ de** vouch for.

garanti, ~e /gaʀɑ̃ti/ adj guaranteed.

garantie /gaʀɑ̃ti/ nf guarantee; **~s** (de police d'assurance) cover. **garantir** **2** vt guarantee; (protéger) protect (**de** from).

garçon /gaʀsɔ̃/ nm boy; (jeune homme) young man; (célibataire) bachelor; **~ (de café)** waiter; **~ d'honneur** best man. **garçonnière** nf bachelor flat.

garde¹ /gaʀd/ nf guard; (d'enfants, de bagages) care; (service) guard (duty); (infirmière) nurse; **de ~** on duty; **~ à vue** (police) custody; **mettre en ~** warn; **prendre ~** be careful (**à** of); **(droit de) ~** custody (**de** of).

garde² /gaʀd/ nm guard; (de propriété, parc) warden; **~ champêtre** village policeman; **~ du corps** bodyguard.

garde-à-vous /gaʀdavu/ nm inv (Mil) **se mettre au ~** stand to attention.

garde-chasse (pl ~s) /gaʀdə-ʃas/ nm gamekeeper.

garde-manger /gaʀdmɑ̃ʒe/ nm inv meat safe; (placard) larder.

garder /gaʀde/ **1** vt (conserver, maintenir) keep; (vêtement) keep on; (surveiller) look after; (défendre) guard; **~ le lit** stay in bed. ■se **~** vpr (denrée) keep; **se ~ de faire** be careful not to do.

garderie /gaʀdəʀi/ nf day nursery.

garde-robe (pl ~s) /gaʀdəʀɔb/ nf wardrobe.

gardien, ~ne /gaʀdjɛ̃, -ɛn/ nm, f (de locaux) security guard; (de prison, réserve) warden; (d'immeuble) caretaker; (de musée) attendant; (de zoo) keeper; (de traditions) guardian; **~ de but** goalkeeper; **~ de la paix** policeman; **~ de nuit** night watchman; **gardienne d'enfants** childminder.

gare /gaʀ/ nf (Rail) station; **~ routière** coach station; (US) bus station. ●interj **~ (à toi)** watch out!

garer /gaʀe/ **1** vt park. ■se **~** vpr park; (s'écarter) move out of the way.

gargouille /gaʀguj/ nf waterspout; (sculptée) gargoyle. **gargouiller** **1** vi gurgle; (stomach) rumble.

garni, ~e /gaʀni/ adj (plat) served with vegetables; **bien ~** (rempli) well-filled.

garnir /gaʀniʀ/ **2** vt (remplir) fill; (décorer) decorate; (couvrir) cover; (doubler) line; (Culin) garnish. **garniture** nf (légumes) vegetables; (ornement) trimming; (de voiture) trim.

gars /gɑ/ nm **1** lad; (adulte) guy, bloke.

gas-oil /gazwal/ nm diesel (oil).

gaspillage /gaspijaʒ/ nm waste. **gaspiller** **1** vt waste.

gastrique /gastʀik/ adj gastric.

g

gastronome /gastʀɔnɔm/ nmf gourmet.

gâteau (pl ~x) /gɑto/ nm cake; ~ **sec** biscuit; (US) cookie; **un papa** ~ a doting dad.

gâter /gɑte/ **1** vt spoil. ■ **se** ~ vpr (viande) go bad; (dent) rot; (temps) get worse.

gâterie /gɑtʀi/ nf little treat.

gâteux, -euse /gɑtø, -z/ adj senile.

gauche /goʃ/ adj left; (maladroit) awkward. ●nf left; **à** ~ on the left; (direction) (to the) left; **la** ~ the left (side); (Pol) the left (wing).

gaucher, -ère /goʃe, -ɛʀ/ adj left handed.

gaufre /gofʀ/ nf waffle. **gaufrette** nf wafer.

gaulois, ~e /golwa, -z/ adj Gallic; (fig) bawdy. **G~, ~e** nm, f Gaul.

gaver /gave/ **1** vt force-feed; (fig) cram. ■ **se** ~ **de** vpr gorge oneself with; (fig) devour.

gaz /gɑz/ nm inv gas; ~ **d'échappement** exhaust fumes; ~ **lacrymogène** tear-gas.

gaze /gɑz/ nf gauze.

gazer /gɑze/ **1** vi **1** **ça gaze?** how's things?

gazette /gɑzɛt/ nf newspaper.

gazeux, -euse /gɑzø, -z/ adj (boisson) fizzy; (eau) sparkling.

gazoduc /gɑzɔdyk/ nm gas pipeline.

gazon /gɑzɔ̃/ nm lawn, grass.

gazouiller /gɑzuje/ **1** vi (oiseau) chirp; (bébé) babble.

GDF abrév m (**Gaz de France**) French gas board.

géant, ~e /ʒeɑ̃, -t/ adj giant. ●nm giant. **géante** nf giantess.

geindre /ʒɛ̃dʀ/ **22** vi groan, moan.

gel /ʒɛl/ nm frost; (produit) gel;

(Comm) freeze; ~ **coiffant** hair gel.

gelée /ʒ(ə)le/ nf frost; (Culin) jelly; ~ **blanche** hoarfrost.

geler /ʒəle/ **6** vt/i freeze; **on gèle** (on a froid) it's freezing; **il ou ça gèle** (il fait froid) it's freezing.

gélule /ʒelyl/ nf (Méd) capsule.

Gémeaux /ʒemo/ nmpl Gemini.

gémir /ʒemiʀ/ **2** vi groan.

gênant, ~e /ʒɛnɑ̃, -t/ adj embarrassing; (irritant) annoying; (incommode) cumbersome.

gencive /ʒɑ̃siv/ nf gum.

gendarme /ʒɑ̃daʀm/ nm policeman, gendarme. ▣**gendarmerie** nf police force; (local) police station.

gendre /ʒɑ̃dʀ/ nm son-in-law.

gène /ʒɛn/ nm gene.

gêne /ʒɛn/ nf discomfort; (confusion) embarrassment; (dérangement) trouble, inconvenience; (pauvreté) poverty.

gêné, ~e /ʒene/ adj embarrassed; (désargenté) short of money.

généalogie /ʒenealɔʒi/ nf genealogy.

gêner /ʒene/ **1** vt bother, disturb; (troubler) embarrass; (entraver) block; (faire mal) hurt.

général, ~e (mpl **-aux**) /ʒeneʀal, -o/ adj general; **en** ~ in general. ●nm (pl **-aux**) general.

généralement /ʒeneʀalmɑ̃/ adv generally.

généraliser /ʒeneʀalize/ **1** vt make general. ●vi generalize. ■ **se** ~ vpr become widespread ou general.

généraliste /ʒeneʀalist/ nmf general practitioner, GP.

généralité /ʒeneʀalite/ nf general point.

génération /ʒeneʀasjɔ̃/ nf generation.

généreux, ~euse /ʒeneʀø, -z/ adj generous.

générique /ʒeneʀik/ nm (au cinéma) credits. ●adj generic.

générosité /ʒeneʀozite/ nf generosity.

génétique /ʒenetik/ adj genetic. ●nf genetics.

Genève /ʒənεv/ npr Geneva.

génial, ∼e (mpl **-iaux**) /ʒenjal, -jo/ adj brilliant; (fantastique **1**) fantastic.

génie /ʒeni/ nm genius; ∼ **civil** civil engineering.

génital, ∼e (mpl **-aux**) /ʒenital, -o/ adj genital.

génocide /ʒenɔsid/ nm genocide.

génoise /ʒenwaz/ nf sponge (cake).

génome /ʒenom/ nm genome.

génothèque /ʒenɔtεk/ nf gene bank.

genou (pl ∼**x**) /ʒənu/ nm knee; **être à** ∼**x** be kneeling.

genre /ʒɑ̃ʀ/ nm sort, kind; (Gram) gender; (allure) **avoir bon/ mauvais** ∼ to look nice/ disreputable; (comportement) **c'est bien son** ∼ it's just like him/her.

gens /ʒɑ̃/ nmpl people.

gentil, ∼**le** /ʒɑ̃ti, -j/ adj kind, nice; (sage) good. **gentillesse** nf kindness. **gentiment** adv kindly.

géographie /ʒeɔgʀafi/ nf geography.

geôlier, -ière /ʒolje, -jεʀ/ nm, f gaoler, jailer.

géologie /ʒeɔlɔʒi/ nf geology.

géomètre /ʒeɔmεtʀ/ nm surveyor.

géométrie /ʒeɔmetʀi/ nf geometry. **géométrique** adj geometric.

gérance /ʒeʀɑ̃s/ nf management.

gérant, ∼**e** /ʒeʀɑ̃, -t/ nm, f manager, manageress; ∼ **d'immeuble** landlord's agent.

gerbe /ʒεʀb/ nf (de fleurs) bunch, bouquet; (d'eau) spray; (de blé) sheaf.

gercer /ʒεʀse/ **10** vt chap; **avoir les lèvres gercées** have chapped lips. ●vi become chapped. **gerçure** nf crack, chap.

gérer /ʒeʀe/ **14** vt manage, run; (traiter: fig) (crise, situation) handle.

germe /ʒεʀm/ nm germ; ∼**s de soja** bean sprouts.

germer /ʒεʀme/ **1** vi germinate.

gestation /ʒεstasjɔ̃/ nf gestation.

geste /ʒεst/ nm gesture.

gesticuler /ʒεstikyle/ **1** vi gesticulate.

gestion /ʒεstjɔ̃/ nf management. **gestionnaire** nmf administrator.

ghetto /gεto/ nm ghetto.

gibier /ʒibje/ nm (animaux) game.

giboulée /ʒibule/ nf shower.

gicler /ʒikle/ **1** vi squirt; **faire** ∼ squirt.

gifle /ʒifl/ nf slap in the face. **gifler** **1** vt slap.

gigantesque /ʒigɑ̃tεsk/ adj gigantic.

gigot /ʒigo/ nm leg (of lamb).

gigoter /ʒigɔte/ **1** vi wriggle; (nerveusement) fidget.

gilet /ʒilε/ nm waistcoat; (cardigan) cardigan; ∼ **de sauvetage** life jacket.

gingembre /ʒε̃ʒɑ̃bʀ/ nm ginger.

girafe /ʒiʀaf/ nf giraffe.

giratoire /ʒiʀatwaʀ/ adj **sens** ∼ roundabout.

girofle /ʒiʀɔfl/ nm **clou de** ∼ clove.

girouette /ʒiʀwεt/ nf weathercock, weathervane.

gisement /ʒizmɑ̃/ nm deposit.

gitan, ∼**e** /ʒitɑ̃, -an/ nm, f gypsy.

gîte* /ʒit/ nm (maison) home; (abri)

shelter; ▣~ **rural** holiday cottage.

givre /ʒivʀ/ nm frost; (sur parebrise) ice.

givré, ~e /ʒivʀe/ adj ▣ crazy.

glace /glas/ nf ice; (crème) ice-cream; (vitre) window; (miroir) mirror; (verre) glass.

glacé, ~e /glase/ adj (vent, accueil) icy; (hands) frozen; (gâteau) iced.

glacer /glase/ ▣ vt freeze; (gâteau, boisson) chill; (pétrifier) chill. ■ **se ~** vpr freeze.

glacier /glasje/ nm (Géog) glacier; (vendeur) ice-cream seller. **glacière** nf coolbox. **glaçon** nm ice-cube.

glaïeul /glajœl/ nm gladiolus.

glaise /glɛz/ nf clay.

gland /glɑ̃/ nm acorn; (ornement) tassel.

glande /glɑ̃d/ nf gland.

glander /glɑ̃de/ ▣ vi ▣ laze around.

glaner /glane/ ▣ vt glean.

glauque /glok/ adj (fig) murky; (street) squalid.

glissade /glisad/ nf (jeu) slide; (dérapage) skid.

glissant, ~e /glisɑ̃, -t/ adj slippery.

glissement /glismɑ̃/ nm sliding; gliding; (fig) shift; **~ de terrain** landslide.

glisser /glise/ ▣ vi slide; (être glissant) be slippery; (sur l'eau) glide; (déraper) slip; (véhicule) skid. ●vt (objet) slip (**dans** into); (remarque) slip in. ■ **se ~** vpr slip (**dans** into).

glissière /glisjɛʀ/ nf slide; **porte à ~** sliding door; **~ de sécurité** (Auto) crash-barrier; **fermeture à ~** zip.

global, ~e (mpl **-aux**) /glɔbal, -o/ adj (entier, général) overall.

globalement adv as a whole.

globe /glɔb/ nm globe; **~ oculaire** eyeball; **~ terrestre** globe.

globule /glɔbyl/ nm (du sang) corpuscle.

gloire /glwaʀ/ nf glory, fame. **glorieux, -ieuse** adj glorious. **glorifier** ⓸⑤ vt glorify.

glose /gloz/ nf gloss.

glossaire /glɔsɛʀ/ nm glossary.

gloussement /glusmɑ̃/ nm chuckle; (de poule) cluck.

glouton, ~ne /glutɔ̃, -ɔn/ adj gluttonous. ●nm, f glutton.

gluant, ~e /glyɑ̃, -t/ adj sticky.

glucose /glykoz/ nm glucose.

glycérine /gliseʀin/ nf glycerin(e).

GO abrév fpl (**grandes ondes**) long wave.

goal /gol/ nm ▣ goalkeeper.

gobelet /gɔblɛ/ nm cup; (en verre) tumbler.

gober /gɔbe/ ▣ vt swallow (whole); **je ne peux pas le ~** ▣ I can't stand him.

goéland /gɔelɑ̃/ nm (sea)gull.

gogo: à ~ /agogo/ loc ▣ galore, in abundance.

goinfre /gwɛ̃fʀ/ nm (glouton ▣) pig. **goinfrer (se)** ▣ vpr ▣ stuff oneself (**de** with).

golf /gɔlf/ nm golf; (terrain) golf course.

golfe /gɔlf/ nm gulf.

gomme /gom/ nf rubber; (US) eraser; (résine) gum. **gommer** ▣ vt rub out.

gond /gɔ̃/ nm hinge; **sortir de ses ~s** ▣ go mad.

gondoler (se) /(sə)gɔ̃dɔle/ ▣ vpr (bois) warp; (métal) buckle.

gonflé, ~e /gɔ̃fle/ adj swollen; **il est ~** ▣ he's got a nerve.

gonflement /gɔ̃fləmɑ̃/ nm swelling.

▣ see A-Z of French life and culture

gonfler /gɔ̃fle/ **1** vt (ballon, pneu) pump up, blow up; (augmenter) increase; (exagérer) inflate. • vi swell.

gorge /gɔʁʒ/ nf throat; (poitrine) breast; (vallée) gorge.

gorgée /gɔʁʒe/ nf sip, gulp.

gorger /gɔʁʒe/ **40** vt fill (**de** with); **gorgé de** full of. ■ se ~ vpr gorge oneself (**de** with).

gorille /gɔʁij/ nm gorilla; (garde **1**) bodyguard.

gosier /gozje/ nm throat.

gosse /gɔs/ nmf **1** kid.

gothique /gɔtik/ adj Gothic.

goudron /gudʁɔ̃/ nm tar. **goudronner 1** vt tarmac.

gouffre /gufʁ/ nm abyss, gulf.

goujat /guʒa/ nm lout, boor.

goulot /gulo/ nm neck; **boire au ~** drink from the bottle.

goulu, ~e /guly/ adj gluttonous. • nm, f glutton.

gourde /guʁd/ nf (à eau) flask; (idiot **1**) fool.

gourer (se) /(sə)guʁe/ **1** vpr **1** make a mistake.

gourmand, ~e /guʁmã, -d/ adj greedy. • nm, f glutton.

gourmandise /guʁmãdiz/ nf greed; **~s** sweets.

gourmet /guʁmɛ/ nm gourmet.

gourmette /guʁmɛt/ nf chain bracelet.

gousse /gus/ nf **~ d'ail** clove of garlic.

goût* /gu/ nm taste; (gré) liking; **prendre ~ à** develop a taste for; **avoir bon ~** (aliment) taste nice; (personne) have good taste; **donner du ~ à** give flavour.

goûter* /gute/ **1** vt taste; (apprécier) enjoy; **~ à ou de** taste. • vi have tea. • nm tea, snack.

goutte /gut/ nf drop; (Méd) gout. **goutte-à-goutte** nm inv drip.

goutter 1 vi drip.

gouttière /gutjɛʁ/ nf gutter.

gouvernail /guvɛʁnaj/ nm rudder; (barre) helm.

gouvernement /guvɛʁnəmã/ nm government.

gouverner /guvɛʁne/ **1** vt/i govern; (dominer) control. **gouverneur** nm governor.

GPS abrév m (**global positioning system**) GPS.

grâce /gʁɑs/ nf (charme) grace; (faveur) favour; (volonté) grace; (Jur) pardon; (Relig) grace; **~ à** thanks to; **rendre (~s) à** give thanks to.

gracier /gʁasje/ **45** vt pardon.

gracieusement /gʁasjøzmã/ adv gracefully; (gratuitement) free (of charge).

gracieux, -ieuse /gʁasjø, -z/ adj graceful.

grade /gʁad/ nm rank; **monter en ~** be promoted.

gradin /gʁadɛ̃/ nm tier, step; **en ~s** terraced; **les ~s** terraces.

gradué, ~e /gʁadye/ adj graded, graduated; **verre ~** measuring jug.

graffiti* /gʁafiti/ nmpl graffiti.

grain /gʁɛ̃/ nm grain; (Naut) squall; **~ de beauté** beauty spot; **~ de café** coffee bean; **~ de poivre** pepper corn; **~ de raisin** grape.

graine /gʁɛn/ nf seed.

graisse /gʁɛs/ nf fat; (lubrifiant) grease. **graisser 1** vt grease. **graisseux, -euse** adj greasy.

grammaire /gʁam(m)ɛʁ/ nf grammar.

gramme /gʁam/ nm gram.

grand, ~e /gʁã, -d/ adj big, large; (haut) tall; (intense, fort) great; (brillant) great; (principal) main; (plus âgé) big, elder; (adulte) grown-up; **au ~ air** in the open air; **au ~ jour** in broad daylight; (fig) in the open; **en ~e partie** largely;

g

~**e banlieue** outer suburbs; ~ **ensemble** housing estate; ~**es lignes** (Rail) main lines; ~ **magasin** department store; ~**e personne** grown-up; ~ **public** general public; ~**e surface** hypermarket; ~**es vacances** summer holidays. ●adv (ouvrir) wide; ~ **ouvert** wide open; **voir** ~ think big. ●nm, f (adulte) grown-up; (enfant) big boy, big girl; (Scol) senior.

grand-chose /gʀɑ̃ʃoz/ pron **pas** ~ not much, not a lot.

Grande-Bretagne /gʀɑ̃dbʀətaɲ/ nf Great Britain.

grandeur /gʀɑ̃dœʀ/ nf greatness; (dimension) size; **folie des** ~**s** delusions of grandeur.

grandir /gʀɑ̃diʀ/ **2** vi grow; (bruit) grow louder. ●vt (talons) make taller; (loupe) magnify.

grand-mère (pl **grands-mères**) /gʀɑ̃mɛʀ/ nf grandmother.

grand-père (pl **grands-pères**) /gʀɑ̃pɛʀ/ nm grandfather.

grands-parents /gʀɑ̃paʀɑ̃/ nmpl grandparents.

grange /gʀɑ̃ʒ/ nf barn.

granulé /gʀanyle/ nm granule.

graphique /gʀafik/ adj graphic; (Ordinat) graphics; **informatique** ~ computer graphics. ●nm graph.

graphologie /gʀafɔlɔʒi/ nf graphology.

grappe /gʀap/ nf cluster; ~ **de raisin** bunch of grapes.

gras, -se /gʀɑ, -s/ adj (gros) fat; (aliment) fatty; (surface, peau, cheveux) greasy; (épais) thick; (caractères) bold; **faire la ~se matinée** sleep late. ●nm (Culin) fat.

gratifiant, ~e /gʀatifjɑ̃, -t/ adj gratifying; (travail) rewarding.

gratifier /gʀatifje/ **45** vt favour, reward (**de** with).

gratin /gʀatɛ̃/ nm gratin (baked dish with cheese topping); (élite **1**) upper crust.

gratis /gʀatis/ adv free.

gratitude /gʀatityd/ nf gratitude.

gratte-ciel* /gʀatsjɛl/ nm inv skyscraper.

gratter /gʀate/ **1** vt/i scratch; (avec un outil) scrape; **ça me gratte 1** it itches. ■ **se** ~ vpr scratch oneself; **se** ~ **la tête** scratch one's head.

gratuiciel /gʀatɥisjɛl/ nm (Internet) freeware.

gratuit, ~e /gʀatɥi, -t/ adj free; (acte) gratuitous. **gratuitement** adv free (of charge).

grave /gʀav/ adj (maladie, accident, problème) serious; (solennel) grave; (voix) deep; (accent) grave. **gravement** adv seriously; gravely.

graver /gʀave/ **1** vt engrave; (sur bois) carve; (Ordinat) burn.

graveur /gʀavœʀ/ nm (Ordinat) burner.

gravier /gʀavje/ nm **du** ~ gravel.

gravité /gʀavite/ nf gravity.

graviter /gʀavite/ **1** vi revolve.

gravure /gʀavyʀ/ nf engraving; (de tableau, photo) print, plate.

gré /gʀe/ nm (volonté) will; (goût) taste; **à son** ~ (agir) as one likes; **de bon** ~ willingly; **bon** ~ **mal** ~ like it or not; **je vous en saurais** ~ I'd be grateful for that.

grec, ~que /gʀɛk/ adj Greek. ●nm (Ling) Greek. **G~, ~que** nm, f Greek.

Grèce nf /gʀɛs/ Greece.

greffe /gʀɛf/ nf graft; (d'organe) transplant. **greffer 1** vt graft; transplant.

greffier, -ière /gʀefje, -jɛʀ/ nm, f clerk of the court.

grêle /gʀɛl/ adj (maigre) spindly; (voix) shrill. ●nf hail.

grêler /gʀele/ **1** vi hail; **il grêle** it's hailing. **grêlon** nm hailstone.

grelot /gʀəlo/ nm (little) bell.

grelotter* /gʀəlɔte/ 🔳 vi shiver.

grenade /gʀənad/ nf (fruit) pomegranate; (explosif) grenade.

grenat /gʀəna/ adj inv dark red.

grenier /gʀənje/ nm attic; (pour grain) loft.

grenouille /gʀənuj/ nf frog.

grès /gʀɛ/ nm sandstone; (poterie) stoneware.

grésiller /gʀezije/ 🔳 vi sizzle; (radio) crackle.

grève /gʀɛv/ nf (rivage) shore; (cessation de travail) strike; **faire ~, être en ~** be on strike; **se mettre en ~** go on strike. **gréviste** nmf striker.

gribouiller /gʀibuje/ 🔳 vt/i scribble.

grief /gʀijɛf/ nm grievance.

grièvement /gʀijɛvmɑ̃/ adv seriously.

griffe /gʀif/ nf claw; (de couturier) label; **coup de ~** scratch.

griffé, ~e /gʀife/ adj (vêtement, article) designer.

griffer /gʀife/ 🔳 vt scratch, claw.

grignoter /gʀiɲɔte/ 🔳 vt/i nibble.

gril /gʀil/ nm (de cuisinière) grill; (plaque) grill pan.

grillade /gʀijad/ nf (viande) grill.

grillage /gʀijaʒ/ nm wire netting.

grille /gʀij/ nf railings; (portail) (metal) gate; (de fenêtre) bars; (de cheminée) grate; (fig) grid. **grille-pain*** nm inv toaster.

griller /gʀije/ 🔳 vt (pain) toast; (viande) grill; (ampoule) blow; (feu rouge) go through; (appareil) burn out. • vi (ampoule) blow; (Culin) **faire ~** (viande) grill; (pain) toast.

grillon /gʀijɔ̃/ nm cricket.

grimace /gʀimas/ nf (funny) face; (de douleur, dégoût) grimace; **faire des ~s** make faces; **faire la ~** pull a face, grimace.

grimper /gʀɛ̃pe/ 🔳 vt climb. • vi climb; **~ sur** ou **dans un arbre** climb a tree.

grincement /gʀɛ̃smɑ̃/ nm creak-(ing).

grincer /gʀɛ̃se/ 🔟 vi creak; **~ des dents** grind one's teeth.

grincheux, -euse /gʀɛ̃ʃø, -z/ adj grumpy.

grippe /gʀip/ nf influenza, flu.

grippé, ~e /gʀipe/ adj **être ~** have (the) flu; (mécanisme) be seized up ou jammed.

gris, ~e /gʀi, -z/ adj grey; (saoul) tipsy.

grivois, ~e /gʀivwa, -z/ adj bawdy.

grog /gʀɔg/ nm hot toddy.

grogner /gʀɔɲe/ 🔳 vi (animal) growl; (personne) grumble.

grognon /gʀɔɲɔ̃/ adj grumpy.

groin /gʀwɛ̃/ nm snout.

gronder /gʀɔ̃de/ 🔳 vi (tonnerre, volcan) rumble; (chien) growl; (conflit) be brewing. • vt scold.

groom /gʀum/ nm bellboy.

gros, ~se /gʀo, -s/ adj big, large; (gras) fat; (important) big; (épais) thick; (lourd) heavy; (buveur, fumeur) heavy; **~ bonnet** 🔟 bigwig; **~ lot** jackpot; **~ mot** swear word; **~ plan** close-up; **~se caisse** bass drum; **~ titre** headline. • nm, f fat man, fat woman. • adv (écrire) big; (risquer, gagner) a lot. • nm **le ~ de** the bulk of; **de ~** (Comm) wholesale; **en ~** roughly; (Comm) wholesale.

groseille /gʀozɛj/ nf redcurrant; **~ à maquereau** gooseberry.

grossesse /gʀosɛs/ nf pregnancy.

grosseur /gʀosœʀ/ nf (volume) size; (enflure) lump.

grossier, -ière /gʀosje, -jɛʀ/ adj (sans finesse) coarse, rough; (rudimentaire) crude; (vulgaire) coarse; (impoli) rude; (erreur) gross. **grossièrement** adv (sommairement) roughly; (vulgairement) coarsely.

grossièreté /nf/ coarseness; crudeness; rudeness; (mot) rude word.

grossir /gʀosiʀ/ 2 vt (faire augmenter) increase, boost; (agrandir) enlarge; (exagérer) exaggerate; ~ **les rangs** *ou* **la foule** swell the ranks. •vi (personne) put on weight; (augmenter) grow.

grossiste /gʀosist/ nmf wholesaler.

grosso modo /gʀosomodo/ adv roughly.

grotesque /gʀɔtɛsk/ adj grotesque; (ridicule) ludicrous.

grotte /gʀɔt/ nf cave; grotto.

grouiller /gʀuje/ 1 vi swarm; ~ **de** be swarming with.

groupe /gʀup/ nm group; (Mus) group, band; ~ **électrogène** generating set; ~ **scolaire** school; ~ **de travail** working party.

groupement /gʀupmɑ̃/ nm grouping.

grouper /gʀupe/ 1 vt put together. ∎ **se** ~ vpr group (together).

grue /gʀy/ nf (machine, oiseau) crane.

gruyère /gʀyjɛʀ/ nm gruyère (cheese).

gué /ge/ nm ford; **passer** *ou* **traverser à** ~ ford.

guenon /gənɔ̃/ nf female monkey.

guépard /gepaʀ/ nm cheetah.

guêpe /gɛp/ nf wasp.

guère /gɛʀ/ adv **ne** ~ hardly; **il n'y a** ~ **d'espoir** there is no hope; **elle n'a** ~ **dormi** she didn't sleep much, she hardly slept.

guérilla /geʀija/ nf guerrilla warfare; (groupe) guerillas.

guérir /geʀiʀ/ 2 vt (personne, maladie, mal) cure (**de** of); (plaie, membre) heal. •vi get better; (blessure) heal; ~ **de** recover

from. **guérison** nf curing; healing; (de personne) recovery.

guerre /gɛʀ/ nf war; **en** ~ at war; **faire la** ~ wage war (**à** against); ~ **civile** civil war; ~ **mondiale** world war.

guerrier, -ière /gɛʀje, -jɛʀ/ adj warlike. •nm, f warrior.

guet /gɛ/ nm watch; **faire le** ~ be on the watch. **guet-apens** (pl **guets-apens**) nm ambush.

guetter /gete/ 1 vt watch; (attendre) watch out for.

gueule /gœl/ nf mouth; (figure 🖪) face; **ta** ~! shut up!; ~ **de bois** 🖪 hangover.

gueuleton /gœltɔ̃/ nm 🖪 blowout, slap-up meal.

gui /gi/ nm mistletoe.

guichet /giʃɛ/ nm window, counter; (de gare) ticket-office; (Théât) box-office; **jouer à** ~**s fermés** (pièce) be sold out; ~ **automatique** cash dispenser.

guide /gid/ nm guide. •nf (fille scout) girl guide.

guider /gide/ 1 vt guide.

guidon /gidɔ̃/ nm handlebars.

guignol /giɲɔl/ nm puppet; (personne) clown; (spectacle) puppet-show.

guillemets /gijmɛ/ nmpl quotation marks, inverted commas; **entre** ~ in inverted commas.

guillotine /gijɔtin/ nf guillotine.

guimauve /gimov/ nf marshmallow; **c'est de la** ~ 🖪 it's slushy *ou* schmaltzy 🖪.

guindé, ~e /gɛ̃de/ adj stiff, formal; (style) stilted.

guirlande /giʀlɑ̃d/ nf garland; tinsel.

guitare /gitaʀ/ nf guitar.

gym /ʒim/ nf gymnastics; (Scol) physical education, PE.

gymnase /ʒimnɑz/ nm

gym(nasium). **gymnastique** nf gymnastics.

gynécologie /ʒinekɔlɔʒi/ nf gynaecology.

Hh

habile /abil/ adj skilful, clever.

habillé, ∼**e** /abije/ adj (vêtement) smart; (soirée) formal.

habillement /abijmã/ nm clothing.

habiller /abije/ **1** vt dress (**de** in); (équiper) clothe; (recouvrir) cover (**de** with). ■ **s'**∼ vpr get dressed; (élégamment) dress up.

habit /abi/ nm (de personnage) outfit; (de cérémonie) tails; ∼**s** clothes.

habitant, ∼**e** /abitã, -t/ nm, f (de maison, quartier) resident; (de pays) inhabitant.

habitat /abita/ nm (mode de peuplement) settlement; (conditions) housing.

habitation /abitasjõ/ nf (logement) house.

habité, ∼**e** /abite/ adj (terre) inhabited.

habiter /abite/ **1** vi live. ● vt live in.

habitude /abityd/ nf habit; **avoir l'**∼ **de** be used to; **d'**∼ usually; **comme d'**∼ as usual.

habitué, ∼**e** /abitɥe/ nm, f (client) regular.

habituel, ∼**le** /abitɥel/ adj usual. **habituellement** adv usually.

habituer /abitɥe/ **1** vt ∼ **qn à** get sb used to. ■ **s'**∼ **à** vpr get used to.

hache /aʃ/ nf axe.

haché, ∼**e** /ˈaʃe/ adj (viande) minced; (phrases) jerky.

hacher /ˈaʃe/ **1** vt mince; (au couteau) chop.

hachis /ˈaʃi/ nm minced meat; (US) ground meat; ∼ **Parmentier** ≈ shepherd's pie.

hachisch /ˈaʃiʃ/ nm hashish.

hachoir /ˈaʃwaʀ/ nm (appareil) mincer; (couteau) chopper; (planche) chopping board.

haie /ˈɛ/ nf hedge; **course de** ∼**s** hurdle race.

haillon /ˈajõ/ nm rag.

haine /ˈɛn/ nf hatred.

haïr /ˈaiʀ/ **36** vt hate.

hâlé, ∼**e** /ˈale/ adj (sun-)tanned.

haleine /alɛn/ nf breath; **travail de longue** ∼ long job.

haleter /ˈalte/ **6** vi pant.

hall /ˈol/ nm hall; (de gare) concourse.

halle /ˈal/ nf market hall; ∼**s** covered market.

halte /ˈalt/ nf stop; **faire** ∼ stop. ● interj stop; (Mil) halt.

haltère /altɛʀ/ nm dumbbell; **faire des** ∼**s** to do weightlifting.

hameau (pl ∼**x**) /ˈamo/ nm hamlet.

hameçon /amsõ/ nm hook.

hanche /ˈãʃ/ nf hip.

handicap /ˈãdikap/ nm handicap. **handicapé,** ∼**e** adj & nm, f disabled (person).

hangar /ˈãgaʀ/ nm shed; (pour avions) hangar.

hanter /ˈãte/ **1** vt haunt.

hantise /'ɑ̃tiz/ nf dread; **avoir la ~ de** dread.

haras /'aʀɑ/ nm stud-farm.

harasser /'aʀase/ **1** vt exhaust.

harcèlement /'aʀsɛlmɑ̃/ nm **~ sexuel** sexual harassment.

harceler /'aʀsəle/ **6** vt harass.

hardi, ~e /'aʀdi/ adj bold.

hareng /'aʀɑ̃/ nm herring.

hargne /'aʀɲ/ nf (aggressive) bad temper.

haricot /'aʀiko/ nm bean; **~ vert** French bean; (US) green bean.

harmonie /aʀmɔni/ nf harmony. **harmonieux, -ieuse** adj harmonious.

harmoniser /aʀmɔnize/ **1** vt harmonize. ∎ **s'~** vpr harmonize.

harnacher /'aʀnaʃe/ **1** vt harness.

harnais /'aʀnɛ/ nm harness.

harpe /'aʀp/ nf harp.

harpon /'aʀpɔ̃/ nm harpoon.

hasard /'azaʀ/ nm chance; (coïncidence) coincidence; **les ~s de** the fortunes of; **au ~** (choisir etc.) at random; (flâner) aimlessly. **hasardeux, -euse** adj risky.

hasarder /'azaʀde/ **1** vt risk; (remarque) venture.

hâte /'ɑt/ nf haste; **à la ~, en ~** hurriedly; **avoir ~ de** look forward to.

hâter /'ɑte/ **1** vt hasten. ∎ **se ~** vpr hurry (**de** to).

hâtif, -ive /'ɑtif, -v/ adj hasty; (précoce) early.

hausse /'os/ nf rise (**de** in); **~ des prix** price rise; **en ~** rising.

hausser /'ose/ **1** vt raise; (épaules) shrug.

haut, ~e /'o, 'ot/ adj high; (de taille) tall; **~e voix** aloud; **~ en couleur** colourful; **plus ~** higher up; (dans un texte) above; **en ~ lieu** in high places. ∎ adv high; **tout ~** out loud. ∎ nm top; **des ~s et des bas** ups and downs; **en ~** (regarder) up; (à l'étage) upstairs; **en ~ de)** at the top (of).

hautbois /'obwa/ nm oboe.

haut-de-forme /'odfɔʀm/ (pl **hauts-de-forme**) nm top hat.

hauteur /'otœʀ/ nf height; (colline) hill; (arrogance) haughtiness; **être à la ~** be up to it; **à la ~ de** (ville) near; **être à la ~ de la situation** be equal to the situation.

haut-le-cœur /'olkœʀ/ nm inv nausea.

haut-parleur* (pl **~s**) /'opaʀlœʀ/ nm loudspeaker.

havre /'ɑvʀ/ nm haven (**de** of).

hayon /'ajɔ̃/ nm (Auto) hatchback.

hebdomadaire /ɛbdɔmadɛʀ/ adj & nm weekly.

hébergement /ebɛʀʒəmɑ̃/ nm accommodation.

héberger /ebɛʀʒe/ **40** vt (ami) put up; (réfugiés) take in.

hébreu (pl **~x**) /ebʀø/ am Hebrew. ∎ nm (Ling) Hebrew; **c'est de l'~!** it's all Greek to me!

Hébreu (pl **~x**) /ebʀø/ nm Hebrew; **les ~x** the Hebrews.

hécatombe /ekatɔ̃b/ nf slaughter.

hectare /ɛktaʀ/ nm hectare (= 10,000 square metres).

hélas /'elɑs/ interj alas. ∎ adv sadly.

hélice /elis/ nf propeller.

hélicoptère /elikɔptɛʀ/ nm helicopter.

helvétique /ɛlvetik/ adj Swiss.

hématome /ematɔm/ nm bruise.

hémorragie /emɔʀaʒi/ nf haemorrhage.

hémorroïdes /emɔʀɔid/ nfpl piles, haemorrhoids.

hennir /'eniʀ/ **2** vi neigh.

hépatite /epatit/ nf hepatitis.

herbe /ɛʀb/ nf grass; (Méd, Culin) herb; **en ~** in the blade; (fig) budding.

héréditaire /eʀeditɛʀ/ adj hereditary.

hérédité /eʀedite/ nf heredity.

hérisser /eʀise/ **1** vt bristle; **~ qn** (fig) ruffle sb. ∎ **se ~** vpr bristle.

hérisson /eʀisɔ̃/ nm hedgehog.

héritage /eʀitaʒ/ nm inheritance; (spirituel) heritage.

hériter /eʀite/ **1** vt/i inherit (**de** from); **~ de qch** inherit sth. **héritier, -ière** nm, f heir, heiress.

hermétique /ɛʀmetik/ adj airtight; (fig) unfathomable.

hernie /ˈɛʀni/ nf hernia.

héroïne /eʀɔin/ nf (femme) heroine; (drogue) heroin.

héroïque /eʀɔik/ adj heroic.

héros /ˈeʀo/ nm hero.

hésiter /ezite/ **1** vi hesitate (**à** to); **j'hésite** I'm not sure.

hétérogène /eteʀɔʒɛn/ adj heterogeneous.

hétérosexuel, ~le /eteʀɔsɛksɥɛl/ nm/ f & adj heterosexual.

hêtre /ˈɛtʀ/ nm beech.

heure /œʀ/ nf time; (soixante minutes) hour; **quelle ~ est-il?** what time is it?; **il est dix ~s** it is ten o'clock; **à l'~** (venir, être) on time; **d'~ en ~** by the hour; **toutes les deux ~s** every two hours; **~ de pointe** rush-hour; **~ de cours** (Scol) period; **~ indue** ungodly hour; **~s creuses** off peak periods; **~s supplémentaires** overtime.

heureusement /œʀøzmɑ̃/ adv fortunately, luckily.

heureux, -euse /œʀø, -z/ adj happy; (chanceux) lucky, fortunate.

heurt /ˈœʀ/ nm collision; (conflit) clash; **sans ~** smoothly.

heurter /ˈœʀte/ **1** vt (cogner) hit; (mur) bump into, hit; (choquer) offend. ∎ **se ~ à** vpr bump into, hit; (fig) come up against.

hexagone /ɛgzagon/ nm hexagon; **l'~** France.

hiberner /ibɛʀne/ **1** vi hibernate.

hibou (pl ~x) /ˈibu/ nm owl.

hier /jɛʀ/ adv yesterday; **~ soir** last night, yesterday evening.

hiérarchie /ˈjeʀaʀʃi/ nf hierarchy.

hilare /ilaʀ/ adj (visage) merry; **être ~** be laughing.

hindou, ~e /ɛ̃du/ adj & nm, f Hindu. **H~, ~e** nm, f Hindu.

hippique /ipik/ adj equestrian; **le concours ~** showjumping.

hippodrome /ipɔdʀom/ nm racecourse.

hippopotame /ipɔpɔtam/ nm hippopotamus.

hirondelle /iʀɔ̃dɛl/ nf swallow.

hisser /ˈise/ **1** vt hoist, haul. ∎ **se ~** vpr heave oneself up.

histoire /istwaʀ/ nf (récit) story; (étude) history; (affaire) business; **~(s)** (chichis) fuss; (ennuis) trouble. **historique** adj historical.

hiver /ivɛʀ/ nm winter. **hivernal, ~e** (mpl **-aux**) adj winter; (glacial) wintry.

H.L.M. abrév m ou f (**habitation à loyer modéré**) block of council flats; (US) low-rent apartment building.

hocher /ˈɔʃe/ **1** vt **~ la tête** (pour dire oui) nod; (pour dire non) shake one's head.

hochet /ˈɔʃɛ/ nm rattle.

hockey /ˈɔkɛ/ nm hockey; **~ sur glace** ice hockey.

hollandais, ~e /ˈɔlɑ̃dɛ, -z/ adj Dutch. ●nm (Ling) Dutch. **H~, ~e** nm, f Dutchman, Dutchwoman.

h

Hollande /'ɔlɑ̃d/ nf Holland.

homard /'ɔmaʀ/ nm lobster.

homéopathie /ɔmeɔpati/ nf homoeopathy.

homicide /ɔmisid/ nm homicide; ~ **involontaire** manslaughter.

hommage /ɔmaʒ/ nm tribute; ~s (salutations) respects; **rendre** ~ **à** pay tribute to.

homme /ɔm/ nm man; (espèce) man (kind); ~ **d'affaires** businessman; ~ **de la rue** man in the street; ~ **d'État** statesman; ~ **politique** politician.

homogène /ɔmɔʒɛn/ adj homogeneous.

homonyme /ɔmɔnim/ nm (personne) namesake.

homosexualité /ɔmɔsɛksɥalite/ nf homosexuality.

homosexuel, ~**le** /ɔmɔsɛksɥɛl/ adj & nm, f homosexual.

Hongrie /'ɔ̃gʀi/ nf Hungary.

hongrois, ~**e** /'ɔ̃gʀwa, -z/ adj Hungarian. ●nm (Ling) Hungarian. **H**~, ~**e** nm, f Hungarian.

honnête /ɔnɛt/ adj honest; (juste) fair. **honnêteté** nf honesty.

honneur /ɔnœʀ/ nm honour; (mérite) credit; **d'**~ (invité, place) of honour; **en l'**~ **de** in honour of; **en quel** ~? 🔢 why?; **faire** ~ **à** (équipe, famille) bring credit to.

honorable /ɔnɔʀabl/ adj honourable; (convenable) respectable.

honoraire /ɔnɔʀɛʀ/ adj honorary. **honoraires** nmpl fees.

honorer /ɔnɔʀe/ 🔟 vt honour; (faire honneur à) do credit to.

honte /'ɔ̃t/ nf shame; **avoir** ~ be ashamed (**de** of); **faire** ~ **à** make ashamed. **honteux, -euse** adj (personne) ashamed (**de** of); (action) shameful.

hôpital (pl **-aux**) /ɔpital, -o/ nm hospital.

hoquet /'ɔkɛ/ nm **le** ~ (the) hiccups.

horaire /ɔʀɛʀ/ adj hourly. ●nm timetable; ~**s libres** flexitime.

horizon /ɔʀizɔ̃/ nm horizon; (Fig) outlook.

horizontal, ~**e** (mpl **-aux**) /ɔʀizɔ̃tal, -o/ adj horizontal.

horloge /ɔʀlɔʒ/ nf clock.

hormis /'ɔʀmi/ prép save.

hormonal, ~**e** (mpl **-aux**) /ɔʀmɔnal, -o/ adj hormonal, hormone.

hormone /ɔʀmon/ nf hormone.

horreur /ɔʀœʀ/ nf horror; **avoir** ~ **de** hate.

horrible /ɔʀibl/ adj horrible.

horrifier /ɔʀifje/ 45 vt horrify.

hors /'ɔʀ/ prép ~ **de** outside, (avec mouvement) out of; ~ **d'atteinte** out of reach; ~ **d'haleine** out of breath; ~ **de prix** extremely expensive; ~ **pair** outstanding; ~ **de soi** beside oneself. **hors-bord*** nm inv speedboat. **hors-d'œuvre** nm inv hors-d'œuvre. **hors-jeu*** adj inv offside. **hors-la-loi** nm inv outlaw. **hors-piste*** nm off-piste skiing. **hors-taxe** adj inv duty-free.

horticulteur, -trice /ɔʀtikyltœʀ, -tʀis/ nm, f horticulturist.

hospice /ɔspis/ nm home.

hospitalier, -ière /ɔspitalje, -jɛʀ/ adj hospitable; (Méd) hospital. **hospitaliser** 🔟 vt take to hospital. **hospitalité** nf hospitality.

hostile /ɔstil/ adj hostile. **hostilité** nf hostility.

hôte /ot/ nm (maître) host; (invité) guest.

hôtel /otɛl/ nm hotel; ~ (**particulier**) (private) mansion; ⚑~ **de ville** town hall.

hôtelier, -ière /otəlje, -jɛR/ adj hotel. ●nm, f hotel keeper. **hôtellerie** nf hotel business.

hôtesse /otɛs/ nf hostess; ~ **de l'air** stewardess.

hotte /ɔt/ nf basket; ~ **aspirante** extractor (hood), (US) ventilator.

houblon /ublɔ̃/ nm **le** ~ hops.

houille /uj/ nf coal; ~ **blanche** hydroelectric power.

houle /ul/ nf swell. **houleux, -euse** adj (mer) rough; (débat) stormy.

housse /us/ nf cover; ~ **de siège** seat cover.

houx /u/ nm holly.

huées /ʮe/ nfpl boos. **huer** ◘ vt boo.

huile /ʮil/ nf oil; (personne ◘) bigwig. **huiler** ◘ vt oil. **huileux, -euse** adj oily.

huis /ʮi/ nm **à** ~ **clos** in camera.

huissier /ʮisje/ nm (Jur) bailiff; (portier) usher.

huit /ʮi(t)/ adj eight; ~ **jours** a week; **lundi en** ~ a week on Monday. ●nm eight. **huitième** adj & nmf eighth.

huître* /ʮitR/ nf oyster.

humain, ~e /ymɛ̃, -ɛn/ adj human; (compatissant) humane. **humanitaire** adj humanitarian. ⚑**humanité** nf humanity.

humble /œbl/ adj humble.

humeur /ymœR/ nf mood; (tempérament) temper; **de bonne/ mauvaise** ~ in a good/ bad mood.

humide /ymid/ adj damp; (chaleur,

climat) humid; (lèvres, yeux) moist. **humidité** nf humidity.

humilier /ymilje/ ◙ vt humiliate.

humoristique /ymɔRistik/ adj humorous.

humour /ymuR/ nm humour; **avoir de l'**~ have a sense of humour.

hurlement /'yRləmɑ̃/ nm howl (ing). **hurler** ◘ vt/i howl.

hutte /'yt/ nf hut.

hydratant, ~e /idRatɑ̃, -t/ adj (lotion) moisturizing.

hydravion /idRavjɔ̃/ nm seaplane.

hydroélectrique /idRɔelɛktRik/ adj hydroelectric.

hydrogène /idRɔʒɛn/ nm hydrogen.

hygiène /iʒjɛn/ nf hygiene. **hygiénique** adj hygienic.

hymne /imn/ nm hymn; ~ **national** national anthem.

hyperlien /ipɛRljɛ̃/ nm (Internet) hyperlink.

hypermarché /ipɛRmaRʃe/ nm (supermarché) hypermarket.

hypertension /ipɛRtɑ̃sjɔ̃/ nf high blood-pressure.

hypertexte /ipɛRtɛkst/ nm (Internet) hypertext.

hypnotiser /ipnɔtize/ ◘ vt hypnotize.

hypocrisie /ipɔkRizi/ nf hypocrisy.

hypocrite /ipɔkRit/ adj hypocritical. ●nmf hypocrite.

hypothèque /ipɔtɛk/ nf mortgage.

hypothèse /ipɔtɛz/ nf hypothesis.

hystérie /isteRi/ nf hysteria.

⚑ *see* A-Z of French life and culture

h

I i

ici /isi/ adv (dans l'espace) here; (dans le temps) now; **d'~ demain** by tomorrow; **d'~ là** in the meantime; **d'~ peu** shortly; **~ même** in this very place; **jusqu'~** until now; (dans le passé) until then.

idéal, ~e (mpl **-aux**) /ideal, -o/ adj & nm ideal. **idéaliser 🔳** vt idealize.

idée /ide/ nf idea; (esprit) mind; **avoir dans l'~ de faire** plan to do; **il ne me viendrait jamais à l'~ de faire** it would never occur to me to do; **~ fixe** obsession; **~ reçue** conventional opinion.

identification /idãtifikasjõ/ nf identification. **identifier 🔳** vt, **s'identifier** vpr identify (**à** with).

identique /idãtik/ adj identical.

identité /idãtite/ nf identity.

idéologie /ideɔlɔʒi/ nf ideology.

idiome /idjom/ nm idiom.

idiot, ~e /idjo, -ɔt/ adj idiotic. •nm, f idiot. **idiotie** nf idiocy; (acte, parole) idiotic thing.

idole /idɔl/ nf idol.

if /if/ nm yew.

ignare /iɲaʀ/ adj ignorant. •nmf ignoramus.

ignoble /iɲɔbl/ adj vile.

ignorance /iɲɔʀɑ̃s/ nf ignorance.

ignorant, ~e /iɲɔʀɑ̃, -t/ adj ignorant. •nm, f ignoramus.

ignorer /iɲɔʀe/ 🔳 vt not know; **je l'ignore** I don't know; (personne) ignore.

il /il/ pron (personne, animal familier) he; (chose, animal) it; (impersonnel) it; ~

est vrai que it is true that; ~ neige/pleut it is snowing/raining; ~ y a there is; (pluriel) there are; (temps) ago; (durée) for; ~ y a 2 ans 2 years ago; ~ y a plus d'une heure que j'attends I've been waiting for over an hour.

île* /il/ nf island; ~ **déserte** desert island; ~**s anglo-normandes** Channel Islands; ~**s Britanniques** British Isles.

illégal, ~e (mpl ~**aux**) /ilegal, -o/ adj illegal.

illégitime /ileʒitim/ adj illegitimate.

illettré, ~e /iletʀe/ adj & nm, f illiterate.

illicite /ilisit/ adj illicit; (Jur) unlawful.

illimité, ~e /ilimite/ adj unlimited.

illisible /ilizibl/ adj illegible; (livre) unreadable.

illogique /ilɔʒik/ adj illogical.

illuminé, ~e /ilymine/ adj lit up; (monument) floodlit.

illusion /ilyzjõ/ nf illusion; **se faire des ~s** delude oneself. **illusoire** adj illusory.

illustre /ilystʀ/ adj illustrious.

illustré, ~e /ilystʀe/ adj illustrated. •nm comic.

illustrer /ilystʀe/ 🔳 vt illustrate. ■**s'~** vpr become famous.

îlot* /ilo/ nm islet; (de maisons) block.

ils /il/ pron they.

image /imaʒ/ nf picture; (métaphore) image; (reflet)

reflection. **imagé,** ~**e** adj full of imagery.

imaginaire /imaʒinɛʀ/ adj imaginary. **imaginatif, -ive** adj imaginative. **imagination** nf imagination.

imaginer /imaʒine/ **1** vt imagine; (inventer) think up. ∎ **s'**~ vpr (se représenter) imagine (**que** that); (croire) think (**que** that).

imbécile /ɛ̃besil/ adj idiotic. ●nmf idiot.

imbiber /ɛ̃bibe/ **1** vt soak (**de** with). ∎ **s'**~ vpr become soaked (**de** with).

imbriqué, ~**e** /ɛ̃bʀike/ adj (lié) interlinked, interlocking; (tuiles) overlapping.

imbu, ~**e** /ɛ̃by/ adj ~ **de** full of.

imitateur, -trice /imitatœʀ, -tʀis/ nm, f imitator; (comédien) impersonator. **imiter 1** vt imitate; (personnage) impersonate; (signature) forge; (faire comme) do the same as.

⚑immatriculation /imatʀikylasjɔ̃/ nf registration.

immatriculer /imatʀikyle/ **1** vt register; **se faire** ~ register; **faire** ~ **une voiture** have a car registered.

immédiat, ~**e** /imedja, -t/ adj immediate. ●nm **dans l'**~ for the time being.

immense /imɑ̃s/ adj huge, immense.

immerger /imɛʀʒe/ **40** vt immerse. ∎ **s'**~ vpr immerse oneself (**dans** in).

immeuble /imœbl/ nm block of flats, building; ~ **de bureaux** office building ou block.

immigrant, ~**e** /imigʀɑ̃, -t/ adj & nm, f immigrant. **immigration** nf immigration. **immigré,** ~**e** adj & nm, f immigrant. **immigrer 1** vi immigrate.

imminent, ~**e** /iminɑ̃, -t/ adj imminent.

immobile /imɔbil/ adj still, motionless.

immobilier, -ière /imɔbilje, -jɛʀ/ adj property; **agence immobilière** estate agent's office; (US) real estate office; **agent** ~ estate agent; (US) real estate agent. ●nm **l'**~ property; (US) real estate.

immobiliser /imɔbilize/ **1** vt immobilize; (stopper) stop. ∎ **s'**~ vpr stop.

immonde /imɔ̃d/ adj filthy.

immoral, ~**e** (mpl **-aux**) /imɔʀal, -o/ adj immoral.

immortel, ~**le** /imɔʀtɛl/ adj immortal.

immuable /imɥabl/ adj unchanging.

immuniser /imynize/ **1** vt immunize; **immunisé contre** (à l'abri de) immune to. **immunité** nf immunity.

impact /ɛ̃pakt/ nm impact.

impair, ~**e** /ɛ̃pɛʀ/ adj (numéro) odd. ●nm blunder, faux pas.

imparfait, ~**e** /ɛ̃paʀfɛ, -t/ adj & nm imperfect.

impasse /ɛ̃pɑs/ nf (rue) dead end; (situation) deadlock.

impatient, ~**e** /ɛ̃pasjɑ̃, -t/ adj impatient.

impatienter /ɛ̃pasjɑ̃te/ **1** vt annoy. ∎ **s'**~ vpr get impatient (**contre qn** with sb).

impayé, ~**e** /ɛ̃peje/ adj unpaid.

impeccable /ɛ̃pekabl/ adj (propre) impeccable, spotless; (soigné) perfect.

impensable /ɛ̃pɑ̃sabl/ adj unthinkable.

impératif, -ive /ɛ̃peʀatif, -v/ adj imperative. ●nm (Gram) imperative; (contrainte) imperative; ~**s** (exigences) requirements, demands (**de** of).

⚑ see A-Z of French life and culture

impératrice /ɛ̃peratris/ nf
empress.

impérial, ~e (mpl **-iaux**)
/ɛ̃perjal, -jo/ adj imperial.

impérieux, -ieuse /ɛ̃perjø, -z/
adj imperious; (pressant) pressing.

imperméable /ɛ̃pɛrmeabl/ adj
impervious (**à** to); (manteau, tissu)
waterproof. ● nm raincoat.

impersonnel, ~le /ɛ̃pɛrsɔnɛl/
adj impersonal.

impertinent, ~e /ɛ̃pɛrtinɑ̃, -t/
adj impertinent.

imperturbable /ɛ̃pɛrtyrbabl/ adj
unshakeable, unruffled.

impétueux, -euse /ɛ̃petɥø, -z/
adj impetuous.

impitoyable /ɛ̃pitwajabl/ adj
merciless.

implant /ɛ̃plɑ̃/ nm implant.

implanter /ɛ̃plɑ̃te/ **1** vt establish,
set up. ■ s'~ vpr become
established.

implication /ɛ̃plikasjɔ̃/ nf
(conséquence) implication;
(participation) involvement.

impliquer /ɛ̃plike/ **1** vt (mêler)
implicate (**dans** in); (signifier)
imply, mean (**que** that);
(nécessiter) involve (**de faire**
doing).

implorer /ɛ̃plɔre/ **1** vt implore,
beg for.

impoli, ~e /ɛ̃pɔli/ adj
impolite, rude.

importance /ɛ̃pɔrtɑ̃s/ nf
importance; (taille) size; (ampleur)
extent; **sans ~** unimportant.

important, ~e /ɛ̃pɔrtɑ̃, -t/ adj
important; (en quantité)
considerable, sizeable, big; (air)
self-important. ● nm l'~ the
important thing.

importateur, -trice /ɛ̃pɔrtatœr,
-tris/ nm, f importer. ● adj
importing. **importation** nf
import.

importer /ɛ̃pɔrte/ **1** vt (Comm)

import. ● vi matter, be important
(**à** to); **il importe que** it is
important that; **n'importe, peu
importe** it does not matter;
n'importe comment anyhow;
n'importe où anywhere;
n'importe qui anybody;
n'importe quoi anything.

importun, ~e /ɛ̃pɔrtœ̃, -yn/ adj
troublesome. ● nm, f nuisance.

imposer /ɛ̃poze/ **1** vt impose (**à**
on); (taxer) tax; **en ~ à qn**
impress sb. ■ s'~ vpr (action) be
essential; (se faire reconnaître) stand
out; (s'astreindre à) **s'~ de faire**
force oneself to do.

imposition /ɛ̃pozisjɔ̃/ nf taxation;
~ des mains laying-on of
hands.

impossible /ɛ̃pɔsibl/ adj
impossible. ● nm **faire l'~** do
one's utmost.

impôt /ɛ̃po/ nm tax; **~s**
(contributions) tax(ation), taxes; **~
sur le revenu** income tax.

impotent, ~e /ɛ̃pɔtɑ̃, -t/ adj
disabled.

imprécis, ~e /ɛ̃presi, -z/ adj
imprecise.

imprégner /ɛ̃preɲe/ **14** vt fill (**de**
with); (imbiber) impregnate (**de**
with). ■ s'~ **de** vpr (fig) immerse
oneself in.

impression /ɛ̃presjɔ̃/ nf
impression; (de livre) printing.
impressionnant, ~e adj
impressive; (choquant) disturbing.
impressionner **1** vt impress;
(choquer) disturb.

imprévisible /ɛ̃previzibl/ adj
unpredictable.

imprévu, ~e /ɛ̃prevy/ adj
unexpected. ● nm unexpected
incident; **sauf ~** unless
anything unexpected happens.

imprimante /ɛ̃primɑ̃t/ nf (Ordinat)
printer; **~ à jet d'encre** ink-jet
printer; **~ (à) laser** laser
printer.

imprimé, ~e /ɛ̃prime/ adj

printed. •nm printed form.

imprimer /ɛ̃pʀime/ **1** vt print; (marquer) imprint. **imprimerie** nf (art) printing; (lieu) printing works. **imprimeur** nm printer.

improbable /ɛ̃pʀɔbabl/ adj unlikely, improbable.

impropre /ɛ̃pʀɔpʀ/ adj incorrect; ∼ **à** unfit for.

improviste: à l'∼ /alɛ̃pʀɔvist/ loc unexpectedly.

imprudence /ɛ̃pʀydɑ̃s/ nf carelessness; (acte) careless action.

imprudent, ∼e /ɛ̃pʀydɑ̃, -t/ adj careless; **il est ∼ de** it is unwise to.

impudent, ∼e /ɛ̃pydɑ̃, -t/ adj impudent.

impuissant, ∼e /ɛ̃pɥisɑ̃, -t/ adj helpless; (Méd) impotent; ∼ **à faire** powerless to do.

impulsif, -ive /ɛ̃pylsif, -v/ adj impulsive. **impulsion** nf (poussée, influence) impetus; (instinct, mouvement) impulse.

impur, ∼e /ɛ̃pyʀ/ adj impure.

imputer /ɛ̃pyte/ **1** vt ∼ **à** attribute to, impute to.

inabordable /inabɔʀdabl/ adj (prix) prohibitive.

inacceptable /inaksɛptabl/ adj unacceptable.

inactif, -ive /inaktif, -v/ adj inactive.

inadapté, ∼e /inadapte/ adj maladjusted. •nm, f (Psych) maladjusted person.

inadmissible /inadmisibl/ adj unacceptable.

inadvertance /inadvɛʀtɑ̃s/ nf **par ∼** by mistake.

inanimé, ∼e /inanime/ adj (évanoui) unconscious; (mort) lifeless; (matière) inanimate.

inaperçu, ∼e /inapɛʀsy/ adj unnoticed.

inapte /inapt/ adj unsuited (à to);

∼ **à faire** incapable of doing; ∼ **au service militaire** unfit for military service.

inattendu, ∼e /inatɑ̃dy/ adj unexpected.

inaugurer /inogyʀe/ **1** vt inaugurate.

incapable /ɛ̃kapabl/ adj incapable (**de qch** of sth); ∼ **de faire** unable to do, incapable of doing. •nmf incompetent.

incapacité /ɛ̃kapasite/ nf inability, incapacity; **être dans l'**∼ **de faire** be unable to do.

incarcérer /ɛ̃kaʀseʀe/ **14** vt imprison, incarcerate.

incarnation /ɛ̃kaʀnasjɔ̃/ nf embodiment, incarnation. **incarné, ∼e** adj (ongle) ingrowing.

incassable /ɛ̃kɑsabl/ adj unbreakable.

incendiaire /ɛ̃sɑ̃djɛʀ/ adj incendiary; (propos) inflammatory. •nmf arsonist.

incendie /ɛ̃sɑ̃di/ nm fire; ∼ **criminel** arson. **incendier** **45** vt set fire to.

incertain, ∼e /ɛ̃sɛʀtɛ̃, -ɛn/ adj uncertain; (contour) vague; (temps) unsettled. **incertitude** nf uncertainty.

inceste /ɛ̃sɛst/ nm incest.

incidence /ɛ̃sidɑ̃s/ nf effect.

incident /ɛ̃sidɑ̃/ nm incident; ∼ **technique** technical hitch.

incinérer /ɛ̃sineʀe/ **14** vt incinerate; (mort) cremate.

inciser /ɛ̃size/ **1** vt make an incision in; (abcès) lance. **incisif, -ive** adj incisive. **incision** nf incision; (d'abcès) lancing.

incitation /ɛ̃sitasjɔ̃/ nf (Jur) incitement (**à** to); (encouragement) incentive. **inciter** **1** vt incite (**à** to); (encourager) encourage.

inclinaison /ɛ̃klinɛzɔ̃/ nf incline; (de la tête) tilt.

inclination /ɛ̃klinasjɔ̃/ nf (penchant) inclination; (geste) (du buste) bow; (de la tête) nod.

incliner /ɛ̃kline/ **1** vt tilt, lean; (courber) bend; (inciter) encourage (**à** to); ~ **la tête** (approuver) nod; (révérence) bow. • vi **à** be inclined to. ■ **s'~** vpr lean forward; (se courber) bow down (**devant** before); (céder) give in, yield (**devant** to); (chemin) slope.

inclure /ɛ̃klyʀ/ **16** vt include; (enfermer) enclose; **jusqu'au lundi inclus** up to and including Monday.

incohérence /ɛ̃kɔeʀɑ̃s/ nf incoherence; (contradiction) discrepancy. **incohérent, ~e** adj incoherent, inconsistent.

incolore /ɛ̃kɔlɔʀ/ adj colourless; (verre) clear.

incommoder /ɛ̃kɔmɔde/ **1** vt inconvenience, bother.

incompatible /ɛ̃kɔ̃patibl/ adj incompatible.

incompétent, ~e /ɛ̃kɔ̃petɑ̃, -t/ adj incompetent.

incomplet, -ète /ɛ̃kɔ̃plɛ, -t/ adj incomplete.

incompréhension /ɛ̃kɔ̃pʀeɑ̃sjɔ̃/ nf lack of understanding.

incompris, ~e /ɛ̃kɔ̃pʀi, -z/ adj misunderstood.

inconcevable /ɛ̃kɔ̃svabl/ adj inconceivable.

incongru, ~e /ɛ̃kɔ̃gʀy/ adj unseemly.

inconnu, ~e /ɛ̃kɔny/ adj unknown (**à** to). • nm, f stranger. • nm **l'~** the unknown.

inconscience /ɛ̃kɔ̃sjɑ̃s/ nf unconsciousness; (folie) madness.

inconscient, ~e /ɛ̃kɔ̃sjɑ̃, -t/ adj unconscious (**de** of); (fou) mad. • nm (Psych) subconscious.

incontestable /ɛ̃kɔ̃tɛstabl/ adj indisputable.

incontrôlable /ɛ̃kɔ̃tʀolabl/ adj unverifiable; (non maîtrisé) uncontrollable.

inconvenant, ~e /ɛ̃kɔ̃vnɑ̃, -t/ adj improper.

inconvénient /ɛ̃kɔ̃venjɑ̃/ nm disadvantage, drawback; (objection) objection.

incorporer /ɛ̃kɔʀpɔʀe/ **1** vt incorporate; (Culin) blend (**à** into); (Mil) enlist.

incorrect, ~e /ɛ̃kɔʀɛkt/ adj (faux) incorrect; (malséant) improper; (impoli) impolite; (déloyal) unfair.

incrédule /ɛ̃kʀedyl/ adj incredulous.

incriminer /ɛ̃kʀimine/ **1** vt (personne) incriminate; (conduite, action) attack.

incroyable /ɛ̃kʀwajabl/ adj incredible.

incruster /ɛ̃kʀyste/ **1** vt inlay (**de** with).

incubateur /ɛ̃kybatœʀ/ nm incubator.

inculpation /ɛ̃kylpasjɔ̃/ nf charge (**de, pour** of). **inculpé, ~e** nm, f accused. **inculper 1** vt charge (**de** with).

inculquer /ɛ̃kylke/ **1** vt instil (**à** into).

inculte /ɛ̃kylt/ adj uncultivated; (personne) uneducated.

incurver /ɛ̃kyʀve/ **1** vt curve, bend. ■ **s'~** vpr curve, bend.

Inde /ɛ̃d/ nf India.

indécent, ~e /ɛ̃desɑ̃, -t/ adj indecent.

indécis, ~e /ɛ̃desi, -z/ adj (de nature) indecisive; (temporairement) undecided.

indéfini, ~e /ɛ̃defini/ adj (Gram) indefinite; (vague) undefined; (sans limites) indeterminate.

indemne /ɛ̃dɛmn/ adj unharmed.

indemniser /ɛ̃dɛmnize/ **1** vt compensate (**de** for).

indemnité /ɛ̃dɛmnite/ nf

indemnity, compensation; (allocation) allowance; ~s de licenciement redundancy payment.

indépendance /ɛ̃depɑ̃dɑ̃s/ nf independence. **indépendant, ~e** adj independent.

indéterminé, ~e /ɛ̃detɛrmine/ adj unspecified.

index /ɛ̃dɛks/ nm forefinger; (liste) index.

indicateur, -trice /ɛ̃dikatœr, -tris/ nm, f (police) informer. •nm (livre) guide; (Tech) indicator.

indicatif, -ve /ɛ̃dikatif, -v/ adj indicative (**de** of). •nm (à la radio) signature tune; (téléphonique) dialling code; (Gram) indicative.

indication /ɛ̃dikasjɔ̃/ nf indication; (renseignement) information; (directive) instruction.

indice /ɛ̃dis/ nm sign; (dans une enquête) clue; (des prix) index; (évaluation) rating; ~ **d'écoute** audience ratings.

indifférence /ɛ̃diferɑ̃s/ nf indifference.

indifférent, ~e /ɛ̃diferɑ̃, -t/ adj indifferent (**à** to); **ça m'est ~** it makes no difference to me.

indigène /ɛ̃diʒɛn/ adj & nmf native, indigenous; (du pays) local. •nmf native.

indigent, ~e /ɛ̃diʒɑ̃, -t/ adj destitute.

indigeste /ɛ̃diʒɛst/ adj indigestible. **indigestion** nf indigestion.

indigne /ɛ̃diɲ/ adj unworthy (**de** of); (acte) vile. **indigner (s')** 1 vpr become indignant (**de** at).

indiqué, ~e /ɛ̃dike/ adj (heure) appointed; (opportun) appropriate; (conseillé) recommended.

indiquer /ɛ̃dike/ 1 vt (montrer) show, indicate; (renseigner sur) point out, tell; (déterminer) give, state, appoint; ~ **du doigt** point to *ou* out *ou* at.

indirect, ~e /ɛ̃dirɛkt/ adj indirect.

indiscipliné, ~e /ɛ̃disipline/ adj unruly.

indiscret, -ète /ɛ̃diskrɛ, -t/ adj (personne) inquisitive; (question) indiscreet.

indiscutable /ɛ̃diskytabl/ adj unquestionable.

indispensable /ɛ̃dispɑ̃sabl/ adj indispensable; **il est ~ qu'il vienne** it is essential that he comes.

individu /ɛ̃dividy/ nm individual.

individuel, ~le /ɛ̃dividɥɛl/ adj (pour une personne) individual; (qui concerne l'individu) personal; **chambre ~le** single room; **maison ~le** detached house.

indolore /ɛ̃dɔlɔr/ adj painless.

Indonésie /ɛ̃dɔnezi/ nf Indonesia.

indu, ~e /ɛ̃dy/ adj **à une heure ~e** at some ungodly hour.

induire /ɛ̃dɥir/ 17 vt infer (**de** from); (inciter) induce (**à faire** to do); ~ **en erreur** mislead.

indulgence /ɛ̃dylʒɑ̃s/ nf indulgence; (de jury) leniency. **indulgent, ~e** adj indulgent; (clément) lenient.

industrialisé, ~e /ɛ̃dystrijalize/ adj industrialized.

industrie /ɛ̃dystri/ nf industry.

industriel, ~le /ɛ̃dystrijɛl/ adj industrial. •nm industrialist.

inédit, ~e /inedi, -t/ adj unpublished; (fig) original.

inefficace /inefikas/ adj (remède, mesure) ineffective; (appareil, système) inefficient.

inégal, ~e (mpl **-aux**) /inegal, -o/ adj unequal; (irrégulier) uneven. **inégalable** adj matchless. **inégalité** nf (injustice) inequality; (irrégularité) unevenness; (disproportion) disparity.

inéluctable /inelyktabl/ adj inescapable.

i

inepte /inɛpt/ adj inept, absurd.

inerte /inɛʁt/ adj inert; (immobile) lifeless; (sans énergie) apathetic. **inertie** nf inertia; (fig) apathy.

inespéré, ~e /inɛspeʁe/ adj unhoped for.

inestimable /inɛstimabl/ adj priceless; (aide) invaluable.

inexact, ~e /inɛgza(kt) , -kt/ adj (imprécis) inaccurate; (incorrect) incorrect.

in extremis* /inɛkstʁemis/ adv (par nécessité) as a last resort; (au dernier moment) at the last minute. ●adj last-minute.

infaillible /ɛ̃fajibl/ adj infallible.

infâme /ɛ̃fɑm/ adj vile.

infantile /ɛ̃fɑ̃til/ adj (puéril) infantile; (maladie) childhood; (mortalité) infant.

infarctus /ɛ̃faʁktys/ nm coronary, heart attack.

infatigable /ɛ̃fatigabl/ adj tireless.

infect, ~e /ɛ̃fɛkt/ adj revolting.

infecter /ɛ̃fɛkte/ ⬛ vt infect. ■s'~ vpr become infected. **infectieux, -ieuse** adj infectious. **infection** nf infection.

inférieur, ~e /ɛ̃feʁjœʁ/ adj (plus bas) lower; (moins bon) inferior (**à** to); ~ **à** (plus petit que) smaller than; (plus bas que) lower than. ●nm, f inferior. **infériorité** nf inferiority.

infernal, ~e (mpl **-aux**) /ɛ̃fɛʁnal, -o/ adj infernal.

infester /ɛ̃fɛste/ ⬛ vt infest.

infidèle /ɛ̃fidɛl/ adj unfaithful (**à** to). **infidélité** nf unfaithfulness; (acte) infidelity.

infiltrer (s') /sɛ̃filtʁe/ ⬛ vpr s'~ (**dans**) (personnes, idées) infiltrate; (liquide) seep through.

infime /ɛ̃fim/ adj tiny, minute.

infini, ~e /ɛ̃fini/ adj infinite. ●nm infinity; **à l'~** endlessly.

infinité /ɛ̃finite/ nf **l'~** infinity;

une ~ **de** an endless number of.

infinitif /ɛ̃finitif/ nm infinitive.

infirme /ɛ̃fiʁm/ adj disabled. ●nmf disabled person. **infirmerie** nf sickbay, infirmary. **infirmier** nm (male) nurse. **infirmière** nf nurse. **infirmité** nf disability.

inflammable /ɛ̃flamabl/ adj inflammable.

inflation /ɛ̃flasjɔ̃/ nf inflation.

infliger /ɛ̃fliʒe/ 🔟 vt inflict; (sanction) impose.

influence /ɛ̃flyɑ̃s/ nf influence. **influencer** 🔟 vt influence. **influent, ~e** adj influential.

influer /ɛ̃flye/ ⬛ vi ~ **sur** influence.

informateur, -trice /ɛ̃fɔʁmatœʁ, -tʁis/ nm, f informant; (pour la police) informer.

informaticien, ~ne /ɛ̃fɔʁmatisjɛ̃, -ɛn/ nm, f computer scientist.

information /ɛ̃fɔʁmasjɔ̃/ nf information; (Jur) inquiry; **une ~** (some) information; (nouvelle) (some) news; **les ~s** the news.

informatique /ɛ̃fɔʁmatik/ nf computer science; (techniques) information technology. **informatiser** ⬛ vt computerize.

informer /ɛ̃fɔʁme/ ⬛ vt inform (**de** about, of). ■s'~ vpr enquire (**de** about).

inforoute /ɛ̃fɔʁut/ nf (Ordinat) information highway.

infortune /ɛ̃fɔʁtyn/ nf misfortune.

infraction /ɛ̃fʁaksjɔ̃/ nf offence; ~ **à** (loi, règlement) breach of.

infrastructure /ɛ̃fʁastʁyktyʁ/ nf infrastructure; (équipements) facilities.

infructueux, -euse /ɛ̃fʁyktɥø, -z/ adj fruitless.

infuser /ɛ̃fyze/ ⬛ vt/i infuse, brew. **infusion** nf herbal tea, infusion.

ingénier (s') /(s)ɛ̃ʒenje/ 45 vpr **s'∼ à** strive to.

ingénieur /ɛ̃ʒenjœʀ/ nm engineer.

ingénieux, -ieuse /ɛ̃ʒenjø, -z/ adj ingenious. **ingéniosité** nf ingenuity.

ingénu, ∼e /ɛ̃ʒeny/ adj naïve.

ingérence /ɛ̃ʒeʀɑ̃s/ nf interference.

ingérer (s') /sɛ̃ʒeʀe/ 14 vpr **s'∼ dans** interfere in.

ingrat, ∼e /ɛ̃gʀa, -t/ adj (personne) ungrateful; (travail) unrewarding, thankless; (visage) unattractive.

ingrédient /ɛ̃gʀedjɑ̃/ nm ingredient.

ingurgiter /ɛ̃gyʀʒite/ 1 vt swallow.

inhabité, ∼e /inabite/ adj uninhabited.

inhabituel, ∼le /inabityɛl/ adj unusual.

inhumain, ∼e /inymɛ̃, -ɛn/ adj inhuman.

inhumation /inymasjɔ̃/ nf burial.

initial, ∼e (mpl **-iaux**) /inisjal, -jo/ adj initial. **initiale** nf initial.

initialisation /inisjalizasjɔ̃/ nf (Ordinat) formatting. **initialiser** 1 vt format.

initiation /inisjasjɔ̃/ nf initiation; (formation) introduction (**à** to); **cours d'∼** introductory course.

initiative /inisjativ/ nf initiative.

initier /inisje/ 45 vt initiate (**à** into); (faire découvrir) introduce (**à** to). ■ **s'∼** vpr **s'∼ à qch** learn sth.

injecter /ɛ̃ʒɛkte/ 1 vt inject; **injecté de sang** bloodshot. **injection** nf injection.

injure /ɛ̃ʒyʀ/ nf insult. **injurier** 45 vt insult. **injurieux, -ieuse** adj insulting.

injuste /ɛ̃ʒyst/ adj unjust, unfair. **injustice** nf injustice.

inné, ∼e /inne/ adj innate, inborn.

innocence /inɔsɑ̃s/ nf innocence. **innocent, ∼e** adj & nm, f innocent. **innocenter** 1 vt clear, prove innocent.

innombrable /inɔ̃bʀabl/ adj countless.

innovateur, -trice /inɔvatœʀ, -tʀis/ nm, f innovator. **innovation** nf innovation. **innover** 1 vi innovate.

inodore /inɔdɔʀ/ adj odourless.

inoffensif, -ive /inɔfɑ̃sif, -v/ adj harmless.

inondation /inɔ̃dasjɔ̃/ nf flood; (action) flooding.

inonder /inɔ̃de/ 1 vt flood; (mouiller) soak; (envahir) inundate (**de** with); **inondé de soleil** bathed in sunlight.

inopiné, ∼e /inɔpine/ adj unexpected; (mort) sudden.

inopportun, ∼e /inɔpɔʀtœ̃, -yn/ adj inopportune, ill-timed.

inoubliable /inublijabl/ adj unforgettable.

inouï, ∼e /inwi/ adj incredible; (événement) unprecedented.

inox® /inɔks/ nm stainless steel.

inoxydable /inɔksidabl/ adj **acier ∼** stainless steel.

inqualifiable /ɛ̃kalifjabl/ adj unspeakable.

inquiet, -iète /ɛ̃kjɛ, -t/ adj worried. **inquiétant, ∼e** adj worrying.

inquiéter /ɛ̃kjete/ 14 vt worry. ■ **s'∼** vpr worry (**de** about). **inquiétude** nf anxiety, worry.

insaisissable /ɛ̃sezisabl/ adj (personne) elusive; (nuance) indefinable.

insalubre /ɛ̃salybʀ/ adj unhealthy.

insatisfaisant, ∼e /ɛ̃satisfəzɑ̃, -t/ adj unsatisfactory. **insatisfait, ∼e** adj (mécontent) dissatisfied; (frustré) unfulfilled.

inscription /ɛ̃skʀipsjɔ̃/ nf

inscription; (immatriculation) enrolment.

inscrire /ɛ̃skʀiʀ/ 🟩 vt write (down); (graver, tracer) inscribe; (personne) enrol; (sur une liste) put down. ■ s'~ vpr put one's name down; **s'~ à** (école) enrol at; (club, parti) join; (examen) enter for.

insecte /ɛ̃sɛkt/ nm insect.

insécurité /ɛ̃sekyʀite/ nf insecurity.

insensé, ~e /ɛ̃sɑ̃se/ adj mad.

insensibilité /ɛ̃sɑ̃sibilite/ nf insensitivity. **insensible** adj insensitive (**à** to); (graduel) imperceptible.

insérer /ɛ̃seʀe/ 🟩 vt insert. ■ s'~ vpr be inserted; **s'~ dans** be part of.

insigne /ɛ̃siɲ/ nm badge; **~s** (d'une fonction) insignia.

insignifiant, ~e /ɛ̃siɲifjɑ̃, -t/ adj insignificant.

insinuation /ɛ̃sinɥasjɔ̃/ nf insinuation.

insinuer /ɛ̃sinɥe/ 🟩 vt insinuate. ■ s'~ vpr (socialement) ingratiate oneself (**auprès de qn** with sb); **s'~ dans** (se glisser) slip into; (idée, nuance) creep into.

insipide /ɛ̃sipid/ adj insipid.

insistance /ɛ̃sistɑ̃s/ nf insistence. **insistant, ~e** adj insistent.

insister /ɛ̃siste/ 🟩 vi insist (**pour faire** on doing); **~ sur** stress.

insolation /ɛ̃sɔlasjɔ̃/ nf (Méd) sunstroke.

insolent, ~e /ɛ̃sɔlɑ̃, -t/ adj insolent.

insolite /ɛ̃sɔlit/ adj unusual.

insolvable /ɛ̃sɔlvabl/ adj insolvent.

insomnie /ɛ̃sɔmni/ nf insomnia.

insonoriser /ɛ̃sɔnɔʀize/ 🟩 vt soundproof.

insouciance /ɛ̃susjɑ̃s/ nf lack of concern. **insouciant, ~e** adj carefree.

insoutenable /ɛ̃sutnabl/ adj unbearable; (argument) untenable.

inspecter /ɛ̃spɛkte/ 🟩 vt inspect. **inspecteur, -trice** nm, f inspector. **inspection** nf inspection.

inspiration /ɛ̃spiʀasjɔ̃/ nf inspiration; (respiration) breath.

inspirer /ɛ̃spiʀe/ 🟩 vt inspire; ~ **la méfiance à qn** inspire distrust in sb. ●vi breathe in. ■ s'~ de vpr be inspired by.

instabilité /ɛ̃stabilite/ nf instability; unsteadiness. **instable** adj unstable; (temps) unsettled.

installation /ɛ̃stalasjɔ̃/ nf installation; (de local) fitting out; (de locataire) settling in. **installations** nfpl facilities.

installer /ɛ̃stale/ 🟩 vt install; (meuble) put in; (étagère) put up; (gaz, téléphone) connect; (équiper) fit out. ■ s'~ vpr settle (down); (emménager) settle in; **s'~ comme** set oneself up as.

instance /ɛ̃stɑ̃s/ nf authority; (prière) entreaty; **avec ~** with insistence; **en ~** pending; **en ~ de** in the course of, on the point of.

instant /ɛ̃stɑ̃/ nm moment, instant; **à l'~** this instant.

instantané, ~e /ɛ̃stɑ̃tane/ adj instantaneous; (café) instant.

instar: à l'~ de /alɛstaʀdə/ loc like.

instaurer /ɛ̃stɔʀe/ 🟩 vt institute.

instigateur, -trice /ɛ̃stigatœʀ, -tʀis/ nm, f instigator.

instinct /ɛ̃stɛ̃/ nm instinct; **d'~** instinctively. **instinctif, -ive** adj instinctive.

instituer /ɛ̃stitɥe/ 🟩 vt establish.

institut /ɛ̃stity/ nm institute; ~ **de beauté** beauty parlour.

instituteur, -trice /ɛ̃stitytœʀ, -tʀis/ nm, f primary-school teacher.

institution /ɛ̃stitysjɔ̃/ nf institution; (école) private school.

instructif, -ive /ɛ̃stryktif, -v/ adj instructive.

instruction /ɛ̃stryksjɔ̃/ nf (formation) education; (Mil) training; (document) directive; ~s (ordres, mode d'emploi) instructions; (Ordinat) (énoncé) instruction; (pas de séquence) statement.

instruire /ɛ̃strɥir/ 🔟 vt teach, educate; ~ de inform of. ∎ s'~ vpr learn, educate oneself; s'~ de enquire about. **instruit, ~e** adj educated.

instrument /ɛ̃strymɑ̃/ nm instrument; (outil) tool; (moyen: fig) instrument; ~ de gestion management tool; ~s de bord (Aviat) controls.

insu: à l'~ de /alɛsydə/ loc without the knowledge of.

insuffisance /ɛ̃syfizɑ̃s/ nf (pénurie) shortage; (médiocrité) inadequacy. **insuffisant, ~e** adj inadequate; (en nombre) insufficient.

insulaire /ɛ̃sylɛr/ adj island. ● nmf islander.

insuline /ɛ̃sylin/ nf insulin.

insulte /ɛ̃sylt/ nf insult. **insulter** 🔟 vt insult.

insupportable /ɛ̃sypɔrtabl/ adj unbearable.

insurger (s') /(s)ɛ̃syrʒe/ 🔟 vpr rebel.

intact, ~e /ɛ̃takt/ adj intact.

intangible /ɛ̃tɑ̃ʒibl/ adj intangible; (principe) inviolable.

intarissable /ɛ̃tarisabl/ adj inexhaustible.

intégral, ~e (mpl **-aux**) /ɛ̃tegral, -o/ adj complete; (texte, édition) unabridged; (paiement) full, in full. **intégralement** adv in full. **intégralité** nf whole.

intègre /ɛ̃tɛgr/ adj upright.

intégrer /ɛ̃tegre/ 🔟 vt integrate. ∎ s'~ vpr (personne) integrate; (maison) fit in.

intégriste /ɛ̃tegrist/ nmf fundamentalist.

intégrité /ɛ̃tegrite/ nf integrity.

intellect /ɛ̃telɛkt/ nm intellect. **intellectuel, ~le** adj & nm, f intellectual.

intelligence /ɛ̃teliʒɑ̃s/ nf intelligence; (compréhension) understanding; (complicité) agreement; **agir d'~ avec qn** act in agreement with sb. **intelligent, ~e** adj intelligent.

intempéries /ɛ̃tɑ̃peri/ nfpl severe weather.

intempestif, -ive /ɛ̃tɑ̃pɛstif, -v/ adj untimely.

intenable /ɛ̃tnabl/ adj unbearable; (enfant) impossible.

intendance /ɛ̃tɑ̃dɑ̃s/ nf (Scol) bursar's office.

intendant, ~e /ɛ̃tɑ̃dɑ̃, -t/ nm (Mil) quartermaster. ● nm, f (Scol) bursar.

intense /ɛ̃tɑ̃s/ adj intense; (circulation) heavy. **intensif, -ive** adj intensive. **intensité** nf intensity.

intenter /ɛ̃tɑ̃te/ 🔟 vt ~ **un procès** ou **une action** institute proceedings (**à**, **contre** against).

intention /ɛ̃tɑ̃sjɔ̃/ nf intention (**de faire** of doing); **à l'~ de qn** for sb. **intentionnel, ~le** adj intentional.

interactif, -ive /ɛ̃tɛraktif, -v/ adj (TV, vidéo) interactive.

interaction /ɛ̃tɛraksjɔ̃/ nf interaction.

intercaler /ɛ̃tɛrkale/ 🔟 vt insert.

intercéder /ɛ̃tɛrsede/ 🔟 vi intercede (**en faveur de** on behalf of).

intercepter /ɛ̃tɛrsɛpte/ 🔟 vt intercept.

interdiction /ɛ̃tɛrdiksjɔ̃/ nf ban; ~ **de fumer** no smoking.

interdire /ɛ̃tɛrdir/ 🔟 vt forbid; (officiellement) ban, prohibit; ~ **à**

qn de faire forbid sb to do.

interdit, ~e /ɛ̃tɛʀdi, -t/ adj prohibited, forbidden; (étonné) dumbfounded.

intéressant, ~e /ɛ̃teʀesɑ̃, -t/ adj interesting; (avantageux) attractive.

intéressé, ~e /ɛ̃teʀese/ adj (en cause) concerned; (pour profiter) self-interested. ●nm, f person concerned.

intéresser /ɛ̃teʀese/ **1** vt interest; (concerner) concern. ■**s'~ à** vpr be interested in.

intérêt /ɛ̃teʀɛ/ nm interest; (égoïsme) self-interest; (**~s**) (Comm) interest; **vous avez ~ à** it is in your interest to.

interface /ɛ̃tɛʀfas/ nf (Ordinat) interface.

intérieur, ~e /ɛ̃teʀjœʀ/ adj inner, inside; (mur, escalier) internal; (vol, politique) domestic; (vie, calme) inner. ●nm interior; (de boîte, tiroir) inside; **à l'~ (de)** inside; (fig) within. **intérieurement** adv inwardly.

intérim /ɛ̃teʀim/ nm interim; **assurer l'~** deputize (**de** for); **par ~** on an interim basis; **président par ~** acting president; **faire de l'~** temp.

intérimaire /ɛ̃teʀimɛʀ/ adj temporary, interim. ●nmf (secrétaire) temp; (médecin) locum.

interjection /ɛ̃tɛʀʒɛksjɔ̃/ nf interjection.

interlocuteur, -trice /ɛ̃tɛʀlɔkytœʀ, -tʀis/ nm, f **son ~** the person one is speaking to.

interloqué, ~e /ɛ̃tɛʀlɔke/ adj **être ~** be taken aback.

intermède /ɛ̃tɛʀmɛd/ nm interlude.

intermédiaire /ɛ̃tɛʀmedjɛʀ/ adj intermediate. ●nmf intermediary. ●nm **sans ~** without an

intermediary, direct; **par l'~ de** through.

interminable /ɛ̃tɛʀminabl/ adj endless.

intermittence /ɛ̃tɛʀmitɑ̃s/ nf **par ~** intermittently.

internat /ɛ̃tɛʀna/ nm boarding-school.

international, ~e (mpl **-aux**) /ɛ̃tɛʀnasjɔnal, -o/ adj international.

internaute /ɛ̃tɛʀnot/ nmf (Ordinat) Netsurfer, Internet user.

interne /ɛ̃tɛʀn/ adj internal; (cours, formation) in-house. ●nmf (Scol) boarder; (Méd) house officer; (US) intern.

internement /ɛ̃tɛʀnəmɑ̃/ nm (Pol) internment. **interner 1** vt (Pol) intern; (Méd) commit.

⚑Internet /ɛ̃tɛʀnɛt/ nm Internet; **sur ~** on the Internet.

interpellation /ɛ̃tɛʀpelasjɔ̃/ nf (Pol) questioning. **interpeller*** **1** vt shout to; (apostropher) shout at; (interroger) question.

interphone /ɛ̃tɛʀfɔn/ nm intercom; (d'immeuble) entry phone.

interposer (s') /(s)ɛ̃tɛʀpoze/ **1** vpr intervene.

interprétariat /ɛ̃tɛʀpʀetaʀja/ nm interpreting. **interprétation** nf interpretation; (d'artiste) performance. **interprète** nmf interpreter; (artiste) performer. **interpréter 14** vt interpret; (jouer) play; (chanter) sing.

interrogateur, -trice /ɛ̃teʀɔgatœʀ, -tʀis/ adj questioning. **interrogatif, -ive** adj interrogative. **interrogation** nf question; (action) questioning; (épreuve) test. **interrogatoire** nm interrogation. **interroger 40** vt question; (élève) test.

interrompre /ɛ̃teʀɔ̃pʀ/ **3** vt break off, interrupt; (personne) interrupt. ■**s'~** vpr break off. **interrupteur** nm switch.

⚑ see A-Z of French life and culture

interruption nf interruption; (arrêt) break.

interurbain, ∼e /ɛ̃tɛRyRbɛ̃, -ɛn/ adj long-distance, trunk.

intervalle /ɛ̃tɛRval/ nm space; (temps) interval; **dans l'**∼ in the meantime.

intervenir /ɛ̃tɛRvəniR/ 58 vi (agir) intervene (**auprès de qn** with sb); (survenir) occur, take place; (Méd) operate. **intervention** nf intervention; (Méd) operation.

intervertir /ɛ̃tɛRvɛRtiR/ 2 vt invert; (rôles) reverse.

interview /ɛ̃tɛRvju/ nf interview. **interviewer** 1 vt interview.

intestin /ɛ̃tɛstɛ̃/ nm intestine.

intime /ɛ̃tim/ adj intimate; (fête, vie) private; (dîner) quiet. ● nmf intimate friend.

intimider /ɛ̃timide/ 1 vt intimidate.

intimité /ɛ̃timite/ nf intimacy; (vie privée) privacy.

intituler /ɛ̃tityle/ 1 vt call, entitle. ■ s'∼ vpr be called ou entitled.

intolérable /ɛ̃tɔleRabl/ adj intolerable. **intolérance** nf intolerance. **intolérant**, ∼e adj intolerant.

intonation /ɛ̃tɔnasjɔ̃/ nf intonation.

intox /ɛ̃tɔks/ nf 🄵 brainwashing.

intoxication /ɛ̃tɔksikasjɔ̃/ nf poisoning; (fig) brainwashing; ∼ **alimentaire** food poisoning. **intoxiquer** 1 vt poison; (fig) brainwash.

intraitable /ɛ̃tRɛtabl/ adj inflexible.

Intranet /ɛ̃tRanɛt/ nm Intranet.

intransigeant, ∼e /ɛ̃tRɑ̃ziʒɑ̃, -t/ adj intransigent.

intransitif, -ive /ɛ̃tRɑ̃zitif, -v/ adj intransitive.

intraveineux, -euse /ɛ̃tRavɛnø, -z/ adj intravenous.

intrépide /ɛ̃tRepid/ adj fearless.

intrigue /ɛ̃tRig/ nf intrigue; (scénario) plot.

intrinsèque /ɛ̃tRɛ̃sɛk/ adj intrinsic.

introduction /ɛ̃tRɔdyksjɔ̃/ nf introduction; (insertion) insertion.

introduire /ɛ̃tRɔdɥiR/ 17 vt introduce, bring in; (insérer) put in, insert; ∼ **qn** show sb in. ■ s'∼ vpr get in; **s'**∼ **dans** get into, enter.

introuvable /ɛ̃tRuvabl/ adj that cannot be found.

introverti, ∼e /ɛ̃tRɔvɛRti/ nm, f introvert. ● adj introverted.

intrus, ∼e /ɛ̃tRy, -z/ nm, f intruder. **intrusion** nf intrusion.

intuitif, -ive /ɛ̃tɥitif, -iv/ adj intuitive. **intuition** nf intuition.

inusable /inyzabl/ adj hardwearing.

inusité, ∼e /inyzite/ adj little used.

inutile /inytil/ adj useless; (vain) needless. **inutilement** adv needlessly. **inutilisable** adj unusable.

invalide /ɛ̃valid/ adj & nmf disabled (person).

invariable /ɛ̃vaRjabl/ adj invariable.

invasion /ɛ̃vazjɔ̃/ nf invasion.

invectiver /ɛ̃vɛktive/ 1 vt abuse.

inventaire /ɛ̃vɑ̃tɛR/ nm inventory; (Comm) stocklist; **faire l'**∼ draw up an inventory; (Comm) do a stocktake.

inventer /ɛ̃vɑ̃te/ 1 vt invent. **inventeur, -trice** nm, f inventor. **inventif, -ive** adj inventive. **invention** nf invention.

inverse /ɛ̃vɛRs/ adj opposite; (ordre) reverse; **en sens** ∼ in ou from the opposite direction. ● nm reverse; **c'est l'**∼ it's the other way round. **inversement** adv conversely. **inverser** 1 vt reverse, invert.

investir /ɛ̃vɛstiʀ/ **2** vt invest.
investissement nm investment.

investiture /ɛ̃vɛstityʀ/ nf (de candidat) nomination; (de président) investiture.

invétéré, ~**e** /ɛ̃vetere/ adj inveterate; (menteur) compulsive; (enraciné) deep-rooted.

invisible /ɛ̃vizibl/ adj invisible.

invitation /ɛ̃vitasjɔ̃/ nf invitation. **invité,** ~**e** nm, f guest. **inviter** **1** vt invite (**à** to).

involontaire /ɛ̃vɔlɔ̃tɛʀ/ adj involuntary; (témoin, héros) unwitting.

invoquer /ɛ̃vɔke/ **1** vt call upon, invoke.

invraisemblable /ɛ̃vʀɛsɑ̃blabl/ adj improbable, unlikely; (incroyable) incredible. **invraisemblance** nf improbability.

iode /jɔd/ nm iodine.

ira, irait /iʀa, iʀɛ/ ▷ ALLER **8**.

Irak /iʀak/ nm Iraq.

Iran /iʀɑ̃/ nm Iran.

iris /iʀis/ nm iris.

irlandais, ~**e** /iʀlɑ̃dɛ, -z/ adj Irish. **I**~, ~**e** nm, f Irishman, Irishwoman.

Irlande /iʀlɑ̃d/ nf Ireland.

IRM abrév m (imagerie par résonance magnétique) magnetic resonance imaging.

ironie /iʀɔni/ nf irony. **ironique** adj ironic.

irrationnel, ~**le** /iʀasjɔnɛl/ adj irrational.

irréalisable /iʀealizabl/ adj (idée, rêve) unachievable; (projet) unworkable.

irrécupérable /iʀekypeʀabl/ adj irretrievable; (capital) irrecoverable.

irréel, ~**le** /iʀeɛl/ adj unreal.

irréfléchi, ~**e** /iʀefleʃi/ adj thoughtless.

irrégulier, -ière /iʀegylje, -jɛʀ/ adj irregular.

irrémédiable /iʀemedjabl/ adj irreparable.

irremplaçable /iʀɑ̃plasabl/ adj irreplaceable.

irréparable /iʀepaʀabl/ adj (objet) beyond repair; (tort, dégâts) irreparable.

irréprochable /iʀepʀɔʃabl/ adj flawless.

irrésistible /iʀezistibl/ adj irresistible; (drôle) hilarious.

irrésolu, ~**e** /iʀezɔly/ adj indecisive; (problème) unsolved.

irrespirable /iʀɛspiʀabl/ adj stifling.

irresponsable /iʀɛspɔ̃sabl/ adj irresponsible.

irrigation /iʀigasjɔ̃/ nf irrigation. **irriguer** **1** vt irrigate.

irritable /iʀitabl/ adj irritable.

irriter /iʀite/ **1** vt irritate. ∎ s'~ vpr get annoyed (**de** at).

irruption /iʀypsjɔ̃/ nf **faire** ~ **dans** burst into.

Islam /islam/ nm Islam. **islamique** adj Islamic.

islamiste /islamist/ adj Islamist, Islamic; nm, f Islamist.

islandais, ~**e** /islɑ̃dɛ, -z/ adj Icelandic. ●nm (Ling) Icelandic. **I**~, ~**e** nm, f Icelander.

Islande /islɑ̃d/ nf Iceland.

isolant /izɔlɑ̃/ nm insulating material. **isolation** nf insulation.

isolé, ~**e** /izɔle/ adj isolated. **isolement** nm isolation.

isoler /izɔle/ **1** vt isolate; (Électr) insulate. ∎ s'~ vpr isolate oneself.

isoloir /izɔlwaʀ/ nm polling booth.

Isorel ® /izɔʀɛl/ nm hardboard.

Israël /isʀaɛl/ nm Israel. **israélien,** ~**ne** adj Israeli.

israélite /israelit/ adj Jewish. ●nmf Jew.

issu, ~e /isy/ adj **être ~ de** (personne) come from; (résulter de) result ou stem from.

issue /isy/ nf (sortie) exit; (résultat) outcome; (fig) solution; **à l'~ de** at the conclusion of; **~ de secours** emergency exit; **rue** ou **voie sans ~** dead end.

Italie /itali/ nf Italy.

italien, ~ne /italjɛ̃, -ɛn/ adj Italian. ●nm (Ling) Italian. **I~, ~ne** nm, f Italian.

italique /italik/ nm italics.

itinéraire /itinerɛr/ nm itinerary, route.

I.U.T. abrév m (**Institut universitaire de technologie**) university institute of technology.

I.V.G. abrév f (**interruption volontaire de grossesse**) abortion.

ivoire /ivwar/ nm ivory.

ivre /ivr/ adj drunk. **ivresse** nf drunkenness; (fig) exhilaration. **ivrogne** nmf drunk(ard).

Jj

j' /ʒ/ ▷JE.

jacinthe /ʒasɛ̃t/ nf hyacinth.

jadis /ʒadis/ adv long ago.

jaillir /ʒajir/ ② vi (liquide) spurt (out); (lumière) stream out; (apparaître) burst forth, spring out.

jalonner /ʒalɔne/ ① vt mark (out).

jalousie /ʒaluzi/ nf jealousy; (store) (venetian) blind. **jaloux, -ouse** adj jealous.

jamais /ʒamɛ/ adv ever; **ne ~** never; **il ne boit ~** he never drinks; **à ~** for ever; **si ~** if ever.

jambe /ʒɑ̃b/ nf leg.

jambon /ʒɑ̃bɔ̃/ nm ham. **jambonneau** (pl **~x**) nm knuckle of ham.

janvier /ʒɑ̃vje/ nm January.

Japon /ʒapɔ̃/ nm Japan.

japonais, ~e /ʒaponɛ, -z/ adj Japanese. ●nm (Ling) Japanese. **J~, ~e** nm, f Japanese.

japper /ʒape/ ① vi yap.

jaquette /ʒakɛt/ nf (de livre, femme) jacket; (d'homme) morning coat.

jardin /ʒardɛ̃/ nm garden; **~ d'enfants** nursery (school); **~ public** public park. **jardinage** nm gardening. **jardiner** ① vi do some gardening, garden. **jardinier, -ière** nm, f gardener.

jardinière /ʒardinjɛr/ nf (meuble) plant-stand; **~ de légumes** mixed vegetables.

jarretelle /ʒartɛl/ nf suspender; (US) garter.

jarretière /ʒartjɛr/ nf garter.

jatte /ʒat/ nf bowl.

jauge /ʒoʒ/ nf capacity; (de navire) tonnage; (compteur) gauge; **~ d'huile** dipstick.

jaune /ʒon/ adj & nm yellow; (péj) scab; **~ d'œuf** (egg) yolk; **rire ~** give a forced laugh. **jaunir** ② vt/i turn yellow. **jaunisse** nf jaundice.

javelot /ʒavlo/ nm javelin.

jazz /dʒaz/ nm jazz.

J.C. abrév m (**Jésus-Christ**) **500 avant/après ~** 500 B.C./A.D.

je, j' /ʒə, ʒ/ pron I.

jean /dʒin/ nm jeans; **un ~** a pair of jeans.

jet¹ /ʒɛ/ nm throw; (de liquide, vapeur) jet; **~ d'eau** fountain.

jet² /dʒɛt/ nm (avion) jet.

jetable /ʒətabl/ adj disposable.

jetée /ʒəte/ nf pier.

jeter /ʒəte/ 38 vt throw; (au rebut) throw away; (regard, ancre, lumière) cast; (cri) utter; (bases) lay; **~ un coup d'œil** have ou take a look (**à** at). ■ **se ~** vpr **se ~ contre** crash ou bash into; **se ~ dans** (fleuve) flow into; **se ~ sur** (se ruer sur) rush at.

jeton /ʒətɔ̃/ nm token; (pour compter) counter; (au casino) chip.

jeu (pl **~x**) /ʒø/ nm game; (amusement) play; (au casino) gambling; (Théât) acting; (série) set; (de lumière, ressort) play; **en ~** (honneur, ressort) at stake; (forces) at work; **~ de cartes** (paquet) pack of cards; **~d'échecs** (boîte) chess set; **~ de mots** pun; **~ télévisé** tv game show; **~ vidéo** video game; **~x de grattage** scratch cards; **les ~x olympiques/ paralympiques** the Olympic Games/Paralympic Games.

jeudi /ʒødi/ nm Thursday.

jeun: à ~ /aʒœ̃/ loc on an empty stomach.

jeune /ʒœn/ adj young; **~ fille** girl; **~ pousse** (Comm) start-up; **~s mariés** newlyweds. ●nmf young person; **les ~s** young people.

jeûne /ʒøn/ nm fast.

jeunesse /ʒœnɛs/ nf youth; (apparence) youthfulness; **la ~** (jeunes) the young.

joaillerie /ʒɔajʀi/ nf jewellery; (magasin) jeweller's shop.

joie /ʒwa/ nf joy.

joindre /ʒwɛ̃dʀ/ 22 vt join (**à** to); (mains, pieds) put together; (efforts) combine; (contacter) contact; (dans une enveloppe) enclose. ■ **se ~ à** vpr join.

joint, ~e /ʒwɛ̃, -t/ adj (efforts) joint; (pieds) together. ●nm joint; (de robinet) washer.

joli, ~e /ʒɔli/ adj pretty, nice; (somme, profit) nice; **c'est du ~!** (ironique) charming! **c'est bien ~ mais** that is all very well but.

joncher /ʒɔ̃ʃe/ 1 vt litter, be strewn over; **jonché de** littered with.

jonction /ʒɔ̃ksjɔ̃/ nf junction.

jongleur, -euse /ʒɔ̃glœʀ, øz/ nm, f juggler.

jonquille /ʒɔ̃kij/ nf daffodil.

joue /ʒu/ nf cheek.

jouer /ʒwe/ 1 vt/i play; (Théât) act; (au casino) gamble; (fonctionner) work; (film, pièce) put on; (cheval) back; (être important) count; **~ à** (jeu, Sport) play; **~ de** (Mus) play; **~ la comédie** put on an act; **bien joué!** well done!

jouet /ʒwɛ/ nm toy; (personne: fig) plaything; (victime) victim.

joueur, -euse /ʒwœʀ, -øz/ nm, f player; (parieur) gambler.

joufflu, ~e /ʒufly/ adj chubby-cheeked; (visage) chubby.

jouir /ʒwiʀ/ 2 vi (sexe) come; **~ de** (droit, avantage) enjoy; (bien, concession) enjoy the use of. **jouissance** nf pleasure; (usage) use (**de qch** of sth).

joujou (pl **~x**) /ʒuʒu/ nm 1 toy.

jour /ʒuʀ/ nm day; (opposé à nuit) day (time); (lumière) daylight; (aspect) light; (ouverture) gap; **de nos ~s** nowadays; **du ~ au lendemain** overnight; **il fait ~** it is daylight; **~ chômé ou férié** public holiday; **~ de fête** holiday; **~ ouvrable, ~ de travail** working day; **mettre à ~** update; **mettre au ~** uncover; **au grand ~** in the open; **donner le ~** give birth; **voir le ~** be born; **vivre au ~ le jour** live from day to day.

journal | juvénile

journal (pl **-aux**) /ʒuʀnal, -o/ nm (news)paper; (spécialisé) journal; (intime) diary; (à la radio) news; ~ **de bord** log-book.

journalier, -ière /ʒuʀnalje, -jɛʀ/ adj daily.

journalisme /ʒuʀnalism/ nm journalism. **journaliste** nmf journalist.

journée /ʒuʀne/ nf day.

jovial, ~e (mpl **-iaux**) /ʒɔvjal, -jo/ adj jovial.

joyau (pl ~**x**) /ʒwajo/ nm gem.

joyeux, -euse /ʒwajø, -z/ adj merry, joyful; ~ **anniversaire** happy birthday.

jubiler /ʒybile/ **1** vi be jubilant.

jucher /ʒyʃe/ **1** vt perch. ■ **se** ~ vpr perch.

judaïsme /ʒydaism/ nm Judaism.

judiciaire /ʒydisjɛʀ/ adj judicial.

judicieux, -ieuse /ʒydisjø, -z/ adj judicious.

judo /ʒydo/ nm judo.

juge /ʒyʒ/ nm judge; (arbitre) referee; ~ **de paix** Justice of the Peace; ~ **de touche** linesman.

jugé: au ~ /oʒyʒe/ loc by guesswork.

jugement /ʒyʒmɑ̃/ nm judgement; (criminel) sentence.

juger /ʒyʒe/ **40** vt/i judge; (estimer) consider (**que** that); ~ **de** judge.

juguler /ʒygyle/ **1** vt stamp out; curb.

juif, -ive /ʒɥif, -v/ adj Jewish. ●nm, f Jew.

juillet /ʒɥijɛ/ nm July.

juin /ʒɥɛ̃/ nm June.

jumeau, -elle (mpl ~**x**) /ʒymo, -ɛl/ adj & nm, f twin. **jumeler** **38** vt (villes) twin.

jumelles /ʒymɛl/ nfpl binoculars.

jument /ʒymɑ̃/ nf mare.

junior /ʒynjɔʀ/ adj & nmf junior.

jupe /ʒyp/ nf skirt.

jupon /ʒypɔ̃/ nm slip, petticoat.

juré, ~e /ʒyʀe/ nm, f juror. ●adj sworn.

jurer /ʒyʀe/ **1** vt swear (**que** that). ●vi (pester) swear; (contraster) clash (**avec** with).

juridiction /ʒyʀidiksjɔ̃/ nf jurisdiction; (tribunal) court of law.

juridique /ʒyʀidik/ adj legal.

juriste /ʒyʀist/ nmf legal expert.

juron /ʒyʀɔ̃/ nm swearword.

jury /ʒyʀi/ nm (Jur) jury; (examinateurs) panel of judges.

jus /ʒy/ nm juice; (de viande) gravy; ~ **de fruit** fruit juice.

jusque /ʒysk(ə)/ prép **jusqu'à** (up) to, as far as; (temps) until, till; (limite) up to; (y compris) even; **jusqu'à ce que** until; **jusqu'à présent** until now; **jusqu'en** until; **jusqu'où?** how far?; ~ **dans, ~ sur** as far as.

juste /ʒyst/ adj fair, just; (légitime) just; (correct, exact) right; (vrai) true; (vêtement) tight; (quantité) on the short side; **le** ~ **milieu** the happy medium. ●adv rightly, correctly; (chanter) in tune; (seulement, exactement) just; (**un peu**) ~ (calculer, mesurer) a bit fine ou close; **au** ~ exactly; **c'était** ~ (presque raté) it was a close thing. **justement** adv (précisément) precisely; (à l'instant) just; (avec justesse) correctly; (légitimement) justifiably.

justesse /ʒystɛs/ nf accuracy; **de** ~ just, narrowly.

justice /ʒystis/ nf justice; (autorités) law; (tribunal) court.

justifier /ʒystifje/ **45** vt justify. ●vi ~ **de** prove. ■ **se** ~ vpr justify oneself.

juteux, -euse /ʒytø, -z/ adj juicy.

juvénile /ʒyvenil/ adj youthful; (délinquance, mortalité) juvenile.

j

Kk

kaki /kaki/ adj inv & nm khaki.

kangourou /kãguʀu/ nm kangaroo.

karaté /kaʀate/ nm karate.

kart /kaʀt/ nm go-cart.

kascher /kaʃɛʀ/ adj inv kosher.

kayak /kajak/ nm kayak.

képi /kepi/ nm kepi.

kermesse /kɛʀmɛs/ nf fête.

kidnapper /kidnape/ **1** vt kidnap.

kilo /kilo/ nm kilo.

kilogramme /kilɔgʀam/ nm kilogram.

kilométrage /kilɔmetʀaʒ/ nm ≈ mileage. **kilomètre** nm kilometre.

kinésithérapeute /kineziteʀapøt/ nmf physiotherapist. **kinésithérapie** nf physiotherapy.

kiosque /kjɔsk/ nm kiosk; ∼ **à musique** bandstand.

kit /kit/ nm kit; ∼ **mains libres conducteur** hands-free kit.

klaxon® /klaksɔn/ nm (Auto) horn. **klaxonner** **1** vi sound one's horn.

Ko abrév m (**kilo-octet**) (Ordinat) KB.

KO abrév m (**knock-out***) KO **1**.

K-way® /kawɛ/ nm inv windcheater.

kyste /kist/ nm cyst.

Ll

l', la /l, la/ ▷LE.

là /la/
● adverb
····▸ (dans ce lieu) there; (ici) here; (chez soi) in; **c'est** ∼ **que** this is where; ∼ **où** where; **par** ∼ (dans cette direction) this way; (dans cette zone) around there; **de** ∼ hence.
····▸ (à ce moment) then; **c'est** ∼ **que** that's when.
····▸ **cet homme-**∼ that man; **ces maisons-**∼ those houses.
● interjection
····▸ ∼ **1** **c'est fini** there (now), it's all over!

là-bas /labɑ/ adv there; (à l'endroit que l'on indique) over there.

label /labɛl/ nm seal, label.

laboratoire /labɔʀatwaʀ/ nm laboratory.

laborieux, -ieuse /labɔʀjø, -z/ adj laborious; (personne) industrious; **classes laborieuses** working classes.

labour /labuʀ/ nm ploughing; (US) plowing. **labourer** **1** vt plough; (US) plow; (déchirer) rip at.

labyrinthe /labiʀɛ̃t/ nm maze, labyrinth.

lac /lak/ nm lake.

lacer /lase/ **10** vt lace up.

lacet /lasɛ/ nm (de chaussure) (shoe-)lace; (de route) sharp bend.

lâche /lɑʃ/ adj cowardly/ (détendu) loose; (sans rigueur) lax. ●nmf coward.

lâcher /lɑʃe/ **1** vt let go of; (laisser tomber) drop; (abandonner) give up; (laisser) leave; (libérer) release; (flèche, balle) fire; (juron, phrase) come out with; (desserrer) loosen; **~ prise** let go. ●vi give way.

lâcheté /lɑʃte/ nf cowardice.

lacrymogène /lakʀimɔʒɛn/ adj **gaz ~** tear gas.

lacune /lakyn/ nf gap.

là-dedans /lad(ə)dɑ̃/ adv (près) in here; (plus loin) in there.

là-dessous /lad(ə)su/ adv (près) under here; (plus loin) under there.

là-dessus /lad(ə)sy/ adv (sur une surface) on here; (plus loin) on there; (sur ce) with that; (quelque temps après) after that; **qu'avez-vous à dire ~?** what have you got to say about it?

ladite /ladit/ ▷ **ledit**.

lagune /lagyn/ nf lagoon.

là-haut /lao/ adv (en hauteur) up here; (plus loin) up there; (à l'étage) upstairs.

laïc /laik/ nm layman.

laid, ~e /lɛ, lɛd/ adj ugly; (action) vile. **laideur** nf ugliness.

lainage /lɛnaʒ/ nm woollen garment.

laine /lɛn/ nf wool; **de ~** woollen.

laïque /laik/ adj (état, loi) secular; (habit, personne) lay; (école) nondenominational. ●nmf layman, laywoman.

laisse /lɛs/ nf lead, leash; **tenir en ~** keep on a lead.

laisser /lese/ **1** vt (déposer) leave, drop off; (confier) leave (**à qn** with sb); (abandonner) leave; (rendre) **~ qn perplexe/froid** leave sb puzzled/cold; **~ qch à qn** (céder, prêter) let sb have sth;

(donner) (choix, temps) give sb sth. ■ **se ~** vpr **se ~ persuader/ insulter** let oneself be persuaded/insulted; **elle ne se laisse pas faire** she won't be pushed around; **laisse-toi faire** leave it to me/him/her etc.; **se ~ aller** let oneself go. ●v aux **~ qn/qch faire** let sb/sth do; **laisse-moi faire** (ne m'aide pas) let me do it; (je m'en occupe) leave it to me; **laisse faire!** so what! **laisser-aller** nm inv carelessness; (dans la tenue) scruffiness. **laissez-passer** nm inv pass.

lait /lɛ/ nm milk; **~ longue conservation** long-life ou UHT milk; **frère/sœur de ~** foster-brother/-sister. **laitage** nm milk product. **laiterie** nf dairy. **laiteux, -euse** adj milky.

laitier, -ière /letje, -jɛʀ/ adj dairy. ●nm, f (livreur) milkman, milkwoman.

laiton /lɛtɔ̃/ nm brass.

laitue /lety/ nf lettuce.

lama /lama/ nm llama.

lambeau (pl **~x**) /lɑ̃bo/ nm shred; **en ~x** in shreds.

lame /lam/ nf blade; (lamelle) strip; (vague) wave; **~ de fond** ground swell; **~ de rasoir** razor blade.

lamentable /lamɑ̃tabl/ adj deplorable. **lamenter (se)** **1** vpr moan (**sur** about, over).

lampadaire /lɑ̃padɛʀ/ nm standard lamp; (de rue) street lamp.

lampe /lɑ̃p/ nf lamp; (ampoule) bulb; (de radio) valve; **~ (de poche)** torch; (US) flashlight; **~ à souder** blowlamp; **~ de chevet** bedside lamp; **~ solaire, ~ à bronzer** sunlamp.

lance /lɑ̃s/ nf spear; (de tournoi) lance; (tuyau) hose; **~ d'incendie** fire hose.

lancement /lɑ̃smɑ̃/ nm throwing; (de navire, de missile, mise sur le marché) launch.

lance-missiles* /lɑ̃smisil/ nm inv missile launcher.

lance-pierres* /lɑ̃spjɛʀ/ nm inv catapult.

lancer /lɑ̃se/ [10] vt throw; (avec force) hurl; (navire, idée, artiste) launch; (émettre) give out; (regard) cast; (moteur) start. ■ se ∼ vpr (Sport) gain momentum; (se précipiter) rush; **se ∼ dans** (explication) launch into; (passetemps) take up. ● nm throw; (action) throwing.

lancinant, ∼e /lɑ̃sinɑ̃, -t/ adj (douleur) shooting; (problème) nagging.

landau /lɑ̃do/ nm pram; (US) baby carriage.

lande /lɑ̃d/ nf heath, moor.

langage /lɑ̃gaʒ/ nm language; ∼ **machine/de programmation** machine/programming language.

langouste /lɑ̃gust/ nf spiny lobster. **langoustine** nf Dublin Bay prawn.

langue /lɑ̃g/ nf (Anat) tongue; (Ling) language; **il m'a tiré la ∼** he stuck his tongue out at me; **de ∼ anglaise** (personne) English-speaking; (journal) English-language; ∼ **maternelle** mother tongue; ∼ **vivante** modern language.

lanière /lanjɛʀ/ nf strap.

lanterne /lɑ̃tɛʀn/ nf lantern; (électrique) lamp; (de voiture) sidelight.

lapin /lapɛ̃/ nm rabbit; **poser un ∼ à qn** [1] stand sb up; **le coup du ∼** rabbit punch; (en voiture) whiplash injury.

lapsus /lapsys/ nm slip (of the tongue).

laque /lak/ nf lacquer; (pour cheveux) hairspray; (peinture) gloss paint.

laquelle /lakɛl/ ▷LEQUEL.

lard /laʀ/ nm streaky bacon.

large /laʀʒ/ adj wide, broad; (grand) large; (généreux) generous; **avoir les idées ∼s** be broad-minded; ∼ **d'esprit** broad-minded. ● adv (calculer, mesurer) on the generous side; **voir ∼** think big. ● nm **faire 10 cm de ∼** be 10 cm wide; **le ∼** (mer) the open sea; **au ∼ de** (Naut) off.

largement adv widely; (ouvrir) wide; (amplement) amply; (généreusement) generously; (au moins) easily.

largesse /laʀʒɛs/ nf generous gift.

largeur /laʀʒœʀ/ nf width, breadth; ∼ **d'esprit** broad-mindedness.

larguer /laʀge/ [1] vt drop; ∼ **les amarres** cast off.

larme /laʀm/ nf tear; (goutte [1]) drop; **en ∼s** in tears.

larmoyant, ∼e /laʀmwajɑ̃, -t/ adj full of tears. **larmoyer** [31] vi (yeux) water; (pleurnicher) whine.

larynx /laʀɛ̃ks/ nm larynx.

las, ∼se /lɑ, lɑs/ adj weary.

lasagnes* /lazaɲ/ nfpl lasagna.

laser /lazɛʀ/ nm laser.

lasser /lɑse/ [1] vt weary. ■ se ∼ vpr grow tired, get weary (de of).

latéral, ∼e (mpl -aux) /lateʀal, -o/ adj lateral.

latin, ∼e /latɛ̃, -in/ adj Latin. ● nm (Ling) Latin.

latte /lat/ nf lath; (de plancher) board; (de siège) slat; (de mur, plafond) lath.

lauréat, ∼e /lɔʀea, -t/ adj prizewinning. ● nm, f prize-winner.

laurier /lɔʀje/ nm (Bot) laurel; (Culin) bay-leaves.

lavable /lavabl/ adj washable.

lavabo /lavabo/ nm wash-basin; ∼**s** toilet(s).

lavage /lavaʒ/ nm washing; ∼ **de cerveau** brainwashing.

lavande /lavɑ̃d/ nf lavender.

lave /lav/ nf lava.

lave-glace (pl ~s) /lavglas/ nm windscreen washer.

lave-linge* /lavlɛ̃ʒ/ nm inv washing machine.

laver /lave/ **1** vt wash; ~ **qn de** (fig) clear sb of. ▪ **se** ~ vpr wash (oneself); **se** ~ **les mains** wash one's hands.

laverie /lavʀi/ nf ~ **(automatique)** launderette; (US) laundromat.

lave-vaisselle* /lavvɛsɛl/ nm inv dishwasher.

laxatif, -ive /laksatif, -v/ adj & nm laxative.

layette /lɛjɛt/ nf baby clothes.

le, la, l' (pl **les**) /lə, la, l, le/

❗ **l'** before vowel or mute h.

● déterminant
⋯▸ the.
⋯▸ (notion générale) **aimer la musique** like music; **l'amour** love.
⋯▸ (possession) **avoir les yeux verts** have green eyes; **il s'est cassé la jambe** he broke his leg.
⋯▸ (prix) **10 euros** ~ **kilo** 10 euros a kilo.
⋯▸ (temps) ~ **lundi** on Mondays; **tous les mardis** every Tuesday.
⋯▸ (avec nom propre) **les Dury** the Durys; **la reine Margot** Queen Margot; **la Belgique** Belgium.
⋯▸ (avec adjectif) the; **je veux la rouge** I want the red one; **les riches** the rich.
● pronom
⋯▸ (homme) him; (femme) her; (chose, animal) it; (au pluriel) them.
⋯▸ (remplaçant une phrase) **je te l'avais bien dit** I told you so; **je** ~ **croyais aussi** I thought so too.

lécher /leʃe/ **14** vt lick; (flamme) lick; (mer) lap.

lèche-vitrines /lɛʃvitʀin/ nm inv **faire du** ~ go window-shopping.

leçon /ləsɔ̃/ nf lesson; **faire la** ~ **à** lecture sb; ~ **particulière** private lesson; ~**s de conduite** driving lessons.

lecteur, -trice /lɛktœʀ, -tʀis/ nm, f reader; (Univ) foreign language assistant; ~ **de cassettes** cassette player; ~ **de disquettes** (disk) drive; ~ **laser** CD player; ~ **optique** optical scanner.

lecture /lɛktyʀ/ nf reading.

ledit, ladite (pl **lesdit(e)s**) /lədi, ladit, ledi(t)/ adj the aforementioned.

légal, ~e (mpl **-aux**) /legal, -o/ adj legal. **légaliser** **1** vt legalize. **légalité** nf legality; (loi) law.

légendaire /leʒɑ̃dɛʀ/ adj legendary. **légende** nf (histoire, inscription) legend; (de carte) key; (d'illustration) caption.

léger, -ère /leʒe, -ɛʀ/ adj light; (bruit, faute, maladie) slight; (café, argument) weak; (imprudent) thoughtless; (frivole) fickle; **à la légère** thoughtlessly. **légèrement** adv lightly; (agir) thoughtlessly; (un peu) slightly. **légèreté** nf lightness; thoughtlessness.

légion /leʒjɔ̃/ nf legion.

légionellose /leʒjɔnɛloz/ nf (Méd) legionnaire's disease.

législatif, -ive /leʒislatif, -v/ adj legislative; **élections législatives** general election.

législature /leʒislatyʀ/ nf term of office.

légitime /leʒitim/ adj (Jur) legitimate; (fig) rightful; **agir en état de** ~ **défense** act in self-defence. **légitimité** nf legitimacy.

legs /lɛg/ nm legacy; (d'effets

personnels) bequest.

léguer /lege/ 🔢 vt bequeath.

légume /legym/ nm vegetable.

lendemain /lɑ̃dmɛ̃/ nm **le ~** the next day; (fig) the future; **le ~ de** the day after; **le ~ matin/ soir** the next morning/evening; **du jour au ~** from one day to the next.

lent, ~e /lɑ̃, -t/ adj slow. **lentement** adv slowly. **lenteur** nf slowness.

lentille /lɑ̃tij/ nf (Culin) lentil; (verre) lens; **~s de contact** contact lenses.

léopard /leopaʀ/ nm leopard.

lèpre /lɛpʀ/ nf leprosy.

lequel, laquelle (pl lesquel(le)s, auquel (pl auxquel(le)s, duquel (pl desquel(le)s) /ləkɛl, lakɛl, lekɛl, ɔkɛl, dykɛl, dekɛl/

> **!** à + lequel = auquel,
> **▪** à + lesquel(le)s = auxquel(le)s;
> de + lequel = duquel,
> de + lesquel(le)s = desquel(le)s

● pronom
••••▸ (relatif) (personne) who; (complément indirect) whom; (autres cas) which; **l'ami auquel tu as écrit** the friend to whom you wrote; **les voisins chez lesquels Sophie est allée** the neighbours whose house Sophie went to.
••••▸ (interrogatif) which; **~ tu veux?** which one do you want?
● adjectif
••••▸ **auquel cas** in which case.

les /le/ ▷LE.

lesbienne /lɛsbjɛn/ nf lesbian.

léser /leze/ 🔢 vt wrong.

lésiner /lezine/ 🔢 vi **ne pas ~ sur** not stint on.

lesquels, lesquelles /lekɛl/ ▷LEQUEL.

lessive /lesiv/ nf (poudre) washing-

powder; (liquide) washing liquid; (linge, action) washing.

leste /lɛst/ adj agile, nimble; (grivois) coarse.

Lettonie /letɔni/ nf Latvia.

lettre /lɛtʀ/ nf letter; **à la ~, au pied de la ~** literally; **en toutes ~s** in full; **les ~s** (Univ) (the) arts.

leucémie /løsemi/ nf leukaemia.

leur (pl ~s) /lœʀ/
● pronom personnel invariable
••••▸ them; **donne-le ~** give it to them; **je ~ fais confiance** I trust them.
● adjectif possessif
••••▸ their; **~s enfants** their children; **à ~ arrivée** when they arrived.
● **le leur, la leur,** (pl **les leurs**) pronom possessif
••••▸ theirs; **chacun le ~** one each; **je suis des ~s** I am one of them.

levain /ləvɛ̃/ nm leaven.

levé, ~e /ləve/ adj (debout) up.

levée /ləve/ nf (de peine, de sanctions) lifting; (de courrier) collection; (de troupes, d'impôts) levying.

lever /ləve/ 🔢 vt lift (up), raise; (interdiction) lift; (séance) close; (armée, impôts) levy. ● vi (pâte) rise. ▪ **se ~** vpr get up; (soleil, rideau) rise; (jour) break. ● nm **au ~** on getting up; **~ du jour** daybreak; **~ de rideau** (Théât) curtain (up); **~ du soleil** sunrise.

levier /ləvje/ nm lever; **~ de changement de vitesse** gear lever.

lèvre /lɛvʀ/ nf lip.

lévrier /levʀije/ nm greyhound.

levure /ləvyʀ/ nf yeast; **~ chimique** baking powder.

lexique /lɛksik/ nm vocabulary; (glossaire) lexicon.

lézard /lezaʀ/ nm lizard.

lézarde /lezaʀd/ nf crack.

liaison /ljezɔ̃/ nf connection; (transport, Ordinat) link; (contact) contact; (Gram, Mil) liaison; (amoureuse) affair; **être en ~ avec** be in contact with; **assurer la ~ entre** liaise between.

liane /ljan/ nf creeper.

Liban /libɑ̃/ nm Lebanon.

libeller /libele/ ① vt (chèque) write; (contrat) draw up; **libellé à l'ordre de** made out to.

libellule /libelyl/ nf dragonfly.

libéral, ~e (mpl **-aux**) /liberal, -o/ adj liberal; **les professions ~es** the professions.

libérateur, -trice /liberatœʀ, -tʀis/ adj liberating. ● nm, f liberator. **libération** nf release; (de pays) liberation.

libérer /libere/ ⑭ vt (personne) free, release; (pays) liberate, free; (bureau, lieux) vacate; (gaz) release. ■ se ~ vpr free oneself.

liberté /libɛʀte/ nf freedom, liberty; (loisir) free time; **être/ mettre en ~** be/set free; **~ conditionnelle** parole; **~ provisoire** provisional release (pending trial); **~ surveillée** probation; **~s publiques** civil liberties.

Libertel /libɛʀtɛl/ nm (Internet) Freenet.

libraire /libʀɛʀ/ nmf bookseller. **librairie** nf bookshop.

libre /libʀ/ adj free; (place, pièce) vacant, free; (passage) clear; (école) private (usually religious); **~ de qch/de faire** free from sth/to do. **libre-échange** nm free trade. **libre-service** (pl **libres-services**) nm (magasin) self-service shop; (restaurant) self-service restaurant.

🔲**licence** /lisɑ̃s/ nf licence; (Univ) degree.

licencié, ~e /lisɑ̃sje/ nm, f graduate; **~ ès lettres/sciences** Bachelor of Arts/Science.

licenciements /lisɑ̃simɑ̃/ nm redundancy; (pour faute) dismissal. **licencier** ㊺ vt make redundant; (pour faute) dismiss.

licorne /likɔʀn/ nf unicorn.

liège /ljɛʒ/ nm cork.

lien /ljɛ̃/ nm (rapport) link; (attache) bond, tie; (corde) rope; **~s affectifs/de parenté** emotional/family ties.

lier /lje/ ㊺ vt tie (up), bind; (relier) link; (engager, unir) bind; **~ conversation** strike up a conversation; **ils sont très liés** they are very close. ■ se ~ avec vpr make friends with.

lierre /ljɛʀ/ nm ivy.

lieu (pl **~x**) /ljø/ nm place; **~x** (locaux) premises; (d'un accident) scene; **sur les ~x** at the scene; **au ~ de** instead of; **avoir ~** take place; **donner ~ à** give rise to; **tenir ~ de** serve as; **s'il y a ~** if necessary; **en premier ~** firstly; **en dernier ~** lastly; **~ commun** commonplace; **~ de rencontre** meeting place.

lièvre /ljɛvʀ/ nm hare.

lifting /liftiŋ/ nm face-lift.

ligne /liɲ/ nf line; (trajet) route; (de métro, train) line; (formes) figure; (de femme) figure; **en ~** (joueurs) lined up; (au téléphone) on the phone; (Ordinat) on line; **~ spécialisée** (Internet) dedicated line.

ligoter /ligɔte/ ① vt tie up.

ligue /lig/ nf league. **liguer (se)** ① vpr join forces (**contre** against).

lilas /lila/ nm & a inv lilac.

limace /limas/ nf slug.

limande /limɑ̃d/ nf (poisson) dab.

lime /lim/ nf file; **~ à ongles** nail file.

limitation /limitasjɔ̃/ nf limitation; **~ de vitesse** speed limit.

🔲 see A-Z of French life and culture

limite /limit/ nf limit; (de jardin, champ) boundary; **à la ~ de** (fig) verging on, bordering on; **à la ~** if it comes to it, at a pinch; **dans une certaine ~** up to a point; **dans la ~ du possible** as far as possible. ● adj (vitesse, âge) maximum; **cas ~** borderline case; **date ~** deadline; **date ~ de vente** sell-by date.

limiter /limite/ **1** vt limit; (délimiter) form the border of. ■ **se ~** vpr limit oneself (**à** to).

limonade /limɔnad/ nf lemonade.

limpide /lɛ̃pid/ adj limpid, clear.

lin /lɛ̃/ nm (tissu) linen.

linge /lɛ̃ʒ/ nm linen; (lessive) washing; (torchon) cloth; **~ (de corps)** underwear. **lingerie** nf underwear. **lingette** nf wipe.

lingot /lɛ̃go/ nm ingot.

linguistique /lɛ̃gɥistik/ adj linguistic. ● nf linguistics.

lion /ljɔ̃/ nm lion; **le L~** Leo. **lionceau** (pl **~x**) nm lion cub. **lionne** nf lioness.

liquidation /likidasjɔ̃/ nf liquidation; (vente) (clearance) sale; **entrer en ~** go into liquidation.

liquide /likid/ adj liquid. ● nm (argent) ready money; **payer en ~** pay cash; **~ de frein** brake fluid.

liquider /likide/ **1** vt liquidate; (vendre) sell.

lire /liʀ/ **39** vt/i read. ● nf lira.

lis¹ /li/ ▷**LIRE 39**.

lis² /lis/ nm (fleur) lily.

lisible /lizibl/ adj legible; (roman) readable.

lisière /lizjɛʀ/ nf edge.

lisse /lis/ adj smooth.

liste /list/ nf list; **~ d'attente** waiting list; **~ électorale** register of voters; **être sur (la) ~ rouge** be ex-directory.

listing /listiŋ/ nm printout.

lit /li/ nm bed; **se mettre au ~** get into bed; **~ de camp** camp-bed; **~ d'enfant** cot; **~ d'une personne** single bed; **~ de deux personnes, grand ~** double bed.

literie /litʀi/ nf bedding.

litière /litjɛʀ/ nf litter.

litige /litiʒ/ nm dispute.

litre /litʀ/ nm litre.

littéraire /liteʀɛʀ/ adj literary; (études, formation) arts.

littéral, ~e (mpl **-aux**) /literal, -o/ adj literal.

littérature /literatyʀ/ nf literature.

littoral (pl **-aux**) /litɔʀal, -o/ nm coast.

Lituanie /litɥani/ nf Lithuania.

livide /livid/ adj deathly pale.

livraison /livʀɛzɔ̃/ nf delivery.

livre /livʀ/ nf (monnaie, poids) pound. ● nm book; **~ de bord** log-book; **~ de compte** books; **~ de poche** paperback.

livrer /livʀe/ **1** vt (Comm) deliver; (abandonner) give over (**à** to); (remettre) (coupable, document) hand over (**à** to); **livré à soi-même** left to oneself. ■ **se ~** vpr (se rendre) give oneself up (**à** to); **se ~ à** (boisson, actes) indulge in; (ami) confide in.

livret /livʀɛ/ nm book; (Mus) libretto; **~ de caisse d'épargne** savings book; **~ scolaire** school report (book).

livreur, -euse /livʀœʀ, -øz/ nm, f delivery man, delivery woman.

local¹, ~e (mpl **-aux**) /lɔkal, -o/ adj local.

local² (pl **-aux**) /lɔkal, -o/ nm premises; **locaux** premises.

localement /lɔkalmɑ̃/ adv locally.

localisation /lɔkalizasjɔ̃/ nf localization.

localiser /lɔkalize/ **1** vt (repérer) locate; (circonscrire) localize.

locataire /lɔkatɛʀ/ nmf tenant; (de chambre) lodger.

location /lɔkasjɔ̃/ nf (de maison) renting; (de voiture, de matériel) hire, rental; (de place) booking, reservation; (par propriétaire) renting out; hiring out; **en ~** (voiture) on hire, rented; (habiter) in rented accommodation.

locomotive /lɔkɔmɔtiv/ nf engine, locomotive.

locution /lɔkysjɔ̃/ nf phrase.

loft /lɔft/ nm loft (apartment).

loge /lɔʒ/ nf (de concierge, de francmaçons) lodge; (d'acteur) dressingroom; (de spectateur) box.

logement /lɔʒmɑ̃/ nm accommodation; (appartement) flat; (habitat) housing.

loger /lɔʒe/ 40 vt (réfugié, famille) house; (ami) put up; (client) accommodate. ●vi live. ■ **se ~** vpr live; **trouver à se ~** find accommodation; **se ~ dans** (balle) lodge itself in.

logiciel /lɔʒisjɛl/ nm software; **~ contributif** shareware; **~ d'application** application software; **~ de groupe** groupware; **~ de jeux** games software; **~ de navigation** browser; **~ public** freeware.

logique /lɔʒik/ adj logical. ●nf logic.

logis /lɔʒi/ nm dwelling.

logistique /lɔʒistik/ nf logistics.

loi /lwa/ nf law.

loin /lwɛ̃/ adv far (away); **au ~** far away; **de ~** from far away; (de beaucoup) by far; **~ de là** far from it; **plus ~** further; **il revient de ~** (fig) he had a close shave.

lointain, ~e /lwɛ̃tɛ̃, -ɛn/ adj distant. ●nm distance; **dans le ~** in the distance.

loisir /lwaziʀ/ nm (spare) time; **~s** (temps libre) leisure, spare time; (distractions) leisure activities; **à ~** at one's leisure;

avoir le ~ de faire have time to do.

londonien, ~ne /lɔ̃dɔnjɛ̃, -ɛn/ adj London. **L~, ~e** nm, f Londoner.

Londres /lɔ̃dʀ/ npr London.

long, longue /lɔ̃, lɔ̃g/ adj long; **à ~ terme** long-term; **être à ~ faire** be a long time doing. ●nm **de ~** (mesure) long; **de ~ en large** back and forth; **(tout) le ~ de** (all) along. ●adv **en dire ~ sur qn/qch** say a lot about sb/sth; **en savoir plus ~ sur** know more about.

longer /lɔ̃ʒe/ 40 vt go along; (limiter) border.

longitude /lɔ̃ʒityd/ nf longitude.

longtemps /lɔ̃tɑ̃/ adv a long time; **avant ~** before long; **trop ~** too long; **ça prendra ~** it will take a long time; **prendre plus ~ que prévu** take longer than anticipated.

longuement /lɔ̃gmɑ̃/ adv (longtemps) for a long time; (en détail) at length.

longueur /lɔ̃gœʀ/ nf length; **~s** (de texte) over-long parts; **à ~ de journée** all day long; **en ~** lengthwise; **~ d'onde** wavelength.

lopin /lɔpɛ̃/ nm **~ de terre** patch of land.

loque /lɔk/ nf **~s** rags; **~ (humaine)** (human) wreck.

loquet /lɔkɛ/ nm latch.

lors de /lɔʀdə/ prép (au moment de) at the time of; (pendant) during.

lorsque /lɔʀsk(ə)/ conj when.

losange /lɔzɑ̃ʒ/ nm diamond.

lot /lo/ nm (portion) share; (aux enchères) lot; (Ordinat) batch; (destin) lot; **gagner le gros ~** hit the jackpot.

loterie /lɔtʀi/ nf lottery.

lotion /lɔsjɔ̃/ nf lotion.

lotissement /lɔtismɑ̃/ nm (à

construire) building plot; (construit) (housing) development.

louable /luabl/ adj praiseworthy. **louange** nf praise.

louche /luʃ/ adj shady, dubious. • nf ladle.

loucher /luʃe/ 🔳 vi squint.

louer /lwe/ 🔳 vt (approuver) praise (**de** for); (prendre en location) (maison) rent; (voiture, matériel) hire, rent; (place) book, reserve; (donner en location) (maison) rent out; (matériel) rent, hire out; **à ~** to let, for rent (US).

loufoque /lufɔk/ adj 🔳 crazy.

loup /lu/ nm wolf.

loupe /lup/ nf magnifying glass.

louper /lupe/ 🔳 vt 🔳 miss; (examen) flunk 🔳.

lourd, ~e /luʀ, -d/ adj heavy; (faute) serious; **~ de dangers** fraught with danger; **il fait ~** it's close ou muggy.

loutre /lutʀ/ nf otter.

louveteau (pl **~x**) /luvto/ nm wolf cub; (scout) Cub (Scout).

loyal, ~e (mpl **-aux**) /lwajal, -o/ adj loyal, faithful; (honnête) fair. **loyauté** nf loyalty; fairness.

loyer /lwaje/ nm rent.

lu /ly/ ▷LIRE 39.

lubrifiant /lybʀifjɑ̃/ nm lubricant.

lucide /lysid/ adj lucid. **lucidité** nf lucidity.

lucratif, -ive /lykʀatif, -v/ adj lucrative; **à but non ~** non-profitmaking.

ludiciel /lydisjɛl/ nm (Ordinat) games software.

lueur /lɥœʀ/ nf (faint) light, glimmer; (fig) glimmer, gleam.

luge /lyʒ/ nf toboggan.

lugubre /lygybʀ/ adj gloomy.

lui /lɥi/
• pronom
····▸ (masculin) (sujet) he; **~, il est à l'étranger** he's abroad; **c'est ~!** it's him!; (objet) him; (animal) it; **c'est à ~** it's his; **elle conduit mieux que ~** she's a better driver than he is.
····▸ (féminin) her; **je ~ ai annoncé** I told her.
····▸ (masculin/féminin) **donne-le-~** give it to him/her.

lui-même /lɥimɛm/ pron himself; (animal) itself.

luire /lɥiʀ/ 🔳 vi shine; (reflet humide) glisten; (reflet chaud, faible) glow.

lumière /lymjɛʀ/ nf light; **~s** (connaissances) knowledge; **faire (toute) la ~ sur une affaire** clear a matter up.

luminaire /lyminɛʀ/ nm lamp.

lumineux, -euse /lyminø, -z/ adj luminous; (éclairé) illuminated; (rayon) of light; (radieux) radiant; **source lumineuse** light source.

lunaire /lynɛʀ/ adj lunar.

lunatique /lynatik/ adj temperamental.

lunch /lœnʃ/ nm buffet lunch.

lundi /lœdi/ nm Monday.

lune /lyn/ nf moon; **~ de miel** honeymoon.

lunettes /lynɛt/ nfpl glasses; (de protection) goggles; **~ de ski/natation** ski/swimming goggles; **~ noires** dark glasses; **~ de soleil** sun-glasses.

lustre /lystʀ/ nf (éclat) lustre; (objet) chandelier.

lutin /lytɛ̃/ nm goblin.

lutte /lyt/ nf fight, struggle; (Sport) wrestling. **lutter** 🔳 vi fight, struggle; (Sport) wrestle. **lutteur, -euse** nm, f fighter; (Sport) wrestler.

luxe /lyks/ nm luxury; **de ~**

luxury; (produit) de luxe.
⚑Luxembourg /lyksɑ̃buʁ/ nm
Luxembourg.

luxer (se) /(sə)lykse/ **1** vpr **se ∼
le genou** dislocate one's knee.

luxueux, -euse /lyksɥø, -z/ adj
luxurious.

⚑lycée /lise/ nm (secondary)

school. **lycéen, ∼ne** nm, f pupil
(at secondary school).

lyophilisé, ∼e /ljɔfilize/ adj
freeze-dried.

lyrique /liʁik/ adj (poésie) lyric;
(passionné) lyrical; **artiste/
théâtre ∼** opera singer/house.

lys /lis/ nm lily.

Mm

m' /m/ ▷**ME**.

ma /ma/ ▷**MON**.

macabre /makabʁ/ adj macabre.

macadam /makadam/ nm
Tarmac®.

macaron /makaʁɔ̃/ nm (gâteau)
macaroon; (insigne) badge.

macédoine /masedwan/ nf mixed
diced vegetables; **∼ de fruits**
fruit salad.

macérer /masere/ **14** vt/i soak;
(dans du vinaigre) pickle.

mâcher /mɑʃe/ **1** vt chew; **ne
pas ∼ ses mots** not mince
one's words.

machin /maʃɛ̃/ nm **1** (chose)
thing; (dont on ne trouve pas le nom)
whatsit **1**.

machinal, ∼e (mpl **-aux**)
/maʃinal, -o/ adj automatic.
machinalement adv
mechanically, automatically.

machination /maʃinasjɔ̃/ nf plot;
des ∼s machinations.

machine /maʃin/ nf machine;
(d'un train, navire) engine; **∼ à
écrire** typewriter; **∼ à laver/
coudre** washing-/sewing-
machine; **∼ à sous** fruit
machine; (US) slot machine.
machine-outil (pl **machines-
outils**) nf machine tool.
machinerie nf machinery.

machiniste /maʃinist/ nm (Théât)
stage-hand; (conducteur) driver.

mâchoire /mɑʃwaʁ/ nf jaw.

mâchonner /mɑʃone/ **1** vt chew.

maçon /masɔ̃/ nm (entrepreneur)
builder; (poseur de briques)
bricklayer; (qui construit en pierre)
mason. **maçonnerie** nf (briques)
brickwork; (pierres) stonework,
masonry; (travaux) building.

madame (pl **mesdames**)
/madam, medam/ nf (à une inconnue)
(dans une lettre) **M∼** Dear Madam;
bonjour, ∼ good morning;
mesdames et messieurs ladies
and gentlemen; (à une femme dont
on connaît le nom) (dans une lettre)
Chère M∼ Dear Mrs ou Ms X;
bonjour, ∼ good morning Mrs
ou Ms X; **oui M∼ le Ministre**
yes Minister; (formule de respect)
oui M∼ yes madam.

mademoiselle (pl
mesdemoiselles) /madmwazɛl,
medmwazɛl/ nf (à une inconnue)
(dans une lettre) **M∼** Dear Madam;
bonjour, ∼ good morning;
entrez mesdemoiselles come
in (ladies); (à une jeune fille dont on
connaît le nom) (dans une lettre) **Chère
M∼** Dear Ms ou Miss X;
bonjour, ∼ good morning Miss
ou Ms X.

⚑ see A-Z of French life and culture

magasin /magazɛ̃/ nm shop, store; (entrepôt) warehouse; (d'une arme) magazine; **en ~** in stock.

magazine /magazin/ nm magazine; (émission) programme.

Maghreb /magʀɛb/ nm North Africa.

magicien, ~ne /maʒisjɛ̃, -ɛn/ nm, f magician.

magie /maʒi/ nf magic. **magique** adj magic; (mystérieux) magical.

magistral, ~e (mpl **-aux**) /maʒistʀal, -o/ adj masterly; (grand: hum) tremendous; **cours ~** lecture.

magistrat /maʒistʀa/ nm magistrate.

magistrature /maʒistʀatyʀ/ nf judiciary; (fonction) public office.

magner (se) /(sə)maɲe/ ▣ vpr ✖ get a move on.

magnétique /maɲetik/ adj magnetic. **magnétiser** ▣ vt magnetize. **magnétisme** nm magnetism.

magnétophone /maɲetɔfɔn/ nm tape recorder; (à cassettes) cassette recorder.

magnétoscope /maɲetɔskɔp/ nm video recorder.

magnificence /maɲifisɑ̃s/ nf magnificence. **magnifique** adj magnificent.

magot /mago/ nm ▣ hoard (of money).

magouille /maguj/ nf ▣ scheming, skulduggery.

magret /magʀɛ/ nm **~ de canard** duck breast.

mai /mɛ/ nm May.

maigre /mɛgʀ/ adj thin; (viande) lean; (yaourt) low-fat; (fig) poor, meagre; **faire ~** abstain from meat. **maigreur** nf thinness; leanness; (fig) meagreness.

maigrir /megʀiʀ/ ▣ vi get

- -
✖ *see A-Z of French life and culture*

thin(ner); (en suivant un régime) slim. ●vt make thin(ner).

maille /mɑj/ nf stitch; (de filet) mesh; **~ qui file** ladder, run; **avoir ~ à partir avec qn** have a brush with sb.

maillet /majɛ/ nm mallet.

maillon /majɔ̃/ nm link.

maillot /majo/ nm (Sport) shirt, jersey; **~ (de corps)** vest; (US) undershirt; **~ (de bain)** (swimming) costume.

main /mɛ̃/ nf hand; **donner la ~ à qn** hold sb's hand; **se donner la ~** hold hands; **en ~s propres** in person; **en bonnes ~s** in good hands; **~ courante** handrail; **se faire la ~** get the hang of it; **perdre la ~** lose one's touch; **sous la ~** to hand; **vol à ~ armée** armed robbery; **fait (à la) ~** handmade; **haut les ~s!** hands up! **main-d'œuvre** (pl **mains-d'œuvre**) nf labour; (ouvriers) labour force.

main-forte* /mɛ̃fɔʀt/ nf inv **prêter ~ à qn** come to sb's aid.

maint, ~e /mɛ̃, mɛ̃t/ adj many a (+ sg); **~s** many; **à ~es reprises** many times.

maintenant /mɛ̃t(ə)nɑ̃/ adv now; (de nos jours) nowadays; (l'époque actuelle) today.

maintenir /mɛ̃t(ə)niʀ/ ▣ vt keep, maintain; (soutenir) support, hold up; (affirmer) maintain; (decision) stand by. ■ **se ~** vpr (tendance) persist; (prix, malade) remain stable.

maintien /mɛ̃tjɛ̃/ nm (attitude) bearing; (conservation) maintenance.

maire /mɛʀ/ nm mayor.

mairie /meʀi/ nf town hall; (administration) town council.

mais /mɛ/ conj but; **~ oui** of course; **~ non** of course not.

maïs /mais/ nm maize, corn; (Culin) sweetcorn.

maison /mɛzɔ̃/ nf house; (foyer)

home; (immeuble) building; (~ **de commerce**) firm; **à la** ~ at home; **rentrer** ou **aller à la** ~ go home; ~ **des jeunes (et de la culture)** youth club; ~ **de repos** rest home; ~ **de convalescence** convalescent home; ~ **de retraite** old people's home; ~ **mère** parent company. ● adj inv (Culin) home-made.

maître*, -esse* /mɛtʀ, -ɛs/ adj (qui contrôle) **être** ~ **de soi** be one's own master; ~ **de la situation** in control of the situation; (principal) (idée, qualité) key, main. ● n, m (Scol) teacher; (d'animal) owner, master. ● nm (expert, guide) master; (dirigeant) leader; ~ **de conférences** senior lecturer; ~ **d'hôtel** head waiter; (domestique) butler. **maître-assistant*, ~ e** (pl **maîtres-assistants**) nm, f lecturer. **maître-chanteur*** (pl **maîtres-chanteurs**) nm blackmailer. **maître-nageur*** (pl **maîtres-nageurs**) nm swimming instructor. **maîtresse** nf (amante) mistress.

maîtrise* /mɛtʀiz/ nf mastery; (contrôle) control; (Mil) supremacy; (Univ) master's degree; (~ **de soi**) self-control.

maîtriser* /mɛtʀize/ vt (sujet, technique) master; (incendie, sentiment, personne) control. ■ se ~ vpr have self-control.

maïzena® /maizena / nf cornflour.

majesté /maʒɛste/ nf majesty.

majestueux, -euse /maʒɛstɥø, z/ adj majestic.

majeur, ~e /maʒœʀ/ adj major, main; (Jur) of age; **en ~e partie** mostly; **la ~e partie de** most of. ● nm middle finger.

majoration /maʒɔʀasjɔ̃/ nf increase (**de** in). **majorer** vt increase.

majoritaire /maʒɔʀitɛʀ/ adj

majority; **être** ~ be in the majority. **majorité** nf majority; **en** ~ chiefly.

Majorque /maʒɔʀk/ nf Majorca.

majuscule /maʒyskyl/ adj capital. ● nf capital letter.

mal¹ /mal/ adv badly; (incorrectement) wrong(ly); (personne) **aller** ~ be unwell; (affaires) go badly; ~ **entendre/comprendre** not hear/understand properly; ~ **en point** in a bad state; **pas** ~ quite a lot. ● adj inv bad, wrong; **c'est** ~ **de** it is wrong ou bad to; **ce n'est pas** ~ 🔲 it's not bad; **Nick n'est pas** ~ 🔲Nick is not bad-looking.

mal² (pl **maux**) /mal, mo/ nm evil; (douleur) pain, ache; (maladie) disease; (effort) trouble; (dommage) harm; (malheur) misfortune; **avoir** ~ **à la tête/à la gorge** have a headache/a sore throat; **avoir le** ~ **de mer/du pays** be seasick/ homesick; **faire** ~ hurt; **se faire** ~ hurt oneself; **j'ai** ~ it hurts; **faire du** ~ **à** hurt, harm; **se donner du** ~ **pour faire qch** go to a lot of trouble to do sth.

malade /malad/ adj sick, ill; (bras, œil) bad; (plante, poumons, côlon) diseased; **tomber** ~ fall ill; (fou 🔲) mad. ● nmf sick person; (d'un médecin) patient; ~ **mental** mentally ill person.

maladie /maladi/ nf illness, disease; (manie 🔲) mania.

maladif, -ive /maladif, -v/ adj sickly; (jalousie, peur) pathological.

maladresse /maladʀɛs/ nf clumsiness; (erreur) blunder.

maladroit, ~e /maladʀwa, -t/ adj clumsy; (sans tact) tactless.

malaise /malɛz/ nm feeling of faintness; (gêne) uneasiness; (état de crise) unrest.

malaisé, ~e /maleze/ adj difficult.

Malaisie /malɛzi/ nf Malaysia.

malaria /malaʀja/ nf malaria.

malaxer /malakse/ **1** vt (pétrir)
knead; (mêler) mix.

malchance /malʃɑ̃s/ nf
misfortune. **malchanceux,
-euse** adj unlucky.

mâle /mɑl/ adj male; (viril) manly.
●nm male.

malédiction /malediksjɔ̃/ nf
curse.

maléfice /malefis/ nm evil spell.
maléfique adj evil.

malentendant, ~e /malɑ̃tɑ̃dɑ̃,
-t/ adj hard of hearing.

malentendu /malɑ̃tɑ̃dy/ nm
misunderstanding.

malfaçon /malfasɔ̃/ nf defect.

malfaisant, ~e /malfəzɑ̃, -t/ adj
harmful; (personne) evil.

malfaiteur /malfɛtœʀ/ nm
criminal.

malformation /malfɔʀmasjɔ̃/ nf
malformation.

malgré /malgʀe/ prép in spite of,
despite; **~ tout** nevertheless.

malheur /malœʀ/ nm misfortune;
(accident) accident; **par ~**
unfortunately; **faire un ~** **1** be
a big hit; **porter ~** be ou bring
bad luck.

malheureusement /malœ
ʀøzmɑ̃/ adv unfortunately.

malheureux, -euse /malœʀø,
-z/ adj unhappy; (regrettable)
unfortunate; (sans succès)
unlucky; (insignifiant) paltry,
pathetic. ●nm, f (poor) wretch.

malhonnête /malɔnɛt/ adj
dishonest. **malhonnêteté** nf
dishonesty.

malice /malis/ nf mischief; **sans
~** harmless; **avec ~**
mischievously. **malicieux,
-ieuse** adj mischievous.

malignité /maliɲite/ nf
malignancy. **malin, -igne** adj
clever, smart; (méchant) malicious;
(tumeur) malignant; (difficile **1**)
difficult.

malingre /malɛ̃gʀ/ adj puny.

malle /mal/ nf (valise) trunk; (Auto)
boot; (US) trunk.

mallette /malɛt/ nf (small)
suitcase; (pour le bureau) briefcase.

malmener /malməne/ **6** vt
manhandle; (fig) give a rough
ride to.

malnutrition /malnytʀisjɔ̃/ nf
malnutrition.

malodorant, ~e /malɔdɔʀɑ̃, -t/
adj smelly, foul-smelling.

malpoli, ~e /malpɔli/ adj rude,
impolite.

malpropre /malpʀɔpʀ/ adj dirty.

malsain, ~e /malsɛ̃, -ɛn/ adj
unhealthy.

malt /malt/ nm malt.

Malte /malt/ nf Malta.

maltraiter /maltʀete/ **1** vt
illtreat.

malveillance /malvɛjɑ̃s/ nf
malice. **malveillant, ~e** adj
malicious.

maman /mamɑ̃/ nf mum(my),
mother; (US) mom(my).

mamelle /mamɛl/ nf teat.

mamelon /mamlɔ̃/ nm (Anat)
nipple; (colline) hillock.

mamie /mami/ nf **1** granny.

mammifère /mamifɛʀ/ nm
mammal.

manche /mɑ̃ʃ/ nf sleeve; (Sport,
Pol) round. ●nm (d'un instrument)
handle; **~ à balai** broomstick;
(Aviat) joystick. **M~** nf **la M~**
the Channel; **le tunnel sous la M~**
the Channel tunnel.

manchette /mɑ̃ʃɛt/ nf cuff; (de
journal) headline.

manchot, ~te /mɑ̃ʃo, -ɔt/ nm, f
one-armed person; (sans bras)
armless person. ●nm (oiseau)
penguin.

mandarine /mɑ̃daʀin/ nf
tangerine, mandarin (orange).

mandat /mɑ̃da/ nm (postal) money

order; (Pol) mandate; (procuration) proxy; (de police) warrant; ~ **d'arrêt** arrest warrant.

mandataire /mɑ̃datɛʀ/ nm representative; (Jur) proxy.

manège /manɛʒ/ nm riding school; (à la foire) merry-go-round; (manœuvre) trick, ploy.

manette /manɛt/ nf lever; (de jeu) joystick.

mangeable /mɑ̃ʒabl/ adj edible.

mangeoire /mɑ̃ʒwaʀ/ nf trough; (pour oiseaux) feeder.

manger /mɑ̃ʒe/ 40 vt eat; (fortune) go through; (profits) eat away at; (économies) use up; (ronger) eat into. ●vi eat; **donner à ~ à** feed. ●nm food.

mangue /mɑ̃g/ nf mango.

maniable /manjabl/ adj easy to handle.

maniaque /manjak/ adj fussy. ●nmf fusspot; (fou) maniac; (fanatique) fanatic; **un ~ de l'ordre** a stickler for tidiness.

manie /mani/ nf habit; (marotte) obsession.

maniement /manimɑ̃/ nm handling. **manier** 45 vt handle.

manière /manjɛʀ/ nf way, manner; ~**s** (politesse) manners; (chichis) fuss; **à la ~ de** in the style of; **de ~ à** so as to; **de toute ~** anyway, in any case.

maniéré, ~e /manjeʀe/ adj affected.

manif /manif/ nf 🔲 demo.

manifestant, ~e /manifɛstɑ̃, -t/ nm, f demonstrator.

manifestation /manifɛstasjɔ̃/ nf expression, manifestation; (de maladie, phénomène) appearance; (Pol) demonstration; (événement) event; ~ **culturelle** cultural event.

manifeste /manifɛst/ adj obvious. ●nm manifesto.

manifester /manifɛste/ 1 vt

show, manifest; (désir, crainte) express. ●vi (Pol) demonstrate. ■ **se ~** vpr (sentiment) show itself; (apparaître) appear; (répondre à un appel) come forward.

manigance /manigɑ̃s/ nf little plot. **manigancer** 10 vt plot.

manipulation /manipylasjɔ̃/ nf handling; (péj) manipulation.

manivelle /manivɛl/ nf handle, crank.

mannequin /mankɛ̃/ nm (personne) model; (statue) dummy.

manœuvrer /manœvʀe/ 1 vt manoeuvre; (machine) operate. ●vi manoeuvre.

manoir /manwaʀ/ nm manor.

manque /mɑ̃k/ nm lack (**de** of); (lacune) gap; ~ **à gagner** loss of earnings; **en (état de) ~** having withdrawal symptoms.

manqué /mɑ̃ke/ adj (écrivain) failed; **garçon ~** tomboy.

manquement /mɑ̃kmɑ̃/ nm ~ **à** breach of.

manquer /mɑ̃ke/ 1 vt miss; (gâcher) spoil; ~ **à** (devoir) fail in; ~ **de** be short of, lack; **il/ça lui manque** he misses him/it; ~ **(de) faire** (faillir) nearly do; **ne manquez pas de** be sure to; ~ **à sa parole** break one's word. ●vi be short ou lacking; (être absent) be absent; (en moins, disparu) be missing; **il me manque 20 euros** I'm 20 euros short.

mansarde /mɑ̃saʀd/ nf attic (room).

manteau (pl ~**x**) /mɑ̃to/ nm coat.

manucure /manykyʀ/ nmf manicurist. ●nf (soins) manicure.

manuel, ~le /manɥɛl/ adj manual. ●nm (livre) manual; (Scol) textbook.

manufacture /manyfaktyʀ/ nf factory; (fabrication) manufacture. **manufacturer** 1 vt manufacture.

manuscrit, ~e /manyskʀi, -t/ adj

handwritten. •nm manuscript.

mappemonde /mapmɔ̃d/ nf
world map; (sphère) globe.

maquereau (pl ~x) /makʁo/ nm
(poisson) mackerel; Ⓣ pimp.

maquette /makɛt/ nf (scale)
model; ~ **(de mise en page)**
paste-up.

maquillage /makijaʒ/ nm
make-up.

maquiller /makije/ 🚹 vt make
up; (truquer) doctor, fake. ∎ se ∎
vpr make (oneself) up.

maquis /maki/ nm (paysage) scrub;
(Mil) Maquis, underground.

maraîcher*, -ère /maʁeʃe, -ɛʁ/
nm, f market gardener; (US) truck
farmer.

marais /maʁɛ/ nm marsh.

marasme /maʁasm/ nm slump,
stagnation; **dans le ~** in the
doldrums.

marbre /maʁbʁ/ nm marble.

marc /maʁ/ nm (eau-de-vie) marc; ~
de café coffee grounds.

marchand, ~e /maʁʃɑ̃, -d/ adj
(valeur) market. •nm, f trader; (de
charbon, vins) merchant; ~ **de
couleurs** ironmonger; (US)
hardware merchant; ~ **de
journaux** newsagent; ~ **de
légumes** greengrocer; ~ **de
poissons** fishmonger.

marchander /maʁʃɑ̃de/ 🚹 vt
haggle over. •vi haggle.

marchandise /maʁʃɑ̃diz/ nf
goods.

marche /maʁʃ/ nf (démarche, trajet)
walk; (rythme) pace; (Mil, Mus, Pol)
march; (d'escalier) step; (Sport)
walking; (de machine) operation,
working; (de véhicule) running; **en
~** (train) moving; (moteur, machine)
running; **faire ~ arrière**
(véhicule) reverse; **mettre en ~**
start (up); **se mettre en ~** start
moving.

···
Ⓖ *see A-Z of French life and culture*

Ⓖ**marché** /maʁʃe/ nm market;
(contrat) deal; **faire son ~** do
one's shopping; ~ **aux puces**
flea market; ~ **noir** black
market.

marchepied /maʁʃəpje/ nm (de
train, camion) step.

marcher /maʁʃe/ 🚹 vi walk; (poser
le pied) tread (**sur** on); (aller) go;
(fonctionner) work, run; (prospérer)
go well; (film, livre) do well;
(consentir Ⓣ) agree; **faire ~ qn** Ⓣ
pull sb's leg.

mardi /maʁdi/ nm Tuesday; **M ~
gras** Shrove Tuesday.

mare /maʁ/ nf (étang) pond;
(flaque) pool.

marécage /maʁekaʒ/ nm marsh;
(sous les tropiques) swamp.

maréchal (pl **-aux**) /maʁeʃal, -o/
nm field marshal.

maréchal-ferrant (pl **-aux-
ferrants** /maʁeʃalferɑ̃/ nm
blacksmith.

marée /maʁe/ nf tide; (poissons)
fresh fish; ~ **haute/basse** high/
low tide; ~ **noire** oil slick.

marelle /maʁɛl/ nf hopscotch.

margarine /maʁgaʁin/ nf
margarine.

marge /maʁʒ/ nf margin; **en ~
de** (à l'écart de) on the fringe(s)
of; ~ **bénéficiaire** profit
margin.

marginal, ~e (mpl **-aux**)
/maʁʒinal, -o/ adj marginal. •nm, f
drop-out.

marguerite /maʁgəʁit/ nf daisy;
(qui imprime) daisy-wheel.

mari /maʁi/ nm husband.

mariage /maʁjaʒ/ nm marriage;
(cérémonie) wedding.

marié, ~e /maʁje/ adj married.
•nm, f (bride) groom, bride; **les
~s** the bride and groom.

marier /maʁje/ 🔢 vt marry. ∎ se
~ vpr get married, marry; **se ~
avec** marry, get married to.

marin, ~e /maʀɛ̃, -in/ adj sea. ●nm sailor.

marine /maʀin/ nf navy; ~ **marchande** merchant navy. ●adj inv navy (blue).

marionnette /maʀjɔnɛt/ nf puppet; (à fils) marionette.

maritalement /maʀitalmɑ̃/ adv (vivre) as husband and wife.

maritime /maʀitim/ adj maritime, coastal; (agent, compagnie) shipping.

marmaille /maʀmaj/ nf ☐ brats.

marmelade /maʀməlad/ nf stewed fruit; ~ **d'oranges** (orange) marmalade.

marmite /maʀmit/ nf (cooking-)pot.

marmonner /maʀmɔne/ ☐ vt mumble.

marmot /maʀmo/ nm ☐ kid.

Maroc /maʀɔk/ nm Morocco.

maroquinerie /maʀɔkinʀi/ nf (magasin) leather goods shop.

marquant, ~e /maʀkɑ̃, -t/ adj (remarquable) outstanding; (qu'on n'oublie pas) memorable.

marque /maʀk/ nf mark; (de produits) brand, make; (décompte) score; **à vos ~s!** (Sport) on your marks!; **de ~** (Comm) brand name; (fig) important; ~ **de fabrique** trademark; ~ **déposée** registered trademark.

marquer /maʀke/ ☐ vt mark; (indiquer) show, say; (écrire) note down; (point, but) score; (joueur) mark; (influencer) leave its mark on; (exprimer) (volonté, sentiment) show. ●vi (laisser une trace) leave a mark; (évènement) stand out; (Sport) score.

marquis, ~e /maʀki, -z/ nm, f marquis, marchioness.

marraine /maʀɛn/ nf godmother.

marrant, ~e /maʀɑ̃, -t/ adj ☐ funny.

marre /maʀ/ adv **en avoir ~** ☐ be fed up (**de** with).

marrer (se) /(sə)maʀe/ ☐ vpr ☐ laugh, have a (good) laugh.

marron /maʀɔ̃/ nm chestnut; (couleur) brown; (coup ☐) thump; ~ **d'Inde** horse chestnut. ●adj inv brown.

mars /maʀs/ nm March.

marteau (pl ~x) /maʀto/ nm hammer; ~ **(de porte)** (door) knocker; ~ **piqueur** ou **pneumatique** pneumatic drill; **être ~** ☐ be mad.

marteler /maʀtəle/ ☐ vt hammer; (poings, talons) pound; (scander) rap out.

martial, ~e (mpl -iaux) /maʀsjal, -jo/ adj military; (art) martial.

martien, ~ne /maʀsjɛ̃, -ɛn/ adj & nm, f Martian.

martyr, ~e /maʀtiʀ/ nm, f martyr. ●adj martyred; (enfant) battered.

martyre /maʀtiʀ/ nm (Relig) martyrdom; (fig) agony, suffering.

martyriser /maʀtiʀize/ ☐ vt (Relig) martyr; (torturer) torture; (enfant) batter.

marxisme /maʀksism/ nm Marxism. **marxiste** adj & nmf Marxist.

masculin, ~e /maskylɛ̃, -in/ adj masculine; (sexe) male; (mode, équipe) men's. ●nm masculine.

masochisme /mazɔʃism/ nm masochism.

masochiste /mazɔʃist/ nmf masochist. ●adj masochistic.

masque /mask/ nm mask; ~ **de beauté** face pack. **masquer** ☐ vt (cacher) hide, conceal (**à** from); (lumière) block (off).

massacre /masakʀ/ nm massacre. **massacrer** ☐ vt massacre; (abîmer ☐) ruin.

massage /masaʒ/ nm massage.

masse /mas/ nf (volume) mass; (gros morceau) lump, mass; (outil)

m

sledge-hammer; **en** ~ (vendre) in bulk; (venir) in force; **produire en** ~ mass-produce; **la** ~ (foule) the masses of; **une** ~ **de** 🄸 masses of; **la** ~ **de** the majority of.

masser /mase/ **1** vt (assembler) assemble; (pétrir) massage. ■ **se** ~ vpr (gens, foule) mass.

massif, -ive /masif, -v/ adj massive; (or, argent) solid. ●nm (de fleurs) clump; (parterre) bed; (Géog) massif. **massivement** adv (en masse) in large numbers.

massue /masy/ nf club, bludgeon.

mastic /mastik/ nm putty; (pour trous) filler.

mastiquer /mastike/ **1** vt (mâcher) chew.

mat /mat/ adj (couleur) matt; (bruit) dull; (teint) olive; **être** ~ (aux échecs) be in checkmate.

mât /mɑ/ nm mast; (pylône) pole; ~ **de drapeau** flagpole.

match /matʃ/ nm match; (US) game; **faire** ~ **nul** tie, draw; ~ **aller** first leg; ~ **retour** return match.

matelas /matla/ nm mattress; ~ **pneumatique** air bed.

matelassé, ~e /matlase/ adj padded; (tissu) quilted.

matelot /matlo/ nm sailor.

mater /mate/ **1** vt (révolte) put down; (personne) bring into line.

matérialiser (se) /(sə)materjalize/ **1** vpr materialize.

matérialiste /materjalist/ adj materialistic. ●nmf materialist.

matériau (pl ~x) /materjo/ nm material.

matériel, ~le /materjɛl/ adj material. ●nm equipment, materials; ~ **informatique** hardware.

maternel, ~le /maternɛl/ adj maternal; (comme d'une mère) motherly. **maternelle** nf nursery school.

maternité /maternite/ nf maternity hospital; (état de mère) motherhood; **de** ~ maternity.

mathématicien, ~ne /matematisjɛ̃, -ɛn/ nm, f mathematician.

mathématique /matematik/ adj mathematical. **mathématiques** nfpl mathematics (+ sg).

maths /mat/ nfpl 🄸 maths (+ sg).

matière /matjɛʀ/ nf matter; (produit) material; (sujet) subject; **en** ~ **de** as regards; ~ **plastique** plastic; ~s **grasses** fat content; ~s **premières** raw materials.

matin /matɛ̃/ nm morning; **de bon** ~ early in the morning.

matinal, ~e (mpl **-aux**) /matinal, -o/ adj morning; (de bonne heure) early; **être** ~ be up early; (d'habitude) be an early riser.

matinée /matine/ nf morning; (spectacle) matinée.

matou /matu/ nm tomcat.

matraque /matʀak/ nf (de police) truncheon; (US) billy (club). **matraquer** **1** vt club, beat; (produit, chanson) plug.

matrimonial, ~e (mpl **-iaux**) /matʀimɔnjal, -jo/ adj matrimonial; **agence** ~e marriage bureau.

maturité /matyʀite/ nf maturity.

maudire /modiʀ/ **41** vt curse.

maudit, ~e /modi, -t/ adj 🄸 blasted, damned.

maugréer /mogʀee/ **15** vi grumble.

mausolée /mozɔle/ nm mausoleum.

maussade /mosad/ adj gloomy.

mauvais, ~e /mɔvɛ, -z/ adj bad; (erroné) wrong; (malveillant) evil; (désagréable) nasty, bad; (mer) rough; **le** ~ **moment** the wrong time; ~e **herbe** weed; ~e **langue** gossip; ~e **passe** tight spot; ~ **traitements** ill-treatment. ● adv (sentir) bad; **il fait** ~ the weather is bad. ● nm **le bon et le** ~ the good and the bad.

mauve /mov/ adj & nm mauve.

mauviette /movjɛt/ nf weakling, wimp.

maux /mo/ ▷ **MAL²**.

maximal, ~e (mpl **-aux**) /maksimal, -o/ adj maximum.

maxime /maksim/ nf maxim.

maximum /maksimɔm/ adj maximum. ● nm maximum; **au** ~ as much as possible; (tout au plus) at most; **faire le** ~ do one's utmost.

mazout /mazut/ nm (fuel) oil.

me, m' /mə, m/ pron me; (indirect) (to) me; (réfléchi) myself.

méandre /meɑ̃dʀ/ nm meander.

mec /mɛk/ nm 🗓 bloke, guy.

mécanicien, ~ne /mekanisjɛ̃, -jɛn/ nm, f mechanic. ● nm train driver.

mécanique /mekanik/ adj mechanical; (jouet) clockwork; **problème** ~ engine trouble. ● nf mechanics (+ sg); (mécanisme) mechanism. **mécaniser** 🗓 vt mechanize.

mécanisme /mekanism/ nm mechanism.

méchamment /meʃamɑ̃/ adv spitefully. **méchanceté** nf nastiness; (action) wicked action.

méchant, ~e /meʃɑ̃, -t/ adj (cruel) wicked; (désagréable, grave) nasty; (enfant) naughty; (chien) vicious; (sensationnel 🗓) terrific. ● nm, f (enfant) naughty child.

mèche /mɛʃ/ nf (de cheveux) lock; (de bougie) wick; (d'explosif) fuse; (outil) drill bit; **de** ~ **avec** in league with.

méconnaissable /mekɔnɛsabl/ adj unrecognizable.

méconnaître* /mekɔnɛtʀ/ 🔢 vt misunderstand, misread; (mésestimer) underestimate.

méconnu, ~e /mekɔny/ adj unrecognized; (artiste) neglected.

mécontent, ~e /mekɔ̃tɑ̃, -t/ adj dissatisfied (**de** with); (irrité) annoyed (**de** at, with). **mécontentement** nm dissatisfaction; annoyance. **mécontenter** 🗓 vt dissatisfy; (irriter) annoy.

médaille /medaj/ nf medal; (insigne) badge; (bijou) medallion. **médaillé, ~e** nm, f medallist.

médaillon /medajɔ̃/ nm medallion; (bijou) locket.

médecin /medsɛ̃/ nm doctor.

médecine /medsin/ nf medicine.

média /medja/ nm medium; **les** ~**s** the media.

médiateur, -trice /medjatœʀ, -tʀis/ nm, f mediator.

médiatique /medjatik/ adj (événement, personnalité) media.

médical, ~e (mpl **-aux**) /medikal, -o/ adj medical.

médicament /medikamɑ̃/ nm medicine, drug.

médico-légal*, ~e (mpl **-aux**) /medikɔlegal, -o/ adj forensic.

médiéval, ~e (mpl **-aux**) /medjeval, -o/ adj medieval.

médiocre /medjɔkʀ/ adj mediocre, poor. **médiocrité** nf mediocrity.

médire /mediʀ/ 🔢 vi ~ **de** speak ill of, malign.

médisance /medizɑ̃s/ nf ~**(s)** malicious gossip.

méditer /medite/ 🗓 vi meditate (**sur** on). ● vt contemplate; (paroles, conseils) mull over; ~ **de** plan to.

Méditerranée /mediteʀane/ nf **la** ~ the Mediterranean.

méditerranéen, ~ne /mediteʀaneɛ̃, -ɛn/ adj Mediterranean.

médium /medjɔm/ nm (personne) medium.

méduse /medyz/ nf jellyfish.

meeting /mitiŋ/ nm meeting.

méfait /mefɛ/ nm misdeed; **les ~s de** (conséquences) the ravages of.

méfiance /mefjɑ̃s/ nf suspicion, distrust. **méfiant, ~e** adj suspicious, distrustful.

méfier (se) /(sə)mefje/ 45 vpr be wary ou careful; **se ~ de** distrust, be wary of.

mégaoctet /megaɔkte/ nm (Ordinat) megabyte.

mégère /meʒɛR/ nf (femme) shrew.

mégot /mego/ nm cigarette end.

meilleur, ~e /mɛjœR/ adj (comparatif) better (**que** than); (superlatif) best; **le ~ livre** the best book; **mon ~ ami** my best friend; **~ marché** cheaper. ● nm, f **le ~, la ~e** the best (one). ● adv (sentir) better; **il fait ~** the weather is better.

mél /mel/ nm email; **envoyer un ~** send an email.

mélancolie /melɑ̃kɔli/ nf melancholy.

mélange /melɑ̃ʒ/ nm mixture, blend.

mélanger /melɑ̃ʒe/ 40 vt mix; (thés, parfums) blend. ■ **se ~** vpr mix; (thés, parfums) blend; (idées) get mixed up.

mélasse /melas/ nf black treacle; (US) molasses.

mêlée /mele/ nf free for all; (au rugby) scrum.

mêler /mele/ 1 vt mix (**à** with); (qualités) combine; (embrouiller) mix up; **~ qn à** (impliquer dans) involve sb in. ■ **se ~** vpr mix; combine; **se ~ à** (se joindre à) mingle with; (participer à) join in; **se ~ de** meddle in; **mêle-toi de ce qui te regarde** mind your own business.

méli-mélo* (pl **mélis-mélos**)

/melimelo/ nm jumble.

mélo /melo/ 1 nm melodrama. ● adj inv slushy, schmaltzy 1.

mélodie /melɔdi/ nf melody. **mélodieux, -ieuse** adj melodious. **mélodique** adj melodic.

mélodramatique /melɔdramatik/ adj melodramatic. **mélodrame** nm melodrama.

mélomane /melɔman/ nmf music lover.

melon /məlɔ̃/ nm melon; **(chapeau) ~** bowler (hat).

membrane /mɑ̃bran/ nf membrane.

membre /mɑ̃bʀ/ nm (Anat) limb; (adhérent) member.

même /mɛm/ adj same; **ce livre ~** this very book; **la bonté ~** kindness itself; **en ~ temps** at the same time. ● pron **le ~, la ~** the same (one). ● adv even; **à ~** (sur) directly on; **à ~ de** in a position to; **de ~** (aussi) too; (de la même façon) likewise; **de ~ que** just as; **~ si** even if.

mémé /meme/ 1 nf granny.

mémo /memo/ nm note, memo.

mémoire /memwaR/ nm (rapport) memorandum; (Univ) dissertation; **~s** (souvenirs écrits) memoirs. ● nf memory; **à la ~ de** to the memory of; **de ~** from memory; **~ morte/vive** (Ordinat) ROM/RAM.

mémorable /memɔrabl/ adj memorable.

menace /mənas/ nf threat. **menacer** 10 vt threaten (**de faire** to do).

ménage /menaʒ/ nm (couple) couple; (travail) housework; (famille) household; **se mettre en ~** set up house.

ménagement /menaʒmɑ̃/ nm **avec ~s** gently; **sans ~s** (dire) bluntly; (jeter, pousser) roughly.

ménager¹, -ère /menaʒe, -ɛR/ adj

household, domestic; **travaux ~s** housework.

ménager² /menaʒe/ 40 vt be gentle with, handle carefully; (utiliser) be careful with; (organiser) prepare (carefully); **ne pas ~ ses efforts** spare no effort.

ménagère /menaʒɛʀ/ nf housewife.

ménagerie /menaʒʀi/ nf menagerie.

mendiant, ~e /mɑ̃djɑ̃, -t/ nm, f beggar.

mendier /mɑ̃dje/ 45 vt beg for. ● vi beg.

mener /məne/ 6 vt lead; (entreprise, pays) run; (étude, enquête) carry out; (politique) pursue; **~ à** (accompagner à) take to; (faire aboutir) lead to; **~ à bien** see through. ● vi lead.

méningite /menɛ̃ʒit/ nf meningitis.

menotte /mənɔt/ nf 🔢 hand; **~s** handcuffs.

mensonge /mɑ̃sɔ̃ʒ/ nm lie; (action) lying. **mensonger, -ère** adj untrue, false.

mensualité /mɑ̃sɥalite/ nf monthly payment.

mensuel, ~le /mɑ̃sɥɛl/ adj monthly. ● nm monthly (magazine). **mensuellement** adv monthly.

mensurations /mɑ̃syʀasjɔ̃/ nfpl measurements.

mental, ~e (mpl **-aux**) /mɑ̃tal, -o/ adj mental; **malade ~** mentally ill person; **handicapé ~** mentally handicapped person.

mentalité /mɑ̃talite/ nf mentality.

menteur, -euse /mɑ̃tœʀ, -øz/ nm, f liar. ● adj untruthful.

menthe /mɑ̃t/ nf mint.

mention /mɑ̃sjɔ̃/ nf mention; (annotation) note; (Scol) grade; **rayer la ~ inutile** delete as appropriate. **mentionner** 🔢 vt mention.

mentir /mɑ̃tiʀ/ 46 vi lie.

menton /mɑ̃tɔ̃/ nm chin.

menu, ~e /məny/ adj (petit) tiny; (fin) fine; (insignifiant) minor. ● adv (couper) fine. ● nm (carte) menu; (repas) meal; (Ordinat) menu; **~ déroulant** pull-down menu.

menuiserie /mənɥizʀi/ nf carpentry, joinery. **menuisier** nm carpenter, joiner.

méprendre (se) /(sə)mepʀɑ̃dʀ/ 50 vpr **se ~ sur** be mistaken about.

mépris /mepʀi/ nm contempt, scorn (**de** for); **au ~ de** regardless of.

méprisable /mepʀizabl/ adj contemptible, despicable.

méprise /mepʀiz/ nf mistake.

méprisant, ~e /mepʀizɑ̃, -t/ adj scornful. **mépriser** 🔢 vt scorn, despise.

mer /mɛʀ/ nf sea; (marée) tide; **en pleine ~** out at sea.

mercenaire /mɛʀsənɛʀ/ nm & a mercenary.

mercerie /mɛʀs(ə)ʀi/ nf haberdashery; (US) notions store. **mercier, -ière** nm, f haberdasher; (US) notions seller.

merci /mɛʀsi/ interj thank you, thanks (**de, pour** for); **~ beaucoup, ~ bien** thank you very much. ● nm thank you. ● nf mercy.

mercredi /mɛʀkʀədi/ nm Wednesday; **~ des Cendres** Ash Wednesday.

merde /mɛʀd/ nf 🔲 shit 🔲.

mère /mɛʀ/ nf mother; **~ de famille** mother.

méridional, ~e (mpl **-aux**) /meʀidjɔnal, -o/ adj southern. ● nm, f Southerner.

mérite /meʀit/ nm merit; **avoir du ~ à faire** deserve credit for doing.

mériter /meʀite/ 🔢 vt deserve; **~**

m

d'**être lu** be worth reading.

méritoire /meʁitwaʁ/ adj
commendable.

merlan /mɛʁlɑ̃/ nm whiting.

merle /mɛʁl/ nm blackbird.

merveille /mɛʁvɛj/ nf wonder,
marvel; **à ~** wonderfully; **faire
des ~s** work wonders.

merveilleux, -euse /mɛʁvɛjø,
-z/ adj wonderful, marvellous.

mes /me/ ▷MON.

mésange /mezɑ̃ʒ/ nf tit(mouse).

mésaventure /mezavɑ̃tyʁ/ nf
misadventure; **par ~** by some
misfortune.

mesdames /medam/ ▷MADAME.

mesdemoiselles /medmwazɛl/
▷MADEMOISELLE.

mésentente /mezɑ̃tɑ̃t/ nf
disagreement.

mesquin, -e /mɛskɛ̃, -in/ adj
mean-minded, petty; (chiche)
mean. **mesquinerie** nf
meanness.

message /mesaʒ/ nm message; **un
~ électronique** an email; **~
texte** text message.

messager, -ère /mesaze, -ɛʁ/ nm,
f messenger. •nm **~ de poche**
pager.

messagerie /mesaʒʁi/ nf
(transports) freight forwarding;
(télécommunications) messaging; **~
électronique** electronic mail; **~
vocale** voice mail.

messe /mɛs/ nf (Relig) mass.

messieurs /mesjø/ ▷MONSIEUR.

mesure /məzyʁ/ nf measurement;
(quantité, unité) measure; (disposition)
measure, step; (cadence) time; **en
~** in time; (modération)
moderation; **à ~ que** as; **dans
la ~ où** in so far as; **dans une
certaine ~** to some extent; **en
~ de** in a position to; **sans ~** to
excess; (fait) **sur ~** made-
to-measure.

mesuré, ~e /məzyʁe/ adj

measured; (attitude) moderate.

mesurer /məzyʁe/ **1** vt measure;
(juger) assess; (argent, temps) ration.
•vi **~ 15 mètres de long** be 15
metres long. ■**se ~ avec** vpr pit
oneself against.

met /mɛ/ ▷METTRE **42**.

métal (pl **-aux**) /metal, -o/ nm
metal. **métallique** adj (objet)
metal; (éclat) metallic.

métallurgie /metalyʁʒi/ nf
(industrie) metalworking industry.

métamorphoser /metamɔʁfoze/
1 vt transform. ■**se ~** vpr be
transformed; **se ~ en**
metamorphose into.

métaphore /metafɔʁ/ nf
metaphor.

météo /meteo/ nf (bulletin) weather
forecast.

météore /meteɔʁ/ nm meteor.

météorologie /meteɔʁɔlɔʒi/ nf
meteorology.

météorologique /meteɔʁɔlɔʒik/
adj meteorological; **conditions
~s** weather conditions.

méthode /metɔd/ nf method;
(ouvrage) course, manual.
méthodique adj methodical.

méticuleux, -euse /metikylø,
-z/ adj meticulous.

métier /metje/ nm job; (manuel)
trade; (intellectuel) profession;
(expérience) experience, skill; **~ (à
tisser)** loom; **remettre qch sur
le ~** rework sth.

métis, ~se /metis/ adj mixed
race. •nm, f person of mixed race.

métrage /metʁaʒ/ nm length;
court ~ short (film); **long ~**
feature-length film.

mètre /mɛtʁ/ nm metre; (règle)
rule; **~ ruban** tape-measure.

métreur, -euse /metʁœʁ, -øz/ nm,
f quantity surveyor.

métrique /metʁik/ adj metric.

métro /metʁo/ nm underground;
(US) subway.

métropole /metʀɔpɔl/ nf metropolis; (pays) mother country. **métropolitain, ~e** adj metropolitan.

mets /mɛ/ nm dish. ●▷ **METTRE 42**.

mettable /mɛtabl/ adj wearable.

metteur /mɛtœʀ/ nm ~ **en scène** director.

mettre /mɛtʀ/ **42** vt put; (radio, chauffage) put ou switch on; (réveil) set; (installer) put in; (revêtir) put on; (porter habituellement) (vêtement, lunettes) wear; (prendre) take; (investir, dépenser) put; (écrire) write, say; **elle a mis deux heures** it took her two hours; ~ **la table** lay the table; ~ **en question** question; ~ **en valeur** highlight; (terrain) develop; **mettons que** let's suppose that. ●vi ~ **bas** (animal) give birth. ■se ~ vpr (vêtement, maquillage) put on; (se placer) (objet) go; (personne) (debout) stand; (assis) sit; (couché) lie; **se ~ en short** put shorts on; **se ~ debout** stand up; **se ~ au lit** go to bed; **se ~ à table** sit down at table; **se ~ en ligne** line up; **se ~ du sable dans les yeux** get sand in one's eyes; **se ~ au chinois/tennis** take up Chinese/tennis; **se ~ au travail** set to work; **se ~ à faire** start to do.

meuble /mœbl/ nm piece of furniture; ~**s** furniture.

meublé /mœble/ nm furnished flat.

meubler /mœble/ **1** vt furnish; (fig) fill. ■se ~ vpr buy furniture.

meugler /møgle/ **1** vi moo.

meule /møl/ nf millstone; ~ **de foin** haystack.

meunier, -ière /mønje, -jɛʀ/ nm, f miller.

meurs, meurt /mœʀ/ ▷ **MOURIR 43**.

meurtre /mœʀtʀ/ nm murder.

meurtrier, -ière /mœʀtʀije, -jɛʀ/ adj deadly. ●nm, f murderer, murderess.

meurtrir /mœʀtʀiʀ/ **2** vt bruise.

meute /møt/ nf pack of hounds.

Mexique /mɛksik/ nm Mexico.

mi- /mi/ préf mid-, half-; **à mi-chemin** half-way; **à mi-pente** half-way up the hill; **à la mi-juin** in mid-June.

miauler /mjole/ **1** vi miaow.

micro /mikʀo/ nm microphone, mike; (Ordinat) micro.

microbe /mikʀɔb/ nm germ.

microfilm /mikʀɔfilm/ nm microfilm.

micro-onde /mikʀoɔ̃d/ nf microwave; **un four à ~s** microwave (oven). **micro-ondes** nm inv microwave (oven).

micro-ordinateur (pl ~**s**) /mikʀoɔʀdinatœʀ/ nm personal computer.

microphone /mikʀɔfɔn/ nm microphone.

microprocesseur /mikʀɔpʀɔsesœʀ/ nm microprocessor.

microscope /mikʀɔskɔp/ nm microscope.

midi /midi/ nm twelve o'clock, midday, noon; (déjeuner) lunch-time; (sud) south. **Midi** nm **le M~** the South of France.

mie /mi/ nf soft part (of the loaf); **un pain de ~** a sandwich loaf.

miel /mjɛl/ nm honey.

mielleux, -euse /mjɛlø, -z/ adj unctuous.

mien, ~ne /mjɛ̃, -ɛn/ pron **le ~, la ~ne, les ~(ne)s** mine.

miette /mjɛt/ nf crumb; (fig) scrap; **en ~s** in pieces.

mieux /mjø/ adj inv better (**que** than); **le** ou **la** ou **les ~** (the) best. ●nm best; (progrès) improvement; **faire de son ~** do one's best; **le ~ serait de**

the best thing would be to. •adv better; **le** ou **la** ou **les ~** (de deux) the better; (de plusieurs) the best; **elle va ~** she is better; **j'aime ~ rester** I'd rather stay; **il vaudrait ~ partir** it would be best to leave; **tu ferais ~ de faire** you would be best to do.

mièvre /mjɛvʀ/ adj insipid.

mignon, ~ne /miɲɔ̃, -ɔn/ adj cute; (gentil) kind.

migraine /migʀɛn/ nf headache; (plus fort) migraine.

migration /migʀasjɔ̃/ nf migration.

mijoter /miʒɔte/ **1** vt/i simmer; (tramer **1**) cook up.

mil /mil/ nm a thousand.

milice /milis/ nf militia.

milieu (pl ~x) /miljø/ nm middle; (environnement) environment; (appartenance sociale) background; (groupe) circle; (voie) middle way; (criminel) underworld; **au ~ de** in the middle of; **en plein** ou **au beau ~ de** right in the middle (of).

militaire /militɛʀ/ adj military. •nm soldier, serviceman.

militant, ~e /militɑ̃, -t/ nm, f militant.

militer /milite/ **1** vi be a militant; **~ pour** militate in favour of.

mille[1] /mil/ adj & nm inv a thousand; **deux ~** two thousand; **mettre dans le ~** (fig) hit the nail on the head.

mille[2] /mil/ nm **~ (marin)** (nautical) mile.

millénaire /milenɛʀ/ nm millennium. •adj a thousand years old.

mille-pattes* /milpat/ nm inv centipede.

millésime /milezim/ nm date; (de vin) vintage.

millet /mijɛ/ nm millet.

milliard /miljaʀ/ nm thousand million, billion. **milliardaire** nmf multimillionaire.

millième /miljɛm/ adj & nmf thousandth.

millier /milje/ nm thousand; **un ~ (de)** about a thousand.

millimètre /milimɛtʀ/ nm millimetre.

million /miljɔ̃/ nm million; **deux ~s (de)** two million. **millionnaire** nmf millionaire.

mime /mim/ nmf mime-artist. •nm (art) mime. **mimer 1** vt mime; (imiter) mimic.

mimique /mimik/ nf expressions and gestures.

minable /minabl/ adj **1** (logement) shabby; (médiocre) pathetic, crummy.

minauder /minode/ **1** vi simper.

mince /mɛ̃s/ adj thin; (svelte) slim; (faible) (espoir, majorité) slim. •interj **1** blast **1**, darn it **1**. **minceur** nf thinness; slimness.

mincir /mɛ̃siʀ/ **2** vi get slimmer; **ça te mincit** it makes you look slimmer.

mine /min/ nf expression; (allure) appearance; **avoir bonne ~** look well; **faire ~ de** make as if to; (exploitation, explosif) mine; (de crayon) lead; **~ de charbon** coalmine.

miner /mine/ **1** vt (saper) undermine; (garnir d'explosifs) mine.

minerai /minʀɛ/ nm ore.

minéral, ~e (mpl -aux) /mineʀal, -o/ adj mineral. •nm (pl -aux) mineral.

minéralogique /mineʀalɔʒik/ adj **plaque ~** numberplate; (US) license plate.

minet, ~te /minɛ, -t/ nm, f (chat **1**) pussy(cat).

mineur, ~e /minœʀ/ adj minor; (Jur) under age. •nm, f (Jur) minor. •nm (ouvrier) miner.

miniature /minjatyʀ/ nf & adj miniature.

minier, -ière /minje, -jɛʀ/ adj mining.

minimal, ~**e** (mpl -**aux**) /minimal, o/ adj minimal, minimum.

minime /minim/ adj minimal, minor. •nmf (Sport) junior.

minimum /minimɔm/ adj minimum. •nm minimum; **au** ~ (pour le moins) at the very least; **en faire un** ~ do as little as possible.

ministère /ministɛʀ/ nm ministry; (gouvernement) government; ~ **public** public prosecutor's office. **ministériel,** ~**le** adj ministerial, government.

ministre /ministʀ/ nm minister; (au Royaume-Uni) Secretary of State; (US) Secretary.

⊞Minitel® /minitɛl/ nm Minitel (telephone videotext system).

minorer /minɔʀe/ **1** vt reduce.

minoritaire /minɔʀitɛʀ/ adj minority; **être** ~ be in the minority. **minorité** nf minority.

minuit /minɥi/ nm midnight.

minuscule /minyskyl/ adj minute. •nf **(lettre)** ~ lower case.

minute /minyt/ nf minute; **'talons** ~**'** 'heels repaired while you wait'.

minuterie /minytʀi/ nf time-switch.

minutie /minysi/ nf meticulousness.

minutieux, -ieuse /minysjø, -z/ adj meticulous.

mioche /mjɔʃ/ nm, f **⊞** kid.

mirabelle /miʀabɛl/ nf (mirabelle) plum.

miracle /miʀakl/ nm miracle; **par** ~ miraculously.

miraculeux, -euse /miʀakylø, -z/ adj miraculous.

mirage /miʀaʒ/ nm mirage.

mire /miʀ/ nf (fig) centre of attraction; (TV) test card.

mirobolant, ~**e** /miʀɔbɔlã, -t/ adj **⊞** marvellous.

miroir /miʀwaʀ/ nm mirror.

miroiter /miʀwate/ **1** vi shimmer, sparkle.

mis, ~**e** /mi, miz/ adj **bien** ~ welldressed. •▷METTRE **42**.

mise /miz/ nf (argent) stake; (tenue) attire; ~ **à feu** blast-off; ~ **au point** adjustment; (fig) clarification; ~ **de fonds** capital outlay; ~ **en garde** warning; ~ **en plis** set; ~ **en scène** direction.

miser /mize/ **1** vt (argent) bet, stake (**sur** on). •vi ~ **sur** (parier) place a bet on; (compter sur) bank on.

misérable /mizeʀabl/ adj miserable, wretched; (indigent) destitute; (minable) seedy, squalid.

misère /mizeʀ/ nf destitution; (malheur) trouble, woe. **miséreux, -euse** nm, f destitute person.

miséricorde /mizeʀikɔʀd/ nf mercy.

missel /misɛl/ nm missal.

missile /misil/ nm missile.

mission /misjõ/ nm mission. **missionnaire** nmf missionary.

missive /misiv/ nf missive.

mistral /mistʀal/ nm (vent) mistral.

mitaine /mitɛn/ nf fingerless mitt.

mite /mit/ nf (clothes-)moth.

mi-temps /mitã/ nf inv (arrêt) half-time; (période) half. •nm inv part-time work; **à** ~ part-time.

miteux, -euse /mitø, -z/ adj shabby.

mitigé, ~**e** /mitiʒe/ adj (modéré)

──────────────────
⊞ *see A-Z of French life and culture*

lukewarm; (succès) qualified.

mitonner /mitɔne/ **1** vt cook slowly with care; (fig) cook up.

mitoyen, **~ne** /mitwajɛ̃, -ɛn/ adj **mur ~** party wall.

mitrailler /mitʀɑje/ **1** vt machine-gun; (fig) bombard.

mitraillette /mitʀɑjɛt/ nf submachine gun. **mitrailleuse** nf machine gun.

mi-voix: à ~ /amivwa/ loc in a low voice.

mixeur /miksœʀ/ nm liquidizer, blender; (batteur) mixer.

mixte /mikst/ adj mixed; (commission) joint; (école) coeducational; (peau) combination.

mobile /mɔbil/ adj mobile; (pièce) moving; (feuillet) loose. ●nm (art) mobile; (raison) motive.

mobilier /mɔbilje/ nm furniture.

mobilisation /mɔbilizasjɔ̃/ nf mobilization. **mobiliser** **1** vt mobilize.

mobilité /mɔbilite/ nf mobility.

mobylette® /mɔbilɛt/ nf moped.

moche /mɔʃ/ adj **1** (laid) ugly; (mauvais) lousy.

modalités /mɔdalite/ nfpl (conditions) terms; (façon de fonctionner) practical details.

mode /mɔd/ nf fashion; (coutume) custom; **à la ~** fashionable. ●nm method, mode; (genre) way; **~ d'emploi** directions (for use).

modèle /mɔdɛl/ adj model. ●nm model; (exemple) example; (Comm) (type) model; (taille) size; (style) style; **~ familial** family size; **~ réduit** (small-scale) model.

modeler /mɔdle/ **6** vt model (**sur** on). ■ **se ~ sur** vpr model oneself on.

modem /mɔdɛm/ nm modem.

modérateur, **-trice** /mɔdeʀatœʀ, -tʀis/ adj

moderating. **modération** nf moderation.

modéré, **~e** /mɔdeʀe/ adj & nm, f moderate.

modérer /mɔdeʀe/ **14** vt (propos) moderate; (désirs, sentiments) curb. ■ **se ~** vpr restrain oneself.

moderne /mɔdɛʀn/ adj modern. **moderniser** **1** vt modernize.

modeste /mɔdɛst/ adj modest. **modestie** nf modesty.

modification /mɔdifikasjɔ̃/ nf modification.

modifier /mɔdifje/ **45** vt change, modify. ■ **se ~** vpr change, alter.

modique /mɔdik/ adj modest.

modiste /mɔdist/ nf milliner.

moduler /mɔdyle/ **1** vt modulate; (adapter) adjust.

moelle /mwal/ nf marrow; **~ épinière** spinal cord; **~ osseuse** bone marrow.

moelleux, **-euse** /mwalø, -z/ adj soft; (onctueux) smooth.

mœurs /mœʀ(s)/ nfpl (morale) morals; (usages) customs; (manières) habits, ways.

moi /mwa/ pron me; (indirect) (to) me; (sujet) I. ●nm self.

moignon /mwaɲɔ̃/ nm stump.

moi-même /mwamɛm/ pron myself.

moindre /mwɛ̃dʀ/ adj (moins grand) lesser; **le** ou **la ~**, **les ~s** the slightest, the least.

moine /mwan/ nm monk.

moineau (pl **~x**) /mwano/ nm sparrow.

moins /mwɛ̃/ prép minus; (pour dire l'heure) to; **une heure ~** dix ten to one. ●adv less (**que** than); **le** ou **la** ou **les ~** the least; **le ~ grand/haut** the smallest/lowest; **~ de** (avec un nom non dénombrable) less (**que** than); **~ de dix euros** less than ten euros; **~ de livres** fewer books; **au ~**, **du ~** at least; **à ~ que** unless; **de ~**

less; **de ~ en ~** less and less; **en ~** less; (manquant) missing.

mois /mwa/ nm month.

moisi, ~e /mwazi/ adj mouldy. • nm mould; **de ~** (odeur) musty. **moisir** 2 vi go mouldy. **moisissure** nf mould.

moisson /mwasɔ̃/ nf harvest.

moissonner /mwasɔne/ 1 vt harvest, reap. **moissonneur, -euse** nm, f harvester.

moite /mwat/ adj sticky, clammy.

moitié /mwatje/ nf half; (milieu) halfway mark; **s'arrêter à la ~** stop halfway through; **à ~ vide** half empty; **à ~ prix** (at) half-price; **la ~ de** half (of). **moitié-moitié** adv half-and-half.

mol /mɔl/ ▷MOU.

molaire /mɔlɛʀ/ nf molar.

molécule /mɔlekyl/ nf molecule.

molester /mɔlɛste/ 1 vt manhandle, rough up.

molle /mɔl/ ▷MOU.

mollement /mɔlmɑ̃/ adv softly; (faiblement) feebly. **mollesse** nf softness; (faiblesse) feebleness; (apathie) listlessness.

mollet /mɔlɛ/ nm (de jambe) calf.

mollir /mɔliʀ/ 2 vi soften; (céder) yield.

môme /mom/ nmf 1 kid.

moment /mɔmɑ̃/ nm moment; (période) time; **(petit) ~** short while; **au ~ où** when; **par ~s** now and then; **du ~ où** ou **que** (pourvu que) as long as, provided that; (puisque) since; **en ce ~** at the moment.

momentané, ~e /mɔmɑ̃tane/ adj momentary. **momentanément** adv momentarily; (en ce moment) at present.

momie /mɔmi/ nf mummy.

mon, ma (**mon** before vowel or mute h) (pl **mes**) /mɔ̃, ma, mɔ̃n, me/ adj my.

Monaco /mɔnako/ npr Monaco.

monarchie /mɔnaʀʃi/ nf monarchy.

monarque /mɔnaʀk/ nm monarch.

monastère /mɔnastɛʀ/ nm monastery.

monceau (pl ~x) /mɔ̃so/ nm heap, pile.

mondain, ~e /mɔ̃dɛ̃, -ɛn/ adj society, social.

monde /mɔ̃d/ nm world; **du ~** (a lot of) people; (quelqu'un) somebody; **le (grand) ~** (high) society; **se faire (tout) un ~ de qch** make a great deal of fuss about sth; **pas le moins du ~** not in the least.

mondial, ~e (mpl **-iaux**) /mɔ̃djal, -jo/ adj world; (influence) worldwide. **mondialement** adv the world over.

mondialisation /mɔ̃djalizasjɔ̃/ nf globalisation.

monétaire /mɔnetɛʀ/ adj monetary.

moniteur, -trice /mɔnitœʀ, -tʀis/ nm, f instructor; (de colonie de vacances) group leader; (US) (camp) counselor.

monnaie /mɔnɛ/ nf currency; (pièce) coin; (appoint) change; **faire la ~ de** get change for; **faire de la ~ à qn** give sb change; **menue** ou **petite ~** small change.

monnayer /mɔneje/ 31 vt convert into cash.

monologue /mɔnɔlɔg/ nm monologue.

monoparental, ~e /mɔnɔpaʀɑ̃tal/ adj **famille ~e** single-parent family.

monopole /mɔnɔpɔl/ nm monopoly. **monopoliser** 1 vt monopolize.

monospace /mɔnɔspas/ nm (Auto) people carrier.

monotone /mɔnɔtɔn/ adj

monotonous. **monotonie** nf monotony.

Monseigneur (pl **Messeigneurs**) /mɔ̃sɛɲœʀ/ nm (à un duc, archevêque) Your Grace; (à un prince) Your Highness.

monsieur (pl **messieurs**) /məsjø, mesjø/ nm (homme) man; (formule de respect) sir; (à un inconnu) (dans une lettre) **M~** Dear Sir; **bonjour, ~** good morning; **mesdames et messieurs** ladies and gentlemen; (à un homme dont on connaît le nom) (dans une lettre) **Cher M~** Dear Mr X; **bonjour, ~** good morning Mr X; **M~ le curé** Father X; **oui M~ le ministre** yes Minister.

monstre /mɔ̃stʀ/ nm monster. ●adj [1] colossal.

monstrueux, -euse /mɔ̃stʀyø, -z/ adj monstrous. **monstruosité** nf monstrosity.

mont /mɔ̃/ nm mountain; **le ~ Everest** Mount Everest; **être toujours par ~s et par vaux** be always on the move.

montage /mɔ̃taʒ/ nm (assemblage) assembly; (au cinéma) editing.

montagne /mɔ̃taɲ/ nf mountain; (région) mountains; **~s russes** roller-coaster. **montagneux, -euse** adj mountainous.

montant, -e /mɔ̃tɑ̃, -t/ adj rising; (col) high; (chemin) uphill. ●nm amount; (pièce de bois) upright.

mont-de-piété (pl **monts-de-piété**) /mɔ̃dpjete/ nm pawnshop.

monte-charge* /mɔ̃tʃaʀʒ/ nm inv goods lift.

montée /mɔ̃te/ nf ascent, climb; (de prix) rise; (de coûts, risques) increase; (côte) hill.

monter /mɔ̃te/ [1] vt (aux. avoir) take up; (à l'étage) take upstairs; (escalier, rue, pente) go up; (assembler) assemble; (tente, échafaudage) put up; (col, manche) set in; (organiser) (pièce) stage; (société) set up;

(attaque, garde) mount. ●vi (aux. être) go ou come up; (à l'étage) go ou come upstairs; (avion) climb; (route) go uphill, climb; (augmenter) rise; (marée) come up; **~ sur** (trottoir, toit) get up on; (cheval, bicyclette) get on; **~ à l'échelle/l'arbre** climb the ladder/tree; **~ dans** (voiture) get in; (train, bus, avion) get on; **~ à bord** climb on board; **~ (à cheval)** ride; **~ à bicyclette/ moto** ride a bike/motorbike.

monteur, -euse /mɔ̃tœʀ, -øz/ nm, f (Tech) fitter; (au cinéma) editor.

montre /mɔ̃tʀ/ nf watch; **faire ~ de** show.

montrer /mɔ̃tʀe/ [1] vt show (à to); **~ du doigt** point to. ■se **~** vpr show oneself; (être) be; (s'avérer) prove to be.

monture /mɔ̃tyʀ/ nf (cheval) mount; (de lunettes) frames (+ pl); (de bijou) setting.

monument /mɔnymɑ̃/ nm monument; **~ aux morts** war memorial. **monumental, ~e** (mpl **-aux**) adj monumental.

moquer (se) /(sə)mɔke/ [1] vpr se **~ de** make fun of; **je m'en moque** [1] I couldn't care less. **moquerie** nf mockery. **moqueur, -euse** adj mocking.

moquette /mɔkɛt/ nf fitted carpet; (US) wall-to-wall carpeting.

moral, ~e (mpl **-aux**) /mɔʀal, -o/ adj moral. ●nm (pl **-aux**) morale; **ne pas avoir le ~** feel down; **avoir le ~** be in good spirits; **ça m'a remonté le ~** it gave me a boost.

morale /mɔʀal/ nf moral code; (mœurs) morals; (de fable) moral; **faire la ~ à** lecture. **moralité** nf (de personne) morals (+ pl); (d'action, œuvre) morality; (de fable) moral.

moralisateur, -trice /mɔʀalizatœʀ, -tʀis/ adj moralizing.

morbide /mɔʀbid/ adj morbid.

morceau (pl ~x) /mɔʀso/ nm
piece, bit; (de sucre) lump; (de
viande) cut; (passage) passage;
manger un ~ ⛶ have a bite to
eat; **mettre en ~x** smash *ou*
tear to bits.

morceler /mɔʀsəle/ ⑥ vt
divide up.

mordant, ~e /mɔʀdɑ̃, -t/ adj
scathing; (froid) biting. ●nm
vigour, energy.

mordiller /mɔʀdije/ ① vt
nibble at.

mordre /mɔʀdʀ/ ③ vi bite (**dans**
into); **~ sur** (ligne) go over;
(territoire) encroach on; **~ à
l'hameçon** bite. ●vt bite.

mordu, ~e /mɔʀdy/ ⛶ nm, f fan.
●adj smitten; **~ de** crazy about.

morfondre (se) /(sə)mɔʀfɔ̃dʀ/ ③
vpr wait anxiously; (languir) mope.

morgue /mɔʀg/ nf morgue,
mortuary; (attitude) arrogance.

moribond, ~e /mɔʀibɔ̃, -d/ adj
dying.

morne /mɔʀn/ adj dull.

morphine /mɔʀfin/ nf morphine.

mors /mɔʀ/ nm (de cheval) bit.

morse /mɔʀs/ nm (animal) walrus;
(code) Morse code.

morsure /mɔʀsyʀ/ nf bite.

mort¹ /mɔʀ/ nf death.

mort², ~e /mɔʀ, -t/ adj dead; **~
de fatigue** dead tired. ●nm, f
dead man, dead woman; **les ~s**
the dead.

mortalité /mɔʀtalite/ nf
mortality; **(taux de) ~**
death rate.

mortel, ~le /mɔʀtɛl/ adj mortal;
(accident) fatal; (poison, silence)
deadly. ●nm, f mortal.
mortellement adv mortally.

mortifié, ~e /mɔʀtifje/ adj
mortified.

mort-né, ~e /mɔʀne/ adj
stillborn.

mortuaire /mɔʀtɥɛʀ/ adj

(cérémonie) funeral.

morue /mɔʀy/ nf cod.

mosaïque /mozaik/ nf mosaic.

mosquée /mɔske/ nf mosque.

mot /mo/ nm word; (lettre, message)
note; **~ d'ordre** watchword; **~
de passe** password; **~s croisés**
crossword (puzzle).

motard /mɔtaʀ/ nm biker; (policier)
police motorcyclist.

moteur, -trice /mɔtœʀ, -tʀis/ adj
(Méd) motor; (force) driving; **à 4
roues motrices** 4-wheel drive.
●nm engine, motor; **barque à ~**
motor launch; **~ de recherche**
(Internet) search engine.

motif /mɔtif/ nm (raisons) grounds
(+ pl); (cause) reason; (Jur) motive;
(dessin) pattern.

motion /mosjɔ̃/ nf motion.

motivation /mɔtivasjɔ̃/ nf
motivation. **motiver** ① vt
motivate.

moto /mɔto/ nf motor cycle.
motocycliste nmf motorcyclist.

motorisé, ~e /mɔtɔʀize/ adj
motorized.

motrice /mɔtʀis/ ▷**MOTEUR**.

motte /mɔt/ nf lump; (de beurre)
slab; (de terre) clod; **~ de
gazon** turf.

mou (**mol** before vowel or mute h),
molle /mu, mɔl/ adj soft; (ventre)
flabby; (sans conviction) feeble;
(apathique) sluggish, listless. ●nm
slack; **avoir du ~** be slack.

mouchard, ~e /muʃaʀ, -d/ nm, f
informer; (Scol) sneak.

mouche /muʃ/ nf fly; (de cible)
bull's eye.

moucher (se) /(sə)muʃe/ ① vpr
blow one's nose.

moucheron /muʃʀɔ̃/ nm midge.

moucheté, ~e /muʃte/ adj
speckled.

mouchoir /muʃwaʀ/ nm
handkerchief, hanky; **~ en
papier** tissue.

m

moue /mu/ nf pout; **faire la ~** pout.

mouette /mwɛt/ nf (sea)gull.

moufle /mufl/ nf (gant) mitten.

mouillé, ~e /muje/ adj wet.

mouiller /muje/ **1** vt wet, make wet; **~ l'ancre** drop anchor. ■ se **~** vpr get (oneself) wet.

moulage /mulaʒ/ nm cast.

moule /mul/ nf (coquillage) mussel. ●nm mould; **~ à gâteau** cake tin; **~ à tarte** flan dish. **mouler 1** vt mould; (statue) cast.

moulin /mulɛ̃/ nm mill; **~ à café** coffee grinder; **~ à poivre** pepper mill; **~ à vent** windmill.

moulinet /mulinɛ/ nm (de canne à pêche) reel; **faire des ~s avec qch** twirl sth around.

moulinette® /mulinɛt/ nf vegetable mill.

moulu, ~e /muly/ adj ground; (fatigué **1**) worn out.

moulure /mulyʀ/ nf moulding.

mourant, ~e /muʀɑ̃, -t/ adj dying. ●nm, f dying person.

mourir /muʀiʀ/ **43** vi (aux. être) die; **~ d'envie de** be dying to; **~ de faim** be starving; **~ d'ennui** be dead bored.

mousquetaire /muskətɛʀ/ nm musketeer.

mousse /mus/ nf moss; (écume) froth, foam; (de savon) lather; (dessert) mousse; **~ à raser** shaving foam. ●nm ship's boy.

mousseline /muslin/ nf muslin; (de soie) chiffon.

mousser /muse/ **1** vi froth, foam; (savon) lather.

mousseux, -euse /musø, -z/ adj frothy. ●nm sparkling wine.

mousson /musɔ̃/ nf monsoon.

moustache /mustaʃ/ nf moustache; **~s** (d'animal) whiskers.

moustique /mustik/ nm mosquito.

moutarde /mutaʀd/ nf mustard.

mouton /mutɔ̃/ nm sheep; (peau) sheepskin; (viande) mutton.

mouvant, ~e /muvɑ̃, -t/ adj changing; (terrain) shifting, unstable.

mouvement /muvmɑ̃/ nm movement; (agitation) bustle; (en gymnastique) exercise; (impulsion) impulse; (tendance) tend, tendency; **en ~** in motion.

mouvementé, ~e /muvmɑ̃te/ adj eventful.

moyen, ~ne /mwajɛ̃, -ɛn/ adj average; (médiocre) poor; **de taille moyenne** medium-sized. ●nm means, way; **~s** means; (dons) ability; **au ~ de** by means of; **il n'y a pas ~ de** it is not possible to. **Moyen Âge** nm Middle Ages (+ pl).

moyennant /mwajɛnɑ̃/ prép (pour) for; (grâce à) with.

moyenne /mwajɛn/ nf average; (Scol) pass-mark; **en ~** on average; **~ d'âge** average age. **moyennement** adv moderately.

Moyen-Orient /mwajɛnɔʀjɑ̃/ nm Middle East.

moyeu (pl **~x**) /mwajø/ nm hub.

mû, mue /my/ adj driven (**par** by).

mucoviscidose /mykɔvisidoz/ nf cystic fibrosis.

mue /my/ nf moulting; (de voix) breaking of the voice.

muer /mɥe/ **1** vi moult; (voix) break. ■ se **~ en** vpr change into.

muet, ~te /mɥɛ, -t/ adj (Méd) dumb; (fig) speechless (**de** with); (silencieux) silent. ●nm, f mute.

mufle /myfl/ nm nose, muzzle; (personne **1**) boor, lout.

mugir /myʒiʀ/ **2** vi (vache) moo; (bœuf) bellow; (fig) howl.

muguet /mygɛ/ nm lily of the valley.

mule /myl/ nf (female) mule; (pantoufle) mule.

mulet /mylɛ/ nm (male) mule.

multicolore /myltikɔlɔʀ/ adj multicoloured.

multimédia /myltimedja/ adj & nm multimedia.

multinational, ~e (mpl -aux) /myltinasjɔnal, -o/ adj multinational. **multinationale** nf multinational (company).

multiple /myltipl/ nm multiple. ●adj numerous, many; (naissances) multiple.

multiplication /myltiplikasjɔ̃/ nf multiplication.

multiplicité /myltiplisite/ nf multiplicity.

multiplier /myltiplije/ 45 vt multiply; (risques) increase. ■ se ~ vpr multiply; (accidents) be on the increase; (difficultés) increase.

multitude /myltityd/ nf multitude, mass.

municipal, ~e (mpl -aux) /mynisipal, -o/ adj municipal; **conseil ~** town council. **municipalité** nf (ville) municipality; (conseil) town council.

munir /myniʀ/ 2 vt ~ **de** provide with. ■ se ~ **de** vpr (apporter) bring; (emporter) take.

munitions /mynisjɔ̃/ nfpl ammunition.

mur /myʀ/ nm wall; ~ **du son** sound barrier.

mûr, ~e /myʀ/ adj ripe; (personne) mature.

muraille /myʀɑj/ nf (high) wall.

mural, ~e (mpl -aux) /myʀal, -o/ adj wall; **peinture ~e** mural.

mûre* /myʀ/ nf blackberry.

mûrir* /myʀiʀ/ 2 vi ripen; (abcès) come to a head; (personne, projet) mature. ●vt (fruit) ripen; (personne) mature.

murmure /myʀmyʀ/ nm murmur.

muscade /myskad/ nf **noix ~** nutmeg.

muscle /myskl/ nm muscle. **musclé, ~e** adj muscular. **musculaire** adj muscular.

musculation /myskylasjɔ̃/ nf bodybuilding.

musculature /myskylatyʀ/ nf muscles (+ pl).

museau (pl ~**x**) /myzo/ nm muzzle; (de porc) snout.

musée /myze/ nm museum; (de peinture) art gallery.

muselière /myzəljɛʀ/ nf muzzle.

musette /myzɛt/ nf haversack.

muséum /myzeɔm/ nm natural history museum.

musical, ~e (mpl -aux) /myzikal, -o/ adj musical.

musicien, ~ne /myzisjɛ̃, -ɛn/ adj musical. ●nm, f musician.

musique /myzik/ nf music; (orchestre) band.

must /myst/ nm 🆃 must.

musulman, ~e /myzylmã, -an/ adj & nm, f Muslim.

mutation /mytasjɔ̃/ nf change; (biologique) mutation; (d'un employé) transfer.

muter /myte/ 1 vt transfer. ●vi mutate.

mutilation /mytilasjɔ̃/ nf mutilation. **mutiler** 1 vt mutilate. **mutilé, ~e** nm, f disabled person.

mutin, ~e /mytɛ̃, -in/ adj mischievous. ●nm mutineer; (prisonnier) rioter.

mutinerie /mytinʀi/ nf mutiny; (de prisonniers) riot.

mutisme /mytism/ nm silence.

mutuel, ~le /mytɥɛl/ adj mutual. **mutuelle** nf mutual insurance company. **mutuellement** adv

m

mutually; (l'un l'autre) each other.

myope /mjɔp/ adj short-sighted.
myopie nf short-sightedness.

myosotis /mjozɔtis/ nm forget-me-not.

myrtille /miʀtij/ nf bilberry, blueberry.

mystère /mistɛʀ/ nm mystery.

mystérieux, -ieuse /misteʀjø, -z/ adj mysterious.

mystification /mistifikasjɔ̃/ nf hoax.

mysticisme /mistisism/ nm mysticism.

mystique /mistik/ adj mystic(al). •nmf mystic. •nf mystique.

mythe /mit/ nm myth. **mythique** adj mythical.

mythologie /mitɔlɔʒi/ nf mythology.

Nn

n' /n/ ▷NE.

nacre /nakʀ/ nf mother-of-pearl.

nage /naʒ/ nf swimming; (manière) stroke; **traverser à la ~** swim across; **en ~** sweating.

nageoire /naʒwaʀ/ nf fin; (de mammifère) flipper.

nager /naʒe/ [40] vt/i swim. **nageur, -euse** nm, f swimmer.

naguère /nagɛʀ/ adv (autrefois) formerly.

naïf, -ive /naif, -v/ adj naïve.

nain, ~e /nɛ̃, nɛn/ nm, f & adj dwarf.

naissance /nɛsɑ̃s/ nf birth; **donner ~ à** give birth to; (fig) give rise to.

naître* /nɛtʀ/ [44] vi be born; (résulter) arise (**de** from); **faire ~** (susciter) give rise to.

naïveté /naivte/ nf naïvety.

nappe /nap/ nf tablecloth; (de pétrole, gaz) layer; **~ phréatique** ground water.

napperon /napʀɔ̃/ nm (cloth) tablemat.

narco-dollars /naʀkodɔlaʀ/ nmpl drug money.

narcotique /naʀkɔtik/ adj & nm narcotic. **narco(-)trafiquant, ~e** (pl ~s) nm, f drug trafficker.

narguer /narge/ [1] vt taunt; (autorité) flout.

narine /naʀin/ nf nostril.

nasal, ~e (mpl -aux) /nazal, -o/ adj nasal.

naseau (pl ~x) /nazo/ nm nostril.

natal, ~e (mpl ~s) /natal/ adj native.

natalité /natalite/ nf birth rate.

natation /natasjɔ̃/ nf swimming.

natif, -ive /natif, -v/ adj native.

nation /nasjɔ̃/ nf nation.

national, ~e (mpl -aux) /nasjɔnal, -o/ adj national. **nationale** nf A road; (US) highway. **nationaliser** [1] vt nationalize.

nationalité /nasjɔnalite/ nf nationality.

natte /nat/ nf (de cheveux) plait; (US) braid; (tapis de paille) mat.

nature /natyʀ/ nf nature; **~ morte** still life; **de ~ à** likely to; **payer en ~** pay in kind. •adj inv plain; (yaourt) natural; (thé) black.

naturel, ~le /natyʀɛl/ adj

natural. •nm nature; (simplicité)
naturalness; (Culin) **au ~** plain;
(thon) in brine. **naturellement**
adv naturally; (bien sûr) of course.

naufrage /nofʀaʒ/ nm shipwreck;
faire ~ be shipwrecked; (bateau)
be wrecked.

nauséabond, ~e /nozeabɔ̃, -d/
adj nauseating.

nausée /noze/ nf nausea.

nautique /notik/ adj nautical;
sports ~s water sports.

naval, ~e (mpl ~s) /naval/ adj
naval; **chantier ~** shipyard.

navet /navɛ/ nm turnip; (film: péj)
flop; (US) turkey.

navette /navɛt/ nf shuttle (service);
faire la ~ shuttle back and
forth.

navigateur, -trice /navigatœʀ,
-tʀis/ nm, f sailor; (qui guide)
navigator; (Internet) browser.
navigation nf navigation; (trafic)
shipping; (Internet) browsing.

naviguer /navige/ 1 vi sail;
(piloter) navigate; (Internet) browse;
~ dans l'Internet surf the
Internet.

navire /naviʀ/ nm ship.

navré, ~e /navʀe/ adj sorry
(**de** to).

---

ne, n' /nə, n/

⚠ n' before vowel or mute h.

● adverb

····▸ **je n'ai que 10 euros** I've
only got 10 euros.

····▸ **tu n'avais qu'à le dire!**
you only had to say so!

····▸ **je crains qu'il ~ parte** I
am afraid he will leave.

▶ Pour les expressions comme
ne... guère, ne... jamais,
ne... pas, ne... plus, etc.
▶ **guère, jamais, pas, plus,** etc.

---

né, ~e /ne/ adj born; **~e Martin**
née Martin; (dans composés)

dernier-~ last-born.
● ▷ **NAÎTRE** 44.

néanmoins /neɑ̃mwɛ̃/ adv
nevertheless.

néant /neɑ̃/ nm nothingness;
réduire à ~ (effet, efforts) negate,
nullify; (espoir) dash; **'revenus:
~'** 'income: nil'.

nécessaire /nesesɛʀ/ adj
necessary. •nm (sac) bag; (trousse)
kit; **le ~** (l'indispensable) the
necessities ou essentials; **faire
le ~** do what is necessary.

nécessité /nesesite/ nf necessity;
de première ~ vital.

nécessiter /nesesite/ 1 vt
necessitate.

néerlandais, ~e /neɛʀlɑ̃dɛ, -z/
adj Dutch. •nm (Ling) Dutch. **N~,
~e** nm, f Dutchman,
Dutchwoman.

néfaste /nefast/ adj harmful
(**à** to).

négatif, -ive /negatif, -v/ adj & nm
negative.

négligé, ~e /negliʒe/ adj (travail)
careless; (tenue) scruffy. •nm
(tenue) negligee.

négligent, ~e /negliʒɑ̃, -t/ adj
careless, negligent.

négliger /negliʒe/ 40 vt neglect;
(ne pas tenir compte de) ignore,
disregard; **~ de faire** fail to do.
■ **se ~** vpr neglect oneself.

négoce /negɔs/ nm business,
trade. **négociant, ~e** nm, f
merchant.

négociation /negɔsjasjɔ̃/ nf
negotiation. **négocier** 45 vt/i
negotiate.

nègre /nɛgʀ/ adj (musique, art)
Negro. •nm (écrivain) ghost writer.

neige /nɛʒ/ nf snow. **neiger** 40
vi snow.

nénuphar* /nenyfaʀ/ nm
waterlily.

nerf /nɛʀ/ nm nerve; (vigueur)
stamina; **être sur les ~s** be
on edge.

nerveux, -euse /nɛʀvø, -z/ adj nervous; (irritable) nervy; (centre, cellule) nerve; (voiture) responsive. **nervosité** nf nervousness; (irritabilité) touchiness.

net, ~te /nɛt/ adj (clair, distinct) clear; (propre) clean; (notable) marked; (soigné) neat; (prix, poids) net. ● **N~** nm (Ordinat) net. ● adv (s'arrêter) dead; (refuser) flatly; (parler) plainly; (se casser) cleanly; (tuer) outright. **nettement** adv (expliquer) clearly; (augmenter, se détériorer) markedly; (indiscutablement) distinctly, decidedly. **netteté** nf clearness.

netéconomie /nɛtekɔnɔmi/ nf e-economy.

nétiquette /netikɛt/ nf netiquette.

nettoyage /nɛtwajaʒ/ nm cleaning; **à sec** dry-cleaning; **produit de ~** cleaner; **~ ethnique** ethnic cleansing.

nettoyer /nɛtwaje/ **31** vt clean.

neuf[1] /nœf/ (/nœv/ before vowels and mute h) adj inv & nm nine.

neuf[2]**, -euve** /nœf, -v/ adj new; **tout ~** brand new. ● nm new; **remettre à ~** brighten up; **du ~** a new development; **quoi de ~?** what's new?

neutre /nøtʀ/ adj neutral; (Gram) neuter. ● nm (Gram) neuter.

neuve /nœv/ ▷NEUF[2].

neuvième /nœvjɛm/ adj & nm, f ninth.

neveu (pl **~x**) /nəvø/ nm nephew.

névrose /nevʀoz/ nf neurosis. **névrosé, ~e** adj & nm, f neurotic.

nez /ne/ nm nose; **~ à ~** face to face; **~ retroussé** turned-up nose.

ni /ni/ conj neither, nor; **~ grand ~ petit** neither big nor small; **~ l'un ~ l'autre ne fument** neither (one nor the other) smokes; **sortir sans manteau ~ chapeau** go without a coat or hat; **elle n'a dit ~ oui ~ non** she didn't say either yes or no.

niais, ~e /njɛ, -z/ adj silly.

niche /niʃ/ nf (de chien) kennel; (cavité) niche.

nicher /niʃe/ **1** vi nest. ■ **se ~** vpr nest; (se cacher) hide.

nicotine /nikɔtin/ nf nicotine.

nid /ni/ nm nest; **faire un ~** build a nest. **nid-de-poule** (pl **nids-de-poule**) nm pot-hole.

nièce /njɛs/ nf niece.

nier /nje/ **45** vt deny.

nigaud, ~e /nigo, -d/ nm, f fool.

nippon, ~ne /nipɔ̃, -ɔn/ adj Japanese. **N~, ~ne** nm, f Japanese.

niveau (pl **~x**) /nivo/ nm level; (compétence) standard; (étage) storey; (US) story; **au ~** up to standard; **mettre à ~** (Ordinat) upgrade; **~ à bulle** (d'air) spirit level; **~ de vie** standard of living.

niveler /nivle/ **6** vt level.

noble /nɔbl/ adj noble. ● nm, f nobleman, noblewoman. **noblesse** nf nobility.

noce /nɔs/ nf (fête **1**) party; (invités) wedding guests; **~s** wedding; **faire la ~** **1** live it up.

nocif, -ive /nɔsif, -v/ adj harmful.

nocturne /nɔktyʀn/ adj nocturnal. ● nm (Mus) nocturne. ● nf (Sport) evening fixture; (de magasin) late-night opening.

Noël /nɔɛl/ nm Christmas.

nœud /nø/ nm (Naut) knot; (pour lier) knot; (pour orner) bow; **~s** (fig) ties; **~ coulant** slipknot, noose; **~ papillon** bow-tie.

noir, ~e /nwaʀ/ adj black; (obscur, sombre) dark; (triste) gloomy. ● nm black; (obscurité) dark; **travail au ~** moonlighting. ● nm, f (personne) Black.

noircir /nwaʀsiʀ/ **2** vt blacken; **~ la situation** paint a black

picture of the situation. ●vi
(banane) go black; (mur) get dirty;
(métal) tarnish. ■ se ~ vpr (ciel)
darken.

noire /nwaʀ/ nf (Mus) crotchet.

noisette /nwazɛt/ nf hazelnut; (de
beurre) knob.

noix /nwa/ nf nut; (du noyer)
walnut; (de beurre) knob; ~ **de
cajou** cashew nut; ~ **de coco**
coconut; **à la ~** 🅸 useless.

nom /nɔ̃/ nm name; (Gram) noun;
au ~ de on behalf of; ~ **et
prénom** full name; ~ **déposé**
registered trademark; ~ **de
famille** surname; ~ **de jeune
fille** maiden name; ~ **de plume**
pen name; ~ **propre**
proper noun.

nomade /nɔmad/ adj nomadic;
(worker, Internet) mobile. ●nmf
nomad.

nombre /nɔ̃bʀ/ nm number; **au ~
de** (parmi) among; (l'un de) one of;
en (grand) ~ in large numbers;
sans ~ countless.

nombreux, -euse /nɔ̃bʀø, -z/ adj
(en grand nombre) many, numerous;
(important) large; **de ~ enfants**
many children; **nous étions
très ~** there were a great many
of us.

nombril /nɔ̃bʀil/ nm navel.

nomination /nɔminasjɔ̃/ nf
appointment.

nommer /nɔme/ **1** vt name; (élire)
(à une poste) appoint; (à un lieu)
post. ■ **se ~** vpr (s'appeler) be
called.

non /nɔ̃/ adv no; (pas) not; ~ **(pas)
que** not that; **il vient, ~?** he is
coming, isn't he?; **moi ~ plus**
neither am/do/can/*etc.* I. ●nm
inv no.

non- /nɔ̃/ préf non-; ~**-fumeur**
non-smoker.

nonante /nɔnɑ̃t/ adj & nm ninety.

non-sens /nɔ̃sɑ̃s/ nm inv absurdity.

nord /nɔʀ/ adj inv (façade, côte)

north; (frontière, zone) northern.
●nm north; **le ~ de l'Europe**
northern Europe; **vent de ~**
northerly (wind); **aller vers le
~** go north; **le Nord** the North;
du Nord northern. **nord-est** nm
north-east.

nordique /nɔʀdik/ adj
Scandinavian.

nord-ouest /nɔʀwɛst/ nm
north-west.

normal, ~e (mpl **-aux**) /nɔʀmal,
-o/ adj normal. **normale** nf
normality; (norme) norm;
(moyenne) average.

normand, ~e /nɔʀmɑ̃, -d/ adj
Norman. **N~, ~e** nm, f Norman.

Normandie /nɔʀmɑ̃di/ nf
Normandy.

norme /nɔʀm/ nf norm; (de
production) standard; ~**s de
sécurité** safety standards.

Norvège /nɔʀvɛʒ/ nf Norway.

norvégien, ~ne /nɔʀveʒjɛ̃, -ɛn/
adj Norwegian. **N~, ~ne** nm, f
Norwegian.

nos /no/ ▷**NOTRE.**

nostalgie /nɔstalʒi/ nf nostalgia;
avoir la ~ de son pays be
homesick. **nostalgique** adj
nostalgic.

notaire /nɔtɛʀ/ nm notary public.

notamment /nɔtamɑ̃/ adv
notably.

note /nɔt/ nf (remarque) note;
(chiffrée) mark, grade; (facture) bill;
(Mus) note; ~ **(de service)**
memorandum.

noter /nɔte/ **1** vt note, notice;
(écrire) note (down); (devoir) mark;
(US) grade; **bien/mal noté**
(employé) highly/poorly rated.

notice /nɔtis/ nf note; (mode
d'emploi) instructions, directions.

notifier /nɔtifje/ **45** vt notify
(**à** to).

notion /nɔsjɔ̃/ nf notion; **avoir
des ~s de** have a basic
knowledge of.

notoire /nɔtwaʀ/ adj well-known; (criminel) notorious.

notre (pl **nos**) /nɔtʀ, no/ adj our.

nôtre /notʀ/ pron **le** ou **la ~, les ~s** ours.

nouer /nwe/ **1** vt tie, knot; (relations) strike up.

nouille /nuj/ nf (Culin) noodle; **des ~s** noodles, pasta; (idiot **1**) idiot.

nounours /nunuʀs/ nm **1** teddy bear.

nourri, ~e /nuʀi/ adj **être logé ~** have bed and board; **~ au sein** breastfed.

nourrice /nuʀis/ nf childminder.

nourrir /nuʀiʀ/ **2** vt feed; (espoir, crainte) harbour; (projet) nurture; (passion) fuel. •vi be nourishing. ■ **se ~** vpr eat; **se ~ de** feed on.
nourrissant, ~e adj nourishing.

nourrisson /nuʀisɔ̃/ nm infant.

nourriture /nuʀityʀ/ nf food.

nous /nu/ pron (sujet) we; (complément) us; (indirect) (to) us; (réfléchi) ourselves; (l'un l'autre) each other; **la voiture est à ~** the car is ours. **nous-mêmes** pron ourselves.

nouveau (**nouvel** before vowel or mute h), **nouvelle** (mpl **~x**) /nuvo, nuvɛl/ adj new; **nouvel an** new year; **~x mariés** newly-weds; **~ venu, nouvelle venue** newcomer. •nm, f (élève) new boy, new girl. •nm **du ~** (fait nouveau) a new development; **de ~, à ~** again. **nouveau-né** (pl **~s**) nm newborn baby.

nouveauté /nuvote/ nf novelty; (chose) new thing; (livre) new publication; (disque) new release.

nouvelle /nuvɛl/ nf (piece of) news; (récit) short story; **~s** news.

Nouvelle-Zélande /nuvɛlzelɑ̃d/ nf New Zealand.

novembre /nɔvɑ̃bʀ/ nm November.

noyade /nwajad/ nf drowning.

noyau (pl **~x**) /nwajo/ nm (de fruit) stone; (US) pit; (de cellule) nucleus; (groupe) group; (centre: fig) core.

noyer /nwaje/ **31** vt drown; (inonder) flood. ■ **se ~** vpr drown; (volontairement) drown oneself; **se ~ dans un verre d'eau** make a mountain out of a molehill. •nm walnut-tree.

nu*, ~e /ny/ adj (corps, personne) naked; (mains, mur, fil) bare; **à l'œil ~** to the naked eye. •nm nude; **mettre à ~** expose.

nuage /nyaʒ/ nm cloud.

nuance /nyɑ̃s/ nf shade; (de sens) nuance; (différence) difference. **nuancer** **10** vt (opinion) qualify.

nucléaire /nykleɛʀ/ adj nuclear. •nm **le ~** nuclear energy.

nudisme /nydism/ nm nudism.

nudité /nydite/ nf nudity; (de lieu) bareness.

nuée /nye/ nf swarm, host.

nues /ny/ nfpl **tomber des ~** be amazed; **porter qn aux ~** praise sb to the skies.

nuire /nɥiʀ/ **17** vi **~ à** harm.

nuisible /nɥizibl/ adj harmful (**à** to).

nuit /nɥi/ nf night; **cette ~** tonight; (hier) last night; **il fait ~** it is dark; **~ blanche** sleepless night; **la ~, de ~** at night; **~ de noces** wedding night.

nul, ~le /nyl/ adj (aucun) no; (zéro) nil; (qui ne vaut rien) useless; (non valable) null; (contrat) void; (testament) invalid; **match ~** draw; **~ en sciences** no good at science; **nulle part** nowhere; **~ autre** no one else. •pron no one. **nullement** adv not at all. **nullité** nf uselessness; (personne) nonentity.

numérique /nymeʀik/ adj numerical; (montre, horloge) digital.

numériser /nymeʀize/ vt digitize.

numéro /nymeʀo/ nm number; (de journal) issue; (spectacle) act; ~ **de téléphone** telephone number; ~ **vert** freephone number. **numéroter 1** vt number.

nuque /nyk/ nf nape (of the neck).

nurse /nœʀs/ nf nanny.

nutritif, -ive /nytʀitif, -v/ adj nutritious; (valeur) nutritional.

oasis /ɔazis/ nf oasis.

obéir /ɔbeiʀ/ **2** vt ~ **à** obey. •vi obey. **obéissance** nf obedience. **obéissant, ~e** adj obedient.

obèse /ɔbɛz/ adj obese.

objecter /ɔbʒɛkte/ **1** vt object.

objectif, -ive /ɔbʒɛktif, -v/ adj objective. •nm objective; (Photo) lens.

objection /ɔbʒɛksjɔ̃/ nf objection; **soulever des ~s** raise objections.

objet /ɔbʒɛ/ nm (chose) object; (sujet) subject; (but) purpose, object; **être ou faire l'~ de** be the subject of; ~ **d'art** objet d'art; ~**s trouvés** lost property; (US) lost and found.

obligation /ɔbligasjɔ̃/ nf obligation; (Comm) bond; **être dans l'~ de** be under obligation to.

obligatoire /ɔbligatwaʀ/ adj compulsory. **obligatoirement** adv (par règlement) of necessity; (inévitablement) inevitably.

obligeance /ɔbliʒɑ̃s/ nf **avoir l'~ de faire** be kind enough to do.

obliger /ɔbliʒe/ **40** vt compel, force (**à faire** to do); (aider) oblige; **être obligé de** have to (**de** for).

oblique /ɔblik/ adj oblique; **regard** ~ sidelong glance; **en** ~ at an angle.

oblitérer /ɔblitere/ **14** vt (timbre) cancel.

obnubilé, ~e /ɔbnybile/ adj obsessed.

obscène /ɔpsɛn/ adj obscene.

obscur, ~e /ɔpskyʀ/ adj dark; (confus, humble) obscure; (vague) vague.

obscurcir /ɔpskyʀsiʀ/ **2** vt make dark; (fig) obscure. ■ s'~ vpr (ciel) darken.

obscurité /ɔpskyʀite/ nf dark-(ness); (de passage, situation) obscurity.

obsédant, ~e /ɔpsedɑ̃, -t/ adj (problème) nagging; (musique, souvenir) haunting.

obsédé, ~e /ɔpsede/ nm, f ~ **(sexuel)** sex maniac; ~ **du ski/ jazz** ski/jazz freak.

obséder /ɔpsede/ **14** vt obsess.

obsèques /ɔpsɛk/ nfpl funeral.

observateur, -trice /ɔpsɛʀvatœʀ, -tʀis/ adj observant. •nm, f observer.

observation /ɔpsɛʀvasjɔ̃/ nf observation; (remarque) remark, comment; (reproche) criticism; (obéissance) observance; **en** ~ under observation.

observer /ɔpsɛʀve/ **1** vt (regarder) observe; (surveiller) watch, observe; (remarquer) notice, observe; **faire** ~ **qch** point sth out (**à** to).

obsession /ɔpsesjɔ̃/ nf obsession.

obstacle /ɔpstakl/ nm obstacle; (pour cheval) fence, jump; (pour athlète) hurdle; **faire ~ à** stand in the way of, obstruct.

obstétrique /ɔpstetʀik/ nf obstetrics (+ sg).

obstiné, ~e /ɔpstine/ adj obstinate.

obstiner (s') /(s)ɔpstine/ **1** vpr persist (**à** in).

obstruction /ɔpstʀyksjɔ̃/ nf obstruction; (de conduit) blockage.

obstruer /ɔpstʀye/ **1** vt obstruct.

obtenir /ɔptəniʀ/ **58** vt get, obtain. **obtention** nf obtaining.

obus /ɔby/ nm shell.

occasion /ɔkazjɔ̃/ nf opportunity (**de faire** of doing); (circonstance) occasion; (achat) bargain; (article non neuf) second-hand buy; **à l'~** sometimes; **d'~** second-hand. **occasionnel, ~le** adj occasional.

occasionner /ɔkazjɔne/ **1** vt cause.

occident /ɔksidɑ̃/ nm (direction) west; **l'O~** the West.

occidental, ~e (mpl **~aux**) /ɔksidɑ̃tal, -o/ adj western. **O~, ~e** (mpl **~aux**) nm, f westerner.

occulte /ɔkylt/ adj occult.

occupant, ~e /ɔkypɑ̃, -t/ nm, f occupant. •nm (Mil) forces of occupation.

occupation /ɔkypasjɔ̃/ nf occupation.

occupé, ~e /ɔkype/ adj busy; (place, pays) occupied; (téléphone) engaged, busy; (toilettes) engaged.

occuper /ɔkype/ **1** vt occupy; (poste) hold; (espace, temps) take up. ∎**s'~** vpr (s'affairer) keep busy (**à faire** doing); **s'~ de** (personne, problème) take care of; (bureau, firme) be in charge of; (se mêler) **occupe-toi de tes affaires** mind your own business.

occurrence: en l'~ /ɑ̃lɔkyʀɑ̃s/ loc in this case.

océan /ɔseɑ̃/ nm ocean.

Océanie /ɔseani/ nf Oceania.

ocre /ɔkʀ/ adj inv ochre.

octante /ɔktɑ̃t/ adj eighty.

octet /ɔktɛ/ nm byte.

octobre /ɔktɔbʀ/ nm October.

octogone /ɔktɔgɔn/ nm octagon.

octroyer /ɔktʀwaje/ **31** vt grant.

oculaire /ɔkylɛʀ/ adj **témoin ~** eye-witness; **troubles ~s** eye trouble.

oculiste /ɔkylist/ nmf ophthalmologist.

odeur /ɔdœʀ/ nf smell.

odieux, -ieuse /ɔdjø, -z/ adj odious.

odorant, ~e /ɔdɔʀɑ̃, -t/ adj sweetsmelling.

odorat /ɔdɔʀa/ nm sense of smell.

œil (pl **yeux**) /œj, jø/ nm eye; **à l'~** **1** for free; **à mes yeux** in my view; **faire de l'~ à** make eyes at; **faire les gros yeux à** glare at; **ouvrir l'~** keep one's eyes open; **~ poché** black eye; **fermer les yeux** shut one's eyes; (fig) turn a blind eye.

œillères /œjɛʀ/ nfpl blinkers.

œillet /œjɛ/ nm (plante) carnation; (trou) eyelet.

œuf (pl **~s**) /œf, ø/ nm egg; **~ à la coque/dur/sur le plat** boiled/ hard-boiled/fried egg.

œuvre /œvʀ/ nf (ouvrage, travail) work; **~ d'art** work of art; (**~ de bienfaisance**) charity; **être à l'~** be at work; **mettre en ~** (réforme, moyens) implement; **mise en ~** implementation. •nm (ensemble spécifié) **l'~ entier de Beethoven** the complete works of Beethoven.

œuvrer /œvʀe/ **1** vi work.

offense /ɔfɑ̃s/ nf insult.

offenser /ɔfɑ̃se/ **1** vt offend. ∎**s'~** vpr take offence (**de** at).

offensive /ɔfɑ̃siv/ nf offensive.

offert, ~e /ɔfɛʀ, -t/ ▷**OFFRIR 21**.

office /ɔfis/ nm office; (Relig)

service; (de cuisine) pantry; **faire ∼ de** act as; **d'∼** without consultation, automatically; **∼ du tourisme** tourist information office.

officiel, ∼le /ɔfisjɛl/ adj official. ●nm official.

officier /ɔfisje/ 45 vi (Relig) officiate. ●nm officer.

officieux, -ieuse /ɔfisjø, -z/ adj unofficial.

offre /ɔfʀ/ nf offer; (aux enchères) bid; **l'∼ et la demande** supply and demand; **'∼s d'emploi'** 'situations vacant'.

offrir /ɔfʀiʀ/ 21 vt offer (**de faire** to do); (cadeau) give; (acheter) buy; **∼ à boire à** (chez soi) give a drink to; (au café) buy a drink for. ■ **s'∼** vpr (se proposer) offer oneself (**comme** as); (solution) present itself; (s'acheter) treat oneself to.

ogive /ɔʒiv/ nf **∼ nucléaire** nuclear warhead.

OGM (**organisme génétiquement modifié**) genetically modified organism.

oie /wa/ nf goose.

oignon* /ɔɲɔ̃/ nm (légume) onion; (de fleur) bulb.

oiseau (pl **∼x**) /wazo/ nm bird.

oisif, -ive /wazif, -v/ adj idle.

olive /ɔliv/ nf & adj inv olive. **olivier** nm olive tree.

olympique /ɔlɛ̃pik/ adj Olympic.

ombrage /ɔ̃bʀaʒ/ nm shade; **prendre ∼ de** take offence at. **ombragé, ∼e** adj shady.

ombre /ɔ̃bʀ/ nf (pénombre) shade; (contour) shadow; (soupçon: fig) hint, shadow; **dans l'∼** (agir, rester) behind the scenes; **faire de l'∼ à qn** be in sb's light.

ombrelle /ɔ̃bʀɛl/ nf parasol.

omelette /ɔmlɛt/ nf omelette.

omettre /ɔmɛtʀ/ 42 vt omit, leave out.

omnibus /ɔmnibys/ nm stopping *ou* local train.

omoplate /ɔmɔplat/ nf shoulder blade.

on /ɔ̃/ pron (tu, vous) you; (nous) we; (ils, elles) they; (les gens) people, they; (quelqu'un) someone; (indéterminé) one, you; **∼ dit** people say, they say, it is said; **∼ m'a demandé mon avis** I was asked for my opinion.

oncle /ɔ̃kl/ nm uncle.

onctueux, -euse /ɔktɥø, -z/ adj smooth.

onde /ɔ̃d/ nf wave; **∼s courtes/ longues** short/long wave; **sur les ∼s** on the air.

on-dit /ɔ̃di/ nm inv **les ∼** hearsay.

onduler /ɔ̃dyle/ 1 vi undulate; (cheveux) be wavy.

onéreux, -euse /ɔneʀø, -z/ adj costly.

ONG abrév f (**organisation non gouvernmentale**) NGO, non-governmental organization.

ongle /ɔ̃gl/ nm (finger) nail; **∼ de pied** toenail; **se faire les ∼s** do one's nails.

ont /ɔ̃/ ▷AVOIR 5.

ONU abrév f (**Organisation des Nations unies**) UN.

onze /ɔ̃z/ adj & nm eleven. **onzième** adj & nm eleventh.

OPA abrév f (**offre publique d'achat**) takeover bid.

opéra /ɔpeʀa/ nm opera; (édifice) opera house. **opéra-comique** (pl **opéras-comiques**) nm light opera.

opérateur, -trice /ɔpeʀatœʀ, -tʀis/ nm, f operator.

opération /ɔpeʀasjɔ̃/ nf operation; (Comm) deal; (calcul) calculation; **∼ escargot** slow-moving protest convoy.

opératoire /ɔpeʀatwaʀ/ adj (Méd) surgical; **bloc ∼** operating suite.

opérer /ɔpeʀe/ 14 vt (personne)

operate on; (exécuter) carry out, make; **∼ qn d'une tumeur** operate on sb to remove a tumour; **se faire ∼** have surgery ou an operation. •vi (Méd) operate; (faire effet) work. ∎ **s'∼** vpr (se produire) occur.

opiniâtre /ɔpinjɑtʀ/ adj tenacious.

opinion /ɔpinjɔ̃/ nf opinion.

opportuniste /ɔpɔʀtynist/ nmf opportunist.

opposant, ∼e /ɔpozɑ̃, -t/ nm, f opponent.

opposé, ∼e /ɔpoze/ adj (sens, angle, avis) opposite; (factions) opposing; (intérêts) conflicting; **être ∼ à** be opposed to. •nm opposite; **à l'∼ de** (contrairement à) contrary to, unlike.

opposer /ɔpoze/ **1** vt (objets) place opposite each other; (personnes) match, oppose; (contraster) contrast; (résistance, argument) put up. ∎ **s'∼** vpr (personnes) confront each other; (styles) contrast; **s'∼ à** oppose.

opposition /ɔpozisjɔ̃/ nf opposition; **par ∼ à** in contrast with; **entrer en ∼ avec** come into conflict with; **faire ∼ à un chèque** stop a cheque.

oppressant, ∼e /ɔpʀesɑ̃, -t/ adj oppressive.

opprimer /ɔpʀime/ **1** vt oppress.

opter /ɔpte/ **1** vi **∼ pour** opt for.

opticien, ∼ne /ɔptisjɛ̃, -ɛn/ nm, f optician.

optimisme /ɔptimism/ nm optimism.

optimiste /ɔptimist/ nmf optimist. •adj optimistic.

option /ɔpsjɔ̃/ nf option.

optique /ɔptik/ adj (verre) optical. •nf (science) optics (+ sg); (perspective) perspective.

or[1] /ɔʀ/ nm gold; **d'∼** golden; **en ∼** gold; (occasion) golden.

or[2] /ɔʀ/ conj now, well; (indiquant une

opposition) and yet.

orage /ɔʀaʒ/ nm (thunder)storm. **orageux, -euse** adj stormy.

oral, ∼e (mpl **-aux**) /ɔʀal, -o/ adj oral. •nm (pl **-aux**) oral.

orange /ɔʀɑ̃ʒ/ adj inv orange; (Aut) (feu) amber; (US) yellow. •nf orange. **orangeade** nf orangeade. **oranger** nm orange tree.

orateur, -trice /ɔʀatœʀ, -tʀis/ nm, f speaker.

orbite /ɔʀbit/ nf orbit; (d'œil) socket.

orchestre /ɔʀkɛstʀ/ nm orchestra; (de jazz) band; (parterre) stalls.

ordinaire /ɔʀdinɛʀ/ adj ordinary; (habituel) usual; (qualité) standard; (médiocre) very average. •nm **l'∼** the ordinary; (nourriture) the standard fare; **d'∼, à l'∼** usually. **ordinairement** adv usually.

ordinateur /ɔʀdinatœʀ/ nm computer; **∼ personnel/de bureau** personal/desktop computer; **∼ portable** laptop (computer); **∼ hôte** (Internet) host.

ordonnance /ɔʀdɔnɑ̃s/ nf (ordre, décret) order; (de médecin) prescription.

ordonné, ∼e /ɔʀdɔne/ adj tidy.

ordonner /ɔʀdɔne/ **1** vt order (**à qn de** sb to); (agencer) arrange; (Méd) prescribe; (prêtre) ordain.

ordre /ɔʀdʀ/ nm order; (propreté) tidiness; **aux ∼s de qn** at sb's disposal; **avoir de l'∼** be tidy; **en ∼** tidy, in order; **de premier ∼** first-rate; **d'∼ officiel** of an official nature; **l'∼ du jour** (programme) agenda; **mettre de l'∼ dans** tidy up; **jusqu'à nouvel ∼** until further notice; **un ∼ de grandeur** an approximate idea.

ordure /ɔʀdyʀ/ nf filth; **∼s** (détritus) rubbish; (US) garbage;

~s **ménagères** household refuse.

oreille /ɔʀɛj/ nf ear.

oreiller /ɔʀeje/ nm pillow.

oreillons /ɔʀejɔ̃/ nmpl mumps.

orfèvre /ɔʀfɛvʀ/ nm goldsmith.

organe /ɔʀgan/ nm organ.

organigramme /ɔʀganigʀam/ nm organization chart; (Ordinat) flowchart.

organique /ɔʀganik/ adj organic.

organisateur, -trice /ɔʀganizatœʀ, -tʀis/ nm, f organizer.

organisation /ɔʀganizasjɔ̃/ nf organization.

organiser /ɔʀganize/ **1** vt organize. ■ **s'**~ vpr organize oneself, get organized.

organisme /ɔʀganism/ nm body, organism.

orge /ɔʀʒ/ nf barley.

orgelet /ɔʀʒəlɛ/ nm sty.

orgue /ɔʀg/ nm organ; ~ **de Barbarie** barrel-organ. **orgues** nfpl organ.

orgueil /ɔʀgœj/ nm pride. **orgueilleux, -euse** adj proud.

orient /ɔʀjã/ nm (direction) east; **l'O**~ the Orient.

oriental, ~e (mpl -aux) /ɔʀjãtal, -o/ adj eastern; (de l'Orient) oriental. **O**~, ~**e** (mpl -aux) nm, f Asian.

orientation /ɔʀjãtasjɔ̃/ nf direction; (tendance politique) leanings (+ pl); (de maison) aspect; (Sport) orienteering; ~ **professionnelle** careers advice; ~ **scolaire** curriculum counselling.

orienter /ɔʀjãte/ **1** vt position; (personne) direct. ■ **s'**~ vpr (se repérer) find one's bearings; **s'**~ **vers** turn towards.

origan /ɔʀigã/ nm oregano.

originaire /ɔʀiʒinɛʀ/ adj **être** ~ **de** be a native of.

original, ~e (mpl -aux) /ɔʀiʒinal, -o/ adj original; (curieux) eccentric. ● nm (œuvre) original. ● nm, f eccentric. **originalité** nf originality; eccentricity.

origine /ɔʀiʒin/ nf origin; **à l'**~ originally; **d'**~ (pièce, pneu) original; **être d'**~ **noble** come from a noble background.

originel, ~le /ɔʀiʒinɛl/ adj original.

orme /ɔʀm/ nm elm.

ornement /ɔʀnəmã/ nm ornament.

orner /ɔʀne/ **1** vt decorate.

orphelin, ~e /ɔʀfəlɛ̃, -in/ nm, f orphan. ● adj orphaned. **orphelinat** nm orphanage.

orteil /ɔʀtɛj/ nm toe.

orthodoxe /ɔʀtɔdɔks/ adj orthodox.

orthographe /ɔʀtɔgʀaf/ nf spelling.

ortie /ɔʀti/ nf nettle.

os /ɔs, o/ nm inv bone.

OS abrév m ▶**OUVRIER SPÉCIALISÉ**.

osciller /ɔsile/ **1** vi sway; (Tech) oscillate; (hésiter) waver; (fluctuer) fluctuate.

osé, ~e /oze/ adj daring.

oseille /ozɛj/ nf (plante) sorrel.

oser /oze/ **1** vi dare.

osier /ozje/ nm wicker.

ossature /ɔsatyʀ/ nf skeleton, frame.

ossements /ɔsmã/ nmpl bones, remains.

osseux, -euse /ɔsø, -z/ adj bony; (Méd) bone.

otage /ɔtaʒ/ nm hostage.

OTAN /ɔtã/ abrév f (**Organisation du traité de l'Atlantique Nord**) NATO.

otarie /ɔtaʀi/ nf eared seal.

ôter /ote/ **1** vt remove (**à qn**

o

from sb); (déduire) take away.

otite /ɔtit/ nf ear infection.

ou /u/ conj or; ~ **bien** or else; ~ **(bien)... ~ (bien)...** either... or...; **vous ~ moi** either you or me.

où /u/ pron where; (dans lequel) in which; (sur lequel) on which; (auquel) at which; **d'~** from which; (pour cette raison) hence; **par ~** through which; **~ qu'il soit** wherever he may be; **juste au moment** ~ just as; **le jour ~** the day when. ●adv where; **d'~?** where from?

ouate /wat/ nf cotton wool; (US) absorbent cotton.

oubli /ubli/ nm forgetfulness; (trou de mémoire) lapse of memory; (négligence) oversight; **tomber dans l'~** sink into oblivion.

oublier /ublije/ 45 vt forget; (omettre) leave out, forget. ▪ s'~ vpr (chose) be forgotten.

ouest /wɛst/ adj inv (façade, côte) west; (frontière, zone) western. ●nm west; **l'~ de l'Europe** western Europe; **vent d'~** westerly (wind); **aller vers l'~** go west; **l'O~** the West; **de l'O~** western.

oui /wi/ adv & nm inv yes.

ouï-dire: par ~ /parwidir/ loc by hearsay.

ouïe /wi/ nf hearing; (de poisson) gill.

ouragan /uragã/ nm hurricane.

ourlet /urlɛ/ nm hem.

ours /urs/ nm bear; ~ **blanc** polar bear; **~ en peluche** teddy bear.

outil /uti/ nm tool. **outillage** nm tools (+ pl). **outiller** 1 vt equip.

outrage /utraʒ/ nm (grave) insult.

outrance /utrãs/ nf **à ~** excessively. **outrancier, -ière** adj extreme.

outre /utr/ prép besides. ●adv

passer ~ pay no heed; **~ mesure** unduly; **en ~** in addition. **outre-mer** adv overseas.

outrepasser /utrəpase/ 1 vt exceed.

outrer /utre/ 1 vt exaggerate; (indigner) incense.

ouvert, ~e /uvɛr, -t/ adj open; (gaz, radio) on. ●▶OUVRIR 21.

ouverture /uvɛrtyr/ nf opening; (Mus) overture; (Photo) aperture; **~s** (offres) overtures; **~ d'esprit** open-mindedness.

ouvrable /uvrabl/ adj **jour ~** working day; **aux heures ~s** during business hours.

ouvrage /uvraʒ/ nm (travail, livre) work; (couture) (piece of) needlework.

ouvre-boîtes* /uvrəbwat/ nm inv tin-opener.

ouvre-bouteilles* /uvrəbutɛj/ nm inv bottle-opener.

ouvreur, -euse /uvrœr, -øz/ nm, f usherette.

ouvrier, -ière /uvrije, -jɛr/ nm, f worker; **~ qualifié/spécialisé** skilled/unskilled worker. ●adj working-class; (conflit) industrial; **syndicat ~** trade union.

ouvrir /uvrir/ 21 vt open (up); (gaz, robinet) turn on. ●vi open (up). ▪ s'~ vpr open (up); **s'~ à qn** open one's heart to sb.

ovaire /ɔvɛr/ nm ovary.

ovale /ɔval/ adj & nm oval.

ovni /ɔvni/ abrév m (**objet volant non-identifié**) UFO.

ovule /ɔvyl/ nm (à féconder) ovum; (gynécologique) pessary.

oxygène /ɔksiʒɛn/ nm oxygen.

oxygéner (s') /(s)ɔksiʒene/ 14 vpr get some fresh air.

ozone /ozon/ nf ozone; **la couche d'~** the ozone layer.

Pp

pacifique /pasifik/ adj peaceful; (personne) peaceable; (Géog) Pacific. **P~** nm **le P~** the Pacific.

pacotille /pakɔtij/ nf junk, rubbish.

PACS abrév nm (**pacte de solidarité**) contract of civil union.

pacser (se) /səpakse/ **1** vpr sign a contract of civil union (PACS).

pagaie /pagɛ/ nf paddle.

pagaille /pagaj/ nf **1** mess, shambles (+ sg).

page /paʒ/ nf page; **mise en ~** layout; **tourner la ~** turn over a new leaf; **être à la ~** be up to date; **~ d'accueil** (Internet) home page.

paie /pɛ/ nf pay.

paiement /pɛmɑ̃/ nm payment.

païen, ~ne /pajɛ̃, -ɛn/ adj & nm, f pagan.

paillasson /pajasɔ̃/ nm doormat.

paille /paj/ nf straw. ●adj (cheveux) straw-coloured.

paillette /pajɛt/ nf (sur robe) sequin; (de savon) flake.

pain /pɛ̃/ nm bread; (miche) loaf (of bread); (de savon, cire) bar; **~ d'épices** gingerbread; **~ grillé** toast.

pair, ~e /pɛʀ/ adj (nombre) even. ●nm (personne) peer; **aller de ~** go together (**avec** with); **au ~** (jeune fille) au pair. **paire** nf pair.

paisible /pezibl/ adj peaceful.

paître* /pɛtʀ/ **44** vi graze.

paix /pɛ/ nf peace; **fiche-moi la ~!** **1** leave me alone!

Pakistan /pakistɑ̃/ nm Pakistan.

palace /palas/ nm luxury hotel.

palais /palɛ/ nm palace; (Anat) palate; **~ de Justice** law courts; **~ des sports** sports stadium.

pâle /pɑl/ adj pale.

Palestine /palɛstin/ nf Palestine.

palier /palje/ nm (d'escalier) landing; (étape) stage.

pâlir /pɑliʀ/ **2** vt/i (turn) pale.

palissade /palisad/ nf fence.

pallier /palje/ **45** vt compensate for.

palmarès /palmaʀɛs/ nm list of prize-winners.

palme /palm/ nf palm leaf; (de nageur) flipper. **palmé, ~e** adj (patte) webbed.

palmier /palmje/ nm palm (tree).

palper /palpe/ **1** vt feel.

palpiter /palpite/ **1** vi (battre) pound; (frémir) quiver.

paludisme /palydism/ nm malaria.

pamplemousse /pɑ̃pləmus/ nm grapefruit.

panaché, ~e /panaʃe/ adj (bariolé, mélangé) motley; **glace ~e** mixed-flavour ice cream. ●nm shandy.

pancarte /pɑ̃kaʀt/ nf sign; (de manifestant) placard.

pané, ~e /pane/ adj breaded.

panier /panje/ nm basket; (de basket-ball) basket; **mettre au ~** **1** throw out; **~ à salade** salad shaker; (fourgon **1**) police van.

panique /panik/ nf panic. **paniquer** **1** vi panic.

panne /pan/ nf breakdown; **être**

en ~ have broken down; **être en ~ sèche** have run out of petrol; **~ d'électricité** *ou* **de courant** power failure.

panneau (pl **~x**) /pano/ nm sign; (publicitaire) hoarding; (de porte) panel; (**~ d'affichage**) notice board; (**~ de signalisation**) road sign.

panoplie /panɔpli/ nf (jouet) outfit; (gamme) range.

pansement /pɑ̃smɑ̃/ nm dressing; **~ adhésif** plaster. **panser** 1 vt (plaie) dress; (personne) dress the wound(s) of; (cheval) groom.

pantalon /pɑ̃talɔ̃/ nm trousers (+ pl).

panthère /pɑ̃tɛʀ/ nf panther.

pantin /pɑ̃tɛ̃/ nm puppet.

pantomime /pɑ̃tɔmim/ nf mime; (spectacle) mime show.

pantoufle /pɑ̃tufl/ nf slipper.

paon /pɑ̃/ nm peacock.

papa /papa/ nm dad(dy).

pape /pap/ nm pope.

paperasse /papʀas/ nf (péj) bumf.

papeterie* /papetʀi/ nf (magasin) stationer's shop.

papier /papje/ nm paper; (formulaire) form; **~s (d'identité)** (identity) papers; **~ absorbant** kitchen paper; **~ aluminium** tin foil; **~ buvard** blotting paper; **~ cadeau** wrapping paper; **~ calque** tracing paper; **~ carbone** carbon paper; **~ collant** adhesive tape; **~ hygiénique** toilet paper; **~ journal** newspaper; **~ à lettres** writing paper; **~ mâché** papier mâché; **~ peint** wallpaper; **~ de verre** sandpaper.

papillon /papijɔ̃/ nm butterfly; (contravention 🔢) parking-ticket; **~ de nuit** moth.

papoter /papote/ 1 vi 🔢 chatter.

paquebot /pakbo/ nm liner.

pâquerette /pɑkʀɛt/ nf daisy.

Pâques /pɑk/ nfpl & nm Easter.

paquet /pakɛ/ nm packet; (de cartes) pack; (colis) parcel; **un ~ de** (beaucoup 🔢) a mass of.

par /paʀ/ prép by; (à travers) through; (motif) out of, from; (provenance) from; **commencer/finir ~ qch** begin/end with sth; **commencer/finir ~ faire** begin by/end up (by) doing; **~ an/mois** a *ou* per year/month; **~ jour** a day; **~ personne** each, per person; **~ avion** (lettre) (by) airmail; **~ci, ~là** here and there; **~ contre** on the other hand; **~ ici/là** this/that way.

parachute /paʀaʃyt/ nm parachute. **parachutiste** nmf parachutist; (Mil) paratrooper.

parader /paʀade/ 1 vi show off.

paradis /paʀadi/ nm (Relig) heaven; (lieu idéal) paradise; **~ fiscal** tax haven.

paradoxal, ~e (mpl **-aux**) /paʀadɔksal, -o/ adj paradoxical.

paraffine /paʀafin/ nf paraffin wax.

parages /paʀaʒ/ nmpl **dans les ~** around.

paragraphe /paʀagʀaf/ nm paragraph.

paraître* /paʀɛtʀ/ 🔢 vi (se montrer) appear; (sembler) seem, appear; (ouvrage) be published, come out; **faire ~** (ouvrage) bring out; **il paraît qu'ils...** apparently they...; **oui, il paraît** so I hear.

parallèle /paʀalɛl/ adj parallel; (illégal) unofficial. ●nm parallel; **faire le ~** make a connection. ●nf parallel (line).

paralyser /paʀalize/ 1 vt paralyse. **paralysie** nf paralysis.

paramètre /paʀamɛtʀ/ nm parameter.

parapente /paʀapɑ̃t/ nm paraglider; (activité) paragliding.

parapharmacie /paʀafaʀmasi/ nf toiletries and vitamins (tpl.)

parapher /paʀafe/ **1** vi initial; (signer) sign.

parapluie /paʀaplɥi/ nm umbrella.

parasite /paʀazit/ nm parasite; ~**s** (radio) interference (+ sg).

parasol /paʀasɔl/ nm sunshade.

paratonnerre /paʀatɔnɛʀ/ nm lightning conductor ou rod.

paravent /paʀavã/ nm screen.

parc /paʀk/ nm park; (de bétail) pen; (de bébé) play-pen; (entrepôt) depot; ~ **de loisirs** theme park; ~ **relais** park and ride; ~ **de stationnement** car park.

parce que /paʀsk(ə)/ conj because.

parchemin /paʀʃəmɛ̃/ nm parchment.

parcmètre /paʀkmɛtʀ/ nm parking meter.

parcourir /paʀkuʀiʀ/ **20** vt travel ou go through; (distance) travel; (des yeux) glance at ou over.

parcours /paʀkuʀ/ nm route; (voyage) journey.

par-delà /paʀdəla/ prép beyond.

par-derrière /paʀdɛʀjɛʀ/ adv (attaquer) from behind; (critiquer) behind sb's back.

par-dessous /paʀdəsu/ prép & adv under (neath).

pardessus /paʀdəsy/ nm overcoat.

par-dessus /paʀdəsy/ prép & adv over; ~ **bord** overboard; ~ **le marché 1** into the bargain; ~ **tout** above all.

par-devant /paʀdəvã/ adv (passer) by the front.

pardon /paʀdɔ̃/ nm forgiveness; **(je vous demande)** ~**!** (I am) sorry!; (pour demander qch) excuse me.

pardonner /paʀdɔne/ **1** vt forgive; ~ **qch à qn** forgive sb for sth.

pare-brise* /paʀbʀiz/ nm inv windscreen.

pare-chocs* /paʀʃɔk/ nm inv bumper.

pareil, ~le /paʀɛj/ adj similar (**à** to); (tel) such (a); **c'est** ~ it's the same; **ce n'est pas** ~ it's not the same thing. ● nm, f equal. ● adv **1** the same.

parent, ~e /paʀã, -t/ adj related (**de** to). ● nm, f relative, relation; ~**s** (père et mère) parents; ~ **isolé** single parent; **réunion de** ~**s d'élèves** parents' evening.

parenté /paʀãte/ nf relationship.

parenthèse /paʀãtɛz/ nf bracket, parenthesis; (fig) digression.

parer /paʀe/ **1** vt (esquiver) parry; (orner) adorn. ● vi ~ **à** deal with; ~ **au plus pressé** tackle the most urgent things first.

paresse /paʀɛs/ nf laziness.

paresseux, -euse /paʀɛsø, -z/ adj lazy. ● nm, f lazy person.

parfait, ~e /paʀfɛ, -t/ adj perfect. **parfaitement** adv perfectly; (bien sûr) absolutely.

parfois /paʀfwa/ adv sometimes.

parfum /paʀfœ̃/ nm (senteur) scent; (substance) perfume, scent; (goût) flavour. **parfumé, ~e** adj fragrant; (savon) scented; (thé) flavoured.

parfumer /paʀfyme/ **1** vt (embaumer) scent; (gâteau) flavour. ■ **se** ~ vpr put on one's perfume. **parfumerie** nf (produits) perfumes; (boutique) perfume shop.

pari /paʀi/ nm bet.

Paris /paʀi/ npr Paris.

parisien, ~ne /paʀizjɛ̃, -ɛn/ adj Parisian; (banlieue) Paris. **P~,** ~**ne** nm, f Parisian.

parking /paʀkiŋ/ nm car park.

parlement /paʀləmã/ nm parliament.

parlementaire /paʀləmɑ̃tɛʀ/ adj parliamentary. ● nmf Member of Parliament.

p

parlementer /parləmɑ̃te/ **1** vi
negotiate.

parler /parle/ **1** vi talk (**à** to); ~
de talk about; **tu parles d'un
avantage!** call that a benefit!;
de quoi ça parle? what is it
about? •vt (langue) speak; (politique,
affaires) talk. ∎ **se** ~ vpr (personnes)
talk (to each other); (langue) be
spoken. •nm speech; (dialecte)
dialect.

parmi /parmi/ prép among(st).

paroi /parwa/ nf wall; ~
rocheuse rock face.

paroisse /parwas/ nf parish.

parole /parɔl/ nf (mot, promesse)
word; (langage) speech;
demander la ~ ask to speak;
prendre la ~ (begin to) speak;
tenir ~ keep one's word; **croire
qn sur** ~ take sb's word for it.

parquet /parkε/ nm (parquet)
floor; **lame de** ~ floorboard; **le**
~ (Jur) prosecution.

parrain /parɛ̃/ nm godfather; (fig)
sponsor.

parsemer /parsəme/ **6** vt strew
(**de** with).

part /par/ nf share, part; **à** ~ (de
côté) aside; (séparément) separate;
(excepté) apart from; **d'une** ~ on
the one hand; **d'autre** ~ on the
other hand; (de plus) moreover;
de la ~ **de** from; **de toutes** ~s
from all sides; **de** ~ **et d'autre**
on both sides; **faire** ~ **à qn**
inform sb (**de** of); **faire la** ~
des choses make allowances;
prendre ~ **à** take part in; (joie,
douleur) share; **pour ma** ~ as
for me.

partage /partaʒ/ nm (division)
dividing; (répartition) sharing out;
recevoir qch en ~ be left sth in
a will.

partager /partaʒe/ **40** vt divide;
(distribuer) share out; (avoir en
commun) share. ∎ **se** ~ **qch** vpr
share sth.

partenaire /partənεr/ nmf
partner.

parterre /partεr/ nm flower bed;
(Théât) stalls.

parti /parti/ nm (Pol) party;
(décision) decision; (en mariage)
match; ~ **pris** bias; **prendre** ~
get involved; prendre ~ **pour
qn** side with sb; **j'en ai pris
mon** ~ I've come to terms
with that.

partial, -e (mpl **-iaux**) /parsjal,
-jo/ adj biased.

participe /partisip/ nm (Gram)
participle.

participant, ~e /partisipɑ̃, -t/
nm, f participant (**à** in).

participation /partisipasjɔ̃/ nf
participation; (financière)
contribution; (d'un artiste)
appearance.

participer /partisipe/ **1** vi ~ **à**
take part in, participate in;
(profits, frais) share.

particule /partikyl/ nf particle.

particulier, -ière /partikylje,
-jεr/ adj (spécifique) particular;
(bizarre) unusual; (privé) private;
rien de ~ nothing special. •nm
private individual; **en** ~ in
particular, particularly.
particulièrement adv
particularly.

partie /parti/ nf part; (cartes, Sport)
game; (Jur) party; **une** ~ **de
pêche** a fishing trip; **en** ~
partly, in part; **en grande** ~
largely; **faire** ~ **de** be part of;
(adhérer à) be a member of; **faire**
~ **intégrante de** be an integral
part of.

partiel, ~le /parsjεl/ adj partial.
•nm (Univ) exam based on a
module.

partir /partir/ **46** vi (aux être) go;
(quitter un lieu) leave, go; (tache)
come out; (bouton) come off; (coup
de feu) go off; (commencer) start; ~
pour le Brésil leave for Brazil;
~ **du principe que** work on the

assumption that; **à ~de** from; **à ~ de maintenant** from now on.

partisan, ~e /paʀtizɑ̃, -an/ nm, f supporter. ●nm (Mil) partisan; **être ~ de** be in favour of.

partition /paʀtisjɔ̃/ nf (Mus) score.

partout /paʀtu/ adv everywhere; **~ où** wherever.

paru /paʀy/ ▷**PARAÎTRE** 18.

parure /paʀyʀ/ nf finery; (bijoux) set of jewels; (de draps) set.

parution /paʀysjɔ̃/ nf publication.

parvenir /paʀvəniʀ/ 58 vi (aux être) **~ à** reach; **~ à faire** manage to do; **faire ~** send.

parvenu, ~e /paʀvəny/ nm, f upstart.

pas¹ /pɑ/

▶ Pour les expressions comme **pas encore, pas mal**, etc. ▷**encore, mal** etc.

● adverbe
····▸ not; **ne ~** not; **je ne sais ~** I don't know; **je ne pense ~** I don't think so; **il a aimé, moi ~** he liked it, I didn't; **~ cher/ poli** cheap/impolite.

····▸ **~ du tout** not at all; **~ de chance!** tough luck!

····▸ **on a bien ri, ~ vrai?** 1 we had a good laugh, didn't we?

! In spoken colloquial French ■ ne... pas is often shortened to **pas**. You will hear **j'ai pas compris** instead of **je n'ai pas compris** (I didn't understand). NB This is not correct written French.

pas² /pɑ/ nm step; (bruit) footstep; (trace) footprint; (vitesse) pace; **à deux ~ (de)** a step away (from); **marcher au ~** march; **rouler au ~** move very slowly; **à ~ de loup** stealthily; **faire les cent ~** walk up and down; **faire le premier ~** make the first move; **~ de porte** doorstep; **~**

de vis (Tech) thread.

passage /pɑsaʒ/ nm (traversée) crossing; (visite) visit; (chemin) way, passage; (d'une œuvre) passage; **de ~** (voyageur) visiting; (amant) casual; **la tempête a tout emporté sur son ~** the storm swept everything away; **~ clouté** pedestrian crossing; **~ interdit** (panneau) no thoroughfare; **~ à niveau** level crossing; **~ souterrain** subway.

passager, -ère /pɑsaʒe, -ɛʀ/ adj temporary. ●nm, f passenger; **~ clandestin** stowaway.

passant, ~e /pɑsɑ̃, -t/ adj (rue) busy. ●nm, f passer-by. ●nm (anneau) loop.

passe /pɑs/ nf pass; **bonne/mauvaise ~** good/bad patch; **en ~ de** on the road to.

passé, ~e /pɑse/ adj (révolu) past; (dernier) last; (fané) faded; **~ de mode** out of fashion. ●nm past. ●prép after.

passe-partout* /pɑspaʀtu/ nm inv master-key. ●adj inv for all occasions.

passeport /pɑspɔʀ/ nm passport.

passer /pɑse/ 1 vi (aux être ou avoir) go past, pass; (aller) go; (venir) come; (temps, douleur) pass; (film) be on; (couleur) fade; **laisser ~** let through; (occasion) miss; **~ devant** (à pied) walk past; (en voiture) drive past; **~ par** go through; **où est-il passé?** where did he get to?; **~ outre** take no notice; **passons!** let's forget about it!; **passons aux choses sérieuses** let's turn to serious matters; **~ dans la classe supérieure** go up a year; **~ pour un idiot** look a fool. ●vt (aux avoir) (franchir) pass, cross; (donner) pass, hand; (temps) spend; (enfiler) slip on; (vidéo, disque) put on; (examen) take, sit; (commande) place; (faire) **~ le temps** while away the time; **~ l'aspirateur** hoover; **~ un coup de fil à qn** give sb a ring; **je vous passe**

Mme X (par le standard) I'll put you through to Mrs X; (en donnant l'appareil) I'll pass you over to Mrs X; ~ **qch en fraude** smuggle sth. ■ **se** ~ vpr happen, take place; (s'écouler) go by; **se** ~ **de** go *ou* do without.

passerelle /pasʀɛl/ nf footbridge; (de navire) gangway; (d'avion) (passenger) footbridge; (Internet) gateway.

passe-temps* /pɑstɑ̃/ nm inv pastime.

passif, -ive /pasif, -v/ adj passive. ●nm (Comm) liabilities.

passion /pasjɔ̃/ nf passion. **passionnant,** ~**e** adj fascinating.

passionné, ~**e** /pasjɔne/ adj passionate; **être** ~ **de** have a passion for.

passionner /pasjɔne/ ▪ vt fascinate. ■ **se** ~ **pour** vpr have a passion for.

passoire /paswaʀ/ nf (à thé) strainer; (à légumes) colander.

pastèque /pastɛk/ nf watermelon.

pasteur /pastœʀ/ nm (Relig) minister.

pastille /pastij/ nf (médicament) pastille, lozenge.

patate /patat/ nf 🔢 spud; ~ **(douce)** sweet potato.

patauger /patoʒe/ 🔢 vi splash about.

pâte /pɑt/ nf paste; (à gâteau) dough; (à tarte) pastry; (à frire) batter; ~**s (alimentaires)** pasta (+ sg.) ~ **à modeler** Plasticine®; ~ **d'amandes** marzipan.

pâté /pate/ nm (Culin) pâté; (d'encre) blot; (de sable) sandpie; ~ **en croûte** ≈ pie; ~ **de maisons** block (of houses).

pâtée /pate/ nf feed, mash.

patente /patɑ̃t/ nf trade licence.

paternel, ~**le** /patɛʀnɛl/ adj paternal. **paternité** nf paternity.

pathétique /patetik/ adj moving.

patience /pasjɑ̃s/ nf patience. **patient,** ~**e** adj & nm, f patient. **patienter** ▪ vi wait.

patin /patɛ̃/ nm skate; ~ **à roulettes** roller-skate.

patinage /patinaʒ/ nm skating. **patiner** ▪ vi skate; (roue) spin. **patinoire** nf ice rink.

pâtisserie /pɑtisʀi/ nf cake shop; (gâteau) pastry; (secteur) cake making. **pâtissier, -ière** nm, f confectioner, pastry-cook.

patrie /patʀi/ nf homeland.

patrimoine /patʀimwan/ nm heritage.

patriote /patʀijɔt/ adj patriotic. ●nmf patriot.

patron, ~**ne** /patʀɔ̃, -ɔn/ nm, f employer, boss; (propriétaire) owner, boss; (saint) patron saint. ●nm (couture) pattern. **patronal,** ~**e** (mpl -**aux**) adj employers'. **patronat** nm employers (+ pl).

patrouille /patʀuj/ nf patrol.

patte /pat/ nf leg; (pied) foot; (de chat) paw; ~**s** (favoris) sideburns; **marcher à quatre** ~**s** walk on all fours; (bébé) crawl; ~**s de derrière** hind legs.

paume /pom/ nf (de main) palm.

paumé, ~**e** /pome/ nm, f 🔢 misfit.

paupière /popjɛʀ/ nf eyelid.

pause /poz/ nf pause; (halte) break.

pauvre /povʀ/ adj poor. ●nmf poor man, poor woman. **pauvreté** nf poverty.

pavé /pave/ nm cobblestone.

pavillon /pavijɔ̃/ nm (maison) house; (drapeau) flag.

payant, ~**e** /pɛjɑ̃, -t/ adj (hôte) paying; **c'est** ~ you have to pay to get in.

payer /peje/ 🔢 vt/i pay; (service, travail) pay for; ~ **qch à qn** buy sb sth; **faire** ~ **qn** charge sb; **il me le paiera!** he'll pay for this.

■ se ∼ vpr **se ∼ qch** buy oneself sth; **se ∼ la tête de** make fun of.

pays /pei/ nm country; (région) region; **du ∼** local.

paysage /peizaʒ/ nm landscape.

paysan, ∼ne /peizã, -an/ nm, f farmer, country person; (péj) peasant. ●adj (agricole) farming; (rural) country.

Pays-Bas /peibɑ/ nmpl **les ∼** the Netherlands.

PCV abrév m (**paiement contre vérification**) **téléphoner en ∼** reverse the charges.

PDG abrév m (**président-directeur général**) chairman and managing director.

péage /peaʒ/ nm toll; (lieu) tollgate.

peau (pl ∼x) /po/ nf skin; (cuir) hide; **∼ de chamois** shammy (leather); **∼de mouton** sheepskin; **être bien/mal dans sa ∼** be/not be at ease with oneself.

pêche /pɛʃ/ nf (fruit) peach; (activité) fishing; (poissons) catch; **∼ à la ligne** angling.

péché /peʃe/ nm sin.

pêcher /peʃe/ vt (poisson) catch; (dénicher) dig up. ●vi fish. **pêcheur** nm fisherman; (à la ligne) angler.

pécuniaire /pekynjɛʀ/ adj financial.

pédagogie /pedagoʒi/ nf education.

pédale /pedal/ nf pedal.

pédalo® /pedalo/ nm pedal boat.

pédant, ∼e /pedã, -t/ adj pedantic.

pédestre /pedɛstʀ/ adj **faire de la randonnée ∼** go walking ou hiking.

pédiatre /pedjatʀ/ nmf paediatrician.

pédicure /pedikyʀ/ nmf chiropodist.

peigne /pɛɲ/ nm comb.

peigner /peɲe/ ❶ vt comb; (personne) comb the hair of. ■ se ∼ vpr comb one's hair.

peignoir /peɲwaʀ/ nm dressing gown.

peindre /pɛ̃dʀ/ ㉒ vt paint.

peine /pɛn/ nf sadness, sorrow; (effort, difficulté) trouble; (Jur) sentence; **avoir de la ∼** feel sad; **faire de la ∼ à** hurt; **ce n'est pas la ∼ de sonner** you don't need to ring the bell; **j'ai de la ∼ à le croire** I find it hard to believe; **se donner** ou **prendre la ∼ de faire** go to the trouble of doing; **∼ de mort** death penalty. ●adv **à ∼** hardly.

peiner /pene/ ❶ vi struggle. ●vt sadden.

peintre /pɛ̃tʀ/ nm painter; **∼ en bâtiment** house painter.

peinture /pɛ̃tyʀ/ nf painting; (matière) paint; **∼ à l'huile** oil painting.

péjoratif, -ive /peʒɔʀatif, -v/ adj pejorative.

pelage /pəlaʒ/ nm coat, fur.

pêle-mêle* /pɛlmɛl/ adv in a jumble.

peler /pəle/ ❻ vt/i peel.

pèlerinage /pɛlʀinaʒ/ nm pilgrimage.

pelle /pɛl/ nf shovel; (d'enfant) spade.

pellicule /pelikyl/ nf film; **∼s** (cheveux) dandruff.

pelote /pəlɔt/ nf (of wool) ball.

peloton /p(ə)lɔtɔ̃/ nm platoon; (Sport) pack; **∼ d'exécution** firing squad.

pelotonner (se) /(sə)plɔtɔne/ ❶ vpr curl up.

pelouse /p(ə)luz/ nf lawn.

p

❖ see A-Z of French life and culture

peluche /p(ə)lyʃ/ nf (matière) plush; (jouet) cuddly toy; **en ~** (lapin, chien) fluffy.

pénal, ~e (mpl **-aux**) /penal, -o/ adj penal. **pénaliser** 🔟 vt penalize. **pénalité** nf penalty.

penchant /pɑ̃ʃɑ̃/ nm inclination; (goût) liking (**pour** for).

pencher /pɑ̃ʃe/ 🔟 vt tilt; **~ pour** favour. •vi lean (over), tilt. ∎ **se ~** vpr lean (forward); **se ~ sur** (problème) examine.

pendaison /pɑ̃dɛzɔ̃/ nf hanging.

pendant¹ /pɑ̃dɑ̃/ prép (au cours de) during; (durée) for; **~ que** while.

pendant², ~e /pɑ̃dɑ̃, -t/ adj hanging; **jambes ~es** with one's legs dangling. •nm (contrepartie) matching piece (**de** to); **~ d'oreille** drop earring.

pendentif /pɑ̃dɑ̃tif/ nm pendant.

penderie /pɑ̃dRi/ nf wardrobe.

pendre /pɑ̃dR/ 🔟 vt/i hang. ∎ **se ~** vpr hang (**à** from); (se tuer) hang oneself.

pendule /pɑ̃dyl/ nf clock. •nm pendulum.

pénétrer /penetRe/ 🔟 vi **~ (dans)** enter; **faire ~ une crème** rub a cream in. •vt penetrate.

pénible /penibl/ adj (travail) hard; (nouvelle) painful; (enfant) tiresome.

péniche /peniʃ/ nf barge.

pénitence /penitɑ̃s/ nf (Relig) penance; (punition) punishment; **faire ~** repent.

pénitentiaire /penitɑ̃sjɛR/ adj (établissement) penal.

pénombre /penɔ̃bR/ nf half-light.

pensée /pɑ̃se/ nf (idée) thought; (fleur) pansy.

penser /pɑ̃se/ 🔟 vt/i think; **~ à** (réfléchir à) think about; (se souvenir de, prévoir) think of; **~ faire** think of doing; **faire ~ à** remind one of.

pensif, -ive /pɑ̃sif, -v/ adj pensive.

pension /pɑ̃sjɔ̃/ nf (Scol) boarding school; (repas, somme) board; (allocation) pension; **(~ de famille)** guest house; **~ alimentaire** (Jur) alimony. **pensionnaire** nmf (Scol) boarder; (d'hôtel) guest. **pensionnat** nm boarding school.

pente /pɑ̃t/ nf slope; **en ~** sloping.

Pentecôte /pɑ̃tkot/ nf **la ~** Whitsun.

pénurie /penyRi/ nf shortage.

pépin /pepɛ̃/ nm (graine) pip; (ennui 🔟) hitch.

pépinière /pepinjɛR/ nf (tree) nursery.

perçant, ~e /pɛRsɑ̃, -t/ adj (cri) shrill; (regard) piercing.

perce-neige /pɛRsəneʒ/ nm or f inv snowdrop.

percepteur /pɛRsɛptœR/ nm tax inspector.

percer /pɛRse/ 🔟 vt pierce; (avec perceuse) drill; (mystère) penetrate. •vi break through; (dent) come through. **perceuse** nf drill.

percevoir /pɛRsəvwaR/ 🔟 vt perceive; (impôt) collect.

perche /pɛRʃ/ nf (bâton) pole.

percher (se) /(sə)pɛRʃe/ 🔟 vpr perch.

percolateur /pɛRkɔlatœR/ nm coffee machine.

percuter /pɛRkyte/ 🔟 vt (véhicule) crash into.

perdant, ~e /pɛRdɑ̃, -t/ adj losing. •nm, f loser.

perdre /pɛRdR/ 🔟 vt/i lose; (gaspiller) waste; **~ ses poils** (chat) moult; **se ~** vpr get lost; (rester inutilisé) go to waste.

perdrix /pɛRdRi/ nf partridge.

perdu, ~e /pɛRdy/ adj lost; (endroit) isolated; (balle) stray;

c'est du temps ~ it's a waste of time.

père /pɛʀ/ nm father; ~ **de famille** father, family man; ~ **spirituel** father figure; **le** ~ **Noël** Santa Claus.

perfection /pɛʀfɛksjɔ̃/ nf perfection.

perfectionner /pɛʀfɛksjɔne/ 🚹 vt (technique) perfect; (art) refine. ■ **se** ~ vpr improve; **se** ~ **en anglais** improve one's English.

perforer /pɛʀfɔʀe/ 🚹 vt perforate; (billet, bande) punch.

performance /pɛʀfɔʀmɑ̃s/ nf performance.

perfusion /pɛʀfyzjɔ̃/ nf drip; **sous** ~ on a drip.

péridurale /peʀidyʀal/ nf epidural.

péril /peʀil/ nm peril; **à tes risques et** ~**s** at your own risk.

périlleux, -euse /peʀijø, -z/ adj perilous.

périmé, ~e /peʀime/ adj (produit) past its use-by date; (désuet) outdated.

période /peʀjɔd/ nf period.

périodique /peʀjɔdik/ adj periodic(al). ●nm (journal) periodical.

péripétie /peʀipesi/ nf (unexpected) event, adventure.

périphérique /peʀifeʀik/ adj peripheral. ●nm (**boulevard**) ~ ring road.

périple /peʀipl/ nm journey.

périr /peʀiʀ/ 🔁 vi perish, die.

perle /pɛʀl/ nf (d'huître) pearl; (de verre) bead.

permanence /pɛʀmanɑ̃s/ nf permanence; (Scol) study room; **de** ~ on duty; **en** ~ permanently; **assurer une** ~ keep the office open.

permanent, ~e /pɛʀmanɑ̃, -t/ adj permanent; (constant) constant; **formation** ~**e** continuous

education. **permanente** nf (coiffure) perm.

permettre /pɛʀmɛtʀ/ 42 vt allow; ~ **à qn de** allow sb to. ■ **se** ~ vpr (achat) afford; **se** ~ **de faire** take the liberty of doing.

permis, ~e /pɛʀmi, -z/ adj allowed. ●nm licence, permit; 🆑~ (**de conduire**) driving licence.

permission /pɛʀmisjɔ̃/ nf permission; **en** ~ (Mil) on leave.

Pérou /peʀu/ nm Peru.

perpendiculaire /pɛʀpɑ̃dikylɛʀ/ adj & nf perpendicular.

perpétuité /pɛʀpetɥite/ nf **à** ~ for life.

perplexe /pɛʀplɛks/ adj perplexed.

perquisition /pɛʀkizisjɔ̃/ nf (police) search.

perron /pɛʀɔ̃/ nm (front) steps.

perroquet /pɛʀɔke/ nm parrot.

perruche /pɛʀyʃ/ nf budgerigar.

perruque /pɛʀyk/ nf wig.

persécuter /pɛʀsekyte/ 🚹 vt persecute.

persévérance /pɛʀseveʀɑ̃s/ nf perseverance. **persévérer** 14 vi persevere.

persienne /pɛʀsjɛn/ nf (outside) shutter.

persil /pɛʀsi/ nm parsley.

persistance /pɛʀsistɑ̃s/ nf persistence. **persistant, ~e** adj persistent; (feuillage) evergreen.

persister /pɛʀsiste/ 🚹 vi persist (**à faire** in doing).

personnage /pɛʀsɔnaʒ/ nm character; (personne célèbre) personality.

personnalité /pɛʀsɔnalite/ nf personality.

personne /pɛʀsɔn/ nf person; ~**s** people. ●pron nobody, no-one; **je**

n'ai vu ～ I didn't see anybody.

personnel, ～le /pɛʀsɔnɛl/ adj personal; (égoïste) selfish. ●nm staff.

perspective /pɛʀspɛktiv/ nf (art, point de vue) perspective; (vue) view; (éventualité) prospect.

perspicace /pɛʀspikas/ adj shrewd. **perspicacité** nf shrewdness.

persuader /pɛʀsɥade/ [1] vt persuade (**de faire** to do).

persuasif, -ive /pɛʀsɥazif, -v/ adj persuasive.

perte /pɛʀt/ nf loss; (ruine) ruin; **à ～ de vue** as far as the eye can see; **～ de** (temps, argent) waste of; **～ sèche** total loss; **～s** (Méd) discharge.

pertinent, ～e /pɛʀtinɑ̃, -t/ adj pertinent.

perturbateur, -trice /pɛʀtyʀbatœʀ, -tʀis/ nm, f disruptive element. **perturbation** nf disruption. **perturber** [1] vt disrupt; (personne) perturb.

pervers, ～e /pɛʀvɛʀ, -s/ adj (dépravé) perverted; (méchant) wicked.

pervertir /pɛʀvɛʀtiʀ/ [2] vt pervert.

pesant, ～e /pəzɑ̃, -t/ adj heavy.

pesanteur /pəzɑ̃tœʀ/ nf heaviness; **la ～** (force) gravity.

pesée /pəze/ nf weighing; (effort) pressure.

pèse-personne (pl ～s) /pɛzpɛʀsɔn/ nm (bathroom) scales.

peser /pəze/ [6] vt/i weigh; **～ sur** bear upon.

pessimiste /pesimist/ adj pessimistic. ●nmf pessimist.

peste /pɛst/ nf plague; (personne [I]) pest.

pet /pɛ/ nm [I] fart [I].

pétale /petal/ nm petal.

pétard /petaʀ/ nm banger.

péter /pete/ [14] vi [I] fart [I], go bang; (casser) snap.

pétillant, ～e /petijɑ̃, -t/ adj (boisson) sparkling; (personne) bubbly.

pétiller /petije/ [1] vi (feu) crackle; (champagne, yeux) sparkle; **～ d'intelligence** sparkle with intelligence.

petit, ～e /p(ə)ti, -t/ adj small; (avec nuance affective) little; (jeune) young, small; (défaut) minor; (mesquin) petty; **en ～** in miniature; **～ à ～** little by little; **un ～ peu** a little bit; **～ ami** boyfriend; **～e amie** girlfriend; **～es annonces** small ads; **～e cuillère** teaspoon; **～ déjeuner** breakfast; **～ pois** garden pea. ●nm, f little child; (Scol) junior; **～s** (de chat) kittens; (de chien) pups. **petite-fille** (pl **petites-filles**) nf granddaughter. **petit-fils** (pl **petits-fils**) nm grandson.

pétition /petisjɔ̃/ nf petition.

petits-enfants /pətizɑ̃fɑ̃/ nmpl grandchildren.

pétrin /petʀɛ̃/ nm **dans le ～** [I] in a fix [I].

pétrir /petʀiʀ/ [2] vt knead.

pétrole /petʀɔl/ nm oil; **～ brut** crude oil.

pétrolier, -ière /petʀɔlje, -jɛʀ/ adj oil. ●nm (navire) oil-tanker.

peu /pø/ adv (**～ de**) (quantité) little, not much; (nombre) few, not many; **～ intéressant** not very interesting; **il mange ～** he doesn't eat very much. ●pron few. ●nm little; **un ～ (de)** a little; **à ～ près** more or less; **de ～** only just; **～ à ～** gradually; **～ après** shortly after/before; **de chose** not much; **～ nombreux** few; **～ souvent** seldom; **pour ～ que** if.

peuple /pœpl/ nm people. **peupler** [1] vt populate.

peuplier /pøplije/ nm poplar.

peur /pœʀ/ nf fear; **avoir ～** be

afraid (**de** of); **de ~ de** for fear
of; **faire ~ à** frighten. **peureux,
-euse** adj fearful.

peut /pø/ ▷POUVOIR 49.

peut-être /pøtɛtʀ/ adv perhaps,
maybe; **~ qu'il viendra** he
might come.

peux /pø/ ▷POUVOIR 49.

phare /faʀ/ nm (tour) lighthouse;
(de véhicule) headlight; **~
antibrouillard** fog lamp.

pharmacie /faʀmasi/ nf (magasin)
chemist's (shop), pharmacy;
(science) pharmacy; (armoire)
medicine cabinet. **pharmacien,
~ne** nm, f chemist, pharmacist.

phénomène /fenɔmɛn/ nm
phenomenon; (personne)
eccentric.

philosophe /filozof/ nmf
philosopher. ●adj philosophical.
philosophie nf philosophy.
philosophique adj
philosophical.

phobie /fɔbi/ nf phobia.

phonétique /fɔnetik/ adj
phonetic. ●nf phonetics.

phoque /fɔk/ nm (animal) seal.

photo /fɔto/ nf photo; (art)
photography; **prendre en ~**
take a photo of; **~ d'identité**
passport photograph.

photocopie /fɔtɔkɔpi/ nf
photocopy. **photocopier** 45 vt
photocopy.

photographe /fɔtɔgʀaf/ nmf
photographer. **photographie** nf
photograph; (art) photography.
photographier 45 vt take a
photo of.

phrase /fʀaz/ nf sentence.

physicien, ~ne /fizisjɛ̃, -ɛn/ nm, f
physicist.

physique /fizik/ adj physical. ●nm
physique; **au ~** physically. ●nf
physics (+ sg.)

piano /pjano/ nm piano.

pianoter /pjanɔte/ 1 vi tinkle; **~**

sur (ordinateur) tap at.

PIB abrév m (**produit intérieur
brut**) GDP.

pic /pik/ nm (outil) pickaxe; (sommet)
peak; (oiseau) woodpecker; **à ~**
(falaise) sheer; (couler) straight to
the bottom; **tomber à ~**
come just at the right time.

pichet /piʃɛ/ nm jug.

picorer /pikɔʀe/ 1 vt/i peck.

picotement /pikɔtmɑ̃/ nm
tingling. **picoter** 1 vt sting;
(yeux) sting.

pie /pi/ nf magpie.

pièce /pjɛs/ nf (d'habitation) room;
(de monnaie) coin; (Théât) play; (pour
raccommoder) patch; (écrit)
document; (morceau) piece; (**~ de
théâtre**) play; **dix euros la ~**
ten euros each; **~ détachée**
part; **~ d'identité** identity
paper; **~s jointes** enclosures;
(courrier électronique) attachments;
~s justificatives written proof;
~ montée tiered cake; **~ de
rechange** spare part; **un deux-
~s** a two-room flat.

pied /pje/ nm foot; (de meuble) leg;
(de lampe) base; (de verre) stem;
(d'appareil photo) stand; **être ~s
nus** be barefoot; **à ~** on foot; **au
~ de la lettre** literally; **avoir ~**
be able to touch the bottom;
jouer au tennis comme un ~
 be hopeless at tennis; **mettre
sur ~** set up; **sur un ~
d'égalité** on an equal footing;
mettre les ~s dans le plat
put one's foot in it; **c'est le ~**
it's great. **pied-bot** (pl **pieds-
bots**) nm club-foot.

piédestal /pjedɛstal/ nm pedestal.

piège /pjɛʒ/ nm trap.

piéger /pjeʒe/ 14 40 vt trap;
lettre/voiture piégée letter/
car bomb.

piercing /piʀsiŋ/ nm body
piercing.

······················ *see* A-Z of French life and culture

pierre | piste

212

pierre /pjɛʀ/ nf stone; ~ **précieuse** precious stone; ~ **tombale** tombstone.

piétiner /pjetine/ **1** vi (avancer lentement) shuffle along; (fig) make no headway; ~ **d'impatience** hop up and down with impatience. ●vt trample (on).

piéton /pjetɔ̃/ nm pedestrian.

pieu (pl ~**x**) /pjø/ nm post, stake.

pieuvre /pjœvʀ/ nf octopus.

pieux, -ieuse /pjø, -z/ adj pious.

pigeon /piʒɔ̃/ nm pigeon.

piger /piʒe/ **40** vt/i **1** understand, get (it).

pile /pil/ nf (tas) pile; (Électr) battery; ~ **ou face?** heads or tails? ●adv (s'arrêter **1**) dead; **à dix heures** ~ **1** at ten on the dot.

pilier /pilje/ nm pillar.

pillage /pijaʒ/ nm looting. **pillard, ~e** nm, f looter. **piller 1** vt loot.

pilote /pilɔt/ nm (Aviat, Naut) pilot; (Auto) driver. ●adj pilot. **piloter 1** vt (Aviat, Naut) pilot; (Auto) drive.

pilule /pilyl/ nf pill; **la** ~ the pill.

piment /pimɑ̃/ nm hot pepper; (fig) spice. **pimenté, ~e** adj spicy.

pin /pɛ̃/ nm pine.

pinard /pinaʀ/ nm **1** plonk **1**, cheap wine.

pince /pɛ̃s/ nf (outil) pliers (+ pl); (levier) crowbar; (de crabe) pincer; (à sucre) tongs (+ pl); ~ **à épiler** tweezers (+ pl); ~ **à linge** clothes peg.

pinceau (pl ~**x**) /pɛ̃so/ nm paintbrush.

pincée /pɛ̃se/ nf pinch (**de** of).

pincer /pɛ̃se/ **10** vt pinch; (attraper **1**) catch. ■ **se** ~ vpr catch oneself; **se** ~ **le doigt** catch one's finger.

pince-sans-rire /pɛ̃ssɑ̃ʀiʀ/ nmf inv

c'est un ~ he has a deadpan sense of humour.

pingouin /pɛ̃gwɛ̃/ nm penguin.

pingre /pɛ̃gʀ/ adj **1** stingy.

pintade /pɛ̃tad/ nf guinea fowl.

piocher /pjɔʃe/ **1** vt/i dig; (étudier **1**) study hard, slog away (at).

pion /pjɔ̃/ nm (de jeu) counter; (aux échecs) pawn; (Scol **1**) supervisor.

pipe /pip/ nf pipe; **fumer la** ~ smoke a pipe.

piquant, ~e /pikɑ̃, -t/ adj (barbe) prickly; (goût) pungent; (remarque) cutting. ●nm prickle.

pique /pik/ nm (aux cartes) spades.

pique-nique* (pl ~**s**) /piknik/ nm picnic.

piquer /pike/ **1** vt (épine) prick; (épice) burn, sting; (abeille, ortie) sting; (serpent, moustique) bite; (enfoncer) stick; (coudre) (machine-) stitch; (curiosité) excite; (voler **1**) pinch. ●vi (avion) dive; (goût) be hot. ■ **se** ~ vpr prick oneself.

piquet /pikɛ/ nm stake; (de tente) peg; (de parasol) pole; ~ **de grève** (strike) picket.

piqûre* /pikyʀ/ nf prick; (d'abeille) sting; (de serpent) bite; (point) stitch; (Méd) injection, jab; **faire une** ~ **à qn** give sb an injection.

pirate /piʀat/ nm pirate; ~ **informatique** computer hacker; ~ **de l'air** hijacker.

pire /piʀ/ adj worse (**que** than); **les** ~**s mensonges** the most wicked lies. ●nm **le** ~ the worst; **au** ~ at worst.

pis /pi/ nm (de vache) udder. ●adj inv & adv worse; **aller de mal en** ~ go from bad to worse.

piscine /pisin/ nf swimming pool; ~ **couverte** indoor swimming-pool.

pissenlit /pisɑ̃li/ nm dandelion.

pistache /pistaʃ/ nf pistachio.

piste /pist/ nf track; (de personne,

d'animal) track, trail; (Aviat) runway; (de cirque) ring; (de ski) slope; (de danse) floor; (Sport) racetrack; **~ cyclable** cycle lane.

pistolet /pistɔlɛ/ nm gun, pistol; (de peintre) spray-gun.

piteux, -euse /pitø, -z/ adj pitiful.

pitié /pitje/ nf pity; **il me fait ~** I feel sorry for him.

piton /pitɔ̃/ nm (à crochet) hook; (sommet pointu) peak.

pitoyable /pitwajabl/ adj pitiful.

pitre /pitʀ/ nm clown; **faire le ~** clown around.

pittoresque /pitɔʀɛsk/ adj picturesque.

pivot /pivo/ nm pivot. **pivoter** [1] vi revolve; (personne) swing round.

placard /plakaʀ/ nm cupboard; (affiche) poster. **placarder** [1] vt (affiche) post up; (mur) cover with posters.

place /plas/ nf place; (espace libre) room, space; (siège) seat, place; (prix d'un trajet) fare; (esplanade) square; (emploi) position; (de parking) space; **à la ~ de** instead of; **en ~, à sa ~** in its place; **faire ~ à** give way to; **sur ~** on the spot; **remettre qn à sa ~** put sb in his place; **ça prend de la ~** it takes up a lot of room; **se mettre à la ~ de qn** put oneself in sb's shoes *ou* place.

placement /plasmɑ̃/ nm (d'argent) investment.

placer /plase/ [10] vt place; (invité, spectateur) seat; (argent) invest. ■ se ~ vpr (personne) take up a position.

plafond /plafɔ̃/ nm ceiling.

plage /plaʒ/ nf beach; **~ horaire** time slot.

plagiat /plaʒja/ nm plagiarism.

plaider /plede/ [1] vt/i plead. **plaidoirie** nf (défence) speech. **plaidoyer** nm plea.

plaie /plɛ/ nf wound; (personne [1]) nuisance.

plaignant, ~e /plɛɲɑ̃, -t/ nm, f plaintiff.

plaindre /plɛ̃dʀ/ [22] vt pity. ■ se ~ vpr complain (**de** about); **se ~ de** (souffrir de) complain of.

plaine /plɛn/ nf plain.

plainte /plɛ̃t/ nf complaint; (gémissement) groan. **plaintif, -ive** adj plaintive.

plaire /plɛʀ/ [47] vi **~ à** please; **ça lui plaît** he likes it; **elle lui plaît** he likes her; **ça me plaît de faire** I like doing; **s'il vous plaît** please. ■ se ~ vpr **il se plaît ici** he likes it here.

plaisance /plɛzɑ̃s/ nf **la (navigation de) ~** boating.

plaisant, ~e /plɛzɑ̃, -t/ adj pleasant; (drôle) amusing.

plaisanter /plɛzɑ̃te/ [1] vi joke. **plaisanterie** nf joke. **plaisantin** nm joker.

plaisir /plɛziʀ/ nm pleasure; **faire ~ à** please; **pour le ~ for fun** *ou* pleasure.

plan /plɑ̃/ nm plan; (de ville) map; (de livre) outline; **~ d'eau** artificial lake; **~ social** planned redundancy programme; **premier ~** foreground.

planche /plɑ̃ʃ/ nf board, plank; (gravure) plate; **~ à repasser** ironing-board; **~ à voile** windsurfing board; (Sport) windsurfing.

plancher /plɑ̃ʃe/ nm floor.

planer /plane/ [1] vi glide; **~ sur** (mystère, danger) hang over.

planète /planɛt/ nf planet.

planeur /planœʀ/ nm glider.

planifier /planifje/ [45] vt plan.

plant /plɑ̃/ nm seedling; (de légumes) patch.

plante /plɑ̃t/ nf plant; **~ d'appartement** houseplant; **~ des pieds** sole (of the foot).

planter /plɑ̃te/ **1** vt (plante) plant; (enfoncer) drive in; (tente) put up; **rester planté** 🔢 stand still.

plaque /plak/ nf plate; (de marbre) slab; (insigne) badge; ~ **chauffante** hotplate; ~ **commémorative** plaque; ~ **minéralogique** numberplate; ~ **de verglas** patch of ice.

plaquer /plake/ **1** vt (bois) veneer; (aplatir) flatten; (rugby) tackle; (abandonner 🔢) ditch 🔢; **tout** ~ chuck it all.

plastique /plastik/ adj & nm plastic; **en** ~ plastic.

plastiquer /plastike/ **1** vt blow up.

plat, ~e /pla, -t/ adj flat. •nm (Culin) dish; (partie de repas) course; (de la main) flat. •**à plat** adv (poser) flat; (batterie, pneu) flat; **à ~ ventre** flat on one's face.

platane /platan/ nm plane tree.

plateau (pl ~**x**) /plato/ nm tray; (de cinéma) set; (de balance) pan; (Géog) plateau; ~ **de fromages** cheeseboard; ~ **de fruits de mer** seafood platter. **plate-bande*** (pl **plates-bandes**) nf flower bed.

platine /platin/ nm platinum. •nf (tourne-disque) turntable; ~ **laser** compact disc player.

plâtre /plɑtR/ nm plaster; (Méd) (plaster) cast.

plein, ~e /plɛ̃, -ɛn/ adj full (**de** of); (total) complete. •nm **faire le ~ (d'essence)** fill up (the tank); **à ~** fully; **à ~ temps** full-time; **en ~ air** in the open air; **en ~ milieu/ visage** right in the middle/the face; **en ~e nuit** in the middle of the night. •adv **avoir des idées ~ la tête** be full of ideas. **pleinement** adv fully.

pleurer /plœRe/ **1** vi cry, weep (**sur** over); (yeux) water. •vt mourn.

pleurnicher /plœRniʃe/ **1** vi 🔢 snivel.

pleurs /plœR/ nmpl tears; **en** ~ in tears.

pleuvoir /pløvwaR/ 48 vi rain; (fig) rain ou shower down; **il pleut** it is raining; **il pleut à verse** ou **des cordes** it is pouring.

pli /pli/ nm fold; (de jupe) pleat; (de pantalon) crease; (lettre) letter; (habitude) habit; **(faux)** ~ crease.

pliant, ~e /plijɑ̃, -t/ adj folding. •nm folding stool, camp-stool.

plier /plije/ 45 vt fold; (courber) bend; (soumettre) submit (**à** to). •vi bend. ■ **se** ~ vpr fold; **se** ~ **à** submit to.

plinthe /plɛ̃t/ nf skirting-board.

plissé, ~e /plise/ adj (jupe) pleated.

plisser /plise/ **1** vt crease; (yeux) screw up.

plomb /plɔ̃/ nm lead; (fusible) fuse; ~**s** (de chasse) lead shot; **de** ou **en** ~ lead. **plombage** nm filling.

plomberie /plɔ̃bRi/ nf plumbing. **plombier** nm plumber.

plongée /plɔ̃ʒe/ nf diving; **en** ~ (sous-marin) submerged.

plongeoir /plɔ̃ʒwaR/ nm diving board.

plonger /plɔ̃ʒe/ 40 vi dive; (route) plunge. •vt plunge. ■ **se** ~ vpr plunge into; **se** ~ **dans** (fig) (lecture) bury oneself in. **plongeur, -euse** n, f diver; (de restaurant) dishwasher.

plu /ply/ ▷PLAIRE 47, PLEUVOIR 48.

pluie /plɥi/ nf rain; (averse) shower; ~ **battante/diluvienne** driving/torrential rain.

plume /plym/ nf feather; (pointe) nib.

plumeau (pl ~**x**) /plymo/ nm feather duster.

plumier /plymje/ nm pencil box.

plupart: la ~ /laplypaR/ loc **la** ~ **des** (gens, cas) most; **la** ~ **du**

temps most of the time; **pour la ∼** for the most part.

pluriel, ∼le /plyʀjɛl/ adj & nm plural.

plus /ply, plys, plyz/
● adverbe de comparaison
····▸ more (**que**); **∼ âgé**/**tard** older/later; **∼ beau** more beautiful; **∼ j'y pense...** the more I think about it...; **deux fois ∼** twice as much; **deux fois ∼ cher** twice as expensive.
····▸ **le ∼** the most; **le ∼ grand** the biggest; (de deux) the bigger.
····▸ **∼ de** (pain) more; (dix jours) more than; **il est ∼ de 8 heures** it is after 8 o'clock.
····▸ **de ∼** more (**que**); (en outre) moreover; **les enfants de ∼ de 10 ans** children over 10 years old; **de ∼ en ∼** more and more.
····▸ **en ∼** on top of that; **c'est en ∼** it's extra; **en ∼ de** in addition to.
····▸ **∼ ou moins** more or less.
····▸ **au ∼ tard** at the latest.
● adverbe de négation
····▸ **ne ∼** (temps) no longer, not any more; **je n'y vais ∼** I don't go there any longer ou any more.
····▸ **ne ∼ de** (quantité) no more; **il n'y a ∼ de pain** there is no more bread.
····▸ **∼ que deux jours!** only two days left!
● préposition & nm masculin
····▸ (maths) plus.

plusieurs /plyzjœʀ/ adj & pron several.

plus-value (pl **∼s**) /plyvaly/ nf (bénéfice) profit.

plutôt /plyto/ adv rather (**que** than).

pluvieux, -ieuse /plyvjø, -z/ adj rainy.

PME abrév f (**petites et moyennes entreprises**) SME.

PNB abrév m (**produit national brut**) GNP.

pneu (pl **∼s**) /pnø/ nm tyre. **pneumatique** adj inflatable.

pneumonie /pnømɔni/ nf pneumonia; **∼ atypique** severe acute respiratory syndrome.

poche /pɔʃ/ nf pocket; (sac) bag; **∼s** (sous les yeux) bags.

pocher /pɔʃe/ ☐ vt (œuf) poach.

pochette /pɔʃɛt/ nf (de documents) folder; (sac) bag, pouch; (d'allumettes) book; (de disque) sleeve; (mouchoir) pocket handkerchief.

poêle /pwal/ nf (**∼ à frire**) frying-pan. ● nm stove.

poème /pɔɛm/ nm poem. **poésie** nf poetry; (poème) poem. **poète** nm poet. **poétique** adj poetic.

poids /pwa/ nm weight; **∼ coq**/**lourd**/**plume** bantamweight/heavyweight/featherweight; **∼ lourd** (camion) lorry, juggernaut; (US) truck.

poignard /pwaɲaʀ/ nm dagger. **poignarder** ☐ vt stab.

poigne /pwaɲ/ nf **avoir de la ∼** have a strong grip.

poignée /pwaɲe/ nf (de porte) handle; (quantité) handful; **∼ de main** handshake.

poignet /pwaɲɛ/ nm wrist; (de chemise) cuff.

poil /pwal/ nm hair; (pelage) fur; (de brosse) bristle; **∼s** (de tapis) pile; **à ∼** ☐ naked; **∼ à gratter** itching powder. **poilu, ∼e** adj hairy.

poinçon /pwɛ̃sɔ̃/ nm awl; (marque) hallmark. **poinçonner** ☐ vt (billet) punch.

poing /pwɛ̃/ nm fist.

point /pwɛ̃/ nm (endroit, Sport) point; (marque visible) spot, dot; (de couture) stitch; (pour évaluer) mark; **enlever un ∼ par faute** take a mark off for each mistake; **à ∼** (Culin) medium; (arriver) at the

p

right time; **faire le** ~ take stock; **mettre au** ~ (photo) focus; (technique) develop; **mettre les choses au** ~ get things clear; **Camille n'est pas encore au** ~ **pour ses examens** Camille is not ready for her exams; **sur le** ~ about to; **au** ~ **que** to the extent that; (~ **final**) full stop, period; **deux** ~s colon; ~ **d'interrogation/ d'exclamation** question/ exclamation mark; ~s **de suspension** suspension points; ~ **virgule** semicolon; ~ **culminant** peak; ~ **du jour** daybreak; ~ **mort** (Auto) neutral; ~ **de repère** landmark; ~ **de suture** (Méd) stitch; ~ **de vente** point of sale; ~ **de vue** point of view. ●adv **(ne)** ~ not.

pointe /pwɛ̃t/ nf point, tip; (clou) tack; (de grille) spike; (fig) touch (**de** of); **de** ~ (industrie) high-tech; **en** ~ pointed; **heure de** ~ peak hour; **sur la** ~ **des pieds** on tiptoe.

pointer /pwɛte/ **1** vt (cocher) tick off; (diriger) point, aim. ●vi (employé) (en arrivant) clock in; (en sortant) clock out. ■ **se** ~ vpr **1** turn up.

pointillé /pwɛ̃tije/ nm dotted line.

pointilleux, -euse /pwɛ̃tijø, -z/ adj fastidious, particular.

pointu, ~e /pwɛ̃ty/ adj pointed; (aiguisé) sharp.

pointure /pwɛ̃tyʀ/ nf size.

poire /pwaʀ/ nf pear.

poireau (pl ~**x**) /pwaʀo/ nm leek.

poirier /pwaʀje/ nm pear tree.

pois /pwa/ nm pea; (motif) dot; **robe à** ~ polka dot dress.

poison /pwazɔ̃/ nm poison.

poisseux, -euse /pwasø, -z/ adj sticky.

poisson /pwasɔ̃/ nm fish; ~ **rouge** goldfish; ~ **d'avril** April

fool; **les P**~**s** Pisces.

poissonnerie nf fish shop.

poissonnier, -ière nm, f fishmonger.

poitrine /pwatʀin/ nf chest; (seins) bosom.

poivre /pwavʀ/ nm pepper.

poivré, ~e adj peppery.

poivrière nf pepper-pot.

poivron /pwavʀɔ̃/ nm sweet pepper.

polaire /polɛʀ/ adj polar. ●nf (veste) fleece.

pôle /pol/ nm pole.

polémique /polemik/ nf debate. ●adj controversial.

poli, ~e /poli/ adj (personne) polite.

police /polis/ nf (force) police (+ pl); (discipline) (law and) order; (d'assurance) policy.

policier, -ière /polisje, -jɛʀ/ adj police; (roman) detective. ●nm policeman.

polir /poliʀ/ **2** vt polish.

politesse /polites/ nf politeness; (parole) polite remark.

politicien, ~ne /politisjɛ̃, -ɛn/ nm, f (péj) politician.

politique /politik/ adj political; **homme** ~ politician. ●nf politics; (ligne de conduite) policy.

pollen /polɛn/ nm pollen.

polluant, ~e /polɥɑ̃, -t/ adj polluting. ●nm pollutant.

polluer /polɥe/ **1** vt pollute.

pollution nf pollution.

polo /polo/ nm (Sport) polo; (vêtement) polo shirt.

Pologne /polɔɲ/ nf Poland.

polonais, ~e /polonɛ, -z/ adj Polish. ●nm (Ling) Polish. P~, ~e nm, f Pole.

poltron, ~ne /poltʀɔ̃, -ɔn/ adj cowardly. ●nm, f coward.

polygame /poligam/ nmf polygamist.

polyvalent, ~e /polivalɑ̃, -t/ adj

● see A-Z of French life and culture

varied; (personne) versatile.

pommade /pɔmad/ nf ointment.

pomme /pɔm/ nf apple; (d'arrosoir) rose; ~ **d'Adam** Adam's apple; ~ **de pin** pine cone; ~ **de terre** potato; ~**s frites** chips; (US) French fries; **tomber dans les** ~**s** Ⓘ pass out.

pommette /pɔmɛt/ nf cheekbone.

pommier /pɔmje/ nm apple tree.

pompe /pɔ̃p/ nf pump; (splendeur) pomp; ~ **à incendie** fire engine; ~**s funèbres** undertaker's (+ sg).

pomper /pɔ̃pe/ Ⓘ vt pump; (copier Ⓘ) copy, crib; ~ **l'air à qn** Ⓘ get on sb's nerves.

pompier /pɔ̃pje/ nm fireman.

pomponner (se) /(sə)pɔ̃pɔne/ Ⓘ vpr get dolled up.

poncer /pɔ̃se/ Ⓘ vt sand.

ponctuation /pɔ̃ktɥasjɔ̃/ nf punctuation.

ponctuel, ~**le** /pɔ̃ktɥɛl/ adj punctual.

pondre /pɔ̃dʀ/ Ⓘ vt/i lay.

poney /pɔnɛ/ nm pony.

pont /pɔ̃/ nm bridge; (de navire) deck; (de graissage) ramp; **faire le** ~ get an extended weekend; ~ **aérien** airlift. **pont-levis** (pl **ponts-levis**) nm drawbridge.

populaire /pɔpylɛʀ/ adj popular; (expression) colloquial; (quartier, origine) working-class. **popularité** nf popularity.

population /pɔpylasjɔ̃/ nf population.

porc /pɔʀ/ nm pig; (viande) pork.

porcelaine /pɔʀsəlɛn/ nf china, porcelain.

porc-épic (pl **porcs-épics**) /pɔʀkepik/ nm porcupine.

porcherie /pɔʀʃəʀi/ nf pigsty.

pornographie /pɔʀnɔgʀafi/ nf pornography.

port /pɔʀ/ nm port, harbour; **à** **bon** ~ safely; ~ **maritime** seaport; (transport) carriage; (d'armes) carrying; (de barbe) wearing.

portable /pɔʀtabl/ nm (Ordinat) laptop (computer); (telephone) mobile (phone).

portail /pɔʀtaj/ nm gate.

portatif, -ive /pɔʀtatif, -v/ adj portable.

porte /pɔʀt/ nf door; (passage) doorway; (de jardin, d'embarquement) gate; **mettre à la** ~ throw out; ~ **d'entrée** front door.

porté, ~**e** /pɔʀte/ adj ~ **à** inclined to; ~ **sur** keen on.

porte-avions* /pɔʀtavjɔ̃/ nm inv aircraft carrier.

porte-bagages* /pɔʀtbagaʒ/ nm inv (de vélo) carrier.

porte-bonheur* /pɔʀtbɔnœʀ/ nm inv lucky charm.

porte-clefs /pɔʀtəkle/ nm inv key ring.

porte-documents* /pɔʀtdɔkymɑ̃/ nm inv briefcase.

portée /pɔʀte/ nf (d'une arme) range; (de voûte) span; (d'animaux) litter; (impact) significance; (Mus) stave; **à** ~ **de (la) main** within (arm's) reach; **hors de** ~ **(de)** out of reach (of); **à la** ~ **de qn** at sb's level.

porte-fenêtre (pl **portes-fenêtres**) /pɔʀtfənɛtʀ/ nf French window.

portefeuille /pɔʀtəfœj/ nm wallet; (de ministre) portfolio.

porte-jarretelles* /pɔʀtʒaʀtɛl/ nm inv suspender belt.

portemanteau (pl ~**x**) /pɔʀtmɑ̃to/ nm coat ou hat stand.

porte-monnaie* /pɔʀtmɔnɛ/ nm inv purse.

porte-parole* /pɔʀtpaʀɔl/ nm inv spokesperson.

porter /pɔʀte/ Ⓘ vt carry; (vêtement, bague) wear; (fruits,

responsabilité, nom) bear; (coup)
strike; (amener) bring; (inscrire)
enter. ●vi (bruit) carry; (coup) hit
home; ~ **sur** rest on; (concerner)
be about. ■ **se** ~ vpr **bien se** ~
be *ou* feel well; **se** ~ **candidat**
stand as a candidate.

porteur, -euse /pɔʀtœʀ, -øz/ nm, f
(de nouvelles) bearer; (Méd) carrier.
●nm (Rail) porter.

portier /pɔʀtje/ nm doorman.

portière /pɔʀtjɛʀ/ nf door.

porto /pɔʀto/ nm port (wine).

portrait /pɔʀtʀɛ/ nm portrait.
portrait-robot (pl **portraits-
robots**) nm identikit®, photofit®.

portuaire /pɔʀtɥɛʀ/ adj port.

portugais, ~e /pɔʀtygɛ, -z/ adj
Portuguese. ●nm (Ling)
Portuguese. P~, ~e nm, f
Portuguese.

Portugal /pɔʀtygal/ nm Portugal.

pose /poz/ nf installation; (attitude)
pose; (Photo) exposure.

posé, ~e /poze/ adj calm, serious.

poser /poze/ **1** vt put (down);
(installer) install, put in; (fondations)
lay; (question) ask; (problème) pose;
~ **sa candidature** apply (**à** for).
●vi (modèle) pose. ■ **se** ~ vpr (avion,
oiseau) land; (regard) fall; (se
présenter) arise.

positif, -ive /pozitif, -v/ adj
positive.

position /pozisjɔ̃/ nf position;
prendre ~ take a stand.

posologie /pozɔlɔʒi/ nf dosage.

posséder /posede/ **14** vt (propriété)
own, possess; (diplôme) have.

possessif, -ive /posesif, -v/ adj
possessive.

possession /posesjɔ̃/ nf
possession; **prendre** ~ **de** take
possession of.

possibilité /posibilite/ nf
possibility.

....

☒ *see A-Z of French life and culture*

possible /posibl/ adj possible; **dès
que** ~ as soon as possible; **le
plus tard** ~ as late as possible.
●nm **le** ~ what is possible; **faire
son** ~ do one's utmost.

postal, ~e (mpl **-aux**) /postal, -o/
adj postal.

☒ poste /post/ nf (service) post;
(bureau) post office; ~ **aérienne**
airmail; **mettre à la** ~ post; ~
restante poste restante. ●nm
(lieu, emploi) post; (de radio, télévision)
set; (téléphone) extension
(number); ~ **d'essence** petrol
station; ~ **d'incendie** fire point;
~ **de pilotage** cockpit; ~ **de
police** police station; ~ **de
secours** first-aid post.

poster[1] /poste/ **1** vt (lettre,
personne) post.

poster[2] /postɛʀ/ nm poster.

postérieur, ~e /posteʀjœʀ/ adj
later; (partie) back; ~ **à** after. ●nm
1 posterior.

posthume /postym/ adj
posthumous.

postiche /postiʃ/ adj false.

postier, -ière /postje, -jɛʀ/ nm, f
postal worker.

post-scriptum* /postskʀiptɔm/
nm inv postscript.

postuler /postyle/ **1** vt/i apply (**à**
for); (principe) postulate.

pot /po/ nm pot; (en plastique)
carton; (en verre) jar; (chance **1**)
luck; (boisson **1**) drink; ~
catalytique catalytic converter;
~ **d'échappement**
exhaust pipe.

potable /potabl/ adj **eau** ~
drinking water.

potage /potaʒ/ nm soup.

potager, -ère /potaʒe, -ɛʀ/ adj
vegetable. ●nm vegetable garden.

pot-au-feu /potofø/ nm inv stew.
(plat) stew.

pot-de-vin (pl **pots-de-vin**)
/podvɛ̃/ nm bribe.

poteau (pl ~**x**) /poto/ nm post;

(télégraphique) pole; ~ **indicateur** signpost.

potelé, ~e /pɔtle/ adj plump.

potentiel, ~le /pɔtɑ̃sjɛl/ adj & nm potential.

poterie /pɔtʀi/ nf pottery; (objet) piece of pottery. **potier** nm potter.

potins /pɔtɛ̃/ nmpl gossip (+ sg).

potiron /pɔtiʀɔ̃/ nm pumpkin.

pou (pl ~x) /pu/ nm louse.

poubelle /pubɛl/ nf dustbin.

pouce /pus/ nm thumb; (de pied) big toe; (mesure) inch.

poudre /pudʀ/ nf powder; (~ **à canon**) gunpowder; **en** ~ (lait) powdered; (chocolat) drinking.

poudrier /pudʀije/ nm (powder) compact.

pouf /puf/ nm pouffe.

poulailler /pulaje/ nm henhouse.

poulain /pulɛ̃/ nm foal; (protégé) protégé.

poule /pul/ nf hen; (Culin) fowl; (femme ✖) tart.

poulet /pulɛ/ nm chicken.

pouliche /puliʃ/ nf filly.

poulie /puli/ nf pulley.

pouls /pu/ nm pulse.

poumon /pumɔ̃/ nm lung.

poupe /pup/ nf stern.

poupée /pupe/ nf doll.

pour /puʀ/ prép for; (envers) to; (à la place de) on behalf of; (comme) as; ~ **cela** for that reason; ~ **cent** per cent; ~ **de bon** for good; ~ **faire** (in order) to do; ~ **que** so that; ~ **moi** (à mon avis) as for me; **trop poli** ~ too polite to; ~ **ce qui est de** as for; **être** ~ be in favour. ● nm inv **le** ~ **et le contre** the pros and cons.

pourboire /puʀbwaʀ/ nm tip.

pourcentage /puʀsɑ̃taʒ/ nm percentage.

pourparlers /puʀpaʀle/ nmpl talks.

pourpre /puʀpʀ/ adj & nm crimson; (violet) purple.

pourquoi /puʀkwa/ conj & adv why. ● nm inv **le** ~ **et le comment** the why and the wherefore.

pourra, pourrait /puʀa, puʀɛ/ ▶POUVOIR 49.

pourri, ~e /puʀi/ adj rotten. **pourrir** ② vt/i rot. **pourriture** nf rot.

poursuite /puʀsɥit/ nf pursuit (**de** of); ~s (Jur) legal action (+ sg).

poursuivre /puʀsɥivʀ/ 57 vt pursue; (continuer) continue (with); ~ **(en justice)** take to court; (droit civil) sue. ● vi continue. ■ **se** ~ vpr continue.

pourtant /puʀtɑ̃/ adv yet.

pourvoir /puʀvwaʀ/ 63 vi ~ **à** provide for; **pourvu de** supplied with.

pourvu que /puʀvyk(ə)/ conj (condition) provided (that); (souhait) let us hope (that).

pousse /pus/ nf growth; (bourgeon) shoot.

poussé, ~e /puse/ adj (études) advanced; (enquête) thorough.

poussée /puse/ nf pressure; (coup) push; (de prix) upsurge; (Méd) attack.

pousser /puse/ ① vt push; (cri) let out; (soupir) heave; (continuer) continue; (exhorter) urge (**à** to); (forcer) drive (**à** to). ● vi push; (grandir) grow; **faire** ~ (cheveux) let grow; (plante) grow. ■ **se** ~ vpr move over ou up; **pousse-toi!** move over!

poussette /pusɛt/ nf pushchair.

poussière /pusjɛʀ/ nf dust. **poussiéreux**, -euse adj dusty.

poussin /pusɛ̃/ nm chick.

poutre /putʀ/ nf beam; (en métal) girder.

p

pouvoir /puvwaʀ/ 49 v aux
(possibilité) can, be able; (permission,
éventualité) may, can; **il peut/
pouvait/pourrait venir** he can/
could/might come; **je n'ai pas
pu** I couldn't; **j'ai pu faire** (réussi
à) I managed to do; **je n'en
peux plus** I am exhausted; **il se
peut que** it may be that. ●nm
power; (gouvernement) government;
au ~ in power; **~s publics**
authorities.

prairie /pʀeʀi/ nf meadow.

praticien, ~ne /pʀatisjɛ̃, -ɛn/ nm,
f practitioner.

pratiquant, ~e /pʀatikɑ̃, -t/ adj
practising. ●nm, f churchgoer.

pratique /pʀatik/ adj practical.
●nf (expérience)
experience; **la ~ du golf/du
cheval** golfing/riding.
pratiquement adv (en pratique) in
practice; (presque) practically.

pratiquer /pʀatike/ 1 vt/i
practise; (Sport) play; (faire) make.

pré /pʀe/ nm meadow.

pré-affranchi, ~e /pʀeafʀɑ̃ʃi/
adj postage-paid.

préalable /pʀealabl/ adj
preliminary, prior. ●nm
precondition; **au ~** first.

préambule /pʀeɑ̃byl/ nm
preamble.

préavis /pʀeavi/ nm notice.

précaire /pʀekɛʀ/ adj precarious.
précarité nf (d'emploi) insecurity.

précaution /pʀekosjɔ̃/ nf (mesure)
precaution; (prudence) caution.

précédent, ~e /pʀesedɑ̃, -t/ adj
previous. ●nm precedent.

précéder /pʀesede/ 14 vt/i
precede.

précepteur, -trice /pʀesɛptœʀ,
-tʀis/ nm, f (private) tutor.

prêcher /pʀeʃe/ 1 vt/i preach.

précieux, -ieuse /pʀesjø, -z/ adj
precious.

....
⧉ *see* A-Z of French life and culture

précipitamment /pʀesipitamɑ̃/
adv hastily. **précipitation** nf
haste.

précipiter /pʀesipite/ 1 vt throw,
precipitate; (hâter) hasten. ■**se ~**
vpr (se dépêcher) rush (**sur** at, on
to); (se jeter) throw oneself;
(s'accélérer) speed up.

précis, ~e /pʀesi, -z/ adj precise,
specific; (mécanisme) accurate; **dix
heures ~es** ten o'clock sharp.
●nm summary.

préciser /pʀesize/ 1 vt specify;
précisez votre pensée could
you be more specific. ■**se ~** vpr
become clear(er). **précision** nf
precision; (détail) detail.

précoce /pʀekɔs/ adj (enfant)
precocious.

préconiser /pʀekɔnize/ 1 vt
advocate.

précurseur /pʀekyʀsœʀ/ nm
forerunner.

prédicateur /pʀedikatœʀ/ nm
preacher.

prédilection /pʀedilɛksjɔ̃/ nf
preference.

prédire /pʀediʀ/ 37 vt predict.

prédominer /pʀedɔmine/ 1 vi
predominate.

préface /pʀefas/ nf preface.

⧉préfecture /pʀefɛktyʀ/ nf
prefecture; **~ de police** police
headquarters.

préféré, ~e /pʀefeʀe/ adj & nm, f
favourite.

préférence /pʀefeʀɑ̃s/ nf
preference; **de ~** preferably.

préférentiel, ~le /pʀefeʀɑ̃sjɛl/
adj preferential.

préférer /pʀefeʀe/ 14 vt prefer (**à**
to); **~ faire** prefer to do; **je ne
préfère pas** I'd rather not;
j'aurais préféré ne pas savoir
I wish I hadn't found out.

⧉préfet /pʀefɛ/ nm prefect; **~ de
police** prefect *ou* chief of police.

préfixe /pʀefiks/ nm prefix.

préhistorique /pReistɔRik/ adj prehistoric.

préjudice /pReʒydis/ nm harm, prejudice; **porter ~ à** harm.

préjugé /pReʒyʒe/ nm prejudice; **être plein de ~s** be very prejudiced.

prélasser (se) /(sə)pRelɑse/ 🚹 vpr loll (about).

prélèvement /pRelɛvmɑ̃/ nm deduction; (de sang) sample. **prélever** 🖪 vt deduct (**sur** from); (sang) take.

préliminaire /pReliminɛR/ adj & nm preliminary; **~s** (sexuels) foreplay.

prématuré, ~e /pRematyRe/ adj premature. •nm premature baby.

premier, -ière /pRəmje, -jɛR/ adj first; (rang) front, first; (enfance) early; (nécessité, souci) prime; (qualité) top, prime; **de ~ ordre** first-rate; 🖪**~ ministre** Prime Minister. •nm, f first (one). •nm (date) first; (étage) first floor; **en ~** first. **première** nf (Rail) first class; (exploit jamais vu) first; (cinéma, Théât) première; (Aut) (vitesse) first (gear). **premièrement** adv firstly.

prémunir /pRemyniR/ 🗷 vt protect (**contre** against).

prenant, ~e /pRənɑ̃, -t/ adj (activité) engrossing; (enfant) demanding.

prénatal, ~e (mpl ~s) /pRenatal/ adj antenatal.

prendre /pRɑ̃dR/ 🗐 vt take; (attraper) catch, get; (acheter) get; (repas) have; (engager, adopter) take on; (poids) put on; (chercher) pick up; **qu'est-ce qui te prend?** what's the matter with you? •vi (liquide) set; (feu) catch; (vaccin) take. ∎**se ~** vpr **se ~ pour** think one is; **s'en ~ à** attack; (rendre responsable) blame; **s'y ~** set about (it).

preneur, -euse /pRənœR, -øz/ nm, f buyer; **être ~** be willing to

buy; **trouver ~** find a buyer.

prénom /pRenɔ̃/ nm first name.

prénommer /pRenɔme/ 🚹 vt call. ∎**se ~** vpr be called.

préoccupation /pReɔkypasjɔ̃/ nf (souci) worry; (idée fixe) preoccupation.

préoccuper /pReɔkype/ 🚹 vt worry; (absorber) preoccupy. ∎**se ~ de** vpr think about.

préparation /pRepaRasjɔ̃/ nf preparation. **préparatoire** adj preparatory.

préparer /pRepaRe/ 🚹 vt prepare; (repas, café) make; **plats préparés** ready-cooked meals. ∎**se ~** vpr prepare oneself (**à** for); (s'apprêter) get ready; (être proche) be brewing.

préposé, ~e /pRepoze/ nm, f employee; (des postes) postman, postwoman.

préposition /pRepozisjɔ̃/ nf preposition.

préretraite /pRerətRɛt/ nf early retirement.

près /pRɛ/ adv near, close; **~ de** near (to), close to; (presque) nearly; **à cela ~** except that; **de ~** closely.

présage /pRezaʒ/ nm omen.

presbyte /pRɛsbit/ adj longsighted, far-sighted.

prescrire /pRɛskRiR/ 🗟 vt prescribe.

préséance /pReseɑ̃s/ nf precedence.

présence /pRezɑ̃s/ nf presence; (Scol) attendance.

présent, ~e /pRezɑ̃, -t/ adj present. •nm (temps, cadeau) present; **à ~** now.

présentateur, -trice /pRezɑ̃tatœR, -tRis/ nm, f presenter.

présentation /pRezɑ̃tasjɔ̃/ nf (de personne) introduction; (exposé) presentation.

p

....

🖪 *see A-Z of French life and culture*

présenter /prezɑ̃te/ **1** vt present; (personne) introduce (**à** to); (montrer) show. •vi ~ **bien** have a pleasing appearance. ∎ **se** ~ vpr introduce oneself (**à** to); (aller) go; (apparaître) appear; (candidat) come forward; (occasion) arise; **se** ~ **à** (examen) sit for; (élection) stand for; **se** ~ **bien** look good.

préservatif /prezɛrvatif/ nm condom.

préserver /prezɛrve/ **1** vt protect.

présidence /prezidɑ̃s/ nf (d'État) presidency; (de société) chairmanship.

▣ président, ~**e** /prezidɑ̃, -t/ nm, f president; (de société, comité) chairman, chairwoman; ~-**directeur général** managing director.

présidentiel, ~**le** /prezidɑ̃sjɛl/ adj presidential.

présider /prezide/ **1** vt preside.

présomptueux, -**euse** /prezɔ̃ptɥø, -z/ adj presumptuous.

presque /prɛsk(ə)/ adv almost, nearly; ~ **jamais** hardly ever; ~ **rien** hardly anything; ~ **pas** (**de**) hardly any.

presqu'île* /prɛskil/ nf peninsula.

pressant, ~**e** /prɛsɑ̃, -t/ adj pressing, urgent.

presse /prɛs/ nf (journaux, appareil) press.

pressentiment /prɛsɑ̃timɑ̃/ nm premonition. **pressentir** **46** vt have a premonition of.

pressé, ~**e** /prese/ adj in a hurry; (orange, citron) freshly squeezed.

presser /prese/ **1** vt squeeze, press; (appuyer sur, harceler) press; (hâter) hasten; (inciter) urge (**de** to). •vi (temps) press; (affaire) be pressing. ∎ **se** ~ vpr (se hâter) hurry; (se grouper) crowd.

··

▣ see A-Z of French life and culture

pressing /presiŋ/ nm (teinturerie) dry-cleaner's.

pression /presjɔ̃/ nf pressure; (bouton) press-stud.

prestance /prɛstɑ̃s/ nf (imposing) presence.

prestation /prɛstasjɔ̃/ nf allowance; (d'artiste) performance.

prestidigitation /prɛstidiʒita-sjɔ̃/ nf conjuring.

prestige /prɛstiʒ/ nm prestige. **prestigieux**, -**ieuse** adj prestigious.

présumé, **e** /prezyme/ adj alleged.

présumer /prezyme/ **1** vt presume; ~ **que** assume that; ~ **de** overrate.

prêt, ~**e** /prɛ, -t/ adj ready (**à qch** for sth, **à faire** to do). •nm loan. **prêt-à-porter** nm inv ready-to-wear clothes.

prétendre /pretɑ̃dr/ **3** vt claim (**que** that); (vouloir) intend; **on le prétend riche** he is said to be very rich. **prétendu**, ~**e** adj so-called. **prétendument** adv supposedly, allegedly.

prétentieux, -**ieuse** /pretɑ̃sjø, -z/ adj pretentious.

prêter /prete/ **1** vt lend (**à** to); (attribuer) attribute; ~ **son aide à qn** give sb some help; ~ **attention** pay attention; ~ **serment** take an oath. •vi ~ **à** lead to.

prêteur, -**euse** /pretœr, -øz/ nm, f (money-)lender; ~ **sur gages** pawnbroker.

prétexte /pretɛkst/ nm pretext, excuse.

prêtre /prɛtr/ nm priest.

preuve /prœv/ nf proof; **des** ~**s** evidence (+ sg); **faire** ~ **de** show; **faire ses** ~**s** prove oneself.

prévaloir /prevalwar/ **60** vi prevail.

prévenant, ~e /pʀevnɑ̃, -t/ adj thoughtful.

prévenir /pʀevniʀ/ 58 vt (menacer) warn; (informer) tell; (médecin) call; (éviter, anticiper) prevent.

préventif, -ive /pʀevɑ̃tif, -v/ adj preventive.

prévention /pʀevɑ̃sjɔ̃/ nf prevention; **faire de la ~** take preventive action; **~ routière** road safety.

prévenu, ~e /pʀevny/ nm, f defendant.

prévisible /pʀevizibl/ adj predictable. **prévision** nf prediction; (météorologique) forecast.

prévoir /pʀevwaʀ/ 63 vt foresee; (temps) forecast; (organiser) plan (for), provide for; (envisager) allow (for); **prévu pour** (jouet) designed for; **comme prévu** as planned.

prévoyance /pʀevwajɑ̃s/ nf foresight. **prévoyant, ~e** adj farsighted.

prier /pʀije/ 45 vi pray. •vt pray to; (demander à) ask (**de** to); **je vous en prie** please; (il n'y a pas de quoi) don't mention it.

prière /pʀijɛʀ/ nf prayer; (demande) request; **~ de** (vous êtes prié de) will you please.

primaire /pʀimɛʀ/ adj primary.

prime /pʀim/ nf free gift; (d'employé) bonus; (subvention) subsidy; (d'assurance) premium.

primé, ~e /pʀime/ adj prizewinning.

primeurs /pʀimœʀ/ nfpl early fruit and vegetables.

primevère /pʀimvɛʀ/ nf primrose.

primitif, -ive /pʀimitif, -v/ adj primitive; (d'origine) original. •nm, f primitive.

primordial, ~e (mpl **-iaux**) /pʀimɔʀdjal, -jo/ adj essential.

prince /pʀɛ̃s/ nm prince.

princesse nf princess.

principal, ~e (mpl **-aux**) /pʀɛ̃sipal, -o/ adj main, principal. •nm headmaster; (chose) main thing.

principe /pʀɛ̃sip/ nm principle; **en ~** in theory; (d'habitude) as a rule.

printanier, -ière /pʀɛ̃tanje, -jɛʀ/ adj spring(-like).

printemps /pʀɛ̃tɑ̃/ nm spring.

prioritaire /pʀijɔʀitɛʀ/ adj priority; **être ~** have priority. **priorité** nf priority; (Auto) right of way.

pris, ~e /pʀi, -z/ adj (place) taken; (personne, journée) busy; (nez) stuffed up; **~ de** (peur, fièvre) stricken with; **~ de panique** panic-stricken. •▷PRENDRE 50.

prise /pʀiz/ nf hold, grip; (animal attrapé) catch; (Mil) capture; (**~ de courant**) (mâle) plug; (femelle) socket; **~ multiple** multiplug adapter; **avoir ~ sur qn** have a hold over sb; **aux ~s avec** to grapple with; **~ de conscience** awareness; **~ de contact** first contact, initial meeting; **~ de position** stand; **~ de sang** blood test.

prisé, ~e /pʀize/ adj popular.

prison /pʀizɔ̃/ nf prison, jail; (réclusion) imprisonment. **prisonnier, -ière** nm, f prisoner.

privation /pʀivasjɔ̃/ nf deprivation; (sacrifice) hardship.

privatiser /pʀivatize/ 1 vt privatize.

privé, ~e /pʀive/ adj private. •nm (Comm) private sector; (Scol) private schools (+ pl); **en ~** in private.

priver /pʀive/ 1 vt **~ de** deprive of. ■ **se ~** (**de**) vpr go without.

privilège /pʀivilɛʒ/ nm privilege. **privilégié, ~e** nm, f privileged person.

prix /pʀi/ nm price; (récompense) prize; **à tout ~** at all costs; **au**

p

~ **de** (fig) at the expense of; ~
coûtant, ~ **de revient** cost
price; **à** ~ **fixe** set price.

probabilité /prɔbabilite/ nf
probability. **probable** adj
probable, likely. **probablement**
adv probably.

probant, ~**e** /prɔbã, -t/ adj
convincing, conclusive.

problème /prɔblɛm/ nm problem.

procédé /prɔsede/ nm process;
(manière d'agir) practice.

procéder /prɔsede/ 14 vi proceed;
~ **à** carry out.

procès /prɔsɛ/ nm (criminel) trial;
(civil) lawsuit, proceedings (+ pl).

processus /prɔsesys/ nm process;
~ **de paix** peace process.

procès-verbal (pl **procès-
verbaux**) /prɔsɛvɛrbal, -o/ nm
minutes (+ pl); (contravention)
ticket.

prochain, ~**e** /prɔʃɛ̃, -ɛn/ adj
(suivant) next; (proche) imminent;
(avenir) near. ● nm fellow man.
prochainement adv soon.

proche /prɔʃ/ adj near, close;
(avoisinant) neighbouring; (parent,
ami) close; ~ **de** close to; **de** ~ **en** ~ gradually; **dans un**
~ **avenir** in the near future;
être ~ (imminent) be approaching.
● nm close relative; (ami) close
friend.

Proche-Orient /prɔʃɔrjɑ̃/ nm
Near East.

proclamation /prɔklamasjɔ̃/ nf
declaration, proclamation.
proclamer 1 vt declare,
proclaim.

procuration /prɔkyrasjɔ̃/ nf
proxy.

procurer /prɔkyre/ 1 vt bring (**à**
to). ■ **se** ~ vpr obtain.

procureur /prɔkyrœr/ nm public
prosecutor.

prodige /prɔdiʒ/ nm (fait) marvel;
(personne) prodigy; **enfant/
musicien** ~ child/musical

prodigy. **prodigieux**, **-ieuse** adj
tremendous, prodigious.

prodigue /prɔdig/ adj wasteful;
fils ~ prodigal son.

producteur, **-trice** /prɔdyktœr,
-tris/ adj producing. ● nm, f
producer. **productif**, **-ive** adj
productive. **production** nf
production; (produit) product.
productivité nf productivity.

produire /prɔdɥir/ 17 vt produce.
■ **se** ~ vpr (survenir) happen;
(acteur) perform.

produit /prɔdɥi/ nm product; ~**s**
(de la terre) produce (+ sg); ~
chimique chemical; ~**s
alimentaires** foodstuffs; ~ **de
consommation** consumer
goods; ~ **intérieur brut** gross
domestic product; ~ **national
brut** gross national product.

proéminent, ~**e** /prɔeminã, -t/
adj prominent.

profane /prɔfan/ adj secular. ● nmf
lay person.

proférer /prɔfere/ 14 vt utter.

professeur /prɔfesœr/ nm
teacher; (Univ) lecturer; (avec
chaire) professor.

profession /prɔfesjɔ̃/ nf
occupation; ~ **libérale**
profession.

professionnel, ~**le**
/prɔfesjɔnɛl/ adj professional;
(école) vocational. ● nm, f
professional.

profil /prɔfil/ nm profile.

profit /prɔfi/ nm profit; **au** ~ **de**
in aid of. **profitable** adj
profitable.

profiter /prɔfite/ 1 vi ~ **à**
benefit; ~ **de** take advantage of.

profond, ~**e** /prɔfɔ̃, -d/ adj deep;
(sentiment, intérêt) profound; (causes)
underlying; **au plus** ~ **de** in the
depths of. **profondément** adv
deeply; (différent, triste) profoundly;
(dormir) soundly. **profondeur** nf
depth.

progéniture /pʀɔʒenityʀ/ nf
offspring.

progiciel /pʀɔʒisjɛl/ nm (Ordinat)
package.

programmation /pʀɔgʀamasjɔ̃/
nf programming.

programme /pʀɔgʀam/ nm
programme; (Scol) (d'une matière)
syllabus; (général) curriculum;
(Ordinat) program. **programmer**
1 vt (ordinateur, appareil) program;
(émission) schedule.
programmeur, -euse nm, f
computer programmer.

progrès /pʀɔgʀɛ/ nm & nmpl
progress; **faire des ~** make
progress. **progresser** **1** vi
progress. **progressif, -ive** adj
progressive. **progression** nf
progression.

prohibitif, -ive /pʀɔibitif, -v/ adj
prohibitive.

proie /pʀwa/ nf prey; **en ~ à**
tormented by.

projecteur /pʀɔʒɛktœʀ/ nm
floodlight; (Mil) searchlight;
(cinéma) projector.

projectile /pʀɔʒɛktil/ nm missile.

projection /pʀɔʒɛksjɔ̃/ nf
projection; (séance) show.

projet /pʀɔʒɛ/ nm plan; (ébauche)
draft; **~ de loi** bill.

projeter /pʀɔʒte/ **38** vt (prévoir)
plan (**de** to); (film) project, show;
(jeter) hurl, project.

prolétaire /pʀɔletɛʀ/ nmf
proletarian.

prologue /pʀɔlɔg/ nm prologue.

prolongation /pʀɔlɔ̃gasjɔ̃/ nf
extension; **~s** (football)
extra time.

prolonger /pʀɔlɔ̃ʒe/ **40** vt extend.
■ **se ~** vpr go on.

promenade /pʀɔmnad/ nf walk;
(à bicyclette, à cheval) ride; (en auto)
drive, ride; **faire une ~** go for
a walk.

promener /pʀɔmne/ **6** vt take

for a walk; **~ son regard sur**
cast an eye over. ■ **se ~** vpr walk;
(aller) se ~ go for a walk.
promeneur, -euse nm, f walker.

promesse /pʀɔmɛs/ nf promise.

prometteur, -euse /pʀɔmɛtœʀ,
-øz/ adj promising.

promettre /pʀɔmɛtʀ/ **42** vt/i
promise. ●vi be promising. ■ **se**
~ de vpr resolve to.

promoteur /pʀɔmɔtœʀ/ nm
(immobilier) property developer.

promotion /pʀɔmɔsjɔ̃/ nf
promotion; (Univ) year; (Comm)
special offer.

prompt, ~e /pʀɔ̃, -t/ adj swift.

promu, ~e /pʀɔmy/ adj **être ~**
be promoted.

prôner /pʀone/ **1** vt extol.

pronom /pʀɔnɔ̃/ nm pronoun.
pronominal, ~e (mpl **-aux**) adj
pronominal.

prononcé, ~e /pʀɔnɔ̃se/ adj
strong.

prononcer /pʀɔnɔ̃se/ **10** vt
pronounce; (discours) make. ■ **se**
~ vpr (mot) be pronounced;
(personne) make a decision (**pour**
in favour of). **prononciation** nf
pronunciation.

pronostic /pʀɔnɔstik/ nm
forecast; (Méd) prognosis.

propagande /pʀɔpagɑ̃d/ nf
propaganda.

propager /pʀɔpaʒe/ **40** vt spread.
■ **se ~** vpr spread.

prophète /pʀɔfɛt/ nm prophet.
prophétie nf prophecy.

propice /pʀɔpis/ adj favourable.

proportion /pʀɔpɔʀsjɔ̃/ nf
proportion; (en mathématiques)
ratio; **toutes ~s gardées**
relatively speaking.
proportionné, ~e adj
proportionate (**à** to).
proportionnel, ~le adj
proportional.
proportionnellement adv
proportionately.

p

propos /pʀɔpo/ nm intention; (sujet) subject; **à ～** at the right time; (dans un dialogue) by the way; **à ～ de** about; **à tout ～** at every possible occasion. • nmpl (paroles) remarks.

proposer /pʀɔpoze/ **1** vt suggest, propose; (offrir) offer. ■ se ～ vpr volunteer (**pour** to). **proposition** nf proposal; (affirmation) proposition; (Gram) clause.

propre /pʀɔpʀ/ adj (non sali) clean; (soigné) neat; (honnête) decent; (à soi) own; (sens) literal; (qui convient) suited to; (spécifique) particular to. • nm **mettre au ～** write out again neatly; **c'est du ～!** (ironique) well done!

proprement /pʀɔpʀəmɑ̃/ adv (avec soin) neatly; (au sens strict) strictly; **le bureau ～ dit** the office itself.

propreté /pʀɔpʀəte/ nf cleanliness.

propriétaire /pʀɔpʀijetɛʀ/ nmf owner; (Comm) proprietor; (qui loue) landlord, landlady.

propriété /pʀɔpʀijete/ nf property; (droit) ownership.

propulser /pʀɔpylse/ **1** vt propel.

proroger /pʀɔʀɔʒe/ **40** vt (contrat) defer; (passeport) extend.

proscrire /pʀɔskʀiʀ/ **30** vt proscribe.

proscrit, ～e /pʀɔskʀi, -t/ adj proscribed. • nm, f (exilé) exile.

prose /pʀoz/ nf prose.

prospectus /pʀɔspɛktys/ nm leaflet.

prospère /pʀɔspɛʀ/ adj flourishing, thriving. **prospérer** **14** vi thrive, prosper. **prospérité** nf prosperity.

prosterner (se) /(sə)pʀɔstɛʀne/ **1** vpr prostrate oneself; **prosterné devant** prostrate before.

prostituée /pʀɔstitɥe/ nf

prostitute. **prostitution** nf prostitution.

protecteur, -trice /pʀɔtɛktœʀ, -tʀis/ nm, f protector. • adj protective.

protection /pʀɔtɛksjɔ̃/ nf protection.

protégé, ～e /pʀɔteʒe/ nm, f protégé.

protéger /pʀɔteʒe/ **40** vt protect. ■ se ～ vpr protect oneself.

protéine /pʀɔtein/ nf protein.

protestant, ～e /pʀɔtɛstɑ̃, -t/ adj & nm, f Protestant.

protestation /pʀɔtɛstasjɔ̃/ nf protest. **protester** **1** vt/i protest.

protocole /pʀɔtɔkɔl/ nm protocol.

protubérant, ～e /pʀɔtybeʀɑ̃/ adj protruding.

proue /pʀu/ nf bow, prow.

prouesse /pʀuɛs/ nf feat, exploit.

prouver /pʀuve/ **1** vt prove.

provenance /pʀɔvnɑ̃s/ nf origin; **en ～ de** from.

provençal, ～e (mpl -aux) /pʀɔ-vɑ̃sal, -o/ adj & nm, f Provençal.

provenir /pʀɔvniʀ/ **58** vi ～ **de** come from.

proverbe /pʀɔvɛʀb/ nm proverb.

province /pʀɔvɛ̃s/ nf province; **de ～** provincial; **la ～** the provinces (+ pl). **provincial, ～e** (mpl -iaux) adj & nm, f provincial.

proviseur /pʀɔvizœʀ/ nm headmaster, principal.

provision /pʀɔvizjɔ̃/ nf supply, store; (sur un compte) credit (balance); (acompte) deposit; ～**s** (vivres) food shopping.

provisoire /pʀɔvizwaʀ/ adj provisional.

provocant, ～e /pʀɔvɔkɑ̃, -t/ adj provocative. **provocation** nf provocation. **provoquer** **1** vt cause; (sexuellement) arouse; (défier) provoke.

proxénète /pʀɔksenɛt/ nm pimp, procurer.

proximité /pʀɔksimite/ nf proximity; **à ~ de** close to.

prude /pʀyd/ adj prudish.

prudemment /pʀydamɑ̃/ adv (conduire) carefully; (attendre) cautiously. **prudence** nf caution. **prudent, ~e** adj (au volant) careful; (à agir) cautious; (sage) wise.

prune /pʀyn/ nf plum.

pruneau (pl ~x) /pʀyno/ nm prune.

prunelle /pʀynɛl/ nf (pupille) pupil; (fruit) sloe.

prunier /pʀynje/ nm plum tree.

psaume /psom/ nm psalm.

pseudonyme /psødɔnim/ nm pseudonym.

psychanalyse /psikanaliz/ nf psychoanalysis. **psychanalyste** nmf psychoanalyst.

psychiatre /psikjatʀ/ nmf psychiatrist. **psychiatrie** nf psychiatry. **psychiatrique** adj psychiatric.

psychique /psiʃik/ adj mental, psychological.

psychologie /psikɔlɔʒi/ nf psychology. **psychologique** adj psychological. **psychologue** nmf psychologist.

pu /py/ ▷ POUVOIR 49.

puant, ~e /pɥɑ̃, -t/ adj stinking.

pub /pyb/ nf 1 **la ~** advertising; **une ~** an advert.

puberté /pybɛʀte/ nf puberty.

public, -que /pyblik/ adj public. ●nm public; (assistance) audience; (Scol) state schools (+ pl); **en ~** in public.

publication /pyblikasjɔ̃/ nf publication.

publicitaire /pyblisitɛʀ/ adj publicity. **publicité** nf publicity, advertising; (annonce) advertisement.

publier /pyblije/ 45 vt publish.

publiquement /pyblikmɑ̃/ adv publicly.

puce /pys/ nf flea; (électronique) chip; **marché aux ~s** flea market.

pudeur /pydœʀ/ nf modesty.

pudibond, ~e /pydibɔ̃, -d/ adj prudish.

pudique /pydik/ adj modest.

puer /pɥe/ 1 vi stink. ●vt stink of.

puéricultrice /pɥeʀikyltʀis/ nf pediatric nurse.

puéril, ~e /pɥeʀil/ adj puerile.

puis /pɥi/ adv then.

puiser /pɥize/ 1 vt draw (**dans** from). ●vi ~ **dans qch** dip into sth.

puisque /pɥisk(ə)/ conj since, as.

puissance /pɥisɑ̃s/ nf power; **en ~** potential.

puissant, ~e /pɥisɑ̃, -t/ adj powerful.

puits /pɥi/ nm well; (de mine) shaft.

pull(-over)* /pyl(ɔvɛʀ) / nm pullover, jumper.

pulpe /pylp/ nf pulp.

pulsation /pylsasjɔ̃/ nf (heart-) beat.

pulvériser /pylveʀize/ 1 vt pulverize; (liquide) spray.

punaise /pynɛz/ nf (insecte) bug; (clou) drawing pin.

punch¹* /pɔ̃ʃ/ nm (boisson) punch.

punch² /pœnʃ/ nm **avoir du ~** have drive.

punir /pyniʀ/ 2 vt punish. **punition** nf punishment.

pupille /pypij/ nf (de l'œil) pupil. ●nmf (enfant) ward.

pupitre /pypitʀ/ nm (Scol) desk; ~

p

à musique music stand.

pur /pyʀ/ adj pure; (whisky) neat.

purée /pyʀe/ nf purée; (de pommes de terre) mashed potatoes (+ pl).

pureté /pyʀte/ nf purity.

purgatoire /pyʀgatwaʀ/ nm purgatory.

purge /pyʀʒ/ nf purge. **purger** 40 vt (Pol, Méd) purge; (peine: Jur) serve.

purifier /pyʀifje/ 45 vt purify.

puritain, ~e /pyʀitɛ̃, -ɛn/ nm, f puritan. ● adj puritanical.

pur-sang /pyʀsɑ̃/ nm inv (cheval) thoroughbred.

pus /py/ nm pus.

putain /pytɛ̃/ nf p whore.

puzzle /pœzl/ nm jigsaw (puzzle).

P-V abrév m (**procès-verbal**) ticket, traffic fine.

pyjama /piʒama/ nm pyjamas (+ pl); **un ~** a pair of pyjamas.

pylône /pilon/ nm pylon.

Pyrénées /piʀene/ nfpl **les ~** the Pyrenees.

pyromane /piʀɔman/ nmf arsonist.

Qq

QG abrév m (**quartier général**) HQ.

QI abrév m (**quotient intellectuel**) IQ.

qu' /k/ ▷**QUE**.

quadriller /kadʀije/ 1 vt (armée) take control of; (police) spread one's net over; **papier quadrillé** squared paper.

quadrupède /kwadʀypɛd/ nm quadruped.

quadruple /kwadʀypl/ adj quadruple. ● nm **le ~ de** four times. **quadrupler** 1 vt/i quadruple.

quai /ke/ nm (de gare) platform; (de port) quay; (de rivière) bank.

qualification /kalifikasjɔ̃/ nf qualification; (compétence pratique) skills (+ pl).

qualifié, ~e /kalifje/ adj (diplômé) qualified; (main-d'œuvre) skilled.

qualifier /kalifje/ 45 vt qualify; (décrire) describe (**de** as). ■ **se ~** vpr qualify (**pour** for).

qualité /kalite/ nf quality; (titre) occupation; (fonction) position; **en sa ~ de** in his ou her capacity as.

quand /kɑ̃/ adv when; **~ même** all the same. ● conj when; (toutes les fois que) whenever; **~ bien même** even if.

quant à /kɑ̃ta/ prép as for.

quantité /kɑ̃tite/ nf quantity; **une ~ de** a lot of; **des ~s (de)** masses ou lots (of).

quarantaine /kaʀɑ̃tɛn/ nf (Méd) quarantine; **une ~ de** about forty; **avoir la ~** be in one's forties.

quarante /kaʀɑ̃t/ adj & nm forty.

quart /kaʀ/ nm quarter; (Naut) watch; **onze heures moins le ~** quarter to eleven; **~ (de litre)** quarter litre; **~ de finale** quarter- final; **~ d'heure** quarter of an hour; **~ de tour** ninety-degree turn.

quartier /kaʀtje/ nm area, district; (zone ethnique) quarter; (de lune, pomme, bœuf) quarter; (d'une orange) segment; **~s** (Mil) quarters; **de ~, du ~** local; **~ général** headquarters; **avoir ~ libre** be free.

quasiment /kazimã/ adv almost, practically.

quatorze /katɔrz/ adj & nm fourteen.

quatre /katr(ə)/ adj & nm four. **quatre-vingt(s)** adj & nm eighty. **quatre-vingt-dix** adj & nm ninety.

quatre-quatre /katrkatr/ nm four-wheel drive.

quatrième /katrijɛm/ adj & nmf fourth. ●nf (Auto) fourth gear.

quatuor /kwatɥɔr/ nm quartet.

que, qu' /kə, k/

❗ **qu'** before vowel or mute h.

●conjonction
····▸ that; **je crains ~...** I'm worried that...
····▸ (souhait, volonté) **je veux ~ tu viennes** I want you to come; **~ tu viennes ou non** whether you come or not; **qu'il entre** let him come in.
····▸ (comparaison) than; **plus grand ~ toi** taller than you.
●pronom interrogatif
····▸ what; **~ voulez-vous manger?** what would you like to eat?
●pronom relatif
····▸ (personne) whom, that; **l'homme ~ j'ai rencontré** the man (whom) I met.
····▸ (chose) that, which; **le cheval ~ Nick m'a offert** the horse (which) Nick gave me.
●adverbe
····▸ **que c'est joli!** it's so pretty!; **~ de monde!** what a lot of people!

Québec /kebɛk/ nm Quebec.

quel, quelle (pl quel(le)s) /kɛl/
●adjectif interrogatif
····▸ which, what; **~ auteur a écrit...?** which writer wrote...?; **~ jour sommes-nous?** what day is it today?
●adjectif exclamatif
····▸ what; **~ idiot!** what an idiot!; **quelle horreur!** that's horrible!
●adjectif relatif
····▸ **~ que soit son âge** whatever his age; **quelles que soient tes raisons** whatever your reasons; **~ que soit le gagnant** whoever the winner is.

quelconque /kɛlkɔ̃k/ adj any, some; (banal) ordinary; (médiocre) poor, second rate.

quelque /kɛlkə/ adj some; **~s** a few, some. ●adv (environ) about, some; **et ~** ⊡ and a bit; **~ chose** something; (dans les phrases interrogatives) anything; **~ part** somewhere; **~ peu** somewhat.

quelquefois /kɛlkəfwa/ adv sometimes.

quelques-uns, -unes /kɛlkəzœ̃, -yn/ pron some, a few.

quelqu'un /kɛlkœ̃/ pron someone, somebody; (dans les phrases interrogatives) anyone, anybody.

querelle /kərɛl/ nf quarrel. **quereller (se)** ❶ vpr quarrel. **querelleur, -euse** adj quarrelsome.

question /kɛstjɔ̃/ nf question; (affaire) matter, question; **poser une ~** ask a question; **en ~** in question; **il est ~ de** (cela concerne) it is about; (on parle de) there is talk of; **il n'en est pas ~** it is out of the question; **pas ~!** no way!

questionnaire /kɛstjɔnɛr/ nm questionnaire.

questionner /kɛstjɔne/ ❶ vt question.

quête /kɛt/ nf (Relig) collection;

q

(recherche) search; **en ~ de** in search of.

queue /kø/ nf tail; (de poêle) handle; (de fruit) stalk; (de fleur) stem; (file) queue; (US) line; (de train) rear; **faire la ~** queue (up); (US) line up; **~ de cheval** ponytail; **faire une ~ de poisson à qn** (Auto) cut in front of sb.

qui /ki/
● pronom interrogatif
····➤ (sujet) who; **~ a fait ça?** who did that?
····➤ (complément) whom; **à ~ est ce livre?** whose book is this?
● pronom relatif
····➤ (personne sujet) who; **c'est Isabelle qui vient d'appeler** it's Isabelle who's just called.
····➤ (autres cas) that, which; **qu'est-ce ~ te prend?** what is the matter with you?; **invite ~ tu veux** invite whoever you want; **~ que ce soit** whoever it is, anybody.

quiche /kiʃ/ nf quiche.

quiconque /kikɔ̃k/ pron whoever; (n'importe qui) anyone.

quille /kij/ nf (de bateau) keel; (jouet) skittle.

quincaillerie /kɛ̃kɑjʀi/ nf hardware; (magasin) hardware shop. **quincaillier*, -ière** nm, f hardware dealer.

quintal (pl **-aux**) /kɛ̃tal, -o/ nm quintal, one hundred kilos.

quinte /kɛ̃t/ nf **~ de toux** coughing fit.

quintuple /kɛ̃typl/ adj quintuple. ● nm **le ~ de** five times.

quintupler 1 vt/i quintuple, increase fivefold.

quinzaine /kɛ̃zɛn/ nf **une ~ (de)** about fifteen.

quinze /kɛ̃z/ adj & nm inv fifteen; **~ jours** two weeks.

quiproquo /kipʀɔko/ nm misunderstanding.

quittance /kitɑ̃s/ nf receipt.

quitte /kit/ adj quits (**envers** with); **~ à faire** even if it means doing.

quitter /kite/ 1 vt leave; (vêtement) take off; **ne quittez pas!** hold the line, please! ■ se **~** vpr part.

qui-vive /kiviv/ nm inv **être sur le ~** be alert.

quoi /kwa/ pron what; (après une préposition) which; **de ~ vivre** (assez) enough to live on; **de ~ écrire** something to write with; **~ qu'il dise** whatever he says; **~ que ce soit** anything; **il n'y a pas de ~** my pleasure; **il n'y a pas de ~ s'inquiéter** there's nothing to worry about.

quoique /kwak(ə)/ conj although, though.

quota /kɔta/ nm quota.

quote-part* (pl **quotes-parts**) /kɔtpaʀ/ nf share.

quotidien, ~ne /kɔtidjɛ̃, -ɛn/ adj daily; (banal) everyday. ● nm daily (paper); (vie quotidienne) everyday life. **quotidiennement** adv daily.

q

Rr

rabâcher /ʀabaʃe/ **1** vt keep repeating.

rabais /ʀabɛ/ nm reduction, discount. **rabaisser 1** vt (déprécier) belittle; (réduire) reduce.

rabat-joie* /ʀabaʒwa/ nm inv killjoy.

rabattre /ʀabatʀ/ **11** vt (chapeau, visière) pull down; (refermer) shut; (diminuer) reduce; (déduire) take off; (col, drap) turn down. ■ **se ~** vpr (se refermer) close; (véhicule) cut back in; **se ~ sur** make do with.

rabot /ʀabo/ nm plane.

rabougri, ~e /ʀabugʀi/ adj stunted.

racaille /ʀakɑj/ nf rabble.

raccommoder /ʀakɔmɔde/ **1** vt mend; (personnes 1) reconcile.

raccompagner /ʀakɔ̃paɲe/ **1** vt see ou take back (home).

raccord /ʀakɔʀ/ nm link; (de papier peint) join; (retouche) touch-up. **raccorder 1** vt connect, join.

raccourci /ʀakuʀsi/ nm short cut; **en ~** in short.

raccourcir /ʀakuʀsiʀ/ **2** vt shorten. ● vi get shorter.

raccrocher /ʀakʀɔʃe/ **1** vt hang back up; (passant) grab hold of; (relier) connect; **~ le combiné** ou **le téléphone** hang up. ● vi hang up. ■ **se ~ à** vpr cling to; (se relier à) be connected to ou with.

race /ʀas/ nf race; (animale) breed; **de ~** (chien) pedigree; (cheval) thoroughbred.

racheter /ʀaʃte/ **6** vt buy (back); (acheter encore) buy more; (nouvel objet) buy another; (société) buy out; **~ des chaussettes** buy new socks. ■ **se ~** vpr make amends.

racial, ~e (mpl **-iaux**) /ʀasjal, -o/ adj racial.

racine /ʀasin/ nf root; **~ carrée/ cubique** square/cube root.

racisme /ʀasism/ nm racism. **raciste** adj & nmf racist.

racket /ʀakɛt/ nm racketeering.

raclée /ʀakle/ nf 1 thrashing.

racler /ʀakle/ **1** vt scrape. ■ **se ~ la gorge** vpr clear one's throat.

racolage /ʀakɔlaʒ/ nm soliciting.

raconter /ʀakɔ̃te/ **1** vt (histoire) tell; (vacances) tell about; (vie, épisode) describe; **~ à qn que** tell sb that, say to sb that; **qu'est-ce que tu racontes?** what are you talking about?

radar /ʀadaʀ/ nm radar; (automatique) speed camera.

radeau (pl **~x**) /ʀado/ nm raft.

radiateur /ʀadjatœʀ/ nm radiator; (électrique) heater.

radiation /ʀadjasjɔ̃/ nf radiation.

radical, ~e (mpl **-aux**) /ʀadikal, -o/ adj radical. ●nm (pl **-aux**) radical.

radieux, -ieuse /ʀadjø, -z/ adj radiant.

radin, ~e /ʀadɛ̃, -in/ adj 1 stingy 1.

radio /ʀadjo/ nf radio; **à la ~** on the radio; (radiographie) X-ray.

radioactif, -ive /ʀadjɔaktif, -v/ adj radioactive. **radioactivité** nf radioactivity.

radiocassette /ʀadjɔkasɛt/ nf radio cassette player.

r

radiodiffuser /ʀadjɔdifyze/ **1** vt broadcast.

radiographie /ʀadjɔgʀafi/ nf (photographie) X-ray.

radiomessageur /ʀadjɔmesaʒœʀ/ nm pager.

radis /ʀadi/ nm radish; **ne pas avoir un ~** **1** be broke.

radoter /ʀadɔte/ **1** vi **1** talk drivel.

radoucir (se) /(sə)ʀadusiʀ/ **2** vpr (humeur) improve; (temps) become milder.

rafale /ʀafal/ nf (de vent) gust; (de mitraillette) burst.

raffermir /ʀafɛʀmiʀ/ **2** vt strengthen. ■ **se ~** vpr become stronger.

raffiné, ~e /ʀafine/ adj refined. **raffinement** nm refinement.

raffiner /ʀafine/ **1** vt refine. **raffinerie** nf refinery.

raffoler /ʀafɔle/ **1** vt **1** **~ de** be crazy about.

raffut /ʀafy/ nm **1** din.

rafle /ʀafl/ nf (police) raid.

rafraîchir /ʀafʀeʃiʀ/ **2** vt cool (down); (mur) give a fresh coat of paint to; (personne, mémoire) refresh. ■ **se ~** vpr (boire) refresh oneself; (temps) get cooler. **rafraîchissant*, ~e** adj refreshing.

rafraîchissement* /ʀafʀeʃismɑ̃/ nm (boisson) cold drink; **~s** refreshments.

ragaillardir /ʀagajaʀdiʀ/ **2** vt **1** cheer up.

rage /ʀaʒ/ nf rage; (maladie) rabies; **faire ~** (bataille, incendie) rage; (maladie) be rife; **~ de dents** raging toothache. **rageant, ~e** adj infuriating.

ragots /ʀago/ nmpl **1** gossip.

ragoût* /ʀagu/ nm stew.

raid /ʀɛd/ nm (Mil) raid; (Sport) trek.

raide /ʀɛd/ adj stiff; (côte) steep; (corde) tight; (cheveux) straight. ● adv (monter, descendre) steeply.

raideur nf stiffness; steepness.

raidir /ʀediʀ/ **2** vt (corps) tense. ■ **se ~** vpr tense up; (position) harden; (corde) tighten.

raie /ʀɛ/ nf (ligne) line; (bande) strip; (de cheveux) parting; (poisson) skate.

raifort /ʀɛfɔʀ/ nm horseradish.

rail /ʀaj/ nm rail, track; **le ~** (transport) rail.

raisin /ʀezɛ̃/ nm **le ~** grapes; **~ sec** raisin; **un grain de ~** a grape.

raison /ʀezɔ̃/ nf reason; **à ~ de** at the rate of; **avec ~** rightly; **avoir ~** be right (**de faire** to do); **avoir ~ de qn** get the better of sb; **donner ~ à** prove right; **en ~ de** because of; **~ de plus** all the more reason; **perdre la ~** lose one's mind.

raisonnable /ʀezɔnabl/ adj reasonable, sensible.

raisonnement /ʀezɔnmɑ̃/ nm reasoning; (propositions) argument.

raisonner /ʀezɔne/ **1** vi think. ● vt (personne) reason with.

rajeunir /ʀaʒœniʀ/ **2** vt **~ qn** make sb (look) younger; (moderniser) modernize; (Méd) rejuvenate. ● vi (personne) look younger.

rajuster /ʀaʒyste/ **1** vt straighten; (salaires) (re)adjust.

ralenti, ~e /ʀalɑ̃ti/ adj slow. ● nm (au cinéma) slow motion; **tourner au ~** tick over, idle.

ralentir /ʀalɑ̃tiʀ/ **2** vt/i slow down. ■ **se ~** vpr slow down.

ralentisseur /ʀalɑ̃tisœʀ/ nm speed ramp.

râler /ʀɑle/ **1** vi groan; (protester **1**) moan.

rallier /ʀalje/ **45** vt rally; (rejoindre) rejoin. ■ **se ~** vpr rally; **se ~ à** (avis) come round to; (parti) join.

rallonge /ʀalɔ̃ʒ/ nf (de table) leaf;

(de fil électrique) extension lead.
rallonger 40 vt lengthen; (séjour, fil, table) extend.

rallumer /ʀalyme/ 1 vt (feu) relight; (lampe) switch on again; (ranimer: fig) revive.

rallye /ʀali/ nm rally.

ramassage /ʀamasaʒ/ nm (cueillette) gathering; (d'ordures) collection; ∼ **scolaire** school bus service.

ramasser /ʀamase/ 1 vt pick up; (récolter) gather; (recueillir, rassembler) collect. ∎ **se** ∼ vpr huddle up, curl up.

rame /ʀam/ nf (aviron) oar; (train) train.

ramener /ʀamne/ 1 vt (rapporter, faire revenir) bring back; (reconduire) take back; ∼ **à** (réduire à) reduce to. ∎ **se** ∼ vpr 1 turn up; **se** ∼ **à** (problème) come down to.

ramer /ʀame/ 1 vi row.

ramollir /ʀamɔliʀ/ 2 vt soften. ∎ **se** ∼ vpr become soft.

ramoneur /ʀamɔnœʀ/ nm (chimney) sweep.

rampe /ʀɑ̃p/ nf banisters; (pente) ramp; (d'accès) (Auto) slip road; ∼ **de lancement** launching pad.

ramper /ʀɑ̃pe/ 1 vi crawl.

rancard /ʀɑ̃kaʀ/ nm 1 date.

rancart /ʀɑ̃kaʀ/ nm **mettre** *ou* **jeter au** ∼ 1 scrap.

rance /ʀɑ̃s/ adj rancid.

rancœur /ʀɑ̃kœʀ/ nf resentment.

rançon /ʀɑ̃sɔ̃/ nf ransom. **rançonner** 1 vt rob, extort money from.

rancune /ʀɑ̃kyn/ nf grudge; **sans** ∼**!** no hard feelings! **rancunier, -ière** adj vindictive.

randonnée /ʀɑ̃dɔne/ nf walk, ramble; **la** ∼ **à cheval** pony trekking; **faire une** ∼ go walking *ou* rambling.

rang /ʀɑ̃/ nm row; (hiérarchie, condition) rank; **se mettre en** ∼

line up; **au premier** ∼ in the first row; (fig) at the forefront; **de second** ∼ (péj) second-rate.

rangée /ʀɑ̃ʒe/ nf row.

rangement /ʀɑ̃ʒmɑ̃/ nm (de pièce) tidying (up); (espace) storage space.

ranger /ʀɑ̃ʒe/ 40 vt put away; (chambre) tidy (up); (disposer) place. ∎ **se** ∼ vpr (véhicule) park; (s'écarter) stand aside; (conducteur) pull over; (s'assagir) settle down; **se** ∼ **à** (avis) accept.

ranimer /ʀanime/ 1 vt revive; (Méd) resuscitate. ∎ **se** ∼ vpr come round.

rapace /ʀapas/ nm bird of prey. ●adj grasping.

rapatriement /ʀapatʀimɑ̃/ nm repatriation. **rapatrier** 45 vt repatriate.

rap /ʀap/ nm rap (music).

râpe /ʀɑp/ nf (Culin) grater; (lime) rasp.

râpé, ∼e /ʀɑpe/ adj (vêtement) threadbare; (fromage) grated.

râper /ʀɑpe/ 1 vt grate; (bois) rasp.

rapide /ʀapid/ adj fast, rapid. ●nm (train) express (train); (cours d'eau) rapids (+ pl). **rapidement** adv fast, rapidly. **rapidité** nf speed.

rappel /ʀapɛl/ nm recall; (deuxième avis) reminder; (de salaire) back pay; (Méd) booster; (de diplomate) recall; (de réservistes) call-up; (Théât) curtain call.

rappeler /ʀaple/ 38 vt (par téléphone) call back; (réserviste) call up; (diplomate) recall; (évoquer) recall; ∼ **qch à qn** remind sb of sth. ∎ **se** ∼ vpr remember, recall.

rappeur, -euse /ʀapœœːʀ, -øz/ nmf rapper.

rapport /ʀapɔʀ/ nm connection; (compte-rendu) report; (profit) yield; ∼**s** (relations) relations; **en** ∼ **avec** (accord) in keeping with; **mettre/se mettre en** ∼ **avec**

r

put/get in touch with; **par ~ à** (comparé à) compared with; (vis-à-vis de) with regard to; **~s (sexuels)** intercourse.

rapporter /Rapɔʀte/ **1** vt (ici) bring back; (là-bas) take back, return; (profit) bring in; (dire, répéter) report. ●vi (Comm) bring in a good return; (moucharder **1**) tell tales. ■ se ~ à vpr relate to.

rapporteur, -euse /RapɔʀtœR, -øz/ nm, f (mouchard) tell-tale. ●nm protractor.

rapprochement /RapʀɔʃmÃ/ nm reconciliation; (Pol) rapprochement; (rapport) connection; (comparaison) parallel.

rapprocher /Rapʀɔʃe/ vt move closer (**de** to); (réconcilier) bring together; (comparer) compare; (date, rendez-vous) bring forward. ■ se ~ vpr get *ou* come closer (**de** to); (personnes, pays) come together; (s'apparenter) be close (**de** to).

rapt /Rapt/ nm abduction.

raquette /Rakɛt/ nf (de tennis) racket; (de ping-pong) bat.

rare /RaR/ adj rare; (insuffisant) scarce. **rarement** adv rarely, seldom. **rareté** nf rarity; scarcity.

ras, ~e /Rα, Rαz/ adv **coupé ~** cut short. ●adj (herbe, poil) short; **à ~ de terre** very close to the ground; **en avoir ~ le bol** **1** be really fed up; **~e campagne** open country; **à ~ bord** to the brim.

raser /Raze/ **1** vt shave; (cheveux, barbe) shave off; (frôler) skim; (abattre) raze. ■ se ~ vpr shave.

rasoir /RazwaR/ nm razor. ●adj inv **1** boring.

rassasier /Rasazje/ **45** vt satisfy, fill up; **être rassasié de** have had enough of.

rassemblement /RasÃbləmÃ/ nm gathering; (manifestation) rally.

rassembler /RasÃble/ **1** vt gather; (forces, courage) summon

up; (idées) collect. ■ se ~ vpr gather.

rassis, ~e /Rasi, -z/ adj (pain) stale.

rassurer /RasyRe/ **1** vt reassure. ■ se ~ vpr reassure oneself; **rassure-toi** don't worry.

rat /Ra/ nm rat.

rate /Rat/ nf spleen.

raté, ~e /Rate/ nm, f (personne) failure. ●nm **avoir des ~s** (voiture) backfire.

râteau (pl ~x) /Rαto/ nm rake.

râtelier /Rαtəlje/ nm hayrack; (dentier **1**) dentures.

rater /Rate/ **1** vt (train, rendez-vous, cible) miss; (gâcher) make a mess of, spoil; (examen) fail. ●vi fail.

ratio /Rasjo/ nm ratio.

rationaliser /Rasjɔnalize/ **1** vt rationalize.

rationnel, ~le /Rasjɔnɛl/ adj rational.

rationnement /RasjɔnmÃ/ nm rationing.

ratisser /Ratise/ **1** vt rake; (fouiller) comb.

rattacher /Rataʃe/ **1** vt (lacets) tie up again; (ceinture de sécurité, collier) refasten; (relier) link; (incorporer) join.

rattrapage /RatRapaʒ/ nm (Comm) adjustment; **cours de ~** remedial lesson.

rattraper /RatRape/ **1** vt catch; (rejoindre) catch up with; (retard, erreur) make up for. ■ se ~ vpr catch up; (se dédommager) make up for it; **se ~ à** catch hold of.

rature /RatyR/ nf deletion.

rauque /Rok/ adj raucous, harsh.

ravager /Ravaʒe/ **40** vt devastate, ravage.

ravages /Ravaʒ/ nmpl **faire des ~** wreak havoc.

ravaler /Ravale/ **1** vt (façade) clean; (colère) swallow.

ravi, ~e /ʀavi/ adj delighted (**que** that).

ravin /ʀavɛ̃/ nm ravine.

ravir /ʀaviʀ/ **2** vt delight; **~ qch à qn** rob sb of sth.

ravissant, ~e /ʀavisɑ̃, -t/ adj beautiful.

ravisseur, -euse /ʀavisœʀ, -øz/ nm, f kidnapper.

ravitaillement /ʀavitajmɑ̃/ nm provision of supplies (**de** to); (denrées) supplies; **~ en essence** refuelling.

ravitailler /ʀavitaje/ **1** vt provide with supplies; (avion) refuel. ■ **se ~** vpr stock up.

raviver /ʀavive/ **1** vt revive; (feu, colère) rekindle.

rayé, ~e /ʀeje/ adj striped.

rayer /ʀeje/ **31** vt scratch; (biffer) cross out; **'~ la mention inutile'** 'delete as appropriate'.

rayon /ʀejɔ̃/ nm ray; (étagère) shelf; (de magasin) department; (de roue) spoke; (de cercle) radius; **~ d'action** range; **~ de miel** honeycomb; **~ X** X-ray; **en connaître un ~** Ⓘ know one's stuff Ⓘ.

rayonnement /ʀejɔnmɑ̃/ nm (éclat) radiance; (influence) influence; (radiations) radiation.

rayonner /ʀejɔne/ **1** vi radiate; (de joie) beam; (se déplacer) tour around (from a central point).

rayure /ʀejyʀ/ nf scratch; (dessin) stripe; **à ~s** striped.

raz-de-marée /ʀɑdmaʀe/ nm inv tidal wave; **~ électoral** electoral landslide.

réacteur /ʀeaktœʀ/ nm jet engine; (nucléaire) reactor.

réaction /ʀeaksjɔ̃/ nf reaction; **~ en chaîne** chain reaction; **moteur à ~** jet engine.

réagir /ʀeaʒiʀ/ **2** vi react; **~ sur** have an effect on.

réalisateur, -trice /ʀealizatœʀ,

-tʀis/ nm, f (au cinéma) director; (TV) producer.

réalisation /ʀealizasjɔ̃/ nf (de rêve) fulfilment; (œuvre) achievement; (TV, cinéma) production; **projet en ~** project in progress.

réaliser /ʀealize/ **1** vt carry out; (effort, bénéfice, achat) make; (rêve) fulfil; (film) direct; (capital) realize; (se rendre compte de) realize. ■ **se ~** vpr be fulfilled.

réalisme /ʀealism/ nm realism.

réaliste /ʀealist/ adj realistic. • nmf realist.

réalité /ʀealite/ nf reality.

réanimation /ʀeanimasjɔ̃/ nf resuscitation; **service de ~** intensive care. **réanimer** **1** vt resuscitate.

réarmement /ʀeaʀməmɑ̃/ nm rearmament.

rébarbatif, -ive /ʀebaʀbatif, -v/ adj forbidding, off-putting.

rebelle /ʀəbɛl/ adj rebellious; (soldat) rebel; **~ à** resistant to. • nmf rebel.

rébellion /ʀebeljɔ̃/ nf rebellion.

rebondir /ʀəbɔ̃diʀ/ **2** vi bounce; rebound; (fig) get moving again.

rebondissement /ʀəbɔ̃dismɑ̃/ nm (new) development.

rebord /ʀəbɔʀ/ nm edge; **~ de la fenêtre** window ledge ou sill.

rebours: à ~ /aʀəbuʀ/ loc (compter, marcher) backwards.

rebrousse-poil: à ~ /aʀəbʀuspwal/ loc the wrong way; (fig) **prendre qn à ~** rub sb up the wrong way.

rebrousser /ʀəbʀuse/ **1** vt **~ chemin** turn back.

rebut /ʀəby/ nm **mettre** ou **jeter au ~** scrap.

rebutant, ~e /ʀəbytɑ̃, -t/ adj offputting.

recaler /ʀəkale/ **1** vt Ⓘ fail; **se faire ~, être recalé** fail.

recel /Rəsɛl/ nm receiving.
receler* 6 vt (objet volé) receive; (cacher) conceal.

récemment /Resamɑ̃/ adv recently.

recensement /Rəsɑ̃smɑ̃/ nm census; (inventaire) inventory.
recenser 1 vt (population) take a census of; (objets) list.

récent, ~e /Resɑ̃, -t/ adj recent.

récépissé /Resepise/ nm receipt.

récepteur /Resɛptœr/ nm receiver.

réception /Resɛpsjɔ̃/ nf reception; (de courrier) receipt.
réceptionniste nmf receptionist.

récession /Resesjɔ̃/ nf recession.

recette /Rəsɛt/ nf (Culin) recipe; (argent) takings; ~s (Comm) receipts.

receveur, -euse /Rəs(ə)vœr, -øz/ nm, f (de bus) conductor; ~ des contributions tax collector.

recevoir /Rəs(ə)vwaR/ 52 vt receive, get; (client, malade) see; (invités) welcome, receive; être reçu à un examen pass an exam.

rechange: de ~ /dəRəʃɑ̃ʒ/ loc (roue, vêtements) spare; (solution) alternative.

réchapper /Reʃape/ 1 vt/i ~ de come through, survive.

recharge /RəʃaRʒ/ nf (de stylo) refill.

réchaud /Reʃo/ nm stove.

réchauffement /Reʃofmɑ̃/ nm (de température) rise (de in); le ~ de la planète global warming.

réchauffer /Reʃofe/ 1 vt warm up. ■ se ~ vpr warm oneself up; (temps) get warmer.

rêche /Rɛʃ/ adj rough.

recherche /RəʃɛRʃ/ nf search (de for); (raffinement) meticulousness; ~(s) (Univ) research; ~s (enquête) investigations; ~ d'emploi jobhunting.

recherché, ~e /RəʃɛRʃe/ adj in great demand; (style) original, recherché (péj); ~ pour meurtre wanted for murder.

rechercher /RəʃɛRʃe/ 1 vt search for.

rechute /Rəʃyt/ nf (Méd) relapse; faire une ~ have a relapse.

récidiver /Residive/ 1 vi commit a second offence.

récif /Resif/ nm reef.

récipient /Resipjɑ̃/ nm container.

réciproque /Resiprɔk/ adj mutual, reciprocal.

réciproquement /Resiprɔkmɑ̃/ adv each other; et ~ and vice versa.

récit /Resi/ nm (compte-rendu) account, story; (histoire) story.

réciter /Resite/ 1 vt recite.

réclamation /Reklamasjɔ̃/ nf complaint; (demande) claim.

réclame /Reklam/ nf advertisement; faire de la ~ advertise; en ~ on offer.

réclamer /Reklame/ 1 vt call for, demand. ●vi complain.

reclus, ~e /Rəkly, -z/ nm, f recluse. ●adj reclusive.

réclusion /Reklyzjɔ̃/ nf imprisonment.

récolte /Rekɔlt/ nf (action) harvest; (produits) crop, harvest; (fig) crop.
récolter 1 vt harvest, gather; (fig) collect, get.

recommandation /Rəkɔmɑ̃dasjɔ̃/ nf recommendation.

recommandé /Rəkɔmɑ̃de/ nm registered letter; envoyer en ~ send by registered post.

recommander /Rəkɔmɑ̃de/ 1 vt recommend.

recommencer /Rəkɔmɑ̃se/ 10 vt (reprendre) begin ou start again; (refaire) repeat. ●vi start ou begin again; ne recommence pas don't do it again.

récompense /Rekɔ̃pɑ̃s/ nf reward; (prix) award. **récompenser** 1 vt reward (**de** for).

réconcilier /Rekɔ̃silje/ 45 vt reconcile. ■ **se ~** vpr become reconciled (**avec** with).

reconduire /Rəkɔ̃dɥiR/ 17 vt see home; (à la porte) show out; (renouveler) renew.

réconfort /Rekɔ̃fɔR/ nm comfort.

reconnaissance /Rəkɔnɛsɑ̃s/ nf gratitude; (fait de reconnaître) recognition; (Mil) reconnaissance. **reconnaissant, ~e** adj grateful (**de** for).

reconnaître* /RəkɔnɛtR/ 18 vt recognize; (admettre) admit (**que** that); (Mil) reconnoitre; (enfant, tort) acknowledge. ■ **se ~** vpr (s'orienter) know where one is; (l'un l'autre) recognize each other.

reconstituer /Rəkɔ̃stitɥe/ 1 vt reconstitute; (crime) reconstruct; (époque) recreate.

reconversion /Rəkɔ̃vɛRsjɔ̃/ nf (de main-d'œuvre) redeployment.

recopier /Rəkɔpje/ 45 vt copy out.

record /RəkɔR/ nm & a inv record.

recouper /Rəkupe/ 1 vt confirm. ■ **se ~** vpr check, tally, match up.

recourbé, ~e /Rəkurbe/ adj curved; (nez) hooked.

recourir /RəkuRiR/ 20 vi **~ à** (expédient, violence) resort to; (remède, méthode) have recourse to.

recours /RəkuR/ nm resort; **avoir ~ à** have recourse to, resort to; **avoir ~ à qn** turn to sb.

recouvrer /Rəkuvre/ 1 vt recover.

recouvrir /RəkuvRiR/ 21 vt cover.

récréation /RekReasjɔ̃/ nf recreation; (Scol) break; (US) recess.

recroqueviller (se) /(sə)RəkRɔkvije/ 1 vpr curl up.

recrudescence /RəkRydesɑ̃s/ nf new outbreak.

recrue /RəkRy/ nf recruit.

recrutement /RəkRytmɑ̃/ nm recruitment. **recruter** 1 vt recruit.

rectangle /Rɛktɑ̃gl/ nm rectangle. **rectangulaire** adj rectangular.

rectifier /Rɛktifje/ 45 vt correct, rectify.

recto /Rɛkto/ nm **au ~** on the front of the page.

reçu, ~e /Rəsy/ adj accepted; (candidat) successful. ● nm receipt. ● ▶RECEVOIR 52.

recueil /Rəkœj/ nm collection.

recueillement /Rəkœjmɑ̃/ nm meditation.

recueillir /RəkœjiR/ 25 vt collect; (prendre chez soi) take in. ■ **se ~** vpr meditate.

recul /Rəkyl/ nm retreat; (éloignement) distance; (déclin) decline; **avoir un mouvement de ~** recoil; **être en ~** be on the decline; **avec le ~** with hindsight.

reculé, ~e /Rəkyle/ adj (région) remote.

reculer /Rəkyle/ 1 vt move back; (véhicule) reverse; (différer) postpone. ● vi move back; (voiture) reverse; (armée) retreat; (régresser) fall; (céder) back down; **~ devant** (fig) shrink from. ■ **se ~** vpr move back.

récupération /RekypeRasjɔ̃/ nf (de l'organisme, de dette) recovery; (d'objets) salvage.

récupérer /RekypeRe/ 14 vt recover; (vieux objets) salvage. ● vi recover.

récurer /RekyRe/ 1 vt scour; **poudre à ~** scouring powder.

récuser /Rekyze/ 1 vt challenge. ■ **se ~** vpr state that one is not qualified to judge.

recyclage /Rəsiklaʒ/ nm (de personnel) retraining; (de matériau) recycling.

recycler /Rəsikle/ 1 vt (personne)

r

retrain; (chose) recycle. ■ se ~ vpr retrain.

rédacteur, -trice /ʀedaktœʀ, -tʀis/ nm, f author, writer; (de journal, magazine) editor.

rédaction /ʀedaksjɔ̃/ nf writing; (Scol) essay, composition; (personnel) editorial staff.

redevable /ʀədəvabl/ adj **être ~ à qn de** (argent) owe sb; (fig) be indebted to sb for.

redevance /ʀədəvɑ̃s/ nf (de télévision) licence fee; (de téléphone) rental charge.

rédiger /ʀediʒe/ 🔟 vt write; (contrat) draw up.

redire /ʀədiʀ/ 27 vt repeat; **avoir ou trouver à ~ à** find fault with.

redondant, ~e /ʀədɔ̃dɑ̃, -t/ adj superfluous.

redonner /ʀədɔne/ 🔱 vt (rendre) give back; (donner davantage) give more; (donner de nouveau) give again.

redoubler /ʀəduble/ 🔱 vt increase; (classe) repeat; **~ de prudence** be even more careful. ● vi (Scol) repeat a year; (s'intensifier) intensify.

redoutable /ʀədutabl/ adj formidable.

redouter /ʀədute/ 🔱 vt dread.

redressement /ʀədʀɛsmɑ̃/ nm (reprise) recovery; **~ judiciaire** receivership.

redresser /ʀədʀese/ 🔱 vt straighten (out ou up); (situation) right, redress; (économie, entreprise) turn around. ■ se ~ vpr (personne) straighten (oneself) up; (se remettre debout) stand up; (pays, économie) recover.

réduction /ʀedyksjɔ̃/ nf reduction.

réduire /ʀeduiʀ/ 17 vt reduce (**à** to). ■ se ~ vpr be reduced ou cut; **se ~ à** (revenir à) come down to.

réduit, ~e /ʀedui, -t/ adj (objet) small-scale; (limité) limited. ●nm cubbyhole.

rééducation /ʀeedykasjɔ̃/ nf (de handicapé) rehabilitation; (Méd) physiotherapy. **rééduquer** 🔱 vt (personne) rehabilitate; (membre) restore normal movement to.

réel, ~le /ʀeɛl/ adj real. ●nm reality. **réellement** adv really.

réexpédier /ʀeɛkspedje/ 45 vt forward; (retourner) send back.

refaire /ʀəfɛʀ/ 33 vt do again; (erreur, voyage) make again; (réparer) do up, redo.

réfectoire /ʀefɛktwaʀ/ nm refectory.

référence /ʀefeʀɑ̃s/ nf reference.

référendum /ʀefeʀɛ̃dɔm/ nm referendum.

référer /ʀefeʀe/ 14 vi **en ~ à** consult. ■ se ~ à vpr refer to, consult.

refermer /ʀəfɛʀme/ 🔱 vt close (again). ■ se ~ vpr close (again).

réfléchi, ~e /ʀefleʃi/ adj (personne) thoughtful; (verbe) reflexive.

réfléchir /ʀefleʃiʀ/ 2 vi think (**à, sur** about). ●vt reflect. ■ se ~ vpr be reflected.

reflet /ʀəflɛ/ nm reflection; (nuance) sheen.

refléter /ʀəflete/ 14 vt reflect. ■ se ~ vpr be reflected.

réflexe /ʀeflɛks/ adj reflex. ●nm reflex; (réaction) reaction.

réflexion /ʀeflɛksjɔ̃/ nf (pensée) thought, reflection; (remarque) remark, comment; **à la ~** on second thoughts.

refluer /ʀəflye/ 🔱 vi flow back; (foule) retreat; (inflation) go down.

reflux /ʀəfly/ nm (marée) ebb, tide.

réforme /ʀefɔʀm/ nf reform. **réformer** 🔱 vt reform; (soldat) invalid out.

refouler /ʀəfule/ 🔱 vt (larmes) hold back; (désir) repress;

(souvenir) suppress.

refrain /RəfRɛ̃/ nm chorus; **le même** ~ the same old story.

refréner* /Rəfʀene/ 14 vt curb, check.

réfrigérateur /RefʀiʒeʀatœR/ nm refrigerator.

refroidir /RəfʀwadiR/ 2 vt/i cool (down). ■ **se** ~ vpr (personne, temps) get cold. **refroidissement** nm cooling; (rhume) chill.

refuge /Rəfyʒ/ nm refuge; (chalet) mountain hut.

réfugié, ~**e** /Refyʒje/ nm, f refugee. **réfugier (se)** 45 vpr take refuge.

refus /Rəfy/ nm refusal; **ce n'est pas de** ~ 1 I wouldn't say no.

refuser /Rəfyze/ 1 vt refuse (**de** to); (client, spectateur) turn away; (recaler) fail; (à un poste) turn down. ■ **se** ~ à vpr (évidence) reject; **se** ~ **à faire** refuse to do.

regain /Rəgɛ̃/ nm ~ **de** renewal *ou* revival of; (Comm) rise.

régal (pl ~**s**) /Regal/ nm treat, delight.

régaler /Regale/ 1 vt ~ **qn de** treat sb to. ■ **se** ~ vpr (de nourriture) **je me régale** it's delicious.

regard /RəgaR/ nm (expression, coup d'œil) look; (vue) eye; (yeux) eyes; ~ **fixe** stare; **au** ~ **de** with regard to; **en** ~ **de** compared with.

regardant, ~**e** /Rəgardɑ̃, -t/ adj ~ **avec son argent** careful with money; **peu** ~ (**sur**) not fussy (about).

regarder /Rəgarde/ 1 vt look at; (observer) watch; (considérer) consider; (concerner) concern; ~ **fixement** stare at; ~ **à** think about, pay attention to. ● vi look. ■ **se** ~ vpr (soi-même) look at oneself; (personnes) look at each other.

régate /Regat/ nf regatta.

régie /Reʒi/ nf ~ **d'État** public corporation; (radio, TV) control room; (au cinéma) production; (Théât) stage management.

régime /Reʒim/ nm (organisation) system; (Pol) regime; (Méd) diet; (de moteur) speed; (de bananes) bunch; **se mettre au** ~ go on a diet; **à ce** ~ at this rate.

régiment /Reʒimɑ̃/ nm regiment.

🄰**région** /Reʒjɔ̃/ nf region. **régional**, ~**e**, (mpl -**aux**) adj regional.

régir /ReʒiR/ 2 vt govern.

régisseur /ReʒisœR/ nm (Théât) stage manager; ~ **de plateau** (TV) floor manager; (au cinéma) studio manager.

registre /RəʒistR/ nm register.

réglage /Reglaʒ/ nm adjustment; (de moteur) tuning.

règle /Regl/ nf rule; (instrument) ruler; ~**s** (de femme) period; **en** ~ in order.

réglé, ~**e** /Regle/ adj (vie) ordered; (arrangé) settled; (papier) ruled.

règlement /Regləmɑ̃/ nm (règles) regulations; (solution) settlement; (paiement) payment. **réglementaire*** adj (uniforme) regulation. **réglementation*** nf regulation, rules. **réglementer*** 1 vt regulate, control.

régler /Regle/ 14 vt settle; (machine) adjust; (programmer) set; (facture) settle; (personne) settle up with; ~ **son compte à** 1 settle a score with.

réglisse /Reglis/ nf liquorice.

règne /Rɛɲ/ nm reign; (végétal, animal, minéral) kingdom.

regret /RəgRɛ/ nm regret; **à** ~ with regret.

regretter /RəgRete/ 1 vt regret; (personne) miss; (pour s'excuser) be sorry.

regrouper /RəgRupe/ 1 vt group

r

....
🄰 *see* A-Z of French life and culture

ou bring together. ■ se ~ vpr gather *ou* group together.

régularité /ʀegylaʀite/ nf regularity; (de rythme, progrès) steadiness; (de surface, écriture) evenness.

régulier, -ière /ʀegylje, -jɛʀ/ adj regular; (qualité, vitesse) steady, even; (ligne, paysage) even; (légal) legal; (honnête) honest.

rehausser /ʀaose/ ■ vt raise; (faire valoir) enhance.

rein /ʀɛ̃/ nm kidney; ~s (dos) small of the back.

reine /ʀɛn/ nf queen.

réinsertion /ʀeɛ̃sɛʀsjɔ̃/ nf reintegration.

réintégrer /ʀeɛ̃tegʀe/ 14 vt (lieu) return to; (Jur) reinstate; (personne) reintegrate.

réitérer /ʀeiteʀe/ 14 vt repeat.

rejaillir /ʀəʒajiʀ/ 2 vi ~ sur splash back onto; ~ sur qn (succès) reflect on sb.

rejet /ʀəʒɛ/ nm rejection; ~s (déchets) waste.

rejeter /ʀəʒte/ 38 vt throw back; (refuser) reject; (déverser) discharge; ~ une faute sur qn shift the blame for a mistake onto sb.

rejoindre /ʀəʒwɛ̃dʀ/ 22 vt go back to, rejoin; (rattraper) catch up with; (rencontrer) join, meet up with. ■ se ~ vpr (personnes) meet up; (routes) join, meet.

réjoui, ~e /ʀeʒwi/ adj joyful.

réjouir /ʀeʒwiʀ/ 2 vt delight. ■ se ~ vpr be delighted (de at). **réjouissances** nfpl festivities. **réjouissant, ~e** adj cheering.

relâche /ʀəlɑʃ/ nm (repos) break, rest; **faire ~** (Théât) be closed.

relâcher /ʀəlɑʃe/ ■ vt slacken; (personne) release; (discipline) relax. ■ se ~ vpr slacken.

relais* /ʀəlɛ/ nm (Sport) relay; (hôtel) hotel; (intermédiaire) intermediary; **prendre le ~ de** take over from.

relancer /ʀəlɑ̃se/ 10 vt boost, revive; (renvoyer) throw back.

relatif, -ive /ʀəlatif, -v/ adj relative; ~ à relating to.

relation /ʀəlasjɔ̃/ nf relationship; (ami) acquaintance; (personne puissante) connection; ~s relations; ~s extérieures foreign affairs; **en ~ avec qn** in touch with sb.

relativement /ʀəlativmɑ̃/ adv relatively; ~ à in relation to.

relativité /ʀəlativite/ nf relativity.

relax /ʀəlaks/ adj inv 1 laid-back.

relaxer (se) /(sə)ʀəlakse/ ■ vpr relax.

relayer /ʀəleje/ 31 vt relieve; (émission) relay. ■ se ~ vpr take over from one another.

reléguer /ʀəlege/ 14 vt relegate.

relent /ʀəlɑ̃/ nm stink; (fig) whiff.

relève /ʀəlɛv/ nf relief; **prendre *ou* assurer la ~** take over (de from).

relevé, ~e /ʀəlve/ adj spicy. ●nm (de compteur) reading; (facture) bill; ~ **bancaire, ~ de compte** bank statement; **faire le ~ de** list.

relever /ʀəlve/ 6 vt pick up; (personne tombée) help up; (remonter) raise; (col) turn up; (compteur) read; (défi) accept; (relayer) relieve; (remarquer, noter) note; (plat) spice up; (rebâtir) rebuild; ~ **de** come within the competence of; (Méd) recover from. ■ se ~ vpr (personne) get up (again); (pays, économie) recover.

relief /ʀəljɛf/ nm relief; **mettre en ~** highlight.

relier /ʀəlje/ 45 vt link (up) (à to); (livre) bind.

religieux, -ieuse /ʀəliʒjø, -z/ adj religious. ●nm, f monk, nun.

religion /ʀəliʒjɔ̃/ nf religion.

reliure /ʀəljyʀ/ nf binding.

reluire /ʀəlɥiʀ/ 17 vi shine.

remaniement /ʀəmanimɑ̃/ nm revision; ~ **ministériel** cabinet reshuffle.

remarquable /ʀəmaʀkabl/ adj remarkable.

remarque /ʀəmaʀk/ nf remark; (par écrit) comment.

remarquer /ʀəmaʀke/ **1** vt notice; (dire) say; **faire** ~ point out (**à** to); **se faire** ~ draw attention to oneself; **remarque(z)** mind you.

remblai /ʀɑ̃blɛ/ nm embankment.

remboursement /ʀɑ̃buʀsəmɑ̃/ nm (d'emprunt, dette) repayment; (Comm) refund.

rembourser /ʀɑ̃buʀse/ **1** vt (dette, emprunt) repay; (billet, frais) refund; (client) give a refund to; (ami) pay back.

remède /ʀəmɛd/ nm remedy; (médicament) medicine.

remédier /ʀəmedje/ **45** vi ~ **à** remedy.

remerciements /ʀəmɛʀsimɑ̃/ nmpl thanks. **remercier** **45** vt thank (**de** for); (licencier) dismiss.

remettre /ʀəmɛtʀ/ **42** vt put back; (vêtement) put back on; (donner) hand over; (devoir, démission) hand in; (faire fonctionner) switch back on; (restituer) give back; (différer) put off; (ajouter) add; (se rappeler) remember; ~ **en cause** ou **en question** call into question. ■ se ~ vpr (guérir) recover; **se** ~ **au tennis** take up tennis again; **se** ~ **au travail** get back to work; **se** ~ **à faire** start doing again; **s'en** ~ **à** leave it to.

remise /ʀəmiz/ nf (abri) shed; (rabais) discount; (transmission) handing over; (ajournement) postponement; ~ **en cause** ou **en question** calling into question; ~ **des prix** prizegiving; ~ **des médailles** medals ceremony; ~ **de peine** remission.

remontant /ʀəmɔ̃tɑ̃/ nm tonic.

remontée /ʀəmɔ̃te/ nf ascent; (d'eau, de prix) rise; ~ **mécanique** ski lift.

remonte-pente (pl ~**s**) /ʀəmɔ̃tpɑ̃t/ nm ski tow.

remonter /ʀəmɔ̃te/ **1** vi go ou come (back) up; (prix, niveau) rise (again); (revenir) go back (**à** to); ~ **dans le temps** go back in time. ●vt (rue, escalier) go ou come (back) up; (relever) raise; (montre) wind up; (objet démonté) put together again; (personne) buck up.

remontoir /ʀəmɔ̃twaʀ/ nm winder.

remords /ʀəmɔʀ/ nm remorse; **avoir du** or **des** ~ feel remorse.

remorque /ʀəmɔʀk/ nf trailer; **en** ~ on tow. **remorquer** **1** vt tow.

remous /ʀəmu/ nm eddy; (de bateau) backwash; (fig) turmoil.

rempart /ʀɑ̃paʀ/ nm rampart.

remplaçant, ~**e** /ʀɑ̃plasɑ̃, -t/ nm, f replacement; (joueur) reserve, substitute.

remplacement /ʀɑ̃plasmɑ̃/ nm replacement; **faire des** ~**s** do supply teaching. **remplacer** **10** vt replace.

rempli, ~**e** /ʀɑ̃pli/ adj full (**de** of); (journée) busy.

remplir /ʀɑ̃pliʀ/ **2** vt fill (up); (formulaire) fill in ou out; (condition) fulfil; (devoir, tâche, rôle) carry out. ■ se ~ vpr fill (up). **remplissage** nm filling up; (de texte) padding.

remporter /ʀɑ̃pɔʀte/ **1** vt take back; (victoire) win.

remuant, ~**e** /ʀəmɥɑ̃, -t/ adj boisterous.

remue-ménage* /ʀəmymenaʒ/ nm inv commotion, bustle.

remuer /ʀəmɥe/ **1** vt move; (thé, café) stir; (passé) rake up. ●vi move; (gigoter) fidget. ■ se ~ vpr move.

rémunération /ʀemyneʀasjɔ̃/ nf payment.

r

renaissance /ʀənɛsɑ̃s/ nf rebirth.

renard /ʀənaʀ/ nm fox.

renchérir /ʀɑ̃ʃeʀiʀ/ ❷ vi (dans une vente) raise the bidding; ~ **sur** go one better than. • vt increase, put up.

rencontre /ʀɑ̃kɔ̃tʀ/ nf meeting; (de routes) junction; (Mil) encounter; (match) match; (US) game.

rencontrer /ʀɑ̃kɔ̃tʀe/ ❶ vt meet; (heurter) hit; (trouver) find. ■ se ~ vpr meet.

rendement /ʀɑ̃dmɑ̃/ nm yield; (travail) output.

rendez-vous /ʀɑ̃devu/ nm appointment; (d'amoureux) date; (lieu) meeting-place; **prendre** ~ (**avec**) make an appointment (with).

rendormir (se) /(sə)ʀɑ̃dɔʀmiʀ/ ❹❻ vpr go back to sleep.

rendre /ʀɑ̃dʀ/ ❸ vt give back, return; (donner en retour) return; (monnaie) give; (justice) dispense; (jugement) pronounce; ~ **heureux/possible** make happy/possible; (vomir ❶) vomit; ~ **compte de** report on; ~ **service (à)** help; ~ **visite à** visit. • vi (terres) yield; (activité) be profitable. ■ se ~ vpr (capituler) surrender; (aller) go (**à** to); **se** ~ **utile** make oneself useful.

rêne /ʀɛn/ nf rein.

renfermé, ~**e** /ʀɑ̃fɛʀme/ adj withdrawn. • nm **sentir le** ~ smell musty.

renflé, ~**e** /ʀɑ̃fle/ adj bulging.

renforcer /ʀɑ̃fɔʀse/ ❿ vt reinforce.

renfort /ʀɑ̃fɔʀ/ nm reinforcement; **à grand** ~ **de** with a great deal of.

renier /ʀənje/ ❹❺ vt (personne, œuvre) disown; (foi) renounce.

renifler /ʀənifle/ ❶ vt/i sniff.

▭ *see A-Z of French life and culture*

renne /ʀɛn/ nm reindeer.

renom /ʀənɔ̃/ nm renown; (réputation) reputation. **renommé**, ~**e** adj famous. **renommée** nf (célébrité) fame; (réputation) reputation.

renoncement /ʀənɔ̃smɑ̃/ nm renunciation.

renoncer /ʀənɔ̃se/ ❿ vi ~ **à** (habitude, ami) give up, renounce; (projet) abandon; ~ **à faire** abandon the idea of doing.

renouer /ʀənwe/ ❶ vt tie up (again); (amitié) renew; ~ **avec qn** get back in touch with sb; (après une dispute) make up with sb.

renouveau (pl ~**x**) /ʀənuvo/ nm revival.

renouveler /ʀənuvle/ ❸❽ vt renew; (réitérer) repeat; (remplacer) replace. ■ se ~ vpr be renewed; (incident) recur, happen again.

renouvellement* /ʀənuvɛlmɑ̃/ nm renewal.

rénovation /ʀenɔvasjɔ̃/ nf (d'édifice) renovation; (d'institution) reform.

renseignement /ʀɑ̃sɛɲ(ə)mɑ̃/ nm ~(**s**) information; (**bureau des**) ~**s** information desk; (**service des**) ~**s téléphoniques** directory enquiries.

renseigner /ʀɑ̃seɲe/ ❶ vt inform, give information to. ■ se ~ vpr enquire, make enquiries, find out.

rentabilité /ʀɑ̃tabilite/ nf profitability. **rentable** adj profitable.

rente /ʀɑ̃t/ nf (private) income; (pension) annuity. **rentier, -ière** nm, f person of private means.

▭**rentrée** /ʀɑ̃tʀe/ nf return; (revenu) income; **la** ~ (**des classes**) the start of the new school year; **faire sa** ~ make a comeback.

rentrer /ʀɑ̃tʀe/ ❶ vi (aux être) go *ou* come back home, return home; (entrer) go *ou* come in; (entrer à nouveau) go *ou* come back in; (revenu) come in; (élèves) go back (to school); ~ **dans** (heurter) smash into; **tout est rentré dans l'ordre** everything is back to normal; ~ **dans ses frais** break even. •vt (aux avoir) bring in; (griffes) draw in; (vêtement) tuck in.

renverser /ʀɑ̃vɛʀse/ **1** vt knock over ou down; (piéton) knock down; (liquide) upset, spill; (mettre à l'envers) turn upside down; (gouvernement) overthrow; (inverser) reverse. ■ se ~ vpr (véhicule) overturn; (verre, vase) fall over.

renvoi /ʀɑ̃vwa/ nm return; (d'employé) dismissal; (d'élève) expulsion; (report) postponement; (dans un livre, fichier) cross-reference; (rot) burp.

renvoyer /ʀɑ̃vwaje/ **32** vt send back, return; (employé) dismiss; (élève) expel; (ajourner) postpone; (référer) refer; (réfléchir) reflect.

repaire /ʀəpɛʀ/ nm den.

répandre /ʀepɑ̃dʀ/ **3** vt (liquide) spill; (étendre, diffuser) spread; (odeur) give off. ■ se ~ vpr spread; (liquide) spill; **se ~ en injures** let out a stream of abuse.

répandu, ~e /ʀepɑ̃dy/ adj widespread.

réparateur, -trice /ʀepaʀatœʀ, -tʀis/ nm engineer. **réparation** nf repair; (compensation) compensation. **réparer** **1** vt repair, mend; (faute) make amends for; (remédier à) put right.

repartie* /ʀəpaʀti/ nf retort; **avoir de la ~** always have a ready reply.

repartir /ʀəpaʀtiʀ/ **46** vi start again; (voyageur) set off again; (s'en retourner) go back; (secteur économique) pick up again.

répartir /ʀepaʀtiʀ/ **2** vt distribute; (partager) share out; (étaler) spread. **répartition** nf distribution.

C repas /ʀəpɑ/ nm meal.

repassage /ʀəpasaʒ/ nm ironing.

repasser /ʀəpase/ **1** vi come ou go back; ~ **devant qch** go past sth again. •vt (linge) iron; (examen) retake, resit; (film) show again.

repêcher /ʀəpeʃe/ **1** vt recover, fish out; (candidat) allow to pass.

repentir¹ /ʀəpɑ̃tiʀ/ nm repentance.

repentir² (se) /(sə)ʀəpɑ̃tiʀ/ **2** vpr (Relig) repent (**de** of); **se ~ de** (regretter) regret.

répercuter /ʀepɛʀkyte/ **1** vt (bruit) send back. ■ se ~ vpr echo; **se ~ sur** have repercussions on.

repère /ʀəpɛʀ/ nm mark; (jalon) marker; (événement) landmark; (référence) reference point.

repérer /ʀəpeʀe/ **14** vt locate, spot. ■ se ~ vpr get one's bearings.

répertoire /ʀepɛʀtwaʀ/ nm (artistique) repertoire; (liste) directory; ~ **téléphonique** telephone directory; (personnel) telephone book. **répertorier** **45** vt index.

répéter /ʀepete/ **14** vt repeat; (Théât) rehearse. •vi rehearse. ■ se ~ vpr be repeated; (personne) repeat oneself.

répétition /ʀepetisjɔ̃/ nf repetition; (Théât) rehearsal.

répit /ʀepi/ nm respite, break.

replier /ʀəplije/ **45** vt fold (up); (ailes, jambes) tuck in. ■ se ~ vpr withdraw (**sur soi-même** into oneself).

réplique /ʀeplik/ nf reply; (riposte) retort; (objection) objection; (Théât) line; (copie) replica. **répliquer** **1** vt/i reply; (riposter) retort; (objecter) answer back.

répondeur /ʀepɔ̃dœʀ/ nm answering machine.

répondre /ʀepɔ̃dʀ/ **3** vt (injure, bêtise) reply with; ~ **que** answer

....

C *see A-Z of French life and culture*

r

ou reply that; ~ **à** (être conforme à) answer; (affection, sourire) return; (avances, appel, critique) respond to; ~ **de** answer for. •vi answer, reply; (être insolent) answer back; (réagir) respond (**à** to).

réponse /repõs/ nf answer, reply; (fig) response.

report /ʀəpɔʀ/ nm (transcription) transfer; (renvoi) postponement.

reportage /ʀəpɔʀtaʒ/ nm report; (par écrit) article.

reporter[1] /ʀəpɔʀte/ **1** vt take back; (ajourner) put off; (transcrire) transfer. ■ se ~ **à** vpr refer to.

reporter[2] /ʀəpɔʀtɛʀ/ nm reporter.

repos /ʀəpo/ nm rest; (paix) peace. **reposant**, ~**e** adj restful.

reposer /ʀəpoze/ **1** vt put down again; (délasser) rest. •vi rest (**sur** on); **laisser** ~ (pâte) leave to stand. ■ se ~ vpr rest; **se** ~ **sur** rely on.

repousser /ʀəpuse/ **1** vt push back; (écarter) push away; (dégoûter) repel; (décliner) reject; (ajourner) postpone, put back. •vi grow again.

reprendre /ʀəpʀãdʀ/ **50** vt take back; (confiance, conscience) regain; (souffle) get back; (évadé) recapture; (recommencer) resume; (redire) repeat; (modifier) alter; (blâmer) reprimand; ~ **du pain** take some more bread; **on ne m'y reprendra pas** I won't be caught out again. •vi (recommencer) resume; (affaires) pick up. ■ se ~ vpr (se ressaisir) pull oneself together; (se corriger) correct oneself.

représailles /ʀəpʀezaj/ nfpl reprisals.

représentant, ~**e** /ʀəpʀezãtã, -t/ nm, f representative.

représentation /ʀəpʀezãtasjõ/ nf representation; (Théât) performance.

représenter /ʀəpʀezãte/ **1** vt represent; (figures) depict, show;

(pièce de théâtre) perform. ■ se ~ vpr (s'imaginer) imagine.

répression /ʀepʀesjõ/ nf repression; (d'élan) suppression.

réprimande /ʀepʀimãd/ nf reprimand.

réprimer /ʀepʀime/ **1** vt (peuple) repress; (sentiment) suppress; (fraude) crack down on.

reprise /ʀəpʀiz/ nf resumption; (Théât) revival; (TV) repeat; (de tissu) darn, mend; (essor) recovery; (Comm) part-exchange, trade-in; **à plusieurs** ~**s** on several occasions.

repriser /ʀəpʀize/ **1** vt darn, mend.

reproche /ʀəpʀɔʃ/ nm reproach; **faire des** ~**s à** find fault with.

reprocher /ʀəpʀɔʃe/ **1** vt ~ **qch à qn** reproach *ou* criticize sb for sth.

reproducteur, -trice /ʀəpʀɔdyktœʀ, -tʀis/ adj reproductive.

reproduire /ʀəpʀɔdɥiʀ/ **17** vt reproduce; (répéter) repeat. ■ se ~ vpr reproduce; (se répéter) recur.

reptile /ʀɛptil/ nm reptile.

repu, ~**e** /ʀəpy/ adj satiated, replete.

républicain, ~**e** /ʀepyblikɛ̃, -ɛn/ adj & nm, f republican.

république /ʀepyblik/ nf republic; ~ **populaire** people's republic.

répudier /ʀepydje/ **45** vt repudiate; (droit) renounce.

répugnance /ʀepyɲãs/ nf repugnance; (hésitation) reluctance; **avoir de la** ~ **pour** loathe. **répugnant**, ~**e** adj repulsive.

répugner /ʀepyɲe/ **1** vt be repugnant to, disgust; ~ **à** (effort, violence) be averse to; ~ **à faire** be reluctant to do.

répulsion /ʀepylsjõ/ nf repulsion.

réputation /ʀepytasjɔ̃/ nf reputation.

réputé, ~e /ʀepyte/ adj renowned (**pour** for); (école, compagnie) reputable; ~ **pour être** reputed to be.

requérir /ʀəkeʀiʀ/ 7 vt require, demand.

requête /ʀəkɛt/ nf request; (Jur) petition.

requin /ʀəkɛ̃/ nm shark.

requis, ~e /ʀəki, -z/ adj (exigé) required; (nécessaire) necessary.

RER abrév m (**réseau express régional**) Parisian rapid transit rail system.

rescapé, ~e /ʀɛskape/ nm, f survivor. ● adj surviving.

rescousse /ʀɛskus/ nf **à la** ~ to the rescue.

réseau (pl ~x) /ʀezo/ nm network; ~ **local** local area network, LAN; **le** ~ **des** ~**x** (Ordinat) Internet.

réservation /ʀezɛʀvasjɔ̃/ nf reservation, booking.

réserve /ʀezɛʀv/ nf reserve; (restriction) reservation, reserve; (indienne) reservation; (entrepôt) store-room; **en** ~ in reserve; **les** ~**s** (Mil) the reserves.

réserver /ʀezɛʀve/ 1 vt reserve; (place) reserve, book. ■ **se** ~ vpr **se** ~ **qch** save sth for oneself; **se** ~ **pour** save oneself for; **se** ~ **le droit de** reserve the right to.

réservoir /ʀezɛʀvwaʀ/ nm tank; (lac) reservoir.

résidence /ʀezidɑ̃s/ nf residence; ~ **secondaire** second home; ~ **universitaire** hall of residence.

résident, ~e /ʀezidɑ̃, -t/ nm, f resident; (étranger) foreign resident.

résider /ʀezide/ 1 vi reside; ~ **dans qch** (difficulté) lie in.

résigner (se) /(sə)ʀeziɲe/ 1 vpr

se ~ **à faire** resign oneself to doing.

résilier /ʀezilje/ 45 vt terminate.

résine /ʀezin/ nf resin.

résistance /ʀezistɑ̃s/ nf resistance; (fil électrique) element. **résistant, ~e** adj tough.

résister /ʀeziste/ 1 vi resist; ~ **à** (agresseur, assaut, influence, tentation) resist; (corrosion, chaleur) withstand.

résolu, ~e /ʀezɔly/ adj resolute; ~ **à faire** determined to do. ● ▷ **RÉSOUDRE** 53.

résolution /ʀezɔlysjɔ̃/ nf (fermeté) resolution; (d'un problème) solving.

résonner /ʀezɔne/ 1 vi resound.

résorber /ʀezɔʀbe/ 1 vt reduce. ■ **se** ~ vpr be reduced.

résoudre /ʀezudʀ/ 53 vt solve; (crise, conflit) resolve. ■ **se** ~ vpr (se décider) resolve to; (se résigner) resign oneself to.

respect /ʀɛspɛ/ nm respect. **respectabilité** nf respectability.

respecter /ʀɛspɛkte/ 1 vt respect; **faire** ~ (loi, décision) enforce.

respectueux, -euse /ʀɛspɛktɥø, -z/ adj respectful; ~ **de l'environnement** environmentally friendly.

respiration /ʀɛspiʀasjɔ̃/ nf breathing; (haleine) breath. **respiratoire** adj respiratory, breathing.

respirer /ʀɛspiʀe/ 1 vi breathe; (se reposer) catch one's breath. ● vt breathe (in); (exprimer) radiate.

resplendir /ʀɛsplɑ̃diʀ/ 2 vi shine (**de** with). **resplendissant, ~e** adj brilliant, radiant.

responsabilité /ʀɛspɔ̃sabilite/ nf responsibility; (légale) liability.

responsable /ʀɛspɔ̃sabl/ adj responsible (**de** for); ~ **de** (chargé de) in charge of. ● nmf person in charge; (coupable) person responsible.

r

resquiller /rɛskije/ 🔢 vi 🔢 (dans le train) fare-dodge; (au spectacle) get in without paying; (dans la queue) jump the queue.

ressaisir (se) /(sə)rəsezir/ 🔢 vpr pull oneself together; (équipe sportive, valeurs boursières) make a recovery.

ressemblance /rəsɑ̃blɑ̃s/ nf resemblance.

ressemblant, **~e** /rəsɑ̃blɑ̃, -t/ adj **être ~** (portrait) be a good likeness.

ressembler /rəsɑ̃ble/ 🔢 vi **~ à** resemble, look like. ■ **se ~** vpr be alike; (physiquement) look alike.

ressentiment /rəsɑ̃timɑ̃/ nm resentment.

ressentir /rəsɑ̃tir/ 🔢 vt feel. ■ **se ~ de** vpr feel the effects of.

resserrer /rəsere/ 🔢 vt tighten; (contracter) compress; (vêtement) take in. ■ **se ~** vpr tighten; (route) narrow; (se regrouper) move closer together.

ressort /rəsɔr/ nm (objet) spring; (fig) energy; **être du ~ de** be the province of; (Jur) be within the jurisdiction of; **en dernier ~** as a last resort.

ressortir /rəsɔrtir/ 🔢 vi go *ou* come back out; (se voir) stand out; (film, disque) be re-released; **faire ~** bring out; **il ressort que** it emerges that. ●vt take out again; (redire) come out with again; (disque, film) re-release.

ressortissant, **~e** /rəsɔrtisɑ̃, -t/ nm, f national.

ressource /rəsurs/ nf resource; **~s** resources; **à bout de ~** at one's wits' end.

ressusciter /rɛsysite/ 🔢 vi come back to life. ●vt bring back to life; (fig) revive.

restant, **~e** /rɛstɑ̃, -t/ adj remaining. ●nm remainder.

....

🔳 *see A-Z of French life and culture*

🔳**restaurant** /rɛstɔrɑ̃/ nm restaurant.

restauration /rɛstɔrasjɔ̃/ nf restoration; (hôtellerie) catering.

restaurer /rɛstɔre/ 🔢 vt restore. ■ **se ~** vpr eat.

reste /rɛst/ nm rest; (d'une soustraction) remainder; **~s** remains (**de** of); (nourriture) leftovers; **un ~ de poulet** some left-over chicken; **au ~**, **du ~** moreover, besides.

rester /rɛste/ 🔢 vi (aux être) stay, remain; (subsister) be left, remain; **il reste du pain** there is some bread left (over); **il me reste du pain** I have some bread left (over); **il me reste à** it remains for me to; **en ~ à** go no further than; **en ~ là** stop there.

restituer /rɛstitɥe/ 🔢 vt (rendre) return; (recréer) reproduce; (rétablir) reconstruct.

restreindre /rɛstrɛ̃dr/ 🔢 vt restrict. ■ **se ~** vpr (dans les dépenses) cut back.

restriction /rɛstriksjɔ̃/ nf restriction.

résultat /rezylta/ nm result.

résulter /rezylte/ 🔢 vi **~ de** result from, be the result of.

résumé /rezyme/ nm summary; **en ~** in short; (pour finir) to sum up. **résumer** 🔢 vt summarize.

résurrection /rezyrɛksjɔ̃/ nf resurrection; (renouveau) revival.

rétablir /retablir/ 🔢 vt restore; (personne) restore to health. ■ **se ~** vpr (ordre, silence) be restored; (guérir) recover. **rétablissement** nm restoration; (de malade, monnaie) recovery.

retard /rətar/ nm lateness; (sur un programme) delay; (infériorité) backwardness; **avoir du ~** be late; (montre) be slow; **en ~** late; (retardé) behind; **en ~ sur l'emploi du temps** behind schedule; **rattraper** *ou* **combler**

son ~ catch up; **prendre du** ~ fall behind.

retardataire /RətaRdatɛR/ nmf latecomer. ● adj late.

retarder /RətaRde/ **1** vt ~ **qn/qch** delay sb/sth, hold sb/sth up; (par rapport à une heure convenue) make sb/sth late; (montre) put back. ● vi (montre) be slow; (personne) be out of touch.

retenir /Rətnir/ **59** vt hold back; (souffle, attention, prisonnier) hold; (eau, chaleur) retain, hold; (larmes) hold back; (garder) keep; (retarder) detain, hold up; (réserver) book; (se rappeler) remember; (déduire) deduct; (accepter) accept. ■ se ~ vpr (se contenir) restrain oneself; **se** ~ **à** hold on to; **se** ~ **de faire** stop oneself from doing.

rétention /Retɑ̃sjɔ̃/ nf retention.

retentir /Rətɑ̃tir/ **2** vi ring out, resound; ~ **sur** have an impact on. **retentissant, ~e** adj resounding. **retentissement** nm (effet) effect.

retenue /Rətny/ nf restraint; (somme) deduction; (Scol) detention.

réticent, ~e /Retisɑ̃, -t/ adj (hésitant) hesitant; (qui rechigne) reluctant; (réservé) reticent.

rétine /Retin/ nf retina.

retiré, ~e /Rətire/ adj (vie) secluded; (lieu) remote.

retirer /Rətire/ **1** vt (sortir) take out; (ôter) take off; (argent, offre, candidature) withdraw; (écarter) (main, pied) withdraw; (billet, bagages) collect, pick up; (avantage) derive; ~ **à qn** take away from sb. ■ se ~ vpr withdraw, retire.

retombées /Rətɔ̃be/ nfpl (conséquences) effects; ~ **radioactives** nuclear fall-out.

retomber /Rətɔ̃be/ **1** vi (faire une chute) fall again; (retourner au sol) land, come down; ~ **dans** (erreur) fall back into.

retouche /Rətuʃ/ nf alteration; (de

photo, tableau) retouch.

retour /Rətur/ nm return; **être de** ~ be back (**de** from); ~ **en arrière** flashback; **par** ~ **du courrier** by return of post; **en** ~ in return.

retourner /Rəturne/ **1** vt (aux avoir) turn over; (vêtement) turn inside out; (maison) turn upside down; (lettre, compliment) return; (émouvoir **1**) shake, upset. ● vi (aux être) go back, return. ■ se ~ vpr turn round; (dans son lit) twist and turn; **s'en** ~ go back; **se** ~ **contre** turn against.

retrait /Rətrɛ/ nm withdrawal; (des eaux) receding; **être (situé) en** ~ **(de)** be set back (from).

retraite /Rətrɛt/ nf retirement; (pension) (retirement) pension; (fuite, refuge) retreat; **mettre à la** ~ pension off; **prendre sa** ~ retire.

retraité, ~e /Rətrete/ adj retired. ● nm, f (old-age) pensioner.

retrancher /Rətrɑ̃ʃe/ **1** vt remove; (soustraire) deduct, subtract. ■ se ~ vpr (Mil) entrench oneself; **se** ~ **derrière** take refuge behind.

retransmettre /Rətrɑ̃smɛtr/ **42** vt broadcast.

rétrécir /Retresir/ **2** vt make narrower; (vêtement) take in. ● vi (tissu) shrink. ■ se ~ vpr (rue) narrow.

rétribution /Retribysjɔ̃/ nf payment.

rétroactif, -ive /Retrɔaktif, -v/ adj retrospective; **augmentation à effet** ~ backdated pay rise.

retrousser /Rətruse/ **1** vt pull up; (manche) roll up.

retrouvailles /Rətruvaj/ nfpl reunion.

retrouver /Rətruve/ **1** vt find (again); (rejoindre) meet (again); (forces, calme) regain; (lieu) be back in; (se rappeler) remember. ■ se ~ vpr find oneself (back); (se réunir)

r

meet (again); (être présent) be found; **s'y ~** (s'orienter, comprendre) find one's way; (rentrer dans ses frais 🔟) break even.

rétroviseur /ʀetʀɔvizœʀ/ nm (Auto) (rear-view) mirror.

réunion /ʀeynjɔ̃/ nf meeting; (rencontre) gathering; (après une séparation) réunion; (d'objets) collection.

réunir /ʀeyniʀ/ ② vt gather, collect; (rapprocher) bring together; (convoquer) call together; (raccorder) join; (qualités) combine. ■ se ~ vpr meet.

réussi, ~e /ʀeysi/ adj successful.

réussir /ʀeysiʀ/ ② vi succeed, be successful; **~ à faire** succeed in doing, manage to do; **~ à un examen** pass an exam; **~ à qn** (méthode) work well for sb; (climat, mode de vie) agree with sb. ●vt (vie) make a success of.

réussite /ʀeysit/ nf success; (jeu) patience.

revaloir /ʀəvalwaʀ/ ⑥⓪ vt **je vous revaudrai cela** (en mal) I'll pay you back for this; (en bien) I'll repay you some day.

revanche /ʀəvɑ̃ʃ/ nf revenge; (Sport) return ou revenge match; **en ~** on the other hand.

rêvasser /ʀɛvase/ ① vi daydream.

rêve /ʀɛv/ nm dream; **faire un ~** have a dream.

réveil /ʀevɛj/ nm waking up, (fig) awakening; (pendule) alarm clock.

réveillé, ~e /ʀeveje/ adj awake.

réveille-matin* /ʀevɛjmatɛ̃/ nm inv alarm clock.

réveiller /ʀeveje/ ① vt wake (up); (sentiment, souvenir) awaken; (curiosité) arouse. ■ se ~ vpr wake up.

réveillon /ʀevɛjɔ̃/ nm (Noël) Christmas Eve; (nouvel an) New Year's Eve. **réveillonner** ① vi see Christmas ou the New Year in.

révéler /ʀevele/ ⑭ vt reveal. ■ se ~ vpr be revealed; **se ~ facile** turn out to be easy, prove easy.

revendeur, -euse /ʀəvɑ̃dœʀ, -øz/ nm, f dealer, stockist; **~ de drogue** drug dealer.

revendication /ʀəvɑ̃dikasjɔ̃/ nf claim. **revendiquer** ① vt claim.

revendre /ʀəvɑ̃dʀ/ ③ vt sell (again); **avoir de l'énergie à ~** have energy to spare.

revenir /ʀəvniʀ/ ⑤⑧ vi (aux être) come back, return (**à** to); **~ à** (activité) go back to; (se résumer à) come down to; (échoir à) fall to; **~ à 100 euros** cost 100 euros; **~ de** (maladie, surprise) get over; **~ sur ses pas** retrace one's steps; **faire ~** (Culin) brown; **ça me revient!** now I remember!; **je n'en reviens pas!** 🔟 I can't get over it!

revenu /ʀəvny/ nm income; (de l'État) revenue.

rêver /ʀeve/ ① vt/i dream (**à** of; **de faire** of doing).

réverbère /ʀevɛʀbɛʀ/ nm street lamp.

révérence /ʀeveʀɑ̃s/ nf reverence; (salut d'homme) bow; (salut de femme) curtsy.

rêverie /ʀɛvʀi/ nf daydream; (activité) daydreaming.

revers /ʀəvɛʀ/ nm reverse; (de main) back; (d'étoffe) wrong side; (de veste) lapel; (de pantalon) turn-up; (de manche) cuff; (tennis) backhand; (fig) set-back.

revêtement /ʀəvɛtmɑ̃/ nm covering; (de route) surface; **~ de sol** floor covering. **revêtir** ⑥⓵ vt cover; (habit) put on; (prendre, avoir) assume.

rêveur, -euse /ʀɛvœʀ, -øz/ adj dreamy. ●nm, f dreamer.

réviser /ʀevize/ ① vt revise; (machine, véhicule) service. **révision** nf revision; service.

revivre /ʀəvivʀ/ ⑥② vi come alive again. ●vt relive.

révocation /Revɔkasjɔ̃/ nf repeal; (d'un fonctionnaire) dismissal.

revoir¹ /RəvwaR/ 63 vt see (again); (réviser) revise.

revoir² /RəvwaR/ nm au ~ goodbye.

révolte /Revɔlt/ nf revolt. **révolté, ~e** nm, f rebel.

révolter /Revɔlte/ 1 vt appal, revolt. ■ se ~ vpr revolt.

révolu /Revɔly/ adj past; **avoir 21 ans ~s** be over 21 years of age.

révolution /Revɔlysjɔ̃/ nf revolution. **révolutionnaire** adj & nmf revolutionary. **révolutionner** 1 vt revolutionize.

revolver* /RevɔlvɛR/ nm revolver, gun.

révoquer /Revɔke/ 1 vt repeal; (fonctionnaire) dismiss.

revue /Rəvy/ nf (examen, défilé) review; (magazine) magazine; (spectacle) variety show.

rez-de-chaussée /Redʃose/ nm inv ground floor; (US) first floor.

RF abrév f (**République Française**) French Republic.

rhinocéros /RinɔseRɔs/ nm rhinoceros.

rhubarbe /RybaRb/ nf rhubarb.

rhum /Rɔm/ nm rum.

rhumatisme /Rymatism/ nm rheumatism.

rhume /Rym/ nm cold; ~ **des foins** hay fever.

ri /Ri/ ▷ **RIRE** 54.

ricaner /Rikane/ 1 vi snigger.

riche /Riʃ/ adj rich (**en** in). ●nmf rich man, rich woman.

richesse /Riʃɛs/ nf wealth; (de sol, décor) richness; ~**s** wealth; (ressources) resources.

ride /Rid/ nf wrinkle; (sur l'eau) ripple.

rideau (pl ~**x**) /Rido/ nm curtain;

(métallique) shutter; (fig) screen.

ridicule /Ridikyl/ adj ridiculous. ●nm (d'une situation) absurdity; (le grotesque) **le** ~ ridicule. **ridiculiser** 1 vt ridicule.

rien /Rjɛ̃/ pron nothing; (quoi que ce soit) anything; **de** ~! don't mention it!; ~ **de bon** nothing good; **elle n'a** ~ **dit** she didn't say anything; ~ **d'autre/de plus** nothing else/more; ~ **du tout** nothing at all; ~ **que** (seulement) just, only; **trois fois** ~ next to nothing; **il n'y est pour** ~ he has nothing to do with it; ~ **à faire!** (c'est impossible) it's no good!; (refus) no way! ⚑. ●nm **un** ~ **de** a touch of; **être puni pour un** ~ be punished for the slightest thing; **se disputer pour un** ~ fight over nothing; **en un** ~ **de temps** in next to no time.

rieur, -euse /RijœR, -øz/ adj cheerful; (yeux) laughing.

rigide /Riʒid/ adj rigid.

rigolade /Rigɔlad/ nf fun.

rigoler /Rigɔle/ 1 vi laugh; (s'amuser) have some fun; (plaisanter) joke.

rigolo, ~te /Rigɔlo, -ɔt/ adj ⚑ funny. ●nm, f ⚑ joker.

rigoureux, -euse /RiguRø, -z/ adj rigorous; (hiver) harsh; (sévère) strict; (travail, recherches) meticulous.

rigueur /RigœR/ nf rigour; **à la** ~ at a pinch; **être de** ~ be obligatory; **tenir** ~ **à qn de qch** bear sb a grudge for sth.

rime /Rim/ nf rhyme.

rimer /Rime/ 1 vi rhyme (**avec** with); **cela ne rime à rien** it makes no sense.

rinçage /Rɛ̃saʒ/ nm rinse; (action) rinsing.

rincer /Rɛ̃se/ 10 vt rinse.

riposte /Ripɔst/ nf retort.

riposter /Ripɔste/ 1 vi retaliate;

$\sim$ **à** (attaque) counter; (insulte) reply to. •vt retort (**que** that).

rire /ʀiʀ/ 54 vi laugh (**de** at); (plaisanter) joke; (s'amuser) have fun; **c'était pour** $\sim$ it was a joke. •nm laugh; **des** $\sim$**s** laughter.

risée /ʀize/ nf **la** $\sim$ **de** the laughing stock of.

risque /ʀisk/ nm risk. **risqué,** $\sim$**e** adj risky; (osé) daring.

risquer /ʀiske/ 1 vt risk (**de faire** of doing); (être passible de) face; **il risque de pleuvoir** it might rain; **tu risques de te faire mal** you might hurt yourself. ■ **se** $\sim$ **à/dans** vpr venture to/into.

ristourne /ʀistuʀn/ nf discount.

rite /ʀit/ nm rite; (habitude) ritual. **rituel,** $\sim$**le** adj & nm ritual.

rivage /ʀivaʒ/ nm shore.

rival, $\sim$**e** (mpl **-aux**) /ʀival, -o/ adj & nm, f rival. **rivaliser** 1 vi compete (**avec** with). **rivalité** nf rivalry.

rive /ʀiv/ nf (de fleuve) bank; (de lac) shore.

riverain, $\sim$**e** /ʀivʀɛ̃, -ɛn/ adj riverside. •nm, f riverside resident; (d'une rue) resident.

rivière /ʀivjɛʀ/ nf river.

riz /ʀi/ nm rice. **rizière** nf paddy field.

robe /ʀɔb/ nf (de femme) dress; (de juge) robe; (de cheval) coat; $\sim$ **de chambre** dressing-gown.

robinet /ʀɔbinɛ/ nm tap; (US) faucet.

robot /ʀɔbo/ nm robot; $\sim$ **ménager** food processor.

robuste /ʀɔbyst/ adj robust.

roche /ʀɔʃ/ nf rock.

rocher /ʀɔʃe/ nm rock.

rock /ʀɔk/ nm (Mus) rock.

rodage /ʀɔdaʒ/ nm **en** $\sim$ (Auto) running in.

roder /ʀɔde/ 1 vt (Auto) run in; **être rodé** (personne) have got the hang of things.

rôder /ʀode/ 1 vi roam; (suspect) prowl.

rogne /ʀɔɲ/ nf 1 anger; **en** $\sim$ in a temper.

rogner /ʀɔɲe/ 1 vt trim; $\sim$ **sur** cut down on.

rognon /ʀɔɲɔ̃/ nm (Culin) kidney.

roi /ʀwa/ nm king; **les R** $\sim$ **mages** the Magi; **la fête des R**$\sim$ Twelfth Night.

rôle /ʀol/ nm role, part.

roller /ʀɔlɛʀ/ nm (patin) rollerblade®; (activité) rollerblading.

romain, $\sim$**e** /ʀɔmɛ̃, -ɛn/ adj Roman. **R**$\sim$**,** $\sim$**e** nm, f Roman. **romaine** nf (laitue) cos.

roman /ʀɔmɑ̃/ nm novel; (genre) fiction.

romance /ʀɔmɑ̃s/ nf ballad.

romancier, -ière /ʀɔmɑ̃sje, -jɛʀ/ nm, f novelist.

romanesque /ʀɔmanɛsk/ adj romantic; (fantastique) fantastic; (récit) fictional; **œuvres** $\sim$**s** novels, fiction.

romantique /ʀɔmɑ̃tik/ adj & nmf romantic. **romantisme** nm romanticism.

rompre /ʀɔ̃pʀ/ 3 vt break; (relations) break off. •vi (se séparer) break up; $\sim$ **avec** (fiancé) break up with; (parti) break away from; (tradition) break with. ■ **se** $\sim$ vpr break.

ronce /ʀɔ̃s/ nf bramble.

rond, $\sim$**e** /ʀɔ̃, -d/ adj round; (gras) plump; (ivre) 1 drunk. •nm (cercle) ring; (tranche) slice; **en** $\sim$ in a circle; **il n'a pas un** $\sim$ 1 he hasn't got a penny.

ronde /ʀɔ̃d/ nf (de policier) beat; (de soldat, gardien) watch; (Mus) semibreve.

rondelle /ʀɔ̃dɛl/ nf (Tech) washer; (tranche) slice.

rondement /ʀɔ̃dmɑ̃/ adv promptly; (franchement) frankly.

rondeur /ʀɔ̃dœʀ/ nf roundness; (franchise) frankness; (embonpoint) plumpness.

rondin /ʀɔ̃dɛ̃/ nm log.

rond-point* (pl **ronds-points**) /ʀɔ̃pwɛ̃/ nm roundabout; (US) traffic circle.

ronfler /ʀɔ̃fle/ **1** vi snore; (moteur) purr.

ronger /ʀɔ̃ʒe/ **40** vt gnaw (at); (vers, acide) eat into. ■ se ~ vpr **se ~ les ongles** bite one's nails.

rongeur /ʀɔ̃ʒœʀ/ nm rodent.

ronronner /ʀɔ̃ʀɔne/ **1** vi purr.

rosbif /ʀɔsbif/ nm roast beef.

rose /ʀoz/ nf rose. ● adj & nm pink.

rosé, ~e /ʀoze/ adj pinkish. ● nm rosé.

roseau (pl ~**x**) /ʀozo/ nm reed.

rosée /ʀoze/ nf dew.

rosier /ʀozje/ nm rose bush.

rossignol /ʀɔsiɲɔl/ nm nightingale.

rotatif, -ive /ʀɔtatif, -v/ adj rotary.

roter /ʀɔte/ **1** vi 🔲 burp.

rôti /ʀoti/ nm joint; (cuit) roast; ~ **de porc** roast pork.

rotin /ʀɔtɛ̃/ nm (rattan) cane.

rôtir /ʀotiʀ/ **2** vt roast.

rôtissoire /ʀotiswaʀ/ nf roasting spit.

rotule /ʀɔtyl/ nf kneecap.

rouage /ʀwaʒ/ nm (Tech) wheel; **les ~s** the works; (d'une organisation: fig) wheels.

roucouler /ʀukule/ **1** vi coo.

roue /ʀu/ nf wheel; ~ **dentée** cog (wheel); ~ **de secours** spare wheel.

rouer /ʀwe/ **1** vt ~ **de coups** thrash.

rouge /ʀuʒ/ adj red; (fer) red-hot. ● nm red; (vin) red wine; (fard) blusher; ~ **à lèvres** lipstick. ● nmf (Pol) red. **rouge-gorge** (pl **rouges-gorges**) nm robin.

rougeole /ʀuʒɔl/ nf measles (+ sg).

rouget /ʀuʒɛ/ nm red mullet.

rougeur /ʀuʒœʀ/ nf redness; (tache) red blotch.

rougir /ʀuʒiʀ/ **2** vi turn red; (de honte) blush.

rouille /ʀuj/ nf rust. **rouillé, ~e** adj rusty.

rouiller /ʀuje/ **1** vi rust. ■ se ~ vpr get rusty.

rouleau (pl ~**x**) /ʀulo/ nm roll; (outil, vague) roller; ~ **à pâtisserie** rolling pin; ~ **compresseur** steamroller.

roulement /ʀulmɑ̃/ nm rotation; (bruit) rumble; (alternance) rotation; (de tambour) roll; ~ **à billes** ballbearing; **travailler par ~** work in shifts.

rouler /ʀule/ **1** vt roll; (ficelle, manches) roll up; (pâte) roll out; (duper 🔲) cheat. ● vi (véhicule, train) go, travel; (conducteur) drive. ■ se ~ **dans** vpr (herbe) roll in; (couverture) roll oneself up in.

roulette /ʀulɛt/ nf (de meuble) castor; (de dentiste) drill; (jeu) roulette; **comme sur des ~s** very smoothly.

roulotte /ʀulɔt/ nf caravan.

roumain, ~e /ʀumɛ̃, -ɛn/ adj Romanian. **R~, ~e** nm, f Romanian.

Roumanie /ʀumani/ nf Romania.

rouquin, ~e /ʀukɛ̃, -in/ 🔲 adj redhaired. ● nm, f redhead.

rouspéter /ʀuspete/ **14** vi 🔲 grumble, moan.

r

rousse /ʀus/ ▸ROUX.

roussir /ʀusiʀ/ ❷ vt scorch. ●vi turn brown.

route /ʀut/ nf road; (Naut, Aviat) route; (direction) way; (voyage) journey; (chemin: fig) path; **en ~** on the way; **en ~!** let's go!; **mettre en ~** start; ⬛**~ nationale** trunk road, main road; **se mettre en ~** set out.

routier, -ière /ʀutje, -jɛʀ/ adj road. ●nm long-distance lorry ou truck driver; (restaurant) transport café; (US) truck stop.

routine /ʀutin/ nf routine.

roux, rousse /ʀu, ʀus/ adj red, russet; (personne) red-haired; (chat) ginger. ●nm, f redhead.

royal, ~e (mpl **-aux**) /ʀwajal, -jo/ adj royal; (cadeau) fit for a king.

royaume /ʀwajom/ nm kingdom.

Royaume-Uni /ʀwajomyni/ nm United Kingdom.

royauté /ʀwajote/ nf royalty.

RTT abrév f (**réduction du temps de travail**) reduction in working hours.

ruban /ʀybɑ̃/ nm ribbon; (de chapeau) band; **~ adhésif** sticky tape; **~ magnétique** magnetic tape.

rubéole /ʀybeɔl/ nf German measles (+ sg).

rubis /ʀybi/ nm ruby.

rubrique /ʀybʀik/ nf heading; (article) column.

ruche /ʀyʃ/ nf beehive.

rude /ʀyd/ adj (au toucher) rough; (pénible) tough; (grossier) coarse; (fameux ⬛) tremendous.

rudement /ʀydmɑ̃/ adv (frapper) hard; (traiter) harshly; (très ⬛) really.

rudimentaire /ʀydimɑ̃tɛʀ/ adj rudimentary.

rue /ʀy/ nf street.

ruée /ʀɥe/ nf rush.

ruer /ʀɥe/ ❶ vi (cheval) buck. ■ **se ~** vpr rush (**dans** into; **vers** towards); **se ~ sur** pounce on.

rugby /ʀygbi/ nm rugby.

rugir /ʀyʒiʀ/ ❷ vi roar.

rugueux, -euse /ʀygø, -z/ adj rough.

ruine /ʀɥin/ nf ruin; **en (~s)** in ruins. **ruiner** ❶ vt ruin.

ruisseau (pl **~x**) /ʀɥiso/ nm stream; (rigole) gutter.

rumeur /ʀymœʀ/ nf (nouvelle) rumour; (son) murmur, hum.

ruminer /ʀymine/ ❶ vi (animal) ruminate; (méditer) meditate.

rupture /ʀyptyʀ/ nf break; (action) breaking; (de contrat) breach; (de pourparlers) breakdown; (de relations) breaking off; (de couple, coalition) break-up.

rural, ~e (mpl **-aux**) /ʀyʀal, -o/ adj rural.

ruse /ʀyz/ nf cunning; **une ~** a trick, a ruse. **rusé, ~e** adj cunning.

russe /ʀys/ adj Russian. ●nm (Ling) Russian. **R~** nmf Russian.

Russie /ʀysi/ nf Russia.

rustique /ʀystik/ adj rustic.

rythme /ʀitm/ nm rhythm; (vitesse) rate; (de la vie) pace. **rythmique** adj rhythmical.

⬛ see A-Z of French life and culture

Ss

s' /s/ ▷SE.

sa /sa/ ▷SON¹.

SA abrév f (**société anonyme**) PLC.

sabbatique /sabatik/ adj (année) sabbatical year.

sable /sɑbl/ nm sand; ~**s mouvants** quicksands. **sabler** vt **1** grit.

sablier /sablije/ nm (Culin) eggtimer.

sablonneux, -euse /sablɔnø, -z/ adj sandy.

sabot /sabo/ nm (de cheval) hoof; (chaussure) clog; (de frein) shoe; ~ **de Denver**® (wheel) clamp.

saboter /sabɔte/ **1** vt sabotage; (bâcler) botch.

sac /sak/ nm bag; (grand, en toile) sack; **mettre à** ~ (maison) ransack; (ville) sack; ~ **à dos** rucksack; ~ **à main** handbag; ~ **de couchage** sleeping-bag; **mettre dans le même** ~ lump together.

saccadé, -e /sakade/ adj jerky.

saccager /sakaʒe/ **40** vt (abîmer) wreck; (maison) ransack; (ville, pays) sack.

saccharine* /sakaʀin/ nf saccharin.

sachet /saʃɛ/ nm (small) bag; (d'aromates) sachet; ~ **de thé** teabag.

sacoche /sakɔʃ/ nf bag; (de vélo) saddlebag.

sacre /sakʀ/ nm (de roi) coronation; (d'évêque) consecration. **sacré, ~e** adj sacred; (maudit **1**) damned. **sacrement** nm sacrament. **sacrer** **1** vt crown; consecrate.

sacrifice /sakʀifis/ nm sacrifice.

sacrifier /sakʀifje/ **45** vt sacrifice; ~ **à** conform to. ■ **se** ~ vpr sacrifice oneself.

sacrilège /sakʀilɛʒ/ nm sacrilege. ● adj sacrilegious.

sadique /sadik/ adj sadistic. ● nmf sadist.

sage /saʒ/ adj wise; (docile) good, well behaved. ● nm wise man.

sage-femme* (pl sages-femmes) /saʒfam/ nf midwife.

sagesse /saʒɛs/ nf wisdom.

Sagittaire /saʒitɛʀ/ nm **le** ~ Sagittarius.

saignant, ~e /sɛɲɑ̃, -t/ adj (Culin) rare.

saigner /seɲe/ **1** vt/i bleed; ~ **du nez** have a nosebleed.

saillant, ~e /sajɑ̃, -t/ adj prominent.

sain, ~e /sɛ̃, sɛn/ adj healthy; (moralement) sane; ~ **et sauf** safe and sound.

saindoux /sɛ̃du/ nm lard.

saint, ~e /sɛ̃, -t/ adj holy; (bon, juste) saintly. ● nm, f saint. **Saint-Esprit** nm Holy Spirit. **sainteté** nf holiness; (d'un lieu) sanctity. **Sainte Vierge** nf Blessed Virgin. **Saint-Sylvestre** nf New Year's Eve.

sais /sɛ/ ▷SAVOIR **55**.

saisie /sezi/ nf (Jur) seizure; (Comput) keyboarding; ~ **de données** data capture.

saisir /seziʀ/ **2** vt grab (hold of); (proie) seize; (occasion, biens) seize; (comprendre) grasp; (frapper) strike; (Ordinat) keyboard, capture; **saisi de** (peur) stricken by, overcome

S

by. ∎ se ~ de vpr seize.
saisissant, ~e adj (spectacle) gripping.

saison /sɛzɔ̃/ nf season; **la morte ~** the off season. saisonnier, -ière adj seasonal.

sait /sɛ/ ▷ SAVOIR 55.

salade /salad/ nf (plat) salad; (plante) lettuce. saladier nm salad bowl.

salaire /salɛʀ/ nm wages (+ pl), salary.

salarié, ~e /salaʀje/ adj wageearning. ●nm, f wage earner.

sale /sal/ adj dirty; (mauvais) nasty.

salé, ~e /sale/ adj (goût) salty; (plat) salted; (opposé à sucré) savoury; (grivois 🛈) spicy; (excessif 🛈) steep. saler 🗌 vt salt.

saleté /salte/ nf dirtiness; (crasse) dirt; (obscénité) obscenity; ~(s) (camelote) rubbish; (détritus) mess.

salir /saliʀ/ 🗌 vt (make) dirty; (réputation) tarnish. ∎ se ~ vpr get dirty. salissant, ~e adj dirty; (étoffe) easily dirtied.

salive /saliv/ nf saliva.

salle /sal/ nf room; (grande, publique) hall; (de restaurant) dining room; (Théât, cinéma) auditorium; **cinéma à trois ~s** three-screen cinema; ~ **à manger** dining room; ~ **d'attente** waiting room; ~ **de bains** bathroom; ~ **de causette** chatroom. ~ **de séjour** living room; ~ **de classe** classroom; ~ **d'embarquement** departure lounge; ~ **d'opération** operating theatre; ~ **des ventes** saleroom.

salon /salɔ̃/ nm lounge; (de coiffure, beauté) salon; (exposition) show; ~ **de thé** tea-room; ~ **virtuel** chatroom.

salopette /salɔpɛt/ nf dungarees (+ pl); (d'ouvrier) overalls (+ pl).

saltimbanque /saltɛ̃bɑ̃k/ nmf (street) acrobat.

salubre /salybʀ/ adj healthy.

saluer /salɥe/ 🗌 vt greet; (en partant) take one's leave of; (de la tête) nod to; (de la main) wave to; (Mil) salute; (accueillir favorablement) welcome.

salut /saly/ nm greeting; (de la tête) nod; (de la main) wave; (Mil) salute; (rachat) salvation. ●interj (bonjour 🛈) hello; (au revoir 🛈) bye.

salutation /salytasjɔ̃/ nf greeting.

samedi /samdi/ nm Saturday.

🅲 SAMU /samy/ abrév m (**Service d'assistance médicale d'urgence**) ≈ mobile accident unit.

sanction /sɑ̃ksjɔ̃/ nf sanction. sanctionner 🗌 vt sanction; (punir) punish.

sandale /sɑ̃dal/ nf sandal.

sang /sɑ̃/ nm blood; **se faire du mauvais ~ ou un ~ d'encre** be worried stiff. **sang-froid** nm inv self-control. **sanglant, ~e** adj bloody.

sangle /sɑ̃gl/ nf strap.

sanglier /sɑ̃glije/ nm wild boar.

sanglot /sɑ̃glo/ nm sob. sangloter 🗌 vi sob.

sanguin, ~e /sɑ̃gɛ̃, -in/ adj (groupe) blood.

sanguinaire /sɑ̃ginɛʀ/ adj bloodthirsty.

sanitaire /sanitɛʀ/ adj (directives) health; (conditions) sanitary; (appareils, installations) bathroom, sanitary. **sanitaires** nmpl bathroom.

sans /sɑ̃/ prép without; ~ **ça,** ~ **quoi** otherwise; ~ **arrêt** nonstop; ~ **encombre/faute*/ tarder** without incident/fail/ delay; ~ **fin/goût/limite** endless/tasteless/limitless; ~ **importance/pareil/**

précédent/travail unimportant/ unparalleled/ unprecedented/ unemployed; **j'ai aimé mais ~ plus** it was good, it wasn't great.

sans-abri* /sɑ̃zabʀi/ nmf inv homeless person.

sans-gêne* /sɑ̃ʒɛn/ adj inv inconsiderate, thoughtless. ●nm inv thoughtlessness.

sans-papiers* /sɑ̃papje/ nm inv illegal immigrant.

santé /sɑ̃te/ nf health; **à ta** ou **votre ~!** cheers!

saoul, ~e /su, sul/ ▷SOUL.

sapin /sapɛ̃/ nm fir (tree); **~ de Noël** Christmas tree.

sarcasme /saʀkasm/ nm sarcasm. **sarcastique** adj sarcastic.

sardine /saʀdin/ nf sardine.

sas /sɑs/ nm (Naut, Aviat) airlock.

satané, ~e /satane/ adj 🔢 damned.

satellite /satelit/ nm satellite.

satin /satɛ̃/ nm satin.

satire /satiʀ/ nf satire.

satisfaction /satisfaksjɔ̃/ nf satisfaction.

satisfaire /satisfɛʀ/ 33 vt satisfy. ●vi **~ à** fulfil. **satisfaisant, ~e** adj (acceptable) satisfactory. **satisfait, ~e** adj satisfied (**de** with).

saturer /satyʀe/ 1 vt saturate.

sauce /sos/ nf sauce; **~ tartare** tartar sauce. **saucière** nf sauceboat.

saucisse /sosis/ nf sausage.

saucisson /sosisɔ̃/ nm (slicing) sausage.

sauf¹ /sof/ prép except; **~ erreur** if I'm not mistaken; **~ imprévu** unless anything unforeseen happens; **~ avis contraire** unless otherwise stated.

sauf², ~ve /sof, sov/ adj safe, unharmed.

sauge /soʒ/ nf (Culin) sage.

saule /sol/ nm willow; **~ pleureur** weeping willow.

saumon /somɔ̃/ nm salmon. ●adj inv salmon(-pink).

sauna /sona/ nm sauna.

saupoudrer /sopudʀe/ 1 vt sprinkle (**de** with).

saut /so/ nm jump; **faire un ~ chez qn** pop round to sb's (place); **le ~** (Sport) jumping; **~ en hauteur/longueur** high/ long jump; **~ périlleux** somersault; **au ~ du lit** on getting up.

sauté, ~e /sote/ adj & nm (Culin) sauté.

saute-mouton* /sotmutɔ̃/ nm inv leap-frog.

sauter /sote/ 1 vi jump; (exploser) blow up; (fusible) blow; (se détacher) come off; **faire ~** (détruire) blow up; (fusible) blow; (casser) break; **~ à la corde** skip; **~ aux yeux** be obvious; **~ au cou de qn** fling one's arms round sb; **~ sur une occasion** jump at an opportunity. ●vt jump (over); (page, classe) skip.

sauterelle /sotʀɛl/ nf grasshopper.

sautiller /sotije/ 1 vi hop.

sauvage /sovaʒ/ adj wild; (primitif, cruel) savage; (farouche) unsociable; (illégal) unauthorized. ●nmf unsociable person; (brute) savage.

sauve /sov/ ▷SAUF².

sauvegarder /sovgaʀde/ 1 vt safeguard; (Ordinat) back up.

sauver /sove/ 1 vt save; (d'un danger) rescue, save; (matériel) salvage. ■ **se ~** vpr (fuir) run away; (partir 1) be off. **sauvetage** nm rescue.

sauveteur nm rescuer. **sauveur** nm saviour.

savant, **∼e** /savɑ̃, -t/ adj learned; (habile) skilful. •nm scientist.

saveur /savœʀ/ nf flavour; (fig) savour.

savoir /savwaʀ/ ⑤ vt know; **elle sait conduire/nager** she can drive/ swim; **faire ∼ à qn que** inform sb that; **(pas) que je sache** (not) as far as I know; **à ∼** namely. •nm learning.

savon /savɔ̃/ nm soap; **passer un ∼ à qn** ① give sb a telling-off. **savonnette** nf bar of soap.

savourer /savuʀe/ ① vt savour. **savoureux**, **-euse** adj tasty; (fig) spicy.

scandale /skɑ̃dal/ nm scandal; (tapage) uproar; (en public) noisy scene; **faire ∼** shock people; **faire un ∼** make a scene. **scandaleux**, **-euse** adj scandalous. **scandaliser** ① vt scandalize, shock.

scander /skɑ̃de/ ① vt (vers) scan; (slogan) chant.

scandinave /skɑ̃dinav/ adj Scandinavian. **S∼** nmf Scandinavian.

Scandinavie /skɑ̃dinavi/ nf Scandinavia.

scarabée /skaʀabe/ nm beetle.

sceau (pl ∼**x**) /so/ nm seal.

scélérat /selera/ nm scoundrel.

sceller /sele/ ① vt seal.

scène /sɛn/ nf scene; (estrade, art dramatique) stage; **mettre en ∼** (pièce) stage; (film) direct; **mise en ∼** direction; **∼ de ménage** domestic dispute.

scepticisme /sɛptisism/ nm scepticism.

sceptique /sɛptik/ adj sceptical. •nmf sceptic.

schéma /ʃema/ nm diagram. **schématique** adj schematic; (sommaire) sketchy. **schématiser** ① vt simplify.

schizophrène /skizɔfʀɛn/ adj & nmf schizophrenic.

sciatique /sjatik/ adj (nerf) sciatic. •nf sciatica.

scie /si/ nf saw.

sciemment /sjamɑ̃/ adv knowingly.

science /sjɑ̃s/ nf science; (savoir) knowledge.

science-fiction /sjɑ̃sfiksjɔ̃/ nf science fiction.

scientifique /sjɑ̃tifik/ adj scientific. •nmf scientist.

scier /sje/ ⑮ vt saw.

scintiller /sɛ̃tije/ ① vi glitter; (étoile) twinkle.

scission /sisjɔ̃/ nf split.

sclérose /skleʀoz/ nf sclerosis; **∼ en plaques** multiple sclerosis.

scolaire /skɔlɛʀ/ adj school. **scolarisé**, **∼e** adj going to school. **scolarité** nf schooling.

score /skɔʀ/ nm score.

scorpion /skɔʀpjɔ̃/ nm scorpion; **le S∼** Scorpio.

scotch* /skɔtʃ/ nm (boisson) Scotch (whisky); (ruban adhésif)® Sellotape®.

scout, **∼e** /skut/ nm & adj scout.

scrupule /skʀypyl/ nm scruple. **scrupuleux**, **-euse** adj scrupulous.

scruter /skʀyte/ ① vt examine, scrutinize.

scrutin /skʀytɛ̃/ nm (vote) ballot; (élections) polls (+ pl).

sculpter /skylte/ ① vt sculpt, carve. **sculpteur** nm sculptor. **sculpture** nf sculpture.

SDF abrév m (**sans domicile fixe**) homeless person.

se, s' /sə, s/

! **s'** before vowel or mute h.

● pronom
····▸ himself, (féminin) herself; (indéfini) oneself; (non humain) itself; (au pluriel) themselves; ~ **laver les mains** wash one's hands; (réciproque) each other, one another; **ils se détestent** they hate each other.

! The translation of **se** will vary according to which verb it is associated with. You should therefore refer to the verb to find it. For example, **se promener, se taire** will be treated respectively under **promener** and **taire**.

séance /seɑ̃s/ nf session; (Théât, cinéma) show; ~ **de pose** sitting; ~ **tenante** forthwith.

seau (pl ~x) /so/ nm bucket, pail.

sec, sèche /sɛk, sɛʃ/ adj dry; (fruits) dried; (coup, bruit) sharp; (cœur) hard; (whisky) neat. ●nm **à** ~ (sans eau) dry; (sans argent) broke; **au** ~ in a dry place.

sèche-cheveux* /sɛʃʃəvø/ nm inv hairdrier.

sèchement /sɛʃmɑ̃/ adv drily.

sécher /seʃe/ 14 vt/i dry; (cours: 🔢) skip; (ne pas savoir 🔢) be stumped. ■ **se** ~ vpr dry oneself. **sécheresse*** nf (de climat) dryness; (temps sec) drought. **séchoir** nm drier.

second, ~e /səɡɔ̃, -d/ adj & nm, f second. ●nm (adjoint) second in command; (étage) second floor. **secondaire** adj secondary. **seconde** nf (instant) second; (vitesse) second gear.

seconder /səɡɔ̃de/ 1 vt assist.

secouer /səkwe/ 1 vt shake; (poussière, torpeur) shake off. ■ **se** ~ vpr 🔢 (se dépêcher) get a move on; (réagir) shake oneself up.

secourir /səkuRiR/ 20 vt assist,

help. **secouriste** nmf first-aid worker.

secours /səkuR/ nm assistance, help; **au** ~! help!; **de** ~ (sortie) emergency; (équipe, opération) rescue. ●nmpl (Méd) first aid.

secousse /səkus/ nf jolt, jerk; (séisme) tremor.

secret, -ète /səkRɛ, -t/ adj secret. ●nm secret; (discrétion) secrecy; **le** ~ **professionnel** professional confidentiality; ~ **de Polichinelle** open secret; **en** ~ in secret, secretly.

secrétaire /səkRetɛR/ nmf secretary; ~ **de direction** personal assistant. ●nm (meuble) writing desk; ~ **d'État** junior minister.

secrétariat /səkRetaRja/ nm secretarial work; (bureau) secretariat.

sectaire /sɛktɛR/ adj sectarian.

secte /sɛkt/ nf sect.

secteur /sɛktœR/ nm area; (Comm) sector; (circuit: Électr) mains (+ pl).

section /sɛksjɔ̃/ nf section; (Scol) stream; (Mil) platoon. **sectionner** 1 vt sever.

sécuriser /sekyRize/ 1 vt reassure.

sécurisé, e /sekyRize/ adj (Ordinat) secure; **une ligne** ~e a secure line.

sécurité /sekyRite/ nf security; (absence de danger) safety; **en** ~ safe, secure; **Sécurité sociale** nf social services, social security services; ~ **des frontières** homeland security.

sédatif /sedatif/ nm sedative.

sédentaire /sedɑ̃tɛR/ adj sedentary.

séducteur, -trice /sedyktœR, -tRis/ adj seductive. ●nm, f seducer. **séduction** nf seduction; (charme) charm.

séduire /seduiR/ 17 vt charm; (plaire à) appeal to; (sexuellement)

seduce. **séduisant, ∼e** adj
attractive.

ségrégation /segʀegasjɔ̃/ nf
segregation.

seigle /sɛgl/ nm rye.

seigneur /sɛɲœʀ/ nm lord; **le S∼**
the Lord.

sein /sɛ̃/ nm breast; **au ∼ de**
within.

séisme /seism/ nm earthquake.

seize /sɛz/ adj & nm sixteen.

séjour /seʒuʀ/ nm stay; (pièce)
living room. **séjourner 1** vi stay.

sel /sɛl/ nm salt; (piquant) spice.

sélectif, -ive /selɛktif, -v/ adj
selective.

sélection /selɛksjɔ̃/ nf selection.
sélectionner 1 vt select.

selle /sɛl/ nf saddle; **∼s** (Méd)
stools.

sellette /sɛlɛt/ nf **sur la ∼**
(personne) in the hot seat.

selon /səlɔ̃/ prép according to; **∼
que** depending on whether.

semaine /səmɛn/ nf week; **en ∼**
during the week.

sémantique /semãtik/ adj
semantic. ●nf semantics.

semblable /sãblabl/ adj similar
(**à** to). ●nm fellow (creature).

semblant /sãblã/ nm **faire ∼ de**
pretend to; **un ∼ de** a
semblance of.

sembler /sãble/ **1** vi seem (**à** to;
que that); **il me semble que** it
seems to me that.

semelle /səmɛl/ nf sole; **∼
compensée** wedge heel.

semence /s(ə)mãs/ nf seed.

semer /s(ə)me/ **6** vt (graine, doute)
sow; (jeter, parsemer) strew; (personne
1) lose; **∼ la panique** spread
panic.

semestre /səmɛstʀ/ nm half year;
(Univ) semester. **semestriel, ∼le**

adj (revue) biannual; (examen) end-
of-semester.

séminaire /seminɛʀ/ nm (Relig)
seminary; (Univ) seminar.

semi-remorque
/s(ə)miʀ(ə)mɔʀk/ nm articulated
lorry.

semis /s(ə)mi/ nm seedling.

semoule /s(ə)mul/ nf semolina.

🔲**sénat** /sena/ nm senate. **sénateur**
nm senator.

sénile /senil/ adj senile.

senior* /senjɔʀ/ adj (âgé) senior;
(mode, publication) for senior
citizens. ●nmf senior citizen.

sens /sãs/ nm (Méd) sense;
(signification) meaning, sense;
(direction) direction; **à mon ∼** to
my mind; **à ∼ unique** (rue) one-
way; **ça n'a pas de ∼** it doesn't
make sense; **∼ commun**
common sense; **∼ giratoire**
roundabout; **∼ interdit** no-entry
sign; (rue) one-way street; **dans
le ∼ des aiguilles d'une
montre** clockwise; **dans le ∼
inverse des aiguilles d'une
montre** anticlockwise; **∼
dessus dessous** upside down;
∼ devant derrière back to
front.

sensation /sãsasjɔ̃/ nf feeling,
sensation; **faire ∼** create a
sensation. **sensationnel, ∼le** adj
sensational.

sensé, ∼e /sãse/ adj sensible.

sensibiliser /sãsibilize/ **1** vt **∼
l'opinion** increase people's
awareness (**à qch** to sth).

sensibilité /sãsibilite/ nf
sensitivity. **sensible** adj sensitive
(**à** to); (appréciable) noticeable.
sensiblement adv noticeably.

sensoriel, ∼le /sãsɔʀjɛl/ adj
sensory.

sensualité /sãsɥalite/ nf
sensuousness; sensuality.
sensuel, ∼le adj sensual.

sentence /sãtãs/ nf sentence.

---

senteur /sɑ̃tœʀ/ nf scent.

sentier /sɑ̃tje/ nm path.

sentiment /sɑ̃timɑ̃/ nm feeling; **faire du ~** sentimentalize; **j'ai le ~ que...** I get the feeling that... **sentimental, ~e** (mpl **-aux**) adj sentimental.

sentir /sɑ̃tiʀ/ ⁴⁶ vt feel; (odeur) smell; (pressentir) sense; **~ la lavande** smell of lavender; **je ne peux pas le ~** ① I can't stand him. •vi smell. ■ **se ~** vpr **se ~ fier/mieux** feel proud/ better.

séparation /separasjɔ̃/ nf separation.

séparatiste /separatist/ adj & nmf separatist.

séparé, ~e /separe/ adj separate; (conjoints) separated.

séparer /separe/ ① vt separate; (en deux) split. ■ **se ~** vpr separate, part (**de** from); (se détacher) split; **se ~ de** (se défaire de) part with.

sept /sɛt/ adj & nm seven.

septante /sɛptɑ̃t/ adj & nm seventy.

septembre /sɛptɑ̃bʀ/ nm September.

septentrional, ~e (mpl **-aux**) /sɛptɑ̃tʀijɔnal, -o/ adj northern.

septième /sɛtjɛm/ adj & nmf seventh.

sépulture /sepyltyʀ/ nf burial; (lieu) burial place.

séquelles /sekɛl/ nfpl (maladie) after-effects; (fig) aftermath.

séquence /sekɑ̃s/ nf sequence.

séquestrer /sekɛstʀe/ ① vt confine (illegally).

sera, serait /səʀa, səʀɛ/ ▷ÊTRE ④.

serbe /sɛʀb/ adj Serbian. **S~** nmf Serbian.

Serbie /sɛʀbi/ nf Serbia.

serein, ~e /səʀɛ̃, -ɛn/ adj serene.

sérénité /seʀenite/ nf serenity.

sergent /sɛʀʒɑ̃/ nm sergeant.

série /seʀi/ nf series (+ sg); (d'objets) set; **de ~** (véhicule etc.) standard; **fabrication** ou **production en ~** mass production.

sérieusement /seʀjøzmɑ̃/ adv seriously.

sérieux, -ieuse /seʀjø, -z/ adj serious; (digne de confiance) reliable; (chances, raison) good. •nm seriousness; **garder son ~** keep a straight face; **prendre au ~** take seriously.

serin /səʀɛ̃/ nm canary.

seringue /səʀɛ̃g/ nf syringe.

serment /sɛʀmɑ̃/ nm oath; (promesse) vow.

sermon /sɛʀmɔ̃/ nm sermon. **sermonner** ① vt lecture.

séropositif, -ive /seʀɔpozitif, -v/ adj HIV positive.

serpent /sɛʀpɑ̃/ nm snake; **~ à sonnettes** rattlesnake.

serpillière* /sɛʀpijɛʀ/ nf floorcloth.

serre /sɛʀ/ nf (de jardin) greenhouse; (griffe) claw.

serré, ~e /seʀe/ adj (habit, nœud, écrou) tight; (personnes) packed, crowded; (lutte, mailles) close; (écriture) cramped; (cœur) heavy.

serrer /seʀe/ ① vt (saisir) grip; (presser) squeeze; (vis, corde, ceinture) tighten; (poing, dents) clench; **~ qn dans ses bras** hug sb; **~ les rangs** close ranks; **~ qn** (vêtement) be tight on sb; **~ qn de près** follow sb closely; **~ la main à** shake hands with. •vi **~ à droite** keep over to the right. ■ **se ~** vpr (se rapprocher) squeeze (up).

serrure /seʀyʀ/ nf lock. **serrurier** nm locksmith.

servante /sɛʀvɑ̃t/ nf (maid) servant.

serveur, -euse /sɛʀvœʀ, -øz/ nm, f (homme) waiter; (femme) waitress.

●nm (Ordinat) server.

serviable /sɛʀvjabl/ adj helpful.

service /sɛʀvis/ nm service; (fonction, temps de travail) duty; (pourboire) service (charge); (dans une société) department; (~ **non**) **compris** service (not) included; **être de** ~ be on duty; **pendant le** ~ (when) on duty; **rendre** ~ **à qn** be a help to sb; ~ **à thé** tea set; ~ **d'ordre** stewards (+ pl); ~ **aprèsvente** after-sales service; ~ **militaire** military service; **les** ~**s secrets** the secret service (+ sg).

serviette /sɛʀvjɛt/ nf (de toilette) towel; (cartable) briefcase; (~ **de table**) serviette, napkin; ~ **hygiénique** sanitary towel.

servir /sɛʀviʀ/ 46 vt/i serve; (être utile) be of use, serve; ~ **qn** (à **table**) wait on sb; **ça sert à** (outil, récipient) it is used for; **ça me sert à/de** I use it to/as; **ça ne sert à rien** (action) it is pointless; ~ **de** serve as, be used as; ~ **à qn de guide** act as a guide for sb. ■**se** ~ vpr (à table) help oneself (**de** to); **se** ~ **de** use. **serviteur** nm servant.

ses /se/ ▷ SON¹.

session /sesjɔ̃/ nf session.

seuil /sœj/ nm doorstep; (entrée) doorway; (fig) threshold.

seul, ~**e** /sœl/ adj alone, on one's own; (unique) only; **un** ~ **exemple** only one example; **pas un** ~ **ami** not a single friend; **lui** ~ **le sait** only he knows; **dans le** ~ **but de** with the sole aim of; **parler tout** ~ talk to oneself; **faire qch tout** ~ do sth on one's own. ●nm, f **le** ~ **la** ~**e** the only one. **seulement** adv only.

sève /sɛv/ nf sap.

sévère /sevɛʀ/ adj severe. **sévérité** nf severity.

sévices /sevis/ nmpl physical abuse.

sévir /seviʀ/ 2 vi (fléau) rage; ~ **contre** punish.

sevrer /səvʀe/ 6 vt wean.

sexe /sɛks/ nm sex; (organes) genitals (+ pl). **sexiste** adj sexist. **sexualité** nf sexuality. **sexuel**, ~**le** adj sexual.

shampooing* /ʃɑ̃pwɛ̃/ nm shampoo.

shérif /ʃeʀif/ nm sheriff.

short /ʃɔʀt/ nm shorts (+ pl).

si (**s'** before il, ils) /si, s/ conj if; (interrogation indirecte) if, whether; ~ **on allait se promener?** what about a walk?; **s'il vous** ou **te plaît** please; ~ **oui** if so; ~ **seulement** if only. ●adv (tellement) so; (oui) (yes); **un** ~ **bon repas** such a good meal; ~ **habile qu'il soit** however skilful he may be; ~ **bien que** with the result that.

sida /sida/ nm (Méd) Aids.

sidérurgie /sideʀyʀʒi/ nf steel industry.

siècle /sjɛkl/ nm century; (époque) age.

siège /sjɛʒ/ nm seat; (Mil) siege; ~ **éjectable** ejector seat; ~ **social** head office, headquarters (+ pl). **siéger** 14 40 vi (assemblée) sit.

sien, ~**ne** /sjɛ̃, -ɛn/ pron **le** ~, **la** ~**ne**, **les** (~**ne**)**s** (homme) his; (femme) hers; (chose) its; **les** ~**s** (famille) one's family.

sieste /sjɛst/ nf nap, siesta.

sifflement /sifləmɑ̃/ nm whistling; **un** ~ a whistle.

siffler /sifle/ 1 vi whistle; (avec un sifflet) blow one's whistle; (serpent, gaz) hiss. ●vt (air) whistle; (chien) whistle to ou for; (acteur) hiss.

sifflet /siflɛ/ nm whistle; ~**s** (huées) boos.

sigle /sigl/ nm acronym.

signal (pl **-aux**) /siɲal, -o/ nm signal; ~ **sonore** (de répondeur) tone.

signalement /siɲalmɑ̃/ nm
description.

signaler /siɲale/ 🔟 vt indicate;
(par une sonnerie, un écriteau) signal;
(dénoncer, mentionner) report; (faire
remarquer) point out.

signalisation /siɲalizasjɔ̃/ nf
signalling, signposting; (signaux)
signals (+ pl).

signataire /siɲatɛʀ/ nmf
signatory.

signature /siɲatyʀ/ nf signature;
(action) signing; ~ **électronique**
digital signature.

signe /siɲ/ nm sign; (de ponctuation)
mark; **faire ~ à qn** wave at sb;
(contacter) contact; **faire ~ à qn
de** beckon sb to; **faire ~ que
non** shake one's head; **faire ~
que oui** nod.

signer /siɲe/ 🔟 vt sign. ■ **se ~** vpr
(Relig) cross oneself.

signet /siɲɛ/ nm (pour livre, Internet)
bookmark; ~**s favoris** (Internet)
hotlist.

significatif, -ive /siɲifikatif, -v/
adj significant.

signification /siɲifikasjɔ̃/ nf
meaning. **signifier** 45 vt mean,
signify; (faire connaître) make
known (**à** to).

silence /silɑ̃s/ nm silence; (Mus)
rest; **garder le ~** keep silent.

silencieux, -ieuse /silɑ̃sjø, -z/
adj silent. ●nm silencer.

silex /silɛks/ nm inv flint.

silhouette /silwɛt/ nf outline,
silhouette.

sillon /sijɔ̃/ nm furrow; (de disque)
groove.

sillonner /sijɔne/ 🔟 vt crisscross.

similaire /similɛʀ/ adj similar.
similitude nf similarity.

simple /sɛ̃pl/ adj simple; (non
double) single. ●nm ~ **dames/
messieurs** ladies'/men's singles
(+ pl). **simple d'esprit** nmf
simpleton. **simplement** adv

simply. **simplicité** nf simplicity;
(naïveté) simpleness.

simplification /sɛ̃plifikasjɔ̃/ nf
simplification. **simplifier** 45 vt
simplify.

simpliste /sɛ̃plist/ adj simplistic.

simulacre /simylakʀ/ nm
pretence, sham.

simulation /simylasjɔ̃/ nf
simulation. **simuler** 🔟 vt
simulate.

simultané, ~e /simyltane/ adj
simultaneous.

sincère /sɛ̃sɛʀ/ adj sincere.
sincérité nf sincerity.

singe /sɛ̃ʒ/ nm monkey; (grand)
ape. **singer** 40 vt mimic, ape.

singulier, -ière /sɛ̃gylje, -jɛʀ/ adj
peculiar, remarkable; (Gram)
singular. ●nm (Gram) singular.

sinistre /sinistʀ/ adj sinister. ●nm
disaster; (incendie) blaze;
(dommages) damage.

sinistré, ~e /sinistʀe/ adj
stricken. ●nm, f disaster victim.

sinon /sinɔ̃/ conj (autrement)
otherwise; (sauf) except (**que**
that); **difficile ~ impossible**
difficult if not impossible.

sinueux, -euse /sinɥø, -z/ adj
winding; (fig) tortuous.

sirène /siʀɛn/ nf (appareil) siren;
(femme) mermaid.

sirop /siʀo/ nm (de fruits, Méd)
syrup; (boisson) cordial.

sismique /sismik/ adj seismic.

site /sit/ nm site; ~ **touristique**
place of interest; ~ **Internet** or
Web Website.

sitôt /sito/ adv ~ **entré**
immediately after coming in; ~
que as soon as; **pas de ~** not
for a while.

situation /sitɥasjɔ̃/ nf situation;
(emploi) job, position; ~ **de
famille** marital status.

situé, ~e /sitɥe/ adj situated.

situer /sitɥe/ 🔟 vt situate, locate.

■ **se** ~ vpr (se trouver) be situated.

six /sis/ (/si/ before consonant, /siz/ before vowel) adj & nm six. **sixième** adj & nmf sixth.

sketch* (pl ~**es**) /skɛtʃ/ nm (Théât) sketch.

ski /ski/ nm (matériel) ski; (Sport) skiing; **faire du** ~ ski; ~ **de fond** cross-country skiing; ~ **nautique** water skiing. **skier** 45 vi ski.

slave /slav/ adj Slav; (Ling) Slavonic.

slip /slip/ nm (d'homme) underpants (+ pl); (de femme) knickers (+ pl); ~ **de bain** (swimming) trunks (+ pl); (du bikini) bikini bottom.

slogan /slɔgã/ nm slogan.

Slovaquie /slɔvaki/ nf Slovakia.

Slovénie /slɔveni/ nf Slovenia.

smoking /smɔkiŋ/ nm dinner jacket.

SNCF abrév f (**Société nationale des Chemins de fer français**) French national railway company.

snob /snɔb/ nmf snob. ●adj snobbish. **snobisme** nm snobbery.

sobre /sɔbʀ/ adj sober.

social, ~e (mpl **-iaux**) /sɔsjal, -jo/ adj social.

socialisme /sɔsjalism/ nm socialism. **socialiste** nmf & a socialist.

société /sɔsjete/ nf society; (entreprise) company; ~ **point com** dot-com.

socle /sɔkl/ nm (de colonne, statue) plinth; (de lampe) base.

socquette /sɔkɛt/ nf ankle sock.

soda /sɔda/ nm fizzy drink.

sœur /sœʀ/ nf sister.

soi /swa/ pron oneself; **derrière** ~ behind one; **en** ~ in itself; **aller de** ~ be obvious.

soi-disant /swadizã/ adj inv so-called. ●adv supposedly.

soie /swa/ nf silk.

soif /swaf/ nf thirst; **avoir** ~ be thirsty; **donner** ~ make one thirsty.

soigné, ~e /swaɲe/ adj (apparence) tidy, neat; (travail) carefully done.

soigner /swaɲe/ ■ vt (s'occuper de) look after, take care of; (tenue, style) take care over; (maladie) treat. ■ **se** ~ vpr look after oneself.

soigneusement /swaɲøzmã/ adv carefully. **soigneux, -euse** adj careful (**de** about); (ordonné) tidy.

soi-même /swamɛm/ pron oneself.

soin /swɛ̃/ nm care; (ordre) tidiness; ~**s** care; (Méd) treatment; **avec** ~ carefully; **avoir** ou **prendre** ~ **de qn/de faire** take care of sb/to do; **premiers** ~**s** first aid (+ sg).

soir /swaʀ/ nm evening; **à ce** ~ see you tonight.

soirée /swaʀe/ nf evening; (réception) party.

soit /swa/ conj (à savoir) that is to say; ~... ~ either... or.
●▷ÊTRE 4.

soixante /swasãt/ adj & nm sixty. **soixante-dix** adj & nm seventy.

soja /sɔʒa/ nm (graines) soya beans (+ pl); (plante) soya.

sol /sɔl/ nm ground; (de maison) floor; (terrain agricole) soil.

solaire /sɔlɛʀ/ adj solar; (huile, filtre) sun.

soldat /sɔlda/ nm soldier.

solde¹ /sɔld/ nf (salaire) pay.

solde² /sɔld/ nm (Comm) balance; **les** ~**s** the sales; ~**s** (écrit en vitrine) sale; **en** ~ (acheter) at sale price.

solder /sɔlde/ ■ vt sell off at sale price; (compte) settle. ■ **se** ~ **par** vpr (aboutir à) end in.

....

S see A-Z of French life and culture

sole /sɔl/ nf (poisson) sole.

soleil /sɔlɛj/ nm sun; (fleur) sunflower; **il y a du ~** it's sunny.

solennel, ~le /sɔlanɛl/ adj solemn.

solfège /sɔlfɛʒ/ nm musical theory.

solidaire /sɔlidɛʀ/ adj (mécanismes) interdependent; (collègues) (mutually) supportive; **être ~ de qn** support sb. **solidarité** nf solidarity.

solide /sɔlid/ adj solid; (personne) strong. ● nm solid.

solidifier /sɔlidifje/ 45 vt solidify. ■ **se ~** vpr solidify.

solitaire /sɔlitɛʀ/ adj solitary. ● nmf (personne) loner. **solitude** nf solitude.

solliciter /sɔlisite/ 1 vt seek; (faire appel à) call upon; **être très sollicité** be very much in demand.

sollicitude /sɔlisityd/ nf concern.

solo /sɔlo/ nm & a inv (Mus) solo.

solution /sɔlysjɔ̃/ nf solution.

solvable /sɔlvabl/ adj solvent.

solvant /sɔlvɑ̃/ nm solvent.

sombre /sɔ̃bʀ/ adj dark; (triste) sombre.

sombrer /sɔ̃bʀe/ 1 vi sink (**dans** into).

sommaire /sɔmɛʀ/ adj (exécution) summary; (description) rough. ● nm contents (+ pl); **au ~** on the programme.

sommation /sɔmasjɔ̃/ nf (Mil) warning; (Jur) notice.

somme /sɔm/ nf sum; **en ~, ~ toute** in short; **faire la ~ de** add (up), total (up). ● nm nap.

sommeil /sɔmɛj/ nm sleep; **avoir ~** be *ou* feel sleepy; **en ~** (projet) put on ice. **sommeiller** 1 vi doze; (fig) lie dormant.

sommelier /sɔməlje/ nm wine steward.

sommer /sɔme/ 1 vt summon.

sommes /sɔm/ ▷ÊTRE 4.

sommet /sɔmɛ/ nm top; (de montagne) summit; (de triangle) apex; (gloire) height.

sommier /sɔmje/ nm bed base.

somnambule /sɔmnɑ̃byl/ nm sleepwalker.

somnifère /sɔmnifɛʀ/ nm sleeping pill.

somnolent, ~e /sɔmnɔlɑ̃, -t/ adj drowsy. **somnoler** 1 vi doze.

somptueux, -euse /sɔ̃ptɥø, -z/ adj sumptuous.

son¹ , sa /sɔ̃, sa/ (**son** before vowel or mute h) (pl **ses**) adj (homme) his; (femme) her; (chose) its; (indéfini) one's.

son² /sɔ̃/ nm (bruit) sound; (de blé) bran; **baisser le ~** turn the volume down.

sondage /sɔ̃daʒ/ nm **~ (d'opinion)** (opinion) poll.

sonde /sɔ̃d/ nf (de forage) drill; (Méd) (d'évacuation) catheter; (d'examen) probe.

sonder /sɔ̃de/ 1 vt (population) poll; (explorer) sound; (terrain) drill; (intentions) sound out.

songe /sɔ̃ʒ/ nm dream.

songer /sɔ̃ʒe/ 40 vt **~ que** think that; **~ à** think about. **songeur, -euse** adj pensive.

sonné, ~e /sɔne/ adj (étourdi) groggy; 1 crazy.

sonner /sɔne/ 1 vt/i ring; (clairon, glas) sound; (heure) strike; (domestique) ring for; **midi sonné** well past noon; **~ de** (clairon) sound, blow.

sonnerie /sɔnʀi/ nf ringing; (de clairon) sounding; (sonnette) bell.

sonnet /sɔnɛ/ nm sonnet.

sonnette /sɔnɛt/ nf bell.

sonore /sɔnɔʀ/ adj resonant; (onde, effets) sound; (rire) resounding.

sonorisation /sɔnɔʀizasjɔ̃/ nf

(matériel) public address system.

sonorité /sɔnɔrite/ nf resonance; (d'un instrument) tone.

sont /sɔ̃/ ▷ ÊTRE **4**.

sophistiqué, ∼e /sɔfistike/ adj sophisticated.

sorcellerie /sɔrsɛlri/ nf witchcraft. **sorcier** nm (guérisseur) witch doctor; (maléfique) sorcerer. **sorcière** nf witch.

sordide /sɔrdid/ adj sordid; (lieu) squalid.

sort /sɔr/ nm (destin, hasard) fate; (condition) lot; (maléfice) spell; **tirer (qch) au ∼** draw lots (for sth).

sortant, ∼e /sɔrtɑ̃, -t/ adj (président etc.) outgoing.

sorte /sɔrt/ nf sort, kind; **de ∼ que** so that; **en quelque ∼** in a way; **de la ∼** in this way; **faire en ∼ que** make sure that.

sortie /sɔrti/ nf exit; (promenade, dîner) outing; (déclaration **1**) remark; (parution) publication; (de disque, film) release; (d'un ordinateur) output; **∼s** (argent) outgoings.

sortilège /sɔrtilɛʒ/ nm (magic) spell.

sortir /sɔrtir/ **46** vi (aux être) go out, leave; (venir) come out; (aller au spectacle) go out; (livre, film) come out; (plante) come up; **∼ de** (pièce) leave; (milieu social) come from; (limites) go beyond; **∼ du commun** ou **de l'ordinaire** be out of the ordinary. •vt (aux avoir) take out; (livre, modèle) bring out; (dire **1**) come out with; **∼ qn de** get sb out of; **être sorti d'affaire** be in the clear. ∎ **s'en ∼** vpr cope, manage.

sosie /sozi/ nm double.

sot, ∼te /so, sɔt/ adj silly.

sottise /sɔtiz/ nf silliness; (action, remarque) foolish thing; **faire des ∼s** be naughty.

sou /su/ nm **1** **∼s** money; **sans le ∼** without a penny; **près de ses ∼s** tight-fisted.

soubresaut /subrəso/ nm (sudden) start.

souche /suʃ/ nf (d'arbre) stump; (de famille) stock; (de carnet) counterfoil.

souci /susi/ nm (inquiétude) worry; (préoccupation) concern; (plante) marigold; **se faire du ∼** worry.

soucier (se) /(sə)susje/ **45** vpr **se ∼ de** care about. **soucieux, -ieuse** adj concerned (**de** about).

soucoupe /sukup/ nf saucer; **∼ volante** flying saucer.

soudain, ∼e /sudɛ̃, -ɛn/ adj sudden. •adv suddenly.

soude /sud/ nf soda.

souder /sude/ **1** vt weld, solder; **famille très soudée** close-knit family. ∎ **se ∼** vpr (os) knit (together).

soudoyer /sudwaje/ **31** vt bribe.

souffle /sufl/ nm (haleine) breath; (respiration) breathing; (explosion) blast; (vent) breath of air; **le ∼ coupé** out of breath; **à couper le ∼** breathtaking.

souffler /sufle/ **1** vi blow; (haleter) puff. •vt (bougie) blow out; (poussière, fumée) blow; (verre) blow; (par explosion) destroy; (chuchoter) whisper; **∼ la réplique à** prompt. **souffleur, -euse** nm, f (Théât) prompter.

souffrance /sufrɑ̃s/ nf suffering; **en ∼** (affaire) pending. **souffrant, ∼e** adj unwell.

souffrir /sufrir/ **21** vi suffer (**de** from). •vt (endurer) suffer; **il ne peut pas le ∼** he cannot stand ou bear him.

soufre /sufr/ nm sulphur.

souhait /swɛ/ nm wish; **à tes ∼s!** bless you!; **paisible à ∼** incredibly peaceful. **souhaitable** adj desirable.

souhaiter /swete/ **1** vt **∼ qch à qn** wish sb sth; **∼ que/faire** hope that/to do; **∼ la bienvenue à qn** welcome sb.

soûl*, ~e /su, sul/ adj drunk. •nm
tout son ~ as much as one can.

soulagement /sulaʒmɑ̃/ nm
relief. **soulager** 40 vt relieve.

soûler* /sule/ 1 vt make drunk.
■ **se** ~ vpr get drunk.

soulèvement /sulɛvmɑ̃/ nm
uprising.

soulever /sulve/ 6 vt lift, raise;
(question, poussière) raise;
(enthousiasme) arouse; (foule) stir
up. ■ **se** ~ vpr lift ou raise
oneself up; (se révolter) rise up.

soulier /sulje/ nm shoe.

souligner /suliɲe/ 1 vt
underline; (yeux) outline; (taille)
emphasize.

soumettre /sumɛtR/ 42 vt
(assujettir) subject (**à** to); (présenter)
submit (**à** to). ■ **se** ~ vpr submit
(**à** to). **soumis**, ~e adj
submissive. **soumission** nf
submission.

soupape /supap/ nf valve.

soupçon /supsɔ̃/ nm suspicion; **un**
~ **de** (un peu de) a touch of.
soupçonner 1 vt suspect.
soupçonneux, -euse adj
suspicious.

soupe /sup/ nf soup.

souper /supe/ 6 vi have supper.
•nm supper.

soupeser /supəze/ 1 vt judge the
weight of; (fig) weigh up.

soupière /supjɛR/ nf (soup)
tureen.

soupir /supiR/ nm sigh; **pousser
un** ~ heave a sigh.

soupirer /supiRe/ 1 vi sigh.

souple /supl/ adj supple; (règlement,
caractère) flexible. **souplesse** nf
suppleness; (de règlement)
flexibility.

source /suRs/ nf (de rivière, origine)
source; (eau) spring; **prendre sa**
~ **à** rise in; **de** ~ **sûre** from a
reliable source; ~ **thermale** hot
spring.

sourcil /suRsi/ nm eyebrow.

sourciller /suRsije/ 1 vi **sans** ~
without batting an eyelid.

sourd, ~e /suR, -d/ adj deaf; (bruit,
douleur) dull; **faire la ~e oreille**
turn a deaf ear. •nm, f deaf
person.

sourd-muet (pl **sourds-muets**).

sourde-muette pl **sourdes-
muettes**) /suRmɥɛ, suRdmɥɛt/ adj
deaf and dumb. •nm, f deafmute.

souricière /suRisjɛR/ nf
mousetrap; (fig) trap.

sourire /suRiR/ 54 vi smile (**à** at);
~ **à** (fortune) smile on. •nm smile;
garder le ~ keep smiling.

souris /suRi/ nf mouse; **des**
~ mice.

sournois, ~e /suRnwa, -z/ adj sly,
underhand.

sous /su/ prép under, beneath; ~
la main handy; ~ **la pluie** in
the rain; ~ **peu** shortly; ~ **terre**
underground.

sous-alimenté, ~e /suzalimɑ̃te/
adj undernourished.

souscription /suskRipsjɔ̃/ nf
subscription. **souscrire** 30 vi ~ **à**
subscribe to.

sous-entendre /suzɑ̃tɑ̃dR/ 3 vt
imply. **sous-entendu** nm
innuendo, insinuation.

sous-estimer /suzɛstime/ 1 vt
underestimate.

sous-jacent, ~e /suʒasɑ̃, -t/ adj
underlying.

sous-marin, ~e /sumaRɛ̃, -in/ adj
underwater; (plongée) deep-sea.
•nm submarine.

soussigné, ~e /susiɲe/ adj & nm, f
undersigned.

sous-sol /susɔl/ nm (cave)
basement.

sous-titre /sutitR/ nm subtitle.

soustraction /sustRaksjɔ̃/ nf
(déduction) subtraction.

soustraire /sustRɛR/ 29 vt (déduire)
subtract; (retirer) take away (**à**

from). ■ **se** ∼ **à** vpr escape from.

sous-traitant /sutʀɛtɑ̃/ nm subcontractor.

sous-verre /suvɛʀ/ nm inv glass mount.

sous-vêtement /suvɛtmɑ̃/ nm underwear.

soute /sut/ nf (de bateau) hold; ∼ **à charbon** coal-bunker.

soutenir /sutniʀ/ 59 vt support; (effort, rythme) sustain; (résister à) withstand; ∼ **que** maintain that.

soutenu, ∼**e** /sutny/ adj (constant) sustained; (style) formal.

souterrain, ∼**e** /sutɛʀɛ̃, -ɛn/ adj underground. ●nm underground passage.

soutien /sutjɛ̃/ nm support.

soutien-gorge (pl **soutiens-gorge**) /sutjɛ̃gɔʀʒ/ nm bra.

soutirer /sutiʀe/ 1 vt ∼ **à qn** extract from sb.

souvenir[1] /suvniʀ/ nm memory, recollection; (objet) memento; (cadeau) souvenir; **en** ∼ **de** in memory of.

souvenir[2] **(se)** /(sə)suvniʀ/ 59 vpr **se** ∼ **de** remember; **se** ∼ **que** remember that.

souvent /suvɑ̃/ adv often.

souverain, ∼**e** /suvʀɛ̃, -ɛn/ adj sovereign. ●nm, f sovereign.

soviétique /sɔvjetik/ adj Soviet.

soyeux, -euse /swajø, -z/ adj silky.

spacieux, -ieuse /spasjø, -z/ adj spacious.

sparadrap /spaʀadʀa/ nm (sticking) plaster.

spatial, ∼**e** (mpl **-iaux**) /spasjal, -jo/ adj space.

speaker, ∼**ine** /spikœʀ, -kʀin/ nm, f announcer.

spécial, ∼**e** (mpl **-iaux**) /spesjal, -jo/ adj special; (bizarre) odd.
spécialement adv·(exprès) specially; (très) especially.

spécialiser (se) /səspesjalize/ 1 vpr specialize (**dans** in).
spécialiste nmf specialist.
spécialité nf speciality; (US) specialty.

spécifier /spesifje/ 45 vt specify.

spécifique /spesifik/ adj specific.

spécimen /spesimɛn/ nm specimen.

spectacle /spɛktakl/ nm show; (vue) sight, spectacle.

spectaculaire /spɛktakylɛʀ/ adj spectacular.

spectateur, -trice /spɛktatœʀ, -tʀis/ nm, f (Sport) spectator; (témoin oculaire) onlooker; **les** ∼**s** (Théât) the audience (+ sg).

spectre /spɛktʀ/ nm (revenant) spectre; (images) spectrum.

spéculateur, -trice /spekylatœʀ, -tʀis/ nm, f speculator.
spéculation nf speculation.
spéculer 1 vi speculate.

spéléologie /speleɔlɔʒi/ nf cave exploration, pot-holing.

spermatozoïde /spɛʀmatozoid/ nm spermatozoon. **sperme** nm sperm.

sphère /sfɛʀ/ nf sphere.

spirale /spiʀal/ nf spiral.

spirituel, ∼**le** /spiʀituɛl/ adj spiritual; (amusant) witty.

spiritueux /spiʀituø/ nm (alcool) spirit.

splendeur /splɑ̃dœʀ/ nf splendour. **splendide** adj splendid.

sponsoriser /spɔ̃sɔʀize/ 1 vt sponsor.

spontané, ∼**e** /spɔ̃tane/ adj spontaneous. **spontanéité** nf spontaneity.

sport /spɔʀ/ adj inv (vêtements) casual. ●nm sport; **veste/voiture de** ∼ sports jacket/car.

sportif, -ive /spɔʀtif, -v/ adj

(personne) sporty; (physique) athletic; (résultats) sports. ● nm, f sportsman, sportswoman.

spot /spɔt/ nm spotlight; ~ **(publicitaire)** ad.

square /skwaʀ/ nm small public garden.

squatter /skwate/ 🕮 vt squat in.

squelette /skəlɛt/ nm skeleton. **squelettique** adj skeletal.

SRAS abrév m **(syndrome respiratoire aigu sévère)** SARS.

SSII abrév f **(société de services et d'ingénierie informatiques)** computer services company

stabiliser /stabilize/ 🕮 vt stabilize. **stable** adj stable.

stade /stad/ nm (Sport) stadium; (phase) stage.

stage /staʒ/ nm (cours) course; (professionnel) placement. **stagiaire** nmf course member; (apprenti) trainee.

stagner /stagne/ 🕮 vi stagnate.

stand /stɑ̃d/ nm stand; (de fête foraine) stall.

standard /stɑ̃daʀ/ nm switchboard. ● adj inv standard. **standardiser** 🕮 vt standardize.

standardiste /stɑ̃daʀdist/ nmf switchboard operator.

standing /stɑ̃diŋ/ nm status, standing; **de** ~ (hôtel) luxury.

starter /staʀtɛʀ/ nm (Auto) choke.

station /stasjɔ̃/ nf station; (halte) stop; ~ **debout** standing position; ~ **de taxis** taxi rank; ~ **balnéaire/de ski** seaside/ski resort; ~ **thermale** spa.

stationnaire /stasjɔnɛʀ/ adj stationary.

stationnement /stasjɔnmɑ̃/ nm parking. **stationner** 🕮 vi park.

station-service (pl **stations-service**) /stasjɔ̃sɛʀvis/ nf service station.

statique /statik/ adj static.

statistique /statistik/ nf statistic; (science) statistics (+ sg.) ● adj statistical.

statue /staty/ nf statue.

statuer /statɥe/ 🕮 vi ~ **sur** give a ruling on.

statut /staty/ nm status. **statutaire** adj statutory.

sténo /steno/ nf (sténographie) shorthand. **sténodactylo** nf shorthand typist. **sténographie** nf shorthand.

stéréo /stereo/ nf & adj inv stereo.

stéréotype /stereotip/ nm stereotype.

stérile /steʀil/ adj sterile.

stérilet /steʀilɛ/ nm coil, IUD.

stérilisation /steʀilizasjɔ̃/ nf sterilization. **stériliser** 🕮 vt sterilize.

stéroïde /steʀɔid/ adj & nm steroid.

stimulant /stimylɑ̃/ nm stimulus; (médicament) stimulant.

stimulateur /stimylatœʀ/ nm ~ **cardiaque** (Méd) pacemaker.

stimuler /stimyle/ 🕮 vt stimulate.

stipuler /stipyle/ 🕮 vt stipulate.

stock /stɔk/ nm stock. **stocker** 🕮 vt stock.

stoïque /stɔik/ adj stoical. ● nmf stoic.

stop /stɔp/ interj stop. ● nm stop sign; (feu arrière) brake light; **faire du** ~ 🕮 hitch-hike. **stopper** 🕮 vt/i stop.

store /stɔʀ/ nm blind; (de magasin) awning.

strapontin /stʀapɔ̃tɛ̃/ nm folding seat, jump seat.

stratégie /stʀateʒi/ nf strategy. **stratégique** adj strategic.

stress /stʀɛs/ nm stress. **stressant, ~e** adj stressful.

stressé, ~e adj stressed.
stresser [1] vt put under stress.

strict /stʀikt/ adj strict; (tenue, vérité) plain; **le ~ minimum** the bare minimum. **strictement** adv strictly.

strident, ~e /stʀidɑ̃, -t/ adj shrill.

strophe /stʀɔf/ nf stanza, verse.

structure /stʀyktyʀ/ nf structure.

studieux, -ieuse /stydjø, -z/ adj studious.

studio /stydjo/ nm (d'artiste, de télévision) studio; (logement) studio flat.

stupéfaction /stypefaksjɔ̃/ nf amazement. **stupéfait, ~e** adj amazed.

stupéfiant, ~e /stypefjɑ̃, -t/ adj astounding. ●nm drug, narcotic.

stupéfier /stypefje/ [45] vt amaze.

stupeur /stypœʀ/ nf amazement; (Méd) stupor.

stupide /stypid/ adj stupid. **stupidité** nf stupidity.

style /stil/ nm style.

styliste /stilist/ nmf fashion designer.

stylo /stilo/ nm pen; **~ (à) bille** ballpoint pen; **~ (à) encre** fountain pen.

su /sy/ ▷SAVOIR [55].

suave /sɥav/ adj sweet.

subalterne /sybaltɛʀn/ adj & nmf subordinate.

subconscient /sypkɔ̃sjɑ̃/ nm subconscious.

subir /sybiʀ/ [2] vt be subjected to; (traitement, expériences) undergo.

subit, ~e /sybi, -t/ adj sudden.

subjectif, -ive /sybʒɛktif, -v/ adj subjective.

subjonctif /sybʒɔ̃ktif/ nm subjunctive.

subjuguer /sybʒyge/ [1] vt (charmer) captivate.

sublime /syblim/ adj sublime.

submerger /sybmɛʀʒe/ [40] vt submerge; (fig) overwhelm.

subordonné, ~e /sybɔʀdɔne/ adj & nm, f subordinate.

subside /sybzid/ nm grant.

subsidiaire /sybzidjɛʀ/ adj subsidiary; **question ~** tiebreaker.

subsistance /sybzistɑ̃s/ nf subsistence. **subsister** [1] vi subsist; (durer, persister) exist.

substance /sypstɑ̃s/ nf substance.

substantiel, ~le /sypstɑ̃sjɛl/ adj substantial.

substantif /sypstɑ̃tif/ nm noun.

substituer /sypstitɥe/ [1] vt substitute (**à** for). ■ **se ~ à** vpr (remplacer) substitute for.

substitut nm substitute; (Jur) deputy public prosecutor.

subtil, ~e /syptil/ adj subtle.

subtiliser /syptilize/ [1] vt ~ **qch (à qn)** steal sth (from sb).

subvenir /sybvəniʀ/ [59] vi ~ **à** provide for.

subvention /sybvɑ̃sjɔ̃/ nf subsidy. **subventionner** [1] vt subsidize.

subversif, -ive /sybvɛʀsif, -v/ adj subversive.

suc /syk/ nm juice.

succédané /syksedane/ nm substitute (**de** for).

succéder /syksede/ [14] vi ~ **à** succeed. ■ **se ~** vpr succeed one another.

succès /syksɛ/ nm success; **à ~** (film, livre) successful; **avoir du ~** be a success.

successeur /syksesœʀ/ nm successor. **successif, -ive** adj successive. **succession** nf succession; (Jur) inheritance.

succinct, ~e /syksɛ̃, -t/ adj succinct.

succomber /sykɔ̃be/ [1] vi die; ~ **à** succumb to.

succulent, ~e /sykylã, -t/ adj
delicious.

succursale /sykyʀsal/ nf (Comm)
branch.

sucer /syse/ 10 vt suck.

sucette /sysɛt/ nf (bonbon)
lollipop; (tétine) dummy; (US)
pacifier.

sucre /sykʀ/ nm sugar; **~ d'orge**
barley sugar; **~ en poudre**
caster sugar; **~ glace** icing
sugar; **~ roux** brown sugar.

sucré /sykʀe/ adj sweet; (additionné
de sucre) sweetened. **sucrer** 1 vt
sugar, sweeten. **sucreries** nfpl
sweets.

sucrier, -ière /sykʀije, -jɛʀ/ adj
sugar. •nm (récipient) sugar-bowl.

sud /syd/ nm south. •adj inv south;
(partie) southern.

sud-est /sydɛst/ nm south-east.

sud-ouest /sydwɛst/ nm
southwest.

Suède /sɥɛd/ nf Sweden.

suédois, ~e /sɥedwa, -z/ adj
Swedish. •nm (Ling) Swedish. **S~,**
~e nm, f Swede.

suer /sɥe/ 1 vt/i sweat; **faire ~**
qn 🛈 get on sb's nerves.

sueur /sɥœʀ/ nf sweat; **en ~**
covered in sweat.

suffire /syfiʀ/ 57 vi be enough (**à**
qn for sb); **il suffit de compter**
all you have to do is count; **une**
goutte suffit a drop is enough;
~ à (besoin) satisfy. ■ **se ~** vpr **se**
~ à soi-même be self-
sufficient.

suffisamment /syfizamã/ adv
sufficiently; **~ de qch** enough
of sth. **suffisance** nf (vanité)
conceit. **suffisant, ~e** adj
sufficient; (vaniteux) conceited.

suffixe /syfiks/ nm suffix.

suffoquer /syfɔke/ 1 vt/i choke,
suffocate.

suffrage /syfʀaʒ/ nm (voix: Pol)
vote; (système) suffrage.

suggérer /sygʒeʀe/ 14 vt suggest.
suggestion nf suggestion.

suicidaire /sɥisidɛʀ/ adj suicidal.
suicide nm suicide. **suicider (se)**
1 vpr commit suicide.

suinter /sɥɛ̃te/ 1 vi ooze.

suis /sɥi/ ▸ÊTRE 4, ▸SUIVRE 57.

Suisse /sɥis/ nf Switzerland. •nmf
Swiss. **suisse** adj Swiss.

suite /sɥit/ nf continuation, rest;
(d'un film) sequel; (série) series;
(appartement, escorte) suite; (résultat)
consequence; **à la ~, de ~**
(successivement) in a row; **à la ~**
de (derrière) behind; **à la ~ de,**
par ~ de (en conséquence) as a
result of; **faire ~ (à)** follow; **par**
la ~ afterwards; **~ à votre**
lettre du further to your letter
of the; **des ~s de** as a result of.

suivant¹, ~e /sɥivã, -t/ adj
following, next. •nm, f following
ou next person.

suivant² /sɥivã/ prép (selon)
according to.

suivi, ~e /sɥivi/ adj (effort) steady,
sustained; (cohérent) consistent;
peu/très ~ (cours) poorly/well
attended.

suivre /sɥivʀ/ 57 vt/i follow;
(comprendre) follow; **faire ~**
(courrier) forward. ■ **se ~** vpr
follow each other.

sujet, ~te /syʒɛ, -t/ adj **~ à** liable
ou subject to. •nm (d'un royaume)
subject; (question) subject; (motif)
cause; (Gram) subject; **au ~ de**
about.

super /sypɛʀ/ nm (essence)
fourstar. •adj inv 🛈 (très) great.
•adv 🛈 ultra, really.

superbe /sypɛʀb/ adj superb.

supérette /sypeʀɛt/ nf
minimarket.

superficie /sypɛʀfisi/ nf area.

superficiel, ~le /sypɛʀfisjɛl/ adj
superficial.

superflu /sypɛʀfly/ adj

superfluous. ●nm (excédent)
surplus.

supérieur, ~e /syperjœr/ adj
(plus haut) upper; (quantité, nombre)
greater (**à** than); (études, principe)
higher (**à** than); (meilleur, hautain)
superior (**à** to). ●nm, f superior.
supériorité nf superiority.

superlatif, -ive /syperlatif, -v/
adj & nm superlative.

supermarché /sypermarʃe/ nm
supermarket.

superposer /syperpoze/ 🔟 vt
superimpose; **lits superposés**
bunk beds.

superproduction
/syperprɔdyksjɔ̃/ nf (film)
blockbuster.

superpuissance /syperpɥisɑ̃s/ nf
superpower.

superstitieux, -ieuse
/syperstisjø, -z/ adj superstitious.

superviser /sypervize/ 🔟 vt
supervise.

suppléant, ~e /sypleɑ̃, -t/ nmf &
adj (**professeur**) ~ supply
teacher; (**juge**) ~ deputy (judge).

suppléer /syplee/ 🔟 vt (remplacer)
fill in for. ●vi ~ **à** (compenser)
make up for.

supplément /syplemɑ̃/ nm
(argent) extra charge; (de frites,
légumes) extra portion; **en ~**
extra; **un ~ de** (travail)
additional; **payer un ~** pay a
supplement. **supplémentaire** adj
extra, additional.

supplice /syplis/ nm torture.

supplier /syplije/ 🔟 vt beg,
beseech (**de** to).

support /sypɔr/ nm support;
(Ordinat) medium.

supportable /sypɔrtabl/ adj
bearable.

supporter¹ /sypɔrte/ 🔟 vt
(privations) bear; (personne) put up
with; (structure: Ordinat) support; **il
ne supporte pas les enfants**/

de perdre he can't stand
children/losing.

supporter²* /sypɔrter/ nm (Sport)
supporter.

supposer /sypoze/ 🔟 vt suppose;
(impliquer) imply; **à ~ que**
supposing that.

suppression /sypresjɔ̃/ nf (de
taxe) abolition; (de sanction) lifting;
(de mot) deletion. **supprimer** 🔟
vt (allocation) withdraw; (contrôle)
lift; (train) cancel; (preuve)
suppress.

suprématie /sypremasi/ nf
supremacy.

suprême /syprem/ adj supreme.

sur /syr/ prép on, upon; (pardessus)
over; (au sujet de) about, on;
(proportion) out of; (mesure) by; ~
la photo in the photograph;
mettre/jeter ~ put/throw on
to; ~ **mesure** made to measure;
~ **place** on the spot; ~ **ce, je
pars** with that, I must go; ~ **le
moment** at the time.

sûr /syr/ adj certain, sure; (sans
danger) safe; (digne de confiance)
reliable; (main) steady; (jugement)
sound; **être ~ de soi** be self-
confident; **j'en étais ~!** I
knew it!

surabondance /syrabɔ̃dɑ̃s/ nf
overabundance.

surcharge /syrʃarʒ/ nf
overloading; (poids) excess load.
surcharger 🔟 vt overload; (texte)
alter.

surchauffer /syrʃofe/ 🔟 vt
overheat.

surcroît* /syrkrwa/ nm increase
(**de** in); **de ~** in addition.

surdité /syrdite/ nf deafness.

surélever /syrelve/ 🔟 vt raise.

sûrement /syrmɑ̃/ adv certainly;
(sans danger) safely; **il a ~ oublié**
he must have forgotten.

surenchère /syrɑ̃ʃer/ nf higher
bid. **surenchérir** 🔟 vi bid higher
(**sur** than).

surestimer /syʀɛstime/ 1 vt
overestimate.

sûreté* /syʀte/ nf safety; (de pays)
security; (d'un geste) steadiness;
être en ~ be safe; **S~
(nationale)** police (+ pl).

surexcité, ~e /syʀɛksite/ adj
very excited.

surf /sœʀf/ nm surfing.

surface /syʀfas/ nf surface; **faire
~** (sous-marin, fig) surface; **en ~**
on the surface.

surfait, ~e /syʀfɛ, -t/ adj
overrated.

surfer /sœʀfe/ 1 vi go surfing; **~
sur l'Internet** surf the Internet.

surgelé, ~e /syʀʒəle/ adj (deep-)
frozen; **aliments ~s**
frozen food.

surgir /syʀʒiʀ/ 2 vi appear
(suddenly); (difficulté) crop up.

sur-le-champ /syʀləʃɑ̃/ adv
right away.

surlendemain /syʀlɑ̃dmɛ̃/ nm **le
~** two days later; **le ~ de** two
days after.

surligneur /syʀliɲœʀ/ nm
highlighter (pen).

surmenage /syʀmənaʒ/ nm
overwork.

surmonter /syʀmɔ̃te/ 1 vt
(vaincre) overcome, surmount;
(être au-dessus de) surmount, top.

surnaturel, ~le /syʀnatyʀɛl/ adj
supernatural.

surnom /syʀnɔ̃/ nm nickname.
surnommer 1 vt nickname.

surpeuplé, ~e /syʀpœple/ adj
overpopulated.

surplomber /syʀplɔ̃be/ 1 vt/i
overhang.

surplus /syʀply/ nm surplus.

surprenant, ~e /syʀpʀənɑ̃, -t/
adj surprising. **surprendre** 50 vt
(étonner) surprise; (prendre au
dépourvu) catch, surprise; (entendre)
overhear. **surpris, ~e** adj
surprised (**de** at).

surprise /syʀpʀiz/ nf surprise.

surréaliste /syʀʀealist/ adj & nmf
surrealist.

sursaut /syʀso/ nm start, jump;
en ~ with a start; **~ de** (regain)
burst of. **sursauter** 1 vi
start, jump.

sursis /syʀsi/ nm reprieve; (Mil)
deferment; **deux ans (de
prison) avec ~** a two-year
suspended sentence.

surtaxe /syʀtaks/ nf surcharge.

surtout /syʀtu/ adv especially;
(avant tout) above all; **~ pas**
certainly not.

surveillance /syʀvɛjɑ̃s/ nf watch;
(d'examen) supervision; (de la police)
surveillance. **surveillant, ~e** nm,
f (de prison) warder; (au lycée)
supervisor (in charge of
discipline). **surveiller** 1 vt
watch; (travaux, élèves) supervise.

survenir /syʀvəniʀ/ 59 vi occur,
take place; (personne) turn up.

survêtement /syʀvɛtmɑ̃/ nm
(Sport) tracksuit.

survie /syʀvi/ nf survival.

survivant, ~e /syʀvivɑ̃, -t/ adj
surviving. ●nm, f survivor.

survivre /syʀvivʀ/ 63 vi survive;
~ à (conflit) survive; (personne)
outlive.

survoler /syʀvɔle/ 1 vt fly over;
(livre) skim through.

sus: en ~ /ɑ̃sys/ loc in addition.

susceptible /syseptibl/ adj
touchy; **~ de faire** likely to do.

susciter /sysite/ 1 vt (éveiller)
arouse; (occasionner) create.

suspect, ~e /syspɛ, -ɛkt/ adj
(individu, faits) suspicious;
(témoignage) suspect; **~ de**
suspected of. ●nm, f suspect.
suspecter 1 vt suspect.

suspendre /syspɑ̃dʀ/ 3 vt
(accrocher) hang (up); (interrompre,
destituer) suspend; **suspendu à**
hanging from. ■ **se ~ à** vpr
hang from.

S

suspens: en ∼ /ãsyspã/ loc (affaire) outstanding; (dans l'indécision) in suspense.

suspense /syspɛns/ nm suspense.

suture /sytyʀ/ nf **point de ∼** stitch.

svelte /svɛlt/ adj slender.

S.V.P. abrév (**s'il vous plaît**) please.

syllabe /silab/ nf syllable.

symbole /sɛ̃bɔl/ nm symbol. **symboliser** [1] vt symbolize.

symétrie /simetʀi/ nf symmetry.

sympa /sɛ̃pa/ adj inv [1] nice; **sois ∼** be a pal.

sympathie /sɛ̃pati/ nf (goût) liking; (compassion) sympathy; **avoir de la ∼ pour** like. **sympathique** adj nice, pleasant. **sympathisant, ∼e** nm, f sympathizer. **sympathiser** [1] vi get on well (**avec** with).

symphonie /sɛ̃fɔni/ nf symphony.

symptôme /sɛ̃ptom/ nm symptom.

synagogue /sinagɔg/ nf synagogue.

synchroniser /sɛ̃kʀɔnize/ [1] vt synchronize.

syncope /sɛ̃kɔp/ nf (Méd) blackout.

syndic /sɛ̃dik/ nm ∼ **(d'immeuble)** property manager.

syndicaliste /sɛ̃dikalist/ nmf (trade-)unionist. ● adj (trade-) union.

syndicat /sɛ̃dika/ nm (trade) union; ∼ **d'initiative** tourist office.

syndiqué, ∼e /sɛ̃dike/ adj **être ∼** be a (trade-)union member.

synonyme /sinɔnim/ adj synonymous. ● nm synonym.

syntaxe /sɛ̃taks/ nf syntax.

synthèse /sɛ̃tɛz/ nf synthesis. **synthétique** adj synthetic.

synthé(tiseur) /sɛ̃te(tizœʀ)/ nm synthesizer.

systématique /sistematik/ adj systematic.

système /sistɛm/ nm system; **le ∼ D** [1] resourcefulness.

Tt

t' /t/ ▷TE.

ta /ta/ ▷TON [1].

🗗**tabac** /taba/ nm tobacco; (magasin) tobacconist's shop.

table /tabl/ nf table; **à ∼!** dinner is ready!; ∼ **de nuit** bedside table; ∼ **des matières** table of contents; ∼ **à repasser** ironing board; ∼ **roulante** (tea-)trolley; (US) (serving) cart.

tableau (pl ∼**x**) /tablo/ nm picture; (peinture) painting;

....

🗗 *see A-Z of French life and culture*

(panneau) board; (graphique) chart; (Scol) blackboard; ∼ **d'affichage** notice-board; ∼ **de bord** dashboard.

tablette /tablɛt/ nf shelf; ∼ **de chocolat** bar of chocolate.

tableur /tablœʀ/ nm spreadsheet.

tablier /tablije/ nm apron; (de pont) platform; (de magasin) shutter.

tabou /tabu/ nm & adj taboo.

tabouret /tabuʀɛ/ nm stool.

tache /taʃ/ nf mark, spot; (salissure) stain; **faire ∼ d'huile** spread; ∼

de rousseur freckle.

tâche /taʃ/ nf task, job.

tacher /taʃe/ **1** vt stain. ■ se ~ vpr (personne) get oneself dirty.

tâcher /taʃe/ **1** vi ~ **de faire** try to do.

tacheté, ~e /taʃte/ adj spotted.

tact /takt/ nm tact.

tactique /taktik/ adj tactical. ● nf (Mil) tactics; **une** ~ a tactic.

taie /tɛ/ nf ~ **(d'oreiller)** pillowcase.

taille /taj/ nf (milieu du corps) waist; (hauteur) height; (grandeur) size; **de** ~ sizeable; **être de** ~ **à faire** be up to doing.

taille-crayons* /tajkrɛjɔ̃/ nm inv pencil-sharpener.

tailler /taje/ **1** vt cut; (arbre) prune; (crayon) sharpen; (vêtement) cut out. ■ se ~ vpr **1** clear off.

tailleur /tajœr/ nm (costume) woman's suit; (couturier) tailor; **en** ~ cross-legged; ~ **de pierre** stone-cutter.

taire /tɛr/ **47** vt not to reveal; **faire** ~ silence. ■ se ~ vpr be silent ou quiet; (devenir silencieux) fall silent.

talc /talk/ nm talcum powder.

talent /talɑ̃/ nm talent. **talentueux, -euse** adj talented, gifted.

talon /talɔ̃/ nm heel; (de chèque) stub.

tambour /tɑ̃bur/ nm drum; (d'église) vestibule.

Tamise /tamiz/ nf Thames.

tampon /tɑ̃pɔ̃/ nm (de bureau) stamp; (ouate) wad, pad; ~ **(hygiénique)** tampon.

tamponner /tɑ̃pɔne/ **1** vt (document) stamp; (véhicule) crash into; (plaie) swab.

tandem /tɑ̃dɛm/ nm (vélo) tandem; (personnes: fig) duo.

tandis que /tɑ̃dik(ə)/ conj while.

tanière /tanjɛr/ nf den.

tant /tɑ̃/ adv (travailler, manger) so much; ~ **de** (quantité) so much; (nombre) so many; ~ **que** as long as; **en** ~ **que** as; ~ **mieux!** all the better!; ~ **pis!** too bad!

tante /tɑ̃t/ nf aunt.

tantôt /tɑ̃to/ adv sometimes.

tapage /tapaʒ/ nm din.

tape /tap/ nf slap. **tape-à-l'œil** adj inv flashy, tawdry.

taper /tape/ **1** vt hit; (prendre **1**) scrounge; ~ **(à la machine)** type. ● vi (cogner) bang; (soleil) beat down; ~ **dans** (puiser dans) dig into; ~ **sur** hit; ~ **sur l'épaule de qn** tap sb on the shoulder. ■ se ~ vpr (corvée **1**) get stuck with **1**.

tapis /tapi/ nm carpet; (petit) rug; ~ **de bain** bathmat; ~ **roulant** (pour objets) conveyor belt; (pour piétons) moving walkway.

tapisser /tapise/ **1** vt (wall) paper; (fig) cover (**de** with). **tapisserie** nf tapestry; (papier peint) wallpaper.

taquin, -in /takɛ̃, -in/ adj fond of teasing. ● nm, f tease(r).

tard /tar/ adv late; **au plus** ~ at the latest; **plus** ~ later; **sur le** ~ late in life.

tarder /tarde/ **1** vi (être lent à venir) be a long time coming; ~ **(à faire)** take a long time (doing), delay (doing); **sans (plus)** ~ without (further) delay; **il me tarde de** I'm longing to.

tardif, -ive /tardif, -v/ adj late.

tare /tar/ nf (défaut) defect.

tarif /tarif/ nm rate; (de train, taxi) fare; **plein** ~ full price.

tarir /tarir/ **2** vt/i dry up. ■ se ~ vpr dry up.

tarte /tart/ nf tart. ● adj inv (ridicule **1**) ridiculous.

tartine /tartin/ nf slice of bread; ~ **de beurre** slice of bread and butter. **tartiner** 1 vt spread.

tartre /taʀtʀ/ nm (de bouilloire) fur, scale; (sur les dents) tartar.

tas /tɑ/ nm pile, heap; **un ou des ~ de** 1 lots of.

tasse /tɑs/ nf cup; **~ à thé** teacup.

tasser /tɑse/ 1 vt pack, squeeze; (terre) pack (down). ■ **se ~** vpr (terrain) sink; (se serrer) squeeze up.

tâter /tɑte/ 1 vt feel; (opinion: fig) sound out. • vi **~ de** try out.

tatillon, ~ne /tatijɔ̃, -jɔn/ adj finicky.

tâtonnements /tɑtɔnmɑ̃/ nmpl (essais) trial and error (+ sg).

tâtons: à ~ /atɑtɔ̃/ loc **avancer à ~** grope one's way along.

tatouage /tatwaʒ/ nm (dessin) tattoo.

taupe /top/ nf mole.

taureau (pl ~x) /tɔʀo/ nm bull; **le T~** Taurus.

taux /to/ nm rate.

taxe /taks/ nf tax.

taxi /taksi/ nm taxi(-cab); (personne 1) taxi driver.

taxiphone ® /taksifɔn/ nm pay phone.

Tchécoslovaquie /tʃekɔslɔvaki/ nf Czechoslovakia.

tchèque /tʃɛk/ adj Czech; **République ~** Czech Republic. **T~** nmf Czech.

te, t' /tə, t/ pron you; (indirect) (to) you; (réfléchi) yourself.

technicien, ~ne /tɛknisjɛ̃, -ɛn/ nm, f technician.

technique /tɛknik/ adj technical. • nf technique.

techno /tɛkno/ nf (Mus) techno.

technologie /tɛknɔlɔʒi/ nf technology.

teindre /tɛ̃dʀ/ 22 vt dye. ■ **se ~** vpr **se ~ les cheveux** dye one's hair.

teint /tɛ̃/ nm complexion.

teinte /tɛ̃t/ nf shade. **teinter** 1 vt (verre) tint; (bois) stain.

teinture /tɛ̃tyʀ/ nf (produit) dye.

teinturier, -ière /tɛ̃tyʀje, -jɛʀ/ nm, f dry-cleaner.

tel, ~le /tɛl/ adj such; **un ~ livre** such a book; **~ que** such as, like; (ainsi que) (just) as; **~ ou ~** such-and-such; **~ quel** (just) as it is.

télé /tele/ nf 1 TV; **~ réalité** nf reality TV.

télécharger /teleʃaʀʒe/ 40 vt (Ordinat) download.

télécommande /telekɔmɑ̃d/ nf remote control.

télécommunications /telekɔmynikasjɔ̃/ nfpl telecommunications.

téléconférence /telekɔ̃feʀɑ̃s/ nf teleconferencing.

télécopie /telekɔpi/ nf fax. **télécopieur** nm fax machine.

téléfilm /telefilm/ nm TV film.

télégramme /telegʀam/ nm telegram.

télégraphier /telegʀafje/ 45 vt/i **~ (à)** cable.

téléguidé, ~e /telegide/ adj radiocontrolled.

télématique /telematik/ nf telematics (+ sg).

téléphérique /teleferik/ nm cable car.

téléphone /telefɔn/ nm (tele-)phone; **~ à carte** cardphone. **téléphoner** 1 vt/i **~ (à)** (tele)phone.

téléphonie /telefɔni/ nf telephony; **~ mobile** mobile telephony. **téléphonique** adj (tele)phone.

télé-réalité /teleʀealite/ nf reality TV.

téléserveur /telesɛʀvœʀ/ nm (Internet) remote server.

télésiège /telesjɛʒ/ nm chairlift.

téléski /teleski/ nm ski tow.

téléspectateur, -trice /telespɛktatœʀ, -tʀis/ nm, f (tv) viewer.

télévente /televɑ̃t/ nf telesales (+ pl).

télévisé, ~e /televize/ adj (débat) televised; **émission ~e** television programme. **télévision** nf television.

télex /telɛks/ nm telex.

tellement /tɛlmɑ̃/ adv (tant) so much; (si) so; **~ de** (quantité) so much; (nombre) so many.

téméraire /temeʀɛʀ/ adj (personne) reckless.

témoignage /temwaɲaʒ/ nm testimony, evidence; (récit) account; **~ de** (marque) token of.

témoigner /temwaɲe/ 1 vi testify (**de** to). •vt (montrer) show; **~ que** testify that.

témoin /temwɛ̃/ nm witness; (Sport) baton; **être ~ de** witness; **~ oculaire** eyewitness.

tempe /tɑ̃p/ nf (Anat) temple.

tempérament /tɑ̃peʀamɑ̃/ nm temperament, disposition.

température /tɑ̃peʀatyʀ/ nf temperature.

tempête /tɑ̃pɛt/ nf storm; **~ de neige** snowstorm.

temple /tɑ̃pl/ nm temple; (protestant) church.

temporaire /tɑ̃pɔʀɛʀ/ adj temporary.

temps /tɑ̃/ nm (notion) time; (Gram) tense; (étape) stage; **à ~ partiel/plein** part-/full-time; **ces derniers ~** lately; **dans le ~** at one time; **dans quelque ~** in a while; **de ~ en ~** from time to time; **~ d'arrêt** pause; **avoir tout son ~** have plenty of time; (météo) weather; **~ de chien** filthy weather; **quel ~ fait-il?** what's the weather like?

tenace /tənas/ adj stubborn.

tenaille /tənaj/ nf pincers (+ pl).

tendance /tɑ̃dɑ̃s/ nf tendency; (évolution) trend; **avoir ~ à** tend to.

tendon /tɑ̃dɔ̃/ nm tendon.

tendre[1] /tɑ̃dʀ/ 3 vt stretch; (piège) set; (bras) stretch out; (main) hold out; (cou) crane; **~ qch à qn** hold sth out to sb; **~ l'oreille** prick up one's ears. •vi **~ à** tend to.

tendre[2] /tɑ̃dʀ/ adj tender; (couleur, bois) soft. **tendresse** nf tenderness.

tendu, ~e /tɑ̃dy/ adj (corde) tight; (personne, situation) tense.

ténèbres /tenɛbʀ/ nfpl darkness.

teneur /tənœʀ/ nf content.

tenir /təniʀ/ 59 vt hold; (pari, promesse, hôtel) keep; (place) take up; (propos) utter; (rôle) play; **~ de** (avoir reçu de) have got from; **~ pour** regard as; **~ chaud** keep warm; **~ compte de** take into account; **~ le coup** hold out; **~ tête à** stand up to. •vi hold; **~ à** be attached to; **~ à faire** be anxious to do; **~ bon** stand firm; **~ dans** fit into; **~ de qn** take after sb; **tiens!** (surprise) hey! ■ **se ~** vpr (debout) stand; (avoir lieu) be held; **se ~ à** hold on to; **s'en ~ à** (se limiter à) confine oneself to.

tennis /tenis/ nm tennis; **~ de table** table tennis. •nmpl (chaussures) sneakers.

ténor /tenɔʀ/ nm tenor.

tension /tɑ̃sjɔ̃/ nf tension; **avoir de la ~** have high blood pressure.

tentation /tɑ̃tasjɔ̃/ nf temptation.

tentative /tɑ̃tativ/ nf attempt.

tente /tɑ̃t/ nf tent.

tenter /tɑ̃te/ 1 vt (allécher) tempt; (essayer) try (**de faire** to do).

tenture /tɑ̃tyʀ/ nf curtain; **~s** draperies.

tenu, ~e /təny/ adj **bien ~** well

kept; ~ **de** required. ●▷TENIR 58.

tenue /təny/ nf (habillement) dress; (de maison) upkeep; (conduite) (good) behaviour; (maintien) posture; ~ **de soirée** evening dress.

Tergal ® /tɛʀgal/ nm Terylene®.

terme /tɛʀm/ nm (mot) term; (date limite) time-limit; (fin) end; **né avant** ~ premature; **à long/ court** ~ long-/short-term; **en bons** ~**s** on good terms (**avec** with).

terminaison /tɛʀminɛzɔ̃/ nf (Gram) ending.

terminal, ~e (mpl **-aux**) /tɛʀmi-nal, -o/ adj terminal. ●nm terminal. **terminale** nf (Scol) ≈ sixth form; (US) twelfth grade.

terminer /tɛʀmine/ 1 vt/i finish; (discours) end, finish. ■**se** ~ vpr end (**par** with).

terne /tɛʀn/ adj dull, drab.

ternir /tɛʀniʀ/ 2 vt/i tarnish. ■**se** ~ vpr tarnish.

terrain /tɛʀɛ̃/ nm ground; (parcelle) piece of land; (à bâtir) plot; ~ **d'aviation** airfield; ~ **de camping** campsite; ~ **de golf** golf course; ~ **de jeu** playground; ~ **vague** waste ground.

terrasse /tɛʀas/ nf terrace; **à la** ~ (d'un café) outside (a café).

terrasser /tɛʀase/ 1 vt (adversaire) knock down; (maladie) strike down.

terre /tɛʀ/ nf (planète, matière) earth; (étendue, pays) land; (sol) ground; **à** ~ (Naut) ashore; **par** ~ (dehors) on the ground; (dedans) on the floor; ~ **(cuite)** terracotta; **la** ~ **ferme** dry land; ~ **glaise** clay. **terreau** (pl ~**x**) nm compost. **terre-plein*** (pl **terres-pleins**) nm platform; (de route) central reservation.

terrestre /tɛʀɛstʀ/ adj (animaux) land; (de notre planète) of the Earth.

terreur /tɛʀœʀ/ nf terror.

terrible /tɛʀibl/ adj terrible; (formidable 1) terrific.

terrier /tɛʀje/ nm (trou) burrow; (chien) terrier.

terrifier /tɛʀifje/ 45 vt terrify.

territoire /tɛʀitwaʀ/ nm territory.

terroir /tɛʀwaʀ/ nm land; **du** ~ local.

terroriser /tɛʀɔʀize/ 1 vt terrorize.

terrorisme /tɛʀɔʀism/ nm terrorism. **terroriste** nmf terrorist.

tertiaire /tɛʀsjɛʀ/ adj (secteur) service.

tes /te/ ▷TON¹.

test /tɛst/ nm test.

testament /tɛstamɑ̃/ nm (Jur) will; (politique, artistique) testament; **Ancien/Nouveau T**~ Old/New Testament.

tétanos /tetanos/ nm tetanus.

têtard /tɛtaʀ/ nm tadpole.

tête /tɛt/ nf head; (visage) face; (cheveux) hair; **à la** ~ **de** at the head of; **à** ~ **reposée** at one's leisure; **de** ~ (calculer) in one's head; **faire la** ~ sulk; **tenir** ~ **à qn** stand up to sb; **il n'en fait qu'à sa** ~ he does just as he pleases; **en** ~ (Sport) in the lead; **faire une** ~ (au football) head the ball; **une forte** ~ a rebel; **la** ~ **la première** head first; **de la** ~ **aux pieds** from head to toe.

tête-à-tête /tɛtatɛt/ nm inv tête-à-tête; **en** ~ in private.

tétée /tete/ nf feed.

tétine /tetin/ nf (de biberon) teat; (sucette) dummy; (US) pacifier.

têtu, ~e /tety/ adj stubborn.

texte /tɛkst/ nm text; (de leçon) subject; (morceau choisi) passage.

texteur /tɛkstœʀ/ nm (Ordinat) word-processor.

textile /tɛkstil/ nm & adj textile.

texto /tɛksto/ nm ▣ text message.

TGV abrév m (**train à grande vitesse**) TGV, high-speed train.

thé /te/ nm tea.

théâtre /teɑtʀ/ nm theatre; (d'un crime) scene; **faire du ~** act.

théière /tejɛʀ/ nf teapot.

thème /tɛm/ nm theme; (traduction: Scol) prose.

théorie /teɔʀi/ nf theory. **théorique** adj theoretical.

thérapie /teʀapi/ nf therapy.

thermique /tɛʀmik/ adj thermal.

thermomètre /tɛʀmɔmɛtʀ/ nm thermometer.

thermos® /tɛʀmos/ nm ou f Thermos® (flask).

thermostat /tɛʀmɔsta/ nm thermostat.

thèse /tɛz/ nf thesis.

thon /tɔ̃/ nm tuna.

thym /tɛ̃/ nm thyme.

tibia /tibja/ nm shinbone.

tic /tik/ nm (contraction) tic, twitch; (manie) habit.

ticket /tikɛ/ nm ticket.

tiède /tjɛd/ adj lukewarm; (nuit) warm.

tiédir /tjediʀ/ ❷ vt/i (**faire**) ~ warm up.

tien, ~ne /tjɛ̃, -ɛn/ pron **le ~, la ~ne, les ~(ne)s** yours; **à la ~ne!** cheers!

tiens, tient /tjɛ̃/ ▷TENIR 59.

tiercé /tjɛʀse/ nm place-betting.

tiers, tierce /tjɛʀ, tjɛʀs/ adj third. •nm (fraction) third; (personne) third party. **tiers-monde** nm Third World.

tige /tiʒ/ nf (Bot) stem, stalk; (en métal) shaft, rod.

tigre /tigʀ/ nm tiger.

tigresse /tigʀɛs/ nf tigress.

tilleul /tijœl/ nm lime tree.

timbre /tɛ̃bʀ/ nm stamp; (sonnette) bell; (de voix) tone. ~ **poste** (pl ~s **poste**) nm postage stamp. **timbrer** ❶ vt stamp.

timide /timid/ adj shy, timid. **timidité** nf shyness.

timoré, ~e /timɔʀe/ adj timorous.

tintement /tɛ̃tmɑ̃/ nm (de sonnette) ringing; (de clés) jingling.

tique /tik/ nf tick.

tir /tiʀ/ nm (Sport) shooting; (action de tirer) firing; (feu, rafale) fire; ~ **à l'arc** archery; ~ **au pigeon** clay pigeon shooting.

tirage /tiʀaʒ/ nm (de photo) printing; (de journal) circulation; (de livre) edition; (Ordinat) hard copy; (de cheminée) draught; ~ **au sort** draw.

tire-bouchon* (pl ~s) /tiʀbuʃɔ̃/ nm corkscrew.

tirelire /tiʀliʀ/ nf piggy bank.

tirer /tiʀe/ ❶ vt pull; (langue) stick out; (conclusion, trait, rideaux) draw; (coup de feu) fire; (gibier) shoot; (photo) print; ~ **de** (sortir) take *ou* get out of; (extraire) extract from; (plaisir, nom) derive from; ~ **parti de** take advantage of; ~ **profit de** profit from; **se faire ~ l'oreille** get told off. •vi shoot, fire (**sur** at); ~ **sur** (corde) pull at; (couleur) verge on; ~ **à sa fin** be drawing to a close; ~ **au clair** clarify; ~ **au sort** draw lots (for). ■ **se** ~ vpr ▣ clear off; **se** ~ **de** get out of; **s'en** ~ (en réchapper) pull through; (réussir ▣) cope.

tiret /tiʀɛ/ nm dash.

tireur /tiʀœʀ/ nm gunman; ~ **d'élite** marksman; ~ **isolé** sniper.

tiroir /tiʀwaʀ/ nm drawer. **tiroir-caisse** (pl **tiroirs-caisses**) nm till, cash register.

tisane /tizan/ nf herbal tea.

....

G see A-Z of French life and culture

tissage /tisaʒ/ nm weaving. **tisser** 1 vt weave. **tisserand** nm weaver.

tissu /tisy/ nm fabric, material; (biologique) tissue; **un ~ de mensonges** (fig) a pack of lies. **tissu-éponge** (pl **tissus-éponge**) nm towelling.

titre /titʀ/ nm title; (diplôme) qualification; (Comm) bond; **~s** (droits) claims; **(gros) ~s** headlines; **à ~ d'exemple** as an example; **à juste ~** rightly; **à ~ privé** in a private capacity; **à ~ double** on two accounts; **~ de propriété** title deed.

tituber /titybe/ 1 vi stagger.

titulaire /titylɛʀ/ adj **être ~** be a permanent staff member; **être ~ de** hold. ●nmf (de permis) holder. **titulariser** 1 vt give permanent status to.

toast /tost/ nm (pain) piece of toast; (canapé, allocution) toast.

toboggan /tɔbɔgã/ nm (de jeu) slide; (Auto) flyover.

toi /twa/ pron you; (réfléchi) yourself; **dépêche-~** hurry up.

toile /twal/ nf cloth; (tableau) canvas; **~ d'araignée** cobweb; **~ de fond** (fig) backdrop; **la ~** (Internet) the Web.

toilette /twalɛt/ nf (habillement) outfit; **~s** (cabinets) toilet(s); **de ~** (articles, savon) toilet; **faire sa ~** have a wash.

toi-même /twamɛm/ pron yourself.

toit /twa/ nm roof; **~ ouvrant** (Auto) sunroof.

toiture /twatyʀ/ nf roof.

tôle /tol/ nf (plaque) iron sheet; **~ ondulée** corrugated iron.

tolérant, ~e /tɔleʀã, -t/ adj tolerant. **tolérer** 14 vt tolerate.

tomate /tɔmat/ nf tomato.

tombe /tɔ̃b/ nf grave; (pierre) gravestone.

tombeau (pl **~x**) /tɔ̃bo/ nm tomb.

tomber /tɔ̃be/ 1 vi (aux être) fall; (fièvre, vent) drop; **faire ~** knock over; (gouvernement) bring down; **laisser ~** (objet, amoureux) drop; (collègue) let down; (activité) give up; **laisse ~!** 1 forget it!; **~ à l'eau** (projet) fall through; **~ bien** ou **à point** come at the right time; **~ en panne** break down; **~ en syncope** faint; **~ sur** (trouver) run across.

tombola /tɔ̃bɔla/ nf tombola; (US) lottery.

tome /tɔm/ nm volume.

ton¹, ta (**ton** before vowel or mute h) (pl **tes**) /tɔ̃, ta, tɔ̃, te/ adj your.

ton² /tɔ̃/ nm (hauteur de voix) pitch; **d'un ~ sec** drily; **de bon ~** in good taste.

tonalité /tɔnalite/ nf (Mus) key; (de téléphone) dialling tone; (US) dial tone.

tondeuse /tɔ̃døz/ nf (à moutons) shears (+ pl); (à cheveux) clippers (+ pl); **~ à gazon** lawn-mower. **tondre** 3 vt (herbe) mow; (mouton) shear; (cheveux) clip.

tonne /tɔn/ nf tonne.

tonneau (pl **~x**) /tɔno/ nm barrel; (en voiture) somersault.

tonnerre /tɔnɛʀ/ nm thunder.

tonton /tɔ̃tɔ̃/ nm 1 uncle.

tonus /tɔnys/ nm energy.

torche /tɔʀʃ/ nf torch.

torchon /tɔʀʃɔ̃/ nm (pour la vaisselle) tea towel.

tordre /tɔʀdʀ/ 3 vt twist. ■ se ~ vpr **se ~ la cheville** twist one's ankle; **se ~ de douleur** writhe in pain; **se ~ (de rire)** split one's sides.

tordu, ~e /tɔʀdy/ adj twisted, bent; (esprit) warped, twisted.

torpille /tɔʀpij/ nf torpedo.

torrent /tɔʀã/ nm torrent.

torride /tɔʀid/ adj torrid; (chaleur) scorching.

torse /tɔʀs/ nm chest; (Anat) torso.

tort /tɔʀ/ nm wrong; **avoir ~** be wrong (**de faire** to do); **donner ~ à** harm; **à ~** wrongly; **être dans son ~** be in the wrong; **faire (du) ~ à** harm; **à ~ et à travers** without thinking.

torticolis /tɔʀtikɔli/ nm stiff neck.

tortiller /tɔʀtije/ **1** vt twist, twirl. ■ **se ~** vpr wriggle.

tortionnaire /tɔʀsjɔnɛʀ/ nm torturer.

tortue /tɔʀty/ nf tortoise; (d'eau) turtle.

tortueux, -euse /tɔʀtɥø, -z/ adj (chemin) twisting; (explication) tortuous.

torture /tɔʀtyʀ/ nf torture. **torturer** **1** vt torture.

tôt /to/ adv early; **au plus ~** at the earliest; **le plus ~ possible** as soon as possible; **~ ou tard** sooner or later; **ce n'est pas trop ~!** it's about time!

total, ~e (mpl **-aux**) /tɔtal, -o/ adj total. ●nm (pl **-aux**) total; **au ~** all in all. **totalement** adv totally. **totaliser** **1** vt total. **totalitaire** adj totalitarian.

totalité /tɔtalite/ nf **la ~ de** all of.

touche /tuʃ/ nf (de piano) key; (de peinture) touch; **(ligne de) ~** (Sport) touchline.

toucher /tuʃe/ **1** vt touch; (émouvoir) move, touch; (contacter) get in touch with; (cible) hit; (argent) draw; (chèque) cash; (concerner) affect. ●vi **à** touch; (question) touch on; (fin, but) approach; **je vais lui en ~ deux mots** I'll talk to him about it. ■ **se ~** vpr (lignes) touch. ●nm (sens) touch.

touffe /tuf/ nf (de poils, d'herbe) tuft; (de plantes) clump.

toujours /tuʒuʀ/ adv always; (encore) still; (de toute façon) anyway; **pour ~** for ever; **~ est-**

il que the fact remains that.

toupet /tupɛ/ nm (culot 🆒) cheek, nerve.

tour /tuʀ/ nf tower; (immeuble) tower block; (échecs) rook; **~ de contrôle** control tower. ●nm (mouvement, succession, tournure) turn; (excursion) trip; (à pied) walk; (en auto) drive; (artifice) trick; (circonférence) circumference; (Tech) lathe; **~ (de piste)** lap; **à ~ de rôle** in turn; **à mon ~** when it is my turn; **c'est mon ~ de** it is my turn to; **faire le ~ de** go round; (question) survey; **~ d'horizon** overview; **~ de potier** potter's wheel; **~ de taille** waist measurement; (ligne) waistline.

tourbillon /tuʀbijɔ̃/ nm whirlwind; (d'eau) whirlpool; (fig) swirl.

tourisme /tuʀism/ nm tourism; **faire du ~** do some sightseeing.

touriste /tuʀist/ nmf tourist. **touristique** adj tourist; (route) scenic.

tourmenter /tuʀmɑ̃te/ vt torment. ■ **se ~** vpr worry.

tournant, ~e /tuʀnɑ̃, -t/ adj (qui pivote) revolving. ●nm bend; (fig) turning-point.

tourne-disque (pl **~s**) /tuʀnədisk/ nm record-player.

tournée /tuʀne/ nf (d'artiste) tour; **c'est ma ~** I'll buy this round; (de facteur, au café) round.

tourner /tuʀne/ **1** vt turn; (film) shoot, make; **~ le dos à** turn one's back on; **~ en dérision** mock. ●vi turn; (toupie, tête) spin; (moteur, usine) run; **~ autour de** go round; (personne, maison) hang around; (terre) revolve round; (question) centre on; **~ de l'œil** 🆒 faint; **mal ~** (affaire) turn out badly. ■ **se ~** vpr turn.

tournesol /tuʀnəsɔl/ nm sunflower.

t

tournevis /tuʀnəvis/ nm
screwdriver.

tournoi /tuʀnwa/ nm tournament.

tourte /tuʀt/ nf pie.

tourterelle /tuʀtəʀɛl/ nf
turtle dove.

Toussaint /tusɛ̃/ nf **la ~** All
Saints' Day.

tousser /tuse/ **1** vi cough.

tout, ~e (pl **tous, toutes**) /tu,
tut/ nm (ensemble) whole; **en ~** in
all; **pas du ~!** not at all! ●adj all;
(n'importe quel) any; **~ le pays** the
whole country, all the country;
~e la nuit/journée the whole
night/day; **~ un paquet** a
whole pack; **tous les jours**
every day; **tous les deux ans**
every two years; **~ le monde**
everyone; **tous les deux,
toutes les deux** both of them;
tous les trois all three (of
them). ●pron everything; all;
anything; **tous** /tus/, **toutes** all;
tous ensemble all together;
prends ~ take everything; **~ ce
que tu veux** everything you
want. ●adv (très) very; (entièrement)
all; **~ au bout/début** right at
the end/beginning; **~ en
marchant** while walking; **~ à
coup** all of a sudden; **~ à fait**
quite, completely; **~ à l'heure**
in a moment; (passé) a moment
ago; **~ au** ou **le long de**
throughout; **~ au plus/moins**
at most/least; **~ de même** all
the same; **~ de suite** straight
away; **~ entier** whole; **~ neuf**
brand new; **~ nu** stark naked.
tout-à-l'égout nm inv main
drainage.

toutefois /tutfwa/ adv however.

tout(-)terrain /tuteʀɛ̃/ adj inv all
terrain.

toux /tu/ nf cough.

toxicomane /tɔksikɔman/ nmf
drug addict.

toxique /tɔksik/ adj toxic.

trac /tʀak/ nm **le ~** nerves; (Théât)
stage fright.

tracas /tʀaka/ nm worry.

trace /tʀas/ nf (trainée, piste) trail;
(d'animal, de pneu) tracks; **~s de
pas** footprints.

tracer /tʀase/ **10** vt draw; (écrire)
write; (route) open up.

trachée-artère /tʀaʃeaʀtɛʀ/ nf
windpipe.

tracteur /tʀaktœʀ/ nm tractor.

tradition /tʀadisjɔ̃/ nf tradition.
traditionnel, ~le adj
traditional.

traducteur, -trice /tʀadyktœʀ,
-tʀis/ nm, f translator. **traduction**
nf translation.

traduire /tʀaduiʀ/ **17** vt translate;
~ en justice take to court.

trafic /tʀafik/ nm (commerce,
circulation) traffic.

trafiquant, ~e /tʀafikɑ̃, -t/ nm, f
trafficker; (d'armes, de drogues)
dealer.

trafiquer /tʀafike/ **1** vi traffic.
●vt **1** (moteur) fiddle with.

tragédie /tʀaʒedi/ nf tragedy.
tragique adj tragic.

trahir /tʀaiʀ/ **2** vt betray.
trahison nf betrayal; (Mil)
treason.

train /tʀɛ̃/ nm (Rail) train; (allure)
pace; **aller bon ~** walk briskly;
en ~ de faire (busy) doing; **~
d'atterrissage** undercarriage; **~
électrique** (jouet) electric train
set; **~ de vie** lifestyle.

traîne* /tʀɛn/ nf (de robe) train; **à
la ~** lagging behind.

traîneau* (pl **~x**) /tʀɛno/ nm
sleigh.

traînée* /tʀɛne/ nf (trace) trail;
(longue) streak; (femme: péj) slut.

traîner* /tʀɛne/ **1** vt drag
(along); **~ les pieds** drag one's
feet. ●vi (pendre) trail; (rester en
arrière) trail behind; (flâner) hang
about; (papiers, affaires) lie around;

~ (en longueur) drag on. ■ se **~** vpr (par terre) crawl.

traire /tʀɛʀ/ 28 vt milk.

trait /tʀɛ/ nm line; (en dessinant) stroke; (caractéristique) feature, trait; **~s** (du visage) features; **avoir ~ à** relate to; **d'un ~** (boire) in one gulp; **~ d'union** hyphen; (fig) link.

traite /tʀɛt/ nf (de vache) milking; (Comm) draft; **d'une (seule) ~** in one go, at a stretch.

traité /tʀete/ nm (pacte) treaty; (ouvrage) treatise.

traitement /tʀɛtmɑ̃/ nm treatment; (salaire) salary; **~ de données** data processing; **~ de texte** word processing.

traiter /tʀete/ 1 vt treat; (affaire) deal with; (données, produit) process; **~ qn de lâche** call sb a coward. ● vi deal (**avec** with); **~ de** (sujet) deal with.

traiteur /tʀɛtœʀ/ nm caterer; (boutique) delicatessen.

traître, -esse* /tʀɛtʀ, -ɛs/ adj treacherous. ● nm, f traitor.

trajectoire /tʀaʒɛktwaʀ/ nf path.

trajet /tʀaʒɛ/ nm (voyage) journey; (itinéraire) route.

trame /tʀam/ nf (de tissu) weft.

tramway /tʀamwɛ/ nm tram; (US) streetcar.

tranchant, ~e /tʀɑ̃ʃɑ̃, -t/ adj sharp; (fig) cutting. ● nm cutting edge; **à double ~** two-edged.

tranche /tʀɑ̃ʃ/ nf (rondelle) slice; (bord) edge; (d'âge, de revenu) bracket.

tranchée /tʀɑ̃ʃe/ nf trench.

trancher /tʀɑ̃ʃe/ 1 vt cut; (question) decide; (contraster) contrast (**sur** with).

tranquille /tʀɑ̃kil/ adj quiet; (esprit) at rest; (conscience) clear; **être/laisser ~** be/leave in peace; **tiens-toi ~!** be quiet!

tranquillisant nm tranquillizer.

tranquilliser 1 vt reassure.

tranquillité nf (peace and) quiet; (d'esprit) peace of mind.

transcription /tʀɑ̃skʀipsjɔ̃/ nf transcription; (copie) transcript.

transcrire 30 vt transcribe.

transe /tʀɑ̃s/ nf **en ~** in a trance.

transférer /tʀɑ̃sfeʀe/ 14 vt transfer.

transfert /tʀɑ̃sfɛʀ/ nm transfer; **~ d'appel** (au téléphone) call diversion.

transformation /tʀɑ̃sfɔʀmasjɔ̃/ nf change; transformation.

transformer /tʀɑ̃sfɔʀme/ 1 vt change; (radicalement) transform; (vêtement) alter. ■ se **~** vpr change; (radicalement) be transformed; **(se) ~ en** turn into.

transgénique /tʀɑ̃sʒenik/ adj genetically modified.

transiger /tʀɑ̃ziʒe/ 40 vi compromise.

transiter /tʀɑ̃zite/ 1 vt/i **~ par** pass through.

transitif, -ive /tʀɑ̃zitif, -v/ adj transitive.

translucide /tʀɑ̃slysid/ adj translucent.

transmettre /tʀɑ̃smɛtʀ/ 42 vt (savoir, maladie) pass on; (ondes) transmit; (à la radio) broadcast.

transmission nf transmission; (radio) broadcasting.

transparence /tʀɑ̃spaʀɑ̃s/ nf transparency. **transparent, ~e** adj transparent.

transpercer /tʀɑ̃spɛʀse/ 10 vt pierce.

transpiration /tʀɑ̃spiʀasjɔ̃/ nf perspiration. **transpirer** 1 vi perspire.

transplanter /tʀɑ̃splɑ̃te/ 1 vt (Bot, Méd) transplant.

transport /tʀɑ̃spɔʀ/ nm transport(ation); **durant le ~** in transit; **les ~s** transport (+ sg); **les ~s en commun** public

t

transport (+ sg). **transporter** /tʀɑ̃spɔʀte/ **1** vt transport; (à la main) carry. **transporteur** nm haulier; (US) trucker.

transversal, ~e (mpl -aux) /tʀɑ̃svɛʀsal, -o/ adj cross, transverse.

trapu, ~e /tʀapy/ adj stocky.

traumatisant, ~e /tʀomatizɑ̃, -t/ adj traumatic. **traumatiser** vt **1** traumatize. **traumatisme** nm trauma.

travail (pl -aux) /tʀavaj, -o/ nm work; (emploi, tâche) job; (façonnage) working; **travaux** work (+ sg); (routiers) roadworks; ~ **à la chaîne** production line work; **travaux dirigés** (Scol) practical; **travaux forcés** hard labour; **travaux manuels** handicrafts; **travaux ménagers** housework.

travailler /tʀavaje/ **1** vi work; (se déformer) warp. ●vt (façonner) work; (étudier) work at ou on.

travailleur, -euse /tʀavajœʀ, -øz/ nm, f worker. ●adj hardworking.

travailliste /tʀavajist/ adj Labour. ●nmf Labour party member.

travers /tʀavɛʀ/ nm (défaut) failing; **à** ~ through; **au** ~ **(de)** through; **de** ~ (chapeau, nez) crooked; (regarder) askance; **j'ai avalé de** ~ it went down the wrong way; **en** ~ **(de)** across.

traversée /tʀavɛʀse/ nf crossing.

traverser /tʀavɛʀse/ **1** vt cross; (transpercer) go (right) through; (période, forêt) go ou pass through.

traversin /tʀavɛʀsɛ̃/ nm bolster.

travesti /tʀavɛsti/ nm transvestite.

trébucher /tʀebyʃe/ **1** vi stumble, trip (over); **faire** ~ trip (up).

trèfle /tʀɛfl/ nm (plante) clover; (cartes) clubs.

treillis /tʀeji/ nm trellis; (en métal) wire mesh; (tenue militaire) combat uniform.

treize /tʀɛz/ adj & nm thirteen.

tréma /tʀema/ nm diaeresis.

tremblement /tʀɑ̃bləmɑ̃/ nm shaking; ~ **de terre** earthquake. **trembler** **1** vi shake, tremble; (lumière, voix) quiver.

tremper /tʀɑ̃pe/ **1** vt/i soak; (plonger) dip; (acier) temper; **faire** ~ soak; ~ **dans** (fig) be mixed up. ■ **se** ~ vpr (se baigner) have a dip.

tremplin /tʀɑ̃plɛ̃/ nm springboard.

trente /tʀɑ̃t/ adj & nm thirty; **se mettre sur son** ~ **et un** dress up; **tous les** ~-**six du mois** once in a blue moon.

trépied /tʀepje/ nm tripod.

très /tʀɛ/ adv very; ~ **aimé/ estimé** much liked/esteemed.

trésor /tʀezɔʀ/ nm treasure; **le T**~ **public** the revenue department.

trésorerie /tʀezɔʀʀi/ nf (bureaux) accounts department; (du Trésor public) revenue office; (argent) funds (+ pl); (gestion) accounts (+ pl). **trésorier, -ière** nm, f treasurer.

tressaillement /tʀesajmɑ̃/ nm quiver; start.

tresse /tʀɛs/ nf braid, plait.

trêve /tʀɛv/ nf truce; (fig) respite; ~ **de plaisanteries** that's enough joking.

tri /tʀi/ nm (classement) sorting; (sélection) selection; **faire le** ~ **de** (classer) sort; (choisir) select; **centre de** ~ sorting office.

triangle /tʀijɑ̃gl/ nm triangle.

tribal, ~e (mpl -aux) /tʀibal, -o/ adj tribal.

tribord /tʀibɔʀ/ nm starboard.

tribu /tʀiby/ nf tribe.

tribunal (mpl -aux) /tʀibynal, -o/ nm court.

tribune /tʀibyn/ nf (de stade) grandstand; (d'orateur) rostrum; (débat) forum; (d'église) gallery.

tribut /tʀiby/ nm tribute.

tributaire /tʀibytɛʀ/ adj ~ **de** dependent on.

tricher /tʀiʃe/ **1** vi cheat. **tricheur, -euse** nm, f cheat.

tricolore /tʀikɔlɔʀ/ adj three-coloured; (écharpe) red, white and blue; (équipe) French.

tricot /tʀiko/ nm (activité) knitting; (pull) sweater; **en ~** knitted; **~ de corps** vest; (US) undershirt. **tricoter 1** vt/i knit.

trier /tʀije/ **45** vt (classer) sort; (choisir) select.

trimestre /tʀimɛstʀ/ nm quarter; (Scol) term. **trimestriel, ~le** adj quarterly; (bulletin) end-of-term.

tringle /tʀɛ̃gl/ nf rail.

trinquer /tʀɛ̃ke/ **1** vi clink glasses.

triomphant, ~e /tʀijɔ̃fɑ̃, -t/ adj triumphant. **triomphe** nm triumph. **triompher 1** vi triumph (**de** over); (jubiler) be triumphant.

tripes /tʀip/ nfpl (mets) tripe (+ sg); (entrailles **1**) guts.

triple /tʀipl/ adj triple, treble. ● nm **le ~** three times as much (**de** as). **triplés, -es** nm, fpl triplets.

tripot /tʀipo/ nm gambling den.

tripoter /tʀipɔte/ **1** vt **1** (personne) grope; (objet) fiddle with.

trisomique /tʀizɔmik/ adj **être ~** have Down's syndrome.

triste /tʀist/ adj sad; (rue, temps, couleur) dreary; (lamentable) dreadful. **tristesse** nf sadness; dreariness.

trivial, ~e (mpl **-iaux**) /tʀivjal, -jo/ adj coarse.

troc /tʀɔk/ nm exchange; (Comm) barter.

trognon /tʀɔɲɔ̃/ nm (de fruit) core.

trois /tʀwɑ/ adj & nm three; **hôtel ~ étoiles** three-star hotel. **troisième** adj & nmf third.

trombone /tʀɔ̃bɔn/ nm (Mus) trombone; (agrafe) paperclip.

trompe /tʀɔ̃p/ nf (d'éléphant) trunk; (Mus) horn.

tromper /tʀɔ̃pe/ **1** vt deceive, mislead; (déjouer) elude. ▪ **se ~** vpr be mistaken; **se ~ de route/ d'heure** take the wrong road/ get the time wrong.

trompette /tʀɔ̃pɛt/ nf trumpet.

trompeur, -euse /tʀɔ̃pœʀ, -øz/ adj (apparence) deceptive.

tronc /tʀɔ̃/ nm trunk; (boîte) collection box.

tronçon /tʀɔ̃sɔ̃/ nm section.

tronçonneuse /tʀɔ̃sɔnøz/ nf chain saw.

trône /tʀon/ nm throne. **trôner 1** vi (vase) have pride of place (**sur** on).

trop /tʀo/ adv (grand, loin) too; (boire, marcher) too much; **~ (de)** quantité) too much; (nombre) too many; **ce serait ~ beau** one should be so lucky; **de ~ en ~** too much; too many; **il a bu un verre de ~** he's had one too many; **se sentir de ~** feel one is in the way.

trophée /tʀɔfe/ nm trophy.

tropical, ~e (mpl **-aux**) /tʀɔpikal, -o/ adj tropical. **tropique** nm tropic.

trop-plein (pl **~s**) /tʀɔplɛ̃/ nm excess; (dispositif) overflow.

troquer /tʀɔke/ **1** vt exchange; (Comm) barter (**contre** for).

trot /tʀo/ nm trot; **aller au ~** trot. **trotter 1** vi trot.

trotteuse /trotøz/ nf (de montre) second hand.

trottoir /trotwar/ nm pavement; (US) sidewalk; ~ **roulant** moving walkway.

trou /tru/ nm hole; (moment) gap; (lieu: péj) dump; ~ **(de mémoire)** memory lapse; ~ **de serrure** keyhole; **faire son** ~ carve one's niche.

trouble /trubl/ adj (eau, image) unclear; (louche) shady. •nm (émoi) emotion; ~**s** (Pol) disturbances; (Méd) disorder (+ sg). **troubler** /truble/ **1** vt disturb; (eau) make cloudy; (inquiéter) trouble. ■se ~ vpr (personne) become flustered.

trouer /true/ **1** vt make a hole ou holes in; **mes chaussures sont trouées** my shoes have got holes in them.

troupe /trup/ nf troop; (d'acteurs) company.

troupeau (pl ~**x**) /trupo/ nm herd; (de moutons) flock.

trousse /trus/ nf case, bag; **aux ~s de** hot on sb's heels; ~ **de toilette** toilet bag.

trousseau (pl ~**x**) /truso/ nm (de clefs) bunch; (de mariée) trousseau.

trouver /truve/ **1** vt find; (penser) think; **il est venu me** ~ he came to see me. ■se ~ vpr (être) be; (se sentir) feel; **il se trouve que** it happens that; **si ça se trouve** maybe; **se** ~ **mal** faint.

truand /tryã/ nm gangster.

truc /tryk/ nm (moyen) way; (artifice) trick; (chose **ℹ**) thing. **trucage** nm (cinéma) special effect.

truffe /tryf/ nf (champignon, chocolat) truffle; (de chien) nose.

truffer /tryfe/ **1** vt (fig) fill, pack (**de** with).

truie /trui/ nf (animal) sow.

truite /truit/ nf trout.

truquer /tryke/ **1** vt fix, rig;

(photo) fake; (résultats) fiddle.

tsar /tsar/ nm tsar, czar.

tu /ty/ pron (parent, ami, enfant) you. ▷TAIRE **47**.

tuba /tyba/ nm (Mus) tuba; (Sport) snorkel.

tube /tyb/ nm tube.

tuberculose /tyberkyloz/ nf tuberculosis.

tuer /tɥe/ **1** vt kill; (d'une balle) shoot, kill; (épuiser) exhaust; ~ **par balles** shoot dead. ■se ~ vpr kill oneself; (accident) be killed.

tuerie /tyri/ nf killing.

tue-tête: à ~ /atytɛt/ loc at the top of one's voice.

tuile /tɥil/ nf tile; (malchance **ℹ**) (stroke of) bad luck.

tulipe /tylip/ nf tulip.

tumeur /tymœr/ nf tumour.

tumulte /tymylt/ nm commotion; (désordre) turmoil.

tunique /tynik/ nf tunic.

Tunisie /tynizi/ nf Tunisia.

tunnel /tynɛl/ nm tunnel.

turbo /tyrbo/ adj turbo. •nf (voiture) turbo.

turbulent, ~**e** /tyrbulã, -t/ adj boisterous, turbulent.

turc, -que /tyrk/ adj Turkish. •nm (Ling) Turkish. T~, **-que** Turk.

turfiste /tyrfist/ nmf racegoer.

Turquie /tyrki/ nf Turkey.

tutelle /tytɛl/ nf (Jur) guardianship; (fig) protection.

tuteur, -trice /tytœr, -tris/ nm, f (Jur) guardian. •nm (bâton) stake.

tutoiement /tytwamã/ nm use of the 'tu' form. **tutoyer** **31** vt address using the 'tu' form.

tuyau (pl ~**x**) /tɥijo/ nm pipe;

(conseil 1) tip; ~ **d'arrosage** hosepipe.

TVA abrév f (**taxe à la valeur ajoutée**) VAT.

tympan /tɛ̃pɑ̃/ nm ear-drum.

type /tip/ nm (genre, traits) type;

(individu 1) bloke, guy; **le ~ même de** a classic example of. • adj inv typical.

typique /tipik/ adj typical.

tyran /tiʀɑ̃/ nm tyrant. **tyrannie** nf tyranny. **tyranniser** 1 vt oppress, tyrannize.

Uu

UE abrév f (**Union européenne**) European Union.

Ukraine /ykʀɛn/ nf Ukraine.

ulcère /ylsɛʀ/ nm (Méd) ulcer.

ULM abrév m (**ultraléger motorisé**) microlight.

ultérieur, ~e /ylteʀjœʀ/ adj later. **ultérieurement** adv later.

ultime /yltim/ adj final.

un, une /œ̃, yn/
• déterminant
⋯▸ a; (devant voyelle) an; ~ **animal** an animal; ~ **jour** one day; **pas ~arbre** not a single tree; **il fait ~ froid!** it's so cold!
• pronom
⋯▸ one; **l'~ d'entre nous** one of us; **les ~s croient que...** some believe...
⋯▸ **la une** the front page.
⋯▸ **j'en veux une** I want one.
• adjectif
⋯▸ one, a, an; **j'ai ~ garçon et deux filles** I have a ou one boy and two girls; **il est une heure** it is one o'clock.
• nom masculin & féminin
⋯▸ ~ **par** ~ one by one.

unanime /ynanim/ adj unanimous.

unanimité /ynanimite/ nf unanimity; **à l'~** unanimously.

uni, ~e /yni/ adj united; (couple)

close; (surface) smooth; (tissu) plain.

unième /ynjɛm/ adj -first; **vingt et ~** twenty-first; **cent ~** one hundred and first.

unifier /ynifje/ 45 vt unify.

uniforme /ynifɔʀm/ nm uniform. • adj uniform. **uniformiser** 1 vt standardize. **uniformité** nf uniformity.

unilatéral, ~e (mpl -aux) /ynilateʀal, -o/ adj unilateral.

union /ynjɔ̃/ nf union; **l'U~ européenne** the European Union.

unique /ynik/ adj (seul) only; (prix, voie) one; (incomparable) unique; **enfant ~** only child; **sens ~** oneway street. **uniquement** adv only, solely.

unir /yniʀ/ 2 vt unite. ∎ **s'~** vpr unite, join.

unité /ynite/ nf unit; (harmonie) unity; ~ **centrale** (Ordinat) processor.

univers /ynivɛʀ/ nm universe.

universel, ~le /ynivɛʀsɛl/ adj universal.

universitaire /ynivɛʀsitɛʀ/ adj (résidence) university; (niveau) academic. • nmf academic.

université /ynivɛʀsite/ nf university.

uranium /yʀanjɔm/ nm uranium.

urbain, ~e /yʀbɛ̃, -ɛn/ adj urban. **urbanisme** nm town planning.

urgence /yʀʒɑ̃s/ nf (cas) emergency; (de situation, tâche) urgency; **d'**~ (mesure) emergency; (transporter) urgently; **les** ~**s** casualty (+ sg). **urgent**, ~e adj urgent.

urine /yʀin/ nf urine. **urinoir** nm urinal.

urne /yʀn/ nf (électorale) ballot box; (vase) urn; **aller aux** ~**s** go to the polls.

urticaire /yʀtikɛʀ/ nf hives (+ pl), urticaria.

us /ys/ nmpl **les** ~ **et coutumes** habits and customs.

usage /yzaʒ/ nm use; (coutume) custom; (de langage) usage; **à l'**~ **de** for; **d'**~ (habituel) customary; **faire** ~ **de** make use of.

usagé, ~e /yzaʒe/ adj worn.

usager /yzaʒe/ nm user.

usé, ~e /yze/ adj worn (out); (banal) trite.

user /yze/ **1** vt wear (out). •vi ~ **de** use. ▪ **s'**~ vpr (tissu) wear (out).

usine /yzin/ nf factory, plant; ~ **sidérurgique** ironworks (+ pl).

usité, ~e /yzite/ adj common.

ustensile /ystɑ̃sil/ nm utensil.

usuel, ~**le** /yzɥɛl/ adj ordinary, everyday.

usure /yzyʀ/ nf (détérioration) wear (and tear).

utérus /yteʀys/ nm womb, uterus.

utile /ytil/ adj useful.

utilisable /ytilizabl/ adj usable. **utilisation** nf use. **utiliser** **1** vt use.

utopie /ytɔpi/ nf Utopia; (idée) Utopian idea. **utopique** adj Utopian.

UV[1] abrév f (**unité de valeur**) course unit.

UV[2] abrév mpl (**ultraviolets**) ultraviolet rays; **faire des** ~ use a sunbed.

Vv

va /va/ ▷ ALLER **8**.

vacance /vakɑ̃s/ nf (poste) vacancy.

vacances /vakɑ̃s/ nfpl holiday(s); (US) vacation; **en** ~ on holiday; ~ **d'été, grandes** ~ summer holidays. **vacancier, -ière** nm, f holidaymaker; (US) vacationer.

vacant, ~e /vakɑ̃, -t/ adj vacant.

vacarme /vakaʀm/ nm din.

vaccin /vaksɛ̃/ nm vaccine. **vacciner** **1** vt vaccinate.

vache /vaʃ/ nf cow. •adj (méchant **1**) nasty.

vaciller /vasije/ **1** vi sway, wobble; (lumière) flicker; (hésiter) falter; (santé, mémoire) fail.

vadrouiller /vadʀuje/ **1** vi **1** wander about.

va-et-vient /vaevjɛ̃/ nm inv toing and froing; (de personnes) comings and goings; **faire le** ~ go to and fro; (interrupteur) two-way switch.

vagabond, ~e /vagabɔ̃, -d/ nm, f vagrant.

vagin /vaʒɛ̃/ nm vagina.

vague /vag/ adj vague. •nm **regarder dans le** ~ stare into space; **il est resté dans le** ~ he was vague about it. •nf wave; ~ **de fond** ground swell; ~ **de**

froid cold spell; **~ de chaleur** heatwave.

vaillant, **~e** /vajɑ̃, -t/ adj brave; (vigoureux) strong.

vaille /vaj/ ▷ VALOIR 60.

vain, **~e** /vɛ̃, vɛn/ adj vain, futile; **en ~** in vain.

vaincre /vɛ̃kʀ/ 59 vt defeat; (surmonter) overcome. **vaincu**, **~e** nm, f (Sport) loser. **vainqueur** nm victor; (Sport) winner.

vais /vɛ/ ▷ ALLER 8.

vaisseau (pl **~x**) /vɛso/ nm ship; (veine) vessel; **~ spatial** spaceship.

vaisselle /vɛsɛl/ nf crockery; (à laver) dishes; **faire la ~** do the washing-up, wash the dishes; **liquide ~** washing-up liquid.

valable /valabl/ adj valid; (de qualité) worthwhile.

valet /valɛ/ nm (aux cartes) jack; **~ (de chambre)** manservant.

valeur /valœʀ/ nf value; (mérite) worth, value; **~s** (Comm) stocks and shares; **avoir de la ~** be valuable; **prendre/perdre de la ~** go up/down in value; **objets de ~** valuables; **sans ~** worthless.

valide /valid/ adj (personne) fit; (billet) valid. **valider** 1 vt validate.

valise /valiz/ nf (suit) case; **faire ses ~s** pack (one's bags).

vallée /vale/ nf valley.

valoir /valwaʀ/ 60 vi (mériter) be worth; (égaler) be as good as; (être valable) (règle) apply; **faire ~** (mérite, qualité) emphasize; (terrain) cultivate; (droit) assert; **se faire ~** put oneself forward; **~ cher/100 euros** be worth a lot/100 euros; **que vaut ce vin?** what's this wine like?; **ne rien ~** be useless ou no good; **ça ne me dit rien qui vaille** I don't like the sound of that; **~ la peine** or **le coup** [1] be worth it; **il vaut/vaudrait mieux faire** it

is/would be better to do. ●vt **~ qch à qn** (éloges, critiques) earn sb sth; (admiration) win sb sth. ■ **se ~** vpr (être équivalents) be as good as each other; **ça se vaut** it's all the same.

valoriser /valɔʀize/ 1 vt add value to; (produit) promote; (profession) make attractive; (région, ressources) develop.

valse /vals/ nf waltz.

vandale /vɑ̃dal/ nmf vandal.

vanille /vanij/ nf vanilla.

vanité /vanite/ nf vanity. **vaniteux, -euse** adj vain, conceited.

vanne /van/ nf (d'écluse) sluicegate; (propos [1]) dig [1]

vantard, **~e** /vɑ̃taʀ, -d/ adj boastful. ●nm, f boaster.

vanter /vɑ̃te/ 1 vt praise. ■ **se ~** vpr boast (**de** about); **se ~ de faire** pride oneself on doing.

vapeur /vapœʀ/ nf (eau) steam; (brume, émanation) vapour; **~s** fumes; **à ~** (bateau, locomotive) steam; **faire cuire à la ~** steam.

vaporisateur /vapɔʀizatœʀ/ nm spray, atomizer. **vaporiser** 1 vt spray.

varappe /vaʀap/ nf rock-climbing.

variable /vaʀjabl/ adj variable; (temps) changeable.

varicelle /vaʀisɛl/ nf chickenpox.

varié, **~e** /vaʀje/ adj (non monotone, étendu) varied; (divers) various; **sandwichs ~s** a selection of sandwiches.

varier /vaʀje/ 45 vt/i vary.

variété /vaʀjete/ nf variety; **spectacle de ~s** variety show.

vase /vɑz/ nm vase. ●nf silt, mud.

vaseux, -euse /vɑzø, -z/ adj (confus [1]) woolly, hazy.

vaste /vast/ adj vast, huge.

vaurien, **~ne** /voʀjɛ̃, -ɛn/ nm, f

V

good-for-nothing.

vautour /votuʀ/ nm vulture.

vautrer (se) /(sə)votʀe/ **1** vpr sprawl; **se ~ dans** (vice, boue) wallow in.

veau (pl ~x) /vo/ nm calf; (viande) veal; (cuir) calfskin.

vécu, ~e /veky/ adj (réel) true, real. ▷VIVRE 82.

vedette /vədɛt/ nf (artiste) star; **en ~** (objet) in a prominent position; (personne) in the limelight; **joueur ~** star player; (bateau) launch.

végétal (mpl **-aux**) /veʒetal, -o/ adj plant. • nm (pl **-aux**) plant.

végétalien, ~ne /veʒetaljɛ̃, -ɛn/ adj & nm, f vegan.

végétarien, ~ne /veʒetaʀjɛ̃, -ɛn/ adj & nm, f vegetarian.

végétation /veʒetasjɔ̃/ nf vegetation; **~s** (Méd) adenoids.

véhicule /veikyl/ nm vehicle.

veille /vɛj/ nf (état) wakefulness; (jour précédent) **la ~ (de)** the day before; **la ~ de Noël** Christmas Eve; **à la ~ de** on the eve of; **la ~ au soir** the previous evening.

veillée /veje/ nf evening (gathering).

veiller /veje/ **1** vi stay up; (monter la garde) be on watch. • vt (malade) watch over; **~ à** attend to; **~ sur** watch over.

veilleur /vɛjœʀ/ nm **~ de nuit** night-watchman.

veilleuse /vɛjøz/ nf night light; (de véhicule) sidelight; (de réchaud) pilot light; **mettre qch en ~** put sth on the back burner.

veine /vɛn/ nf (Anat) vein; (nervure, filon) vein; (chance **1**) luck; **avoir de la ~ 1** be lucky.

véliplanchiste /veliplɑ̃ʃist/ nmf windsurfer.

vélo /velo/ nm bike; (activité) cycling; **faire du ~** go cycling; **~ tout terrain** mountain bike.

vélomoteur /velomotœʀ/ nm moped.

velours /v(ə)luʀ/ nm velvet; **~ côtelé** corduroy.

velouté, ~e /vəlute/ adj smooth. • nm (Culin) **~ d'asperges** cream of asparagus soup.

vendanges /vɑ̃dɑ̃ʒ/ nfpl grape harvest.

vendeur, -euse /vɑ̃dœʀ, -øz/ nm, f shop assistant; (marchand) salesman, saleswoman; (Jur) vendor, seller.

vendre /vɑ̃dʀ/ **3** vt sell; **à ~** for sale. ■ **se ~** vpr (être vendu) be sold; (trouver acquéreur) sell; **se ~ bien** sell well.

vendredi /vɑ̃dʀədi/ nm Friday; **V~ saint** Good Friday.

vénéneux, -euse /venenø, -z/ adj poisonous.

vénérer /venere/ **14** vt revere.

vénérien, ~ne /veneʀjɛ̃, -ɛn/ adj **maladie ~ne** venereal disease.

vengeance /vɑ̃ʒɑ̃s/ nf revenge, vengeance.

venger /vɑ̃ʒe/ **40** vt avenge. ■ **se ~** vpr take ou get one's revenge (**de qch** for sth; **de qn** on sb).

vengeur, -eresse /vɑ̃ʒœʀ, -əʀɛs/ adj vengeful. • nm, f avenger.

venimeux, -euse /vənimø, -z/ adj poisonous, venomous.

venin /vənɛ̃/ nm venom.

venir /vəniʀ/ **58** vi (aux être) come (**de** from); **faire ~ qn** send for sb, call sb; **en ~ à** come to; **en ~ aux mains** come to blows; **où veut-elle en ~?** what is she driving at?; **il m'est venu à l'esprit** or **à l'idée que** it occurred to me that; **s'il venait à pleuvoir** if it should rain; **dans les jours à ~** in the next few days. • v aux ~ **de faire** have just done; **il vient/venait d'arriver** he has/had just arrived; **~ faire** come to do; **viens voir** come and see.

vent /vɑ̃/ nm wind; **il fait du ~** it is windy; **être dans le ~** 🗓 be trendy.

vente /vɑ̃t/ nf sale; **~ (aux enchères)** auction; **en ~** on ou for sale; **mettre qch en ~** put sth up for sale; **~ de charité** (charity) bazaar; **~ au détail/en gros** retailing/wholesaling; **équipe de ~** sales team.

ventilateur /vɑ̃tilatœʀ/ nm fan, ventilator. **ventiler** 🗓 vt ventilate.

ventouse /vɑ̃tuz/ nf suction pad; (pour déboucher) plunger.

ventre /vɑ̃tʀ/ nm stomach; (d'animal) belly; (utérus) womb; **avoir du ~** have a paunch.

venu, ~e /vəny/ adj **bien ~** (à propos) apt, timely; **mal ~** badly timed; **il serait mal ~ de faire** it wouldn't be a good idea to do. ● ▷ VENIR 59

venue /vəny/ nf coming.

ver /vɛʀ/ nm worm; (dans la nourriture) maggot; (du bois) woodworm; **~ luisant** glow-worm; **~ à soie** silkworm; **~ solitaire** tapeworm; **~ de terre** earthworm.

verbal, ~e (mpl **-aux**) /vɛʀbal, -o/ adj verbal.

verbe /vɛʀb/ nm verb.

verdir /vɛʀdiʀ/ 🗓 vi turn green.

véreux, -euse /veʀø, -z/ adj wormy; (malhonnête) shady.

verger /vɛʀʒe/ nm orchard.

verglas /vɛʀɡlɑ/ nm black ice.

véridique /veʀidik/ adj true.

vérification /veʀifikasjɔ̃/ nf check(ing), verification.

vérifier /veʀifje/ 45 vt check, verify; (confirmer) confirm.

véritable /veʀitabl/ adj true, real; (authentique) real.

vérité /veʀite/ nf truth; (de tableau, roman) realism; **en ~** in fact, actually.

vermine /vɛʀmin/ nf vermin.

verni, ~e /vɛʀni/ adj (chaussures) patent (leather); (chanceux 🗓) lucky.

vernir /vɛʀniʀ/ 🗓 vt varnish. ▪■ se **~** vpr se **~ les ongles** apply nail polish.

vernis /vɛʀni/ nm varnish; (de poterie) glaze; **~ à ongles** nail polish.

verra, verrait /vɛʀa, vɛʀɛ/ ▷ VOIR 64

verre /vɛʀ/ nm glass; (de lunettes) lens; **~ à vin** wine glass; **prendre** ou **boire un ~** have a drink; **~ de contact** contact lens; **~ dépoli** frosted glass.

verrière /vɛʀjɛʀ/ nf (toit) glass roof; (paroi) glass wall.

verrou /vɛʀu/ nm bolt; **sous les ~s** behind bars.

verrouillage /veʀujaʒ/ nm **~ central** ou **centralisé (des portes)** central locking.

verrue /vɛʀy/ nf wart; **~ plantaire** verruca.

vers[1] /vɛʀ/ prép towards; (aux environs de) (temps) about; (lieu) near, around; (période) towards; **~ le soir** towards evening.

vers[2] /vɛʀ/ nm (poésie) line of verse.

versatile /vɛʀsatil/ adj unpredictable, volatile.

verse: à ~ /avɛʀs/ loc in torrents.

Verseau /vɛʀso/ nm **le ~** Aquarius.

versement /vɛʀsəmɑ̃/ nm payment; (échelonné) instalment.

verser /vɛʀse/ 🗓 vt/i pour; (larmes, sang) shed; (payer) pay. ● vi pour; (voiture) overturn; **~ dans** (fig) lapse into.

version /vɛʀsjɔ̃/ nf version; (traduction) translation.

verso /vɛʀso/ nm back (of the page); **voir au ~** see overleaf.

vert, ~e /vɛʀ, -t/ adj green; (vieillard) sprightly. • nm green; **les ~s** the Greens.

vertèbre /vɛʀtɛbʀ/ nf vertebra; **se déplacer une ~** slip a disc.

vertical, ~e (mpl -aux) /vɛʀtikal, -o/ adj vertical.

vertige /vɛʀtiʒ/ nm dizziness; ~s dizzy spells; **avoir le ~** feel dizzy. **vertigineux, -euse** adj dizzy; (très grand) staggering.

vertu /vɛʀty/ nf virtue; **en ~ de** in accordance with. **vertueux, -euse** adj virtuous.

verveine /vɛʀvɛn/ nf verbena.

vessie /vesi/ nf bladder.

veste /vɛst/ nf jacket.

vestiaire /vɛstjɛʀ/ nm cloakroom; (Sport) changing-room; (US) locker-room.

vestibule /vɛstibyl/ nm hall; (Théât, d'hôtel) foyer.

vestige /vɛstiʒ/ nm (objet) relic; (trace) vestige.

veston /vɛstɔ̃/ nm jacket.

vêtement /vɛtmã/ nm article of clothing; ~s clothes, clothing.

vétéran /veteʀã/ nm veteran.

vétérinaire /veteʀinɛʀ/ nmf vet, veterinary surgeon, (US) veterinarian.

vêtir /vetiʀ/ **61** vt dress. ■ se ~ vpr dress.

veto* /veto/ nm inv veto.

vêtu, ~e /vety/ adj dressed (**de** in).

veuf, veuve /vœf, -vœf/ adj widowed. • nm, f widower, widow.

veuille /vœj/ ▷VOULOIR **64**.

veut, veux /vø/ ▷VOULOIR **64**.

vexation /vɛksasjɔ̃/ nf humiliation.

vexer /vɛkse/ **1** vt upset, hurt. ■ se ~ vpr be upset, be hurt.

viable /vjabl/ adj viable; (projet) feasible.

viande /vjãd/ nf meat.

vibrer /vibʀe/ **1** vi vibrate; **faire ~** (âme, foules) stir.

vicaire /vikɛʀ/ nm curate.

vice /vis/ nm (moral) vice; (physique) defect.

vicier /visje/ **45** vt contaminate; (air) pollute.

vicieux, -ieuse /visjø, -z/ adj depraved. • nm, f pervert.

victime /viktim/ nf victim; (d'un accident) casualty.

victoire /viktwaʀ/ nf victory; (Sport) win. **victorieux, -ieuse** adj victorious; (équipe) winning.

vidange /vidãʒ/ nf emptying; (Auto) oil change; (tuyau) waste pipe ou outlet.

vide /vid/ adj empty. • nm (absence, manque) vacuum, void; (espace) space; (trou) gap; (sans air) vacuum; **à ~** empty; **emballé sous ~** vacuum packed; **suspendu dans le ~** dangling in space.

vide-greniers* /vidgʀənje/ nm inv bric-a-brac sale.

vidéo /video/ adj inv video; **jeu ~** video game. • nf video. **vidéocassette** nf video (tape). **vidéoclip** nm music video. **vidéoconférence** nf videoconferencing; (séance) videoconference. **vidéodisque** nm videodisc. **vidéophone** nm videophone.

vide-ordures* /vidɔʀdyʀ/ nm inv rubbish chute.

vidéothèque /videotɛk/ nf video library.

vider /vide/ **1** vt empty; (poisson) gut; (expulser **1**) throw out. ■ se ~ vpr empty.

vie /vi/ nf life; (durée) lifetime; **à ~, pour la ~** for life; **donner la ~ à** give birth to; **en ~** alive; **la ~ est chère** the cost of living is high.

vieil /vjɛj/ ▷ VIEUX.

vieillard /vjɛjaʀ/ nm old man.

vieille /vjɛj/ ▷ VIEUX.

vieillesse /vjɛjɛs/ nf old age.

vieillir /vjɛjiʀ/ **2** vi grow old, age; (mot, idée) become old-fashioned. ●vt age. **vieillissement** nm ageing.

viens, vient /vjɛ̃/ ▷ VENIR 59.

vierge /vjɛʀʒ/ nf virgin; **la V~** Virgo. ●adj virgin; (feuille, cassette) blank; (cahier, pellicule) unused, new.

vieux (**vieil** before vowel or mute h), **vieille** (mpl **vieux**) /vjø, vjɛj/ adj old. ●nm, f old man, old woman; **petit ~** little old man; **les ~** old people; **vieille fille** (péj) spinster; **~ garçon** old bachelor. **vieux jeu** adj inv old-fashioned.

vif, vive /vif, viv/ adj (animé) lively; (émotion, vent) keen; (froid) biting; (lumière) bright; (douleur, contraste, parole) sharp; (souvenir, style, teint) vivid; (succès, impatience) great; **brûler/enterrer ~** burn/bury alive; **de vive voix** personally. ●nm **à ~** (plaie) open; **avoir les nerfs à ~** be on edge; **blessé au ~** cut to the quick.

vigie /viʒi/ nf lookout.

vigilant, ~e /viʒilɑ̃, -t/ adj vigilant.

Vigipirate /viʒipiʀat/ nm government public security measures.

vigne /viɲ/ nf (plante) vine; (vignoble) vineyard. **vigneron, ~ne** nm, f wine-grower.

vignette /viɲɛt/ nf (étiquette) label; (Auto) road tax disc.

vignoble /viɲɔbl/ nm vineyard.

vigoureux, -euse /viguʀø, -z/ adj vigorous, sturdy.

vigueur /vigœʀ/ nf vigour; **être/ entrer en ~** (loi) be/come into force; **en ~** current.

VIH abrév m (**virus**

immunodéficitaire humain) HIV.

vilain, ~e /vilɛ̃, -ɛn/ adj (mauvais) nasty; (laid) ugly. ●nm, f naughty boy, naughty girl.

villa /villa/ nf detached house.

village /vilaʒ/ nm village.

villageois, ~e /vilaʒwa, -z/ adj village. ●nm, f villager.

ville /vil/ nf town; (importante) city; **~ d'eaux** spa.

vin /vɛ̃/ nm wine; **~ d'honneur** reception.

vinaigre /vinɛgʀ/ nm vinegar. **vinaigrette** nf oil and vinegar dressing, vinaigrette.

vingt /vɛ̃/ (/vɛ̃t/ before vowel and in numbers 22-29) adj & nm twenty.

vingtaine /vɛ̃tɛn/ nf **une ~ (de)** about twenty.

vingtième /vɛ̃tjɛm/ adj & nmf twentieth.

vinicole /vinikɔl/ adj wine(- producing).

viol /vjɔl/ nm (de femme) rape; (de lieu, loi) violation.

violemment /vjɔlamɑ̃/ adv violently.

violence /vjɔlɑ̃s/ nf violence; (acte) act of violence. **violent, ~e** adj violent.

violer /vjɔle/ **1** vt rape; (lieu, loi) violate.

violet, ~te /vjɔlɛ, -t/ adj purple. ●nm purple. **violette** nf violet.

violon /vjɔlɔ̃/ nm violin; **~ d'Ingres** hobby.

violoncelle /vjɔlɔ̃sɛl/ nm cello.

vipère /vipɛʀ/ nf viper, adder.

virage /viʀaʒ/ nm bend; (en ski) turn; (changement d'attitude: fig) change of course.

virée /viʀe/ nf **1** trip, tour; (en voiture) drive; (à vélo) ride.

virement /viʀmɑ̃/ nm (Comm) (credit) transfer; **~**

automatique standing order.

virer /viʀe/ **1** vi turn; **~ de bord** tack; (fig) do a U-turn; **~ au rouge** turn red. • vt (argent) transfer; (expulser **1**) throw out; (élève) expel; (licencier **1**) fire.

virgule /viʀgyl/ nf comma; (dans un nombre) (decimal) point.

viril, ~e /viʀil/ adj virile.

virtuel, ~le /viʀtɥɛl/ adj (potentiel) potential; (mémoire, réalité) virtual.

virulent, ~e /viʀylã, -t/ adj virulent.

virus /viʀys/ nm virus.

vis[1] /vi/ ▷VIVRE 62, ▷VOIR 63.

vis[2] /vis/ nf screw.

visa /viza/ nm visa.

visage /vizaʒ/ nm face.

vis-à-vis /vizavi/ prép **~ de** (en face de) opposite; (à l'égard de) in relation to; (comparé à) compared to, beside. • nm inv (personne) person opposite; **en ~** opposite each other.

visée /vize/ nf aim; **avoir des ~s sur** have designs on.

viser /vize/ **1** vt (cible, centre) aim at; (poste, résultats) aim for; (concerner) be aimed at; (document) stamp; **~ à** aim at; (mesure, propos) be aimed at; **~ à faire** aim to do. • vi aim.

viseur /vizœʀ/ nm (d'arme) sights (+ pl); (Photo) viewfinder.

visière /vizjɛʀ/ nf (de casquette) peak; (de casque) visor.

vision /vizjõ/ nf vision.

visite /vizit/ nf visit; (pour inspecter) inspection; (personne) visitor; **heures de ~** visiting hours; **~ guidée** guided tour; **~ médicale** medical; **rendre ~ à, faire une ~ à** pay a visit; **être en ~ (chez qn)** be visiting (sb); **avoir de la ~** have visitors.

visiter /vizite/ **1** vt visit; (appartement) view. **visiteur, -euse** nm, f visitor.

visser /vise/ vt screw (on).

visuel, ~le /vizɥɛl/ adj visual. • nm (Ordinat) visual display unit, VDU.

vit /vi/ ▷VIVRE 62, ▷VOIR 63.

vital, ~e (mpl **-aux**) /vital, -o/ adj vital.

vitamine /vitamin/ nf vitamin.

vite /vit/ adv fast, quickly; (tôt) soon; **~!** quick!; **faire ~** be quick; **au plus ~, le plus ~ possible** as quickly as possible.

vitesse /vites/ nf speed; (régime: Auto) gear; **à toute ~** at top speed; **en ~** in a hurry, quickly; **boîte à cinq ~s** five-speed gearbox.

viticole /vitikɔl/ adj (industrie) wine; (région) wine-producing. **viticulteur** nm wine-grower.

vitrage /vitʀaʒ/ nm (vitres) windows; **double ~** double glazing.

vitrail (pl **-aux**) /vitʀaj, -o/ nm stained-glass window.

vitre /vitʀ/ nf (window) pane; (de véhicule) window.

vitrine /vitʀin/ nf (shop) window; (meuble) display cabinet.

vivace /vivas/ adj (plante) perennial; (durable) enduring.

vivacité /vivasite/ nf liveliness; (agilité) quickness; (d'émotion, d'intelligence) keenness; (de souvenir, style, teint) vividness.

vivant, ~e /vivã, -t/ adj (example, symbole) living; (en vie) alive, living; (actif, vif) lively. • nm **un bon ~** a bon viveur; **de son ~** in his lifetime; **les ~s** the living.

vive[1] /viv/ ▷VIF.

vive[2] /viv/ interj **~ le roi!** long live the king!

vivement /vivmã/ adv (fortement) strongly; (vite, sèchement) sharply; (avec éclat) vividly; (beaucoup) greatly; **~ la fin!** I'll be glad when it's the end!

vivier /vivje/ nm fish pond; (artificiel) fish tank.

vivifier /vivifje/ ⁴⁵ vt invigorate.

vivre /vivʀ/ ⁶³ vi live; ~ **de** (nourriture) live on; ~ **encore** be still alive; **faire** ~ (famille) support. •vt (vie) live; (période, aventure) live through.

vivres /vivʀ/ nmpl supplies.

VO abrév f (**version originale**) **en** ~ in the original language.

vocabulaire /vɔkabylɛʀ/ nm vocabulary.

vocal, ~e (mpl **-aux**) /vɔkal, -o/ adj vocal.

vœu (pl ~**x**) /vø/ nm (souhait) wish; (promesse) vow; **meilleurs ~x** best wishes.

vogue /vɔg/ nf fashion, vogue; **en** ~ in fashion ou vogue.

voguer /vɔge/ ¹ vi sail.

voici /vwasi/ prép here is, this is; (au pluriel) here are, these are; **me** ~ here I am; ~ **un an** (temps passé) a year ago; ~ **un an que** it is a year since.

voie /vwa/ nf (route) road; (partie de route) lane; (chemin) way; (moyen) means, way; (rails) track; (quai) platform; **en** ~ **de** in the process of; **en** ~ **de développement** (pays) developing; **espèce en** ~ **de disparition** endangered species; **par la** ~ **des airs** by air; **par** ~ **orale** orally; **sur la bonne/ mauvaise** ~ (fig) on the right/ wrong track; **montrer la** ~ lead the way; ~ **de dégagement** slip-road; ~ **ferrée** railway; (US) railroad; **V~ lactée** Milky Way; ~ **navigable** waterway; ~ **publique** public highway; ~ **sans issue** (sur panneau) no through road; (fig) dead end.

voilà /vwala/ prép here is, that is; (au pluriel) there are, those are; (voici) here is, here are; **le** ~ there he is; ~**!** right!; (en offrant

qch) there you are!; ~ **un an** (temps passé) a year ago; ~ **un an que** it is a year since; **tu en veux? en** ~ do you want some? here you are; **en** ~ **des histoires!** what a fuss!; **et** ~ **que** and then.

voilage /vwalaʒ/ nm net curtain.

voile /vwal/ nf (de bateau) sail; (Sport) sailing. •nm veil; (tissu léger) net.

voilé, ~e /vwale/ adj (allusion, femme) veiled; (flou) hazy.

voiler /vwale/ ¹ vt (dissimuler) veil; (déformer) buckle. ■ **se** ~ vpr (devenir flou) become hazy; (se déformer) (roue) buckle.

voilier /vwalje/ nm sailing ship.

voir /vwaʀ/ ⁶⁴ vt see; **faire** ~ **qch à qn** show sth to sb; **laisser** ~ show; **avoir quelque chose à** ~ **avec** have something to do with; **ça n'a rien à** ~ that's got nothing to do with it; **je ne peux pas le** ~ ⁣☒ I can't stand him. •vi **y** ~ be able to see; **je n'y vois rien** I cannot see; ~ **trouble** have blurred vision; **voyons** let's see now; **voyons, soyez sages!** come on now, behave yourselves! ■ **se** ~ vpr (dans la glace) see oneself; (être visible) show; (se produire) be seen; (se trouver) find oneself; (se fréquenter, se rencontrer) see each other; (être vu) be seen.

voire /vwaʀ/ adv or even, not to say.

voirie /vwaʀi/ nf (service) highway maintenance.

voisin, ~e /vwazɛ̃, -in/ adj (de voisinage) neighbouring; (proche) nearby; (adjacent) next (**de** to); (semblable) similar (**de** to). •nm, f neighbour; **le** ~ the man next door, the neighbour. **voisinage** nm neighbourhood; (proximité) proximity.

voiture /vwatyʀ/ nf (motor) car; (wagon) coach, carriage; **en** ~**!** all aboard!; ~ **bélier** ramraiding car; ~ **à cheval** horse-drawn carriage; ~ **de course** racing car; ~ **école** driving school car; ~ **d'enfant** pram; (US) baby carriage; ~ **de tourisme** saloon car.

voix /vwa/ nf voice; (suffrage) vote; **à ~ basse** in a whisper.

vol /vɔl/ nm (d'avion, d'oiseau) flight; (groupe d'oiseaux) flock, flight; (délit) theft; (hold-up) robbery; ~ **à l'étalage** shoplifting; ~ **à la tire** pickpocketing; **à ~ d'oiseau** as the crow flies; **de haut** ~ high-ranking; ~ **libre** hang-gliding; ~ **à voile** gliding.

volaille /vɔlaj/ nf **la ~** (poules) poultry; **une ~** a fowl.

volant /vɔlɑ̃/ nm (steering-)wheel; (de jupe) flounce; (de badminton) shuttlecock; **donner un coup de ~** turn the wheel sharply.

volcan /vɔlkɑ̃/ nm volcano.

volée /vɔle/ nf flight; (oiseaux) flight, flock; (de coups, d'obus, au tennis) volley; **à toute ~** hard; **à la ~** in flight, in mid-air.

voler /vɔle/ **1** vi (oiseau) fly; (dérober) steal (**à** from). •vt steal; ~ **qn** rob sb; **il ne l'a pas volé** he deserved it.

volet /vɔlɛ/ nm (de fenêtre) shutter; (de document) (folded ou tear-off) section; **trié sur le ~** hand-picked.

voleur, -euse /vɔlœr, -øz/ nm, f thief; **au ~!** stop thief! •adj thieving.

volley-ball* /vɔlɛbol/ nm volleyball.

volontaire /vɔlɔ̃tɛr/ adj (délibéré) voluntary; (opiniâtre) determined. •nmf volunteer. **volontairement** adv voluntarily; (exprès) intentionally.

volonté /vɔlɔ̃te/ nf (faculté, intention) will; (souhait) wish; (énergie) willpower; **à ~** (comme on veut) as required; **du vin à ~** unlimited wine; **bonne ~** goodwill; **mauvaise ~** ill will.

volontiers /vɔlɔ̃tje/ adv (de bon gré) with pleasure, willingly, gladly; (admettre) readily.

volt /vɔlt/ nm volt.

volte-face* /vɔltəfas/ nf inv (fig) U-turn; **faire ~** do a U-turn.

voltige /vɔltiʒ/ nf acrobatics (+ pl).

volume /vɔlym/ nm volume.

volumineux, -euse /vɔlyminø, -z/ adj bulky; (livre, dossier) thick.

volupté /vɔlypte/ nf voluptuousness.

vomi /vɔmi/ nm vomit.

vomir /vɔmir/ **2** vt vomit; (fig) belch out. •vi be sick, vomit.

vomissement /vɔmismɑ̃/ nm vomiting; ~**s du matin** morning sickness.

vont /vɔ̃/ ▷ALLER **8**.

vorace /vɔras/ adj voracious.

vos /vo/ ▷VOTRE.

votant, ~e /vɔtɑ̃, -t/ nm, f voter.

vote /vɔt/ nm (action) voting; (suffrage) vote; ~ **d'une loi** passing of a bill; ~ **par correspondance/procuration** postal/proxy vote.

voter /vɔte/ **1** vi vote. •vt vote for; (adopter) pass; (crédits) vote.

votre (pl **vos**) /vɔtr, vo/ adj your.

vôtre /votr/ pron **le** ou **la ~, les ~s** yours.

vouer /vwe/ **1** vt (vie, temps) dedicate (**à** to); **voué à l'échec** doomed to failure.

vouloir /vulwar/ **64** vt (exiger) want (**faire** to do); (souhaiter) want; **que veux-tu boire?** what

V

would you like to drink?; **je voudrais bien y aller** I'd really like to go; **je veux bien venir** I'm happy to come; **comme tu voudras** as you wish; (accepter) **veuillez vous asseoir** please sit down; **veuillez patienter** (au téléphone) please hold the line; (signifier) ∼ **dire** mean; **qu'est-ce que cela veut dire?** what does that mean?; **en** ∼ **à qn** bear a grudge against sb. ▪ **s'en** ∼ vpr regret; **je m'en veux de lui avoir dit** I really regret having told her.

voulu, ∼**e** /vuly/ adj (délibéré) intentional; (requis) required.

vous /vu/ pron (sujet, complément) you; (indirect) (to) you; (réfléchi) yourself; (pluriel) yourselves; (l'un l'autre) each other. **vous-même** pron yourself. **vous-mêmes** pron yourselves.

voûte* /vut/ nf (plafond) vault; (porche) archway.

vouvoiement /vuvwamɑ̃/ nm use of the 'vous' form. **vouvoyer** 31 vt address using the 'vous' form.

voyage /vwajaʒ/ nm trip; (déplacement) journey; (par mer) voyage; ∼**(s)** (action) travelling; ∼ **d'affaires** business trip; ∼ **d'études** study trip; ∼ **de noces** honeymoon; ∼ **organisé** (package) tour.

voyager /vwajaʒe/ 40 vi travel.

voyageur, -euse /vwajaʒœʀ, -øz/ nm, f traveller; (passager) passenger; ∼ **de commerce** travelling salesman.

voyant, ∼**e** /vwajɑ̃, -t/ adj gaudy. ● nm (signal) (warning) light.

voyelle /vwajɛl/ nf vowel.

voyou /vwaju/ nm hooligan.

vrac: en ∼ /ɑ̃vʀak/ loc (pêle-mêle) haphazardly; (sans emballage) loose; (en gros) in bulk.

vrai, ∼**e** /vʀɛ/ adj true; (authentique) real. ● nm truth; **à** ∼ **dire** to tell the truth; **pour de** ∼ for real. **vraiment** adv really.

vraisemblable /vʀɛsɑ̃blabl/ adj (probable) likely; (excuse, histoire) plausible. **vraisemblablement** adv probably. **vraisemblance** nf likelihood, plausibility.

vrombir /vʀɔ̃biʀ/ 2 vi roar.

VRP abrév m (**voyageur représentant placier**) rep, representative.

VTC abrév m (**vélo tous chemins**) hybrid bike.

VTT abrév m (**vélo tout terrain**) mountain bike.

vu, ∼**e** /vy/ adj **bien** ∼ well thought of; **ce serait plutôt mal** ∼ it wouldn't go down well; **bien** ∼**!** good point! ● prép in view of; ∼ **que** seeing that. ● ▷ **VOIR** 64.

vue /vy/ nf (spectacle) sight; (vision) (eye) sight; (panorama, idée, image, photo) view; **avoir en** ∼ have in mind; **à** ∼ (tirer) on sight; (payable) at sight; **de** ∼ by sight; **perdre de** ∼ lose sight of; **en** ∼ (proche) in sight; (célèbre) in the public eye; **en** ∼ **de faire** with a view to doing; **à** ∼ **d'œil** visibly; **avoir des** ∼s **sur** have designs on.

vulgaire /vylgɛʀ/ adj (grossier) vulgar; (ordinaire) common.

vulnérable /vylneʀabl/ adj vulnerable.

V

Ww

wagon /vagɔ̃/ nm (de voyageurs) carriage; (de marchandises) wagon. **wagon-lit** (pl **wagons-lits**) nm sleeper. **wagon-restaurant** (pl **wagons-restaurants**) nm restaurant car.

walkman® /wokman/ nm personal stereo, walkman®.

waters* /watɛʀ/ nmpl toilets.

watt /wat/ nm watt.

wc /(dublə)vese/ nmpl toilet (+ sg).

Web /wɛb/ nm Web; **un site** ~ a website; **une page** ~ web page.

webcam /wɛbkam/ nf webcam.

webmestre /wɛbmɛstʀ/ nm webmaster.

week-end* /wikɛnd/ nm weekend.

whisky* (pl **-ies**) /wiski/ nm whisky.

Xx

xénophobe /gzenɔfɔb/ adj xenophobic. •nmf xenophobe.

xérès /gzeʀɛs/ nm sherry.

xylophone /ksilɔfon/ nm xylophone.

W

Yy

y /i/
- adverbe
····▸ there; (dessus) on it; (pluriel) on them; (dedans) in it; (pluriel) in them; **j'∼ vais** I'm on my way; **n'∼ va pas** don't go; **du lait? il n'∼ en a pas** milk? there's none; **tu n'∼ arriveras jamais** you'll never manage it.
- pronom
····▸ **s'∼ habituer** get used to it.
····▸ **s'∼ attendre** expect it.
····▸ **∼ penser** think about it.
····▸ **∼ être pour qch** have sth to do with it.

yaourt /'jauʀ(t)/ nm yoghurt.
  yaourtière nf yoghurt-maker.

yard /'jaʀd/ nm yard (= 91,44 cm).

yen /'jɛn/ nm yen.

yeux /jø/ ▷ ŒIL.

yoga /'jɔga/ nm yoga.

yougoslave /'jugɔslav/ adj Yugoslav. **Y∼** nmf Yugoslav.

Yougoslavie /'jugɔslavi/ nf Yugoslavia.

yo-yo®* /'jojo/ nm inv yo-yo®.

Zz

zapper /zape/ **1** vi (à la télévision) channel-hop.

zèbre /zɛbʀ/ nm zebra.

zèle /zɛl/ nm zeal.

zéro /zeʀo/ nm nought, zero; (température) zero; (Sport) nil; (tennis) love; (personne) nonentity; **partir de ∼** start from scratch; **repartir à ∼** start all over again.

zeste /zɛst/ nm peel; **un ∼ de** (fig) a touch of.

zézayer /zezeje/ **31** vi lisp.

zigzag /zigzag/ nm zigzag; **en ∼** winding.

zinc /zɛ̃g/ nm (métal) zinc; (comptoir 1) bar.

zizanie /zizani/ nf discord; **semer la ∼** put the cat among the pigeons.

zizi /zizi/ nm 1 willy.

zodiaque /zɔdjak/ nm zodiac.

zona /zona/ nm (Méd) shingles (+ sg).

zone /zon/ nf zone, area; (banlieue pauvre) slums; **∼ bleue** restricted parking zone; **∼ euro** eurozone.

zoo /zo(o)/ nm zoo.

zoom /zum/ nm zoom lens.

zut /zyt/ interj 1 damn 1.

Test yourself with word games

This section contains a number of word games which will help you to use your dictionary more effectively and to build up your knowledge of French vocabulary and usage in an entertaining way. You will find answers to all puzzles and games at the end of the section.

1 Madame Irma

Madame Irma is very good at predicting the future, but she is not very good at conjugating French verbs in the future tense. Help her to replace all the verbs in brackets with the correct future form.

Lion 23 juillet–22 août

Cette semaine, les Lions (être) à la fête.
Travail: Il ne (falloir) pas vous laisser
démoraliser par les problèmes et les
discussions qui (pouvoir) surgir en début
de semaine. Les 19 et 20 avril vous (offrir) la
possibilité d'un changement radical dans votre
carrière. Pourquoi ne pas saisir votre chance? **Santé**: Le
stress ne vous (épargner) pas, surtout le 18. Attention!
Pour décompresser, faites un peu de sport et tout (aller)
bien. **Amitié**: Vous êtes très sociable et cette semaine,
vous vous (faire) encore de nouveaux amis. **Côté cœur**:
Vénus (veiller) sur vous. Une nouvelle rencontre
(survenir) peut-être. Si vous avez un partenaire,
votre relation (être) au beau fixe.

---

2 Power cut

Unfortunately, there was a power cut while Jean was writing a computer manual for his office staff. He had just begun to label his diagram of a computer. Can you help Jean unscramble the letters and get on with his labelling?

TURANIDORE

VARICLE

ROUSSI

QUITTEDES

NARCE

RUCRUSE

MOCR-D

3 The odd meaning out

Watch out: one word can have different meanings. In the following exercise, only two of the suggested translations are correct. Use the dictionary to spot the odd one out, then find the correct French translation for it.

example:

blindé   ❑ armoured
           ☑ blind
           ❑ immune

blind = aveugle

gauche   ❑ left
          ❑ gauge
          ❑ awkward

lentille ❑ lentil
         ❑ lens
         ❑ lent

porte   ❑ door
         ❑ carry
         ❑ port (wine)

duvet   ❑ duvet
         ❑ down
         ❑ sleeping-bag

4 Word magnets

Antoine's brother took all his magnets off the fridge door to wipe it clean. He put them back the wrong way round. Can you help Antoine rewrite the correct sentences?

| heure | hier | suis | me | levé | bonne | de | je |

_____

| dit | pourtant | je | fois | lui | plusieurs | ai | le |

_____

| sur | sortant | table | les | prends | clés | en | la |

_____

| ira | Portugal | elle | prochaine | au | vacances | l'année | en |

_____

| film | voir | un | allés | cinéma | sommes | nous | au |

_____

| voisine | de | là | frère | pas | le | la | n'est |

_____

5 What are they like?

Here are two lists of adjectives you can use to describe people's characteristics. Each word in the second column is the opposite of one of the adjectives in the first column. Can you link them?

1. grand	**A.** intelligent
2. blond	**B.** méchant
3. bête	**C.** gros
4. énervé	**D.** petit
5. gentil	**E.** sympathique
6. timide	**F.** brun
7. patient	**G.** calme
8. désagréable	**H.** extraverti
9. poli	**I.** impatient
10. maigre	**J.** malpoli

example: 1.D. *grand* est le contraire de *petit*.

Answers

1

seront	ira
faudra	ferez
pourront	veillera
offriront	surviendra
épargnera	sera

2

ordinateur	écran
clavier	curseur
souris	cd-rom
disquette	

3

lent = prêté
port = porto
gauge = jauge
duvet = couette

4

Hier, je me suis levé de bonne heure.
Pourtant, je le lui ai dit plusieurs fois.
Prends les clés sur la table en sortant.
l'année prochaine, elle ira en vacances au Portugal.
Nous sommes allés voir un film au cinéma.
Le frère de la voisine n'est pas là.

5

1. D. *grand* est le contraire de *petit*.
2. F. *blond* est le contraire de *brun*.
3. A. *bête* est le contraire d'*intelligent*.
4. G. *énervé* est le contraire de *calme*.
5. B. *gentil* est le contraire de *méchant*.
6. H. *timide* est le contraire d'*extraverti*.
7. I. *patient* est le contraire d'*impatient*.
8. E. *désagréable* est le contraire de *sympathique*.
9. J. *poli* est le contraire de *malpoli*.
10. C. *maigre* est le contraire de *gros*.

Calendar of French traditions, festivals, and holidays

January

1	8	15	22	29
2	9	16	23	30
3	10	17	24	31
4	11	18	25	
5	12	19	26	
6	13	20	27	
7	14	21	28	

February

1	8	15	22
2	9	16	23
3	10	17	24
4	11	18	25
5	12	19	26
6	13	20	27
7	14	21	28

March

1	8	15	22	29
2	9	16	23	30
3	10	17	24	31
4	11	18	25	
5	12	19	26	
6	13	20	27	
7	14	21	28	

April

1	8	15	22	29
2	9	16	23	30
3	10	17	24	31
4	11	18	25	
5	12	19	26	
6	13	20	27	
7	14	21	28	

May

1	8	15	22	29
2	9	16	23	30
3	10	17	24	31
4	11	18	25	
5	12	19	26	
6	13	20	27	
7	14	21	28	

June

1	8	15	22	29
2	9	16	23	30
3	10	17	24	
4	11	18	25	
5	12	19	26	
6	13	20	27	
7	14	21	28	

July

1	8	15	22	29
2	9	16	23	30
3	10	17	24	31
4	11	18	25	
5	12	19	26	
6	13	20	27	
7	14	21	28	

August

1	8	15	22	29
2	9	16	23	30
3	10	17	24	31
4	11	18	25	
5	12	19	26	
6	13	20	27	
7	14	21	28	

September

1	8	15	22	29
2	9	16	23	30
3	10	17	24	
4	11	18	25	
5	12	19	26	
6	13	20	27	
7	14	21	28	

October

1	8	15	22	29
2	9	16	23	30
3	10	17	24	31
4	11	18	25	
5	12	19	26	
6	13	20	27	
7	14	21	28	

November

1	8	15	22	29
2	9	16	23	30
3	10	17	24	
4	11	18	25	
5	12	19	26	
6	13	20	27	
7	14	21	28	

December

1	8	15	22	29
2	9	16	23	30
3	10	17	24	31
4	11	18	25	
5	12	19	26	
6	13	20	27	
7	14	21	28	

1 January

le jour de l'an (New Year's Day) is a public holiday and a day of family celebration, with a large lunch, traditionally featuring seafood of various kinds.

6 January

la Fête des Rois (Epiphany or Twelfth Night). Around this time, most families have a *galette des Rois*, a rich pastry cake filled with *frangipane* (almond paste). The cake contains a *fève*, literally a bean, as this is what was originally used. Nowadays the *fève* takes the form of a tiny plastic or ceramic figure. The person who gets the *fève* in their portion puts on the cardboard crown which comes with the cake.

2 February

la Chandeleur (Candlemas) is celebrated in the church but is not a public holiday. However, it is traditional to eat *crêpes* (pancakes) on this day.

14 February

la Saint Valentin (St Valentine's Day). As in many other countries, people celebrate a romantic relationship with gifts of flowers or chocolates.

1 April

le premier avril (April Fool's Day). The French also take advantage of this occasion to play tricks on one another, calling out *poisson d'avril!* (literally 'April fish').

1 May

La Fête du Travail (International Labour Day) is a public holiday.

8 May

le 8 mai or **la Fête de la Victoire** is a public holiday commemorating Victory in Europe on 8 May 1945.

24 June

la Saint-Jean (Midsummer's Day). In many areas, bonfires (*les feux de la Saint-Jean*) are lit on Midsummer's Night. People are supposed to jump over these, re-enacting a pagan custom intended to ward off the cold of winter.

14 July

la Fête Nationale or **le 14 juillet** is usually called Bastille Day in English and is a public holiday in France. It commemorates the taking of the Bastille prison in Paris and the liberation of its prisoners by the people of Paris in 1789, one of the first events of the Revolution. All over France there are parades on the day of the 14th and firework displays and *bals* (local dances) either on the night of the 13th or of the 14th.

15 August

l'Assomption (Feast of the Assumption) is a public holiday. Many people in France are either setting off on holiday around the 15th or else returning home, so this is traditionally a very busy time on the roads.

1 November

la Toussaint (All Saints' Day) is a public holiday and the day when people remember their dead relatives and friends, although properly speaking it is All Souls' Day the following day that is set aside for this in the church. People take flowers to the cemetery, particularly chrysanthemums, as these are in bloom at this time. Because of this association, it is best to avoid taking chrysanthemums as a gift for someone. Schoolchildren have a two-week holiday around this time.

11 November

le 11 novembre is a public holiday to commemorate the Armistice of 1918 and a day of remembrance for those who died in the two world wars and in subsequent conflicts. All towns and villages hold parades in which war veterans accompany local officials and a brass band to lay wreaths on the war memorial. In Paris, the President lays a wreath on the tomb of the unknown soldier beneath the *Arc de Triomphe* on the *Champs-Élysées*.

8 December

la fête de l'Immaculée Conception (Feast of the Immaculate Conception). In the city of Lyons, this is celebrated as **la Fête de la Lumière** (Festival of Light) said to commemorate the Virgin's intervention to prevent the plague reaching Lyons in the Middle Ages. People put rows of candles in coloured glass jars on the outsides of their windowsills, so that all the buildings in the centre of the city are illuminated.

24 December

la veille de Noël (Christmas Eve) is the time when most people exchange presents. Many people go to *la messe de minuit* (midnight mass).

25 December

Noël (Christmas) is a public holiday and a day of eating and drinking. Lunch will often start with a variety of seafood, oysters being particularly popular. Turkey is often eaten as a main course, sometimes with chestnut stuffing. A variety of cheeses will be followed by *la bûche de Noël*, a rich chocolate cake in the form of a snow-covered log. French people do not usually send Christmas cards, the custom being to send wishes for the coming year to more distant friends and relatives during the month of January.

26 December

There is no particular name for the day after Christmas Day and it is not a public holiday.

31 December

la Saint-Sylvestre (New Year's Eve). Many people have parties to celebrate *le réveillon du Nouvel An* (New Year's Eve Party). Once again, food plays a major part and, as at Christmas, this is a time to splash out on luxury foods such as *foie gras*. There will often be dancing and the New Year will be welcomed in with champagne.

Movable feasts and holidays

Mardi gras

Shrove Tuesday, the last day of carnival before the beginning of Lent on Ash Wednesday. Traditionally, *crêpes* (pancakes) are eaten for supper. In many areas of France, sugared fritters called *bugnes* in and around Lyons and *oreillettes* farther south, are eaten between *la fête des Rois* and *mardi gras*.

le Vendredi saint

Good Friday is celebrated in the church, but is not a public holiday.

Pâques

Easter Sunday, *le dimanche de Pâques*, is for many people the occasion for a big family lunch. Easter hunts are organised for children, with chocolate eggs, rabbits, hens, or fish traditionally hidden in the family garden. *Le lundi de Pâques* (Easter Monday) is a public holiday.

l'Ascension

the Thursday forty days after Easter is a public holiday in France.

la Pentecôte

(Whitsun) on the seventh Sunday after Easter represents for many people the first long weekend of the summer, as *le lundi de la Pentecôte* (Whit Monday) is a public holiday. Many families go to stay with friends or relatives in the country.

la Fête des mères

(Mother's Day) is the Sunday after *Pentecôte*. This is another occasion for a big family meal, with presents for the mother.

La fête des pères

(Father's Day) is celebrated in similar fashion two weeks later.

A–Z of French life and culture

Académie française
A learned body whose main role nowadays is to monitor new developments in the French language and to make decisions as to what is acceptable and what is not, although these decisions are not always taken entirely seriously by the public at large. Its 40 members are elected for life on the basis of their contribution to scholarship or literature.

Alliance Française
A private organization which aims to spread awareness of French language and culture. It has centres in cities throughout the world, providing classes and a variety of cultural activities.

année scolaire
The French school year starts with the RENTRÉE *des classes* in early September and ends in early July. There is a week's holiday in late October/early November around *la Toussaint* (All Saints' Day, 1 November), two weeks around Christmas and New Year, two weeks in February, and two weeks in April.

Antenne 2 ▶ FRANCE 2

arrondissement
The three largest cities in France – Paris, Lyons, and Marseilles – are divided into numbered administrative areas called *arrondissements*. Each has its own mayor and council, and the number of the *arrondissement* is usually part of the postcode. The system makes for a convenient way for people to talk about which part of the city they live in e.g. '*le neuvième arrondissement*' or simply '*le neuvième*'.

An arrondissement is also a sub-division of a DÉPARTEMENT.

ARTE
A television channel, run jointly by France and Germany, which provides a high standard of cultural programmes.

Assemblée Nationale
The lower house of the French parliament, also called the *Chambre des députés*. There are 577 DÉPUTÉS, elected for a five-year term, often after two rounds of voting, as at least 50% of the vote must be obtained.

Astérix
A hugely popular comic-book character invented by cartoonists Goscinny and Uderzo. *Astérix* is a tiny but invincible village leader in the ancient province of Gaul, whose fictional adventures with his fellow-villagers often involve fighting and outwitting the occupying Romans and make for gentle mockery of cultures outside Gaul. The *Astérix* books have been translated into 40 languages.

autoroute
France has an extensive motorway system, largely financed by tolls calculated according to the distance travelled and the vehicle type. Tickets are obtained and tolls paid at *péages*

(tollgates). There is a speed limit for standard vehicles of 130 km/h (approx. 80 mph) and 110 km/h (approx. 70 mph) in wet weather.

baccalauréat

The *baccalauréat*, generally known informally as the *Bac*, is the examination sat in the final year of the LYCÉE (*la terminale*), so usually at age 17 or 18. Students sit exams in a fairly broad range of subjects in a particular category: the *Bac S* places emphasis on the sciences, for example, whilst the *Bac L* has a literary bias. Some categories cater for students specializing in more directly job-based subjects such as agriculture. The final result is given as a single overall mark or grade out of 20, although the scores for individual subjects are also given. It is common to use the *Bac* as a point of reference in job advertisements, so that *Bac + 4* would mean a person who had completed 4 years of full-time study after the *Bac*, with appropriate diplomas to show for it.

bachelier

The holder of the BACCALAURÉAT, entitled to enrol for university courses.

bande dessinée (BD)

Comic books of all sorts and for a wide variety of age and interest groups are immensely popular in France and form an important part of French culture. Cartoon characters such as *Astérix*, *Lucky Luke*, and *Tintin* are household names and older comic books are often collectors' items.

Basque

The Basque country extends on both sides of the Pyrenees with about one quarter of a million Basques living in France and ten times that number in Spain. The French Basque region (*le Pays basque français*) does not have any autonomous status nor is Basque recognized as an official language. It is, however, taught in some schools, and there are an estimated 40,000 Basque speakers in France.

Bison Futé

Devised by the French traffic information service, *Bison Futé* reports on travel conditions nationally and recommends alternative routes (*les itinéraires 'bis'*) for travellers wishing to avoid traffic jams. *Bison Futé* traffic tips are made known through the media and appear on road signs in yellow on a green background.

boules

A type of bowls, also called PÉTANQUE, played all over France, using metal *boules* and a jack known as a *cochonnet*. Special areas (*terrains de boules*) are set aside for the game in towns and villages, although one of the obvious attractions of the game is that it can be played virtually anywhere. There are some regional variations, notably in the size and form of the playing area and the size of the bowls.

brasserie

The original meaning of *brasserie* is 'brewery', and although the word is still used in this sense, it has come also to mean a type of bar-restaurant, usually serving simple, traditional French food at reasonable prices.

Most *brasseries* offer a fixed-price menu, especially at lunchtime.

Breton

The ancient Celtic language of Brittany (*Bretagne*). It is related to Welsh, Irish, Scottish Gaelic, and Cornish. Recent decades have seen a revival of interest in the language, going hand in hand with the assertion of a regional cultural identity and a movement for independence from France. Breton is fairly widely spoken and is taught in secondary schools in the region, although it is not recognized as an official language in France.

Brevet d'études professionnelles (BEP)

A vocational qualification awarded at the end of a two-year, practically-based course in a LYCÉE specializing in providing teaching directly related to the workplace.

Brevet de technicien (BT)

A vocational qualification awarded at the end of a three-year course in a special section of a LYCÉE. There is considerable competition for entry to courses, and the standards required result in a high dropout rate.

Brevet de technicien supérieur (BTS)

A vocational qualification awarded at the end of a two-year course after the BACCALAURÉAT in a specific professional field.

Brevet des collèges

A general educational qualification taken in a range of subjects by students aged around 15 in the final year of COLLÈGE.

bureau de tabac

Tobacconists are either individual shops or else are to be found in a *bar-tabac* or *café-tabac*. They are also often combined with a newsagents (*marchand de journaux*). As well as being licensed to sell tobacco and cigarettes, they have a state licence to sell stamps, LOTO tickets, the *vignette* (road tax disc for motor vehicles), and certain other official documents.

Canal Plus (Canal+)

A privately-owned French television channel broadcasting mainly feature films. Viewers pay a subscription and access the channel using a decoder.

CAPES – certificat d'aptitude au professorat de l'enseignement du second degré

The qualification normally required in order to teach in a secondary school. Qualification is by means of a competitive examination (CONCOURS) usually at the end of a two-year course in a specialist teacher-training institute (*IUFM: Institut universitaire pour la formation des maîtres*).

Carte bleue

A credit card issued by French banks as part of the international Visa network.

Carte grise

The registration document for a motor vehicle. It is an offence not to carry it when driving the vehicle, and police checks are frequent. Vehicle registration numbers depend on the DÉPARTEMENT in which the owner lives and have to be changed if the owner moves to a different one.

Carte nationale d'identité

Although not obligatory, most French citizens possess a *carte nationale d'identité* (national identity card), obtained from their local MAIRIE, PREFECTUR, or *commissariat de police* (police station), as proof of identity is often required, for example when paying by cheque. It is also accepted as a travel document by all EU countries.

Catalan

The language spoken by 25 per cent of people in Spain and by some people in the Perpignan area of southwest France. It is taught in schools in the area but is not recognized as an official language in France.

CDI – Centre de documentation et d'information

A resource and information centre providing library and IT facilities in a school or college. The term has largely replaced *bibliothèque* (library) in this context.

CE – cycle élémentaire

Also called *cours élémentaire*, this is the programme for the two years of primary school for children aged 7 to 9 (*CE1* and *CE2*).

Césars

Prizes awarded annually for achievements in the film industry, so the French equivalent of the Oscars.

Chambre des députés

▶ ASSEMBLÉE NATIONALE

champignons

The French use the word *champignons* (mushrooms) to refer to any of the types of mushroom-like fungi that are to be found in the countryside, whether edible or not. Cultivated button mushrooms are called *champignons de Paris*. Hunting for edible *champignons* is almost a national leisure activity, and many varieties are highly prized. Advice on whether a *champignon* is edible or not can usually be obtained in a PHARMACIE.

Champs-Élysées

The world-famous avenue in central Paris, known for its luxury shops, hotels, and clubs. At one end is the *Arc de Triomphe*, the scene of the remembrance ceremony each year for the Armistice of 1918 and under which is the tomb of an unknown soldier, killed in World War I.

charcuterie

A shop or supermarket counter selling a wide variety of pork products. As well as cuts of pork, *charcutiers* usually sell chicken, both raw and ready-cooked, and there will be various types of raw and cooked ham, a variety of pâtés, often homemade in small shops, and a selection of *saucissons*. Most *charcuteries* also offer a variey of salads, various types of savoury pastries, and a number of dishes, different every day, which can be reheated at home or on the premises. Some also offer a catering service, in which case the shop will probably call itself a *charcutier-traiteur*. The word *charcuterie* is also used to mean pork products such as ham and *saucisson*.

chasse

La chasse (hunting) is a widely practised sport in France. Legislation as to the rights of hunters to hunt over privately-owned land varies according to the region and the amount of land concerned. During the hunting season, hunting is permitted on Thursdays, Saturdays, and Sundays. It is advisable not to stray from public footpaths when walking in the countryside on these days. The hunters (*les chasseurs*) are a powerful political lobby and are represented in the ASSEMBLÉE NATIONALE.

Cinquième

La Cinquième is an educational television channel which broadcasts on the ARTE channel during the day.

Cinquième république

This is the present régime in France. The constitution was established in 1958 according to principles put forward by Charles de Gaulle.

classe de neige

A period, generally a week, which a school class, usually of under-twelves, spends in a mountain area. Ski tuition is integrated with normal school work.

classe préparatoire

An intensive two-year course, provided by some prestigious LYCÉES, which prepares students for the competitive examinations (CONCOURS) by means of which students are selected for the GRANDES ÉCOLES.

classes

In French schools, after CM, classes go in reverse order, starting at age 11–12 in *sixième* and progressing through *cinquième*, *quatrième*, *troisième*, *seconde*, *première*, and ending in *terminale* at age 17 or 18, the year in which the BACCALAURÉAT is taken. Education in France is compulsory up to the end of *seconde*.

CM – Cycle moyen

Also called *Cours moyen* this is the programme for the two years of primary school for children aged 9 to 11 (*CM1* and *CM2*).

collège

A state school for pupils between the ages of 11 and 15, between the ÉCOLE PRIMAIRE and the LYCÉE. The organization of the school and the curriculum followed are laid down at national level.

colonie de vacances

A holiday village or summer camp for children. Originally set up as a means of giving poorer city children a way of getting out into the countryside, these are still largely state-subsidized. The informal word for them is *colo*.

commune

The *commune* is the smallest administrative unit of French local government. Each has its own MAIRE (mayor).

concours

Entry into many areas of the public services, including the teaching profession, as well as the most prestigious institutes of higher education, depends on succeeding in a competitive examination or *concours*.

The number of candidates admitted depends on the number of posts or places available in a given year.

conduite accompagnée (CA)

A learner driver who has passed the theory part of the driving test (*code de la route*) in a state-approved driving school is allowed to practise driving a vehicle accompanied by a qualified driver over the age of 28. Such drivers are not allowed to drive on AUTOROUTES and are required to have a white sticker with a red 'A' displayed on the rear of their vehicle.

conseil de classe

A committee representing each class in a COLLÈGE or LYCÉE consisting of the class teachers, two elected parent members, and two elected class members. It is chaired by the head teacher. The *conseil de classe* meets regularly to discuss the progress of the class and any problems that have arisen.

CP – Cycle préparatoire

Also called *Cours préparatoire*, this is the first year of primary school, starting a child's formal education off at the statutory age of 6.
Most children will have already attended an ÉCOLE MATERNELLE.

CRS – compagnies républicaines de sécurité

Special police units trained in public order techniques and riot control. They also police the AUTOROUTES and support mountain rescue and lifeguard work.

département

An administrative unit of government in France. Each *département* has a number and this appears as the first two digits in postcodes for addresses within the département and as the two-digit number at the end of registration numbers on motor vehicles.

député

An elected member of the ASSEMBLÉE NATIONALE.

droguerie

As a shop or supermarket section, there seems little connection between the name, which might be literally translated as 'drugstore', and the merchandise displayed. However, *drogue* can also mean the raw ingredients of dyes, and *droguistes* were originally dye merchants. Nowadays you will find not only dyes but household products and cleaning utensils, candles, and a variey of other useful household items.

école libre

Private sector school education, provided predominantly by the Catholic Church.

école maternelle

A school providing free nursery education from age 2 to 6. Many children start at 2 and virtually all children attend between the ages of 4 and 6, which is the statutory school starting age and the time at which children move into the ÉCOLE PRIMAIRE.

école primaire

A primary school for children between the ages of 6, the statutory minimum age for starting school, and 11.

école secondaire

Secondary education in France consists of two phases: COLLÈGE

(11–15 years) AND LYCÈE (15/16 –17/18 years).

Élysée ▶ PALAIS DE L' ÉLYSÉE

Europe 1

A popular commercial French-language radio station, which broadcasts news, popular music, sport, and light entertainment from the Saarland in Germany.

Événement du jeudi – l'Événement du jeudi

A popular weekly news magazine.

Express – l'Express

A weekly news magazine offering in-depth coverage of political and cultural matters.

faculté

La faculté – and more usually and informally *la fac* – is the way that students refer to their university, particularly the location itself, so that *aller à la fac* would be the equivalent of 'to go into college'.

Figaro – le Figaro

A right-wing national daily newspaper with a wide circulation.

France 2

This is the main publicly-owned television channel and aims to provide a wide range of quality programmes.

France 3

A state-owned television channel which is regionally based and is required to promote regional diversity and to cover a wide range of beliefs and opinions.

France Culture

A 24-hour RADIO FRANCE radio station featuring serious talk programmes on a wide variety of cultural and social topics.

France Info

A 24-hour radio news station run by RADIO FRANCE.

France Inter

A RADIO FRANCE radio station broadcasting mainly light entertainment, including a considerable proportion of studio comedy shows, but also offering good news coverage.

France Musiques

A 24-hour RADIO FRANCE radio station. Its main focus is classical music but it also provides considerable coverage of jazz and world music.

Gendarmerie nationale

A section of the military which provides police services outside the major towns.

gîte rural

A farmhouse or other building in the country which has been turned into a holiday cottage. Houses displaying the official *gîte de France* sign must conform to certain standards.

grande école

A prestigious higher education establishment admitting students on the results of a CONCOURS. They have different areas of specialization and competition for entry is fierce, as they are widely believed to offer the highest level of education available and thus a guarantee of subsequent career success.

hôtel de ville ▶ MAIRIE

Humanité – l'Humanité
The communist national daily newspaper.

immatriculation ▶ PLAQUE D'IMMATRICULATION

Internet
A wealth of useful information on French culture, society, and current affairs can be obtained on the Internet. All the main French newspapers have websites (e.g. http://www.lemonde.fr), as do the television channels (e.g. http://www.france3.fr and http://www.tf1.fr). The *Louvre* museum has an interesting site at http://web.culture.fr/ louvre.

Légion d'honneur
The system of honours awarded by the state for meritorious achievement. The *Président de la République* is the *Grand maître*. The basic rank is *Chevalier*. Holders of the *Légion d'honneur* are entitled to wear *une rosette* (a small red lapel ribbon).

Libération
A left-wing national daily newspaper published in Paris. A separate edition is published for Lyons.

licence
A university degree awarded after a year's study following the DEUG.

Loto
The French national lottery. People play the *Loto* using special machines which can be found in BUREAUX DE TABAC throughout France.

Luxembourg ▶ PALAIS DU LUXEMBOURG

lycée
A school providing the last three years of secondary education after COLLÈGE. The first year is *seconde* at the age of 15/16, going through *première*, and ending with *terminale* at age 17/18. As well as those which provide a conventional academic education, there are a number of different types of *lycée* offering a more vocationally-based education.

M6
A popular, privately-owned, commercial television channel.

magasins
Opening and closing times of shops (*les magasins*) vary according to the type of shop and the location. Department stores (*les grands magasins*) are generally open all day from 9 a.m. to 7 p.m. In larger towns, most other shops, with the exception of small food shops, are also open all day. Privately-owned food shops such as butchers and fishmongers generally open at 8 a.m. and do not close in the evening until 7 or 7.30. Most, however, are closed between midday and 2 or 3 p.m. In small towns, all the shops, with the exception of bakers, generally close for 2 or 3 hours in the middle of the day. In both small and large towns, it is always possible to find all types of

food shops open on Sunday mornings until midday. In smaller towns, however, many of the shops are closed on Mondays.

maire

The chief officer of a COMMUNE, he or she represents state authority locally, officiates at marriages, and supervises local elections.

mairie

The *mairie* (town hall) is the administrative headquarters of the CONSEIL MUNICIPAL. In larger towns the *mairie* is often called the *hôtel de ville*.

Maison des jeunes et de la culture

The *Maison des jeunes et de la culture* (*MJC*) is an organization which provides community arts, sports and leisure activities for young people. Attached to the Ministry of Sport, the *MJC* was founded in 1964 to enable young people in rural communities to take part in cultural activities in winter.

marchés

All towns in France have a weekly market with stalls selling a variety of produce, and some areas in big cities have a market every day. Many stalls are held by local people selling their own produce. Despite supermarkets, many people do much of their food shopping *au marché*.

Marianne

The symbolic female figure often used to represent the French Republic. There are statues of her in public places all over France, and she also appears on the standard French stamp. She is always depicted wearing the Phrygian bonnet, a pointed cap which became one of the symbols of liberty as represented by the 1789 Revolution.

Marseillaise

The French national anthem, so called because it was the marching song of a group of republican volunteers from Marseilles a few years after the 1789 revolution.

Matignon

The *Hôtel Matignon* is the official residence and office of the French prime minister, situated in the *rue de Varenne*, Paris. The word *Matignon* is often used to refer to the prime minister's office. See ÉLYSÉE.

Médecins du monde

A charitable organization which provides medical and humanitarian aid in areas stricken by war, famine, or natural disaster.

Médecins sans frontières

A charitable organization which sends medical teams anywhere in the world where they are needed to cope with the effects on people of war and disaster.

Minitel

A computer terminal available in a variety of models to the subscribers of FRANCE TÉLÉCOM. It gives users access to the *Télétel* network, which has a huge variety of services, payable at different rates, including the telephone directory. It can now be accessed via the Internet.

MJC – Maison des jeunes et de la culture

A community youth centre offering a wide variety of services and activities.

Monde – le Monde

A national daily newspaper. Its political stance is left of centre, and it is entirely owned by its staff. It provides full coverage of national and international news and is known for its in-depth analysis of current issues. It is unusual in publishing virtually no photographs of current events.

Nouvel Observateur – le Nouvel Observateur

A left-wing weekly magazine providing in-depth articles on current political issues and good coverage of culture and the arts.

Palais Bourbon

A large eighteenth-century residence on the left bank of the Seine which is now the seat of the ASSEMBLÉE NATIONALE.

Palais de l'Élysée

The official residence and office of the French President, situated just off the CHAMPS-ÉLYSÉES in Paris.

Palais du Luxembourg

A seventeenth century palace in the *jardin du Luxembourg* in Paris. It is now the seat of the SÉNAT.

paysan

Since *paysan* can be used in French to mean both 'small farmer' and, more offensively, 'peasant', small farmers are generally referred to as *agriculteurs*. However, many small farmers take pride in their identity as *paysans*, particularly in the more remote areas of the country, where small farms are still the usual form of cultivation. The difficulty of making a living with a limited amount of land has, however, led to many such farms being abandoned or amalgamated into larger units and a general movement of the traditional rural population towards the towns.

permis de conduire

A driving licence can be issued to a person over the age of 18 who has passed both parts of the driving test. The first part is the theory test (*code de la route*) and consists of forty questions based on the highway code. This can be sat from the age of 16 onwards and gives the right to CONDUITE ACCOMPAGNÉE. The practical driving test has to be taken within two years of the theory test. It is compulsory to carry your driving licence with you when you are driving a vehicle.

pétanque ▶ BOULES

pharmacie

Pharmacies in France generally sell only medicines and closely related products such as toiletries and some brands of make-up and perfume. The products of the major perfume houses are to be found in *parfumeries*. Pharmacists traditionally play an active paramedical role, and people will often consult them rather than a doctor in the case of minor ailments and accidents. Pharmacies are easily spotted by the green cross, which is lit up when the pharmacy is open. A *pharmacie de garde* (duty chemist) can dispense medicines outside normal opening hours as part of a local rota.

plaque d'immatriculation

A vehicle's registration plate. The last two figures indicate the number of the DÉPARTEMENT in which the owner lives. If you move into another *département*, you are obliged by law to change your registration plate accordingly.

Point – le Point

A centre-right weekly news magazine offering in-depth coverage of politics and economics.

police

There are three principal police forces: the *police municipale* who are responsible for routine local policing such as traffic offences, who are locally organized and are not armed, the *police nationale* who are nationally organized and generally armed, and the *gendarmerie nationale* which is a branch of the military.

Poste – La Poste

The state monopoly postal service. Postboxes in France are yellow.

préfecture

The administrative headquarters of a DÉPARTEMENT.

préfet

The most senior offical responsible for representing the state within the DÉPARTEMENT.

Premier ministre

The chief minister of the government, appointed by the PRÉSIDENT DE LA RÉPUBLIQUE and responsible for the overall management of government affairs.

Président de la République

The president is the head of state and is elected for a term of 7 years. Under the constitution of the CINQUIÈME RÉPUBLIQUE the president plays a strong executive role in the governing of the country.

Priorité à droite

Except at roundabouts, and unless there are other indications or regulations in force, French drivers must always give way to traffic approaching from the right.

Quai d'Orsay

The *ministère des Affaires étrangères* (ministry of Foreign Affairs) is situated here, so *Quai d'Orsay* is often used by journalists to mean the ministry.

Radio France

The state-owned radio broadcasting company.

région

The largest administrative unit in France, consisting of a number of DÉPARTEMENTS. Each has its own *conseil régional* (regional council) which has responsibilities in education and economic planning.

rentrée

The week at the beginning of September when the new school year starts and around which much of French administrative life revolves. The preceding weeks see intensive advertising of associated merchandise, from books and stationery to clothes and sports equipment. *La rentrée littéraire* marks the start of the literary year and *la rentrée parlementaire* signals the reassembly of parliament after the recess.

repas

Traditionally the midday meal was the

big meal of the day, and for people who live in country areas this is still largely the case. Even in big cities many people continue to eat a big meal in the middle of the day, though they are tending more and more to have a snack lunch and to eat their main meal in the evening. In either case, the main meal virtually always consists of a number of courses, typically a starter such as pâté, *saucisson*, or salad, then meat or fish with a vegetable dish, followed by cheese and dessert. Cheese is virtually always eaten and is served before the dessert. In town and country alike, Sunday is the day for a big family meal in the middle of the day, and the PÂTISSERIES are usually crowded on Sunday mornings as people queue up to buy a large tart or cake for their hosts or guests.

restaurants

France is rightly famed for the quality of its restaurants. It is always possible to find restaurants and BRASSERIES offering fixed-price menus which are generally good value for money. A basket of bread is usually included in the price of the meal, and most restaurants will have several inexpensive house wines, available in *pichets* (jugs) of ¼, ½, and 1 litre. Service is included in the bill, although many people do leave a tip if the meal and the service have been good.

route départementale

These are signalled on French road maps as 'D' followed by a number and are marked in yellow. They are roads maintained by the DÉPARTEMENT and are secondary roads, not intended to be used for fast travel from place to place. Many of them have stretches marked in green on maps to highlight areas or views of particular beauty.

route nationale

A *route nationale* forms part of the state-maintained road network, outside the AUTOROUTES but providing fast roads for travel between towns and cities. They are signalled by 'N' followed by the road number and are marked in red on French road maps.

SAMU – service d'aide médicale d'urgence

A 24 hour service coordinated by each DÉPARTEMENT to provide mobile medical services and staff, ambulances, and helicopters to accident scenes and emergencies.

Sénat

The upper house of parliament which meets in the PALAIS DU LUXEMBOURG. It consists of 321 elected *sénateurs*. It votes laws and the state budget.

SNCF – Société nationale des chemins de fer français

The state-owned railway company, which also has access to private finance.

tabac ▶ BUREAU DE TABAC

télécarte

A phone card for use in telephone kiosks, widely available from *France Télécom* (the state owned telephone company), *bureaux de poste*, *tabacs* and *marchands de journaux*.

TF1 – Télévision française 1

Originally a state-controlled television channel, now privately-owned, *TF1* has an obligation to ensure that 50% of its programmes are of French origin.

TGV – train à grande vitesse

The new-generation high-speed electric train. It runs on special tracks and can reach speeds of up to 300 km/h.

Tintin

A comic-book character invented by the Belgian cartoonist Hergé in 1929. Tintin's adventures with the irrepressible Capitaine Haddock are still bestsellers and have been translated into more than 40 languages.

Tour de France

Probably the most famous cycle race in the world, the *Tour de France* takes place over a different route each year but always ends on the CHAMPS ÉLYSÉES towards the end of July. The overall winner after each section of the race is entitled to wear *le maillot jaune* (yellow jersey).

Treizième mois

An addition to an employee's salary, equal to his/her usual monthly payment, which some employees receive at the end of the calendar year.

Verlan

A form of French slang which reverses the order of syllables in many common words. The term itself is derived from the word *l'envers* the syllables of which are reversed to create *vers-l'en* (*verlan*). Single syllable words are also converted so *femme* becomes *meuf*, *mec* becomes *keum*, etc.

Wallon

A regional Romance language spoken in Southern Belgium (*Wallonie*). It belongs to the same linguistic family as the French language, and is sometimes considered a French dialect. *Wallon* should not be confused with Belgian French, which differs from the French of France in pronunciation and vocabulary only.

Letter-writing

Holiday postcard

■ Beginnings (informal): *Cher* is used for a man, *Chère* for a woman. A letter to two males or to a male and female begins with *Chers*. For two female correspondents *Chères Madeleine et Hélène*. For friends and relatives: *Chers amis, Chers cousins*, etc. For a family: *Chers tous*.

■ Address: On an envelope Mr, Mrs, and Miss can be abbreviated to *M., Mme, Mlle*, although the full forms are considered preferable in more formal letters. There is no direct equivalent for Ms. If you do not know a woman's marital status use *Madame (Mme)*.

Road names such as *rue, avenue, place* are not generally given capital letters.

The name of the town comes after the postcode and on the same line.

---

14. 7. 2007

Cher Alexandre,

Grosses bises d'Edimbourg! Cela fait trois jours que nous sommes ici et nous n'avons pas encore vu la pluie! Espérons que ça va durer. La vieille ville est très belle et du château on a une vue splendide jusqu'à l'estuaire. Et en Normandie, comment ça va?

A bientôt pour des retrouvailles parisiennes.

Marie et Dominique

M. A. Pilnard

38 rue Glacière

75013 Paris

■ Endings (informal): *Bien amicalement, Amitiés; A bientôt* = see you soon.

Christmas and New Year wishes (informal)

- On most personal letters French speakers do not put their address at the top of the letter. The date is given preceded by *le*. For the first day of the month *le 1er* is used. Generally, the name of the town in which the letter is written is placed before the date.

  1 The tradition of Christmas cards is much less widespread in France than in Great Britain. While Christmas greetings may be sent, it is more customary to send best wishes for the New Year in January.

  2 In the year 2006/2007 etc. = *en l'an 2006/2007* etc., but *bonne année 2006/2007* etc.

---

le 18 décembre 2006 **1**

Chers Steve et Michelle,

Nous vous souhaitons un Joyeux Noël **1** et une très bonne année 2007 **2** ! En espérant que ce nouveau millénaire vous apportera tout ce que vous désirez et que nous trouverons une occasion pour nous revoir!

Bises à vous deux,

Gérard

New Year wishes (formal)

le 5 janvier 2007

Je vous **1** présente mes meilleurs vœux pour l'année 2007. Que cette année vous apporte, à vous et à votre famille, bonheur et prospérité.

Pierre Carlier

---

1 Note the use of the formal form *vous*.

Invitation (informal)

Invitations to parties are usually by word of mouth, but for more formal events such as weddings, invitations are sent out.

1 Note the use of the informal form *tu* betweeen good friends.

Paris, le 28/04/07

Cher Denis,

Que fais-tu 1 cet été? Pascal et moi avons décidé d'inviter tous les copains d'Orléans à nous rejoindre dans notre maison de Dordogne pour le weekend du 14 juillet. Il y aura fête au village avec bal populaire et feu d'artifice. Le petit vin du pays n'est pas mal non plus!

Nous comptons sur toi pour venir trinquer avec nous,

Bises,

Martine

■ Endings (informal): *Bises* (= lots of love) is very informal and is appropriate for very good friends and family. Alternatives for close friends and family include *Bien à toi, Bons baisers* or affectionately *Je t'embrasse*. If the letter is addressed to more than one person use *Bien à vous* or *Je vous embrasse*.

Booking a hotel room

Miss Sylvia Daley
The Willows
49 North Terrace
Kings Barton
Nottinghamshire
NG8 4LQ
England

Hôtel Beauséjour
Chemin des Mimosas
06100 Grasse

le 8 avril 2007

Madame,

J'ai bien reçu le dépliant de votre hôtel et je vous en remercie.

Je souhaite réserver une chambre calme avec salle de bains, en pension complète **1** pour la période du 7 au 18 juin. Pour les arrhes, je vous prie de m'informer de leur montant et des modalités de paiement possibles depuis la Grande-Bretagne.

En vous remerciant d'avance, je vous prie de croire, Madame, en mes sentiments les meilleurs.

S. Daley

---

1 Or *une chambre avec douche en demi-pension* or *avec petit déjeuner*. The term *en suite* does not exist for bathroom facilities in French.

Cancelling a reservation

Mrs J. Warrington
Downlands
Steyning
West Sussex
BN44 6LZ

Hôtel des Voyageurs
9 cours Gambetta
91949 Les Ulis

le 15 février 2007

Monsieur,

Je suis au regret de devoir annuler la réservation de chambre pour deux personnes pour la nuit du 24 au 25 mars, que j'avais effectuée par téléphone le 18 janvier dernier. **1**

Je vous remercie de votre compréhension et vous prie d'agréer, Monsieur, l'expression de mes sentiments distingués.

J. Warrington

1 If reasons for the cancellation are specified these could include: *pour raisons de santé/de famille, en raison d'un décès dans la famille*, etc.

Sending an email

File Edit View Text Mail Attach User Tools Window

Fichier Edition Vue Texte Message Rattacher Agent Outil Fenêtre

Fichier Edition Vue Texte Message Rattacher

To: toothild@scene.co.uk
Cc: itumoran@ecosse.ac.uk
Subject: tu es connectée?

Cher Daniel,

J'ai bien reçu ton mél [1]. Je suis ravie que nous puissions communiquer par Internet. N'oublie pas de joindre à ton prochain message le fichier sur l'argot que tu m'as promis!

Salut,[2]

Clare

1 Note that *mél* is an abbreviated form of *message électronique*. To send an attachment = *joindre un fichier*.
2 Endings (informal): An alternative could be *A bientôt* or simply *Bises* to a close friend in an informal context.

Texting

The basic principles governing French SMS abbreviations are similar to those governing English SMS. Certain words or syllables can be represented by letters or numbers that sound the same but take up less space. Also, points, accents and other diacritics are generally omitted altogether. For example, the syllables '-pé' and '-té' can be replaced by the letters P and T, the word 'sans' by '100', and the conjunction 'que' by 'ke'. Another way of shortening words is simply to omit certain letters, especially vowels. For example, 'bonjour' becomes 'bjr' and 'quand' becomes 'qd'.

As in English, 'emoticons' are very popular, and some of the more established ones are included in the table below.

Glossary of French SMS abbreviations

Abbreviation	Full word	Abbreviation	Full word	Emoticons*	
1mn	juste une minute	kekina	qu'est-ce qu'il ya?	:-)	sourire
100	sans	kfé	café	;-)	clin d'œil
5pa	sympa	ki	qui	:-(	pas content, déçu
6né	cinéma	koi29	quoi de neuf	:-D	je rigole
@+	à plus tard	l8	lui	:-X	motus et bouche cousue
@2m1	à demain	L	elle		
ap	après	mat1	matin	:-|	indifférent
aprM, AM	après-midi	MDR	mort de rire	:'(	je pleure
bi1to	bientôt	MSG	message	|I	endormi
bjr	bonjour	pb	problème	:|	hmmm...
bsr	bonsoir	pk	pourquoi	:-o	oh!
C	c'est	pr	pour	:-@	hurlant
cad	c'est à dire	qd	quand	:-P	lapsus (ma langue a fourché)
dak	d'accord	ri1	rien		
d1ngue	dingue	rstp	réponds s'il te plaît	0:-)	un ange
dzolé	désolé			:-*	bisou
entouK	en tout cas	seur	sœur	:[	abattu
fet	fête	slt cv?	salut ça va?	@-'-,—	une rose
frR	frère	strC	stressé		
G	j'ai	svp	s'il vous plaît	*NB: the '-' which depicts the nose is often omitted or replaced by an 'o' eg. :) or :o)
IR	hier	tjr	toujours		
jamé	jamais	TOK	t'es OK?		
jenémar	j'en ai marre	TOQP	t'es occupé?		
je t'M	je t'aime	Vlo	vélo		
ke	que	vs	vous		
		we	week-end		

The French words you must know

A
à
accepter
accompagner
acheter
addition *l'* (f)
adolescent *l'* (m)
adresse *l'* (f)
aéroport *l'* (m)
affreux
âge *l'* (m)
agent de police *l'* (m)
agréable
aider
aimer
alcool *l'* (m)
alimentation *l'* (f)
aller
*allô
alors
ami *l'* (m); amie *l'* (f)
amour *l'* (m)
amusant
an *l'* (m)
anglais
Angleterre *l'* (f)
animal *l'* (m)
année *l'* (f)
anniversaire *l'* (m)
*août
appareil-photo *l'* (m)
appeler, s'
apprendre
après
*après-midi *l'* (m/f)
arrêter
arrivée *l'* (f)
arriver
assez
attendre

attention *l'* (f)
au revoir
au secours
aujourd'hui
aussi
autobus *l'* (m)
automne *l'* (m)
autoroute *l'* (f)
autre
avant
avec
avion *l'* (m)
avoir
avril

B
bain *le*
banane *la*
banlieue *la*
banque *la*
bar *le*
bâtiment *le*
beau
beaucoup
besoin *le*
bête
bibliothèque *la*
bic *le*
bien
bien sûr
bientôt
bière *la*
billet *le*
blanc
bleu
boire
boisson *la*
*boîte *la*
bon
bon anniversaire
bon appétit
bonjour

bonne année
bonsoir
bouche *la*
boucherie *la*
boulangerie *la*
bouteille *la*
boutique *la*
bras *le*
brosse à dents *la*
brouillard *le*
bruit *le*
brun
bureau *le*
bureau de renseignements *le*
bus *le*

C
ça
cadeau *le*
café *le*
caisse *la*
campagne *la*
camping *le*
cantine *la*
car *le*
carnet *le*
carrefour *le*
carte *la*
carte postale *la*
casser
célèbre
célibataire
centre *le*
centre-ville *le*
cependant
chaise *la*
chambre *la*
chance *la*
changer
chanter
chaque

chat *le*
château *le*
chaud
chauffeur *le*
chaussette *la*
chaussure *la*
chemise *la*
cher
chercher
cheveux *les* (m)
chez
chic
chien *le*
chocolat *le*
choisir
choix *le*
chose *la*
cinéma *le*
circulation *la*
clé/clef *la*
cœur *le*
coiffeur *le*
coin *le*
combien
commander
comme
commencer
comment
commissariat *le*
composer
composter
comprendre
comprimés *les* (m)
concours *le*
conducteur *le*
conduire
confiture *la*
confortable
*connaître
content
continuer
contre

copain *le*
copine *la*
corps *le*
correspondant *le*
côte *la*
coucher, se
couleur *la*
couper
courses *les* (f)
couteau *le*
*coûter
croire
cuiller/cuillière *la*
cuisine *la*

D

d'abord
d'accord
d'habitude
dans
date *la*
de
début *le*
décembre
décider
défense de
déjà
déjeuner *le*
délicieux
demain
demander
demi
dentiste *le*
départ *le*
(se) dépêcher
depuis
dernier
derrière
descendre
désolé
dessert *le*
destination *la*
devant
devoir
difficile
dimanche
*dîner *le*
dire

direction *la*
discuter
disputer, se
disque compact *le*
docteur *le*
donc
donner
dormir
dos *le*
douche *la*
droit
droite *la*
drôle
dur

E

eau *l'* (f)
eau minérale *l'* (f)
échange *l'* (m)
écossais
Ecosse *l'* (f)
écouter
écrire, s'
église *l'* (f)
embouteillage *l'* (m)
émission *l'* (f)
emploi *l'* (m)
en
en retard
en ville
enchanté
encore
enfant *l'* (m/f)
enfin
entendre, s'
entre
entrée *l'* (f)
entrer
environ
envoyer
épicerie *l'* (f)
équipe *l'* (f)
escalier *l'* (m)
espérer
essayer (de)
essence *l'* (f)
est *l'* (m)

et
étage *l'* (m)
été *l'* (m)
étranger *l'* (m)
être
étudiant *l'* (m)
euro *l'* (m)
exactement
excuser, s'
exemple *l'* (m);
  par exemple
*extra

F

facile
faim *la*; avoir faim
faire
famille *la*
fatigué
faux
femme *la*
fenêtre *la*
fermer
février
fille *la*
film *le*
fils *le*
fin *la*
finir
fleur *la*
fois *la*
foot *le*
fourchette *la*
*frais/fraîche
fraise *la*
framboise *la*
français
France *la*
frère *le*
frigo *le*
froid
fromage *le*
fruit *le*
fumer

G

gagner
gallois

garçon *le*
gare *la*
gâteau *le*
gauche
gens *les* (m)
gentil
glace *la*
gorge *la*
grand
Grande-Bretagne *la*
grand-mère *la*
grand-père *le*
gras
gratuit
grave
grippe *la*
gris
gros
guichet *le*

H

habiter
haut
heure *l'* (f)
heureux
hier
histoire *l'* (f)
hiver *l'* (m)
homme *l'* (m)
hôpital *l'* (m)
horaire *l'* (m)
hôtel *l'* (m)
huile *l'* (f)
hypermarché *l'* (m)

I

ici
idée *l'* (f)
idiot
*île *l'* (f)
il y a
impoli
important
informations *les* (f)
instant *l'* (m)
intelligent
interdit

intéressant
intéresser, s'
irlandais
Irlande l' (f)

J
jamais
jambe la
janvier
jardin le
jaune
jeu le
jeudi
jeune
joli
jouer
jour le
journal le
journée la
juillet
juin
jusqu'à
juste

L
là
là-bas
lait le
large
laver, se
lent
lettre la
lever, se
libre
lieu le; avoir lieu
lire
lit le
livre le
loin
long
louer
lundi
lunettes les (f)

M
madame
mademoiselle
magasin le

mai
main la
maintenant
mais
maison la
mal: avoir mal
malade
malheureusement
manger
marché le
marcher
mardi
mari le
mars
matin le
mauvais
méchant
meilleur
même
menu le
mer la
merci
mercredi
mère la
météo la
métier le
métro le
mettre
midi
mieux
minuit
minute la
miroir le
moche
mode la
moins, au moins
mois le
moment le
monde le
monnaie la
monsieur
montagne la
monter
montre la
montrer
mort
mot le
mur le

musique la

N
nager
neige la
nettoyer
Noël
noir
nom le
non
nord le
nourriture la
nouveau
novembre
nuage le
nuit la
numéro le

O
octobre
*œil l' (m)
*œuf l' (m)
oignon l' (m)
oiseau l' (m)
oncle l' (m)
ordinateur l' (m)
oreille l' (f)
ou
où
oublier
ouest l' (m)
oui
ouvert

P
pain le
papier le
Pâques
par
parapluie le
parce que
pardon
parfait
parking le
parler
partie la
partir
partout

pas
pas encore
passer, se
*passe-temps le
passionnant
pauvre
payer
pays le
Pays de Galles le
péage le
pendant
penser
perdre
père le
permis (de
    conduire) le
personne la
petit
petit ami le/petite
    amie la
petit déjeuner le
peu
peur la; avoir peur
peut-être
pièce la
pied le; à pied
piscine la
plage la
plan le
plein
pluie la
plus tard
poire la
poisson le
poivre le
police la
pomme la
pomme de terre la
pont le
porc le
porte la
portefeuille le
*porte-monnaie le
porter
possible
poste la
poubelle la
poulet le

pour
pourquoi
pousser
pouvoir
premier
prendre
prénom *le*
préparer
près tout; près
presque
prêt
printemps *le*
privé
prix *le*
problème *le*
prochain
professeur *le*
promenade *la*
promener, se
propre
public
puis

Q

quai *le*
quand
que
quelque chose
quelque(s)
quelquefois
quelqu'un
question *la*
qui
quitter
quoi

R

raconter
radio *la*
raison *la*;
  avoir raison
ranger
rapide
rappeler
récemment
recevoir

regarder
règle *la*
rencontrer, se
rentrer
repas *le*
réserver
rester
retour *le*
réveiller, se
rez-de-chaussée *le*
rhume *le*
riche
rien
rire
*rond-point *le*
rose
roue *la*
rouge
route *la*
Route Nationale *la*
Royaume-Uni *le*
rue *la*

S

sac *le*
sac à main *le*
sage
saison *la*
salade *la*
sale
salle *la*
salon *le*
salut
samedi
sans
sauf
savoir
savon *le*
secours *le*
secrétaire *le/la*
séjour *le*
sel *le*
semaine *la*
sentir
septembre
serveur *le*

serviette *la*
servir
seul
seulement
si
sœur *la*
soif *la*; avoir soif
soir *le*
soirée *la*
soldes *les* (m)
soleil *le*
sortie *la*
sortir
soudain
sourire
sous
souvent
sport *le*
station *la*
stylo *le*
sud *le*
super
supermarché *le*
sur
sympa

T

table *la*
taille *la*
tante *la*
tard
tasse *la*
téléphone
  (portable) *le*
téléphoner
télévision *la*
température *la*
temps *le*
tête *la*
thé *le*
timbre *le*
tirer
toilettes *les* (f)
tôt
toujours
tous les jours

tout
tout de suite
tout le monde
train *le*
travail *le*
travailler
très
triste
trop
trouver, se

U

utile

V

vacances *les* (f)
vaisselle *la*
vendredi
venir
verre *le*
vert
vêtements *les* (m)
vie *la*
vieux
village *le*
ville *la*
vin *le*
violet
visage *le*
visiter
vite
vivre
voici
voilà
voir, se
voiture *la*
voyager
vrai
vraiment

Y

yeux *les* (m)

Z

zéro

---

*alternative spelling

a /eɪ, ə/ determiner

! **an** avant voyelle ou h muet.

▶ For expressions such as **make a noise, make a fortune** ▷ NOISE, FORTUNE.

····▶ un/une. **∼ tree** un arbre; **∼ chair** une chaise.
····▶ (per) **two euros ∼ kilo** deux euros le kilo; **three times ∼ day** trois fois par jour.

! When talking about what people are or do, **a** is not translated into French: **she's a teacher** elle est professeur; **he's a widower** il est veuf.

aback adv **taken ∼** déconcerté.

abandon vt abandonner. •n abandon m.

abate vi (flood, fever) baisser; (storm) se calmer. •vt diminuer.

abbey n abbaye f.

abbot n abbé m.

abbreviate vt abréger. **abbreviation** n abréviation f.

abdicate vt/i abdiquer.

abdomen n abdomen m.

abduct vt enlever. **abductor** n ravisseur/-euse m/f.

abhor vt (pt **abhorred**) exécrer.

abide vt supporter; **∼ by** respecter.

ability n capacité f (**to do** à faire); (talent) talent m.

abject adj (state) misérable; (coward) abject.

ablaze adj en feu.

able adj (skilled) compétent; **be ∼ to do** pouvoir faire; (know how to)

savoir faire. **ably** adv avec compétence.

abnormal adj anormal. **abnormality** n anomalie f.

aboard adv à bord. •prep à bord de.

abode n demeure f; **of no fixed ∼** sans domicile fixe.

abolish vt abolir.

Aborigine n aborigène mf (d'Australie).

abort vt faire avorter; (Comput) abandonner. •vi avorter.

abortion n avortement m; **have an ∼** se faire avorter.

abortive adj (attempt) avorté; (coup) manqué.

about adv (approximately) environ; **∼ the same** à peu près pareil; **there was no-one ∼** il n'y avait personne. •prep **it's ∼ ...** il s'agit de ...; **what I like ∼ her is** ce que j'aime chez elle c'est; **to wander ∼ the streets** errer dans les rues; **how/what ∼ some tea?** et si on prenait un thé?; **what ∼ you?** et toi? •adj **be ∼ to do** être sur le point de faire; **be up and ∼** être debout. **∼-face, ∼-turn** n (fig) volte-face f inv.

above prep au-dessus de; **he is not ∼ lying** il n'est pas incapable de mentir; **∼ all** surtout. •adv **the apartment ∼** l'appartement du dessus; **see ∼** voir ci-dessus. **∼-board** adj honnête. **∼-mentioned** adj susmentionné.

abrasive adj abrasif; (manner) mordant. •n abrasif m.

abreast adv de front; **keep ∼ of** se tenir au courant de.

abroad adv à l'étranger.

a

abrupt adj (sudden, curt) brusque; (steep) abrupt. **abruptly** adv (suddenly) brusquement; (curtly) avec brusquerie.

abscess n abcès m.

abseil vi descendre en rappel.

absence n absence f; (lack) manque m; **in the ~ of** faute de.

absent adj absent.

absentee n absent/-e m/f.

absent-minded adj distrait.

absolute adj (monarch, majority) absolu; (chaos, idiot) véritable. **absolutely** adv absolument.

absolve vt **~ sb of sth** décharger qn de qch.

absorb vt absorber.

abstain vi s'abstenir (**from** de).

abstract[1] /'æbstrækt/ adj abstrait. • n (summary) résumé m; **in the ~** dans l'abstrait.

abstract[2] /əb'strækt/ vt tirer.

absurd adj absurde.

abundance n abondance f. **abundant** adj abondant. **abundantly** adv (entirely) tout à fait.

abuse[1] /ə'bjuːz/ vt (position) abuser de; (person) maltraiter; (insult) injurier.

abuse[2] /ə'bjuːs/ n (misuse) abus m (**of** de); (cruelty) mauvais traitement m; (insults) injures fpl.

abusive adj (person) grossier; (language) injurieux.

abysmal adj épouvantable.

abyss n abîme m.

academic adj (career) universitaire; (year) académique; (scholarly) intellectuel; (theoretical) théorique. • n universitaire mf.

academy n (school) école f; (society) académie f.

accelerate vi (speed up) s'accélérer; (Auto) accélérer. **accelerator** n accélérateur m.

accent[1] /'æksent/ n accent m.

accent[2] /æk'sent/ vt accentuer.

accept vt accepter. **acceptable** adj acceptable. **acceptance** n (of offer) acceptation f; (of proposal) approbation f.

access n accès m. **accessible** adj accessible.

accessory adj accessoire. • n (Jur) complice mf (**to** de).

accident n accident m; (chance) hasard m; **by ~** par hasard. **accidental** adj (death) accidentel; (meeting) fortuit. **accidentally** adv accidentellement; (by chance) par hasard.

acclaim vt applaudir. • n louanges fpl.

acclimatize vt/i (s')acclimater (**to** à).

accommodate vt loger; (adapt to) s'adapter à; (satisfy) satisfaire. **accommodating** adj accommodant. **accommodation** n logement m.

accompaniment n accompagnement m. **accompany** vt accompagner.

accomplice n complice mf (**in, to** de).

accomplish vt accomplir; (objective) réaliser. **accomplished** adj très compétent. **accomplishment** n (feat) réussite f; (talent) talent m.

accord vi concorder (**with** avec). • vt accorder (**sb sth** qch à qn). • n accord m; **of my own ~** de moi-même.

accordance n **in ~ with** conformément à.

according adv **~ to** (principle, law) selon; (person, book) d'après. **accordingly** adv en conséquence.

accordion n accordéon m.

accost vt aborder.

account n (Comm) compte m; (description) compte-rendu m; **on ~**

of à cause de; **on no** ~ en aucun cas; **take into** ~ tenir compte de; **it's of no** ~ peu importe. ■ ~ **for** (explain) expliquer; (represent) représenter. **accountability** n responsabilité f. **accountable** adj responsable (**for** de; **to** envers).

accountancy n comptabilité f. **accountant** n comptable mf. **accounts** npl comptabilité f, comptes mpl.

accumulate vt/i (s')accumuler.

accuracy n (of figures) justesse f; (of aim) précision f; (of forecast) exactitude f. **accurate** adj juste, précis. **accurately** adv exactement, précisément.

accusation n accusation f.

accuse vt accuser; **the** ~**d** l'accusé/-e m/f.

accustomed adj accoutumé; **become** ~ **to** s'accoutumer à.

ace n (card, person) as m.

ache n douleur f. ●vi (person) avoir mal; **my leg** ~**s** ma jambe me fait mal.

achieve vt (aim) atteindre; (result) obtenir; (ambition) réaliser. **achievement** n (feat) réussite f; (fulfilment) réalisation f (**of** de).

acid adj & n acide (m). **acidity** n acidité f. ~ **rain** n pluies fpl acides.

acknowledge vt (error, authority) reconnaître. (letter) accuser réception de. **acknowledgement** n reconnaissance f.

acne n acné f.

acorn n (Bot) gland m.

acoustic adj acoustique. **acoustics** npl acoustique f.

acquaint vt ~ **sb with sth** mettre qn au courant de qch; **be** ~**ed with** (person) connaître; (fact) savoir. **acquaintance** n connaissance f.

acquire vt acquérir; (habit) prendre.

acquit vt (pt **acquitted**) (Jur) acquitter. **acquittal** n acquittement m.

acre n acre f, ≈ demi-hectare m.

acrid adj âcre.

acrimonious adj acrimonieux.

acrobat n acrobate mf. **acrobatics** npl acrobaties fpl.

acronym n acronyme m.

across adv & prep (side to side) d'un côté à l'autre (de); (on other side) de l'autre côté (**from** de); **go** or **walk** ~ traverser; **lie** ~ **the bed** se coucher en travers du lit; ~ **the world** partout dans le monde.

act n acte m; (Jur, Pol) loi f; **put on an** ~ jouer la comédie. ●vi agir; (Theat) jouer; ~ **as** servir de. ●vt (part, role) jouer.

acting n (Theat) jeu m. ● adj (temporary) intérimaire.

action n action f; (Mil) combat m; **out of** ~ hors service; **take** ~ agir.

activate vt (machine) faire démarrer; (alarm) déclencher.

active adj actif; (volcano) en activité; **take an** ~ **interest in** s'intéresser activement à. **activist** n activiste mf. **activity** n activité f.

actor n acteur m. **actress** n actrice f.

actual adj réel; **the** ~ **words** les mots exacts; **in the** ~ **house** (the house itself) dans la maison elle-même. **actuality** n réalité f. **actually** adv (in fact) en fait; (really) vraiment.

acute adj (anxiety) vif; (illness) aigu; (shortage) grave; (mind) pénétrant.

ad n (TV) pub f 🔲; **small** ~ petite annonce f.

AD abbr (**Anno Domini**) ap. J.-C.

adamant adj catégorique.

adapt vt/i (s')adapter (**to** à).
adaptability n adaptabilité f.
adaptable adj souple.
adaptation n adaptation f.
adaptor n (Electr) adaptateur m.

add vt/i ajouter (**to** à); (in maths)
additionner. ■ ~ **up** (facts, figures)
s'accorder; ~ **sth up**
additionner qch; ~ **up to**
s'élever à.

adder n vipère f.

addict n toxicomane mf; (fig) accro
mf 🔢.

addicted adj be ~ avoir une
dépendance (**to** à); (fig) être
accro (**to** à). **addiction** n
(Med) dépendance f (**to** à);
passion f (**to** pour). **addictive** adj
qui crée une dépendance.

addition n (item) ajout m; (in
maths) addition f; **in** ~ en plus.
additional adj supplémentaire.

additive n additif m.

address n adresse f; (speech)
discours m. ●vt (letter) mettre
l'adresse sur; (crowd) s'adresser à;
~ **sth to** adresser qch à.
addressee n destinataire mf.

adequate adj suffisant;
(satisfactory) satisfaisant.

adhere vi (lit, fig) adhérer (**to** à);
~ **to** (policy) observer.

adjacent adj contigu; ~ **to**
attenant à.

adjective n adjectif m.

adjoin vt être contigu à.
adjoining adj (room) voisin.

adjourn vt (trial) ajourner; **the
session was** ~**ed** la séance a
été levée. ●vi s'arrêter; (Parliament)
lever la séance; ~ **to** passer à.

adjust vt (level, speed) régler; (price)
ajuster; (clothes) rajuster. ●vt/i ~
(oneself) to s'adapter à.
adjustable adj réglable.
adjustment n (of rates)
rajustement m; (of control) réglage
m; (of person) adaptation f.

ad lib vt/i (pt **ad libbed**)
improviser.

administer vt administrer.

administration n
administration f. **administrative**
adj administratif. **administrator**
n administrateur/-trice m/f.

admiral n amiral m.

admiration n admiration f.
admire vt admirer. **admirer** n
admirateur/-trice m/f.

admission n (to a place) entrée f;
(confession) aveu m.

admit vt (pt **admitted**)
(acknowledge) reconnaître,
admettre; (crime) avouer; (new
member) admettre; ~ **to**
reconnaître. **admittance** n
entrée f. **admittedly** adv il
est vrai.

ado n **without more** ~ sans plus
de cérémonie.

adolescence n adolescence f.
adolescent n & a adolescent/-e
m/f .

adopt vt adopter. **adopted** adj
(child) adoptif. **adoption** n
adoption f. **adoptive** adj adoptif.

adorable adj adorable.
adoration n adoration f. **adore**
vt adorer.

adorn vt orner.

adrift adj & adv à la dérive.

adult adj & n adulte (mf).

adultery n adultère m.

adulthood n âge m adulte.

advance vt (sum) avancer; (tape,
career) faire avancer; (interests)
servir. ●vi (lit) avancer; (progress)
progresser. ●n avance f; (progress)
progrès m; **in** ~ à l'avance.
advanced adj avancé; (studies)
supérieur.

advantage n avantage m; **take** ~
of profiter de; (person) exploiter.
advantageous adj avantageux.

adventure n aventure f.

adventurer n aventurier-ière m/f.
adventurous adj aventureux.

adverb n adverbe m.

adverse adj défavorable.

advert n annonce f; (TV) pub f 🄐.

advertise vt faire de la publicité pour; (car, house, job) mettre une annonce pour. •vi faire de la publicité; (for staff) passer une annonce. **advertisement** n publicité f; (in newspaper) annonce f. **advertiser** n annonceur m. **advertising** n publicité f.

advice n conseils mpl; **some ~, a piece of ~** un conseil.

advise vt conseiller; (inform) aviser; **~ against** déconseiller. **adviser** n conseiller/-ère m/f. **advisory** adj consultatif.

advocate¹ /'ædvəkət/ n (Jur) avocat m; (supporter) partisan m.

advocate² /'ædvəkeɪt/ vt recommander.

aerial adj aérien. •n antenne f.

aerobics n aérobic m.

aeroplane n avion m.

aerosol n bombe f aérosol.

aesthetic adj esthétique.

afar adv **from ~** de loin.

affair n (matter) affaire f; (romance) liaison f.

affect vt affecter.

affection n affection f. **affectionate** adj affectueux.

affinity n affinité f.

afflict vt affliger.

affluence n richesse f.

afford vt avoir les moyens d'acheter; (provide) fournir; **can you ~ the time?** avez-vous le temps?

afloat adj & adv (boat) à flot.

afoot adv **sth is ~** il se prépare qch.

afraid adj **be ~** (frightened) avoir peur (**of, to** de; **that** que); (worried) craindre (**that** que); **I'm ~ I can't come** je suis désolé mais je ne peux pas venir.

Africa n Afrique f.

African n Africain/-e m/f. •adj africain.

after adv & prep après; **soon ~** peu après; **be ~ sth** rechercher qch; **~ all** après tout. •conj après que; **~ doing** après avoir fait.

aftermath n conséquences fpl (**of** de).

afternoon n après-midi m or f inv; **in the ~** (dans) l'après-midi.

after: ~ shave n après-rasage m. **~ thought** n pensée f après coup.

afterwards adv après, par la suite.

again adv encore; **~ and ~** à plusieurs reprises; **start ~** recommencer; **she never saw him ~** elle ne l'a jamais revu.

against prep contre; **~ the law** illégal.

age n âge m; (era) ère f, époque f; **I've been waiting for ~s** j'attends depuis des heures. •vt/i (pres p **ageing**) vieillir.

aged¹ /'eɪdʒd/ adj **~ six** âgé de six ans.

aged² /'eɪdʒɪd/ adj âgé.

ageism n discrimination f en raison de l'âge.

agency n agence f.

agenda n ordre m du jour; (fig) programme m.

agent n agent m.

aggravate vt (make worse) aggraver; (annoy) exaspérer. **aggravation** n (worsening) aggravation f; (annoyance) ennuis mpl.

aggression n agression f. **aggressive** adj agressif. **aggressiveness** n agressivité f. **aggressor** n agresseur m.

agitate vt agiter.

ago adv il y a; **a month ~** il y a un mois; **long ~** il y a longtemps; **how long ~?** il y a

a

combien de temps?

agonize vi se tourmenter (**over** à propos de). **agonized** adj angoissé. **agonizing** adj déchirant. **agony** n douleur f atroce; (mental) angoisse f.

agree vi être d'accord (**on** sur; **with** avec); ~ **to** consentir à; ~ **with** (approve of) approuver. •vt être d'accord (**that** sur le fait que); (admit) convenir (**that** que); (date, solution) se mettre d'accord sur.

agreeable adj agréable; **be** ~ (willing) être d'accord.

agreed adj (time, place) convenu; **we're** ~ nous sommes d'accord.

agreement n accord m; **in** ~ d'accord.

agricultural adj agricole. **agriculture** n agriculture f.

aground adv **run** ~ (ship) s'échouer.

ahead adv (in front) en avant, devant; (in advance) à l'avance; **be 10 points** ~ avoir 10 points d'avance; ~ **of time** en avance; **go** ~! allez-y!

aid vt aider. •n aide f; **in** ~ **of** au profit de.

aide n aide mf.

Aids n (Med) sida m.

aim vt (gun) braquer (**at** sur); **be** ~ **ed at sb** (campaign, remark) viser qn. •vi ~ **for/at sth** viser qch; ~ **to do** avoir l'intention de. •n but m; **take** ~ viser. **aimless** adj sans but.

air n air m; **by** ~ par avion; **on the** ~ à l'antenne. •vt aérer; (views) exprimer. •adj (base, disaster) aérien; (pollution, pressure) atmosphérique. ~ **bed** n matelas m pneumatique. ~ **conditioning** n climatisation f. ~**craft** n inv avion m. ~**craft carrier** n porteavions m inv. ~**field** n terrain m d'aviation. ~ **force** n armée f de l'air. ~ **freshener** n désodorisant m d'atmosphère. ~

hostess n hôtesse f de l'air. ~**lift** vt transporter par pont aérien. ~**line** n compagnie f aérienne. ~**liner** n avion m de ligne. ~**lock** n (in pipe) bulle f d'air; (chamber) sas m. ~**mail** n (**by**) ~**mail** par avion. ~**plane** n (US) avion m. ~**port** n aéroport m. ~ **raid** n attaque f aérienne. ~**tight** adj hermétique. ~ **traffic controller** n contrôleur/-euse m/f aérien/-ne. ~**waves** npl ondes fpl.

airy adj (**-ier, -iest**) (room) clair et spacieux.

aisle n (of church) allée f centrale; (in train) couloir m.

ajar adv & adj entrouvert.

akin adj ~ **to** semblable à.

alarm n alarme f; (clock) réveil m; (feeling) frayeur f. •vt inquiéter. ~ **clock** n réveil m.

alas interj hélas.

Albania n Albanie f.

album n album m.

alcohol n alcool m.

alcoholic adj alcoolique; (drink) alcoolisé. •n alcoolique mf.

ale n bière f.

alert adj alerte; (watchful) vigilant. •n alerte f; **on the** ~ sur le qui-vive. •vt alerter; ~ **sb to** prévenir qn de. **alertness** n vivacité f; vigilance f.

A-level n ≈ baccalauréat m

algebra n algèbre f.

Algeria n Algérie f.

alias n (pl ~**es**) faux nom m. •prep alias.

alibi n alibi m.

alien n & a étranger/-ère (m/f) (**to** à).

alienate vt éloigner.

alight adj en feu, allumé.

alike adj semblable. •adv de la même façon; **look** ~ se ressembler.

alive adj vivant; ∼ **to** conscient de; ∼ **with** grouillant de.

all /ɔːl/
● pronoun
····▸ (everything) tout; **is that** ∼? c'est tout?; **that was** ∼ **(that) he said** c'est tout ce qu'il a dit; **I ate it** ∼ j'ai tout mangé.

❗ Use the translation **tous** for a group of masculine or mixed gender people or objects and **toutes** for a group of feminine gender: **we were all delighted** *nous étions tous ravis*; **'where are the cups?'—'they're all in the kitchen'** *'où sont les tasses?'-'elles sont toutes dans la cuisine'*.

● determiner
····▸ tout/toute/tous/toutes; ∼ **the time** tout le temps; ∼ **his life** toute sa vie; ∼ **of us** nous tous; ∼ **(the) women** toutes les femmes.

● adverb
····▸ (completely) tout; **they were** ∼ **alone** ils étaient tout seuls; **tell me** ∼ **about it** raconte-moi tout; ∼ **for** tout à fait pour; **not** ∼ **that well** pas si bien que ça; ∼ **too** bien trop.

❗ When the adjective that follows is in the feminine and begins with a consonant, the translation is *toute/toutes*: **she was all alone** *elle était toute seule*.

allege vt prétendre. ∼**d** adj présumé; **allegedly** adv prétendument.

allergic adj allergique (**to** à). **allergy** n allergie f.

alleviate vt alléger.

alley n (street) ruelle f.

alliance n alliance f.

allied adj allié.

alligator n alligator m.

allocate vt (funds) affecter; (time) accorder; (task) assigner.

allot vt (pt **allotted**) (money) attribuer; (task) assigner. **allotment** n attribution f; (land) parcelle f de terre.

all-out adj (effort) acharné; (strike) total.

allow vt (authorize) autoriser à; (let) laisser; (enable) permettre; (concede) accorder; ∼ **for** tenir compte de.

allowance n allocation f; **make** ∼**s for sth** tenir compte de qch; **make** ∼**s for sb** essayer de comprendre qn.

alloy n alliage m.

all right adj (not bad) pas mal; **are you** ∼? ça va?; **is it** ∼ **if ...?** est-ce que ça va si ...? ● adv (see) bien; (function) comme il faut. ● interj d'accord.

ally[1] /'ælaɪ/ n allié/-e m/f.

ally[2] /ə'laɪ/ vt allier; ∼ **oneself with** s'allier avec.

almighty adj tout-puissant; (very great) formidable.

almond n amande f. ∼ **tree** n amandier m.

almost adv presque; **he** ∼ **died** il a failli mourir.

alone adj & adv seul.

along prep le long de; **walk** ∼ **the beach** marcher sur la plage. ● adv **come** ∼ venir; **walk** ∼ marcher; **push/pull sth** ∼ pousser/tirer qch; **all** ∼ (time) depuis le début; ∼ **with** avec.

alongside adv à côté; **come** ∼ (Naut) accoster. ● prep (next to) à côté de; (all along) le long de.

aloof adj distant.

aloud adv à haute voix.

alphabet n alphabet m. **alphabetical** adj alphabétique.

alpine adj (landscape) alpestre; (climate) alpin.

already adv déjà.

alright a & adv ▷**ALL RIGHT**.

Alsatian n (dog) berger m allemand.

also adv aussi.

altar n autel m.

alter vt/i changer; (building) transformer; (garment) retoucher. **alteration** n changement m; (to building) transformation f; (to garment) retouche f.

alternate¹ /ˈɔːltəneɪt/ vt/i alterner.

alternate² /ɔːlˈtɜːnət/ adj en alternance; **on ~ days** un jour sur deux. **alternately** adv alternativement.

alternative adj autre; (solution) de rechange. ●n (specified option) alternative f; (possible option) choix m. **alternatively** adv sinon.

alternator n alternateur m.

although conj bien que.

altitude n altitude f.

altogether adv (completely) tout à fait; (on the whole) tout compte fait.

aluminium n aluminium m.

always adv toujours.

am ▷**BE**.

a.m. adv du matin.

amalgamate vt/i (merge) fusionner; (metals) (s')amalgamer.

amateur n & adj amateur (m).

amaze vt stupéfaire. **amazed** adj stupéfait. **amazement** n stupéfaction f. **amazing** adj stupéfiant; (great) exceptionnel.

ambassador n ambassadeur m.

amber n ambre m; (Auto) orange m.

ambiguity n ambiguïté f.

ambiguous adj ambigu.

ambition n ambition f. **ambitious** adj ambitieux.

ambulance n ambulance f.

ambush n embuscade f. ●vt tendre une embuscade à.

amenable adj obligeant; **~ to** (responsive) sensible à.

amend vt modifier. **amendment** n (to rule) amendement m.

amends npl **make ~** réparer son erreur.

amenities npl équipements mpl.

America n Amérique f.

American n Américain/-e m/f. ●adj américain.

amiable adj aimable.

amicable adj amical.

amid(st) prep au milieu de.

amiss adj **there is something ~** il y a quelque chose qui ne va pas.

ammonia n (gas) ammoniac m; (solution) ammoniaque f.

ammunition n munitions fpl.

amnesty n amnistie f.

among(st) prep parmi; (affecting a group) chez; **be ~ the poorest** être un des plus pauvres; **be ~ the first** être dans les premiers.

amorous adj amoureux.

amount n quantité f; (total) montant m; (sum of money) somme f. ●vi **~ to** (add up to) s'élever à; (be equivalent to) revenir à.

amp n ampère m.

amphibian n amphibie m.

ample adj (resources) largement suffisant; (proportions) généreux.

amplifier n amplificateur m.

amputate vt amputer.

amuse vt amuser.

amusement n (mirth) amusement m; (diversion) distraction f. **~ arcade** n salle f de jeux.

an ▷**A**.

anaemia n anémie f.

anaesthetic n anesthésique m.

analyse vt analyser. **analysis** n (pl

-yses) analyse f. **analyst** n analyste mf.

anarchist n anarchiste mf.

anatomical adj anatomique. **anatomy** n anatomie f.

ancestor n ancêtre m.

anchor n ancre f. •vt mettre à l'ancre. •vi jeter l'ancre.

anchovy n anchois m.

ancient adj ancien.

ancillary adj auxiliaire.

and conj et; **two hundred ~ sixty** deux cent soixante; **go ~ see him** allez le voir; **richer ~ richer** de plus en plus riche.

anew adv (once more) encore, de nouveau; (in a new way) à nouveau.

angel n ange m.

anger n colère f. •vt mettre en colère, fâcher.

angle n angle m. •vi pêcher (à la ligne); **~ for** (fig) quêter. **angler** n pêcheur/-euse m/f.

Anglo-Saxon adj anglo-saxon. •n Anglo-Saxon/-ne m/f.

angry adj (-ier, -iest) fâché, en colère; **get ~** se fâcher, se mettre en colère (**with** contre); **make sb ~** mettre qn en colère.

anguish n angoisse f.

animal n & adj animal (m).

animate¹ /'ænɪmət/ adj (person) vivant; (object) animé.

animate² /'ænɪmeɪt/ vt animer.

aniseed n anis m.

ankle n cheville f. **~ sock** n socquette f.

annex vt annexer.

anniversary n anniversaire m.

announce vt annoncer (**that** que). **announcement** n (spoken) annonce f; (written) avis m. **announcer** n (radio, TV) speaker/-ine m/f.

annoy vt agacer, ennuyer.

annoyance n contrariété f. **annoyed** adj fâché (**with** contre); **get ~ed** se fâcher. **annoying** adj ennuyeux.

annual adj annuel. •n publication f annuelle. **annually** adv (earn, produce) par an; (do, inspect) tous les ans.

annul vt (pt **annulled**) annuler.

anonymity n anonymat m. **anonymous** adj anonyme.

anorak n anorak m.

another det & pron un/-e autre; **~ coffee** (one more) encore un café; **~ ten minutes** encore dix minutes, dix minutes de plus; **can I have ~?** est-ce que je peux en avoir un autre?

answer n réponse f; (solution) solution f; (phone) **there's no ~** ça ne répond pas. •vt répondre à; (prayer) exaucer; **~ the door** ouvrir la porte. •vi répondre. ■ **~ back** répondre; **~ for** répondre de; **~ to** (superior) dépendre de; (description) répondre à. **answerable** adj responsable (**for** de; **to** devant). **answering machine** n répondeur m.

ant n fourmi f.

antagonism n antagonisme m. **antagonize** vt provoquer l'hostilité de.

Antarctic n **the ~** l'Antarctique m. •adj antarctique.

antenatal adj prénatal.

antenna n (pl **-ae**) (of insect) antenne f; (pl **-as**; aerial: US) antenne f.

anthem n (Relig) motet m; (of country) hymne m national.

anthrax n charbon m.

antibiotic n & adj antibiotique (m).

antibody n anticorps m.

anticipate vt (foresee, expect) prévoir, s'attendre à.

anticipation n attente f; **in ~ of**

a

en prévision *or* attente de.

anticlimax n (let-down) déception f.

anticlockwise adv & adj dans le sens inverse des aiguilles d'une montre.

antics npl pitreries fpl.

antifreeze n antigel m.

antiquated adj (idea) archaïque; (building) vétuste.

antique adj (old) ancien; (old-style) à l'ancienne. ●n objet m ancien, antiquité f. ~ **dealer** n antiquaire mf. ~ **shop** n magasin m d'antiquités.

anti-Semitic adj antisémite.

antiseptic adj & n antiseptique (m).

antisocial adj asocial, antisocial; (reclusive) sauvage.

antlers npl bois mpl.

anxiety n (worry) anxiété f; (eagerness) impatience f.

anxious adj (troubled) anxieux; (eager) impatient (**to** de).

any det (some) du, de l', de la, des; (after negative) de, d'; (every) tout; (no matter which) n'importe quel; **at ~ moment** à tout moment; **have you ~ water?** avez-vous de l'eau? ●pron (no matter which one) n'importe lequel; (any amount of it or them) en; **I do not have ~** je n'en ai pas; **did you see ~ of them?** en avez-vous vu? ●adv (a little) un peu; **do you have ~ more?** en avez-vous encore?; **do you have ~ more tea?** avez-vous encore du thé?; **I don't do it ~ more** je ne le fais plus.

anybody pron (no matter who) n'importe qui; (somebody) quelqu'un; (after negative) personne; **he did not see ~** il n'a vu personne.

anyhow adv (anyway) de toute façon; (carelessly) n'importe comment.

anyone pron ▷ANYBODY.

anything pron (no matter what) n'importe quoi; (something) quelque chose; (after negative) rien; **he did not see ~** il n'a rien vu; **~ but** nullement; **~ you do** tout ce que tu fais.

anyway adv de toute façon.

anywhere adv (no matter where) n'importe où; (somewhere) quelque part; (after negative) nulle part; **he does not go ~** il ne va nulle part; **~ you go** partout où tu vas, où que tu ailles; **~ else** partout ailleurs.

apart adv (on or to one side) à part; (separated) séparé; (into pieces) en pièces; **~ from** à part, excepté; **ten metres ~** à dix mètres l'un de l'autre; **come ~** (break) tomber en morceaux; (machine) se démonter; **legs ~** les jambes écartées; **keep ~** séparer; **take ~** démonter.

apartment n (US) appartement m.

ape n singe m. ●vt singer.

aperitif n apéritif m.

apex n sommet m.

apologetic adj (tone) d'excuse; **be ~** s'excuser. **apologetically** adv en s'excusant.

apologize vi s'excuser (**for** de; **to** auprès de).

apology n excuses fpl.

apostrophe n apostrophe f.

appal vt (pt **appalled**) horrifier. **appalling** adj épouvantable.

apparatus n appareil m.

apparent adj apparent. **apparently** adv apparemment.

appeal n appel m; (attractiveness) attrait m, charme m. ●vi (Jur) faire appel; **~ to sb** (beg) faire appel à qn; (attract) plaire à qn; **~ to sb for sth** demander qch à qn. **appealing** adj (attractive) attirant.

appear vi apparaître. (arrive) se présenter; (seem, be published) paraître. (Theat) jouer; **~ on TV**

passer à la télé. **appearance** n
apparition f; (aspect) apparence f.

appease vt apaiser.

appendix n (pl **-ices**)
appendice m.

appetite n appétit m.

appetizer n (snack) amuse-gueule
m inv; (drink) apéritif m.

appetizing adj appétissant.

applaud vt/i applaudir; (decision)
applaudir à. **applause** n
applaudissements mpl.

apple n pomme f; **~-tree** n
pommier m.

appliance n appareil m.

applicable adj valable; **if** ~ le
cas échéant.

applicant n candidat/-e m/f
(**for** à).

application n application f;
(request, form) demande f; (for job)
candidature f.

apply vt appliquer. ●vi ~ **to** (refer)
s'appliquer à; (ask) s'adresser à;
~ **for** (job) postuler pour; (grant)
demander; ~ **oneself to**
s'appliquer à.

appoint vt (to post) nommer; (fix)
désigner; **well-~ed** bien équipé.

appointment n nomination f;
(meeting) rendez-vous m inv; (job)
poste m; **make an** ~ prendre
rendez-vous (**with** avec).

appraisal n évaluation f.
appraise vt évaluer.

appreciate vt (like) apprécier;
(understand) comprendre; (be grateful
for) être reconnaissant de. ●vi
prendre de la valeur.
appreciation n appréciation f;
(gratitude) reconnaissance f; (rise)
augmentation f. **appreciative** adj
reconnaissant; (audience)
enthousiaste.

apprehend vt (arrest)
appréhender; (understand)
comprendre. **apprehension** n
(arrest) appréhension f; (fear)
crainte f.

apprehensive adj inquiet; **be** ~
of craindre.

apprentice n apprenti m. ●vt
mettre en apprentissage.

approach vt (s')approcher de;
(accost) aborder; (with request)
s'adresser à. ●vi (s')approcher. ●n
approche f; **an** ~ **to** (problem) une
façon d'aborder; (person) une
démarche auprès de.
approachable adj abordable.

appropriate[1] /əˈprəʊprɪeɪt/ vt
s'approprier.

appropriate[2] /əˈprəʊprɪət/ adj
approprié, propre.
appropriately adv à propos.

approval n approbation f; **on** ~ à
or sous condition.

approve vt approuver. ●vi ~ **of**
approuver. **approving** adj
approbateur.

approximate[1] /əˈprɒksɪmeɪt/ vi
~ **to** se rapprocher de.

approximate[2] /əˈprɒksɪmət/ adj
approximatif. **approximately**
adv environ. **approximation** n
approximation f.

apricot n abricot m.

April n avril m. ~ **Fools Day** n le
premier avril.

apron n tablier m.

apt adj (suitable) approprié; **be** ~
to avoir tendance à.

aptitude n aptitude f.

aptly adv à propos.

Aquarius n Verseau m.

aquatic adj aquatique; (Sport)
nautique.

Arab n Arabe mf. ●adj arabe.

Arabian adj d'Arabie.

Arabic adj & n (Ling) arabe (m).

arbitrary adj arbitraire.

arbitrate vi arbitrer. **arbitration**
n arbitrage m. **arbitrator** n
médiateur/-trice m/f.

arcade n (shops) galerie f; (arches)
arcades fpl.

arch n arche f; (of foot) voûte f plantaire. • vt/i (s')arquer. • adj (playful) malicieux.

archaeological adj archéologique. **archaeologist** n archéologue mf. **archaeology** n archéologie f.

archbishop n archevêque m.

archery n tir m à l'arc.

architect n architecte mf; (of plan) artisan m. **architectural** adj architectural. **architecture** n architecture f.

archives npl archives fpl.

archway n voûte f.

Arctic n the ~ l'Arctique m. • adj (climate) arctique; (expedition) polaire; (conditions) glacial.

ardent adj ardent.

are ▷BE.

area n (region) région f; (district) quartier m; (fig) domaine m; (in geometry) aire f; **parking/picnic ~** aire f de parking/de pique-nique.

arena n arène f.

aren't ▷ARE NOT.

Argentina n Argentine f.

arguable adj discutable. **arguably** adv selon certains.

argue vi (quarrel) se disputer; (reason) argumenter. • vt (debate) discuter; ~ **that** alléguer que.

argument n dispute f; (reasoning) argument m; (discussion) débat m. **argumentative** adj ergoteur.

Aries n Bélier m.

arise vi (pt **arose**; pp **arisen**) (problem) survenir; (question) se poser; ~ **from** résulter de.

aristocrat n aristocrate mf.

arithmetic n arithmétique f.

ark n (Relig) arche f.

arm n bras m; ~ **in arm** bras dessus bras dessous. • vt armer; ~**ed robbery** vol m à main armée.

armament n armement m.

arm: ~**-band** n brassard m. ~**chair** n fauteuil m.

armour n armure f. **armoured** adj blindé. **armoury** n arsenal m.

armpit n aisselle f.

arms npl (weapons) armes fpl. ~ **dealer** n trafiquant m d'armes.

army n armée f.

aroma n arôme m. **aromatic** adj aromatique.

arose ▷ARISE.

around adv (tout) autour; (here and there) çà et là. • prep autour de; ~ **here** par ici.

arouse vt (awaken, cause) éveiller; (excite) exciter.

arrange vt arranger; (time, date) fixer; ~ **to** s'arranger pour.

arrangement n arrangement m; (agreement) entente f; **make ~s** prendre des dispositions.

array n **an ~ of** (display) un étalage impressionnant de.

arrears npl arriéré m; **in ~** (rent) arriéré; **he is in ~** il a des retards dans ses paiements.

arrest vt arrêter; (attention) retenir. • n arrestation f; **under ~** en état d'arrestation.

arrival n arrivée f; **new ~** nouveau venu m, nouvelle venue f.

arrive vi arriver; ~ **at** (destination) arriver à; (decision) parvenir à.

arrogance n arrogance f.

arrow n flèche f.

arse n ▣ cul m ▣.

arson n incendie m criminel. **arsonist** n incendiaire mf.

art n art m; (fine arts) beaux-arts mpl.

artery n artère f.

art gallery n (public) musée m (d'art); (private) galerie f (d'art).

arthritis n arthrite f.

artichoke n artichaut m.

article n article m; ~ **of clothing** vêtement m.

articulate adj (person) capable de s'exprimer clairement; (speech) distinct.

articulated lorry n semiremorque m.

artificial adj artificiel.

artist n artiste mf.

arts npl **the** ~ les arts mpl; (Univ) lettres fpl.

artwork n (of book) illustrations fpl.

as conj comme; (while) pendant que; (over gradual period of time) au fur et à mesure que; ~ **she grew older** au fur et à mesure qu'elle vieillissait; **do** ~ **I say** fais ce que je dis; ~ **usual** comme d'habitude. •prep ~ **a mother** en tant que mère; ~ **a gift** en cadeau; ~ **from Monday** à partir de lundi; ~ **for,** ~ **to** quant à; ~ **if** comme si; **you look** ~ **if you're tired** vous avez l'air (d'être) fatigué. •adv ~ **tall** ~ aussi grand que; ~ **much** ~, ~ **many** ~ autant que; ~ **soon** ~ aussitôt que; ~ **well** ~ aussi bien que; ~ **wide** ~ **possible** aussi large que possible.

asbestos n amiante f.

ascend vt gravir. •vi monter.

ascertain vt établir (**that** que).

ash n cendre f; ~**(-tree)** frêne m.

ashamed adj **be** ~ avoir honte (**of** de).

ashore adv à terre.

ashtray n cendrier m.

Asia n Asie f.

Asian n Asiatique mf. •adj asiatique.

aside adv de côté; ~ **from** à part. •n aparté m.

ask vt/i demander; (a question) poser; (invite) inviter; ~ **sb sth** demander qch à qn; ~ **sb to do** demander à qn de faire; ~ **about** (thing) se renseigner sur; (person) demander des nouvelles de; ~ **for** demander.

asleep adj endormi; (numb) engourdi. •adv **fall** ~ s'endormir.

asparagus n(plant) asperge f; (Culin) asperges fpl.

aspect n aspect m; (direction) orientation f.

asphyxiate vt/i (s')asphyxier.

aspire vi aspirer (**to** à; **to do** à faire).

aspirin n aspirine® f.

ass n âne m; (person ▯) idiot/-e m/f.

assail vt attaquer. **assailant** n agresseur m.

assassin n assassin m. **assassinate** vt assassiner. **assassination** n assassinat m.

assault n (Mil) assaut m; (Jur) agression f. •vt (person: Jur) agresser.

assemble vt(construct) assembler; (gather) rassembler. •vi se rassembler.

assembly n assemblée f. ~ **line** n chaîne f de montage.

assent n assentiment m. •vi consentir.

assert vt affirmer; (rights) revendiquer. **assertion** n affirmation f. **assertive** adj assuré.

assess vt évaluer; (payment)

déterminer le montant de.
assessment n évaluation f.
assessor n (valuer) expert m.

asset n (advantage) atout m;
(financial) bien m; **~s** (Comm)
actif m.

assign vt (allot) assigner; **~ sb to**
(appoint) affecter qn à.

assignment n (task) mission f;
(diplomatic) poste m; (academic)
devoir m.

assist vt/i aider. **assistance** n
aide f.

assistant n aide mf; (in shop)
vendeur/-euse m/f. • adj (manager)
adjoint.

associate[1] /əˈsəʊʃɪət/ n & adj
associé/-e (m/f).

associate[2] /əˈsəʊʃɪeɪt/ vt associer.
• vi **~ with** fréquenter.
association n association f.

assorted adj divers; (foods)
assorti.

assortment n assortiment m; (of
people) mélange m.

assume vt supposer; (power,
attitude) prendre; (role, burden)
assumer.

assurance n assurance f.

assure vt assurer.

asterisk n astérisque m.

asthma n asthme m.

astonish vt étonner.

astound vt stupéfier.

astray adv **go ~** s'égarer; **lead ~**
égarer.

astride adv & prep à califourchon
(sur).

astrologer n astrologue mf.
astrology n astrologie f.

astronaut n astronaute mf.

astronomer n astronome mf.

asylum n asile m.

at /æt, ət/
• preposition

▷ For expressions such as
laugh at, look at
▷**laugh, look.**

····▶ (in position or place) à; **he's
~ his desk** il est à son bureau;
she's ~ work/school elle est
au travail/à l'école.

····▶ (at someone's house or
business) chez; **~ Mary's/the
dentist's** chez Mary/le dentiste.

····▶ (in times, ages) à; **~ four
o'clock** à quatre heures; **~ two
years of age** à l'âge de deux
ans.

····▶ (in email addresses) arobase f

ate ▷**EAT.**

atheist n athée mf.

athlete n athlète mf. **athletic** adj
athlétique. **athletics** npl
athlétisme m; (US) sports mpl.

Atlantic adj atlantique. • n **the ~
(Ocean)** l'Atlantique m.

atlas n atlas m.

atmosphere n (air) atmosphère f;
(mood) ambiance f. **atmospheric**
adj atmosphérique; d'ambiance.

atom n atome m.

atrocious adj atroce.

atrocity n atrocité f.

attach vt/i (s')attacher; (letter)
joindre (**to** à).

attaché n (Pol) attaché/-e m/f. **~
case** n attaché-case m.

attached adj **be ~ to** (like) être
attaché à; **the ~ letter** la lettre
ci-jointe.

attachment n (accessory)
accessoire m; (affection)
attachement m; (e-mail) pièces fpl
jointes.

attack n attaque f; (Med) crise f.
• vt attaquer.

attain vt atteindre (à); (gain)
acquérir.

attempt vt tenter. • n tentative f;

an ~ **on sb's life** un attentat contre qn.

attend vt assister à; (class) suivre; (school, church) aller à. •vi assister; ~ **(to)** (look after) s'occuper de.

attendance n présence f; (people) assistance f.

attendant n employé/-e m/f. •adj associé.

attention n attention f; ~! (Mil) garde-à-vous! **pay** ~ faire or prêter attention (**to** à).

attentive adj attentif; (considerate) attentionné. **attentively** adv attentivement. **attentiveness** n attention f.

attest vt/i ~ **(to)** attester.

attic n grenier m.

attitude n attitude f.

attorney n (US) avocat/-e m/f.

attract vt attirer. **attraction** n attraction f; (charm) attrait m.

attractive adj attrayant, séduisant. **attractively** adv agréablement. **attractiveness** n attrait m, beauté f.

attribute[1] /ə'trɪbju:t/ vt ~ **to** attribuer à.

attribute[2] /'ætrɪbju:t/ n attribut m.

aubergine n aubergine f.

auction n vente f aux enchères. •vt vendre aux enchères. **auctioneer** n commissaire priseur m.

audacious adj audacieux.

audience n (theatre, radio) public m; (interview) audience f.

audiovisual adj audiovisuel.

audit n vérification f des comptes. •vt vérifier.

audition n audition f. •vt/i auditionner (**for** pour).

auditor n commissaire m aux comptes.

August n août m.

aunt n tante f.

auspicious adj favorable.

Australia n Australie f.

Australian n Australien/-ne m/f. •adj australien.

Austria n Autriche f.

Austrian n Autrichien/-ne m/f. •adj autrichien.

authentic adj authentique.

author n auteur m.

authoritarian adj autoritaire.

authoritative adj (credible) qui fait autorité; (manner) autoritaire.

authority n autorité f; (permission) autorisation f.

authorization n autorisation f. **authorize** vt autoriser.

autistic adj (person) autiste; (response) autistique.

autograph n autographe m. •vt signer, dédicacer.

automate vt automatiser.

automatic adj automatique. •n (Auto) voiture f automatique.

automobile n (US) auto(mobile) f.

autonomous adj autonome.

autumn n automne m.

auxiliary adj & n auxiliaire (mf); ~ **(verb)** auxiliaire m.

avail vt ~ **oneself of** profiter de. •n **of no** ~ inutile; **to no** ~ sans résultat.

availability n disponibilité f. **available** adj disponible.

avenge vt venger; ~ **oneself** se venger (**on** de).

avenue n avenue f; (line of approach:fig) voie f.

average n moyenne f; **on** ~ en moyenne. •adj moyen. •vt faire la moyenne de; (produce, do) faire en moyenne.

aviary n volière f.

avocado n avocat m.

avoid vt éviter. **avoidance** n (of

injuries) **prévention** f; (of responsibility) **refus** m.

await vt attendre.

awake vt/i (pt **awoke**; pp **awoken**) (s')éveiller. ●adj **be ~** ne pas dormir, être (r)éveillé.

award vt (grant) attribuer; (prize) décerner; (points) accorder. ●n récompense f,prix m; (scholarship) bourse f; **pay ~** augmentation f (de salaire).

aware adj (well-informed) averti; **be ~ of** (danger) être conscient de; (fact) savoir; **become ~ of** prendre conscience de. **awareness** n conscience f.

away adv (far) (au) loin; (absent) absent, parti; **~ from** loin de; **move ~** s'écarter; (to new home) déménager; **six kilometres ~** à six kilomètres (de distance); **take ~** emporter; **he was snoring ~** il ronflait. ●adj & n **~ (match)** match m à l'extérieur.

awe n crainte f (révérencielle).

awe-inspiring adj impressionnant.

awesome adj redoutable.

awful adj affreux. **awfully** adv (badly) affreusement; (very 🛈) rudement.

awkward adj difficile; (inconvenient) inopportun; (clumsy) maladroit; (embarrassing) gênant; (embarrassed) gêné. **awkwardly** adv maladroitement; avec gêne. **awkwardness** n maladresse f; (discomfort) gêne f.

awning n auvent m; (of shop) store m.

awoke, awoken ▷AWAKE.

axe n hache f. ●vt (pres p **axing**) réduire; (eliminate) supprimer; (employee) renvoyer.

axis n (pl **axes**) axe m.

axle n essieu m.

Bb

BA abbr ▷BACHELOR OF ARTS.

babble vi babiller; (stream) gazouiller. ●n babillage m.

baby n bébé m. **~ carriage** n (US) voiture f d'enfant. **~-sit** vi faire du babysitting, garder des enfants. **~-sitter** n baby-sitter mf.

bachelor n célibataire m. **B~ of Arts** licencié/-e m/f ès lettres.

back n (of person, hand, page, etc.) dos m; (of house) derrière m; (of vehicle) arrière m; (of room) fond m; (of chair) dossier m; (in football) arrière m; **at the ~ of the book** à la fin du livre; **in ~ of** (US) derrière. ●adj (leg, wheel) arrière inv; (door, gate) de derrière; (taxes) arriéré. ●adv en arrière; (returned) de retour, rentré; **come ~** revenir; **give ~** rendre; **take ~** reprendre; **I want it ~** je veux le récupérer. ●vt (support) appuyer; (bet on) miser sur; (vehicle) faire reculer. ●vi (of person, vehicle) reculer. **~ down** céder; **~ out** se désister; (Auto) sortir en marche arrière; **~ up** (support) appuyer. **~ache** n mal m de dos. **~-bencher** n (Pol) député m. **~bone** n colonne f vertébrale. **~date** vt antidater. **~fire** vi (Auto) pétarader; (fig) mal tourner. **~gammon** n trictrac m.

background n fond m, arrièreplan m; (context) contexte m; (environment) milieu m; (experience) formation f. ●adj (music, noise) de fond.

backhand n revers m.
  backhander n (bribe) pot-de-vin m.

backing n soutien m.

back: ~**lash** n retour m de bâton; réaction f violente (**against** contre). ~**log** n retard m. ~**number** n vieux numéro m. ~**pack** n sac m à dos. ~**side** n (buttocks 🄵) derrière m. ~**stage** adj & adv dans les coulisses. ~**stroke** n dos m crawlé. ~**track** vi rebrousser chemin; (change one's opinion) faire marche arrière.

backup n soutien m; (Comput) sauvegarde f. ●adj de secours; (Comput) de sauvegarde.

backward adj (step etc.) en arrière; (retarded) arriéré.

backwards adv en arrière; (walk) à reculons; (read) à l'envers; **go ~ and forwards** aller et venir.

bacon n lard m; (in rashers) bacon m.

bacteria npl bactéries fpl.

bad adj (**worse, worst**) mauvais; (wicked) méchant; (ill) malade; (accident) grave; (food) gâté; **feel ~** se sentir mal; **go ~** se gâter; ~ **language** gros mots mpl; **too ~!** tant pis!; (I'm sorry) dommage!

badge n badge m; (coat of arms) insigne m.

badger n blaireau m. ●vt harceler.

badly adv mal; (hurt) gravement; **want ~** avoir grande envie de.

badminton n badminton m.

bad-tempered adj irritable.

baffle vt déconcerter.

bag n sac m; ~**s** (luggage) bagages mpl; (under eyes 🄵) valises fpl; ~**s of** plein de.

baggage n bagages mpl; ~ **reclaim** réception f des bagages.

baggy adj large.

bagpipes npl cornemuse f.

bail n caution f; **on ~** sous caution; (cricket) bâtonnet m. ●vt mettre en liberté provisoire.

bailiff n huissier m.

bait n appât m. ●vt appâter; (fig) tourmenter.

bake vt faire cuire au four; ~ **a cake** faire un gâteau. ●vi cuire; (person) faire du pain. **baked beans** npl haricots mpl blancs à la tomate. **baked potato** n pomme f de terre en robe des champs. **baker** n boulanger/-ère m/f. **bakery** n boulangerie f.

balance n équilibre m; (scales) balance f; (outstanding sum: Comm) solde m; (of payments, of trade) balance f; (remainder) restant m. ●vt mettre en équilibre; (weigh up, also Comm) balancer; (budget) équilibrer; (to compensate) contrebalancer. ●vi être en équilibre.

balcony n balcon m.

bald adj chauve; (tyre) lisse; (fig) simple.

balk vt contrecarrer. ●vi ~ **at** reculer devant.

ball n (golf, tennis, etc.) balle f; (football) ballon m; (billiards) bille f; (of wool) pelote f; (sphere) boule f; (dance) bal m.

ballet n ballet m.

balloon n ballon m.

ballot n scrutin m. ●vt consulter par vote (**on** sur). ~ **box** n urne f. ~ **paper** n bulletin m de vote.

ballpoint pen n stylo m (à) bille.

ban vt (pt **banned**) interdire; ~ **sb from** exclure qn de; ~ **sb from doing** interdire à qn de faire. ●n interdiction f (**on** de).

banal adj banal.

banana n banane f.

band n (strip, group of people) bande f; (pop group) groupe m; (brass band) fanfare f. ●vi ~ **together** se réunir.

bandage n bandage m. ●vt bander.

B and B abbr ▷BED AND BREAKFAST.

bandit n bandit m.

bandstand n kiosque m à musique.

bang n (blow, noise) coup m; (explosion) détonation f; (of door) claquement m. ●vt/i taper; (door) claquer; ~ **one's head** se cogner la tête. ●interj vlan. ●adv 🔲 ~ **in the middle** en plein milieu; ~ **on time** à l'heure pile.

banger n (firework) pétard m; (Culin) saucisse f; **(old)** ~ (car 🔲) guimbarde f.

banish vt bannir.

banister n rampe f d'escalier.

bank n (Comm) banque f; (of river) rive f; (of sand) banc m. ●vt mettre en banque. ●vi (Aviat) virer; ~ **with** avoir un compte à; ~ **on** compter sur. ~ **account** n compte m en banque. ~ **card** n carte f bancaire. ~ **holiday** n jour m férié.

banking n opérations fpl bancaires; (as career) la banque.

banknote n billet m de banque.

bankrupt adj **be** ~ être en faillite; **go** ~ faire faillite. ●n failli/-e m/f. ●vt mettre en faillite. **bankruptcy** n faillite f.

bank statement n relevé m de compte.

banner n bannière f.

baptism n baptême m. **baptize** vt baptiser.

bar n (of metal) barre f; (on window, cage) barreau m; (of chocolate) tablette f; (pub) bar m; (counter) comptoir m; (Mus) mesure f; (fig) obstacle m; ~ **of soap** savonnette f; **the** ~ (Jur) le barreau. ●vt (pt **barred**) (obstruct) barrer; (prohibit) interdire; (exclude) exclure. ●prep sauf.

barbecue n barbecue m. ●vt faire au barbecue.

barbed wire n fil m de fer barbelé.

barber n coiffeur m (pour hommes).

bar code n code m (à) barres.

bare adj nu; (cupboard) vide. ●vt mettre à nu. ~**foot** adj nu-pieds inv, pieds nus. **barely** adv à peine.

bargain n (deal) marché m; (cheap thing) occasion f. ●vi négocier; (haggle) marchander; **not** ~ **for** ne pas s'attendre à.

barge n péniche f. ●vi ~ **in** interrompre; (into room) faire irruption.

bark n (of tree) écorce f; (of dog) aboiement m. ●vi aboyer.

barley n orge f.

bar: ~**maid** n serveuse f. ~**man** n (pl -**men**) barman m.

barn n grange f.

barracks npl caserne f.

barrel n tonneau m; (of oil) baril m; (of gun) canon m.

barren adj stérile.

barricade n barricade f. ●vt barricader.

barrier n barrière f; **ticket** ~ guichet m.

barrister n avocat m.

bartender n (US) barman m.

barter n troc m. ●vt troquer (**for** contre).

base n base f. ●vt baser (**on** sur; **in** à). ●adj ignoble. **baseball** n base-ball m.

basement n sous-sol m.

bash 🔲 vt cogner; ~**ed in** enfoncé. ●n coup m violent; **have a** ~ **at** s'essayer à.

basic adj fondamental, élémentaire; **the** ~**s** l'essentiel m. **basically** adv au fond.

basil n basilic m.

basin n (for liquids) cuvette f; (for food) bol m; (for washing) lavabo m; (of river) bassin m.

basis n (pl **bases**) base f.

bask vi se prélasser (**in** à).

basket n corbeille f; (with handle) panier m. **basketball** n basket (-ball) m.

Basque n (person) Basque mf; (Ling) basque m. • adj basque.

bass¹ /beɪs/ adj (voice, part) de basse; (sound, note) grave. • n (pl **basses**) basse f.

bass² /bæs/ n inv (freshwater fish) perche f; (sea) bar m.

bassoon n basson m.

bastard n (illegitimate) bâtard/-e m/f; (insult ⊠) salaud m ⊠.

bat n (cricket etc.) batte f; (table tennis) raquette f; (animal) chauvesouris f. • vt (pt **batted**) (ball) frapper; **not ~ an eyelid** ne pas sourciller.

batch n (of cakes, people) fournée f; (of goods, text *also* Comput) lot m.

bath n (pl **-s**) bain m; (tub) baignoire f; **have a ~** prendre un bain; (swimming) **~s** piscine f. • vt donner un bain à.

bathe vt baigner. • vi se baigner; (US) prendre un bain.

bathing n baignade f. **~-costume** n maillot m de bain.

bath: **~robe** n (US) robe f de chambre. **~room** n salle f de bains.

baton n (policeman's) matraque f; (Mus) baguette f.

batter vt battre. • n (Culin) pâte f (à frire).

battery n (Mil, Auto) batterie f; (of torch, radio) pile f.

battle n bataille f; (fig) lutte f. • vi se battre. **~field** n champ m de bataille.

baulk vt/i ▸BALK.

bay n (Bot) laurier m; (Geog, Archit) baie f; (area) aire f; (bark) aboiement m; **keep** or **hold at ~** tenir à distance. • vi aboyer. **~-leaf** n feuille f de laurier. **~**

window n fenêtre f en saillie.

bazaar n (shop, market) bazar m; (sale) vente f.

BC abbr (**before Christ**) avant J.-C.

BBS abbr (**Bulletin Board System**) (Internet) babillard m électronique, BBS m.

---

be /biː/

! present **am, is, are**; past **was, were**; past participle **been**.

• intransitive verb

····▸ être; **I am tired** je suis fatigué; **it's me** c'est moi.

····▸ (feelings) avoir; **I am hot** j'ai chaud; **he is hungry/thirsty** il a faim/soif; **her hands are cold** elle a froid aux mains.

····▸ (age) avoir; **I am 15** j'ai 15 ans.

····▸ (weather) faire; **it's warm** il fait chaud; **it's 25°** il fait 25°.

····▸ (health) aller; **how are you?** comment allez-vous or comment vas-tu?

····▸ (visit) aller; **I've never been to Italy** je ne suis jamais allé en Italie.

• auxiliary verb

····▸ (in tenses) **I am working** je travaille; **he was writing to his mother** il écrivait à sa mère; **she is to do it at once** (obligation) elle doit le faire tout de suite.

····▸ (in passives) **he was killed** il a été tué; **the window has been fixed** on a réparé la fenêtre.

····▸ (in tag questions) **their house is lovely, isn't it?** leur maison est très jolie, n'est-ce pas?

····▸ (in short answers) **'I am a painter'—'are you?'** 'je suis peintre'—'ah oui?'; **'are you a doctor?'—'yes, I am'** 'êtes-vous médecin?'—'oui'; **'you're not going out'—'yes I am'** 'tu ne sors pas'—'si'.

beach n plage f.

b

beacon n (lighthouse) phare m; (marker) balise f.

bead n perle f.

beak n bec m.

beaker n gobelet m.

beam n (timber) poutre f; (of light) rayon m; (of torch) faisceau m. •vi rayonner. •vt (broadcast) transmettre.

bean n haricot m.

bear n ours m. •vt (pt **bore**; pp **borne**) (carry, show, feel) porter; (endure, sustain) supporter; (child) mettre au monde. •vi ~ **left** (go) prendre à gauche; ~ **in mind** tenir compte de. ■ ~ **out** confirmer; ~ **up** tenir le coup. **bearable** adj supportable.

beard n barbe f.

bearer n porteur/-euse m/f.

bearing n (behaviour) maintien m; (relevance) rapport m; **get one's** ~s s'orienter.

beast n bête f; (person) brute f.

beat vt/i (pt **beat**; pp **beaten**) battre; ~ **a retreat** battre en retraite; ~ **it!** dégage! 🗊; **it** ~s **me** 🗊 ça me dépasse. •n (of drum, heart) battement m; (of policeman) ronde f. ■ ~ **off** repousser; ~ **up** tabasser. **beating** n raclée f.

beautiful adj beau.

beauty n beauté f. ~ **parlour** n institut m de beauté. ~ **spot** n grain m de beauté; (place) site m pittoresque.

beaver n castor m.

became ▷ BECOME.

because conj parce que; ~ **of** à cause de.

become vt/i (pt **became**; pp **become**) devenir; (befit) convenir à; **what has** ~ **of her?** qu'est-ce qu'elle est devenue?

bed n lit m; (layer) couche f; (of sea) fond m; (of flowers) parterre m; **go to** ~ (aller) se coucher. •vi (pt bedded) ~ **down** se coucher. ~ **and breakfast** n chambre f avec petit déjeuner, chambre f d'hôte. ~ **bug** n punaise f. ~**clothes** npl couvertures fpl.

bedding n literie f.

bed: ~**ridden** adj cloué au lit. ~**room** n chambre f (à coucher). ~**side** n chevet m. ~**sit**, ~**sitter** n chambre f meublée, studio m. ~**spread** n dessus m de lit. ~**time** n heure f du coucher.

bee n abeille f; **make a** ~**-line for** aller tout droit vers.

beech n hêtre m.

beef n bœuf m. ~**burger** n hamburger m.

beehive n ruche f.

been ▷ BE.

beer n bière f.

beetle n scarabée m.

beetroot n inv betterave f.

before prep (time) avant; (place) devant; **the day** ~ **yesterday** avant-hier. •adv avant; (already) déjà; **the day** ~ la veille. •conj ~ **leaving** avant de partir; ~ **I forget** avant que j'oublie. **beforehand** adv à l'avance.

beg vt (pt **begged**) (food, money, favour) demander (**from** à); ~ **sb to do** supplier qn de faire. •vi mendier; **it is going** ~**ging** personne n'en veut.

began ▷ BEGIN.

beggar n mendiant/-e m/f.

begin vt/i (pt **began**, pp **begun**, pres p **beginning**) commencer (**to do** à faire). **beginner** n débutant/-e m/f. **beginning** n commencement m, début m.

begun ▷ BEGIN.

behalf n **on** ~ **of** (act, speak, campaign) pour; (phone, write) de la part de.

behave vi se conduire; ~ (**oneself**) se conduire bien.

behaviour , (US) **behavior** n

comportement m (**towards** envers).

behead vt décapiter.

behind prep derrière; (in time) en retard sur. ●adv derrière; (late) en retard; **leave ~** oublier. ●n (buttocks 🖸) derrière m 🖸.

beige adj & n beige (m).

being n (person) être m.

belch vi avoir un renvoi. ●vt **~ out** (smoke) s'échapper. ●n renvoi m.

Belgian n Belge mf. ●adj belge. **Belgium** n Belgique f.

belief n conviction f; (trust) confiance f; (faith: Relig) foi f.

believe vt/i croire; **~ in** croire à; (deity) croire en. **believer** n croyant/-e m/f.

bell n cloche f; (small) clochette f; (on door) sonnette f.

belly n ventre m. **~ button** n nombril m.

belong vi **~ to** appartenir à; (club) être membre de.

belongings npl affaires fpl.

beloved adj & n bien-aimé/-e (m/f).

below prep sous, au-dessous de; (fig) indigne de. ●adv en dessous; (on page) ci-dessous.

belt n ceinture f; (Tech) courroie f; (fig) zone f. ●vt (hit 🖸) rosser. ●vi (rush 🖸) **~ in/out** entrer/sortir à toute vitesse.

beltway n (US) périphérique m.

bemused adj perplexe.

bench n banc m; **the ~** (Jur) la magistrature (assise).

bend vt (pt **bent**) (knee, arm, wire) plier; (head, back) courber. ●vi (road) tourner; (person) **~ down/ over** se pencher. ●n courbe f; (in road) virage m; (of arm, knee) pli m.

beneath prep sous, au-dessous de; (fig) indigne de. ●adv en dessous.

benefactor n bienfaiteur/- trice m/f.

beneficial adj bénéfique.

benefit n avantage m; (allowance) allocation f. ●vt (be useful to) profiter à; (do good to) faire du bien à. ●vi profiter; **~ from** tirer profit de.

benign adj (kindly) bienveillant; (Med) bénin.

bent ▷BEND. ●n (talent) aptitude f; (inclination) penchant m. ●adj tordu; 🖾 corrompu; **~ on doing** décidé à faire.

bequest n legs m.

bereaved adj endeuillé; **the ~** la famille endeuillée. **bereavement** n deuil m.

berry n baie f.

berserk adj fou furieux.

berth n (in train, ship) couchette f; (anchorage) mouillage m; **give a wide ~ to** éviter. ●vi mouiller.

beside prep à côté de; **~ oneself** hors de soi; **~ the point** sans rapport.

besides prep en plus de. ●adv en plus.

besiege vt assiéger.

best adj meilleur; **the ~ book** le meilleur livre; **the ~ part of** la plus grande partie de; **the ~ thing is to** le mieux est de. ●adv **(the) ~** (behave, play) le mieux. ●n **the ~** le meilleur, la meilleure; **do one's ~** faire de son mieux; **make the ~ of** s'accommoder de. **~ man** n témoin. **~-seller** n bestseller m, livre m à succès.

bet n pari m. ●vt/i (pt **bet** or **betted**, pres p **betting**) parier (**on** sur).

betray vt trahir.

better adj meilleur; **the ~ part of** la plus grande partie de; **get ~** s'améliorer; (recover) se remettre. ●adv mieux; **I had ~ go** je ferais mieux de partir. ●vt (improve) améliorer; (do better than) surpasser. •n **get the ~ of** l'emporter sur; **so much the ~** tant mieux. **~ off** adj (richer) plus riche; **he is/would be ~ off at home** il est/serait mieux chez lui.

betting shop n bureau m du PMU.

between prep entre. •adv **in ~ au** milieu.

beverage n boisson f.

beware vi prendre garde (**of** à).

bewilder vt déconcerter.

beyond prep au-delà de; (control, reach) hors de; (besides) excepté. •adv au-delà; **it is ~ me** ça me dépasse.

bias n (inclination) tendance f; (prejudice) parti m pris. •vt (pt **biased**) influer sur. **biased** adj partial.

bib n bavoir m.

Bible n Bible f.

biceps n biceps m.

bicycle n vélo m, bicyclette f. •adj (bell, chain) de vélo; (pump, clip) à vélo.

bid n (at auction) enchère f; (attempt) tentative f. •vt/i (pt **bade**, pp **bidden** or **bid**, pres p **bidding**) (offer) offrir, mettre une enchère (de) (**for** pour); **~ sb good morning** dire bonjour à qn; **~ sb farewell** faire ses adieux à qn.

bidding n (at auction) enchères fpl; **he did my ~** il a fait ce que je lui ai dit.

bifocals npl verres mpl à double foyer.

big adj (**bigger, biggest**) grand; (in bulk) gros.

bike n vélo m.

bikini n bikini m.

bilberry n myrtille f.

bilingual adj bilingue.

bill n (invoice) facture f; (in hotel, for

gas) note f; (in restaurant) addition f; (of sale) acte m; (Pol) projet m de loi; (banknote: US) billet m de banque; (Theat) **on the ~** à l'affiche; (of bird) bec m. •vt (person: Comm) envoyer la facture à. **~board** n panneau m d'affichage.

billet n cantonnement m. •vt (pt **billeted**) cantonner (**on** chez).

billiards n billard m.

billion n billion m; (US) milliard m.

bin n (for rubbish) poubelle f; (for storage) casier m.

bind vt (pt **bound**) attacher; (book) relier; **be bound by** être tenu par. •n (bore) corvée f.

binding n reliure f. •adj (agreement, contract) qui lie.

binge n (drinking) beuverie f; (eating) gueuleton m.

binoculars npl jumelles fpl.

biochemistry n biochimie f.

biodegradable adj biodégradable.

biographer n biographe mf. **biography** n biographie f.

biological adj biologique.

biologist n biologiste mf.

biology n biologie f.

bioterrorism n bioterrorisme m.

birch n (tree) bouleau m; (whip) fouet m.

bird n oiseau m; (girl 🅴) nana f.

Biro® n stylo m à bille, bic® m.

birth n naissance f; **give ~** accoucher. **~ certificate** n acte m de naissance. **~control** n contraception f. **~day** n anniversaire m. **~mark** n tache f de naissance. **~-rate** n taux m de natalité.

biscuit n biscuit m; (US) petit pain m (au lait).

bishop n évêque m.

bit ▷ BITE. •n morceau m; (of horse)

mors m; (of tool) mèche f; **a ~** (a little) un peu; (Comput) bit m.

bitch n chienne f; (woman) garce f . •vi dire du mal (**about** de).

bite vt/i (pt **bit**; pp **bitten**) mordre; **~ one's nails** se ronger les ongles. •n morsure f; (by insect) piqûre f; (mouthful) bouchée f; **have a ~** manger un morceau.

bitter adj amer; (weather) glacial. •n bière f. **bitterly** adv amèrement; **it is ~ly cold** il fait un temps glacial.

bizarre adj bizarre.

black adj noir; **~ and blue** couvert de bleus. •n (colour) noir m; **B~** (person) Noir/-e m/f. •vt noircir; (goods) boycotter. **~berry** n mûre f. **~bird** n merle m. **~board** n tableau m noir. **~currant** n cassis m.

blacken vt/i noircir.

black: ~ eye n œil m poché. **~head** n point m noir. **~ ice** n verglas m. **~leg** n jaune m.

blacklist n liste f noire. •vt mettre à l'index.

blackmail n chantage m. •vt faire chanter. **blackmailer** n maître-chanteur m.

black: ~ market n marché m noir. **~out** n panne f de courant; (Med) syncope f. **~ pudding** n boudin m. **~ sheep** n brebis f galeuse. **~smith** n forgeron m. **~ spot** n point m noir.

bladder n vessie f.

blade n (of knife) lame f; (of propeller, oar) pale f; **~ of grass** brin m d'herbe.

blame vt accuser; **~ sb for sth** reprocher qch à qn; **he is to ~** il est responsable (**for** de). •n responsabilité f (**for** de).

bland adj (insipid) fade.

blank adj (page) blanc; (screen) vide; (cheque) en blanc; **to look ~** avoir l'air ébahi. •n blanc m; **~ (cartridge)** cartouche f à blanc.

blanket n couverture f; (layer) couche f.

blasphemous adj blasphématoire; (person) blasphémateur.

blast n explosion f; (wave of air) souffle m; (of wind) rafale f; (noise from siren etc.) coup m. •vt (blow up) faire sauter. **~ off** décoller. **~ furnace** n haut-fourneau m. **~off** n lancement m.

blatant adj (obvious) flagrant; (shameless) éhonté.

blaze n feu m; (accident) incendie m. •vt **~ a trail** faire œuvre de pionnier. •vi (fire) brûler; (sky, eyes) flamboyer.

bleach n (for cleaning) eau f de Javel; (for hair, fabric) décolorant m. •vt/i blanchir; (hair) décolorer.

bleak adj (landscape) désolé; (outlook, future) sombre.

bleed vt/i (pt **bled**) saigner.

bleep n bip m.

blemish n imperfection f; (on fruit, reputation) tache f. •vt entacher.

blend vt mélanger. •vi se fondre ensemble; **to ~ with** se marier à. •n mélange m. **blender** n mixeur n, mixer n.

bless vt bénir; **be ~ed with** jouir de; **~ you!** à vos souhaits! **blessed** adj (holy) saint; (damned) sacré. **blessing** n bénédiction f; (benefit) avantage m; (stroke of luck) chance f.

blew ▷**BLOW**

blight n (disease: Bot) rouille f; (fig) plaie f.

blind adj aveugle (**to** à;) (corner, bend) sans visibilité. •vt aveugler. •n (on window) store m; **the ~** les aveugles mpl.

blindfold adj **be ~** avoir les yeux bandés. •adv les yeux bandés. •n bandeau m. •vt bander les yeux à.

blindness n (Med) cécité f; (fig) aveuglement m.

blind spot n (Auto) angle m mort.

blink vi cligner des yeux; (light) clignoter.

bliss n délice m. **blissful** adj délicieux.

blister n ampoule f; (on paint) cloque f. ●vi cloquer.

blitz n (Aviat) raid m éclair. ●vt bombarder.

blob n (drop) (grosse) goutte f; (stain) tache f.

block n bloc m; (buildings) pâté m de maisons; (in pipe) obstruction f; **~ (of flats)** immeuble m; **~ letters** majuscules fpl. ●vt bloquer.

blockade n blocus m. ●vt bloquer.

blockage n obstruction f.

blockbuster n gros succès m.

bloke n 🆃 type m.

blond adj & n blond (m).

blonde adj & n blonde (f).

blood n sang m. ●adj (donor, bath) de sang; (bank, poisoning) du sang; (group, vessel) sanguin. **~-pressure** n tension f artérielle. **~shed** n effusion f de sang. **~shot** adj injecté de sang. **~stream** n sang m. ● **test** n prise f de sang.

bloody adj (-ier, -iest) sanglant; 🆇 sacré. ●adv 🆇 vachement 🆃. **~-minded** adj 🆃 hargneux, obstiné.

bloom n fleur f. ●vi fleurir; (person) s'épanouir.

blossom n fleur(s) f (pl). ●vi fleurir; (person) s'épanouir.

blot n tache f. ●vt (pt **blotted**) tacher; (dry) sécher; **~ out** effacer.

blotch n tache f.

blouse n chemisier m.

blow vt/i (pt **blew**; pp **blown**) souffler; (fuse) (faire) sauter; (squander 🆇) claquer; (opportunity) rater; **~ one's nose** se moucher; **~ a whistle** siffler. ●n coup m. ■ **~ away** or **off** emporter; **~ out** souffler; **~ over** passer; **~ up** (faire) sauter; (tyre) gonfler; (Photo) agrandir.

blow-dry n brushing m. ●vt faire un brushing à.

blown ▷BLOW.

bludgeon n matraque f. ●vt matraquer.

blue adj bleu; (movie) porno. ●n bleu m; **come out of the ~** être inattendu; **have the ~s** avoir le cafard. **~bell** n jacinthe f des bois. **~print** n projet m.

bluff vt/i bluffer. ●n bluff m; **call sb's ~** dire chiche à qn. ●adj (person) carré.

blunder vi faire une bourde; (move) avancer à tâtons. ●n gaffe f.

blunt adj (knife) émoussé; (person) brusque. ●vt émousser. **bluntly** adv carrément.

blur n image f floue. ●vt (pt **blurred**) brouiller.

blurb n résumé m publicitaire.

blush vi rougir. ●n rougeur f. **blusher** n fard m à joues.

blustery adj **~ wind** bourrasque f.

boar n sanglier m.

board n planche f; (for notices) tableau m; (food) pension f; **full ~** pension f complète; **half ~** demipension f; (committee) conseil m; **~ of directors** conseil m d'administration; **go by the ~** tomber à l'eau; **on ~** à bord. ●vt/i (bus, train) monter dans; (Naut) monter à bord (de); **~ with** être en pension chez.

boarding-school n école f privée avec internat.

boast vi se vanter (**about** de). ●vt s'enorgueillir de. ●n vantardise f.

boat n bateau m; (small) canot m; **in the same ~** logé à la même enseigne.

bode vi ~ **well/ill** être de bon/ mauvais augure.

bodily adj (need, well-being) physique; (injury) corporel. ●adv physiquement; (in person) en personne.

body n corps m; (mass) masse f; (organization) organisme m; ~ **part** n partie f de corps; ~**(work)** (Auto) carrosserie f; **the main ~ of** le gros de. ~**-building** n culturisme m. ~**guard** n garde m du corps.

bog n marais m. ●vt (pt **bogged**) **get ~ged down** s'enliser dans.

bogus adj faux.

boil n furoncle m; **bring to the ~** porter à ébullition. ●vt/i bouillir. ■ ~ **down to** se ramener à; ~ **over** déborder. **boiled** adj (egg) à la coque; (potatoes) à l'eau.

boiler n chaudière f; ~ **suit** n bleu m (de travail).

boisterous adj tapageur; (child) turbulent.

bold adj hardi; (cheeky) effronté; (type) gras.

Bolivia n Bolivie f.

bollard n (on road) balise f.

bolt n (on door) verrou m; (for nut) boulon m; (lightning) éclair m. ●vt (door) verrouiller; (food) engouffrer. ●vi s'emballer.

bomb n bombe f; ~ **scare** alerte f à la bombe. ●vt bombarder.

bomber n (aircraft) bombardier m; (person) plastiqueur m.

bombshell n **be a ~** tomber comme une bombe.

bond n (agreement) engagement m; (link) lien m; (Comm) obligation f, bon m; **in ~** (entreposé) en douane.

bone n os m; (of fish) arête f. ●vt désosser. ~**-dry** adj tout à fait sec.

bonfire n feu m; (for celebration) feu m de joie.

bonnet n (hat) bonnet m; (of vehicle) capot m.

bonus n prime f.

bony adj (**-ier, -iest**) (thin) osseux; (fish) plein d'arêtes.

boo interj hou. ●vt/i huer. ●n huée f.

booby trap n mécanisme m piégé. ●vt (pt **-trapped**) piéger.

book n livre m; (exercise) cahier m; (of tickets etc.) carnet m; ~**s** (Comm) comptes mpl. ●vt (reserve) réserver; (driver) dresser un PV à; (player) prendre le nom de; (write down) inscrire. ●vi retenir des places; (**fully**) ~**ed** complet. ~**case** n bibliothèque f. **booking-office** n guichet m. ~**keeping** n comptabilité f. **booklet** n brochure f. ~**maker** n bookmaker m. ~**mark** n (for book, Internet) signet m. ~**seller** n libraire mf. ~**shop** n librairie f. ~**stall** n kiosque m (à journaux).

boom vi (gun, wind, etc.) gronder; (trade) prospérer. ●n grondement m; (Comm) boom m, prospérité f.

boost vt stimuler; (morale) remonter; (price) augmenter; (publicize) faire de la réclame pour.

boot n (knee-length) botte f; (anklelength) chaussure f (montante); (for walking) chaussure f de marche; (Sport) chaussure f de sport; (of vehicle) coffre m; **get the ~** ⊠ se faire virer. ●vt/i ~ **up** (Comput) amorcer.

booth n (for telephone) cabine f; (at fair) baraque f.

booze vi 🅣 boire (beaucoup). ●n 🅣 alcool m.

border n (edge) bord m; (frontier) frontière f; (in garden) bordure f. ●vi ~ **on** être voisin de, avoisiner.

bore vt ennuyer; **be ~d** s'ennuyer; ▷BEAR. ●vi (Tech) forer. ●n raseur/-euse m/f; (thing) ennui

m. **boredom** n ennui m. **boring** adj ennuyeux.

born adj né; **be** ~ naître.

borne ▷BEAR.

borough n municipalité f.

borrow vt emprunter (**from** à).

Bosnia n Bosnie f.

Bosnian adj bosniaque. •n Bosniaque.

bosom n poitrine f; ~ **friend** ami/-e m/f intime.

boss n 🔲 patron/-ne m/f. •vt ~ **(about)** 🔲 mener par le bout du nez.

bossy adj autoritaire.

botch vt bâcler, saboter.

both det les deux; ~ **the books** les deux livres. •pron tous/toutes (les) deux, l'un/-e et l'autre; **we ~ agree** nous sommes tous les deux d'accord; **I bought ~ (of them)** j'ai acheté les deux; **I saw ~ of you** je vous ai vus tous les deux; ~ **Paul and Anne** (et) Paul et Anne. •adv à la fois.

bother vt (annoy, worry) ennuyer; (disturb) déranger. •vi se déranger; **don't ~ (calling)** ce n'est pas la peine d'appeler); **don't ~ about us** ne t'inquiète pas pour nous; **I can't be ~ed** j'ai la flemme 🔲. •n ennui m; (effort) peine f; **it's no ~** ce n'est rien.

bottle n bouteille f; (for baby) biberon m. •vt mettre en bouteille. ■ ~ **up** contenir. ~ **bank** n collecteur m (de verre usagé). ~**neck** n (traffic jam) embouteillage m. ~**opener** n ouvre-bouteilles m inv.

bottom n fond m; (of hill, page, etc.) bas m; (buttocks) derrière m 🔲. •adj inférieur, du bas.

bought ▷BUY.

bounce vi rebondir; (person) faire des bonds, bondir; (cheques 🔳) être refusé. •vt faire rebondir. •n rebond m.

bound vi (leap) bondir; ~**ed by** limité par; ▷BIND. •n bond m. •adj **be** ~ **for** être en route pour, aller vers; ~ **to** (obliged) obligé de; (certain) sûr de.

boundary n limite f.

bounds npl limites fpl; **out of** ~ être interdit d'accès.

bout n période f; (Med) accès m; (boxing) combat m.

bow[1] /bəʊ/ n (weapon) arc m; (of violin) archet m; (knot) nœud m.

bow[2] /baʊ/ n salut m; (of ship) proue f. •vt/i (s')incliner.

bowels npl intestins mpl; (fig) profondeurs fpl.

bowl n (for washing) cuvette f; (for food) bol m; (for soup) assiette f creuse. •vt/i (cricket) lancer; ■ ~ **over** bouleverser.

bowler n (cricket) lanceur m; ~ **(hat)** (chapeau) melon m.

bowling n (ten-pin) bowling m; (on grass) jeu m de boules. ~**-alley** n bowling m.

bow tie n nœud m papillon.

box n boîte f; (cardboard) carton m; (Theat) loge f; **the** ~ 🔲 la télé. •vt mettre en boîte; (Sport) boxer; ~ **sb's ears** gifler qn; ~ **in** enfermer.

boxing n boxe f. •adj de boxe. **B**~ **Day** n le lendemain de Noël.

box office n guichet m.

boy n garçon m; ~ **band** boys band m.

boycott vt boycotter. •n boycottage m.

boyfriend n (petit) ami m.

bra n soutien-gorge m.

brace n (fastener) attache f; (dental) appareil m; (tool) vilebrequin m; ~**s** (for trousers) bretelles fpl. •vt soutenir; ~ **oneself** rassembler ses forces.

bracket n (for shelf etc.) tasseau m, support m; (group) tranche f; **in** ~**s** entre parenthèses. •vt mettre entre parenthèses *or* crochets.

braid n (trimming) galon m; (of hair) tresse f.

brain n cerveau m; **~s** (fig) intelligence f. •vt assommer. **brainless** adj stupide. **~wash** vt faire subir un lavage de cerveau à. **~wave** n idée f géniale, trouvaille f. **brainy** adj (-ier, -iest) doué.

brake n (Auto *also* fig) frein m. •vt/i freiner. **~ light** n feu m stop.

bran n son m.

branch n (of tree) branche f; (of road) embranchement m; (Comm) succursale f; (of bank) agence f. •vi **~ (off)** bifurquer.

brand n marque f. •vt **~ sb as sth** désigner qn comme qch.

brand-new adj tout neuf.

brandy n cognac m.

brass n cuivre m; **get down to ~ tacks** en venir aux choses sérieuses; **the ~** (Mus) les cuivres mpl; **top ~** ⊠ galonnés mpl.

brat n ① môme mf ①.

brave adj courageux; (smile) brave. •n (American Indian) brave m. •vt braver. **bravery** n courage m.

brawl n bagarre f. •vi se bagarrer.

Brazil n Brésil m.

breach n (of copyright, privilege) violation f; (in relationship) rupture f; (gap) brèche f. •vt ouvrir une brèche dans.

bread n pain m; **~ and butter** tartine f. **~-bin**, (US) **~-box** n boîte f à pain. **~crumbs** npl chapelure f.

breadth n largeur f.

bread-winner n soutien m de famille.

break vt (pt **broke**, pp **broken**) casser; (smash into pieces) briser; (vow, silence, rank, etc.) rompre; (law) violer; (a record) battre; (news) révéler; (journey) interrompre; (heart, strike, ice) briser; **~ one's arm** se casser le bras. •vi (se) casser; se briser. **~ rupture f; (in relationship, continuity) rupture f; (interval) interruption f; (at school) récréation f, récré f; (for coffee) pause f; (luck ①) chance f. **■ ~ away** se détacher; **~ down** vi (collapse) s'effondrer; (negotiations) échouer; (machine) tomber en panne; vt (door) enfoncer; (analyse) analyser; **~ even** rentrer dans ses frais; **~ into** cambrioler; **~ off** (se) détacher; (suspend) rompre; (stop talking) s'interrompre; **~ out** (fire, war, etc.) éclater; (faire) cesser; (couple) rompre; (marriage) disperser; (schools) être en vacances. **breakable** adj fragile. **breakage** n casse f.

breakdown n (Tech) panne f; (Med) dépression f; (of figures) analyse f. •adj (Auto) de dépannage.

breakfast n petit déjeuner m.

break : **~-in** n cambriolage m. **~through** n percée f.

breast n sein m; (chest) poitrine f. **~-feed** vt (pt **-fed**) allaiter. **~-stroke** n brasse f.

breath n souffle m, haleine f; **out of ~** à bout de souffle; **under one's ~** tout bas.

breathalyser® n alcootest m.

breathe vt/i respirer. **■ ~ in** inspirer; **~ out** expirer.

breathless adj à bout de souffle.

breathtaking adj à vous couper le souffle.

bred ▷BREED.

breed vt (pt **bred**) élever; (give rise to) engendrer. •vi se reproduire. •n race f.

breeze n brise f.

brew vt (beer) brasser; (tea) faire infuser. •vi (beer) fermenter; (tea) infuser; (fig) se préparer. •n décoction f. **brewer** n brasseur m.

brewery n brasserie f.

bribe n pot-de-vin m. •vt soudoyer. **bribery** n corruption f.

brick n brique f. **∼layer** n maçon m.

bridal adj (dress) de mariée; (car, chamber) des mariés.

bride n mariée f. **∼groom** n marié m. **∼smaid** n demoiselle f d'honneur.

bridge n pont m; (Naut) passerelle f; (of nose) arête f; (card game) bridge m. •vt **∼ a gap** combler une lacune.

bridle n bride f. •vt brider. **∼-path** n piste f cavalière.

brief adj bref. •n instructions fpl; (Jur) dossier m. •vt donner des instructions à.

briefcase n serviette f.

briefs npl slip m.

bright adj brillant, vif; (day, room) clair; (cheerful) gai; (clever) intelligent.

brighten vt égayer. •vi (weather) s'éclaircir; (face) s'éclairer.

brilliant adj (student, career) brillant; (light) éclatant; (very good 🗉) super.

brim n bord m. •vi (pt **brimmed**); **∼ over** déborder (**with** de).

bring vt (pt **brought**) (thing) apporter; (person, vehicle) amener; **∼ to bear** (pressure etc.) exercer. ∎ **∼ about** provoquer; **∼ back** (return with) rapporter; (colour, shine) redonner; **∼ down** faire tomber; (shoot down, knock down) abattre; **∼ forward** avancer; **∼ off** réussir; **∼ out** (take out) sortir; (bring out) faire ressortir; (book) publier; **∼ round** faire revenir à soi; **∼ up** (child) élever; (Med) vomir; (question) aborder.

brink n bord m.

brisk adj vif.

bristle n poil m. •vi se hérisser; **bristling with** hérissé de.

Britain n Grande-Bretagne f.

British adj britannique; **the ∼** les Britanniques mpl.

Briton n Britannique mf.

Brittany n Bretagne f.

brittle adj fragile.

broad adj large; (choice, range) grand. **∼ bean** n fève f.

broadband adj à haut débit. •n ADSL m haut débit m.

broadcast vt/i (pt **broadcast**) diffuser; (person) parler à la television or à la radio. •n émission f.

broadly adv en gros.

broad-minded adj large d'esprit.

broccoli n inv brocoli m.

brochure n brochure f.

broke ▷BREAK. •adj (penniless 🗉) fauché.

broken ▷BREAK. •adj **∼ English** mauvais anglais m.

bronchitis n bronchite f.

bronze n bronze m.

brooch n broche f.

brood n nichée f, couvée f. •vi méditer tristement.

broom n balai m.

broth n bouillon m.

brothel n maison f close.

brother n frère m. **∼hood** n fraternité f. **∼-in-law** n (pl **∼s-in-law**) beau-frère m.

brought ▷BRING.

brow n front m; (of hill) sommet m.

brown adj (object) marron; (hair) brun; **∼ bread** pain m complet; **∼ sugar** sucre m roux. •n marron m; brun m. •vt/i brunir; (Culin) (faire) dorer.

Brownie n jeannette f.

browse vi flâner; (animal) brouter. •vt (Comput) naviguer. **browser** n (Comput) navigateur m.

bruise n bleu m. •vt (knee, arm etc.)

brush n brosse f; (skirmish) accrochage m; (bushes) broussailles fpl. ●vt brosser. ∎ ~ **against** frôler; ~ **aside** (dismiss) repousser; ∎ ~ **up (on)** se remettre à.

Brussels n Bruxelles. ~ **sprouts** npl choux mpl de Bruxelles.

brutal adj brutal.

brute n brute f; **by ~ force** par la force.

BSE abbr (**Bovine Spongiform Encephalopathy**) encéphalopathie f spongiforme bovine, ESB f.

bubble n bulle f; **blow ~s** faire des bulles. ●vi bouillonner; ∎ ~ **over** déborder. ~ **bath** n bain m moussant.

buck n mâle m; (US, 🔲) dollar m; **pass the ~** rejeter la responsabilité (**to** sur). ●vi (horse) ruer; ∎ ~ **up** 🔲 prendre courage; (hurry 🔲) se grouiller 🔲.

bucket n seau m (**of** de).

buckle n boucle f. ●vt/i (fasten) (se) boucler; (bend) voiler.

bud n bourgeon m. ●vi (pt **budded**) bourgeonner.

Buddhism n bouddhisme m.

budding adj (talent) naissant; (athlete) en herbe.

budge vt/i (faire) bouger.

budgerigar n perruche f.

budget n budget m. ●vi ~ **for** prévoir (dans son budget).

buff n (colour) chamois m; 🔲 fanatique mf.

buffalo n (pl -**oes** or -**o**) buffle m; (US) bison m.

buffer n tampon m; ~ **zone** zone f tampon.

buffet¹ /'bʊfeɪ/ n (meal, counter) buffet m; ~ **car** buffet m.

buffet² /'bʌfɪt/ n (blow) soufflet m. ●vt (pt **buffeted**) souffleter.

bug n (bedbug) punaise f; (any small insect) bestiole f; (germ) microbe m; (stomachache 🔲) ennuis mpl gastriques; (device) micro m; (defect) défaut m; (Comput) bogue f, bug m. ●vt (pt **bugged**) mettre des micros dans; 🔲 embêter.

buggy n poussette f.

build vt/i (pt **built**) bâtir, construire. ●n carrure f. ∎ ~ **up** (increase) augmenter, monter; (accumulate) (s')accumuler. **builder** n entrepreneur m en bâtiment; (workman) ouvrier m du bâtiment.

building n (structure) bâtiment m; (dwelling) immeuble m. ~ **society** n caisse f d'épargne.

build-up n accumulation f; (fig) publicité f.

built ▷BUILD.

built-in adj encastré.

built-up area n agglomération f, zone f urbanisée.

bulb n (Bot) bulbe m; (Electr) ampoule f.

Bulgaria n Bulgarie f.

Bulgarian n (person) Bulgare mf; (Ling) bulgare m. ●adj bulgare.

bulge n renflement m. ●vi se renfler, être renflé; **be bulging with** être gonflé or bourré de.

bulimia n boulimie f.

bulk n volume f; **in ~** (buy, sell) en gros; (transport) en vrac; **the ~ of** la majeure partie de.

bull n taureau m. ~**dog** n bouledogue m. ~**doze** vt raser au bulldozer.

bullet n balle f.

bulletin n bulletin m.

bullet-proof adj (vest) pare-balles inv; (vehicle) blindé.

bullfight n corrida f.

bullion n or m or argent m en lingots.

bullring n arène f.

bull's-eye n mille m.

b

bully n (child) petite brute f; (adult) tyran m. •vt maltraiter.

bum n 🇽 derrière m 🇹; (US, 🇽) vagabond/-e m/f.

bumble-bee n bourdon m.

bump n (swelling) bosse f; (on road) bosse f. •vt/i cogner, heurter. ■ ∼ **along** cahoter; ∼ **into** (hit) rentrer dans; (meet) tomber sur.

bumper n pare-chocs m inv. •adj exceptionnel.

bumpy adj (road) accidenté.

bun n (cake) petit pain m; (hair) chignon m.

bunch n (of flowers) bouquet m; (of keys) trousseau m; (of people) groupe m; (of bananas) régime m; ∼ **of grapes** grappe f de raisin.

bundle n paquet m. •vt mettre en paquet; (push) fourrer.

bung n bouchon m. •vt (stop up) boucher; (throw 🇽) flanquer 🇹.

bunion n (Med) oignon m.

bunk n (on ship, train) couchette f. ∼**-beds** npl lits mpl superposés.

buoy n bouée f. •vt ∼ **up** (hearten) soutenir, encourager.

buoyancy n (of floating object) flottabilité f; (cheerfulness) gaieté f.

burden n fardeau m. •vt ennuyer (**with** de).

bureau n (pl **-eaux**) bureau m.

bureaucracy n bureaucratie f.

burglar n cambrioleur m; ∼ **alarm** alarme f. **burglarize** vt (US) cambrioler. **burglary** n cambriolage m. **burgle** vt cambrioler.

Burgundy n (wine) bourgogne m.

burial n enterrement m.

burn vt/i (pt **burned** or **burnt**) brûler. •n brûlure f. ■ ∼ **down** être réduit en cendres. **burner** n (on cooker) brûleur m; (on computer) graveur m. **burning** adj en flammes; (fig) brûlant.

burnt ▷BURN.

burp n 🇹 rot m. •vi 🇹 roter.

burrow n terrier m. •vt creuser.

bursar n intendant/-e m/f. **bursary** n bourse f.

burst vt/i (pt **burst**) (balloon, bubble) crever; (pipe) (faire) éclater. •n explosion f; (of laughter) éclat m; (surge) élan m. ■ ∼ **into** (room) faire irruption dans; ∼ **into tears** fondre en larmes; ∼ **out** ∼ **out laughing** éclater de rire; ∼ **with** be ∼**ing with** déborder de.

bury vt (person etc.) enterrer; (hide, cover) enfouir; (engross, thrust) plonger.

bus n (pl **buses**) (auto)bus m. •vt transporter en bus. •vi (pt **bussed**) prendre l'autobus.

bush n (shrub) buisson m; (land) brousse f.

business n (task, concern) affaire f; (commerce) affaires fpl; (line of work) métier m; (shop) commerce m; **he has no** ∼ **to** il n'a pas le droit de; **mean** ∼ être sérieux; **that's none of your** ∼**!** ça ne vous regarde pas! ∼**like** adj sérieux. ∼**man** n homme m d'affaires.

busker n musicien/-ne m/f des rues.

bus-stop n arrêt m d'autobus.

bust n (statue) buste m; (bosom) poitrine f. •vt/i (pt **busted** or **bust**) (burst 🇽) crever; (break 🇽) (se) casser. •adj (broken, finished 🇽) fichu; **go** ∼ 🇽 faire faillite.

bustle vi s'affairer. •n affairement m, remue-ménage m.

busy adj (**-ier**, **-iest**) (person) occupé; (street) animé; (day) chargé. •vt ∼ **oneself with** s'occuper à.

but conj mais. •prep sauf; ∼ **for** sans; **nobody** ∼ personne d'autre que; **nothing** ∼ rien que. ●adv (only) seulement.

butcher n boucher m. ●vt massacrer.

butler n maître m d'hôtel.

butt n (of gun) crosse f; (of cigarette) mégot m; (of joke) cible f; (barrel) tonneau m; (US, 🔲) derrière m 🔲. ●vi ~ **in** interrompre.

butter n beurre m. ●vt beurrer. ~**-bean** n haricot m blanc. ~**cup** n bouton-d'or m.

butterfly n papillon m.

buttock n fesse f.

button n bouton m. ●vt/i ~ **(up)** (se) boutonner.

buttonhole n boutonnière f. ●vt accrocher.

buy vt (pt **bought**) acheter (**from** à); ~ **sth for sb** acheter qch à qn, prendre qch pour qn; (believe 🔀) croire, avaler.

buzz n bourdonnement m. ●vi bourdonner. **buzzer** n sonnerie f.

by prep par, de; (near) à côté de; (before) avant; (means) en, à, par; ~ **bike** à vélo; ~ **car** en auto; ~ **day** de jour; ~ **the kilo** au kilo; ~ **running** en courant; ~ **sea** par mer; ~ **that time** à ce moment-là; ~ **the way** à propos; ~ **oneself** tout seul. ●adv **close** ~ tout près; ~ **and large** dans l'ensemble.

bye(-bye) interj 🔲 au revoir, salut 🔲.

by-election n élection f partielle.

Byelorussia n Biélorussie f.

by-law n arrêté m municipal.

bypass n (Auto) rocade f; (Med) pontage m. ●vt contourner.

by-product n dérivé m; (fig) conséquence f.

byte n octet m.

Cc

cab n taxi m; (of lorry, train) cabine f.

cabbage n chou m.

cabin n (hut) cabane f; (in ship, aircraft) cabine f.

cabinet n petit placard m; (glassfronted) vitrine f; (Pol) cabinet m.

cable n câble m. ●vt câbler. ~**-car** n téléphérique m. ~ **television** n télévision f par câble.

cache n (hoard) cache f; (place) cachette f.

cackle n (of hen) caquet m; (laugh) ricanement m. ●vi caqueter; (laugh) ricaner.

cactus n (pl **-ti** or ~**es**) cactus m.

cadet n élève m officier.

Caesarean adj ~ **(section)** césarienne f.

café n café m, snack-bar m.

caffeine n caféine f.

cage n cage f. ●vt mettre en cage.

cagey adj réticent.

cagoule n K-way® m.

cajole vt ~ **sb into doing sth** amener qn à faire qch par la cajolerie.

cake n gâteau m; (of soap) pain m. ●vi former une croûte (**on** sur).

calculate vt calculer; (estimate) évaluer. **calculated** adj délibéré; (risk) calculé. **calculating** adj calculateur. **calculation** n calcul m. **calculator** n calculatrice f.

calculus n (pl **-li** *or* ~**es**) calcul m.

calendar n calendrier m.

calf n (pl **calves**) (young cow or bull) veau m; (of leg) mollet m.

calibre n calibre m.

call vt/i appeler; (loudly) crier; **he's** ~**ed John** il s'appelle John; ~ **sb stupid** traiter qn d'imbécile. •n appel m; (of bird) cri m; (visit) visite f; **make/pay a** ~ **on** rendre visite à; **be on** ~ être de garde; ~ **box** cabine f téléphonique. ~ **centre** n centre m d'appels. ∎~ **back** rappeler; (visit) repasser; ~ **for** (help) appeler à; (demand) demander; (require) exiger; (collect) passer prendre; ~ **in** passer. ~ **off** annuler. ~ **on** (visit) rendre visite à; (urge) demander à (**to do** de faire). ~ **out (to)** appeler. ~ **round** venir. ~ **up** appeler.

calling n vocation f.

callous adj inhumain.

calm adj calme. •n calme m. •vt/i ~ **(down)** (se) calmer.

calorie n calorie f.

camcorder n caméscope® m.

came ▷COME.

camel n chameau m.

camera n appareil(-photo) m; (TV, cinema) caméra f; **in** ~ à huis clos. ~**man** n (pl **-men**) cadreur m, cameraman m.

camouflage n camouflage m. •vt camoufler.

camp n camp m. •vi camper.

campaign n campagne f. •vi faire campagne.

camper n campeur/-euse m/f. ~ **(-van)** n camping-car m.

camping n camping m; **go** ~ faire du camping.

campsite n camping m.

campus n (pl ~**es**) campus m.

can¹ /kæn, kən/

! infinitive **be able to**; present **can**; present negative **can't**, **cannot** (*formal*); past **could**; past participle **been able to**

• auxiliary verb

····▶ pouvoir; **where** ~ **I buy stamps?** où est-ce que je peux acheter des timbres?; **she can't come** elle ne peut pas venir.

····▶ (be allowed to) pouvoir; ~ **I smoke?** est-ce que je peux fumer?

····▶ (know how to) savoir; **she** ~ **swim** elle sait nager; **he can't drive** il ne sait pas conduire.

····▶ (with verbs of perception) **I** ~ **hear you** je t'entends; ~ **they see us?** est-ce qu'ils nous voient?

can² /kæn/ n (for food) boîte f; (of petrol) bidon m. •vt (pt **canned**) mettre en conserve.

Canada n Canada m.

Canadian n Canadien/-ne m/f. •adj canadien.

canal n canal m.

canary n canari m.

cancel vt/i (pt **cancelled**) (call off, revoke) annuler; (cross out) barrer; (a stamp) oblitérer; ∎~ **out** (se) neutraliser. **cancellation** n annulation f.

cancer n cancer m; **have** ~ avoir un cancer.

Cancer n Cancer m.

cancerous adj cancéreux.

candid adj franc.

candidate n candidat/-e m/f.

candle n bougie f; (in church) cierge m. ~**stick** n bougeoir m.

candy n (US) bonbon(s) m(pl). ~**-floss** n barbe f à papa.

cane n canne f; (for baskets) rotin m; (for punishment) badine f. •vt donner des coups de badine à.

canister n boîte f.

cannabis n cannabis m.

cannibal n cannibale mf.

cannon n (pl ~ or ~s) canon m. ~-**ball** n boulet m de canon.

cannot ▷ CAN NOT.

canoe n canoë m. ●vi faire du canoë. **canoeist** n canoéiste mf.

canon n (clergyman) chanoine m; (rule) canon m.

can-opener n ouvre-boîtes m inv.

canopy n dais m; (for bed) baldaquin m.

can't ▷ CAN NOT.

canteen n (restaurant) cantine f; (flask) bidon m.

canter n petit galop m. ●vi aller au petit galop.

canvas n toile f.

canvass vt/i (Comm, Pol) faire du démarchage (auprès de); ~ **opinion** sonder l'opinion.

canyon n cañon m.

cap n (hat) casquette f; (of bottle, tube) bouchon m; (of beer or milk bottle) capsule f; (of pen) capuchon m; (for toy gun) amorce f. ●vt (pt **capped**) couronner.

capability n capacité f.

capable adj (person) compétent; ~ **of doing** capable de faire.

capacity n capacité f; **in my ~ as a doctor** en ma qualité de médecin.

cape n (cloak) cape f; (Geog) cap m.

caper vi gambader. ●n (leap) cabriole f; (funny film) comédie f; (Culin) câpre f.

capital adj (letter) majuscule; (offence) capital. ●n (town) capitale f; (money) capital m; ~ **(letter)** majuscule f.

capitalism n capitalisme m.

capitalize vi ~ **on** tirer parti de.

capitulate vi capituler.

Capricorn n Capricorne m.

capsize vt/i (faire) chavirer.

capsule n capsule f.

captain n capitaine m.

caption n (under photo) légende f; (subtitle) sous-titre m.

captivate vt captiver.

captive adj & n captif/-ive (m/f.) **captivity** n captivité f.

capture vt (person, animal) capturer; (moment, likeness) saisir. ●n capture f.

car n voiture f. ●adj (industry, insurance) automobile; (accident, phone) de voiture; (journey, chase) en voiture.

caravan n caravane f.

carbohydrate n hydrate m de carbone.

carbon n carbone m.

carburettor n carburateur m.

card n carte f.

cardboard n carton m.

cardiac adj cardiaque; ~ **arrest** arrêt m du cœur.

cardigan n cardigan m.

cardinal adj (sin) capital; (rule) fondamental; (number) cardinal. ●n cardinal m.

card index n fichier m.

care n (attention) soin m, attention f; (worry) souci m; (looking after) soins mpl; **take ~ of** (deal with) s'occuper de; (be careful with) prendre soin de; **take ~ to do sth** faire bien attention à faire qch. ●vi ~ **about** s'intéresser à; ~ **for** s'occuper de; (invalid) soigner; ~ **to do** vouloir faire; **I don't ~** ça m'est égal.

career n carrière f. ●vi ~ **in/out** entrer/sortir à toute vitesse.

carefree adj insouciant.

careful adj prudent; (research, study) méticuleux; **(be) ~!** (fais) attention! **carefully** adv avec soin; (cautiously) prudemment.

careless adj négligent; (work) bâclé.

carer n (relative) *personne ayant un parent handicapé ou un malade à charge;* (professional) aide f à la domicile.

caress n caresse f. ●vt caresser.

caretaker n concierge mf. ●adj (president) par intérim.

car ferry n ferry m.

cargo n (pl ∼es) chargement m; (Naut) cargaison f.

Caribbean adj des Caraïbes, des Antilles. ●n **the** ∼ (sea) la mer des Antilles; (islands) les Antilles fpl.

caring adj affectueux.

carnation n œillet m.

carnival n carnaval m.

carol n chant m de Noël.

carp n inv carpe f. ●vi maugréer.

car-park n parc m de stationnement, parking m.

carpenter n (joiner) menuisier m; (builder) charpentier m. **carpentry** n menuiserie f; (structural) charpenterie f.

carpet n (fitted) moquette f; (loose) tapis m. ●vt (pt **carpeted**) mettre de la moquette dans.

carriage n (rail) wagon m; (ceremonial) carrosse m; (of goods) transport m; (cost) port m.

carriageway n chaussée f.

carrier n transporteur m; (Med) porteur/-euse m/f; ∼ **(bag)** sac m en plastique.

carrot n carotte f.

carry vt/i porter; (goods) transporter; (involve) comporter; (motion) voter; **be carried away** s'emballer. ■∼ **off** emporter; (prize) remporter; ■∼ **on** (continue) continuer; (business) conduire; (conversation) mener; ∼ **out** (order, plan) exécuter; (duty) remplir; (experiment, operation, repair) effectuer. ∼-**cot** n portebébé m.

car sharing n covoiturage m.

cart n charrette f. ●vt (heavy bag 🄘) trimballer 🄘.

carton n (box) boîte f; (of yoghurt, cream) pot m; (of cigarettes) cartouche f.

cartoon n dessin m humoristique; (cinema) dessin m animé; (strip cartoon) bande f dessinée.

cartridge n cartouche f.

carve vt tailler; (meat) découper.

car-wash n lavage m automatique.

cascade n cascade f. ●vi tomber en cascade.

case n (instance) cas m; (Jur) affaire f; (suitcase) valise f; (crate) caisse f; (for spectacles) étui m; **(just) in** ∼ au cas où; **in** ∼ **he comes** au cas où il viendrait; **in** ∼ **of fire** en cas d'incendie; **in any** ∼ de toute façon; **the** ∼ **for sth** les arguments mpl en faveur de qch; **the** ∼ **for the defence** la défense.

cash n espèces fpl, argent m; **in** ∼ en espèces. ●adj (price) comptant. ●vt encaisser; ∼ **in (on)** profiter (de). ∼-**back** n retrait m d'argent à la caisse. ∼ **desk** n caisse f. ∼ **dispenser** n distributeur m de billets.

cashew n cajou m.

cash flow n marge f brute d'auto-financement.

cashier n caissier/-ière m/f.

cashmere n cachemire m.

cash: ∼**point** n distributeur m de billets. ∼ **point card** n carte f de retrait. ∼ **register** n caisse f enregistreuse.

casino n casino m.

casket n (box) coffret m; (coffin) cercueil m.

casserole n (pan) daubière f; (food) ragoût m.

cassette n cassette f.

cast vt (pt **cast**) (object, glance) jeter; (shadow) projeter; (metal) couler;

~ (off) (shed) se dépouiller de; **~ one's vote** voter; **~ iron** fonte f. ● n (cinema, Theat, TV) distribution f; (Med) plâtre m.

castaway n naufragé/-e m/f.

cast-iron adj de fonte; (fig) en béton.

castle n château m; (chess) tour f.

cast-offs npl vieux vêtements mpl.

castor n (wheel) roulette f.

castrate vt châtrer.

casual adj (informal) décontracté; (remark) désinvolte; (acquaintance) de passage; (work) temporaire.
casually adv (remark) d'un air détaché; (dress) simplement.

casualty n victime f; (part of hospital) urgences fpl.

cat n chat m; (feline) félin m.

catalogue n catalogue m. ● vt dresser un catalogue de.

catalyst n catalyseur m.

catalytic adj **~ converter** pot m catalytique.

catapult n lance-pierres m inv. ● vt projeter.

cataract n (Med, Geog) cataracte f.

catarrh n catarrhe m.

catastrophe n catastrophe f.

catch vt (pt **caught**) attraper; (bus, plane) prendre; (understand) saisir; **~ sb doing** surprendre qn en train de faire; **~ fire** prendre feu; **~ sight of** apercevoir; **~ sb's attention/eye** attirer l'attention de qn. ● vi (get stuck) se prendre (**in** dans); (start to burn) prendre. ● n (fastening) fermeture f; (drawback) piège m; (in sport) prise f. ■ **~ on** devenir populaire. **~ out** prendre de court. **~ up** rattraper son retard; **~ up with sb** rattraper qn.

catching adj contagieux.

catchment n **~ area** (School) secteur m.

catch-phrase n formule f favorite.

catchy adj entraînant.

category n catégorie f.

cater vi organiser des réceptions; **~ for/to** (guests) accueillir; (needs) pourvoir à; (reader) s'adresser à. **caterer** n traiteur m.

caterpillar n chenille f.

cathedral n cathédrale f.

catholic adj éclectique. **Catholic** adj & n catholique (mf). **Catholicism** n catholicisme m.

Catseye® n plot m rétroréfléchissant.

cattle npl bétail m.

caught ▷CATCH.

cauliflower n chou-fleur m.

cause n cause f; (reason) raison f, motif m. ● vt causer; **~ sth to grow/move** faire pousser/ bouger qch.

causeway n chaussée f.

caution n prudence f; (warning) avertissement m. ● vt avertir. **cautious** adj prudent. **cautiously** adv prudemment.

cave n grotte f. ● vi **~ in** s'effondrer; (agree) céder. **~man** n (pl **-men**) homme m des cavernes.

cavern n caverne f.

caviare n caviar m.

caving n spéléologie f.

CCTV abbr (closed circuit television) télévision f en circuit fermé.

CD abbr (**compact disc**) disque m compact, CD m.

CD-ROM n disque m optique compact, CD-ROM m.

cease vt/i cesser. **~-fire** n cessez-le-feu m inv.

cedar n cèdre m.

cedilla n cédille f.

ceiling n plafond m.

celebrate vt (occasion) fêter; (Easter, mass) célébrer. ● vi faire la fête. **celebrated** adj célèbre.

celebration n fête f.

celebrity n célébrité f.

celery n céleri m.

cell n cellule f; (Electr) élément m.

cellar n cave f.

cellist n violoncelliste mf. **cello** n violoncelle m.

cellphone n (téléphone m) portable.

Celt n Celte mf.

cement n ciment m. •vt cimenter. ∼-**mixer** n bétonnière f.

cemetery n cimetière m.

censor n censeur m. •vt censurer.

censure n censure f. •vt critiquer.

census n recensement m.

cent n cent m.

centenary n centenaire m.

centigrade adj centigrade.

centilitre, (US) **centiliter** n centilitre m.

centimetre, (US) **centimeter** n centimètre m.

centipede n millepattes m inv.

central adj central; ∼ **heating** chauffage m central; ∼ **locking** fermeture f centralisée des portes. **centralize** vt centraliser. **centrally** adv (situated) au centre.

centre , (US) **center** n centre m. •vt (pt **centred**) centrer. •vi ∼ **on** tourner autour de.

century n siècle m.

ceramic adj (art) céramique; (object) en céramique.

cereal n céréale f.

ceremonial adj (dress) de cérémonie. •n cérémonial m. **ceremony** n cérémonie f.

certain adj certain; **for** ∼ avec certitude; **make** ∼ **of** s'assurer de. **certainly** adv certainement. **certainty** n certitude f.

certificate n certificat m.

certify vt certifier.

cesspit, cesspool n fosse f d'aisances.

chafe vt/i frotter (contre).

chagrin n dépit m.

chain n chaîne f; ∼ **reaction** réaction f en chaîne; ∼ **store** magasin m à succursales multiples. •vt enchaîner. ∼-**smoke** vi fumer sans arrêt.

chair n chaise f; (armchair) fauteuil m; (Univ) chaire f; (chairperson) président/-e m/f. •vt (preside over) présider. ∼**man** n (pl -**men**) président/-e m/f. ∼**woman** n (pl -**women** présidente f.

chalk n craie f.

challenge n défi m; (opportunity) challenge m. •vt (summon) défier (**to do** de faire); (question truth of) contester. **challenger** n (Sport) challenger m. **challenging** adj stimulant.

chamber n (old use) chambre f. ∼**maid** n femme f de chambre. ∼ **music** n musique f de chambre. ∼-**pot** n pot m de chambre.

champagne n champagne m.

champion n champion/-ne m/f. •vt défendre. **championship** n championnat m.

chance n (luck) hasard m; (opportunity) occasion f; (likelihood) chances fpl; (risk) risque m; **by** ∼ par hasard; **by any** ∼ par hasard; ∼**s are that** il est probable que. •adj fortuit. •vt ∼ **doing** prendre le risque de faire; ∼ **it** tenter sa chance.

chancellor n chancelier m; **C**∼ **of the Exchequer** Chancelier de l'échiquier.

chandelier n lustre m.

change vt (alter) changer; (exchange) échanger (**for** contre). (money) changer; ∼ **trains/one's dress** changer de train/de robe; ∼ **one's mind** changer d'avis. •vi changer; (change clothes) se changer; ∼ **into** se transformer en; ~ **over** passer (**to** à). •n changement m; (money) monnaie f; **a ~ for the better** une amélioration; **a ~ for the worse** un changement en pire; **a ~ of clothes** des vêtements de rechange; **for a ~** pour changer.

changeable adj changeant.

changing room n (in shop) cabine f d'essayage; (Sport) vestiaire m.

channel n (for liquid, information) canal m; (TV) chaîne f; (groove) rainure f. •vt (pt **channelled**) canaliser. C~ **the (English) C~** la Manche; **the C~ tunnel** le tunnel sous la Manche; **the C~ Islands** les îles fpl Anglo-Normandes

chant n (Relig) mélopée f; (of demonstrators) chant m scandé. •vt/i scander; (Relig) psalmodier.

chaos n chaos m.

chap n (man 🄸) type m 🄸

chapel n chapelle f.

chaplain n aumônier m.

chapped adj gercé.

chapter n chapitre m.

char vt (pt **charred**) carboniser.

character n caractère m; (in novel, play) personnage m; **of good ~** de bonne réputation.

characteristic adj & n caractéristique (f).

charcoal n charbon m de bois; (art) fusain m.

charge n (fee) frais mpl; (Mil) charge f; (Jur) inculpation f; (task, custody) charge f; **in ~ of** responsable de; **take ~ of** prendre en charge, se charger de. •vt (customer) faire payer; (enemy, gun) charger; (Jur) inculper (**with** de); ~ **£20 an hour** prendre 20 livres de l'heure; ~ **card** carte f d'achat. •vi faire payer; (bull) foncer; (person) se précipiter.

charisma n charisme m.

charismatic adj charismatique.

charitable adj charitable. **charity** n charité f; (organization) organisation f caritative.

charm n charme m; (trinket) amulette f. •vt charmer.

charming adj charmant.

chart n (graph) graphique m; (table) tableau m; (map) carte f. •vt (route) porter sur la carte.

charter n charte f; ~ **(flight)** charter m. •vt affréter; ~**ed accountant** expert-comptable m.

chase vt poursuivre; ~ **away or off** chasser. •vi courir (**after** après). •n chasse f.

chassis n châssis m.

chastise vt châtier.

chat n conversation f; (on Internet) causette f, bavardage m; **have a ~** bavarder; ~ **show** talk-show m. ~**room** n salle f de causette, salle f de bavardage. •vi (pt **chatted**) bavarder. ■ ~ **up** 🄸 draguer 🄸

chatter n bavardage m. •vi bavarder; **his teeth are ~ing** il claque des dents. ~**box** n bavard/-e m/f.

chatty adj bavard.

chauffeur n chauffeur m.

chauvinist n chauvin/-e m/f. macho m.

cheap adj bon marché inv; (fare, rate) réduit; (joke, gimmick) facile; ~**er** meilleur marché inv. **cheapen** vt déprécier. **cheaply** adv à bas prix.

cheat vi tricher. •vt tromper. •n tricheur/-euse m/f.

check vt/i vérifier; (tickets, rises, inflation) contrôler; (stop) arrêter; (tick off: US) cocher. •n contrôle m; (curb) frein m; (chess) échec m; (pattern) carreaux mpl; (bill: US) addition f; (cheque: US) chèque m. ■ ~ **in** remplir la fiche; (at airport) enregistrer; ~ **out** partir; ~ **sth out** vérifier qch. ~ **up** vérifier. ~ **up on** (story) vérifier; (person) faire une enquête sur.

check: ~-**in** n enregistrement m. **checking account** n (US) compte m courant. ~-**list** n liste f de contrôle. ~-**mate** n échec m et mat. ~-**out** n caisse f. ~-**point** n contrôle m. ~-**up** n examen m médical.

cheek n joue f; (impudence) culot m 🅸. **cheeky** adj effronté.

cheer n gaieté f; ~s acclamations fpl; (when drinking) à la vôtre. •vt/i applaudir; ~ **sb (up)** (gladden) remonter le moral à qn; ~ **up** prendre courage. **cheerful** adj joyeux. **cheerfulness** n gaieté f.

cheerio interj 🅸 salut 🅸.

cheese n fromage m.

cheetah n guépard m.

chef n chef m.

chemical adj chimique. •n produit m chimique.

chemist n pharmacien/-ne m/f; (scientist) chimiste mf; ~**'s (shop)** pharmacie f. **chemistry** n chimie f.

cheque n chèque m. ~-**book** n chéquier m. ~ **card** n carte f bancaire.

chequered adj (pattern) à damiers; (fig) en dents de scie.

cherish vt chérir; (hope) caresser.

cherry n cerise f; (tree, wood) cerisier m.

chess n échecs mpl. ~-**board** n échiquier m.

chest n (Anat) poitrine f; (box) coffre m; ~ **of drawers** commode f.

chestnut n (nut) marron m, châtaigne f; (tree) marronnier m; (sweet) châtaignier m.

chew vt mâcher.

chic adj chic inv.

chick n poussin m.

chicken n poulet m. •adj 🆇 froussard. •vi ~ **out** 🆇 se dégonfler. ~-**pox** n varicelle f.

chick-pea n pois m chiche.

chicory n (for salad) endive f; (in coffee) chicorée f.

chief n chef m. •adj principal. **chiefly** adv principalement.

chilblain n engelure f.

child n (pl **children**) enfant mf. ~-**birth** n accouchement m. **childhood** n enfance f. **childish** adj puéril. **childless** adj sans enfants. **childlike** adj enfantin. ~-**minder** n nourrice f.

Chile n Chili m.

chill n froid m; (Med) refroidissement m. •adj froid. •vt (person) faire frissonner; (wine) rafraîchir; (food) mettre à refroidir.

chilli n (pl ~**es**) piment m.

chilly adj froid; **it's** ~ il fait froid.

chime n carillon m. •vt/i carillonner.

chimney n cheminée f. ~-**sweep** n ramoneur m.

chimpanzee n chimpanzé m.

chin n menton m.

china n porcelaine f.

China n Chine f.

Chinese n (person) Chinois/-e m/f; (Ling) chinois m. •adj chinois.

chip n (on plate) ébréchure f; (piece) éclat m; (of wood) copeau m; (Culin) frite f; (Comput) puce f; **(potato)** ~**s** (US) chips fpl. •vt/i (pt **chipped**) (s')ébrécher; ~ **in** 🅸 dire son mot; (with money) contribuer.

chiropodist n pédicure mf.

chirp n pépiement m. •vi pépier. **chirpy** adj gai.

chisel n ciseau m. •vt (pt **chiselled**) ciseler.

chit n note f; (voucher) bon m.

chitchat n 🅸 bavardage m.

chivalrous adj galant.

chives npl ciboulette f.

chlorine n chlore m.

choc ice n esquimau m.

chock-a-block adj plein à craquer.

chocolate n chocolat m.

choice n choix m. •adj de choix.

choir n chœur m. ∼**boy** n jeune choriste m.

choke vt/i (s')étrangler; ∼ **(up)** boucher. •n starter m.

cholesterol n cholestérol m.

choose vt/i (pt **chose**, pp **chosen**) choisir; ∼ **to do** décider de faire. **choosy** adj difficile.

chop vt/i (pt **chopped**) (wood) couper; (food) hacher; **chopping board** planche f à découper; ∼ **down** abattre. •n (meat) côtelette f. **chopper** n hachoir m. 🔲 hélico m 🔲.

choppy adj (sea) agité.

chopstick n baguette f (chinoise).

chord n (Mus) accord m.

chore n (routine) tâche f; (unpleasant) corvée f.

chortle n gloussement m. •vi glousser.

chorus n chœur m; (of song) refrain m.

chose, chosen ▷CHOOSE.

Christ n le Christ.

christen vt baptiser. **christening** n baptême m.

Christian adj & n chrétien/-ne (m/f). ∼ **name** nom m de baptême. **Christianity** n christianisme m.

Christmas n Noël m; ∼ **Day/Eve** le jour/la veille de Noël. •adj (card, tree) de Noël.

chronic adj (situation, disease) chronique; (bad 🔲) nul.

chronicle n chronique f.

chronological adj chronologique.

chrysanthemum n chrysanthème m.

chubby adj (**-ier, -iest**) potelé.

chuck vt 🔲 lancer; ∼ **away** or **out** 🔲 balancer.

chuckle n gloussement m. •vi glousser.

chuffed adj 🔲 vachement content 🔲.

chunk n morceau m. **chunky** adj (sweater, jewellery) gros; (person) costaud.

church n église f. ∼ **goer** n pratiquant/-e m/f. ∼**yard** n cimetière m.

churn n baratte f; (milk-can) bidon m. •vt baratter; ∼ **out** produire en série.

chute n toboggan m; (for rubbish) vide-ordures m inv.

chutney n condiment m aigredoux.

cider n cidre m.

cigar n cigare m.

cigarette n cigarette f; ∼ **end** mégot m.

cinder n cendre f.

cinema n cinéma m.

cinnamon n cannelle f.

circle n cercle m; (Theat) balcon m. •vt (go round) tourner autour de; (word, error) encercler. •vi tourner en rond.

circuit n circuit m. ∼ **board** n carte f de circuit imprimé. ∼**-breaker** n disjoncteur m.

circuitous adj indirect.

circular adj & n circulaire (f).

circulate vt/i (faire) circuler. **circulation** n circulation f; (of newspaper) tirage m.

circumcise vt circoncire.

circumference n circonférence f.

circumflex n circonflexe m.

circumstance n circonstance f; ∼**s** (financial) situation f; **under no** ∼**s** en aucun cas.

circus n cirque m.

cistern n réservoir m.

citizen n citoyen/-ne m/f; (of town) habitant/-e m/f. **citizenship** n nationalité f.

citrus adj ~ **fruit(s)** agrumes mpl; ~ **tree** citrus m.

city n (grande) ville f.

civic adj (official) municipal; (pride, duty) civique.

civil adj civil. ~ **disobedience** n résistance f passive. ~ **engineer** n ingénieur m des travaux publics.

civilian adj & n civil/-e (m/f).

civilization n civilisation f. **civilize** vt civiliser.

civil: ~ **law** n droit m civil. ~ **liberties** npl libertés fpl individuelles. ~ **rights** npl droits mpl civils. ~ **servant** n fonctionnaire mf. ~ **service** n fonction f publique. ~ **war** n guerre f civile.

claim vt (demand) revendiquer; (assert) prétendre. ●n revendication f; (assertion) affirmation f; (for insurance) réclamation f; (right) droit m. **claimant** n (of benefits) demandeur/-euse m/f.

clairvoyant n voyant/-e m/f.

clam n palourde f.

clamber vi grimper.

clammy adj (-ier, -iest) moite.

clamour n clameur f. ●vi ~ **for** réclamer.

clamp n valet m; (Med) pince f; **(wheel)** ~ sabot m de Denver. ●vt cramponner; (jaw) serrer; (car) mettre un sabot de Denver à; ~ **down on** faire de la répression contre.

clan n clan m.

clang n son m métallique.

clap vt/i (pt **clapped**) applaudir; (put forcibly) mettre; ~ **one's hands** frapper dans ses mains. ●n applaudissement m; (of thunder) coup m.

claret n bordeaux m rouge.

clarification n clarification f. **clarify** vt/i (se) clarifier.

clarinet n clarinette f.

clarity n clarté f.

clash n choc m; (fig) conflit m. ●vi (metal objects) s'entrechoquer; (armies) s'affronter; (meetings) avoir lieu en même temps; (colours) jurer.

clasp n (fastener) fermoir m. ●vt serrer.

class n classe f. ●vt classer; ~ **sb/sth as** assimiler qn/qch à.

classic adj & n classique (m). ~**s** (Univ) lettres fpl classiques. **classical** adj classique.

classified adj (information) secret; ~ **(ad)** petite annonce f.

classroom n salle f de classe.

clatter n cliquetis m. ●vi cliqueter.

clause n clause f; (Gram) proposition f.

claw n (of animal, small bird) griffe f; (of bird of prey) serre f; (of lobster) pince f. ●vt griffer.

clay n argile f.

clean adj propre; (shape, stroke) net. ●adv complètement. ●vt nettoyer; ~ **one's teeth** se brosser les dents. ●vi ~ **up** faire le nettoyage. **cleaner** n (at home) femme f de ménage; (industrial) agent m de nettoyage; (of clothes) teinturier/-ière m/f. **cleanliness** n propreté f. **cleanly** adv proprement; (sharply) nettement.

cleanse vt nettoyer; (fig) purifier.

clean-shaven adj glabre.

clear adj (explanation) clair; (need, sign) évident; (glass) transparent; (profit) net; (road) dégagé; **make sth** ~ être très clair sur qch; ~ **of** (away from) à l'écart de. ●adv complètement; **stand** ~ **of** s'éloigner de. ●vt (free) dégager (**of** de). (table) débarrasser; (building) évacuer; (cheque) compenser; (jump over) franchir; (debt) liquider; (Jur) disculper. •vi (fog) se dissiper; (cheque) être compensé. ∎ ~ **away** or **off** (remove) enlever. ~ **off** or **out** 🔳 décamper. ~ **out** (clean) nettoyer. ~ **up** (tidy) ranger; (weather) s'éclaircir.

clearance n (permission) autorisation f; (space) espace m; ~ **sale** liquidation f.

clear-cut adj net.

clearing n clairière f.

clearly adv clairement.

clef n (Mus) clé f.

cleft n fissure f.

clench vt serrer.

clergy n clergé m. ~**man** n (pl -**men**) ecclésiastique m.

cleric n clerc m. **clerical** adj (Relig) clérical; (staff, work) de bureau.

clerk n employé/-e m/f de bureau; (US) **(sales)** ~ vendeur/-euse m/f.

clever adj intelligent; (skilful) habile.

click n déclic m; (Comput) clic m. •vi faire un déclic; (people 🔳) sympathiser; (Comput) cliquer (**on** sur.) •vt (heels, tongue) faire claquer.

client n client/-e m/f.

clientele n clientèle f.

cliff n falaise f.

climate n climat m.

climax n (of story, contest) point m culminant; (sexual) orgasme m.

climb vt grimper; (steps) monter; (tree, ladder) grimper à; (mountain) faire l'ascension de. •vi grimper; ~ **into** (car) monter dans; ~ **into bed** se mettre au lit. •n (of mountain) escalade f; (steep hill, rise) montée f. ∎ ~ **down** (fig) reculer. **climber** n (Sport) alpiniste mf.

clinch vt (deal) conclure; (victory, order) décrocher.

cling vi (pt **clung**) se cramponner

(**to** à.) (stick) coller. ~**-film** n scellofrais® m.

clinic n centre m médical; (private) clinique f. **clinical** adj clinique.

clink n tintement m. •vt/i (faire) tinter.

clip n (for paper) trombone m; (for hair) barrette f; (for tube) collier m; (of film) extrait m. •vt (pt **clipped**) (fasten) attacher (**to** à). (cut) couper.

clippers npl tondeuse f; (for nails) coupe-ongles m inv.

clipping n (from press) coupure f de presse.

cloak n cape f; (man's) houppelande f. ~**room** n vestiaire m; (toilet) toilettes fpl.

clobber n 🔳 attirail m. •vt (hit 🔳) tabasser 🔳.

clock n pendule f; (large) horloge f. •vi ~ **on/in** or **off/out** pointer; ~ **up** (miles) faire. ~**-tower** n beffroi m. ~**wise** adj & adv dans le sens des aiguilles d'une montre.

clockwork n mécanisme m. •adj mécanique.

clog n sabot m. •vt/i (pt **clogged**) (se) boucher.

cloister n cloître m.

clone n clone m. •vt cloner.

close¹ /kləʊs/ adj (friend, relative) proche (**to** de). (link, collaboration) étroit; (examination) minutieux; (result, match) serré; (weather) lourd; ~ **together** (crowded) serrés; ~ **by**, ~ **at hand** tout près; **have a** ~ **shave** l'échapper belle; **keep a** ~ **watch on** surveiller de près. •adv près. •n (street) impasse f.

close² /kləʊz/ vt fermer; (meeting, case) mettre fin à. •vi se fermer; (shop) fermer; (meeting, play) prendre fin. •n fin f.

closely adv (follow) de près. **closeness** n proximité f.

closet n (US) placard m.

close-up n gros plan m.

closure n fermeture f.

clot n (of blood) caillot m; (in sauce) grumeau m. ●vt/i (pt **clotted**) (se) coaguler.

cloth n (fabric) tissu m; (duster) chiffon m; (table-cloth) nappe f.

clothe vt vêtir.

clothes npl vêtements mpl. **~-hanger** n cintre m. **~-line** n corde f à linge.

clothing n vêtements mpl.

cloud n nuage m. ●vi ~ **over** se couvrir (de nuages); (face) s'assombrir. **cloudy** adj (sky) couvert; (liquid) trouble.

clout n (blow) coup m de poing; (power) influence f. ●vt frapper.

clove n clou m de girofle; ~ **of garlic** gousse f d'ail.

clover n trèfle m.

clown n clown m. ●vi faire le clown.

club n (group) club m; (weapon) massue f; **(golf)** ~ club m (de golf); **~s** (cards) trèfle m. ●vt/i (pt **clubbed**) matraquer. ■ ~ **together** cotiser.

cluck vi glousser.

clue n indice m; (in crossword) définition f; **I haven't a ~** 🔲 je n'en ai pas la moindre idée.

clump n massif m.

clumsy adj (**-ier, -iest**) maladroit; (tool) peu commode.

clung ▷CLING.

cluster n (of people, islands) groupe m; (of flowers, berries) grappe f. ●vi se grouper.

clutch vt (hold) serrer fort; (grasp) saisir. ●vi ~ **at** (try to grasp) essayer de saisir. ●n (Auto) embrayage m; (of eggs) couvée f; (of people) groupe m.

clutter n désordre m. ●vt ~ **(up)** encombrer.

coach n autocar m; (of train) wagon m; (horse-drawn) carrosse m; (Sport)

entraîneur/-euse m/f. ●vt (team) entraîner; (pupil) donner des leçons particulières à.

coal n charbon m. **~field** n bassin m houiller. **~-mine** n mine f de charbon.

coarse adj grossier.

coast n côte f. ●vi (car, bicycle) descendre en roue libre. **coastal** adj côtier.

coast: **~guard** n (person) gardecôte m; (organization) gendarmerie f maritime. **~line** n littoral m.

coat n manteau m; (of animal) pelage m; (of paint) couche f; ~ **of arms** armoiries fpl. ●vt enduire, couvrir; (with chocolate) enrober (**with** de). **coating** n couche f.

coax vt cajoler.

cob n (of corn) épi m.

cobbler n cordonnier m.

cobblestones npl pavés mpl.

cobweb n toile f d'araignée.

cocaine n cocaïne f.

cock n (rooster) coq m. (oiseau) mâle m. ●vt (gun) armer; (ears) dresser.

cockerel n jeune coq m.

cockle n (Culin) coque f.

cock: **~pit** n poste m de pilotage. **~roach** n cafard m. **~tail** n cocktail m.

cocky adj (**-ier, -iest**) trop sûr de soi.

cocoa n cacao m.

coconut n noix f de coco.

COD abbr (**cash on delivery**) envoi m contre remboursement.

cod n inv morue f; **~-liver oil** huile f de foie de morue.

code n code m. ●vt coder.

coerce vt contraindre.

coexist vi coexister.

coffee n café m. ~ **bar** n café m. ~ **bean** n grain m de café. **~pot**

n cafetière f. **~-table** n table f basse.

coffin n cercueil m.

cog n pignon m; (fig) rouage m.

cognac n cognac m.

coil vt/i (s')enrouler. ●n (of rope) rouleau m; (of snake) anneau m; (contraceptive) stérilet m.

coin n pièce f (de monnaie). ●vt (word) inventer.

coincide vi coïncider. **coincidence** n coïncidence f. **coincidental** adj dû à une coïncidence.

colander n passoire f.

cold adj froid; (person) **be or feel ~** avoir froid; **it is ~** il fait froid; **get ~ feet** avoir les jetons 🅸; ●n froid m; (Med) rhume m; **~-blooded** adj (lit) à sang froid; (fig) sans pitié. **coldness** n froideur f. **~ sore** n bouton m de fièvre.

coleslaw n salade f de chou cru.

colic n coliques fpl.

collaborate vi collaborer.

collapse vi s'effondrer; (person) s'écrouler; (fold) se plier. ●n effondrement m.

collar n col m; (of dog) collier m. **~-bone** n clavicule f.

collateral n nantissement m.

colleague n collègue mf.

collect vt rassembler; (pick up) ramasser; (call for) passer prendre; (money, fare) encaisser; (taxes, rent) percevoir; (as hobby) collectionner. ●vi se rassembler; (dust) s'amasser. ●adv **call ~** (US) appeler en PCV. **collection** n collection f; (of money) collecte f; (in church) quête f; (of mail) levée f.

collective adj collectif.

collector n (as hobby) collectionneur/-euse m/f; (of taxes) percepteur m; (of rent, debt) encaisseur m.

college n (for higher education)

établissement m d'enseignement supérieur; (within university) collège m; **be at ~** faire des études supérieures.

collide vi entrer en collision (**with** avec).

colliery n houillère f.

collision n collision f.

colloquial adj familier. **colloquialism** n expression f familière.

Colombia n Colombie f.

colon n (Gram) deux-points m inv; (Anat) côlon m.

colonel n colonel m.

colonial adj & n colonial/-e (m/f).

colour, (US) **color** n couleur f. ●adj (photo) en couleur; (TV set) couleur inv. ●vt colorer; (with crayon) colorier. **~-blind** adj daltonien. **coloured** adj de couleur. **colourful** adj aux couleurs vives; (fig) haut en couleur. **colouring** n (of skin) teint m; (in food) colorant m.

colt n poulain m.

column n colonne f.

coma n coma m.

comb n peigne m. ●vt peigner; **~ one's hair** se peigner; **~ a place** passer un lieu au peigne fin.

combat n combat m. ●vt (pt **combated**) combattre.

combination n combinaison f.

combine[1] /kəmˈbaɪn/ vt/i (se) combiner, (s')unir.

combine[2] /ˈkɒmbaɪn/ n (Comm) groupe m; **~ harvester** moissonneuse-batteuse f.

come vi (pt **came**, pp **come**) venir; (bus, letter) arriver; (postman) passer; **~ and look!** viens voir!; **~ in** (size, colour) exister; **when it ~s to** lorsqu'il s'agit de. ▪ **~ about** survenir. **~ across** (meaning) passer; **~ across sth** tomber sur qch. **~ away** (leave) partir; (come off) se détacher. ~ **back** revenir. ~ **by** obtenir. ~ **down** descendre; (price) baisser; ~ **forward** se présenter. ~ **in** entrer; ~ **in useful** être utile. ~ **in for** recevoir. ~ **into** (money) hériter de. ~ **off** (succeed) réussir; (fare) s'en tirer; (detach) se détacher. ~ **on** (actor) entrer en scène; (light) s'allumer; (improve) faire des progrès; ~ **on!** allez!. ~ **out** sortir. ~ **round** reprendre connaissance; (change mind) changer d'avis; ~ **through** s'en tirer. ~ **to** reprendre connaissance; ~ **to sth** (amount) revenir à qch; (decision, conclusion) arriver à qch. ~ **up** (problem) être soulevé; (opportunity) se présenter; (sun) se lever; ~ **up against** se heurter à. ~ **up with** trouver.

comedian n comique m.

comedy n comédie f.

comfort n confort m; (consolation) réconfort m. ●vt consoler. **comfortable** adj (chair, car) confortable; (person) à l'aise; (wealthy) aisé.

comfortably adv confortablement; ~ **off** aisé.

comfy adj 🔢 ▷COMFORTABLE.

comic adj comique. ●n (person) comique m; ~ **(book)**, ~ **strip** bande f dessinée.

coming n arrivée f; ~**s and goings** allées et venues fpl. ●adj à venir.

comma n virgule f.

command n (authority) commandement m; (order) ordre m; (mastery) maîtrise f. ●vt ordonner à (**to do** de faire); (be able to use) disposer de; (respect) inspirer. **commandeer** vt réquisitionner. **commander** n commandant m. **commanding** adj imposant. **commandment** n commandement m.

commando n commando m.

commemorate vt commémorer.

commence vt/i commencer.

commend vt (praise) louer; (entrust) confier.

commensurate adj proportionné.

comment n commentaire m. ●vi faire des commentaires; ~ **on** commenter. **commentary** n commentaire m; (radio, TV) reportage m. **commentate** vi faire un reportage. **commentator** n commentateur/-trice m/f.

commerce n commerce m.

commercial adj commercial; (traveller) de commerce. ●n publicité f.

commiserate vi compatir (**with** avec).

commission n commission f; (order for work) commande f; **out of** ~ hors service. ●vt (order) commander; (Mil) nommer officier; ~ **to do** charger de faire. **commissioner** n préfet m (de police); (in EU) membre m de la Commission européenne.

commit vt (pt **committed**) commettre; (entrust) confier; ~ **oneself** s'engager; ~ **perjury** se parjurer; ~ **suicide** se suicider; ~ **to memory** apprendre par cœur. **commitment** n engagement m.

committee n comité m.

commodity n article m.

common adj (shared by all) commun (**to** à); (usual) courant; (vulgar) vulgaire, commun; **in** ~ en commun; ~ **people** le peuple; ~ **sense** bon sens m. ●n terrain m communal; **the C**~**s** Chambre f des Communes.

commoner n roturier/-ière m/f.

common law n droit m coutumier.

commonly adv communément.

commonplace adj banal. ●n banalité f.

common-room n salle f de détente.

Commonwealth n **the** ~ le Commonwealth m.

commotion n (noise) vacarme m; (disturbance) agitation f.

communal adj (shared) commun; (life) collectif.

commune n (group) communauté f.

communicate vt/i communiquer. **communication** n communication f. **communicative** adj communicatif.

communion n communion f.

Communism n communisme m. **Communist** adj & n communiste (mf).

community n communauté f.

commute vi faire la navette. •vt (Jur) commuer. **commuter** n navetteur/-euse m/f.

compact adj compact; (lady's case) poudrier m.

compact disc n disque m compact. ~ **player** n platine f laser.

companion n compagnon/-agne m/f. **companionship** n camaraderie f.

company n (companionship, firm) compagnie f; (guests) invités/-es m/fpl.

comparative adj (study, form) comparatif; (comfort) relatif.

compare vt comparer (**with, to** à). ~**d with** par rapport à. •vi être comparable. **comparison** n comparaison f.

compartment n compartiment m.

compass n (for direction) boussole f; (scope) portée f; **a pair of** ~**es** un compas.

compassionate adj compatissant.

compatible adj compatible.

compel vt (pt **compelled**) contraindre. **compelling** adj irrésistible.

compensate vt/i (financially) dédommager (**for** de). ~ **for sth** compenser qch. **compensation** n compensation f; (financial) dédommagement m.

compete vi concourir; ~ **with** rivaliser avec.

competent adj compétent.

competition n (contest) concours m; (Sport) compétition f; (Comm) concurrence f.

competitive adj (prices) compétitif; (person) qui a l'esprit de compétition.

competitor n concurrent/-e m/f.

compile vt (list) dresser; (book) rédiger.

complacency n suffisance f.

complain vi se plaindre (**about, of** de). **complaint** n plainte f; (official) réclamation f; (illness) maladie f.

complement n complément m. •vt compléter. **complementary** adj complémentaire.

complete adj complet; (finished) achevé; (downright) parfait. •vt achever; (a form) remplir. **completely** adv complètement. **completion** n achèvement m.

complex adj complexe. •n (Psych) complexe m.

complexion n (of face) teint m; (fig) caractère m.

compliance n (agreement) conformité f.

complicate vt compliquer. **complicated** adj compliqué. **complication** n complication f.

compliment n compliment m. •vt complimenter. **complimentary** adj (offert) à titre gracieux; (praising) flatteur.

comply vi ~ **with** se conformer à, obéir à.

component n (of machine) pièce f;

(chemical substance) composant m; (element: fig) composante f. ● adj constituant.

compose vt composer; ~ **oneself** se calmer. **composed** adj calme. **composer** n (Mus) compositeur m. **composition** n composition f.

composure n calme m.

compound n (substance, word) composé m; (enclosure) enclos m. ● adj composé.

comprehend vt comprendre. **comprehension** n compréhension f.

comprehensive adj étendu, complet; (insurance) tous risques inv. ~ **school** n collège m d'enseignement secondaire.

compress vt comprimer.

comprise vt comprendre, inclure.

compromise n compromis m. ● vt compromettre. ● vi transiger, arriver à un compromis.

compulsive adj (Psych) compulsif; (liar, smoker) invétéré.

compulsory adj obligatoire.

compute vt calculer.

computer n ordinateur m; ~ **science** informatique f. **computerize** vt informatiser.

comrade n camarade mf.

con[1] /kɒn/ vt (pt **conned** ⊠) rouler ⊠, escroquer (**out of** de.) ● n ⊠ escroquerie f.

con[2] /kɒn/ ▷PRO.

conceal vt dissimuler (**from** à.)

concede vt concéder. ● vi céder.

conceited adj vaniteux.

conceive vt/i concevoir; ~ **of** concevoir.

concentrate vt/i (se) concentrer. **concentration** n concentration f.

concept n concept m.

conception n conception f.

concern n (interest, business) affaire f; (worry) inquiétude f; (firm: Comm) entreprise f, affaire f. ● vt concerner; ~ **oneself with, be** ~**ed with** s'occuper de. **concerned** adj inquiet. **concerning** prep en ce qui concerne.

concert n concert m.

concession n concession f.

conciliation n conciliation f.

concise adj concis.

conclude vt conclure. ● vi se terminer. **conclusion** n conclusion f. **conclusive** adj concluant.

concoct vt confectionner; (invent: fig) fabriquer. **concoction** n mélange m.

concourse n (Rail) hall m.

concrete n béton m. ● adj de béton; (fig) concret. ● vt bétonner.

concur vi (pt **concurred**) être d'accord.

concurrently adv simultanément.

concussion n commotion f (cérébrale).

condemn vt condamner.

condensation n (on walls) condensation f; (on windows) buée f. **condense** vt/i (se) condenser.

condition n condition f; **on** ~ **that** à condition que. ● vt conditionner. **conditional** adj conditionnel.

conditioner n après-shampooing m.

condolences npl condoléances fpl.

condom n préservatif m.

condone vt pardonner, fermer les yeux sur.

conducive adj ~ **to** favorable à.

conduct[1] /'kɒndʌkt/ n conduite f.

conduct[2] /kən'dʌkt/ vt conduire; (orchestra) diriger. **conductor** n chef m d'orchestre; (of bus) receveur m; (on train: US) chef m de train; (Electr) conducteur m. conductress f.

cone n cône m. (of ice-cream) cornet m.

confectioner n confiseur/-euse m/f. **confectionery** n confiserie f.

confer vt/i (pt **conferred**) conférer.

conference n conférence f.

confess vt/i avouer; (Relig) (se) confesser. **confession** n confession f; (of crime) aveu m.

confide vt confier. •vi ~ **in** se confier à.

confidence n (trust) confiance f. (boldness) confiance f en soi; (secret) confidence f; **in** ~ en confidence. **confident** adj sûr.

confidential adj confidentiel.

configuration n configuration f. **configure** vt configurer.

confine vt enfermer; (limit) limiter; ~**d space** espace m réduit; ~**d to** limité à.

confirm vt confirmer. **confirmed** adj (bachelor) endurci; (smoker) invétéré.

confiscate vt confisquer.

conflict[1] /ˈkɒnflɪkt/ n conflit m.

conflict[2] /kənˈflɪkt/ vi (statements, views) être en contradiction (**with** avec); (appointments) tomber en même temps (**with** que). **conflicting** adj contradictoire.

conform vt/i (se) conformer.

confound vt confondre.

confront vt affronter; ~ **with** confronter avec.

confuse vt (bewilder) troubler; (mistake, confound) confondre; **become** ~**d** s'embrouiller; **I am** ~**d** je m'y perds. **confusing** adj déroutant. **confusion** n confusion f.

congeal vt/i (se) figer.

congested adj (road) embouteillé;

(passage) encombré; (Med) congestionné. **congestion** n (traffic) encombrement(s) m(pl); (Med) congestion f.

congratulate vt féliciter (**on** de). **congratulations** npl félicitations fpl.

congregate vi se rassembler. **congregation** n assemblée f.

congress n congrès m. **C** ~ (US) le Congrès.

conjugate vt conjuguer. **conjugation** n conjugaison f.

conjunction n (Ling) conjonction f. **in** ~**with** conjointement avec.

conjunctivitis n conjonctivite f.

conjure vi faire des tours de passe-passe. •vt ~ **up** faire apparaître. **conjuror** n prestidigitateur/-trice m/f.

con man n ⊠ escroc m.

connect vt/i (se) relier; (in mind) faire le rapport entre; (install, wire up to mains) brancher; ~ **with** (of train) assurer la correspondance avec; ~**ed** (idea, event) lié; **be** ~**ed with** avoir rapport à.

connection n rapport m. (Rail) correspondance f; (phone call) communication f; (Electr) contact m; (joining piece) raccord m; ~**s** (Comm) relations fpl.

connive vi ~ **at** se faire le complice de.

conquer vt vaincre; (country) conquérir. **conqueror** n conquérant n.

conquest n conquête f.

conscience n conscience f. **conscientious** adj consciencieux.

conscious adj conscient; (deliberate) voulu. **consciously** adv consciemment. **consciousness** n conscience f; (Med) connaissance f.

conscript n appelé m.

consecutive adj consécutif.

consensus n consensus m.

consent vi consentir (**to** à). ●n consentement m.

consequence n conséquence f. **consequently** adv par conséquent.

conservation n préservation f. ~ **area** zone f protégée. **conservationist** n défenseur m de l'environnement.

conservative adj conservateur; (estimate) minimal.

Conservative Party n parti m conservateur.

conservatory n (greenhouse) serre f; (room) véranda f.

conserve vt conserver; (energy) économiser.

consider vt considérer; (allow for) tenir compte de; (possibility) envisager (**doing** de faire).

considerable adj considérable; (much) beaucoup de.

considerate adj prévenant, attentionné. **consideration** n considération f; (respect) égard(s) m(pl)

considering prep compte tenu de.

consignment n envoi m.

consist vi consister (**of** en; **in doing** à faire).

consistency n (of liquids) consistance f; (of argument) cohérence f.

consistent adj cohérent; ~ **with** conforme à.

consolation n consolation f.

consolidate vt/i (se) consolider.

consonant n consonne f.

conspicuous adj (easily seen) en évidence; (showy) voyant; (noteworthy) remarquable.

conspiracy n conspiration f.

constable n agent m de police, gendarme m.

constant adj (questions) incessant; (unchanging) constant; (friend) fidèle. ●n constante f.

constantly adv constamment.

constellation n constellation f.

constipation n constipation f.

constituency n circonscription f électorale.

constituent adj constitutif. ●n élément m constitutif; (Pol) électeur/-trice m/f.

constitution n constitution f.

constrain vt contraindre. **constraint** n contrainte f.

constrict vt (flow) comprimer; (movement) gêner.

construct vt construire. **construction** n construction f. **constructive** adj constructif.

consulate n consulat m.

consult vt consulter. ●vi ~ **with** conférer avec. **consultant** n conseiller/-ère m/f; (Med) spécialiste mf. **consultation** n consultation f.

consume vt consommer; (destroy) consumer. **consumer** n consommateur/-trice m/f.

consummate vt consommer.

consumption n consommation f; (Med) phtisie f.

contact n contact m; (person) relation f. ●vt contacter. ~ **lenses** npl lentilles fpl (de contact).

contagious adj contagieux.

contain vt contenir; ~ **oneself** se contenir. **container** n récipient m; (for transport) container m.

contaminate vt contaminer.

contemplate vt (gaze at) contempler; (think about) envisager.

contemporary adj & n contemporain/-e (m/f).

contempt n mépris m. **contemptible** adj méprisable. **contemptuous** adj méprisant.

contend vt soutenir. •vi ~ **with** (compete) rivaliser avec; (face) faire face à. **contender** n adversaire mf.

content¹ /'kɒntent/ n (of letter) contenu m. (amount) teneur f; ~**s** contenu m.

content² /kən'tent/ adj satisfait. •vt contenter. **contented** adj satisfait. **contentment** n contentement m.

contest¹ /'kɒntest/ n (competition) concours m. (struggle) lutte f.

contest² /kən'test/ vt contester; (compete for or in) disputer. **contestant** n concurrent/-e m/f.

context n contexte m.

continent n continent m; **the C** ~ l'Europe f (continentale). **continental** adj continental, européen. **continental quilt** n couette f.

contingency n éventualité f. ~ **plan** plan m d'urgence.

continual adj continuel.

continuation n continuation f. (after interruption) reprise f; (new episode) suite f.

continue vt/i continuer; (resume) reprendre. **continued** adj continu.

continuous adj continu. **continuously** adv (without a break) sans interruption; (repeatedly) continuellement.

contort vt tordre; ~ **oneself** se contorsionner.

contour n contour m.

contraband n contrebande f.

contraception n contraception f. **contraceptive** adj & n contraceptif (m).

contract¹ /'kɒntrækt/ n contrat m.

contract² /kən'trækt/ vt/i (se) contracter. **contraction** n contraction f.

contractor n entrepreneur/-euse m/f.

contradict vt contredire. **contradictory** adj contradictoire.

contrary¹ /'kɒntrərɪ/ adj contraire (**to** à). •n contraire m. **on the** ~ au contraire. •adv ~ **to** contrairement à.

contrary² /kən'treərɪ/ adj entêté.

contrast¹ /'kɒntrɑːst/ n contraste m.

contrast² /kən'trɑːst/ vt/i contraster.

contravention n infraction f.

contribute vt donner. •vi ~ **to** contribuer à; (take part) participer à; (newspaper) collaborer à. **contribution** n contribution f. **contributor** n collaborateur/-trice m/f.

contrive vt imaginer; ~ **to do** trouver moyen de faire.

control vt (pt **controlled**) (firm) diriger; (check) contrôler; (restrain) maîtriser. •n contrôle m. (mastery) maîtrise f. ~**s** commandes fpl. (knobs) boutons mpl; **have under** ~ (event) avoir en main; **in** ~ **of** maître de. ~ **tower** n tour f de contrôle.

controversial adj discutable, discuté. **controversy** n controverse f.

conurbation n agglomération f, conurbation f.

convalesce vi être en convalescence.

convene vt convoquer. •vi se réunir.

convenience n commodité f. ~**s** toilettes fpl; **all modern** ~**s** tout le confort moderne; **at your** ~ quand cela vous conviendra, à votre convenance. ~ **foods** npl plats mpl tout préparés.

convenient adj commode, pratique; (time) bien choisi; **be** ~ **for** convenir à.

convent n couvent m.

convention n (assembly, agreement) convention f. (custom) usage m.

conventional adj conventionnel.

conversation n conversation f.
conversational adj (tone) de la conversation; (French) de tous les jours.

converse[1] /kən'vɜːs/ vi s'entretenir, converser (**with** avec).

converse[2] /'kɒnvɜːs/ adj & n inverse (m). **conversely** adv inversement.

conversion n conversion f.

convert[1] /kən'vɜːt/ vt convertir; (house) aménager. • vi ~ **into** se transformer en.

convert[2] /'kɒnvɜːt/ n converti/-e m/f.

convertible adj convertible. • n (car) décapotable f.

convey vt (wishes, order) transmettre; (goods, people) transporter; (idea, feeling) communiquer. **conveyor belt** n tapis m roulant.

convict[1] /kən'vɪkt/ vt déclarer coupable.

convict[2] /'kɒnvɪkt/ n prisonnier/-ière m/f.

conviction n (Jur) condamnation f; (opinion) conviction f.

convince vt convaincre.

convoke vt convoquer.

convoy n convoi m.

convulse vt convulser; (fig) bouleverser; **be ~d with laughter** se tordre de rire.

cook vt/i (faire) cuire; (of person) faire la cuisine; ~ **up** ▣ fabriquer. • n cuisinier/-ière m/f. **cooker** n (stove) cuisinière f. **cookery** n cuisine f.

cookie n (US) biscuit m.

cooking n cuisine f. • adj de cuisine.

cool adj frais; (calm) calme; (unfriendly) froid. • n fraîcheur f. (calmness ▣) sang-froid m; **in the**
~ au frais. • vt/i rafraîchir. ~ **box** n glacière f.

coolly adv calmement, froidement.

coop n poulailler m. • vt ~ **up** enfermer.

cooperate vi coopérer. **cooperation** n coopération f.

cooperative adj coopératif. • n coopérative f.

coordinate vt coordonner.

cop vt (pt **copped**) ▣ piquer. • n (policeman) ▣ flic m. ■ ~ **out** ▣ se dérober.

cope vi s'en sortir ▣, se débrouiller; ~ **with** (problem) faire face à.

copper n cuivre m. (coin) sou m; ▣ flic m. • adj de cuivre.

copulate vi s'accoupler.

copy n copie f. (of book, newspaper) exemplaire m; (print: Photo) épreuve f. • vt/i copier.

copyright n droit m d'auteur, copyright m.

copy-writer n rédacteur-concepteur m, rédactrice-conceptrice f.

cord n (petite) corde f; (of curtain, pyjamas) cordon m; (Electr) cordon m électrique; (fabric) velours m côtelé.

cordial adj cordial. • n (drink) sirop m.

corduroy n velours m côtelé.

core n (of apple) trognon m; (of problem) cœur m; (Tech) noyau m. • vt (apple) évider.

cork n liège m. (for bottle) bouchon m. • vt boucher. **corkscrew** n tire-bouchon m.

corn n blé m. (maize: US) maïs m; (seed) grain m; (hard skin) cor m.

cornea n cornée f.

corner n coin m; (bend in road) virage m; (football) corner m. • vt coincer, acculer; (market) accaparer. ● vi prendre un virage.

cornflour n farine f de maïs.

cornice n corniche f.

corny adj (-ier, -iest) (joke) éculé.

corollary n corollaire m.

coronary n infarctus m.

coronation n couronnement m.

corporal n caporal m. ∼ **punishment** n châtiment m corporel.

corporate adj (ownership) en commun; (body) constitué.

corporation n (Comm) société f.

corpse n cadavre m.

corpuscle n globule m.

correct adj (right) exact, juste, correct; (proper) correct; **you are** ∼ vous avez raison. ● vt corriger.

correction n correction f.

correlate vt/i (faire) correspondre.

correspond vi correspondre. **correspondence** n correspondance f.

corridor n couloir m.

corrode vt/i (se) corroder.

corrugated adj ondulé; ∼ **iron** tôle f ondulée.

corrupt adj corrompu. ● vt corrompre. **corruption** n corruption f.

Corsica n Corse f.

cosh n matraque f. ● vt matraquer.

cosmetic n produit m de beauté. ● adj cosmétique; (fig, pej) superficiel. ∼ **surgery** n chirurgie f esthétique.

cosmopolitan adj & n cosmopolite (mf).

cosmos n cosmos m.

cost vt (pt cost) coûter. (pt costed) établir le prix de. ● n coût m. ∼**s** (Jur) dépens mpl. **at all** ∼**s** à tout prix; **to one's** ∼ à ses dépens; ∼ **price** prix m de

revient; ∼ **of living** coût m de la vie. ∼**-effective** adj rentable.

costly adj (-ier, -iest) coûteux; (valuable) précieux.

costume n costume m. (for swimming) maillot m. ∼ **jewellery** npl bijoux mpl de fantaisie.

cosy adj (-ier, -iest) confortable, intime.

cot n lit m d'enfant; (camp-bed: US) lit m de camp.

cottage n petite maison f de campagne; (thatched) chaumière f. ∼ **pie** n hachis m Parmentier.

cotton n coton m. (for sewing) fil m (à coudre). ● vi ∼ **on** ✗ piger. ∼ **wool** n coton m hydrophile.

couch n canapé m. ● vt (express) formuler.

cough vi tousser. ● n toux f. ■ ∼ **up** ✗ cracher, payer.

could ▷CAN¹.

couldn't ▷COULD NOT.

council n conseil m. ∼ **house** n maison f louée par la municipalité, ≈ H.L.M. m or f.

councillor n conseiller/-ère m/f municipal/-e.

counsel n conseil m. ● n inv (Jur) avocat/-e m/f. **counsellor** n conseiller/-ère m/f.

count vt/i compter. ● n (numerical record) décompte m; (nobleman) comte m. ∼ **on** compter sur.

counter n comptoir m. (in bank) guichet m; (token) jeton m. ● adv ∼ **to** à l'encontre de. ● adj opposé. ● vt opposer; (blow) parer. ● vi riposter.

counteract vt neutraliser.

counterbalance n contrepoids m. ● vt contrebalancer.

counterfeit adj & n faux (m). ● vt contrefaire.

counterfoil n souche f.

counter-productive adj qui produit l'effet contraire.

countess n comtesse f.

countless adj innombrable.

country n (land, region) pays m. (homeland) patrie f; (countryside) campagne f.

countryman n (pl **-men**) campagnard m; (fellow citizen) compatriote m.

countryside n campagne f.

county n comté m.

coup n (achievement) joli coup m. (Pol) coup m d'état.

couple n (people, animals) couple m. **a ~ of** (two or three) deux ou trois. •vt/i (s')accoupler.

coupon n coupon m; (for shopping) bon m or coupon m de réduction.

courage n courage m.

courgette n courgette f.

courier n messager/-ère m/f; (for tourists) guide m.

course n cours m; (for training) stage m; (series) série f; (Culin) plat m; (for golf) terrain m; (at sea) itinéraire m. **change ~** changer de cap; **~ (of action)** façon f de faire; **during the ~ of** pendant; **in due ~** en temps utile; **of ~** bien sûr.

court n cour f; (tennis) court m; **go to ~** aller devant les tribunaux. •vt faire la cour à; (danger) rechercher.

courteous adj courtois.

courtesy n courtoisie f; **by ~ of** avec la permission de.

courthouse n (US) palais m de justice.

court-martial vt (pt **-martialled**) faire passer en conseil de guerre. •n cour f martiale.

court: **~room** n salle f de tribunal. **~ shoe** n escarpin m. **~yard** n cour f.

cousin n cousin/-e m/f. **first ~** cousin/-e m/f germain/-e.

cove n anse f, crique f.

covenant n convention f.

cover vt couvrir. •n (for bed, book) couverture f. (lid) couvercle m; (for furniture) housse f; (shelter) abri m; **take ~** se mettre à l'abri. ■ **~ up** cacher; (crime) couvrir; **~ up for** couvrir.

coverage n reportage m.

covering n enveloppe f. **~ letter** lettre f d'accompagnement.

covert adj (activity) secret; (threat) voilé; (look) dérobé.

cover-up n opération f de camouflage.

cow n vache f.

coward n lâche mf.

cowboy n cow-boy m.

cowshed n étable f.

coy adj (faussement) timide, qui fait le or la timide.

cozy US ▷cosy.

crab n crabe m. **~-apple** n pomme f sauvage.

crack n fente f; (in glass) fêlure f; (noise) craquement m; (joke ▣) plaisanterie f. •adj ▣ d'élite. •vt/i (break partially) (se) fêler; (split) (se) fendre; (nut) casser; (joke) raconter; (problem) résoudre; **get ~ing** ▣ s'y mettre. ■ **~ down on** ▣ sévir contre. **~ up** ▣ craquer.

cracker n (Culin) biscuit m (salé); (for Christmas) diablotin f.

crackle vi crépiter. •n crépitement m.

cradle n berceau m. •vt bercer.

craft n métier m artisanal; (technique) art m; (boat) bateau m.

craftsman n (pl **-men**) artisan m. **craftsmanship** n art m.

crafty adj (**-ier**, **-iest**) rusé.

crag n rocher m à pic.

cram vt/i (pt **crammed**). (for an exam) bachoter (**for** pour;) **~ into** (pack) (s')entasser dans; **~ with** (fill) bourrer de.

cramp n crampe f.

cramped adj à l'étroit.

cranberry n canneberge f.

crane n grue f. • vt (neck) tendre.

crank n excentrique mf; (Tech) manivelle f.

crap n (nonsense 🗙) conneries fpl 🗙; (faeces 🗙) merde f 🗙.

crash n accident m; (noise) fracas m; (of thunder) coup m; (of firm) faillite f. • vt/i avoir un accident (avec); (of plane) s'écraser; (two vehicles) se percuter; ~ **into** rentrer dans. ~ **course** n cours m intensif. ~-**helmet** n casque m (anti-choc). ~-**land** vi atterrir en catastrophe.

crate n cageot m.

cravat n foulard m.

crave vt/i ~ **for** désirer ardemment. **craving** n envie f irrésistible.

crawl vi (insect) ramper; (vehicle) se traîner; **be** ~**ing with** grouiller de. • n (pace) pas m; (swimming) crawl m.

crayfish n inv écrevisse f.

crayon n craie f grasse.

craze n engouement m.

crazy adj (-**ier**, -**iest**) fou; ~ **about** (person) fou de; (thing) fana or fou de.

creak n grincement m. • vi grincer.

cream n crème f. • adj crème inv. • vt écrémer.

crease n pli m. • vt/i (se) froisser.

create vt créer. **creation** n création f. **creative** adj (person) créatif; (process) créateur. **creator** n créateur/-trice m/f.

creature n créature f.

crèche n garderie f.

credentials npl (identity) pièces fpl d'identité; (competence) références fpl.

credibility n crédibilité f.

credit n (credence) crédit m; (honour) honneur m; **in** ~ créditeur; ~**s** (cinema) générique m. • adj (balance) créditeur. • vt croire; (Comm) créditer; ~ **sb with** attribuer à qn. ~ **card** n carte f de crédit. ~ **note** n avoir m.

creditor n créancier/-ière m/f.

creditworthy adj solvable.

creed n credo m.

creek n (US) ruisseau m. **up the** ~ 🗙 dans le pétrin 🗙.

creep vi (pt **crept**) (insect, cat) ramper; (fig) se glisser. • n (person 🗙) pauvre type m 🔳. **give sb the** ~**s** faire frissonner qn. **creeper** n liane f.

cremate vt incinérer. **cremation** n incinération f. **crematorium** n (pl -**ia**) crématorium m.

crêpe n crêpe m. ~ **paper** n papier m crêpon.

crept ▷CREEP.

crescent n croissant m; (of houses) rue f en demi-lune.

cress n cresson m.

crest n crête f. (coat of arms) armoiries fpl.

cretin n crétin/-e m/f.

crevice n fente f.

crew n (of plane, ship) équipage m; (gang) équipe f. ~ **cut** n coupe f en brosse. ~ **neck** n (col) ras du cou m.

crib n lit m d'enfant. • vt/i (pt **cribbed**) copier.

cricket n (Sport) cricket m. (insect) grillon m.

crime n crime m; (minor) délit m; (acts) criminalité f.

criminal adj & n criminel/-le (m/f).

crimson adj & n cramoisi (m).

cringe vi reculer; (fig) s'humilier.

crinkle vt/i (cloth) (se) froisser. • n pli m.

cripple n infirme mf. • vt estropier; (fig) paralyser.

crisis n (pl **crises**) crise f.

crisp adj (Culin) croquant; (air, reply) vif. **crisps** npl chips fpl.

criss-cross adj entrecroisé. ●vt/i (s')entrecroiser.

criterion n (pl **-ia**) critère m.

critic n critique m. **critical** adj critique. **critically** adv d'une manière critique; (ill) gravement.

criticism n critique f.

criticize vt/i critiquer.

croak n (bird) croassement m; (frog) coassement m. ●vi croasser; coasser.

Croatia n Croatie f.

Croatian n Croate mf. ●adj Croate.

crochet n crochet m. ●vt faire du crochet.

crockery n vaisselle f.

crocodile n crocodile m.

crook n (criminal 🔲) escroc m; (stick) houlette f.

crooked adj tordu; (winding) tortueux; (askew) de travers; (dishonest: fig) malhonnête.

crop n récolte f; (fig) quantité f. ●vt (pt **cropped**) couper. ●vi ~ **up** se présenter.

cross n croix f; (hybrid) hybride m. ●vt/i traverser; (legs, animals) croiser; (cheque) barrer; (paths) se croiser;~ **sb's mind** venir à l'esprit de qn. ●adj en colère, fâché (**with** contre). **talk at** ~ **purposes** parler sans se comprendre. ■ ~ **off** or **out** rayer. ~**-check** vt vérifier (pour confirmer). ~**-country** (running) n cross m. ~**-examine** vt faire subir un contre-interrogatoire à. ~**-eyed** adj **be** ~**-eyed** loucher. ~**fire** n feux mpl croisés.

crossing n (by boat) traversée f; (on road) passage m clouté.

crossly adv avec colère.

cross: ~**-reference** n renvoi m.

~**roads** n carrefour m. ~**word** n mots mpl croisés.

crotch n (of garment) entrejambes m inv.

crouch vi s'accroupir.

crow n corbeau m; **as the** ~ **flies** à vol d'oiseau. ●vi (of cock) chanter; (fig) jubiler. ~**bar** n pied-de-biche m.

crowd n foule f. **crowded** adj plein.

crown n couronne f; (top part) sommet m. ●vt couronner.

Crown Court n Cour f d'assises.

crucial adj crucial.

crucifix n crucifix m.

crucify vt crucifier.

crude adj (raw) brut; (rough, vulgar) grossier.

cruel adj (**crueller**, **cruellest**) cruel.

cruise n croisière f. ●vi (ship) croiser; (tourists) faire une croisière; (vehicle) rouler; **cruising speed** vitesse f de croisière.

crumb n miette f.

crumble vt/i (s')effriter; (bread) (s')émietter; (collapse) s'écrouler.

crumple vt/i (se) froisser.

crunch vt croquer. ●n (event) moment m critique; **when it comes to the** ~ quand ça devient sérieux.

crusade n croisade f. **crusader** n (knight) croisé m; (fig) militant/-e m/f.

crush vt écraser; (clothes) froisser. ●n (crowd) presse f; **a** ~ **on** 🔲 le béguin pour.

crust n croûte f. **crusty** adj croustillant.

crutch n béquille f; (crotch) entrejambes m inv.

crux n **the** ~ **of** (problem) le point crucial de. ●

cry n cri m. ●vi (weep) pleurer; (call

out) crier. ∎ ∼ **off** se décommander.

crying adj (need) urgent; **a ∼ shame** une vraie honte. ●n pleurs mpl.

cryptic adj énigmatique.

crystal n cristal m. ∼-**clear** adj parfaitement clair.

cub n petit m; **Cub (Scout)** louveteau m.

Cuba n Cuba f.

cube n cube m. **cubic** adj cubique; (metre) cube.

cubicle n (in room, hospital) box m; (at swimming-pool) cabine f.

cuckoo n coucou m.

cucumber n concombre m.

cuddle vt câliner. ●vi **(kiss and) ∼** s'embrasser. ●n caresse f. **cuddly** adj câlin; **cuddly toy** peluche f.

cue n signal m; (Theat) réplique f; (billiards) queue f.

cuff n manchette f; (US: on trousers) revers m; **off the ∼** impromptu. ●vt gifler. ∼-**link** n bouton m de manchette.

cul-de-sac n (pl **culs-de-sac**) impasse f.

cull vt (select) choisir; (kill) massacrer.

culminate vi **∼ in** se terminer par. **culmination** n point m culminant.

culprit n coupable mf.

cult n culte m.

cultivate vt cultiver. **cultivation** n culture f.

cultural adj culturel.

culture n culture f. **cultured** adj cultivé.

cumbersome adj encombrant.

cunning adj rusé. ●n astuce f, ruse f.

cup n tasse f; (prize) coupe f; **Cup final** finale f de la coupe.

cupboard n placard m.

cup-tie n match m de coupe.

curate n vicaire m.

curator n (of museum) conservateur m.

curb n (restraint) frein m; (of path) (US) bord m du trottoir. ●vt (desires) refréner; (price increase) freiner.

cure vt guérir; (fig) éliminer; (Culin) fumer; (in brine) saler. ●n (recovery) guérison f; (remedy) remède m.

curfew n couvre-feu m.

curiosity n curiosité f. **curious** adj curieux.

curl vt/i (hair) boucler. ●n boucle f. ∎ ∼**up** se pelotonner; (shrivel) se racornir.

curler n bigoudi m.

curly adj (-ier, -iest) bouclé.

currant n raisin m de Corinthe.

currency n (money) monnaie f; (of word) fréquence f; **foreign ∼** devises fpl étrangères.

current adj (term, word) usité; (topical) actuel; (year) en cours. ●n courant m. ∼ **account** n compte m courant. ∼ **events** npl l'actualité f.

currently adv actuellement.

curriculum n (pl **-la**) programme m scolaire. ∼ **vitae** n curriculum vitae m.

curry n curry m. ●vt ∼ **favour with** chercher les bonnes grâces de.

curse n (spell) malédiction f; (swearword) juron m. ●vt maudire. ●vi (swear) jurer.

cursor n curseur m.

curt adj brusque.

curtain n rideau m.

curve n courbe f. ●vi (line) s'incurver; (edge) se recourber; (road) faire une courbe. ●vt courber.

cushion n coussin m. ●vt (a blow) amortir; (fig) protéger.

custard n crème f anglaise; (set) flan m.

custody n (of child) garde f; (Jur) détention f préventive.

custom n coutume f; (patronage: Comm) clientèle f. **customary** adj habituel.

customer n client/-e m/f; (person 🔟) type m.

customize vt personnaliser.

custom-made adj fait sur mesure.

customs npl douane f. ●adj douanier. ~ **officer** n douanier m.

cut vt/i (pt **cut**, pres p **cutting**) vt couper; (hedge) tailler; (prices) réduire. ●vi couper. ●n (wound) coupure f; (of clothes) coupe f; (in surgery) incision f; (share) part f; (in prices) réduction f. ■~ **back** vi faire des économies. vt réduire. ~ **down (on)** réduire. ~ **in** (in conversation) intervenir. ~ **off** couper; (tide, army) isoler; ~ **out** vt découper; (leave out) supprimer; vi (engine) s'arrêter. ~ **short** (visit) écourter. ~ **up** couper; (carve) découper.

cutback n réduction f.

cute adj 🔟 mignon.

cutlery n couverts mpl.

cutlet n côtelette f.

cut-price adj à prix réduit.

cutting adj cinglant. ●n (from newspaper) coupure f; (plant) bouture f.

CV abbr ▷ CURRICULUM VITAE.

cyanide n cyanure m.

cyberspace n cyberspace m.

cycle n cycle m; (bicycle) vélo m. ●vi aller à vélo.

cycling n cyclisme m. ~ **shorts** npl cycliste m.

cyclist n cycliste mf.

cylinder n cylindre m.

cymbal n cymbale f.

cynic n cynique mf. **cynical** adj cynique. **cynicism** n cynisme m.

cypress n cyprès m.

Cypriot n Cypriote mf. ●adj cypriote.

Cyprus n Chypre f.

cyst n kyste m.

czar n tsar m.

Czech n (person) Tchèque mf; (Ling) tchèque m. ~ **Republic** n République f tchèque.

Dd

dab vt (pt **dabbed**) tamponner; ~ **sth on** appliquer qch par petites touches. ●n touche f.

dabble vi ~ **in sth** faire qch en amateur.

dad n 🔟 papa m. **daddy** n 🔟 papa m.

daffodil n jonquille f.

daft adj bête.

dagger n poignard m.

daily adj quotidien. ●adv tous les jours. ●n (newspaper) quotidien m.

dainty adj (-ier, -iest) (lace, food) délicat; (shoe, hand) mignon.

dairy n (on farm) laiterie f; (shop) crémerie f. ●adj (farm, cow, product) laitier; (butter) fermier.

daisy n pâquerette f.

dam n barrage m.

damage n (to property) dégâts mpl; (Med) lésions fpl; **to do sth ~** (cause, trade) porter atteinte à; **~s** (Jur) dommages-intérêts mpl. •vt (property) endommager; (health) nuire à; (reputation) porter atteinte à. **damaging** adj (to health) nuisible; (to reputation) préjudiciable.

damn vt (Relig) damner; (condemn: fig) condamner. •interj 🔲 zut 🔲, merde 🔲. •n **not give/care a ~ about** se ficher de 🔲. •adj fichu 🔲. •adv franchement.

damp n humidité f. •adj humide. **dampen** vt (lit) humecter; (fig) refroidir. **dampness** n humidité f.

dance vt/i danser. •n danse f; (gathering) bal m; **~ hall** dancing m. **dancer** n danseur/-euse m/f.

dandelion n pissenlit m.

dandruff n pellicules fpl.

Dane n Danois/-e m/f.

danger n danger m; (risk) risque m; **be in ~ of** risquer de. **dangerous** adj dangereux.

dangle vt (object) balancer; (legs) laisser pendre. •vi (object) se balancer (**from** à).

Danish n (Ling) danois m. •adj danois.

dare vt oser (**(to) do** faire); **~ sb to do** défier qn de faire. •n défi m. **daring** adj audacieux.

dark adj (day, colour, suit, mood, warning) sombre; (hair, eyes, skin) brun; (secret, thought) noir. •n noir m; (nightfall) tombée f de la nuit; **in the ~** (fig) dans le noir. **darken** vt/i (sky) (s')obscurcir; (mood) (s')assombrir. **darkness** n obscurité f. **~room** n chambre f noire.

darling adj & n chéri/-e (m/f).

dart n fléchette f; **~s** (game) fléchettes fpl. •vi **~ in/away** entrer/filer comme une flèche.

dash vi se précipiter; **~ off** se sauver. •vt (hope) anéantir; **~ sth against** projeter qch contre. •n course f folle; (of liquid) goutte f; (of colour) touche f; (in punctuation) tiret m.

dashboard n tableau m de bord.

data npl données fpl. **~base** n base f de données. **~ capture** n saisie f de données. **~ processing** n traitement m des données. **~ protection** n protection f de l'information.

date n date f; (meeting) rendezvous m; (fruit) datte f; **out of ~** (old-fashioned) démodé; (passport) périmé; **to ~** à ce jour; **up to ~** (modern) moderne; (list) à jour. •vt/i dater; (go out with) sortir avec; **~ from** dater de. **dated** adj démodé.

daughter n fille f. **~-in-law** n (pl **~s-in-law**) belle-fille f.

daunt vt décourager.

dawdle vi flâner, traînasser 🔲.

dawn n aube f. •vi (day) se lever; **it ~ed on me that** je me suis rendu compte que.

day n jour m; (whole day) journée f; (period) époque f; **the ~ before** la veille; **the following** or **next ~** le lendemain. **~break** n aube f.

daydream n rêves mpl. •vi rêvasser (**about** de).

day: ~light n jour m. **~time** n journée f. **~ trader** n spéculateur m à la journée, scalpeur m.

daze n **in a ~** (from blow) étourdi; (from drug) hébété. **dazed** adj (by blow) abasourdi; (by news) ahuri.

dazzle vt éblouir.

dead adj mort; (numb) engourdi. •adv complètement; **in ~ centre** au beau milieu; **stop ~** s'arrêter net. •n **in the ~ of** au cœur de; **the ~** les morts. **deaden** vt (sound, blow) amortir; (pain) calmer. **~ end** n impasse f. **~line** n date f limite. **~lock** n impasse f.

deadly adj (-ier, -iest) mortel; (weapon) meurtrier.

deaf adj sourd. **deafen** vt assourdir. **deafness** n surdité f.

deal vt (pt **dealt**) donner; (blow) porter. ●vi (trade) être en activité; ~ **in** être dans le commerce de. ●n affaire f; (cards) donne f; **a great** or **good** ~ beaucoup (**of** de). ■ ~ **with** (handle, manage) s'occuper de; (be about) traiter de. **dealer** n marchand/-e m/f; (agent) concessionnaire mf. **dealings** npl relations fpl.

dear adj cher; ~ **Sir/Madam** Monsieur/Madame. ~ **(my)** ~ mon chéri/ma chérie m/f. ●adv cher. ●interj **oh** ~**!** oh mon Dieu!

death n mort f; ~ **penalty** peine f de mort.

debatable adj discutable.

debate n (formal) débat m; (informal) discussion f. ●vt (formally) débattre de; (informally) discuter.

debit n débit m. ●adj (balance) débiteur. ●vt (pt **debited**) débiter.

debris n débris mpl; (rubbish) déchets mpl.

debt n dette f; **be in** ~ avoir des dettes.

debug vt (Comput) déboguer.

decade n décennie f.

decadent adj décadent.

decaffeinated adj décaféiné.

decay vi (vegetation) pourrir; (tooth) se carier; (fig) décliner. ●n pourriture f; (of tooth) carie f; (fig) déclin m.

deceased adj décédé. ●n défunt/-e m/f.

deceit n tromperie f. **deceitful** adj trompeur.

deceive vt tromper.

December n décembre m.

decent adj (respectable) comme il faut; (adequate) convenable; (good) bon; (kind) gentil; (not indecent) décent. **decently** adv convenablement.

deception n tromperie f. **deceptive** adj trompeur.

decide vt/i décider (**to do** de faire); (question) régler; ~ **on** se décider pour. **decided** adj (firm) résolu; (clear) net. **decidedly** adv nettement.

decimal adj décimal. ●n décimale f; ~ **point** virgule f.

decipher vt déchiffrer.

decision n décision f.

decisive adj (conclusive) décisif; (firm) décidé.

deck n pont m; (of cards: US) jeu m; (of bus) étage m. ~**-chair** n chaise f longue.

declaration n déclaration f. **declare** vt déclarer.

decline vt/i refuser; (fall) baisser. ●n (waning) déclin m; (drop) baisse f; **in** ~ sur le déclin.

decode vt décoder.

decommission vt (arms) mettre hors service; (reactor) démanteler.

decompose vt/i (se) décomposer.

decor n décor m.

decorate vt décorer; (room) refaire, peindre. **decoration** n décoration f. **decorative** adj décoratif.

decorator n peintre m; **(interior)** ~ décorateur/-trice m/f.

decoy n (person, vehicle) leurre m; (for hunting) appeau m.

decrease¹ /dɪˈkriːs/ vt/i diminuer.

decrease² /ˈdiːkriːs/ n diminution f.

decree n (Pol, Relig) décret m; (Jur) jugement m. ●vt (pt **decreed**) décréter.

decrepit adj (building) délabré; (person) décrépit.

dedicate vt dédier; ~ **oneself to** se consacrer à.

dedicated adj dévoué; ∼ **line** (Internet) ligne f spécialisée.

dedication n dévouement m; (in book) dédicace f.

deduce vt déduire.

deduct vt déduire; (from wages) retenir.

deed n acte m.

deem vt considérer.

deep adj profond; (mud, carpet) épais. •adv profondément; ∼ **in thought** absorbé dans ses pensées. **deepen** vt/i (admiration, concern) augmenter.

deep-freeze n congélateur m. •vt congeler.

deep vein thrombosis n thrombose f veineuse profonde.

deer n inv cerf m; (doe) biche f.

deface vt dégrader.

default vi (Jur) ∼ **(on payments)** ne pas régler ses échéances. •n (on payments) non-remboursement m; **by** ∼ par défaut; **win by** ∼ gagner par forfait. •adj (Comput) par défaut.

defeat vt vaincre; (thwart) faire échouer. •n défaite f.

defect[1] /ˈdiːfekt/ n défaut m.

defect[2] /dɪˈfekt/ vi faire défection; ∼ **to** passer à.

defective adj défectueux.

defector n transfuge mf.

defence n défense f.

defend vt défendre. **defendant** n (Jur) accusé-e m/f. **defender** défenseur m.

defensive adj défensif. •n défensive f.

defer vt (pt **deferred**) (postpone) reporter; (judgement) suspendre; (payment) différer.

deference n déférence f. **deferential** adj déférent.

defiance n défi m; **in** ∼ **of** contre. **defiant** adj rebelle.

defiantly adv avec défi.

deficiency n insuffisance f; (fault) défaut m.

deficient adj insuffisant; **be** ∼ **in** manquer de.

deficit n déficit m.

define vt définir.

definite adj (exact) précis; (obvious) net; (firm) ferme; (certain) certain. **definitely** adv certainement; (clearly) nettement.

definition n définition f.

deflate vt dégonfler.

deflect vt (missile) dévier; (criticism) détourner.

deforestation n déforestation f.

deform vt déformer.

defraud vt (client, employer) escroquer; (state, customs) frauder; ∼ **sb of sth** escroquer qch à qn.

defrost vt dégivrer.

deft adj adroit.

defunct adj défunt.

defuse vt désamorcer.

defy vt défier; (attempts) résister à.

degenerate[1] /dɪˈdʒenəreɪt/ vi dégénérer (**into** en).

degenerate[2] /dɪˈdʒenərət/ adj & n dégénéré-e m/f.

degrade vt (humiliate) humilier; (damage) dégrader.

degree n degré m; (Univ) diplôme m universitaire; (Bachelor's degree) licence f; **to such a** ∼ **that** à tel point que.

dehydrate vt/i (se) déshydrater.

deign vt ∼ **to do** daigner faire.

dejected adj découragé.

delay vt (flight) retarder; (decision) différer; ∼ **doing** attendre pour faire. •n (of plane, post) retard m; (time lapse) délai m.

delegate[1] /ˈdelɪgət/ n délégué-e m/f.

delegate[2] /ˈdelɪgeɪt/ vt déléguer.

d

delegation n délégation f.

delete vt supprimer; (Comput) effacer; (with pen) barrer. **deletion** n suppression f; (with line) rature f.

deliberate[1] /dɪˈlɪbəreɪt/ vi délibérer.

deliberate[2] /dɪˈlɪbərət/ adj délibéré; (steps, manner) mesuré. **deliberately** adv (do, say) exprès; (sarcastically, provocatively) délibérément.

delicacy n délicatesse f; (food) mets m raffiné.

delicate adj délicat.

delicatessen n épicerie f fine.

delicious adj délicieux.

delight n joie f, plaisir m. ●vt ravir. ●vi ~ **in** prendre plaisir à. **delighted** adj ravi. **delightful** adj charmant/-e.

delinquent adj & n délinquant/-e (m/f).

delirious adj délirant.

deliver vt (message) remettre; (goods) livrer; (speech) faire; (baby) mettre au monde; (rescue) délivrer. **delivery** n (of goods) livraison f; (of mail) distribution f; (of baby) accouchement m.

delude vt tromper; ~ **oneself** se faire des illusions.

deluge n déluge m. ●vt submerger (**with** de).

delusion n illusion f.

delve vi fouiller.

demand vt (request, require) demander; (forcefully) exiger. ●n (request) demande f; (pressure) exigence f; **in** ~ très demandé; **on** ~ à la demande. **demanding** adj exigeant.

demean vt ~ **oneself** s'abaisser.

demeanour, (US)**demeanor** n comportement m.

demented adj fou.

demise n disparition f.

demo n (demonstration 🔲) manif f 🔲.

democracy n démocratie f.

democrat n démocrate mf. **democratic** adj démocratique.

demolish vt démolir.

demon n démon m.

demonstrate vt démontrer; (concern, skill) manifester. ●vi (Pol) manifester. **demonstration** n démonstration f; (Pol) manifestation f. **demonstrative** adj démonstratif. **demonstrator** n manifestant/-e m/f.

demoralize vt démoraliser.

demote vt rétrograder.

den n (of lion) antre m; (room) tanière f.

denial n (of rumour) démenti m; (of rights) négation f; (of request) rejet m.

denim n jean m; ~**s** (jeans) jean m.

Denmark n Danemark m.

denomination n (Relig) confession f; (money) valeur f.

denounce vt dénoncer.

dense adj dense. **densely** adv (packed) très. **density** n densité f.

dent n bosse f. ●vt cabosser.

dental adj dentaire; ~ **floss** fil m dentaire; ~ **surgeon** chirurgien-dentiste m.

dentist n dentiste mf. **dentistry** n médecine f dentaire.

dentures npl dentier m.

deny vt nier (**that** que); (rumour) démentir; ~ **sb sth** refuser qch à qn.

deodorant n déodorant m.

depart vi partir; ~ **from** (deviate) s'éloigner de.

department n (in shop) rayon m; (in hospital, office) service m; (Univ) département m; **D**~ **of Health** ministère m de la Santé; ~ **store** grand magasin m.

departure n départ m; **a ∼ from** (custom, truth) une entorse à.

depend vi dépendre (**on** de). **∼ on** (rely on) compter sur; **it (all) ∼s** ça dépend; **∼ing on the season** suivant la saison. **dependable** adj (person) digne de confiance. **dependant** n personne f à charge. **dependence** n dépendance f.

dependent adj dépendant; **be ∼ on** dépendre de.

depict vt (describe) dépeindre; (in picture) représenter.

deplete vt réduire.

deport vt expulser.

depose vt déposer.

deposit vt (pt **deposited**) déposer. ●n (in bank) dépôt m; (on house) versement m initial; (on holiday) acompte m; (against damage) caution f; (on bottle) consigne f; (of mineral) gisement m; **∼ account** compte m de dépôt. **depositor** n (Comm) déposant/-e m/f.

depot n dépôt m; (US) gare f.

depreciate vt/i (se) déprécier.

depress vt déprimer. **depressing** adj déprimant. **depression** n dépression f; (Econ) récession f.

deprivation n privation f.

deprive vt ∼ **of** priver de. **deprived** adj démuni.

depth n profondeur f; (of knowledge, ignorance) étendue f; (of colour, emotion) intensité f.

deputize vi ∼ **for** remplacer.

deputy n adjoint/-e m/f. ●adj adjoint; **∼ chairman** vice-président m.

derail vt faire dérailler. **derailment** n déraillement m.

deranged adj dérangé.

derelict adj abandonné.

deride vt ridiculiser. **derision** n moqueries fpl. **derisory** adj dérisoire.

derivative adj & n dérivé (m).

derive vt ∼ **sth from** tirer qch de. ●vi ∼ **from** découler de.

derogatory adj (word) péjoratif; (remark) désobligeant.

descend vt/i descendre; **be ∼ed from** descendre de. **descendant** n descendant/-e m/f. **descent** n descente f; (lineage) origine f.

describe vt décrire; ∼ **sb as sth** qualifier qn de qch. **description** n description f. **descriptive** adj descriptif.

desert[1] /'dezət/ n désert m.

desert[2] /dɪ'zɜːt/ vt/i abandonner; (cause) déserter. **deserted** adj désert. **deserter** n déserteur m.

deserts npl **get one's ∼** avoir ce qu'on mérite.

deserve vt mériter (**to** de). **deservedly** adv à juste titre. **deserving** adj (person) méritant; (action) louable.

design n (sketch) plan m; (idea) conception f; (pattern) motif m; (art of designing) design m; (aim) dessein m. ●vt (sketch) dessiner; (devise, intend) concevoir.

designate vt désigner.

designer n concepteur/-trice m/f; (of fashion, furniture) créateur/-trice m/f. ●adj (clothes) de haute couture; (sunglasses, drink) de dernière mode.

desirable adj (outcome) souhaitable; (person) désirable.

desire n désir m. ●vt désirer.

desk n bureau m; (of pupil) pupitre m; (in hotel) réception f; (in bank) caisse f.

desolate adj (place) désolé; (person) affligé.

despair n désespoir m. ●vi désespérer (**of** de).

desperate adj désespéré; (criminal) prêt à tout; **be ∼ for** avoir désespérément besoin de. **desperately** adv désespérément; (worried) terriblement; (ill) gravement.

d

d

desperation n désespoir m; **in ~** en désespoir de cause.

despicable adj méprisable.

despise vt mépriser.

despite prep malgré.

despondent adj découragé.

dessert n dessert m. **~spoon** n cuillère f à dessert.

destination n destination f.

destiny n destin m.

destitute adj sans ressources.

destroy vt détruire; (animal) abattre. **destroyer** n (warship) contre-torpilleur m.

destruction n destruction f. **destructive** adj destructeur.

detach vt détacher; **~ed house** maison f (individuelle).

detail n détail m; **go into ~** entrer dans les détails. • vt (plans) exposer en détail.

detain vt retenir; (in prison) placer en détention. **detainee** n détenu/-e m/f.

detect vt (error, trace) déceler; (crime, mine, sound) détecter. **detection** n détection f. **detective** n inspecteur/-trice m/f; (private) détective m.

detention n détention f; (School) retenue f.

deter vt (pt **deterred**) dissuader (**from** de).

detergent adj & n détergent (m).

deteriorate vi se détériorer.

determine vt déterminer; **~ to do** résoudre de faire. **determined** adj (person) décidé; (air) résolu.

deterrent n moyen m de dissuasion. • adj (effect) dissuasif.

detest vt détester.

detonate vt/i (faire) détoner. **detonation** n détonation f. **detonator** n détonateur m.

detour n détour m.

detract vi **~ from** (success, value) porter atteinte à; (pleasure) diminuer.

detriment n **to the ~ of** au détriment de. **detrimental** adj nuisible (**to** à).

devalue vt dévaluer.

devastate vt (place) ravager; (person) accabler.

develop vt (plan) élaborer; (mind, body) développer; (land) mettre en valeur; (illness) attraper; (habit) prendre. • vi (child, country, plot, business) se développer; (hole, crack) se former.

development n développement m; **(housing) ~** lotissement m; **(new) ~** fait m nouveau.

deviate vi dévier; **~ from** (norm) s'écarter de.

device n appareil m; (means) moyen m; (bomb) engin m explosif.

devil n diable m.

devious adj (person) retors.

devise vt (scheme) concevoir; (product) inventer.

devoid adj **~ of** dépourvu de.

devolution n (Pol) régionalisation f.

devote vt consacrer (**to** à). **devoted** adj dévoué. **devotion** n dévouement m; (Relig) dévotion f.

devour vt dévorer.

devout adj fervent.

dew n rosée f.

diabetes n diabète m.

diabolical adj diabolique; (bad 🛈) atroce.

diagnose vt diagnostiquer. **diagnosis** n (pl **-oses**) diagnostic m.

diagonal adj diagonal. • n diagonale f.

diagram n schéma m.

dial n cadran m. • vt (pt **dialled**)

(number) faire; (person) appeler; **dialling code** indicatif m; **dialling tone** tonalité f.

dialect n dialecte m.

dialogue n dialogue m.

diameter n diamètre m.

diamond n diamant m; (shape) losange m; (baseball) terrain m; ~**s** (cards) carreau m.

diaper n (US) couche f.

diaphragm n diaphragme m.

diarrhoea, (US) **diarrhea** n diarrhée f.

diary n (for appointments) agenda m; (journal) journal m intime.

dice n inv dé m. •vt (food) couper en dés.

dictate vt/i dicter.

dictation n dictée f.

dictator n dictateur m. **dictatorship** n dictature f.

dictionary n dictionnaire m.

did ▷ DO.

didn't ▷ DID NOT.

die vi (pres p **dying**) mourir; (plant) crever; **be dying to do** mourir d'envie de faire. ∎ ~ **down** diminuer. ~ **out** disparaître.

diesel n gazole m; ~ **engine** moteur m diesel.

diet n (usual food) alimentation f; (restricted) régime m. •vi être au régime. **dietary** adj alimentaire. **dietician** n diététicien/-ne m/f.

differ vi différer (**from** de).

difference n différence f; (disagreement) différend m. **different** adj différent (**from, to** de).

differentiate vt différencier. •vi faire la différence (**between** entre).

differently adv différemment (**from** de).

difficult adj difficile. **difficulty** n difficulté f.

diffuse[1] /dɪˈfjuːs/ adj diffus.

diffuse[2] /dɪˈfjuːz/ vt diffuser.

dig vt/i (pt **dug**; pres p **digging**) (excavate) creuser; (in garden) bêcher. •n (poke) coup m de coude; (remark) pique f 🗓; (Archeol) fouilles fpl. ∎ ~ **up** déterrer.

digest vt/i digérer. **digestible** adj digestible. **digestion** n digestion f.

digger n excavateur m.

digit n chiffre m. **digitize** vt numériser.

digital adj (clock) à affichage numérique; (display, recording) numérique. ~ **audio tape** n cassette f audionumérique. ~ **camera** n appareil m photo numérique.

dignified adj digne.

dignitary n dignitaire m.

dignity n dignité f.

digress vi faire une digression.

dilapidated adj délabré.

dilate vt/i (se) dilater.

dilemma n dilemme m.

diligent adj appliqué.

dilute vt diluer.

dim adj (**dimmer, dimmest**) (weak) faible; (dark) sombre; (indistinct) vague; 🗓 stupide. •vt/i (pt **dimmed**) (light) baisser.

dime n (US) (pièce f de) dix cents.

dimension n dimension f.

diminish vt/i diminuer.

dimple n fossette f.

din n vacarme m.

dine vi dîner. **diner** n dîneur/-euse m/f; (US) restaurant m à service rapide.

dinghy n dériveur m.

dingy adj (**-ier, -iest**) minable.

dining room n salle f à manger.

dinner n (evening meal) dîner m; (lunch) déjeuner m; **have** ~ dîner.

~**jacket** n smoking m. ~ **party**
n dîner m.

dinosaur n dinosaure m.

dip vt/i (pt **dipped**) plonger; ~
into (book) feuilleter; (savings)
puiser dans; ~ **one's**
headlights se mettre en code.
● n (slope) déclivité f; (in sea) bain
m rapide.

diploma n diplôme m (**in** en).

diplomacy n diplomatie f.
diplomat n diplomate mf.
diplomatic adj (Pol)
diplomatique; (tactful) diplomate.

dire adj affreux; (need, poverty)
extrême.

direct adj direct. ● adv
directement. ● vt diriger; (letter,
remark) adresser; (a play) mettre
en scène; ~ **sb to** indiquer à qn
le chemin de; (order) signifier à
qn de.

direction n direction f; (Theat)
mise f en scène; ~**s** indications
fpl; **ask** ~**s** demander le chemin;
~**s for use** mode m d'emploi.

directly adv directement; (at once)
tout de suite. ● conj dès que.

director n directeur/-trice m/f;
(Theat) metteur m en scène.

directory n (phone book) annuaire
m. ~ **enquiries** npl
renseignements mpl
téléphoniques.

dirt n saleté f; (earth) terre f; ~
cheap ▨ très bon marché inv.
~-**track** n (Sport) cendrée f.

dirty adj (-**ier**, -**iest**) sale; (word)
grossier; **get** ~ se salir. ● vt/i (se)
salir.

disability n handicap m.

disable vt rendre infirme.
disabled adj handicapé.

disadvantage n désavantage m.
disadvantaged adj défavorisé.

disagree vi ne pas être d'accord
(**with** avec). ~ **with sb** (food,
climate) ne pas convenir à qn.
disagreement n désaccord m;

(quarrel) différend m.

disappear vi disparaître.
disappearance n disparition f
(**of** de).

disappoint vt décevoir.
disappointment n déception f.

disapproval n désapprobation f
(**of** de).

disapprove vi ~ (**of**)
désapprouver.

disarm vt/i désarmer.
disarmament n désarmement m.

disarray n désordre m.

disaster n désastre m. **disastrous**
adj désastreux.

disband vi disperser. ● vt
dissoudre.

disbelief n incrédulité f.

disc n disque m; (Comput) ▷DISK.

discard vt se débarrasser de;
(beliefs) abandonner.

discharge vt (unload) décharger;
(liquid) déverser; (duty) remplir;
(dismiss) renvoyer; (prisoner)
libérer. ● vi (of pus) s'écouler.

disciple n disciple m.

disciplinary adj disciplinaire.

discipline n discipline f. ● vt
discipliner; (punish) punir.

disc jockey n disc-jockey m,
animateur m.

disclaimer n démenti m.

disclose vt révéler. **disclosure** n
révélation f (**of** de).

disco n (club ▨) discothèque f;
(event) soirée f disco.

discolour vt/i (se) décolorer.

discomfort n gêne f.

disconcert vt déconcerter.

disconnect vt détacher; (unplug)
débrancher; (cut off) couper.

discontent n mécontentement m.

discontinue vt (service)
supprimer; (production) arrêter.

discord n discorde f; (Mus)
discordance f.

discount¹ /'dɪskaʊnt/ n remise f; (on minor purchase) rabais m.

discount² /dɪs'kaʊnt/ vt (advice) ne pas tenir compte de; (possibility) écarter.

discourage vt décourager.

discourse n discours m.

discourteous adj peu courtois.

discover vt découvrir. **discovery** n découverte f.

discreet adj discret.

discrepancy n divergence f.

discretion n discrétion f.

discriminate vt/i distinguer; ~ **against** faire de la discrimination contre. **discriminating** adj qui a du discernement. **discrimination** n discernement m; (bias) discrimination f.

discus n disque m.

discuss vt (talk about) discuter de; (in writing) examiner. **discussion** n discussion f.

disdain n dédain m.

disease n maladie f.

disembark vt/i débarquer.

disenchanted adj désabusé.

disentangle vt démêler.

disfigure vt défigurer.

disgrace n (shame) honte f; (disfavour) disgrâce f. •vt déshonorer. **disgraced** adj (in disfavour) disgracié. **disgraceful** adj honteux.

disgruntled adj mécontent.

disguise vt déguiser. •n déguisement m; **in ~** déguisé.

disgust n dégoût m. •vt dégoûter.

dish n plat m; **the ~es** (crockery) la vaisselle. •vt **~ out** 🗊 distribuer; **~ up** servir.

dishcloth n lavette f; (for drying) torchon m.

dishearten vt décourager.

dishevelled adj échevelé.

dishonest adj malhonnête.

dishonour, (US) **dishonor** n déshonneur m.

dishwasher n lave-vaisselle m inv.

disillusion vt désabuser. **disillusionment** n désillusion f.

disincentive n **be a ~ to** décourager.

disinclined adj ~ **to** peu disposé à.

disinfect vt désinfecter. **disinfectant** n désinfectant m.

disintegrate vt/i (se) désintégrer.

disinterested adj désintéressé.

disjointed adj (talk) décousu.

disk n (US) ▷DISC; (Comput) disque m. ~ **drive** n drive m, lecteur m de disquettes.

diskette n disquette f.

dislike n aversion f. •vt ne pas aimer.

dislocate vt (limb) disloquer.

dislodge vt (move) déplacer; (drive out) déloger.

disloyal adj déloyal (**to** envers).

dismal adj morne, triste.

dismantle vt démonter, défaire.

dismay n consternation f (**at** devant). •vt consterner.

dismiss vt renvoyer; (appeal) rejeter; (from mind) écarter. **dismissal** n renvoi m.

dismount vi descendre, mettre pied à terre.

disobedient adj désobéissant.

disobey vt désobéir à. •vi désobéir.

disorder n désordre m; (ailment) trouble(s) m(pl). **disorderly** adj désordonné.

disorganized adj désorganisé.

disown vt renier.

disparaging adj désobligeant.

dispassionate adj impartial;

(unemotional) calme.

dispatch vt (send, complete) expédier; (troops) envoyer. ●n expédition f. envoi m; (report) dépêche f.

dispel vt (pt **dispelled**) dissiper.

dispensary n (in hospital) pharmacie f; (in pharmacy) officine f.

dispense vt distribuer; (medicine) préparer. ●vi ~ **with** se passer de. **dispenser** n (container) distributeur m.

disperse vt/i (se) disperser.

display vt montrer, exposer; (feelings) manifester. ●n exposition f; manifestation f; (Comm) étalage m; (of computer) visuel m.

displeased adj mécontent (**with** de).

disposable adj jetable.

disposal n (of waste) évacuation f; **at sb's** ~ à la disposition de qn.

dispose vt disposer. ●vi ~ **of** se débarrasser de; **well** ~**d to** bien disposé envers.

disposition n disposition f; (character) naturel m.

disprove vt réfuter.

dispute vt contester. ●n discussion f; (Pol) conflit m; **in** ~ contesté.

disqualify vt rendre inapte; (Sport) disqualifier; ~ **from driving** retirer le permis à.

disquiet n inquiétude f. **disquieting** adj inquiétant.

disregard vt ne pas tenir compte de. ●n indifférence f (**for** à).

disrepair n délabrement m.

disreputable adj peu recommandable.

disrepute n discrédit m.

disrespect n manque m de respect. **disrespectful** adj irrespectueux.

disrupt vt (disturb, break up) perturber; (plans) déranger. **disruption** n perturbation f. **disruptive** adj perturbateur.

dissatisfied adj mécontent.

dissect vt disséquer.

disseminate vt diffuser.

dissent vi différer (**from** de). ●n dissentiment m.

dissertation n mémoire m.

disservice n **do a** ~ **to sb** rendre un mauvais service à qn.

dissident adj & n dissident/-e (m/f).

dissimilar adj dissemblable, différent.

dissipate vt/i (se) dissiper. **dissipated** adj (person) dissolu.

dissolve vt/i (se) dissoudre.

dissuade vt dissuader.

distance n distance f; **from a** ~ de loin; **in the** ~ au loin. **distant** adj éloigné, lointain; (relative) éloigné; (aloof) distant.

distaste n dégoût m. **distasteful** adj désagréable.

distil vt (pt **distilled**) distiller.

distinct adj distinct; (definite) net; **as** ~ **from** par opposition à. **distinction** n distinction f; (in exam) mention f très bien. **distinctive** adj distinctif.

distinguish vt/i distinguer.

distort vt déformer. **distortion** n distorsion f; (of facts) déformation f.

distract vt distraire. **distracted** adj (distraught) éperdu. **distracting** adj gênant. **distraction** n (lack of attention, entertainment) distraction f.

distraught adj éperdu.

distress n douleur f; (poverty, danger) détresse f. ●vt peiner. **distressing** adj pénible.

distribute vt distribuer.

district n région f; (of town) quartier m.

distrust n méfiance f. ●vt se méfier de.

disturb vt déranger; (alarm, worry) troubler. **disturbance** n dérangement m (**of** de); (noise) tapage m. **disturbances** npl (Pol) troubles mpl. **disturbed** adj troublé; (psychologically) perturbé. **disturbing** adj troublant.

disused adj désaffecté.

ditch n fossé m. ●vt ⊠ abandonner.

ditto adv idem.

dive vi plonger; (rush) se précipiter. ●n plongeon m; (of plane) piqué m; (place ⊠) bouge m. **diver** n plongeur/-euse m/f.

diverge vi diverger. **divergent** adj divergent.

diverse adj divers.

diversion n détournement m; (distraction) diversion f; (of traffic) déviation f. **divert** vt détourner; (traffic) dévier.

divide vt/i (se) diviser.

dividend n dividende m.

divine adj divin.

diving: ~-**board** n plongeoir m. ~-**suit** n scaphandre m.

division n division f.

divorce n divorce m (**from** avec). ●vt/i divorcer (d'avec).

divulge vt divulguer.

DIY abbr ▶DO-IT-YOURSELF.

dizziness n vertige m.

dizzy adj (**-ier, -iest**) vertigineux; **be** or **feel** ~ avoir le vertige.

---

do /du:/

❗ present **do, does**; present negative **don't, do not**; past **did**; past participle **done**

● transitive and intransitive verb
····▸ faire; **she is doing her**

homework elle fait ses devoirs.

····▸ (progress, be suitable) aller; **how are you doing?** comment ça va?

····▸ (be enough) suffire; **will five dollars ~?** cinq dollars, ça suffira?

● auxiliary verb
····▸ (in questions) ~ **you like Mozart?** aimes-tu Mozart?, est-ce que tu aimes Mozart?; **did your sister phone?** est-ce que ta sœur a téléphoné?, ta sœur a-t-elle téléphoné?

····▸ (in negatives) **I don't like Mozart** je n'aime pas Mozart.

····▸ (emphatic uses) **I ~ like your dress** j'aime beaucoup ta robe; **I ~ think you should go** je pense vraiment que tu devrais y aller.

····▸ (referring back to another verb) **I live in Orford and so does Lily** j'habite à Orford et Lily aussi; **she gets paid more than I ~** elle est payée plus que moi; **'I don't like carrots'—'neither ~ I'** 'je n'aime pas les carottes'—'moi non plus'.

····▸ (imperatives) **don't shut the door** ne ferme pas la porte; ~ **be quiet** tais-toi!

····▸ (short questions and answers) **you like fish, don't you?** tu aimes le poisson, n'est-ce pas?; **Lola didn't phone, did she?** Lola n'a pas téléphoné par hasard?; **'does he play tennis?'—'no he doesn't/yes he does'** 'est-ce qu'il joue au tennis?'—'non/oui'; **'Marion didn't say that'—'yes she did'** 'Marion n'a pas dit ça'—'si'.

■ **do away with** supprimer. ■ **do up** (fasten) fermer; (house) refaire. ■ **do with it's to ~ with** c'est à propos de; **it's nothing to ~ with** ça n'a rien à voir avec. ■ **do without** se passer de.

docile adj docile.

dock n (Jur) banc m des accusés; dock m. •vi arriver au port. •vt mettre à quai; (wages) faire une retenue sur.

doctor n médecin m, docteur m; (Univ) docteur m. •vt (cat) châtrer; (fig) altérer.

doctorate n doctorat m.

document n document m. **documentary** adj & n documentaire (m). **documentation** n documentation f.

dodge vt esquiver. •vi faire un saut de côté. •n mouvement m de côté.

dodgems npl autos fpl tamponneuses.

dodgy adj (-ier, -iest) (🛈: difficult) épineux, délicat; (untrustworthy) louche 🛈.

doe n (deer) biche f.

does ▷ DO.

doesn't ▷ DOES NOT.

dog n chien m. •vt (pt **dogged**) poursuivre. **~-collar** n col m romain. **~-eared** adj écorné.

dogged adj obstiné.

dogma n dogme m. **dogmatic** adj dogmatique.

dogsbody n bonne f à tout faire.

do-it-yourself n bricolage m.

doldrums npl **be in the ~** (person) avoir le cafard.

dole vt ~ **out** distribuer. •n 🛈 indemnité f de chômage; **on the ~** 🛈 au chômage.

doll n poupée f. •vt ~ **up** 🛈 bichonner.

dollar n dollar m.

dollop n (of food 🛈) gros morceau m.

dolphin n dauphin m.

domain n domaine m.

dome n dôme m.

domestic adj familial; (trade, flights) intérieur; (animal) domestique. **domesticated** adj (animal) domestiqué.

domestic science n arts mpl ménagers.

dominant adj dominant.

dominate vt/i dominer. **domination** n domination f.

domineering adj dominateur.

domino n (pl **~es**) domino m; **~es** (game) dominos mpl.

donate vt faire don de. **donation** n don m.

done ▷ DO.

donkey n âne m. ~ **work** n travail m pénible.

donor n donateur/-trice m/f; (of blood) donneur/-euse m/f.

don't ▷ DO NOT.

doodle vi griffonner.

doom n (ruin) ruine f; (fate) destin m. •vt **be ~ed to** être destiné or condamné à; **~ed (to failure)** voué à l'échec.

door n porte f; (of vehicle) portière f, porte f. **~bell** n sonnette f. **~man** n (pl **-men**) portier m. **~mat** n paillasson m. **~step** n pas m de (la) porte, seuil m. **~way** n porte f.

dope n 🛈 cannabis m; (idiot 🗷) imbécile mf. •vt doper. **dopey** adj (foolish 🗷) imbécile.

dormant adj en sommeil.

dormitory n dortoir m; (Univ, US) résidence f.

dosage n dose f; (on label) posologie f.

dose n dose f.

dot n point m; **on the ~** 🛈 à l'heure pile.

dot-com n (société) point com f; ~ **millionaire** n millionaire mf de l'Internet. ~ **shares** npl actions fpl des sociétés point com.

dote vi ~ **on** adorer.

dotted adj (fabric) à pois; ~ **line** pointillé m; ~ **with** parsemé de.

double adj double; (room, bed) pour deux personnes; ~ **the size** deux fois plus grand. ●adv deux fois; **pay** ~ payer le double. ●n double m; (stuntman) doublure f; ~**s** (tennis) double m; **at** or **on the** ~ au pas de course. ●vt/i doubler; (fold) plier en deux. ~**-bass** n (Mus) contrebasse f. ~**-check** vt revérifier. ~ **chin** n double menton m. ~**-cross** vt tromper. ~**-decker** n autobus m à impériale.

doubt n doute m. ●vt douter de; ~ **if** or **that** douter que. **doubtful** adj incertain, douteux; (person) qui a des doutes. **doubtless** adv sans doute.

dough n pâte f; (money) fric m 🄸.

doughnut n beignet m.

douse vt arroser; (light, fire) éteindre.

dove n colombe f.

Dover n Douvres.

dowdy adj (-ier, -iest) (clothes) sans chic, monotone; (person) sans élégance.

down adv en bas; (of sun) couché; (lower) plus bas; **come** or **go** ~ descendre; **go** ~ **to the post office** aller à la poste; ~ **under** aux antipodes; ~ **with** à bas. ●prep en bas de; (along) le long de. ●vt (knock down, shoot down) abattre; (drink) vider. ●n (fluff) duvet m.

down: ~**-and-out** n clochard/-e m/f. ~**cast** adj démoralisé. ~**fall** n chute f. ~**grade** vt déclasser. ~**-hearted** adj découragé.

downhill adv **go** ~ descendre; (pej) baisser.

down: ~**load** vt (Comput) télécharger. ~**-market** adj bas de gamme. ~ **payment** n acompte m. ~**pour** n grosse averse f.

downright adj (utter) véritable; (honest) franc. ●adv carrément.

downstairs adv en bas. ●adj d'en bas.

down: ~**stream** adv en aval. ~**-to-earth** adj pratique.

downtown adj (US) du centre-ville; ~ **Boston** le centre de Boston.

downward adj & adv, **downwards** adv vers le bas.

doze vi somnoler; ~ **off** s'assoupir. ●n somme m.

dozen n douzaine f; **a** ~ **eggs** une douzaine d'œufs; ~**s of** 🄸 des dizaines de.

Dr abbr (**Doctor**) Docteur.

drab adj terne.

draft n (outline) brouillon m; (Comm) traite f; **the** ~ (Mil, US) la conscription; **a** ~ **treaty** un projet de traité; (US) ▷DRAUGHT. ●vt faire le brouillon de; (draw up) rédiger.

drag vt/i (pt **dragged**) traîner; (river) draguer; (pull away) arracher; ~ **on** s'éterniser. ●n (task 🄸) corvée f; (person 🄸) raseur/-euse m/f; **in** ~ en travesti.

dragon n dragon m.

drain vt (land) drainer; (vegetables) égoutter; (tank, glass) vider; (use up) épuiser; ~ **(off)** (liquid) faire écouler. ●vi ~ **(off)** (of liquid) s'écouler. ●n (sewer) égout m; ~**(-pipe)** tuyau m d'écoulement; **a** ~ **on** une ponction sur. **draining-board** n égouttoir m.

drama n art m dramatique, théâtre m; (play, event) drame m. **dramatic** adj (situation) dramatique; (increase) spectaculaire. **dramatist** n dramaturge m. **dramatize** vt adapter pour la scène; (fig) dramatiser.

drank ▷DRINK.

drape vt draper. **drapes** npl (US) rideaux mpl.

drastic adj sévère.

draught n courant m d'air; **~s** (game) dames fpl. **~ beer** n bière f pression.

draughty adj plein de courants d'air.

draw vt (pt **drew**; pp **drawn**) (picture) dessiner; (line) tracer; (pull) tirer; (attract) attirer. ●vi dessiner; (Sport) faire match nul; (come, move) venir. ●n (Sport) match m nul; (in lottery) tirage m au sort. ■ **~ back** reculer. **~ near** (s')approcher (**to** de). **~ out** (money) retirer. **~ up** vi (stop) s'arrêter; vt (document) dresser; (chair) approcher.

drawback n inconvénient m.

drawbridge n pont-levis m.

drawer n tiroir m.

drawing n dessin m. **~-board** n planche f à dessin. **~-pin** n punaise f. **~-room** n salon m.

drawl n voix f traînante.

drawn ▷DRAW. ●adj (features) tiré; (match) nul.

dread n terreur f, crainte f. ●vt redouter. **dreadful** adj épouvantable, affreux. **dreadfully** adv terriblement.

dream n rêve m. ●vt/i (pt **dreamed** or **dreamt**) rêver; **~ up** imaginer. ●adj (ideal) de ses rêves.

dreary adj (-ier, -iest) triste; (boring) monotone.

dredge vt (river) draguer; **~ sth up** (fig) exhumer.

dregs npl lie f.

drench vt tremper.

dress n robe f; (clothing) tenue f. ●vt/i (s')habiller; (food) assaisonner; (wound) panser; **~ up as** se déguiser en; **get ~ed** s'habiller. **~ circle** n premier balcon m.

dresser n (furniture) buffet m; **be a stylish ~** s'habiller avec chic.

dressing n (sauce) assaisonnement m; (bandage) pansement m. **~-gown** n robe f de chambre. **~-room** n (Sport) vestiaire m; (Theat) loge f. **~-table** n coiffeuse f.

dressmaker n couturière f. **dressmaking** n couture f.

dress rehearsal n répétition f générale.

dressy adj (-ier, -iest) chic inv.

drew ▷DRAW .

dribble vi (liquid) dégouliner; (person) baver; (football) dribbler.

dried adj (fruit) sec.

drier n séchoir m.

drift vi aller à la dérive; (pile up) s'amonceler; **~ towards** glisser vers. ●n dérive f. amoncellement m; (of events) tournure f; (meaning) sens m; **snow ~** congère f. **driftwood** n bois m flotté.

drill n (tool) perceuse f; (for teeth) roulette f; (training) exercice m; (procedure ▣) marche f à suivre; **(pneumatic) ~** marteau m piqueur. ●vt percer; (train) entraîner. ●vi être à l'exercice.

drink vt/i (pt **drank**; pp **drunk**) boire. ●n (liquid) boisson f; (glass of alcohol) verre m; **a ~ of water** un verre d'eau. **drinking water** n eau f potable.

drip vi (pt **dripped**) (é)goutter; (washing) s'égoutter. ●n goutte f; (person ▣) lavette f.

drip-dry vt laisser égoutter. ●adj sans essorage.

drive vt (pt **drove**; pp **driven**) (vehicle) conduire; (sb somewhere) chasser, pousser; (machine) actionner; **~ mad** rendre fou. ●vi conduire. ●n promenade f en voiture; (private road) allée f; (fig) énergie f; (Psych) instinct m; (Pol) campagne f; (Auto) traction f; (golf, Comput) drive m; **it's a two-hour ~** il y a deux heures de route; **lefthand ~** conduite f à gauche. ■ **~ at** en venir à.

drivel n bêtises fpl.

driver n conducteur/-trice m/f, chauffeur m. ~'s **license** n (US) permis m de conduire.

driving n conduite f; **take one's ~ test** passer son permis. ●adj (rain) battant; (wind) cinglant. ~ **licence** n permis m de conduire. ~ **school** n auto-école f.

drizzle n bruine f. ●vi bruiner.

drone n (of engine) ronronnement m; (of insects) bourdonnement m. ●vi ronronner; bourdonner.

drool vi baver (**over** sur).

droop vi pencher, tomber.

drop n goutte f; (fall, lowering) chute f. ●vt/i (pt **dropped**) (laisser) tomber; (decrease, lower) baisser; ~ **(off)** (person from car) déposer; ~ **a line** écrire un mot (**to** à). ■ ~ **in** passer (**on** chez). ~ **off** (doze) s'assoupir. ~ **out** se retirer (**of** de); (of student) abandonner.

dropout n marginal/-e m/f, raté/-e m/f.

droppings npl crottes fpl.

drought n sécheresse f.

drove ▷DRIVE.

droves npl foules fpl.

drown vt/i (se) noyer.

drowsy adj somnolent; **be** or **feel ~** avoir envie de dormir.

drug n drogue f; (Med) médicament m. ●vt (pt **drugged**) droguer. ~ **addict** n drogué/-e m/f. **drugstore** n (US) drugstore m.

drum n tambour m; (for oil) bidon m; ~**s** batterie f. ●vi (pt **drummed**) tambouriner. ●vt ~ **into sb** répéter sans cesse à qn; ~ **up** (support) susciter; (business) créer. **drummer** n tambour m; (in pop group) batteur m.

drumstick n baguette f de tambour; (of chicken) pilon m.

drunk ▷DRINK. ●adj ivre; **get ~** s'enivrer. ●n ivrogne/-esse m/f.

drunkard n ivrogne/-esse m/f.

drunken adj ivre. **drunkenness** n ivresse f.

dry adj (**drier, driest**) sec; (day) sans pluie; **be** or **feel ~** avoir soif. ●vt/i (faire) sécher; ~ **up** (dry dishes) essuyer la vaisselle; (of supplies) (se) tarir; (be silent [I]) se taire. ~-**clean** vt nettoyer à sec. ~-**cleaner** n teinturier m. ~ **run** n galop m d'essai.

DTD abbr (**Document Type Definition**) DTD f.

dual adj double. ~ **carriageway** n route f à quatre voies. ~-**purpose** adj qui fait double emploi.

dub vt (pt **dubbed**) (film) doubler (**into** en); (nickname) surnommer.

dubious adj (pej) douteux; **be ~ about** avoir des doutes sur.

duck n canard m. ●vi se baisser subitement. ●vt (head) baisser; (person) plonger dans l'eau.

duct n conduit m.

dud adj (tool 🗷) mal fichu; (coin 🗷) faux; (cheque 🗷) sans provision. ●n **be a ~** (not work 🗷) ne pas marcher.

due adj (owing) dû; (expected) attendu; (proper) qui convient; ~ **to** à cause de; (caused by) dû à; **she's ~ to leave now** il est prévu qu'elle parte maintenant; **in ~ course** (at the right time) en temps voulu; (later) plus tard. ●adv ~ **east** droit vers l'est. ●n dû m; ~**s** droits mpl; (of club) cotisation f.

duel n duel m.

duet n duo m.

dug ▷DIG.

duke n duc m.

dull adj ennuyeux; (colour) terne; (weather) maussade; (sound) sourd. ●vt (pain) atténuer; (shine) ternir.

duly adv comme il convient; (as expected) comme prévu.

dumb adj muet; (stupid 🔲) bête. ■ ~ **down** (course, TV coverage) baisser le niveau intellectuel de.

dumbfound vt sidérer, ahurir.

dummy n (of tailor) mannequin m; (of baby) sucette f. ●adj factice. ~ **run** n galop m d'essai.

dump vt déposer; (get rid of 🔲) se débarrasser de. ●n tas m d'ordures; (refuse tip) décharge f; (Mil) dépôt m; (dull place 🔲) trou m 🔲; **be in the ~s** 🔲 avoir le cafard.

dune n dune f.

dung n (excrement) bouse f, crotte f; (manure) fumier m.

dungarees npl salopette f.

dungeon n cachot m.

duplicate¹ /ˈdjuːplɪkət/ n double m. ●adj identique.

duplicate² /ˈdjuːplɪkeɪt/ vt faire un double de; (on machine) polycopier.

durable adj (tough) résistant; (enduring) durable.

duration n durée f.

during prep pendant.

dusk n crépuscule m.

dusky adj (-ier, -iest) foncé.

dust n poussière f. ●vt/i épousseter; (sprinkle) saupoudrer (**with** de). ~**bin** n poubelle f.

duster n chiffon m.

dust: ~**man** n (pl -**men**) éboueur m. ~**pan** n pelle f (à poussière).

dusty adj (-ier, -iest) poussiéreux.

Dutch adj néerlandais; **go** ~ partager les frais. ●n (Ling) néerlandais m. ~**man** n Néerlandais m. ~**woman** n Néerlandaise f.

dutiful adj obéissant.

duty n devoir m; (tax) droit m; (of official) fonction f; **on** ~ de service. ~-**free** adj hors-taxe.

duvet n couette f.

dwarf n nain/-e m/f. ●vt rapetisser.

dwell vi (pt **dwelt**) demeurer; ~ **on** s'étendre sur. **dweller** n habitant/-e m/f. **dwelling** n habitation f.

dwindle vi diminuer.

dye vt teindre. ●n teinture f.

dying adj mourant; (art) qui se perd.

dynamic adj dynamique.

dynamite n dynamite f.

dysentery n dysenterie f.

dyslexia n dyslexie f. **dyslexic** adj & n dyslexique (mf).

Ee

each det chaque inv; ~ **one** chacun/-e m/f. ●pron chacun/-e m/f; **oranges at 30p** ~ des oranges à 30 pence pièce.

each other pron l'un/l'une l'autre, les uns/les unes les autres; **know** ~ se connaître; **love** ~ s'aimer.

eager adj impatient (**to** de); (person, acceptance) enthousiaste; ~ **for** avide de.

eagle n aigle m.

ear n oreille f; (of corn) épi m. ~**ache** n mal m à l'oreille. ~-**drum** n tympan m.

earl n comte m.

early (-**ier**, -**iest**) adv tôt, de

bonne heure; (ahead of time) en avance; **as I said earlier** comme je l'ai déjà dit. ●adj (attempt, years) premier; (hour) matinal; (fruit) précoce; (retirement) anticipé; **have an ~ dinner** dîner tôt; **in ~ summer** au début de l'été; **at the earliest** au plus tôt.

earmark vt désigner (**for** pour).

earn vt gagner; (interest: Comm) rapporter.

earnest adj sérieux; **in ~** sérieusement.

earnings npl salaire m; (profits) gains mpl.

ear: ~phones npl casque m. **~-ring** n boucle f d'oreille. **~shot** n **within/in ~shot** à portée de voix.

earth n terre f; **why/how/where on ~...?** pourquoi/comment/où diable...? ●vt (Electr) mettre à la terre. **earthenware** n faïence f. **~quake** n tremblement m de terre.

ease n facilité f; (comfort) bien-être m; **at ~** à l'aise; (Mil) au repos; **with ~** facilement. ●vt (pain, pressure) atténuer; (congestion) réduire; (transition) faciliter. ●vi (pain, pressure) s'atténuer; (congestion, rain) diminuer.

easel n chevalet m.

east n est m; **the E~** (Orient) l'Orient m. ●adj (side, coast) est; (wind) d'est. ●adv à l'est.

Easter n Pâques m; **~ egg** œuf m de Pâques.

easterly adj (wind) d'est; (direction) de l'est.

eastern de l'est; **~ France** l'est de la France.

eastward adj (side) est inv; (journey) vers l'est.

easy adj (-ier, -iest) facile; **go ~ with** 🄘 y aller doucement avec; **take it ~** ne te fatigue pas. **~going** adj accommodant.

eat vt/i (pt **ate**; pp **eaten**) manger; **~ into** ronger.

eavesdrop vi (pt **-dropped**) écouter aux portes.

ebb n reflux m. ●vi descendre; (fig) décliner.

EC abbr (**European Commission**) CE f.

eccentric adj & n excentrique (mf).

echo n (pl **-oes**) écho m. ●vt répercuter; (idea, opinion) reprendre. ●vi retentir, résonner (**to, with** de).

eclipse n éclipse f. ●vt éclipser.

ecological adj écologique.

ecology n écologie f.

e-commerce n commerce m électronique, commerce m en ligne.

economic adj économique; (profitable) rentable; **~ refugee** réfugié/-e m/f économique. **economical** adj économique; (person) économe. **economics** n économie f, sciences fpl économiques. **economist** n économiste mf.

economize vi **~ (on)** économiser.

economy n économie f. **~-class syndrome** n syndrome m de la classe économique.

ecosystem n écosystème m.

ecstasy n extase f; (drug) ecstasy m.

edge n bord m; (of town) abords mpl; (of knife) tranchant m; **have the ~ on** 🄘 l'emporter sur; **on ~** énervé. ●vt (trim) border. ●vi **~ forward** avancer doucement.

edgeways adv **I can't get a word in ~** je n'arrive pas à placer un mot.

edgy adj énervé.

edible adj comestible.

edit vt (pt **edited**) (newspaper, page) être le rédacteur/la rédactrice de; (check) réviser; (cut) couper; (TV, cinema) monter.

edition n édition f.

editor n (writer) rédacteur/-trice m/f; (of works, anthology) éditeur/-trice m/f; (TV, cinema) monteur/-teuse m/f; **the ~ (in chief)** le rédacteur en chef.

editorial adj de la rédaction. •n éditorial m.

educate vt instruire; (mind, public) éduquer. **educated** adj instruit. **education** n éducation f; (schooling) études fpl. **educational** adj éducatif; (establishment, method) d'enseignement.

eel n anguille f.

eerie adj (**-ier, -iest**) sinistre.

effect n effet m; **come into ~** entrer en vigueur; **in ~** effectivement; **take ~** agir. •vt effectuer.

effective adj efficace; (actual) effectif. **effectively** adv efficacement; (in effect) en réalité. **effectiveness** n efficacité f.

effeminate adj efféminé.

effervescent adj effervescent.

efficiency n efficacité f; (of machine) rendement m. **efficient** adj efficace. **efficiently** adv efficacement.

effort n efforts mpl; **make an ~** faire un effort; **be worth the ~** en valoir la peine. **effortless** adj facile.

effusive adj expansif.

e.g. abbr par ex.

egg n œuf m. •vt ~ **on** pousser. **~-cup** n coquetier m. **~-plant** n (US) aubergine f. **~shell** n coquille f d'œuf.

ego n amour-propre m; (Psych) moi m. **egotism** n égotisme m. **egotist** n égotiste mf.

Egypt n Égypte f.

eiderdown n édredon m.

eight adj & n huit (m). **eighteen** adj & n dix-huit (m). **eighth** adj & n huitième (mf). **eighty** adj & n quatre-vingts (m).

either det & pron l'un/une ou l'autre; (with negative) ni l'un/une ni l'autre; **you can take ~** tu peux prendre n'importe lequel/laquelle. •adv non plus. •conj **~...or** ou (bien)...ou (bien); (with negative) ni...ni.

eject vt (troublemaker) expulser; (waste) rejeter.

elaborate[1] /ɪˈlæbərət/ adj compliqué.

elaborate[2] /ɪˈlæbəreɪt/ vt élaborer. •vi préciser; ~ **on** s'étendre sur.

elastic adj & n élastique (m); ~ **band** élastique m. **elasticity** n élasticité f.

elated adj transporté de joie.

elbow n coude m; ~ **room** espace m vital.

elder adj & n aîné/-e (m/f); (tree) sureau m.

elderly adj âgé; **the ~** les personnes fpl âgées.

eldest adj & n aîné/-e (m/f).

elect vt élire; ~ **to do** choisir de faire. •adj (president etc.) futur. **election** n élection f. **elector** n électeur/-trice m/f. **electoral** adj électoral. **electorate** n électorat m.

electric adj électrique; ~ **blanket** couverture f chauffante. **electrical** adj électrique. **electrician** n électricien/-ne m/f. **electricity** n électricité f. **electrify** vt électrifier; (excite) électriser. **electrocute** vt électrocuter.

electronic adj électronique. ~ **publishing** n édition f. **electronics** n électronique f.

elegance n élégance f.

element n élément m; (of heater etc.) résistance f. **elementary** adj élémentaire.

elephant n éléphant m.

elevate vt élever. **elevation** n

élévation f. **elevator** n (US) ascenseur m.

eleven adj & n onze (m). **eleventh** adj & n onzième (mf).

elicit vt obtenir (**from** de).

eligible adj admissible (**for** à); **be ~ for** (entitled to) avoir droit à.

eliminate vt éliminer.

elm n orme m.

elongate vt allonger.

elope vi s'enfuir (**with** avec). **elopement** n fugue f (amoureuse).

eloquence n éloquence f.

else adv d'autre; **somebody/nothing ~** quelqu'un/rien d'autre; **everybody ~** tous les autres; **somewhere/something ~** part/chose; **or ~** ou bien. **elsewhere** adv ailleurs.

elude vt échapper à.

elusive adj insaisissable.

email n (medium) courrier m électronique; (item) e-mail m, mél m; **~ sb** envoyer un e-mail à qn; **~ sth** envoyer qch par courrier électronique.

emancipate vt émanciper.

embankment n (of river) quai m; (of railway) remblai m.

embark vt embarquer. •vi (Naut) embarquer; **~ on** (journey) entreprendre; (campaign, career) se lancer dans.

embarrass vt plonger dans l'embarras; **be/feel ~ed** être/se sentir gêné. **embarrassment** n confusion f, gêne f.

embassy n ambassade f.

embed vt (pt **embedded**) enfoncer (**in** dans).

embellish vt embellir.

embers npl braises fpl.

embezzle vt détourner (**from** de). **embezzlement** n détournement m de fonds.

emblem n emblème m.

embodiment n incarnation f. **embody** vt incarner; (legally) incorporer.

emboss vt (metal) repousser; (paper) gaufrer.

embrace vt (person) étreindre; (religion) embrasser; (include) comprendre. •n étreinte f.

embroider vt broder. **embroidery** n broderie f.

embryo n embryon m.

emerald n émeraude f.

emerge vi (person) sortir (**from** de); **it ~d that** il est apparu que. **emergence** n apparition f.

emergency n (crisis) crise f; (urgent case: Med) urgence f; **in an ~** en cas d'urgence. **~ exit** n sortie f de secours; **~ landing** n atterrissage m forcé. **~ room** n (US) salle f des urgences.

emigrant n émigrant/-e m/f. **emigrate** vi émigrer.

eminence n éminence f. **eminent** adj éminent.

emission n émission f.

emit vt (pt **emitted**) émettre.

emotion n émotion f. **emotional** adj (development) émotif; (reaction) émotionel; (film, scene) émouvant.

emotive adj qui soulève les passions.

emperor n empereur m.

emphasis n accent m; **lay ~ on** mettre l'accent sur. **emphasize** vt mettre l'accent sur. **emphatic** adj catégorique; (manner) énergique.

empire n empire m.

employ vt employer. **employee** n employé/-e m/f. **employer** n employeur/-euse m/f.

employment n emploi m; **find ~** trouver du travail.

empower vt autoriser (**to do** à faire).

e

empty adj (**-ier, -iest**) vide; (street) désert; (promise) vain; **on an ~ stomach** à jeun. •vt/i (se) vider. **~-handed** adj les mains vides.

emulate vt imiter.

enable vt **~ sb to** permettre à qn de.

enamel n émail m. •vt (pt **enamelled**) émailler.

encase vt revêtir, recouvrir (**in** de).

enchant vt enchanter.

enclose vt entourer; (land) clôturer; (with letter) joindre. **enclosed** adj (space) clos; (with letter) ci-joint. **enclosure** n enceinte f; (with letter) pièce f jointe.

encompass vt inclure.

encore interj & n bis (m).

encounter vt rencontrer. •n rencontre f.

encourage vt encourager.

encroach vi **~ upon** empiéter sur.

encyclopedia n encyclopédie f. **encyclopaedic** adj encyclopédique.

end n fin f; (farthest part) bout m; **come to an ~** prendre fin; **~-product** produit m fini; **in the ~** finalement; **no ~ of** 🔲 énormément de; **on ~** (upright) debout; (in a row) de suite; **put an ~to** mettre fin à. •vt (marriage) mettre fin à; **~ one's days** finir ses jours. •vi se terminer; **~ up doing** finir par faire.

endanger vt mettre en danger.

endearing adj attachant.

endeavour, (US) **endeavor** n (attempt) tentative f; (hard work) effort m. •vi faire tout son possible (**to do** pour faire).

ending n fin f.

endive n chicorée f.

endless adj interminable; (supply) inépuisable; (patience) infini.

endorse vt (candidate, decision) appuyer; (product, claim) approuver; (cheque) endosser.

endurance n endurance f.

endure vt supporter. •vi durer. **enduring** adj durable.

enemy n & adj ennemi/-e (m/f).

energetic adj énergique. **energy** n énergie f.

enforce vt (rule, law) appliquer, faire respecter; (silence, discipline) imposer (**on** à); **~d** forcé.

engage vt (staff) engager; (attention) retenir; **be ~d in** se livrer à. •vi **~ in** se livrer à. **engaged** adj fiancé; (busy) occupé; **get ~d** se fiancer. **engagement** n fiançailles fpl; (meeting) rendezvous m; (undertaking) engagement m.

engaging adj attachant, engageant.

engine n moteur m; (of train) locomotive f; (of ship) machines fpl. **~-driver** n mécanicien m.

engineer n ingénieur m; (repairman) technicien m; (on ship) mécanicien m. •vt (contrive) manigancer.

engineering n ingénierie f; (industry) mécanique f; **civil ~** génie m civil.

England n Angleterre f.

English adj anglais. •n (Ling) anglais m; **the ~** les Anglais mpl. **~man** n Anglais m. **~-speaking** adj anglophone. **~woman** n Anglaise f.

engrave vt graver.

engrossed adj absorbé (**in** dans).

engulf vt engouffrer.

enhance vt (prospects, status) améliorer; (price, value) augmenter.

enjoy vt aimer (**doing** faire); (benefit from) jouir de; **~ oneself** s'amuser; **~ your meal!** bon

appétit! **enjoyable** adj agréable.
enjoyment n plaisir m.

enlarge vt agrandir. •vi
s'agrandir; (pupil) se dilater; ∼
on s'étendre sur. **enlargement**
n agrandissement m.

enlighten vt éclairer (**on** sur).
enlightenment n instruction f;
(information) éclaircissement m.

enlist vt (person) recruter; (fig)
obtenir. •vi s'engager.

enmity n inimitié f.

enormous adj énorme.
enormously adv énormément.

enough adv & n assez; **have** ∼ **of**
en avoir assez de. •det assez de;
∼ **glasses**/**time** assez de verres/
de temps.

enquire ▷INQUIRE.
enquiry▷INQUIRY.

enrage vt mettre en rage, rendre
furieux.

enrol vt/i (pt **enrolled**)
(s')inscrire. **enrolment** n
inscription f.

ensure vt garantir; ∼ **that**
(ascertain) s'assurer que.

entail vt entraîner.

entangle vt emmêler.

enter vt (room, club, phase) entrer
dans; (note down, register) inscrire;
(data) entrer, saisir. •vi entrer
(**into** dans); ∼ **for** s'inscrire à.

enterprise n entreprise f;
(boldness) initiative f.
enterprising adj entreprenant.

entertain vt amuser, divertir;
(guests) recevoir; (ideas)
considérer. **entertainer** n artiste
mf. **entertaining** adj divertissant.
entertainment n divertissement
m; (performance) spectacle m.

enthral vt (pt **enthralled**)
captiver.

enthusiasm n enthousiasme m
(**for** pour).

enthusiast n passionné/-e m/f
(**for** de). **enthusiastic** adj

(supporter) enthousiaste; **be** ∼**ic**
about être enthousiasmé par.
enthusiastically adv avec
enthousiasme.

entice vt attirer; ∼ **sb to do**
entraîner qn à faire.

entire adj entier. **entirely** adv
entièrement. **entirety** n **in its**
∼**ty** en entier.

entitle vt donner droit à (**to sth**
à qch); **to do** de faire); ∼**d** (book)
intitulé; **be** ∼**d to sth** avoir
droit à qch.

entrance[1] /'entrəns/ n (entering, way
in) entrée f (**to** de); (right to enter)
admission f. •adj (charge, exam)
d'entrée.

entrance[2] /ɪn'trɑːns/ vt
transporter.

entrant n (Sport) concurrent/-e
m/f; (in exam) candidat/-e m/f.

entrenched adj (opinion)
inébranlable; (Mil) retranché.

entrepreneur n entrepreneur/-
euse m/f.

entrust vt confier; ∼ **sb with sth**
confier qch à qn.

entry n entrée f; ∼ **form** fiche f
d'inscription.

envelop vt (pt **enveloped**)
envelopper.

envelope n enveloppe f.

envious adj envieux (**of** de).

environment n (ecological)
environnement m; (social) milieu
m. **environmental** adj du milieu;
de l'environnement.
environmentalist n
écologiste mf.

envisage vt prévoir (**doing** de
faire).

envoy n envoyé/-e m/f.

envy n envie f. •vt envier; ∼ **sb**
sth envier qch à qn.

epic n épopée f. •adj épique.

epidemic n épidémie f.

epilepsy n épilepsie f.

episode n épisode m.

epitome n modèle m. **epitomize** vt incarner.

equal adj & n égal/-e (m/f); ~ **opportunities/rights** égalité f des chances/droits; ~ **to** (task) à la hauteur de. •vt (pt **equalled**) égaler. **equality** n égalité f. **equalize** vt/i égaliser. **equalizer** n (goal) but m égalisateur. **equally** adv (divide) en parts égales; (just as) tout aussi.

equanimity n sérénité f.

equate vt assimiler (**with** à). **equation** n équation f.

equator n équateur m.

equilibrium n équilibre m.

equip vt (pt **equipped**) équiper (**with** de). **equipment** n équipement m.

equity n équité f.

equivalence n équivalence f.

era n ère f, époque f.

eradicate vt éliminer; (disease) éradiquer.

erase vt effacer. **eraser** n (rubber) gomme f.

erect adj droit. •vt ériger. **erection** n érection f.

erode vt éroder; (fig) saper. **erosion** n érosion f.

erotic adj érotique.

errand n commission f, course f.

erratic adj (behaviour, person) imprévisible; (performance) inégal.

error n erreur f.

erupt vi (volcano) entrer en éruption; (fig) éclater.

escalate vt intensifier. •vi (conflict) s'intensifier. **escalation** n intensification f. **escalator** n escalier m mécanique, escalator® m.

escapade n frasque f.

escape vt échapper à. •vi s'enfuir, s'évader; (gas) fuir. •n fuite f,
évasion f; (of gas etc.) fuite f; **have a lucky** or **narrow** ~ l'échapper belle.

escapism n évasion f (du réel).

escort[1] /'eskɔːt/ n (guard) escorte f; (companion) compagnon/compagne m/f.

escort[2] /ɪˈskɔːt/ vt escorter.

Eskimo n Esquimau/-de m/f.

especially adv en particulier.

espionage n espionnage m.

espresso n (café) express m.

essay n (in literature) essai m; (School) rédaction f; (Univ) dissertation f.

essence n essence f.

essential adj essentiel; **the** ~**s** l'essentiel m. **essentially** adv essentiellement.

establish vt établir; (business) fonder.

establishment n (process) instauration f; (institution) établissement m; **the E**~ l'ordre m établi.

estate n (house and land) domaine m; (possessions) biens mpl; (housing estate) cité f; ~ **agent** n agent m immobilier. ~ **car** n break m.

esteem n estime f.

esthetic adj (US) ▷AESTHETIC.

estimate[1] /'estɪmət/ n (calculation) estimation f; (Comm) devis m.

estimate[2] /'estɪmeɪt/ vt évaluer; ~ **that** estimer que. **estimation** n (esteem) estime f; (judgment) opinion f.

Estonia n Estonie f.

estuary n estuaire m.

eternal adj éternel.

eternity n éternité f.

ethic n éthique f; ~**s** moralité f. **ethical** adj éthique.

ethnic adj ethnique. ~ **cleansing** n nettoyage m ethnique.

EU abbr (**European Union**) UE f, Union f européenne.

euphoria n euphorie f.

euro n euro m. ~ **zone** n zone f euro.

Europe n Europe f.

European adj & n européen/-ne (m/f); ~ **Community** Communauté f européenne.

eurosceptic n eurosceptique mf.

euthanasia n euthanasie f.

evacuate vt évacuer.

evade vt (blow) esquiver; (question) éluder.

evaluation n évaluation f.

evaporate vi s'évaporer; ~**d milk** lait m condensé.

evasion n fuite f (**of** devant); (excuse) faux-fuyant m; **tax** ~ évasion f fiscale. **evasive** adj évasif.

eve n veille f (**of** de).

even adj (surface, voice, contest) égal; (teeth, hem) régulier; (number) pair; **get** ~ **with** se venger de. ●adv même; ~ **better**/etc. (still) encore mieux/etc.; ~ **so** quand même. ■ ~ **out** (differences) s'atténuer; ~ **sth out** (inequalities) réduire qch; ~ **up** équilibrer.

evening n soir m; (whole evening, event) soirée f.

evenly adv (spread, apply) uniformément; (breathe) régulièrement; (equally) en parts égales.

event n événement m; (Sport) épreuve f; **in the** ~ **of** en cas de. **eventful** adj mouvementé.

eventual adj (outcome, decision) final; (aim) à long terme. **eventuality** n éventualité f. **eventually** adv finalement; (in future) un jour ou l'autre.

ever adv jamais; (at all times) toujours.

evergreen n arbre m à feuilles persistantes.

everlasting adj éternel.

ever since prep & adv depuis.

every adj ~ **house/window** toutes les maisons/les fenêtres; ~ **time/minute** chaque fois/minute; ~ **day** tous les jours; ~ **other day** tous les deux jours. **everybody** pron tout le monde. **everyday** adj quotidien. **everyone** pron tout le monde. **everything** pron tout. **everywhere** adv partout; ~**where he goes** partout où il va.

evict vt expulser (**from** de).

evidence n (proof) preuves fpl (**that** que; **of, for** de); (testimony) témoignage m; (traces) trace f (**of** de); **give** ~ témoigner; **be in** ~ être visible. **evident** adj manifeste. **evidently** adv (apparently) apparemment; (obviously) manifestement.

evil adj malfaisant. ●n mal m.

evoke vt évoquer.

evolution n évolution f.

evolve vi évoluer. ●vt élaborer.

ewe n brebis f.

ex- pref ex-, ancien.

exact adj exact; **the** ~ **opposite** exactement le contraire. ●vt exiger (**from** de). **exactly** adv exactement.

exaggerate vt/i exagérer.

exalted adj élevé.

exam n Ⓘ examen m.

examination n examen m.

examine vt examiner; (witness) interroger. **examiner** n examinateur/-trice m/f.

example n exemple m; **for** ~ par exemple; **make an** ~ **of** punir pour l'exemple.

exasperate vt exaspérer.

excavate vt fouiller. **excavations** npl fouilles fpl.

exceed vt dépasser. **exceedingly** adv extrêmement.

excel vi (pt **excelled**) exceller (**at,**

in en; **at doing** à faire). ●vt surpasser.

excellence n excellence f. **excellent** adj excellent.

except prep sauf, excepté; ~ **for** à part. ●vt excepter. **excepting** prep sauf, excepté.

exception n exception f; **take** ~ **to** s'offusquer de. **exceptional** adj exceptionnel.

excerpt n extrait m.

excess¹ /ɪk'ses/ n excès m.

excess² /'ekses/ adj ~ **weight** excès m de poids; ~ **baggage** excédent m de bagages.

excessive adj excessif.

exchange vt échanger (**for** contre). ●n échange m; (between currencies) change m; ~ **rate** taux m de change; **telephone** ~ central m téléphonique.

Exchequer n (Pol) ministère m britannique des finances.

excise n excise f, taxe f.

excite vt exciter; (enthuse) enthousiasmer. **excited** adj excité; **get** ~**d** s'exciter. **excitement** n excitation f. **exciting** adj passionnant.

exclaim vt s'exclamer.

exclamation n exclamation f; ~ **mark** or **point** (US) point m d'exclamation.

exclude vt exclure.

exclusive adj (club) fermé; (rights) exclusif; (news item) en exclusivité; ~ **of meals** repas non compris. **exclusively** adv exclusivement.

excruciating adj atroce.

excursion n excursion f.

excuse¹ /ɪk'skju:z/ vt excuser; ~ **from** (exempt) dispenser de; ~ **me!** excusez-moi!, pardon!

excuse² /ɪk'skju:s/ n (reason) excuse f; (pretext) prétexte m (**for sth** à qch; **for doing** pour faire).

ex-directory adj sur liste rouge.

execute vt exécuter. **executioner** n bourreau m.

executive n (person) cadre m; (committee) exécutif m. ●adj exécutif.

exemplary adj exemplaire.

exemplify vt illustrer.

exempt adj exempt (**from** de). ●vt exempter.

exercise n exercice m; ~ **book** cahier m. ●vt exercer; (restraint, patience) faire preuve de. ●vi faire de l'exercice.

exert vt exercer; ~ **oneself** se fatiguer. **exertion** n effort m.

exhaust vt épuiser. ●n (Auto) pot m d'échappement.

exhaustive adj exhaustif.

exhibit vt exposer; (fig) manifester. ●n objet m exposé.

exhibition n exposition f; (of skill) démonstration f. **exhibitionist** n exhibitionniste mf.

exhibitor n exposant/-e m/f.

exhilarate vt griser.

exile n exil m; (person) exilé/-e m/f. ●vt exiler.

exist vi exister. **existence** n existence f; **be in** ~**ence** exister. **existing** adj actuel.

exit n sortie f. ●vt/i (also Comput) sortir (de).

exodus n exode m.

exonerate vt disculper.

exotic adj exotique.

expand vt développer; (workforce) accroître. ●vi se développer; (population) s'accroître; (metal) se dilater.

expanse n étendue f.

expansion n développement m; (Pol, Comm) expansion f.

expatriate adj & n expatrié/-e (m/f).

expect vt s'attendre à; (suppose) supposer; (demand) exiger; (baby) attendre.

expectancy n attente f.

expectant adj ~ **mother** future maman f.

expectation n (assumption) prévision f; (hope) aspiration f; (demand) exigence f.

expedient adj opportun. •n expédient m.

expedition n expédition f.

expel vt (pt **expelled**) expulser; (pupil) renvoyer.

expend vt consacrer.

expenditure n dépenses fpl.

expense n frais mpl; **at sb's ~** aux frais de qn; ~ **account** frais mpl de représentation. **expensive** adj cher; (tastes) de luxe. **expensively** adv luxueusement.

experience n expérience f. •vt (undergo) connaître; (feel) éprouver; ~**d** expérimenté.

experiment n expérience f. •vi expérimenter, faire des essais.

expert n spécialiste mf. •adj spécialisé, expert. **expertise** n compétence f. **expertly** adv de manière experte.

expire vi expirer; ~**d** périmé. **expiry** n expiration f.

explain vt expliquer. **explanation** n explication f. **explanatory** adj explicatif.

explicit adj explicite.

explode vt/i (faire) exploser.

exploit[1] /'eksplɔɪt/ n exploit m.

exploit[2] /ɪk'splɔɪt/ vt exploiter.

exploration n exploration f. **exploratory** adj (talks) exploratoire. **explore** vt explorer; (fig) étudier. **explorer** n explorateur/-trice m/f.

explosion n explosion f. **explosive** adj & n explosif (m).

exponent n avocat/-e m/f (**of** de).

export[1] /ɪk'spɔːt/ vt exporter.

export[2] /'ekspɔːt/ n (process) exportation f; (product) produit m d'exportation.

expose vt exposer; (disclose) révéler.

exposure n révélation f; (Photo) pose f; **die of ~** mourir de froid.

express vt exprimer. •adj exprès. •adv **send sth ~** envoyer qch en exprès. •n (train) rapide m. **expression** n expression f. **expressive** adj expressif. **expressly** adv expressément.

exquisite adj exquis.

extend vt (visit) prolonger; (house) agrandir; (range) élargir; (arm, leg) étendre. •vi (stretch) s'étendre; (in time) se prolonger. **extension** n (of line, road) prolongement m; (of visa, loan) prorogation f; (building) addition f; (phone number) poste m; (cable) rallonge f.

extensive adj vaste; (study) approfondi; (damage) considérable. **extensively** adv (much) beaucoup; (very) très.

extent n (size, scope) étendue f; (degree) mesure f; **to some ~** dans une certaine mesure; **to such an ~ that** à tel point que.

extenuating adj atténuant.

exterior adj & n extérieur (m).

exterminate vt exterminer.

external adj extérieur; (cause, medical use) externe.

extinct adj (species) disparu; (volcano, passion) éteint.

extinguish vt éteindre. **extinguisher** n extincteur m.

extol vt (pt **extolled**) louer, chanter les louanges de.

extort vt extorquer (**from** à). **extortion** n (Jur) extorsion f. **extortionate** adj exorbitant.

extra adj supplémentaire; ~ **charge** supplément m; ~ **time** (football) prolongation f; ~ **strong** extrafort. •adv encore; plus. •n supplément m; (cinema) figurant/-e m/f.

extract¹ /ɪkˈstrækt/ vt sortir (**from** de); (tooth) extraire; (promise) arracher.

extract² /ˈekstrækt/ n extrait m.

extra-curricular adj parascolaire.

extradite vt extrader.

extramarital adj extraconjugal.

extramural adj (Univ) hors faculté.

extraordinary adj extraordinaire.

extravagance n prodigalité f. **extravagant** adj (person) dépensier; (claim) extravagant.

extreme adj & n extrême (m). **extremely** adv extrêmement.

extremist n extrémiste mf.

extremity n extrémité f.

extricate vt dégager.

extrovert n extraverti/-e m/f.

exuberance n exubérance f.

exude vt (charm) respirer; (smell) exhaler.

eye n œil m (pl yeux); **keep an ∼ on** surveiller. ●vt (pt eyed; pres p eyeing) regarder. ∼**ball** n globe m oculaire. ∼**brow** n sourcil m. ∼**-catching** adj attrayant. ∼**lash** n cil m. ∼**lid** n paupière f. ∼**-opener** n révélation f. ∼**-shadow** n ombre f à paupières. ∼**sight** n vue f. ∼**sore** n horreur f. ∼**witness** n témoin m oculaire.

Ff

fable n fable f.

fabric n (cloth) tissu m.

fabulous adj fabuleux; (marvellous 🄸) formidable.

face n visage m, figure f; (expression) air m; (appearance, dignity) face f; (of clock) cadran m; (Geol) face f; (of rock) paroi f; **in the ∼ of** face à; **make a (funny) ∼** faire la grimace; **∼ to ∼** face à face. ●vt être en face de; (risk) devoir affronter; (confront) faire face à; (deal with) **I can't ∼ him** je n'ai pas le courage de le voir. ●vi (person) regarder; (chair) être tourné vers; (window) donner sur; **∼ up to** faire face à; **∼d with** face à.

facelift n lifting m; **give a ∼ to** donner un coup de neuf à.

face value n valeur f nominale; **take sth at ∼** prendre qch au pied de la lettre.

facial adj (hair) du visage; (injury) au visage. ●n soin m du visage.

facility n (building) complexe m; (feature) fonction f; **facilities** (equipment) équipements mpl.

facsimile n fac-similé m.

fact n fait m; **as a matter of ∼, in ∼** en fait; **know for a ∼ that** savoir de source sûre que; **owing/due to the ∼ that** étant donné que.

factor n facteur m.

factory n usine f.

factual adj (account, description) basé sur les faits; (evidence) factuel.

faculty n faculté f.

fade vi (sound) s'affaiblir; (memory) s'effacer; (flower) se faner; (material) se décolorer; (colour) passer.

fail vi échouer; (grow weak) (s'af)faiblir; (run short) manquer; (engine) tomber en panne. ●vt (exam) échouer à; **∼ to do** (not do) ne pas faire; (not be able) ne pas réussir à faire; **without ~** à coup sûr.

failing n défaut m; **~ that/this** sinon.

failure n échec m; (person) raté-e m/f; (breakdown) panne f; **~ to do** (inability) incapacité f de faire.

faint adj léger, faible; **feel ~** (ill) se sentir mal; **I haven't the ~est idea** je n'en ai pas la moindre idée. ● vi s'évanouir. ● n évanouissement m; **~-hearted** adj timide.

fair n foire f. ● adj (hair, person) blond; (skin) clair; (weather) beau; (amount, quality) raisonnable; (just) juste, équitable. ● adv (play) loyalement.

fairground n champ m de foire.

fairly adv (justly) équitablement; (rather) assez.

fairness n justice f.

fairy n fée f. **~ story, ~-tale** n conte m de fées.

faith n (belief) foi f; (confidence) confiance f.

faithful adj fidèle.

fake n (forgery) faux m; (person) imposteur m; **it is a ~** c'est un faux. ● adj faux. ● vt (signature) contrefaire; (results) falsifier; (illness) feindre.

falcon n faucon m.

fall vi (pt **fell**; pp **fallen**) tomber; **~ short** être insuffisant. ● n chute f; (autumn: US) automne m; **Niagara F~s** chutes fpl du Niagara. ■ **~ back on** se rabattre sur. **~ behind** prendre du retard. **~ down or off** tomber. **~ for** (person 🔲) tomber amoureux de; (a trick 🔲) se laisser prendre à. **~ in** (Mil) se mettre en rangs. **~ off** (decrease) diminuer. **~ out** se brouiller (with avec). **~ over** tomber (par terre). **~ through** (plans) tomber à l'eau.

fallacy n erreur f.

false adj faux. **~ teeth** npl dentier m.

falter vi (courage) faiblir; (when speaking) bafouiller 🔲.

fame n renommée f. **famed** adj célèbre (**for** pour).

familiar adj familier; **be ~ with** connaître.

family n famille f.

famine n famine f.

famished adj affamé.

famous adj célèbre (**for** pour).

fan n (mechanical) ventilateur m; (hand-held) éventail m; (of person) fan mf 🔲, admirateur-trice m/f; (enthusiast) fervent-e m/f, passionné-e m/f. ● vt (pt **fanned**) (face) éventer; (fig) attiser. ● vi **~ out** se déployer en éventail.

fanatic n fanatique mf.

fan belt n courroie f de ventilateur.

fancy n (whim, fantasy) fantaisie f; **take a ~ to sb** se prendre d'affection pour qn; **it took my ~** ça m'a plu. ● adj (buttons etc.) fantaisie inv; (prices) extravagant; (impressive) impressionnant. ● vt s'imaginer; (want 🔲) avoir envie de; (like 🔲) aimer. **~ dress** n déguisement m.

fang n (of dog) croc m; (of snake) crochet m.

fantasize vi fantasmer.

fantastic adj fantastique.

fantasy n fantaisie f; (daydream) fantasme m.

fanzine n magazine m des fans, fanzine m.

FAQ abbr (**Frequently Asked Questions**) (Internet) FAQ f, foire f aux questions.

far adv loin; (much) beaucoup; (very) très; **~ away, ~ off** au loin; **as ~ as** (up to) jusqu'à; **as ~ as I know** autant que je sache; **by ~** de loin; **~ from** loin de. ● adj lointain; (end, side) autre. **~away** adj lointain.

farce n farce f.

fare n (prix du) billet m; (food) nourriture f. •vi (progress) aller; (manage) se débrouiller.

Far East n Extrême-Orient m.

farewell interj & n adieu (m).

farm n ferme f. •vt cultiver; ~ **out** céder en sous-traitance. •vi être fermier. **farmer** n fermier m. ~**house** n ferme f. **farming** n agriculture f. ~**yard** n basse-cour f.

fart 🔲 vi péter 🔲. •n pet m 🔲.

farther adv plus loin. •adj plus éloigné.

farthest adv le plus loin. •adj le plus éloigné.

fascinate vt fasciner.

Fascism n fascisme m.

fashion n (current style) mode f; (manner) façon f; **in** ~ à la mode; **out of** ~ démodé. •vt façonner. **fashionable** adj à la mode.

fast adj rapide; (colour) grand teint inv; (firm) fixe, solide; **be** ~ (of a clock) avancer. •adv vite; (firmly) ferme; **be** ~ **asleep** dormir d'un sommeil profond. •vi jeûner. •n jeûne m.

fasten vt/i (s')attacher. **fastener**, **fastening** n attache f, fermeture f.

fast food n fast-food m. restauration f rapide.

fat n graisse f; (on meat) gras m. •adj (fatter, fattest) gros, gros; (meat) gras; (profit) gros; **a** ~ **lot** 🔲 bien peu (**of** de).

fatal adj mortel; (fateful, disastrous) fatal. **fatality** n mort m. **fatally** adv mortellement.

fate n sort m. **fateful** adj fatidique.

father n père m. ~**hood** n paternité f. ~**-in-law** n (pl ~**s-in-law**) beau-père m.

fathom n brasse f (= 1.8 m). •vt ~ **(out)** comprendre.

fatigue n épuisement m; (Tech) fatigue f. •vt fatiguer.

fatten vt/i engraisser. **fattening** adj qui fait grossir.

fatty adj (food) gras; (tissue) adipeux.

faucet n (US) robinet m.

fault n (defect, failing) défaut m; (blame) faute f; (Geol) faille f; **at** ~ fautif; **find** ~ **with** critiquer. •vt ~ **sth/sb** prendre en défaut qn/qch. **faulty** adj défectueux.

favour, (US) **favor** n faveur f; **do sb a** ~ rendre service à qn; **in** ~ **of** pour. •vt favoriser; (support) être en faveur de; (prefer) préférer. **favourable** adj favorable.

favourite adj & n favori/-te (m/f).

fawn n (animal) faon m; (colour) beige m foncé. •vi ~ **on** flagorner.

fax n fax m, télécopie f. •vt faxer, envoyer par télécopie. ~ **machine** n fax m. télécopieur m; (for public use) Publifax® m.

FBI abbr (**Federal Bureau of Investigation**) (US) Police f judiciaire fédérale.

fear n crainte f, peur f; (fig) risque m; **for** ~ **of/that** de peur de/que. •vt craindre.

feasible adj faisable; (likely) plausible.

feast n festin m; (Relig) fête f. •vi festoyer. •vt régaler (**on** de).

feat n exploit m.

feather n plume f. •vt ~ **one's nest** s'enrichir.

feature n caractéristique f; (of person, face) trait m; (film) long métrage m; (article) article m de fond. •vt (advert) représenter; (give prominence to) mettre en vedette. •vi figurer (**in** dans).

February n février m.

fed ▷ FEED. •adj **be** ~ **up** 🔲 en avoir marre 🔲 (**with** de).

federal adj fédéral.

fee n (for entrance) prix m; **~(s)** (of doctor) honoraires mpl; (of actor, artist) cachet m; (for tuition) frais mpl; (for enrolment) droits mpl.

feeble adj faible.

feed vt (pt **fed**) nourrir, donner à manger à; (suckle) allaiter; (supply) alimenter. •vi se nourrir (**on** de). **~ in information** rentrer des données. •n nourriture f; (of baby) tétée f.

feedback n réaction (s) f(pl); (Med, Tech) feed-back m.

feel vt (pt **felt**) (touch) tâter; (be conscious of) sentir; (emotion) ressentir; (experience) éprouver; (think) estimer. •vi (tired, lonely) se sentir; **~ hot/thirsty** avoir chaud/soif; **~ as if** avoir l'impression que; **~ awful** (ill) se sentir malade; **~ like** (want 🔲) avoir envie de.

feeler n antenne f; **put out ~s** tâter le terrain.

feeling n (emotion) sentiment m; (physical) sensation f; (impression) impression f.

feet ▷FOOT.

feign vt feindre.

fell ▷FALL. •vt (cut down) abattre.

fellow n compagnon m, camarade m; (of society) membre m; (man 🔲) type m 🔲. **~-countryman** n compatriote m. **~-passenger** n compagnon m de voyage.

fellowship n camaraderie f; (group) association f.

felony n crime m.

felt ▷FEEL. •n feutre m. **~-tip** n feutre m.

female adj (animal) femelle; (voice, sex) féminin. •n femme f; (animal) femelle f.

feminine adj & n féminin (m). **femininity** n féminité f. **feminist** n féministe mf.

fence n barrière f; **sit on the ~**

ne pas prendre position. •vt **~ (in)** clôturer. •vi (Sport) faire de l'escrime. **fencing** n escrime f.

fend vi **~ for oneself** se débrouiller tout seul. •vt **~ off** (blow, attack) parer.

fender n (for fireplace) garde-cendre m; (mudguard: US) garde-boue m inv.

ferment[1] /'fɜːment/ n ferment m; (excitement: fig) agitation f.

ferment[2] /fə'ment/ vt/i (faire) fermenter.

fern n fougère f.

ferocious adj féroce.

ferret n (animal) furet m. •vi **~ about** fureter. •vt **~ out** dénicher.

ferry n (long-distance) ferry m; (short-distance) bac m. •vt transporter.

fertile adj fertile; (person, animal) fécond. **fertilizer** n engrais m.

festival n festival m; (Relig) fête f.

festive adj de fête, gai; **~ season** période f des fêtes. **festivity** n réjouissances fpl.

fetch vt (go for) aller chercher; (bring person) amener; (bring thing) apporter; (be sold for) rapporter.

fête n fête f; (church) kermesse f. •vt fêter.

fetish n (object) fétiche m; (Psych) obsession f.

feud n querelle f.

fever n fièvre f. **feverish** adj fiévreux.

few det peu de; **a ~ houses** quelques maisons; **quite a ~ people** un bon nombre de personnes. •pron quelques-uns/ quelques-unes.

fewer det moins de; **be ~** être moins nombreux (**than** que). **fewest** det le moins de.

fiancé n fiancé m. **fiancée** n fiancée f.

fibre, (US) **fiber** n fibre f. **~glass** n fibre f de verre.

fiction n fiction f; **(works of)** ~ romans mpl. **fictional** adj fictif.

fiddle n 🎻 violon m; (swindle 🎻) combine f. •vi ✖ frauder. •vt 🎻 falsifier; ~ **with** 🎻 tripoter 🎻.

fidget vi gigoter sans cesse.

field n champ m; (Sport) terrain m; (fig) domaine m. •vt (ball: cricket) bloquer.

fierce adj féroce; (storm, attack) violent.

fiery adj (-ier, -iest) (hot) ardent; (spirited) fougueux.

fifteen adj & n quinze (m).

fifth adj & n cinquième (mf).

fifty adj & n cinquante (m).

fig n figue f.

fight vi (pt **fought**) se battre; (struggle: fig) lutter; (quarrel) se disputer. •vt se battre avec; (evil: fig) lutter contre. •n (struggle) lutte f; (quarrel) dispute f; (brawl) bagarre f; (Mil) combat m. ■ ~ **back** se défendre (**against** contre). ~ **off** surmonter. ~ **over** se disputer qch. (sth) **fighter** n (determined person) lutteur/-euse m/f; (plane) avion m de chasse. **fighting** n combats mpl.

figment n **a** ~ **of the imagination** un produit de l'imagination.

figure n (number) chiffre m; (diagram) figure f; (shape) forme f; (body) ligne f; ~s arithmétique f. •vt s'imaginer. •vi (appear) figurer; **that** ~s (US, 🎻) c'est logique; ■ ~ **out** comprendre; ~ **of speech** n façon f de parler.

file n (tool) lime f. dossier m, classeur m; (Comput) fichier m; (row) file f. •vt limer; (papers) classer; (Jur) déposer. ■ ~ **in** entrer en file. ~ **past** défiler devant.

filing cabinet n classeur m.

fill vt/i (se) remplir. •n **have had one's** ~ en avoir assez. ■ ~ **in** (form) remplir. ~ **out** prendre du poids. ~ **up** (Auto) faire le plein (de carburant); (bath, theatre) (se) remplir.

fillet n filet m. •vt découper en filets.

filling n (of tooth) plombage m; (of sandwich) garniture f. ~ **station** n station-service f.

film n film m; (Photo) pellicule f. •vt filmer. ~-**goer** n cinéphile mf. ~**star** n vedette f de cinéma.

filter n filtre m; (traffic signal) flèche f. •vt/i filtrer; (of traffic) suivre la flèche. ~ **coffee** n café m filtre.

filth n crasse f. **filthy** adj crasseux.

fin n (of fish, seal) nageoire f; (of shark) aileron m.

final adj dernier; (conclusive) définitif. •n (Sport) finale f.

finale n (Mus) finale m.

finalize vt mettre au point, fixer.

finally adv (lastly, at last) enfin, finalement; (once and for all) définitivement.

finance n finance f. •adj financier. •vt financer. **financial** adj financier.

find vt (pt **found**) trouver; (sth lost) retrouver. •n trouvaille f; ~ **out** vt découvrir; vi se renseigner (**about** sur). **findings** npl conclusions fpl.

fine adj fin; (excellent) beau; ~ **arts** beaux-arts mpl. •n amende f. •vt condamner à une amende.

finger n doigt m. •vt palper. ~-**nail** n ongle m. ~**print** n empreinte f digitale. ~**tip** n bout m du doigt.

finish vt/i finir; ~ **doing** finir de faire; ~ **up doing** finir par faire; ~ **up in** se retrouver à. •n fin f; (of race) arrivée f; (appearance) finition f.

finite adj fini.

Finland n Finlande f. **Finn** n Finlandais/-e m/f.

Finnish adj finlandais. •n (Ling) finnois m.

fir n sapin m.

fire n (element) feu m; (blaze) incendie m; (heater) radiateur m; **set ~ to** mettre le feu à. ●vt (bullet) tirer; (dismiss) renvoyer; (fig) enflammer. ●vi tirer (**at** sur). ~ **a gun** tirer un coup de revolver/de fusil. ~ **alarm** n alarme f incendie. ~**arm** n arme f à feu. ~ **brigade** n pompiers mpl. ~ **engine** n voiture f de pompiers. ~ **escape** n escalier m de secours. ~ **extinguisher** n extincteur m. ~**man** n (pl **-men**) pompier m. ~**place** n cheminée f. ~ **station** n caserne f de pompiers. ~**wall** n mur m coupe-feu; (Internet) pare-feu m inv. ~**wood** n bois m de chauffage. ~**work** n feu m d'artifice.

firing squad n peloton m d'exécution.

firm n entreprise f, société f. ●adj ferme; (belief) solide.

first adj premier; **at ~ hand** de première main; **at ~ sight** à première vue; ~ **of all** tout d'abord. ●n premier/-ière m/f. ●adv d'abord, premièrement; (arrive) le premier, la première; **at ~** d'abord. ~ **aid** n premiers soins mpl. ~**class** adj de première classe. ~ **floor** n premier étage m; (US) rez-de-chaussée m inv. ~ **gear** n première (vitesse) f. F~ **Lady** n (US) épouse f du Président.

firstly adv premièrement.

first name n prénom m.

fish n poisson m. ~ **shop** poissonnerie f. ●vi pêcher; ~ **for** (cod) pêcher; ~ **out** (from water) repêcher; (take out 🚩) sortir. **fisherman** n (pl **-men**) n pêcheur m.

fishing n pêche f; **go ~** aller à la pêche. ~ **rod** n canne f à pêche.

fishmonger n poissonnier/-ière m/f.

fist n poing m.

fit n accès m, crise f; **be a good ~**

(dress) être à la bonne taille. ●adj (**fitter, fittest**) en bonne santé; (proper) convenable; (good enough) bon; (able) capable; **in no ~ state to do** pas en état de faire. ●vt/i (pt **fitted**) (into space) aller; (install) poser. ■ ~ **in** vt caser; vi (newcomer) s'intégrer. ~ **out,** ~ **up** équiper.

fitness n forme f; (of remark) justesse f.

fitted adj (wardrobe) encastré. ~ **carpet** n moquette f.

fitting adj approprié. ●n essayage m. ~ **room** n cabine f d'essayage.

five adj & n cinq (m).

fix vt (make firm, attach, decide) fixer; (mend) réparer; (deal with) arranger; ~ **sb up with sth** trouver qch à qn.

fixture n (Sport) match m; ~**s** (in house) installations fpl.

fizz vi pétiller. ●n pétillement m. **fizzy** adj gazeux.

flabbergast vt sidérer.

flabby adj flasque.

flag n drapeau m; (Naut) pavillon m. ●vt (pt **flagged**) ~ (**down**) faire signe de s'arrêter à. ●vi (weaken) faiblir; (sick person) s'affaiblir. ~**pole** n mât m. ~**stone** n dalle f.

flake n flocon m; (of paint, metal) écaille f. ●vi s'écailler.

flamboyant adj (colour) éclatant; (manner) extravagant.

flame n flamme f; **burst into ~s** exploser; **go up in ~s** brûler. ●vi flamber.

flamingo n flamant m (rose).

flammable adj inflammable.

flan n tarte f; (custard tart) flan m.

flank n flanc m. ●vt flanquer.

flannel n (material) flanelle f; (for face) gant m de toilette.

flap vi (pt **flapped**) battre. ●vt ~ **its wings** battre des ailes. ●n (of pocket) rabat m; (of table) abattant m.

flare vi ~ **up** (fighting) éclater. • n flamboiement m; (Mil) fusée f éclairante; (in skirt) évasement m. **flared** adj évasé.

flash vi briller; (on and off) clignoter; ~ **past** passer à toute vitesse. • vt faire briller; (aim torch) diriger (**at** sur); (flaunt) étaler; ~ **one's headlights** faire un appel de phares. • n (of news, camera) flash m; **in a** ~ en un éclair. ~**back** n retour m en arrière. ~**light** n lampe f de poche.

flask n (for chemicals) flacon m; (for drinks) thermos® m or f inv.

flat adj (**flatter, flattest**) plat; (tyre) à plat; (refusal) catégorique. (fare, rate) fixe. • adv (say) carrément. • n (rooms) appartement m; (tyre 🇬🇧) crevaison f; (Mus) bémol m.

flat out adv (drive) à toute vitesse; (work) d'arrache-pied.

flatten vt/i (s')aplatir.

flatter vt flatter.

flaunt vt étaler, afficher.

flavour, (US) **flavor** n goût m; (of ice-cream) parfum m. • vt parfumer (**with** à), assaisonner (**with** de). **flavouring** n arôme m artificiel.

flaw n défaut m.

flea n puce f. ~ **market** n marché m aux puces.

fleck n petite tache f.

fled ▷FLEE.

flee vt/i (pt **fled**) fuir.

fleece n toison f; (garment) polaire f. • vt plumer.

fleet n (Naut, Aviat) flotte f; **a** ~ **of vehicles** (in reserve) parc m; (on road) convoi m.

fleeting adj très bref.

Flemish adj flamand. • n (Ling) flamand m.

flesh n chair f; **one's (own)** ~ **and blood** la chair de sa chair.

flew ▷FLY.

flex vt (knee) fléchir; (muscle) faire jouer. • n (Electr) fil m.

flexible adj flexible.

flexitime n horaire m variable.

flick n petit coup m. • vt donner un petit coup à; ~ **through** feuilleter.

flight n (of bird, plane) vol m; ~ **of stairs** escalier m; (fleeing) fuite f; **take** ~ prendre la fuite. ~**deck** n poste m de pilotage.

flimsy adj (**-ier, -iest**) (pej) mince, peu solide.

flinch vi (wince) broncher; (draw back) reculer.

fling vt (pt **flung**) jeter.

flint n (rock) silex m.

flip vt (pt **flipped**) donner un petit coup à; ~ **through** feuilleter. • n chiquenaude f.

flippant adj désinvolte.

flipper n (of seal) nageoire f; (of swimmer) palme f.

flirt vi flirter. • n flirteur/-euse m/f.

float vt/i (faire) flotter. • n flotteur m; (cart) char m.

flock n (of sheep) troupeau m; (of people) foule f. • vi affluer.

flog vt (pt **flogged**) (beat) fouetter; (sell 🇬🇧) vendre.

flood n inondation f; (fig) flot m. • vt inonder. • vi (building) être inondé; (river) déborder; (people: fig) affluer.

floodlight n projecteur m. • vt (pt **floodlit**) illuminer.

floor n sol m, plancher m; (for dancing) piste f; (storey) étage m. • vt (knock down) terrasser; (baffle) stupéfier. ~**board** n planche f.

flop vi (pt **flopped**) (drop)

s'affaler; (fail 🔢) échouer; (head) tomber. ●n 🔢 échec m, fiasco m.

floppy adj lâche, flasque. ●n ~ **(disk)** disquette f.

florist n fleuriste mf.

flounder vi (animal, person) se débattre (**in** dans); (economy) stagner. ●n flet m; (US) poisson m plat.

flour n farine f.

flourish vi prospérer. ●vt brandir. ●n geste m élégant.

flout vt se moquer de.

flow vi couler; (circulate) circuler; (traffic) s'écouler; (hang loosely) flotter; ~ **in** affluer; ~ **into** (of river) se jeter dans. ●n (of liquid, traffic) écoulement m; (of tide) flux m; (of orders, words: fig) flot m. ~ **chart** n organigramme m.

flower n fleur f. ●vi fleurir.

flown ▷FLY.

flu n grippe f.

fluctuate vi varier.

fluent adj (style) aisé; **be ~ (in a language)** parler (une langue) couramment.

fluff n peluche(s) f(pl); (down) duvet m.

fluid adj & n fluide (m).

fluke n coup m de chance.

flung ▷FLING.

fluoride n fluor m.

flush vi rougir. ●vt nettoyer à grande eau; ~ **the toilet** tirer la chasse d'eau. ●n (blush) rougeur f; (fig) excitation f. ●adj ~ **with** (level with) au ras de. ∎~ **out** chasser.

fluster vt énerver.

flute n flûte f.

flutter vi voleter; (of wings) battre. ●n (wings) battement m; (fig)

agitation f; (bet 🔢) pari m.

flux n changement m continuel.

fly n mouche f; (of trousers) braguette f. ●vi (pt **flew**; pp **flown**) voler; (passengers) voyager en avion; (flag) flotter; (rush) filer. ●vt (aircraft) piloter; (passengers, goods) transporter par avion; (flag) arborer. ∎~ **off** s'envoler.

flyer n (person) aviateur m; (circular) prospectus m.

flying adj (saucer) volant; **with ~ colours** haut la main; ~ **start** excellent départ m; ~ **visit** visite f éclair (adj inv). ●n (activity) aviation f.

flyover n pont m (routier).

foal n poulain m.

foam n écume f, mousse f; ~ **(rubber)** caoutchouc m mousse. ●vi écumer, mousser.

focus n (pl ~**es** or **-ci**) foyer m; (fig) centre m; **be in/out of** ~être/ne pas être au point. ●vt/i (faire) converger; (instrument) mettre au point; (with camera) faire la mise au point (**on** sur); (fig) (se) concentrer. ~ **group** n groupe m de discussion.

fodder n fourrage m.

foe n ennemi/-e m/f.

foetus n fœtus m.

fog n brouillard m. ●vt/i (pt **fogged**) (window) (s')embuer.

foggy adj brumeux; **it is ~** il fait du brouillard.

foil n (tin foil) papier m d'aluminium; (deterrent) repoussoir m. ●vt (thwart) déjouer.

fold vt/i (paper, clothes) (se) plier; (arms) croiser; (fail) s'effondrer. ●n pli m; (for sheep) parc m à moutons; (Relig) bercail m. **folder** n (file) chemise f; (leaflet) dépliant m. **folding** adj pliant.

foliage n feuillage m.

folk n gens mpl; ~**s** parents mpl.
• adj (dance) folklorique;
(music) folk.

folklore n folklore m.

follow vt/i suivre; **it** ~**s that** il
s'ensuit que; ~ **suit** en faire
autant; ~ **up** (letter) donner suite
à. **follower** n partisan m.

following n partisans mpl. • adj
suivant; ~ **day** lendemain. • prep
à la suite de.

fond adj (loving) affectueux; (hope)
cher; **be** ~ **of** aimer.

fondle vt caresser.

fondness n affection f; (for things)
attachement m.

food n nourriture f; **French** ~ la
cuisine française. • adj
alimentaire. ~ **processor** n
robot m (ménager).

fool n idiot/-e m/f. • vt duper. • vi ~
around faire l'idiot; **foolish** adj
idiot.

foot n (pl **feet**) pied m; (measure)
pied m (=30.48 cm); (of stairs, page)
bas m; **on** ~ à pied; **on** or **to**
one's feet debout; **under sb's**
feet dans les jambes de qn. • vt
(bill) payer.

foot-and-mouth disease n
fièvre f aphteuse.

football n (ball) ballon m; (game)
football m. **footballer** n
footballeur m.

foot: ~**bridge** n passerelle f;
~**hold** n prise f.

footing n **on an equal** ~ sur un
pied d'égalité; **be on a friendly**
~ **with sb** avoir des rapports
amicaux avec qn; **lose one's** ~
perdre pied.

foot: ~**note** n note f (en bas de la
page). ~**path** n (in countryside)
sentier m; (in town) chemin m.
~**print** n empreinte f (de pied).
~**step** n pas m. ~**wear** n
chaussures fpl.

for /fɔː(r)/
• preposition
⋯▸ pour; ~ **me** pour moi; **music**
~ **dancing** de la musique pour
danser; **what is it** ~**?** ça sert
à quoi?
⋯▸ (with a time period that is still
continuing) depuis; **I've been**
waiting ~ **two hours** j'attends
depuis deux heures; **I haven't**
seen him ~ **ten years** je ne
l'ai pas vu depuis dix ans.
⋯▸ (with a time period that has
ended) pendant; **I waited** ~
two hours j'ai attendu pendant
deux heures.
⋯▸ (with a future time period)
pour; **I'm going to Paris** ~ **six**
weeks je vais à Paris pour six
semaines.
⋯▸ (with distances) pendant; **I**
drove ~ **50 kilometres** j'ai
roulé pendant 50 kilomètres.

forbid vt (pt **forbade**; pp
forbidden) interdire, défendre
(**sb to do** à qn de faire). ~ **sb**
sth interdire or défendre qch à
qn; **you are forbidden to**
leave il vous est interdit de
partir. **forbidding** adj menaçant.

force n force f; **come into** ~
entrer en vigueur; **the** ~**s** les
forces fpl armées. • vt forcer. ■ ~
into faire entrer de force. ~ **on**
imposer à. **forced** adj forcé.

force-feed vt (pt **-fed**) (person)
nourrir de force; (animal) gaver.

forceful adj énergique.

ford n gué m. • vt passer à gué.

forearm n avant-bras m inv.

forecast vt (pt **forecast**) prévoir.
• n weather ~ météo f.

forecourt n (of garage) devant m;
(of station) cour f.

forefinger n index m.

forefront n **at/in the** ~ **of** à la
pointe de.

foregone adj **it's a** ~
conclusion c'est couru d'avance.

foreground n premier plan m.

forehead n front m.

foreign adj étranger; (trade) extérieur; (travel) à l'étranger. **foreigner** n étranger/-ère m/f.

foreman n (pl **-men**) contremaître m.

foremost adj le plus éminent. • adv **first and ~** tout d'abord.

forensic adj médico-légal; ~ **medicine** médecine f légale.

foresee vt (pt **-saw**; pp **-seen**) prévoir.

forest n forêt f. **forestry** n sylviculture f.

foretaste n avant-goût m.

forever adv toujours.

foreword n avant-propos m inv.

forfeit n (penalty) peine f; (in game) gage m. • vt perdre.

forgave ▷ FORGIVE.

forge n forge f. • vt (metal, friendship) forger; (copy) contrefaire, falsifier. • vi ~ **ahead** aller de l'avant, avancer. **forger** n faussaire m. **forgery** n faux m, contrefaçon f.

forget vt/i (pt **forgot**; pp **forgotten**) oublier; ~ **oneself** s'oublier. **forgetful** adj distrait. ~ **-me-not** n myosotis m.

forgive vt (pt **forgave**; pp **forgiven**) pardonner (**sb for sth** qch à qn).

fork n fourchette f; (for digging) fourche f; (in road) bifurcation f. • vi (road) bifurquer; ∎ ~ **out** 🄵 payer. **forked** adj fourchu. ~ **-lift truck** n chariot m élévateur.

form n forme f; (document) formulaire m; (School) classe f; **on** ~ en forme. • vt/i (se) former.

formal adj officiel, en bonne et due forme; (person) compassé, cérémonieux; (dress) de cérémonie; (denial, grammar) formel; (language) soutenu. **formality** n cérémonial m;

(requirement) formalité f.

format n format m. • vt (pt **formatted**) (disk) formater.

former adj ancien; (first of two) premier. • n **the** ~ celui-là, celle-là. **formerly** adv autrefois.

formula n (pl **-ae** or **-as**) formule f. **formulate** vt formuler.

fort n (Mil) fort m; **to hold the** ~ s'occuper de tout.

forth adv **from this day** ~ à partir d'aujourd'hui; **and so** ~ et ainsi de suite; **go back and** ~ aller et venir.

forthcoming adj à venir, prochain; (sociable 🄵) communicatif.

forthright adj direct.

forthwith adv sur-le-champ.

fortnight n quinze jours mpl, quinzaine f.

fortnightly adj bimensuel. • adv tous les quinze jours.

fortunate adj heureux; **be** ~ avoir de la chance. **fortunately** adv heureusement.

fortune n fortune f; **make a** ~ faire fortune; **have the good** ~ **to** avoir la chance de. ~ **-teller** n diseur/-euse m/f de bonne aventure.

forty adj & n quarante (m). ~ **winks** un petit somme.

forward adj en avant; (advanced) précoce; (bold) effronté. • n (Sport) avant m. • adv en avant; **come** ~ se présenter; **go** ~ avancer. • vt (letter, e-mail) faire suivre; (goods) expédier; (fig) favoriser. **forwardness** n précocité f. **forwards** adv en avant.

fossil n & adj fossile (m).

foster vt (promote) encourager; (child) élever. • adj (child, parent) adoptif; (family, home) de placement.

fought ▷ FIGHT.

foul adj (smell, weather) infect; (place,

action) immonde; (language)
ordurier. •n (football) faute f. •vt
souiller, encrasser; ~ up 🄸
gâcher. ~-mouthed adj grossier.

found ▷FIND. •vt fonder.

foundation n fondation f; (basis)
fondement m; (make-up) fond m de
teint. **founder** n fondateur/-
trice m/f.

fountain n fontaine f; ~-pen n
stylo m à encre.

four adj & n quatre (m).

fourteen adj & n quatorze (m).

fourth adj & n quatrième (mf).

four-wheel drive n (car) quatre-
quatre m.

fowl n (one bird) poulet m; (group)
volaille f.

fox n renard m. •vt (baffle)
mystifier; (deceive) tromper.

fraction n fraction f.

fracture n fracture f. •vt/i (se)
fracturer.

fragile adj fragile.

fragment n fragment m.

fragrance n parfum m.

frail adj frêle.

frame n (of building, boat) charpente
f; (of picture) cadre m; (of window)
châssis m; (of spectacles) monture f;
~ of mind humeur f. •vt
encadrer; (fig) formuler; (Jur, 🄸)
monter un coup contre. ~work
n structure f; (context) cadre m.

France n France f.

franchise n (Pol) droit m de vote;
(Comm) franchise f.

frank adj franc. •vt affranchir.
frankly adv franchement.

frantic adj frénétique. ~ with
fou de.

fraternity n (bond) fraternité f;
(group, club) confrérie f.

fraud n (deception) fraude f; (person)
imposteur m. **fraudulent** adj
frauduleux.

fray n **the** ~ la bataille. •vt/i
(s')effilocher.

freckle n tache f de rousseur.

free adj libre; (gratis) gratuit;
(lavish) généreux; ~ (of charge)
gratuit(ement); **a** ~ **hand** carte
f blanche. •vt (pt **freed**) libérer;
(clear) dégager.

freedom n liberté f.

free: ~ **enterprise** n la libre
entreprise. ~ **kick** n coup m
franc. ~**lance** adj & n free-lance
(mf), indépendant/-e (m/f).

freely adv librement.

Freemason n franc-maçon m.

Freenet n (Comput) Libertel m.

free: ~**phone (number)** n
numéro m vert. ~-**range** adj
(eggs) de ferme.

Freeware n (Comput) Gratuiciel m.

freeway n (US) autoroute f.

freeze vt/i (pt **froze**; pp **frozen**)
geler; (Culin) (se) congeler;
(wages) bloquer. •n gel m. blocage
m; ~-**dried** adj lyophilisé.

freezer n congélateur m.

freezing adj glacial; **below** ~
au-dessous de zéro.

freight n fret m.

French adj français. •n (Ling)
français m; **the** ~ les Français
mpl; ~ **bean** n haricot m vert; ~
fries npl frites fpl; ~**man** n
Français m; ~-**speaking** adj
francophone; ~ **window** n
porte-fenêtre f; ~**woman** n
Française f.

frenzied adj frénétique. **frenzy** n
frénésie f.

frequent[1] /'fri:kwənt/ adj
fréquent.

frequent[2] /frɪ'kwent/ vt
fréquenter.

fresco n fresque f.

fresh adj frais; (different, additional)
nouveau; (cheeky 🄸) culotté.

freshen vi (weather) fraîchir. ■ ~

up (person) se rafraîchir.

freshly adv nouvellement.

freshness n fraîcheur f.

freshwater adj d'eau douce.

friction n friction f.

Friday n vendredi m.

fridge n frigo m.

fried ▷ FRY. ● adj frit; ~ **eggs** œufs mpl sur le plat.

friend n ami/-e m/f. **friendly** adj (-ier, -iest) amical, gentil. **friendship** n amitié f.

frieze n frise f.

fright n peur f; (person, thing) horreur f.

frighten vt effrayer; ~ **off** faire fuir. **frightened** adj effrayé; **be** ~ed avoir peur (**of** de). **frightening** adj effrayant.

frill n (trimming) fanfreluche f; **with no** ~s très simple.

fringe n (edging, hair) frange f; (of area) bordure f; (of society) marge f. ~ **benefits** npl avantages mpl sociaux.

frisk vt (search) fouiller.

fritter n beignet m. ● vt ~ **away** gaspiller.

frivolity n frivolité f.

frizzy adj crépu.

fro ▷ TO AND FRO.

frog n grenouille f; **a** ~ **in one's throat** un chat dans la gorge.

frolic vi (pt **frolicked**) s'ébattre. ● n ébats mpl.

from prep de; (with time, prices) à partir de, de; (habit, conviction) par; (according to) d'après; **take** ~ **sb** prendre à qn; **take** ~ **one's pocket** prendre dans sa poche.

front n (of car, train) avant m; (of garment, building) devant m; (Mil, Pol) front m; (of book, pamphlet) début m; (appearance: fig) façade f. ● adj de devant, avant inv; (first) premier; ~ **door** porte f d'entrée; **in** ~

(of) devant. **frontage** n façade f.

frontier n frontière f.

frost n gel m, gelée f; (on glass) givre m. ● vt/i (se) givrer. ~**-bite** n gelure f.

frosty adj (weather, welcome) glacial; (window) givré.

froth n (on beer) mousse f; (on water) écume f. ● vi mousser, écumer.

frown vi froncer les sourcils; ~ **on** désapprouver. ● n froncement m de sourcils.

froze ▷ FREEZE.

frozen ▷ FREEZE. ● adj congelé.

fruit n fruit m; (collectively) fruits mpl. **fruitful** adj (discussions) fructueux. ~ **machine** n machine f à sous.

frustrate vt (plan) faire échouer; (person: Psych) frustrer; (upset **ī**) exaspérer. **frustration** n (Psych) frustration f; (disappointment) déception f.

fry vt/i (pt **fried**) (faire) frire. **frying-pan** n poêle f (à frire).

FTP abbr (File Transfer Protocol) (Internet) protocole m FTP.

fudge n caramel m mou. ● vt (issue) esquiver.

fuel n combustible m; (for car engine) carburant m. ● vt (pt **fuelled**) alimenter en combustible.

fugitive n & a fugitif/-ive (m/f).

fulfil vt (pt **fulfilled**) accomplir, réaliser; (condition) remplir; ~ **oneself** s'épanouir. **fulfilling** adj satisfaisant. **fulfilment** n réalisation f. épanouissement m.

full adj plein (**of** de); (bus, hotel) complet; (programme) chargé; (skirt) ample; **be** ~ **(up)** n'avoir plus faim; **at** ~ **speed** à toute vitesse. ● n **in** ~ intégralement; **to the** ~ complètement. ~ **back** n (Sport) arrière m. ~ **moon**

n pleine lune f. ~ **name** n nom m et prénom m. ~**-scale** adj (drawing etc.) grandeur nature inv; (fig) de grande envergure. ~ **stop** n point m. ~**-time** adj & adv à plein temps.

fully adv complètement; ~ **fledged** (member, citizen) à part entière.

fume vi rager. **fumes** npl émanations fpl, vapeurs fpl.

fun n amusement m; **be** ~ être chouette; **for** ~ pour rire; **make** ~ **of** se moquer de.

function n (purpose, duty) fonction f; (event) réception f. ●vi fonctionner.

fund n fonds m. ●vt fournir les fonds pour.

fundamental adj fondamental. **fundamentalist** n intégriste mf.

funeral n enterrement m. ●adj funèbre.

funfair n fête f foraine.

fungus n (pl **-gi**) (plant) champignon m; (mould) moisissure f.

funnel n (for pouring) entonnoir m; (of ship) cheminée f.

funny adj (**-ier**, **-iest**) drôle; (odd) bizarre.

fur n (for garment) fourrure f; (on animal) poils mpl; (in kettle) tartre m.

furious adj furieux.

furnace n fourneau m.

furnish vt (room) meubler; (supply) fournir. **furnishings** npl ameublement m.

furniture n meubles mpl, mobilier m.

furry adj (animal) à fourrure; (toy) en peluche.

further adj plus éloigné; (additional) supplémentaire. ●adv plus loin; (more) davantage. ●vt avancer. ~ **education** n formation f continue.

furthermore adv en outre, de plus.

furthest adj le plus éloigné. ●adv le plus loin.

fury n fureur f.

fuse vt/i (melt) fondre; (unite: fig) fusionner; ~ **the lights** faire sauter les plombs. ●n (of plug) fusible m; (of bomb) amorce f.

fuss n (when upset) histoire(s) f(pl); (when excited) agitation f; **make a** ~ faire des histoires. s'agiter; (about food) faire des chichis; **make a** ~ **of** faire grand cas de. ●vi s'agiter. **fussy** adj (finicky) tatillon; (hard to please) difficile.

future adj futur. ●n avenir m; (Gram) futur m; **in** ~ à l'avenir.

fuzzy adj (hair) crépu; (photograph) flou; (person ⒈) à l'esprit confus.

Gg

Gaelic n gaélique m.

gag n (on mouth) bâillon m; (joke) blague f. ●vt (pt **gagged**) bâillonner.

gain vt (respect, support) gagner; (speed, weight) prendre. ●vi (of clock) avancer. ●n (increase) augmentation f (**in** de); (profit) gain m.

galaxy n galaxie f.

gale n tempête f.

gallery n galerie f; (art) ~ musée m.

Gallic adj français.

gallon n gallon m (imperial = 4.546 litres; Amer. = 3.785 litres).

gallop n galop m. •vi (pt **galloped**) galoper.

galore adv (prizes, bargains) en abondance; (drinks, sandwiches) à gogo 🔲.

gamble vt/i jouer. ~ **on** miser sur. •n (venture) entreprise f risquée; (bet) pari m; (risk) risque m. **gambling** n jeu m.

game n jeu m; (football) match m; (tennis) partie f; (animals, birds) gibier m. •adj (brave) courageux. ~ **for** prêt à. ~**keeper** n gardechasse m.

gammon n jambon m.

gang n (of youths) bande f; (of workmen) équipe f. •vi ~ **up** se liguer (**on, against** contre).

gangmaster n gangmaster m, chef m d'équipe (d'ouvriers saisonniers).

gangway n passage m; (aisle) allée f; (of ship) passerelle f.

gaol n & vt ▷JAIL.

gap n trou m, vide m; (in time) intervalle m; (in education) lacune f; (difference) écart m.

gape vi rester bouche bée. **gaping** adj béant.

garage n garage m. •vt mettre au garage.

garbage n (US) ordures fpl.

garden n jardin m. •vi jardiner. **gardener** n jardinier/-ière m/f. **gardening** n jardinage m.

gargle vi se gargariser.

garish adj (clothes) tape-à-l'œil.

garland n guirlande f.

garlic n ail m.

garment n vêtement m.

garnish vt garnir (**with** de). •n garniture f.

garter n jarretière f.

gas n (pl ~**es**) gaz m; (Med) anesthésie m; (petrol: US) essence f. •adj (mask, pipe) à gaz. •vt asphyxier; (Mil) gazer.

gash n entaille f. •vt entailler.

gasoline n (petrol: US) essence f.

gasp vi haleter; (in surprise: fig) avoir le souffle coupé. •n halètement m.

gate n (in garden, airport) porte f; (of field, level crossing) barrière f. ~**way** n porte f; (Internet) passerelle f.

gather vt (people, objects) rassembler; (pick up) ramasser; (flowers) cueillir; (fig) comprendre; ~ **speed** prendre de la vitesse; (sewing) froncer. •vi (people) se rassembler; (pile up) s'accumuler. **gathering** n réunion f.

gauge n jauge f, indicateur m. •vt (speed, distance) jauger; (reaction, mood) évaluer.

gaunt adj décharné.

gauze n gaze f.

gave ▷GIVE.

gay adj (joyful) gai; (homosexual) gay inv. •n gay mf.

gaze vi ~ **(at)** regarder (fixement). •n regard m (fixe).

GB abbr ▷GREAT BRITAIN.

gear n (equipment) matériel m; (Tech) engrenage m; (Auto) vitesse f; **in** ~ en prise. **out of** ~ au point mort. •vt **to be geared to** s'adresser à. ~**box** n (Auto) boîte f de vitesses. ~-**lever**, (US) ~-**shift** n levier m de vitesse.

geese ▷GOOSE.

gel n (for hair) gel m.

gem n pierre f précieuse.

Gemini n Gémeaux mpl.

gender n (Ling) genre m; (of person) sexe m.

gene n gène m. ~ **library** n génothèque f.

general adj général. •n général m; **in** ~ en général.

general election n élections fpl législatives.

generalization n généralisation f. **generalize** vt/i généraliser.

general practitioner n (Med) généraliste m.

generate vt produire.

generation n génération f.

generator n (Electr) groupe m électrogène.

generosity n générosité f. **generous** adj généreux; (plentiful) copieux.

genetics n génétique f.

Geneva n Genève.

genial adj affable, sympathique.

genitals npl organes mpl génitaux.

genius n (pl ~es) génie m.

genome n génome m.

gentle adj (mild, kind) doux; (pressure, breeze) léger; (reminder, hint) discret.

gentleman n (pl -men) (man) monsieur m; (well-bred) gentleman m.

gently adv doucement.

gents npl (toilets) toilettes fpl; (on sign) 'Messieurs'.

genuine adj (reason, motive) vrai; (jewel, substance) véritable; (person, belief) sincère.

geography n géographie f.

geology n géologie f.

geometry n géométrie f.

geriatric adj gériatrique.

germ n (Med) microbe m.

German n (person) Allemand/-e m/f; (Ling) allemand m. ●adj allemand.

German measles n rubéole f.

Germany n Allemagne f.

gesture n geste m.

get /get/

! past **got**; past participle **got**, **gotten** (US); present participle **getting**

● transitive verb

⋯▸ recevoir. **we got a letter** nous avons reçu une lettre.

⋯▸ (obtain) **I got a job in Paris** j'ai trouvé un travail à Paris. **I'll ~ sth to eat at the airport** je mangerai qch à l'aéroport.

⋯▸ (buy) acheter. **~ sb a present** acheter un cadeau à qn.

⋯▸ (achieve) obtenir. **he got it right** il a obtenu le bon résultat. **~ good grades** avoir de bonnes notes.

⋯▸ (fetch) chercher. **go and ~ a chair** va chercher une chaise.

⋯▸ (transport) prendre. **we can ~ the bus** on peut prendre le bus.

⋯▸ (understand 🛈) comprendre. **now let me ~ this right...** alors si je comprends bien...

⋯▸ (experience) **~ a surprise** être surpris. **~ a shock** avoir un choc.

⋯▸ (illness) **~ measles** attraper la rougeole. **~ a cold** s'enrhumer.

⋯▸ (ask or persuade) **~ him to call me** dis-lui de m'appeler. **I'll ~ her to help me** je lui demanderai de m'aider.

⋯▸ (cause to be done) **~ a TV repaired** faire réparer une télévision. **~ one's hair cut** se faire couper les cheveux.

● intransitive verb

⋯▸ devenir. **he's getting old** il vieillit; **it's getting late** il se fait tard.

⋯▸ (in passives) **~ married** se marier. **~ hurt** être blessé.

⋯▸ (arrive) arriver. **~ to the airport** arriver à l'aéroport.
■ **~ about** (person) se déplacer.
■ **~ along** (manage) se débrouiller; (progress) avancer.

g

■~ **along with** s'entendre avec. ■~ **at** (reach) atteindre; (imply) vouloir dire. ■~ **away** partir; (escape) s'échapper. ■~ **back** vi revenir. •vt récupérer. ■~ **by** vi (manage) se débrouiller. • vt (pass) passer. ■~ **down** vt/i descendre. • vt (depress) déprimer. ■~ **in** entrer. ■~ **into** (car) monter dans; (dress) mettre. ■~ **off** vt (bus) descendre; (remove) enlever. • vi (from bus) descendre; (leave) partir; (Jur) être acquitté. ■~ **on** vi (to bus) monter; (succeed) réussir. • vt (bus) monter. ■~ **on with** (person) s'entendre avec; (job) attaquer. ■~ **out** sortir. ■~ **out of** (fig) se soustraire. ■~ **over** (illness) se remettre de. ■~ **round** (rule) contourner; (person) entortiller. ■~ **through** vi passer; (on phone) ~ **through to sb** avoir qn. • vt traverser. ■~ **up** se lever. ■~ **up to** faire.

getaway n fuite f.

ghastly adj (**-ier, -iest**) affreux.

gherkin n cornichon m.

ghetto n ghetto m.

ghost n fantôme m.

giant n & adj géant (m).

gibberish n baragouin m, charabia m.

giblets npl abats mpl.

giddy adj (**-ier, -iest**) vertigineux. **be** or **feel** ~ avoir le vertige.

gift n (present) cadeau m; (ability) don m.

gifted adj doué.

gift wrap n papier m cadeau.

gigantic adj gigantesque.

giggle vi ricaner (sottement), glousser. •n ricanement m; **the** ~**s** le fou rire.

gimmick n truc m.

gin n gin m.

ginger n gingembre m. •adj (hair) roux. ~ **beer** n boisson f gazeuse au gingembre. ~**bread** n pain m d'épices.

gingerly adv avec précaution.

giraffe n girafe f.

girl n (child) (petite) fille f; (young woman) (jeune) fille f. ~ **band** n girls band m. ~**friend** n amie f; (of boy) petite amie f.

giro n virement m bancaire; (cheque) mandat m.

gist n essentiel m.

give vt (pt **gave**; pp **given**) donner; (gesture) faire; (laugh, sigh) pousser; ~ **sb sth** donner qch à qn. •vi donner; (yield) céder; (stretch) se détendre. •n élasticité f. ■~ **away** donner; (secret) trahir; ~ **back** rendre; ~ **in** (yield) céder (**to** à). ~ **off** (heat, fumes) dégager; (signal, scent) émettre. ~ **out** vt distribuer. ~ **over** (devote) consacrer; (stop 🔢) cesser; ~ **up** vt/i (renounce) renoncer (à); (yield) céder. ~ **oneself up** se rendre. ~ **way** céder; (collapse) s'effondrer.

given ▷GIVE. •adj donné. ~ **name** n prénom m.

glad adj content. **gladly** adv avec plaisir.

glamorous adj séduisant, ensorcelant.

glamour, (US) **glamor** n enchantement m, séduction f.

glance n coup m d'œil. •vi ~ **at** jeter un coup d'œil à.

gland n glande f.

glare vi briller très fort. ~ **at** regarder d'un air furieux. •n (of lights) éclat m (aveuglant); (stare: fig) regard m furieux. **glaring** adj (dazzling) éblouissant; (obvious) flagrant.

glass n verre m. **glasses** npl (spectacles) lunettes fpl.

glaze vt (door) vitrer; (pottery) vernisser. •n vernis m.

gleam n lueur f. •vi luire.

glide vi glisser; (of plane) planer.

glider n planeur m.

glimpse n (insight) aperçu m; **catch a ~ of** entrevoir.

glitter vi scintiller. ●n scintillement m.

global adj (world-wide) mondial; (allembracing) global. **~ warming** n réchauffement m de la planète.

globalization n globalisation f.

globe n globe m.

gloom n obscurité f; (sadness: fig) tristesse f. **gloomy** adj triste; (pessimistic) pessimiste.

glorious adj splendide; (deed, hero) glorieux.

glory n gloire f; (beauty) splendeur f. ●vi **~ in** être très fier de.

gloss n lustre m, brillant m. ●adj brillant. ●vi **~ over** (make light of) glisser sur; (cover up) dissimuler.

glossary n glossaire m.

glossy adj brillant.

glove n gant m. **~ compartment** n (Auto) boîte f à gants.

glow vi (fire) rougeoyer; (person, eyes) rayonner. ●n rougeoiement m, éclat m. **glowing** adj (report) enthousiaste.

glucose n glucose m.

glue n colle f. ●vt (pres p **gluing**) coller.

GM abbr (genetically modified) transgénique.

gnaw vt/i ronger.

GNP abbr (**Gross National Product**) produit m national brut, PNB m.

go /gəʊ/

! present **go, goes;** past **went;** past participle **gone**

● intransitive verb

····➤ aller; **~ to school/town/ market** aller à l'école/en ville/au marché. **~ for a swim/walk** aller nager/se promener.

····➤ (leave) s'en aller. **I must be ~ing** il faut que je m'en aille.

····➤ (vanish) **the money's gone** il n'y a plus d'argent. **my bike's gone** mon vélo n'est plus là.

····➤ (work, function) marcher. **is the car ~ing?** est-ce que la voiture marche?

····➤ (become) devenir. **~ blind** devenir aveugle. **~ pale/red** pâlir/rougir.

····➤ (turn out, progress) aller. **how's it going?** comment ça va? **how did the exam ~ ?** comment s'est passé l'examen?

····➤ (in future tenses) **be ~ing to do** aller faire.

● noun

····➤ (turn) tour m; (try) essai m; **have a ~!** essaie!; **full of ~** dynamique.

■ **go across** traverser. ■ **go after** poursuivre. ■ **go away** partir. **~ away!** va-t'en!, allez-vous-en! ■ **go back** retourner. ■ **back in** rentrer; **~ back to work** reprendre le travail. ■ **go down** (quality, price) baisser; (person) descendre; (sun) se coucher. ■ **go in** entrer. ■ **go in for** (exam) se présenter à. ■ **go off** (leave) partir; (bomb) exploser; (alarm clock) sonner; (milk) tourner; (light) s'éteindre. ■ **go on** (continue) continuer; (light) s'allumer; **~ on doing** continuer à faire; **what's ~ing on?** qu'est-ce qui se passe? ■ **go out** sortir; (light, fire) s'éteindre. ■ **go over** vérifier. ■ **go round** (be enough) être assez; **~ round to see sb** passer voir qn. ■ **go through** (check) examiner; (search) fouiller; **~ through a difficult time** traverser une période difficile. ■ **go together** aller ensemble. ■ **go under** (sink) couler; (fail) échouer. ■ **go up** (person) monter; (price, salary) augmenter. ■ **go without** se passer de.

go-ahead n feu m vert. ●adj dynamique.

goal n but m. ~**keeper** n gardien m de but. ~**post** n poteau m de but.

goat n chèvre f.

gobble vt engouffrer.

go-between n intermédiaire mf.

god n dieu m. ~**child** n (pl -**children**) filleul/-e m/f. ~**daughter** n filleule f.

goddess n déesse f.

god: ~**father** n parrain m. ~**mother** n marraine f. ~**send** n aubaine f. ~**son** n filleul m.

goggles npl lunettes fpl (protectrices).

going n **it is slow/hard ~** c'est lent/difficile. ●adj (price, rate) actuel.

go-kart n kart m.

gold n or m. ●adj en or, d'or.

golden adj en or, d'or; (in colour) doré; (opportunity) unique.

gold: ~**fish** n poisson m rouge. ~**plated** adj plaqué or. ~**smith** n orfèvre m.

golf n golf m. ~**course** n terrain m de golf.

gone ▷GO. ●adj parti. **~ six o'clock** six heures passées. **the butter's all ~** il n'y a plus de beurre.

good adj (**better, best**) bon; (weather) beau; (well-behaved) sage; **as ~ as** (almost) pratiquement. **that's ~ of you** c'est gentil (de ta part). **be ~ with** savoir s'y prendre avec. **feel ~** se sentir bien. **it is ~ for you** ça vous fait du bien. ●n bien m; **do ~** faire du bien. **is it any ~?** est-ce que c'est bien? **it's no ~** ça ne vaut rien. **it is no ~ shouting** ça ne sert à rien de crier. **for ~** pour toujours. ~**afternoon** interj bonjour. ~**bye** interj & n au revoir (m inv). ~**evening** interj bonsoir. **G~**

Friday n Vendredi m saint. ~**looking** adj beau. **~ morning** interj bonjour. **~natured** adj gentil.

goodness n bonté f; **my ~!** mon Dieu!

goodnight interj bonsoir, bonne nuit.

goods npl marchandises fpl.

goodwill n bonne volonté f.

google® vt/i chercher sur (le moteur de recherche) Google®, googler.

goose n (pl **geese**) oie f. ~**berry** n groseille f à maquereau. ~**pimples** npl chair f de poule.

gorge n (Geog) gorge f. ●vt ~ **oneself** se gaver (**on** de).

gorgeous adj magnifique, splendide, formidable.

gorilla n gorille m.

gory adj (**-ier, -iest**) sanglant; (horrific: fig) horrible.

gospel n évangile m; **the G~** l'Évangile m.

gossip n bavardages mpl, commérages mpl; (person) bavard/-e m/f. ●vi bavarder.

got ▷GET. ●**have ~** avoir; **have ~ to do** devoir faire.

govern vt/i gouverner. **governess** n gouvernante f. **government** n gouvernement m. **governor** n gouverneur m.

gown n robe f; (of judge, teacher) toge f.

GP abbr ▷GENERAL PRACTITIONER.

GPS abbr (**Global Positioning System**) GPS m.

grab vt (pt **grabbed**) saisir.

grace n grâce f. ●vt (honour) honorer; (adorn) orner. **graceful** adj gracieux.

gracious adj (kind) bienveillant; (elegant) élégant.

grade n catégorie f; (of goods)

qualité f; (on scale) grade m; (school mark) note f; (class: US) classe f. • vt classer; (school work) noter. ~ **school** n (US) école f primaire.

gradual adj progressif, graduel. **gradually** adv progressivement, peu à peu.

graduate[1] /'grædʒʊət/ n (Univ) diplômé/-e m/f.

graduate[2] /'grædʒʊeɪt/ vi obtenir son diplôme. • vt graduer. **graduation** n remise f des diplômes.

graffiti npl graffiti mpl.

graft n (Med, Bot) greffe f; (work) boulot m. • vt greffer (**on to** sur); (work) trimer.

grain n (seed, quantity, texture) grain m; (in wood) fibre f.

gram n gramme m.

grammar n grammaire f.

grand adj magnifique; (duke, chorus) grand.

grandad n 🔲 papy m.

grand: ~**child** n (girl) petite-fille f; (boy) petit-fils m; **her** ~**children** ses petits-enfants mpl. ~**daughter** n petite-fille f. ~**father** n grand-père m. ~**ma** n ▷GRANNY. ~**mother** n grandmère f. ~**parents** npl grandsparents mpl. ~ **piano** n piano m à queue. ~**son** n petit-fils m. ~**stand** n tribune f.

granny n 🔲mémé f, mamie f.

grant vt (permission) accorder; (request) accéder à; (admit) admettre (**that** que); **take sth for** ~**ed** considérer qch comme une chose acquise. • n subvention f; (Univ) bourse f.

granule n (of sugar, salt) grain m; (of coffee) granulé m.

grape n grain m de raisin. ~**s** raisin(s) m(pl).

grapefruit n inv pamplemousse m.

graph n graphique m.

graphic adj (arts) graphique; (fig) vivant, explicite. **graphics** npl (Comput) graphiques mpl.

grasp vt saisir. • n (hold) prise f; (strength of hand) poigne f; (reach) portée f; (fig) compréhension f.

grass n herbe f. ~**hopper** n sauterelle f. ~**land** n prairie f.

grass roots npl peuple m. • adj (movement) populaire; (support) de base.

grate n (hearth) âtre m; (fire basket) grille f. • vt râper. • vi grincer.

grateful adj reconnaissant.

grater n râpe f.

gratified adj très heureux. **gratify** vt faire plaisir à.

grating n (bars) grille f; (noise) grincement m.

gratitude n reconnaissance f.

gratuity n (tip) pourboire m; (bounty: Mil) prime f.

grave[1] /greɪv/ n tombe f. • adj (serious) grave.

grave[2] /grɑːv/ adj ~ **accent** accent m grave.

gravel n graviers mpl.

grave: ~**stone** n pierre f tombale. ~**yard** n cimetière m.

gravity n (seriousness) gravité f; (force) pesanteur f.

gravy n jus m (de viande).

gray (US) adj & n ▷GREY.

graze vi (eat) paître. • vt (touch) frôler; (scrape) écorcher. • n écorchure f.

grease n graisse f. • vt graisser. **greasy** adj graisseux.

great adj grand; (very good 🔲) génial 🔲, formidable 🔲; (grandfather, grandmother) arrière-.

Great Britain n Grande-Bretagne f.

greatly adv (very) très; (much) beaucoup.

Greece n Grèce f.

greed n avidité f; (for food) gourmandise f. **greedy** adj avide; gourmand.

Greek n (person) Grec/-que m/f; (Ling) grec m. ● adj grec.

green adj vert; (fig) naïf. ● n vert m; (grass) pelouse f; (golf) green m; **~s** légumes mpl verts. **~grocer** n marchand/-e m/f de fruits et légumes.

greenhouse n serre f; **~ effect** effet m de serre.

greet vt (welcome) accueillir; (address politely) saluer. **greeting** n accueil m.

greetings interj salutations 🔼 ● npl (Christmas) vœux mpl. **~ card** n carte f de vœux.

grew ▷GROW.

grey adj gris; (fig) triste; **go ~** (hair, person) grisonner. ● n gris m. **~hound** n lévrier m.

grid n grille f; (network: Electr) réseau m.

grief n chagrin m; **come to ~** (person) avoir un malheur; (fail) tourner mal.

grievance n griefs mpl.

grieve vt/i (s')affliger; **~ for** pleurer.

grill n (cooking device) gril m; (food) grillade f; (Auto) calandre f. ● vt/i (faire) griller; (interrogate) mettre sur la sellette.

grim adj sinistre.

grimace n grimace f. ● vi grimacer.

grime n crasse f.

grin vi (pt **grinned**) sourire. ● n (large) sourire m.

grind vt (pt **ground**) (grain) écraser; (coffee) moudre; (sharpen) aiguiser; **~ one's teeth** grincer des dents. ● vi **~ to a halt** s'immobiliser. ● n corvée f.

grip vt (pt **gripped**) saisir; (interest) passionner. ● n prise f; (strength of hand) poigne f; **come to ~s with**

en venir aux prises avec.

grisly adj (-ier, -iest) (remains) macabre; (sight) horrible.

gristle n cartilage m.

grit n (for roads) sable m; (fig) courage m. ● vt (pt **gritted**) (road) sabler; (teeth) serrer.

groan vi gémir. ● n gémissement m.

grocer n (person) épicier/-ière m/f; (shop) épicerie f. **groceries** npl (shopping) courses fpl; (goods) épicerie f. **grocery** n (shop) épicerie f.

groin n aine f.

groom n marié m; (for horses) palefrenier/-ière /m/f. ● vt (horse) panser; (fig) préparer.

groove n (for door etc.) rainure f; (in record) sillon m.

grope vi tâtonner. **~ for** chercher à tâtons.

gross adj (behaviour) vulgaire; (Comm) brut. ● n inv grosse f.

grotto n (pl **~es**) grotte f.

grouch vi (grumble 🔼) rouspéter, râler.

ground¹ /graʊnd/ n terre f, sol m; (area) terrain m; (reason) raison f; (Electr, US) masse f; **~s** terres fpl, parc m; (of coffee) marc m; **on the ~** par terre. **lose ~** perdre du terrain. ● vt/i (Naut) échouer; (aircraft) retenir au sol.

ground² /graʊnd/ ▷GRIND. ● adj **~ beef** (US) bifteck m haché.

ground: ~ floor n rez-de-chaussée m inv. **~work** n travail m préparatoire.

group n groupe m. ● vt/i (se) grouper. **~ware** n (Comput) logiciel m de groupe.

grovel vi (pt **grovelled**) ramper.

grow vi (pt **grew**; pp **grown**) (person) grandir; (plant) pousser;

(become) devenir; (crime) augmenter. •vt cultiver. ∎ ~ **up** devenir adulte, grandir. **grower** n cultivateur/-trice m/f.

growl vi (dog) gronder; (person) grogner. •n grognement m.

grown ▷GROW. •adj adulte. ~-**up** adj & n adulte (mf).

growth n (of person, plant) croissance f; (in numbers) accroissement m; (of hair, tooth) pousse f; (Med) grosseur f, tumeur f.

grudge vt ~ **doing** faire à contrecœur. ~ **sb sth** (success, wealth) en vouloir à qn de qch. •n rancune f; **have a** ~ **against** en vouloir à.

grumble vi ronchonner, grogner (**at** après).

grumpy adj (-**ier**, -**iest**) grincheux, grognon.

grunt vi grogner. •n grognement m.

guarantee n garantie f. •vt garantir.

guard vt protéger; (watch) surveiller. •vi ~ **against** se protéger contre. •n (Mil) garde f; (person) garde m; (on train) chef m de train.

guardian n gardien/-ne m/f; (of orphan) tuteur/-trice m/f.

guess vt/i deviner; (suppose) penser. •n conjecture f.

guest n invité/-e m/f; (in hotel) client/-e m/f. ~-**house** n pension f. ~-**room** n chambre f d'amis.

guidance n (advice) conseils mpl; (information) information f.

guide n (person, book) guide m; (girl) guide f. •vt guider. ~-**book** n guide m. ~ **dog** n chien d'aveugle. ~**line** n indication f; (advice) conseils mpl.

guillotine n (for execution) guillotine f; (for paper) massicot m.

guilt n culpabilité f. **guilty** adj coupable.

guinea-pig n (animal) cochon m d'Inde; (fig) cobaye m.

guitar n guitare f.

gulf n (part of sea) golfe m; (hollow) gouffre m.

gull n mouette f, (larger) goéland m.

gullible adj crédule.

gully n (ravine) ravin m; (drain) rigole f.

gulp vt ~ (**down**) avaler en vitesse. •vi (from fear etc.) avoir la gorge serrée. •n gorgée f.

gum n (Anat) gencive f; (glue) colle f; (for chewing) chewing-gum m. •vt (pt **gummed**) gommer.

gun n (pistol) revolver m; (rifle) fusil m; (large) canon m. •vt (pt **gunned**) ~ **down** abattre. ~**fire** n fusillade f. ~**powder** n poudre f à canon. ~**shot** n coup m de feu.

gurgle n (of water) gargouillement m; (of baby) gazouillis m. •vi (water) gargouiller; (baby) gazouiller.

gush vi ~ (**out**) jaillir. •n jaillissement m.

gust n rafale f; (of smoke) bouffée f.

gut n (belly ⚠) ventre m. •vt (pt **gutted**) (fish) vider; (of fire) dévaster. **gutted** adj ⚠ abattu.

guts npl ⚠ (insides of human) tripes fpl ⚠; (insides of animal, building) entrailles fpl; (courage) cran m ⚠.

gutter n (on roof) gouttière f. (in street) caniveau m.

guy n (man ⚠) type m.

gym n (place) gymnase m; (activity) gym(nastique) f.

gymnasium n gymnase m.

gymnastics npl gymnastique f.

gynaecologist n gynécologue mf.

gypsy n bohémien/-ne m/f.

Hh

habit n habitude f; (costume: Relig) habit m; **be in/get into the ~ of** avoir/prendre l'habitude de.

habitual adj (usual) habituel; (smoker, liar) invétéré.

hack n (writer) écrivaillon m. ●vi (Comput) pirater; **~ into** s'introduire dans. ●vt tailler. **hacker** n (Comput) pirate m informatique.

hackneyed adj rebattu.

had ▷HAVE.

haddock n inv églefin m.

haemorrhage n hémorragie f.

haggard adj (person) exténué; (face, look) défait.

haggle vi marchander; **~ over sth** discuter du prix de qch.

hail n grêle f. ●vt (greet) saluer; (taxi) héler. ●vi grêler; **~ from** venir de. **~stone** n grêlon m.

hair n (on head) cheveux mpl; (on body, of animal) poils mpl; (single strand on head) cheveu m; (on body) poil m. **~brush** n brosse f à cheveux. **~cut** n coupe f de cheveux. **~-do** n ① coiffure f. **~dresser** n coiffeur/-euse m/f. **~drier** n séchoir m (à cheveux). **~pin** n épingle f à cheveux. **~ remover** n dépilatoire m. **~-style** n coiffure f.

hairy adj (-ier, -iest) poilu; (terrifying) ① horrifiant.

half n (pl halves) (part) moitié f; (fraction) demi m; **~ a dozen** une demi-douzaine; **~ an hour** une demi-heure; **four and a ~** quatre et demi; **an hour and a ~** une heure et demie; **~ and half** moitié moitié; **in ~** en deux. ●adj demi; **~ price** à moitié prix. ●adv à moitié.

~-back n (Sport) demi m. **~-hearted** adj tiède. **~-mast** n **at ~-mast** en berne. **~-term** n vacances fpl de demi-trimestre. **~-time** n mi-temps f. **~-way** adv à mi-chemin. **~wit** n imbécile mf.

hall n (in house) entrée f; (corridor) couloir m; (in airport) hall m; (for events) salle f; **~ of residence** résidence f universitaire.

hallmark n (on gold) poinçon m; (fig) caractéristique f.

hallo ▷HELLO.

Hallowe'en n la veille de la Toussaint.

halt n arrêt m; (temporary) suspension f; (Mil) halte f. ●vt (proceedings) interrompre; (arms sales, experiments) mettre fin à. ●vi (vehicle) s'arrêter; (army) faire halte.

halve vt (time) réduire de moitié; (fruit) couper en deux.

ham n jambon m.

hamburger n hamburger m.

hammer n marteau m. ●vt/i marteler; **~ sth into sth** enfoncer qch dans qch; **~ sth out** (agreement) parvenir à qch.

hammock n hamac m.

hamper n panier m. ●vt gêner.

hamster n hamster m.

hand n main f; (of clock) aiguille f; (writing) écriture f; (worker) ouvrier/-ière m/f; (cards) jeu m; **give sb a ~** donner un coup de main à qn; **at ~** proche; **on ~** disponible; **on the one ~...on the other ~** d'une part...d'autre part; **to ~** à portée de la main. ●vt **~ sb sth, ~sth to sb** donner qch à qn. ■ **~ in or over**

remettre; ~ **out** distribuer.
~**bag** n sac m à main.
~-**baggage** n bagages mpl à
main. ~**book** n manuel m.
~**brake** n frein m à main.
~**cuffs** npl menottes fpl.

handicap n handicap m. •vt (pt
handicapped) handicaper.

handkerchief n (pl ~s)
mouchoir m.

handle n (of door, bag) poignée f;
(of implement) manche m; (of cup,
bucket) anse f; (of frying pan) queue f.
•vt (manage) manier; (deal with)
traiter; (touch) manipuler.

handout n document m; (leaflet)
prospectus m; (money) aumône f.

hands-free kit n kit m mains
libres conducteur.

handshake n poignée f de main.

handsome adj (good looking) beau;
(generous) généreux.

handwriting n écriture f.

handy adj (-ier, -iest) (book, skill)
utile; (size, shape, tool) pratique;
(person) doué. ~**man** n (pl -men)
bricoleur m.

hang vt (pt **hung**) (from hook,
hanger) accrocher; (from rope)
suspendre; (pt **hanged**) (person)
pendre. •vi (from hook) être
accroché; (from rope) être
suspendu; (person) être pendu. •n
get the ~ of doing 🔲 piger
comment faire 🔲. ■ ~ **about**
traîner; ~ **on** 🔲 (hold out) tenir;
(wait) attendre; ~ **on to sth**
s'agripper à qch; ~ **out** vi 🔲 (live)
crécher 🔲; (spend time) passer son
temps; vt (washing) étendre; ~ **up**
(telephone) raccrocher.

hanger n (for clothes) cintre m.

hang-gliding n vol m libre.

hangover n gueule f de bois 🔲.

hang-up n 🔲 complexe m.

haphazard adj peu méthodique.

happen vi arriver, se passer; ~
to sb arriver à qn; **it so ~s that**
il se trouve que.

happily adv joyeusement;
(fortunately) heureusement.

happiness n bonheur m.

happy adj (-ier, -iest) heureux;
I'm not ~ about it je ne suis
pas content; ~ **with sth**
satisfait de qch; ~ **medium**
juste milieu m.

harass vt harceler. **harassment** n
harcèlement m.

harbour, (US) **harbor** n port m.
•vt (shelter) héberger.

hard adj dur; (difficult) difficile,
dur; (evidence, fact) solide; **find it**
~ **to do** avoir du mal à faire; ~
on sb dur envers qn. •adv (work)
dur; (pull, hit, cry) fort; (think, study)
sérieusement. ~**board** n
aggloméré m. ~ **copy** n (Comput)
tirage m. ~ **disk** n disque m dur.

hardly adv à peine; (expect, hope)
difficilement; ~ **ever** presque
jamais.

hardship n (poverty) privations fpl;
(ordeal) épreuve f.

hard: ~ **shoulder** n bande f
d'arrêt d'urgence. ~ **up** adj 🔲
fauché 🔲. ~**ware** n (Comput)
matériel m, hardware m; (goods)
quincaillerie f. ~-**working** adj
travailleur.

hardy adj (-ier, -iest) résistant.

hare n lièvre m.

harm n mal m; **there is no ~ in**
il n'y a pas de mal à. •vt (person)
faire du mal à; (object)
endommager. **harmful** adj
nuisible. **harmless** adj inoffensif.

harmony n harmonie f.

harness n harnais m. •vt (horse)
harnacher; (use) exploiter.

harp n harpe f. •vi ~ **on (about)**
rabâcher.

harrowing adj (experience) atroce;
(story) déchirant.

harsh adj (punishment) sévère;
(person) dur; (light) cru; (voice)
rude; (chemical) corrosif.
harshness n dureté f.

harvest n récolte f; **the wine ~** les vendanges fpl. ●vt (corn) moissonner; (vegetables) récolter.

has ▷HAVE.

hassle n complications fpl. ●vt 🄣 talonner (**about** à propos de); (worry) stresser.

haste n hâte f; **in ~** à la hâte; **make ~** se dépêcher.

hasty adj (-ier, -iest) précipité.

hat n chapeau m.

hatch n (Aviat) panneau m mobile; (Naut) écoutille f; (for food) passeplats m inv. ●vt/i (eggs) (faire) éclore.

hate n haine f. ●vt détester; (violently) haïr; (sport, food) avoir horreur de.

hatred n haine f.

haughty adj (-ier, -iest) hautain.

haul vt tirer. ●n (by thieves) butin m; (by customs) saisie f; **it will be a long ~** l'étape sera longue; **long/short ~** (transport) long/court courrier m. **haulage** n transport m routier. **haulier** n (firm) société f de transports routiers.

haunt vt hanter. ●n lieu m de prédilection.

---

have /hæv/

❗ present **have, has**; past **had**; ▪ past participle **had**

●transitive verb

····▸(possess) avoir; **I ~ (got) a car** j'ai une voiture; **they ~ (got) problems** ils ont des problèmes.

····▸(do sth) **~ a try** essayer; **~ a bath** prendre un bain.

····▸**~ sth done** faire faire qch; **~ your hair cut** se faire couper les cheveux.

●auxiliary verb

····▸(in perfect tenses) avoir; être; **I ~ seen him** je l'ai vu; **she had**

fallen elle était tombée.

····▸(in tag questions) **you've seen her, haven't you?** tu l'as vue, n'est-ce pas?; **you haven't seen her, ~ you?** tu ne l'as pas vue, par hasard?

····▸(in short answers) **'you've never met him'—'yes I ~'** 'tu ne l'as jamais rencontré'—'mais si!'

····▸(must) **~ to** devoir; **I ~ to go** je dois partir; **you don't ~ to do it** tu n'es pas obligé de le faire.

▶ For expressions such as **have a walk, have dinner** ▷walk, dinner.

---

haven n refuge m; (fig) havre m.

havoc n dévastation f.

hawk n faucon m.

hay n foin m; **~ fever** rhume m des foins.

haywire adj **go ~** (plans) dérailler; (machine) se détraquer.

hazard n risque m; **~ (warning) lights** feux mpl de détresse. ●vt hasarder.

haze n brume f.

hazel n (bush) noisetier m. **~nut** n noisette f.

hazy adj (-ier, -iest) (misty) brumeux; (fig) vague.

he pron il; (emphatic) lui; **here ~ is** le voici.

head n tête f; (leader) chef m; (of beer) mousse f; **~s or tails?** pile ou face? ●vt (list) être en tête de; (team) être à la tête de; (chapter) intituler; **~ the ball** faire une tête. ●vi **~ for** se diriger vers.

headache n mal m de tête; **have a ~** avoir mal à la tête.

heading n titre m; (subject category) rubrique f.

head: ~lamp, ~light n phare m. **~line** n gros titre m. **~master** n directeur m. **~mistress** n directrice f. ~ **office** siège m social. ~**on** adj & adv de front. ~**phones** npl casque m. ~**quarters** npl siège m social; (Mil) quartier m général. ~ **rest** n (Auto) repose-tête m inv. ~**strong** adj têtu.

heal vt/i guérir.

health n santé f. ~ **centre** n centre m médico-social. ~ **food** n produits mpl diététiques. ~ **insurance** n assurance f maladie.

healthy adj (person, plant, skin, diet) sain; (air) salutaire.

heap n tas m; ~**s of** ⚠ un tas de. ●vt ~ **(up)** entasser.

hear vt (pt **heard**) entendre; (news, rumour) apprendre; (lecture, broadcast) écouter. ●vi entendre; ~ **from** recevoir des nouvelles de; ~ **of** or **about** entendre parler de.

hearing n ouïe f; (of case) audience f; **give sb a** ~ écouter qn. ~**-aid** n prothèse f auditive.

hearse n corbillard m.

heart n cœur m; ~**s** (cards) cœur m; **at** ~ au fond; **by** ~ par cœur; **be** ~**-broken** avoir le cœur brisé; **lose** ~ perdre courage. ~ **attack** n crise f cardiaque. ~**burn** n brûlures fpl d'estomac. ~**felt** adj sincère.

hearth n foyer m.

heartily adv (greet) chaleureusement; (laugh, eat) de bon cœur.

hearty adj (-**ier**, -**iest**) (sincere) chaleureux; (meal) solide.

heat n chaleur f; (contest) épreuve f éliminatoire. ●vt (house) chauffer; ~ **(up)** (food) faire chauffer; (reheat) réchauffer. **heated** adj (fig) passionné; (lit) (pool) chauffé. **heater** n appareil m de chauffage.

heather n bruyère f.

heating n chauffage m.

heave vt (lift) hisser; (pull) traîner

péniblement; ~ **a sigh** pousser un soupir. ●vi (pull) tirer de toutes ses forces; (retch) avoir un haut-le-cœur.

heaven n ciel m.

heavily adv lourdement; (smoke, drink) beaucoup.

heavy adj (-**ier**, -**iest**) lourd; (cold, work) gros; (traffic) dense. ~ **goods vehicle** n poids m lourd. ~**-handed** adj maladroit. ~**weight** n poids m lourd.

Hebrew n (person) Hébreu m; (Ling) hébreu m. ●adj hébreu; (Ling) hébraïque.

hectic adj (activity) intense; (period, day) mouvementé.

hedge n haie f. ●vi (in answering) se dérober.

hedgehog n hérisson m.

heel n talon m.

hefty adj (-**ier**, -**iest**) (person) costaud ⚠; (object) pesant.

height n hauteur f; (of person) taille f; (of plane, mountain) altitude f; (of fame, glory) apogée m; (of joy, folly, pain) comble m.

heir n héritier/-ière m/f. **heiress** n héritière f. **heirloom** n objet m de famille.

held ▷HOLD.

helicopter n hélicoptère m.

hell n enfer m.

hello interj bonjour!; (on phone) allô!

helmet n casque m.

help vt/i aider (**to do** à faire); ~ **(sb) with a bag/the housework** aider qn à porter un sac/à faire le ménage; ~ **oneself** se servir; **he can't** ~ **it** ce n'est pas de sa faute. ●n aide f. ●interj au secours! **helper** n aide mf. **helpful** adj utile; (person) serviable. **helping** n portion f. **helpless** adj impuissant.

hem n ourlet m. ●vt (pt **hemmed**) faire un ourlet à; ~ **in** cerner.

hen n poule f.

hence | himself

hence adv (for this reason) d'où; (from now) d'ici. **henceforth** adv désormais.

hepatitis n hépatite f.

her pron la, l'; (indirect object) lui; it's ~ c'est elle; **for** ~ pour elle. •adj son, sa; pl ses.

herb n herbe f; ~**s** (Culin) fines herbes fpl.

herd n troupeau m.

here adv ici; ~! (take this) tiens!; tenez!; ~ **is, ~ are** voici; I'm ~ je suis là. **hereabouts** adv par ici. **hereafter** adv après; (in book) ci-après. **hereby** adv par le présent acte; (in letter) par la présente.

herewith adv ci-joint.

heritage n patrimoine m. ~ **tourism** n tourisme m culturel.

hernia n hernie f.

hero n (pl ~**es**) héros m.

heroic adj héroïque.

heroin n héroïne f.

heroine n héroïne f.

heron n héron m.

herring n hareng m.

hers pron le sien, la sienne, les sien(ne)s; **it is** ~ c'est à elle or le sien or la sienne.

herself pron (emphatic) elle-même; (reflexive) se; **proud of** ~ fière d'elle; **by** ~ toute seule.

hesitate vi hésiter. **hesitation** n hésitation f.

heterosexual adj & n hétérosexuel/-le (m/f).

hexagon n hexagone m.

heyday n apogée m.

HGV abbr ▶HEAVY GOODS VEHICLE.

hi interj 🔳 salut! 🔳.

hiccup n hoquet m; (the) ~**s** le hoquet. •vi hoqueter.

hide vt (pt **hid**; pp **hidden**) cacher (**from** à). •vi se cacher (**from** de); **go into hiding** se cacher. •n (skin) peau f.

hideous adj (monster, object) hideux; (noise) affreux.

hiding n **go into** ~ se cacher; **give sb a** ~ administrer une correction à qn.

hierarchy n hiérarchie f.

hi-fi n (chaîne f) hi-fi f inv.

high adj haut; (price, number) élevé; (priest, speed) grand; (voice) aigu; **in the** ~ **season** en pleine saison. •n **a (new)** ~ un niveau record. •adv haut. ~**brow** adj & n intellectuel/-le (m/f). ~ **chair** n chaise f haute. ~ **court** n cour f suprême. **higher education** n enseignement m supérieur. ~**jump** n saut m en hauteur. ~**level** adj à haut niveau.

highlight n (best moment) point m fort; ~**s** (in hair) reflet m; (artificial) mèches fpl; (Sport) résumé m. •vt (emphasize) souligner.

highly adv extrêmement; (paid) très bien; **speak/think** ~ **of** dire/penser beaucoup de bien de.

Highness n Altesse f.

high: ~**-rise (building)** n tour f. ~ **school** n lycée m. ~**-speed** adj (train) à grande vitesse; (film) ultrarapide. ~ **street** n rue f principale. ~**-tech** adj de pointe.

highway n route f nationale; (US) autoroute f; ~ **code** code m de la route.

hijack vt détourner. •n détournement m. **hijacker** n pirate m (de l'air).

hike n randonnée f; **price** ~ hausse f de prix. •vi faire de la randonnée.

hilarious adj désopilant.

hill n colline f; (slope) côte f. **hilly** adj vallonné.

him pron le, l'; (indirect object) lui; it's ~ c'est lui; **for** ~ pour lui.

himself pron (emphatic) lui-même; (reflexive) se; **proud of** ~ fier de lui; **by** ~ tout seul.

hind adj de derrière.

hinder vt (hamper) gêner; (prevent) empêcher. **hindrance** n obstacle m, gêne f.

hindsight n **with ~** rétrospectivement.

Hindu n Hindou/-e m/f. ● adj hindou.

hinge n charnière f. ● vi ~ **on** dépendre de.

hint n allusion f; (of spice, accent) pointe f; (of colour) touche f; (advice) conseil m. ● vt laisser entendre. ● vi ~ **at** faire allusion à.

hip n hanche f.

hippopotamus n (pl ~**es**) hippopotame m.

hire vt (thing) louer; (person) engager. ● n location f. ~**-car** n voiture f de location. ~**-purchase** n achat m à crédit.

his adj son, sa, pl ses. ● pron le sien, la sienne, les sien(ne)s; **it is ~** c'est à lui or le sien or la sienne.

hiss n sifflement m. ● vt/i siffler.

history n histoire f; **make ~** entrer dans l'histoire.

hit vt (pt **hit**; pres p **hitting**) frapper; (collide with) heurter; (find) trouver; (affect, reach) toucher. ● vi ~ **on** (find) tomber sur; ~ **it off** s'entendre bien (**with** avec). ● n (blow) coup m; (fig) succès m; (song) tube m 🔲; (on Internet) (visit) visite f, accès m; (result) page f trouvée, résultat m.

hitch vt (fasten) accrocher; ~ **up** remonter. ● n (snag) anicroche f. ~**-hike** vi faire du stop 🔲. ~**-hiker** n auto-stoppeur/-euse m/f.

hi-tech adj de pointe.

HIV abbr (**human immunodeficiency virus**) VIH m.

hive n ruche f. ● vt ~ **off** séparer; (industry) céder.

HIV-positive adj séropositif.

hoard vt amasser; (supplies) stocker. ● n trésor m; (of provisions) provisions fpl.

hoarse adj enroué.

hoax n canular m.

hobby n passe-temps m inv.

hockey n hockey m.

hog n cochon m. ● vt (pt **hogged**) 🔲 monopoliser.

hold vt (pt **held**) tenir; (contain) contenir; (conversation, opinion) avoir; (shares, record, person) détenir; ~ **(the line), please** ne quittez pas. ● vi (rope, weather) tenir. ● n prise f; **get ~ of** attraper; (ticket) se procurer; (person) (by phone) joindre; **on ~** en attente. ■ ~ **back** (contain) retenir; (hide) cacher; ~ **down** (job) garder; (person) tenir; (costs) limiter; ~ **on** (stand firm) tenir bon; (wait) attendre; ~ **on to** (keep) garder; (cling to) se cramponner à; ~ **out** vt (offer) offrir; vi (resist) tenir le coup; ~ **up** (support) soutenir; (delay) retarder; (rob) attaquer.

holder n détenteur/-trice m/f; (of passport, post) titulaire mf; (for object) support m.

holding n participation f.

hold-up n retard m; (of traffic) embouteillage m; (robbery) hold-up m inv.

hole n trou m.

holiday n vacances fpl; (public) jour m férié; (time off) congé m. ● vi passer ses vacances. ● adj de vacances. ~**-maker** n vacancier/-ière m/f.

Holland n Hollande f.

hollow adj creux; (fig) faux. ● n creux m. ● vt creuser.

holly n houx m.

holy adj (**-ier, -iest**) saint; (water) bénit; **H~ Ghost, H~ Spirit** Saint-Esprit m.

homage n hommage m.

home n (place to live) logement m;

maison f; (institution) maison f; (family base) foyer m; (country) pays m. ●adj de la maison, du foyer; (of family) de famille; (Pol) intérieur; (match, visit) à domicile. ●adv ~ à la maison, chez soi; **come** or **go** ~ rentrer; (from abroad) rentrer dans son pays; **feel at** ~ **with** être à l'aise avec. ~ **computer** n ordinateur m, PC m.

homeland n patrie f; ~ **security** n sécurité f des frontières.

homeless adj sans abri. ●n **the** ~ les sans-abri mpl.

homely adj (-**ier**, -**iest**) (cosy) accueillant; (simple) sans prétention; (person: US) sans attraits.

home: ~-**made** adj (fait) maison. **H**~ **Office** n ministère m de l'Intérieur. ~ **page** n (Internet) page f d'accueil. **H**~ **Secretary** n Ministre m de l'Intérieur. ~**sick** adj **be** ~**sick** avoir le mal du pays. ~**work** n devoirs mpl.

homosexual adj & n homosexuel/-le (m/f).

honest adj (truthful) intègre; (trustworthy) honnête; (sincere) franc. **honestly** adv honnêtement; franchement. **honesty** n honnêteté f.

honey n miel m; (person 🔲) chéri/-e m/f. ~**moon** n voyage m de noces; (fig) lune f de miel.

honk vi klaxonner.

honorary adj (person) honoraire; (degree) honorifique.

honour, (US) **honor** n honneur m. ●vt honorer.

hood n capuchon m; (on car, pram) capote f; (car engine cover: US) capot m.

hoof n (pl ~s) sabot m.

hook n crochet m; (on garment) agrafe f; (for fishing) hameçon m; **off the** ~ tiré d'affaire; (phone) décroché. ●vt accrocher.

hoot n (of owl) (h)ululement m; (of car) coup m de klaxon. ●vi (owl)

(h)ululer; (car) klaxonner; (jeer) huer.

hoover vt ~ **a room** passer l'aspirateur dans une pièce.

Hoover® n aspirateur m.

hop vi (pt **hopped**) sauter (à cloche-pied); ~ **in!** 🔲 vas-y, monte! ●n bond m; ~**s** houblon m.

hope n espoir m. ●vt/i espérer; ~ **for** espérer avoir; **I** ~ **so** je l'espère.

hopeful adj (news, sign) encourageant; (person) plein d'espoir; (mood) optimiste. **hopefully** adv (with luck) avec un peu de chance; (with hope) avec optimisme.

hopeless adj désespéré; (useless: fig) nul 🔲.

horizon n horizon m.

horizontal adj horizontal.

hormone n hormone f.

horn n corne f; (of car) klaxon® m; (Mus) cor m.

horoscope n horoscope m.

horrible adj horrible.

horrid adj horrible.

horrific adj horrifiant.

horrify vt horrifier.

horror n horreur f. ●adj (film, story) d'épouvante.

horse n cheval m. ~**back** n **on** ~**back** à cheval. ~-**chestnut** n marron m (d'Inde). ~**man** n (pl -**men**) cavalier m. ~**power** n puissance f (en chevaux). ~-**race** n course f de chevaux. ~-**radish** n raifort m. ~**shoe** n fer m à cheval. ~ **show** n concours m hippique.

hose n tuyau m. ●vt arroser. ~-**pipe** n tuyau m.

hospitable adj hospitalier.

hospital n hôpital m.

host n (to guests) hôte m; (on TV) animateur m; (Internet) ordinateur m hôte; **a ~ of** une foule de; (Relig) hostie f.

hostage n otage m; **hold sb ~** garder qn en otage.

hostel n foyer m; **(youth) ~** auberge f (de jeunesse).

hostess n hôtesse f.

hostile adj hostile.

hot adj (**hotter, hottest**) chaud; (Culin) épicé; **be** or **feel ~** avoir chaud; **it is ~** il fait chaud; **in ~ water** ⚠ dans le pétrin. •vt/i (pt **hotted**) **~ up** ⚠ chauffer. **~ air balloon** n montgolfière f. **~ dog** n hot-dog m.

hotel n hôtel m.

hot: **~headed** adj impétueux. **~ list** n (Internet) signets mpl favoris. **~plate** n plaque f chauffante. **~ water bottle** n bouillotte f.

hound n chien m de chasse. •vt poursuivre.

hour n heure f.

hourly adj horaire; **on an ~ basis** à l'heure. •adv toutes les heures.

house[1] /haʊs/ n maison f; (Pol) Chambre f; **on the ~** aux frais de la maison.

house[2] /haʊz/ vt loger; (of building) abriter.

household n (house, family) ménage m. •adj ménager.

house: **~keeper** n gouvernante f. **~proud** adj méticuleux. **~warming** n pendaison f de crémaillère. **~wife** n (pl **-wives**) ménagère f. **~work** n travaux mpl ménagers.

housing n logement m; **~ association** service m de logement; **~ development** cité f; (smaller) lotissement m.

hover vi (bird) voleter; (vacillate) vaciller. **hovercraft** n aéroglisseur m.

how adv comment; **~ are you?** comment allez-vous?; **~ long/**

tall is...? quelle est la longueur/ hauteur de...?; **~ many?, ~ much?** combien?; **~ pretty!** comme or que c'est joli!; **~ about a walk?** si on faisait une promenade?; **~ do you do?** (greeting) enchanté.

however adv (nevertheless) cependant; **~ hard I try** j'ai beau essayer; **~ much it costs** quel que soit le prix; **~ young/ poor he is** si jeune/pauvre soit-il; **~ you like** comme tu veux.

howl n hurlement m. •vi hurler.

HP abbr ▷ **HIRE-PURCHASE**.

hp abbr ▷ **HORSEPOWER**.

HQ abbr ▷ **HEADQUARTERS**.

hub n moyeu m; (fig) centre m.

hug vt (pt **hugged**) serrer dans ses bras. •n étreinte f; **give sb a ~** serrer qn dans ses bras.

huge adj énorme.

hull n (of ship) coque f.

hum vt/i (pt **hummed**) (person) fredonner; (insect) bourdonner; (engine) ronronner. •n bourdonnement m; ronronnement m.

human adj humain. •n humain m. **~ being** n être m humain.

humane adj (person) humain; (act) d'humanité; (killing) sans cruauté.

humanitarian adj humanitaire.

humanity n humanité f.

humble adj humble.

humid adj humide.

humiliate vt humilier.

humorous adj humoristique; (person) plein d'humour.

humour, (US) **humor** n humour m; (mood) humeur f. •vt amadouer.

hump n bosse f. •vt ⚠ porter.

hunchback n bossu/-e m/f.

hundred adj & n cent (m); **two ~**

and one deux cent un; **~s of** des centaines de. **hundredth** adj & n centième (mf).

hung ▷**HANG**.

Hungarian n (person) Hongrois/-e m/f; (Ling) hongrois m. •adj hongrois. **Hungary** n Hongrie f.

hunger n faim f. •vi **~ for** avoir faim de.

hungry adj (**-ier, -iest**) affamé; **be ~** avoir faim.

hunt vt/i chasser; **~ for** chercher. •n chasse f. **hunter** n chasseur m. **hunting** n chasse f.

hurdle n (Sport) haie f; (fig) obstacle m.

hurricane n ouragan m.

hurry vi se dépêcher; **~ out** sortir précipitamment. •vt (work) terminer à la hâte; (person) bousculer. •n hâte f; **in a ~** pressé.

hurt vt/i (pt **hurt**) faire mal (à); (injure, offend) blesser. •adj blessé. •n blessure f.

hurtle vi **~ down** dévaler; **~ along a road** foncer sur une route.

husband n mari m.

hush vt faire taire; **~ up** (news) étouffer. •n silence m. •interj chut!

husky adj (**-ier, -iest**) enroué. •n husky m.

hustle vt (push, rush) bousculer. •vi (hurry) se dépêcher; (work: US) se

démener. •n **~ and bustle** agitation f.

hut n cabane f.

hyacinth n jacinthe f.

hydrant n (fire) **~** bouche f d'incendie.

hydraulic adj hydraulique.

hydroelectric adj hydroélectrique.

hydrogen n hydrogène m; **~ bomb** bombe f à hydrogène.

hyena n hyène f.

hygiene n hygiène f. **hygienic** adj hygiénique.

hymn n cantique m; (fig) hymne m.

hype n 🅣 battage m publicitaire. •vt **~ (up)** (film, book) faire du battage pour.

hyperactive adj hyperactif.

hyperlink n hyperlien m.

hypermarket n hypermarché m.

hypertext n hypertexte m.

hyphen n trait m d'union.

hypnosis n hypnose f.

hypocrisy n hypocrisie f. **hypocrite** n hypocrite mf. **hypocritical** adj hypocrite.

hypothesis n (pl **-ses**) hypothèse f.

hysteria n hystérie f. **hysterical** adj hystérique.

hysterics npl crise f de nerfs; **be in ~** rire aux larmes.

Ii

I pron je, j'; (stressed) moi.

ice n glace f; (on road) verglas m. •vt (cake) glacer. •vi **~ (up)** (window) se givrer; (river) geler. **~box** n (US) réfrigérateur m. **~-cream** n

glace f. **~-cube** n glaçon m. **~ hockey** n hockey m sur glace.

Iceland n Islande f. **Icelander** n Islandais/-e m/f. **Icelandic** adj & n islandais (m).

ice: ~ **lolly** n glace f (sur bâtonnet). ~ **rink** n patinoire f. ~ **skate** n patin m à glace.

icicle n stalactite f (de glace).

icing n (sugar) glaçage m.

icy adj (**-ier, -iest**) (hands, wind) glacé; (road) verglacé; (manner, welcome) glacial.

ID n pièce f d'identité; ~ **card** carte f d'identité.

idea n idée f.

ideal adj idéal. • n idéal m.

identical adj identique.

identification n identification f; (papers) pièce f d'identité.

identify vt identifier. • vi ~ **with** s'identifier à.

identikit n ~ **picture** portraitrobot m.

identity n identité f; ~ **theft** vol m d'identité.

ideological adj idéologique.

idiom n (phrase) idiome m; (language) parler m, langue f. **idiomatic** adj idiomatique.

idiosyncrasy n particularité f.

idiot n idiot/-e m/f. **idiotic** adj idiot.

idle adj (lazy) paresseux; (doing nothing) oisif; (boast, threat) vain. • vi (engine) tourner au ralenti. • vt ~ **away** gaspiller.

idol n idole f. **idolize** vt idolâtrer.

idyllic adj idyllique.

i.e. abbr c-à-d, c'est-à-dire.

if conj si.

ignite vt/i (s')enflammer.

ignition n (Auto) allumage m; ~ (**switch**) contact m; ~ **key** clé f de contact.

ignorance n ignorance f. **ignorant** adj ignorant (**of** de). **ignorantly** adv par ignorance.

ignore vt (person) ignorer; (mistake, remark) ne pas relever; (feeling, fact) ne pas tenir compte de.

ill adj malade. • adv mal. • n mal m. ~**-advised** adj malavisé. ~ **at ease** adj mal à l'aise. ~**-bred** adj mal élevé.

illegal adj illégal.

illegible adj illisible.

illegitimate adj illégitime.

ill: ~**-fated** adj malheureux. ~ **feeling** n ressentiment m.

illiterate adj & n analphabète (mf).

illness n maladie f.

ill-treat vt maltraiter.

illuminate vt éclairer; (decorate with lights) illuminer. **illumination** n éclairage m. illumination f.

illusion n illusion f.

illustrate vt illustrer. **illustration** n illustration f. **illustrative** adj qui illustre.

image n image f; (of firm, person) image f de marque. **imagery** n images fpl.

imaginable adj imaginable. **imaginary** adj imaginaire. **imagination** n imagination f. **imaginative** adj plein d'imagination.

imagine vt (s')imaginer (**that** que); ~ **being rich** s'imaginer riche.

imbalance n déséquilibre m.

imitate vt imiter.

immaculate adj impeccable.

immaterial adj sans importance (**to** pour; **that** que).

immature adj (person) immature; (plant) qui n'est pas arrivé à maturité.

immediate adj immédiat.

immediately adv immédiatement. • conj dès que.

immense adj immense. **immensely** adv extrêmement, immensément. **immensity** n immensité f.

immerse vt plonger (**in** dans).

immersion n immersion f;
immersion heater chauffe-eau
m inv électrique.

immigrant n & adj immigré/-e
(m/f); (newly-arrived) immigrant/-e
(m/f). **immigrate** vi immigrer.
immigration n immigration f.

imminent adj imminent.

immobilizer n système m
antidémarrage.

immoral adj immoral.

immortal adj immortel.

immune adj immunisé (**from, to**
contre); (reaction, system)
immunitaire. **immunity** n
immunité f. **immunization** n
immunisation f. **immunize** vt
immuniser.

impact n impact m.

impair vt (performance) affecter;
(ability) affaiblir.

impart vt communiquer,
transmettre.

impartial adj impartial.

impassable adj (barrier)
infranchissable; (road)
impraticable.

impassive adj impassible.

impatience n impatience f.
impatient adj impatient; **get
impatient** s'impatienter.
impatiently adv impatiemment.

impeccable adj impeccable.

impede vt entraver.

impediment n entrave f; **speech**
~ défaut m d'élocution.

impending adj imminent.

imperative adj urgent. •n
impératif m.

imperfect adj incomplet; (faulty)
défectueux. •n (Gram) imparfait
m. **imperfection** n
imperfection f.

imperial adj impérial; (measure)
conforme aux normes
britanniques. **imperialism** n
impérialisme m.

impersonal adj impersonnel.

impersonate vt se faire passer
pour; (mimic) imiter.

impertinent adj impertinent.

impervious adj imperméable
(**to** à).

impetuous adj impétueux.

impetus n impulsion f.

impinge vi ~ **on** affecter;
(encroach) empiéter sur.

implement n instrument m; (tool)
outil m. •vt exécuter, mettre en
application; (software) implanter.
implementation n mise f en
application.

implicit adj (implied) implicite (**in**
dans); (unquestioning) absolu.

imply vt (assume, mean) impliquer;
(insinuate) laisser entendre.

impolite adj impoli.

import[1] /ɪmˈpɔːt/ vt importer.

import[2] /ˈɪmpɔːt/ n (article)
importation f; (meaning)
signification f.

importance n importance f.
important adj important.

impose vt imposer (**on sb** à qn;
on sth sur qch). •vi s'imposer; ~
on sb abuser de la bienveillance
de qn. **imposing** adj imposant.

impossible adj impossible. •n
the ~ l'impossible m.

impotent adj impuissant.

impound vt confisquer, saisir.

impoverish vt appauvrir.

impractical adj peu réaliste.

impregnable adj imprenable.

impress vt impressionner; ~ **sth
on sb** faire bien comprendre
qch à qn. **impression** n
impression f. **impressionable** adj
impressionnable. **impressive** adj
impressionnant.

imprint[1] /ˈɪmprɪnt/ n empreinte f.

imprint[2] /ɪmˈprɪnt/ vt (fix) graver
(**on** dans); (print) imprimer.

imprison vt emprisonner.

improbable adj (not likely) improbable; (incredible) invraisemblable.

improper adj (unseemly) malséant; (dishonest) irrégulier.

improve vt/i (s')améliorer. **improvement** n amélioration f.

improvise vt/i improviser.

impudent adj impudent.

impulse n impulsion f; **on ~** sur un coup de tête. **impulsive** adj impulsif. **impulsively** adv par impulsion.

impurity n impureté f.

in prep (inside, within) dans; (expressing place, position) à, en; (expressing time) en, dans; **~ the box/garden** dans la boîte/le jardin; **~ Paris/school** à Paris/l'école; **~ town** en ville; **~ the country** à la campagne; **~ English** en anglais; **~ India** en Inde; **~ Japan** au Japon; **~ winter** en hiver; **~ spring** au printemps; **~ an hour** (at end of) au bout d'une heure; **~ an hour('s time)** dans une heure; **~ (the space of) an hour** en une heure; **~ doing** en faisant; **~ the evening** le soir; **~ one ~ ten** un sur dix; **~ between** entre les deux; (time) entretemps; **~ a firm voice** d'une voix ferme; **~ blue** en bleu; **~ ink** à l'encre; **~ uniform** en uniforme; **~ a skirt** en jupe; **~ a whisper** en chuchotant; **~ a loud voice** d'une voix forte; **the best ~** le meilleur de; **we are ~ for** on va avoir; **have it ~ for sb** 🖽 avoir qn dans le collimateur. ● adv (inside) dedans; (at home) là, à la maison; (in fashion) à la mode; **come ~** entrer; **run ~** entrer en courant.

inability n incapacité f (**to do** de faire).

inaccessible adj inaccessible.

inaccurate adj inexact.

inactive adj inactif. **inactivity** n inaction f.

inadequate adj insuffisant.

inadvertently adv par mégarde.

inadvisable adj inopportun, à déconseiller.

inane adj idiot, débile.

inanimate adj inanimé.

inappropriate adj inopportun; (term) inapproprié.

inarticulate adj qui a du mal à s'exprimer.

inasmuch as adv dans la mesure où; (because) vu que.

inaugurate vt (open, begin) inaugurer; (person) investir.

inborn adj inné.

inbred adj (inborn) inné.

Inc. abbr (**incorporated**) S.A.

incapable adj incapable (**of doing** de faire).

incapacitate vt immobiliser.

incense[1] /ˈɪnsens/ n encens m.

incense[2] /ɪnˈsens/ vt mettre en fureur.

incentive n motivation f; (payment) prime f.

incessant adj incessant. **incessantly** adv sans cesse.

incest n inceste m. **incestuous** adj incestueux.

inch n pouce m (=2.54 cm.). ● vi **~ towards** se diriger petit à petit vers.

incidence n fréquence f.

incident n incident m. **incidental** adj secondaire. **incidentally** adv à propos; (by chance) par la même occasion.

incinerate vt incinérer. **incinerator** n incinérateur m.

incite vt inciter, pousser.

inclination n (tendency) tendance f; (desire) envie f.

incline[1] /ɪnˈklaɪn/ vt/i (s')incliner;

be ~d to avoir tendance à.

incline² /'ɪŋklaɪn/ n pente f.

include vt comprendre, inclure. **including** prep (y) compris. **inclusion** n inclusion f.

inclusive adj & adv inclus; **~ of delivery** livraison comprise.

income n revenus mpl; **~ tax** impôt m sur le revenu.

incoming adj (tide) montant; (tenant, government) nouveau; (call) qui vient de l'extérieur.

incompatible adj incompatible.

incompetent adj incompétent.

incomplete adj incomplet.

incomprehensible adj incompréhensible.

inconceivable adj inconcevable.

inconclusive adj peu concluant.

incongruous adj déconcertant, surprenant.

inconsiderate adj (person) peu attentif à autrui; (act) maladroit.

inconsistent adj (argument) incohérent; (performance) inégal; (behaviour) changeant; **~ with** en contradiction avec.

inconspicuous adj qui passe inaperçu.

incontinent adj incontinent.

inconvenience n dérangement m; (drawback) inconvénient m. • vt déranger. **inconvenient** adj incommode; **if it's not inconvenient for you** si cela ne vous dérange pas.

incorporate vt incorporer (**into** dans); (contain) comporter.

incorrect adj incorrect.

increase¹ /'ɪŋkriːs/ n augmentation f (**in, of** de). **be on the ~** être en progression.

increase² /ɪn'kriːs/ vt/i augmenter. **increasing** adj croissant. **increasingly** adv de plus en plus.

incredible adj incroyable.

incriminate vt incriminer. **incriminating** adj compromettant.

incubate vt (eggs) couver. **incubation** n incubation f. **incubator** n couveuse f.

incur vt (pt **incurred**) (penalty, anger) encourir; (debts) contracter.

indebted adj **~ to sb** redevable à qn (**for** de); (grateful) reconnaissant à qn.

indecent adj indécent.

indecisive adj indécis; (ending) peu concluant.

indeed adv en effet; (emphatic) vraiment.

indefinite adj vague; (period, delay) illimité. **indefinitely** adv indéfiniment.

indelible adj indélébile.

indemnity n (protection) assurance f; (payment) indemnité f.

indent vt (text) renfoncer. **indentation** n (dent) marque f.

independence n indépendance f. **independent** adj indépendant. **independently** adv de façon indépendante; **independently of** indépendamment de.

index n (pl **~es**) (in book) index m; (in library) catalogue n; (in economy) indice m; **~ card** fiche f; **~ (finger)** index m. • vt classer. **~-linked** adj indexé.

India n Inde f.

Indian n Indien/-ne m/f. • adj indien.

indicate vt indiquer. **indication** n indication f.

indicative adj & n indicatif (m).

indicator n (pointer) aiguille f; (on vehicle) clignotant m; (board) tableau m.

indict vt inculper. **indictment** n accusation f.

indifferent adj indifférent; (not good) médiocre.

indigenous adj indigène.

i

indigestible adj indigeste.
indigestion n indigestion f.

indignant adj indigné.

indirect adj indirect. **indirectly** adv indirectement.

indiscreet adj indiscret. **indiscretion** n indiscrétion f.

indiscriminate adj sans distinction. **indiscriminately** adv sans distinction.

indisputable adj indiscutable.

individual adj individuel; (tuition) particulier. ●n individu m. **individualist** n individualiste mf. **individuality** n individualité f. **individually** adv individuellement.

indoctrinate vt endoctriner. **indoctrination** n endoctrinement m.

indolent adj indolent.

Indonesia n Indonésie f.

indoor adj (clothes) d'intérieur; (pool, court) couvert. **indoors** adv à l'intérieur.

induce vt (influence) persuader; (stronger) inciter (**to do** à faire). **inducement** n (financial) récompense f; (incentive) motivation f.

induction n (Electr) induction f; (inauguration) installation f.

indulge vt (person, whim) céder à; (child) gâter. ●vi ~ **in** se livrer à. **indulgence** n indulgence f; (treat) plaisir m. **indulgent** adj indulgent.

industrial adj industriel; (accident) du travail; ~ **action** grève f; ~ **dispute** conflit m social. **industrialist** n industriel/-le m/f. **industrialized** adj industrialisé.

industrious adj diligent.

industry n industrie f; (zeal) zèle m.

inebriated adj ivre.

inedible adj immangeable.

ineffective adj inefficace.

inefficient adj inefficace; (person) incompétent.

ineligible adj inéligible; **be ~ for** ne pas avoir droit à.

inept adj incompétent; (tactless) maladroit.

inequality n inégalité f.

inescapable adj indéniable.

inevitable adj inévitable.

inexcusable adj inexcusable.

inexhaustible adj inépuisable.

inexpensive adj pas cher.

inexperience n inexpérience f. **inexperienced** adj inexpérimenté.

infallible adj infaillible.

infamous adj (person) tristement célèbre; (deed) infâme.

infancy n petite enfance f; **in its ~** (fig) à ses débuts mpl. **infant** n (baby) bébé m; (at school) enfant m. **infantile** adj infantile.

infatuated adj ~ **with** entiché de. **infatuation** n engouement m.

infect vt contaminer; ~ **sb with sth** transmettre qch à qn. **infection** n infection f. **infectious** adj contagieux.

infer vt (pt **inferred**) (deduce) déduire.

inferior adj inférieur (**to** à). (work, product) de qualité inférieure. ●n inférieur/-e m/f. **inferiority** n infériorité f.

inferno n (hell) enfer m; (blaze) brasier m.

infertile adj infertile.

infest vt infester (**with** de).

infidelity n infidélité f.

infighting n conflits mpl internes.

infinite adj infini. **infinitely** adv infiniment. **infinitive** n infinitif m. **infinity** n infinité f.

infirm adj infirme. **infirmary** n

hôpital m; (sick-bay) infirmerie f.
infirmity n infirmité f.

inflame vt enflammer.
inflammable adj inflammable.
inflammation n inflammation f.
inflammatory adj incendiaire.

inflatable adj gonflable. **inflate**
vt (lit, fig) gonfler.

inflation n inflation f.

inflection n (of word root) flexion f;
(of vowel, voice) inflexion f.

inflict vt infliger (**on** à).

influence n influence f; **under
the ~** (drunk 🔢) éméché. • vt
(person) influencer; (choice) influer
sur. **influential** adj (powerful)
influent; (theory, artist) très suivi.

influenza n grippe f.

influx n afflux m.

inform vt informer (**of** de). **keep
~ed** tenir au courant.

informal adj (simple) simple, sans
façons; (unofficial) officieux;
(colloquial) familier. **informality** n
simplicité f. **informally** adv (dress)
en tenue décontractée; (speak) en
toute simplicité.

informant n indicateur/-trice m/f.

information n renseignements
mpl, informations fpl; **some ~** un
renseignement. **~
superhighway** n autoroute f de
l'information. **~ technology** n
informatique f.

informative adj (book) riche en
renseignements; (visit) instructif.

informer n indicateur/-trice m/f.

infrequent adj rare.

infringe vt (rule) enfreindre;
(rights) ne pas respecter.
infringement n infraction f.

infuriate vt exaspérer.

ingenuity n ingéniosité f.

ingot n lingot m.

ingrained adj (hatred) enraciné;
(dirt) bien incrusté.

ingratiate vt **~ oneself with** se

faire bien voir de.

ingredient n ingrédient m.

inhabit vt habiter. **inhabitable**
adj habitable. **inhabitant** n
habitant/-e m/f.

inhale vt inhaler; (smoke) avaler.
inhaler n inhalateur m.

inherent adj inhérent (**in** à).
inherently adv en soi, par sa
nature.

inherit vt hériter de; **~ sth from
sb** hériter qch de qn.
inheritance n héritage m.

inhibit vt (restrain) inhiber; (prevent)
entraver.

inhospitable adj inhospitalier.

inhuman adj inhumain.

initial n initiale f. • vt (pt
initialled) parapher. • adj initial.

initiate vt (project) mettre en
œuvre; (talks) amorcer; (person)
initier (**into** à). **initiation** n
initiation f; (start) amorce f.

initiative n initiative f.

inject vt injecter (**into** dans). (new
element: fig) insuffler (**into** à).
injection n injection f, piqûre f.

injure vt blesser; (damage) nuire à.
injury n blessure f.

injustice n injustice f.

ink n encre f.

inkling n petite idée f.

inland adj intérieur; **I~ Revenue**
service m des impôts
britannique.

in-laws npl (parents) beaux-parents
mpl; (family) belle-famille f.

inlay[1] /ɪnˈleɪ/ vt (pt **inlaid**)
incruster (**with** de); (on wood)
marqueter.

inlay[2] /ˈɪnleɪ/ n incrustation f; (on
wood) marqueterie f.

inlet n bras m de mer; (Tech)
arrivée f.

inmate n (of asylum) interné/-e m/f;
(of prison) détenu/-e m/f.

innocent adj & n innocent/-e (m/f).

innocuous adj inoffensif.

innovate vi innover.

innuendo n (pl ~es) insinuations fpl; (sexual) allusions fpl grivoises.

innumerable adj innombrable.

inoculate vt vacciner (**against** contre).

inopportune adj inopportun.

in-patient n malade mf hospitalisé/-e.

input n (of energy) alimentation f (**of** en); (contribution) contribution f; (data) données fpl; (computer process) saisie f des données. •vt (data) saisir.

inquest n enquête f.

inquire vi se renseigner (**about, into** sur). •vt demander.

inquiry n demande f de renseignements; (inquest) enquête f.

inquisitive adj curieux.

inroad n **make ~s into** faire une avancée sur.

insane adj fou; (Jur) aliéné. **insanity** n folie f; (Jur) aliénation f mentale.

inscribe vt inscrire. **inscription** n inscription f.

inscrutable adj énigmatique.

insect n insecte m. **insecticide** n insecticide m.

insecure adj (person) qui manque d'assurance; (job) précaire; (lock, property) peu sûr. **insecurity** n (of person) manque m d'assurance; (of situation) insécurité f.

insensitive adj insensible; (remark) indélicat.

inseparable adj inséparable (**from** de).

insert vt insérer (**in** dans).

in-service adj (training) continu.

inshore adj côtier.

inside n intérieur m; **~s** 🄸 entrailles fpl. •adj intérieur. •adv à l'intérieur; **go ~** entrer. •prep à l'intérieur de; (of time) en moins de; **~ out** à l'envers; (thoroughly) à fond.

insight n (perception) perspicacité f; (idea) aperçu m.

insignia npl insigne m.

insignificant adj (cost, difference) négligeable; (person) insignifiant.

insincere adj peu sincère.

insinuate vt insinuer.

insist vt/i insister (**that** pour que). **~ on** exiger; **~ on doing** vouloir à tout prix faire. **insistence** n insistance f. **insistent** adj insistant. **insistently** adv avec insistance.

insofar as adv dans la mesure où.

insolent adj insolent.

insolvent adj insolvable.

insomnia n insomnie f. **insomniac** n insomniaque mf.

inspect vt (school, machinery) inspecter; (tickets) contrôler. **inspection** n inspection f; (of passport, ticket) contrôle m. **inspector** n inspecteur/-trice m/f; (on bus) contrôleur/-euse m/f.

inspiration n inspiration f. **inspire** vt inspirer.

install vt installer.

instalment n (payment) versement m; (of serial) épisode m.

instance n exemple m; (case) cas m; **for ~** par exemple; **in the first ~** en premier lieu.

instant adj immédiat; (food) instantané. •n instant m.

instantaneous adj instantané.
instantly adv immédiatement.

instead adv plutôt; ~ **of doing** au lieu de faire; ~ **of sb** à la place de qn.

instep n cou-de-pied m.

instigate vt (attack) lancer; (proceedings) engager.

instil vt (pt **instilled**) inculquer; (fear) insuffler.

instinct n instinct m. **instinctive** adj instinctif.

institute n institut m. ●vt instituer; (proceedings) engager. **institution** n institution f; (school, hospital) établissement m.

instruct vt (teach) instruire; (order) ordonner; ~ **sb in sth** enseigner qch à qn; ~ **sb to do** donner l'ordre à qn de faire. **instruction** n instruction f. **instructions** npl (for use) mode m d'emploi. **instructive** adj instructif. **instructor** n (skiing, driving) moniteur/-trice m/f.

instrument n instrument m.

instrumental adj instrumental; **be** ~ **in** contribuer à. **instrumentalist** n instrumentaliste mf.

insubordinate adj insubordonné.

insufficient adj insuffisant.

insular adj (Geog) insulaire; (mind, person: fig) borné.

insulate vt (room, wire) isoler.

insulin n insuline f.

insult[1] /ɪnˈsʌlt/ vt insulter.
insult[2] /ˈɪnsʌlt/ n insulte f.

insurance n assurance f (**against** contre).

insure vt assurer; ~ **that** (US) s'assurer que.

intact adj intact.

intake n (of food) consommation f; (School, Univ) admissions fpl.

integral adj intégral (**to** à).

integrate vt/i (s')intégrer (**with** à; **into** dans).

integrity n intégrité f.

intellect n intelligence f.
intellectual adj & n intellectuel/-le (m/f).

intelligence n intelligence f; (Mil) renseignements mpl.
intelligent adj intelligent.
intelligently adv intelligemment.

intend vt (outcome) vouloir; ~ **to do** avoir l'intention de faire. **intended** adj (result) voulu; (visit) projeté.

intense adj intense; (person) sérieux. **intensely** adv (very) extrêmement.

intensify vt/i (s')intensifier.

intensive adj intensif; **in** ~ **care** en réanimation.

intent n intention f. ●adj absorbé; ~ **on doing** résolu à faire.

intention n intention f.
intentional adj intentionnel.

intently adv attentivement.

interact vi (factors) agir l'un sur l'autre; (people) communiquer.
interactive adj (TV, video) interactif.

intercept vt intercepter.

interchange n (road junction) échangeur m; (exchange) échange m.

interchangeable adj interchangeable.

intercom n interphone® m.

interconnected adj (parts) raccordé; (problems) lié.

intercourse n rapports mpl.

interest n intérêt m; ~ **rate** taux m d'intérêt. ●vt intéresser (**in** à). **interested** adj; **be** ~**ed in** s'intéresser à. **interesting** adj intéressant.

interface n interface f.

interfere vi se mêler des affaires

des autres; ~ **in** se mêler de; ~
with (freedom) empiéter sur;
(tamper with) toucher.
interference n ingérence f;
(sound, light waves) brouillage m;
(radio) parasites mpl.
interim n **in the** ~ entre-temps.
● adj (government) provisoire;
(payment) intermédiaire.
interior n intérieur m. ● adj
intérieur.
interjection n interjection f.
interlock vt/i (Tech) (s')emboîter,
(s')enclencher.
interlude n intervalle m; (Theat,
Mus) intermède m.
intermediary adj & n
intermédiaire (mf).
intermediate adj intermédiaire;
(exam, level) moyen.
intermission n (Theat)
entracte m.
intermittent adj intermittent.
intern[1] /ɪnˈtɜːn/ vt interner.
intern[2] /ˈɪntɜːn/ n (US) stagiaire
mf; (Med) interne mf.
internal adj interne; (domestic: Pol)
intérieur; **I**~ **Revenue** (US)
service m des impôts américain.
international adj international.
Internet n Internet m; **on the** ~
sur Internet; ~ **access** accès à
Internet; ~ **service provider**
fournisseur m d'accès Internet.
interpret vt interpréter (**as**
comme). ● vi faire l'interprète.
interpretation n interprétation
f. **interpreter** n interprète mf.
interrelated adj
interdépendant, lié.
interrogate vt interroger.
interrogative adj & n (Ling)
interrogatif (m).
interrupt vt/i interrompre.
interruption n interruption f.
intersect vt/i (lines, roads) (se)
croiser. **intersection** n
intersection f.

interspersed adj parsemé
(**with** de).
intertwine vt/i (s')entrelacer.
interval n intervalle m; (Theat)
entracte m.
intervene vi intervenir; (of time)
s'écouler (**between** entre);
(happen) arriver.
interview n (for job) entretien m;
(by a journalist) interview f. ● vt
(candidate) faire passer un
entretien à; (celebrity) interviewer.
intestine n intestin m.
intimacy n intimité f.
intimate[1] /ˈɪntɪmeɪt/ vt (state)
annoncer; (hint) laisser entendre.
intimate[2] /ˈɪntɪmət/ adj intime.
intimately adv intimement.
intimidate vt intimider.
into prep (put, go, fall) dans; (divide,
translate, change) en; **be** ~ jazz être
fana du jazz 🅸; **8** ~ **24 is 3** 24
divisé par 8 égale 3.
intolerant adj intolérant.
intonation n intonation f.
intoxicate vt enivrer.
intoxicated adj ivre.
intoxication n ivresse f.
intractable adj (person)
intraitable; (problem) rebelle.
intranet n (Comput) intranet m.
intransitive adj intransitif.
intravenous adj (Med)
intraveineux.
intricate adj complexe.
intrigue vt intriguer. ● n intrigue
f. **intriguing** adj fascinant;
(curious) curieux.
intrinsic adj intrinsèque (**to** à).
introduce vt (person, idea,
programme) présenter; (object, law)
introduire (**into** dans).
introduction n introduction f;
(of person) présentation f.
introductory adj (words)
préliminaire.
introvert n introverti/-e m/f.

intrude vi (person) s'imposer (**on sb** à qn), déranger. **intruder** n intrus/-e m/f. **intrusion** n intrusion f.

intuition n intuition f. **intuitive** adj intuitif.

inundate vt inonder (**with** de).

invade vt envahir.

invalid[1] /'ɪnvəli:d/ n malade mf; (disabled) infirme mf.

invalid[2] /ɪn'vælɪd/ adj (passport) pas valable; (claim) sans fondement. **invalidate** vt (argument) infirmer; (claim) annuler.

invaluable adj inestimable.

invariable adj invariable. **invariably** adv invariablement.

invasion n invasion f.

invent vt inventer. **invention** n invention f. **inventive** adj inventif. **inventor** n inventeur/-trice m/f.

inventory n inventaire m.

invert vt (order) intervertir; (image, values) renverser; **~ed commas** guillemets mpl.

invest vt investir; (time, effort) consacrer. •vi faire un investissement; **~ in** (buy) s'acheter.

investigate vt examiner; (crime) enquêter sur. **investigation** n investigation f. **investigator** n (police) enquêteur/-euse m/f.

investment n investissement m; **emotional ~** engagement m personnel. **investor** n investisseur/-euse m/f; (in shares) actionnaire mf.

invigilate vi (exam) surveiller. **invigilator** n surveillant/-e m/f.

invigorate vt revigorer.

invisible adj invisible.

invitation n invitation f. **invite** vt inviter; (ask for) demander. **inviting** adj engageant.

invoice n facture f. •vt facturer.

involuntary adj involontaire.

involve vt impliquer; (person) faire participer (**in** à). **involved** adj (complex) compliqué; (at stake) en jeu; **be ~d in** (work) participer à; (crime) être mêlé à. **involvement** n participation f (**in** à).

inward adj (feeling) intérieur. **inwardly** adv intérieurement. **inwards** adv vers l'intérieur.

iodine n iode m; (antiseptic) teinture f d'iode.

iota n iota m; **not one ~ of** pas un grain de.

IOU abbr (**I owe you**) reconnaissance f de dette.

IQ abbr (**intelligence quotient**) QI m.

Iran n Iran m.

Iraq n Irak m.

irate adj furieux.

IRC abbrev (**Internet Relay Chat**) (Internet) conversation f IRC.

Ireland n Irlande f.

Irish n & adj irlandais (m). **~man** n Irlandais m. **~woman** n Irlandaise f.

iron n fer m; (appliance) fer m (à repasser). •adj (will) de fer; (bar) en fer. •vt repasser.

ironic adj ironique.

iron: ironing-board n planche f à repasser. **~monger** n quincaillier m.

irony n ironie f.

irrational adj irrationnel; (person) pas raisonnable.

irregular adj irrégulier.

irrelevant adj hors de propos.

irreplaceable adj irremplaçable.

irresistible adj irrésistible.

irrespective adj **~ of** sans tenir compte de.

irresponsible adj irresponsable.

irreverent adj irrévérencieux.

irrigate vt irriguer.

irritable adj irritable.

irritate vt irriter. **irritating** adj irritant.

is ▷BE.

ISDN abbr (**integrated services digital network**) RNIS n, réseau m numérique à intégration de services.

Islam n (faith) islam m; (Muslims) Islam m. **Islamic** adj islamique.

island n île f.

isle n île f.

isolate vt isoler. **isolation** n isolement m.

Israel n Israël m.

Israeli n Israélien/-ne m/f. ●adj israélien.

issue n question f; (outcome) résultat m; (of magazine) numéro m; (of stamps) émission f; (offspring) descendance f; **at** ~ en cause. ●vt distribuer; (stamps) émettre; (book) publier; (order) délivrer. ●vi ~ **from** provenir de.

it /ɪt/
●pronoun
····▸ (subject) il, elle; **'where's the book/chair?'— '**~**'s in the kitchen'** 'où est le livre/la chaise?'—'il/elle est dans la cuisine'.
····▸ (object) le, la, l'; ~**'s my**

book and I want ~ c'est mon livre et je le veux; **I liked his shirt, did you notice** ~**?** sa chemise m'a plu, l'as-tu remarquée?; **give** ~ **to me** donne-le-moi.
····▸ (with preposition) **we talked a lot about** ~ on en a beaucoup parlé; **Elliott went to** ~ Elliott y est allé.
····▸ (impersonal) il; ~**'s raining** il pleut; ~ **will snow** il va neiger.

IT abbr ▷INFORMATION TECHNOLOGY.

Italian n (person) Italien/-ne m/f; (Ling) italien m. ●adj italien.

italics npl italique m.

Italy n Italie f.

itch n démangeaison f. ●vi démanger; **my arm** ~**es** j'ai le bras qui me démange; **be** ~**ing to do** mourir d'envie de faire.

item n article m; (on agenda) point m.

itemize vt détailler; ~**d bill** facture f détaillée.

itinerary n itinéraire m.

its det son, sa; pl ses.

it's ▷IT IS, IT HAS.

itself pron lui-même, elle-même; (reflexive) se.

ivory n ivoire m; ~ **tower** tour f d'ivoire.

ivy n lierre m.

Jj

jab vt (pt **jabbed**) ~ **sth into sth** planter qch dans qch. ●n coup m; (injection) piqûre f.

jack n (Auto) cric m; (cards) valet m; (Electr) jack m. ●vt ~ **up** soulever avec un cric.

jacket n veste f, veston m; (of book) jaquette f.

jackknife n couteau m pliant. ●vi (lorry) se mettre en portefeuille.

jackpot n gros lot m; **hit the** ~ gagner le gros lot.

jade n (stone) jade m.

jaded adj (tired) fatigué; (bored) blasé.

jagged adj (rock) déchiqueté; (knife) dentelé.

jail n prison f. ●vt mettre en prison.

jam n confiture f; **(traffic)** ~ embouteillage m. ●vt/i (pt **jammed**) (wedge) (se) coincer; (cram) (s')entasser; (street) encombrer; (radio) brouiller.

Jamaica n Jamaïque f.

jam-packed adj Ⓣ bondé; ~ **with** bourré de.

jangle n tintement m. ●vt/i (faire) tinter.

janitor n (US) gardien m.

January n janvier m.

Japan n Japon m.

Japanese n (person) Japonais/-e m/f; (Ling) japonais m. ●adj japonais.

jar n pot m, bocal m. ●vi (pt **jarred**) rendre un son discordant; (colours) détonner. ●vt ébranler.

jargon n jargon m.

jaundice n jaunisse f.

javelin n javelot m.

jaw n mâchoire f.

jay n geai m.

jazz n jazz m. ●vt ~ **up** (dress) rajeunir; (event) ranimer.

jealous adj jaloux. **jealousy** n jalousie f.

jeans npl jean m.

jeer vt/i ~ **(at)** huer. ●n huée f.

jelly n gelée f. ~**fish** n méduse f.

jeopardize vt (career, chance) compromettre; (lives) mettre en péril.

jerk n secousse f; (fool ⊠) crétin m Ⓣ. ●vt tirer brusquement. ●vi tressaillir. **jerky** adj saccadé.

jersey n (garment) pull-over m; (fabric) jersey m.

jet n (plane, stream) jet m; (mineral) jais m; ~ **lag** décalage m horaire.

jettison vt jeter par-dessus bord; (Aviat) larguer; (fig) rejeter.

jetty n jetée f.

Jew n juif/juive m/f.

jewel n bijou m. **jeweller** n bijoutier/-ière m/f. **jeweller('s)** n (shop) bijouterie f. **jewellery** n bijoux mpl.

Jewish adj juif.

jibe n moquerie f.

jigsaw n puzzle m.

jingle vt/i (faire) tinter. ●n tintement m; (advertising) refrain m publicitaire, sonal m.

jinx n (person) porte-malheur m inv; (curse) sort m.

jitters npl **have the** ~ Ⓣ être nerveux. **jittery** adj nerveux.

job n emploi m; (post) poste m; **out of a** ~ sans emploi; **it is a good** ~ **that** heureusement que; **just the** ~ tout à fait ce qu'il faut. ~ **centre** n bureau m des services nationaux de l'emploi. **jobless** adj sans emploi.

jockey n jockey m.

jog n **go for a** ~ aller faire un jogging. ●vt (pt **jogged**) heurter; (memory) rafraîchir. ●vi faire du jogging. **jogging** n jogging m.

join vt (attach) réunir, joindre; (club) devenir membre de; (company) entrer dans; (army) s'engager dans; (queue) se mettre dans; (in activity) se joindre à qn; (meet) rejoindre qn. ●vi (become member) adhérer; (pieces) se joindre; (roads) se rejoindre. ●n raccord m. ◼ ~ **in** participer; ~ **in sth** participer à qch; ~ **up** (Mil) s'engager; ~ **sth up** relier qch. **joiner** n menuisier/-ière m/f.

joint adj (action) collectif; (measures, venture) commun; (winner) ex aequo inv; (account) joint; ~ **author** coauteur m. ●n (join) joint m; (Anat) articulation f; (Culin) rôti m; **out of** ~ déboîté.

joke n plaisanterie f; (trick) farce f; **it's no** ~ ce n'est pas drôle. ●vi plaisanter. **joker** n blagueur/-euse m/f; (cards) joker m.

jolly adj (**-ier, -iest**) (person) enjoué; (tune) joyeux. ●adv 🆃 drôlement.

jolt vt secouer. ●vi cahoter. ●n secousse f; (shock) choc m.

jostle vt/i (se) bousculer.

jot vt (pt **jotted**) ~ (**down**) noter.

journal n journal m. **journalism** n journalisme m. **journalist** n journaliste mf.

journey n (trip) voyage m; (short or habitual) trajet m. ●vi voyager.

joy n joie f. **joyful** adj joyeux.

joy: ~**riding** n rodéo m à la voiture volée. ~**stick** n (Comput) manette f; (Aviat) manche m à balai.

jubilant adj (person) exultant; (mood) réjoui.

Judaism n judaïsme m.

judge n juge m. ●vt juger; (distance) estimer; **judging by/from** à en juger par. **judg(e)ment** n jugement m.

judicial adj judiciaire. **judiciary** n magistrature f.

judo n judo m.

jug n (glass) carafe f; (pottery) pichet m.

juggernaut n (lorry) poids m lourd.

juggle vt/i jongler (avec). **juggler** n jongleur/-euse m/f.

juice n jus m. **juicy** adj juteux; (details 🆃) croustillant.

jukebox n juke-box m.

July n juillet m.

jumble vt mélanger. ●n (of objects) tas m; (of ideas) fouillis m; ~ **sale** vente f de charité.

jumbo n (also ~ **jet**) gros-porteur m.

jump vt sauter; ~ **the lights** passer au feu rouge; ~ **the**

queue passer devant tout le monde. ●vi sauter; (in surprise) sursauter; (price) monter en flèche; ~ **at** (opportunity) sauter sur. ●n saut m, bond m; (increase) bond m.

jumper n pull(-over) m; (dress: US) robe f chasuble.

jump-leads npl câbles mpl de démarrage.

jumpy adj nerveux.

junction n (of roads) carrefour m; (on motorway) échangeur m.

June n juin m.

jungle n jungle f.

junior adj (young) jeune; (in rank) subalterne; (school) primaire. ●n cadet/-te m/f; (School) élève mf du primaire.

junk n bric-à-brac m inv; (poor quality) camelote f; ~ **food** nourriture f industrielle.

junkie n 🆇 drogué/-e m/f.

junk: ~ **mail** n prospectus mpl. ~**-shop** n boutique f de bric-à-brac.

jurisdiction n compétence f; (Jur) juridiction f.

juror n juré m.

jury n jury m.

just adj (fair) juste. ●adv (immediately, slightly) juste; (simply) tout simplement; (exactly) exactement; **he has/had ~ left** il vient/venait de partir; **have ~ missed** avoir manqué de peu; **I'm ~ leaving** je suis sur le point de partir; **it's ~ a cold** ce n'est qu'un rhume; ~ **as tall/well as** tout aussi grand/bien que; ~ **listen!** écoutez donc!; **it's ~ ridiculous** c'est vraiment ridicule.

justice n justice f; **J~ of the Peace** juge m de paix.

justification n justification f. **justify** vt justifier.

jut vi (pt **jutted**) ~ (**out**)

s'avancer en saillie.

juvenile adj (childish) puéril; (offender) **mineur**; (delinquent) jeune. •n jeune mf; (Jur) mineur/-e m/f.

juxtapose vt juxtaposer.

Kk

kangaroo n kangourou m.

karate n karaté m.

kebab n brochette f.

keel n (of ship) quille f. •vi ~ **over** (boat) chavirer; (person) s'écrouler.

keen adj (interest, wind, feeling) vif; (mind, analysis) pénétrant; (edge, appetite) aiguisé; (eager) enthousiaste; **be ~ on** être passionné de; **be ~ to do** or **on doing** tenir beaucoup à faire. **keenly** adv vivement. **keenness** n enthousiasme m.

keep vt (pt **kept**) garder; (promise, shop, diary) tenir; (family) faire vivre; (animals) élever; (rule) respecter; (celebrate) célébrer; (delay) retenir; ~ **sth clean/ warm** garder qch propre/au chaud; ~ **sb in/out** empêcher qn de sortir/d'entrer; ~ **sb from doing** empêcher qn de faire. •vi (food) se conserver; ~ **(on)** continuer (**doing** à faire). •n pension f; (of castle) donjon m. ∎ ~ **down** rester allongé; ~ **sth down** limiter qch; ~ **your voice down!** baisse la voix!; ~ **to** (road) ne pas s'écarter de; (rules) respecter; ~ **up** (car, runner) suivre; (rain) continuer; ~ **up with sb** (in speed) aller aussi vite que; (class, inflation, fashion, news) suivre.

keeper n gardien/-ne m/f.

keepsake n souvenir m.

kennel n niche f.

kept ▷KEEP.

kerb n bord m du trottoir.

kernel n amande f; ~ **of truth** fond m de vérité.

kettle n bouilloire f.

key n clé f; (of computer, piano) touche f. •adj (industry, figure) clé (inv). •vt ~ **(in)** saisir. ~**board** n clavier m. ~**hole** n trou m de serrure. ~-**pad** n (of telephone) clavier m numérique. ~-**ring** n porte-clés m inv. ~**stroke** n (Comput) frappe f.

khaki adj kaki inv.

kick vt/i donner un coup de pied (à); (horse) botter. •n coup m de pied; (of gun) recul m; **get a ~ out of doing** 🔲 prendre plaisir à faire. ∎ ~ **out** 🔲 virer 🔲.

kick-off n coup m d'envoi.

kid n (goat, leather) chevreau m; (child 🔲) gosse mf 🔲. •vt/i (pt **kidded**) blaguer.

kidnap vt (pt **kidnapped**) enlever. **kidnapping** n enlèvement m.

kidney n rein m; (Culin) rognon m.

kill vt tuer; (rumour: fig) arrêter. •n mise f à mort. **killer** n tueur/-euse m/f. **killing** n meurtre m.

kiln n four m.

kilo n kilo m.

kilobyte n kilo-octet m.

kilogram n kilogramme m.

kilometre, (US) **kilometer** n kilomètre m.

kilowatt n kilowatt m.

kin n parents mpl.

kind n genre m, sorte f; **in** ~ en nature; ~ **of** (somewhat 🛈) assez. ● adj gentil, bon.

kindergarten n jardin m d'enfants.

kindle vt/i (s')allumer.

kindly adj (**-ier, -iest**) (person) gentil; (interest) bienveillant. ● adv avec gentillesse; **would you** ~ **do** auriez-vous l'amabilité de faire.

kindness n bonté f.

king n roi m. **kingdom** n royaume m; (Bot) règne m. ~**fisher** n martin-pêcheur m. ~**-size(d)** adj géant.

kiosk n kiosque m; **telephone** ~ cabine f téléphonique; (Internet) borne f interactive, kiosque m.

kiss n baiser m. ● vt/i (s')embrasser.

kit n (clothing) affaires fpl; (set of tools) trousse f; (for assembly) kit m. ● vt (pt **kitted**) ~ **out** équiper.

kitchen n cuisine f.

kite n (toy) cerf-volant m; (bird) milan m.

kitten n chaton m.

kitty n (fund) cagnotte f.

knack n tour m de main (**of doing** pour faire).

knead vt pétrir.

knee n genou m. ~**cap** n rotule f.

kneel vi (pt **knelt**) ~ (**down**) se mettre à genoux; (in prayer) s'agenouiller.

knew ▷**KNOW**.

knickers npl petite culotte f, slip m.

knife n (pl **knives**) couteau m. ● vt poignarder.

knight n chevalier m; (chess) cavalier m. ● vt anoblir. ~**hood** n titre m de chevalier.

knit vt/i (pt **knitted** or **knit**) tricoter; (bones) (se) souder. **knitting** n tricot m. **knitwear** n tricots mpl.

knob n bouton m.

knock vt/i cogner; (criticize 🛈) critiquer; ~ **sth off/out** faire tomber qch. ● n coup m. ▪ ~ **down** (chair, pedestrian) renverser; (demolish) abattre; (reduce) baisser; ~ **off** (stop work 🛈) arrêter de travailler; ~ **£10 off** faire une réduction de 10 livres; ~ **it off!** 🛈 ça suffit!; ~ **out** assommer; ~ **over** renverser; ~ **up** (meal) préparer en vitesse.

knockout n (boxing) knock-out m.

knot n nœud m. ● vt (pt **knotted**) nouer.

know vt/i (pt **knew**; pp **known**) (answer, reason, language) savoir (**that** que); (person, place, name, rule, situation) connaître; (recognize) reconnaître; ~ **how to do** savoir faire; ~ **about** (event) être au courant de; (subject) s'y connaître en; ~ **of** (from experience) connaître; (from information) avoir entendu parler de. ~**how** n savoir-faire m inv.

knowingly adv (intentionally) délibérément; (meaningfully) d'un air entendu.

knowledge n connaissance f; (learning) connaissances fpl. **knowledgeable** adj savant.

knuckle n jointure f, articulation f.

Koran n Coran m.

Korea n Corée f.

kosher adj casher inv.

k

L1

lab n 🔲 labo m.

label n étiquette f. •vt (pt **labelled**) étiqueter.

laboratory n laboratoire m.

laborious adj laborieux.

labour, (US) **labor** n travail m; (workers) main-d'œuvre f; **in ~** en train d'accoucher. •vi peiner (**to do** à faire). •vt trop insister sur.

Labour n le parti travailliste. •adj travailliste.

laboured adj laborieux.

labourer n ouvrier/-ière m/f; (on farm) ouvrier/-ière m/f agricole.

lace n dentelle f; (of shoe) lacet m. •vt (shoe) lacer; (drink) arroser.

lacerate vt lacérer.

lack n manque m; **for ~ of** faute de. •vt manquer de; **be ~ing** manquer (**in** de).

lad n garçon m, gars m.

ladder n échelle f; (in stocking) maille f filée. •vt/i (stocking) filer.

laden adj chargé (**with** de).

ladle n louche f.

lady n (pl **ladies**) dame f; **ladies and gentlemen** mesdames et messieurs; **young ~** jeune femme or fille f. **~bird** n coccinelle f.

ladylike adj distingué.

lag vi (pt **lagged**) traîner. •vt (pipes) calorifuger. •n (interval) décalage m.

lager n bière f blonde.

lagoon n lagune f.

laid ▷LAY[1]. **~ back** adj décontracté.

lain ▷LIE[2].

lake n lac m.

lamb n agneau m; **leg of ~** gigot m d'agneau.

lame adj boiteux.

lament n lamentation f. •vt/i se lamenter (sur).

laminated adj laminé.

lamp n lampe f. **~post** n réverbère m. **~shade** n abat-jour m inv.

lance vt (Med) inciser.

land n terre f; (plot) terrain m; (country) pays m. •adj terrestre; (policy, reform) agraire. •vt/i débarquer; (aircraft) (se) poser, (faire) atterrir; (fall) tomber; (obtain) décrocher; (a blow) porter; **~ up** se retrouver.

landing n débarquement m; (Aviat) atterrissage m; (top of stairs) palier m. **~-stage** n débarcadère m.

land: ~lady n propriétaire f; (of pub) patronne f. **~lord** n propriétaire m; (of pub) patron m. **~mark** n (point de) repère m. **~mine** n mine f terrestre.

landscape n paysage m. •vt aménager.

landslide n glissement m de terrain; (Pol) raz-de-marée m inv (électoral).

lane n (path, road) chemin m; (strip of road) voie f; (of traffic) file f; (Aviat) couloir m.

language n langue f; (speech, style) langage m. **~ engineering** n ingénierie f des langues. **~ laboratory** n laboratoire m de langue.

lank adj (hair) plat.

lanky adj (-ier, -iest) grand et maigre.

lantern n lanterne f.

lap n genoux mpl; (Sport) tour m (de piste). • vi (pt **lapped**) (waves) clapoter. ■ ~ **up** laper.

lapel n revers m.

lapse vi (decline) se dégrader; (expire) se périmer; ~ **into** retomber dans. • n défaillance f, erreur f; (of time) intervalle m.

laptop n (Comput) portable m.

lard n saindoux m.

larder n garde-manger m inv.

large adj grand, gros; **at** ~ en liberté; **by and** ~ en général. **largely** adv en grande mesure.

lark n (bird) alouette f; (bit of fun 🔢) rigolade f. • vi 🔢 rigoler.

larva n (pl -**vae**) larve f.

laryngitis n laryngite f.

laser n laser m. ~ **printer** n imprimante f laser. ~ **treatment** n (Med) laserothérapie f.

lash vt fouetter. • n coup m de fouet; (eyelash) cil m. ■ ~ **out** (spend) dépenser follement; ~ **out against** attaquer.

lass n jeune fille f.

lasso n lasso m.

last adj dernier; **the** ~ **straw** le comble; **the** ~ **word** le mot de la fin; **on its** ~ **legs** sur le point de rendre l'âme; ~ **night** hier soir. • adv en dernier; (most recently) la dernière fois. • n dernier/-ière m/f; (remainder) reste m; **at (long)** ~ enfin. • vi durer. ~-**ditch** adj ultime. **lasting** adj durable. **lastly** adv en dernier lieu. ~-**minute** adj de dernière minute.

latch n loquet m.

late adj (not on time) en retard; (former) ancien; (hour, fruit) tardif; **the** ~ **Mrs X** feu Mme X. • adv (not early) tard; (not on time) en retard; **in** ~ **July** fin juillet; **of** ~ dernièrement. **lately** adv dernièrement. **latest** adj ▶LATE; (last) dernier.

lathe n tour m.

lather n mousse f. • vt savonner. • vi mousser.

Latin n (Ling) latin m. • adj latin. ~ **America** n Amérique f latine.

latitude n latitude f.

latter adj dernier. • n **the** ~ celui-ci, celle-ci.

Latvia n Lettonie f.

laudable adj louable.

laugh vi rire (**at** de). • n rire m. **laughable** adj ridicule.

laughing stock n risée f.

laughter n (act) rire m; (sound of laughs) rires mpl.

launch vt (rocket) lancer; (boat) mettre à l'eau; ~ **(out) into** se lancer dans. • n lancement m; (boat) vedette f. **launching pad** n aire f de lancement.

launderette n laverie f automatique.

laundry n (place) blanchisserie f; (clothes) linge m.

laurel n laurier m.

lava n lave f.

lavatory n toilettes fpl.

lavender n lavande f.

lavish adj (person) généreux; (lush) somptueux. • vt prodiguer (**on** à). **lavishly** adv luxueusement.

law n loi f; (profession, subject of study) droit m; ~ **and order** l'ordre public. ~-**abiding** adj respectueux des lois. ~-**court** n tribunal m.

lawful adj légal.

lawn n pelouse f, gazon m. ~-**mower** n tondeuse f à gazon.

lawsuit n procès m.

lawyer n avocat m.

lax adj (government) laxiste; (security) relâché.

laxative n laxatif m.

lay¹ /leɪ/ adj (non-clerical) laïque; (worker) non-initié. ●vt (pt **laid**) poser, mettre; (trap) tendre; (table) mettre; (plan) former; (eggs) pondre. ●vi pondre; ~ **waste** ravager. ■ ~ **aside** mettre de côté; ~ **down** (dé)poser; (condition) (im)poser; ~ **off** vt (worker) licencier; vi 🄣 arrêter; ~ **on** (provide) fournir; ~ **out** (design) dessiner; (display) disposer; (money) dépenser.

lay² /leɪ/ ▷LIE².

lay-by n (pl ~**s**) aire f de repos.

layer n couche f.

layman n (pl -**men**) profane m.

layout n disposition f.

laze vi paresser. **laziness** n paresse f. **lazy** adj (-**ier**, -**iest**) paresseux.

lead¹ /liːd/ vt/i (pt **led**) mener; (team) diriger; (life) mener; (induce) amener; ~ **to** conduire à, mener à. ●n avance f; (clue) indice m; (leash) laisse f; (Theat) premier rôle m; (wire) fil m; **in the** ~ en tête. ■ ~ **away** emmener; ~ **up to** (come to) en venir à; (precede) précéder.

lead² /led/ n plomb m; (of pencil) mine f.

leader n chef m; (of country, club) dirigeant/-e m/f; (leading article) éditorial m. **leadership** n direction f.

lead-free adj (petrol) sans plomb.

leading adj principal.

leaf n (pl **leaves**) feuille f; (of table) rallonge f. ●vi ~ **through** feuilleter.

leaflet n prospectus m.

leafy adj feuillu.

league n ligue f; (Sport) championnat m; **in** ~ **with** de mèche avec.

leak n fuite f. ●vi fuir; (news: fig) s'ébruiter. ●vt répandre; (fig) divulguer.

lean¹ /liːn/ adj maigre. ●n (of meat) maigre m.

lean² /liːn/ vt/i (pt **leaned** or **leant**) (rest) (s')appuyer; (slope) pencher. ■ ~ **out** se pencher à l'extérieur; ~ **over** (of person) se pencher.

leaning adj penché. ●n tendance f.

leap vi (pt **leaped** or **leapt**) bondir. ●n bond m. ~ **year** n année f bissextile.

learn vt/i (pt **learned** or **learnt**) apprendre (**to do** à faire). **learned** adj érudit. **learner** n débutant/-e m/f. **learning curve** n courbe f d'apprentissage.

lease n bail m. ●vt louer à bail.

leash n laisse f.

least adj **the** ~ (smallest amount of) le moins de; (slightest) le or la moindre. ●n le moins. ●adv le moins; (with adjective) le or la moins; **at** ~ au moins.

leather n cuir m.

leave vt (pt **left**) laisser; (depart from) quitter; (person) laisser tranquille; **be left (over)** rester. ●n (holiday) congé m; (consent) permission f; **take one's** ~ prendre congé (**of** de); **on** ~ (Mil) en permission. ■ ~ **alone** (thing) ne pas toucher; (person) laisser tranquille; ~ **behind** laisser; ~ **out** omettre.

Lebanon n Liban m.

lecture n cours m, conférence f; (rebuke) réprimande f. ●vt/i faire un cours or une conférence (à); (rebuke) réprimander. **lecturer** n conférencier/-ière m/f; (Univ) enseignant/-e m/f.

led ▷LEAD¹.

ledge n (window) rebord m; (rock) saillie f.

ledger n grand livre m.

leech n sangsue f.

leek n poireau m.

leer vi ~ **(at)** lorgner. ●n regard m sournois.

leeway n (fig) liberté f d'action; (Naut) dérive f.

left ▷LEAVE. ●adj gauche. ●adv à gauche. ●n gauche f. **~-hand** adj à or de gauche. **~-handed** adj gaucher.

left luggage (office) n consigne f.

left-overs npl restes mpl.

left-wing adj de gauche.

leg n jambe f; (of animal) patte f; (of table) pied m; (of chicken) cuisse f; (of lamb) gigot m; (of journey) étape f.

legacy n legs m.

legal adj légal; (affairs) juridique.

legend n légende f.

leggings npl (for woman) caleçon m.

legible adj lisible.

legionnaire n légionnaire m.

legislation n (body of laws) législation f; (law) loi f. **legislature** n corps m législatif.

legitimate adj légitime.

leisure n loisirs mpl; **at one's ~** à tête reposée. ●adj (centre) de loisirs.

leisurely adj lent. ●adv sans se presser.

lemon n citron m.

lemonade n (fizzy) limonade f; (still) citronnade f.

lend vt (pt **lent**) prêter; (credibility) conférer; **~ itself to** se prêter à.

length n longueur f; (in time) durée f; (section) morceau m; **at ~** (at last) enfin; **at (great) ~** longuement.

lengthen vt/i (s')allonger.

lengthways adv dans le sens de la longueur.

lengthy adj long.

lenient adj indulgent.

lens n lentille f; (of spectacles) verre m; (Photo) objectif m.

lent ▷LEND.

Lent n Carême m.

lentil n lentille f.

Leo n Lion m.

leopard n léopard m.

leotard n body m.

leprosy n lèpre f.

lesbian lesbienne f. ●adj lesbien.

less adj (in quantity) moins de (**than** que). ●adv, n & prep moins; **~ than** (with numbers) moins de; **work ~ than** travailler moins que; **ten pounds ~** dix livres de moins; **~ and ~** de moins en moins. **lessen** vt/i diminuer. **lesser** adj moindre.

lesson n leçon f.

let vt (pt **let**; pres p **letting**) laisser; (lease) louer. ●v aux **~ us do, ~'s do** faisons; **~ him do** qu'il fasse; **~ me know the results** informe-moi des résultats. ●n location f. ■ **~ down** baisser; (deflate) dégonfler; (fig) décevoir; **~ go** vt lâcher; vi lâcher prise; **~ sb in/out** laisser or faire entrer/ sortir qn; **~ a dress out** élargir une robe; **~ oneself in for** (task) s'engager à; (trouble) s'attirer; **~ off** (explode, fire) faire éclater or partir; (excuse) dispenser; (not punish) ne pas punir; **~ up** Ⓘ s'arrêter.

let-down n déception f.

lethal adj mortel; (weapon) meurtrier.

letter n lettre f. **~-bomb** n lettre f piégée. **~-box** n boîte f à or aux lettres.

lettering n (letters) caractères mpl.

lettuce n laitue f, salade f.

let-up n répit m.

leukaemia n leucémie f.

level adj plat, uni; (on surface) horizontal; (in height) au même niveau (**with** que); (in score) à égalité. ●n niveau m; **(spirit) ~** niveau m à bulle; **be on the ~**

Ⅰ être franc. ●vt (pt **levelled**) niveler; (aim) diriger. ~ **crossing** n passage m à niveau. ~**-headed** adj équilibré.

lever n levier m. ●vt soulever au moyen d'un levier.

leverage n influence f.

levy vt (tax) prélever. ●n impôt m.

lexicon n lexique m.

liability n responsabilité f; Ⅰ handicap m; **liabilities** (debts) dettes fpl.

liable adj be ~ **to do** avoir tendance à faire, pouvoir faire; ~ **to** (illness) sujet à; (fine) passible de; ~ **for** responsable de.

liaise vi Ⅰ faire la liaison. **liaison** n liaison f.

liar n menteur/-euse m/f.

libel n diffamation f. ●vt (pt **libelled**) diffamer.

liberal adj libéral; (generous) généreux, libéral.

Liberal adj & n (Pol) libéral/-e (m/f).

liberate vt libérer.

liberty n liberté f; **at** ~ **to** libre de; **take liberties** prendre des libertés.

Libra n Balance f.

librarian n bibliothécaire mf.

library n bibliothèque f.

libretto n livret m.

lice ▷**LOUSE**.

licence, (US) **license** n permis m; (for television) redevance f; (Comm) licence f; (Liberty: fig) licence f. ~ **plate** n plaque f minéralogique.

license vt accorder un permis à, autoriser.

lick vt lécher; (defeat Ⅰ) rosser; (fig) **a** ~ **of paint** un petit coup de peinture. ●n coup m de langue.

lid n couvercle m.

lie¹ /laɪ/ n mensonge m. ●vi (pt **lied**; pres p **lying**) (tell lies) mentir.

lie² /laɪ/ vi (pt **lay**; pp **lain**; pres p **lying**) s'allonger; (remain) rester; (be) se trouver, être; (in grave) reposer; **be lying** être allongé. ■ ~ **down** s'allonger; ~ **in** faire la grasse matinée; ~ **low** se cacher.

lieutenant n lieutenant m.

life n (pl **lives**) vie f. ~**belt** n bouée f de sauvetage. ~**boat** n canot m de sauvetage. ~**buoy** n bouée f de sauvetage. ~ **coach** n conseiller/-ère m/f en développement personnel. ~ **cycle** n cycle m de vie. ~**guard** n sauveteur m. ~ **insurance** n assurance-vie f. ~**jacket** n gilet m de sauvetage.

lifeless adj inanimé.

lifelike adj très ressemblant.

life: ~**long** adj de toute la vie. ~ **sentence** n condamnation f à perpétuité. ~**size(d)** adj grandeur nature inv. ~ **story** n vie f. ~**style** n style m de vie. ~ **support machine** n appareil m de respiration artificielle.

lifetime n vie f; **in one's** ~ de son vivant.

lift vt lever; (steal Ⅰ) voler. ●vi (of fog) se lever. ●n (in building) ascenseur m; **give a** ~ **to** emmener (en voiture). ~**-off** n (Aviat) décollage m.

light n lumière f; (lamp) lampe f; (for fire, on vehicle) feu m; (headlight) phare m; **bring to** ~ révéler; **come to** ~ être révélé; **have you got a** ~**?** vous avez du feu? ●adj (not dark) clair; (not heavy) léger. ●vt (pt **lit** or **lighted**) allumer; (room) éclairer; (match) frotter. ■ ~ **up** vi s'allumer; vt (room) éclairer. ~ **bulb** n ampoule f.

lighten vt (give light to) éclairer; (make brighter) éclaircir; (make less heavy) alléger.

lighter n briquet m; (for stove) allume-gaz m inv.

light: ~**-headed** adj (dizzy) qui a un vertige; (frivolous) étourdi. ~**-hearted** adj gai. ~**house** n phare m.

lighting n éclairage m.

lightly adv légèrement.

lightning n éclair m, foudre f. •adj (visit) éclair inv.

lightweight adj léger. •n (boxing) poids m léger.

light year n année f lumière.

like¹ /laɪk/ adj semblable, pareil; **be** ~**-minded** avoir les mêmes sentiments. •prep comme. •conj Ⓘ comme. •n pareil m; **the** ~**s of you** les gens comme vous.

like² /laɪk/ vt aimer (bien); **I should** ~ je voudrais, j'aimerais; **would you** ~? voudriez-vous?, voudrais-tu?; ~**s** goûts mpl. **likeable** adj sympathique.

likelihood n probabilité f.

likely adj (-ier, -iest) probable. •adv probablement; **he is** ~ **to do** il fera probablement; **not** ~! Ⓘ pas question!

likeness n ressemblance f.

likewise adv également.

liking n (for thing) penchant m; (for person) affection f.

lilac n lilas m. •adj lilas inv.

Lilo® n matelas m pneumatique.

lily n lis m, lys m.

limb n membre m.

limber vi ~ **up** faire des exercices d'assouplissement.

limbo n **be in** ~ (forgotten) être tombé dans l'oubli.

lime n (fruit) citron m vert; ~**(-tree)** tilleul m.

limelight n **in the** ~ en vedette.

limestone n calcaire m.

limit n limite f. •vt limiter.

limited company n société f anonyme.

limp vi boiter. •n **have a** ~ boiter. •adj mou.

line n ligne f; (track) voie f; (wrinkle) ride f; (row) rangée f, file f; (of poem) vers m; (rope) corde f; (of goods) gamme f; (queue: US) queue f; **be in** ~ **for** avoir de bonnes chances de; **hold the** ~ ne quittez pas; **in** ~ **with** en accord avec; **stand in** ~ faire la queue. •vt (paper) régler; (streets) border; (garment) doubler; (fill) remplir, garnir. ■~ **up** (s')aligner; (in queue) faire la queue; ~ **sth up** prévoir qch. ~ **dancing** danse f en ligne.

linen n (sheets) linge m; (material) lin m.

liner n paquebot m.

linesman n (football) juge m de touche; (tennis) juge m de ligne.

linger vi s'attarder; (smells) persister.

linguist n linguiste mf.

linguistics n linguistique f.

lining n doublure f.

link n lien m; (of chain) maillon m. •vt relier; (relate) (re)lier; ~ **up** (of roads) se rejoindre. **linkage** n lien m. **links** n inv terrain m de golf. ~**-up** n liaison f.

lino n lino m.

lion n lion m. **lioness** n lionne f.

lip n lèvre f; (edge) rebord m; **pay** ~**-service to** n'approuver que pour la forme. ~**-read** vt/i lire sur les lèvres. ~**salve** n baume m pour les lèvres. ~**stick** n rouge m (à lèvres).

liquid n & adj liquide (m).

liquidation n liquidation f; **go into** ~ déposer son bilan.

liquidize vt passer au mixeur. **liquidizer** n mixeur m.

liquor n alcool m.

liquorice n réglisse f.

lisp n zézaiement m; **with a ~** en zézayant. ● vi zézayer.

list n liste f. ● vt dresser la liste de. ● vi (ship) gîter.

listen vi écouter; **~ to, ~ in (to)** écouter. **listener** n auditeur/-trice m/f.

listless adj apathique.

lit ▷LIGHT.

liter ▷LITRE.

literal adj (meaning) littéral; (translation) mot à mot. **literally** adv littéralement; mot à mot.

literary adj littéraire.

literate adj qui sait lire et écrire.

literature n littérature f; (brochures) documentation f.

Lithuania n Lituanie f.

litigation n litiges mpl.

litre, (US) **liter** n litre m.

litter n (rubbish) détritus mpl, papiers mpl; (animals) portée f. ● vt éparpiller; (make untidy) laisser des détritus dans; **~ed with** jonché de. **~-bin** n poubelle f.

little adj petit; (not much) peu de. ● n peu m; **a ~** un peu (de). ● adv peu.

live¹ /laɪv/ adj vivant; (wire) sous tension; (broadcast) en direct; **be a ~ wire** être très dynamique.

live² /lɪv/ vt/i vivre; (reside) habiter, vivre; **~ it up** mener la belle vie. ■ **~ down** faire oublier; **~ on** (feed oneself on) vivre de; (continue) survivre; **~ up to** se montrer à la hauteur de.

livelihood n moyens mpl d'existence.

lively adj (-ier, -iest) vif, vivant.

liven vt/i **~ up** (s')animer; (cheer up) (s')égayer.

liver n foie m.

livestock n bétail m.

livid adj livide; (angry) furieux.

living adj vivant. ● n vie f; **make a**

~ gagner sa vie; **~ conditions** conditions fpl de vie. **~-room** n salle f de séjour.

lizard n lézard m.

load n charge f; (loaded goods) chargement m, charge f; (weight, strain) poids m; **~s of** 🛈 des tas de 🛈. ● vt charger.

loaf n (pl **loaves**) pain m. ● vi **~ (about)** fainéanter.

loan n prêt m; (money borrowed) emprunt m. ● vt prêter.

loathe vt détester (**doing** faire). **loathing** n dégoût m.

lobby n entrée f, vestibule m; (Pol) lobby m, groupe m de pression. ● vt faire pression sur.

lobster n homard m.

local adj local; (shops) du quartier; **~ government** administration f locale. ● n personne f du coin; (pub 🛈) pub m du coin.

localization n localisation f.

locally adv localement; (nearby) dans les environs.

locate vt (situate) situer; (find) repérer.

location n emplacement m; **on ~** (cinema) en extérieur.

lock n (of door) serrure f; (on canal) écluse f; (of hair) mèche f. ● vt/i fermer à clef; (wheels: Auto) (se) bloquer. ■ **~ in or up** (person) enfermer; **~ out** (by mistake) enfermer dehors.

locker n casier m.

locket n médaillon m.

locksmith n serrurier m.

locum n (doctor) remplaçant/-e m/f.

lodge n (house) pavillon m (de gardien or de chasse); (of porter) loge f. ● vt (accommodate) loger; (money, complaint) déposer. ● vi être logé (**with** chez); (become fixed) se loger. **lodger** n locataire mf, pensionnaire mf. **lodgings** n logement m.

loft n grenier m.

lofty adj (-ier, -iest) (tall, noble) élevé; (haughty) hautain.

log n (of wood) bûche f; ~ (~**book**) (Naut) journal m de bord; (Auto) ≈ carte f grise. ●vt (pt **logged**) noter; (distance) parcourir. ■~ **on** (Comput) se connecter; ~ **off** (Comput) se déconnecter.

logic adj logique. **logical** adj logique.

logistics n logistique f.

loin n (Culin) filet m; ~**s** reins mpl.

loiter vi traîner.

loll vi se prélasser.

lollipop n sucette f.

London n Londres. **Londoner** n Londonien/-ne m/f.

lone adj solitaire.

lonely adj (-ier, -iest) solitaire; (person) seul, solitaire.

long adj long; **how ~ is?** quelle est la longueur de?; (in time) quelle est la durée de?; **how ~?** combien de temps?; **a ~ time** longtemps. ●adv longtemps; **he will not be ~** il n'en a pas pour longtemps; **as** or **so ~ as** pourvu que; **before ~** avant peu; **I no ~er do** je ne fais plus. ●vi avoir bien or très envie (**for, to** de); ~ **for sb** (pine for) se languir de qn. ~**distance** adj (flight) sur long parcours; (phone call) interurbain; (runner) de fond. ~ **face** n grimace f. ~**hand** n écriture f courante.

longing n envie f (**for** de); (nostalgia) nostalgie f (**for** de).

longitude n longitude f.

long: ~ **jump** n saut m en longueur. ~**-range** adj (missile) à longue portée; (forecast) à long terme. ~**-sighted** adj presbyte. ~**-standing** adj de longue date. ~**-term** adj à long terme. ~ **wave** n grandes ondes fpl. ~**-winded** adj verbeux.

loo n 🄸 toilettes fpl.

look vi regarder; (seem) avoir l'air; ~ **like** ressembler à, avoir l'air de. ●n regard m; (appearance) air m, aspect m; (good) ~**s** beauté f. ■~ **after** s'occuper de, soigner; ~ **at** regarder; ~ **back on** repenser à; ~ **down on** mépriser; ~ **for** chercher; ~ **forward to** attendre avec impatience; ~ **in on** passer voir; ~ **into** examiner; ~ **out** faire attention; ~ **out for** (person) guetter; (symptoms) guetter l'apparition de; ~ **round** se retourner; ~ **up** (word) chercher; (visit) passer voir; ~ **up to** respecter.

lookout n (Mil) poste m de guet; (person) guetteur m; **be on the ~ for** rechercher.

loom vi surgir; (war) menacer; (interview) être imminent. ●n métier m à tisser.

loony n & adj 🄸 fou, folle (mf).

loop n boucle f. ●vt boucler. ~**hole** n lacune f.

loose adj (knot) desserré; (page) détaché; (clothes) ample, lâche; (tooth) qui bouge; (lax) relâché; (not packed) en vrac; (inexact) vague; (pej) immoral; **at a ~ end** désœuvré; **come ~** bouger. **loosely** adv sans serrer; (roughly) vaguement. **loosen** vt (slacken) desserrer; (untie) défaire.

loot n butin m. ●vt piller.

lord n seigneur m; (British title) lord m; **the L~** le Seigneur; (good) **L~!** mon Dieu!

lorry n camion m.

lose vt/i (pt **lost**) perdre; **get lost** se perdre. **loser** n perdant/-e m/f.

loss n perte f; **be at a ~** être perplexe; **be at a ~ to** être incapable de; **heat ~** déperdition f de chaleur.

lost ▷LOSE. ●adj perdu. ~ **property** n objets mpl trouvés.

lot n **the ~** (le) tout m; (people) tous mpl, toutes fpl; **a ~ (of), ~s**

(of) ▢ beaucoup (de); **quite a ~ (of)** ▢ pas mal (de); (fate) sort m; (at auction) lot m; (land) lotissement m.

lotion n lotion f.

lottery n loterie f.

loud adj bruyant, fort. •adv fort; **out ~** tout haut. **loudly** adv fort. **~speaker** n haut-parleur m.

lounge vi paresser. •n salon m.

louse n (pl **lice**) pou m.

lousy adj (-ier, -iest) ▢ infect.

lout n rustre m.

lovable adj adorable.

love n amour m; (tennis) zéro m; **in ~** amoureux (**with** de); **make ~** faire l'amour. •vt (person) aimer; (like greatly) aimer (beaucoup) (**to do** faire). **~ affair** n liaison f amoureuse. **~ life** n vie f amoureuse.

lovely adj (-ier, -iest) joli; (delightful) très agréable.

lover n (male) amant m; (female) maîtresse f; (devotee) amateur m (**of** de).

loving adj affectueux.

low adj & adv bas; **~ in sth** à faible teneur en qch. •n (low pressure) dépression f; **reach a (new) ~** atteindre son niveau le plus bas. •vi meugler. **~-calorie** adj basses-calories. **~-cut** adj décolleté.

lower adj & adv ▷LOW. •vt baisser; **~ oneself** s'abaisser.

low: ~-fat adj (diet) sans matières grasses; (cheese) allégé. **~-key** adj modéré; (discreet) discret. **~lands** npl plaine(s) f(pl). **~-lying** adj à faible altitude.

loyal adj loyal (**to** envers).

loyalty n fidélité f. **~ card** n carte f de fidélité.

lozenge n (shape) losange m; (tablet) pastille f.

LP n (disque m) 33 tours m.

Ltd. abbr (**Limited**) SA.

lubricant n lubrifiant m.

lubricate vt lubrifier.

luck n chance f; **bad ~** malchance f; **good ~!** bonne chance!

luckily adv heureusement.

lucky adj (-ier, -iest) qui a de la chance, heureux; (event) heureux; (number) qui porte bonheur; **it's ~ that** heureusement que.

ludicrous adj ridicule.

lug vt (pt **lugged**) traîner.

luggage n bagages mpl. **~-rack** n porte-bagages m inv.

lukewarm adj tiède.

lull vt **he ~ed them into thinking that** il leur a fait croire que. •n accalmie f.

lullaby n berceuse f.

lumber n bois m de charpente. •vt ▢ **~ sb with** (chore) coller à qn ▢. **~jack** n bûcheron m.

luminous adj lumineux.

lump n morceau m; (swelling on body) grosseur f; (in liquid) grumeau m. •vt **~ together** réunir. **~ sum** n somme f globale.

lunacy n folie f.

lunar adj lunaire.

lunatic n fou/folle m/f.

lunch n déjeuner m. •vi déjeuner.

luncheon n déjeuner m. **~ voucher** n chèque-repas m.

lung n poumon m.

lunge vi bondir (**at** sur; **forward** en avant).

lurch n **leave in the ~** planter là, laisser en plan. •vi (person) tituber.

lure vt appâter, attirer. •n (attraction) attrait m, appât m.

lurid adj choquant, affreux; (gaudy) voyant.

lurk vi se cacher; (in ambush) s'embusquer; (prowl) rôder;

(suspicion, danger) menacer.

luscious adj appétissant.

lush adj luxuriant.

lust n luxure f.

Luxemburg n Luxembourg m.

luxurious adj luxueux.

luxury n luxe m. ●adj de luxe.

lying ▷LIE¹, ▷LIE². ●n mensonges mpl.

lyric adj lyrique. **lyrical** adj lyrique. **lyrics** npl paroles fpl.

Mm

MA abbr ▷MASTER OF ARTS.

mac n 🔢 imper m.

machine n machine f. ●vt (sew) coudre à la machine; (Tech) usiner. **~-gun** n mitrailleuse f.

mackerel n inv maquereau m.

mackintosh n imperméable m.

mad adj (**madder, maddest**) fou; (foolish) insensé; (dog) enragé; (angry 🔢) furieux; **be ~ about** se passionner pour; (person) être fou de; **drive sb ~** exaspérer qn; **like ~** comme un fou. **~ cow disease** n maladie f de la vache folle.

madam n madame f; (unmarried) mademoiselle f.

made ▷MAKE.

madly adv (interested, in love) follement; (frantically) comme un fou.

madman n (pl **-men**) fou m.

madness n folie f.

magazine n revue f, magazine m; (of gun) magasin m.

maggot n (in fruit) ver m, (for fishing) asticot m.

magic n magie f. ●adj magique.

magician n magicien/-ne m/f.

magistrate n magistrat m.

magnet n aimant m. **magnetic** adj magnétique.

magnificent adj magnifique.

magnify vt grossir; (sound) amplifier; (fig) exagérer. **magnifying glass** n loupe f.

magpie n pie f.

mahogany n acajou m.

maid n (servant) bonne f; (in hotel) femme f de chambre.

maiden n (old use) jeune fille f. ●adj (aunt) célibataire; (voyage) premier. **~ name** n nom m de jeune fille.

mail n (postal service) poste f; (letters) courrier m; (armour) cotte f de mailles. ●adj (bag, van) postal. ●vt envoyer par la poste. **~ box** n boîte f aux lettres; (Comput) boîte f aux lettres électronique. **mailing list** n liste f d'adresses. **~man** n (pl **-men**) (US) facteur m. **~ order** n vente f par correspondance. **~ shot** n publipostage m.

main adj principal; **a ~ road** une grande route. ●n (water/gas) ~ conduite f d'eau/de gaz; **the ~s** (Electr) le secteur; **in the ~** en général. **~frame** n unité f centrale. **~land** n continent m. **~stream** n tendance f principale, ligne f.

maintain vt (continue, keep, assert) maintenir; (house, machine, family) entretenir; (rights) soutenir.

maintenance n (care) entretien m; (continuation) maintien m; (allowance) pension f alimentaire.

maisonette n duplex m.

maize n maïs m.

majestic adj majestueux.

majesty n majesté f.

major adj majeur. ●n commandant m. ●vi ∼ **in** (Univ, US) se spécialiser en.

majority n majorité f; **the** ∼ **of people** la plupart des gens. ●adj majoritaire.

make vt/i (pt **made**) faire; (manufacture) fabriquer; (friends) se faire; (money) gagner; (decision) prendre; (place, position) arriver à; (cause to be) rendre; ∼ **sb do sth** faire faire qch à qn; (force) obliger qn à faire qch; **be made of** être fait de; ∼ **oneself at home** se mettre à l'aise; ∼ **sb happy** rendre qn heureux; ∼ **it** arriver; (succeed) réussir; **I** ∼ **it two o'clock** j'ai deux heures; **I** ∼ **it 150** d'après moi, ça fait 150; **I cannot** ∼ **anything of it** je n'y comprends rien; **can you** ∼ **Friday?** vendredi, c'est possible?; ∼ **as if to** faire mine de. ●n (brand) marque f. ■ ∼ **do** (manage) se débrouiller (**with** avec); ∼ **for** se diriger vers; (cause) tendre à créer; ∼ **good** vi réussir; vt compenser; (repair) réparer; ∼ **off** filer (**with** avec); ∼ **out** distinguer; (understand) comprendre; (draw up) faire; (assert) prétendre; ∼ **up** vt faire, former; (story) inventer; (deficit) combler; vi se réconcilier; ∼ **up for** compenser; (time) rattraper; ∼ **up one's mind** se décider.

make-believe adj feint, illusoire. ●n fantaisie f.

maker n fabricant m.

makeshift adj improvisé.

make-up n maquillage m; (of object) constitution f; (Psych) caractère m.

malaria n paludisme m.

Malaysia n Malaisie f.

male adj (voice, sex) masculin; (Bot, Tech) mâle. ●n mâle m.

malfunction n mauvais fonctionnement m. ●vi mal fonctionner.

malice n méchanceté f. **malicious** adj méchant.

malignant adj malveillant; (tumour) malin.

mall n **(shopping)** ∼ (in suburbs) centre m commercial; (in town) galerie f marchande.

malnutrition n sousalimentation f.

Malta n Malte f.

mammal n mammifère m.

mammoth n mammouth m. ●adj (task) gigantesque; (organization) géant.

man n (pl **men**) homme m; (in sports team) joueur m; (chess) pièce f; ∼ **to man** d'homme à homme. ●vt (pt **manned**) (desk) tenir; (ship) armer; (guns) servir; (be on duty at) être de service à.

manage vt (project, organization) diriger; (shop, affairs) gérer; (handle) manier; **I could** ∼ **another drink** 🔲 je prendrais bien encore un verre; **can you** ∼ **Friday?** vendredi, c'est possible? ●vi se débrouiller; ∼ **to do** réussir à faire. **manageable** adj (tool, size, person) maniable; (job) faisable.

management n (managers) direction f; (of shop) gestion f.

manager n directeur/-trice m/f; (of shop) gérant/-e m/f; (of actor) impresario m.

mandate n mandat m.

mandatory adj obligatoire.

mane n crinière f.

mango n (pl ∼**es**) mangue f.

manhandle vt maltraiter, malmener.

man: ∼**hole** n regard m. ∼**hood** n âge m d'homme; (quality) virilité f.

maniac n maniaque mf, fou m, folle f.

manicure n manucure f. •vt soigner, manucurer.

manifest adj manifeste. •vt manifester.

manipulate vt (tool, person) manipuler.

mankind n genre m humain.

manly adj viril.

man-made adj (fibre) synthétique; (pond) artificiel; (disaster) d'origine humaine.

manned adj (spacecraft) habité.

manner n manière f; (attitude) attitude f; (kind) sorte f; ~s (social behaviour) manières fpl.

mannerism n particularité f; (quirk) manie f.

manoeuvre n manœuvre f. •vt/i manœuvrer.

manor n manoir m.

manpower n main-d'œuvre f.

mansion n (in countryside) demeure f; (in town) hôtel m particulier.

manslaughter n homicide m involontaire.

mantelpiece n (manteau m de) cheminée.

manual adj (labour) manuel; (typewriter) mécanique. •n (handbook) manuel m.

manufacture vt fabriquer. •n fabrication f.

manure n fumier m.

many adj & n beaucoup (de); **a great** or **good** ~ un grand nombre (de); ~ **a** bien des.

map n carte f; (of streets) plan m. •vt (pt **mapped**) faire la carte de; ~ **out** (route) tracer; (arrange) organiser.

mar vt (pt **marred**) gâcher.

marble n marbre m; (for game) bille f.

March n mars m.

march vi (Mil) marcher (au pas). •vt ~ **off** (lead away) emmener. •n marche f.

margin n marge f.

marginal adj marginal; (increase) léger, faible; (seat: Pol) disputé.

marinate vt faire mariner (**in** dans).

marine adj marin. •n (shipping) marine f; (sailor) fusilier m marin.

marital adj conjugal. ~ **status** n situation f de famille.

mark n (currency) mark m; (stain) tache f; (trace) marque f; (School) note f; (target) but m. •vt marquer; (exam) corriger; ~ **out** délimiter; (person) désigner; ~ **time** marquer le pas.

marker n (pen) marqueur m; (tag) repère m; (School, Univ) examinateur/-trice m/f.

market n marché m; **on the** ~ en vente. •vt (sell) vendre; (launch) commercialiser. ~ **research** n étude f de marché.

marmalade n confiture f d'oranges.

maroon n bordeaux m inv. •adj bordeaux inv.

marooned adj abandonné; (snowbound) bloqué.

marquee n grande tente f; (of circus) chapiteau m; (awning: US) auvent m.

marriage n mariage m (**to** avec).

married adj marié (**to** à); (life) conjugal; **get** ~ se marier (**to** avec).

marrow n (of bone) moelle f; (vegetable) courge f.

marry vt épouser; (give or unite in marriage) marier. •vi se marier.

marsh n marais m.

marshal n maréchal m; (at event) membre m du service d'ordre. •vt (pt **marshalled**) rassembler.

martyr n martyr/-e m/f. •vt martyriser.

marvel n merveille f. •vi (pt **marvelled**) s'émerveiller (**at** de).

marvellous adj merveilleux.

marzipan n pâte f d'amandes.

masculine adj & n masculin (m).

mash n (potatoes 🔢) purée f. •vt écraser. **mashed potatoes** npl purée f (de pommes de terre).

mask n masque m. •vt masquer.

Mason n franc-maçon m.

masonry n maçonnerie f.

mass n (Relig) messe f; masse f; **the ~es** les masses fpl. •vt/i (se) masser.

massacre n massacre m. •vt massacrer.

massage n massage m. •vt masser.

massive adj (large) énorme; (heavy) massif.

mass media n médias mpl.

mass-produce vt fabriquer en série.

mast n (on ship) mât m; (for radio, TV) pylône m.

master n maître m; (in secondary school) professeur m; **M~ of Arts** titulaire d'une maîtrise ès lettres. •vt maîtriser.

masterpiece n chef-d'œuvre m.

mastery n maîtrise f.

mat n (petit) tapis m; (at door) paillasson m.

match n (for lighting fire) allumette f; (Sport) match m; (equal) égal/-e m/f; (marriage) mariage m; (sb to marry) parti m; **be a ~ for** pouvoir tenir tête à. •vt opposer; (go with) aller avec; (cups) assortir; (equal) égaler. •vi (be alike) être

assorti. **matchbox** n boîte f à allumettes.

matching adj assorti.

mate n camarade mf; (of animal) compagnon m, compagne f; (assistant) aide mf; (chess) mat m. •vt/i (s')accoupler (**with** avec).

material n matière f; (fabric) tissu m; (documents, for building) matériau(x) m(pl); **~s** (equipment) matériel m. •adj matériel; (fig) important. **materialistic** adj matérialiste.

materialize vi se matérialiser, se réaliser.

maternal adj maternel.

maternity n maternité f. •adj (clothes) de grossesse. **~ hospital** n maternité f. **~ leave** n congé m maternité.

mathematics n & npl mathématiques fpl.

maths, (US) **math** n maths fpl.

mating n accouplement m.

matrimony n mariage m.

matron n (married, elderly) dame f âgée; (in hospital) infirmière f en chef.

matt adj mat.

matter n (substance) matière f; (affair) affaire f; **as a ~ of fact** en fait; **what is the ~?** qu'est-ce qu'il y a? •vi importer; **it does not ~** ça ne fait rien; **no ~ what happens** quoi qu'il arrive.

mattress n matelas m.

mature adj (psychologically) mûr; (plant) adulte. •vt/i (se) mûrir. **maturity** n maturité f.

mauve adj & n mauve (m).

maverick n non-conformiste mf.

maximize vt porter au maximum.

maximum adj & n (pl **-ima**) maximum (m).

m

may /meɪ/

! past **might**

● auxiliary verb

····▸ (possibility) **they ~ be able to come** ils pourront peut-être venir; **she ~ not have seen him** elle ne l'a peut-être pas vu; **it ~ rain** il risque de pleuvoir; **'will you come?'—'I might'** 'tu viendras?'—'peut-être'.

····▸ (permission) **you ~ leave** vous pouvez partir; **~ I smoke?** puis-je fumer?

····▸ (wish) **~ he be happy** qu'il soit heureux.

May n mai m.

maybe adv peut-être.

mayhem n (havoc) ravages mpl.

mayonnaise n mayonnaise f.

mayor n maire m.

maze n labyrinthe m.

Mb abbr (**megabyte**) (Comput) Mo.

me pron me, m'; (after prep.) moi; (indirect object) me, m'; **he knows ~** il me connaît.

meadow n pré m.

meagre adj maigre.

meal n repas m; (grain) farine f.

mean adj (poor) misérable; (miserly) avare; (unkind) méchant; (average) moyen. ●n milieu m; (average) moyenne f; **in the ~-time** en attendant. ●vt (pt **meant**) vouloir dire, signifier; (involve) entraîner; **I ~ that!** je suis sérieux; **be meant for** être destiné à; **~ to do** avoir l'intention de faire.

meaning n sens m, signification f. **meaningful** adj significatif. **meaningless** adj dénué de sens.

means n moyen(s) m (pl;) **by ~ of sth** au moyen de qch. ●npl (wealth) moyens mpl financiers; **by all ~** certainement; **by no ~** nullement.

meant ▷MEAN.

meantime, meanwhile adv en attendant.

measles n rougeole f.

measure n mesure f; (ruler) règle f. ●vt/i mesurer; **~ up to** être à la hauteur de. **measurement** n mesures fpl.

meat n viande f. **meaty** adj de viande; (fig) substantiel.

mechanic n mécanicien/-ne m/f.

mechanical adj mécanique.

mechanism n mécanisme m.

medal n médaille f.

meddle vi (interfere) se mêler (**in** de); (tinker) toucher (**with** à).

media n ▷MEDIUM. ●npl **the ~** les média mpl; **talk to the ~** parler à la presse.

median adj médian. ●n médiane f.

mediate vi servir d'intermédiaire.

medical adj médical; (student) en médecine. ●n visite f médicale.

medication n médicaments mpl.

medicine n (science) médecine f; (substance) médicament m.

medieval adj médiéval.

mediocre adj médiocre.

meditate vt/i méditer.

Mediterranean adj méditerranéen. ●n **the ~** la Méditerranée f.

medium n (pl **media**) (mid-point) milieu m; (for transmitting data) support m; (pl **mediums**) (person) médium m. ●adj moyen.

medley n mélange m; (Mus) potpourri m.

meet vt (pt **met**) rencontrer; (see again) retrouver; (be introduced to) faire la connaissance de; (face) faire face à; (requirement) satisfaire. ●vi se rencontrer; (see each other again) se retrouver; (in session) se réunir.

meeting n réunion f; (between two people) rencontre f.

megabyte n (Comput) mégaoctet m.

melancholy n mélancolie f. ●adj mélancolique.

mellow adj (fruit) mûr; (sound, colour) moelleux, doux; (person) mûri. ●vt/i (mature) mûrir; (soften) (s')adoucir.

melody n mélodie f.

melon n melon m.

melt vt/i (faire) fondre.

member n membre m. **M~ of Parliament** n député m. **membership** n adhésion f; (members) membres mpl; (fee) cotisation f.

memento n (pl ~es) (object) souvenir m.

memo n note f.

memoir n (record, essay) mémoire m.

memorandum n note f.

memorial n monument m. ●adj commémoratif.

memorize vt apprendre par cœur.

memory n (mind, in computer) mémoire f; (thing remembered) souvenir m; **from ~** de mémoire; **in ~ of** à la mémoire de.

men ▷MAN.

menace n menace f; (nuisance) peste f. ●vt menacer.

mend vt réparer; (darn) raccommoder; **~ one's ways** s'amender. ●n raccommodage m; **on the ~** en voie de guérison.

meningitis n méningite f.

menopause n ménopause f.

mental adj mental; (hospital) psychiatrique.

mentality n mentalité f.

mention vt mentionner; **don't ~ it!** il n'y a pas de quoi!, je vous en prie! ●n mention f.

menu n (food, on computer) menu m; (list) carte f.

MEP abbr (**Member of the European Parliament**) député m au Parlement européen.

mercenary adj & n mercenaire (m.)

merchandise n marchandises fpl.

merchant n marchand m. ●adj (ship, navy) marchand. **~ bank** n banque f de commerce.

merciful adj miséricordieux.

mercury n mercure m.

mercy n pitié f; **at the ~ of** à la merci de.

mere adj simple. **merest** adj moindre.

merge vt/i (se) mêler (**with** à) (companies: Comm) fusionner. **merger** n fusion f.

mermaid n sirène f.

merrily adv (happily) joyeusement; (unconcernedly) avec insouciance.

merry adj (-ier, -iest) gai; **make ~** faire la fête. **~-go-round** n manège m.

mesh n maille f; (fabric) tissu m à mailles; (network) réseau m.

mesmerize vt hypnotiser.

mess n désordre m, gâchis m; (dirt) saleté f; (Mil) mess m; **make a ~ of** gâcher. ●vt **~ up** gâcher.; ●vi **~ about** s'amuser; (dawdle) traîner; **~ with** (tinker with) tripoter.

message n message m.

messenger n messager/-ère m/f.

messy adj (-ier, -iest) en désordre; (dirty) sale.

met ▷MEET.

metal n métal m. ●adj de métal. **metallic** adj métallique; (paint, colour) métallisé.

metallurgy n métallurgie f.

metaphor n métaphore f.

meteor n météore m.

meteorite n météorite m.

meteorology n météorologie f.

meter n compteur m; (US) ▷METRE.

method n méthode f.

methylated spirit(s) n alcool m à brûler.

meticulous adj méticuleux.

metre, (US) **meter** n mètre m.

metric adj métrique.

metropolis n métropole f. **metropolitan** adj métropolitain.

mew n miaulement m. •vi miauler.

mews npl appartements mpl chic aménagés dans d'anciennes écuries.

Mexico n Mexique m.

miaow n & vi ▷MEW.

mice ▷MOUSE.

mickey n **take the ~ out of** 🔲 se moquer de.

microchip n puce f; circuit m intégré.

microlight n ULM m.

microprocessor n microprocesseur m.

microscope n microscope m.

microwave n micro-onde f; ~ **(oven)** four m à micro-ondes. •vt passer au four à micro-ondes.

mid adj **in ~ air** en plein ciel; **in ~ March** à la mi-mars; **~ afternoon** milieu m de l'après-midi; **he's in his ~ twenties** il a environ vingt-cinq ans.

midday n midi m.

middle adj (door, shelf) du milieu; (size) moyen. •n milieu m; **in the ~ of** au milieu de. **~-aged** adj d'âge mûr. **M~ Ages** n Moyen âge m. **~ class** n classe f moyenne. **M~ East** n Moyen-Orient m.

midge n moucheron m.

midget n nain/-e m/f. •adj minuscule.

midnight n minuit f; **it's ~** il est minuit.

midst n **in the ~ of** au beau milieu de; **in our ~** parmi nous.

midsummer n milieu m de l'été; (solstice) solstice m d'été.

midway adv **~ between/along** à mi-chemin entre/le long de.

midwife n (pl **-wives**) sage-femme f.

might¹ /maɪt/ v aux **I ~ have been killed!** j'aurais pu être tué; **you ~ try doing sth** vous pourriez faire qch; ▷MAY.

might² /maɪt/ n puissance f.

mighty adj puissant; (huge 🔲) énorme. •adv 🔲 vachement 🔲.

migrant adj & n (bird) migrateur (m); (worker) migrant/-e (m/f).

migrate vi émigrer. **migration** n migration f.

mild adj (surprise, taste, tobacco, attack) léger; (weather, cheese, soap, person) doux; (case, infection) bénin.

mile n mile m (= 1,6 km); **walk for ~s** marcher pendant des kilomètres; **~s better** 🔲 bien meilleur. **mileage** n nombre m de miles, kilométrage m.

milestone n (lit) borne f; (fig) étape f importante.

military adj militaire.

militia n milice f.

milk n lait m. •vt (cow) traire; (fig) pomper.

milkman n (pl **-men**) laitier m.

milky adj (skin, colour) laiteux; (tea) au lait; **M~ Way** Voie f lactée.

mill n moulin m; (factory) usine f. •vt moudre. •vi **~ around** grouiller.

millennium n (pl **~s**) millénaire m.

millimetre, (US) **millimeter** n millimètre m.

million n million m; **a ~ pounds** un million de livres. **millionaire** n millionnaire m.

millstone n meule f; (fig) boulet m.

mime n (actor) mime mf; (art) mime m. •vt/i mimer.

mimic vt (pt **mimicked**) imiter. •n imitateur/-trice m/f.

mince vt hacher; **not to ~ matters** ne pas mâcher ses mots. •n viande f hachée.

mind n esprit m; (sanity) raison f; (opinion) avis m; **be on sb's ~** préoccuper qn; **bear that in ~** ne l'oubliez pas; **change one's ~** changer d'avis; **make up one's ~** se décider (**to** à). •vt (have charge of) s'occuper de; (heed) faire attention à; **I do not ~ the noise** le bruit ne me dérange pas; **I don't ~** ça m'est égal; **would you ~ checking?** je peux vous demander de vérifier?

minder n (bodyguard) garde m de corps; **(child)** ~ nourrice f.

mindless adj (programme) bête; (work) abrutissant; (vandalism) gratuit.

mine n mine f. •vt extraire; (Mil) miner. •pron le mien, la mienne, les mien(ne)s; **the blue car is ~** la voiture bleue est la mienne or à moi.

minefield n (lit) champ m de mines; (fig) terrain m miné.

miner n mineur m.

mineral n & adj minéral (m); ~ **water** eau f minérale.

minesweeper n (ship) dragueur m de mines.

mingle vt/i (se) mêler (**with** à).

minibus n minibus m.

minicab n taxi m (non agréé).

minimal adj minimal.

minimize vt minimiser; (Comput) réduire.

minimum adj & n (pl-**ima**) minimum (m).

minister n ministre m.

ministerial adj ministériel.
ministry n ministère m.

mink n vison m.

minor adj (change, surgery) mineur; (injury, burn) léger; (road) secondaire. •n (Jur) mineur/-e m/f.

minority n minorité f; **in the ~** en minorité. •adj minoritaire.

mint n (Bot, Culin) menthe f; (sweet) bonbon m à la menthe; (fortune 🔢) fortune f. •vt frapper; **in ~ condition** à l'état neuf.

minus prep moins; (without 🔢) sans. •n moins m; (drawback) inconvénient m.

minute[1] /'mɪnɪt/ n minute f; **~s** (of meeting) compte-rendu m.

minute[2] /maɪˈnjuːt/ adj (object) minuscule; (risk, variation) minime.

miracle n miracle m.

mirror n miroir m, glace f; (Auto) rétroviseur m. •vt refléter.

misbehave vi se conduire mal.

miscalculation n (lit) erreur f de calcul; (fig) mauvais calcul m.

miscarriage n fausse couche f; ~ **of justice** erreur f judiciaire.

miscellaneous adj divers.

mischief n (playfulness) espièglerie f; (by children) bêtises fpl.
mischievous adj espiègle; (malicious) méchant.

misconduct n mauvaise conduite f.

misconstrue vt mal interpréter.

misdemeanour, (US) **misdemeanor** n (Jur) délit m.

miser n avare mf.

miserable adj (sad) malheureux; (wretched) misérable; (performance, result) lamentable.

misery n (unhappiness) souffrance f; (misfortune) misère f; (person 🔢) rabat-joie mf inv.

misfit n inadapté/-e m/f.

misfortune n malheur m.

misgiving n (doubt) doute m; (apprehension) crainte f.

misguided adj (foolish) imprudent; (mistaken) erroné; **be ~** (person) se tromper.

mishap n incident m.

misjudge vt (distance, speed) mal évaluer; (person) mal juger.

mislay vt (pt **mislaid**) égarer.

mislead vt (pt **misled**) tromper. **misleading** adj trompeur.

misplace vt mal ranger; (lose) égarer. **misplaced** adj (fear, criticism) déplacé.

misprint n coquille f, faute f typographique.

misread vt (pt **misread**) mal lire; (intentions) mal interpréter.

miss vt/i manquer; (bus) rater; **he ~es her/Paris** elle/Paris lui manque; **you're ~ing the point** tu n'as rien compris; **~ sth out** omettre qch; **~ out on sth** laisser passer qch. ● n coup m manqué; **it was a near ~** on l'a échappé belle.

Miss n Mademoiselle f; **~ Smith** (written) Mlle Smith.

misshapen adj difforme.

missile n (Mil) missile m; (thrown) projectile m.

mission n mission f. **missionary** n missionnaire mf.

misspell vt (pt **misspelt** or **misspelled**) mal écrire.

mist n brume f; (on window) buée f. ● vt/i (s')embuer.

mistake n erreur f; **by ~** par erreur; **make a ~** faire une erreur. ● vt (pt **mistook**; pp **mistaken**) (meaning) mal interpréter; **~ for** prendre pour.

mistaken adj (enthusiasm) mal placé; **be ~** avoir tort.

mistletoe n gui m.

mistreat vt maltraiter.

mistress n maîtresse f.

misty adj (-ier, -iest) brumeux; (window) embué.

misunderstanding n malentendu m.

misuse vt (word) mal employer; (power) abuser de; (equipment) faire mauvais usage de.

mitten n moufle f.

mix n mélange m. ● vt mélanger; (drink) préparer; (cement) malaxer. ● vi se mélanger; (socially) être sociable; **~ with sb** fréquenter qn. ■ **~ up** (confuse) confondre; (jumble up) mélanger; **get ~ed up in** se trouver mêlé à.

mixed adj (school) mixte; (collection, diet) varié; (nuts, sweets) assorti.

mixer n (Culin) batteur m électrique; **be a good ~** être sociable; **~ tap** mélangeur m.

mixture n mélange m.

mix-up n confusion f (**over** sur).

moan n gémissement m. ● vi gémir; (complain) râler 🗊.

mob n (crowd) foule f; (gang) gang m; **the M~** la Mafia. ● vt (pt **mobbed**) assaillir.

mobile adj mobile; **~ phone** téléphone m portable. ● n mobile m.

mobilize vt/i mobiliser.

mock vt/i se moquer (de). ● adj faux.

mockery n moquerie f; **a ~ of** une parodie de.

mock-up n maquette f.

mode n mode m.

model n (Comput, Auto) modèle m; (scale representation) maquette f; (person showing clothes) mannequin m. ● adj modèle; (car) modèle réduit inv; (railway) miniature. ● vt (pt **modelled**) modeler; (clothes) présenter. ● vi être mannequin; (pose) poser. **modelling** n métier m de mannequin.

modem n modem m.

moderate adj & n modéré/-e (m/f).

moderation n modération f; **in ~** avec modération.

modern adj moderne; **~ languages** langues fpl vivantes. **modernize** vt moderniser.

modest adj modeste. **modesty** n modestie f.

modification n modification f. **modify** vt modifier.

module n module m.

moist adj (soil) humide; (skin, palms) moite; (cake) moelleux. **moisten** vt humecter. **moisture** n humidité f. **moisturizer** n crème f hydratante.

molar n molaire f.

mold (US) ▷MOULD.

mole n grain m de beauté; (animal) taupe f.

molecule n molécule f.

molest vt (pester) importuner; (sexually) agresser sexuellement.

moment n (short time) instant m; (point in time) moment m. **momentarily** adv momentanément; (soon: US) très bientôt. **momentary** adj momentané.

momentum n élan m.

monarch n monarque m. **monarchy** n monarchie f.

Monday n lundi m.

monetary adj monétaire.

money n argent m; **make ~** (person) gagner de l'argent; (business) rapporter de l'argent. **~-box** n tirelire f. **~ order** n mandat m postal.

monitor n dispositif m de surveillance; (Comput) moniteur m. •vt surveiller; (broadcast) être à l'écoute de.

monk n moine m.

monkey n singe m.

monopolize vt monopoliser.

monopoly n monopole m.

monotonous adj monotone. **monotony** n monotonie f.

monsoon n mousson f.

monster n monstre m. **monstrous** adj monstrueux.

month n mois m.

monthly adj mensuel. •adv (pay) au mois; (publish) tous les mois. •n (periodical) mensuel m.

monument n monument m.

moo vi meugler.

mood n humeur f; **in a good/ bad ~** de bonne/mauvaise humeur. **moody** adj d'humeur changeante.

moon n lune f.

moonlight n clair m de lune. **moonlighting** n 𝕀 travail m au noir.

moor n lande f. •vt amarrer.

mop n balai m à franges; **~ of hair** crinière f 𝕀. •vt (pt mopped) **~ (up)** éponger.

moped n vélomoteur m.

moral adj moral. •n morale f; **~s** moralité f.

morale n moral m.

morbid adj morbide.

more adv plus; **~ serious** plus sérieux; **work ~** travailler plus; **sleep ~ and ~** dormir de plus en plus; **once ~** une fois de plus; **I don't go there any ~** je n'y vais plus; **~ or less** plus ou moins. •det plus de; **a little ~ wine** un peu plus de vin; **~ bread** encore un peu de pain; **there's no ~ bread** il n'y a plus de pain; **nothing ~** rien de plus. •pron plus; **cost ~ than** coûter plus cher que; **I need ~ of it** il m'en faut davantage.

moreover adv de plus.

morning n matin m; (whole morning) matinée f.

Morocco n Maroc m.

morsel n morceau m.

mortal adj & n mortel/-le (m/f).

mortgage n emprunt-logement m. • vt hypothéquer.

mortuary n morgue f.

mosaic n mosaïque f.

mosque n mosquée f.

mosquito n (pl ~es) moustique m.

moss n mousse f.

most det (nearly all) la plupart de; ~ **people** la plupart des gens; **the** ~ **votes/money** le plus de voix/d'argent. • n le plus. • pron la plupart; ~ **of us** la plupart d'entre nous; ~ **of the money** la plus grande partie de l'argent. **the** ~ **I can do is ...** tout ce que je peux faire c'est ... • adv **the** ~ **beautiful house/hotel in Oxford** la maison la plus belle/ l'hôtel le plus beau d'Oxford; ~ **interesting** très intéressant; **what I like** ~ **(of all) is** ce que j'aime le plus c'est. **mostly** adv surtout.

moth n papillon m de nuit; (in cloth) mite f.

mother n mère f. • vt (lit) materner; (fig) dorloter. **motherhood** n maternité f. ~**-in-law** n (pl ~**s-in-law**) belle-mère f. ~**-of-pearl** n nacre f. **M~'s Day** n la fête des mères. ~**-to-be** n future maman f. ~ **tongue** n langue f maternelle.

motion n mouvement m; (proposal) motion f; ~ **picture** (US) film m. • vt/i ~ **(to) sb to** faire signe à qn de. **motionless** adj immobile.

motivate vt motiver.

motive n motif m; (Jur) mobile m.

motor n moteur m; (car) auto f. • adj (industry, insurance, vehicle) automobile; (activity, disorder: Med) moteur. ~**bike** n moto f. ~ **car** n auto f. ~**-cyclist** n motocycliste mf. ~ **home** n autocaravane f.

motorist n automobiliste mf.

motorway n autoroute f.

mottled adj tacheté.

motto n (pl ~s) devise f.

mould n (shape) moule m; (fungus) moisissure f. • vt mouler; (influence) former. **moulding** n moulure f. **mouldy** adj moisi.

mount n (hill) mont m; (horse) monture f. • vt (stairs) gravir; (platform, horse, bike) monter sur; (jewel, picture, campaign, exhibit) monter. • vi monter; (number, toll) augmenter; (concern) grandir.

mountain n montagne f; ~ **bike** (vélo) tout terrain m, VTT m. **mountaineer** n alpiniste mf.

mourn vt/i ~ **(for)** pleurer. **mournful** adj mélancolique. **mourning** n deuil m.

mouse n (pl mice) souris f. ~**trap** n souricière f.

mouth n bouche f; (of dog, cat) gueule f; (of cave, tunnel) entrée f. **mouthful** n bouchée f. ~**wash** n eau f dentifrice. ~**watering** adj appétissant.

move vt (object) déplacer; (limb, head) bouger; (emotionally) émouvoir; ~ **house** déménager. • vi bouger; (vehicle) rouler; (change address) déménager; (act) agir. • n mouvement m; (in game) coup m; (player's turn) tour m; (step, act) manœuvre f; (house change) déménagement m; **on the** ~ en mouvement. ■ ~ **back** reculer; ~ **in** emménager; ~ **in with** s'installer avec; ~ **on** (person) se mettre en route; (vehicle) repartir; (time) passer; ~ **sth on** faire avancer qch; ~ **sb on** faire circuler qn; ~ **over** or **up** se pousser.

movement n mouvement m.

movie n (US) film m; **the** ~s le cinéma.

moving adj (vehicle) en marche; (part, target) mobile; (staircase) roulant; (touching) émouvant.

mow vt (pp **mowed** or **mown**)

(lawn) tondre; (hay) couper; ~ **down** faucher. **mower** n tondeuse f.

MP abbr ▸MEMBER OF PARLIAMENT.

Mr n (pl **Messrs**) ~ **Smith** Monsieur or M. Smith; ~ **President** Monsieur le Président.

Mrs n (pl **Mrs**) ~ **Smith** Madame or Mme Smith.

Ms n Mme.

much adv beaucoup; **too** ~ trop; **very** ~ beaucoup; **I like them as** ~ **as you (do)** je les aime autant que toi. • pron beaucoup; **not** ~ pas grand-chose; **he didn't say** ~ il n'a pas dit grand-chose; **I ate so** ~ **that** j'ai tellement mangé que. • det beaucoup de; **too** ~ **money** trop d'argent; **how** ~ **time is left?** combien de temps reste-t-il?

muck n saletés fpl; (manure) fumier m. ■ ~ **about** 🆃 faire l'imbécile. **mucky** adj sale.

mud n boue f.

muddle n (mix-up) malentendu m; (mess) pagaille f 🆃; **get into a** ~ s'embrouiller. ■ ~ **through** se débrouiller; ~ **up** embrouiller.

muddy adj couvert de boue.

muffle vt emmitoufler; (bell) assourdir; (voice) étouffer.

mug n grande tasse f; (for beer) chope f; (face 🆃) gueule f 🆇; (fool 🆃) poire f 🆃. • vt (pt **mugged**) agresser. **mugger** n agresseur m.

muggy adj lourd.

mule n mulet m.

multicoloured adj multicolore.

multiple adj & n multiple (m); ~ **sclerosis** sclérose f en plaques.

multiplication n multiplication f. **multiply** vt/i (se) multiplier.

multistorey adj (car park) à niveaux multiples.

mum n 🆃 maman f.

mumble vt/i marmonner.

mummy n (mother 🆃) maman f; (embalmed body) momie f.

mumps n oreillons mpl.

munch vt mâcher.

mundane adj terre-à-terre.

municipal adj municipal.

mural adj mural. • n peinture f murale.

murder n meurtre m. • vt assassiner. **murderer** n meurtrier m, assassin m.

murky adj (-ier, -iest) (water) glauque; (past) trouble.

murmur n murmure m. • vt/i murmurer.

muscle n muscle m. • vi ~ **in** 🆃 s'imposer (**on** dans).

muscular adj (tissue, disease) musculaire; (body, person) musclé.

museum n musée m.

mushroom n champignon m. • vi (town) proliférer; (demand) s'accroître rapidement.

music n musique f.

musical adj (person) musicien; (voice) mélodieux; (accompaniment) musical; (instrument) de musique. • n comédie f musicale.

musician n musicien/-ne m/f.

Muslim n Musulman/-e m/f. • adj musulman.

mussel n moule f.

must v aux devoir; **you** ~ **go** vous devez partir, il faut que vous partiez; **she** ~ **be consulted** il faut la consulter; **he** ~ **be old** il doit être vieux; **I** ~ **have done it** j'ai dû le faire. • n **be a** ~ 🆃 être indispensable.

mustard n moutarde f.

musty adj (-ier, -iest) (room) qui sent le renfermé; (smell) de moisi.

mute adj & n muet/-te (m/f). **muted** adj (colour) sourd; (response) tiède; (celebration) mitigé.

mutilate vt mutiler.

mutter vt/i marmonner.

mutton n mouton m.

mutual adj (reciprocal) réciproque; (common) commun; (consent) mutuel. **mutually** adv mutuellement.

muzzle n (snout) museau m; (device) muselière f; (of gun) canon m. •vt museler.

my adj mon, ma, pl mes.

myself pron (reflexive) me, m'; **I've hurt ~** je me suis fait mal; (emphatic) moi-même; **I did it ~** je l'ai fait moi-même; (after preposition) moi, moi-même; **I am proud of ~** je suis fier de moi.

mysterious adj mystérieux.

mystery n mystère m.

mystic adj & n mystique (mf). **mystical** adj mystique.

myth n mythe m. **mythical** adj mythique. **mythology** n mythologie f.

Nn

nag vt/i (pt **nagged**) critiquer; (pester) harceler. **nagging** adj persistant.

nail n clou m; (of finger, toe) ongle m; **on the ~** sans tarder, tout de suite. •vt clouer. **~ polish** n vernis m à ongles.

naïve adj naïf.

naked adj nu; **to the ~ eye** à l'œil nu.

name n nom m; (fig) réputation f. •vt nommer; (terms) fixer; **be ~d after** porter le nom de.

namely adv à savoir.

nanny n nurse f.

nap n somme m.

nape n nuque f.

napkin n serviette f.

nappy n couche f.

narcotic adj & n narcotique (m).

narrative n récit m. **narrator** n narrateur/-trice m/f.

narrow adj étroit. •vt/i (se) rétrécir; (limit) (se) limiter; **~ down the choices** limiter les choix. **~-minded** adj à l'esprit étroit; (ideas) étroit.

nasal adj nasal.

nasty adj (-ier, -iest) mauvais, désagréable; (malicious) méchant.

nation n nation f.

national adj national. •n ressortissant/-e m/f.

nationality n nationalité f.

nationalize vt nationaliser.

nationally adv à l'échelle nationale.

native n (local inhabitant) autochtone mf; (non-European) indigène mf; **be a ~ of** être originaire de. •adj indigène; (country) natal; **~ language** langue f maternelle; **~ speaker of French** personne f de langue maternelle française.

natural adj naturel.

naturally adv (normally, of course) naturellement; (by nature) de nature.

nature n nature f.

naughty adj (-ier, -iest) vilain, méchant; (indecent) grivois.

nausea n nausée f. **nauseous** adj (smell) écœurant.

nautical adj nautique.

naval adj (battle) naval; (officer) de marine.

navel n nombril m.

navigate vt (sea) naviguer sur; (ship) piloter. •vi naviguer.
navigation n navigation f.

navy n marine f. •adj ~ **(blue)** bleu inv marine.

near adv près; **draw ~** (s')approcher (**to** de). •prep près de. •adj proche; ~ **to** près de. •vt approcher de.

nearby adj proche. •adv à proximité.

nearly adv presque; **I ~ forgot** j'ai failli oublier; **not ~ as pretty as** loin d'être aussi joli que.

nearness n proximité f.

nearside adj (Auto) du côté du passager.

neat adj soigné, net; (room) bien rangé; (clever) habile; (drink) sec.
neatly adv avec soin; habilement.

necessarily adv nécessairement.

necessary adj nécessaire.

necessitate vt nécessiter.

necessity n nécessité f; (thing) chose f indispensable.

neck n cou m; (of dress) encolure f.
~ **and neck** adj à égalité. ~**lace** n collier m. ~**line** n encolure f.
~**tie** n cravate f.

nectarine n brugnon m, nectarine f.

need n besoin m. •vt avoir besoin de; (demand) demander; **you ~ not come** vous n'êtes pas obligé de venir.

needle n aiguille f.

needless adj inutile.

needlework n couture f; (object) ouvrage m (à l'aiguille).

needy adj (-ier, -iest) nécessiteux. •n **the ~** les indigents.

negative adj négatif. •n (of photograph) négatif m; (word: Gram) négation f; **in the ~** (answer) par la négative; (Gram) à la forme négative.

neglect vt négliger, laisser à l'abandon; ~ **to do** négliger de faire. •n manque m de soins; **(state of)** abandon m.

negligent adj négligent.

negotiate vt/i négocier.
negotiation n négociation f.

neigh n hennissement m. •vi hennir.

neighbour, (US) **neighbor** n voisin/-e m/f. **neighbourhood** n voisinage m, quartier m; **in the ~hood of** aux alentours de.
neighbouring adj voisin.
neighbourly adj amical.

neither adj & pron aucun/-e des deux, ni l'un/-e ni l'autre. •adv ni; ~ **big nor small** ni grand ni petit. •conj (ne) non plus; ~ **am I coming** je ne viendrai pas non plus.

nephew n neveu m.

nerve n nerf m; (courage) courage m; (calm) sang-froid m; (impudence 🛈) culot m; ~**s** (before exams) trac m. ~**-racking** adj éprouvant.

nervous adj nerveux; **be or feel ~** (afraid) avoir peur; ~ **breakdown** dépression f nerveuse. **nervousness** n nervosité f; (fear) crainte f.

nest n nid m. •vi nicher. ~**-egg** n pécule m.

nestle vi se blottir.

net n filet m; (Comput) net m, Internet m. •vt (pt **netted**) prendre au filet. •adj (weight) net.
~**ball** n netball m.

Netherlands n **the ~** les Pays-Bas mpl.

netiquette n nétiquette f.

Netsurfer n Internaute mf.

nettle n ortie f.

network n réseau m.

n

neurotic adj & n névrosé/-e (m/f).

neuter adj & n neutre (m). •vt (castrate) castrer.

neutral adj neutre; **~ (gear)** (Auto) point m mort.

never adv (ne) jamais; **he ~ refuses** il ne refuse jamais; **I ~ saw him** 🇬🇧 je ne l'ai pas vu; **~ again** plus jamais; **~ mind** (don't worry) ne vous en faites pas; (it doesn't matter) peu importe.

nevertheless adv néanmoins, toutefois.

new adj nouveau; (brand-new) neuf. **~-born** adj nouveau-né. **~comer** n nouveau venu m, nouvelle venue f.

newly adv nouvellement. **~-weds** npl jeunes mariés mpl.

news n nouvelle(s) f(pl); (radio, press) informations fpl; (TV) actualités fpl, informations fpl. **~ agency** n agence f de presse. **~agent** n marchand/-e m/f de journaux. **~caster** n présentateur/-trice m/f. **~group** n (Internet) forum m de discussion. **~letter** n bulletin m. **~paper** n journal m.

new year n nouvel an m. **New Year's Day** n le jour de l'an. **New Year's Eve** n la Saint-Sylvestre.

New Zealand n Nouvelle-Zélande f.

next adj prochain; (adjoining) voisin; (following) suivant; **~ to** à côté de; **~ door** à côté (**to** de). •adv la prochaine fois; (afterwards) ensuite. •n suivant/-e m/f; (e-mail) message m suivant. **~-door** adj d'à côté. **~ of kin** n parent m le plus proche.

nib n plume f.

nibble vt/i grignoter.

nice adj agréable, bon; (kind) gentil; (pretty) joli; (respectable) bien inv; (subtle) délicat. **nicely** adv agréablement; gentiment; (well) bien.

nicety n subtilité f.

niche n (recess) niche f; (fig) place f, situation f.

nick n petite entaille f; **be in good/bad ~** 🇬🇧 être en bon/mauvais état. •vt (steal, arrest 🇬🇧) piquer.

nickel n (metal) nickel m; (US) pièce f de cinq cents.

nickname n surnom m. •vt surnommer.

nicotine n nicotine f.

niece n nièce f.

niggling adj (person) tatillon; (detail) insignifiant.

night n nuit f; (evening) soir m. •adj de nuit. **~-cap** n boisson f (avant d'aller se coucher). **~-club** n boîte f de nuit. **~-dress** n chemise f de nuit. **~fall** n tombée f de la nuit. **nightie** n chemise f de nuit.

nightingale n rossignol m.

nightly adj & adv (de) chaque nuit or soir.

night : **~mare** n cauchemar m. **~-time** n nuit f.

nil n (Sport) zéro m. •adj (chances, risk) nul.

nimble adj agile.

nine adj & n neuf (m).

nineteen adj & n dix-neuf (m).

ninety adj & n quatre-vingt-dix (m).

ninth adj & n neuvième (mf).

nip vt/i (pt **nipped**) (pinch) pincer; (rush 🇬🇧) courir; **~ out/back** sortir/rentrer rapidement. •n pincement m.

nipple n mamelon m; (of baby's bottle) tétine f.

nippy adj (-ier, -iest) (air) piquant; (car) rapide.

nitrogen n azote m.

no det aucun/-e; pas de; ~ **man** aucun homme; ~ **money/time** pas d'argent/de temps; ~ **one** ▷NOBODY; ~ **smoking/entry** défense de fumer/d'entrer; ~ **way!** 🆘 pas question! • adv non. • n (pl **noes**) non m inv.

nobility n noblesse f.

noble adj noble. ~**man** n (pl -**men**) noble m.

nobody pron (ne) personne; **he knows** ~ il ne connaît personne. • n nullité f.

nocturnal adj nocturne.

nod vt/i (pt **nodded**) ~ **(one's head)** faire un signe de tête; ~ **off** s'endormir. • n signe m de tête.

noise n bruit m; **make a** ~ faire du bruit. **noisily** adv. bruyamment. **noisy** adj (-**ier**, -**iest**) bruyant.

no man's land n no man's land m.

nominal adj symbolique, nominal; (value) nominal.

nominate vt nommer; (put forward) proposer.

none pron aucun/-e; ~ **of us** aucun/-e de nous; **I have** ~ je n'en ai pas.

non-existent adj inexistant.

nonplussed adj perplexe.

nonsense n absurdités fpl.

non-smoker n non-fumeur m.

non-stick adj antiadhésif.

non-stop adj (train, flight) direct. • adv sans arrêt.

noodles npl nouilles fpl.

noon n midi m.

nor adv ni. • conj (ne) non plus; ~ **shall I come** je ne viendrai pas non plus.

norm n norme f.

normal adj normal.

Norman n Normand/-e m/f. • adj (village) normand; (arch) roman.

north n nord m. • adj nord inv, du nord. • adv vers le nord.

North America n Amérique f du Nord.

north-east n nord-est m.

northerly adj (wind, area) du nord; (point) au nord.

northern adj (accent) du nord; (coast) nord. **northerner** n habitant/-e m/f du nord.

northward adj (side) nord inv; (journey) vers le nord.

north-west n nord-ouest m.

Norway n Norvège f.

Norwegian n (person) Norvégien/-ne m/f; (language) norvégien m. • adj norvégien.

nose n nez m. • vi ~ **about** fouiner.

nosedive n piqué m. • vi descendre en piqué.

nostalgia n nostalgie f.

nostril n narine f; (of horse) naseau m.

nosy adj (-**ier**, -**iest**) 🆘 curieux, indiscret.

not adv (ne) pas; **I do** ~ **know** je ne sais pas; ~ **at all** pas du tout; ~ **yet** pas encore; **I suppose** ~ je suppose que non.

notably adv notamment.

notch n entaille f. • vt ~ **up** (score) marquer.

note n note f; (banknote) billet m; (short letter) mot m. • vt noter; (notice) remarquer. ~**book** n carnet m.

nothing pron (ne) rien; **he eats** ~ il ne mange rien; ~ **else** rien d'autre; ~ **much** pas grand-

chose; **for** ~ pour rien, gratis.
● **rien** n m; (person) nullité f. ● adv
nullement.

notice n avis m, annonce f; (poster)
affiche f; **(advance)** ~ préavis m;
at short ~ dans des délais très
brefs; **give in one's** ~ donner
sa démission; **take** ~ faire
attention (**of** à). ● vt remarquer,
observer. **noticeable** adj visible.
~**-board** n tableau m d'affichage.

notify vt (inform) aviser; (make
known) notifier.

notion n idée f, notion f.

notorious adj (criminal) notoire;
(district) mal famé; (case)
tristement célèbre.

notwithstanding prep malgré.
● adv néanmoins.

nought n zéro m.

noun n nom m.

nourish vt nourrir. **nourishing**
adj nourrissant. **nourishment** n
nourriture f.

novel n roman m. ● adj nouveau.
novelist n romancier/-ière m/f.
novelty n nouveauté f.

November n novembre m.

now adv maintenant. ● conj
maintenant que; **just** ~
maintenant; (a moment ago) tout à
l'heure; ~ **and again,** ~ **and
then** de temps à autre.

nowadays adv de nos jours.

nowhere adv nulle part.

nozzle n (tip) embout m; (of hose)
jet m.

nuclear adj nucléaire.

nude adj nu. ● n nu/-e m/f; **in the**
~ tout nu.

nudge vt pousser du coude. ● n
coup m de coude.

nudism n nudisme m. **nudity** n
nudité f.

nuisance n (thing, event) ennui m;
(person) peste f; **be a** ~ être
embêtant.

null adj nul.

numb adj engourdi (**with** par).
● vt engourdir.

number n nombre m; (of ticket,
house, page) numéro m; (written
figure) chiffre m; **a** ~ **of people**
plusieurs personnes. ● vt
numéroter; (count, include)
compter. ~**-plate** n plaque f
d'immatriculation.

numeral n chiffre m.

numerate adj qui sait compter.

numerical adj numérique.

numerous adj nombreux.

nun n religieuse f.

nurse n infirmier/-ière m/f; (nanny)
nurse f. ● vt soigner; (hope)
nourrir.

nursery n (room) chambre f
d'enfants; (for plants) pépinière f;
(day) ~ crèche f. ~ **rhyme** n
comptine f. ~ **school** n (école)
maternelle f.

nursing home n maison f de
retraite.

nut n (walnut, Brazil nut) noix f;
(hazelnut) noisette f; (peanut)
cacahuète f; (Tech) écrou m.
~**crackers** npl casse-noix m inv.

nutmeg n muscade f.

nutrient n substance f nutritive.

nutritious adj nutritif.

nuts adj (crazy 🆃) cinglé.

nutshell n coquille f de noix; **in a**
~ en un mot.

nylon n nylon m.

Oo

oak n chêne m.

OAP abbr (**old-age pensioner**) retraité/-e m/f.

oar n rame f.

oath n (promise) serment m; (swearword) juron m.

oats npl avoine f.

obedience n obéissance f. **obedient** adj obéissant. **obediently** adv docilement.

obese adj obèse.

obey vt/i obéir (à).

object[1] /ˈɒbdʒɪkt/ n (thing) objet m; (aim) but m; (Gram) complément m d'objet; **money is no ~** l'argent n'est pas un problème.

object[2] /əbˈdʒekt/ vi protester. •vt **~ that** objecter que; **~ to** (behaviour) désapprouver; (plan) protester contre. **objection** n objection f; (drawback) inconvénient m.

objective adj & n objectif (m)

obligation n devoir m.

obligatory adj obligatoire.

oblige vt obliger (**to do** à faire).

oblivion n oubli m. **oblivious** adj inconscient (**to, of** de).

oblong adj oblong. •n rectangle m.

obnoxious adj odieux.

oboe n hautbois m.

obscene adj obscène.

obscure adj obscur. •vt obscurcir; (conceal) cacher.

observance n (of law) respect m; (of sabbath) observance f. **observant** adj observateur.

observation n observation f.

observe vt observer; (remark) remarquer.

obsess vt obséder. **obsession** n obsession f. **obsessive** adj (person) maniaque; (thought) obsédant; (illness) obsessionnel.

obsolete adj dépassé.

obstacle n obstacle m.

obstinate adj obstiné.

obstruct vt (road) bloquer; (view) cacher; (progress) gêner. **obstruction** n (act) obstruction f; (thing) obstacle m; (in traffic) encombrement m.

obtain vt obtenir. •vi avoir cours. **obtainable** adj disponible.

obvious adj évident. **obviously** adv manifestement.

occasion n occasion f; (big event) événement m; **on ~** à l'occasion.

occasional adj (event) qui a lieu de temps en temps; **the ~ letter** une lettre de temps en temps. **occasionally** adv de temps à autre.

occupation n (activity) occupation f; (job) métier m, profession f. **occupational therapy** n ergothérapie f.

occupier n occupant/-e m/f.

occupy vi occuper.

occur vi (pt **occurred**) se produire; (arise) se présenter; **~ to sb** venir à l'esprit de qn.

occurrence n (event) fait m; (instance) occurrence f.

ocean n océan m.

Oceania n Océanie f.

o'clock adv **it is six ~** il est six heures; **at one ~** à une heure.

October n octobre m.

O

octopus n (pl ~es) pieuvre f.

odd adj bizarre; (number) impair; (left over) qui reste; (sock) dépareillé; **write the ~ article** écrire un article de temps en temps; **~ jobs** menus travaux mpl; **twenty ~** vingt et quelques. **oddity** n bizarrerie f.

odds npl chances fpl; (in betting) cote f (**on** de); **at ~** en désaccord; **it makes no ~** ça ne fait rien; **~ and ends** des petites choses.

odour, (US) **odor** n odeur f. **odourless** adj inodore.

of /ɒv/

▶ For expressions such as **of course, consist of** ▷**course, consist.**

● preposition
⋯▸ de; **a photo ~ the dog** une photo du chien; **the king ~ the beasts** le roi des animaux; **(made) ~ gold** en or; **it's kind ~ you** c'est très gentil de votre part; **some ~ us** quelques-uns d'entre nous; **~ it/them** en; **have you heard ~ it?** est-ce que tu en as entendu parler?

off adv **be ~** partir, s'en aller; **I'm ~** je m'en vais; **30 metres ~** à 30 mètres; **a month ~** dans un mois. ● adj (gas, water) coupé; (tap) fermé; (light, TV) éteint; (party, match) annulé; (bad) (food) avarié; (milk) tourné; **Friday is my day ~** je ne travaille pas le vendredi; **25% ~** 25% de remise. ● prep **3 metres ~ the ground** 3 mètres (au-dessus) du sol; **just ~ the kitchen** juste à côté de la cuisine; **that is ~ the point** là n'est pas la question.

offal n abats mpl.

offence n (Jur) infraction f; **give ~ to** offenser; **take ~** s'offenser (**at** de).

offend vt offenser; **be ~ed** s'offenser (**at** de). ● vi (Jur) commettre une infraction. **offender** n délinquant/-e m/f.

offensive adj (remark) injurieux; (language) grossier; (smell) repoussant; (weapon) offensif. ● n offensive f.

offer vt (pt **offered**) offrir. ● n offre f; **on ~** en promotion.

offhand adj désinvolte. ● adv à l'improviste.

office n bureau m; (duty) fonction f; **in ~** au pouvoir. ● adj de bureau.

officer n (army) officier m; (**police**) **~** policier m; (**government**) **~** fonctionnaire m.

official adj officiel. ● n (civil servant) fonctionnaire m/f; (of party, union) officiel/-le m/f; (of police, customs) agent m.

off: **~licence** n magasin m de vins et spiritueux. **~line** adj autonome; (switched off) déconnecté; (Comput) hors connexion. **~load** vt (stock) écouler; (Comput) décharger. **~peak** adj (call) au tarif réduit; (travel) en période creuse. **~putting** adj rebutant. **~set** vt (pt **-set**; pres p **-setting**) compenser. **~shore** adj (out to sea) au large, en mer; (towards the sea) de terre; **an ~ breeze** une brise de terre. ● adv (funds) hors-lieu inv. **~side** adj (Sport) hors jeu inv; (Auto) du côté du conducteur. **~spring** n progéniture f.

often adv souvent; **how ~ do you meet?** vous vous voyez tous les combien?; **every so ~** de temps en temps.

oil n (for lubrication, cooking) huile f; (for fuel) pétrole m; (for heating) mazout m. ● vt huiler. **~ field** n gisement m pétrolifère. **~painting** n peinture f à l'huile. **~skins** npl ciré m. **~tanker** n pétrolier m.

oily adj graisseux.

ointment n pommade f.

OK, okay adj d'accord; **is it ~ if...?** ça va si...?; **feel ~** aller bien.

old adj vieux; (person) vieux, âgé; (former) ancien; **how ~ is he?** quel âge a-t-il?; **he is eight years ~** il a huit ans; **~er, ~est** aîné. **~ age** n vieillesse f. **~-age pensioner** n retraité/-e m/f. **~-fashioned** adj démodé; (person) vieux jeu inv. **~ man** n vieillard m, vieux m. **~ woman** n vieille f.

olive n olive f; **~ oil** huile f d'olive. ● adj olive inv.

Olympic adj olympique. **~ Games** npl Jeux mpl olympiques.

omelette n omelette f.

omen n augure m.

ominous adj (presence, cloud) menaçant; (sign) de mauvais augure.

omission n omission f. **omit** vt (pt **omitted**) omettre.

on prep sur; **~ the table** sur la table; **put the key ~ it** mets la clé dessus; **~ 22 March** le 22 mars; **~ Monday** lundi; **~ TV** à la télé; **~ video** en vidéo; **be ~ steroids** prendre des stéroïdes; **~ arriving** en arrivant. ● adj (TV, oven, light) allumé; (dishwasher, radio) en marche; (tap) ouvert; (lid) mis; **the match is still ~** le match aura lieu quand même; **the news is ~ in 10 minutes** les informations sont dans 10 minutes. ● adv **have sth ~** porter qch; **20 years ~** 20 ans plus tard; **from that day ~** à partir de ce jour-là; **further ~** plus loin; **~ and off** (occasionally) de temps en temps; **go ~ and ~** (person) parler pendant des heures.

once adv une fois; (formerly) autrefois. ● conj une fois que; **all at ~** tout d'un coup.

oncoming adj (vehicle) qui approche.

one det & n un/-e (m/f). ● pron un/-e m/f; (impersonal) on; **~ (and only)** seul (et unique); **a big ~** un grand/une grande; **this/that ~** celui-ci/-là, celle-ci/-là; **~ another** l'un/-e l'autre. **~-off** adj 🔢 unique, exceptionnel. **~self** pron soi-même; (reflexive) se. **~-way** adj (street) à sens unique; (ticket) simple.

ongoing adj (process) continu; **be ~** être en cours.

onion n oignon m.

on-line adj & adv en ligne.

onlooker n spectateur/-trice m/f.

only adj seul; **~ son** fils unique. ● adv seulement; **he is ~ six** il n'a que six ans.

onset n début m.

onward(s) adv en avant.

open adj ouvert; (view) dégagé; (free to all) public; (undisguised) manifeste; (question) en attente; **in the ~ air** en plein air. ● vt/i (door) (s')ouvrir; (shop, play) ouvrir; **~ out** or **up** (s')ouvrir. **~-ended** adj (stay) de durée indéterminée; (debate, question) ouvert. **~-heart** adj (surgery) à cœur ouvert.

opening n (of book) début m; (of exhibition, shop) ouverture f; (of film) première f; (in market) débouché m; (job) poste m (disponible).

open: ~-minded adj **be ~-minded** avoir l'esprit ouvert. **~-plan** adj paysagé.

opera n opéra m.

operate vt/i opérer; (Tech) (faire) fonctionner; **~ on** (Med) opérer; **operating theatre** n salle f d'opération.

operation n opération f; **have an ~** se faire opérer; **in ~** (plan) en vigueur; (mine) en service.

operative n employé/-e m/f. ● adj (law) en vigueur.

operator n opérateur/-trice m/f; (telephonist) standardiste mf.

opinion n opinion f, avis m.

O

opinionated adj qui a des avis sur tout.

opponent n adversaire mf.

opportunity n occasion f (**to do** de faire).

oppose vt s'opposer à; **as ~d to** par opposition à. **opposing** adj opposé.

opposite adj (direction, side) opposé; (building) d'en face. ●n contraire m. ●adv en face. ●prep ~ (**to**) en face de.

opposition n opposition f.

oppress vt opprimer. **oppressive** adj (cruel) oppressif; (heat) oppressant.

opt vi ~ **for** opter pour; ~ **out** refuser de participer (**of** à); ~ **to do** choisir de faire.

optical adj optique. ~ **illusion** n illusion f d'optique. ~ **scanner** n lecteur m optique.

optician n opticien/-ne m/f.

optimism n optimisme m. **optimist** n optimiste mf. **optimistic** adj optimiste.

option n option f; (choice) choix m.

optional adj facultatif; ~ **extras** accessoires mpl en option.

or conj ou; (with negative) ni.

oral n & adj oral (m).

orange n (fruit) orange f; (colour) orange m. ●adj (colour) orange inv.

orbit n orbite f. ●vt décrire une orbite autour de.

orchard n verger m.

orchestra n orchestre m.

orchid n orchidée f.

ordeal n épreuve f.

order n ordre m; (Comm) commande f; **in ~** (tidy) en ordre; (document) en règle; **in ~ that** pour que; **in ~ to** pour. ●vt ordonner; (goods) commander; ~ **sb to** ordonner à qn de.

orderly adj (tidy) ordonné; (not unruly) discipliné. ●n (Mil) planton m; (Med) aide-soignant/-e m/f.

ordinary adj (usual) ordinaire; (average) moyen.

ore n minerai m.

organ n organe m; (Mus) orgue m.

organic adj organique; (produce) biologique.

organization n organisation f.

organize vt organiser.

organizer n organisateur/-trice m/f; **electronic ~** agenda m électronique.

orgasm n orgasme m.

Orient n **the ~** l'Orient m. **oriental** adj oriental.

origin n origine f.

original adj original; (inhabitant) premier; (member) originaire. **originality** n originalité f. **originally** adv (at the outset) à l'origine.

originate vi (plan) prendre naissance; ~ **from** provenir de; (person) venir de. ●vt être l'auteur de. **originator** n (of idea) auteur m; (of invention) créateur/-trice m/f.

ornament n (decoration) ornement m; (object) objet m décoratif.

orphan n orphelin/-e m/f. ●vt rendre orphelin. **orphanage** n orphelinat m.

orthopaedic adj orthopédique.

ostentatious adj tape-à-l'œil inv.

osteopath n ostéopathe mf.

ostrich n autruche f.

other adj autre; **the ~ one** l'autre mf. ●n & pron autre mf; (**some**) ~**s** d'autres. ●adv ~ **than** (apart from) à part; (otherwise than) autrement que. **otherwise** adv autrement.

otter n loutre f.

ouch interj aïe!

ought v aux devoir; **you ~ to stay** vous devriez rester; **he ~**

to succeed il devrait réussir; **I ~ to have done it** j'aurais dû le faire.

ounce n once f (= 28.35 g).

our adj notre, pl nos.

ours poss le or la nôtre, les nôtres.

ourselves pron (reflexive) nous; (emphatic) nous-mêmes; (after preposition) **for ~** pour nous, pour nous-mêmes.

out adv dehors; **he's ~** il est sorti; **further ~** plus loin; **be ~** (book) être publié; (light) être éteint; (sun) briller; (flower) être épanoui; (tide) être bas; (player) être éliminé; **~ of** hors de; **go/walk/ get ~ of** sortir de; **~ of pity** par pitié; **made ~ of** fait de; **5 ~ of 6** 5 sur 6. **~break** n (of war) déclenchement m; (of violence, boils) éruption f. **~burst** n explosion f. **~cast** n paria m. **~class** vt surclasser. **~come** n résultat m. **~cry** n tollé m. **~dated** adj démodé. **~door** adj (activity) de plein air; (pool) en plein air. **~doors** adv dehors.

outer adj extérieur; **~ space** espace m extra-atmosphérique.

outfit n (clothes) tenue f.

outgoing adj (minister, tenant) sortant; (sociable) ouvert. **outgoings** npl dépenses fpl.

outgrow vt (pt **-grew**; pp **-grown**) (clothes) devenir trop grand pour; (habit) dépasser.

outing n sortie f.

outlaw n hors-la-loi m inv. ●vt déclarer illégal.

outlet n (for water, gas) tuyau m de sortie; (for goods) débouché m; (for feelings) exutoire m.

outline n contour m; (of plan) grandes lignes fpl; (of essay) plan m. ●vt tracer le contour de; (summarize) exposer brièvement.

out: ~live vt survivre à. **~look** n perspective f. **~number** vt surpasser en nombre. **~ of date** adj démodé; (expired) périmé. **~**

of hand adj incontrôlable. **~ of order** adj en panne. **~ of work** adj sans travail. **~patient** n malade mf externe.

output n rendement m; (Comput) sortie f. ●vt/i (Comput) sortir.

outrage n (anger) indignation f; (atrocity) attentat m; (scandal) outrage m. ●vt (morals) outrager; (person) scandaliser. **outrageous** adj scandaleux.

outright adv (completely) catégoriquement; (killed) sur le coup. ●adj (majority) absolu; (ban) catégorique; (hostility) pur et simple.

outset n début m.

outside n extérieur m. ●adv dehors. ●prep en dehors de; (in front of) devant. ●adj extérieur. **outsider** n étranger/-ère m/f; (Sport) outsider m.

out: ~ skirts npl périphérie f. **~spoken** adj franc. **~standing** adj exceptionnel; (not settled) en suspens.

outward adj & adv vers l'extérieur; (sign) extérieur. (journey) d'aller. **outwards** adv vers l'extérieur.

oval n & adj ovale (m).

ovary n ovaire m.

oven n four m.

over prep (across) par-dessus; (above) au-dessus de; (covering) sur; (more than) plus de; **it's ~ the road** c'est de l'autre côté de la rue; **~ here/there** par ici/là; **children ~ six** les enfants de plus de six ans; **~ the weekend** pendant le weekend; **all ~ the house** partout dans la maison. ●adj, adv (term) terminé; (war) fini; **get sth ~ with** en finir avec qch; **ask sb ~** inviter qn; **~ and ~ (again)** à plusieurs reprises; **five times ~** cinq fois de suite.

overall adj global, d'ensemble;

(length) total. ● adv globalement.

overalls npl combinaison f.

over: ~**board** adv par-dessus bord. ~**cast** adj couvert. ~**charge** vt faire payer trop cher à. ~**coat** n pardessus m.

overcome vt (pt **-came**. pp **-come**) (enemy) vaincre; (difficulty, fear) surmonter; ~ **by** accablé de.

overcrowded adj bondé; (country) surpeuplé.

overdo vt (pt **-did**; pp **-done**) (Culin) trop cuire; ~ **it** (overwork) en faire trop.

over: ~ **dose** n surdose f, overdose f. ~ **draft** n découvert m. ~ **draw** vt (pt **-drew**. pp **-drawn**) faire un découvert sur. ~ **due** adj en retard; (bill) impayé.

overflow[1] /əʊvəˈfləʊ/ vi déborder.

overflow[2] /ˈəʊvəfləʊ/ n (outlet) trop-plein m. ~ **car park** n parking m de délestage.

overhaul vt réviser.

overhead[1] /əʊvəˈhed/ adv au-dessus; (in sky) dans le ciel.

overhead[2] /ˈəʊvəhed/ adj aérien; ~ **projector** rétroprojecteur m. **overheads** npl frais mpl généraux.

over: ~**hear** vt (pt **-heard**) entendre par hasard. ~**lap** vt/i (pt **-lapped**) (se) chevaucher. ~**leaf** adv au verso. ~**load** vt surcharger. ~**look** vt (window) donner sur; (miss) ne pas voir.

overnight[1] /əʊvəˈnaɪt/ adv dans la nuit; (instantly: fig) du jour au lendemain.

overnight[2] /ˈəʊvənaɪt/ adj (train) de nuit; (stay) d'une nuit; (fig) soudain.

over: ~**power** vt (thief) maîtriser; (army) vaincre; (fig) accabler.

~**-priced** adj trop cher. ~**rate** vt surestimer. ~**react** vi réagir de façon excessive. ~**riding** adj (consideration) numéro un; (importance) primordial. ~**rule** vt (decision) annuler.

overrun vt (pt **-ran**; pp **-run**; pres p **-running**) (country) envahir; (budget) dépasser. ● vi (meeting) durer plus longtemps que prévu.

overseas adj étranger. ● adv outre-mer, à l'étranger.

over: ~**see** vt (pt **-saw**. pp **-seen**) surveiller. ~**sight** n omission f. ~**sleep** vi (pt **-slept**) se réveiller trop tard. ~**take** vt/i (pt **-took**; pp **-taken**) dépasser; (fig) frapper. ~**time** n heures fpl supplémentaires. ~**turn** vt/i (se) renverser. ~**weight** adj trop gros.

overwhelm vt (enemy) écraser; (shame) accabler. **overwhelmed** adj (with offers, calls) submergé (**with, by** de); (with shame, work) accablé; (by sight) ébloui. **overwhelming** adj (heat, grief) accablant; (defeat, victory) écrasant; (urge) irrésistible.

overwork vt/i (se) surmener. ● n surmenage m.

owe vt devoir. **owing** adj dû; **owing to** en raison de.

owl n hibou m.

own adj propre. ● pron **my** ~ le mien, la mienne; **a house of one's** ~ sa propre maison; **on one's** ~ tout seul. ● vt posséder; ~ **up (to)** Ⅰ avouer. **owner** n propriétaire mf. **ownership** n propriété f; (of land) possession f.

oxygen n oxygène m.

oyster n huître f.

ozone n ozone m; ~ **layer** couche f d'ozone.

Pp

PA abbr ▷ PERSONAL ASSISTANT.

pace n pas m; (speed) allure f; **keep
~ with** suivre. ●vt (room)
arpenter. ●vi ~ **(up and down)**
faire les cent pas.

Pacific n ~ **(Ocean)** océan m
Pacifique.

pack n paquet m; (Mil) sac m; (of
hounds) meute f; (of thieves) bande
f; (of lies) tissu m. ●vt (into case)
mettre dans une valise; (into box,
crate) emballer; (for sale)
conditionner; (crowd) remplir
complètement; ~ **one's
suitcase** faire sa valise. ●vi faire
ses valises. ~ **into** (cram)
s'entasser dans; ~ **off** expédier;
send ~ing envoyer promener.

package n paquet m; (Comput)
progiciel m; ~ **deal** offre f
globale; ~ **holiday** voyage m
organisé. ●vt empaqueter.

packed adj (crowded) bondé; ~
lunch repas m froid.

packet n paquet m.

packing n (action, material)
emballage m.

pad n (of paper) bloc m; (to protect)
protection f; (for ink) tampon m;
(launch) ~ rampe f de
lancement. ●vt (pt **padded**)
rembourrer; (text: fig) délayer. ●vi
(pt **padded**) (walk) marcher à pas
feutrés. **padding** n
rembourrage m.

paddle n pagaie f. ●vt ~ **a canoe**
pagayer. ●vi patauger.

padlock n cadenas m. ●vt
cadenasser.

paediatrician n pédiatre mf.

pagan adj & n païen/-ne (m/f).

page n (of book) page f. ●vt (on

pager) rechercher; (over speaker)
faire appeler. **pager** n
radiomessageur m.

pain n douleur f; ~s efforts mpl;
be in ~ souffrir; **take ~s to** se
donner du mal pour. ●vt (grieve)
peiner. **painful** adj douloureux;
(laborious) pénible. ~-**killer** n
analgésique m. **painless** adj
(operation) indolore; (death) sans
souffrance; (trouble-free) sans
peine. **painstaking** adj
minutieux.

paint n peinture f; ~s (in tube, box)
couleurs fpl. ●vt/i peindre. ~
brush n pinceau m. **painter** n
peintre m. **painting** n peinture f.
~**work** n peintures fpl.

pair n paire f; (of people) couple m;
a ~ of trousers un pantalon.
●vi ~ **off** former un couple.

pajamas npl (US) ▷ PYJAMAS.

Pakistan n Pakistan m.

palace n palais m.

palatable adj (food) savoureux;
(solution) acceptable. **palate** n
palais m.

pale adj pâle. ●vi pâlir.

Palestine n Palestine f.

pallid adj pâle.

palm n (of hand) paume f; (tree)
palmier m; (symbol) palme f. ■ ~
off 🔟 ~ **sth off as** faire passer
qch pour; ~ **sth off on sb**
refiler qch à qn 🔟.

palpitate vi palpiter.

paltry adj (-ier, -iest) dérisoire,
piètre.

pamper vt choyer.

pamphlet n brochure f.

pan n casserole f; (for frying) poêle f.

p

pancake n crêpe f.

pandemonium n tohu-bohu m.

pander vi ~ **to** (person, taste) flatter bassement.

pane n carreau m, vitre f.

panel n (of door) panneau m; (of experts, judges) commission f; (on discussion programme) invités mpl; (**instrument**) ~ tableau m de bord.

pang n serrement m au cœur; ~**s of conscience** remords mpl.

panic n panique f. ● vt/i (pt **panicked**) (s')affoler. ~**-stricken** adj pris de panique, affolé.

pansy n (Bot) pensée f.

pant vi haleter.

panther n panthère f.

pantomime n (show) spectacle m de Noël; (mime) mime m.

pantry n garde-manger m inv.

pants npl (underwear) slip m; (trousers: US) pantalon m.

paper n papier m; (newspaper) journal m; (exam) épreuve f; (essay) exposé m; (wallpaper) papier m peint; (identity) ~**s** papiers mpl (d'identité); **on** ~ par écrit. ● vt (room) tapisser. ~**back** n livre m de poche. ~**-clip** n trombone m. ~ **feed tray** n (Comput) bac m d'alimentation en papier. ~ **work** n (work) travail m administratif; (documentation) documents mpl.

par n (golf) par m. **be below** ~ ne pas être en forme; **on a** ~ **with** (performance) comparable à; (person) l'égal de.

parachute n parachute m. ● vi descendre en parachute.

parade n (procession) parade f; (Mil) défilé m. ● vi défiler. ● vt faire étalage de.

paradise n paradis m.

paradox n paradoxe m.

paraffin n pétrole m (lampant); (wax) paraffine f.

paragliding n parapente m.

paragon n modèle m.

paragraph n paragraphe m.

parallel adj parallèle. ● n parallèle m; (maths) parallèle f.

Paralympics npl **the** ~ les jeux paralympiques.

paralyse vt paralyser. **paralysis** n paralysie f.

paramedic n auxiliaire mf médical/-e.

parameter n paramètre m.

paramount adj suprême.

paranoia n paranoïa f. **paranoid** adj paranoïaque; (Psych) paranoïde.

paraphernalia n attirail m.

parasol n ombrelle f; (on table, at beach) parasol m.

paratrooper n (Mil) parachutiste mf.

parcel n paquet m.

parchment n parchemin m.

pardon n pardon m; (Jur) grâce f; **I beg your** ~ je vous demande pardon. ● vt (pt **pardoned**) pardonner (**sb for sth** qch à qn); (Jur) gracier.

parent n parent m.

parenthesis n (pl **-theses**) parenthèse f.

parenthood n (fatherhood) paternité f; (motherhood) maternité f.

Paris n Paris.

parish n (Relig) paroisse f; (municipal) commune f.

park n parc m. ● vt/i (se) garer; (remain parked) stationner. ~ **and ride** n parc m relais.

parking n stationnement m; **no** ~ stationnement interdit. ~ **lot** n (US) parking m. ~ **meter** n parcmètre m. ~ **ticket** n (fine) contravention f, PV m⬛.

parliament n parlement m. **parliamentary** adj parlementaire.

parlour, (US) **parlor** n salon m.

parody n parodie f. ●vt parodier.

parole n **on ~** en liberté conditionnelle.

parrot n perroquet m.

parry vt (Sport) parer; (question) éluder. ●n parade f.

parsley n persil m.

parsnip n panais m.

part n partie f; (of serial) épisode m; (of machine) pièce f; (Theat) rôle m; (side in dispute) parti m; **in ~** en partie; **on the ~ of** de la part de; **take ~ in** participer à. ●adj partiel. ●adv en partie. ●vt/i (separate) (se) séparer; **~ with** se séparer de.

part-exchange n reprise f; **take sth in ~** reprendre qch.

partial adj partiel; (biased) partial; **be ~ to** avoir un faible pour.

participant n participant/-e m/f. **participate** vi participer (**in** à). **participation** n participation f.

participle n participe m.

particular n détail m; **~s** détails mpl; **in ~** en particulier. ●adj particulier; (fussy) difficile; (careful) méticuleux; **that ~ man** cet homme-là. **particularly** adv particulièrement.

parting n séparation f; (in hair) raie f. ●adj d'adieu.

partition n (of room) cloison f; (Pol) partition f. ●vt (room) cloisonner; (country) partager.

partly adv en partie.

partner n (professional) associé/-e m/f; (economic, sporting) partenaire mf; (spouse) époux/-se m/f; (unmarried) partenaire mf. **partnership** n association f.

partridge n perdrix f.

part-time adj & adv à temps partiel.

party n fête f; (formal) réception f; (group) groupe m; (Pol) parti m; (Jur) partie f.

pass vt/i (pt passed) passer; (overtake) dépasser; (in exam) réussir; (approve) (candidate) admettre; (invoice) approuver; (remark) faire; (judgement) prononcer; (law, bill) adopter; **~ (by)** (building) passer devant; (person) croiser. ●n (permit) laisser-passer m inv; (ticket) carte f d'abonnement; (Geog) col m; (Sport) passe f; **~ (mark)** (in exam) moyenne f. ■ **~ away** mourir; **~ out** (faint) s'évanouir; **~ sth out** distribuer qch; **~ over** (overlook) délaisser; **~ up** (forego) laisser passer.

passage n (way through, text) passage m; (voyage) traversée f; (corridor) couloir m.

passenger n (in car, plane, ship) passager/-ère m/f; (in train, bus, tube) voyageur/-euse m/f.

passer-by n (pl passers-by) passant/-e m/f.

passing adj (motorist) qui passe; (whim) passager; (reference) en passant.

passion n passion f. **passionate** adj passionné.

passive adj passif.

passport n passeport m.

password n mot m de passe.

past adj (times, problems) passé; (president) ancien; **the ~ months** ces derniers mois. ●n passé m. ●prep (beyond) après; **walk/go ~ sth** passer devant qch; **10 ~ 6** six heures dix; **it's ~ 11** il est 11 heures passées. ●adv **go/walk ~** passer.

pasta n pâtes fpl (alimentaires).

paste n (glue) colle f; (dough) pâte f; (of fish, meat) pâté m; (jewellery) strass m. ●vt coller.

pasteurize vt pasteuriser.

pastime n passe-temps m inv.

pastry n (dough) pâte f; (tart) pâtisserie f.

pat vt (pt **patted**) tapoter. ●n petite tape f.

patch n pièce f; (over eye) bandeau m; (spot) tache f; (of snow, ice) plaque f; (of vegetables) carré m; **bad ~** période f difficile. ■ **~ up** (trousers) rapiécer; (quarrel) résoudre.

patent adj (obvious) manifeste; (patented) breveté; **~ leather** cuir m verni. ●n brevet m. ●vt faire breveter.

path n sentier m, chemin m; (in park) allée f; (of rocket) trajectoire f.

pathetic adj misérable; (bad 🎵) lamentable.

patience n patience f.

patient adj patient. ●n patient/-e m/f. **patiently** adv patiemment.

patriotic adj patriotique; (person) patriote.

patrol n patrouille f; **~ car** voiture f de police. ●vt/i patrouiller (dans).

patron n (of the arts) mécène m; (customer) client/-e m/f. **patronage** n clientèle f; (support) patronage m. **patronize** vt (person) traiter avec condescendance; (establishment) fréquenter.

patter n (of steps) bruit m; (of rain) crépitement m.

pattern n motif m, dessin m; (for sewing) patron m; (for knitting) modèle m.

paunch n ventre m.

pause n pause f. ●vi faire une pause; (hesitate) hésiter.

pave vt paver; **~ the way** ouvrir la voie (**for** à).

pavement n trottoir m; (US) chaussée f.

paving stone n pavé m.

paw n patte f. ●vt (animal) donner des coups de patte à; (touch 🎵) peloter 🎵.

pawn n pion m. ●vt mettre en gage. **~broker** n prêteur/-euse m/f sur gages. **~-shop** n mont-de-piété m.

pay vt (pt **paid**) payer; (interest) rapporter; (compliment, attention) faire; (visit, homage) rendre. ●vi payer; (business) rapporter; **~ for sth** payer qch. ●n salaire m; **~ rise** augmentation f (de salaire). ■ **~ back** rembourser; **~ in** déposer; **~ off** (loan) rembourser; (worker) congédier; (succeed) être payant; **~ out** payer, débourser.

payable adj payable; **~ to** (cheque) à l'ordre de.

payment n paiement m; (regular) versement m; (reward) récompense f.

payroll n fichier m des salaires; **be on the ~ of** être employé par.

PC abbr ▶ PERSONAL COMPUTER.

PDA abbr (**personal digital assistant**) assistant m personnel numérique.

PE abbr (**physical education**) éducation f physique, EPS f.

pea n (petit) pois m.

peace n paix f; **~ of mind** tranquillité f d'esprit. **peaceful** adj (tranquil) paisible; (peaceable) pacifique.

peach n pêche f.

peacock n paon m.

peak n (of mountain) pic m; (of cap) visière f; (maximum) maximum m; (on graph) sommet m; (of career) apogée m; (of fitness) meilleur m; **~ hours** heures fpl de pointe.

peal n (of bells) carillon m; (of laughter) éclat m.

peanut n cacahuète f; **~s** (money) 🎵 clopinettes fpl 🎵.

pear n poire f.

pearl n perle f.

peasant n paysan/-ne m/f.

peat n tourbe f.

pebble n caillou m; (on beach) galet m.

peck vt/i (food) picorer; (attack) donner des coups de bec (à). ●n coup m de bec; **a ~ on the cheek** une bise.

peckish adj be ~ 🄸 avoir faim.

peculiar adj (odd) bizarre; (special) particulier (**to** à). **peculiarity** n bizarrerie f.

pedal n pédale f. ●vi pédaler.

pedantic adj pédant.

peddle vt colporter; (drugs) faire du trafic de.

pedestrian n piéton m. ●adj (precinct, street) piétonnier; (fig) prosaïque; ~ **crossing** passage m pour piétons.

pedigree n (of animal) pedigree m; (of person) ascendance f. ●adj (dog) de pure race.

pee vi 🄸 faire pipi 🄸.

peek vi & n ▶PEEP.

peel n (on fruit) peau m; (removed) épluchures fpl. ●vt (fruit, vegetables) éplucher; (prawn) décortiquer. ●vi (of skin) peler; (of paint) s'écailler.

peep vi jeter un coup d'œil (furtif) (**at** à). ●n coup m d'œil (furtif). ~**hole** n judas m.

peer vi ~ (**at**) regarder fixement. ●n (equal, noble) pair m. **peerage** n pairie f.

peg n (for clothes) pince f à linge; (to hang coats) patère f; (for tent) piquet m. ●vt (pt **pegged**) (clothes) accrocher avec des pinces; (prices) indexer.

pejorative adj péjoratif.

pelican n pélican m; ~ **crossing** passage m pour piétons.

pellet n (round mass) boulette f; (for gun) plomb m.

pelt vt bombarder (**with** de). ●n (skin) peau f.

pelvis n (Anat) bassin m.

pen n stylo m; (for sheep) enclos m; (for baby, cattle) parc m.

penal adj pénal. **penalize** vt pénaliser.

penalty n peine f; (fine) amende f; (in football) penalty m.

penance n pénitence f.

pence ▶PENNY.

pencil n crayon m. ●vt (pt **pencilled**) crayonner; ~ **in** noter provisoirement. ~**-sharpener** n taille-crayons m inv.

pending adj (matter) en souffrance; (Jur) en instance. ●prep (until) en attendant.

penetrate vt pénétrer; (silence, defences) percer; (organization) infiltrer. ●vi pénétrer. **penetrating** adj pénétrant.

pen-friend n correspondant/-e m/f.

penguin n manchot m, pingouin m.

pen: ~**knife** n (pl -**knives**) canif m. ~**name** n pseudonyme m.

penniless adj sans le sou.

penny n (pl **pennies** or **pence**) (unit of currency) penny m; (small amount) centime m.

pension n (from state) pension f; (from employer) retraite f; ~ **scheme** plan m de retraite. ●vt ~ **off** mettre à la retraite. **pensioner** n retraité/-e m/f.

pensive adj songeur.

penthouse n appartement m de luxe (au dernier étage).

penultimate adj avant-dernier.

people npl gens mpl, personnes fpl; **English ~** les Anglais mpl; ~ **say** on dit. ●n peuple m. ●vt peupler. ~ **carrier** n monospace m.

pepper n poivre m; (vegetable) poivron m. ●vt (Culin) poivrer.

peppermint n (plant) menthe f

poivrée; (sweet) bonbon m à la menthe.

per prep par; ~ **annum** par an; ~ **cent** pour cent; ~ **kilo** le kilo; **ten km ~ hour** dix km à l'heure.

percentage n pourcentage m.

perception n perception f. **perceptive** adj perspicace.

perch n (of bird) perchoir m. •vi (se) percher.

perennial adj perpétuel; (plant) vivace.

perfect[1] /pəˈfekt/ vt perfectionner.

perfect[2] /ˈpɜːfɪkt/ adj parfait. •n (Ling) parfait m.

perfection n perfection f; **to ~** à la perfection.

perfectly adv parfaitement.

perforate vt perforer.

perform vt (task) exécuter; (function) remplir; (operation) procéder à; (play) jouer; (song) chanter. •vi (actor, musician, team) jouer; ~ **well/badly** (candidate, business) avoir de bons/de mauvais résultats. **performance** n interprétation f; (of car, team) performance f; (show) représentation f; (fuss) histoire f. **performer** n artiste mf.

perfume n parfum m.

perhaps adv peut-être.

peril n péril m. **perilous** adj périlleux.

perimeter n périmètre m.

period n période f; (era) époque f; (lesson) cours m; (Gram) point m; (Med) règles fpl. •adj d'époque. **periodical** n périodique m.

peripheral adj (vision, suburb) périphérique; (issue) annexe. •n (Comput) périphérique m.

perish vi périr; (rubber) se détériorer.

perjury n faux témoignage m.

perk n 🔢 avantage m. •vt/i ~ **up**

🔢 (se) remonter. **perky** adj 🔢 gai.

perm n permanente f. •vt **have one's hair ~ed** se faire faire une permanente.

permanent adj permanent. **permanently** adv (happy) en permanence; (employed) de façon permanente.

permissible adj permis.

permission n permission f.

permissive adj libéral; (pej) permissif.

permit[1] /pəˈmɪt/ vt (pt **permitted**) permettre (**sb to** qn de), autoriser (**sb to** qn à).

permit[2] /ˈpɜːmɪt/ n permis m.

perpendicular adj perpendiculaire.

perpetrator n auteur m.

perpetuate vt perpétuer.

perplexed adj perplexe.

persecute vt persécuter.

perseverance n persévérance f. **persevere** vi persévérer.

persist vi persister (**in doing** à faire). **persistence** n persistance f. **persistent** adj (cough, snow) persistant; (obstinate) obstiné; (noise, pressure) continuel.

person n personne f; **in ~** en personne.

personal adj (life, problem, opinion) personnel; (safety, freedom, insurance) individuel. ~ **ad** n petite annonce f. ~ **assistant** n secrétaire mf de direction. ~ **computer** n ordinateur m (personnel), microordinateur m.

personality n personnalité f; (star) vedette f.

personal: ~ **organizer** n agenda m. ~ **stereo** n baladeur m.

personnel n personnel m.

perspiration n (sweat) sueur f; (sweating) transpiration f. **perspire** vi transpirer.

persuade vt persuader (**to** de).
persuasion n persuasion f.
persuasive adj persuasif.

pertinent adj pertinent.

perturb vt troubler.

Peru n Pérou m.

pervasive adj (smell) pénétrant;
(feeling) envahissant.

perverse adj (desire) pervers;
(refusal, attitude) illogique.
perversion n perversion f.

pervert[1] /pə'vɜːt/ vt (truth)
travestir; (values) fausser; (justice)
entraver.

pervert[2] /'pɜːvɜːt/ n pervers/-e m/f.

pessimist n pessimiste mf.
pessimistic adj pessimiste.

pest n (insect) insecte m nuisible;
(animal) animal m nuisible; (person
🔟) enquiquineur/-euse m/f 🔟.

pester vt harceler.

pet n animal m de compagnie;
(favourite) chouchou/-te m/f. • adj
(theory, charity) favori; ~ **hate** bête
f noire; ~ **name** petit nom m. • vt
(pt **petted**) caresser; (spoil)
chouchouter 🔟.

petal n pétale m.

peter vi ~ **out** (conversation) tarir;
(supplies) s'épuiser.

petite adj (woman) menue.

petition n pétition f. • vt adresser
une pétition à.

petrol n essence f. ~ **bomb** n
cocktail m molotov. ~ **station** n
station-service f. ~ **tank** n
réservoir m d'essence.

petticoat n jupon m.

petty adj (**-ier, -iest**) (minor) petit;
(mean) mesquin; ~ **cash** petite
caisse f.

pew n banc m (d'église).

pharmacist n pharmacien/-ne
m/f. **pharmacy** n pharmacie f.

phase n phase f. • vt ~ **in/out**
introduire/supprimer peu à peu.

PhD abbr (**Doctor of Philosophy**)
doctorat m.

pheasant n faisan/-e m/f.

phenomenon n (pl **-ena**)
phénomène m.

phew interj ouf.

philosopher n philosophe mf.
philosophical adj philosophique;
(resigned) philosophe. **philosophy**
n philosophie f.

phlegm n (Med) mucosité f.

phobia n phobie f.

phone n téléphone m; **on the** ~
au téléphone. • vt (person)
téléphoner à; ~ **England**
téléphoner en Angleterre. • vi
téléphoner; ~ **back** rappeler. ~
book n annuaire m. ~ **booth**, ~
box n cabine f téléphonique. ~
call n coup m de fil 🔟. ~**card** n
télécarte f. ~**in** n émission f à
ligne ouverte. ~ **number** n
numéro m de téléphone.

phonetic adj phonétique.

phoney adj (**-ier, -iest**) 🔟 faux.
• n (person) charlatan m; **it's a** ~
c'est un faux.

photocopier n photocopieuse f.

photocopy n photocopie f. • vt
photocopier.

photograph n photographie f.
• vt photographier.
photographer n photographe mf.

phrase n expression f; (idiom)
locution f. • vt exprimer,
formuler. ~**-book** n guide m de
conversation.

physical adj physique.

physicist n physicien/-ne m/f.

physics n physique f.

physiotherapist n
kinésithérapeute mf.
physiotherapy n
kinésithérapie f.

physique n physique m.

piano n piano m.

pick n choix m; (best) meilleur/-e

p

m/f; (tool) pioche f. •vt choisir;
(flower) cueillir; (lock) crocheter;
~ **a quarrel with** chercher
querelle à; ~ **one's nose** se
curer le nez. ∎ ~ **on** harceler; ~
out choisir; (identify) distinguer; ~
up vt ramasser; (sth fallen)
relever; (weight) soulever; (habit,
passenger, speed) prendre; (learn)
apprendre; vi s'améliorer.

pickaxe n pioche f.

picket n (striker) gréviste mf; (stake)
piquet m; ~ **(line)** piquet m de
grève. •vt (pt **picketed**) installer
un piquet de grève devant.

pickle n conserves fpl au vinaigre;
(gherkin) cornichon m. •vt
conserver dans du vinaigre.

pick-up n (stylus-holder) lecteur m;
(on guitar) capteur m; (collection)
ramassage m; (improvement)
reprise f.

picnic n pique-nique m. •vi (pt
picnicked) pique-niquer.

pictorial adj (magazine) illustré;
(record) graphique.

picture n image f; (painting)
tableau m; (photograph) photo f;
(drawing) dessin m; (film) film m;
(fig) description f; **the** ~**s** le
cinéma. •vt s'imaginer; **be** ~**d**
(shown) être représenté.

picturesque adj pittoresque.

pie n (sweet) tarte f; (savoury)
tourte f.

piece n morceau m; (of string, ribbon)
bout m; (of currency, machine) pièce f;
a ~ **of advice/furniture** un
conseil/meuble; **go to** ~**s** (fig)
s'effondrer; **take to** ~**s**
démonter.

pier n jetée f.

pierce vt percer.

pig n porc m, cochon m.

pigeon n pigeon m. ~**-hole** n
casier m.

pig-headed adj entêté.

pigsty n porcherie f.

pigtail n natte f.

pike n inv (fish) brochet m.

pile n (heap) tas m; (stack) pile f; (of
carpet) poil m; ~**s of** 🔲 un tas de
🔲. •vt ~ **(up)** entasser. •vi ~
into s'engouffrer dans; ~ **up**
(snow, leaves) s'entasser; (debts,
work) s'accumuler. ~**-up** n (Auto)
carambolage m.

pilgrim n pèlerin m. **pilgrimage**
n pèlerinage m.

pill n pilule f.

pillar n pilier m. ~**-box** n boîte f
aux lettres.

pillion n siège m de passager;
ride ~ monter en croupe.

pillow n oreiller m. ~**case** n taie f
d'oreiller.

pilot n pilote m. •adj pilote. •vt (pt
piloted) piloter. ~**-light** n
veilleuse f.

pimple n bouton m.

pin n épingle f; (of plug) fiche f; (for
wood, metal) goujon m; (in surgery)
broche f; **have** ~**s and needles**
avoir des fourmis. •vt (pt
pinned) épingler, attacher; (trap)
coincer; ~ **sb down** (fig) forcer
qn à se décider; ~ **up** accrocher.

pinafore n tablier m.

pincers npl tenailles fpl.

pinch vt pincer; (steal 🔲) piquer.
•vi (be too tight) serrer. •n (mark)
pinçon m; (of salt) pincée f; **at a** ~
à la rigueur.

pine n (tree) pin m. •vi ~ **(away)**
dépérir; ~ **for** languir après.

pineapple n ananas m.

pinecone n pomme f de pin.

pink adj & n rose (m).

pinpoint vt (problem, cause, location)
indiquer; (time) déterminer.

pint n pinte f (GB = 0.57 litre; US =
0.47 litre).

pin-up n 🔲 pin-up f inv. 🔲

pioneer n pionnier m. •vt ~ **the
use of** être le premier à utiliser.

pious adj pieux.

pip n (seed) pépin m; (sound) top m.

pipe n tuyau m; (to smoke) pipe f; (Mus) chalumeau m; ~s cornemuse f. ● vt transporter par tuyau. ■ ~ **down** se taire.

pipeline n oléoduc m; **in the** ~ en cours.

piping n tuyauterie f; ~ **hot** fumant.

pirate n pirate m. ● vt pirater.

Pisces n Poissons mpl.

pistol n pistolet m.

pit n fosse f; (mine) puits m; (quarry) carrière f; (for orchestra) fosse f; (of stomach) creux m; (of cherry: US) noyau m. ● vt (pt **pitted**) marquer; (fig) opposer; ~ **oneself against** se mesurer à.

pitch n (Sport) terrain m; (of voice, note) hauteur f; (degree) degré m; (Mus) ton m; (tar) brai m. ● vt jeter; (tent) planter. ● vi (ship) tanguer. ■ ~ **in** 🅸 contribuer.

pitfall n écueil m.

pitiful adj pitoyable. **pitiless** adj impitoyable.

pit stop n arrêt m mécanique.

pittance n **earn a** ~ gagner trois fois rien.

pity n pitié f; (regrettable fact) dommage m; **take** ~ **on** avoir pitié de; **what a** ~! quel dommage! ● vt avoir pitié de.

pivot n pivot m. ● vi (pt **pivoted**) pivoter.

placard n affiche f.

place n endroit m, lieu m; (house) maison f; (seat, rank) place f; **at** or **to my** ~ chez moi; **change** ~s changer de place; **in the first** ~ d'abord; **out of** ~ déplacé; **take** ~ avoir lieu. ● vt placer; (order) passer; (remember) situer; **be** ~d (in race) se placer. ~-**mat** n set m.

placid adj placide.

plagiarism n plagiat m. **plagiarize** vt/i plagier.

plague n (bubonic) peste f;

(epidemic) épidémie f; (of ants, locusts) invasion f. ● vt harceler.

plaice n inv carrelet m.

plain adj (obvious) clair; (candid) franc; (simple) simple; (not pretty) sans beauté; (not patterned) uni; ~ **chocolate** chocolat m noir; **in** ~ **clothes** en civil. ● adv franchement. ● n plaine f. **plainly** adv clairement; franchement; simplement.

plaintiff n (Jur) plaignant/-e m/f.

plaintive adj plaintif.

plait vt tresser. ● n natte f.

plan n projet m, plan m; (diagram) plan m. ● vt (pt **planned**) projeter (**to do** de faire); (timetable, day) organiser; (economy, work) planifier. ● vi prévoir; ~ **on** s'attendre à.

plane n (level) plan m; (aeroplane) avion m; (tool) rabot m. ● adj plan. ● vt raboter.

planet n planète f.

plank n planche f.

planning n (of economy, work) planification f; (of holiday, party) organisation f; (of town) urbanisme m; **family** ~ planning m familial; ~ **permission** permis m de construire.

plant n plante f; (Tech) matériel m; (factory) usine f. ● vt planter; (bomb) placer.

plaster n plâtre m; (adhesive) sparadrap m. ● vt plâtrer; (cover) couvrir (**with** de).

plastic adj en plastique; (art, substance) plastique; ~ **surgery** chirurgie f esthétique. ● n plastique m.

plate n assiette f; (of metal) plaque f; (silverware) argenterie f; (in book) gravure f. ● vt (metal) plaquer.

plateau n (pl ~x) plateau m; (fig) palier m.

platform n (stage) estrade f; (for speaking) tribune f; (Rail) quai m; (Pol) plate-forme f.

p

platoon n (Mil) section f.

play vt/i jouer; (instrument) jouer de; (record) mettre; (game) jouer à; (opponent) jouer contre; (match) disputer; **~ safe** ne pas prendre de risques. ●n jeu m; (Theat) pièce f. ∎ **~ down** minimiser; **~ on** (fears) exploiter; **~ up** 🔢 commencer à faire des siennes 🔢; **~ up sth** mettre l'accent sur qch.

playful adj (remark) taquin; (child) joueur.

play: ~ground n cour f de récréation. **~-group, ~-school** n garderie f.

playing n (Sport) jeu m; (Theat) interprétation f. **~-card** n carte f à jouer. **~-field** n terrain m de sport.

play: ~-pen n parc m (pour bébé). **~wright** n auteur m dramatique.

plc abbr (**public limited company**) SA.

plea n (for mercy, tolerance) appel m; (for food, money) demande f; (reason) excuse f; **make a ~ of guilty** plaider coupable.

plead vt/i supplier; (Jur) plaider.

pleasant adj agréable.

please vt/i plaire (à), faire plaisir (à); **~ oneself, do as one ~s** faire ce qu'on veut. ●adv s'il vous or te plaît. **pleased** adj content (**with** de). **pleasing** adj agréable.

pleasure n plaisir m; **with ~** avec plaisir; **my ~** je vous en prie.

pleat n pli m. ●vt plisser.

pledge n (token) gage m; (promise) promesse f. ●vt promettre; (pawn) mettre en gage.

plentiful adj abondant.

plenty n abondance f; **~ (of)** (a great deal) beaucoup (de); (enough) assez (de).

pliers npl pinces fpl.

plight n détresse f.

plinth n socle m.

plod vi (pt **plodded**) avancer péniblement.

plonk n 🔢 pinard m 🔢.

plot n (conspiracy) complot m; (of novel) intrigue f; **~ (of land)** terrain m. ●vt/i (pt **plotted**) (plan) comploter; (mark out) tracer.

plough n charrue f. ●vt/i labourer. ∎ **~ back** réinvestir; **~ through** avancer péniblement dans.

plow n & vt/i (US) ▸PLOUGH.

ploy n stratagème m.

pluck vt (flower, fruit) cueillir; (bird) plumer; (eyebrows) épiler; (strings: Mus) pincer; **~ up courage** prendre son courage à deux mains. **plucky** adj courageux.

plug n (for sink) bonde f; (Electr) fiche f, prise f. ●vt (pt **plugged**) (hole) boucher; (publicize 🔢) faire du battage autour de. ∎ **~ in** brancher. **~-hole** n bonde f.

plum n prune f; **~ pudding** (plum-)pudding m.

plumber n plombier m.

plume n (of feathers) panache m.

plummet vi tomber, plonger.

plump adj potelé, dodu.

plunge vt/i (dive, thrust) plonger; (fall) tomber. ●n plongeon m; (fall) chute f; **take the ~** se jeter à l'eau. **plunger** n (for sink) ventouse f.

plural adj pluriel; (noun) au pluriel; (ending) du pluriel. ●n pluriel m.

plus prep plus; **ten ~** plus de dix. ●adj (Electr & fig) positif. ●n signe m plus; (fig) atout m.

ply vt (tool) manier; (trade) exercer. ●vi faire la navette; **~ sb with drink** offrir continuellement à boire à qn.

plywood n contreplaqué m.

p.m. adv de l'après-midi or du soir.

pneumatic drill n

marteaupiqueur m.

pneumonia n pneumonie f.

PO abbr ▷POST OFFICE.

poach vt/i (game) braconner; (staff) débaucher; (Culin) pocher.

PO Box n boîte f postale.

pocket n poche f; **be out of ~** avoir perdu de l'argent. ●adj de poche. ●vt empocher. **~-book** n (notebook) carnet m; (wallet: US) portefeuille m; (handbag: US) sac m à main. **~-money** n argent m de poche.

pod n (peas) cosse f; (vanilla) gousse f.

podgy adj (-ier, -iest) dodu.

poem n poème m. **poet** n poète m. **poetic** adj poétique. **poetry** n poésie f.

point n (position) point m; (tip) pointe f; (decimal point) virgule f; (remark) remarque f; **good ~s** qualités fpl; **on the ~ of** sur le point de; **~ in time** moment m; **~ of view** point m de vue; **to the ~** pertinent; **what is the ~?** à quoi bon? ●vt (aim) braquer; (show) indiquer; **~ out** signaler. ●vi indiquer du doigt; **~ out that, make the ~ that** faire remarquer que. **~-blank** adj & adv à bout portant.

pointed adj (sharp) pointu; (window) en pointe; (remark) lourd de sens.

pointless adj inutile.

poise n (confidence) assurance f; (physical elegance) aisance f.

poison n poison m. ●vt empoisonner. **poisonous** adj (substance) toxique; (plant) vénéneux; (snake) venimeux.

poke vt/i (push) pousser; (fire) tisonner; (thrust) fourrer; **~ fun at** se moquer de. ●n (petit) coup m. ■ **~ out** (head) sortir.

poker n (for fire) tisonnier m; (cards) poker m.

Poland n Pologne f.

polar adj polaire.

pole n (stick) perche f; (for flag) mât m; (Geog) pôle m.

Pole n Polonais/-e m/f.

pole-vault n saut m à la perche.

police n police f. ●vt faire la police dans. **~ constable** n agent m de police. **~man** n (pl -men) agent m de police. **~ station** n commissariat m de police. **~woman** n (pl -women) femme-agent f.

policy n politique f; (insurance) police f (d'assurance).

polish vt polir; (shoes, floor) cirer. ●n (for shoes) cirage m; (for floor) encaustique f; (for nails) vernis m; (shine) poli m; (fig) raffinement m. ■ **~ off** finir en vitesse; **~ up** (language) perfectionner.

Polish adj polonais. ●n (Ling) polonais m.

polished adj raffiné.

polite adj poli.

political adj politique.

politician n homme m politique, femme f politique.

politics n politique f.

poll n (vote casting) scrutin m; (survey) sondage m; **go to the ~s** aller aux urnes. ●vt (votes) obtenir.

pollen n pollen m.

polling booth n isoloir m.

polling station n bureau m de vote.

pollution n pollution f.

polo n polo m. **~ neck** n col m roulé.

pomegranate n grenade f.

pomp n pompe f.

pompous adj pompeux.

pond n étang m; (artificial) bassin m; (stagnant) mare f.

ponder vt/i réfléchir (à), méditer (sur).

p

pong n (stink 🔲) puanteur f. •vi 🔲 puer.

pony n poney m. ~**tail** n queue f de cheval.

poodle n caniche m.

pool n (puddle) flaque f; (pond) étang m; (of blood) mare f; (for swimming) piscine f; (fund) fonds m commun; (of ideas) réservoir m; (snooker) billard m américain; ~**s** pari m mutuel sur le football. •vt mettre en commun.

poor adj (not wealthy) pauvre; (not good) médiocre, mauvais.

poorly adj malade. •adv mal.

pop n (noise) pan m; (music) pop m. •adj pop inv. •vt/i (pt **popped**) (burst) crever; (put) mettre; ~ **in/out/off** entrer/sortir/partir. ■~ **up** surgir. ~**-up** n fenêtre f pop-up.

pope n pape m.

poppy n pavot m; (wild) coquelicot m.

popular adj populaire; (in fashion) en vogue; **be** ~ **with** plaire à.

population n population f.

porcelain n porcelaine f.

porcupine n porc-épic m.

pork n porc m.

pornography n pornographie f.

port n (harbour) port m; (left: Naut) bâbord m; ~ **of call** escale f; (wine) porto m.

portable adj portable.

porter n (carrier) porteur m; (doorkeeper) portier m.

portfolio n (Pol, Comm) portefeuille m.

portion n (at meal) portion f; (part) partie f.

portrait n portrait m.

portray vt représenter.

Portugal n Portugal m.

Portuguese n (Ling) portugais m; (person) Portugais/-e m/f. •adj portugais.

pose vt/i poser; ~ **as** (expert) se poser en. •n pose f.

poser n (person) frimeur/-euse m/f; (puzzle) colle f.

posh adj 🔲 chic inv.

position n position f; (job, state) situation f. •vt placer.

positive adj positif; (sure) sûr, certain; (real) réel, vrai.

possess vt posséder.

possession n possession f; **take** ~ **of** prendre possession de.

possessive adj possessif.

possible adj possible.

possibly adv peut-être; **if I** ~ **can** si cela m'est possible; **I cannot** ~ **leave** il m'est impossible de partir.

post n (pole) poteau m; (station, job) poste m; (mail service) poste f; (letters) courrier m. •adj postal. •vt (letter) poster; **keep** ~**ed** tenir au courant; ~ **(up)** (a notice) afficher; (appoint) affecter.

postage n affranchissement m; tarif m postal.

postal adj postal. ~ **order** n mandat m.

post: ~**box** n boîte f aux lettres. ~**card** n carte f postale. ~ **code** n code m postal.

poster n (for information) affiche f; (for decoration) poster m.

postgraduate n étudiant/-e m/f de troisième cycle.

posthumous adj posthume.

post: ~**man** n (pl -**men**) facteur m. ~**mark** n cachet m de la poste.

post-mortem n autopsie f.

post office n poste f.

postpone vt remettre.

postscript n (to letter) postscriptum m inv.

posture n posture f. •vi prendre des poses.

pot n pot m; (drug 🔲) hasch m; **go**

to ~ 🔲 aller à la ruine; **take ~ luck** tenter sa chance. •vt (plants) mettre en pot.

potato n (pl ~es) pomme f de terre.

pot-belly n bedaine f.

potential adj & n potentiel (m).

pothole n (in rock) caverne f; (in road) nid m de poule. **pot-holing** n spéléologie f.

potter n potier m. •vi bricoler. **pottery** n (art) poterie f; (objects) poteries fpl.

potty adj (-ier, -iest) (crazy 🔲) toqué. •n pot m.

pouch n poche f; (for tobacco) blague f.

poultry n volailles fpl.

pounce vi bondir (**on** sur). •n bond m.

pound n (weight) livre f (= 454 g); (money) livre f; (for dogs, cars) fourrière f. •vt (crush) piler; (bombard) pilonner. •vi frapper fort; (of heart) battre fort; (walk) marcher à pas lourds.

pour vt verser. •vi couler, ruisseler (**from** de); (rain) pleuvoir à torrents. ■ **~ in/out** (people) arriver/sortir en masse; **~ off** or **out** vider. **pouring rain** n pluie f torrentielle.

pout vi faire la moue.

poverty n misère f, pauvreté f.

powder n poudre f. •vt poudrer.

power n (strength) puissance f; (control) pouvoir m; (energy) énergie f; (Electr) courant m. •vt (engine) faire marcher; (plane) propulser; **~ed by** (engine) propulsé par; (generator) alimenté par. **~ cut** n coupure f de courant.

powerful adj puissant.

powerless adj impuissant.

power: ~point n prise f de courant. **~-station** n centrale f électrique.

practical adj pratique. **~ joke** n farce f.

practice n (procedure) pratique f; (of profession) exercice m; (Sport) entraînement m; **in ~** (in fact) en pratique; (well-trained) en forme; **out of ~** rouillé; **put into ~** mettre en pratique.

practise vt/i (musician, typist) s'exercer (à); (Sport) s'entraîner (à); (put into practice) pratiquer; (profession) exercer.

practitioner n praticien/-ienne m/f; **dental ~** dentiste mf.

praise vt faire l'éloge de; (God) louer. •n éloges mpl, louanges fpl.

pram n landau m.

prance vi caracoler.

prawn n crevette f rose.

pray vi prier. **prayer** n prière f.

preach vt/i prêcher; **~ at** or **to** prêcher.

precarious adj précaire.

precaution n précaution f.

precede vt précéder.

precedence n (in importance) priorité f; (in rank) préséance f.

precedent n précédent m.

precinct n quartier m commerçant; (pedestrian area) zone f piétonne; (district: US) circonscription f.

precious adj précieux.

precipitate vt (person, event, chemical) précipiter.

précis n résumé m.

precise adj précis; (careful) méticuleux. **precision** n précision f.

precocious adj précoce.

preconceived adj préconçu.

predator n prédateur m.

predicament n situation f difficile.

predict vt prédire. **predictable** adj prévisible. **prediction** n prédiction f.

p

predispose vt prédisposer **to do** à faire).

predominant adj prédominant.

pre-empt vt (anticipate) anticiper; (person) devancer.

preface n (to book) préface f; (to speech) préambule m.

prefect n (pupil) élève m/f chargé/-e de la discipline; (official) préfet m.

prefer vt (pt **preferred**) préférer (**to do** faire). **preferably** adv de préférence. **preference** n préférence f. **preferential** adj préférentiel.

prefix n préfixe m.

pregnancy n grossesse f.

pregnant adj (woman) enceinte; (animal) pleine; (pause) éloquent.

prehistoric adj préhistorique.

prejudge vt (issue) préjuger de; (person) juger d'avance.

prejudice n préjugé(s) m(pl); (harm) préjudice m. •vt (claim) porter préjudice à; (person) léser. **prejudiced** adj partial; (person) qui a des préjugés.

premature adj prématuré.

premeditated adj prémédité.

premises npl locaux mpl; **on the ~** sur les lieux.

premium n (insurance) prime f; **be at a ~** être précieux.

preoccupied adj préoccupé.

preparation n préparation f; **~s** préparatifs mpl.

preparatory adj préparatoire. **~ school** n école f primaire privée; (US) école f secondaire privée.

prepare vt/i (se) préparer (**for** à); **be ~d for** (expect) s'attendre à; **~d to** prêt à.

preposition n préposition f.

preposterous adj absurde, ridicule.

prep school n ▷**PREPARATORY SCHOOL**.

prerequisite n condition f préalable.

prescribe vt prescrire.

prescription n (Med) ordonnance f.

presence n présence f; **~ of mind** présence f d'esprit.

present¹ /'preznt/ adj présent. •n présent m; (gift) cadeau m; **at ~** à présent; **for the ~** pour le moment.

present² /prɪ'zent/ vt présenter; (film, concert) donner; **~ sb with** offrir à qn. **presentation** n présentation f. **presenter** n présentateur/-trice m/f.

preservation n (of food) conservation f; (of wildlife) préservation f.

preservative n (Culin) agent m de conservation.

preserve vt préserver; (Culin) conserver. •n réserve f; (fig) domaine m; (jam) confiture f.

presidency n présidence f.

president n président/-e m/f.

press vt/i (button) appuyer (sur); (squeeze) presser; (iron) repasser; (pursue) poursuivre; **be ~ed for** (time) manquer de; **~ for sth** faire pression pour avoir qch; **~ sb to do sth** pousser qn à faire qch; **~ on** continuer (**with sth** qch). •n (newspapers, machine) presse f; (for wine) pressoir m. **~ cutting** n coupure f de presse.

pressing adj pressant.

press: ~ release n communiqué m de presse. **~-stud** n bouton-pression m. **~-up** n pompe f.

pressure n pression f. •vt faire pression sur. **~-cooker** n cocotte-minute f. **~ group** n groupe m de pression.

pressurize vt (cabin) pressuriser; (person) faire pression sur.

prestige n prestige m.

presumably adv

vraisemblablement.

presume vt (suppose) présumer.

pretence, (US) **pretense** n feinte f, simulation f; (claim) prétention f; (pretext) prétexte m.

pretend vt/i faire semblant (**to do** de faire); ~ **to** (lay claim to) prétendre à.

pretentious adj prétentieux.

pretext n prétexte m.

pretty adj (-ier, -iest) joli. ●adv assez; ~ **much** presque.

prevail vi (be usual) prédominer; (win) prévaloir; ~ **on** persuader (**to do** de faire). **prevailing** adj actuel; (wind) dominant.

prevalent adj répandu.

prevent vt empêcher (**from doing** de faire). **prevention** n prévention f. **preventive** adj préventif.

preview n avant-première f; (fig) aperçu m.

previous adj précédent, antérieur; ~ **to** avant. **previously** adv auparavant.

prey n proie f; **bird of** ~ rapace m. ●vi ~ **on** faire sa proie de; (worry) préoccuper.

price n prix m. ●vt fixer le prix de. **priceless** adj inestimable; (amusing 🇬🇧) impayable 🇬🇧.

prick vt (with pin) piquer; ~ **up one's ears** dresser l'oreille. ●n piqûre f.

prickle n piquant m.

pride n orgueil m; (satisfaction) fierté f; ~ **of place** place f d'honneur. ●vpr ~ **oneself on** s'enorgueillir de.

priest n prêtre m.

prim adj (**primmer, primmest**) guindé, méticuleux.

primarily adv essentiellement.

primary adj (school, elections) primaire; (chief, basic) premier, fondamental. ●n (Pol: US) primaire f.

prime adj principal, premier; (first-rate) excellent. ●vt (pump, gun) amorcer; (surface) apprêter. **P~ Minister** n Premier Ministre m.

primitive adj primitif.

primrose n primevère f (jaune).

prince n prince m. **princess** n princesse f.

principal adj principal. ●n (of school) directeur/-trice m/f.

principle n principe m; **in/on** ~ en/par principe.

print vt imprimer; (write in capitals) écrire en majuscules; ~**ed matter** imprimés mpl. ●n (of foot) empreinte f; (letters) caractères mpl; (photograph) épreuve f; (engraving) gravure f; **in** ~ disponible; **out of** ~ épuisé. **printer** n (person) imprimeur m; (Comput) imprimante f.

prion n prion m.

prior adj précédent. ●n (Relig) prieur m. ~ **to** prep avant (de).

priority n priorité f; **take** ~ avoir la priorité (**over** sur).

prise vt forcer; ~ **open** ouvrir en forçant.

prison n prison f. **prisoner** n prisonnier/-ière m/f. ~ **officer** n gardien/-ne m/f de prison.

pristine adj **be in** ~ **condition** être comme neuf.

privacy n intimité f, solitude f.

private adj privé; (confidential) personnel; (lessons, house) particulier; (ceremony) intime; **in** ~ en privé; (of ceremony) dans l'intimité. ●n (soldier) simple soldat m. **privately** adv en privé; dans l'intimité; (inwardly) intérieurement.

privilege n privilège m. **privileged** adj privilégié; **be** ~**d to** avoir le privilège de.

prize n prix m. ●vt (value) priser.

pro n **the** ~**s and cons** le pour et le contre.

probable adj probable. **probably** adv probablement.

probation n (testing) essai m; (Jur) liberté f surveillée.

probe n (device) sonde f; (fig) enquête f. •vt sonder. •vi ~ **into** sonder.

problem n problème m. •adj difficile. **problematic** adj problématique.

procedure n procédure f; (way of doing sth) démarche f à suivre.

proceed vi (go) aller, avancer; (pass) passer (**to** à); (act) procéder; ~ **(with)** continuer; ~ **to do** se mettre à faire.

proceedings npl (discussions) débats mpl; (meeting) réunion f; (report) actes mpl; (Jur) poursuites fpl.

proceeds npl (profits) produit m, bénéfices mpl.

process n processus m; (method) procédé m; **in** ~ en cours; **in the** ~ **of doing** en train de faire. ~**or** n (Culin) robot m (ménager); (Comput) unité f centrale. •vt (material, data) traiter.

procession n défilé m.

procrastinate vi différer, tergiverser.

procure vt obtenir.

prod vt/i (pt **prodded**) pousser doucement. •n petit coup m.

prodigy n prodige m.

produce[1] /'prɒdjuːs/ n produits mpl.

produce[2] /prə'djuːs/ vt/i produire; (bring out) sortir; (show) présenter; (cause) provoquer; (Theat, TV), mettre en scène; (radio) réaliser; (cinema) produire. **producer** n metteur m en scène; réalisateur m; producteur m.

product n produit m.

production n production f; (Theat, TV) mise f en scène; (radio) réalisation f.

productive adj productif. **productivity** n productivité f.

profession n profession f.

professional adj professionnel; (of high quality) de professionnel; (person) qui exerce une profession libérale. •n professionnel/-le m/f.

professor n professeur m (titulaire d'une chaire).

proficient adj compétent.

profile n (of face) profil m; (of body, mountain) silhouette f; (by journalist) portrait m.

profit n profit m, bénéfice m. •vi ~ **by** tirer profit de. **profitable** adj rentable.

profound adj profond.

profusely adv (bleed) abondamment; (apologize) avec effusion. **profusion** n profusion f.

program n (US) ▷PROGRAMME; **(computer)** ~ programme m. •vt (pt **programmed**) programmer.

programme n programme m; (broadcast) émission f.

programmer n programmeur/-euse m/f.

programming n (Comput) programmation f.

progress[1] /'prəʊgres/ n progrès m (pl) (**in** ~) en cours; **make** ~ faire des progrès; ~ **report** compte-rendu m.

progress[2] /prə'gres/ vi (advance, improve) progresser.

progressive adj progressif; (reforming) progressiste.

prohibit vt interdire (**sb from doing** à qn de faire).

project[1] /prə'dʒekt/ vt projeter. •vi (jut out) être en saillie.

project[2] /'prɒdʒekt/ n (plan) projet m; (undertaking) entreprise f; (School) dossier m.

projection n projection f ; saillie f; (estimate) prévision f.

p

projector n projecteur m.

proliferate vi proliférer.

prolong vt prolonger.

prominent adj (projecting) proéminent; (conspicuous) bien en vue; (fig) important.

promiscuous adj de mœurs faciles.

promise n promesse f. •vt/i promettre. **promising** adj prometteur; (person) qui promet.

promote vt promouvoir; (advertise) faire la promotion de. **promotion** n promotion f.

prompt adj rapide; (punctual) à l'heure, ponctuel. •adv (on the dot) pile. •vt inciter; (cause) provoquer; (Theat) souffler à. •n (Comput) message m guide-opérateur. **prompter** n souffleur/-euse m/f. **promptly** adv rapidement; ponctuellement.

prone adj ∼ **to** sujet à.

pronoun n pronom m.

pronounce vt prononcer. **pronunciation** n prononciation f.

proof n (evidence) preuve f; (test, trial copy) épreuve f; (of alcohol) teneur f en alcool. •adj ∼ **against** à l'épreuve de.

prop n support m; (Theat) accessoire m. •vt (pt **propped**) ∼ **(up)** (support) étayer; (lean) appuyer.

propaganda n propagande f.

propel vt (pt **propelled**) (vehicle, ship) propulser; (person) pousser.

propeller n hélice f.

proper adj correct, bon; (adequate) convenable; (real) vrai; (thorough 🔢) parfait. **properly** adv correctement, comme il faut; (adequately) convenablement.

proper noun n nom m propre.

property n (house) propriété f; (things owned) biens mpl, propriété f. •adj immobilier, foncier.

prophecy n prophétie f.

prophet n prophète m.

proportion n (ratio, dimension) proportion f; (amount) partie f.

proposal n proposition f; (of marriage) demande f en mariage.

propose vt proposer. •vi faire une demande en mariage; ∼ **to do** se proposer de faire.

proposition n proposition f; (matter 🔢) affaire f. •vt 🔢 faire des propositions malhonnêtes à.

proprietor n propriétaire mf.

propriety n (correct behaviour) bienséance f.

prose n prose f; (translation) thème m.

prosecute vt poursuivre en justice. **prosecution** n poursuites fpl. **prosecutor** n procureur m.

prospect[1] /'prɒspekt/ n (outlook) perspective f; (chance) espoir m.

prospect[2] /prə'spekt/ vt/i prospecter.

prospective adj (future) futur; (possible) éventuel.

prospectus n brochure f; (Univ) livret m de l'étudiant.

prosperity n prospérité f. **prosperous** adj prospère.

prostitute n prostituée f.

prostrate adj (prone) à plat ventre; (exhausted) prostré.

protect vt protéger. **protection** n protection f. **protective** adj protecteur; (clothes) de protection.

protein n protéine f.

protest[1] /'prəʊtest/ n protestation f; **under** ∼ en protestant.

protest[2] /prə'test/ vt/i protester.

Protestant adj & n protestant/-e (m/f).

protester n manifestant/-e m/f.

protocol n protocole m.

protrude vi dépasser.

proud adj fier, orgueilleux.

prove vt prouver. •vi ~ **(to be) easy** se révéler facile; ~ **oneself** faire ses preuves. **proven** adj éprouvé.

proverb n proverbe m.

provide vt fournir (**sb with sth** qch à qn). •vi ~ **for** (allow for) prévoir; (guard against) parer à; (person) pourvoir aux besoins de.

provided conj ~ **that** à condition que.

providing conj ▷PROVIDED.

province n province f; (fig) compétence f.

provision n (stock) provision f; (supplying) fourniture f; (stipulation) dispositions fpl; ~s (food) provisions fpl.

provisional adj provisoire.

provocative adj provocant.

provoke vt provoquer.

prow n proue f.

prowess n prouesses fpl.

prowl vi rôder.

proxy n **by** ~ par procuration.

prudish adj pudibond, prude.

prune n pruneau m. •vt (cut) tailler.

pry vi ~ **into** mettre son nez dans.

psalm n psaume m.

pseudonym n pseudonyme m.

psychiatric adj psychiatrique. **psychiatrist** n psychiatre mf. **psychiatry** n psychiatrie f.

psychic adj (phenomenon) métapsychique; (person) doué de télépathie.

psychoanalyse vt psychanalyser.

psychological adj psychologique. **psychologist** n psychologue mf. **psychology** n psychologie f.

PTO abbr (**please turn over**) TSVP.

pub n pub m.

puberty n puberté f.

public adj public; (library) municipal; **in** ~ en public.

publican n patron/-ne m/f de pub.

publication n publication f.

public house n pub m.

publicity n publicité f.

publicize vt faire connaître au public.

public: ~ **relations** n relations fpl publiques. ~ **school** n école f privée; (US) école f publique. ~ **transport** n transports mpl en commun.

publish vt publier. **publisher** n éditeur m. **publishing** n édition f.

pudding n dessert m; (steamed) pudding m.

puddle n flaque f d'eau.

puff n (of smoke) bouffée f; (of breath) souffle m. •vt/i souffler. ■ ~ **at** (cigar) tirer sur. ~ **out** (swell) (se) gonfler.

pull vt/i tirer; (muscle) se froisser. ~ **a face** faire une grimace; ~ **one's weight** faire sa part du travail; ~ **sb's leg** faire marcher qn. •n traction f; (fig) attraction f; (influence) influence f; **give a** ~ tirer. ■ ~ **away** (Auto) démarrer; ~ **back** or **out** (withdraw) (se) retirer; ~ **down** (building) démolir; ~ **in** (enter) entrer; (stop) s'arrêter; ~ **off** enlever; (fig) réussir; ~ **out** (from bag) sortir; (extract) arracher; (Auto) déboîter; ~ **over** (Auto) se ranger (sur le côté); ~ **through** s'en tirer; ~ **oneself together** se ressaisir.

pull-down menu n (Comput) menu m déroulant.

pulley n poulie f.

pullover n pull(-over) m.

pulp n (of fruit) pulpe f; (for paper) pâte f à papier.

pulpit n chaire f.

pulsate vi battre.

pulse n (Med) pouls m.

pump n pompe f; (plimsoll) chaussure f de sport. •vt/i pomper; (person) soutirer des renseignements à; ~ **up** gonfler.

pumpkin n citrouille f.

pun n jeu m de mots.

punch vt donner un coup de poing à; (ticket) poinçonner. •n coup m de poing; (vigour ▣) punch m; (device) poinçonneuse f; (drink) punch m. ~-**line** n chute f.

punctual adj à l'heure; (habitually) ponctuel.

punctuation n ponctuation f.

puncture n crevaison f. •vt/i crever.

pungent adj âcre.

punish vt punir (**for sth** de qch). **punishment** n punition f.

punk n (music, fan) punk m; (US: ▣) voyou m.

punt n (boat) barque f; (Hist) (Irish pound) livre f irlandaise.

puny adj -**ier**, -**iest** chétif.

pupil n (person) élève mf; (of eye) pupille f.

puppet n marionnette f.

puppy n chiot m.

purchase vt acheter (**from sb** à qn). •n achat m.

pure adj pur.

purgatory n purgatoire m.

purge vt purger (**of** de). •n purge f.

purification n (of water, air) épuration f; (Relig) purification f. **purify** vt épurer; purifier.

puritan n puritain/-e m/f.

purity n pureté f.

purple adj & n violet (m).

purpose n but m; (determination) résolution f; **on** ~ exprès; **to no** ~ sans résultat.

purr n ronronnement m. •vi ronronner.

purse n porte-monnaie m inv; (handbag: US) sac m à main. •vt (lips) pincer.

pursue vt poursuivre.

pursuit n poursuite f; (hobby) activité f, occupation f.

pus n pus m.

push vt/i pousser; (button) appuyer sur; (thrust) enfoncer; (recommend ▣) proposer avec insistance; **be** ~**ed for** (time) manquer de; **be** ~**ing thirty** ▣ friser la trentaine; ~ **sb around** bousculer qn. •n poussée f; (effort) gros effort m; (drive) dynamisme m; **give the** ~ **to** ▣ flanquer à la porte ▣. ▪ ~ **in** resquiller; ~ **on** continuer; ~ **up** (lift) relever; (prices) faire monter.

pushchair n poussette f.

pusher n revendeur/-euse m/f (de drogue).

push-up n pompe f.

put vt/i (pt **put**; pres p **putting**) mettre, placer, poser; (question) poser; ~ **the damage at a million** estimer les dégâts à un million; ~ **sth tactfully** dire qch avec tact. ▪ ~ **across** communiquer; ~ **away** ranger; (in hospital, prison) enfermer; ~ **back** (postpone) remettre; (delay) retarder; ~ **down** (dé)poser; (write) inscrire; (pay) verser; (suppress) réprimer; ~ **forward** (plan) soumettre; ~ **in** (insert) introduire; (fix) installer; (submit) soumettre; ~ **in for** faire une demande de; ~ **off** (postpone) renvoyer à plus tard; (disconcert) déconcerter; (displease) rebuter; ~ **sb off sth** dégoûter qn de qch; ~ **on** (clothes, radio) mettre; (light) allumer; (accent, weight) prendre; ~ **out** sortir; (stretch) (é)tendre; (extinguish) éteindre; (disconcert) déconcerter; (inconvenience) déranger; ~ **up** lever, remonter;

(building) construire; (notice) mettre; (price) augmenter; (guest) héberger; (offer) offrir; ~ **up with** supporter.

putt vi putter. •n putt m.

putty n mastic m.

puzzle n énigme f; (game) casse-tête m inv; (jigsaw) puzzle m. •vt rendre perplexe. •vi se creuser la tête.

pyjamas npl pyjama m.

pylon n pylône m.

Qq

quack n (of duck) coin-coin m inv; (doctor) charlatan m.

quadrangle (of college) n cour f.

quadruple adj & n quadruple (m). •vt/i quadrupler.

quail n (bird) caille f.

quaint adj pittoresque; (old) vieillot; (odd) bizarre.

qualification n diplôme m; (ability) compétence f; (fig) réserve f, restriction f.

qualified adj diplômé; (able) qualifié (**to do** pour faire); (fig) conditionnel.

qualify vt qualifier; (modify) mettre des réserves à; (statement) nuancer. •vi obtenir son diplôme (**as** de); (Sport) se qualifier; ~ **for** remplir les conditions requises pour.

quality n qualité f.

qualm n scrupule m.

quantity n quantité f.

quarantine n quarantaine f.

quarrel n dispute f, querelle f. •vi (pt **quarrelled**) se disputer.

quarry n (excavation) carrière f; (prey) proie f. •vt extraire.

quart n ≈ litre m.

quarter n quart m; (of year) trimestre m; (25 cents: US) quart m de dollar; (district) quartier m; ~**s** logement m; **from all** ~**s** de toutes parts. •vt diviser en quatre; (troops) cantonner.

quarterly adj trimestriel. •adv tous les trois mois.

quartet n quatuor m.

quartz n quartz m. •adj (watch) à quartz.

quash vt (suppress) étouffer; (Jur) annuler.

quaver vi trembler, chevroter. •n (Mus) croche f.

quay n (Naut) quai m.

queasy adj **feel** ~ avoir mal au cœur.

queen n reine f; (cards) dame f.

queer adj étrange; (dubious) louche; ⊠ homosexuel.

quench vt éteindre; (thirst) étancher; (desire) étouffer.

query n question f. •vt mettre en question.

quest n recherche f.

question n question f; **in** ~ en question; **out of the** ~ hors de question. •vt interroger; (doubt) mettre en question, douter de. ~ **mark** point m d'interrogation.

questionnaire n questionnaire m.

queue n queue f. •vi (pres p **queuing**) faire la queue.

quibble vi ergoter.

quick adj rapide; (clever) vif/vive; **be ~** (hurry) se dépêcher. • adv vite. • n **cut to the~** piquer au vif. **quicken** vt/i (s')accélérer. **quickly** adv rapidement, vite. **~sand** n sables mpl mouvants.

quid n inv £ livre f sterling.

quiet adj (calm, still) tranquille; (silent) silencieux; (gentle) doux; (discreet) discret; **keep ~** se taire. • n tranquillité f; **on the ~** en cachette. **quieten** vt/i (se) calmer. **quietly** adv (speak) doucement; (sit) en silence.

quilt n édredon m; **(continental) ~** couette f.

quirk n bizarrerie f.

quit vt (pt **quitted**) quitter; (smoking) arrêter de. • vi abandonner; (resign) démissionner; **~ doing** (US) cesser de faire.

quite adv tout à fait, vraiment; (rather) assez; **~ a few** un bon nombre (de).

quits adj quitte (**with** envers); **call it ~** en rester là.

quiver vi trembler.

quiz n (pl **quizzes**) test m; (game) jeu-concours m. • vt (pt **quizzed**) questionner.

quotation n citation f; (price) devis m; (stock exchange) cotation f; **~ marks** guillemets mpl.

quote vt citer; (reference, number) rappeler; (price) indiquer; (share price) coter. • vi **~ for** faire un devis pour; **~ from** citer. • n (quotation) citation f; (estimate) devis m; **in ~s** £ entre guillemets.

Rr

rabbi n rabbin m.

rabbit n lapin m.

rabies n (disease) rage f.

race n (contest) course f; (group) race f. • adj racial; **~ relations** relations fpl inter-raciales. • vt (compete with) faire la course avec; (horse) faire courir. • vi courir; (pulse) battre précipitamment; (engine) s'emballer. **~course** n champ m de courses. **~horse** n cheval m de course. **~track** n piste f; (for horses) champ m de courses.

racing n courses fpl; **~ car** voiture f de course.

racism n racisme m. **racist** adj & n raciste (mf).

rack n (shelf) étagère f; (for clothes) portant m; (for luggage) compartiment m à bagages; (for dishes) égouttoir m. • vt **~ one's brains** se creuser la cervelle.

racket n (Sport) raquette f; (noise) vacarme m; (swindle) escroquerie f; (crime) trafic m.

radar n & adj radar (m).

radial n **~ (tyre)** pneu m radial.

radiate vt (happiness) rayonner de; (heat) émettre. • vi rayonner (**from** de). **radiation** n (radioactivity) radiation f. **radiator** n radiateur m.

radical n & a radical/-e (m/f).

radio n radio f; **on the ~** à la radio. • vt (message) envoyer par radio; (person) appeler par radio.

radioactive adj radioactif.

radiographer n manipulateur/-trice m/f radiographe.

radish n radis m.

radius n (pl **-dii**) rayon m.

raffle n tombola f.

rag n chiffon m; ~**s** loques fpl.

rage n rage f, colère f; **be all the ~** faire fureur. ●vi (person) tempêter; (storm, battle) faire rage.

ragged adj (clothes) en loques; (person) dépenaillé.

raid n (Mil, on stock market) raid m; (by police) rafle f; (by criminals) hold-up m inv. ●vt faire un raid or une rafle or un hold-up dans. **raider** n (thief) pillard m; (Mil) commando m; (corporate) raider m.

rail n (on balcony) balustrade f; (stairs) rampe f; (for train) rail m; (for curtain) tringle f; **by ~** par chemin de fer.

railing n (also ~**s**) grille f.

railway, (US) **railroad** n chemin m de fer. **~ line** n voie f ferrée. **~ station** n gare f.

rain n pluie f. ●vi pleuvoir. ~**bow** n arc-en-ciel m. ~**coat** n imperméable m. ~**fall** n précipitation f. **~ forest** n forêt f tropicale.

rainy adj (**-ier, -iest**) pluvieux; (season) des pluies.

raise vt (barrier, curtain) lever; (child, cattle) élever; (question) soulever; (price, salary) augmenter. ●n (US) augmentation f.

raisin n raisin m sec.

rake n râteau m. ●vt (garden) ratisser; (search) fouiller dans. ■ ~ **in** (money) amasser; ~ **up** (past) remuer.

rally vt/i (se) rallier; (strength) reprendre; (after illness) aller mieux; **~ round** venir en aide. ●n rassemblement m; (Auto) rallye m; (tennis) échange m.

ram n bélier m. ●vt (pt **rammed**) (thrust) enfoncer; (crash into) rentrer dans.

RAM abbr (**random access memory**) RAM f.

ramble n randonnée f. ●vi faire

une randonnée. ■ ~ **on** discourir.

ramp n (slope) rampe f; (in garage) pont m de graissage.

rampage[1] /ræm'peɪdʒ/ vi se déchaîner (**through** dans).

rampage[2] /'ræmpeɪdʒ/ n **go on the ~** tout saccager.

ran ▷RUN.

rancid adj rance.

random adj (fait) au hasard. ●n **at ~** au hasard.

rang ▷RING[2].

range n (of prices, products) gamme f; (of people, beliefs) variété f; (of radar, weapon) portée f; (of aircraft) autonomie f; (of mountains) chaîne f. ●vi aller; (vary) varier.

rank n rang m; (Mil) grade m. ●vt/i **~ among** (se) classer parmi.

ransack vt (search) fouiller; (pillage) mettre à sac.

ransom n rançon f.

rap n coup m sec; (Mus) rap m. ●vi (pt **rapped**) donner des coups secs (**on** sur).

rape vt violer. ●n viol m.

rapid adj rapide.

rapist n violeur m.

rapturous adj (delight) extasié; (welcome) enthousiaste.

rare adj rare; (Culin) saignant. **rarely** adv rarement.

rascal n coquin/-e m/f.

rash n (Med) rougeurs fpl. ●adj irréfléchi.

raspberry n framboise f.

rat n rat m. ●vi (pt **ratted**) **~ on** (desert) lâcher; (inform on) dénoncer.

rate n (ratio, level) taux m; (speed) rythme m; (price) tarif m; (of exchange) taux m; **at any ~** en tout cas. ●vt (value) estimer; (deserve) mériter; **~ sth highly** admirer beaucoup qch. ●vi **~ as**

être considéré comme.

rather adv (by preference) plutôt; (fairly) assez, plutôt; (a little) un peu; **I would ~ go** j'aimerais mieux partir; **~ than go** plutôt que de partir.

rating n (score, value) cote f; **the ~s** (TV) l'indice m d'écoute, l'audimat® m.

ratio n proportion f.

ration n ration f. • vt rationner.

rational adj rationnel; (person) sensé.

rationalize vt justifier; (organize) rationaliser.

rattle vi (bottles, chains) s'entrechoquer; (window) vibrer. • vt (bottles, chains) faire s'entrechoquer; (fig, 🎅) énerver. • n cliquetis m; (toy) hochet m. **~snake** n serpent m à sonnette, crotale m.

rave vi (enthuse) s'emballer; (in fever) délirer; (in anger) tempêter.

raven n corbeau m.

ravenous adj **be ~** avoir une faim de loup.

ravine n ravin m.

raving adj **~ lunatic** fou m furieux, folle f furieuse.

ravishing adj ravissant.

raw adj cru; (not processed) brut; (wound) à vif; (immature) inexpérimenté; **get a ~ deal** être mal traité; **~ material** matière f première.

ray n (of light) rayon m; **~ of hope** lueur f d'espoir.

razor n rasoir m. **~-blade** n lame f de rasoir.

re prep au sujet de; (at top of letter) objet.

reach vt (place, level) atteindre; (decision) arriver à; (contact) joindre; (audience, market) toucher. • vi **~ up/down** lever/baisser le bras; **~ across** étendre le bras. • n portée f; **within ~ of** à

portée de; (close to) à proximité de.

react vi réagir. **reaction** n réaction f. **reactor** n réacteur m.

read vt/i (pt **read**) lire; (study) étudier; (instrument) indiquer; **~ about sb** lire quelque chose sur qn; **~ out** lire à haute voix. **reader** n lecteur/-trice m/f. **reading** n lecture f; (measurement) indication f; (interpretation) interprétation f.

readjust vt rajuster. • vi se réadapter (**to** à).

read-only memory, ROM n mémoire f morte.

ready adj (-ier, -iest) prêt; (quick) prompt. **~-made** adj tout fait. **~-to-wear** adj prêt-à-porter.

real adj (not imaginary) véritable, réel; (not artificial) vrai; **it's a ~ shame** c'est vraiment dommage. **~ estate** n biens mpl immobiliers.

realism n réalisme m. **realistic** adj réaliste.

reality n réalité f. **~ TV** n télé-réalité f.

reasonable adj raisonnable.

realize vt se rendre compte de, comprendre; (fulfil, turn into cash) réaliser; (price) atteindre.

really adv vraiment.

reap vt (crop) recueillir; (benefits) récolter.

reappear vi reparaître.

rear n arrière m; (of person) derrière m. 🎅 • adj (seat) arrière inv; (entrance) de derrière. • vt élever. • vi (horse) se cabrer. **~-view mirror** n rétroviseur m.

reason n raison f (**to do, for doing** de faire); **within ~** dans la limite du raisonnable.

reassurance n réconfort m. **reassure** vt rassurer.

rebate n (refund) remboursement m; (discount) remise f.

rebel[1] /'rebl/ n & adj rebelle (mf).

rebel[2] /rɪ'bel/ vi (pt **rebelled**) se rebeller. **rebellion** n rébellion f.

rebound[1] /rɪ'baʊnd/ vi rebondir; ~ **on** (backfire) se retourner contre.

rebound[2] /'riːbaʊnd/ n rebond m.

rebuke vt réprimander. ●n réprimande f.

recall vt (remember) se souvenir de; (call back) rappeler. ●n (memory) mémoire f; (Comput, Mil) rappel m.

recap vt/i (pt **recapped**) récapituler. ●n récapitulation f.

recede vi s'éloigner; **his hair is receding** son front se dégarnit.

receipt n (written) reçu m; (of letter) réception f; ~**s** (Comm) recettes fpl.

receive vt recevoir; (stolen goods) receler. **receiver** n (telephone) combiné m; (TV) récepteur m.

recent adj récent. **recently** adv récemment.

receptacle n récipient m.

reception n réception f; **give sb a warm** ~ donner un accueil chaleureux à qn.

recess n (alcove) alcôve m; (for door) embrasure f; (Jur, Pol) vacances fpl; (School, US) récréation f.

recession n récession f.

recharge vt recharger.

recipe n recette f.

recipient n (of honour) récipiendaire mf; (of letter) destinataire mf.

reciprocate vt (compliment) retourner; (kindness) payer de retour. ●vi en faire autant.

recite vi réciter.

reckless adj imprudent.

reckon vt/i calculer; (judge) considérer; (think) penser; ~ **on/with** compter sur/avec. **reckoning** n (guess) estimation f; (calculation) calculs mpl.

reclaim vt récupérer; (flooded land) assécher.

recline vi s'allonger; (seat) s'incliner.

recluse n reclus/-e m/f.

recognition n reconnaissance f; **beyond** ~ méconnaissable; **gain** ~ être reconnu.

recognize vt reconnaître.

recollect vt se souvenir de, se rappeler. **recollection** n souvenir m.

recommend vt recommander. **recommendation** n recommandation f.

reconcile vt (people) réconcilier; (facts) concilier; ~ **oneself to** se résigner à.

recondition vt remettre à neuf.

reconsider vt réexaminer. ●vi réfléchir.

reconstruct vt reconstruire; (crime) faire une reconstitution de.

record[1] /rɪ'kɔːd/ vt/i (in register, on tape) enregistrer; (in diary) noter; ~ **that** rapporter que.

record[2] /'rekɔːd/ n (of events) compte-rendu m; (official) procès-verbal m; (personal, administrative) dossier m; (historical) archives fpl; (past history) réputation f; (Mus) disque m; (Sport) record m; **(criminal)** ~ casier m judiciaire; **off the** ~ officieusement. ●adj record inv.

recorder n (Mus) flûte f à bec.

recording n enregistrement m.

record-player n tourne-disque m.

recover vt récupérer. ●vi se remettre; (economy) se redresser. **recovery** n (Med) rétablissement m; (of economy) relance f.

recreation n récréation f.

recruit n recrue f. ●vt recruter. **recruitment** n recrutement m.

rectangle n rectangle m.

rectify vt rectifier.

recuperate vt récupérer. •vi se rétablir.

recur vi (pt **recurred**) se reproduire.

recycle vt recycler.

red adj (**redder, reddest**) rouge; (hair) roux. •n rouge m; **in the ~** en déficit. **R~ Cross** n Croix-Rouge f. **~currant** n groseille f.

redecorate vt repeindre, refaire.

redeploy vt réorganiser; (troops) répartir.

red: ~-handed adj en flagrant délit. **~-hot** adj brûlant.

redirect vt (traffic) dévier; (letter) faire suivre.

redness n rougeur f.

redo vt (pt **-did**; pp **-done**) refaire.

redress vt (wrong) redresser; (balance) rétablir. •n réparation f.

reduce vt réduire; (temperature) faire baisser. **reduction** n réduction f.

redundancy n licenciement m.

redundant adj superflu; (worker) licencié; **make ~** licencier.

reed n (plant) roseau m.

reef n récif m, écueil m.

reel n (of thread) bobine f; (of film) bande f; (winding device) dévidoir m. •vi chanceler. •vt **~ off** réciter.

refectory n réfectoire m.

refer vt/i (pt **referred**) **~ to** (allude to) faire allusion à; (concern) s'appliquer à; (consult) consulter; (direct) renvoyer à.

referee n (Sport) arbitre m. •vt (pt **refereed**) arbitrer.

reference n référence f; (mention) allusion f; (person) personne f pouvant fournir des références; **in** or **with ~ to** en ce qui concerne; (Comm) suite à.

referendum n (pl **~s**) référendum m.

refill[1] /riːˈfɪl/ vt (glass) remplir à nouveau; (pen) recharger.

refill[2] /ˈriːfɪl/ n recharge f.

refine vt raffiner.

reflect vt refléter; (heat, light) renvoyer. •vi réfléchir (**on** à); **~ well/badly on sb** faire honneur/du tort à qn.

reflection n réflexion f; (image) reflet m; **on ~** à la réflexion.

reflective adj (surface) réfléchissant; (person) réfléchi.

reflector n (on car) catadioptre m.

reflex adj & n réflexe (m).

reflexive adj (Gram) réfléchi.

reform vt réformer. •vi (person) s'amender. •n réforme f.

refrain n refrain m. •vi s'abstenir (**from** de).

refresh vt (drink) rafraîchir; (rest) reposer. **refreshments** npl rafraîchissements mpl.

refrigerate vt réfrigérer. **refrigerator** n réfrigérateur m.

refuel vt/i (pt **refuelled**) (se) ravitailler.

refuge n refuge m; **take ~** se réfugier. **refugee** n réfugié/-e m/f.

refund[1] /riːˈfʌnd/ vt rembourser.

refund[2] /ˈriːfʌnd/ n remboursement m.

refurbish vt remettre à neuf.

refuse[1] /rɪˈfjuːz/ vt/i refuser.

refuse[2] /ˈrefjuːs/ n ordures fpl.

regain vt retrouver; (lost ground) regagner.

regard vt considérer; **as ~s** en ce qui concerne. •n égard m, estime f; **in this ~** à cet égard; **~s** amitiés fpl. **regarding** prep en ce qui concerne.

regardless adv malgré tout; **~ of** sans tenir compte de.

regime n régime m.

regiment n régiment m.

r

region n région f; **in the ~ of** environ.

register n registre m. ●vt (record) enregistrer; (vehicle) faire immatriculer; (birth) déclarer; (letter) recommander; (indicate) indiquer; (express) exprimer. ●vi (enrol) s'inscrire; (at hotel) se présenter; (fig) être compris.

registrar n officier m de l'état civil; (Univ) responsable m du bureau de la scolarité.

registration n (of voter, student) inscription f; (of birth) déclaration f; **~ (number)** (Auto) numéro m d'immatriculation.

registry office n bureau m de l'état civil.

regret n regret m. ●vt (pt regretted) regretter (**to do** de faire). **regretfully** adv à regret.

regular adj régulier; (usual) habituel. ●n habitué/-e m/f. **regularity** n régularité f. **regularly** adv régulièrement.

regulate vt régler. **regulation** n (rule) règlement m; (process) réglementation f.

rehabilitate vt (in public esteem) réhabiliter; (prisoner) réinsérer.

rehearsal n répétition f. **rehearse** vt/i répéter.

reign n règne m. ●vi régner (**over** sur).

reimburse vt rembourser.

reindeer n inv renne m.

reinforce vt renforcer. **reinforcement** n renforcement m; **~s** renforts mpl.

reinstate vt (person) réintégrer; (law) rétablir.

reject[1] /'riːdʒekt/ n marchandise f de deuxième choix.

reject[2] /rɪ'dʒekt/ vt (offer, plea) rejeter; (goods) refuser. **rejection** n (personal) rejet m; (of candidate, work) refus m.

rejoice vi se réjouir.

relapse n rechute f. ●vi rechuter; **~ into** retomber dans.

relate vt raconter; (associate) associer. ●vi **~ to** se rapporter à; (get on with) s'entendre avec. **related** adj (ideas) lié; **we are ~d** nous sommes parents.

relation n rapport m; (person) parent/-e m/f. **relationship** n relations fpl; (link) rapport m.

relative n parent/-e m/f. ●adj relatif; (respective) respectif.

relax vt (grip) relâcher; (muscle) décontracter; (discipline) assouplir. ●vi (person) se détendre; (grip) se relâcher. **relaxation** n détente f. **relaxing** adj délassant.

relay[1] /'riːleɪ/ n (also **~ race**) course f de relais.

relay[2] /riː'leɪ/ vt relayer.

release vt (prisoner) libérer; (fastening) faire jouer; (object, hand) lâcher; (film) faire sortir; (news) publier. ●n libération f; (of film) sortie f; (new record, film) nouveauté f.

relevance n pertinence f, intérêt m.

relevant adj pertinent; **be ~ to** avoir rapport à.

reliability n (of firm) sérieux m; (of car) fiabilité f; (of person) honnêteté f. **reliable** adj (firm) sérieux; (person, machine) fiable.

reliance n dépendance f.

relic n vestige m; (object) relique f.

relief n soulagement m (**from** à); (assistance) secours m; (outline) relief m; **~ road** route f de délestage.

relieve vt soulager; (help) secourir; (take over from) relayer.

religion n religion f. **religious** adj religieux.

relish n plaisir m; (Culin) condiment m. ●vt (food) savourer; (idea) se réjouir de.

relocate vt muter. ●vi (company)

déménager; (worker) être muté.
relocation n délocalisation f.

reluctance n répugnance f.

reluctant adj (person) peu
enthousiaste; (consent) accordé à
contrecœur; ~ **to** peu disposé à.
reluctantly adv à contrecœur.

rely vi ~ **on** (count) compter sur;
(be dependent) dépendre de.

remain vi rester. **remainder** n
reste m.

remand vt mettre en détention
provisoire. •n **on** ~ en
détention provisoire.

remark n remarque f. •vt
remarquer. •vi ~ **on** faire des
remarques sur. **remarkable** adj
remarquable.

remedy n remède m. •vt
remédier à.

remember vt se souvenir de, se
rappeler; ~ **to do** ne pas oublier
de faire. **remembrance** n
souvenir m.

remind vt rappeler (**sb of sth**
qch à qn); ~ **sb to do** rappeler à
qn de faire. **reminder** n
rappel m.

reminisce vi évoquer ses
souvenirs.

remission n (Med) rémission f;
(Jur) remise f.

remnant n reste m; (trace) vestige
m; (of cloth) coupon m.

remodel vt (pt **remodelled**)
remodeler.

remorse n remords m.

remote adj (place, time) lointain;
(person) **distant**; (slight) vague; ~
control télécommande f.

removable adj amovible.

removal n (of employee) renvoi m;
(of threat) **suppression** f; (of troops)
retrait m; (of stain) détachage m;
(from house) déménagement m; ~
men déménageurs mpl.

remove vt enlever; (dismiss)
renvoyer; (do away with)

supprimer; (Comput) effacer.

remunerate vt rémunérer.
remuneration n rémunération f.

render vt rendre.

renegade n renégat/-e m/f.

renew vt renouveler; (resume)
reprendre. **renewable** adj
renouvelable.

renounce vt renoncer à; (disown)
renier.

renovate vt rénover.

renown n renommée f.

rent n loyer m. •vt louer; **for** ~ à
louer. **rental** n prix m de
location.

reopen vt/i rouvrir.

reorganize vt réorganiser.

rep n (Comm) représentant/-e m/f.

repair vt réparer. •n réparation f;
in good/**bad** ~ en bon/mauvais
état.

repatriate vt rapatrier.
repatriation n rapatriement m.

repay vt (pt **repaid**) rembourser;
(reward) récompenser.
repayment n remboursement m.

repeal vt abroger. •n abrogation f.

repeat vt/i répéter; (renew)
renouveler; ~ **itself**, ~ **oneself**
se répéter. •n répétition f;
(broadcast) reprise f.

repel vt (pt **repelled**) repousser.

repent vi se repentir (**of** de).

repercussion n répercussion f.

repetition n répétition f.

replace vt (put back) remettre; (take
the place of) remplacer.
replacement n remplacement m
(**of** de); (person) remplaçant/-e
m/f; (new part) pièce f de rechange.

replay n (Sport) match m rejoué;
(recording) répétition f immédiate.

replenish vt (refill) remplir;
(renew) renouveler.

replica n copie f exacte.

reply vt/i répondre. •n réponse f.

report vt rapporter, annoncer (**that** que); (notify) signaler; (denounce) dénoncer. •vi faire un rapport; ~ **(on)** (news item) faire un reportage sur; ~ **to** (go) se présenter chez. •n rapport m; (in press) reportage m; (School) bulletin m. **reporter** n reporter m.

repossess vt reprendre.

represent vt représenter.

representation n représentation f; **make ~s to** protester auprès de.

representative adj représentatif, typique (**of** de). •n représentant/-e m/f.

repress vt réprimer.

reprieve n (delay) sursis m; (pardon) grâce f. •vt accorder un sursis à; gracier.

reprimand vt réprimander. •n réprimande f.

reprisals npl représailles fpl.

reproach vt reprocher (**sb for sth** qch à qn). •n reproche m.

reproduce vt/i (se) reproduire. **reproduction** n reproduction f. **reproductive** adj reproducteur.

reptile n reptile m.

republic n république f. **republican** adj & n républicain/-e (m/f).

repudiate vt répudier; (contract) refuser d'honorer.

reputable adj honorable, de bonne réputation.

reputation n réputation f.

repute n réputation f.

request n demande f. •vt demander (**of, from** à).

require vt (of thing) demander; (of person) avoir besoin de; (demand, order) exiger. **required** adj requis. **requirement** n exigence f; (condition) condition f (requise).

rescue vt sauver. •n sauvetage m (**of** de); (help) secours m.

research n recherche(s) f(pl). •vt/i faire des recherches (sur). **researcher** n chercheur/-euse m/f.

resemblance n ressemblance f. **resemble** vt ressembler à.

resent vt être indigné de, s'offenser de. **resentment** n ressentiment m.

reservation n (doubt) réserve f; (booking) réservation f; (US) réserve f (indienne); **make a ~** réserver.

reserve vt réserver. •n (stock, land) réserve f; (Sport) remplaçant/-e m/f; **in ~** en réserve; **the ~s** (Mil) les réserves fpl. **reserved** adj (person, room) réservé.

reshuffle vt (Pol) remanier. •n (Pol) remaniement m (ministériel).

residence n résidence f; (of students) foyer m; **in ~** (doctor) résidant.

resident adj résidant; **be ~** résider. •n habitant/-e m/f; (foreigner) résident/-e m/f; (in hotel) pensionnaire mf. **residential** adj résidentiel.

resign vt abandonner; (job) démissionner de. •vi démissionner; ~ **oneself to** se résigner à. **resignation** n résignation f; (from job) démission f. **resigned** adj résigné.

resilience n élasticité f; ressort m.

resin n résine f.

resist vt/i résister (à). **resistance** n résistance f. **resistant** adj (Med) rebelle; (metal) résistant.

resolution n résolution f.

resolve vt résoudre (**to do** faire). •n résolution f.

resort vi ~ **to** avoir recours à. •n (recourse) recours m; (place) station f; **in the last ~** en dernier ressort.

resource n ressource f; ~**s** (wealth) ressources fpl.

resourceful adj ingénieux.

respect n respect m; (aspect) égard m; **with ~ to** à l'égard de, relativement à. •vt respecter.

respectability n respectabilité f. **respectable** adj respectable.

respectful adj respectueux.

respective adj respectif.

respite n répit m.

respond vi répondre (**to** à); **~ to** (react to) réagir à. **response** n réponse f.

responsibility n responsabilité f. **responsible** adj responsable; (job) qui comporte des responsabilités.

responsive adj réceptif.

rest vt/i (se) reposer; (lean) (s')appuyer (**on** sur); (be buried, lie) reposer; (remain) demeurer. •n repos m; (support) support m; **have a ~** se reposer; **the ~** (remainder) le reste (**of** de); (other people) les autres.

restaurant n restaurant m.

restless adj agité.

restoration n rétablissement m; restauration f.

restore vt rétablir; (building) restaurer; **~ sth to sb** restituer qch à qn.

restrain vt contenir; **~ sb from** retenir qn de. **restrained** adj (moderate) mesuré; (in control of self) maître de soi.

restrict vt restreindre. **restriction** n restriction f.

rest room n (US) toilettes fpl.

result n résultat m. •vi résulter; **~ in** aboutir à.

resume vt/i reprendre.

résumé n résumé m; (of career: US) CV m, curriculum vitae m.

resurrect vt ressusciter.

resuscitate vt réanimer.

retail n détail m. •adj & adv au détail. •vt/i (se) vendre (au détail). **retailer** n détaillant/- e m/f.

retain vt (hold back, remember) retenir; (keep) conserver.

retaliate vi riposter. **retaliation** n représailles fpl.

retch vi avoir un haut-le-cœur.

retire vi (from work) prendre sa retraite; (withdraw) se retirer; (go to bed) se coucher. **retired** adj retraité. **retirement** n retraite f.

retort vt/i répliquer. •n réplique f.

retrace vt **~ one's steps** revenir sur ses pas.

retract vt/i (se) rétracter.

retrain vt/i (se) recycler.

retreat vi (Mil) battre en retraite. •n retraite f.

retrieval n (Comput) extraction f. **retrieve** vt (object) récupérer; (situation) redresser; (data) extraire.

retrospect n **in ~** rétrospectivement.

return vi (come back) revenir; (go back) retourner; (go home) rentrer. •vt (give back) rendre; (bring back) rapporter; (send back) renvoyer; (put back) remettre. •n retour m; (yield) rapport m; **~s** (Comm) bénéfices mpl; **in ~ for** en échange de. **~ ticket** n allerretour m.

reunion n réunion f.

reunite vt réunir.

rev n (Auto 🔲) tour m. •vt/i (pt **revved**) **~ (up)** (engine 🔲) (s')emballer.

reveal vt révéler; (allow to appear) laisser voir.

revelation n révélation f.

revenge n vengeance f. •vt venger.

revenue n revenu m.

reverberate vi (sound, light) se répercuter.

r

reverend adj révérend.

reversal n renversement m; (of view) revirement m.

reverse adj contraire, inverse. •n contraire m; (back) revers m, envers m; (gear) marche f arrière. •vt (situation, bracket) renverser; (order) inverser; (decision) annuler; ~ **the charges** appeler en PCV. •vi (Auto) faire marche arrière.

review n (inspection, magazine) revue f; (of book) critique f. •vt passer en revue; (situation) réexaminer; faire la critique de. **reviewer** n critique m.

revise vt réviser; (text) revoir. **revision** n révision f.

revival n (of economy) reprise f; (of interest) regain m.

revive vt (person, hopes) ranimer; (custom) rétablir. •vi se ranimer.

revoke vt révoquer.

revolt vt/i (se) révolter. •n révolte f. **revolting** adj dégoûtant.

revolution n révolution f.

revolve vi tourner.

revolver n revolver m.

revolving door n porte f à tambour.

reward n récompense f. •vt récompenser (**for** de). **rewarding** adj rémunérateur; (worthwhile) qui (en) vaut la peine.

rewind vt (pt **rewound**) rembobiner.

rewire vt refaire l'installation électrique de.

rhetorical adj (de) rhétorique; (question) de pure forme.

rheumatism n rhumatisme m.

rhinoceros n (pl ~ **es**) rhinocéros m.

rhubarb n rhubarbe f.

rhyme n rime f; (poem) vers mpl. •vt/i (faire) rimer.

rhythm n rythme m. **rhythmic(al)** adj rythmique.

rib n côte f.

ribbon n ruban m; **in ~s** en lambeaux.

rice n riz m. ~ **pudding** n riz m au lait.

rich adj riche.

rid vt (pt **rid**; pres p **ridding**) débarrasser (**of** de); **get ~ of** se débarrasser de.

ridden ▷RIDE.

riddle n énigme f. •vt ~ **with** (bullets) cribler de; (mistakes) bourrer de.

ride vi (pt **rode**; pp **ridden**) aller (à bicyclette, à cheval); (in car) rouler; (on a horse as sport) monter à cheval. •vt (a particular horse) monter; (distance) parcourir. •n promenade f, tour m; (distance) trajet m; **give sb a ~** (US) prendre qn en voiture; **go for a ~** aller faire un tour (à bicyclette, à cheval). **rider** n cavalier/-ière m/f; (in horse race) jockey m; (cyclist) cycliste mf; (motorcyclist) motocycliste mf.

ridge n arête f, crête f.

ridiculous adj ridicule.

riding n équitation f.

rifle n fusil m. •vt (rob) dévaliser.

rift n (crack) fissure f; (between people) désaccord m.

rig vt (pt **rigged**) (equip) équiper; (election, match) truquer. •n (for oil) derrick m. ■ ~ **out** habiller; ~ **up** (arrange) arranger.

right adj (morally) bon; (fair) juste; (best) bon, qu'il faut; (not left) droit; **be ~** (person) avoir raison (**to** de); (calculation, watch) être exact; **put ~** arranger, rectifier. •n (entitlement) droit m; (not left) droite f; (not evil) le bien; **be in the ~** avoir raison; **on the ~** à droite. •vt (a wrong, sth fallen) redresser. • adv (not left) à droite; (directly) tout droit; (exactly) bien, juste; (completely) tout (à fait); ~ **away** tout de suite; ~ **now** (at once) tout de suite; (at present) en ce moment.

righteous adj vertueux.

rightful adj légitime.

right-handed adj droitier.

rightly adv correctement; (with reason) à juste titre.

right of way n (Auto) priorité f.

right wing adj de droite.

rigid adj rigide.

rigorous adj rigoureux.

rim n bord m.

rind n (on cheese) croûte f; (on bacon) couenne f; (on fruit) écorce f.

ring¹ /rɪŋ/ n (hoop) anneau m; (jewellery) bague f; (circle) cercle m; (boxing) ring m; **(wedding)** ~ alliance f. •vt entourer; (word in text) entourer d'un cercle.

ring² /rɪŋ/ vt/i (pt **rang**; pp **rung**) sonner; (of words) retentir; ~ **the bell** sonner. •n sonnerie f; **give sb a** ~ donner un coup de fil à qn. ▪ ~ **back** rappeler; ~ **off** raccrocher; ~ **up** téléphoner (à).

ring road n périphérique m.

rink n patinoire f.

rinse vt rincer; ~ **out** rincer. •n rinçage m.

riot n émeute f; (of colours) profusion f; **run** ~ se déchaîner. •vi faire une émeute.

rip vt/i (pt **ripped**) (se) déchirer; **let** ~ (not check) laisser courir; ~ **off** ⚠ rouler. •n déchirure f.

ripe adj mûr. **ripen** vt/i mûrir.

rip-off n ⚠ vol m; arnaque f ⚠.

ripple n ride f, ondulation f. •vt/i (water) (se) rider.

rise vi (pt **rose**; pp **risen**) (go upwards, increase) monter, s'élever; (stand up, get up from bed) se lever; (rebel) se soulever; (sun) se lever; (water) monter; ~ **up** se soulever. •n (slope) pente f; (increase) hausse

f; (in pay) augmentation f; (progress, boom) essor m; **give** ~ **to** donner lieu à.

risk n risque m; **at** ~ menacé. •vt risquer; ~ **doing** (venture) se risquer à faire. **risky** adj risqué.

rite n rite m; **last** ~s derniers sacrements mpl.

rival n rival/-e m/f. •adj rival; (claim) opposé. •vt (pt **rivalled**) rivaliser avec.

river n rivière f; (flowing into sea) fleuve m. •adj (fishing, traffic) fluvial.

rivet n (bolt) rivet m. •vt (pt **riveted**) river, riveter.

Riviera n **the (French)** ~ la Côte d'Azur.

road n route f; (in town) rue f; (small) chemin m; **the** ~ **to** (glory: fig) le chemin de. •adj (sign, safety) routier. ~**-map** n carte f routière. ~ **rage** n violence f au volant. ~**worthy** adj en état de marche.

roam vi errer. •vt (streets, seas) parcourir.

roar n hurlement m; (of lion, wind) rugissement m; (of lorry, thunder) grondement m. •vt/i hurler; (lion, wind) rugir; (lorry, thunder) gronder; ~ **with laughter** rire aux éclats.

roast vt/i rôtir. •n (meat) rôti m. •adj rôti. ~ **beef** n rôti m de bœuf.

rob vt (pt **robbed**) voler (**sb of sth** qch à qn); (bank, house) dévaliser; (deprive) priver (**of** de). **robber** n voleur/-euse m/f. **robbery** n vol m.

robe n (of judge) robe f; (dressinggown) peignoir m.

robin n rouge-gorge m.

robot n robot m.

robust adj robuste.

rock n roche f; (rock face, boulder) rocher m; (hurled stone) pierre f; (sweet) sucre m d'orge; (Mus) rock

r

m; **on the ~s** (drink) avec des
glaçons; (marriage) en crise. •vt/i
(se) balancer; (shake) (faire)
trembler; (child) bercer.
~-climbing n varappe f.

rocket n fusée f.

rocking-chair n fauteuil m à
bascule.

rocky adj (**-ier, -iest**) (ground)
rocailleux; (hill) rocheux; (shaky:
fig) branlant.

rod n (metal) tige f; (wooden)
baguette f; (for fishing) canne f à
pêche.

rode ▷RIDE.

roe n œufs mpl de poisson.

rogue n (dishonest) bandit m;
(mischievous) coquin/-e m/f.

role n rôle m.

roll vt/i rouler; **~ (about)** (child,
dog) se rouler; **be ~ing (in
money)**🗉 rouler sur l'or. •n
rouleau m; (list) liste f; (bread)
petit pain m; (of drum, thunder)
roulement m; (of ship) roulis m.
■**~ out** étendre; **~ over** se
retourner; **~ up** (sleeves)
retrousser.

roll-call n appel m.

roller n rouleau m. **~ blade** n
patin m en ligne, roller m.
~-coaster n montagnes fpl
russes. **~-skate** n patin m à
roulettes.

ROM abbr (**read-only memory**)
mémoire f morte.

Roman adj & n romain/-e (m/f). **~
Catholic** adj & n catholique (mf).

romance n (novel) roman m
d'amour; (love) amour m; (affair)
idylle f; (fig) poésie f.

Romania n Roumanie f.

Romanian adj roumain. •n
(person) Roumain/-e m/f; (language)
roumain m.

romantic adj (love) romantique;
(of the imagination) romanesque.

roof n toit m; (of mouth) palais m.

•vt recouvrir. **~-rack** n galerie f.
~-top n toit m.

room n pièce f; (bedroom) chambre
f; (large hall) salle f; (space) place f;
~ for manoeuvre marge f de
manœuvre. **~-mate** n camarade
mf de chambre.

roomy adj spacieux; (clothes)
ample.

root n racine f; (source) origine f;
take ~ prendre racine. •vt/i
(s')enraciner. ■**~ about**
fouiller; **~ for** (US 🗉)
encourager; **~ out** extirper.

rope n corde f; **know the ~s** être
au courant. •vt attacher; **~ in**
(person) enrôler.

rose n rose f. •• ▷RISE.

rosé n rosé m.

rosy adj (**-ier, -iest**) rose; (hopeful)
plein d'espoir.

rot vt/i (pt **rotted**) pourrir.

rota n liste f (de service).

rotary adj rotatif.

rotate vt/i (faire) tourner; (change
round) alterner.

rotten adj pourri; (tooth) gâté; (bad
🗉) mauvais, sale.

rough adj (manners) rude; (to touch)
rugueux; (ground) accidenté;
(violent) brutal; (bad) mauvais;
(estimate) approximatif. •adv (live)
à la dure.

roughage n fibres fpl.

roughly adv rudement;
(approximately) à peu près.

round adj rond. •n (circle) rond m;
(slice) tranche f; (of visits, drinks)
tournée f; (competition) partie f,
manche f; (boxing) round m; (of
talks) série f; **~ of applause**
applaudissements mpl; **go the
~s** circuler. •prep autour de; **she
lives ~ here** elle habite par ici;
~ the clock vingt-quatre heures
sur vingt-quatre. •adv autour; **~
about** (nearby) par ici; (fig) à peu
près; **go or come ~ to** (a friend)
passer chez; **enough to go ~**

r

assez pour tout le monde. •vt (object) arrondir; (corner) tourner. ∎ ~ **off** terminer; ~ **up** rassembler

roundabout n (in fairground) manège m; (for traffic) rond-point m (à sens giratoire). •adj indirect.

round trip n voyage m aller-retour.

round-up n rassemblement m; (of suspects) rafle f.

route n itinéraire m, parcours m; (Naut, Aviat) route f.

routine n routine f. •adj de routine.

row¹ /rəʊ/ n rangée f, rang m; **in a ~** (consecutive) consécutif. •vi ramer; (Sport) faire de l'aviron. •vt **a boat up the river** remonter la rivière à la rame.

row² /raʊ/ n (noise 🔲) tapage m; (quarrel 🔲) dispute f. •vi 🔲 se disputer.

rowdy adj (-ier, -iest) tapageur.

rowing n aviron m. ~-**boat** n bateau m à rames.

royal adj royal. **royalty** n famille f royale; **royalties** droits mpl d'auteur.

RSI abbr (**repetitive strain injury**) TMS m, trouble m musculo-squelettique.

rub vt/i (pt **rubbed**) frotter; ~ **it in** insister, en rajouter. •n friction f. ~ **out** (s')effacer.

rubber n caoutchouc m; (eraser) gomme f. ~ **band** n élastique m. ~ **stamp** n tampon m.

rubbish n (refuse) ordures fpl; (junk) saletés fpl; (fig) bêtises fpl.

rubble n décombres mpl.

ruby n rubis m.

rucksack n sac m à dos.

rude adj impoli, grossier; (improper) indécent; (blow) brutal.

ruffle vt (hair) ébouriffer; (clothes) froisser; (person) contrarier. •n (frill) ruche f.

rug n petit tapis m.

rugby n rugby m.

rugged adj (surface) rude, rugueux; (ground) accidenté; (character, features) rude.

ruin n ruine f. •vt (destroy) ruiner; (damage) abîmer; (spoil) gâter.

rule n règle f; (regulation) règlement m; (Pol) gouvernement m; **as a ~** en règle générale. •vt gouverner; (master) dominer; (decide) décider; ~ **out** exclure. •vi régner. **ruler** n dirigeant/-e m/f, gouvernant m; (measure) règle f.

ruling adj (class) dirigeant; (party) au pouvoir. •n décision f.

rum n rhum m.

rumble vi gronder; (stomach) gargouiller. •n grondement m; gargouillement m.

rumour, (US) **rumor** n bruit m, rumeur f; **there's a ~ that** le bruit court que.

rump n (of animal) croupe f; (of bird) croupion m; (steak) romsteck m.

run vi (pt **ran**; pp **run**; pres p **running**) courir; (flow) couler; (pass) passer; (function) marcher; (melt) fondre; (extend) s'étendre; (of bus) circuler; (of play) se jouer; (last) durer; (of colour in washing) déteindre; (in election) être candidat. •vt (manage) diriger; (event) organiser; (risk, race) courir; (house) tenir; (temperature, errand) faire; (Comput) exécuter. •n course f; (journey) parcours m; (outing) promenade f; (rush) ruée f; (series) série f; (for chickens) enclos m; (in cricket) point m; **in the long ~** avec le temps; **on the ~** en fuite. ∎ ~ **across** rencontrer par hasard; ~ **away** s'enfuir; ~ **down** descendre en courant; (of vehicle) renverser; (production) réduire progressivement; (belittle) dénigrer; ~ **into** (hit) heurter; ~ **off** (copies) tirer; ~ **out** (be used up) s'épuiser; (of lease) expirer; ~ **out of** manquer de; ~ **over** (of vehicle) écraser; (details) revoir; ~ **through** regarder qch rapidement; **~ sth through sth** passer qch à travers qch; **~ up** (bill) accumuler.

runaway n fugitif/-ive m/f. ●adj fugitif; (horse, vehicle) fou; (inflation) galopant.

rung ▷RING². ●n (of ladder) barreau m.

runner n coureur/-euse m/f. **~ bean** n haricot m d'Espagne. **~-up** n second/-e m/f.

running n course f à pied; (of business) gestion f; (of machine) marche f; **be in the ~ for** être sur les rangs pour. ●adj (commentary) suivi; (water) courant; **four days ~** quatre jours de suite.

runway n piste f.

rural adj rural.

rush vi (move) se précipiter; (be in a hurry) se dépêcher. ●vt (person) bousculer; (Mil) prendre d'assaut; **~ to** envoyer d'urgence à. ●n ruée f; (haste) bousculade f; (plant) jonc m; **in a ~** pressé. **~-hour** n heure f de pointe.

Russia n Russie f.

Russian adj russe. ●n (person) Russe mf; (language) russe.

rust n rouille f. ●vt/i rouiller.

rustle vt/i (papers) froisser.

rusty adj rouillé.

ruthless adj impitoyable.

rye n seigle m.

Ss

sabbath n (Jewish) sabbat m; (Christian) jour m du seigneur.

sabbatical adj (Univ) sabbatique.

sabotage n sabotage m. ●vt saboter.

saccharin n saccharine f.

sack n (bag) sac m; **get the ~** 🅣 être renvoyé. ●vt 🅣 renvoyer; (plunder) saccager. **sacking** n (cloth) toile f à sac; (dismissal 🅣) renvoi m.

sacrament n sacrement m.

sacred adj sacré.

sacrifice n sacrifice m. ●vt sacrifier.

sad adj (**sadder, saddest**) triste.

saddle n selle f. ●vt (horse) seller.

sadist n sadique mf. **sadistic** adj sadique.

sadly adv tristement; (unfortunately) malheureusement.

sadness n tristesse f.

safe adj (not dangerous) sans danger; (reliable) sûr; (out of danger) en sécurité; (after accident) sain et sauf; **~ from** à l'abri de. ●n coffre-fort m.

safeguard n sauvegarde f. ●vt sauvegarder.

safely adv sans danger; (in safe place) en sûreté.

safety n sécurité f. **~-belt** n ceinture f de sécurité. **~-pin** n épingle f de sûreté. **~-valve** n soupape f de sûreté.

saffron n safran m.

sag vi (pt **sagged**) (beam, mattress) s'affaisser; (flesh) être flasque.

sage n (herb) sauge f.

Sagittarius n Sagittaire m.

said ▷SAY.

sail n voile f; (journey) tour m en bateau. ●vi (person) voyager en bateau; (as sport) faire de la voile; (set off) prendre la mer; **~ across**

traverser. •vt (boat) piloter; (sea) traverser. **sailing-boat, sailing-ship** n voilier m.

sailor n marin m.

saint n saint/-e m/f.

sake n **for the ~ of** pour.

salad n salade f.

salaried adj salarié.

salary n salaire m.

sale n vente f; **for ~** à vendre; **on ~** en vente; (reduced) en solde; **~s** (reductions) soldes mpl; **~s assistant**, (US) **~s clerk** vendeur/-euse m/f.

salesman n (pl **-men**) (in shop) vendeur m; (traveller) représentant m.

saline adj salin. •n sérum m physiologique.

saliva n salive f.

salmon n inv saumon m.

salon n salon m.

saloon n (on ship) salon m; **~ (car)** berline f.

salt n sel m. •vt saler. **salty** adj salé.

salutary adj salutaire.

salute n salut m. •vt saluer. •vi faire un salut.

salvage n sauvetage m; (of waste) récupération f. •vt sauver; (for re-use) récupérer.

same adj même (**as que**). •pron **the ~** le même, la même, les mêmes; **at the ~ time** en même temps; **the ~ (thing)** la même chose.

sample n échantillon m; (of blood) prélèvement m. •vt essayer; (food) goûter.

sanctimonious adj (pej) supérieur.

sanction n sanction f. •vt sanctionner.

sanctity n sainteté f.

sanctuary n (safe place) refuge m; (Relig) sanctuaire m; (for animals) réserve f.

sand n sable m; **~s** (beach) plage f.

sandal n sandale f.

sandpaper n papier m de verre. •vt poncer.

sandpit n bac m à sable.

sandwich n sandwich m; **~ course** cours m avec stage pratique.

sandy adj (beach) de sable; (soil) sablonneux; (hair) blond roux inv.

sane adj (view) sensé; (person) sain d'esprit.

sang ▷ SING.

sanitary adj (clean) hygiénique; (system) sanitaire; **~ towel** serviette f hygiénique.

sanitation n installations fpl sanitaires.

sanity n équilibre m mental; (sense) bon sens m.

sank ▷ SINK.

Santa (Claus) n le père Noël.

sapphire n saphir m.

sarcasm n sarcasme m. **sarcastic** adj sarcastique.

sash n (on uniform) écharpe f; (on dress) ceinture f.

sat ▷ SIT.

satchel n cartable m.

satellite n & adj satellite (m); **~ dish** antenne f parabolique.

satire n satire f. **satirical** adj satirique.

satisfaction n satisfaction f.

satisfactory adj satisfaisant.

satisfy vt satisfaire; (convince) convaincre.

satphone n téléphone m satellite.

saturate vt saturer. **saturated** adj (wet) trempé.

Saturday n samedi m.

sauce n sauce f.

saucepan n casserole f.

saucer n soucoupe f.

Saudi Arabia n Arabie f saoudite.

sausage n (for cooking) saucisse f; (ready to eat) saucisson m.

savage adj (blow, temper) violent; (attack) sauvage. ●n sauvage mf. ●vt attaquer sauvagement.

save vt sauver; (money) économiser; (time) gagner; (keep) garder; ~ **(sb) doing sth** éviter (à qn) de faire qch. ●n (football) arrêt m. **saver** n épargnant/-e m/f. **saving** n économie f. **savings** npl économies fpl.

saviour, (US) **savior** n sauveur m.

savour, (US) **savor** n saveur f. ●vt savourer. **savoury** adj (tasty) savoureux; (Culin) salé.

saw ▷SEE. ●n scie f. ●vt (pt **sawed**; pp **sawn** or **sawed**) scier.

sawdust n sciure f.

saxophone n saxophone m.

say vt/i (pt **said**) dire; (prayer) faire. ●n **have a** ~ dire son mot; (in decision) avoir voix au chapitre. **saying** n proverbe m.

scab n croûte f.

scaffolding n échafaudage m.

scald vt (injure, cleanse) ébouillanter. ●n brûlure f.

scale n (for measuring) échelle f; (extent) étendue f; (Mus) gamme f; (on fish) écaille f; **on a small** ~ sur une petite échelle; ~ **model** maquette f. ●vt (climb) escalader; ~ **down** réduire. **scales** npl (for weighing) balance f.

scallop n coquille f Saint-Jacques.

scalp n cuir m chevelu.

scampi npl (fresh) langoustines fpl; (breaded) scampi mpl.

scan vt (pt **scanned**) scruter; (quickly) parcourir. ●n (ultrasound) échographie f; (CAT) scanner m.

scandal n scandale m; (gossip) potins mpl ⚠.

Scandinavia n Scandinavie f.

scanty adj (-ier, -iest) maigre; (clothing) minuscule.

scapegoat n bouc m émissaire.

scar n cicatrice f. ●vt (pt **scarred**) marquer.

scarce adj rare. **scarcely** adv à peine.

scare vt faire peur à; **be** ~**d** avoir peur. ●n peur f; **bomb** ~ alerte f à la bombe. **scarecrow** n épouvantail m.

scarf n (pl **scarves**) écharpe f; (over head) foulard m.

scarlet adj écarlate; ~ **fever** scarlatine f.

scary adj (-ier, -iest) ⚠ qui fait peur.

scathing adj cinglant.

scatter vt (throw) éparpiller, répandre; (disperse) disperser. ●vi se disperser.

scavenge vi fouiller (dans les ordures). **scavenger** n (animal) charognard m.

scene n scène f; (of accident, crime) lieu m; (sight) spectacle m; **behind the** ~**s** en coulisse. **scenery** n paysage m; (Theat) décors mpl. **scenic** adj panoramique.

scent n (perfume) parfum m; (trail) piste f. ●vt flairer; (make fragrant) parfumer.

sceptic n sceptique mf. **sceptical** adj sceptique. **scepticism** n scepticisme m.

schedule n horaire m; (for job) planning m; **behind** ~ en retard; **on** ~ dans les temps. ●vt prévoir; ~**d flight** vol m régulier.

scheme n projet m; (dishonest) combine f; **pension** ~ plan m de retraite. ●vi comploter.

schizophrenic adj & n schizophrène (mf).

scholar n érudit/-e m/f.

school n école f; **go to** ~ aller à

l'école. ●adj (age, year, holidays) scolaire. ~**boy** n élève m. ~**girl** n élève f. **schooling** n scolarité f. ~**teacher** n (primary) instituteur/-trice m/f; (secondary) professeur m.

science n science f; **teach** ~ enseigner les sciences. **scientific** adj scientifique. **scientist** n scientifique mf.

scissors npl ciseaux mpl.

scold vt gronder.

scoop n (shovel) pelle f; (measure) mesure f; (for ice cream) cuillère f à glace; (news) exclusivité f.

scooter n (child's) trottinette f; (motor cycle) scooter m.

scope n étendue f; (competence) compétence f; (opportunity) possibilité f.

scorch vt brûler; (iron) roussir.

score n score m; (Mus) partition f; **on that** ~ à cet égard. ●vt marquer; (success) remporter. ●vi marquer un point; (football) marquer un but; (keep score) marquer les points. **scorer** n (Sport) marqueur m.

scorn n mépris m. ●vt mépriser.

Scorpio n Scorpion m.

Scot n écossais/-e m/f.

Scotland n écosse f.

Scottish adj écossais.

scoundrel n gredin m.

scour vt (pan) récurer; (search) parcourir. **scourer** n tampon m à récurer.

scourge n fléau m.

scout n éclaireur m. ●vi ~ **around for** rechercher.

scowl n air m renfrogné. ●vi prendre un air renfrogné.

scramble vi (clamber) grimper. ●vt (eggs) brouiller. ●n (rush) course f.

scrap n petit morceau m; ~**s** (of metal, fabric) déchets mpl; (of food) restes mpl; (fight 🅸) bagarre f. ●vt (pt **scrapped**) abandonner; (car) détruire.

scrape vt gratter; (damage) érafler. ●vi ~ **against** érafler. ■ ~ **through** réussir de justesse.

scrap: ~**paper** n papier m brouillon. ~**yard** n casse f.

scratch vt/i (se) gratter; (with claw, nail) griffer; (graze) érafler; (mark) rayer. ●n (on body) égratignure f; (on surface) éraflure f; **start from** ~ partir de zéro; **up to** ~ à la hauteur. ~ **card** n jeu m de grattage.

scrawl n gribouillage m. ●vt/i gribouiller.

scrawny adj (**-ier, -iest**) décharné.

scream vt/i crier. ●n cri m (perçant).

screech vi (scream) hurler; (tyres) crisser. ●n cri m strident; (of tyres) crissement m.

screen n écran m; (folding) paravent m. ●vt masquer; (protect) protéger; (film) projeter; (candidates) filtrer; (Med) faire subir un test de dépistage. **screening** n (cinema) projection f; (Med) dépistage m.

screen: ~**play** n scénario m. ~ **saver** n protecteur m d'écran.

screw n vis f. ●vt visser; ~ **up** (eyes) plisser; (ruin 🅸) cafouiller 🅸. ~**driver** n tournevis m.

scribble vt/i griffonner. ●n griffonnage m.

script n script m; (of play) texte m.

scroll n rouleau m. ●vt/i (Comput) (faire) défiler. ~ **bar** n barre f de défilement.

scrounge 🅸 vt (favour) quémander; (cigarette) piquer 🅸; ~ **money from sb** taper de l'argent à qn. ●vi ~ **off sb** vivre sur le dos de qn.

scrub n (land) broussailles fpl. ●vt/i (pt **scrubbed**) nettoyer (à la brosse), frotter.

s

scruffy adj (-ier, -iest) ⊞ dépenaillé.

scrum n (rugby) mêlée f.

scruple n scrupule m.

scrutinize vt scruter. **scrutiny** n examen m minutieux.

scuba-diving n plongée f sousmarine.

scuffle n bagarre f.

sculpt vt/i sculpter. **sculptor** n sculpteur m.

sculpture n sculpture f.

scum n (on liquid) mousse f; (people: pej) racaille f.

scurry vi se précipiter, courir (**for** pour chercher); ~ **off** se sauver.

sea n mer f; **at** ~ en mer; **by** ~ par mer. ●adj (air) marin; (bird) de mer; (voyage) par mer. ~**food** n fruits mpl de mer. ~**gull** n mouette f.

seal n (animal) phoque m; (insignia) sceau m; (with wax) cachet m. ●vt sceller; cacheter; (stick down) coller. ■~ **off** (area) boucler.

seam n (in cloth) couture f; (of coal) veine f.

search vt/i (examine) fouiller; (seek) chercher; (study) examiner; (Comput) rechercher. ●n fouille f; (quest) recherches fpl; (Comput) recherche f; **in** ~ **of** à la recherche de. ~ **engine** n (Internet) moteur m de recherche. ~**light** n projecteur m. ~**warrant** n mandat m de perquisition.

sea: ~**shell** n coquillage m. ~**shore** n (coast) littoral m; (beach) plage f.

seasick adj **be** ~ avoir le mal de mer.

seaside n bord m de la mer.

season n saison f; ~ **ticket** carte f d'abonnement. ●vt assaisonner. **seasonal** adj saisonnier. **seasoning** n assaisonnement m.

seat n siège m; (place) place f; (of

trousers) fond m; **take a** ~ asseyez-vous. ●vt (put) placer; **the room** ~**s 30** la salle peut accueillir 30 personnes. ~**belt** n ceinture f (de sécurité)

seaweed n algue f marine.

secluded adj retiré.

seclusion n isolement m.

second[1] /'sekənd/ adj deuxième, second; **a** ~ **chance** une nouvelle chance; **have** ~ **thoughts** avoir des doutes. ●n deuxième mf; (unit of time) seconde f; ~**s** (food) rab m. ⊞ ●adv (in race) deuxième; (secondly) deuxièmement. ●vt (proposal) appuyer.

second[2] /sɪ'kɒnd/ vt (transfer) détacher (**to** à).

secondary adj secondaire; ~ **school** lycée m, école f secondaire.

second-best n pis-aller m.

second-class adj (Rail) de deuxième classe; (post) au tarif lent.

second hand n (on clock) trotteuse f.

second-hand adj & adv (article) d'occasion; (information) de seconde main.

secondly adv deuxièmement.

second-rate adj médiocre.

secrecy n secret m.

secret adj secret. ●n secret m; **in** ~ en secret.

secretarial adj (work) de secrétaire.

secretary n secrétaire mf; **S**~ **of State** ministre m; (US) ministre m des Affaires étrangères.

secrete vt (Med) sécréter; (hide) cacher.

secretive adj secret. **secretly** adv secrètement.

sect n secte f. **sectarian** adj sectaire.

section n partie f; (in store) rayon

sector n secteur m.

secular adj (school) laïque; (art, music) profane.

secure adj (safe) sûr; (job, marriage) stable; (knot, lock) solide; (window) bien fermé; (feeling) de sécurité; (person) sécurisé. ●vt attacher; (obtain) s'assurer; (ensure) assurer.

security n (safety) sécurité f; (for loan) caution f; ~ **guard** vigile m.

sedate adj calme. ●vt donner un sédatif à. **sedative** n sédatif m.

seduce vt séduire. **seducer** n séducteur/-trice m/f. **seduction** n séduction f. **seductive** adj séduisant.

see vt/i (pt **saw**; pp **seen**) voir; **see you (soon)!** à bientôt!; ~**ing that** vu que. ∎ ~ **out** (person) raccompagner à la porte; ~ **through** (deception) déceler; (person) percer à jour; ~ **sth through** mener qch à bonne fin; ~ **to** s'occuper de; ~ **to it that** veiller à ce que.

seed n graine f; (collectively) graines fpl; (origin: fig) germe m; (tennis) tête f de série. **seedling** n plant m.

seek vt (pt **sought**) chercher.

seem vi sembler; **he ~s to think** il a l'air de croire.

seen ▷SEE.

seep vi suinter; ~ **into** s'infiltrer dans.

see-saw n tapecul m. ●vt osciller.

seethe vi ~ **with** (anger) bouillir de; (people) grouiller de.

segment n segment m; (of orange) quartier m.

segregate vt séparer.

seize vt saisir; (territory, prisoner) s'emparer de. ●vi ~ **on** (chance) saisir; ~ **up** (engine) se gripper.

seizure n (Med) crise f.

seldom adv rarement.

select vt sélectionner. ●adj privilégié. **selection** n sélection f. **selective** adj sélectif.

self n (pl **selves**) moi m; (on cheque) moi-même. ~**-assured** adj plein d'assurance. ~**-catering** adj (holiday) en location. ~**-centred**, (US) ~**-centered** adj égocentrique. ~**-confident** adj sûr de soi. ~**-conscious** adj timide. ~**-contained** adj (flat) indépendant. ~**-control** n sangfroid m. ~**-defence** n autodéfense f; (Jur) légitime défense f. ~**-employed** adj qui travaille à son compte. ~**-esteem** n amour-propre m. ~**-governing** adj autonome. ~**-indulgent** adj complaisant. ~**-interest** n intérêt m personnel.

selfish adj égoïste.

selfless adj désintéressé.

self: ~**-portrait** n autoportrait m. ~**-reliant** adj autosuffisant. ~**-respect** n respect m de soi. ~**-righteous** adj satisfait de soi. ~**-sacrifice** n abnégation f. ~**-satisfied** adj satisfait de soi. ~**-seeking** adj égoïste. ~**-service** n & adj libre-service (m).

sell vt/i (pt **sold**) vendre; ~ **well** se vendre bien. ∎ ~ **off** liquider; ~ **out** (items) se vendre; **have sold out** avoir tout vendu.

Sellotape® n scotch® m.

sell-out n (betrayal) 🄸 revirement m; **be a** ~ (show) afficher complet.

semester n (Univ) semestre m.

semicircle n demi-cercle m.

semicolon n point-virgule m.

semi-detached adj ~ **house** maison f jumelée.

semifinal n demi-finale f.

seminar n séminaire m.

semolina n semoule f.

senate n sénat m. **senator** n sénateur m.

send vt/i (pt **sent**) envoyer. ■ ~
away (dismiss) renvoyer; ~
(away or **off) for** commander
(par la poste); ~ **back** renvoyer;
~ **for** (person, help) envoyer
chercher; ~ **up** 🇬🇧 parodier.

senile adj sénile.

senior adj plus âgé (**to** que); (in
rank) haut placé; **be** ~ **to sb** être
le supérieur de qn. ●n aîné/-e
m/f. ~ **citizen** personne f âgée.
~ **school** n lycée m.

sensation n sensation f.
sensational adj sensationnel.

sense n sens m; (mental impression)
sentiment m; (common sense) bon
sens m; ~**s** (mind) raison f;
there's no ~ **in doing** cela ne
sert à rien de faire; **make** ~
avoir un sens; **make** ~ **of**
comprendre. ●vt (pres)sentir.
senseless adj insensé; (Med) sans
connaissance.

sensible adj raisonnable; (clothing)
pratique.

sensitive adj sensible (**to** à);
(issue) difficile.

sensory adj sensoriel.

sensual adj sensuel. **sensuality** n
sensualité f.

sensuous adj sensuel.

sent ▷ SEND.

sentence n phrase f; (punishment:
Jur) peine f. ●vt ~ **to**
condamner à.

sentiment n sentiment m.
sentimental adj sentimental.

sentry n sentinelle f.

separate[1] /'seprət/ adj (piece) à
part; (issue) autre; (sections)
différent; (organizations) distinct.

separate[2] /'sepəreɪt/ vt/i (se)
séparer.

separately adv séparément.

separation n séparation f.

September n septembre m.

septic adj (wound) infecté; ~ **tank**
fosse f septique.

sequel n suite f.

sequence n (order) ordre m; (series)
suite f; (in film) séquence f.

Serb adj serbe. ●n (person) Serbe
mf; (Ling) serbe m.

Serbia n Serbie f.

sergeant n (Mil) sergent m;
(policeman) brigadier m.

serial n feuilleton m. ●adj (Comput)
série inv.

series n inv série f.

serious adj sérieux; (accident, crime)
grave.

seriously adv sérieusement; (ill)
gravement; **take** ~ prendre au
sérieux.

sermon n sermon m.

serpent n serpent m.

serrated adj dentelé.

serum n sérum m.

servant n domestique mf.

serve vt/i servir; faire; (transport,
hospital) desservir; ~ **as/to** servir
de/à; ~ **a purpose** être utile; ~
a sentence (Jur) purger une
peine. ●n (tennis) service m.

server n serveur m; **remote** ~
téléserveur m.

service n service m; (maintenance)
révision f; (Relig) office m; ~**s**
(Mil) forces fpl armées. ●vt (car)
réviser. ~ **area** n (Auto) aire f de
services. ~ **charge** n service m.
~ **station** n station-service f.

session n séance f; **be in** ~ (Jur)
tenir séance.

set vt (pt **set**; pres p **setting**)
placer; (table) mettre; (limit) fixer;
(clock) mettre à l'heure; (example,
task) donner; (TV), (cinema) situer;
~ **fire to** mettre le feu à; ~
free libérer; ~ **to music** mettre
en musique. ●vi (sun) se coucher;
(jelly) prendre; ~ **sail** partir. ●n
(of chairs, stamps) série f; (of knives,
keys) jeu m; (of people) groupe m;
(TV), (radio) poste m; (Theat) décor
m; (tennis) set m; (mathematics)

ensemble m. ●adj (time, price) fixe; (procedure) bien determiné; (meal) à prix fixe; (book) au programme; **~ against sth** opposé à; **be ~ on doing** tenir absolument à faire. ■**~ about** se mettre à; **~ back** (delay) retarder; (cost Ⅱ) coûter; **~ in** (take hold) s'installer, commencer; **~ off** or **out** partir; **~ off** (panic, riot) déclencher; (bomb) faire exploser; **~ out** (state) présenter; (arrange) disposer; **~ out to do sth** chercher à faire qch; **~ up** (stall) monter; (equipment) assembler; (experiment) préparer; (company) créer; (meeting) organiser. **~-back** n revers m.

settee n canapé m.

setting n cadre m; (on dial) position f.

settle vt (arrange, pay) régler; (date) fixer; (nerves) calmer. ●vi (come to rest) (bird) se poser; (dust) se déposer; (live) s'installer. ■**~ down** se calmer; (marry etc.) se ranger; **~ for** accepter; **~ in** s'installer; **~ up (with)** régler.

settlement n règlement m (**of** de); (agreement) accord m; (place) colonie f.

settler n colon m.

seven adj & n sept (m).

seventeen adj & n dix-sept (m).

seventh adj & n septième (mf).

seventy adj & n soixante-dix (m).

sever vt (cut) couper; (relations) rompre.

several adj & pron plusieurs; **~ of us** plusieurs d'entre nous.

severe adj (harsh) sévère; (serious) grave.

sew vt/i (pt **sewed**; pp **sewn** or **sewed**) coudre.

sewage n eaux fpl usées.

sewer n égout m.

sewing n couture f. **~-machine** n machine f à coudre.

sewn ▷SEW.

sex n sexe m; **have ~** avoir des rapports (sexuels). ●adj sexuel. **sexist** adj & n sexiste (mf). **sexual** adj sexuel.

shabby adj (**-ier, -iest**) (place, object) miteux; (person) habillé de façon miteuse; (treatment) mesquin.

shack n cabane f.

shade n ombre f; (of colour, opinion) nuance f; (for lamp) abat-jour m inv; **a ~ bigger** légèrement plus grand. ●vt (tree) ombrager; (hat) projeter une ombre sur.

shadow n ombre f. ●vt (follow) filer. **S~ Cabinet** n cabinet m fantôme.

shady adj (**-ier, -iest**) ombragé; (dubious) véreux.

shaft n (of tool) manche m; (of arrow) tige f; (in machine) axe m; (of mine) puits m; (of light) rayon m.

shake vt (pt **shook**; pp **shaken**) secouer; (bottle) agiter; (belief) ébranler; **~ hands with** serrer la main à; **~ one's head** dire non de la tête. ●vi trembler. ●n secousse f; **give sth a ~** secouer qch. ■**~ off** se débarrasser de. **~-up** n (Pol) remaniement m.

shaky adj (**-ier, -iest**) (hand, voice) tremblant; (ladder) branlant; (weak: fig) instable.

shall v aux **I ~ do** je ferai; **we ~ see** nous verrons; **~ we go...?** si on allait... ?

shallow adj peu profond; (fig) superficiel.

shame n honte f; **it's a ~** c'est dommage. ●vt faire honte à.

shampoo n shampooing m. ●vt faire un shampooing à.

shandy n panaché m.

shan't ▷SHALL NOT.

shanty n (shack) baraque f; **~ town** bidonville m.

shape n forme f. ●vt (clay) modeler; (rock) façonner; (future: fig) déterminer; **~ sth into balls**

faire des boules avec qch. •vi ~
up (plan) prendre tournure;
(person) faire des progrès.

share n part f; (Comm) action f. •vt/
i partager; (feature) avoir en
commun. ~**holder** n actionnaire
mf. ~**ware** n (Comput) logiciel m
contributif.

shark n requin m.

sharp adj (knife) tranchant; (pin)
pointu; (point, angle, cry) aigu;
(person, mind) vif; (tone) acerbe.
•adv (stop) net; (sing, play) trop
haut; **six o'clock** ~ six heures
pile. •n (Mus) dièse m.

sharpen vt aiguiser; (pencil)
tailler.

shatter vt (glass) fracasser; (hope)
briser. •vi (glass) voler en éclats.

shave vt/i (se) raser. •n **have a** ~
se raser. **shaver** n rasoir m
électrique.

shaving n (of wood) copeau m. •adj
(cream, foam, gel) à raser.

shawl n châle m.

she pron elle. •n (animal) femelle f.

shear vt (pp **shorn** or **sheared**)
(sheep) tondre; ~ **off** se
détacher.

shears npl cisaille f.

shed n remise f. •vt (pt **shed**; pres p
shedding) perdre; (light, tears)
répandre.

sheen n lustre m.

sheep n inv mouton m. ~**-dog** n
chien m de berger.

sheepish adj penaud.

sheepskin n peau f de mouton.

sheer adj pur; (steep) à pic; (fabric)
très fin. •adv à pic.

sheet n drap m; (of paper) feuille f;
(of glass, ice) plaque f.

shelf n (pl **shelves**) étagère f; (in
shop, fridge) rayon m; (in oven)
plaque f.

shell n coquille f; (on beach)
coquillage m; (of building) carcasse

f; (explosive) obus m. •vt (nut)
décortiquer; (peas) écosser; (Mil)
bombarder.

shellfish npl (lobster etc.) crustacés
mpl; (mollusc) coquillages mpl.

shelter n abri m. •vt/i (s')abriter;
(give lodging to) donner asile à.

shelve vt (plan) mettre en
suspens.

shepherd n berger m; ~**'s pie**
hachis m Parmentier. •vt (people)
guider.

sherry n xérès m.

shield n bouclier m; (screen) écran
m. •vt protéger.

shift vt/i (se) déplacer, bouger;
(exchange, alter) changer de. •n
changement m; (workers) équipe f;
(work) poste m; ~ **work** travail m
posté, travail m par roulement.

shifty adj (**-ier, -iest**) louche.

shimmer vi chatoyer. •n
chatoiement m.

shin n tibia m.

shine vt (pt **shone**) (torch) braquer
(**on** sur). •vi (light, sun, hair)
briller; (brass) reluire. •n
lustre m.

shingle n (pebbles) galets mpl; (on
roof) bardeau m.

shingles npl (Med) zona m.

shiny adj (**-ier, -iest**) brillant.

ship n bateau m, navire m. •vt (pt
shipped) transporter. **shipment**
n (by sea) cargaison f; (by air, land)
chargement m. **shipping** n (ships)
navigation f. ~**wreck** n épave f;
(event) naufrage m.

shirt n chemise f; (woman's)
chemisier m.

shiver vi frissonner. •n frisson m.

shock n choc m; (Electr) décharge f;
in ~ en état de choc; ~
absorber amortisseur m. •adj
(result) choc inv; (tactics) de choc.
•vt choquer.

shoddy adj (**-ier, -iest**) mal fait;
(behaviour) mesquin.

shoe n chaussure f; (of horse) fer m; **(brake)** ~ sabot m (de frein). ●vt (pt **shod**; pres p **shoeing**) (horse) ferrer. ~**lace** n lacet m. ~**size** n pointure f.

shone ▷ SHINE.

shook ▷ SHAKE.

shoot vt (pt **shot**) (gun) tirer un coup de; (bullet) tirer; (missile, glance) lancer; (person) tirer sur; (kill) abattre; (execute) fusiller; (film) tourner. ●vi tirer (**at** sur). ●n (Bot) pousse f. ■ ~ **down** abattre; ~ **out** (rush) sortir en vitesse; ~ **up** (spurt) jaillir; (grow) pousser vite.

shooting n (killing) meurtre m (par arme à feu) **hear** ~ entendre des coups de feu.

shop n magasin m; (small) boutique f; (workshop) atelier m. ●vi (pt **shopped**) faire ses courses; ~ **around** comparer les prix. ~ **assistant** n vendeur/-euse m/f. ~**floor** n (workers) ouvriers mpl. ~**keeper** n commerçant/-e m/f. ~**lifter** n voleur/-euse m/f à l'étalage.

shopper n acheteur/-euse m/f.

shopping n (goods) achats mpl; **go** ~ (for food) faire les courses; (for clothes etc.) faire les magasins. ~ **bag** n sac m à provisions. ~ **centre**, (US) ~ **center** n centre m commercial.

shop window n vitrine f.

shore n côte f, rivage m; **on** ~ à terre.

short adj court; (person) petit; (brief) court, bref; (curt) brusque; **be** ~ **(of)** manquer (de); **everything** ~ **of** tout sauf; **nothing** ~ **of** rien de moins que; **cut** ~ écourter; **cut sb** ~ interrompre qn; **fall** ~ ne pas arriver à; **he is called Tom for** ~ son diminutif est Tom; **in** ~ en bref. ●adv (stop) net. ●n (Electr) court-circuit m; (film) courtmétrage m; ~**s** (trousers) short m.

shortage n manque m.

short: ~**bread** n sablé m. ~**change** vt (cheat) rouler 🔳. ~ **circuit** n court-circuit m. ~**coming** n défaut m. ~ **cut** n raccourci m.

shorten vt raccourcir.

shortfall n déficit m.

shorthand n sténographie f; ~ **typist** sténodactylo f.

short: ~ **list** n liste f des candidats choisis. ~**-lived** adj de courte durée.

shortly adv bientôt.

short: ~**-sighted** adj myope. ~**-staffed** adj à court de personnel; ~ **story** n nouvelle f. ~**-term** adj à court terme.

shot ▷ SHOOT. ●n (firing, attempt) coup m de feu; (person) tireur m; (bullet) balle f; (photograph) photo f; (injection) piqûre f; **like a** ~ sans hésiter. ~**gun** n fusil m de chasse.

should v aux devoir; **you** ~ **help me** vous devriez m'aider; **I** ~ **have stayed** j'aurais dû rester; **I** ~ **like to** j'aimerais bien; **if he** ~ **come** s'il venait.

shoulder n épaule f. ●vt (responsibility) endosser; (burden) se charger de. ~ **bag** n sac m à bandoulière. ~ **blade** n omoplate f.

shout n cri m. ●vt/i crier (**at** après); ~ **sth out** lancer qch à haute voix.

shove n **give sth a** ~ pousser qch. ●vt/i pousser; ~ **off!** 🔳 tire-toi! 🔳.

shovel n pelle f. ●vt (pt **shovelled**) pelleter.

show vt (pt **showed**; pp **shown**) montrer; (dial, needle) indiquer; (put on display) exposer; (film) donner; (conduct) conduire; ~ **sb in/out** faire entrer/sortir qn. ●vi (be visible) se voir. ●n (exhibition) exposition f, salon m; (Theat) spectacle m; (cinema) séance f; (of strength) démonstration f; **for ~** pour l'effet; **on ~** exposé. ∎ **~ off** faire le fier/la fière; **~ sth/sb off** exhiber qch/qn; **~ up** se voir; (appear) se montrer; **~ sb up** faire honte à qn.

shower n douche f; (of rain) averse f. ●vt **~ with** couvrir de. ●vi se doucher.

showing n performance f; (cinema) séance f.

show-jumping n concours m hippique.

shown ▷SHOW.

show: **~-off** n m'as-tu-vu mf inv 🔲. **~room** n salle f d'exposition.

shrank ▷SHRINK.

shrapnel n éclats mpl d'obus.

shred n lambeau m; (least amount: fig) parcelle f. ●vt (pt **shredded**) déchiqueter; (Culin) râper.

shrewd adj (person) habile; (move) astucieux.

shriek n hurlement m. ●vt/i hurler.

shrill adj (voice) perçant; (tone) strident.

shrimp n crevette f.

shrine n (place) lieu m de pèlerinage.

shrink vt/i (pt **shrank**; pp **shrunk**) rétrécir; (lessen) diminuer; **~ from** reculer devant.

shrivel vt/i (pt **shrivelled**) (se) ratatiner.

shroud n linceul m. ●vt (veil) envelopper.

Shrove Tuesday n mardi m gras.

shrub n arbuste m.

shrug vt (pt **shrugged**) **~ one's shoulders** hausser les épaules; **~ sth off** ignorer qch.

shrunk ▷SHRINK.

shudder vi frémir. ●n frémissement m.

shuffle vt (feet) traîner; (cards) battre. ●vi traîner les pieds.

shun vt (pt **shunned**) fuir.

shut vt (pt **shut**; pres p **shutting**) fermer. ●vi (door) se fermer; (shop) fermer. ∎ **~ in** or **up** enfermer; **~ up** 🔲 se taire; **~ sb up** faire taire qn.

shutter n volet m; (Photo) obturateur m.

shuttle n (bus) navette f; **~ service** navette f. ●vi faire la navette. ●vt transporter.

shuttlecock n (badminton) volant m.

shy adj timide. ●vi **~ away from** se tenir à l'écart de.

sibling n frère/sœur m/f.

sick adj malade; (humour) macabre; (mind) malsain; **be ~** (vomit) vomir; **be ~ of** 🔲 en avoir assez or marre de 🔲; **feel ~** avoir mal au cœur. **~-leave** n congé m de maladie.

sickly adj (-ier,-iest) (person) maladif; (taste, smell) écœurant.

sickness n maladie f.

sick-pay n indemnité f de maladie.

side n côté m; (of road, river) bord m; (of hill, body) flanc m; (Sport) équipe f; (TV 🔲) chaîne f; **~ by ~** côte à côte. ●adj latéral. ●vi **~ with** se ranger du côté de. **~board** n buffet m. **~ effect** n effet m secondaire. **~light** n (Auto) feu m de position. **~line** n activité f secondaire. **~show** n attraction f. **~step** vt (pt **-stepped**) éviter. **~street** n rue f latérale. **~track** vt fourvoyer. **~walk** n (US) trottoir m.

sideways adj (look) de travers. ●adv (move) latéralement; (look at) de travers.

siding n voie f de garage.

sidle vi s'avancer furtivement (**up to** vers).

siege n siège m.

siesta n sieste f.

sieve n tamis m; (for liquids) passoire f. ●vt tamiser.

sift vt tamiser. ●vi ~ **through** examiner.

sigh n soupir m. ●vt/i soupirer.

sight n vue f; (scene) spectacle m; (on gun) mire f; **at** or **on** ~ à vue; **catch** ~ **of** apercevoir; **in** ~ visible; **lose** ~ **of** perdre de vue. ●vt apercevoir.

sightseeing n tourisme m.

sign n signe m; (notice) panneau m. ●vt/i signer. ■ ~ **on** (as unemployed) pointer au chômage; ~ **up** (s')engager.

signal n signal m. ●vt (pt **signalled**) (gesture) faire signe (**that** que); (indicate) indiquer.

signatory n signataire mf.

signature n signature f; ~ **tune** indicatif m.

significance n importance f; (meaning) signification f. **significant** adj important; (meaningful) significatif. **significantly** adv (much) sensiblement.

signify vt signifier.

signpost n panneau m indicateur.

silence n silence m. ●vt faire taire.

silent adj silencieux; (film) muet. **silently** adv silencieusement.

silhouette n silhouette f. ●vt be ~d **against** se profiler contre.

silicon n silicium m; ~ **chip** puce f électronique.

silk n soie f.

silly adj (-**ier**, -**iest**) bête, idiot.

silver n argent m; (silverware) argenterie f. ●adj en argent.

similar adj semblable (**to** à). **similarity** n ressemblance f. **similarly** adv de même.

simile n comparaison f.

simmer vt/i (soup) mijoter; (water) (laisser) frémir.

simple adj simple.

simplicity n simplicité f.

simplify vt simplifier.

simplistic adj simpliste.

simply adv simplement; (absolutely) absolument.

simulate vt simuler.

simultaneous adj simultané.

sin n péché m. ●vi (pt **sinned**) pécher.

---

since /sɪns/
● preposition
····▸ depuis; **I haven't seen him** ~ **Monday** je ne l'ai pas vu depuis lundi; **I've been waiting** ~ **yesterday** j'attends depuis hier; **she had been living in Paris** ~ **1985** elle habitait Paris depuis 1985.
● conjunction
····▸ (in time expressions) depuis que; ~ **she's been working here** depuis qu'elle travaille ici; ~ **she left** depuis qu'elle est partie or depuis son départ.
····▸ (because) comme; ~ **he was ill, he couldn't go** comme il était malade, il ne pouvait pas y aller.
● adverb
····▸ depuis; **he hasn't been seen** ~ on ne l'a pas vu depuis.

---

sincere adj sincère. **sincerely** adv sincèrement. **sincerity** n sincérité f.

sinful adj immoral; ~ **man** pécheur m.

sing vt/i (pt **sang**; pp **sung**) chanter.

singe vt (pres p **singeing**) brûler légèrement; (with iron) roussir.

singer n chanteur/-euse m/f.

single adj seul; (not double) simple; (unmarried) célibataire; (room, bed) pour une personne; (ticket) simple; **in** ~ **file** en file indienne. ●n (ticket) aller simple m; (record) 45 tours m inv; ~**s** (tennis) simple m. ●vt ~ **out**

S

choisir. ~-handed adj tout seul.
~-minded adj tenace. ~ parent
n parent m isolé.

singular n singulier m. ●adj
(strange) singulier; (noun) au
singulier.

sinister adj sinistre.

sink vt (pt sank; pp sunk) (boat)
couler; (well) forer; (post)
enfoncer. ●vi (boat) couler; (sun,
level) baisser; (wall) s'effondrer.
●n (in kitchen) évier m; (wash-basin)
lavabo m. ■ ~ in (news) faire son
chemin.

sinner n pécheur/-eresse m/f.

sip n petite gorgée f. ●vt (pt
sipped) boire à petites gorgées.

siphon n siphon m. ●vt ~ off
siphonner.

sir n Monsieur m; Sir (title) Sir m.

siren n sirène f.

sirloin n aloyau m.

sister n sœur f; (nurse) infirmière f
en chef. ~-in-law n (pl ~s-in-
law) belle-sœur f.

sit vt/i (pt sat; pres p sitting)
(s')asseoir; (committee) siéger; ~
(for) (exam) se présenter à; be
~ting être assis. ■ ~ around ne
rien faire; ~ down s'asseoir.

site n emplacement m; (building)
~ chantier m. ●vt construire.

sitting n séance f; (in restaurant)
service m. ~-room n salon m.

situate vt situer; be ~d être
situé. situation n situation f.

six adj & n six (m).

sixteen adj & n seize (m).

sixth adj & n sixième (mf).

sixty adj & n soixante (m).

size n dimension f; (of person,
garment) taille f; (of shoes) pointure
f; (of sum, salary) montant m; (extent)
ampleur f. ■ ~ up (person) se
faire une opinion de; (situation)
évaluer. sizeable adj assez grand.

skate n patin m; (fish) raie f. ●vi
patiner.

skateboard n skateboard m,
planche f à roulettes. ●vi faire du
skateboard.

skating n patinage m.

skeleton n squelette m; ~ staff
effectifs mpl minimums.

sketch n esquisse f; (hasty) croquis
m; (Theat) sketch m. ●vt faire une
esquisse or un croquis de. ●vi
faire des esquisses.

sketchy adj (-ier, -iest) (details)
insuffisant; (memory) vague.

skewer n brochette f.

ski n ski m. ●adj de ski. ●vi (pt
ski'd or skied; pres p skiing)
skier; (go skiing) faire du ski.

skid vi (pt skidded) déraper. ●n
dérapage m.

skier n skieur/-euse m/f.

skiing n ski m.

ski jump n saut m à ski.

skilful adj habile.

ski lift n remontée f mécanique.

skill n habileté f; (craft)
compétence f; ~s connaissances
fpl. skilled adj (worker) qualifié;
(talented) consommé.

skim vt (pt skimmed) écumer;
(milk) écrémer; (pass over)
effleurer. ●vi ~ through
parcourir.

skimpy adj (clothes) étriqué.

skin n peau f. ●vt (pt skinned)
(animal) écorcher; (fruit) éplucher.

skinny adj (-ier, -iest) 🔳 maigre.

skip vi (pt skipped) sautiller; (with
rope) sauter à la corde. ●vt (page,
class) sauter. ●n petit saut m;
(container) benne f.

skipper n capitaine m.

skirmish n escarmouche f.

skirt n jupe f. ●vt contourner.
skirting-board n plinthe f.

skittle n quille f.

skull n crâne m.

sky n ciel m. ~-blue adj & n bleu

ciel m inv. ~ **marshal** n garde m armé (*à bord d'un avion.*) ~**scraper** n gratte-ciel m inv.

slab n (of stone) dalle f.

slack adj (not tight) détendu; (person) négligent; (period) creux. •n (in rope) mou m. •vi se relâcher.

slacken vt (rope) donner du mou à; (grip) relâcher; (pace) réduire. •vi (grip, rope) se relâcher; (activity) ralentir; (rain) se calmer.

slam vt/i (pt **slammed**) (door) claquer; (throw) flanquer; (criticize 🔲) critiquer. •n (noise) claquement m.

slander n (offence) diffamation f; (statement) calomnie f. •vt calomnier; (Jur) diffamer. **slanderous** adj diffamatoire.

slang n argot m.

slant vt/i (faire) pencher; (news) présenter sous un certain jour. •n inclinaison f; (bias) angle m. **slanted** adj (biased) orienté; (sloping) en pente.

slap vt (pt **slapped**) (strike) donner une tape à; (face) gifler; (put) flanquer 🔲. •n claque f; (on face) gifle f. •adv tout droit.

slapdash adj (person) brouillon 🔲; (work) bâclé 🔲.

slash vt (picture, tyre) taillader; (face) balafrer; (throat) couper; (fig) réduire (radicalement). •n lacération f.

slat n (in blind) lamelle f; (on bed) latte f.

slate n ardoise f. •vt 🔲 taper sur 🔲.

slaughter vt massacrer; (animal) abattre. •n massacre m; abattage m.

slave n esclave mf. •vi trimer 🔲. **slavery** n esclavage m.

sleazy adj (-ier, -iest) 🔲 (story) scabreux; (club) louche.

sledge n luge f; (horse-drawn) traîneau m.

sleek adj (hair) lisse, brillant; (shape) élégant.

sleep n sommeil m; **go to** ~ s'endormir. •vi (pt **slept**) dormir; (spend the night) coucher; ~ **in** faire la grasse matinée. •vt loger.

sleeper n (Rail) (berth) couchette f; (on track) traverse f.

sleeping-bag n sac m de couchage.

sleeping-pill n somnifère m.

sleep-walker n somnambule mf.

sleepy adj (-ier, -iest) somnolent; **be** ~ avoir sommeil.

sleet n neige f fondue.

sleeve n manche f; (of record) pochette f; **up one's** ~ en réserve.

sleigh n traîneau m.

slender adj (person) mince; (majority) faible.

slept ▶ SLEEP.

slice n tranche f. •vt couper (en tranches).

slick adj (adept) habile; (insincere) roublard 🔲. •n (oil) ~ marée f noire.

slide vt/i (pt **slid**) glisser; ~ **into** (go silently) se glisser dans. •n glissade f; (fall: fig) baisse f; (in playground) toboggan m; (for hair) barrette f; (Photo) diapositive f.

sliding adj (door) coulissant; ~ **scale** échelle f mobile.

slight adj petit, léger; (slender) mince; (frail) frêle. •vt (insult) offenser. •n affront m. **slightest** adj moindre. **slightly** adv légèrement, un peu.

slim adj (**slimmer, slimmest**) mince. •vi (pt **slimmed**) maigrir.

slime n dépôt m gluant; (on riverbed) vase f. **slimy** adj visqueux; (fig) servile.

sling n (weapon, toy) fronde f; (bandage) écharpe f. •vt (pt **slung**) jeter, lancer.

slip vt/i (pt **slipped**) glisser; ~**ped**

disc hernie f discale; ~ **sb's mind** échapper à qn. •n (mistake) erreur f; (petticoat) combinaison f; (paper) bout m de papier; ~ **of the tongue** lapsus m. ■~ **away** s'esquiver; ~ **into** (go) se glisser dans; (clothes) mettre; ~ **up** 🔲 faire une gaffe 🔲.

slipper n pantoufle f.

slippery adj glissant.

slip road n bretelle f.

slit n fente f. •vt (pt **slit**; pres p **slitting**) déchirer; ~ **sth open** ouvrir qch; ~ **sb's throat** égorger qn.

slither vi glisser.

sliver n (of glass) éclat m; (of soap) reste m.

slobber vi 🔲 baver.

slog 🔲 vt (pt **slogged**) (hit) frapper dur. •vi (work) bosser 🔲. •n (work) travail m dur.

slogan n slogan m.

slope vi être en pente; (handwriting) pencher. •n pente f; (of mountain) flanc m.

sloppy adj (-ier, -iest) (food) liquide; (work) négligé; (person) négligent.

slosh vt 🔲 répandre; (hit 🔲) frapper. •vi clapoter.

slot n fente f. •vt/i (pt **slotted**) (s')insérer.

sloth n paresse f.

slot-machine n distributeur m automatique; (for gambling) machine f à sous.

slouch vi être avachi.

Slovakia n Slovaquie f.

Slovenia n Slovénie f.

slovenly adj débraillé.

slow adj lent; **be** ~ (clock) retarder; **in** ~ **motion** au ralenti. •adv lentement. •vt/i ralentir. **slowly** adv lentement. **slowness** n lenteur f.

sludge n vase f.

slug n (mollusc) limace f; (bullet 🔲) balle f; (blow 🔲) coup m.

sluggish adj (person) léthargique; (circulation) lent.

slum n taudis m.

slump n (Econ) effondrement m; (in support) baisse f. •vi (demand, trade) chuter; (economy) s'effondrer; (person) s'affaler.

slung ▷SLING.

slur vt/i (pt **slurred**) (words) mal articuler. •n calomnie f (**on** sur).

slush n (snow) neige f fondue. ~ **fund** n caisse f noire.

sly adj (crafty) rusé; (secretive) sournois. •n **on the** ~ en cachette.

smack n tape f; (on face) gifle f. •vt donner une tape à; gifler. •vi ~ **of sth** sentir qch. •adv 🔲 tout droit.

small adj petit. •n ~ **of the back** creux m des reins. •adv (cut) menu. ~ **ad** n petite annonce f. ~ **business** n petite entreprise f. ~ **change** n petite monnaie f. ~**pox** n variole f. ~ **print** n petits caractères mpl. ~ **talk** n banalités fpl.

smart adj élégant; (clever 🔲) malin, habile; (restaurant) chic inv; (Comput) intelligent. •vi (wound) brûler.

smarten vt/i ~ (**up**) embellir; ~ (**oneself**) **up** s'arranger.

smash vt/i (se) briser, (se) fracasser; (opponent, record) pulvériser. •n (noise) fracas m; (blow) coup m; (car crash) collision f; (hit record 🔲) tube m. 🔲

smashing adj 🔲 épatant.

SME abbr (**small and medium enterprises**) PME.

smear vt (stain) tacher; (coat) enduire; (discredit: fig) diffamer. •n tache f; (effort to discredit) propos m diffamatoire; ~ (**test**) frottis m.

smell n odeur f; (sense) odorat m. •vt/i (pt **smelt** or **smelled**) sentir; ~ **of** sentir. **smelly** adj qui sent mauvais.

smelt ▷ SMELL.

smile n sourire m. ●vi sourire.

smiley n (Internet) binette f.

smirk n petit sourire m satisfait.

smitten adj (in love) fou d'amour.

smog n smog m.

smoke n fumée f; **have a ~** fumer. ●vt/i fumer. **smoked** adj fumé. **smokeless** adj (fuel) non polluant. **smoker** n fumeur/-euse m/f. **smoky** adj (air) enfumé.

smooth adj lisse; (movement) aisé; (manners) onctueux; (flight) sans heurts. ●vt lisser; (process) faciliter.

smoothly adv (move, flow) doucement; (brake, start) en douceur; **go ~** marcher bien.

smother vt (stifle) étouffer; (cover) couvrir.

smoulder vi (lit) se consumer; (fig) couver.

smudge n trace f. ●vt/i (ink) (s')étaler.

smug adj (**smugger, smuggest**) suffisant.

smuggle vt passer (en contrebande). **smuggler** n contrebandier/-ière m/f. **smuggling** n contrebande f.

smutty adj grivois.

snack n casse-croûte m inv.

snag n inconvénient m; (in cloth) accroc m.

snail n escargot m.

snake n serpent m.

snap vt/i (pt **snapped**) (whip, fingers) (faire) claquer; (break) (se) casser net; (say) dire sèchement. ●n claquement m; (Photo) photo f. ●adj soudain. ■ ~ **up** (buy) sauter sur.

snapshot n photo f.

snare n piège m.

snarl vi gronder (en montrant les dents). ●n grondement m. **~-up** n embouteillage m.

snatch vt (grab) attraper; (steal) voler; (opportunity) saisir; ~ **sth from sb** arracher qch à qn. ●n (theft) vol m; (short part) fragment m.

sneak vi aller furtivement. ●n 🔲 rapporteur/-euse m/f.

sneer n sourire m méprisant. ●vi sourire avec mépris.

sneeze n éternuement m. ●vi éternuer.

snide adj narquois.

sniff vt/i renifler. ●n reniflement m.

snigger n ricanement m. ●vi ricaner.

snip vt (pt **snipped**) couper.

sniper n tireur m embusqué.

snippet n bribe f.

snivel vi (pt **snivelled**) pleurnicher.

snob n snob mf.

snooker n snooker m.

snoop vi 🔲 fourrer son nez partout.

snooty adj (**-ier, -iest**) 🔲 snob inv, hautain.

snooze n petit somme m. ●vi sommeiller.

snore n ronflement m. ●vi ronfler.

snorkel n tuba m.

snort n grognement m. ●vi (person) grogner; (horse) s'ébrouer.

snout n museau m.

snow n neige f. ●vi neiger; **be ~ed under with** être submergé de.

snowball n boule f de neige. ●vi faire boule de neige.

snow: ~**board** n snowboard m. ~**boarding** n surf m des neiges. ~**bound** adj bloqué par la neige. ~**drift** n congère f. ~**drop** n perce-neige m or f inv. **~flake** n flocon de neige. **~man** n (pl **-men**) bonhomme m de neige. **~-plough** n chasse-neige m inv.

snub vt (pt **snubbed**) rembarrer. ● n rebuffade f.

snuffle vi renifler.

snug adj (**snugger, snuggest**) (cosy) confortable; (tight) bien ajusté.

snuggle vi se pelotonner.

so adv si, tellement; (thus) ainsi; **~ am I** moi aussi; **~ good as** aussi bon que; **that is ~** c'est ça; **I think ~** je pense que oui; **five or ~** environ cinq; **~ as to** de manière à; **~ far** jusqu'ici; **~ long!** 🔲 à bientôt!; **~ many, ~ much** tant (de); **~ that** pour que. ● conj donc, alors.

soak vt/i (faire) tremper (**in** dans). ■ **~ in** pénétrer; **~ up** absorber. **soaking** adj trempé.

soap n savon m. ● vt savonner. **~ opera** n feuilleton m. **~ powder** n lessive f.

soar vi monter (en flèche).

sob n sanglot m. ● vi (pt **sobbed**) sangloter.

sober adj qui n'a pas bu d'alcool; (serious) sérieux. ● vi **~ up** dessoûler.

soccer n football m.

sociable adj sociable.

social adj social. ● n réunion f (amicale), fête f.

socialism n socialisme m. **socialist** adj & n socialiste (mf).

socialize vi se mêler aux autres; **~ with** fréquenter.

socially adv socialement; (meet) en société.

social: ~ security n aide f sociale. **~ worker** n travailleur/-euse m/f social/-e.

society n société f.

sociological adj sociologique. **sociologist** n sociologue mf.

sociology n sociologie f.

sock n chaussette f. ● vt (hit 🔲) flanquer un coup (de poing) à.

socket n (for lamp) douille f; (Electr) prise f (de courant); (of eye) orbite f.

soda n soude f; **~(-water)** eau f de Seltz.

sodden adj détrempé.

sofa n canapé m. **~ bed** n canapé-lit m.

soft adj (gentle, lenient) doux; (not hard) doux, mou; (heart, wood) tendre; (silly) ramolli. **~ drink** n boisson f non alcoolisée.

soften vt/i (se) ramollir; (tone down, lessen) (s')adoucir.

soft spot n **to have a ~ for sb** avoir un faible pour qn.

software n logiciel m.

soggy adj (**-ier, -iest**) (ground) détrempé; (food) ramolli.

soil n sol m, terre f. ● vt/i (se) salir.

sold ▷SELL. ● adj **~ out** épuisé.

solder n soudure f. ● vt souder.

soldier n soldat m. ● vi **~ on** 🔲 persévérer.

sole n (of foot) plante f; (of shoe) semelle f; (fish) sole f. ● adj unique, seul. **solely** adv uniquement.

solemn adj solennel.

solicitor n notaire m; (for court and police work) ≈ avocat/-e m/f.

solid adj solide; (not hollow) plein; (gold) massif; (mass) compact; (meal) substantiel. ● n solide m; **~s** (food) aliments mpl solides.

solidarity n solidarité f.

solidify vt/i (se) solidifier.

solitary adj (alone) solitaire; (only) seul.

solo n solo m. ● adj (Mus) solo inv; (flight) en solitaire.

soluble adj soluble.

solution n solution f.

solve vt résoudre.

solvent adj (Comm) solvable. •n (dis)solvant m.

some /sʌm, səm/
•determiner
····▸ (unspecified amount) du/de l'/de la/des; **I have to buy ~ bread** je dois acheter du pain; **have ~ water** prenez de l'eau; **~ sweets** des bonbons.
····▸ (certain) certains/certaines; **~ people say that** certains disent que.
····▸ (unknown) un/une; **~ man came to the house** un homme est venu à la maison.
····▸ (considerable amount) **we stayed there for ~ time** nous sommes restés là assez longtemps; **it will take ~ doing** ça ne va pas être facile à faire.

▷ In front of a plural adjective *des* changes to *de*: **some pretty dresses** de jolies robes.

•pronoun
····▸ en; **he wants ~** il en veut; **have ~ more** reprenez-en.
····▸ (certain) certains/certaines; **~ are expensive** certains sont chers.
•adverb
····▸ environ; **~ 20 people** environ 20 personnes.

somebody pron quelqu'un. •n **be a ~** être quelqu'un.

somehow adv d'une manière ou d'une autre; (for some reason) je ne sais pas pourquoi.

someone pron & n ▷ SOMEBODY.

someplace adv (US) ▷ SOMEWHERE.

somersault n roulade f. •vi faire une roulade.

something pron & n quelque chose (m); **~ good** quelque chose de bon; **~ like** un peu comme.

sometime adv un jour; **~ in**

June en juin. •adj (former) ancien.

sometimes adv quelquefois, parfois.

somewhat adv quelque peu, un peu.

somewhere adv quelque part.

son n fils m.

song n chanson f; (of bird) chant m.

son-in-law n (pl **sons-in-law**) gendre m.

soon adv bientôt; (early) tôt; **I would ~er stay** j'aimerais mieux rester; **~ after** peu après; **~er or later** tôt ou tard.

soot n suie f.

soothe vt calmer.

sophisticated adj raffiné; (machine) sophistiqué.

sopping adj trempé.

soppy adj (**-ier, -iest**) 🆃 sentimental.

sorcerer n sorcier m.

sordid adj sordide.

sore adj douloureux; (vexed) en rogne (**at, with** contre). •n plaie f.

sorely adv fortement.

sorrow n chagrin m.

sorry adj (**-ier, -iest**) (regretful) désolé (**to** de; **that** que); (wretched) triste; **feel ~ for** plaindre; **~!** pardon!

sort n genre m, sorte f, espèce f; (person 🆃) type m; **what ~ of?** quel genre de?; **be out of ~s** ne pas être dans son assiette. •vt **~ (out)** (classify) trier; **~ out** (tidy) ranger; (arrange) arranger; (problem) régler.

so-so adj & adv comme ci comme ça.

sought ▷ SEEK.

soul n âme f.

sound n son m, bruit m. •adj solide; (healthy) sain; (sensible) sensé. •vt/i sonner; (seem)

S

sembler (**as if** que); (test) sonder; ~ **out** sonder; ~ **a horn** klaxonner; ~ **like** sembler être. ~ **asleep** adj profondément endormi. ~ **barrier** n mur m du son.

soundly adv (sleep) à poings fermés; (built) solidement.

sound-proof adj insonorisé. ●vt insonoriser.

sound-track n bande f sonore.

soup n soupe f, potage m.

sour adj aigre. ●vt/i (s')aigrir.

source n source f.

south n sud m. ●adj sud inv, du sud. ●adv vers le sud.

South Africa n Afrique f du Sud.

South America n Amérique f du Sud.

south-east n sud-est m.

southern adj du sud. **southerner** n habitant/-e m/f du sud.

southward adj (side) sud inv; (journey) vers le sud.

south-west n sud-ouest m.

souvenir n souvenir m.

sovereign n & a souverain/-e (m/f).

sow[1] /saʊ/ vt (pt sowed; pp sowed or sown) (seed) semer; (land) ensemencer.

sow[2] /saʊ/ n (pig) truie f.

soya n soja m. ~ **sauce** n sauce f soja.

spa n station f thermale.

space n espace m; (room) place f; (period) période f. ●adj (research) spatial. ●vt ~ (**out**) espacer. ~**craft** n inv, ~**ship** n engin m spatial. ~**suit** n combinaison f spatiale.

spacious adj spacieux.

spade n (for garden) bêche f; (child's) pelle f; (cards) pique m. ~**work** n (fig) travail m préparatoire.

spaghetti n spaghetti mpl.

spam n (Comput) multipostage m abusif.

Spain n Espagne f.

span n (of arch) portée f; (of wings) envergure f; (of time) durée f. ●vt (pt spanned) enjamber; (in time) embrasser.

Spaniard n Espagnol/-e m/f.

spaniel n épagneul m.

Spanish adj espagnol. ●n (Ling) espagnol m.

spank vt donner une fessée à.

spanner n (tool) clé f (plate); (adjustable) clé f à molette.

spare vt (treat leniently) épargner; (do without) se passer de; (afford to give) donner, accorder. ● adj en réserve; (surplus) de trop; (tyre, shoes) de rechange; (room, bed) d'ami; **are there any ~ tickets?** y a-t-il encore des places? ●n ~ (**part**) pièce f de rechange. ~ **time** n loisirs mpl.

sparing adj frugal. **sparingly** adv en petite quantité.

spark n étincelle f. ● vt ~ **off** (initiate) provoquer.

sparkle vi étinceler. ●n étincellement m. **sparkling** adj (wine) mousseux; (eyes) brillant.

spark-plug n bougie f.

sparrow n moineau m.

sparse adj clairsemé. **sparsely** adv (furnished) peu.

spasm n (of muscle) spasme m; (of coughing, anger) accès m.

spat ▷SPIT.

spate n **a ~ of** (letters) une avalanche de.

spatter vt éclabousser (**with** de).

spawn n frai m, œufs mpl. ●vt pondre. ●vi frayer.

speak vi (pt spoke; pp spoken) parler. ●vt (say) dire; (language) parler. ■ ~ **up** parler plus fort.

speaker n (in public) orateur m;

(Pol) président m; (loudspeaker) baffle m; **be a French/a good ~** parler français/bien.

spear n lance f.

spearmint n menthe f verte.

special adj spécial; (exceptional) exceptionnel.

specialist n spécialiste mf.

speciality, specialty n spécialité f.

specialize vi se spécialiser (**in** en).

specially adv spécialement.

species n inv espèce f.

specific adj précis, explicite.

specification n (of design) spécification f; (of car equipment) caractéristiques fpl. **specify** vt spécifier.

specimen n spécimen m, échantillon m.

speck n (stain) (petite) tache f; (particle) grain m.

specs npl 🖬 lunettes fpl.

spectacle n spectacle m. **spectacles** n lunettes fpl. **spectacular** adj spectaculaire.

spectator n spectateur/-trice m/f.

spectrum n (pl **-tra**) spectre m; (of ideas) gamme f.

speculate vi s'interroger (**about** sur); (Comm) spéculer. **speculation** n conjectures fpl; (Comm) spéculation f. **speculator** n spéculateur/-trice m/f.

speech n (faculty) parole f; (diction) élocution f; (dialect) langage m; (address) discours m. **speechless** adj muet (**with** de).

speed n (of movement) vitesse f; (swiftness) rapidité f. **~ camera** n radar m. **~ dating**® n rencontres fpl rapides, speed dating m. ● vi (pt **sped**) aller vite; (pt **speeded**) (drive too fast) aller trop vite. ■ **~ up** accélérer; (of pace) s'accélérer.

speedboat n vedette f.

speeding n excès m de vitesse.

speed limit n limitation f de vitesse.

speedometer n compteur m (de vitesse).

spell n (magic) charme m, sortilège m; (curse) sort m; (of time) (courte) période f. ● vt/i (pt **spelled** or **spelt**) écrire; (mean) signifier; **~ out** épeler; (explain) expliquer. **~checker** n correcteur m orthographique.

spelling n orthographe f. ● adj (mistake) d'orthographe.

spend vt (pt **spent**) (money) dépenser (**on** pour); (time, holiday) passer; (energy) consacrer (**on** à). ● vi dépenser.

spent ▷SPEND. ● adj (used) utilisé; (person) épuisé.

sperm n (pl **sperms** or **sperm**) sperme m.

sphere n sphère f.

spice n épice f; (fig) piquant m.

spick-and-span adj impeccable.

spicy adj épicé; piquant.

spider n araignée f.

spike n pointe f.

spill vt (pt **spilled** or **spilt**) renverser, répandre. ● vi se répandre; **~ over** déborder.

spin vt/i (pt **spun**; pres p **spinning**) (wool, web) filer; (turn) (faire) tourner; (story) débiter; **~ out** faire durer. ● n (movement, excursion) tour m.

spinach n épinards mpl.

spinal adj vertébral. **~ cord** n moelle f épinière.

spin-drier n essoreuse f.

spine n colonne f vertébrale; (prickle) piquant m.

spin-off n avantage m accessoire; (by-product) dérivé m.

spinster n célibataire f; (pej) vieille fille f.

spiral adj en spirale; (staircase) en

colimaçon. ●n spirale f. ●vi (pt **spiralled**) (prices) monter (en flèche).

spire n flèche f.

spirit n esprit m; (boldness) courage m; **~s** (morale) moral m; (drink) spiritueux mpl. ●vt **~ away** faire disparaître. **spirited** adj fougueux. **~-level** n niveau m à bulle.

spiritual adj spirituel.

spit vt/i (pt **spat** or **spit**; pres p **spitting**) cracher; (of rain) crachiner; **~ out** cracher; **the ~ting image of** le portrait craché or vivant de. ●n crachat(s) m(pl); (for meat) broche f.

spite n rancune f; **in ~ of** malgré. ●vt contrarier.

splash vt éclabousser. ●vi faire des éclaboussures; **~ (about)** patauger. ●n (act, mark) éclaboussure f; (sound) plouf m; (of colour) tache f.

spleen n (Anat) rate f.

splendid adj magnifique, splendide.

splint n (Med) attelle f.

splinter n éclat m; (in finger) écharde f. **~ group** n groupe m dissident.

split vt/i (pt **split**; pres p **splitting**) (se) fendre; (tear) (se) déchirer; (divide) (se) diviser; (share) partager; **~ one's sides** se tordre (de rire). ●n fente f; déchirure f; (share 🄵) part f, partage m; (quarrel) rupture f; (Pol) scission f. ■ **~ up** (couple) rompre. **~ second** n fraction f de seconde.

splutter vi crachoter; (stammer) bafouiller; (engine) tousser.

spoil vt (pt **spoilt** or **spoiled**) (pamper) gâter; (ruin) abîmer; (mar) gâcher, gâter. ●n **~(s)** butin m. **~-sport** n trouble-fête mf inv.

spoke[1] /spəʊk/ n rayon m.

spoke[2], **spoken** ▷ SPEAK.

spokesman n (pl **-men**) porteparole m inv.

sponge n éponge f. ●vt éponger. ●vi **~ on** vivre aux crochets de. **~-bag** n trousse f de toilette. **~-cake** n génoise f.

sponsor n (of concert) parrain m, sponsor m; (surety) garant m; (for membership) parrain m, marraine f. ●vt parrainer, sponsoriser; (member) parrainer. **sponsorship** n patronage m; parrainage m.

spontaneous adj spontané.

spoof n 🄵 parodie f.

spoon n cuiller f, cuillère f.

spoonful n (pl **~s**) cuillerée f.

sport n sport m; **(good) ~** (person 🄵) chic type m; **~s car/coat** voiture/veste f de sport. ●vt (display) exhiber, arborer.

sporting adj sportif; **a ~ chance** une assez bonne chance.

sportsman n (pl **-men**) sportif m.

sporty adj 🄵 sportif.

spot n (mark, stain) tache f; (dot) point m; (in pattern) pois m; (drop) goutte f; (place) endroit m; (pimple) bouton m; **a ~ of** 🄵 un peu de; **on the ~** sur place; (without delay) sur le coup. ●vt (pt **spotted**) 🄵 apercevoir. **~ check** n contrôle m surprise.

spotless adj impeccable.

spotlight n (lamp) projecteur m, spot m.

spotty adj (skin) boutonneux.

spouse n époux m, épouse f.

spout n (of teapot) bec m; (of liquid) jet m; **up the ~** (ruined 🄵) fichu. ●vi jaillir.

sprain n entorse f, foulure f. ●vt **~ one's wrist** se fouler le poignet.

sprang ▷ SPRING.

sprawl vi (town, person) s'étaler. ●n étalement m.

spray n (of flowers) gerbe f; (water) gerbe f d'eau; (from sea) embruns

mpl; (device) bombe f, atomiseur m.
• vt (surface, insecticide, plant)
vaporiser; (person) asperger;
(crops) traiter.

spread vt/i (pt **spread**) (stretch,
extend) (s')étendre; (news, fear) (se)
répandre; (illness) (se) propager;
(butter) (s')étaler. • n propagation
f; (of population) distribution f;
(paste) pâte f à tartiner; (food)
belle table f. ~**-eagled** adj bras
et jambes écartés. ~**sheet** n
tableur m.

spree n **go on a** ~ (have fun 🆃)
faire la noce.

sprig n petite branche f.

sprightly adj (**-ier, -iest**)
alerte, vif.

spring vi (pt **sprang**; pp **sprung**)
bondir. • vt ~ **sth on sb**
annoncer qch de but en blanc à
qn. • n bond m; (device) ressort m;
(season) printemps m; (of water)
source f. ~ **from** provenir de;
■ ~ **up** surgir. ~**board** n
tremplin m. ~ **onion** n oignon m
blanc.

springy adj (**-ier, -iest**) élastique.

sprinkle vt (with liquid) arroser
(**with** de); (with salt, flour)
saupoudrer (**with** de); (sand)
répandre. **sprinkler** n (in garden)
arroseur m; (for fires) extincteur m
(à déclenchement) automatique.

sprint vi (Sport) sprinter. • n
sprint m.

sprout vt/i pousser. • n (on plant)
pousse f; (**Brussels**) ~**s** choux
mpl de Bruxelles.

spruce adj pimpant. • vt ~
oneself up se faire beau. • n
(tree) épicéa m.

sprung ▷SPRING.

spud n 🆃 patate f.

spun ▷SPIN.

spur n (of rider) éperon m; (stimulus)
aiguillon m; **on the** ~ **of the
moment** sous l'impulsion du
moment. • vt (pt **spurred**)
éperonner.

spurious adj faux.

spurn vt repousser.

spurt vi jaillir; (fig) accélérer. • n
jet m; (of energy) sursaut m.

spy n espion/-ne m/f. • vi
espionner. • vt apercevoir.

squabble vi se chamailler. • n
chamaillerie f.

squad n (of soldiers) escouade f;
(Sport) équipe f.

squadron n (Mil) escadron m;
(Aviat) escadrille f.

squalid adj sordide.

squander vt (money, time) gaspiller.

square n carré m; (open space in
town) place f. • adj carré; (honest)
honnête; (meal) solide; (boring 🆃)
ringard; **(all)** ~ (quits) quitte; ~
metre mètre m carré. • vt (settle)
régler; ~ **up to** faire face à.

squash vt écraser; (crowd) serrer.
• n (game) squash m; (marrow: US)
courge f; **lemon** ~ citronnade f;
orange ~ orangeade f.

squat vi (pt **squatted**)
s'accroupir; ~ **in a house**
squatteriser une maison. • adj
(dumpy) trapu. **squatter** n
squatter m.

squawk n cri m rauque. • vi
pousser un cri rauque.

squeak n petit cri m; (of door)
grincement m. • vi crier; grincer.

squeal n cri m aigu. • vi pousser
un cri aigu; ~ **on** (inform on 🆃)
dénoncer.

squeamish adj (trop) délicat.

squeeze vt presser; (hand, arm)
serrer; (extract) exprimer (**from**
de); (extort) soutirer (**from** à). • vi
(force one's way) se glisser. • n
pression f; (Comm) restrictions fpl
de crédit.

squid n calmar m.

squint vi loucher; (with half-shut
eyes) plisser les yeux. • n (Med)
strabisme m.

squirm vi se tortiller.

squirrel n écureuil m.

s

squirt vt/i (faire) jaillir. ●n jet m.

stab vt (pt **stabbed**) (with knife) poignarder. ●n coup m (de couteau); **have a ~ at sth** essayer de faire qch.

stability n stabilité f. **stabilize** vt stabiliser.

stable adj stable. ●n écurie f. **~-boy** n lad m.

stack n tas m. ●vt ~ **(up)** entasser, empiler.

stadium n stade m.

staff n personnel m; (in school) professeurs mpl; (Mil) état-major m; (stick) bâton m. ●vt pourvoir en personnel.

stag n cerf m.

stage n (Theat) scène f; (phase) stade m, étape f; (platform in hall) estrade f; **go on the ~** faire du théâtre. ●vt mettre en scène; (fig) organiser. ~ **door** entrée f des artistes. ~ **fright** n trac m.

stagger vi chanceler. ●vt (shock) stupéfier; (payments) échelonner. **staggering** adj stupéfiant.

stagnate vi stagner.

stag night n soirée f pour enterrer une vie de garçon.

staid adj sérieux.

stain vt tacher; (wood) colorer. ●n tache f; (colouring) colorant m. **stained glass window** n vitrail m.

stainless steel n acier m inoxydable.

stain remover n détachant m.

stair n marche f; **the ~s** l'escalier m. **~case**, **~way** escalier m.

stake n (post) pieu m; (wager) enjeu m; **at ~** en jeu. ●vt (area) jalonner; (wager) jouer; ~ **a claim to** revendiquer.

stale adj pas frais; (bread) rassis; (smell) de renfermé.

stalk n (of plant) tige f. ●vi marcher de façon guindée. ●vt (hunter) chasser; (murderer) suivre.

stall n (in stable) stalle f; (in market) éventaire m; ~**s** (Theat) orchestre m. ●vt/i (Auto) caler; ~ **(for time)** temporiser.

stallion n étalon m.

stamina n résistance f.

stammer vt/i bégayer. ●n bégaiement m.

stamp vt/i ~ **(one's foot)** taper du pied. ●vt (letter) timbrer. ●n (for postage, marking) timbre m; (mark: fig) sceau m. ■ ~ **out** supprimer. ~**-collecting** n philatélie f.

stampede n fuite f désordonnée; (rush: fig) ruée f. ●vi s'enfuir en désordre; se ruer.

stand vi (pt **stood**) être or se tenir (debout); (rise) se lever; (be situated) se trouver; (Pol) être candidat (**for** à); ~ **in line** (US) faire la queue; ~ **to reason** être logique. ●vt mettre (debout); (tolerate) supporter; ~ **a chance** avoir une chance. ●n (stance) position f; (Mil) résistance f; (for lamp) support m; (at fair) stand m; (in street) kiosque m; (for spectators) tribune f; (Jur, US) barre f; **make a ~** prendre position. ■ ~ **back** reculer; ~ **by** or **around** ne rien faire; ~ **by** (be ready) se tenir prêt; (promise, person) rester fidèle à; ~ **down** se désister; ~ **for** représenter; ⊡ supporter; ~ **in for** remplacer; ~ **out** ressortir; ~ **up** se lever; ~ **up for** défendre; ~ **up to** résister à.

standard n norme f; (level) niveau m (voulu); (flag) étendard m; ~**s** (morals) principes mpl. ●adj ordinaire.

standard of living n niveau m de vie.

standby adj de réserve. ●n **be a ~** être de réserve.

stand-in n remplaçant/-e m/f.

standing adj debout inv. ●n réputation f; (duration) durée f. ~ **order** n prélèvement m bancaire.

standpoint n point m de vue.

standstill n **at a ~** immobile; **bring/come to a ~** (s')immobiliser.

stank ▷STINK.

staple n agrafe f. •vt agrafer. •adj principal, de base. **stapler** n agrafeuse f.

star n étoile f; (person) vedette f. •vt (pt **starred**) (film) avoir pour vedette. •vi ~ **in** être la vedette de.

starch n amidon m; (in food) fécule f. •vt amidonner.

stardom n célébrité f.

stare vi ~ **at** regarder fixement. •n regard m fixe.

starfish n étoile f de mer.

stark adj (desolate) désolé; (severe) austère; (utter) complet; (fact) brutal. •adv complètement.

starling n étourneau m.

start vt/i commencer; (machine) (se) mettre en marche; (fashion) lancer; (cause) provoquer; (jump) sursauter; (of vehicle) démarrer; ~ **to do** commencer or se mettre à faire; ~**ing tomorrow** à partir de demain. •n commencement m, début m; (of race) départ m; (lead) avance f; (jump) sursaut m. ■~ **off** commencer (**doing** par faire); ~ **out** partir; ~ **up** (business) lancer. **starter** n (Auto) démarreur m; (runner) partant m; (Culin) entrée f.

starting point n point m de départ.

startle vt (make jump) faire tressaillir; (shock) alarmer.

starvation n faim f.

starve vi mourir de faim. •vt affamer; (deprive) priver.

stash vt cacher.

state n état m; (pomp) apparat m; **S~** état m; **the S~s** les États-Unis; **get into a ~** s'affoler. •adj d'état, de l'état; (school) public.

•vt affirmer (**that** que); (views) exprimer; (fix) fixer.

stately adj (-ier, -iest) majestueux. ~ **home** n château m.

statement n déclaration f; (of account) relevé m.

statesman n (pl **-men**) homme m d'état.

static adj statique. •n (radio, TV) parasites mpl.

station n (Rail) gare f; (TV) chaîne f; (Mil) poste m; (rank) condition f. •vt poster, placer; ~**ed at** or **in** (Mil) en garnison à.

stationary adj immobile, stationnaire; (vehicle) à l'arrêt.

stationery n papeterie f.

station wagon n (US) break m.

statistic n statistique f; ~**s** statistique f.

statue n statue f.

status n (pl ~**es**) situation f, statut m; (prestige) standing m.

statute n loi f; ~**s** (rules) statuts mpl. **statutory** adj statutaire; (holiday) légal.

staunch adj (friend) loyal, fidèle.

stave n (Mus) portée f. •vt ~ **off** éviter, conjurer.

stay vi rester; (spend time) séjourner; (reside) loger. •vt (hunger) tromper. •n séjour m. ■~ **away from** (school) ne pas aller à; ~ **behind** or ~ **on** rester; ~ **in** rester à la maison; ~ **up** veiller, se coucher tard.

stead n **stand sb in good ~** être utile à qn.

steadfast adj ferme.

steady adj (-ier, -iest) stable; (hand, voice) ferme; (regular) régulier; (staid) sérieux. •vt maintenir, assurer; (calm) calmer.

steak n steak m, bifteck m; (of fish) darne f.

steal vt/i (pt **stole**; pp **stolen**)

voler (**from sb** à qn).

steam n vapeur f; (on glass) buée f. •vt (cook) cuire à la vapeur. •vi fumer. ~-**engine** n locomotive f à vapeur

steamer n (Culin) cuit-vapeur m; (boat) (bateau à) vapeur m.

steel n acier m; ~ **industry** sidérurgie f. •vpr ~ **oneself** s'endurcir, se cuirasser.

steep adj raide, rapide; (price: 🔢) excessif. •vt (soak) tremper; ~**ed in** (fig) imprégné de.

steeple n clocher m.

steer vt diriger; (ship) gouverner; (fig) guider. •vi (in ship) gouverner; ~ **clear of** éviter.

steering-wheel n volant m.

stem n tige f; (of glass) pied m. •vi (pt **stemmed**) ~ **from** provenir de. •vt (pt **stemmed**) (check, stop) endiguer, contenir. ~ **cell** n cellule f souche.

stench n puanteur f.

stencil n pochoir m. •vt (pt **stencilled**) décorer au pochoir.

step vi (pt **stepped**) marcher, aller. •n pas m; (stair) marche f; (of train) marchepied m; (action) mesure f; ~**s** (ladder) escabeau m; **in** ~ au pas; (fig) conforme (**with** à). ■ ~ **down** (resign) démissionner; (from ladder) descendre; ~ **forward** faire un pas en avant; ~ **in** (intervene) intervenir; ~ **up** (pressure) augmenter. ~**brother** n demifrère m. ~**daughter** n belle-fille f. ~**father** n beau-père m. ~**-ladder** n escabeau m. ~**mother** n belle-mère f. **stepping-stone** n (fig) tremplin m. ~**sister** n demi-sœur f. ~**son** n beau-fils m.

stereo n stéréo f; (record-player) chaîne f stéréo. •adj stéréo inv.

stereotype n stéréotype m.

sterile adj stérile. **sterility** n stérilité f.

sterilize vt stériliser.

sterling n livre(s) f (pl) sterling. •adj sterling inv; (silver) fin; (fig) excellent.

stern adj sévère. •n (of ship) arrière m.

steroid n stéroïde m.

stew vt/i cuire à la casserole; ~**ed fruit** compote f; ~**ed tea** thé m trop infusé. •n ragoût m.

steward n (of club) intendant m; (on ship) steward m. **stewardess** n hôtesse f.

stick vt (pt **stuck**) (glue) coller; (put 🔢) mettre; (endure 🔢) supporter. •vi (adhere) coller, adhérer; (to pan) attacher; (remain 🔢) rester; (be jammed) être coincé; **be stuck with sb** 🔢 se farcir qn. •n bâton m; (for walking) canne f. ■ ~ **at** persévérer dans; ~ **out** vt (head) sortir; (tongue) tirer; vi (protrude) dépasser; ~ **to** (promise) rester fidèle à; ~ **up for** 🔢 défendre.

sticker n autocollant m.

sticky adj (-ier, -iest) poisseux; (label, tape) adhésif.

stiff adj raide; (limb, joint) ankylosé; (tough) dur; (drink) fort; (price) élevé; (manner) guindé; ~ **neck** torticolis m.

stifle vt/i étouffer.

stiletto adj & n ~**s**, ~ **heels** talons mpl aiguille.

still adj immobile; (quiet) calme, tranquille; **keep** ~! arrête de bouger! •n silence m. •adv encore, toujours; (even) encore; (nevertheless) tout de même.

stillborn adj mort-né.

still life n nature f morte.

stimulate vt stimuler. **stimulation** n stimulation f.

stimulus n (pl **-li**) (spur) stimulant m.

sting n piqûre f; (of insect) aiguillon m. •vt/i (pt **stung**) piquer.

stingy adj (-ier, -iest) avare (**with** de).

stink n puanteur f. ●vi (pt **stank** or **stunk**; pp **stunk**) ~ (**of**) puer.

stipulate vt stipuler.

stir vt/i (pt **stirred**) (move) remuer; (excite) exciter; ~ **up** (trouble) provoquer. ●n agitation f.

stirrup n étrier m.

stitch n point m; (in knitting) maille f; (Med) point m de suture; (muscle pain) point m de côté; **be in ~es** 🄸 avoir le fou rire. ●vt coudre.

stock n réserve f; (Comm) stock m; (financial) valeurs fpl; (family) souche f; (soup) bouillon m; **we're out of ~** il n'y en a plus; **take ~** (fig) faire le point; **in ~** en stock. ●adj (goods) courant. ●vt (shop) approvisionner; (sell) vendre. ●vi ~ **up** s'approvisionner (**with** de). ~**broker** n agent m de change. ~ **cube** n bouillon-cube m. **S~ Exchange** n Bourse f.

stocking n bas m.

stock market n Bourse f.

stockpile n stock m. ●vt stocker; (arms) amasser.

stock-taking n (Comm) inventaire m.

stocky adj (**-ier, -iest**) trapu.

stodgy adj lourd.

stole, stolen ▷STEAL.

stomach n estomac m; (abdomen) ventre m. ●vt (put up with) supporter. ~**ache** n mal m à l'estomac or au ventre.

stone n pierre f; (pebble) caillou m; (in fruit) noyau m; (weight) 6,350 kg. ●adj de pierre; ~**cold/-deaf** complètement froid/sourd. ●vt (throw stones) lapider; (fruit) dénoyauter.

stony adj pierreux.

stood ▷STAND.

stool n tabouret m.

stoop vi (bend) se baisser; (condescend) s'abaisser. ●n **have a ~** être voûté.

stop vt/i (pt **stopped**) arrêter (**doing** de faire); (moving, talking) s'arrêter; (prevent) empêcher (**from** de); (hole, leak) boucher; (pain, noise) cesser; (stay 🄸) rester. ●n arrêt m; (full stop) point m; ~ (**-over**) halte f; (port of call) escale f. ■ ~ **off** s'arrêter; ~ **up** boucher.

stopgap n bouche-trou m. ●adj intérimaire.

stoppage n arrêt m; (of work) arrêt de travail; (of pay) retenue f.

stopper n bouchon m.

stop-watch n chronomètre m.

storage n (of goods, food) emmagasinage m. ~ **heater** n radiateur m électrique à accumulation.

store n réserve f; (warehouse) entrepôt m; (shop) grand magasin m; (US) magasin m; **have in ~ for** réserver à; **set ~ by** attacher du prix à. ●vt (for future) mettre en réserve; (in warehouse, mind) emmagasiner. ~**room** n réserve f.

storey n étage m.

stork n cigogne f.

storm n tempête f, orage m. ●vt prendre d'assaut. ●vi (rage) tempêter.

story n histoire f; (in press) article m; (storey: US) étage m. ~**teller** n conteur/-euse m/f.

stout adj corpulent; (strong) solide. ●n bière f brune.

stove n cuisinière f.

stow vt ~ **away** (put away) ranger; (hide) cacher. ●vi voyager clandestinement.

straddle vt être à cheval sur, enjamber.

straggler n traînard/-e m/f.

straight adj droit; (tidy) en ordre; (frank) franc; ~ **face** visage m sérieux; **get sth ~** mettre qch au clair. ●adv (in straight line) droit; (direct) tout droit; ~ **ahead** or

S

on tout droit; **~ away** tout de suite; •n (Sport) ligne f droite.

straighten vt (nail, situation) redresser; (tidy) arranger.

straightforward adj honnête; (easy) simple.

straight off adj 🔲 sans hésiter.

strain vt (rope, ears) tendre; (limb) fouler; (eyes) fatiguer; (muscle) froisser; (filter) passer; (vegetables) égoutter; (fig) mettre à l'épreuve. •vi fournir des efforts. •n tension f; (fig) effort m; (breed) race f; (of virus) variété f; **~s** (tune: Mus) accents mpl. **strained** adj forcé; (relations) tendu. **strainer** n passoire f.

strait n détroit m; **~s** détroit m; **be in dire ~s** être aux abois. **~-jacket** n camisole f de force.

strand n (thread) fil m, brin m; (of hair) mèche f.

stranded adj (person) en rade; (ship) échoué.

strange adj étrange; (unknown) inconnu. **stranger** n inconnu/-e m/f.

strangle vt étrangler.

stranglehold n **have a ~ on** tenir à la gorge.

strap n (of leather) courroie f; (of dress) bretelle f; (of watch) bracelet m. •vt (pt **strapped**) attacher.

strategic adj stratégique. **strategy** n stratégie f.

straw n paille f; **the last ~** le comble.

strawberry n fraise f.

stray vi s'égarer; (deviate) s'écarter. •adj perdu; (isolated) isolé. •n animal m perdu.

streak n raie f, bande f; (trace) trace f; (period) période f; (tendency) tendance f. •vt (mark) strier. •vi filer à toute allure.

stream n ruisseau m; (current) courant m; (flow) flot m; (in school) classe f (de niveau). •vi ruisseler

(**with** de); (eyes, nose) couler.

streamline vt rationaliser. **streamlined** adj (shape) aérodynamique.

street n rue f. **~car** n (US) tramway m. **~ lamp** n réverbère m. **~ map** n indicateur m des rues.

strength n force f; (of wall, fabric) solidité f; **on the ~ of** en vertu de. **strengthen** vt renforcer, fortifier.

strenuous adj (exercise) énergique; (work) ardu.

stress n (emphasis) accent m; (pressure) pression f; (Med) stress m. •vt souligner, insister sur.

stretch vt (pull taut) tendre; (arm, leg) étendre; (neck) tendre; (clothes) étirer; (truth) forcer; **~ one's legs** se dégourdir les jambes. •vi s'étendre; (person) s'étirer; (clothes) se déformer. •n étendue f; (period) période f; (of road) tronçon m; **at a ~** d'affilée. •adj (fabric) extensible.

stretcher n brancard m.

strew vt (pt **strewed**; pp **strewed** or **strewn**) (scatter) répandre; (cover) joncher.

strict adj strict.

stride vi (pt **strode**; pp **stridden**) faire de grands pas. •n grand pas m.

strife n conflit(s) m(pl).

strike vt (pt **struck**) frapper; (blow) donner; (match) frotter; (gold) trouver. •vi faire grève; (attack) attaquer; (clock) sonner. •n (of workers) grève f; (Mil) attaque f; (find) découverte f; **on ~** en grève. ■**~ off** or **out** rayer; **~ up** (a friendship) lier amitié (**with** avec). **striker** n gréviste mf; (football) attaquant/-e m/f. **striking** adj frappant.

string n ficelle f; (of violin, racket) corde f; (of pearls) collier m; (of lies) chapelet m; **the ~s** (Mus) les cordes; **pull ~s** faire jouer ses relations. •vt (pt **strung**) (thread) enfiler. **stringed** adj (instrument) à cordes.

stringent adj rigoureux, strict.

stringy adj filandreux.

strip vt/i (pt **stripped**) (undress) (se) déshabiller; (deprive) dépouiller. •n bande f.

stripe n rayure f, raie f. **striped** adj rayé.

strip light n néon m.

stripper n strip-teaseur/-euse m/f; (solvent) décapant.

strip-tease n strip-tease m.

strive vi (pt **strove**; pp **striven**) s'efforcer (**to** de).

strode ▷STRIDE.

stroke vt (with hand) caresser. •n coup m; (of pen) trait m; (swimming) nage f; (Med) attaque f, congestion f; **at a ~** d'un seul coup.

stroll vi flâner; **~ in** entrer tranquillement. •n petit tour m. **stroller** n (US) poussette f.

strong adj fort; (shoes, fabric) solide; **be fifty ~** être fort de cinquante personnes. **~hold** n bastion m.

strongly adv (greatly) fortement; (with energy) avec force; (deeply) profondément.

strove ▷STRIVE.

struck ▷STRIKE.

structure n (of cell, poem) structure f; (building) construction f.

struggle vi lutter, se battre. •n lutte f; (effort) effort m; **have a ~ to** avoir du mal à.

strum vt (pt **strummed**) gratter de.

strung ▷STRING. •adj **~ up** (tense) nerveux.

strut n (support) étai m. •vi (pt **strutted**) se pavaner.

stub n bout m; (counterfoil) talon m. •vt (pt **stubbed**) **~ one's toe** se cogner le doigt de pied. ■ **~ out** écraser.

stubble n (on chin) barbe f de plusieurs jours; (remains of wheat) chaume m.

stubborn adj obstiné.

stuck ▷STICK.•adj (jammed) coincé; **I'm ~** (for answer) je sèche. **~-up** adj 🔲 prétentieux.

stud n (on jacket) clou m; (for collar) bouton m; (stallion) étalon m; (horse farm) haras m. •vt (pt **studded**) clouter.

student n (Univ) étudiant/-e m/f; (School) élève mf. •adj (restaurant, life) universitaire.

studio n studio m.

studious adj (person) studieux; (deliberate) étudié.

study n étude f; (office) bureau m. •vt/i étudier.

stuff n substance f; 🔲 chose (s) f (pl). •vt rembourrer; (animal) empailler; (cram) bourrer; (Culin) farcir; (block up) boucher; (put) fourrer. **stuffing** n bourre f; (Culin) farce f.

stuffy adj (**-ier**, **-iest**) mal aéré; (dull 🔲) vieux jeu inv.

stumble vi trébucher; **~ across** or **on** tomber sur. **stumbling block** n obstacle m.

stump n (of tree) souche f; (of limb) moignon m; (of pencil) bout m.

stumped adj embarrassé.

stun vt (pt **stunned**) étourdir; (bewilder) stupéfier.

stung ▷STING.

stunk ▷STINK.

stunning adj (delightful 🔲) sensationnel.

stunt vt (growth) retarder. •n (feat 🔲) tour m de force; (trick 🔲) truc m; (dangerous) cascade f.

stupid adj stúpide, bête. **stupidity** n stupidité f.

sturdy adj (-ier, -iest) robuste.

stutter vi bégayer. •n bégaiement m.

sty n (pigsty) porcherie f; (on eye) orgelet m.

style n style m; (fashion) mode f; (sort) genre m; (pattern) modèle m; **do sth in ~** faire qch avec classe. •vt (design) créer; **~ sb's hair** coiffer qn.

stylish adj élégant.

stylist n (of hair) coiffeur/-euse m/f.

suave adj (urbane) courtois; (smooth: pej) doucereux.

subconscious adj & n inconscient (m), subconscient (m.)

subcontract vt sous-traiter.

subdue vt (feeling) maîtriser; (country) subjuguer. **subdued** adj (person, mood) morose; (light) tamisé; (criticism) contenu.

subject[1] /ˈsʌbdʒɪkt/ adj (state) soumis; **~ to** soumis à; (liable to, dependent on) sujet à. •n sujet m; (focus) objet m; (School, Univ) matière f; (citizen) ressortissant/-e m/f, sujet/-te m/f.

subject[2] /səbˈdʒekt/ vt soumettre.

subjective adj subjectif.

subject-matter n contenu m.

subjunctive adj & n subjonctif (m.)

sublet vt sous-louer.

submarine n sousmarin m.

submerge vt submerger. •vi plonger.

submissive adj soumis.

submit vt/i (pt submitted) (se) soumettre (**to** à).

subordinate adj subalterne; (Gram) subordonné. •n subordonné/-e m/f.

subpoena n (Jur) citation f, assignation f.

subscribe vt/i verser (de l'argent) (**to** à); **~ to** (loan, theory) souscrire à; (newspaper) s'abonner à, être abonné à. **subscriber** n abonné/-e m/f. **subscription** n abonnement m; (membership dues) cotisation f.

subsequent adj (later) ultérieur; (next) suivant. **subsequently** adv par la suite.

subside vi (land) s'affaisser; (flood, wind) baisser.

subsidiary adj accessoire. •n (Comm) filiale f.

subsidize vt subventionner. **subsidy** n subvention f.

substance n substance f.

substandard adj de qualité inférieure.

substantial adj considérable; (meal) substantiel.

substitute n succédané m; (person) remplaçant/-e m/f. •vt substituer (**for** à).

subtitle n sous-titre m.

subtle adj subtil.

subtract vt soustraire.

suburb n faubourg m, banlieue f; **~s** banlieue f. **suburban** adj de banlieue. **suburbia** n la banlieue.

subway n passage m souterrain; (US) métro m.

succeed vi réussir (**in doing** à faire). •vt (follow) succéder à.

success n succès m, réussite f.

successful adj réussi, couronné de succès; (favourable) heureux; (in exam) reçu; **be ~ in doing** réussir à faire.

succession n succession f; **in ~** de suite.

successive adj successif; **six ~ days** six jours consécutifs.

successor n successeur m.

such det & pron tel(le), tel(le)s; (so much) tant(de). •adv si; **~ a book** un tel livre; **~ books** de tels livres; ~ **courage** tant de courage; ~ **a big house** une si grande maison; **as** ~ comme, tel que; **as** ~ en tant que tel; **there's no** ~ **thing** ça n'existe pas. ~**-and-**~ adj tel ou tel.

suck vt sucer. ■ ~ **in** or **up** aspirer. **sucker** n (rubber pad) ventouse f; (person Ⅰ) dupe f.

suction n succion f.

sudden adj soudain, subit; **all of a** ~ tout à coup. **suddenly** adv subitement, brusquement.

sue vt (pres p **suing**) poursuivre (en justice).

suede n daim m.

suffer vt/i souffrir; (loss, attack) subir. **sufferer** n victime f, malade mf. **suffering** n souffrance(s) f(pl).

sufficient adj (enough) suffisamment de; (big enough) suffisant.

suffix n suffixe m.

suffocate vt/i suffoquer.

sugar n sucre m. ●vt sucrer.

suggest vt suggérer. **suggestion** n suggestion f.

suicidal adj suicidaire.

suicide n suicide m; **commit** ~ se suicider.

suit n (man's) costume m; (woman's) tailleur m; (cards) couleur f.●vt convenir à; (garment, style) aller à; (adapt) adapter.

suitable adj qui convient (**for** à), convenable. **suitably** adv convenablement.

suitcase n valise f.

suite n (rooms) suite f; (furniture) mobilier m.

suited adj (**well**) ~ (matched) bien assorti; ~ **to** fait pour, apte à.

sulk vi bouder.

sullen adj maussade.

sultana n raisin m de Smyrne, raisin m sec.

sultry adj (-ier, -iest) étouffant, lourd; (fig) sensuel.

sum n somme f; (in arithmetic) calcul m. ●vt/i (pt **summed**) ~ **up** résumer, récapituler; (assess) évaluer.

summarize vt résumer.

summary n résumé m. ●adj sommaire.

summer n été m. ●adj d'été. ~**time** n (season) été m.

summery adj estival.

summit n sommet m; ~ (**conference**) (Pol) (conférence f au) sommet m.

summon vt appeler; ~ **sb to a meeting** convoquer qn à une réunion; ~ **up** (strength, courage) rassembler.

summons n (Jur) assignation f. ●vt assigner.

sun n soleil m. ●vt (pt **sunned**) ~ **oneself** se chauffer au soleil. ~**burn** n coup m de soleil.

Sunday n dimanche m. ~ **school** n catéchisme m.

sundry adj divers; **sundries** articles mpl divers; **all and** ~ tout le monde.

sunflower n tournesol m.

sung ▷SING.

sun-glasses npl lunettes fpl de soleil.

sunk ▷SINK.

sunken adj (ship) submergé; (eyes) creux.

sunlight n soleil m.

sunny adj (-ier, -iest) ensoleillé.

sun: ~**rise** n lever m du soleil. ~**-roof** n toit m ouvrant. ~**screen** n filtre m solaire. ~**set** n coucher m du soleil. ~**shine** n soleil m. ~**stroke** n insolation f.

sun-tan n bronzage m. ~ **lotion** n lotion f solaire. ~ **oil** n huile f solaire.

super adj Ⅰ formidable.

superb adj superbe.

superficial adj superficiel.

superfluous adj superflu.

superimpose vt superposer (**on** à).

superintendent n directeur/-trice m/f; (of police) commissaire m.

superior adj & n supérieur/-e (m /f).

superlative adj suprême. •n (Gram) superlatif m.

supermarket n supermarché m.

supersede vt remplacer, supplanter.

superstition n superstition f. **superstitious** adj superstitieux.

superstore n hypermarché m.

supervise vt surveiller, diriger. **supervision** n surveillance f. **supervisor** n surveillant/-e m/f; (shop) chef m de rayon; (firm) chef m de service.

supper n dîner m; (late at night) souper m.

supple adj souple.

supplement¹ /'sʌplɪmənt/ n supplément m. **supplementary** adj supplémentaire.

supplement² /'sʌplɪmənt/ vt compléter.

supplier n fournisseur m.

supply vt fournir; (equip) pourvoir; (feed) alimenter (**with** en). •n provision f; (of gas) alimentation f; **supplies** (food) vivres mpl; (material) fournitures fpl.

support vt soutenir; (family) assurer la subsistance de. •n soutien m, appui m; (Tech) support m. **supporter** n partisan/-e m/f; (Sport) supporter m. **supportive** adj qui soutient et encourage.

suppose vt/i supposer; **be ∼d to do** être censé faire, devoir faire; **supposing he comes** supposons qu'il vienne.

supposedly adv soi-disant, prétendument.

suppress vt (put an end to) supprimer; (restrain) réprimer; (stifle) étouffer.

supreme adj suprême.

surcharge n supplément m; (tax) surtaxe f.

sure adj sûr; **make ∼ of** s'assurer de; **make ∼ that** vérifier que. •adv (US 🄸) pour sûr. **surely** adv sûrement.

surf n ressac m. •vi faire du surf; (Internet) surfer.

surface n surface f. •adj superficiel. •vt revêtir. •vi faire surface; (fig) réapparaître.

surfer n surfeur/-euse m/f; (Internet) internaute mf.

surge vi (waves, crowd) déferler; (increase) monter. •n (wave) vague f; (rise) montée f.

surgeon n chirurgien m.

surgery n chirurgie f; (office) cabinet m; (session) consultation f; **need ∼** devoir être opéré.

surgical adj chirurgical. **∼ spirit** n alcool m à 90 degrés.

surly adj (**-ier, -iest**) bourru.

surname n nom m de famille.

surplus n surplus m. •adj en surplus.

surprise n surprise f. •vt surprendre. **surprised** adj surpris (**at** de). **surprising** adj surprenant.

surrender vi se rendre. •vt (hand over) remettre; (Mil) rendre. •n (Mil) reddition f; (of passport) remise f.

surround vt entourer; (Mil) encercler. **surrounding** adj environnant. **surroundings** npl environs mpl; (setting) cadre m.

surveillance n surveillance f.

survey¹ /sə'veɪ/ vt (review) passer

en revue; (inquire into) enquêter sur; (building) inspecter.

survey² /'sɜːveɪ/ n (inquiry) enquête f; inspection f; (general view) vue f d'ensemble.

surveyor n expert m (géomètre).

survival n survie f.

survive vt/i survivre (à). **survivor** n survivant/-e m/f.

susceptible adj sensible (**to** à); ~ **to** (prone to) prédisposé à.

suspect¹ /sə'spekt/ vt soupçonner; (doubt) douter de.

suspect² /'sʌspekt/ n & adj suspect/-e (m/f).

suspend vt (hang, stop) suspendre; (licence) retirer provisoirement. **suspended sentence** n condamnation f avec sursis.

suspender n jarretelle f; ~**s** (braces: US) bretelles fpl. ~ **belt** n porte-jarretelles m.

suspension n suspension f; retrait m provisoire.

suspicion n soupçon m; (distrust) méfiance f.

suspicious adj soupçonneux; (causing suspicion) suspect; **be ~ of** se méfier de. **suspiciously** adv de façon suspecte.

sustain vt supporter; (effort) soutenir; (suffer) subir.

sustenance n (food) nourriture f; (nourishment) valeur f nutritive.

swallow vt/i avaler; ~ **up** (absorb, engulf) engloutir. •n hirondelle f.

swam ▸SWIM.

swamp n marais m. •vt (flood, overwhelm) submerger.

swan n cygne m.

swap vt/i (pt **swapped**) 🔲 échanger. •n 🔲 échange m.

swarm n essaim m. •vi fourmiller; ~ **into** or **round** (crowd) envahir.

swat vt (pt **swatted**) (fly) écraser.

sway vt/i (se) balancer; (influence) influencer. •n balancement m; (rule) empire m.

swear vt/i (pt **swore**; pp **sworn**) jurer (**to sth** de qch); ~ **at** injurier; ~ **by sth** 🔲 ne jurer que par qch. ~ **-word** n juron m.

sweat n sueur f. •vi suer.

sweater n pull-over m.

sweat-shirt n sweat-shirt m.

swede n rutabaga m.

Swede n Suédois/-e m/f. **Sweden** n Suède f.

Swedish adj suédois. •n (Ling) suédois m.

sweep vt/i (pt **swept**) (floor) balayer; (carry away) emporter, entraîner; (chimney) ramoner. •n coup m de balai; (curve) courbe f; (mouvement) geste m, mouvement m; (for chimneys) ramoneur m. ◾ ~ **by** passer rapidement or majestueusement. **sweeper** n (for carpet) balai m mécanique; (football) libero m.

sweet adj (not sour, pleasant) doux; (not savoury) sucré; (charming 🔲) gentil; **have a ~ tooth** aimer les sucreries. •n bonbon m; (dish) dessert m. ~**corn** n maïs m.

sweeten vt sucrer; (fig) adoucir. **sweetener** n édulcorant m.

sweetheart n petit/-e ami/-e m/f; (term of endearment) chéri/-e m/f.

sweetly adv gentiment.

sweetness n douceur f; goût m sucré.

sweet pea n pois m de senteur.

swell vt/i (pt **swelled**; pp **swollen** or **swelled**) (increase) grossir; (expand) (se) gonfler; (hand, face) enfler. •n (of sea) houle f. **swelling** n (Med) enflure f.

sweltering adj étouffant.

swept ▷SWEEP.

swerve vi faire un écart.

swift adj rapide. • n (bird) martinet m.

swim vi (pt **swam**; pp **swum**; pres p **swimming**) nager; (be dizzy) tourner. • vt traverser à la nage; (distance) nager. • n baignade f; **go for a ∼** aller se baigner. **swimmer** n nageur/-euse m/f. **swimming** n natation f.

swimming pool n piscine f.

swimsuit n maillot m (de bain).

swindle vt escroquer. • n escroquerie f.

swine npl (pigs) pourceaux mpl. • n inv (person 🔲) salaud m.

swing vt/i (pt **swung**) (se) balancer; (turn round) tourner; (pendulum) osciller. • n balancement m; (seat) balançoire f; (of opinion) revirement m (**towards** en faveur de); (Mus) rythme m; **be in full ∼** battre son plein. ■∼ **round** (person) se retourner.

swipe vt (hit 🔲) frapper; (steal 🔲) piquer. ∼ **card** n carte f magnétique, badge m.

swirl vi tourbillonner. • n tourbillon m.

Swiss adj suisse. • n inv Suisse mf.

switch n bouton m (électrique), interrupteur m; (shift) changement m, revirement m. • vt (transfer) transférer; (exchange) échanger (**for** contre); (reverse positions of) changer de place; ∼ **trains** (change) changer de train. • vi changer. ■∼ **off** éteindre; ∼ **on** mettre, allumer.

switchboard n standard m.

Switzerland n Suisse f.

swivel vt/i (pt **swivelled**) (faire) pivoter.

swollen ▷SWELL.

swoop vi (bird) fondre; (police) faire une descente, foncer. • n (police raid) descente f.

sword n épée f.

swore ▷SWEAR.

sworn ▷SWEAR. • adj (enemy) juré; (ally) dévoué.

swot vt/i (pt **swotted**) (study 🔲) bûcher 🔲. • n 🔲 bûcheur/-euse m/f🔲

swum ▷SWIM.

swung ▷SWING.

syllabus n (pl ∼**es**) (School, Univ) programme m.

symbol n symbole m. **symbolic(al)** adj symbolique. **symbolize** vt symboliser.

symmetrical adj symétrique.

sympathetic adj compatissant; (fig) compréhensif.

sympathize vi ∼ **with** (pity) plaindre; (fig) comprendre les sentiments de. **sympathizer** n sympathisant/-e m/f.

sympathy n (pity) compassion f; (fig) compréhension f; (solidarity) solidarité f; (condolences) condoléances fpl; (affinity) affinité f; **be in ∼ with** comprendre, être en accord avec.

symptom n symptôme m.

synagogue n synagogue f.

synonym n synonyme m.

synopsis n (pl **-opses**) résumé m.

syntax n syntaxe f.

synthesis n (pl **-theses**) synthèse f.

synthetic adj synthétique.

syringe n seringue f.

syrup n (liquid) sirop m; (treacle) mélasse f raffinée.

system n système m; (body) organisme m; (order) méthode f. **systematic** adj systématique.

systems analyst n analysteprogrammeur/- euse m/f.

Tt

tab n (on can) languette f; (on garment) patte f; (label) étiquette f; (US 🇹) addition f; (Comput) tabulatrice f; (setting) tabulation f.

table n table f; **at (the)** ∼ à table; **lay** or **set the** ∼ mettre la table. • vt (motion) présenter. ∼**-cloth** n nappe f. ∼**-mat** n set m de table. ∼**-spoon** n cuillère f de service.

tablet n (of stone) plaque f; (drug) comprimé m.

table tennis n tennis m de table; ping-pong® m.

taboo n & a tabou (m).

tacit adj tacite.

tack n (nail) clou m; (stitch) point m de bâti; (course of action) voie f. • vt (nail) clouer; (stitch) bâtir; (add) ajouter. • vi (Naut) louvoyer.

tackle n équipement m; (in soccer) tacle m; (in rugby) plaquage m. • vt (problem) s'attaquer à; (player) tacler, plaquer.

tact n tact m. **tactful** adj plein de tact.

tactics npl tactique f.

tadpole n têtard m.

tag n (label) étiquette f. • vt (pt **tagged**) (label) étiqueter. • vi ∼ **along** 🇹 suivre.

tail n queue f; ∼**s** (coat) habit m; ∼**s!** (on coin) pile! • vt (follow) filer. • vi ∼ **away** or **off** diminuer. ∼**-back** n bouchon m. ∼**-gate** n hayon m.

tailor n tailleur m. • vt (garment) façonner; (fig) adapter. ∼**-made** adj fait sur mesure.

take vt/i (pt **took**; pp **taken**) prendre (**from sb** à qn); (carry) emporter, porter (**to** à); (escort) emmener; (contain) contenir;

(tolerate) supporter; (accept) accepter; (prize) remporter; (exam) passer; (precedence) avoir; (view) adopter; ∼ **sb home** ramener qn chez lui; **be taken by** or **with** être impressionné par; **be taken ill** tomber malade; **it** ∼**s time** il faut du temps pour. ■ ∼ **after** tenir de; ∼ **apart** démonter; (fig) descendre en flammes 🇹; ∼ **away** (object) enlever; (person) emmener; (pain) supprimer; ∼ **back** reprendre; (return) rendre; (accompany) raccompagner; (statement) retirer; ∼ **down** (object) descendre; (notes) prendre; ∼ **in** (object) rentrer; (include) inclure; (cheat) tromper; ∼ **off** (Aviat) décoller; ∼ **sth off** enlever qch; ∼ **sb off** imiter qn; ∼ **on** (task, staff, passenger) prendre; (challenger) relever le défi de; ∼ **out** sortir; (stain) enlever; ∼ **over** vt (country, firm) prendre le contrôle de; vi prendre le pouvoir; ∼ **over from** remplacer; ∼ **part** participer (**in** à); ∼ **place** avoir lieu; ∼ **to** se prendre d'amitié pour; (activity) prendre goût à; ∼ **to doing** se mettre à faire; ∼ **up** (object) monter; (hobby) se mettre à; (occupy) prendre; (resume) reprendre; ∼ **up with** se lier avec. ∼**-away** n (meal) repas m à emporter. ∼**-off** n (Aviat) décollage m. ∼**-over** n (Pol) prise f de pouvoir; (Comm) rachat m.

tale n conte m; (report) récit m; (lie) histoire f.

talent n talent m. **talented** adj doué.

talk vt/i parler; (chat) bavarder; ∼ **sb into doing** persuader qn de faire; ∼ **sth over** discuter de qch. • n (talking) propos mpl;

(conversation) conversation f; (lecture) exposé m.

talkative adj bavard.

tall adj (high) haut; (person) grand.

tame adj apprivoisé; (dull) insipide. ●vt apprivoiser; (lion) dompter.

tamper vi ~ **with** (lock, machine) tripoter; (accounts, evidence) trafiquer.

tan vt/i (pt **tanned**) bronzer; (hide) tanner. ●n bronzage m.

tangerine n mandarine f.

tangle vt/i ~ **(up)** s'emmêler. ●n enchevêtrement m.

tank n réservoir m; (vat) cuve f; (for fish) aquarium m; (Mil) char m (de combat).

tanker n (lorry) camion-citerne m; (ship) navire-citerne m; **oil/petrol** ~ pétrolier m.

tantrum n crise f (de colère).

tap n (for water) robinet m; (knock) petit coup m; **on** ~ disponible. ●vt (pt **tapped**) (knock) taper (doucement); (resources) exploiter; (phone) mettre sur écoute.

tape n bande f (magnétique); (cassette) cassette f; (video) cassette f vidéo; (fabric) ruban m; (sticky) scotch ® m. ●vt (record) enregistrer; ~ **sth to sth** coller qch à qch. ~**-measure** n mètre m ruban. ~ **recorder** n magnétophone m.

tapestry n tapisserie f.

tar n goudron m. ●vt (pt **tarred**) goudronner.

target n cible f; (objective) objectif m. ●vt (city) prendre pour cible; (weapon) diriger; (in marketing) viser.

tariff n (price list) tarif m; (on imports) droit m de douane.

tarmac, **Tarmac®** n macadam m; (runway) piste f.

tarpaulin n bâche f.

tarragon n estragon m.

tart n tarte f. ●adj aigrelet.

task n tâche f.

taste n goût m; (experience) aperçu m. ●vt (eat, enjoy) goûter à; (try) goûter; (perceive taste of) sentir (le goût de). ●vi ~ **of** or **like** avoir un goût de. **tasteful** adj de bon goût.

tattoo vt tatouer. ●n tatouage m.

tatty adj (-ier, -iest) 🄣 miteux.

taught ▷TEACH.

taunt vt railler. ●n raillerie f.

Taurus n Taureau m.

tax n (on goods, services) taxe f; (on income) impôt m. ●vt imposer; (put to test: fig) mettre à l'épreuve. **taxable** adj imposable. **taxation** n imposition f; (taxes) impôts mpl.

tax: ~ **collector** n percepteur m. ~**-deductible** adj déductible des impôts. ~ **disc** n vignette f. ~**-free** adj exempt d'impôts. ~ **haven** n paradis m fiscal.

taxi n taxi m. ~ **rank** n station f de taxi.

tax: ~**payer** n contribuable mf. ~ **relief** n dégrèvement m fiscal. ~ **return** n déclaration f d'impôts.

tea n (drink, meal) thé m; (children's snack) goûter m; ~ **bag** sachet m de thé.

teach vt (pt **taught**) apprendre (**sb sth** qch à qn); (in school) enseigner (**sb sth** qch à qn). ●vi enseigner. **teacher** n enseignant/-e m/f; (secondary) professeur m; (primary) instituteur/-trice m/f.

team n équipe f; (of animals) attelage m. ●vi ~ **up** faire équipe (**with** avec).

teapot n théière f.

tear¹ /teə(r)/ vt/i (pt **tore**; pp **torn**) (se) déchirer; (snatch) arracher (**from** à); (rush) aller à toute vitesse. ●n déchirure f.

tear² /tɪə(r)/ n larme f; **in** ~**s** en larmes. ~**-gas** n gaz m lacrymogène.

tease vt taquiner. •n taquin/-e m/f.

tea: ~ **shop** n salon m de thé.
~**spoon** n petite cuillère f.

teat n tétine f.

tea-towel n torchon m.

technical adj technique.

technician n technicien/-ne m/f.

technique n technique f.

techno n (Mus) techno f.

technology n technologie f.

technophobe n technophobe mf.

teddy adj ~ **bear** ours m en
peluche.

tedious adj ennuyeux.

tee n (golf) tee m.

teenage adj (girl, boy) adolescent;
(fashion) des adolescents.
teenager n jeune mf,
adolescent/-e m/f.

teens npl **in one's** ~ adolescent.

teeth ▸TOOTH.

teethe vi faire ses dents.

teetotaller n personne f qui ne
boit pas d'alcool.

telecommunications npl
télécommunications fpl.

telecommuting n télétravail m.

teleconferencing n
téléconférence f.

telegram n télégramme m.

telegraph n télégraphe m. •adj
télégraphique.

telephone n téléphone m. •vt
(person) téléphoner à; (message)
téléphoner. •vi téléphoner. ~
book n annuaire m. ~ **booth**, ~
box n cabine f téléphonique. ~
call n coup m de téléphone. ~
number n numéro m de
téléphone.

telephoto adj ~ **lens**
téléobjectif m.

telescope n télescope m. •vt/i
(se) télescoper.

teletext n télétexte m.

televise vt téléviser.

television n télévision f; ~ **set**
poste m de télévision,
téléviseur m.

teleworking n télétravail m.

telex n télex m. •vt envoyer par
télex.

tell vt (pt **told**) dire (**sb sth** qch à
qn); (story) raconter; (distinguish)
distinguer; ~ **sb to do sth** dire
à qn de faire qch; ~ **sth from**
sth voir la différence entre qch
et qch. •vi (show) avoir un effet;
(know) savoir. ■~ **off** 🔢 gronder.

temp n intérimaire mf. •vi faire de
l'intérim.

temper n humeur f; (anger) colère
f; **lose one's** ~ se mettre en
colère.

temperament n tempérament
m. **temperamental** adj
capricieux.

temperature n température f;
have a ~ avoir de la fièvre *or*
de la température.

temple n temple m; (of head)
tempe f.

temporary adj temporaire,
provisoire.

tempt vt tenter; ~ **sb to do**
donner envie à qn de faire.

ten adj & n dix (m).

tenacious adj tenace.

tenancy n location f. **tenant** n
locataire m.

tend vt s'occuper de. •vi ~ **to** (be
apt to) avoir tendance à; (look after)
s'occuper de. **tendency** n
tendance f.

tender adj tendre; (sore, painful)
sensible. •vt offrir, donner. •vi
faire une soumission. •n (Comm)
soumission f; **be legal** ~ (money)
avoir cours.

tendon n tendon m.

tennis n tennis m. •adj (court,
match) de tennis.

tenor | that

560

tenor n (meaning) sens m général; (Mus) ténor m.

tense n (Gram) temps m. ●adj tendu. ●vt (muscles) tendre, raidir. ●vi (face) se crisper.

tension n tension f.

tent n tente f.

tentative adj provisoire; (hesitant) timide.

tenth adj & n dixième (mf).

tepid adj tiède.

term n (word, limit) terme m; (of imprisonment) temps m; (School) trimestre m; ∼s conditions fpl; **on good/bad** ∼s en bons/ mauvais termes; **in the short/ long** ∼ à court/long terme; **come to** ∼s with sth accepter qch; ∼ **of office** (Pol) mandat m. ●vt appeler.

terminal adj (point) terminal; (illness) incurable. ●n (oil, computer) terminal m; (Rail) terminus m; (Electr) borne f; **air** ∼ aérogare f.

terminate vt mettre fin à. ●vi prendre fin.

terminus n (pl **-ni**) (station) terminus m.

terrace n terrasse f; (houses) rangée f de maisons contiguës; **the** ∼s (Sport) les gradins mpl.

terracotta n terre f cuite.

terrible adj affreux, atroce.

terrific adj (huge) énorme; (great 𝕀) formidable.

terrify vt terrifier; **be terrified of** avoir très peur de.

territory n territoire m.

terror n terreur f.

terrorism n terrorisme m. **terrorist** n terroriste mf.

test n épreuve f; (written exam) contrôle m; (of machine, product) essai m; (of sample) analyse f; **driving** ∼ examen m du permis de conduire. ●vt évaluer; (School) contrôler; (machine, product) essayer; (sample) analyser;

(patience, strength) mettre à l'épreuve. ●vi ∼ **for** faire une recherche de.

testament n testament m; **Old/ New T**∼ Ancien/Nouveau Testament m.

testicle n testicule m.

testify vt/i témoigner (**to** de; **that** que).

testimony n témoignage m.

test tube n éprouvette f.

tetanus n tétanos m.

text n texte m. ●vt ∼ **sb** envoyer un texto à qn. ∼**book** n manuel m. ∼ **message** n texto m.

texture n (of paper) grain m; (of fabric) texture f.

than conj que, qu'; (with numbers) de; **more/less** ∼ **ten** plus/moins de dix.

thank vt remercier; ∼ **you!**, ∼**s!** merci! **thankful** adj reconnaissant (**for** de). **thanks** npl remerciements mpl; ∼**s to** grâce à. **Thanksgiving (Day)** n (US) jour m d'Action de Grâces.

---

that /ðæt/ pl **those**

●determiner
⸱⸱⸱▸ ce, cet, cette, ces; ∼ **dog** ce chien; ∼ **man** cet homme; ∼ **woman** cette femme; **those books** ces livres; **at** ∼ **moment** à ce moment-là.

❗ To distinguish **that/those** from **this/these**, you add **-là** to the noun: **I prefer that car** je préfère cette voiture-là.

●pronoun
⸱⸱⸱▸ cela, ça, ce; **what's** ∼?, **what are those?** qu'est-ce que c'est (que ça)?; **who's** ∼? qui est-ce?; ∼ **is my brother** c'est or voilà mon frère; **those are my parents** ce sont mes parents.
⸱⸱⸱▸ (emphatic) celui-là, celle-là,

ceux-là, celles-là; **all the dresses are nice but I like ∼/those best** toutes les robes sont jolies mais je préfère celle-là/celles-là.

● relative pronoun

····▸ (for subject) qui; **the man ∼ stole the car** l'homme qui a volé la voiture.

····▸ (for object) que; **the girl ∼ I met** la fille que j'ai rencontrée.

❗ With a preposition, use *lequel/laquelle/lesquels/lesquelles*: **the chair ∼ I was sitting on** la chaise sur laquelle j'étais assis.
With a preposition that translates as à, use *auquel/à laquelle/auxquels/auxquelles*: **the girls ∼ I was talking to** les filles auxquelles je parlais.
With a preposition that translates as de, use *dont*: **the people ∼ I've talked about** les personnes dont j'ai parlé.

● conjunction que; **she said ∼ she would do it** elle a dit qu'elle le ferait.

thatched adj de chaume; ∼ **cottage** chaumière f.

thaw vt/i (faire) dégeler; (snow) (faire) fondre. ● n dégel m.

the /ðə, ðɪ:/ determiner

····▸ le, l', la, les; ∼ **dog** le chien; ∼ **tree** l'arbre; ∼ **chair** la chaise; **to** ∼ **shops** aux magasins.

❗ With a preposition that translates as à: à + le = au and à + les = aux.

theatre n théâtre m.

theft n vol m.

their adj leur, pl leurs.

theirs pron le *or* la leur, les leurs.

them pron les; (after preposition) eux, elles; **(to)** ∼ leur; **phone** ∼! téléphone-leur!; **I know** ∼ je les

connais; **both of** ∼ tous/toutes les deux.

theme n thème m. ∼ **park** n parc m de loisirs (à thème).

themselves pron eux-mêmes, elles-mêmes; (reflexive) se; (after preposition) eux, elles.

then adv alors; (next) ensuite, puis; (therefore) alors, donc. ● adj d'alors; **from** ∼ **on** dès lors.

theology n théologie f.

theory n théorie f.

therapy n thérapie f.

there adv là; (with verb) y; (over there) là-bas; **he goes** ∼ il y va; **on** ∼ là-dessus; ∼ **is,** ∼ **are** il y a; (pointing) voilà. ● interj ∼, ∼! allons, allons!

therefore adv donc.

thermal adj thermique.

thermometer n thermomètre m.

Thermos® n thermos ® m or f inv.

thermostat n thermostat m.

thesaurus n (pl **-ri**) dictionnaire m de synonymes.

these ▷THIS.

thesis n (pl **theses**) thèse f.

they pron ils, elles; (emphatic) eux, elles; (people in general) on.

thick adj épais; (stupid) bête; **be 6 cm** ∼ avoir 6 cm d'épaisseur.

thief n (pl **thieves**) voleur/-euse m/f.

thigh n cuisse f.

thin adj (**thinner, thinnest**) mince; (person) maigre, mince; (sparse) clairsemé; (fine) fin. ● vt/i (pt **thinned**) ∼ **(down)** (paint) diluer; (soup) allonger.

thing n chose f; ∼**s** (belongings) affaires fpl; **the best** ∼ **is to** le mieux est de; **the (right)** ∼ ce qu'il faut (**for sb** à qn).

think vt/i (pt **thought**) penser (**about, of** à); (carefully) réfléchir (**about, of** à); (believe) croire; **I** ∼

so je crois que oui; ~ **of doing** envisager de faire. ∎~ **over** bien réfléchir à; ~ **up** inventer.

third adj troisième. •n troisième mf; (fraction) tiers m. **T**~ **World** n tiers-monde m.

thirst n soif f.

thirsty adj **be** ~ avoir soif; **make** ~ donner soif à.

thirteen adj & n treize (m).

thirty adj & n trente (m).

---

this /ðɪs/pl **these**

•determiner
····▸ ce/cet/cette/ces; ~ **dog** ce chien; ~ **man** cet homme; ~ **woman** cette femme; **these books** ces livres.

❗ To distinguish from **that** and **those**, you need to add -ci after the noun: **I prefer this car** je préfère cette voiture-ci.

•pronoun
····▸ ce; **what's** ~?, **what are these?** qu'est-ce que c'est?; **who is** ~? qui est-ce?; ~ **is the kitchen** voici la cuisine; ~ **is Sophie** je te or vous présente Sophie; **these are your things** ce sont tes affaires.
····▸ (emphatic) celui-ci/celle-ci/ceux-ci/celles-ci; **all the dresses are nice but I like** ~/**these best** toutes les robes sont jolies mais je préfère celle-ci/celles-ci.

---

thistle n chardon m.

thorn n épine f.

thorough adj (detailed) approfondi; (meticulous) minutieux. **thoroughly** adv (clean, study) à fond; (very) tout à fait.

those ▷ THAT.

though conj bien que. •adv quand même.

thought ▷ THINK. •n pensée f, idée f. **thoughtful** adj pensif; (kind) prévenant.

thousand adj & n mille (m inv); ~**s**

of des milliers de. **thousandth** adj & n millième (mf).

thread n (yarn & fig) fil m; (of screw) pas m. •vt enfiler; ~ **one's way** se faufiler.

threat n menace f. **threaten** vt/i menacer (**with** de).

three adj & n trois (m).

threw ▷ THROW.

thrill n frisson m; (pleasure) plaisir m. •vt transporter (de joie); **be** ~**ed** être ravi. •vi frissonner (de joie).

thrive vi (pt thrived or throve;pp thrived or thriven) prospérer; **he** ~**s on it** cela lui réussit.

throat n gorge f; **have a sore** ~ avoir mal à la gorge.

throb vi (pt throbbed) (heart) battre; (engine) vibrer. •n (pain) élancement m; (of engine) vibration f. **throbbing** adj (pain) lancinant.

throne n trône m.

through prep à travers; (during) pendant; (by means or way of, out of) par; (by reason of) grâce à, à cause de. •adv à travers; (entirely) jusqu'au bout. •adj (train) direct; **be** ~ (finished) avoir fini; **come** or **go** ~ (cross, pierce) traverser; **I'm putting you** ~ je vous passe votre correspondant.

throughout prep ~ **the country** dans tout le pays; ~ **the day** pendant toute la journée. •adv (place) partout; (time) tout le temps.

throw vt (pt threw; pp thrown) jeter, lancer; (baffle) déconcerter; ~ **a party** faire une fête. •n jet m; (of dice) coup m. ∎~ **away** jeter; ~ **off** (get rid of) se débarrasser de; ~ **out** jeter; (person) expulser; (reject) rejeter; ~ **up** (arms) lever; (vomit 🄸) vomir.

thrust vt (pt thrust) pousser. •n poussée f.

thud n bruit m sourd.

thug n voyou m.

thumb n pouce m. ●vt (book) feuilleter; ~ **a lift** faire de l'autostop. ~-**index** n répertoire m à onglets.

thump vt/i cogner (sur); (heart) battre fort. ●n coup m.

thunder n tonnerre m. ●vi (weather, person) tonner. ~**storm** n orage m.

Thursday n jeudi m.

thus adv ainsi.

thwart vt contrecarrer.

thyme n thym m.

tick n (sound) tic-tac m; (mark) coche f; (moment 🄸) instant m; (insect) tique f.●vi faire tic-tac. ●vt (~ **off**) cocher. ■ ~ **over** tourner au ralenti.

ticket n billet m; (for bus, cloakroom) ticket m; (label) étiquette f. ~-**collector** n contrôleur/-euse m/f. ~-**office** n guichet m.

tickle vt chatouiller; (amuse: fig) amuser.●n chatouillement m.

tidal adj (river) à marées; ~ **wave** raz-de-marée m inv.

tide n marée f; (of events) cours m.

tidy adj (-ier,-iest) (room) bien rangé; (appearance, work) soigné; (methodical) ordonné; (amount 🄸) joli.●vt/i (~ **up**) faire du rangement; ~ **sth** (**up**) ranger qch; ~ **oneself up** s'arranger.

tie vt (pres p **tying**) attacher; (knot) faire; (scarf) nouer; (link) lier.●vi (in football) faire match nul; (in race) être ex aequo.●n (necktie) cravate f; (fastener) attache f; (link) lien m; (draw) match m nul. ■ ~ **down** attacher; ~ **in with** être lié à; ~ **up** attacher; (money) immobiliser; (occupy) occuper.

tier n étage m, niveau m; (in stadium) gradin m.

tiger n tigre m.

tight adj (clothes, budget) serré; (grip) ferme; (rope) tendu; (security) strict; (angle) aigu. ●adv (hold, sleep) bien; (squeeze) fort.

tighten vt/i (se) tendre; (bolt) (se) resserrer; (control) renforcer.

tights npl collant m.

tile n (on wall, floor) carreau m; (on roof) tuile f.● vt carreler; couvrir de tuiles.

till n caisse f (enregistreuse).●vt (land) cultiver. ● prep & conj ▷UNTIL.

timber n bois m (de construction); (trees) arbres mpl.

time n temps m; (moment) moment m; (epoch) époque f; (by clock) heure f; (occasion) fois f; (rhythm) mesure f; ~**s** (multiplying) fois fpl; **any** ~ n'importe quand; **for the** ~ **being** pour le moment; **from** ~ **to** ~ de temps en temps; **have a good** ~ s'amuser; **in no** ~ en un rien de temps; **in** ~ à temps; (eventually) avec le temps; **a long** ~ longtemps; **on** ~ à l'heure; **what's the** ~? quelle heure est-il?; ~ **off** du temps libre. ●vt choisir le moment de; (measure) minuter; (Sport) chronométrer. ~ **limit** n délai m.

timer n minuterie f; (for cooker) minuteur m.

time: ~-**scale** n délais mpl. ~**table** n horaire m. ~ **zone** n fuseau m horaire.

timid adj timide; (fearful) peureux.

tin n étain m; (container) boîte f; ~**(plate)** fer-blanc m. ● vt (pt **tinned**) mettre en boîte. ~**foil** n papier m d'aluminium.

tingle vi picoter. ●n picotement m.

tin-opener n ouvre-boîtes m inv.

tint n teinte f; (for hair) shampooing m colorant. ●vt teinter.

tiny adj (-ier, -iest) tout petit.

tip n (of stick, pen, shoe, ski) pointe f; (of nose, finger, wing) bout m; (gratuity) pourboire m; (advice) tuyau m; (for rubbish) décharge f. ●vt/i (pt **tipped**) (tilt) pencher; (overturn) (faire) basculer; (pour) verser; (empty) déverser; (give money) donner un pourboire à. ∎ ~ **off** prévenir.

tiptoe n **on** ~ sur la pointe des pieds.

tire vt/i (se) fatiguer; ~ **of** se lasser de. •n (US) pneu m.

tired adj fatigué; **be** ~ **of** en avoir assez de.

tiring adj fatigant.

tissue n tissu m; (handkerchief) mouchoir m en papier; ~ **(paper)** papier m de soie.

tit n (bird) mésange f; **give** ~ **for tat** rendre coup pour coup.

title n titre m. ~ **deed** n titre m de propriété.

---

to /tuː, tə/
● preposition
····▸ à; ~ **Paris** à Paris; **give the book** ~ **Jane** donne le livre à Jane; ~ **the office** au bureau; ~ **the shops** aux magasins.
····▸ (with feminine countries) en; ~ **France** en France.
····▸ (to + personal pronoun) me/te/lui/nous/vous/leur; **she gave it** ~ **them** elle le leur a donné; **I'll say it** ~ **her** je vais le lui dire.

> ! à + le = au
> ∎ à + les = aux.

● in an infinitive *to is not translated* (**to go** aller; **to sing** chanter)
····▸ (in order to) pour; **he's gone into town** ~ **buy a shirt** il est parti en ville pour acheter une chemise.
····▸ (after adjectives) à; de; **be easy/difficult** ~ **read** être facile/difficile à lire; **it's easy/difficult to read her writing** c'est facile/difficile de lire son écriture.

▷ For verbal expressions using the infinitive 'to' such as **to tell sb to do sth, to help sb to do sth** ▷tell, help.

---

toad n crapaud m.

toast n pain m grillé, toast m; (drink) toast m. •vt (bread) faire griller; (drink to) porter un toast à. **toaster** n grille-pain m inv.

tobacco n tabac m.

tobacconist n marchand/-e m/f de tabac; ~**'s (shop)** tabac m.

toboggan n toboggan m, luge f.

today n & adv aujourd'hui (m).

toddler n bébé m (qui fait ses premiers pas).

toe n orteil m; (of shoe) bout m; **on one's** ~s vigilant. •vt ~ **the line** se conformer.

together adv ensemble; (at same time) à la fois; ~ **with** avec.

toilet n toilettes fpl.

toiletries npl articles mpl de toilette.

token n (symbol) témoignage m; (voucher) bon m; (coin) jeton m. •adj symbolique.

told ▷TELL.

tolerance n tolérance f.

tolerate vt tolérer.

toll n péage m; **death** ~ nombre m de morts; **take its** ~ faire des ravages. •vi (bell) sonner.

tomato n (pl ~es) tomate f.

tomb n tombeau m.

tomorrow n & adv demain (m); ~ **morning/night** demain matin/ soir; **the day after** ~ après-demain.

ton n tonne f (= 1016 kg); **(metric)** ~ tonne f (= 1000 kg); ~**s of** 🔢 des masses de.

tone n ton m; (of radio, telephone) tonalité f. •vt ~ **down** atténuer. •vi ~ **(in)** s'harmoniser (**with** avec).

tongs npl (for coal) pincettes fpl; (for sugar) pince f; (for hair) fer m.

tongue n langue f.

tonic n (Med) tonique m. •adj

(effect, accent) tonique; ~ **(water)** tonic m, Schweppes® m.

tonight n & adv (evening) ce soir; (night) cette nuit.

tonsil n amygdale f.

too adv trop; (also) aussi; ~ **many people** trop de gens; **I've got** ~**much/many** j'en ai trop; **me** ~ moi aussi.

took▷TAKE.

tool n outil m. ~**bar** n barre f d'outils. ~**box** n boîte f à outils.

toot n coup m de klaxon®. ●vt/i ~ **(the horn)** klaxonner.

tooth n (pl **teeth**) dent f. ~**ache** n mal m de dents. ~**brush** n brosse f à dents. ~**paste** n dentifrice m. ~**pick** n cure-dents m inv.

top n (highest point) sommet m; (upper part) haut m; (upper surface) dessus m; (lid) couvercle m; (of bottle, tube) bouchon m; (of beer bottle) capsule f; (of list) tête f; **on** ~ **of** sur; (fig) en plus de. ●adj (shelf) du haut; (step, floor) dernier; (in rank) premier; (best) meilleur; (distinguished) éminent; (maximum) maximum. ●vt (pt **topped**) (exceed) dépasser; (list) venir en tête de; ~ **up** remplir; ~**ped with** (dome) surmonté de; (cream) recouvert de.

topic n sujet m.

topless adj aux seins nus.

torch n (electric) lampe f de poche; (flaming) torche f.

tore ▷TEAR¹.

torment vt tourmenter.

torn ▷TEAR¹.

torrent n torrent m.

tortoise n tortue f. ~**shell** n écaille f.

torture n torture f; (fig) supplice m.●vt torturer.

Tory n & a tory (mf), conservateur/-trice (m/f).

toss vt lancer; (salad) tourner; (pancake) faire sauter. ●vi se

retourner; ~ **a coin**, ~ **up** tirer à pile ou face (**for** pour).

tot n petit/-e enfant m/f; (drink) petit verre m.

total n & a total (m). ●vt (pt **totalled**) (add up) additionner; (amount to) se monter à.

touch vt toucher; (tamper with) toucher à. ●vi se toucher. ●n (sense) toucher m; (contact) contact m; (of artist, writer) touche f; **a** ~**of** (small amount) un petit peu de; **get in** ~ **with** se mettre en contact avec; **out of** ~ **with** déconnecté de. ■ ~ **down** (Aviat) atterrir; ~ **up** retoucher. ~**down** n atterrissage m; (Sport) essai m. ~ **line** n ligne f de touche. ~**tone** adj (phone) à touches.

tough adj (negotiator) coriace; (law) sévère; (time) difficile; (robust) robuste.

tour n voyage m; (visit) visite f; (by team) tournée f; **on** ~ en tournée. ●vt visiter.

tourist n touriste mf. ●adj touristique. ~ **office** n syndicat m d'initiative.

tournament n tournoi m.

tout vi ~ **(for)** racoler 🎯.●vt (sell) revendre. ●n racoleur/-euse m/f; revendeur/-euse m/f.

tow vt remorquer. ●n remorque f; **on** ~ en remorque.

toward(s) prep vers; (of attitude) envers.

towel n serviette f.

tower n tour f. ●vi ~ **above** dominer.

town n ville f; **in** ~ en ville. ~ **council** n conseil m municipal. ~ **hall** n mairie f.

tow: ~ **path** n chemin m de halage. ~ **truck** n dépanneuse f.

toxic adj toxique.

toy n jouet m. ●vi ~ **with** (object) jouer avec; (idea) caresser.

trace n trace f. ●vt (person)

retrouver; (cause) déterminer; (life) retracer; (draw) tracer; (with tracing paper) décalquer.

track n (of person, car) traces fpl; (of missile) trajectoire f; (path) sentier m; (Sport) piste f; (Rail) voie f; (on disc) morceau m; **keep ~ of** suivre. ●vt suivre la trace or la trajectoire de. ■**~ down** retrouver. **~ suit** n survêtement m.

tractor n tracteur m.

trade n commerce m; (job) métier m; (swap) échange m. ●vi faire du commerce; **~ on** exploiter. ●vt échanger. ●adj (route, deficit) commercial. **~-in** n reprise f. **~ mark** n marque f (de fabrique); (registered) marque f déposée.

trader n commerçant/-e m/f; (on stockmarket) opérateur/-trice m/f.

trade union n syndicat m.

trading n commerce m; (on stockmarket) transactions fpl (boursières).

tradition n tradition f.

traffic n trafic m; (on road) circulation f. ●vi (pt **trafficked**) faire du trafic (**in** de). **~ jam** n embouteillage m. **~-lights** npl feux mpl (de circulation). **~ warden** n contractuel/-le m/f.

trail vt/i traîner; (plant) ramper; (track) suivre; **~ behind** traîner. ●n (of powder) traînée f; (track) piste f; (path) sentier m.

trailer n remorque f; (caravan) caravane f; (film) bande-annonce f.

train n (Rail) train m; (underground) rame f; (procession) file f; (of dress) traîne f. ●vt (instruct, develop) former; (sportsman) entraîner; (animal) dresser; (ear) exercer; (aim) braquer. ●vi être formé, étudier; (Sport) s'entraîner. **trained** adj (skilled) qualifié; (doctor) diplômé. **trainee** n stagiaire mf. **trainer** n (Sport) entraîneur/-euse m/f. **trainers** npl (shoes) chaussures fpl de sport.

training n formation f; (Sport) entraînement m.

tram n tram(way) m.

tramp vi marcher (d'un pas lourd). ●vt parcourir. ●n (vagrant) clochard/-e m/f; (sound) bruit m.

trample vt/i **(on)** piétiner; (fig) fouler aux pieds.

tranquil adj tranquille. **tranquillizer** n tranquillisant m.

transact vt négocier. **transaction** n transaction f.

transcript n transcription f.

transfer[1] /træns'fɜː(r)/ vt (pt **transferred**) transférer; (power) céder; (employee) muter. ●vi être transféré; (employee) être muté.

transfer[2] /'trænsfɜː(r)/ n transfert m; (of employee) mutation f; (image) décalcomanie f.

transform vt transformer.

transitive adj transitif.

translate vt traduire. **translation** n traduction f. **translator** n traducteur/-trice m/f.

transmit vt (pt **transmitted**) transmettre. **transmitter** n émetteur m.

transparency n transparence f; (Photo) diapositive f.

transplant n transplantation f; (Med) greffe f.

transport[1] /træns'pɔːt/ vt transporter.

transport[2] /'trænspɔːt/ n transport m.

trap n piège m. ●vt (pt **trapped**) (jam, pin down) coincer; (cut off) bloquer; (snare) prendre au piège.

trash n (refuse) ordures fpl; (nonsense) idioties fpl. **~-can** n (US) poubelle f.

trauma n traumatisme m. **traumatic** adj traumatisant.

travel vi (pt **travelled**, US **traveled**) voyager; (vehicle, bullet)

t

aller. ●vt parcourir. ●n voyages mpl. ~ **agency** n agence f de voyages.

traveller, (US) **traveler** n voyageur/-euse m/f; **~'s cheque** chèque m de voyage.

trawler n chalutier m.

tray n plateau m; (on office desk) corbeille f.

treacle n mélasse f.

tread vi (pt **trod**; pp **trodden**) marcher (**on** sur). ●vt fouler. ●n (sound) pas m; (of tyre) chape f.

treasure n trésor m. ●vt (gift, memory) chérir; (friendship, possession) tenir beaucoup à.

treasury n trésorerie f; **the T~** le ministère des Finances.

treat vt traiter; **~ sb to sth** offrir qch à qn. ●n (pleasure) plaisir m; (food) gâterie f. **treatment** n traitement n.

treaty n traité m.

treble adj triple; **~ clef** clé f de sol. ●vt/i tripler. ●n (voice) soprano m.

tree n arbre m.

trek n randonnée f. ●vi (pt **trekked**) **~ across/through** traverser péniblement; **go ~king** faire de la randonnée.

tremble vi trembler.

tremendous adj énorme; (excellent) formidable.

tremor n tremblement m; **(earth)** ~ secousse f.

trench n tranchée f.

trend n tendance f; (fashion) mode f. **trendy** adj 🄸 branché 🄸.

trespass vi s'introduire illégalement (**on** dans). **trespasser** n intrus/-e m/f.

trial n (Jur) procès m; (test) essai m; (ordeal) épreuve f. **go on ~** passer en jugement; **by ~ and error** par expérience.

triangle n triangle m.

tribe n tribu f.

tribunal n tribunal m.

tributary n affluent m.

tribute n tribut m; **pay ~ to** rendre hommage à.

trick n tour m; (dishonest) combine f; (knack) astuce f; **do the ~** 🄸 faire l'affaire. ●vt tromper. **trickery** n ruse f.

trickle vi dégouliner; **~ in/out** arriver or partir en petit nombre. ●n filet m; (fig) petit nombre m.

tricky adj (task) difficile; (question) épineux; (person) malin.

trifle n bagatelle f; (cake) diplomate m; **a ~** (small amount) un peu. ●vi **~ with** jouer avec.

trigger n (of gun) gâchette f; (of machine) manette f. ●vt **~ (off)** (initiate) déclencher.

trim adj (**trimmer, trimmest**) soigné; (figure) svelte. ●vt (pt **trimmed**) (hair, grass) couper; (budget) réduire; (decorate) décorer. ●n (cut) coupe f d'entretien; (decoration) garniture f; **in ~** en forme.

trinket n babiole f.

trip vt/i (pt **tripped**) (faire) trébucher. ●n (journey) voyage m; (outing) excursion f.

triple adj triple. ●vt/i tripler. **triplets** npl triplés/-es m/fpl.

tripod n trépied m.

trite adj banal.

triumph n triomphe m. ●vi triompher (**over** de).

trivial adj insignifiant.

trod, trodden ▷TREAD.

trolley n chariot m.

trombone n (Mus) trombone m.

troop n bande f; **~s** (Mil) troupes fpl. ●vi **~ in/out** entrer/sortir en bande.

trophy n trophée m.

tropic n tropique m; ~**s** tropiques mpl.

trot n trot m; **on the ~** 🇬🇧 coup sur coup. • vi (pt **trotted**) trotter.

trouble n problèmes mpl ; ennuis mpl; (pains, effort) peine f; **be in ~** avoir des ennuis; **go to a lot of ~** se donner du mal; **what's the ~?** quel est le problème? • vt (bother) déranger; (worry) tracasser. • vi ~ **(oneself) to do** se donner la peine de faire. ~**maker** n provocateur/-trice m/f. ~**shooter** n conciliateur/-trice m/f; (Tech) expert m.

troublesome adj ennuyeux.

trousers npl pantalon m; **short ~** short m.

trout n inv truite f.

trowel n (garden) déplantoir m; (for mortar) truelle f.

truant n (School) élève mf qui fait l'école buissonnière; **play ~** sécher les cours.

truce n trêve f.

truck n (lorry) camion m; (cart) chariot m; (Rail) wagon m de marchandises. ~**driver** n routier m.

true adj vrai; (accurate) exact; (faithful) fidèle.

truffle n truffe f.

truly adv vraiment; (faithfully) fidèlement; (truthfully) sincèrement.

trumpet n trompette f.

trunk n (of tree, body) tronc m; (of elephant) trompe f; (box) malle f; (Auto, US) coffre m; ~**s** (for swimming) slip m de bain.

trust n confiance f; (association) trust m; **in ~** en dépôt. • vt avoir confiance en; ~ **sb with** confier à qn. • vi ~ **in or to** s'en remettre à. **trustee** n

administrateur/-trice m/f.

trustworthy adj digne de confiance.

truth n (pl **-s**) vérité f. **truthful** adj (account) véridique; (person) qui dit la vérité.

try vt/i (pt **tried**) essayer; (be a strain on) éprouver; (Jur) juger; ~ **on or out** essayer; ~ **to do** essayer de faire. • n (attempt) essai m; (rugby) essai m.

T-shirt n tee-shirt m.

tub n (for flowers) bac m; (of ice cream) pot m; (bath) baignoire f.

tube n tube m; **the ~** 🇬🇧 le métro.

tuberculosis n tuberculose f.

tuck n pli m. • vt (put away, place) ranger; (hide) cacher. • vi ~ **in or into** 🇬🇧 attaquer; ~ **in** (shirt) rentrer; (blanket, person) border.

Tuesday n mardi m.

tug vt (pt **tugged**) tirer. • vi ~ **at/on** tirer sur. • n (boat) remorqueur m.

tuition n cours mpl; (fee) frais mpl pédagogiques.

tulip n tulipe f.

tumble vi (fall) dégringoler. • n chute f. ~-**drier** n sèche-linge m inv.

tumbler n verre m droit.

tummy n 🇬🇧 ventre m.

tumour n tumeur f.

tuna n inv thon m.

tune n air m; **be in ~/out of ~** (instrument) être/ne pas être en accord; (singer) chanter juste/ faux. • vt (engine) régler; (Mus) accorder. • vi ~ **in (to)** (radio), TV écouter. ∎ ~ **up** s'accorder.

Tunisia n Tunisie f.

tunnel n tunnel m; (in mine) galerie f. • vi (pt **tunnelled**) creuser un tunnel (**into** dans).

turf n (pl **turf** or **turves**) gazon m; **the ~** (racing) le turf. ●vt **~ out** ⊡ jeter dehors.

Turk n Turc m, Turque f. **Turkey** n Turquie f.

turkey n dinde f.

Turkish adj turc. ●n (Ling) turc m.

turn vt/i tourner; (person) se tourner; (to other side) retourner; (change) (se) transformer (**into** en); (become) devenir; (deflect) détourner; (milk) tourner. ●n tour m; (in road) tournant m; (of mind, events) tournure f; **do a good ~** rendre service; **in ~** à tour de rôle; **take ~s** se relayer. ■ **~ against** se retourner contre; **~ away** vi se détourner; vt (avert) détourner; (refuse) refuser; (send back) renvoyer; **~ back** vi (return) retourner; (vehicle) faire demi-tour; vt (fold) rabattre; **~ down** refuser; (fold) rabattre; (reduce) baisser; **~ off** (light) éteindre; (engine) arrêter; (tap) fermer; (of driver) tourner; **~ on** (light) allumer; (engine) allumer; (tap) ouvrir; **~ out** vt (light) éteindre; (empty) vider; (produce) produire; vi **it ~s out that** il se trouve que; **~ out well/badly** bien/mal se terminer; **~ over** (se) retourner; **~ round** (person) se retourner; **~ up** vi arriver; (be found) se retrouver; vt (find) déterrer; (collar) remonter.

turning n rue f; (bend) virage m.

turnip n navet m.

turn: **~out** n assistance f. **~over** n (pie) chausson m; (money) chiffre m d'affaires. **~table** n (for record) platine f.

turquoise adj turquoise inv.

turtle n tortue f (de mer). **~-neck** n col m montant.

tutor n (private) professeur m particulier; (Univ) (GB) chargé/-e m/f de travaux dirigés.

tutorial n (Univ) classe f de travaux dirigés.

tuxedo n (US) smoking m.

TV n télé f.

tweezers npl pince f (à épiler).

twelfth adj & n douzième (mf).

twelve adj & n douze (m); **~ (o'clock)** midi m or minuit m.

twentieth adj & n vingtième (mf).

twenty adj & n vingt (m).

twice adv deux fois.

twig n brindille f.

twilight n crépuscule m. ●adj crépusculaire.

twin n & a jumeau/-elle (m/f).●vt (pt **twinned**) jumeler.

twinge n (of pain) élancement m; (of conscience, doubt) accès m.

twinkle vi (star) scintiller; (eye) pétiller. ●n scintillement m; pétillement m.

twinning n jumelage m.

twist vt tordre; (weave together) entortiller; (roll) enrouler; (distort) déformer. ●vi (rope) s'entortiller; (road) zigzaguer. ●n torsion f; (in rope) tortillon m; (in road) tournant m; (in play, story) coup m de théâtre.

twitch vi (person) trembloter; (mouth) trembler; (string) vibrer.●n (tic) tic m; (jerk) secousse f.

two adj & n deux (m); **in ~s** par deux; **break in ~** casser en deux.

tycoon n magnat m.

type n type m, genre m; (print) caractères mpl. ●vt/i (write) taper (à la machine). **~face** n police f (de caractères). **~writer** n machine f à écrire.

typical adj typique.

typist n dactylo mf.

tyrant n tyran m.

tyre n pneu m.

Uu

udder n pis m, mamelle f.

UFO n OVNI m inv.

UHT abbr (**ultra heat treated**) ~ **milk** lait m longue conservation.

ugly adj (-ier, -iest) laid.

UK abbr ▶UNITED KINGDOM.

Ukraine n Ukraine f.

ulcer n ulcère m.

ulterior adj ultérieur; ~ **motive** arrière-pensée f.

ultimate adj dernier, ultime; (definitive) définitif; (basic) fondamental.

ultrasound n ultrason m.

umbilical cord n cordon m ombilical.

umbrella n parapluie m.

umpire n arbitre m. •vt arbitrer.

umpteenth adj 🗓 énième.

UN abbr (**United Nations**) ONU f.

unable adj incapable; (through circumstances) dans l'impossibilité (**to do** de faire).

unacceptable adj (suggestion) inacceptable; (behaviour) inadmissible.

unanimous adj unanime. **unanimously** adv à l'unanimité.

unattended adj sans surveillance.

unattractive adj (idea) peu attrayant; (person) peu attirant.

unauthorized adj non autorisé.

unavoidable adj inévitable.

unbearable adj insupportable.

unbelievable adj incroyable.

unbiased adj impartial.

unblock vt déboucher.

unborn adj (child) à naître; (generation) à venir.

uncalled-for adj injustifié, déplacé.

uncanny adj (-ier, -iest) étrange, troublant.

uncivilized adj barbare.

uncle n oncle m.

uncomfortable adj (chair) inconfortable; (feeling) pénible; **feel** or **be** ~ (person) être mal à l'aise.

uncommon adj rare.

unconscious adj sans connaissance, inanimé; (not aware) inconscient (**of** de). •n inconscient m.

unconventional adj peu conventionnel.

uncouth adj grossier.

uncover vt découvrir.

undecided adj indécis.

under prep sous; (less than) moins de; (according to) selon. •adv au-dessous; ~ **it/there** là-dessous. ~ **age** adj mineur. ~ **cover** adj secret. ~**cut** vt (pt -**cut**; pres p -**cutting**) (Comm) vendre moins cher que. ~**dog** n (Pol) opprimé/-e m/f; (socially) déshérité/-e m/f. ~**done** adj pas assez cuit. ~**estimate** vt sous-estimer. ~**fed** adj sous-alimenté. ~**go** vt (pt -**went**; pp -**gone**) subir. ~**graduate** n étudiant/-e m/f (qui prépare la licence).

underground adj souterrain; (secret) clandestin. •adv sous terre. •n (rail) métro m.

under: ~**line** vt souligner. ~**mine** vt saper.

underneath prep sous. ●adv (en) dessous.

under: ∼**pants** npl slip m. ∼**rate** vt sous-estimer.

understand vt/i (pt **-stood**) comprendre.

understanding adj compréhensif. ●n compréhension f; (agreement) entente f.

undertake vt (pt **-took**; pp **-taken**) entreprendre. ∼**taker** n entrepreneur m de pompes funèbres. ∼**taking** n (task) entreprise f; (promise) promesse f.

underwater adj sous-marin. ●adv sous l'eau.

under: ∼**wear** n sous-vêtements mpl. ∼**world** n (of crime) milieu m, pègre f.

undo vt (pt **-did**; pp **-done**) défaire, détacher; (wrong) réparer; (Comput) annuler.

undress vt/i (se) déshabiller; **get** ∼**ed** se déshabiller.

undue adj excessif.

unearth vt déterrer.

uneasy adj (ill at ease) mal à l'aise; (worried) inquiet; (situation) difficile.

uneducated adj (person) inculte; (speech) populaire.

unemployed adj en chômage. ●npl **the** ∼ les chômeurs mpl.

unemployment n chômage m; ∼ **benefit** allocations fpl de chômage.

uneven adj inégal.

unexpected adj inattendu, imprévu. **unexpectedly** adv (arrive) à l'improviste; (small, fast) étonnamment.

unfair adj injuste.

unfaithful adj infidèle.

unfit adj (Med) pas en forme; (ill) malade; (unsuitable) impropre (**for** à); ∼ **to** (unable) pas en état de.

unfold vt déplier; (expose)

exposer. ●vi se dérouler.

unforeseen adj imprévu.

unforgettable adj inoubliable.

unfortunate adj malheureux; (event) fâcheux.

ungrateful adj ingrat.

unhappy adj (**-ier, -iest**) (person) malheureux; (face) triste; (not pleased) mécontent (**with** de).

unharmed adj indemne, sain et sauf.

unhealthy adj (**-ier, -iest**) (climate) malsain; (person) en mauvaise santé.

unheard-of adj inouï.

unhurt adj indemne.

uniform n uniforme m. ●adj uniforme.

unify vt unifier.

unintentional adj involontaire.

uninterested adj indifférent (**in** à).

union n union f; (trade union) syndicat m; **U**∼ **Jack** drapeau m du Royaume-Uni.

unique adj unique.

unit n unité f; (of furniture) élément m; ∼ **trust** ≈ SICAV f.

unite vt/i (s')unir.

United Kingdom n Royaume-Uni m.

United Nations npl Nations fpl Unies.

United States (of America) npl États-Unis mpl (d'Amérique).

unity n unité f.

universal adj universel.

universe n univers m.

university n université f. ●adj universitaire; (student, teacher) d'université.

unkind adj pas gentil, méchant.

unknown adj inconnu. ●n **the** ∼ l'inconnu m.

unleaded adj sans plomb.

u

unless conj à moins que.

unlike adj différent. • prep contrairement à; (different from) différent de.

unlikely adj improbable.

unload vt décharger.

unlock vt ouvrir.

unlucky adj -ier, -iest malheureux; (number) qui porte malheur.

unmarried adj célibataire.

unnatural adj pas naturel, anormal.

unnecessary adj inutile.

unnoticed adj inaperçu.

unofficial adj officieux.

unpack vt (suitcase) défaire; (contents) déballer. • vi défaire sa valise.

unpleasant adj désagréable (**to** avec).

unplug vt débrancher.

unpopular adj impopulaire; ∼ **with** mal vu de.

unprofessional adj peu professionnel.

unqualified adj non diplômé; (success) total; **be** ∼ **to** ne pas être qualifié pour.

unravel vt (pt **unravelled**) démêler.

unreasonable adj irréaliste.

unrelated adj sans rapport (**to** avec).

unreliable adj peu sérieux; (machine) peu fiable.

unrest n troubles mpl.

unroll vt dérouler.

unruly adj indiscipliné.

unsafe adj (dangerous) dangereux; (person) en danger.

unscheduled adj pas prévu.

unscrupulous adj sans scrupules, malhonnête.

unsettled adj instable.

unsightly adj laid.

unskilled adj (worker) non qualifié.

unsound adj (roof) en mauvais état; (investment) douteux.

unsteady adj (step) chancelant; (ladder) instable; (hand) mal assuré.

unsuccessful adj (result, candidate) malheureux; (attempt) infructueux; **be** ∼ ne pas réussir (**in doing** à faire).

unsuitable adj inapproprié; **be** ∼ ne pas convenir.

unsure adj incertain.

untidy adj (-ier, -iest) (person) désordonné; (room) en désordre; (work) mal soigné.

untie vt (knot, parcel) défaire; (person) détacher.

until prep jusqu'à; **not** ∼ pas avant. • conj jusqu'à ce que; **not** ∼ pas avant que.

untrue adj faux.

unused adj (new) neuf; (not in use) inutilisé.

unusual adj exceptionnel; (strange) insolite, étrange.

unwanted adj (useless) superflu; (child) non désiré.

unwelcome adj fâcheux; (guest) importun.

unwell adj souffrant.

unwilling adj peu disposé (**to** à); (accomplice) malgré soi.

unwind vt/i (pt **unwound**) (se) dérouler; (relax ▣) se détendre.

unwise adj imprudent.

unwrap vt déballer.

up adv en haut, en l'air; (sun, curtain) levé; (out of bed) levé, debout; (finished) fini; **be** ∼ (level, price) avoir monté. • prep (a hill) en haut de; (a tree) dans; (a ladder) sur; **come** *or* **go** ∼ monter; ∼ **in the bedroom** là-haut dans la chambre; ∼ **there** là-haut; ∼ **to**

jusqu'à; (task) à la hauteur de; **it is ~ to you** ça dépend de vous (**to** de); **be ~ to sth** (able) être capable de qch; (plot) préparer qch; **be ~ to** (in book) en être à; **be ~ against** faire face à; **~ to date** moderne; (news) récent. ●n **~s and downs** les hauts et les bas mpl.

up-and-coming adj prometteur.

upbringing n éducation f.

update vt mettre à jour.

upgrade vt améliorer; (person) promouvoir.

upheaval n bouleversement m.

uphill adj qui monte; (fig) difficile. ●adv **go ~** monter.

upholstery n rembourrage m; (in vehicle) garniture f.

upkeep n entretien m.

up-market adj haut-de-gamme.

upon prep sur.

upper adj supérieur; **have the ~ hand** avoir le dessus. ●n (of shoe) empeigne f. **~ class** n aristocratie f. **~most** adj (highest) le plus haut.

upright adj droit. ●n (post) montant m.

uprising n soulèvement m.

uproar n tumulte m.

uproot vt déraciner.

upset[1] /ʌpˈset/ vt (pt upset; pres p upsetting) (overturn) renverser; (plan, stomach) déranger; (person) contrarier, affliger. ●adj peiné.

upset[2] /ˈʌpset/ n dérangement m; (distress) chagrin m.

upside-down adv (lit) à l'envers; (fig) sens dessus dessous.

upstairs adv en haut. ●adj (flat) du haut.

uptight adj 🇬🇧 tendu, coincé 🇬🇧.

up-to-date adj à la mode; (records) à jour.

upward adj & adv, **upwards** adv vers le haut.

urban adj urbain.

urge vt conseiller vivement (**to do** de faire); **~ on** encourager. ●n forte envie f.

urgency n urgence f; (of request, tone) insistance f. **urgent** adj urgent; (request) pressant.

urinal n urinoir m.

urine n urine f.

us pron nous; (**to**) **~** nous; **both of ~** tous/toutes les deux.

US abbr ▷UNITED STATES.

USA abbr ▷UNITED STATES OF AMERICA.

use[1] /juːz/ vt se servir de, utiliser. (consume) consommer; **~ up** épuiser.

use[2] /juːs/ n usage m, emploi m; **in ~** en usage; **it is no ~ doing** ça ne sert à rien de faire; **make ~ of** se servir de; **of ~** utile.

used[1] /juːzd/ adj (car) d'occasion.

used[2] /juːst/ v aux **he ~ to smoke** il fumait (autrefois). ●adj **~ to** habitué à.

useful adj utile.

useless adj inutile; (person) incompétent.

user n (of road, service) usager m; (of product) utilisateur/-trice m/f. **~-friendly** adj facile d'emploi; (Comput) convivial.

usual adj habituel, normal; **as ~** comme d'habitude. **usually** adv d'habitude.

utility n utilité f; (**public**) **~** service m public.

utmost adj (furthest, most intense) extrême; **the ~ care** le plus grand soin. ●n **do one's ~** faire tout son possible.

utter adj complet, absolu. ●vt prononcer.

U-turn n demi-tour m; (fig) volteface f inv.

u

Vv

vacancy n (post) poste m vacant; (room) chambre f disponible.

vacant adj (post) vacant; (seat) libre; (look) vague.

vacate vt quitter.

vacation n vacances fpl.

vaccinate vt vacciner.

vacuum n vide m. ~ **cleaner** n aspirateur m. ~**-packed** adj emballé sous vide.

vagina n vagin m.

vagrant n vagabond/-e m/f.

vague adj vague; (outline) flou; **be ~ about** ne pas préciser.

vain adj (conceited) vaniteux; (useless) vain; **in ~** en vain.

valentine n ~ **(card)** carte f de la Saint-Valentin.

valid adj (argument, ticket) valable; (passport) valide.

valley n vallée f.

valuable adj (object) de valeur; (help) précieux. **valuables** npl objets mpl de valeur.

valuation n (of painting) expertise f; (of house) évaluation f.

value n valeur f; ~ **added tax** taxe f à la valeur ajoutée, TVA f. ● vt (appraise) évaluer; (cherish) attacher de la valeur à.

valve n (Tech) soupape f; (of tyre) valve f; (Med) valvule f.

van n camionnette f.

vandal n vandale mf.

vanguard n **in the ~ of** à l'avantgarde f de.

vanilla n vanille f.

vanish vi disparaître.

vapour n vapeur f.

variable adj variable.

varicose adj ~ **veins** varices fpl.

varied adj varié.

variety n variété f; (entertainment) variétés fpl.

various adj divers.

varnish n vernis m. ● vt vernir.

vary vt/i varier.

vase n vase m.

vast adj (space) vaste; (in quantity) énorme.

vat n cuve f.

VAT abbr **(value added tax)** TVA f.

vault n (roof) voûte f; (in bank) chambre f forte; (tomb) caveau m; (jump) saut m. ● vt/i sauter.

VCR abbr ▷VIDEO CASSETTE RECORDER.

VDU abbr ▷VISUAL DISPLAY UNIT.

veal n veau m.

vegan adj & n végétalien/-ne (m/f).

vegetable n légume m. ● adj végétal.

vegetarian adj & n végétarien/-ne (m/f).

vehicle n véhicule m.

veil n voile m.

vein n (in body, rock) veine f; (on leaf) nervure f.

velvet n velours m.

vending-machine n distributeur m automatique.

veneer n (on wood) placage m; (fig) vernis m.

venereal adj vénérien.

venetian adj ~ **blind** jalousie f.

vengeance n vengeance f; **with a ∼** de plus belle.

venison n venaison f.

venom n venin m.

vent n bouche f, conduit m; (in coat) fente f. • vt (anger) décharger (**on** sur).

ventilate vt ventiler. **ventilator** n ventilateur m.

venture n entreprise f. • vt/i (se) risquer.

venue n lieu m.

verb n verbe m.

verbal adj verbal.

verdict n verdict m.

verge n bord m; **on the ∼ of doing** sur le point de faire. • vi **∼ on** friser, frôler.

verify vt vérifier.

vermin n vermine f.

versatile adj (person) aux talents variés; (mind) souple.

verse n strophe f; (of Bible) verset m; (poetry) vers mpl.

version n version f.

versus prep contre.

vertebra n (pl **-brae**) vertèbre f.

vertical adj vertical.

vertigo n vertige m.

very adv très. • adj (actual) même; **the ∼ day** le jour même; **at the ∼ end** tout à la fin; **the ∼ first** le tout premier; **∼ much** beaucoup.

vessel n vaisseau m.

vest n maillot m de corps; (waistcoat: US) gilet m.

vet n vétérinaire mf. • vt (pt **vetted**) (candidate) examiner (de près).

veteran n vétéran m; **war ∼** ancien combattant m.

veterinary adj vétérinaire; **∼ surgeon** vétérinaire mf.

veto n (pl **∼es**) veto m; (right)

droit m de veto. • vt mettre son veto à.

vibrate vt/i (faire) vibrer.

vicar n pasteur m.

vice n (depravity) vice m; (Tech) étau m.

vicinity n environs mpl; **in the ∼ of** à proximité de.

vicious adj (spiteful) méchant; (violent) brutal; **∼ circle** cercle m vicieux.

victim n victime f.

victor n vainqueur m. **victory** n victoire f.

video adj (game, camera) vidéo inv. • n (recorder) magnétoscope m; (film) vidéo f; **∼ (cassette)** cassette f vidéo. **∼ game** n jeu m vidéo. **∼phone** n vidéophone m. • vt enregistrer.

videotape n bande f vidéo. • vt (programme) enregistrer; (wedding) filmer avec une caméra vidéo.

view n vue f; **in my ∼** à mon avis; **in ∼ of** compte tenu de; **on ∼** exposé; **with a ∼ to** dans le but de. • vt (watch) regarder; (consider) considérer (**as** comme); (house) visiter. **viewer** n (TV) téléspectateur/-trice m/f.

view: ∼finder n viseur m. **∼point** n point m de vue.

vigilant adj vigilant.

vigour, (US) **vigor** n vigueur f.

vile adj (base) vil; (bad) abominable.

villa n pavillon m; (for holiday) villa f.

village n village m.

villain n scélérat m, bandit m; (in story) méchant m.

vindictive adj vindicatif.

vine n vigne f.

vinegar n vinaigre m.

vineyard n vignoble m.

vintage n (year) année f,

V

millésime m. ●adj (wine) de grand cru; (car) d'époque.

viola n (Mus) alto m.

violate vt violer.

violence n violence f. **violent** adj violent.

violet n (Bot) violette f; (colour) violet m.

violin n violon m.

VIP abbr (**very important person**) personnalité f, VIP m.

virgin n (woman) vierge f.

Virgo n Vierge f.

virtual adj quasi-total; (Comput) virtuel. **virtually** adv pratiquement.

virtue n vertu f; (advantage) mérite m; **by ~ of** en raison de.

virus n virus m.

visa n visa m.

visibility n visibilité f. **visible** adj visible.

vision n vision f.

visit vt (pt **visited**) (person) rendre visite à; (place) visiter. ●vi être en visite. ●n (tour, call) visite f; (stay) séjour m. **visitor** n visiteur/-euse m/f; (guest) invité-e m/f.

visual adj visuel. ~ **display unit** n visuel m, console f de visualisation.

visualize vt se représenter; (foresee) envisager.

vital adj vital.

vitamin n vitamine f.

vivacious adj plein de vivacité.

vivid adj (colour, imagination) vif; (description, dream) frappant.

vivisection n vivisection f.

vocabulary n vocabulaire m.

vocal adj vocal; (person) qui s'exprime franchement. ~ **cords** npl cordes fpl vocales.

vocation n vocation f. **vocational** adj professionnel.

voice n voix f. ●vt (express) formuler. ~ **mail** n messagerie f vocale.

void adj vide (**of** de); (not valid) nul. ●n vide m.

volatile adj (person) versatile; (situation) explosif.

volcano n (pl ~**es**) volcan m.

volley n (of blows, in tennis) volée f; (of gunfire) salve f.

volt n (Electr) volt m. **voltage** n tension f.

volume n volume m.

voluntary adj volontaire; (unpaid) bénévole.

volunteer n volontaire mf. ●vi s'offrir (**to do** pour faire); (Mil) s'engager comme volontaire. ●vt offrir.

vomit vt/i (pt **vomited**) vomir. ●n vomi m.

vote n vote m; (right) droit m de vote. ●vt/i voter; ~ **sb in** élire qn. **voter** n électeur/-trice m/f. **voting** n vote m (**of** de); (poll) scrutin m.

vouch vi ~ **for** se porter garant de.

voucher n bon m.

vowel n voyelle f.

voyage n voyage m (en mer).

vulgar adj vulgaire.

vulnerable adj vulnérable.

V

W w

wad n (pad) tampon m; (bundle) liasse f.

wade vi ~ **through** (mud) patauger dans. (book: fig) avancer péniblement dans.

wafer n (biscuit) gaufrette f.

waffle n (talk 🇬🇧) verbiage m; (cake) gaufre f. ● vi 🇬🇧 divaguer.

wag vt/i (pt **wagged**) (tail) remuer.

wage vt (campaign) mener; ~ **war** faire la guerre. ● n (weekly, daily) salaire m; ~**s** salaire m. ~**-earner** n salarié/-e m/f.

wagon n (horse-drawn) chariot m; (Rail) wagon m (de marchandises).

wail vi gémir. ● n gémissement m.

waist n taille f. ~**coat** n gilet m.

wait vt/i attendre; **I can't ~ to start** j'ai hâte de commencer; **let's ~ and see** attendons voir; ~ **for** attendre; ~ **on** servir. ● n attente f.

waiter n garçon m, serveur m.

waiting-list n liste f d'attente.

waiting-room n salle f d'attente.

waitress n serveuse f.

waive vt renoncer à.

wake vt/i (pt **woke**; pp **woken**) ~ **(up)** (se) réveiller. ● n (track) sillage m; **in the ~ of** (after) à la suite de. ~ **up call** n réveil m téléphoné.

Wales n pays m de Galles.

walk vi marcher; (not ride) aller à pied; (stroll) se promener. ● vt (streets) parcourir; (distance) faire à pied; (dog) promener. ● n promenade f, tour m; (gait) démarche f; (pace) marche f, pas m; (path) allée f. **have a ~** faire une promenade. ■ ~ **out** (go away) partir; (worker) faire grève; ~ **out on** abandonner.

walkie-talkie n talkie-talkie m.

walking n marche f (à pied). ● adj (corpse, dictionary: fig) ambulant.

walkman® n walkman® m, baladeur m.

walk: ~**-out** n grève f surprise. ~**-over** n victoire f facile.

wall n mur m; (of tunnel, stomach) paroi f. ● adj mural. **walled** adj (city) fortifié.

wallet n portefeuille m.

wallpaper n papier m peint. ● vt tapisser.

walnut n (nut) noix f; (tree) noyer m.

waltz n valse f. ● vi valser.

wander vi errer; (stroll) flâner; (digress) s'écarter du sujet; (in mind) divaguer.

wane vi décroître.

want vt vouloir (**to do** faire); (need) avoir besoin de (**doing** d'être fait); (ask for) demander; **I ~ you to do it** je veux que vous le fassiez. ● vi ~ **for** manquer de. ● n (need, poverty) besoin m; (desire) désir m; (lack) manque m; **for ~ of** faute de. **wanted** adj (criminal) recherché par la police.

war n guerre f; **at ~** en guerre; **on the ~path** sur le sentier de la guerre.

ward n (in hospital) salle f; (minor: Jur) pupille mf; (Pol) division f électorale. ● vt ~ **off** (danger) prévenir.

warden n directeur/-trice m/f; (of

park) gardien/-ne m/f; (**traffic**) ~ contractuel/-le m/f.

wardrobe n (furniture) armoire f; (clothes) garde-robe f.

warehouse n entrepôt m.

wares npl marchandises fpl.

warfare n guerre f.

warm adj chaud; (hearty) chaleureux; **be** or **feel** ~ avoir chaud; **it is** ~ il fait chaud. •vt/i ~ (**up**) (se) réchauffer; (food) chauffer; (liven up) (s')animer; (exercise) s'échauffer.

warmth n chaleur f.

warn vt avertir, prévenir; ~ **sb off sth** (advise against) mettre qn en garde contre qch; (forbid) interdire qch à qn.

warning n avertissement m; (notice) avis m; **without** ~ sans prévenir. ~ **light** n voyant m. ~ **triangle** n triangle m de sécurité.

warp vt/i (wood) (se) voiler; (pervert) pervertir; (judgment) fausser.

warrant n (for arrest) mandat m (d'arrêt); (Comm) autorisation f. •vt justifier.

warranty n garantie f.

wart n verrue f.

wartime n **in** ~ en temps de guerre.

wary adj (-ier, -iest) prudent.

was ▷ BE.

wash vt/i (se) laver; (flow over) baigner; ~ **one's hands of se** laver les mains de. •n lavage m; (clothes) lessive f; **have a** ~ se laver. ▪ ~ **up** faire la vaisselle; (US) se laver. ~ **basin** n lavabo m.

washer n rondelle f.

washing n lessive f. ~ **machine** n machine f à laver. ~ **powder** n lessive f.

washing-up n vaisselle f. ~ **liquid** n liquide m vaisselle.

wash: ~ **out** n 🄵 fiasco m.

~ **room** n (US) toilettes fpl.

wasp n guêpe f.

wastage n gaspillage m.

waste vt gaspiller; (time) perdre. •vi ~ **away** dépérir. •adj superflu; ~ **products** or **matter** déchets mpl. •n gaspillage m; (of time) perte f; (rubbish) déchets mpl; **lay** ~ dévaster. **wasteful** adj peu économique; (person) gaspilleur.

waste: ~ **land** n (desolate) terre f désolée; (unused) terre f inculte; (in town) terrain m vague. ~ **paper** n vieux papiers mpl. ~ **paper basket** n corbeille f (à papier).

watch vt/i (television) regarder; (observe) observer; (guard, spy on) surveiller; (be careful about) faire attention à. •n (for telling time) montre f; (Naut) quart m; **be on the** ~ guetter; **keep** ~ **on** surveiller. ▪ ~ **out** (take care) faire attention (**for** à); ~ **out for** (keep watch) guetter.

water n eau f; **by** ~ en bateau. •vt arroser. •vi (eyes) larmoyer; **my/his mouth** ~s l'eau me/lui vient à la bouche. ▪ ~ **down** couper (d'eau); (tone down) édulcorer. ~ **colour** n (painting) aquarelle f. ~ **cress** n cresson m (de fontaine). ~ **fall** n chute f d'eau, cascade f. ~ **heater** n chauffe-eau m. **watering-can** n arrosoir m. ~ **lily** n nénuphar m. ~ **melon** n pastèque f. ~ **proof** adj (material) imperméable. ~ **shed** n (in affairs) tournant m décisif. ~ **skiing** n ski m nautique. ~ **tight** adj étanche. ~ **way** n voie f navigable.

watery adj (colour) délavé; (eyes) humide; (soup) trop liquide.

wave n vague f; (in hair) ondulation f; (radio) onde f; (sign) signe m. •vt agiter. •vi faire signe (de la main); (move in wind) flotter.

waver vi vaciller.

W

wavy adj (line) onduleux; (hair) ondulé.

wax n cire f; (for skis) fart m. • vt cirer; farter; (car) lustrer.

way n (road, path) chemin m (**to** de); (distance) distance f; (direction) direction f; (manner) façon f; (means) moyen m; **∼s** (habits) habitudes fpl; **be in the ∼** bloquer le passage; (hindrance: fig) gêner (qn); **be on one's** or **the ∼** être sur son or le chemin; **by the ∼** à propos; **by the ∼side** au bord de la route; **by ∼ of** comme; (via) par; **go out of one's ∼** se donner du mal; **in a ∼** dans un sens; **make one's ∼ somewhere** se rendre quelque part; **push one's ∼ through** se frayer un passage; **that ∼** par là; **this ∼** par ici; **∼ in** entrée f; **∼ out** sortie f. • adv 𝕀 loin.

we pron nous.

weak adj faible; (delicate) fragile.

weakness n faiblesse f; (fault) point m faible; **a ∼ for** (liking) un faible pour.

wealth n richesse f; (riches, resources) richesses fpl; (quantity) profusion f.

wealthy adj (-ier, -iest) riche. • n **the ∼** les riches mpl.

weapon n arme f; **∼s of mass destruction** armes fpl de destruction massive.

wear vt (pt **wore**; pp **worn**) porter; (put on) mettre; (expression) avoir. • vi (last) durer; **∼ (out)** (s')user. • n (use) usage m; (damage) usure f. ∎ **∼ down** user; **∼ off** (colour, pain) passer; **∼ out** (exhaust) épuiser.

weary adj (-ier, -iest) fatigué, las. • vi **∼ of** se lasser de.

weather n temps m; **under the ∼** patraque. • adj météorologique. • vt (survive) réchapper de or à. **∼ forecast** n météo f.

weave vt/i (pt **wove**; pp **woven**) tisser; (basket) tresser; (move) se faufiler. • n (style) tissage m.

web n (of spider) toile f; (on foot) palmure f.

Web n (Comput) Web m. **∼cam** n webcam f. **∼master** n administrateur m de site Internet. **∼ page** n page f Web. **∼ search** n recherche f sur le Web. **∼site** n site m Internet.

wedding n mariage m. **∼-ring** n alliance f.

wedge n (of wood) coin m; (under wheel) cale f. • vt caler; (push) enfoncer; (crowd) coincer.

Wednesday n mercredi m.

weed n mauvaise herbe f. • vt/i désherber; **∼ out** extirper.

week n semaine f; **a ∼ today/ tomorrow** aujourd'hui/demain en huit. **∼day** n jour m de semaine. **∼end** n week-end m, fin f de semaine.

weekly adv toutes les semaines. • adj & n (periodical) hebdomadaire (m).

weep vt/i (pt **wept**) pleurer (**for sb** qn).

weigh vt/i peser; **∼ anchor** lever l'ancre. ∎ **∼ down** lester (avec un poids); (bend) faire plier; (fig) accabler; **∼ up** calculer.

weight n poids m; **lose/put on ∼** perdre/prendre du poids. **∼-lifting** n haltérophilie f. **∼ training** n musculation f en salle.

weird adj bizarre.

welcome adj agréable; (timely) opportun; **be ∼** être le or la bienvenu(e), être les bienvenu(e)s; **you're ∼!** il n'y a pas de quoi; **∼ to do** libre de faire. • interj soyez le or la bienvenu(e), soyez les bienvenu(e)s. • n accueil m. • vt accueillir; (as greeting) souhaiter

W

la bienvenue à; (fig) se
réjouir de.

weld vt souder. •n soudure f.

welfare n bien-être m; (aid) aide f
sociale. W~ State n état-
providence m.

well¹ /wel/ n puits m.

well² /wel/ adv (**better, best**)
bien; **do** ~ (succeed) réussir;
done! bravo! •adj bien inv; **as** ~
aussi; **be** ~ (healthy) aller bien.
•interj eh bien; (surprise) tiens.

well: ~-**behaved** adj sage.
~-**being** n bien-être m inv.

wellington n (boot) botte f de
caoutchouc.

well: ~-**known** adj (bien) connu.
~-**meaning** adj bien
intentionné. ~ **off** adj aisé,
riche. ~-**read** adj instruit. ~-**to-
do** adj riche. ~-**wisher** n
admirateur/-trice m/f.

Welsh adj gallois. •n (Ling)
gallois m.

went ▷GO.

wept ▷WEEP.

were ▷BE.

west n ouest m; **the W**~ (Pol)
l'Occident m. •adj d'ouest. •adv
vers l'ouest.

western adj de l'ouest; (Pol)
occidental. •n (film) western m.
westerner n occidental/-e m/f.

West Indies n Antilles fpl.

westward adj (side) ouest inv;
(journey) vers l'ouest.

wet adj (**wetter, wettest**)
mouillé; (damp, rainy) humide;
(paint) frais; **get** ~ se mouiller.
•vt (pt **wetted**) mouiller. •n **the
~** l'humidité f; (rain) la pluie f.
~**suit** n combinaison f de
plongée.

whale n baleine f.

wharf n quai m.

what /wɒt/
• pronoun
····▷ (in questions as object
pronoun) qu'est-ce que?; ~ **are
we going to do?** qu'est-ce que
nous allons faire?
····▷ (in questions as subject
pronoun) qu'est-ce qui?; ~
happened? qu'est-ce qui s'est
passé?
····▷ (introducing clause as object)
ce que; **I don't know** ~ **he
wants** je ne sais pas ce
qu'il veut.
····▷ (introducing clause as subject)
ce qui; **tell me** ~ **happened**
raconte moi ce qui s'est passé.
····▷ (with prepositions) quoi; ~
are you thinking about? à
quoi penses-tu?
• determiner
····▷ quel/quelle/quels/quelles; ~
train did you catch? quel train
as-tu pris?; ~ **time is it?** quelle
heure est-il?

whatever adj ~ **book** quel que
soit le livre. •pron (no matter what)
quoi que, quoi qu'; (anything that)
tout ce qui; (object) tout ce que
or qu'; ~ **happens** quoi qu'il
arrive; ~ **happened?** qu'est-ce
qui est arrivé?; ~ **the problems**
quels que soient les problèmes;
~ **you want** tout ce que vous
voulez; **nothing** ~ rien du tout.

whatsoever adj & pron
▷WHATEVER.

wheat n blé m, froment m.

wheel n roue f; **at the** ~ (of
vehicle) au volant; (helm) au
gouvernail. •vt pousser. •vi
tourner; ~ **and deal** faire des
combines. ~**barrow** n brouette f.
~**chair** n fauteuil m roulant.

when adv & pron quand. •conj
quand, lorsque; **the day/
moment** ~ le jour/moment où.

whenever conj & adv (at whatever
time) quand; (every time that) chaque
fois que.

where adv, conj & pron où; (whereas) alors que; (the place that) là où.

whereabouts adv (à peu près) où. • n sb's ~ l'endroit où se trouve qn.

whereas conj alors que.

wherever conj & adv où que; (everywhere) partout où; (anywhere) (là) où; (emphatic where) où donc.

whether conj si; **not know ~** ne pas savoir si; ~ **I go or not** que j'aille ou non.

---

which /wɪtʃ/
• pronoun
····▸ (in questions) lequel/laquelle/ lesquels/lesquelles; **there are three peaches, ~ do you want?** il y a trois pêches, laquelle veux-tu?
····▸ (in questions with superlative adjective) quel/quelle/quels/ quelles; ~ **(apple) is the biggest?** quelle est la plus grosse?
····▸ (in relative clauses as subject) qui; **the book ~ is on the table** le livre qui est sur la table.
····▸ (in relative clauses as object) que; **the book ~ Tina is reading** le livre que lit Tina.
• determiner
····▸ quel/quelle/quels/quelles; ~ **car did you choose?** quelle voiture as-tu choisie?

---

whichever adj ~ **book** quel que soit le livre que or qui; **take ~ book you wish** prenez le livre que vous voulez. • pron celui/ celle/ceux/celles qui or que.

while n moment m. • conj (when) pendant que; (although) bien que; (as long as) tant que. • vt ~ **away** (time) passer.

whilst conj ▷WHILE.

whim n caprice m.

whine vi gémir, se plaindre. • n gémissement m.

whip n fouet m. • vt (pt **whipped**) fouetter; (Culin) fouetter, battre; (seize) enlever brusquement. • vi (move) aller en vitesse. ■ ~ **up** exciter; (cause) provoquer; (meal 🄸) préparer.

whirl vt/i (faire) tourbillonner. • n tourbillon m. ~**pool** n tourbillon m. ~**wind** n tourbillon m (de vent).

whisk vt (snatch) enlever or emmener brusquement; (Culin) fouetter. • n (Culin) fouet m.

whiskers npl (of animal) moustaches fpl; (of man) favoris mpl.

whisper vt/i chuchoter. • n chuchotement m; (rumour: fig) rumeur f, bruit m.

whistle n sifflement m; (instrument) sifflet m. • vt/i siffler; ~ **at** or **for** siffler.

white adj blanc. • n blanc m; (person) blanc/-che m/f. ~ **coffee** n café m au lait. ~**collar worker** n employé/-e m/f de bureau. ~ **elephant** n projet m coûteux et peu rentable. ~ **lie** n pieux mensonge m. **W~ Paper** n livre m blanc.

whitewash n blanc m de chaux. • vt blanchir à la chaux; (person: fig) blanchir.

Whitsun n la Pentecôte.

whiz vi (pt **whizzed**) (through air) fendre l'air; (hiss) siffler; (rush) aller à toute vitesse. ~**-kid** n jeune prodige m.

who pron qui.

whoever pron (no matter who) qui que ce soit qui or que; (the one who) quiconque; **tell ~ you want** dites-le à qui vous voulez.

whole adj entier; (intact) intact; **the ~ house** toute la maison. • n totalité f; (unit) tout m; **on the ~** dans l'ensemble. ~**foods** npl aliments mpl naturels et diététiques. ~**-hearted** adj sans réserve. ~**meal** adj complet.

wholesale adj (firm) de gros; (fig)

W

systématique. • adv (in large quantities) en gros; (fig) en masse.

wholesome adj sain.

wholly adv entièrement.

whom pron (that) que, qu'; (after prepositions & in questions) qui; **of ~** dont; **with ~** avec qui.

whooping cough n coqueluche f.

whose pron & a à qui, de qui; **~ hat is this?, ~ is this hat?** à qui est ce chapeau?; **~ son are you?** de qui êtes-vous le fils?; **the man ~ hat I see** l'homme dont je vois le chapeau.

why adv pourquoi; **the reason ~** la raison pour laquelle.

wicked adj méchant, mauvais, vilain.

wide adj large; (ocean) vaste. • adv (fall) loin du but; **open ~** ouvrir tout grand; **~ open** grand ouvert; **~ awake** éveillé. **widely** adv (spread, spaced) largement; (travel) beaucoup; (generally) généralement; (extremely) extrêmement.

widespread adj très répandu.

widow n veuve f. **widowed** adj (man) veuf; (woman) veuve. **widower** n veuf m.

width n largeur f.

wield vt (axe) manier; (power: fig) exercer.

wife n (pl **wives**) femme f, épouse f.

wig n perruque f.

wiggle vt/i remuer; (hips) tortiller; (worm) se tortiller.

wild adj sauvage; (sea, enthusiasm) déchaîné; (mad) fou; (angry) furieux. • adv (grow) à l'état sauvage.

wildlife n faune f.

---

will¹ /wɪl/

! present **will**; present negative **won't, will not**; past **would**

• auxiliary verb
····▸ (in future tense) **he'll come** il viendra; **it ~ be sunny tomorrow** il va faire du soleil demain.
····▸ (inviting and requesting) **~ you have some coffee?** est-ce que vous voulez du café?
····▸ (making assumptions) **they won't know what's happened** ils ne doivent pas savoir ce qui s'est passé.
····▸ (in short questions and answers) **you'll come again, won't you?** tu reviendras, n'est-ce pas?; **'they won't forget'—'yes they ~'** 'ils n'oublieront pas'—'si'.
····▸ (capacity) **the lift ~ hold 12** l'ascenseur peut transporter 12 personnes.
····▸ (ability) **the car won't start** la voiture ne veut pas démarrer.

• transitive verb **~ sb's death** souhaiter ardemment la mort de qn.

---

will² /wɪl/ n volonté f; (document) testament m; **at ~** quand or comme on veut.

willing adj (help, offer) spontané; (helper) bien disposé; **~ to** disposé à. **willingly** adv (with pleasure) volontiers; (not forced) volontairement. **willingness** n empressement m (**to do** à faire).

willow n saule m.

will-power n volonté f.

win vt/i (pt **won**; pres p **winning**) gagner; (victory, prize) remporter; (fame, fortune) acquérir, trouver; **~ round** convaincre. • n victoire f.

winch n treuil m. • vt hisser au treuil.

wind¹ /wɪnd/ n vent m; (breath) souffle m; **get ~ of** avoir vent de; **in the ~** dans l'air. • vt essouffler. ~ **farm** n ferme f d'éoliennes.

wind² /waɪnd/ vt/i (pt **wound**) (s')enrouler; (of path, river) serpenter; ~ **(up)** (clock) remonter; ~ **up** (end) (se) terminer; ~ **up in hospital** finir à l'hôpital.

windmill n moulin m à vent.

window n fenêtre f; (glass pane) vitre f; (in vehicle, train) vitre f; (in shop) vitrine f; (counter) guichet m; (Comput) fenêtre f. ~-**box** n jardinière f. ~-**cleaner** n laveur m de carreaux. ~-**dresser** n étalagiste mf. ~-**ledge** n rebord de (la) fenêtre. ~-**shopping** n lèche-vitrines m. ~-**sill** n (inside) appui m de (la) fenêtre; (outside) rebord m de (la) fenêtre.

windscreen n pare-brise m inv. ~ **wiper** n essuie-glace m.

windshield n (US) ▷**WINDSCREEN.**

windsurfing n planche f à voile.

windy adj (**-ier, -iest**) venteux; **it is** ~ il y a du vent.

wine n vin m. ~-**cellar** n cave f (à vin). ~-**glass** n verre m à vin. ~-**grower** n viticulteur m. ~ **list** n carte f des vins. ~-**tasting** n dégustation f de vins.

wing n aile f; ~**s** (Theat) coulisses fpl; **under one's** ~ sous son aile. ~ **mirror** n rétroviseur m extérieur.

wink vi faire un clin d'œil; (light, star) clignoter. ●n clin m d'œil; clignotement n.

winner n (of game) gagnant/-e m/f; (of fight) vainqueur m.

winning ▷**WIN.** ●adj (number, horse) gagnant; (team) victorieux; (smile) engageant. **winnings** npl gains mpl.

winter n hiver m.

wipe vt essuyer. ●vi ~ **up** essuyer la vaisselle. ●n coup m de torchon or d'éponge. ■ ~ **out** (destroy) anéantir; (remove) effacer.

wire n fil m; (US) télégramme m.

wiring n (Electr) installation f électrique.

wisdom n sagesse f.

wise adj prudent, sage; (look) averti.

wish n (specific) souhait m, vœu m; (general) désir m; **best** ~**es** (in letter) amitiés fpl; (on greeting card) meilleurs vœux mpl. ●vt souhaiter, vouloir, désirer (**to do** faire); (bid) souhaiter. ●vi ~ **for** souhaiter; **I** ~ **he'd leave** je voudrais bien qu'il parte.

wishful adj **it's** ~ **thinking** c'est prendre ses désirs pour des réalités.

wistful adj mélancolique.

wit n intelligence f; (humour) esprit m; (person) homme m d'esprit, femme f d'esprit.

witch n sorcière f.

with prep avec; (having) à; (because of) de; (at house of) chez; **the man** ~ **the beard** l'homme à la barbe; **fill** ~ remplir de; **pleased/shaking** ~ content/ frémissant de.

withdraw vt/i (pt **withdrew**; pp **withdrawn**) (se) retirer. **withdrawal** n retrait m.

wither vt/i (se) flétrir.

withhold vt (pt **withheld**) refuser (de donner); (retain) retenir; (conceal) cacher (**from** à).

within prep & adv à l'intérieur (de); (in distances) à moins de; ~ **a month** (before) avant un mois; ~ **sight** en vue.

without prep sans; ~ **my knowing** sans que je sache.

withstand vt (pt **withstood**) résister à.

witness n témoin m; (evidence) témoignage m; **bear** ~ **to** témoigner de. ●vt être le témoin

W

de, voir. ~ **box**, ~ **stand** n barre f des témoins.

witty adj (-ier, -iest) spirituel.

wives ▷WIFE.

wizard n magicien m; (genius: fig) génie m.

WMD abbr (**weapon of mass destruction**) ADM f.

woke, woken ▷WAKE.

wolf n (pl **wolves**) loup m. ●vt (food) engloutir.

woman n (pl **women**) femme f; ~ **doctor** femme f médecin; ~ **driver** femme f au volant.

women ▷WOMAN.

won ▷WIN.

wonder n émerveillement m; (thing) merveille f; **it is no** ~ ce or il n'est pas étonnant (**that** que). ●vt se demander (**if** si). ●vi s'étonner (**at** de); (reflect) songer (**about** à).

wonderful adj merveilleux.

won't ▷WILL NOT.

wood n bois m.

wooden adj en or de bois. (stiff: fig) raide, comme du bois.

wood: ~**wind** n (Mus) bois mpl. ~**work** n (craft, objects) menuiserie f.

wool n laine f. **woollen** adj de laine. **woollens** npl lainages mpl.

woolly adj laineux; (vague) nébuleux. ●n (garment 🅣) lainage m.

word n mot m; (spoken) parole f, mot m; (promise) parole f; (news) nouvelles fpl; **by** ~ **of mouth** de vive voix; **give/keep one's** ~ donner/tenir sa parole; **have a** ~ **with** parler à; **in other** ~**s** autrement dit. ●vt rédiger. **wording** n termes mpl.

word processing n traitement

m de texte. **word processor** n machine f à traitement de texte.

wore ▷WEAR.

work n travail m; (product, book) œuvre f, ouvrage m; (building work) travaux mpl; ~**s** (Tech) mécanisme m; (factory) usine f. ●vi (person) travailler; (drug) agir; (Tech) fonctionner, marcher. ●vt (Tech) faire fonctionner, faire marcher; (land, mine) exploiter; (shape, hammer) travailler; ~ **sb** (make work) faire travailler qn. ■ ~ **out** vt (solve) résoudre; (calculate) calculer; (elaborate) élaborer; vi (succeed) marcher; (Sport) s'entraîner; ~ **up** vt développer; vi (to climax) monter vers; ~**ed up** (person) énervé.

workaholic n 🅣 bourreau m de travail.

worker n travailleur/-euse m/f; (manual) ouvrier/-ière m/f.

work-force n main-d'œuvre f.

working adj (day, lunch) de travail; ~**s** mécanisme m; **in** ~ **order** en état de marche.

working class n classe f ouvrière. ●adj ouvrier.

workman n (pl -**men**) ouvrier m.

work: ~**out** n séance f de mise en forme. ~**shop** n atelier m. ~-**station** n poste m de travail.

world n monde m; **best in the** ~ meilleur au monde. ●adj (power) mondial; (record) du monde.

world-wide adj universel.

World Wide Web, WWW n World Wide Web m, réseau m des réseaux.

worm n ver m. ●vt ~ **one's way into** s'insinuer dans.

worn ▷WEAR. ●adj usé. ~-**out** adj (thing) complètement usé; (person) épuisé.

worried adj inquiet.

worry vt/i (s')inquiéter. •n souci m.

worse adj pire, plus mauvais; **be ~ off** perdre. •adv plus mal. •n pire m. **worsen** vt/i empirer.

worship n (adoration) culte m. •vt (pt **worshipped**) adorer. •vi faire ses dévotions.

worst adj pire, plus mauvais. •adv **(the) ~** (sing) le plus mal. •n **the ~ (one)** (person, object) le or la pire; **the ~ (thing)** le pire.

worth adj **be ~** valoir; **it is ~ waiting** ça vaut la peine d'attendre; **it is ~ (one's) while** ça (en) vaut la peine. •n valeur f; **ten pence ~ of** (pour) dix pence de. **worthless** adj qui ne vaut rien. **worthwhile** adj qui (en) vaut la peine.

worthy adj (-ier, -iest) digne (**of** de); (laudable) louable.

would v aux **he ~ do/you ~ sing** (conditional tense) il ferait/tu chanterais; **he ~ have done** il aurait fait; **I ~ come every day** (used to) je venais chaque jour; **I ~ like some tea** je voudrais du thé; **~ you come here?** voulez-vous venir ici?; **he wouldn't come** il a refusé de venir. **~-be** adj soidisant.

wound[1] /wuːnd/ n blessure f. •vt blesser; **the ~ed** les blessés mpl.

wound[2] /waʊnd/ ▷WIND[2].

wove, woven ▷WEAVE.

wrap vt (pt **wrapped**) **~ (up)** envelopper. •vi **~ up** (dress warmly) se couvrir; **~ped up in** (engrossed) absorbé dans.

wrapping n emballage m.

wreak vt **~ havoc** faire des ravages.

wreath n (of flowers, leaves) couronne f.

wreck n (sinking) naufrage m; (ship, remains, person) épave f; (vehicle) voiture f accidentée or délabrée. •vt détruire; (ship) provoquer le naufrage de. **wreckage** n (pieces) débris mpl; (wrecked building) décombres mpl.

wrestle vi lutter, se débattre (**with** contre).

wrestling n lutte f; **(all-in) ~** catch m.

wriggle vt/i (se) tortiller.

wring vt (pt **wrung**) (twist) tordre; (clothes) essorer; **~ out of** (obtain from) arracher à.

wrinkle n (crease) pli m; (on skin) ride f. •vt/i (se) rider.

wrist n poignet m.

write vt/i (pt **wrote**; pp **written**) écrire. ■ **~ back** répondre; **~ down** noter; **~ off** (debt) passer aux profits et pertes; (vehicle) considérer bon pour la casse; **~ up** (from notes) rédiger.

write-off n perte f totale.

writer n auteur m, écrivain m; **~ of** auteur de.

write-up n compte-rendu m.

writing n écriture f; **~(s)** (works) écrits mpl; **in ~** par écrit. **~-paper** n papier m à lettres.

written ▷WRITE.

wrong adj (incorrect, mistaken) faux, mauvais. (unfair) injuste; (amiss) qui ne va pas; (clock) pas à l'heure; **be ~** (person) avoir tort (**to** de); (be mistaken) se tromper; **go ~** (err) se tromper; (turn out badly) mal tourner; **it is ~ to** (morally) c'est mal de; **what's ~?** qu'est-ce qui ne va pas?; **what is ~ with you?** qu'est-ce que vous avez? •adv mal. •n injustice f; (evil) mal m; **be in the ~** avoir tort. •vt faire (du) tort à. **wrongful** adj injustifié, injuste. **wrongfully** adv à tort. **wrongly** adv mal; (blame) à tort.

wrote ▷WRITE.

wrought iron n fer m forgé.

wrung ▷WRING.

Xx

Xmas n Noël m.
X-ray n rayon m X; (photograph)
radio (graphie) f. • vt
radiographier.

Yy

yank vt tirer brusquement. • n
coup m brusque.
yard n (measure) yard m (= 0.9144
metre). (of house) cour f; (garden: US)
jardin m; (for storage) chantier m,
dépôt m. ~**stick** n mesure f.
yawn vi bâiller. • n bâillement m.
yeah adv ⊡ ouais.
year n an m, année f; **school/tax**
~ année scolaire/fiscale; **be ten**
~**s old** avoir dix ans.
yearly adj annuel. • adv
annuellement.
yearn vi avoir bien or très envie
(**for, to** de).
yeast n levure f.
yell vt/i hurler. • n hurlement m.
yellow adj jaune; (cowardly ⊡)
froussard. • n jaune m.
yes adv oui; (as answer to negative
question) si. • n oui m inv.
yesterday n & adv hier (m).
yet adv encore; (already) déjà. • conj
pourtant, néanmoins.
yew n if m.
yield vt (produce) produire, rendre;
(profit) rapporter; (surrender) céder.
• n rendement m.
yoga n yoga m.
yoghurt n yaourt m.

yolk n jaune m (d'œuf).
you pron (familiar form) tu, pl vous;
(polite form) vous; (object) te, t', pl
vous; (polite) vous; (after prep.) toi,
pl vous; (polite) vous; (indefinite) on;
(object) vous; **(to)** ~ te, t', pl vous;
(polite) vous; **I gave** ~ **a pen** je
vous ai donné un stylo; **I know**
~ je te connais or je vous
connais.
young adj jeune. • n (people)
jeunes mpl; (of animals) petits mpl.
your adj (familiar form) ton, ta, pl tes;
(polite form, & familiar form pl.) votre,
pl vos.
yours pron (familiar form) le tien, la
tienne, les tien(ne)s; (polite form, &
familiar form pl.) le or la vôtre, les
vôtres; ~ **faithfully/sincerely**
je vous prie d'agréer mes
salutations les meilleures.
yourself pron (familiar form)
toi-même; (polite form) vous-même;
(reflexive & after prepositions) te, t';
vous; **proud of** ~ fier de toi.
yourselves pron vous-mêmes;
(reflexive) vous.
youth n jeunesse f; (young man)
jeune m. ~ **hostel** n auberge f de
jeunesse.
Yugoslav adj yougoslave. • n
Yougoslave mf.
Yugoslavia n Yougoslavie f.

Zz

zap vt 🔢 (kill) descendre; (Comput) enlever.

zeal n zèle m.

zebra n zèbre m. ∼ **crossing** n passage m pour piétons.

zero n zéro m.

zest n (gusto) entrain m; (spice: fig) piment m; (of orange or lemon peel) zeste m.

zip n (vigour) allant m; ∼**(-fastener)** fermeture f

éclair(r). ●vt (pt **zipped**) fermer avec une fermeture éclair(r); (Comput) compresser. **Zip code** (US) n code m postal.

zodiac n zodiaque m.

zone n zone f.

zoo n zoo m.

zoom vi (rush) se précipiter. ■ ∼ **off** or **past** filer (comme une flèche). ∼ **lens** n zoom m.

zucchini n inv (US) courgette f.

z

Summary of French grammar

Grammar provides a useful description of the patterns which make up a language. The following pages offer a summary for reference.

1 NOUNS and GENDER

- All nouns are either *masculine* or *feminine* in French
- The gender is an important feature of each noun
- The gender is shown by the article (*definite* or *indefinite*)

1.1 The definite article (= THE)

	Singular	Plural
Masculine	**le**	**les**
Feminine	**la**	**les**

- **le** and **la** are reduced to **l'** before:
  a singular noun starting with a vowel (**école → l'école**)
  a singular noun starting with a silent h (**hôtel → l'hôtel**)
- **les** is the plural in all cases

1.2 The indefinite article (= A or AN; plural = SOME)

	Singular	Plural
Masculine	**un**	**des**
Feminine	**une**	**des**

- **un** and **une** also indicate the number 1 in counting:
  e.g. **une pomme** = one apple [*see* **NUMBERS** *section 9.1*]
- **des** is the plural in all cases

⚠️ NOTE: Articles are rarely omitted: e.g. **les enfants aiment les bonbons** = children like sweets BUT when specifying someone's occupation, the article is dropped: e.g. **il est boucher** = he is a butcher, **ma sœur est avocat** = my sister is a lawyer

2 NOUNS and NUMBER

- number means *singular* or *plural*
- nouns in most cases add an ending in the plural

2.1 Typical nouns:

Most nouns add -**s** in the plural:
e.g. **chaise → chaises** (= chairs) **chien → chiens** (= dogs)

2.2 Nouns ending in -eu or -eau:

These nouns usually add -**x** in the plural:
e.g. **jeu → jeux** (= games) **bureau → bureaux** (= desks)

2.3 Nouns ending in -ou:

These nouns usually add -**s** in the plural.
BUT there are 6 common exceptions which add -**x**:

bijou → bijoux (= jewels) **genou → genoux** (= knees)
caillou → cailloux (= pebbles) **hibou → hiboux** (= owls)
chou → choux (= cabbages) **joujou → joujoux** (= toys)

2.4 Nouns ending in -al:

These nouns usually change from -**al** to -**aux**:
e.g. **rival → rivaux** (= rivals); **cheval → chevaux** (= horses)
BUT there are exceptions: e.g. **bal → bals** (= dances)

2.5 Nouns ending in -ail:

These nouns usually add -**s**: e.g. **détail → détails** (= details)
BUT there are exceptions: e.g. **travail → travaux** (= works)

2.6 Some nouns have unusual plurals:

These plurals need to be learnt individually:
e.g. **ciel → cieux** (= skies) **œil → yeux** (= eyes)

 NOTE: the group: monsieur → messieurs; madame → mesdames;
mademoiselle → mesdemoiselles; mon-, ma- in these words meant 'my' originally
(as in 'my lord', 'my lady')
[*See* POSSESSIVE ADJECTIVES *section 6*]

2.7 Hyphenated nouns

- The plurals of this group of nouns vary and depend on how the word is formed (*adjective + noun*, *verb + noun*, etc.)

- In cases where there is an ADJECTIVE + NOUN, it is normal for both words in the compound to change:
  e.g. **beau-père → beaux-pères** (= fathers-in-law)

- It is often helpful to translate the compound and find which word will logically become plural:
  e.g. **arc-en-ciel** (= rainbow) **→ arcs-en-ciel** (= rainbows)
  (literally 'arc in the sky' → 'arcs in the sky')

 NOTE: sometimes it is logical to leave the word unchanged in the plural because no noun is present in the make-up of the compound: e.g. **un passe-partout** = skeleton key **→ des passe-partout** = skeleton keys (literally 'a go-everywhere' : VERB + ADVERB)

2.8 Nouns showing no change between singular and plural

Nouns already ending in **-s**: e.g. **bois → bois** (= woods)
Nouns already ending in **-x**: e.g. **voix → voix** (= voices)
Nouns already ending in **-z**: e.g. **nez → nez** (= noses)

3 NOUNS and QUANTITY

- There are many nouns which indicate quantity
  e.g. **un kilo de** = a kilo of…; **une livre de** = a pound of…;
  une bouteille de = a bottle of…

- The word **de** is important in quantity expressions

- Sometimes **de** combines with **le / la / l' / les** to mean 'some'

3.1 The partitive article (= SOME)

de + NOUNS	
de + le → du	e.g. **le pain → du pain** = some bread
de + la → de la	e.g. **la crème → de la crème** = some cream
de + l' → de l'	e.g. **l'huile → de l'huile** = some oil
de + les → des	e.g. **les oranges → des oranges** = some oranges

NOTE: After a negative (*not, no more*, etc.: *see* NEGATIVES *section 12*), only use **de** or **d'**: e.g. **je n'ai plus de pain** = I haven't got any more bread; **il ne prend pas d'huile** = he's not buying any oil. After a quantity expression such as **un kilo de**, do not change **de** to **des**: e.g. **un kilo de pommes** = a kilo of apples

4 NOUNS replaced by PRONOUNS

4.1 Subject pronouns

■ Subject pronouns (*I, we, they*, etc.) replace nouns

■ They refer to people or things

■ They govern verbs (e.g. **je chante** = I sing) [*see* VERBS *section 10.1*]

Singular	Plural
je = I	**nous** = we
tu = you	**vous** = you
il = he /it	**ils** = they [*masculine*]
elle = she / it	**elles** = they [*feminine*]
on = one*	

• **on** is used as a less specific subject pronoun to mean 'one', 'you', 'people', 'we', 'they':
  e.g. **on mange ici?** = shall we eat here?
  on n'aime pas refuser = one doesn't like to refuse
  on parle français là? = do they speak French there?

4.2 Object pronouns

4.2.a Direct object pronouns

■ Direct object pronouns (*it, him, us*, etc.) replace nouns

■ They refer to people or things

■ They are the object (= affected by the action) of verbs:
  e.g. hit the ball; go on, hit it! = **frappe la balle; allez, frappe-la!**

French	English
me / m'	me
te / t'	you [*singular*]
le / l'	him /it
la / l'	her / it
se / s'	himself/ herself/ itself
nous	us
vous	you [*plural*]
les	them
se / s'	themselves

- **m' / t' / l' / s'** are used if the word that follows starts with a vowel or a silent h:
  e.g. **ils l'aiment** = they love her
  elles l'ont humidifié = they sprayed it with water
- object pronouns affect the ending of a past participle [*see* **VERBS** *section 10.1.f*] if the object is feminine or plural:
  e.g. **elle a poli la table → elle l'a polie** (she polished it)

4.2.b Indirect object pronouns

■ Indirect object pronouns (*to it, to him, to us*, etc.) replace nouns

■ They refer to people or things

■ They are the indirect object (= *indirectly* affected by the action) of verbs:
  e.g. **donnez-lui la balle!** = give the ball to him (or to her)!
  il m'a montré la photo = he showed me the photo

French	English
me / m'	(to) me
te / t'	(to) you [*singular*]
lui	(to) him or it
lui	(to) her or it
nous	(to) us
vous	(to) you [*plural*]
leur	(to) them

- (to) shows that the word 'to' is understood in the sentence even though it may not actually be said:
  e.g. give them that! = give that to them! = **donne-le**-leur!

4.2.c Indirect object pronouns: places and quantities

- The indirect object pronoun referring to a place is:
  y (= there) e.g. **j'y vais** = I'm going there

- The indirect object pronoun referring to a quantity is:
  en (= of it, of them, some) e.g. **j'en voudrais 3** = I'd like 3 (of them); **offrez-leur-en** = offer them some

4.3 Order of object pronouns in the sentence

- Object pronouns come before most verb parts:
  e.g. **elle leur rend les livres** = she returns the books to them

- Object pronouns come before an infinitive:
  e.g. **elle va leur rendre les livres** = she is going to return the books to them

- Object pronouns come before the first part of a compound tense (= conjugated with **avoir** or **être**: *see* **VERBS** *section 10.1.f*)
  e.g. **elle leur a rendu les livres** = she returned the books to them

- Object pronouns follow the imperative form of the verb and are linked to it by a hyphen:
  e.g. **rends-leur les livres!** = return the books to them!

- Object pronouns return to normal order even with an imperative if it is negative:
  e.g. **ne les rendez pas!** = don't return them!

- When they occur in multiples in a sentence, object pronouns have a fixed order

OBJECT PRONOUN ORDER (see above tables for meanings):

me					
te	le	lui		y	en
se*	la	leur			
nous	les				
vous					
se*					

- the first column (me, te, se) is also used with reflexive verbs
  [see **VERBS** section 10.1]
- **se** means: (to) himself, (to) herself, (to) oneself, (to) themselves

 NOTE: any combination of object pronouns will fall in this order:
e.g. **ils y en ont mis 6** = they put 6 of them there
il le lui a payé = he bought it for her
ils le leur y ont expliqué = they explained it to them there

4.4 Disjunctive or emphatic pronouns

- Pronouns are sometimes used for emphasis:

Disjunctive Pronouns	
moi	nous
toi	vous
lui	eux
elle	elles

- They take on these spellings:
  * after prepositions:
  e.g. **avec moi** = with me
  * after **que** or **qu'** in comparative sentences [see **COMPARISON** section 8.1]:
  e.g. **plus petit que lui** = smaller than him
  * to emphasize the subject:
  e.g. **lui, il n'aime pas le vin rouge mais elle, elle l'adore**
  = he doesn't like red wine but she loves it
  * with **même** meaning 'self' (*myself, yourself*, etc.):
  e.g. **toi-même** = yourself
  vous-mêmes = yourselves

⚠️ NOTE: that **-s** is added to **même** in the plural

⚠️ NOTE: **moi** and **toi** are also used as 'emphatics' in imperatives when pronouns follow the verb: e.g. **donnez-le-moi**! = give it to me! **mets-toi là**! = sit yourself there!

---

5 ADJECTIVES

- Adjectives qualify nouns
- They usually follow the noun in French
- They reflect the noun in both gender and number
- Many determiners (*this, my, all, three*, etc.) are adjectival
- Some adjectives are used alone as nouns
  e.g. **il est intelligent, le petit** = the little one (= boy) is bright

5.1 Common adjectival endings:

- The masculine form is that given in the dictionary
- Add **-e** to form the feminine:
  e.g. **une jupe courte** = a short skirt
- Add **-s** to the masculine to form the masculine plural:
  e.g. **des voyages intéressants** = interesting journeys
- Add **-s** to the feminine to form the feminine plural
  e.g. **des histoires amusantes** = funny stories

5.2 Adjectives ending in -e

These stay the same in the feminine:
e.g. **aimable** → feminine **aimable**

⚠️ NOTE: unless the **-e** has an acute accent: e.g. **aimé** → feminine **aimée**

-s is added in the normal way in the plural:
e.g. **aimable** → plural **aimables**

⚠️ NOTE: this is true of all adjectives:
unless the ending is **-x** (e.g. **curieux** → masculine plural **curieux**)
unless there is already a final **-s** (**bas** → masculine plural **bas**)

5.3 Table of adjectives showing typical endings and their feminines:

Typical ending	Adjective	Feminine	English
The following double the last letter and add an **-e**			
-as	**bas**	**basse**	low
-eil	**pareil**	**pareille**	similar
-el	**mortel**	**mortelle**	fatal
-en	**ancien**	**ancienne**	ancient
-et	**muet**	**muette**	mute
! *sometimes* !	**inquiet**	**inquiète**	anxious
-on	**bon**	**bonne**	good
-ul	**nul**	**nulle**	no good
The following add a final -e and lengthen the syllable by adding an accent or changing a consonant or consonant group			
-er	**premier**	**première**	first
-ef	**bref**	**brève**	brief
-if	**actif**	**active**	active
-eux	**fameux**	**fameuse**	infamous
-eur	**menteur**	**menteuse**	untruthful
-nc	**blanc**	**blanche**	white
-ic	**public**	**publique**	public
-gu	**aigu**	**aiguë**	acute

The following are examples of irregular adjectives which show additional variations
doux → douce (= sweet); **faux → fausse** (= false)
favori → favorite (= favourite); **frais → fraîche** (= fresh)
gentil → gentille (= kind); **jaloux → jalouse** (= jealous)
malin → maligne (= cunning); **roux → rousse** (= red)
sot → sotte (= silly)

5.4 Position of adjectives

- Most adjectives follow the noun; this is because an adjective distinguishes the noun in some way (colour, shape, etc.) and this position gives more emphasis in French: e.g. **un chocolat chaud** (= a hot chocolate)

- Some adjectives go before the noun: these are usually common adjectives where a distinguishing feature is less pronounced:

e.g. **un vieil ami de la famille** (= an old family friend)
These may almost become part of the noun as a compound:
e.g. **un jeune homme** (= a young man)
les petits enfants (= the little children; the grandchildren)

■ Some adjectives change meaning if they go before the noun:
e.g. **la pauvre fille** (= the poor girl!)
la fille pauvre (= the girl with little money)
la mauvaise clé (= the wrong key)
un animal mauvais (= a vicious animal)
un seul président (= only one president)
elle, seule, le sait (= she alone knows that)

5.4.a beau, nouveau, vieux

■ These 3 adjectives go before the noun

■ They form a group because they have an extra spelling:

Masculine	Masculine with vowel*	Masculine Plural	Feminine	Feminine Plural	English
beau	**bel**	**beaux**	**belle**	**belles**	beautiful
nouveau	**nouvel**	**nouveaux**	**nouvelle**	**nouvelles**	new
vieux	**vieil**	**vieux**	**vieille**	**vieilles**	old

• The extra spelling is used if the noun is masculine and starts with a vowel:
e.g. **arbre → un bel arbre** (= a lovely tree)

Examples: **une belle femme** (= a beautiful woman)
de nouveaux livres (= new books)
de vieilles histoires (= old stories)

⚠ NOTE: **des** changes to **de** in front of a plural adjective

6 POSSESSION

■ Possession is commonly expressed by using **de**

■ The style used is:
'the dog of Paul' = **le chien de Paul** = Paul's dog

'the clothes of Sophie' = **les vêtements de Sophie** = Sophie's clothes

■ Possession is also shown by possessive adjectives (*my*, *your*, etc.):

POSSESSIVE ADJECTIVES			
Masculine	Feminine	Plural	English
mon	**ma**	**mes**	my
ton	**ta**	**tes**	your
son	**sa**	**ses**	his/her/its/one's
notre	**notre**	**nos**	our
votre	**votre**	**vos**	your
leur	**leur**	**leurs**	their

• The word matches the gender and number of the 'thing' possessed NOT the speaker:
  e.g. **ma sœur** = my sister (the speaker may be male)
• **ma**, **ta**, and **sa** end in vowels; therefore they are not used before a vowel:
  e.g. NOT **sa amie** BUT **son amie** = his girlfriend

6.1 mine, yours, etc.

■ These are expressed by possessive pronouns

■ They reflect the gender and number of the 'thing' possessed:

POSSESSIVE PRONOUNS				
Masculine	Feminine	Masculine Plural	Feminine Plural	English
le mien	**la mienne**	**les miens**	**les miennes**	mine
le tien	**la tienne**	**les tiens**	**les tiennes**	yours
le sien	**la sienne**	**les siens**	**les siennes**	his/hers/its
le nôtre	**la nôtre**	**les nôtres**	**les nôtres**	ours
le vôtre	**la vôtre**	**les vôtres**	**les vôtres**	yours
le leur	**la leur**	**les leurs**	**les leurs**	theirs

• The word matches the gender and number of the 'thing' possessed NOT the speaker:
  e.g. **cette chaise est la mienne** = this chair is mine (*the speaker may be male*)

7 ADVERBS

- Adverbs usually give additional information about a verb's action: i.e. they say 'how' (= in what way or manner), 'when', 'where' something happens

- Most adverbs are formed from the feminine adjective by adding **-ment**
  e.g. **heureux → heureuse → heureusement** (= happily, fortunately)

Exceptions include:

7.1 masculine adjectives ending in a vowel

The feminine **-e** is dropped:
e.g. **hardi → hardiment** (= robustly)
résolu → résolument (= resolutely)

7.2 adjectives ending in -ant or -ent

The **-nt** is dropped and the **-m-** is doubled:
e.g. **constant → constamment** (= constantly)
intelligent → intelligemment (= intelligently)
Note however **lent → lentement** (= slowly)

8 COMPARISON

8.1 Comparative of adjectives and adverbs

- The comparative in English is usually expressed by:
  'more…'   (e.g. *more interesting*)
  'as…'   (e.g. *as big*)
  'less…'   (e.g. *less intelligent*)
  or the suffix '-er' (e.g. *bigger*)

- The comparative in French is expressed in most cases by:
  'plus…'   (e.g. **plus intéressant**)
  'aussi…'   (e.g. **aussi grand**)
  'moins…'   (e.g. **moins intelligent**)

- The word for 'than' in French is **que** (or **qu'**)

- The adjective reflects the gender and number of the noun described. Examples:
il est plus grand que toi = he is taller than you
cette rue est moins longue que celle-là = this road is shorter than that one

SOME IRREGULAR COMPARATIVES		
Adjective	Comparative	English
bon = good	**meilleur**	better
mauvais = bad	**pire**	worse
petit = small	**moindre**	lesser, less great,
! *sometimes* !	**plus petit**	smaller
bien = well	**mieux**	better
mal = badly	**pis**	worse
! *sometimes* !	**plus mal**	
peu = little	**moins**	less

8.2 Superlative of adjectives and adverbs

- The superlative in English is usually expressed by 'most...' (e.g. *most interesting*) or the suffix '-est' (e.g. *biggest*)

- The superlative in French is expressed in most cases by: '**le/la/les plus**...' (e.g. **le plus intéressant**)

- The article is repeated reflecting the gender and number of the noun described:
e.g. **la ville la plus belle** = the most beautiful city

- The superlative is often followed by 'in' which is translated by **de**...:
e.g. **la ville la plus belle du monde** = the most beautiful city in the world

9 TIMES

- Time phrases begin with **il est**... (= it is...)

- The French equivalent of 'o' clock' is **heures**
BUT 1 o' clock = **une heure** (i.e. no **-s** required in the singular)

- The 24 hour clock is often used to make a.m. and p.m. clear

- The number of hours is stated first before any minutes are detailed:
  minutes 'past' the hour are simply added to the end of the phrase:

  e.g. **il est sept heures dix**

  'quarter past' is expressed by **et quart**:

  e.g. **il est sept heures et quart**

  minutes 'to' the hour follow the word **moins** (= minus):

  e.g. **il est quatre heures moins cinq** (= five to four)

  'quarter to' is expressed by **moins le quart**:

  e.g. **il est quatre heures moins le quart**

  'half past' is expressed by **et demie**:

  e.g. **il est trois heures et demie**

⚠ NOTE: **midi** (= midday) and **minuit** (= midnight) are masculine; therefore **et demie** changes to **et demi**: e.g. **il est midi et demi**

9.1 The cardinal numbers 1–24

[*see* ORDINAL NUMBERS section 9.5]

1 un/e	**7** sept	**13** treize	**19** dix-neuf
2 deux	**8** huit	**14** quatorze	**20** vingt
3 trois	**9** neuf	**15** quinze	**21** vingt et un/e
4 quatre	**10** dix	**16** seize	**22** vingt-deux
5 cinq	**11** onze	**17** dix-sept	**23** vingt-trois
6 six	**12** douze	**18** dix-huit	**24** vingt-quatre

Examples:

1.00 = **il est une heure**

2.00 = **il est deux heures**

2.10 = **il est deux heures dix**

2.15 = **il est deux heures et quart** [also **il est deux heures quinze**]

2.30 = **il est deux heures et demie** [also **il est deux heures trente**]

2.35 = **il est trois heures moins vingt-cinq** [also **il est deux heures trente-cinq**]

9.2 The numbers 30–100 (in 10s)

30 trente	**70** soixante-dix
40 quarante	**80** quatre-vingts
50 cinquante	**90** quatre-vingt-dix
60 soixante	**100** cent

9.3 Numbers: norms and exceptions

■ Numbers normally count up by linking each digit to 20, 30, etc. by a hyphen: e.g. **vingt-deux, vingt-trois**…

Exceptions worthy of note include:

■ Numbers ending in 1 (*31, 41*, etc.) add **et un** (= and one) to the main number: e.g. 61 = **soixante et un**
EXCEPT for:
81 (**quatre-vingt-un**); 91 (**quatre-vingt-onze**); 101 (**cent un**):

■ Numbers 70–79 are unusual in that they count literally as:
sixty-ten (**soixante-dix**) = 70
sixty-eleven (**soixante et onze**) = 71
sixty-twelve (**soixante-douze**) = 72 etc.

■ Numbers 80–100 are unusual in that they count literally as:
four-twenties (**quatre-vingts**) = 80
four-twenties-one (**quatre-vingt-un**) = 81
four-twenties-two (**quatre-vingt-deux**) = 82 etc.
and over 90…
four-twenties-seventeen (**quatre-vingt-dix-sept**) = 97 etc.

⚠ NOTE: the final **-s** of **vingts** is dropped if any digit follows

■ Over 100, there is no hyphen linking the 100, 200, etc. with following digits: e.g. **trois cent dix-huit** = 318

⚠ NOTE: the final **-s** of **cents** is dropped if any digit follows

9.4 1000 and year dates

The number 1000 = **mille**. However, in written dates, **mille** changes to **mil**:
e.g. 1914 = **mil neuf cent quatorze**

⚠ NOTE: the word **cent** is not omitted

9.4.a Other dates

■ The article **le** is used to specify the day of the month:
e.g. **c'est aujourd'hui le six septembre** = today is the 6th of September

■ The cardinal numbers (**un, deux,** …) are used (NOT the ordinal numbers as in English style: *1st, 2nd*, etc.)

■ sometimes the article **le** goes before the day:
e.g. **c'est** le mardi **deux juillet** = it's Tuesday 2 July

9.5 Ordinal numbers

■ The ordinal numbers count focusing on sequence or priority (*first, second, third,* etc.)

■ Ordinal numbers in French are usually formed by adding -**ième** to the cardinal number:
e.g. **deuxième** (= 2nd), **troisième** (= 3rd), etc.
BUT there are exceptions:
e.g. **premier** = 1st

⚠️ NOTE: numbers like 21st do not follow this change:
e.g. 31st = **trente-et-unième**

■ There is sometimes a spelling change:
e.g. **neuvième** = 9th (-**f**- changes to -**v**-)
onzième = 11th (**onze** drops the final -**e**)

---

10 VERBS

■ Verbs add action to a phrase (**he kicks the ball**) or they describe a state (**she is lazy**)

■ A sentence needs a verb for it to make sense (*he… the dog* → *he strokes the dog*)

■ An infinitive is a verb preceded by 'to' (*I want to go*)

■ A finite verb indicates tense (*will go; went*)

■ Tense is the time at which something happens, exists, etc.

10.1 Regular verbs

■ Some verbs belong to 'regular' groups where they follow the same pattern

■ Regular patterns are identified by the endings -**er**, -**ir**, and -**re**

■ Some regular verbs are REFLEXIVE which means the action involves *oneself*:
e.g. **je me lave** = I wash myself [*see* **PRONOUNS** *section 4.3*]

10.1.a Regular verbs in the present tense

The present tense describes what is happening now (*it is raining*) or what regularly happens (*he plays football on Tuesdays*) or a current truth (*she does love chips*)

---

parler 'to speak' **AN EXAMPLE OF AN -ER VERB**

je parle = I speak   **nous parlons** = we speak
tu parles = you speak   **vous parlez** = you speak
il parle = he speaks   **ils (masc) parlent** = they speak
elle parle = she speaks   **elles (fem) parlent** = they speak

---

- **tu** is used to speak to a child or someone known well
- **vous** is used in polite speech or to more than one person
- **ils** also means 'they' referring to a mixed male and female group
- the translation *I speak*, etc., may also be *I am speaking* and *I do speak*

---

finir 'to finish' **AN EXAMPLE OF AN -IR VERB**

je finis = I finish   **nous finissons** = we finish
tu finis = you finish   **vous finissez** = you finish
il finit = he finishes   **ils (masc) finissent** = they finish
elle finit = she finishes   **elles (fem) finissent** = they finish

---

- note the lengthened stem **-iss-** in the plural

---

vendre 'to sell' **AN EXAMPLE OF AN -RE VERB**

je vends = I sell   **nous vendons** = we sell
tu vends = you sell   **vous vendez** = you sell
il vend = he sells   **ils (masc) vendent** = they sell
elle vend = she sells   **elles (fem) vendent** = they sell

- note the dropped verb ending with **il** and **elle**
  Other present tense patterns are individual to each verb or to a small number of verbs; these are known as 'irregular' verbs. [*see* **VERB TABLES**]

10.1.b Regular verbs in the imperative

- The imperative is a way of ordering, suggesting strongly
- 3 parts of the present tense are used: **tu, nous, vous**
- The **-s** is dropped from the **tu** part of the verb:
  e.g. **parle!** (= talk!); **parlons!** (= let's talk!); **parlez!** (= talk!)
  BUT there are exceptions [see **VERB TABLES**]:
  e.g. **aie!** (= have!); **ayons!** (= let's have!); **ayez!** (= have!)
  sois! (= be!); **soyons!** (= let's be!); **soyez!** (= be!)
  sache! (= know!); **sachons!** (= let's know!); **sachez!** (= know!)

10.1.c Regular verbs in the imperfect tense

The imperfect tense describes what was happening in the past (*it was raining*) or what used to be a fact or occurrence (*he used to like chocolate*; *he used to go to classes*); in French it also expresses what happened regularly (**il jouait au football tous les jeudis** = he played football every Tuesday)

Imperfect tense endings	
-ais	**-ions**
-ais	**-iez**
-ait	**-aient**
-ait	**-aient**

- these endings apply to all verbs
- they are added to a stem
- the stem is taken from the *nous* part of the present tense
  e.g. **nous finissons → finiss- → je finissais**
- the only irregular stem is **ét-** from **être**:
  e.g. **j'étais** (= I was), **tu étais** (= you were)…etc.

10.1.d Regular verbs in the future tense

The future tense describes what will happen (*it will rain*) or what is expected to be a fact (*it will be easy*)

Future tense endings	
-ai	**-ons**
-as	**-ez**
-a	**-ont**
-a	**-ont**

- these endings apply to all verbs

- they are added to a stem: the stem is the infinitive
  e.g. **finir** → **je finirai** (= I shall finish)
  BUT **-re** verbs drop the final **-e**:
  e.g. **vendre** → **je vendrai** (= I shall sell)

- some irregular stems have to be learnt

- the future may also be expressed by:
  the verb ALLER + INFINITIVE = **je vais finir**… (I am going to finish…)

TABLE of irregular future stems: [see VERB TABLES]

Infinitive	Future Stem	Infinitive	Future Stem
avoir	**j'aurai** = I shall have	tenir	**je tiendrai** = I shall hold
être	**je serai** = I shall be	vouloir	**je voudrai** = I shall want
faire	**je ferai** = I shall make	pouvoir	**je pourrai** = I shall be able
savoir	**je saurai** = I shall know	recevoir	**je recevrai** = I shall get
voir	**je verrai** = I shall see	devoir	**je devrai** = I shall have to
envoyer	**j'enverrai** = I shall send	courir	**je courrai** = I shall run
venir	**je viendrai** = I shall come	mourir	**je mourrai** = I shall die

- compounds of the above have the same stem:
  e.g. **retenir** (= to hold back) → **je retiendrai**

10.1.e Regular verbs in the conditional tense

The conditional tense describes what would happen (*it would make*

him angry) or what would be a fact (*it would be easy*)
Formation: = FUTURE STEM + CONDITIONAL ENDINGS

Conditional tense endings	
-ais	**-ions**
-ais	**-iez**
-ait	**-aient**
-ait	**-aient**

■ these endings apply to all verbs
e.g. **il commencerait** (= he would begin)
tu devrais (= you ought to)

■ the word **si** (= if) is often present or understood in the meaning:
e.g. **il le ferait si tu le lui demandais** (= he'd do it if you asked him)

10.1.f Regular verbs in the perfect tense

The perfect tense describes what has happened (*it has snowed*; *they have written*). In French it is also used for what happened and remained the case until a specific point in time (**ils y sont restés jusqu'à mardi** = they stayed there until Tuesday) or to state an action as part of a series, each action being complete in itself (**je me suis approché de la maison, j'ai sonné à la porte**… = I went up to the house, rang the doorbell…)

Formation of the perfect tense:

■ Two common verbs are important in the formation of this tense: AVOIR and ÊTRE

avoir = to have	
j'ai	nous avons
tu as	vous avez
il a	ils ont
elle a	elles ont

être = to be	
je suis	nous sommes
tu es	vous êtes
il est	ils sont
elle est	elles sont

■ 3 parts are needed to make the perfect tense:
SUBJECT + AVOIR/ÊTRE + PAST PARTICIPLE

■ The past participle of regular verbs is made by removing the last syllable of the infinitive (**regarder, choisir, rendre**) and by replacing it with **é, -i, -u** respectively:

e.g. **regarder → regardé → j'ai regardé** (= I have watched)
choisir → choisi → tu as choisi (= you have chosen)
rendre → rendu → il a rendu (= he has given back)
BUT some past participles have to be learnt [see **VERB TABLES**].

TABLE giving common irregular past participles following the auxiliary (= 'helper') verb *avoir*:

Infinitive	Past Participle	Infinitive	Past Participle
avoir	**j'ai eu** = I have had	croire	**j'ai cru** = I have believed
être	**j'ai été** = I have been	savoir	**j'ai su** = I have known
faire	**j'ai fait** = I have made	voir	**j'ai vu** = I have seen
boire	**j'ai bu** = I have drunk	pleuvoir	**il a plu** = it has rained
pouvoir	**j'ai pu** = I have been able	dire	**j'ai dit** = I have said
devoir	**j'ai dû** = I have had to	écrire	**j'ai écrit** = I have written
lire	**j'ai lu** = I have read	mettre	**j'ai mis** = I have put
vouloir	**j'ai voulu** = I have wanted	prendre	**j'ai pris** = I have taken

• the past participle does not change its spelling after **avoir** unless there is a direct object preceding it: e.g. **j'ai vendu la table** (= I sold the table)
BUT **où est la table que tu as vendue**? (= where is the table you've sold?)

■ Most verbs make their perfect tense with **avoir** but the exceptions are: 1 reflexive verbs and 2 a small group of verbs of 'motion'. These take **être** and the past participle behaves like an adjective.

---

1 se laver = to get washed / to wash oneself

je me suis lavé(e) = I got washed
tu t'es lavé(e) = you got washed
il s'est lavé = he got washed
elle s'est lavée = she got washed
nous nous sommes lavé(e)s = we got washed
vous vous êtes lavé(e)(s) = you got washed
ils se sont lavés = they got washed
elles se sont lavées = they got washed

• The alternatives in brackets depend on gender (masculine or feminine) and number (singular or plural)

---

2 VERBS OF MOTION WHICH TAKE ÊTRE

arriver	**je suis arrivé(e)** = I arrived
partir	**je suis parti(e)** = I left
retourner	**je suis retourné(e)** = I returned
rester	**je suis resté(e)** = I stayed
tomber	**je suis tombé(e)** = I fell
mourir	**je suis mort(e)** = I died
naître	**je suis né(e)** = I was born
monter	**je suis monté(e)** = I went up
descendre	**je suis descendu(e)** = I went down
entrer	**je suis entré(e)** = I entered
aller	**je suis allé(e)** = I went
sortir	**je suis sorti(e)** = I went out
venir	**je suis venu(e)** = I came
revenir	**je suis revenu(e)** = I came back

• compounds of the above also take **être** e.g. **devenir** (= to become)
je suis devenu(e)

10.1.g Regular verbs in the pluperfect tense

The pluperfect tense describes what had happened (*it had snowed; they had written*) or what had been the case (*it had been easy*).
Formation: = IMPERFECT TENSE OF AVOIR OR ÊTRE + PAST PARTICIPLE
[*see* **VERB TABLES**]

Examples:
j'avais fini = I had finished
nous avions vendu l'appartement = we had sold the flat
elle s'était réveillée = she had woken up
nous étions partis = we had left

⚠️ NOTE: past participles after **être** behave in the same way as they do for the perfect tense: i.e. they look like adjectives reflecting the gender and number of the subject

10.1.h Regular verbs in the future perfect tense

The future perfect tense describes what will have happened (*he will have arrived*) or what will have been the case (*it will not have been easy*)

Formation: = FUTURE TENSE OF AVOIR OR ÊTRE + PAST PARTICIPLE
[*see* **VERB TABLES**]

Examples:
j'aurai fini = I shall have finished
nous aurons vendu la voiture = we shall have sold the car
nous serons descendus = we shall have gone down

⚠️ NOTE: past participles after **être** behave in the same way as they do for the perfect tense: i.e. they look like adjectives reflecting the gender and number of the subject

10.2 Irregular verbs [see **VERB TABLES**]

11 NEGATIVES

- The negative expresses *not, never, no-one*, etc.
- In French the negative usually has 2 parts:
  e.g. **ne... pas** (= not), **ne... jamais** (= never),
  ne...personne (= nobody), etc.
- If the negative is the SUBJECT (*nobody knows*), then the negative reverses:
  i.e. **ne...personne** → personne ne...
  e.g. **personne ne sait**!
- Usually however with verbs, the 2 parts 'sandwich' the finite verb:
  e.g. **il ne mange pas** = he is not eating

  BUT if an infinitive is present, they exclude the infinitive from the 'sandwich':
  e.g. **il ne veut pas** manger = he doesn't want to eat
  AND in a compound tense (e.g. *perfect, pluperfect*), they only sandwich the first verb:
  e.g. **il n'est pas allé** = he didn't go
  ALSO if object pronouns are present, these 'cling' to the verb within the 'sandwich':
  e.g. **elle l'a acheté** → **elle** ne l'a pas acheté (= she didn't buy it)
- If no verb is present, as in a short response, then the **ne**... is omitted:
  e.g. '**Qui a frappé**?' – '**Personne!**' (= 'Who knocked ?' 'Nobody!')

French verbs

1 chanter

Present indicative

je	chante
tu	chantes
il	chante
nous	chantons
vous	chantez
ils	chantent

Present subjunctive

(que)	je	chante
(que)	tu	chantes
(qu')	il	chante
(que)	nous	chantions
(que)	vous	chantiez
(qu')	ils	chantent

Future indicative

je	chanterai
tu	chanteras
il	chantera
nous	chanterons
vous	chanterez
ils	chanteront

Present conditional

je	chanterais
tu	chanterais
il	chanterait
nous	chanterions
vous	chanteriez
ils	chanteraient

Imperfect indicative

je	chantais
tu	chantais
il	chantait
nous	chantions
vous	chantiez
ils	chantaient

Past participle

chanté/chantée

Perfect indicative

j'	ai	chanté
tu	as	chanté
il	a	chanté
elle	a	chanté
nous	avons	chanté
vous	avez	chanté
ils	ont	chanté
elles	ont	chanté

Pluperfect indicative

j'	avais	chanté
tu	avais	chanté
il	avait	chanté
elle	avait	chanté
nous	avions	chanté
vous	aviez	chanté
ils	avaient	chanté
elles	avaient	chanté

2 finir

Present indicative

je	finis
tu	finis
il	finit
nous	finissons
vous	finissez
ils	finissent

Future indicative

je	finirai
tu	finiras
il	finira
nous	finirons
vous	finirez
ils	finiront

Imperfect indicative

je	finissais
tu	finissais
il	finissait
nous	finissions
vous	finissiez
ils	finissaient

Perfect indicative

j'	ai	fini
tu	as	fini
il	a	fini
elle	a	fini
nous	avons	fini
vous	avez	fini
ils	ont	fini
elles	ont	fini

Present subjunctive

(que)	je	finisse
(que)	tu	finisses
(qu')	il	finisse
(que)	nous	finissions
(que)	vous	finissiez
(qu')	ils	finissent

Present conditional

je	finirais
tu	finirais
il	finirait
nous	finirions
vous	finiriez
ils	finiraient

Past participle

fini/finie

Pluperfect indicative

j'	avais	fini
tu	avais	fini
il	avait	fini
elle	avait	fini
nous	avions	fini
vous	aviez	fini
ils	avaient	fini
elles	avaient	fini

3 attendre

Present indicative

j'	attends
tu	attends
il	attend
nous	attendons
vous	attendez
ils	attendent

Present subjunctive

(que)	j'	attende
(que)	tu	attendes
(qu')	il	attende
(que)	nous	attendions
(que)	vous	attendiez
(qu')	ils	attendent

Future indicative

j'	attendrai
tu	attendras
il	attendra
nous	attendrons
vous	attendrez
ils	attendront

Present conditional

j'	attendrais
tu	attendrais
il	attendrait
nous	attendrions
vous	attendriez
ils	attendraient

Imperfect indicative

j'	attendais
tu	attendais
il	attendait
nous	attendions
vous	attendiez
ils	attendaient

Past participle

attendu/attendue

Pluperfect indicative

j'	avais	attendu
tu	avais	attendu
il	avait	attendu
elle	avait	attendu
nous	avions	attendu
vous	aviez	attendu
ils	avaient	attendu
elles	avaient	attendu

Perfect indicative

j'	ai	attendu
tu	as	attendu
il	a	attendu
elle	a	attendu
nous	avons	attendu
vous	avez	attendu
ils	ont	attendu
elles	ont	attendu

4 être

Present indicative

je	suis
tu	es
il	est
nous	sommes
vous	êtes
ils	sont

Future indicative

je	serai
tu	seras
il	sera
nous	serons
vous	serez
ils	seront

Imperfect indicative

j'	étais
tu	étais
il	était
nous	étions
vous	étiez
ils	étaient

Perfect indicative

j'	ai	été
tu	as	été
il	a	été
elle	a	été
nous	avons	été
vous	avez	été
ils	ont	été
elles	ont	été

Present subjunctive

(que)	je	sois
(que)	tu	sois
(qu')	il	soit
(que)	nous	soyons
(que)	vous	soyez
(qu')	ils	soient

Present conditional

je	serais
tu	serais
il	serait
nous	serions
vous	seriez
ils	seraient

Past participle

été (*invariable*)

Pluperfect indicative

j'	avais	été
tu	avais	été
il	avait	été
elle	avait	été
nous	avions	été
vous	aviez	été
ils	avaient	été
elles	avaient	été

5 avoir

Present indicative	
j'	ai
tu	as
il	a
nous	avons
vous	avez
ils	ont

Present subjunctive		
(que)	j'	aie
(que)	tu	aies
(qu')	il	ait
(que)	nous	ayons
(que)	vous	ayez
(qu')	ils	aient

Future indicative	
j'	aurai
tu	auras
il	aura
nous	aurons
vous	aurez
ils	auront

Present conditional	
j'	aurais
tu	aurais
il	aurait
nous	aurions
vous	auriez
ils	auraient

Imperfect indicative	
j'	avais
tu	avais
il	avait
nous	avions
vous	aviez
ils	avaient

Past participle

eu/eue

Pluperfect indicative		
j'	avais	eu
tu	avais	eu
il	avait	eu
elle	avait	eu
nous	avions	eu
vous	aviez	eu
ils	avaient	eu
elles	avaient	eu

Perfect indicative		
j'	ai	eu
tu	as	eu
il	a	eu
elle	a	eu
nous	avons	eu
vous	avez	eu
ils	ont	eu
elles	ont	eu

[6] acheter
1 j'achète 2 j'achèterai
3 j'achetais 4 que j'achète
5 acheté

[7] acquérir
1 j'acquiers, nous acquérons, ils
acquièrent 2 j'acquerrai
3 j'acquérais 4 que j'acquière
5 acquis

[8] aller
1 je vais, tu vas, il va, nous
allons, vous allez, ils vont 2 j'irai
3 j'allais 4 que j'aille, que nous
allions, qu'ils aillent 5 allé

[9] asseoir
1 j'assois, tu assois, il assoit, nous
assoyons, vous assoyez, ils
assoient 2 j'assoirai 3 j'assoyais
4 que j'assoie, que nous
assoyions, qu'ils assoient 5 assis

[10] avancer
1 nous avançons 3 j'avançais

[11] battre
1 je bats, il bat, nous battons
2 je battrai 3 je battais 4 que je
batte 5 battu

[12] boire
1 je bois, il boit, nous buvons,
ils boivent 2 je boirai 3 je buvais
4 que je boive 5 bu

[13] bouillir
1 je bous, il bout, nous bouillons,
ils bouillent 2 je bouillirai
3 je bouillais 4 que je bouille
5 bouilli

[14] céder
1 je cède, nous cédons,
ils cèdent 2 je céderai 3 je
cédais 4 que je cède 5 cédé

[15] créer
1 je crée, nous créons 2 je
créerai 3 je créais 4 que je crée
5 créé

[16] conclure
1 je conclus, il conclut, nous
concluons, ils concluent
2 je conclurai 3 je concluais
4 que je conclue 5 conclu
(*but* inclus)

[17] conduire
1 je conduis, nous conduisons
2 je conduirai 3 je conduisais
4 que je conduise 5 conduit
(*but* lui, nui)

[18] connaître
1 je connais, il connaît, nous
connaissons 2 je connaîtrai
3 je connaissais 4 que je
connaisse 5 connu

[19] coudre
1 je couds, il coud, nous
cousons, ils cousent 2 je coudrai
3 je cousais 4 que je couse
5 cousu

[20] courir
1 je cours, il court, nous courons,
ils courent 2 je courrai 3 je
courais 4 que je coure 5 couru

[21] couvrir
1 je couvre 2 je couvrirai

---

1 Present Indicative 2 Future Indicative 3 Imperfect Indicative 4 Present Subjunctive 5 Past Participle

3 je couvrais 4 que je couvre
5 couvert

[22] craindre
1 je crains, il craint, nous
craignons, ils craignent
2 je craindrai 3 je craignais
4 que je craigne 5 craint

[23] croire
1 je crois, il croit, nous croyons,
ils croient 2 je croirai
3 je croyais, nous croyions
4 que je croie, que nous croyions
5 cru

[24] croître
1 je croîs, il croît, nous croissons
2 je croîtrai 3 je croissais
4 que je croisse 5 crû/crue (but
accru, décru)

[25] cueillir
1 je cueille 2 je cueillerai 3 je
cueillais 4 que je cueille 5 cueilli

[26] devoir
1 je dois, il doit, nous devons, ils
doivent 2 je devrai 3 je devais
4 que je doive, que nous devions
5 dû/due

[27] dire
1 je dis, il dit, nous disons, vous
dites, ils disent 2 je dirai
3 je disais 4 que je dise 5 dit

[28] dissoudre
1 je dissous, il dissout, nous
dissolvons, ils dissolvent
2 je dissoudrai 3 je dissolvais
4 que je dissolve 5 dissous/
dissoute

[29] distraire
1 je distrais, il distrait, nous
distrayons 2 je distrairai
3 je distrayais 4 que je distraie
5 distrait

[30] écrire
1 j'écris, il écrit, nous écrivons
2 j'écrirai 3 j'écrivais
4 que j'écrive 5 écrit

[31] employer
1 j'emploie, nous employons,
ils emploient 2 j'emploierai
3 j'employais, nous employions
4 que j'emploie, que nous
employions 5 employé

[32] envoyer
1 j'envoie, nous envoyons,
ils envoient 2 j'enverrai
3 j'envoyais, nous envoyions
4 que j'envoie, que nous
envoyions 5 envoyé

[33] faire
1 je fais, nous faisons (say
/fəzɔ̃/), vous faites, ils font
2 je ferai 3 je faisais (say /fəzɛ/)
4 que je fasse, que nous fassions
5 fait

[34] falloir (impersonal)
1 il faut 2 il faudra 3 il fallait
4 qu'il faille 5 fallu

[35] fuir
1 je fuis, nous fuyons 2 je fuirai
3 je fuyais, nous fuyions 4 que je
fuie, que nous fuyions 5 fui

[36] haïr
1 je hais, il hait, nous haïssons,

---

1 Present Indicative 2 Future Indicative 3 Imperfect Indicative 4 Present Subjunctive 5 Past Participle

ils haïssent **2** je haïrai **3** je
haïssais **4** que je haïsse **5** haï

[37] interdire
1 j'interdis, vous interdisez
2 j'interdirai **3** j'interdisais
4 que j'interdise **5** interdit

[38] jeter
1 je jette, nous jetons, ils jettent
2 je jetterai **3** je jetais **4** que je
jette **5** jeté

[39] lire
1 je lis, il lit, nous lisons **2** je lirai
3 je lisais **4** que je lise **5** lu

[40] manger
1 je mange, nous mangeons
2 je mangerai **3** je mangeais
4 que je mange, que nous
mangions **5** mangé

[41] maudire
1 je maudis, il maudit, nous
maudissons **2** je maudirai
3 je maudissais **4** que je
maudisse **5** maudit

[42] mettre
1 je mets, tu mets, nous mettons
2 je mettrai **3** je mettais **4** que
je mette **5** mis

[43] mourir
1 je meurs, il meurt, nous
mourons **2** je mourrai
3 je mourais **4** que je meure
5 mort

[44] naître
1 je nais, il naît, nous naissons
2 je naîtrai **3** je naissais **4** que je
naisse **5** né

[45] oublier
1 j'oublie, nous oublions, ils
oublient **2** j'oublierai
3 j'oubliais, nous oubliions, vous
oubliiez **4** que nous oubliions,
que vous oubliiez **5** oublié

[46] partir
1 je pars, nous partons
2 je partirai **3** je partais
4 que je parte **5** parti

[47] plaire
1 je plais, il plaît (*but* il tait), nous
plaisons **2** je plairai **3** je plaisais
4 que je plaise **5** plu

[48] pleuvoir (*impersonal*)
1 il pleut **2** il pleuvra
3 il pleuvait **4** qu'il pleuve **5** plu

[49] pouvoir
1 je peux, il peut, nous
pouvons, ils peuvent **2** je pourrai
3 je pouvais **4** que je puisse, que
nous puissions **5** pu

[50] prendre
1 je prends, il prend, nous
prenons **2** je prendrai
3 je prenais **4** que je prenne
5 pris

[51] prévoir
1 je prévois, il prévoit, nous
prévoyons, ils prévoient
2 je prévoirai **3** je prévoyais,
nous prévoyions **4** que je
prévoie, que nous prévoyions
5 prévu

[52] recevoir
1 je reçois, il reçoit, nous

---

1 Present Indicative **2** Future Indicative **3** Imperfect Indicative **4** Present Subjunctive **5** Past Participle

recevons, ils reçoivent **2** je recevrai **3** je recevais **4** que je reçoive, que nous recevions **5** reçu

[**53**] **résoudre**
1 je résous, il résout, nous résolvons, ils résolvent
2 je résoudrai **3** je résolvais
4 que je résolve **5** résolu

[**54**] **rire**
1 je ris, nous rions, ils rient
2 je rirai **3** je riais, nous riions
4 que je rie, que nous riions **5** ri

[**55**] **savoir**
1 je sais, il sait, nous savons, ils savent **2** je saurai **3** je savais
4 que je sache, que nous sachions **5** su

[**56**] **suffire**
1 il suffit, ils suffisent **2** il suffira
3 il suffisait **4** qu'il suffise **5** suffi
(*but* frit)

[**57**] **suivre**
1 je suis, il suit, nous suivons
2 je suivrai **3** je suivais **4** que je suive **5** suivi

[**58**] **tenir**
1 je tiens, il tient, nous tenons, ils tiennent **2** je tiendrai **3** je tenais

4 que je tienne, que nous tenions **5** tenu

[**59**] **vaincre**
1 je vaincs, il vainc, nous vainquons, ils vainquent
2 je vaincrai **3** je vainquais
4 que je vainque **5** vaincu

[**60**] **valoir**
1 je vaux, il vaut, nous valons
2 je vaudrai **3** je valais **4** que je vaille, que nous valions **5** valu

[**61**] **vêtir**
1 je vêts, il vêt, nous vêtons
2 je vêtirai **3** je vêtais **4** que je vête **5** vêtu

[**62**] **vivre**
1 je vis, il vit, nous vivons, ils vivent **2** je vivrai **3** je vivais
4 que je vive **5** vécu

[**63**] **voir**
1 je vois, nous voyons, ils voient
2 je verrai **3** je voyais, nous voyions **4** que je voie, que nous voyions **5** vu

[**64**] **vouloir**
1 je veux, il veut, nous voulons, ils veulent **2** je voudrai **3** je voulais **4** que je veuille, que nous voulions **5** voulu

---

What are the equivalent tenses in English

Present indicative
je chante = *I sing, I'm singing*

Future indicative
je chanterai = *I will sing*

Imperfect indicative
je chantais = *I was singing*

Perfect indicative
j'ai chanté
= *I sang, I have sung*

Pluperfect indicative
j'avais chanté = *I had sung*

Present subjunctive
bien que je chante
= *although I sing*

Present conditional
si je pouvais, je chanterais
= *if I could, I would sing*

Past participle
chanté/chantée = *sung*

How to conjugate a reflexive verb

Present indicative and other simple tenses
je me lave
tu te laves
il se lave
elle se lave
nous nous lavons
vous vous lavez
ils se lavent
elles se lavent

in the negative form
je ne me lave pas
tu ne te laves pas
il ne se lave pas
elle ne se lave pas
nous ne nous lavons pas
vous ne vous lavez pas
ils ne se lavent pas
elles ne se lavent pas

Perfect indicative and other compound tenses
(always with auxiliary **être***)*
je me suis lavé
tu t'es lavé
il s'est lavé
elle s'est lavée
nous nous sommes lavés
vous vous êtes lavés
ils se sont lavés
elles se sont lavées

in the negative form
je ne me suis pas lavé
tu ne t'es pas lavé
il ne s'est pas lavé
elle ne s'est pas lavée
nous ne nous sommes pas
lavés
vous ne vous êtes pas lavés
ils ne se sont pas lavés
elles ne se sont pas lavées